SCOTLAND
The Later Middle Ages

THE EDINBURGH HISTORY OF SCOTLAND

General Editor

GORDON DONALDSON, D.Litt.

*Fraser Professor of Scottish History and Palaeography
in the University of Edinburgh*

SCOTLAND

The Later Middle Ages

Ranald Nicholson

The Edinburgh History of Scotland

Volume 2

Oliver & Boyd

OLIVER & BOYD
Croythorn House
23 Ravelston Terrace
Edinburgh EH4 3TJ
A Division of Longman Group Ltd.

Hardback edition first published, 1974
First published in paperback, 1978

ISBN 0 05 003184 8 *paperback*

PRINTED IN HONG KONG BY
COMMONWEALTH PRINTING PRESS LTD

PREFACE

The whole period covered by this volume has figured, and continues to figure, in many popular histories varying in merit and idiosyncrasy. Many aspects of it have been touched upon in the last half century in specialised publications that are scholarly and less popular. But scarcely since Edwardian times has there been an attempt to embody the products of accumulating research in a fresh synthesis of Scotland's history in the later Middle Ages. This is an attempt. The somewhat profuse footnotes (which can be ignored by all save the zealous) draw attention to the useful labours of many scholars, and perhaps disclose that I have occasionally supplemented their work by a little independent research.

It will be obvious that what I have produced is not harmonious in its proportions, that some parts are emaciated and others gross. This has resulted from my inclination to give to the fifteenth century a fuller weight corresponding to the increasing abundance of source material. I have also lingered longest in treating periods that are complex and have paused more briefly at those which may be understood with less detailed exposition. In all cases dates have been rendered in modern reckoning : thus medieval Scottish documents dated between 1 January and 24 March inclusive have been assigned to the year following that stated in the original.

This book would not have taken shape without the co-operation of a succession of secretaries and typists, some of whom sought other employment. Three—Mrs Frederick Law, Mrs William Pollard and Miss Gilian MacPherson—persevered to the end. The publishers, as represented by Mr A. W. R. Seward and Miss Alison Reid, have been skilful, courteous, and patient beyond belief. My present colleagues in the University of Guelph, as well as my former colleagues in the University of Edinburgh, have been helpful and encouraging. Nor should I omit to acknowledge the aid of my parents, whose enduring enthusiasm extended even to the Augean task of proof correction. To three scholars I owe a great deal: Professor Geoffrey Hand of

University College, Dublin, read one-third of the book in typescript; Professor A. A. M. Duncan of the University of Glasgow read half of it; and Professor Gordon Donaldson of the University of Edinburgh read the whole of it. All extricated me from pitfalls, and I am particularly indebted to Professor Donaldson's sagacity.

It need hardly be said that none of my various helpers bears responsibility for the remaining defects in this work, which are entirely my own. It is some consolation that Sir Gilbert Hay opined: 'there is na man withe out sum falt may wret'. And, for the moment, doubts and hesitations must take second place to the kind of relief that Gavin Douglas felt when he wrote: 'heir is endit the lang desparit wark'.

RANALD NICHOLSON

Note on 1978 impression (Paperback edition)

So few scholarly reviews of this book have so far appeared that I have been deprived of the feelings of contrition that might have inspired me to major revision. One exception is a review by Dr Athol L. Murray, who has rightly pointed out that the men whom I described as "commissioners for the assessment of crown lands" were primarily concerned with leasing the lands and ought properly to be styled "commissioners for the leasing of crown lands".

Another review suggested that in view of the latest research I might feel inclined to revise my general opinions regarding the relations of crown and nobility. I do not feel so inclined. I should, however, draw the attention of readers to Professor G. W. S. Barrow's interesting article on "Lothian in the First War of Independence, 1296–1328" (*Scottish Historical Review*, vol. LV, 1976, pp. 151–71), which offers an interpretation somewhat different from my own. Lastly, in view of my predilection for Scotticisms, I regret that I have written of a certain common unit of account as a "mark" rather than a "merk" and would be relieved if readers would bear in mind that the latter is the appropriate Scottish rendering.

RANALD NICHOLSON

CONTENTS

viii CONTENTS

Appendix 2 : Genealogical Tables

LIST OF ABBREVIATIONS USED IN FOOTNOTES

Particulars of works not cited here are given either in the footnotes (if they are of minor relevance) or in the bibliography (if they are of major relevance). In the footnotes numerals in roman type signify the number, or part, of a volume; those in arabic signify pages, unless preceded by 'No.', in which case they refer to a document. When one footnote in which two or more works are cited is followed by a footnote citing the last of those works, the title of that work has been repeated for the sake of clarity, in place of the term *ibid.*

Aberdeen-Banff Illustrations	= *Illustrations of the Topography and Antiquities of the Shires of Aberdeen and Banff* (Spalding Club, 1847–69).
Aberdeen Burgh Recs.	= *Early Records of the Burgh of Aberdeen* (S.H.S., 1957).
Aberdeen Council Register	= *Extracts from the Council Register of the Burgh of Aberdeen* (Spalding Club, 1844).
Aberdeen Fasti	= *Fasti Aberdonenses: Selections from the Records of the University and King's College of Aberdeen* (Spalding Club, 1854).
Aberdeen Registrum	= *Registrum Episcopatus Aberdonensis* (Spalding and Maitland Clubs, 1845).
A.D.A.	= *The Acts of the Lords Auditors of Causes and Complaints, 1466–94*, ed. T. Thomson (London, 1839).
A.D.C.	= *The Acts of the Lords of Council in Civil Causes*, ed. T. Thomson and others (Edinburgh, 1839 and 1918).
A.D.C.P.	= *Acts of the Lords of Council in Public Affairs 1501–1554: Selections from Acta Dominorum Concilii*, ed. R. K. Hannay (1932).
A.P.S.	= *Acts of the Parliaments of Scotland*, ed. T. Thomson and C. Innes (Edinburgh, 1814–75).
Arbroath Liber	= *Liber S. Thome de Aberbrothoc* (Bannatyne Club, 1848–56).
Ayr Burgh Charters	= *Charters of the Royal Burgh of Ayr* (Ayr and Wigton Archaeological Association, 1883).

Balfour-Melville,   = E. W. M. Balfour-Melville, *James I, King of*
   James I   *Scots* (1936).

Barbour, *The Bruce*   = J. Barbour, *The Bruce* (S.T.S., 1894).

Barron, *War of*   = Evan Macleod Barron, *The Scottish War of*
   Independence   *Independence: a Critical Study*, 2nd edn.
                    (1934).

Barrow, *Bruce*   = G. W. S. Barrow, *Robert Bruce and the*
                   Community of the Realm of Scotland (1965).

B.I.H.R.   = *Bulletin of the Institute of Historical Research.*

Blind Harry, *Wallace*   = *The Actis and Deeds of the Illustere and*
      —   *Vailzeand Campioun Schir William Wallace,*
                   Knicht of Ellerslie (S.T.S., 1889).

B.M.   = British Museum.

Boece, *History*   = Hector Boethius, *Scotorum Historiae*, 2nd edn.
                   (Paris, 1574), pp. 1–384 v.

Boece, *Vitae*   = *Hectoris Boetii Murthlacensium et*
                   Aberdonensium Episcoporum Vitae
                   (Bannatyne Club, 1825).

Brechin Registrum   = *Registrum Episcopatus Brechinensis* (Bannatyne
                   Club, 1856).

Brown, *Early Travellers*   = Brown, P. Hume, *Early Travellers in Scotland*
                   (1891).

Buchanan, *History*   = G. Buchanan, *The History of Scotland*,
                   translated J. Aikman (Glasgow and Edinburgh,
                   1827–30).

Burghs Convention Recs.   = *Extracts from the Records of the Convention*
                   of the Royal Burghs of Scotland, ed.
                   J. D. Marwick (1870–90).

Burns, *Basle*   = J. H. Burns, *Scottish Churchmen and the*
                   Council of Basle (1962).

Cal. Close   = *Calendar of the Close Rolls preserved in the*
                   Public Record Office (1900–).

Cal. Docs. Scot.   = *Calendar of Documents relating to Scotland*,
                   ed. J. Bain (1881–8).

Cal. Papal Letters   = *Calendar of Entries in the Papal Registers*
                   relating to Great Britain and Ireland: Papal
                   Letters ed. W. H. Bliss and others (1893–).

Cal. Papal Petitions   = *Calendar of Entries in the Papal Registers*
                   relating to Great Britain and Ireland: Petitions
                   to the Pope, ed. W. H. Bliss (1896).

Cal. Patent   = *Calendar of the Patent Rolls preserved in the*
                   Public Record Office (1901–).

Cal. Scot. Supp.	= *Calendar of Scottish Supplications to Rome* (S.H.S., 1934–71).
Cambuskenneth Registrum	= *Registrum Monasterii S. Marie de Cambuskenneth* (Grampian Club, 1872).
Cameron, *Apostolic Camera*	= *The Apostolic Camera and Scottish Benefices*, ed. A. I. Cameron (1934).
Chron. Anonimalle	= *The Anonimalle Chronicle, 1333–81*, ed. V. H. Galbraith (1927).
Chron. Auchinleck	= *The Auchinleck Chronicle, ane schort memoriale of the scottis corniklis for addicioun*, ed. T. Thomson (Edinburgh, 1819, 1877).
Chron. Baker	= Geoffrey le Baker, *Chronicon*, ed. E. M. Thompson (1889).
Chron. Bower	= *Johannis de Fordun Scotichronicon cum Supplementis et Continuatione Walteri Bower*, ed. W. Goodall (Edinburgh, 1759).
Chron. Fordun	= *J. de Fordun, Cronica Gentis Scotorum*, ed. W. F. Skene (1871–2).
Chron. Froissart	= *The Chronicle of Froissart translated out of French by Sir John Bourchier, Lord Berners, annis 1523–25*, ed. W. P. Ker (1967).
Chron. Knighton	= Henry Knighton, *Chronicon*, ed. J. R. Lumby (R.S., 1889, 1895).
Chron. Lanercost	= *Chronicon de Lanercost* (Maitland Club, 1839).
Chron. Melsa	= *Chronica Monasterii de Melsa*, ed. E. A. Bond (R.S., 1867).
Chron. Pluscarden	= *Liber Pluscardensis*, ed. F. J. H. Skene (1877–80).
Chron. Walsingham	= Thomas Walsingham, *Historia Anglicana*, ed. H. T. Riley (R.S., 1863).
Chron. Wyntoun	=Andrew Wyntoun, *Orygynale Cronykil of Scotland*, ed. D. Laing (1872–79).
Conway, *Henry VII*	= Agnes Conway, *Henry VII's Relations with Scotland and Ireland, 1485–1498* (1932).
Coulton, *Scottish Abbeys*	= G. G. Coulton, *Scottish Abbeys and Social Life* (1933).
Davidson and Gray, *Staple*	= John Davidson and Alexander Gray, *The Scottish Staple at Veere* (1909).
Dowden, *Bishops*	= J. Dowden, *The Bishops of Scotland* (1912).
Dumfriesshire Trans.	= *Transactions of the Dumfriesshire and Galloway Natural History and Antiquarian Society* (1862–).

Dunbar, *Scot. Kings* = A. H. Dunbar, *Scottish Kings: A Revised Chronology of Scottish History*, 2nd edn. (1906).

Duncan, *Nation of Scots* = A. A. M. Duncan, *The Nation of Scots and the Declaration of Arbroath* (Historical Assoc., 1970).

Dunfermline Registrum = *Registrum de Dunfermelyn* (Bannatyne Club, 1842).

Dunlop, *Bishop Kennedy* = Annie I. Dunlop, *The Life and Times of James Kennedy, Bishop of St Andrews* (1950).

Durkan, *Bishop Turnbull* = John Durkan, *William Turnbull, Bishop of Glasgow* (1951).

Easson, *Religious Houses* = D. E. Easson, *Medieval Religious Houses: Scotland* (1957).

Edinburgh Burgh Recs. = *Extracts from the Records of the Burgh of Edinburgh* (S.B.R.S., 1869–92).

Edinburgh City Charters = *Charters and Other Documents Relating to the City of Edinburgh* (S.B.R.S., 1871).

E.H.R. = *English Historical Review*.

E.R. = *The Exchequer Rolls of Scotland*, ed. J. Stuart and others (Edinburgh, 1878–1908).

Extracta = *Extracta e Variis Cronicis Scocie* (Abbotsford Club, 1842).

Ferrerius, *Continuatio* = Hector Boethius, *Scotorum Historiae*, 2nd edn. (Paris, 1574), pp. 385 *et seq.* (*continuatio per Ioannem Ferrerium*).

Fife Court Bk. = *The Sheriff Court Book of Fife* (S.H.S., 1928).

Flodden Papers = *Flodden Papers, Diplomatic correspondence between the Courts of France and Scotland 1507–1517*, ed. Marguerite Wood (S.H.S., 1933).

Foedera = *Foedera, Conventiones, Literae . . . accurante Thoma Rymer*, 3rd edn. (The Hague, 1739–45).

Fraser, *Douglas* = W. Fraser, *The Douglas Book* (1885).

Glasgow Registrum = *Registrum Episcopatus Glasguensis* (Bannatyne and Maitland Clubs, 1843).

Godscroft, *Douglas and Angus* = David Hume of Godscroft, *The History of the Houses of Douglas and Angus* (Edinburgh, 1644).

Grant, *Social and Economic Development* = I. F. Grant, *The Social and Economic Development of Scotland before 1603* (1930).

Gregory, *Western Highlands*	= Donald Gregory, *History of the Western Highlands and Isles of Scotland from ... 1493 to ... 1625* (1881).
Hailes, *Annals*	= Sir David Dalrymple, Lord Hailes, *Annals of Scotland from the Accession of Malcolm III surnamed Canmore to the Restoration of James I*, 3rd edn. (Edinburgh, 1819).
H.B.C.	= *Handbook of British Chronology*, ed. F. M. Powicke and E. B. Fryde (1961).
Highland Papers	= *Highland Papers* (S.H.S., 1914–34).
H.M.C.	= *Reports of the Royal Commission on Historical Manuscripts* (1870–).
Innes, *Scot. Middle Ages*	= Cosmo Innes, *Scotland in the Middle Ages* (1860).
Innes, *Sketches*	= Cosmo Innes, *Sketches of Early Scotch History* (1861).
James I, Life and Death	= *The Life and Death of King James the First of Scotland* (Maitland Club, 1837).
James IV, Letters	= *The Letters of James IV* (S.H.S., 1953).
Kelso Liber	= *Liber S. Marie de Calchou* (Bannatyne Club, 1846).
Knox, *History*	= *John Knox's History of the Reformation in Scotland*, ed. W. C. Dickinson (1949).
Lesley, *History*	= J. Lesley, *The History of Scotland from the Death of King James I in the Year MCCCCXXXVI to the Year MDLXI* (Bannatyne Club, 1830).
Mackenzie, *Highlands and Isles*	= W. C. Mackenzie, *The Highlands and Isles of Scotland: A Historical Survey* (1949).
Mackenzie, *Flodden*	= W. M. Mackenzie, *The Secret of Flodden* (1931).
Mackie, *James IV*	= R. L. Mackie, *King James IV of Scotland, A Brief Survey of His Life and Times* (1958).
MacQueen, *Robert Henryson*	= John MacQueen, *Robert Henryson: A Study of the Major Narrative Poems* (1967).
Major, *History*	= J. Major, *A History of Greater Britain* (S.H.S., 1892).
Melrose Liber	= *Liber Sancte Marie de Melros* (Bannatyne Club, 1837).
Misc.	= *Miscellany* (of S.H.S. etc.).
Monro, *Western Isles*	= *Monro's Western Isles of Scotland and Genealogies of the Clans 1549*, ed. R. W. Munro (1961).

Moray Registrum	= *Registrum Episcopatus Moraviensis* (Bannatyne Club, 1837).
Morton Registrum	= *Registrum Honoris de Morton* (Bannatyne Club, 1853).
Nat. MSS. Scot.	= *Facsimiles of the National Manuscripts of Scotland* (London, 1867–73).
Nicholson, *Edward III*	= Ranald Nicholson, *Edward III and the Scots: the Formative Years of a Military Career, 1327–35* (1965).
Paisley Registrum	= *Registrum Monasterii de Passelet* (Maitland Club, 1832; New Club, 1877).
Palgrave, *Documents*	= *Documents and Records Illustrating the History of Scotland*, ed. F. Palgrave (London, 1837).
Patrick, *Statutes*	= *Statutes of the Scottish Church*, ed. D. Patrick (S.H.S., 1907).
Pinkerton, *History*	= J. Pinkerton, *The History of Scotland from the Accession of the House of Stuart to that of Mary, with Appendixes of Original Papers* (London, 1797).
Pryde, *Burghs*	= G. S. Pryde, *The Burghs of Scotland: A Critical List* (1965).
P.R.O.	= Public Record Office, London.
Pitscottie, *Historie*	= R. Lindesay of Pitscottie, *The Historie and Chronicles of Scotland* (S.T.S., 1899–1911).
Proc. Soc. Antiq. Scot.	= *Proceedings of the Society of Antiquaries of Scotland* (1851–).
Raine, *Letters*	= *Historical Papers and Letters from Northern Registers*, ed. Jas. Raine (R.S., 1873).
Rait, *Parliaments*	= R. S. Rait, *The Parliaments of Scotland* (1924).
Rashdall, *Universities*	= Hastings Rashdall, *The Universities of Europe in the Middle Ages* (1964).
R.M.S.	= *Registrum Magni Sigilli Regum Scotorum*, ed. J. M. Thomson and others (1882–1914).
Robertson, *Concilia*	= *Concilia Scotiae* (Half Title: *Statuta Ecclesiae Scoticanae*), ed. J. Robertson (Bannatyne Club, 1866).
Rot. Parl.	= *Rotuli Parliamentorum ut et Petitiones et Placita in Parliamento* (1783).
Rot. Scot.	= *Rotuli Scotiae in Turri Londinensi et in Domo Capitulari Westmonasteriensi Asservati*, ed. D. Macpherson and others (1814–19).

R.P.C.	= *Register of the Privy Council of Scotland*, ed. J. H. Burton and others (1877–).
R.S.	= Rolls Series.
R.S.S.	= *Registrum Secreti Sigilli Regum Scotorum*, ed. M. Livingstone and others (1908–).
St Andrews Acta	= *Acta Facultatis Artium Universitatis S. Andree 1413–1588* (S.H.S., 1964).
St Andrews Copiale	= *Copiale Prioratus Sanctiandree* ed. J. H. Baxter (1930).
St Andrews Univ. Recs.	= *The Early Records of the University of St Andrews* (S.H.S., 1926).
Scalacronica	= *Scalacronica, by Sir Thomas Gray of Heton, Knight* (Maitland Club, 1836).
S.B.R.S.	= Scottish Burgh Records Society.
Scot. Church Hist. Soc. Recs.	= *Records of the Scottish Church History Society* (1926–).
Scot. Legal Hist.	= *An Introduction to Scottish Legal History* (Stair Soc., 1958).
Scots Peerage	= *The Scots Peerage*, ed. Sir J. Balfour Paul (1904–14).
S.H.R.	= *Scottish Historical Review* (1903–28, 1947–).
S.H.S.	= Scottish History Society.
Sources of Scots Law	= *An Introductory Survey of the Sources and Literature of Scots Law* (Stair Soc., 1936).
Stevenson, *Documents*	= *Documents Illustrative of the History of Scotland*, ed. J. Stevenson (1870).
Stones, *Documents*	= E. L. G. Stones, *Anglo-Scottish Relations, 1174–1328: Some selected documents* (1964).
S.T.S.	= Scottish Text Society.
T.A.	= *Accounts of the Lord High Treasurer of Scotland*, ed. T. Dickson and Sir J. Balfour Paul (1877–1916).
'Trewe Encountre'	= 'A contemporary account of the battle of Flodden', *Proc. Soc. Antiq. Scot.*, VII (1866–7). 141–52.
T.R.H.S.	= *Transactions of the Royal Historical Society.*
Tytler, *History*	= Patrick Fraser Tytler, *The History of Scotland* (1887).
Vita Edwardi	= *Vita Edwardi Secundi monachi cuiusdam Malmesberiensis*, ed. and trs. N. Denholm-Young (1957).

Watt, *Fasti*   = *Fasti Ecclesiae Scoticanae Medii Aevi*, ed.
                                D. E. R. Watt (1969).

Wigtown Charters   = *Wigtownshire Charters* (S.H.S., 1960).

Wittig, *Scottish*   = Kurt Wittig, *The Scottish Tradition in*
  Tradition   *Literature* (1958).

1

SCOTLAND AT THE CLOSE OF THE THIRTEENTH CENTURY: SOCIETY, ECONOMY AND INSTITUTIONS

Despite the alarms and vicissitudes of the years between 1286 and 1296 they were years of lingering peace. Within Scotland there was discord, even civil war, but there was no armed conflict with an external foe, and little to show that the relatively golden age of the Alexanders was about to be followed by one of blood and iron. When it came, the change was unforeseen, sudden and traumatic. With the beginning of the Anglo-Scottish wars in 1296 there was an end, so far as Scotland was concerned, to the formative years of the earlier Middle Ages. Preceding centuries of rapid innovation were succeeded by others of slow and erratic development. The last decade of peace summed up achievements that coming generations had to strive to regain before attempting to surpass. What was characteristic of Scotland during that decade impressed itself as a pattern that was afterwards modified, but which was nonetheless still perceptible centuries later.

The pattern was unique. It showed some features that were common throughout western Europe, together with others that were indigenous. For though the Scots were not wholly isolated, they dwelt (so affirmed the Declaration of Arbroath) in a land 'beyond which there is no habitation', distant by two months journey from the papal court at Rome which was the centre of western Christendom.

Within Scotland itself, geography fostered diversity and particularism. Yet the physical features of the land amounted to hindrances rather than absolute barriers. By horseback the normal day's journey was one of twenty miles; but with relays of horses it was possible for a man to cover eighty. The king's highway, the *via regis*, passed from one royal burgh and royal castle to another, forming a network of recognised routes in the more developed parts of Scotland. The Tweed could be crossed by ford or by bridges at Berwick and Roxburgh. The Tay could be crossed by the bridge at Perth. The Forth could be crossed not only by the bridge at Stirling but by the ferries of Airth, Queensferry and Earlsferry. And a river might be not so much a barrier as a route of communication: the Forth was navigable by seagoing vessels as far as Stirling, the Tay as far as Perth, though the Clyde, not artificially deepened until more modern times, could take ships only as far as Dumbarton, so that Glasgow was no bustling sea-port but a sleepy inland market town and ecclesiastical centre. The importance of water-borne traffic meant that an inland loch might be the nucleus of a parish or barony. Among the sea-lochs and islands of the west, where the population was part Norse in descent, much use was made of galleys propelled by oars and fitted with an auxiliary mast and sail.

Linked together in a scheme of communications which differed from that of the present day was a population of some 400,000 whose distribution corresponded to a society that was agricultural, not industrial. Although there were over fifty burghs, they can have comprised scarce ten per cent of the population, for a typical burgh was rarely more than a street or 'gait' leading to the castle that almost invariably rose beside it. It was the existence of a cathedral which alone conferred the title of 'city' and brought distinction not only to Aberdeen, a leading burgh, but to places like Brechin and Glasgow which perhaps had a few hundred inhabitants apiece. Though townsfolk were few, the rural population was probably as large as at the present day, particularly where the land was fertile—around the estuaries of the Forth and Tay, in the lower reaches of the Tweed valley, and in parts of Moray and Galloway. Even in these areas, however, the typical rural community was not that of a 'nucleated' village, for the population was fairly evenly spread over the land that sustained it.[1] Settlements took the form of steadings (isolated farms) or 'touns' (townships) dispersed over the lands of a barony. Their inhabitants were subject to the baron's court, which had more than a

[1] See Lord Cooper, 'The Numbers and the Distribution of the Population of Medieval Scotland', *S.H.R.*, xxvi. 2–9; G. W. S. Barrow, Rural Settlement in Central and Eastern Scotland: the medieval evidence', *Scottish Studies*, vi. 123–44.

judicial function: it organised and supervised their labours and thereby instilled a sense of community.

The original functional basis of each township was probably the plough-team. The heavy wooden plough needed six or eight oxen to drag it. Almost as many men were needed to urge it on its way. This was reflected in the measurement of land commonly used in the Lowlands: the arable land of a township was normally one plough-gate (or ploughgang) supposedly amounting to 120 English acres or 104 Scots acres, though not necessarily in one compact tract. North of Perth, where the usual measurement was the davoch (comparable to four ploughgates)[2] the underlying concept was not area but productivity. Even the ploughgate seldom represented a measured area, but rather a notion of the amount of land a plough team could cope with. It was made up of eight oxgates (or oxgangs). A husbandman was supposed to contribute two oxen and thus be entitled to two oxgates or one 'husbandland'.[3] But a rich husbandman might possess a whole plough-team of oxen; a poor one might have only a half share in an ox;[4] a more depressed class, the cottars, owned no oxen and were enjoined to use the foot-plough.[5] It was usual for a group of between four and sixteen husbandmen to act as joint tenants and to combine their resources both in tilling the soil and in paying the rent in money, produce and labour services. The various shares in the plough-team probably determined the share that each husbandman paid in rent as well as his share in the common arable lands. These lands were from time to time re-allocated according to the practice of 'run-rig'. Although the word is not found in a written source prior to 1437,[6] the practice it described was doubtless older. The method of ploughing had the effect of dividing the arable land into strips or 'rigs', some twenty or thirty feet wide, and of separating these by shallow ditches, the upcast topsoil of the ditches both raising the height of the rigs and improving their quality.

Rig cultivation was an answer to a main problem of Scottish agriculture, that of drainage. The rigs ran downhill so that the ditches dividing them played the part of field drains. This method could not

[2] *E.R.*, XIII. cxxxix.

[3] An interesting entry in the Colvil MS. states: 'Anno Domini [blank] the erll of Marche causit his servand Sim Samond to divide the haill landis in the Mers in husband landis, ilk husband land xxvj akkeris quhair pluk [plough] & syth may gang.' (*A.P.S.*, I. Notices of Manuscripts, xxiv).

[4] *Ibid.*, II. 8, c. 20.

[5] *Ibid.*, I. 397; II. 8, c. 20.

[6] Grant, *Social and Economic Development*, p. 287, n. 2.

be successfully applied to the level carses or straths that bordered many a Scottish river. These potentially fertile lands were undrained bogs or were used as summer pasture while the plough-teams toiled up and down the rigs on the neighbouring slopes. These received whatever manure was available and were sown year after year with coarse barley (bere) or oats, more rarely with wheat. From time to time the cultivated 'infield' would be expanded when part of the outlying land, the 'outfield', was manured by folding cattle upon it, thereafter being ploughed and cropped until its fertility was exhausted. The higher slopes, the roughest and wettest pieces of ground, were kept for grazing. In both Highlands and Lowlands, however, there were large tracts that were unsuitable even for grazing. Vast peat bogs provided fuel but little else. The Scottish 'forests' were mostly destitute of trees and used as game reserves for hunting, hawking and fishing. These sporting pursuits played an important part in the economy and, particularly in the Highlands, might make the difference between famine and plenty.

Although the Highlands were less suited to arable farming than the Lowlands, the rearing of cattle and sheep was probably of more significance in both areas alike than was the cultivation of crops. There are traces of an official campaign to encourage tillage and to prevent earls, barons and freeholders 'wastand thair landis and the cuntre with multitud of scheip and bestis'.[7] But a sixteenth-century writer could still assert that the country was 'more gevin to store of bestiall than ony production of cornys'.[8] The agrarian difference between Highlands and Lowlands was not so much that the one region was pastoral and the other agricultural, but rather that the Highlands concentrated on cattle-rearing and the Lowlands on sheep-farming.

For mixed farming was universal. A share in the arable lands carried with it grazing rights for so many head of sheep or cattle. Both in Highlands and Lowlands, there was a migration to the summer shielings, usually, but not always, on the upper slopes. There the men guarded the herds and flocks from wolves and foxes and sheared the sheep; the women carded and spun wool and made butter and cheese from the milk of cows and ewes. By the use of summer shielings the animals were removed from the growing crops in the open fields— for the only permanently fenced enclosures were parks for the preservation of game. The practice of transhumance also helped to conserve

[7] *A.P.S.*, I. 382, 397; II. 8, c. 20; *Chron. Wyntoun*, II. 265–6.
[8] Bellenden, cited in *Scot. Legal Hist.*, p. 286.

scarce winter fodder. Even so, it was necessary around Martinmas (11 November) to slaughter most of the cattle, keeping just enough for breeding and to draw the plough. Over winter there was no fresh meat save what could be got by hunting. The population lived on the salted carcases of the 'marts', eked out with oatmeal, barley-bread and salted or dried fish. There were violent fluctuations in the food supply, and it was not easy to relieve wholesale famine by imports of corn from abroad.

In a society whose main concern was land and its produce it was natural that personal status should depend on the amount of land held and the way in which it was held. Landholding, as it affected the whole range of society from serf to king, presented a variety that almost defies classification. The essential dividing line was between the minority, the free tenants (*libere tenentes*), who held their land by homage and fealty, quit of labour service or any other 'dishonourable' burden, and the vast majority who lived and worked upon the land but enjoyed neither secure tenure nor complete personal freedom. Various terms, with different shades of meaning, were used to describe this vast servile or semi-servile class—*nativi*, *bondi*, neyfs, carls, cumlaws, *rustici*, churls and husbandmen. Some were still outright slaves, 'thai that ar of foul kyn',[9] who, if they fled from their master, could be led back by the nose.[10] Many were tied to the soil (*adscripti glebe*) and could not depart from the barony without their lord's permission. In the Gaelic areas there was also a semi-servile class, known in Ireland as *betagh*, relegated to humdrum toil while their betters engaged in the aristocratic pursuits of fighting, hunting, fishing, or steering a galley.

There was, however, a tendency for servile status to disappear, or at least to be mitigated. While the husbandman had to provide boon work, labour for stipulated periods on the demesne lands, and pay the 'heriot' and 'merchet' that signalised his semi-servile condition, he might rise in the world if these obligations were commuted into cash payments. Though this process was not completed until modern times it had already begun on the lands of Kelso Abbey and elsewhere in Scotland.[11] This development held out prospects to the husbandman with capital and initiative. Legislation attributed to

9 *A.P.S.*, i. 401. See also 'A gud were of law', *ibid.*, 753.
10 *Quoniam Attachiamenta, ibid.*, 655.
11 *Kelso Liber*, ii. 455–6.

Alexander II alludes to 'malaris of carls born',[12] men of base descent who paid 'maill' or money rent. Usually the husbandman paid maill for a year at a time and his tenure was secure only for that year; he might have cottars working under him who were his tenants-at-will and could be dismissed without warning from their croft and kail yard. It was possible, however, for a husbandman to obtain a 'tack' (a lease of land) for a number of years (often three or five) in return for a fixed yearly 'ferm' (*firma*) in cash. The 'fermour' (*firmarius*) might be no husbandman but someone of higher status who wished to invest in the exploitation of a large holding of land. Such a tenure might be not merely for a term of years, as in the case of a tack; it could be granted in liferent—it might even be perpetual and heritable, held 'in feu'. So came about the concept of tenure 'in feu-ferm' (*in feudifirma*). This term, already found in ecclesiastical chartularies and in the exchequer rolls, signified a heritable grant of land in return for a fixed and perpetual money rent.[13]

Nonetheless the hybrid feu-ferm tenure was still rare and undefined. It conveyed less authority and prestige than the earlier forms of feudal tenure in which land was held in return for knight-service or a token payment (blench-ferm) or prayers (*in elemosina*). These feudal tenures might be regarded as a superstructure erected over the subordinate forms of Scottish landholding that concerned the bulk of the population. A grant in feudal form, usually made by a written charter issued by the 'superior', conferred upon a vassal a fief which was heritable, held by the vassal and his heirs 'of' the superior and his heirs, and this connection was symbolised by the swearing of fealty and the performance of homage. Though families might come and go, the fiefs that they had held remained. A fief was a continuing entity, theoretically indivisible save in the circumstance of descent to co-heiresses. It was imbued with obligations that might be real or merely nominal, but were always 'honourable'. It was imbued also with inherent privileges, not least economic privileges. If the fief was a barony its holder had the right to exploit its woods, its arable and pasture lands, its fishing waters, its deposits of peat and minerals. He might take tolls from those who used the tracks that ran through it. If he built a watermill the men of the barony were 'thirled' to it and had to pay 'multure' for the compulsory facility of grinding their corn there. There was much concern over what a barony was worth,

[12] *A.P.S.*, I. 401.
[13] A survey of the development of feu-ferm from the twelfth century to the sixteenth is given in *E.R.*, XIII. cxiii–cxxv.

and 'extents' or surveys were often carried out to assess its rental in money and kind. The rental interested not only the holder of the fief but the superior of whom it was held : apart from any service that was stipulated, most fiefs were bound to render to the superior the customary feudal 'aids' and the 'casualties' of wardship, marriage and relief. The specific or implied conditions on which fiefs were held provided a basis for justice, administration, military service and land law. When land and its produce provided the chief source of wealth it was feudal land law that ultimately controlled economic life. Theoretically a vassal might not dispose of his fief save by limited sub-infeudation or resignation to the superior. In practice, however, land could be disposed of in any way by obtaining from the superior (at a price) a charter of confirmation to cover the transaction. Whether homage and oaths of fealty kept their pristine significance is questionable. Often they must have been looked upon only as a form of land registration, the traditional and formal method of completing, or renewing, a business bargain between landlord and tenant.

In England the statute *Quia Emptores* of 1290, drawn up in the interests of the king and the greater landholders, tended to eliminate the intermediate stages between the top and the bottom of the feudal 'pyramid'. In Scotland no such measure ever operated : the pyramid of free tenants existed with its intermediate stages intact. At its apex was the king. Those who held fiefs directly of the king were his tenants-in-chief, who in their turn might have subordinate feudal tenants. The category of tenants-in-chief was wide : it included some persons of relative obscurity and excluded others who might hold broad lands not directly of the king but of a baron. Thus a man's position on the tenurial pyramid did not in itself determine his social or political standing. Wealth, the holding of office, experience in government, administration or warfare, all these counted.

Noble birth counted most of all and was emphasised by the devices of heraldry. Scarcely yet, however, was noble birth marked by the award of titles. In the Gaelic areas illustrious descent and the formal recognition of the immediate kinsfolk was enough to make a man a chief. In the north-east there were some fifty thanes; but the word 'thane' was merely one of office applied to the holders of a particular kind of heritable stewardship. No one was created a baron : anyone who held a barony—a fief with a court in which public justice could be dispensed—simply *was* a baron. Nor were lords created : the term 'lord' could be applied to any baron; and a 'lordship' denoted nothing more than a barony, although in the Gaelic areas it might correspond more closely to the type of petty kingdom known in Ireland as a *tuath*. Knights were certainly created (not necessarily by the king) but the rank they held was military and was granted in recognition, or expectation, of service in war. On the other hand the thirteen earls of Scotland were distinguished by the fact that only they possessed a specific and heritable title of dignity; and this title, conferred by the king upon them or their predecessors, carried a social and political rank nearest to that of the king himself.

The hierarchical structure of lay society was matched by another and more clearly defined hierarchy, that of the kirk, which occupied a place in society far greater than it holds today. No one questioned the literal truth of any passage in the Bible. The saints were not remote [14] and would intervene in this world to punish those who scorned them,[15] or to reward those who venerated their name and their relics.[16] Their feast days, together with pilgrimages to their shrines, were the medieval equivalent of holidays and tourism, although they carried more serious overtones. For the bliss of heaven and the pains of hell were real, and the concept of morality was more broadly based than that of the present day when only one sin attracts attention while its six deadly companions are scarcely remembered : in the Middle Ages each of the seven could earn damnation. It was believed, however, that 'the super-abundant merits of Christ, the Virgin Mary and the Saints formed a celestial treasury, out of which the debts of individual penitents could be paid'. This treasury of merits was at the disposal of the priests who heard confession and through the sacrament of penance granted remission of ever-lasting punishment. Nonetheless the forgiven sinner had to pay the wages of his sin either on earth or in purgatory, the intermediate existence between heaven and hell. The pains of purgatory could in turn be avoided, or mitigated, by good works, by the prayers of monks, by the celebration of the sacrifice of the mass, by indulgences granted by the pope.[17]

Not surprisingly, the influence of the clergy was great. Comparable to the thirteen Scottish earls were the twelve Scottish bishops.

---

[14] Thus in 1459 an inquest found that 'the Blessed Virgin Mary, our Lady, was the last possessor of the lands of Brochton . . . and Sir John Denum, chaplain, took sasine of the said lands on the part of our foresaid Lady with a portrait painted on paper' (cited in Dunlop, *Bishop Kennedy*, p. 421).

[15] See *Chron. Bower*, II. 462.

[16] *Ibid.*, 250.

[17] A. I. Dunlop, 'Remissions and Indulgences in Fifteenth Century Scotland', *Scot. Church Hist. Soc. Recs.*, xv. 153–67, at 154–5.

Comparable to the barons were the abbots, priors, cathedral deans and archdeacons. All of these prelates, together with the earls and barons, were 'magnates' and, under the king, shared in government and administration. Moreover, bishops, abbots and priors controlled the lands and property (the 'temporalities') with which their bishopric, abbey or priory had been endowed. In respect of these temporalities they were tenants-in-chief of the king. In contrast to the lay magnates, however, their position was not hereditary : they held their lands by virtue of their ecclesiastical office. They were elected to that office by the chapter of their cathedral, abbey or priory, usually after the king's approval. They had then to seek confirmation of the election by the pope, to whom they swore obedience. Bishops would be consecrated either at the papal court or by three Scottish bishops specially commissioned by a papal bull—a letter sealed with the pope's seal (*bulla*). The king then invested the new bishop in his temporalities, for which he swore fealty and did homage. Their oaths of fealty to the king and obedience to the pope sometimes involved the prelates in conflicting loyalties; and since the prelates were mostly kinsmen or clients of king or barons the appointments to the great benefices were usually conducted against a background of contesting claims, ambiguity, dispute and intervention. The last word lay with the pope. His powers were not limited to confirmation of an 'elect'. He might quash or disregard an election. In 1233 he had 'provided' a bishop of Dunblane. Of the twelve bishops in office in 1296 five had been provided by the pope.[18]

The *plenitudo potestatis* of the pope—his fulness of power in any spiritual matter—extended beyond appointments. His was the authority to give a final decision and to confer any spiritual benefit. From the decisions of diocesan courts litigants appealed to the papal court (*curia*). Dispensations from the requirements of canon law, indulgences, absolution, spiritual grace in all its forms, could be obtained from the pope. Recourse to the *curia* was costly and often had to be financed by loans from Italian bankers, whose operations extended even to Scotland.[19] Nonetheless, the obstacles of distance and expense did not stop the flow of appeals and petitions to Rome and the return flow of letters of grace and papal bulls.

The process was perhaps encouraged by conditions peculiar to

18 For the growth of papal provisions see George P. Innes, 'Ecclesiastical Patronage in Scotland in the Later Middle Ages', *Scot. Church Hist. Soc. Recs.*, XIII. 73–83.

19 *Rot. Scot.*, I. 6–7.

Scotland :[20] for although it was a distinct ecclesiastical 'province' it had as yet no archbishop to act as metropolitan and supervise its kirk. This anomaly had been recognised in 1192 when a papal bull had made the Scottish kirk a 'special daughter' of Rome. Two bishoprics were excluded from this privilege : the see of Galloway was part of the province of York ; the see of Sodor (or the Isles) was subject to the Norwegian archbishop of Nidaros (Trondheim). The other ten bishops, however, were answerable only to the pope. A bull of 1225 allowed them to hold a provincial council at which it became the practice to choose one bishop as a temporary 'conservator of the privileges of the Scottish kirk'. This device preserved the formal parity of the Scottish bishops. But if all were equal, two, St Andrews and Glasgow, were more equal than the rest, or at least far richer.

The disparity in wealth among the bishoprics was reflected in the scale of their cathedrals (by this time mostly completed) and in the number of canons—a mere handful or more than thirty—who served them.[21] It was also reflected in the complexity or the simplicity of diocesan organisation. St Andrews had two archdeaconries (St Andrews and Lothian) subdivided into eight rural deaneries. The organisation of the diocese of Glasgow was similar.[22] But these two dioceses, with over two hundred parish kirks apiece, were exceptional in Scotland and together included almost half the total of about eleven hundred parishes.

By the end of the thirteenth century Scotland had already obtained almost the full complement of parish kirks that it was to possess down to the Reformation.[23] When a patron built a kirk he also endowed it, often with a ploughgate of land. In addition to the rents obtainable from this kirkland the parson or *rector* had the right to the teinds of the parish. The teinds (tithes) represented a tenth of all annual increase, such as the tenth sheaf in the fields after harvest, or the tenth calf that was born. Apart from the teinds there were offerings, and these, together with mortuary dues and other fees, formed a large part of the parson's income. In 1275 Boiamund de Vitia had arrived as a papal collector and had set down the revenue of each kirk in the so-called 'Bagimond's Roll' to be used as a basis of taxation by the papacy. The resources available from an aggregation of kirks are

[20] *Cal. Scot. Supp. 1418–1422*, p. xii.

[21] See Ian B. Cowan, 'The Organisation of Scottish Secular Cathedral Chapters', *Scot. Church Hist. Soc. Recs.*, XIV. 19–47.

[22] See Watt, *Fasti*, pp. 143–96, 289–332.

[23] See Ian B. Cowan, 'The Development of the Parochial System in Medieval Scotland', *S.H.R.*, XL. 43–55, and his *Parishes of Medieval Scotland*.

shown by the fact that over a six-year period those in the diocese of Glasgow alone produced 'tenths' amounting to £4,575 3s. 6¾d.[24]—a vast sum by contemporary standards.

While monasteries, cathedrals and episcopal households had landed revenues of their own on which to draw, it was largely by the accumulation of parish kirks that they were financed. Arbroath Abbey had been gifted thirty-three parish kirks *in proprios usus*, a term that conveyed to the abbey all the rights and revenues that pertained to the parson (*rector*) of each kirk. If a kirk was 'appropriated' in this way the abbey as *rector* uplifted most of the revenues and appointed a vicar to serve the parish. At this period the latter would normally be a 'vicar perpetual', who had some security of tenure, and his income would include a share in the teinds.[25] But although a statute of the provincial council accorded the vicars a reasonable minimum income of ten marks a year (£6 13s. 4d.)—a fair professional salary for the time—this statute was not always observed. The appropriation system held 'temptations to injustice' and 'risks of friction'.[26] There was a danger that well-qualified men might not be attracted to the sweated labour of an ill-paid parish priest and that the spiritual life of the parishes might suffer. The danger was not, however, widely realised. By 1286 appropriation had gone far and it was still to continue; in 1521 John Major remarked that it had gone 'beyond what was wise'.[27] While only about one third of the English parishes were appropriated, the Scottish parishes were eventually nearly all appropriated.[28] Over a hundred and fifty were already appropriated to five monasteries alone—Arbroath, Paisley, Kelso, Melrose and Holyrood.[29] It was often at the expense of the parishes that monasticism flourished.

By 1273, when Lady Devorgilla Balliol founded Sweetheart Abbey, monastic development in Scotland was virtually complete and all the chief religious orders save the Carthusians were represented.[30]

---

[24] See A. I. Dunlop, 'Bagimond's Roll', *S.H.S. Misc. VI.* 3–77, at 25, also *ibid., V.* 79–106; *X.* 1–9.

[25] Ian B. Cowan, 'Vicarages and the Cure of Souls in Medieval Scotland', *Scot. Church Hist. Soc. Recs.*, XVI. 111–27.

[26] Coulton, *Scottish Abbeys*, pp. 99, 77–80.

[27] Major, *History*, p. 136.

[28] Ian B. Cowan, 'Some Aspects of the Appropriation of Parish Churches in Medieval Scotland', *Scot. Church Hist. Soc. Recs.*, XIII. 203–22, at 205.

[29] See Ian B. Cowan, *The Parishes of Medieval Scotland*. The appendix lists the kirks appropriated to each religious institution.

[30] For details of the religious orders and their Scottish foundations, see Easson, *Religious Houses*.

These orders may be divided into two main groups—the monks and the canons regular. The monks were 'cloistered' and followed the Benedictine rule or the modifications of it that had been adopted at Cluny, Tiron, Cîteaux, or Val des Choux.[31] The Augustinian and Premonstratensian canons regular, like monks, lived according to a rule (*regula*), but one which allowed them to leave the bounds of their cloister, even to serve a parish kirk.[32] In Scotland the Augustinians were comparable in importance to the Cistercians: though the latter possessed eleven abbeys the former were established at Holyrood and Scone; their priory of St Andrews was not only the richest religious house in Scotland but its canons acted as the chapter of the cathedral of St Andrews.

By English or continental standards no Scottish religious house was particularly wealthy; yet in relation to the country's slender resources the religious houses were extremely well endowed. In the thirteenth century when the monastic population reached its peak it can hardly have been more than a thousand. Piety never wholly disappeared; but 'since so much wealth was in so few hands, the social status of the monk was high'; there were 'self-interested converts' and 'the cloister was becoming an almshouse for the nobility'.[33] This was even more true of the few nunneries that provided respectable retreats for well-born ladies whose marriage prospects were blighted.

From the thirteenth century onwards a new ecclesiastical development, the rise of the mendicant orders, supplemented the work of parish priests, monks and canons regular, and overshadowed the lingering eremitical tradition still represented by a few hermits and anchorites.[34] By 1286 the friars preachers (Dominicans or black friars) had at least twelve friaries in Scotland; the friars minor (Franciscans or grey friars) had six; the Carmelites (white friars) had three; and expansion was to continue throughout the Middle Ages.[35] The friaries were invariably established in the burghs, and their relatively small endowments came mainly from burghal rents. While the friars lived a communal life they were not cloistered. Their work (and their mendicant vocation) took them among the people. Whereas the monastic

---

[31] Monastic rules and monastic life are discussed in Coulton, *Scottish Abbeys*.

[32] Ian B. Cowan, 'The Religious and the Cure of Souls in Medieval Scotland', *Scot. Church Hist. Soc. Recs.*, XIV. 215–30.

[33] Coulton, *Scottish Abbeys*, pp. 35, 49, 251.

[34] See D. McRoberts, 'Hermits in Medieval Scotland', *Innes Review*, XVI. 199–216.

[35] Easson, *Religious Houses*, pp. 96–119.

orders stressed prayer, meditation, and a withdrawal from the world, and it was no part of the duty of a monk to preach, the friars preached, acted as confessors, and ministered to the poor and the sick.

It was not, however, the friars alone who were responsible for charitable works. Charity was a means by which any man might acquire spiritual grace. Before the Reformation more than a hundred foundations had been made of leper-houses, almshouses, hospitals and hospices for pilgrims and travellers.[36] Almost half of these had definitely been founded before 1296 and the proportion may well have been higher. In addition, all ecclesiastical establishments were expected to relieve the poor and furnish hospitality to pilgrims and travellers (and the royal household as well).

Another social service that concerned the kirk was teaching, for 'the notion of a purely secular education was unknown'. So also was the idea that even elementary education should be available to all; no systematic attempt was made to provide it on a parochial basis. But if education was 'fostered by the church to subserve the church's ends' [37] it subserved other ends as well. The novice or song schools of the cathedrals and religious houses taught potential monks, canons, friars, vicars-choral and choristers how to sing plain-song and read (if not understand) Latin. These schools, which were probably open, at a price, to boys of the locality,[38] gave the aptest scholars the means of acquiring further learning. Moreover, the chancellor of a cathedral had responsibility for the running of a 'grammar school' in which Latin, the language of higher education, was inculcated. Such grammar schools were not confined to the cathedral precincts but were already to be found in the burghs. As yet, however, there was no *studium generale* entitled to confer a university degree. A degree had to be obtained outside Scotland, usually at Paris, or perhaps at Oxford, where Lady Devorgilla Balliol had recently founded Balliol College and where John Duns, a Scottish Franciscan, was making his mark in Merton College as a theologian and philosopher of lasting repute. It is perhaps difficult to reconcile the view that 'the standard of school education in Scotland was, as compared with England and

---

[36] *Ibid.*, pp. 134–65; John Durkan, 'Care of the Poor: Pre-Reformation Hospitals', *Innes Review*, x. 268–80.

[37] D. E. Easson, 'The Medieval Church in Scotland and Education', *Scot. Church Hist. Soc. Recs.*, VI. 13–26, at 21, 24, 25

[38] *Kelso Liber*, I. No. 173.

France, decidedly low'[39] with the fact that in thirteenth-century Scotland graduates formed 'a normal feature of the social scene'.[40]

The importance of the kirk was not limited to its spiritual and social works: in employing the resources that had been piously bestowed upon it the kirk made a direct and material contribution to the economic development of Scotland, sometimes proving itself a pastor of sheep as well as of souls. The Cistercians in particular specialised in sheep-farming and had granges and shielings on the Galloway moors, the Lammermuir hills and the glens of Angus. Those of Newbattle had even begun to exploit the nearby coal seams and to produce salt at Prestonpans by boiling the sea water. Almost every religious house owned tenements in the burghs and used them to promote its own trade, both local and overseas. Some bishops and abbots obtained royal charters allowing them to set up burghs of their own, such as St Andrews and Glasgow.

Their example was followed by the barons: Robert Bruce had a burgh at Annan, James the Steward had one at Renfrew, and there existed at least eight other baronial burghs.[41] By the late sixteenth century it could be contemptuously assumed that such burghs were 'thrallit to serve ane raice of pepill'[42]—they allegedly served a mere baronial family, whereas the community of burgesses of a royal burgh held their burgh as tenants of the king. In the thirteenth century however, distinctions among the various types of burgh—royal, baronial or ecclesiastical—were not so obvious as at later times: all burghs were 'free' (privileged) burghs,[43] at least in the sense that all burghs enjoyed the 'freedom' of burghal law. Yet distinctions were beginning to be made: the royal burgesses thought themselves by virtue of their tenure to be superior to other burgesses;[44] and they profited from the close connection between the king's burghs, the king's castles, the sheriffdoms, the royal administration and royal finance. For the royal burghs provided the king with various revenues, including 'maills' (rents), the profits of the burgh court, and the tolls or 'petty customs'[45] levied on goods entering the burgh for

[39] D. E. Easson, op. cit., Scot. Church Hist. Soc. Recs., VI. 13–26, at 25.

[40] Donald E. R. Watt, 'University Graduates in Scottish Benefices before 1410', ibid., XV. 77–88, at 77.

[41] See Pryde, Burghs, Section II, and Kirkintilloch Burgh Court Book (S.H.S.), pp. xi–xviii.

[42] Burghs Convention Recs., I. 321.

[43] Kirkintilloch Burgh Court Book (S.H.S.), pp. xxxiv, xxxvii–xl.

[44] See Leges Quatuor Burgorum, cap. xiii (A.P.S., I. 335).

[45] For a list of these see Assisa de Tolloneis (ibid., 667–70).

sale in its market. These miscellaneous revenues might be assessed and the right to collect them granted each year for a stipulated sum (ferm). To the king the ferms forthcoming from his burghs represented a useful, but by no means the foremost, source of revenue : in 1264 his chamberlain accounted for burgh ferms (less allowances) amounting to £675 18s. 2½d. ;[46] as much might be obtained as feudal 'relief' from one important tenant-in-chief.[47]

But distinct from the burgh ferms there was an increasingly important revenue collected *in* the burghs, though not *from* the burghs : whilst there were no import duties, save anchorage dues,[48] the king had begun to levy a 'new custom'[49] (later known as the 'maltote' or 'great custom') on the wool, woolfells (fleeces) and hides exported from Scotland. And these 'staple goods', which, together with fish, were virtually the sole Scottish exports, could be lawfully exported only from a burgh.

Of the king's burghs twenty-three out of the total of thirty-six[50] were situated on the east coast, or had subordinate havens upon it. To these ports came vessels laden with the fine cloth and manufactures of Flanders and Lombardy, the wines of France, timber from the Baltic, oriental luxuries, and the spices that made a winter diet of salt beef palatable. A company of Lombards sought to set up a trading post at Cramond or Queensferry but was thwarted through the opposition of the merchants of Edinburgh, probably already organised in their own merchant gild. Hanseatic merchants and men from Cologne were trading in Scotland,[51] while the Flemings had a trading post in the Red Hall in Berwick. But Scottish merchants were not content to do business only in their own home burghs : when their goods were arrested in Flanders in 1292 the value came to £1,459 8s. 0d.[52]—a sizable figure by contemporary standards.

The enterprise of Scottish merchants was aided by the development of merchant gilds. These were brotherhoods founded upon oath

[46] *E.R.*, I. 10. This sum may be compared with the chamberlain's accounts of proceeds of the crown demesnes (£2,896 18s. 3d.) and the 'common receipts', fines and feudal casualties (£1,808 5s. 0½d.).

[47] In 1293 the relief of the Scottish lands of the Earl of Buchan was put at 1,097 marks, that is £731 6s. 8d. (Stevenson, *Documents*, I. No. cccvii).

[48] See *Custuma Portuum* (*A.P.S.*, I. 671–2).

[49] Documents relating to this export duty are mentioned in a contemporary list of the royal muniments (*ibid.*, 114, 118); see also Stevenson, *Documents*, II. 487.

[50] See Pryde, *Burghs*, Section I.

[51] J. W. Dilley, 'German Merchants in Scotland, 1297–1327', *S.H.R.*, XVII. 142–55.

[52] Stevenson, *Documents*, I. No. ccxlviii.

and pledge, fostered by a gild court, common gatherings, common religious worship, and social benefits limited to the members and their families. The gild was not a national organisation : its trading privileges, such as the exclusive right to deal in staple goods, were based upon a burgh. For each burgh was the centre for a defined trade precinct which, in the case of some royal burghs, might amount to a whole sheriffdom. It was hopefully envisaged that within this trade-precinct goods, or at least staple goods, would invariably go for sale to the burgh market. And if the burgh possessed a merchant gild it was the gild merchants who profited most from this monopoly.

Even in the late thirteenth century there is evidence of the existence of a gild only in the more important burghs—Perth, Aberdeen, Stirling, Dundee, Elgin and Berwick. In the case of Berwick, the most important Scottish burgh, a set of *Statuta Gilde*, rules of the gild, survives, of which the last nine chapters are dated between 1281 and 1294.[53] From these statutes it is evident that the Berwick gild was both a merchant gild and a gild of burgesses, had a connection with the election of the burgh council and magistrates, and thought itself to be the 'community' of the town.[54] A list of the burgesses and community of Berwick who swore fealty to Edward I in 1291 yields only eighty-one names ; a similar list for Perth gives seventy-one ;[55] and a corresponding list for Berwick in 1333 gives forty.[56] If numbers such as these approached the sum total of the burgesses the latter must have composed an exclusive oligarchy among the indwellers of the burgh ; and it was in the merchant gild that this oligarchy was entrenched.

For although there were craftsmen in the burghs, each burgh was first and foremost a *villa mercatoria*, a town whose chief function was trade. Even the craftsman engaged in cloth manufacture was of an inferior and almost servile status : in the mid-thirteenth century, when there was a successful attempt to prevent cloth manufacture becoming a rural industry, it was enacted that any wool-comber leaving a burgh to dwell among 'uplandmen'—countryfolk—was to be imprisoned.[57] More than a century later a man was described in the burgh court of Aberdeen as scarcely human (*semihomo*) because he was a weaver.[58] Not surprisingly, certain craftsmen—fleshers, shoe-

[53] *A.P.S.*, I. 431–38.

[54] *Statuta Gilde* (*A.P.S.*, I. 431–8), *passim*. See also 'of the breder of the Gild' (*ibid.*, 719).

[55] *Cal. Docs. Scot.*, II. No. 508.

[56] *Rot. Scot.*, I. 255–6.

[57] James Mackinnon, *Social and Industrial History of Scotland*, I. 64.

[58] *Aberdeen Burgh Recs.*, pp. 32–3.

makers and fishermen—were excluded from membership of the merchant gild unless they merely supervised the workmen under them and abjured the personal exercise of a craft that soiled their hands.[59] In any case the entrance fee to the Berwick gild was the high sum of forty shillings.[60] When a labourer's daily wage was 2d. and that of a craftsman between 3d. and 6d.[61] the entrance fee alone debarred them from the gild; the entrance fee for burgess-ship may also have debarred all but the more substantial craftsmen even from becoming burgesses.

While the inhabitants of the Scottish burghs were a small minority of the country's population, and while the burgesses were a fraction even of that minority, their influence was surprisingly great. The fact that trade was entirely in their hands had something to do with this. But in addition the influence of the burgesses owed much to the co-operation that existed among them [62] and to the distinct and complex institutions and organisations that the burgesses evolved, of which the gild was only one. The burgesses, and even the underlings in the burghs, were set apart from the rest of the population by their special courts and by the right of the bailies of the burgh to 'repledge' an inhabitant of the burgh from a non-burghal court if the case was one with which the burgh court was competent to deal.

In civil cases, however, there could be an appeal from the burgh court. As chief financial officer of the crown the king's chamberlain had a special responsibility for the king's burghs. One of his duties was to hold a chamberlain ayre, supposedly once a year, passing from one royal burgh to another. Burgh courts, and even the chamberlain on his ayre, might ask counsel from a special advisory body named 'the four burghs'.[63] This was composed of four burgesses from each of the king's burghs of Berwick, Roxburgh, Edinburgh and Stirling, who met at Haddington under the chairmanship of the chamberlain to declare the law on contested points of burghal usage and privilege.[64] Already, however, there existed a written collection entitled the

---

[59] *Leges Quatuor Burgorum,* cap. xciv (*A.P.S.,* I. 351).

[60] *Statuta Gilde,* cap. xi (*ibid.,* 433).

[61] *Cal. Docs. Scot.,* IV. 459. On the basis of such figures the purchasing power of money was about two hundred times greater than at the present day.

[62] See *A.P.S.,* I. 723.

[63] It is so styled when it first appears (*c.* 1270) in the Berne MS. (S.R.O.), similarly in a plea of 1292 (Stevenson, *Documents,* I. 380); not until the fourteenth century is it called a court.

[64] See *A.P.S.,* I. 742, c. 8.

Leges Quatuor Burgorum and a copy of these laws of the four burghs was kept among the royal muniments.[65]

Just as the burghs were administered through the burgh court, the gild court, the chamberlain ayre and the four burghs, the administration of the other communities of the land took a curial form; and the various courts made up the framework of local and central government. For the greater part of the population the court that mattered most was the baron court of their lord. This was the lowest court in which public justice could be dispensed—for proceedings in the baron court were begun in the name of the king. The court could deal with such civil actions as petty debt. In criminal actions it could pass sentence of death if a culprit was caught red-handed committing theft or manslaughter; criminal justice was always summary and there was no appeal from the gallows. But the ordinary stock-in-trade of the baron court was the variety of minor disputes, economic and administrative decisions, that comprehended 'the weill of the tenandis and the keeping of gude nichtbourhede'.[66] It was the baron (or his bailie) who presided over the baron court; but in its proceedings he theoretically took no direct part. The body of the court was made up of the baron's tenants who owed 'suit of court'. Their attendance was enforced by fines, for it was the suitors who acted as judges. If they were numerous they might choose an assize—a jury of men put upon oath (*jurati*)[67]—to declare their knowledge of the case before the court. The forespeaker of the assize announced the joint finding and the dempster of the court declared the 'doom' or judgment.

But a discontented litigant might formally declare that the doom given against him was 'fals, stynkand and rottin'[68] and appeal to the court of the sheriffdom. Scotland was divided into almost thirty sheriffdoms and it was the sheriff court that gave meaning to this territorial organisation. Although the jurisdiction of the sheriff court was not notably greater than that of the baron court the former had the greater prestige : it was a royal court, presided over by the king's sheriff, who was aided by subordinate officers—crowners, mairs and serjeants—and it was held usually at the royal castle which was the *caput*, or legal centre, of the sheriffdom ; its suitors were the barons of

---

[65] *Ibid.*, 114, 329–56.

[66] For the organisation, functions and procedure of a baron court see *The Court Book of the Barony of Carnwath* (S.H.S.), pp. lxxiv–cxii; *Scot. Legal Hist.*, pp. 374–7.

[67] See Ian D. Willock, *The Origins and Development of the Jury in Scotland* (Stair Soc.).   [68] *A.P.S.*, I. 742.

the sheriffdom who were the king's tenants-in-chief; its procedure linked it closely with the central government, for many civil actions could begin only when a plaintiff presented a brieve that he had bought from the king's chancery.[69] A brieve was an instruction written *brevi manu* in Latin and sealed with the king's seal.[70] It ran in the king's name and was addressed to a particular official, usually sheriff or justiciar. It outlined some alleged grievance and ordered investigation by a sworn inquest. By 1292 the royal muniments included two sacks full of rolls of inquests.[71]

Just as the process of appeal linked the baron court to the sheriff court, it linked the latter to the court of the justiciar. There were three justiciars with authority respectively over Lothian, Galloway, and Scotia—the district north of the Forth. In theory each justiciar went on ayre in the spring and in the autumn, holdng his itinerant court (to which the tenants-in-chief owed suit) at the *caput* of each sheriffdom.[72] Apart from dealing with falsed dooms from the sheriff court, the justiciar's court was one of first instance for civil actions raised by brieves. In the course of the ayre administrative matters were also dealt with : the justiciar was to enquire into the probity and efficiency of the sheriffs and other officials. But it was its criminal jurisdiction that made the court so formidable : only it could deal with the four pleas of the crown (murder, rape, robbery and arson) which were withheld from lesser courts. Since the profits of justice— in the shape of fines and amercements—were large, the justice ayre played a significant part in royal finance : the justiciar of Lothian raised almost £550 in 1266.[73] The success of the justice ayre was estimated both by the amount of the fines forthcoming for the king and by the number of criminal corpses left dangling from the gallows.

In civil cases, however, there lay an ultimate resort even higher than the justice ayre : the disappointed litigant could once more false a doom and appeal to the king and his council;[74] and that council might meet *in parliamento*.

[69] For procedure in the sheriff court, see *Scot. Legal Hist.*, pp. 350–5.

[70] For the various brieves and their use see H. McKechnie, *Judicial Process upon Brieves, 1219–1532* (David Murray Lecture, 1956), and *The Register of Brieves* (Stair Soc.).

[71] *A.P.S.*, I. 114.

[72] For a contemporary outline of procedure see *Modus Procedendi in Itinere Justiciarie* (ibid., 705–8). See also *Scot. Legal Hist.*, pp. 408–10.

[73] *E.R.*, I. 27.

[74] Sir Philip J. Hamilton Grierson, 'The Appellate Jurisdiction of the Scottish Parliament', *S.H.R.*, xv. 205–22.

In surviving Scottish documents the first mention of parliament is in July 1290 when burgesses of Berwick applied the word to a contemporary assembly of Scottish magnates at Birgham.[75] The word 'parliament' was a novel term, probably introduced from England, and it did not yet entirely displace the earlier term *colloquium* as a description of the greatest and most formal assemblies of the king and his counsellors.[76] That parliament was the centre of supreme jurisdiction may be inferred from a treatise written in French and probably composed in 1293 for the edification of John Balliol.[77] This treatise mentions occasions when the king has 'common assembly and personal speech with all the prelates, earls and barons of the realm'[78]—a description which might cover both parliament and some other type of council. But a distinction is drawn between the two : certain cases which might involve disinheritance should be decided 'in full parliament and not by a lesser council'.[79] The words 'full parliament' did not signify a parliament that had a full attendance but one that was fully competent to act as a court of law and was formally summoned on forty days' warning.[80] Thus the surviving records of the parliaments of February and August 1293 take the form of rolls of pleas— 'pleas . . . before the king and his council in his first parliament' or 'pleas of parliament . . . before the lord king and his council'.[81] From the decisions of parliament there could be no appeal. And parliament not only applied the law : it could enact new law through its statutes and ordinances.

Besides its judicial and legislative functions parliament had others. There, above all, the king acted in concert with those who by birth or office were the recognised leaders of the kingdom : to the parliament or *colloquium* held at Birgham in March 1290 came twelve bishops, twenty-three abbots, eleven priors, twelve earls and fifty barons; all were magnates; probably all were tenants-in-chief of the king and, as such, owed him suit of court. No one questioned their right to give counsel and reach collective decisions upon *ardua negocia*, the affairs of state affecting the wellbeing of the realm.

While such decisions might be made and publicised in parliament, there existed (or were soon to exist) two other types of council

---

[75] Stevenson, *Documents*, I. No. cix.
[76] A. A. M. Duncan, 'The early parliaments of Scotland', *S.H.R.*, XLV. 36–58.
[77] 'The Scottish King's Household', ed. Mary Bateson, *S.H.S. Misc.* II. 1–43. The editor dates the document 1305 but admits (p. 5) that it might have 'resulted from the work of Alexander III or John Balliol'.
[78] *Ibid.*, 37.   [80] *R.M.S.*, I. No. 446.
[79] *Ibid.*, 43.   [81] *A.P.S.*, I. 445, 448.

that might also make such decisions. One was the 'general council', first styled as such in the later fourteenth century[82] and described simply as a 'council' before that time. This, like parliament, was an assembly of bishops, abbots, priors, earls and barons. Unlike parliament, it scarcely ever functioned as a court : it could be summoned on shorter warning and its procedure was not hampered by judicial formalities or clogged up with litigation. Nonetheless it was just as competent as parliament to deal with any *ardua negocia*, whether administrative, financial or political. Moreover in dealing with the day-to-day problems of government the king relied not on parliaments or on full-scale councils, which might be held only on one or two occasions in the year, but on the advice of a small, informal and speedily convoked royal council, later known as the secret or privy council—secret or privy in the sense that the councillors were sworn not to reveal its deliberations. While this privy council included selected magnates, its basic membership was naturally made up of those who were in fairly constant attendance upon the king, namely the dignitaries and officials of the royal household who composed a rudimentary civil service.

In England there already existed a large and complex civil service, well nourished on fees of office and expense accounts and imbued with *esprit de corps*. Although the English chancery and exchequer had originated in the royal household they were already departments of state established at Westminster rather than departments of the itinerant household. In Scotland, however, this development scarcely took place. Central government was established not in a fixed capital but in the royal household. As the king and his household toured the land so also did the machinery of central government. Catering for the king's household and his miscellaneous entourage in itself involved the delegation of authority, the keeping of accounts and the compilation of many administrative ordinances of the household.[83] There were senior clerks, lesser clerks, ushers and menials, as well as the three great officers of the household—the steward, the constable and the marshal[84]—whose offices had become hereditary and were vested in important baronial families. Those who had the right to be fed at table in the king's hall had duties which

[82] P. 181 below.
[83] Twenty-five rolls and memoranda of these existed among the royal muniments (*A.P.S.*, I. 114).
[84] For their duties and a description of the household as a whole see Mary Bateson, *op. cit.*, *S.H.S. Misc.* II. 1–43.

at the lowest level were purely domestic but which at higher levels merged into the functions of central government.

It was the chancellor and chamberlain who held the key posts in central government. Until 1335 the chancellor was always a cleric. He presided over the king's parliaments and councils and kept the king's great seal, the most solemn means of authenticating documents drawn up in chancery—the royal secretariat. Chancery was formally described as the king's chapel, for the clerics who served in the king's chapel made up the original staff who worked under the chancellor. Apart from an official salary of £100 the chancellor was paid a traditional fee for each brieve issued under the great seal. Besides the formalised legal brieves which set in motion many of the processes of justice, chancery issued charters conveying or confirming grants of land or office. It also issued brieves in the form of precepts or mandates, incorporating some administrative order in the name of the king. Already it was thought that no brieve of this type should be issued under the great seal unless it had first been warranted by a precept under the king's privy seal. The latter was to be entrusted to a wise and knowledgable man, for the office of the privy seal was 'the key and security of the great seal'.[85]

In contrast to the chancellor the chamberlain was usually a layman. The office—which corresponded to that of the English treasurer—was not beneath the notice of an earl and carried a salary of 100 marks. As chief financial officer of the crown the chamberlain was to receive feudal casualties and see to the administration of the king's burghs and the royal demesne lands.[86] The latter were leased out to fermours, and the royal muniments included nineteen rolls containing not only sheriffs' accounts but 'extents' of the demesne lands.[87] Although there existed an assessment of landed revenue, the *Antiqua Taxatio*, on which a land tax could be levied, such taxation was extraordinary and could be resorted to only in accordance with feudal custom for such occasions as the knighting of the king's eldest son. For his various financial activities the chamberlain had to render an account in exchequer. In Scotland the exchequer was not a permanent department of state,[88] though it was not necessarily less efficient than its imposing and unwieldy counterpart in England. Far from being a permanent institution the Scottish exchequer met for only a brief time at intervals that might be anything from six months

[85] *Ibid.*, 32.   [86] *Ibid.*   [87] *A.P.S.*, I. 118.
[88] Its characteristics are outlined by Athol Murray in 'The Procedure of the Scottish Exchequer in the early Sixteenth Century', *S.H.R.*, XL. 89–117.

to several years. The accounts presented by the chamberlain, the sheriffs, custumars, and bailies of burghs, were audited by an *ad hoc* commission that usually comprised the chamberlain, some lay and ecclesiastical magnates and senior clerks. The accounts themselves were drawn up in a simple form : first came the *oneracio*, a list of the revenues collected ; then came the *expense*, a list of what had been spent on behalf of the king. For the royal revenues were not merely collected locally but were used locally : sheriffs, custumars and bailies received precepts ordering them to make miscellaneous payments—for salaries, the upkeep of a royal castle, or pensions or donations to some religious house. In exchequer the surplus or deficit would be reckoned by an abacus and the moving of counters on the painted squares of the exchequer board. Financial reckoning was awkward : Roman numerals were used, so also were the denominations of pounds, shillings and pence, besides the mark (13s. 4d. or two-thirds of a pound), but the pound, the mark, and even the shilling, were merely units of account ; the only coins minted in Scotland were silver pennies equal in value to those of England. And much of the royal income was paid not in cash but in produce, which was stored in the royal castles and manors for the use of the king's itinerant household. It was assumed that the king should 'live of his own', financing his household and government from the traditional crown revenues. No distinction was drawn between the revenues of government and the revenues of the king : it was the king who governed.

By 1286 the Scottish kingdom was a fairly large political unit on the fragmented map of medieval Europe ; but the striking unification that had hitherto taken place was outward rather than inward. Diversity was more obvious than uniformity, local self-sufficiency more obvious than national interdependence. The concept of one race, one law, one tongue, did not apply in medieval Scotland—like Switzerland it became a nation despite its diversity.

In the field of law the diversity was marked. There was a 'confusion and intermingling of customary, Roman, feudal and canon law'.[89] It was acknowledged that all laws either 'ar manis law or Godis law',[90] and God's law was represented by the comprehensive code of canon law administered in the consistory court of a diocese,

[89] A. I. Dunlop, *St Andrews Acta*, I. cliii, n. 6. See also Peter Stein, 'The source of the Romano-canonical part of Regiam Maiestatem', *S.H.R.*, XLVIII. 107–23, and 'Roman Law in Scotland', *Ius Romanum Medii Aevi*, v. 13b, 1–51.
[90] *A.P.S.*, I. 739.

the 'court of Christianity' over which a bishop's 'official' presided. In addition, feudal law, soon to be exemplified in a treatise styled *Regiam Majestatem*,[91] was applicable throughout much of Scotland. There were also the beginnings of a statutory law: in the royal muniments there were rolls of statutes, laws and assizes of the land[92] —among them, no doubt, some obsolescent compilations such as the 'laws of Malcolm Makkenneth'[93] and the 'laws between the Brets and Scots'.[94] Yet law and custom varied from district to district according to the degree to which Celtic or Anglo-Norman tradition prevailed or co-existed. There was still room for Brehon law,[95] for the laws of Galloway,[96] the laws of the forests,[97] the laws of the four burghs, and even the law of Clan MacDuff.[98]

To some extent the diversity of law was mitigated: the king's brieves had the effect of imposing some uniformity; and baron court, sheriff court, justiciar's court and parliament made up a four-tiered structure combining feudal justice and feudal law with royal justice and whatever synthesis currently passed for 'common law'. But this system of inter-relating courts applied only to the 'royalty' of a sheriffdom. In a number of sheriffdoms some barons or religious corporations had been granted the right to hold lands in 'regality'.[99] The regalities were comparable to the English palatinates and were outwith the ordinary judicial system.[100] A grant of land *in regalitatem* was said to take as much out of the crown as the crown was capable of giving. No royal official, not even a justiciar, could exercise his office within a regality; there the king's brieves were of no force.

While the king's officers were excluded from the regalities, there were vast areas, comprising much of the Highlands, where they simply failed to appear, and where military force, the ultimate (and sometimes necessary) political sanction, could scarcely be brought to bear. The Highlands, with their distinctive characteristics, could still almost be equated with the high lands throughout all Scotland save the south-east. Although there were racial affinities between Highlanders and Lowlanders they were separated by an almost insuperable

---

[91] A. A. M. Duncan, 'Regiam Majestatem: a reconsideration', *Juridical Review*, N.S., VI. 199–217.

[92] *A.P.S.*, I. 114, 116–7.   [93] *Ibid.*, 709–12.   [94] *Ibid.*, 663–5.

[95] See John Cameron, *Celtic Law*, and James Mackinnon, *The Constitutional History of Scotland*, pp. 13–32.

[96] *A.P.S.*, I. 187.   [97] *Ibid.*, 687–92.   [98] *Ibid.*, 187.

[99] It has been calculated that prior to 1560 there were fifty-four regalities in Scotland (*Kirkintilloch Burgh Court Book* [S.H.S.], p. xlii, n. 2).

[100] See 'The Franchise Courts and Regalities', *Scot. Legal Hist.*, pp. 374–83.

barrier of language : as late as 1521 John Major was to remark that 'one half of Scotland speaks Irish [Gaelic]'.[101] But to think of a two-fold division of Scotland into Highlands and Lowlands would be something of an over-simplification. Some areas, still Gaelic, were in contact with Anglo-Scoto-Norman society and institutions. Others were far from the influence of any burgh, feudal lordship, or any other novel institution. In effect Scotland, like Gaul, was divided into three parts.

This tripartite division was reflected in the pattern of territorial lordship. In the south-eastern region, approximating to the diocese of St Andrews, government and administration were at their most intensive; the area was relatively fertile and, although it included the earldoms of March and Fife, a typical lordship was one such as the small but rich barony of Dirleton held by the family of De Vaux. Between the completely English-speaking south-east and the completely Gaelic-speaking north-west there stretched a band of earldoms and great lordships that began in Galloway and ended in Caithness. These incorporated lands that were Highland, lands that were Low-land, populations part English-speaking, part Gaelic-speaking. Here were to be found ten of the earldoms, headed by earls at least partly of Gaelic descent; and they, like the royal house itself, formed a link between the Gaelic past and the Anglo-Scoto-Norman present. To the west of this border zone, in the greater part of the West Highlands and Isles, there were four lordships held of the crown. William, Earl of Ross, grandson of Ferquhard MacIntsagairt, held not only Ross but Skye and Lewis. Three descendants of Somerled, onetime 'king' of the Isles, also had lordships : Alexander of Argyll—a MacDougal—held much of mainland Argyll; Angus MacDonald 'of the Isles'[102] was established in Kintyre, Islay and the neighbouring islands; and Alan MacRuaridh held Uist and Garmoran. All four attended the council at Scone in February 1284 where the last three figured among the barons of the realm.[103] But the reality was less baronial than Gaelic : chiefship and an emerging clan spirit were of more impor-tance than homage, fealty, the niceties of feudal land law or royal justice.

Thus most of the region to the west of a line running from Dum-barton to Dornoch was virtually unaffected by the forces that had transformed eastern Scotland. Sheriff courts and justice ayres touched the fringes of this area but did not penetrate it. No burgh was to be found within it. Among the fairly numerous stone castles that

---

[101] Major, *History*, p. 49.   [102] *A.P.S.*, I. 447.   [103] *Ibid.*, 424.

guarded the entrances to glens and sea lochs there was as yet scarcely one that belonged to the king. Even the kirk was ill-represented with one small cathedral at Lismore, one abbey at Iona, another at Saddell, a few struggling priories, no friaries and no hospitals. This area, a third of Scotland, had many chapels but not many more than a hundred parish kirks while the remaining two-thirds had almost a thousand. It was a region that looked southward to Gaelic Ireland rather than eastward to the anglicised Lowlands.

Nonetheless, despite all the factors that made for division, the kingdom of Scotland formed a totality. Its modern equivalent would be a federal rather than a unitary state : the two main cultural groups, Gaelic and English-speaking, were loosely associated under an aristocracy of mixed origins, whose members, more often than not, spoke a neutral language, French, and, in varying degrees, ruled their lands with some autonomy. Unity was at least symbolised (as in England) by the phrase 'community of the realm', which recurs after 1286 in the official documents of the time. It would be unwise to read too much into this phrase or to idealise it ; yet it may be admitted that 'Scotland had evolved during the peaceful thirteenth century a political identity or nationhood' and that this was 'a cause, not a result, of the war for independence'.[104] The sense of political identity was to survive even during the critical years between 1286 and 1292 when the chief agent of unity, the kingship, was in abeyance.

[104] A. A. M. Duncan, 'The Community of the realm of Scotland and Robert Bruce : a review', *S.H.R.*, XLV. 184–201, at 184.

2

A LAND WITHOUT A KING

In 1249, in a discussion that preceded the enthronement of the boy-king Alexander III, Walter Comyn, Earl of Menteith, is said to have remarked that a land without a king lay in as much perplexity as a vessel in the midst of the waves of the ocean without oarsmen or helmsman.[1] The truth of this remark was to be borne out many years later by the events that followed the fateful night of 19 March 1286 when Alexander III was thrown from his horse near Kinghorn. His accidental death was the culmination of a number of family misfortunes: one of his two sons had died in 1281, the other early in 1284; neither left issue; his daughter, Margaret, who had married Eric II of Norway, had died in 1283, leaving the babe-in-arms known as Margaret, the Maid of Norway. The stormy night that saw the death of King Alexander left the infant Maid as the sole surviving descendant in the direct line of the ancient royal dynasty.

Two years before, on 5 February 1284, a council had drawn up a tailzie (entail) to regulate the royal succession. It was then enacted that if King Alexander should die leaving no legitimate son or daughter the magnates would receive the Maid of Norway as 'our lady and rightful heir of our said lord the king of Scotland, of all the kingdom and of the Isle of Man [etc.]'.[2] Elsewhere in Western Europe the claim of a female to inherit a kingdom would almost certainly have been contested. The ill-advised tailzie of 1284 stored up trouble for the future. Its recognition of the Maid as heir presumptive may have been intended by Alexander to facilitate a dynastic union of Scotland and England,[3] or to preserve the existing friendship by a marriage alliance. More probably it was intended to

---

[1] *Chron. Fordun,* I. 293.　　[2] *A.P.S.,* I. 424.　　[3] P. 30 below.

prevent immediate dispute over the succession among magnates distantly related to the royal house and was a stop-gap measure. For after the death of his three children King Alexander still hoped to produce offspring of his own. In 1285 he married for the second time. On his death his widowed queen, Yolande, daughter of the Count of Dreux, claimed to be with child. If Queen Yolande were to bear a posthumous son to King Alexander, that son would have clear right to succeed; if she were to bear a daughter, that daughter would have a better right than the Maid.

Because of Queen Yolande's reported pregnancy there could be no immediate recognition of the Maid, or of anyone else, as the rightful successor to King Alexander. This uncertainty encouraged the ambitions of other possible claimants. When parliament met at Scone on 2 April 1286, Robert Bruce, the aged Lord of Annandale, seems to have denied the right of any female to inherit the kingdom and advanced his own claim as a descendant of David I. After a short adjournment of parliament John Balliol, another descendant of David I, arrived to contest the Bruce claim. There was 'bitter pleading' between Bruce and Balliol but nothing could be determined until the outcome of the queen's pregnancy was known. Parliament sensibly decided that all magnates should swear to keep the peace and take a non-committal oath of fealty to 'the nearest by blood who by right must inherit'. It still remained to be decided who was 'nearest by blood' to the late king. Meanwhile six guardians—William Fraser, Bishop of St Andrews, Robert Wishart, Bishop of Glasgow, Duncan, Earl of Fife, Alexander Comyn, Earl of Buchan, James the Steward and John Comyn, Lord of Badenoch—were chosen to carry on government in the name of the community of the realm and to supervise arrangements for the eventual determination of the succession.[4] Excluded from the regency the Bruces made ready to defy it. Robert Bruce the eldest, Lord of Annandale, and his son, Robert Bruce, Earl of Carrick, met at the latter's castle of Turnberry on 20 September 1286. The earl's son, Robert Bruce the youngest (future King of Scotland), seems to have been absent from the reunion. But other nobles of the Bruce connection were present. They concluded a bond of alliance in which they reserved their allegiance to the King of England—of whom most of them held lands—and their allegiance to the (unspecified) person who would obtain the kingdom of Scot-

---

[4] For this summary see the masterly reconstruction of events by A. A. M. Duncan, *op. cit.*, *S.H.R.*, xlv. 184–201, at 184–6.

land 'by reason of the blood of the Lord Alexander, . . . King of Scotland who last died, . . . and in accordance with the ancient customs hitherto approved and used in the realm of Scotland'.[5] The Bruces thus adhered to the oath of fealty exacted in the Scone parliament, probably hoping that they themselves might turn out to be the beneficiaries.

Although the Turnberry bond was ostensibly devised to give support to Richard de Burgh, Earl of Ulster, it was certainly the prelude to a show of force as soon as it became clear at the end of the year that Queen Yolande's pregnancy was either feigned or had resulted in a still-birth.[6] John Balliol was afterwards to claim that the Lord of Annandale and the Earl of Carrick attacked and seized the royal castles of Dumfries and Wigtown and made some sort of proclamation in the courtyard of the Balliol castle of Buittle in Galloway.[7] In the winter of 1286-7 there was civil war. The guardians called out the host—the able-bodied men obliged to serve in the defence of the land—and were successful in preserving their authority. By over-hasty action the Bruces had compromised their chances of the throne. The guardians 'teetered through two further years on the brink of civil war'.[8] One guardian, Duncan, Earl of Fife, was ambushed and slain in the late summer of 1289. Shortly before, another guardian, the Earl of Buchan, had died a natural death. No one was chosen to fill the two vacancies, probably because agreement was impossible. The question of the succession was left unresolved—stalemate had been reached.

In the immediate aftermath of Alexander III's death the Scottish magnates had thought of Edward I of England as a person who might help them to resolve their difficulties. Scottish embassies followed in Edward's wake as he left for France on 13 May 1286. His response was probably to offer his good services only on condition that the Scots acknowledged him to be lord superior of Scotland.[9] This claim was of ancient origin : Scottish kings were solemnly enthroned on a ceremonial stone in the abbey of Scone;[10] but although they possessed a crown, and wore it, they were not formally crowned ; nor

---

[5] Stevenson, *Documents*, I. No. xxi.
[6] A. A. M. Duncan, *op. cit.*, *S.H.R.*, XLV. 184-201, at 187-8.
[7] Palgrave, *Documents*, I. 42.
[8] A. A. M. Duncan, *op. cit.*, *S.H.R.*, XLV. 184-201, at 188-9.
[9] *Ibid.*, pp. 187, 189.
[10] See M. Dominica Legge, 'La Piere D'Escosse', *S.H.R.*, XXXVIII. 109-13.

were they anointed;[11] it might therefore be questioned whether they were independent kings. The question of coronation and unction was linked to that of the homage that Scottish kings owed to those of England. In 1278 Alexander III had affirmed that he owed such homage only for the lands he held in England (Tynedale and Penrith); Edward had claimed it was due not only for these but for the kingdom of Scotland as well, and had then reserved the right to open the question at a later date.[12] Even in the troubles that followed Alexander III's death the Scots were unwilling to acknowledge the claim to overlordship, and Edward allowed them to simmer for three years in their own juice. In 1284 Alexander III had written to him hinting that the 'indissoluble bond created between you and us' might be strengthened and that 'much good may yet come to pass through your kinswoman, the daughter of your niece . . . the late Queen of Norway'. Alexander had not only hinted at the desirability of a royal marriage between the Maid of Norway and a member of Edward's family but had stressed that the Maid was his heir.[13] It required no great foresight to see that a marriage between the Maid and Edward's own heir, the young Edward of Caernarvon, might result in a union of Scotland and England. To Eric of Norway, moreover, it must have seemed that the chances of his daughter's succeeding to the Scottish kingdom were shadowy unless outside help were forthcoming. On 1 April 1289 an embassy was appointed at Bergen to approach Edward and treat of the marriage of the Maid.[14] On 3 October, at the request of Edward, who had lately returned from France, the guardians appointed the Bishops of St Andrews and Glasgow, John Comyn of Badenoch and the eldest Robert Bruce to treat with the Norwegian envoys in his presence.[15] Apart from the question of the Maid, there were other matters in dispute between the Scots and Norwegians.[16] It seemed that Edward, who had won a reputation for his mediation in continental disputes, was not un-

---

[11] The Information that Edward I supplied to the Paris lawyers whom he consulted during the 'Great Cause' (p. 39 below) began with the statement: 'The king of a certain kingdom [Scotland] was neither anointed nor crowned, but placed in a customary royal seat by the earls, magnates and prelates of the kingdom' (G. J. Hand, 'The Opinions of the Paris Lawyers upon the Scottish Succession *c.* 1292', *Irish Jurist* [New Series], v. 141–55, at 144).

[12] *Dunfermline Registrum*, No. 321; *Foedera*, I. pt. ii, 169, 176.

[13] Stones, *Documents*, No. 13.

[14] *Diplomatarium Norvegicum*, XIX. 230–1.

[15] Stevenson, *Documents*, I. No. lix; *Foedera*, I. pt. iii, 50.

[16] See Ranald Nicholson, 'The Franco-Scottish and Franco-Norwegian Treaties of 1295', *S.H.R.*, XXXVIII. 114–32.

fitted to act as honest broker in the negotiations. Even so, the Scots were anxious as to the topics that might be raised at the forthcoming conference : their envoys were empowered to negotiate only on a basis that would preserve 'the liberty and honour of the realm of Scotland'.[17]

In a meeting at Salisbury there were 'many negotiations and great debates'. The Norwegians had asked Edward's aid and counsel so that his grand-niece should be accorded obedience as 'lady, queen and heiress' by her people of Scotland.[18] By the treaty of Salisbury of 6 November 1289 they won their objective. The Maid was to arrive in Scotland or England before 1 November 1290. She would then come under the custody of her great-uncle, Edward, who would send her into Scotland free of any matrimonial engagement as soon as that country was well secured and in peace. The Scots also conceded that if any of the Scottish guardians or officials should seem 'suspect' to the Norwegian envoys they should be replaced by other Scots. If Scots and Norwegians could not come to agreement English representatives would have the final say. Reports on the state of affairs in Scotland would be made to the Kings of England and Norway.[19]

What the Scottish envoys had conceded was vital. In the treaty of Salisbury they had recognised the right of Edward to intervene in Scotland ; and the basis on which that right rested, whether good neighbourhood, kinship to the Maid, or feudal superiority, had not been clarified. Little had been saved of the honour and liberty of Scotland. Much had been compromised.

On 14 March 1290 an impressive number of Scottish nobles and prelates gathered in a council or parliament at Birgham near Roxburgh to ratify the treaty of Salisbury. Already there were rumours that the pope had granted a dispensation for a marriage between the Maid and Edward's heir. On 17 March the Scots sent a letter to Edward which alluded to his 'good neighbourhood', recounted their joy at the rumour of the dispensation and, in advance, gave consent to the intended match, providing that Edward would meet some reasonable requirements.[20]

The prospect of a marriage between the heir of England and the heiress of Scotland must have caused some heart-searching among responsible Scots. The Scottish clergy had long looked with suspicion on attempts to extend English influence over their kirk. Archbishops of Canterbury and of York had each formerly claimed to be metro-

[17] *Foedera*, I. pt. iii, 50.   [18] Stevenson, *Documents*, I. No. lxxv.
[19] *Ibid*.   [20] *A.P.S.*, I. 85–6.

politan of Scotland; and in the treaty of Falaise of 1174 the issue of the feudal vassalage of the Scottish king had been linked to the issue of the subjection of the Scottish kirk to its English counterpart. The independence granted to the Scottish kirk as a 'special daughter' of Rome in 1192 was something that a future papal bull might conceivably take away. Meanwhile, within the institutions that made up the kirk there were attempts to preserve and assert independence and to reduce outside influence, especially influence from England.[21] It was symptomatic of this attitude that on 1 April 1289 Pope Nicholas IV furiously denounced the 'detestable' custom of admitting only native Scots to serve in the Scottish religious houses.[22] This xenophobic attitude was possibly merely professional in its origins, but it might amount to something like nationalism.

If the attitude of the Scottish prelates towards England was guarded and apprehensive that of the Scottish nobles was perhaps less so. The processes of marriage and heredity that had brought unity to scattered lands within Scotland did not stop short at the Tweed. Although no Scot seems to have held land in the coastal shires stretching from Sussex to Cornwall, reports made to the English exchequer in 1295 show that there were at least twelve Scots who held land in Yorkshire, sixteen in Cumberland, and twenty-four in Northumberland,[23] while John Balliol had manors in seventeen English shires bringing in rents amounting to the large sum of almost £500 a year.[24] Nevertheless the importance of the English lands held by a few of the Scottish nobility should not be exaggerated. Only in the case of the Balliols, Bruces, Comyns and Umfravilles were the holdings of great value. Whether or not these English holdings were of greater value than the Scottish lands of these families it was obvious that even a Bruce or Balliol could play no dominant role in England whilst he might well do so in Scotland. It was Scotland that the Bruces, Balliols and Comyns thought of as the orbit of their ambitions; to that extent at least they were Scots.

Whatever the consensus of their accumulated traditions and vested interests, the Scottish nobles and prelates must also have been influenced in 1290 by the way in which Edward or his agents had dealt with Scottish matters in recent months. Some years previously Pope Gregory X had levied a tax of an annual tenth of clerical in-

---

[21] See Easson, *Religious Houses*, pp. 10–1, 53. The attitude of Scottish Franciscans is shown by W. M. Mackenzie in 'A Prelude to the War of Independence', *S.H.R.*, xxvii. 105–13.

[22] *Foedera*, i. pt. iii, 45.

[23] *Cal. Docs. Scot.*, ii. No. 736.   [24] *Ibid.*

come throughout Christendom to finance a new crusade. Edward
coveted the proceeds from Scotland and a bull of 18 March 1291
was finally to order the Scots clergy to pay the tax and its arrears to
him.[25] Moreover Scottish merchants and other Scots with goods or
property in England were affected by the 'sinister prosecution' set
afoot in English courts by Jean Le Mazun, a Gascon merchant who
was a creditor of the late Alexander III.[26] This and other cases led to
a clash of Scottish and English jurisdiction.[27] In addition Edward's
increasing involvement in Scottish affairs seemed to threaten the
kingdom's territorial integrity. By 4 June 1290 he had assumed control of the Isle of Man [28]—part of the Scottish kingdom. A few weeks
later he empowered the Bishop of Durham to receive the men of the
Isles into his peace and take whatever other measures might be prudently desirable.[29] The Melrose chronicler was not blind to the fate
that had befallen the Welsh, restive under 'the yoke of the English'.[30]
It was, however, unthinkable that Edward could look on Scotland
as another Wales. There had been peace between Scots and English
for at least seventy years. Half of the Scots spoke English. Most of the
Scottish barons were not outlandish figures in cosmopolitan society.
Alexander II had married Edward's aunt. Alexander III had married
Edward's sister. Whatever the technicalities of the relationship between the two realms the spirit of the relationship was one that left
the Scots unaware of subordination. If they had misgivings about the
future they were all the more determined that the status of their kingdom should be preserved.

In July 1290 the Scottish magnates once more gathered at Birgham to negotiate with English envoys a marriage treaty that would
unite the heir of England and the heiress of Scotland and, so it was
expected, lead to a state of affairs in which both realms would share
a common ruler. In this marriage treaty the concern of the Scots was
to keep intact their own rights, customs, laws, liberties and independence. No Scot was to be held to answer outwith the realm for any
legal case that fell within it. No parliament was to be held outwith the

25 *Foedera*, I. pt. iii, 84; F. M. Powicke, *The Thirteenth Century, 1216–1307*
(1953), 264–7, 500; W. E. Lunt, *Financial Relations of the Papacy with England
to 1327* (1939), I. 292, 296, 334, 338; D. E. Easson, 'Scottish Abbeys and the War
of Independence', *Scot. Church Hist. Soc. Recs.*, XI. 63–81, at 68–70.

26 Stevenson, *Documents*, I. Nos. li, civ, cix.

27 *Ibid.*, Nos. li, lvi, lxxix, lxxvii, lxxxix, xc, cxx.

28 *Ibid.*, No. ciii; *Foedera*, I. pt. iii, 74.

29 Stevenson, *Documents*, I. No. cvii.

30 *Chronicle of Melrose* (Facsimile Edition, ed. A. O. Anderson, M. O. Anderson and W. Croft Dickinson, 1936), p. 156.

realm on any matter concerning the status of the realm or its Marches (bounds). Even if Scotland and England were to share the same ruler, the Scottish realm was to remain 'separate and divided from England according to its rightful boundaries, free in itself and without subjection.'[31] This last clause summed up the attitude of the Scots, just as the English attitude was summed up in the words that the English representatives appended to the same clause : 'saving the right of our said lord [Edward I] and of any other, which may pertain to him or to any other, upon matters concerning the Marches or elsewhere before the time of the present concession, or in rightful manner might pertain in time to come'.[32] The treaty ended with a statement that its contents should be so understood that the rights of neither kingdom and neither king should be increased or diminished. This clause was far less a guarantee of Scottish independence than a retention by Edward of the right to deny it. The reservations expressed by the English negotiators nullified the safeguards devised by the Scots and reflected adversely on Edward's goodwill. His aim was not a settlement by which both kingdoms would share a common ruler yet preserve their identity. His ideal was an incorporating union under the English crown, a union in which the kingdom of Scotland would disappear; and he refused to recognise that this was unacceptable to most Scots. Stubborn adherence to an impracticable project was the reverse of statesmanship.

Edward's ratification of the marriage treaty was accompanied by new attempts to extend English influence in Scotland : he appointed the Bishop of Durham to act there as lieutenant on behalf of the Maid of Norway and Edward of Caernarvon and required the Scottish guardians to obey the bishop.[33] The bishop and other English emissaries also demanded custody of the Scottish castles 'on account of certain dangers and suspicions'. All that the guardians could do was obtain a delay of the delivery of castles until the arrival of the Maid.[34]

On 20 May 1290 Edward had despatched a ship from Yarmouth laden with extraordinary delicacies such as rice, sturgeon, ginger and whalemeat. The vessel came back a month later without the Maid. Eleven sailors were sick or dead, probably through food contamination.[35] Eric seems to have insisted that his daughter be sent in one of his own ships to Orkney; and there, on Norwegian territory, the final arrangements would be made for her transfer to Edward's custody.

[31] Stevenson, *Documents*, 1. No. cviii, p. 167.   [32] *Ibid.*
[33] *Foedera*, 1. pt. iii, 72.   [34] *Ibid.*
[35] Stevenson, *Documents*, 1. Nos. xcvi, cxvii.

By 4 October English representatives had arrived in Wick, well equipped with cash for a final diplomatic tussle with the Norwegians.[36] Further travel was unnecessary. The Maid had set sail at the end of September and died after her vessel reached the Orkneys.[37] Scottish affairs were once more in turmoil, and dormant ambitions were stirred to more heedless confusion than ever.

By 7 October 1290 William Fraser, Bishop of St Andrews, one of the four remaining guardians, had heard rumours of the death of the Maid and wrote to Edward announcing that the eldest Robert Bruce had come to Perth with a great following; his adherents, the Earls of Mar and Atholl, were collecting forces; war and slaughter might result unless Edward intervened to allow the Scots to remain true to the oath they had taken on King Alexander's death. The letter ended with a piece of advice :

> If Sir John Balliol comes to your presence we advise you to take care so to treat with him that in any event your honour and advantage be preserved. . . . Let your excellency deign, if you please, to approach toward the Marches for the consolation of the Scottish people and to save the shedding of blood, and set over them for king him who of right ought to have the succession, if so be that he will follow your counsel.[38]

John Balliol's mother, the virtuous Lady Devorgilla, had died early in 1290 and the Balliol claim was strengthened by the fact that it was now indisputably vested in her son. At Gateshead, on 16 November 1290, Balliol issued a charter styling himself 'heir of the kingdom of Scotland' and in that capacity granted to the influential Bishop of Durham the lands in Northumberland and Cumberland that belonged to the Scottish crown.[39]

The eldest Bruce was no more scrupulous than Balliol, though possibly more ingenious. Apart from his threatening moves he instigated a formal protest against two of the guardians, Bishop Fraser and John Comyn of Badenoch, inhibiting them from setting up anyone as king. This protest ran in the name of 'the seven earls of Scotland', presumably holders of the more ancient earldoms who, in association with the 'community', had allegedly the right of 'making a king' and installing him on the royal seat. Bruce's theory, which may have been

---

[36] *Ibid.*, Nos. cxi, cxiv, cxv, cxvi.
[37] Letter of Bishop Audfinn in *Proc. Soc. Antiq. Scot.*, x. 417–9.
[38] *Nat. MSS. Scot.*, i. No. lxx.
[39] Stevenson, *Documents*, i. No. cxxv.

based upon the German imperial practice, was open to question; but it provided a basis on which to challenge any attempt of the surviving guardians to decide the succession. Bruce, the 'legitimate and true heir', was nowise willing to receive justice at the hands of Fraser and Comyn, the partisans of Balliol. Already, in the Turnberry bond of 1286, Bruce and his adherents had reserved their allegiance to the English king; now they placed themselves under the protection of Edward and appealed to the crown of England.[40]

Edward might conclude that those magnates who were enrolled in the rival factions of Bruce and Balliol would welcome his intervention to judge the Scottish succession. He might also conclude that there would be little opposition from those factions, or from the other less vociferous claimants, if he took the opportunity to insist on recognition as lord superior of Scotland. In the opening months of 1291 he gathered extracts from the registers and chronicles of English religious houses as evidence of his overlordship.[41] More significantly, he arranged that English ships would be ready, if need be, to blockade Scotland;[42] he sent to Newcastle 10,000 marks [43] to finance either warfare or diplomacy; he summoned the feudal magnates and the shire levies of northern England to muster at Norham Castle on the English side of Tweed on 2 June 1291.[44] Early in May he himself arrived at Norham and 'declared the reason for his coming as overlord of the land of Scotland before the magnates of Scotland, who, at his request, came to Norham to negotiate certain business touching the land of Scotland, which was then destitute of a king'. The Scots were informed that Edward 'by virtue of the overlordship that belongs to him' had come 'to do justice to everyone as sovereign'. He therefore asked for their 'kind agreement, and for acknowledgment of his overlordship'.[45]

Despite his suave words Edward had come prepared for a tussle; and at first it seemed that there would be one. The Scottish representatives at Norham asked leave to deliberate upon Edward's request for acknowledgment as lord superior. Edward allowed them three weeks, by which time the English levies were expected at Norham. A reply was forthcoming on behalf of those Scots who 'came to Norham the other day at your request, and the others whom they have

---

[40] Stones, *Documents*, No. 14.

[41] Palgrave, *Documents*, I. 56–138; E. L. G. Stones, 'The Appeal to History in Anglo-Scottish Relations between 1291 and 1401: Part I', *Archives*, IX. No. 41, 11–21.

[42] Stevenson, *Documents*, I. No. cxxvi.   [43] *Ibid.*, No. cxxiv.

[44] *Foedera*, I. pt. iii, 86–7.   [45] Stones, *Documents*, No. 15.

been able to consult in so short a time'. This Scottish reply outlined Edward's request for acknowledgment as lord superior and declared that

> the good people who have sent us here make answer that they do not in the least believe that you would ask so great a thing if you were not convinced of your sound right to it. But they have no knowledge of your right, nor did they ever see it claimed and used by you or your ancestors; therefore they answer you . . . that they have no power to reply to your statement, lacking a lord [king] to whom the demand ought to be addressed . . . for he, and no other, will have power to reply and to act in the matter.[46]

Edward took this reply at its face value. The 'good people' of Scotland, who, despite their homely description, were the substantially aristocratic community of the realm,[47] had admitted that they had no authority to answer his request. But an answer might be forthcoming from the claimants to the vacant throne : for someone among the competitors was presumably the rightful king ; if all of them acknowledged Edward to be overlord of Scotland the community of the realm must follow suit. This was the flaw in the reply of the community.

Early in June the various competitors were asked if they acknowledged Edward to be lord superior of Scotland, and whether they would accept his judgment of the succession. The would-be kings, who now included another seven persons besides Bruce and Balliol, announced that Edward had convinced them that he was rightfully lord superior and they would abide by his decision of the succession ;[48] sasine of the land and custody of the royal castles should be delivered to Edward so that he could restore them to the person adjudged to be the rightful king as soon as that person did homage to Edward as lord superior.[49]

At this point Edward encountered obstacles. Fourteen Scottish barons to whom the 'community' had once entrusted custody of the royal castles had scruples about delivering them to Edward. But nothing came of this last-ditch stand on behalf of the community : fortified by the acknowledgment of the competitors, Edward persuaded not only the latter, but the guardians as well, to assent to the

[46] *Ibid.*, No. 16.
[47] A. A. M. Duncan, *op. cit.*, *S.H.R.*, XLV. 184–201, at 190.
[48] Stones, *Documents*, No. 17.
[49] *Nat. MSS. Scot.*, I. No. lxxi.

transfer of the castles. The honour of the scrupulous barons was thus preserved and the castles were handed over to English constables.[50]

The submission of the competitors had weakened the chances of opposition from the Scottish magnates. Nor had there been warfare or even the presence of alien officials to arouse among the common folk any intense resentment at what must have seemed a political transaction involving a mere feudal technicality that could have no effect upon their lives. Thus Edward established his position not only as lord superior but as 'direct lord' of Scotland during the interregnum. He assumed thorough control of the kingdom and its revenues and administration, and ordered the arrest of those who refused to take an oath of fealty.[51] After a fealty-gathering tour as far as Perth he made his way to Berwick on 2 August 1291 to open the first session of the lawsuit known as the 'Great Cause' of the Scottish succession.

In deference to the spirit of thirteenth-century *legalitas* Edward prepared to determine the Great Cause with conspicuous formality. He himself, in theory, was to act only as president of the court and as the mouthpiece of its judgment. The court itself was composed according to a precedent of Roman law, the *judicium centumvirale*,[52] and numbered 104 auditors. Edward himself nominated 24 of the auditors—twelve English barons and twelve English ecclesiastics. Two of the competitors, John Balliol and his brother-in-law John Comyn, the guardian, were allowed to nominate jointly another forty auditors not only on their own behalf but on behalf of those other competitors who would abide by their nomination. Similarly Robert Bruce was allowed to nominate forty auditors on his own behalf and on behalf of those competitors who would abide by his nomination.[53] In practice, however, the choice of auditors reflected the twofold party division within Scotland. From the lists of auditors it is clear that the nobility of Scotland was fairly evenly divided in support of Bruce or Balliol; but the high ecclesiastical backing for Balliol outweighed that given to Bruce.

It is impossible in a brief summary to do justice to the complex issues raised by the proceedings of the court of auditors.[54] These pro-

[50] A. A. M. Duncan, *op. cit.*, *S.H.R.*, XLV. 184–201, at 191–2.
[51] *Cal. Docs. Scot.*, II. No. 508.
[52] G. Neilson, 'Bruce versus Balliol, 1291–2', *S.H.R.*, XVI. 1–14.
[53] Palgrave, *Documents*, I. Illustrations, ii, v–vi.
[54] The most recent survey is by G. W. S. Barrow in *Bruce*, pp. 52–68; see also E. L. G. Stones, 'The Records of the Great Cause of 1291–92', *S.H.R.*, XXXV. 89–109.

ceedings touched upon the nature of the state [55] as well as upon questions of feudal law, Roman civil law, and 'natural law'; Edward canvassed the opinions of doctors of law of the university of Paris [56] to help him through the maze. Some of the competitors (by this time twelve in number) had no hope of immediate success but were merely taking the chance to record their claims for possible future use. More serious claims were presented by Bruce, Balliol, John Hastings, Lord of Abergavenny, and Floris, Count of Holland.

The first three claimed as descendants of David, Earl of Huntingdon, grandson of David I. Earl David had left three daughters, Margaret, Isabella and Ada. John Balliol was the grandson of the eldest daughter, Robert Bruce was son of the second daughter, and John Hastings was grandson of the third daughter.[57] The object of Hastings's claim was not to gain the Scottish crown but to argue that the Scottish kingdom was like a barony which had descended to three co-heiresses: the lands and revenues should therefore be equally divided among the descendants of the co-heiresses. Bruce, for the time being, refuted the claim that the kingdom was partible. The laws observed by subjects, he asserted, were not applicable to the kings who ruled over them or to the kingdom as a legal entity: the law applicable to the Great Cause was that same law which held that a kingdom could not be divided, namely 'the law by which kings reign', which he equated with 'natural law'.[58]

Having thus countered Hastings's claim, Bruce went on to clarify his own. Again and again he stressed that he was one degree nearer the royal line than Balliol. If Balliol's mother had not recently died Bruce's claim would (he affirmed) be self-evident: for although Devorgilla was as near in degree to the royal line as he, and came of a senior branch, nonetheless it was Bruce who would have been preferred because (presumably by natural law) 'male blood is worthier and purer to claim and govern a kingdom than female blood.'[59] Balliol's claim came to him solely from Devorgilla, and since *her* claim was inferior to that of Bruce so also was her son's. Besides, claimed Bruce, Alexander II had once publicly recognised *him* as his heir, as some who were still alive well knew.[60]

[55] B. C. Keeney, 'The Medieval Idea of the State: the Great Cause, 1291–2', *Toronto Law Journal*, VII. 48–71.

[56] G. J. Hand, *op. cit.*, *Irish Jurist* (New Series), V. 141–55.

[57] See Appendix 2, Genealogical Table A.

[58] Palgrave, *Documents*, I. 23, 25.

[59] *Ibid.*, p. 24.

[60] *Ibid.*, pp. 29–30; see also pp. 19–20.

To the minds of many of the auditors Bruce's arguments must have seemed strained. The auditors were familiar with the feudal laws of succession to a barony or an earldom and were unlikely to be eager to follow a wild goose chase after natural law. In this lay the strength of Balliol's case and he exploited it well. He asserted that the case should be tried according to the laws and usages of England and Scotland.[61] After the kingship itself the highest tenures were those of the earldoms. Like a kingdom an earldom could not be divided; and it descended by seniority of line, not by nearness of degree.[62] Thus should it be with a kingdom : Balliol, grandson of the first daughter of Earl David, had a better claim than Bruce, son of the second daughter.

But Floris, Count of Holland, presented an ingenious case that might dispose of all descendants of David, Earl of Huntingdon: Earl David, he claimed, had resigned his possible right of succession to the kingdom, and King William had then declared that if his own line should fail the succession should pass to his sister Ada, whose descendant was Count Floris. The count asserted that there existed in the Scottish treasury written evidence that would prove his case.[63] This gave the opportunity for a breathing-space. On 12 August Edward adjourned the court; it was to meet again at Berwick on 2 June 1292. Meanwhile the Scottish treasury, monasteries, and other likely places, were to be searched (fruitlessly, as it turned out) for documents relevant to Count Floris' case or that of other competitors.[64]

The breathing-space also allowed Edward time to try out the ground for a case of his own. Although recognised as lord superior of Scotland, even as 'direct lord', he was not wholly satisfied. At Norham in June 1291 he had informed the competitors (who did not demur) that he reserved his own hereditary right 'as one among others claiming right to the kingdom',[65] for Edward was a descendant of Malcolm III and Queen Margaret. Moreover as feudal superior he may have contemplated the tantalising possibility that Scotland might be declared a male fief, succession to which could not lie through a female; or alternatively that competitors might be excluded through the remoteness of their relationship to the royal stock; on one of these grounds, if not both, they might then be swept aside

[61] *Ibid.*, p. 28.

[62] *Ibid.*, p. 27.

[63] G. G. Simpson, 'The Claim of Florence, Count of Holland, to the Scottish Throne, 1291-2', *S.H.R.*, xxxvi. 111–24.

[64] Palgrave, *Documents*, I. 35–6.

[65] *Foedera*, I. pt. iii, 96.

after they had served their purpose;[66] the kingdom would then escheat to its lord superior, Edward. In August 1291 £10,000 were to be forwarded to him, ostensibly for the expenses of his household,[67] possibly for other uses : James the Steward and another five Scottish magnates were offered lands worth £100 or 100 marks a year 'if it happens that the realm of Scotland shall remain in the possession of the king and his heirs',[68] and the king in question was Edward. These offers were afterwards cancelled, presumably because no support was forthcoming for his candidature. But before the court of auditors re-assembled at Berwick Edward had tightened his hold on Scotland and had sought to win the good opinion of barons, prelates and burgesses by gracious concessions. After a year of his personal rule it would be difficult for any succeeding king to assert the independent tradition of Scottish monarchy.

When the Great Cause re-opened at Berwick on 2 June 1292 it seemed no nearer determination. Yet another competitor, Eric of Norway, sent procurators who presented a claim that depended not upon descent but upon ascent : if the Maid of Norway was rightful Queen of Scotland then Eric as her father was her rightful heir. But Eric's procurators advanced this dubious claim half-heartedly, possibly only as a bargaining point to give them greater chance of winning other claims upon Scottish revenues that they simultaneously brought before Edward.[69] In any case the court decided on 2 June, without prejudice to the claims of Eric and other competitors, to determine first of all whether Balliol or Bruce had the better claim.

As the aged Bruce sensed that his own claim would founder he clutched at the claim of the Count of Holland, which still drifted like flotsam on the stormy waters. From the first, Bruce and the count had been on good terms.[70] Now, on 14 June, their mutual friends persuaded the two to conclude an indenture : if Floris should become King of Scotland he would convey to Bruce one-third of Scotland; similarly, if Bruce became king he would convey one-third to Floris, partly redeemable, however, by a transfer of the Bruce lands in England to the count.[71] This interesting stipulation suggests that Bruce's interests were centred in Scotland.

---

[66] See G. J. Hand, op. cit., Irish Jurist (New Series), v. 141–55, at 144–5, 147–8, 151–2, 154.

[67] Stevenson, Documents, i. No. cxxiv.

[68] Rot. Scot., i. 3.

[69] Ranald Nicholson, op. cit., S.H.R., xxxviii. 114–32, at 123.

[70] They were associated in the Appeals of the Seven Earls (Palgrave, Documents, pp. 20–1).   [71] Stevenson, Documents, i. No. cclv.

The indenture of 14 June 1292 represented the Lord of Annandale's last-ditch defence against Balliol: if Balliol's claim triumphed over that of Bruce it might yet fail before that of Count Floris, in which event Bruce would at least gain a third of Scotland. By 6 November the court had decided that Balliol had a better claim than Bruce. On the following day the disappointed eldest Bruce transmitted his rejected claim to his posterity—his son, the Earl of Carrick, and *his* heirs. Carrick and his heirs were accorded 'full and free power to sue for the realm, and to prosecute . . . the right which pertains to him in this matter, in the way that seems best to him.' [72] Though the eldest Bruce had failed he impressed upon his family his own burning conviction of the justice of his claim. This conviction was perhaps not shared by the Earl of Carrick, but it certainly was by the latter's son, the youngest Robert Bruce, who now came to the fore by reason of a further shift within the three generations of the Bruce family: on 9 November the Earl of Carrick resigned his earldom to the youngest Bruce,[73] who within fourteen years would seize the kingdom.

The Great Cause was not yet over. On 10 November the lawyers of the eldest Bruce modified his previous argument that the kingdom was indivisible and pleaded that, like Hastings, Bruce should receive a third of the royal demesne. This plea failed when the court decided that neither the kingdom nor its revenues could be divided.[74] Next came the turn of Count Floris to press his claim; Balliol's lawyers had merely to point out that he had produced no evidence to support it and Count Floris withdrew his claim. Another six competitors followed his example; the claims of Eric of Norway, Roger Mandeville and John Comyn of Badenoch were rejected because of their 'failure to sue'.[75] One significant feature of the Great Cause was, in fact, the failure of John Comyn, guardian of Scotland and member of the most powerful Scottish baronial family, to press his own claim, based on direct descent from Donald Bane, who had endured a disputed reign in Scotland between 1093 and 1097. Just as, latterly, Count Floris was in collusion with Bruce, so also John Comyn was in collusion with Balliol, whose sister he had married. If Balliol be-

---

[72] Stones, *Documents*, No. 18. See the question of 'estoppel' in G. J. Hand, *op. cit.*, *Irish Jurist* (New Series), v. 141–55, at 150.

[73] *A.P.S.*, 1. 449.

[74] This was assumed by Edward in the *quaestio* he submitted to the Paris lawyers (G. J. Hand, *op. cit.*, *Irish Jurist* [New Series], v. 141–55, at 144).

[75] Stones, *Documents*, No. 19.

came king the Comyns would undoubtedly be the power behind the throne.

On 17 November 1292 Edward gave judgment in favour of Balliol,[76] who was duly enthroned at Scone on St Andrew's Day. The new king joined Edward at Newcastle for the Christmas festivities and on 26 December did homage to him.[77] When Edward had ordered that Balliol should receive sasine of the kingdom he had qualified the award with a typical Edwardian reservation: 'saving our right and that of our heirs when we shall wish to speak thereupon.'[78] Edward had not given up hope of controlling Scotland directly rather than merely as the lord superior of a vassal king. It was ominous that Balliol was warned to govern justly so that no one should have cause to complain, lest the lord superior of Scotland should be obliged to apply a guiding hand.[79]

[76] *Ibid.*
[77] *Ibid.*, No. 20; Stevenson, *Documents*, I. 372.
[78] *Rot. Scot.*, I. 11; similarly Stones, *Documents*, No. 19.
[79] *Foedera*, I. pt. iii, 111.

3

KING JOHN, THE FRENCH ALLIANCE
AND THE GUARDIANS OF SCOTLAND

It is understandable, though misleading, that the history of Scotland has usually been written from the point of view of the Bruces (who were ultimately successful) rather than from that of the Balliols (who were ultimately unsuccessful). It is even more misleading that John Balliol has gone down in history as Toom Tabard rather than as King John. Balliol set out to be no less a king than his predecessors : his family had had links with Scotland since the twelfth century; there was nothing to hinder the acclimatisation of the new dynasty, particularly since it was backed by the Comyns, not only the most powerful baronial family but one with the best claim to be regarded as 'patriotic'.[1] Almost certainly it was for King John's edification that a treatise was compiled in French outlining the traditional organisation of the Scottish royal household[2] and touching upon Scottish government in general. Between February 1293 and May 1294 at least four parliaments were held.[3] On one occasion parliament was to be the seat of 'the dispensing of justice upon a scale which may have been unprecedented in Scotland', for there was to be public summons before king and council of 'everyone with a complaint . . . to show the injuries and trespasses done to them by whatsoever ill-doers'. In general there is 'remarkable evidence that King John and his council were determined to secure the possessions and authority of the crown'.[4] Not only did King John try to restore royal authority through parliament but he tried to renew the policy of

[1] P. 47 below.
[2] P. 20 above.
[3] A. A. M. Duncan, *op. cit., S.H.R.*, xlv. 36–58, at 40–3.
[4] *Ibid.*, 46.

assimilation that earlier kings had applied to the West Highlands and Isles. In his first parliament in February 1293 he ordained the erection of three new sheriffdoms in Skye, Lorne and Kintyre.[5] What might have proved the culminating stage in the extension of integrating institutions to the West Highlands and Isles achieved nothing: separatism came into its own in the welter of the wars of independence.

The origin of these wars can be traced to the very outset of King John's reign: shortly before he had arrived in Newcastle to perform his homage, judgment had been given there by Edward in a case involving an appeal from a Scottish court. This assumption of appellate jurisdiction followed from Edward's recognised position as lord superior; but the Scots had hoped that he would deal with appeals only on Scottish soil. On behalf of King John a number of Scottish magnates petitioned Edward that he should adhere to the provisions in the marriage treaty of Birgham which would forbid the hearing of such appeals outwith Scotland. On 2 January 1293, however, King John was forced to acknowledge in writing that Edward was released from any restrictions imposed by the treaty of Birgham or by his promises during the interregnum.[6]

Although there followed no flood of appeals from Scotland to England the few that were forthcoming, notably from MacDuff, brother of the late Earl of Fife, brought a crisis. Partly the fault was that of King John, who sought to evade the consequences of his admission of 2 January 1293. Had he sent attorneys to answer in his name to the appeals that were presented he might have avoided the humiliation of appearing in person to defend the judgments given in his own court. Because of John's evasion Edward's council drew up onerous rules to regulate the procedure of appeals from Scotland: the Scottish king must always attend in person to answer such appeals. In November 1293 King John did attend. In vain he affirmed 'that he is king of the realm of Scotland and dare not make answer at the suit of Macduff, nor in anything touching his kingdom without the advice of his people'. He was offered an adjournment to seek such advice but rejected it since that would have been an admission of the competence of the English court. King John was therefore adjudged guilty of contempt of court, and was sentenced to lose his three chief castles and towns. Had he held firm the result would have been war or the bitterest humiliation. He chose the lesser humiliation and

<hr />

[5] *A.P.S.*, I. 447–8.
[6] Barrow, *Bruce*, pp. 70–3.

sought the adjournment that he had previously rejected. The Mac-Duff case dragged on with further adjournments.[7]

Edward himself, in his capacity as Duke of Aquitaine, had occasionally suffered humiliation at the hands of his overlord, the French king. Edward was inclined to treat King John no more gently than Philip IV treated *him*. But the Scottish kingdom, unlike the duchy of Aquitaine, had long possessed at least *de facto* independence and had as much right to be considered a distinct state as England. Edward paid no heed to the fact that the Scots had only reluctantly accepted him as lord superior. And both sides were poles apart in their interpretation of what was implied by Edward's position as lord superior : John was willing to behave as a vassal king ; what Edward wanted was not a vassal king but a mere agent whose every action he might review. John's position was an impossible one : his own subjects regarded him as a king ; Edward regarded him as a subject.

The situation was further complicated by the fact that Edward had been ruling Scotland directly between June 1291 and November 1292. There still remained unsettled matters of finance and justice that he had dealt with during this period ; he assumed that he had a right to see that they were settled. Among the outstanding matters were the respective claims of the Count of Flanders and Eric of Norway to large arrears of dower or dowry that should have been paid from the Scottish revenues. In addition Eric was to claim that the Western Isles, ceded to the Scottish crown in 1266 in return for annual payment of a hundred marks in perpetuity, should revert to Norway since payment was in arrears.[8] To attain his ends in Scotland Eric was working not only through Edward but through the Bruces : in 1293 the widowed Eric married Isabella, sister of the youngest Bruce. This match took place at a time when there was a Bruce-Balliol dispute over the vacant bishopric of Galloway.[9] To King John it must have seemed that Edward, Eric, and the Bruces had banded together to undermine his authority and prestige, perhaps even to dismember his kingdom.

The trend of events can hardly have been hidden from the Scottish magnates. John Comyn, Earl of Buchan, had been among those who from the very first had sensed that the question of appeals

[7] *Ibid.*, pp. 74–83; Stones, *Documents*, No. 21.

[8] Ranald Nicholson, *op. cit.*, S.H.R., XXXVIII. 114–32 at 122–3, 129; *A.P.S.*, I. 448.

[9] A. A. M. Duncan, *op. cit.*, S.H.R., XLV. 36–58, at 45; Robert J. Brentano, 'The Whithorn Vacancy of 1293–94', *Innes Review*, IV. 71–83; Barrow, *Bruce*, pp. 92–3.

menaced what remained of Scottish independence. During the minority of Alexander III, when Henry III of England was trying to control Scotland, the Comyns had acquired intimate experience of Anglo-Scottish relations and in 1258 had made an abortive alliance with the English king's foe, Llewelyn, Prince of Wales.[10] Between September 1294 and March 1295 the Welsh, lately subdued by Edward I, were once more striving for independence under Madog ap Llewelyn. Madog's rising had partly been in response to Edward's order that the Welsh should fight for him against the French.[11] The same demand was presented to the Scots. Their response was less spontaneous than that of the Welsh but it was all the more deliberate and prepared.

The outbreak of war between Edward and Philip IV of France had arisen from a naval incident off the coast of Brittany. As a result Philip eventually denounced his great vassal as contumacious and forfeited Edward's duchy of Aquitaine. Edward sent his defiance and made ready to defend the duchy. In the summer of 1294 King John was present in England at the great council that prepared for war with France and was induced to promise Scottish help.[12] The war had not only made Edward increase his demands upon the Scots but had created a situation in which the Scots were tempted to resist all Edward's demands, both present and past. On 5 July 1295 Scottish envoys were sent to conclude a treaty with the French king.

It was not the first time that the Scots had looked to France for help against the English; but the treaty that was drafted at Paris on 23 October 1295 was to have far more lasting effects than any previous Franco-Scottish pact. It was a defensive and offensive alliance directed against England; neither ally would make a separate peace; the alliance was to be given the more permanence by a projected marriage between the niece of the French king and Edward Balliol, son and heir of King John. The French asked that the treaty should be ratified not only by King John but by the Scottish prelates, barons, knights, and 'communities of the towns'. The Scottish burgesses made their entry into high affairs of state when the seals of six burghs were attached to the Scottish ratification at Dunfermline on 23 February 1296.[13] From the other seals attached to the ratification it is clear that the new alliance had powerful support within Scotland. King John, however, had misgivings. Although his own great seal

[10] D. E. R. Watt, 'The Minority of Alexander III of Scotland', *T.R.H.S.* (5th series), XXI. 1–23, at 17.
[11] Barrow, *Bruce*, p. 88.   [12] *Ibid.*, pp. 87–8.   [13] *A.P.S.*, I. 451–3.

was appended he himself seems to have been unwilling to accept responsibility : at the assembly in July 1295 that had decided to send envoys to France the implementation of the new policy was entrusted to a council of twelve—four bishops, four earls and four barons—which represented the main elements in the political community.[14]

The Franco-Scottish alliance was only one among the many alliances that were being made in Western Europe as Edward aimed at the encirclement of France and Philip built up counter-alliances that threatened England itself. Philip even swept Edward's Norwegian associates into his schemes : on the day before the conclusion of the Franco-Scottish alliance a Franco-Norwegian alliance was also concluded at Paris. The French persuaded both Scots and Norwegians to forget their own disputes for the time being : the aim of French policy was that the Norwegians would provide shipping for a seaborne invasion of England ;[15] the Scots would invade by land.

The Scottish host was summoned to muster at Caddonlea near Selkirk on 11 March 1296.[16] It would be made up, as most Scottish armies were to be made up during the wars of independence, of both 'feudal' and 'national' elements. Feudal military service provided a small number of well-armed and mounted knights, esquires and men-at-arms, but the bulk of the host, the ordinary rank and file, was drawn from the lower classes of society who furnished the *servitium Scoticanum* that dated back to pre-feudal times.[17] This 'Scottish service', known also as *communis exercitus*, 'common army', was the old military service, comparable to the Anglo-Saxon fyrd. It meant that every able-bodied man between the ages of sixteen and sixty could be summoned to join the levies of the sheriffdoms when the king's host was mustered for the defence of the country. There was thus a system of national conscription.

Similar developments had taken place in England ; yet there were vital differences between Scottish and English armies. The man-power of England, with a population five times larger than that of Scotland, was large enough to allow selection by commissioners of array of the best men levied in the shires ; and the commissioners soon learned to recruit men who were proficient in the use of the deadly long-bow. By contrast the Scottish levies turned up with a motley

[14] Barrow, *Bruce*, p. 89.

[15] Ranald Nicholson, *op. cit.*, S.H.R., xxxviii. 114–32, at 116–9. Although the Norwegians never appeared the French made a few naval raids and forced the English to organise coastal defences (A. Z. Freeman, 'A Moat Defensive : the Coast Defence Scheme of 1295', *Speculum*, xlii. 442–62).

[16] Barrow, *Bruce*, p. 93.   [17] *Highland Papers*, ii. 233–5.

assembly of weapons—spears, Lochaber axes, short-bow and sword. The manpower and wealth of the English feudal classes was great enough to allow a large proportion of the English host to be made up of well-armed cavalry; by contrast Scotland was weak in cavalry. In England, as in Scotland, the traditional period of military service was forty days in the year; but the English king was wealthy enough to pay daily wages of war to all his troops, from the haughtiest earl to the humblest groom; those who took the king's wages were more amenable to royal discipline and could be induced to serve longer than forty days. If Scottish troops were paid they were paid by those who sent them, not by the Scottish king. Often Scottish armies could be held together only through the prospect of a share in booty and plunder. Besides the lasting differences that were obvious even in 1296, the Scots had no recent experience of warfare; the English had perfected their military machine in the bitter campaigns that crushed the Welsh.

As the ill-trained Scottish host mustered at Caddonlea there were gaps in the ranks: the eldest Robert Bruce had died in the previous year at the age of eighty-four;[18] neither his son nor his grandson, the new Earl of Carrick, was prepared to fight for Balliol—they joined the Earls of March and Angus who fought for Edward.[19] From the Bruce lordship of Annandale, now held for King John by John Comyn, Earl of Buchan, a force set out on Easter Monday (26 March) to launch an unsuccessful assault on Carlisle,[20] where Bruce senior commanded the garrison. From the very outset of the war Edward could take advantage of Scottish rivalries and use one faction against another.

Before engaging in warfare, Edward had gone through the motions of holding a parliament at Newcastle to which he summoned King John; Edward had also summoned his army to Newcastle; King John understandably failed to appear. Immediately after the Scottish assault on Carlisle the English crossed the Tweed. Berwick, the most important Scottish burgh, refused to open its gates, although the burgesses were assured of good treatment if they capitulated. They had once written flattering letters to Edward; now they insulted him from behind their flimsy palisades. On 30 March 1296 the town was taken by storm and the inhabitants were indiscriminately butchered. In revenge, the Earls of Ross, Menteith and Atholl ravaged Tynedale and Redesdale.[21] Soon the Scots were to be taught for the

[18] *Cal. Docs. Scot.*, II. No. 689.
[20] Barrow, *Bruce*, pp. 97–9.
[19] Stones, *Documents*, No. 22.
[21] *Chron. Lanercost*, pp. 171–5.

first time, but not for the last, the danger of waging pitched battle with the English: at Dunbar on 27 April 1296 the Scottish host was overwhelmed by the Earl of Surrey.[22] This ended the bellicosity of the Scots for the time being. The castles of Dunbar, Roxburgh, Jedburgh and Dumbarton were surrendered by their garrisons. Edinburgh Castle held out against siege machines for only a week. When Edward arrived at Stirling it was to find that the garrison had fled, leaving the gate-keeper to surrender the castle.[23] When he reached Perth the local gentry hastened to submit and swear fealty.[24]

Soon after the fall of Berwick, King John had sent two Franciscan friars to the town to present a final and dignified remonstrance to Edward : the latter had 'caused harm beyond measure to the liberties of ourselves and our kingdom . . . for instance by summoning us outside our realm at the mere beck and call of anybody, as your own whim dictated, and by harassing us unjustifiably'. The friars had renounced the homage and fealty 'which, be it said, were extorted by extreme coercion on your part'.[25] Now came the time for John to eat his brave words. Deserted by all save a few of his Comyn supporters he had fled to the glens of Angus and Mearns and had little alternative save abject surrender. At the royal castle of Kincardine on 2 July 1296 he was obliged to seal a document in which he confessed his wrongdoing and folly in allying himself with the foes of his overlord and surrendered to Edward the land and people of Scotland.[26] Once, King John had been ceremonially made king; now he was to be ceremonially unmade. He was attired in royal splendour for the last time, then the crown was taken from his head, the sceptre and sword from his hands, the ring from his finger, the costly fur from his tabard or surcoat. His tabard was 'toom'—bare or empty—and Balliol, the unmade king, became 'Toom Tabard'.[27] Having 'stamped on Balliol's name an image of perpetual disgrace', Edward marched as far north as Elgin, meeting with no resistance. He returned to Berwick on 26 August 1296. According to a diarist of the expedition, he had 'conquered and serched the kyngdom of Scotteland . . . in xxj

---

[22] *Ibid.*, pp. 175–7.
[23] 'Diary of the Expedition of Edward I into Scotland', *Bannatyne Misc. I.* 264–82, at 276.
[24] *Cal. Docs. Scot.*, II. 178–9.
[25] Stones, *Documents*, No. 23.
[26] *Ibid.*, No. 24.
[27] G. G. Simpson, 'Why was John Balliol called "Toom Tabard"?', *S.H.R.*, XLVII. 196–9.

wekis'.[28] Those weeks had seen the end of decades of peace between Scotland and England. They were to be followed by two and a half centuries of enmity and warfare.

In the course of Edward's progress through Scotland many magnates had hastened to swear fealty to him and to renounce the Franco-Scottish alliance. When he held parliament at Berwick at the end of August 1296 further submissions were received and others were forwarded by the sheriffs he appointed. The names of hundreds of Scots, nobles, prelates and even men of lesser standing, filled the thirty-five membranes of parchment that came to be known as the Ragman Roll.[29] Less concern for such a legalistic recording of Scottish fealties, more concern to secure the real loyalty of the Scots, might have brought Edward better results. As it was, before he left for England in September he had already committed a blunder that alienated many who in course of time might have loyally accepted him. By feudal custom the escheat of a fief to its overlord left unaltered the rights and privileges inherent in the fief; and the escheated fief of Scotland was a kingdom. One course open to Edward was to appoint a new vassal king. Bruce senior was willing enough to step into the position that Balliol had vacated: at the very outset of Edward's Scottish campaign he and his son had joined Edward at Wark, affirming that 'we are, and always have been, faithful'.[30] The chronicler Bower narrates that after the English victory at Dunbar the elder Bruce asked Edward to install him as King of Scotland, only to be snubbed when Edward answered in French: 'Have we nothing to do but win realms for you?'[31] The two Bruces were sent with their tails between their legs to bring their own tenants of Annandale and Carrick to Edward's obedience.[32] There was to be no new vassal King of Scotland. Another course open to Edward after the deposition of Balliol was for him to assume the title of King of Scots himself. Instead, he ruled Scotland in his capacity as King of England. He let it be seen that, at best, the kingdom of Scotland was in abeyance, at worst, it had come to an end: the Scottish regalia and the Scottish muniments were sent to London, the enthronement stone was removed from Scone[33] and installed as a trophy of war in Westminster;

[28] 'Diary of the Expedition of Edward I into Scotland, *Bannatyne Misc. I.* 264–82, at 281.

[29] *Cal. Docs. Scot.*, II. No. 823.   [30] Stones, *Documents*, No. 22.

[31] *Chron. Bower*, II. 166.   [32] Stones, *Documents*, No. 25.

[33] For the history of the 'Stone of Destiny' see W. Douglas Simpson, *Dunstaffnage Castle and the Stone of Destiny* (1958).

Edward referred to Scotland not as a kingdom but as 'the land of Scotland'. The change of status was one that should not have befallen a mere barony, but it embodied Edward's consistent attitude towards Scotland. In his view the British Isles could hold only a single kingdom, that of England. Scotland, after 1296, would be administered separately from England, but no more separately, no more independently, than the lordship of Ireland or the principality of Wales. Although local civil government was left in Scottish hands central government was in English hands. For the first time the full scope of Edward's policy was clear to all Scots. They had once pitied the Welsh. Now they themselves were reduced to the same status. The only alternative to a future of humiliation was to fight for a restoration of the Scottish kingdom.

But who was to lead the fight? Not only John Balliol but many of the Scottish nobles taken prisoner at Dunbar were captive in England. The names of most of the remaining nobles swelled the Ragman Roll; and the English administration can hardly have worried over the absence of the name of William Wallace, esquire, second son of a simple knight, Sir Malcolm Wallace of Elderslie, vassal of James the Steward.

William Wallace was probably among those who had been driven to guerrilla resistance when Edward's justiciar, William Ormsby, was 'following steadfastly the command of the king' and 'outlawed without distinction of person all who were unwilling to take the oath of fealty to the King of England'.[34] After a brawl with the English garrison of Lanark Wallace escaped with the help of his wife (or mistress), who was put to death by his pursuers. In revenge Wallace came back to Lanark, slew the English sheriff, Sir William Hazelrigg,[35] and became the foremost leader of the 'outlaws'.

Wallace's personal grievances against the English occupying forces, and his personal reactions, were probably not unique. Nor was he the only Scot who was keenly aware of the issues raised by Edward's attempt to reduce Scotland to subordinate status. If the Scottish kingdom disappeared the Scottish kirk might well be the next victim. On 1 October 1296 Edward ordered that only English priests should be presented to vacant benefices in Galloway. Less than a year later the same order was applied to all Scotland.[36] By the intru-

---

[34] *The Chronicle of Walter of Guisborough*, ed. H. Rothwell (1957), p. 294.
[35] The traditional account given in Blind Harry's *Wallace* (S.T.S.), pp. 113–8, is supported by English sources.
[36] *Rot. Scot.*, I. 35, 47.

sion of English ecclesiastics the Scottish kirk could gradually be subverted from within, and the last distinctive Scottish institution would be converted into an agency of the English occupation. Although numerous Scottish ecclesiastics had hastened to make their peace with Edward [37] many others held aloof : 'out of a possible total of twelve bishops of Scotland only three are known to have done homage to Edward'.[38] One of the three was Robert Wishart, Bishop of Glasgow, who, according to the Lanercost chronicler, 'conspired with the Steward . . . for a new piece of insolence. . . . Not daring openly to break their pledge to the king, they caused a certain bloody man, William Wallace, who had formerly been chief of brigands in Scotland, to revolt against the king, and assemble the people in his support'.[39] It was probably through the underhand efforts of Wishart and the Steward that Wallace was no longer the mere leader of a band of outlaws but by May 1297 was a joint leader with Sir William Douglas in an attack upon Ormsby the justiciar, who was holding his court at Scone. When Ormsby was put to flight the smouldering resistance that had lasted throughout the winter of 1296–7 flared into a wholesale rising.[40]

Already there were suspicions of the younger Bruce's intentions. Though obliged to take a solemn oath at Carlisle that he would remain loyal to Edward, he assembled his father's vassals, the knights of Annandale, told them that the Carlisle oath had been given under duress, and affirmed : 'No man holds his flesh and blood in hatred, and I am no exception. I must join my own people and the nation in which I was born.' [41] The patriotism thus expressed was doubtless sincere ; but it was coupled with another motive. The younger Bruce, a man of more mettle than his father, saw in the Scottish rising a chance to pursue his grandfather's legacy of the quest for the crown. In 1297 he joined the insurgents, 'aspiring to the kingdom, as was commonly said'.[42]

The Earl of Carrick was with Wishart, Wallace and the Steward in June 1297, when they encountered an English force at Irvine. Wallace and the majority were fighting for the captive Balliol and were at odds with their new ally, who was striving for his own claims. One Scottish knight said that it was folly to fight for men who

[37] *Ibid.*, I. 24–6.
[38] Barrow, *Bruce*, p. 111.
[39] *Chron. Lanercost*, p. 190.
[40] Barron, *War of Independence*, pp. 27–30; Barrow, *Bruce*, pp. 117–8.
[41] Barrow, *Bruce*, pp. 118–19.
[42] A. A. M. Duncan, *op. cit.*, *S.H.R.*, XLV. 184–201, at 194.

were divided against themselves and joined the English. He was followed by Bishop Wishart, the Steward, Bruce, and most of the other Scottish leaders who claimed to act as spokesmen of 'the whole community of the realm'. A document of capitulation was drafted at Irvine on 7 July 1297 [43] outlining the lenient terms on which they were to be pardoned by Edward. The result was to discredit the Scottish magnates politically almost as much as the battle of Dunbar had done militarily.[44] Under the belief that Scotland had been pacified, Edward set sail for Flanders at the end of August, taking with him some of the Dunbar prisoners, who were to have a chance of winning their freedom by good service against the French.[45]

But if William Wallace had been previously a mere agent of Bishop Wishart and the Steward, the capitulation of Irvine released him from tutelage. He had established himself in Selkirk forest, then, and afterwards, a sure retreat for the forces of resistance south of the Forth; and with him he had a force that one of Edward's officials described as 'a large company'.[46] For, so claimed an English chronicler, 'the common folk of the land followed him as their leader and ruler; the retainers of the great lords adhered to him; and even though the lords themselves were present with the [English] king in body, at heart they were on the opposite side'.[47] By August 1297 Wallace had crossed the Tay to besiege the English-held castle of Dundee [48] and to link up with staunch allies in the north, where the rising had gone from strength to strength.

The chief leader of the northern rising was Andrew Moray. Like Wallace he had personal grievances: his father and uncle were Edward's captives; he himself had been imprisoned in Chester Castle until he escaped. Also, like Wallace, Moray was a mere esquire. Yet despite their equal military rank there was a vast difference between the two young men. Wallace was no great landholder. Andrew Moray was heir to his father's large estates in Moray and Cromarty, heir also to his uncle's lordship of Bothwell in Lanarkshire, centred upon Bothwell Castle, one of the new stonebuilt castles in Scotland, and perhaps the most impressive. In the other family castle of Avoch in the Black Isle Andrew Moray assembled his retainers in May 1297 and with Alexander Pilche, a burgess of Inver-

[43] Stevenson, *Documents*, II. No. ccccxlvii.
[44] *Ibid.*, No. ccccliv.
[45] *Rot. Scot.*, I. 44–5.
[46] Stevenson, *Documents*, II. No. ccccliii.
[47] *The Chronicle of Walter of Guisborough*, ed. Harry Rothwell (1957), p. 299.   [48] *Chron. Bower*, II. 171.

ness, planned an attack upon the garrison of Urquhart Castle [49] on the shores of Loch Ness. By the end of July Edward's luke-warm Scottish supporters in Moray were on the defensive; [50] Andrew Moray took advantage of the rugged terrain to wage successful guer-rilla warfare. Well might Edward's treasurer of Scotland write on 5 August that the outcome of the Irvine pacification was obscure in the regions north of the Forth. [51]

No details survive of the campaign that Andrew Moray must have waged in the following five weeks to obtain mastery of the whole region north of Tay; and nothing is known of the circumstances in which Moray's troops linked up with those of Wallace. An English force belatedly set out under the Earl of Surrey and Treasurer Cres-singham, reached Stirling early in September, and found the troops of both Moray and Wallace massed on the Abbey Craig on the northern bank of the Forth. In July Treasurer Cressingham had had as many as 300 heavy cavalry and 10,000 footmen in his pay, [52] and it is unlikely that he and the Earl of Surrey had brought a smaller force to Stirling. On 11 September 1297 the English host, after two previous false starts, began for the third time to cross the narrow wooden bridge on which only two horsemen could ride abreast. [53]

The vanguard reached the northern bank only to be over-whelmed. Cressingham was slain, and the Scots made souvenirs of his skin. [54] Surrey rode post-haste to Berwick in humiliating flight. English losses were immense. The outcome was the utter overthrow of all that Edward had so far achieved in Scotland. An unknown con-temporary writer composed Latin verses to celebrate the Scottish victory that had been attained through Wallace's inspiration: once more King John would be able to reign in his own kingdom. [55]

The same mood of optimism appeared in a letter of 11 October 1297 which Wallace wrote from Haddington to the merchants of Lübeck and Hamburg thanking them for their support and inform-ing them that it was again safe to trade with Scotland, which was now 'recovered by war from the power of the English'. The letter ran

---

[49] *Cal. Docs. Scot.*, II. No. 922.

[50] Barron, *War of Independence*, pp. 37–67.

[51] Stevenson, *Documents*, II. No. cccclxvii.

[52] *Ibid.*, No. ccccliii.

[53] Barrow, *Bruce*, pp. 123–4.

[54] For his career in Scotland see A. Z. Freeman, 'The King's Penny: the Headquarters Paymasters under Edward I, 1295–1307', *Journal of British Studies*, VI. 1–22, at 7–11.

[55] *Chron. Bower*, II. 171.

in the names of Andrew Moray and William Wallace, 'leaders of the army of the kingdom of Scotland, and the community of the same kingdom'.[56] The army of the kingdom was thus accorded precedence over the community; the name of Moray was accorded precedence over that of Wallace. But Moray had been mortally wounded at Stirling bridge.[57] He died leaving a posthumous son and namesake who was to earn even greater fame than his father.

The death of Andrew Moray left Wallace supreme in Scotland. Within a few months one of the Scottish earls dubbed him knight. More than that, he was appointed sole guardian of Scotland and in one of his few known charters styled himself 'William Wallace, knight, guardian of the kingdom of Scotland and commander of its armies in the name of the famous prince the Lord John, by God's grace illustrious King of Scotland, by consent of the community of that realm'.[58] In the last resort, however, Wallace's power rested upon his position as commander of the Scottish army, not upon his position within the aristocratic 'community'.[59] He was 'the leader of a popular movement with a measure of social discontent in its makeup'.[60] And the army that Wallace formed was hardly the kind in which chivalric magnates would feel at home: the stress was laid upon the 'common army'. Lists of those liable to conscription were drawn up in every community from the sheriffdom to the merest rural township. Gallows were erected (and used) to hang those who disobeyed the call to arms; the recruits were formed into military units of five, ten, a hundred or a thousand men, and rigid discipline was demanded.[61] This was a 'New Model Army' comparable to that of Cromwell save in one respect—Wallace was fighting for a king. No one could challenge Wallace's position so long as he was successful in warfare; and at first he was. In November 1297 he led his new army into the north of England: at a time of famine in Scotland the army would be supported upon English booty and provisions.[62]

It was while Edward was absent in Flanders that Wallace had proved himself 'the hammer and scourge of the English'.[63] In March 1298 the king returned to England and immediately began prepara-

[56] *Documents Illustrative of Sir William Wallace, his Life and Times* (Maitland Club), No. xv.

[57] *Chron. Bower*, II. 171.

[58] Barrow, *Bruce*, p. 129

[59] See *Chron. Bower*, II. 174.

[60] A. A. M. Duncan, *Nation of Scots*, p. 16.

[61] *Chron. Bower*, II. 170–1, 172.

[62] *Ibid.*, 172.   [63] *Ibid.*, 169.

tions for a new campaign in Scotland.[64] By the beginning of July he had reached Roxburgh at the head of a powerful army and set out for Edinburgh to meet the supply ships that were expected in the Forth. Contrary winds prevented all but a few of the ships from reaching Leith; and they brought wine rather than victuals. Some of Edward's Welsh troops were drunk or dying; they had no love for their English conquerors and it was suspected they might defect to the Scots. Having advanced some ten miles west of Edinburgh, Edward was faced with the prospect of having to retreat. Then his loyal supporters the Earls of March and Angus arrived in camp with the news that Wallace lay in the wood of Callendar near Falkirk. On 22 July 1298 the two armies confronted one another.[65]

Since the campaign had begun, Wallace's strategy had been the one that was to bring success in future years: he had laid waste the country and burned the towns south of Forth so that they could not be used by the invaders;[66] he had harassed their stragglers, and almost starved the whole army into retreat. Yet this was not the way to win chivalric esteem; and Wallace, the newly dubbed knight, may have been taunted into action to preserve his military laurels. Somewhere near Falkirk he drew up his men in a defensive position protected by a palisade of stakes bound together with ropes. In front lay marsh and loch; on the flanks there was probably broken ground; behind these defences the spearmen were grouped in four great 'schiltrons'. These circular formations, from which spears projected like the spines of a hedgehog, may have been invented by Wallace in his reorganisation of the Scottish army. Between each schiltron were placed the archers of Ettrick forest. In the rear was the cavalry.[67]

Despite Wallace's careful preparations the Scots at Falkirk were far less favourably placed than they had been the year before at the Abbey Craig. It has been rightly said that Falkirk was a battle the Scots should never have fought.[68] They trusted most of all in their infantry spearmen,[69] who had to contend with the overwhelming superiority of the English both in archers and cavalry. Moreover, the small force of Scottish cavalry was contributed by nobles who were

[64] The preparations are detailed in *Scotland in 1298: Documents relating to the Campaign of King Edward the First in that Year, and especially to the Battle of Falkirk* (ed. Henry Gough, London, 1888), afterwards cited as *Scotland in 1298*.

[65] Barrow, *Bruce*, pp. 140–2.

[66] *Chron. Lanercost*, p. 191.

[67] *Scotland in 1298*, pp. xviii, xx, xxv, xxix.

[68] Barron, *War of Independence*, p. 77.

[69] *Chron. Lanercost*, p. 191.

restive under Wallace's command. Few of them stayed to fight.[70] Deprived of cavalry support the spearmen in the schiltrons kept up a dour resistance. They were easy targets for the bowmen and were at last overwhelmed by repeated cavalry charges. English chroniclers narrated that thousands of 'the poor common folk'—and even some priests—were slain at Falkirk;[71] they could not grace their accounts of the English triumph—as they had done in writing of Dunbar and were to do in recounting future English victories—with long lists of Scottish nobles who were slain or captured.

From the slaughter of Falkirk Wallace had escaped with his life; but his power was shattered. On the banks of the Forth he resigned his post as guardian.[72] His meteoric rise had hardly been that of a proletarian hero: folk tradition took pains to stress his gentle birth. Yet Wallace was a member of a social class that had not hitherto shown initiative in affairs of state. His personal dominance, regarded as extreme presumption by his enemies, had briefly been enough to break down traditional feudal ties. As a Scottish Cromwell he might have fashioned Scotland anew. Though he failed to do this, his achievement was nonetheless a fundamental one. He had inspired a patriotic resistance among the common folk that outlasted defeat; and it was this resistance that was to frustrate the ambitions of Plantagenet imperialism.

With Wallace's fall from power the way was open for more traditional leaders to reassert themselves. Within a few months Robert Bruce, Earl of Carrick, grandson of the competitor in the Great Cause, was uneasily associated with John Comyn of Badenoch, the 'Red Comyn', son of the Comyn who had been guardian in 1286. They acted as 'guardians of the kingdom of Scotland in the name of the famous prince the illustrious King John, together with the bishops, abbots, priors, earls, barons and other magnates and the whole community of the realm'.[73] Once more the aristocratic community was to the fore; there was no longer mention of 'the army of the kingdom'— the nation in arms. But for the next five years only south-east Scotland, dominated by the castles of Edinburgh, Berwick and Roxburgh, was under firm English control; elsewhere the guardians re-established a Scottish administration.[74] They were aided by two new bishops: in

---

[70] *Chron. Bower*, II. 170, 175.
[71] *Scotland in 1298*, pp. xv, xvi, xxi, xxiii, xxv.
[72] *Chron. Bower*, II. 176.
[73] Barrow, *Bruce*, p. 148.   [74] *Ibid.*, pp. 148-9.

1297 Wallace had induced the chapter of St Andrews to elect William Lamberton as successor to Bishop William Fraser, who had died in France, and in 1299 David Moray, kinsman of the late Andrew Moray, had been elected to the bishopric of Moray; both Lamberton and Moray received consecration at the papal court and were to urge Boniface VIII to support the Scots.[75]

Lamberton returned to Scotland in time to join the Scottish leaders in a lively conference in the forest of Selkirk on 19 August 1299. According to an English spy who witnessed the proceedings, Sir David Graham 'demanded the lands and goods of Sir William Wallace because he was leaving the kingdom without the leave or approval of the guardians'[76]—Wallace, it seems, was preparing to set out on a self-appointed mission to France or Norway.[77] Sir Malcolm Wallace, who was present in the council, defended his brother. Graham gave him the lie and both drew their daggers. The fracas was enlivened when the Red Comyn 'leapt upon the Earl of Carrick [his fellow-guardian] and seized him by the throat', while the Earl of Buchan grappled with Bishop Lamberton 'until the Steward and others went between and stopped this scuffle'.

The upshot was a new organisation of the guardianship: Bishop Lamberton was to be chief guardian with control of the Scottish castles; Bruce and the Red Comyn were to be associated with him as guardians.[78] On 13 November 1299 the three were in the Tor Wood,[79] evidently besieging Stirling Castle (which fell by the end of the year). By May 1300, however, the Earl of Carrick was ousted from the triumvirate. When a parliament was held at Rutherglen on 10 May 1300 there were further alterations. Finally Comyn and Lamberton were both confirmed in office, and the place vacated by Bruce was given to Sir Ingeram Umfraville, who was associated with Balliol and the Comyns.[80]

When Edward invaded Galloway in the summer of 1300 he was met by the Earl of Buchan and the Red Comyn of Badenoch. The two Comyns proposed peace on condition that John Balliol be restored and that Scotsmen be permitted to buy back their forfeited English estates. Edward angrily rejected these terms. He had just besieged and captured Caerlaverock Castle—an exploit recorded in a chivalric

[75] Dowden, *Bishops*, pp. 21–2, 151–2; T. S. R. Boase, *Boniface VIII* (1933), p. 209; Palgrave, *Documents*, I. No. cxlix.

[76] *Nat. MSS. Scot.*, II. No. viii.   [77] Barrow, *Bruce*, p. 164.

[78] *Nat. MSS. Scot.*, II. No. viii.   [79] *Cal. Docs. Scot.*, II. No. 1109.

[80] G. O. Sayles, 'The Guardians of Scotland and a Parliament at Rutherglen in 1300', *S.H.R.*, xxiv. 245–50.

French poem by a war-correspondent who accompanied the expedition.[81] Edward continued his march through Galloway to the river
Cree, where he put to flight an opposing Scottish force.[82] This encounter, more humiliating than disastrous for the ruling Comyn
party, marked the end of the campaign. By 24 August 1300 the king
had retired to Sweetheart Abbey. There he received the travel-weary
Archbishop Winchelsea of Canterbury who had come to the wilds of
Galloway to present the papal bull *Scimus fili* drawn up by Boniface
VIII on 28 June 1299—the day of David Moray's consecration in the
papal court—and now belatedly released.[83] When Winchelsea burst
into the royal presence with the obnoxious bull Edward cut short his
sermonising and interjected : 'By God's blood! For Zion's sake I will
not be silent, and for Jerusalem's sake I will not be at rest, but with
all my strength I will defend my right that is known to all the world'.[84]

What was known to all the world was less clear to Pope Boniface.
In the bull *Scimus fili* he informed Edward of a new issue : 'We in
no wise doubt it to be contained in the book of your memory how
from ancient times the kingdom of Scotland pertained by full right
. . . to the foresaid Roman Church, and that, as we have understood,
it was not feudally subject to your ancestors . . . nor is it so to you.'[85]
Feudal subjection had been imposed by force and 'the fear which
may befall even the steadfast'. If Edward did indeed claim a right to
the kingdom of Scotland he should send envoys to the papal court
furnished with proof.[86]

The pope's challenge placed Edward in a procedural dilemma.[87]
It was decided that there should be a twofold response : in a counter-
blast to *Scimus fili* the English barons professed themselves wonder-
struck by the pope's allegations ;[88] seven weeks later the result of much
intellectual effort [89] was compressed into Edward's own more courteous reply to Boniface. The latter was informed that English claims
upon Scotland dated from 'the days of Eli and Samuel the prophet',
when fugitives from Troy had extirpated the giants in Albion. From
this mythological history (much more acceptable then than it would
be now) Edward drew important conclusions, which were reinforced

[81] See *The Siege of Caerlaverock*, ed. Nicholas Harris Nicolas (London, 1828).
[82] Barrow, *Bruce*, pp. 158–60.
[83] T. S. R. Boase, *Boniface VIII*, p. 210 and n.
[84] F. M. Powicke, *The Thirteenth Century*, p. 229.
[85] Stones, *Documents*, No. 28.
[86] *Ibid.*   [87] *Ibid.*, No. 29.
[88] F. M. Powicke, *The Thirteenth Century*, pp. 701–2, 705.
[89] *Ibid.*, pp. 701–2, 705.

by an account of more recent history concluding with Balliol's resignation of the realm into Edward's hands.[90]

While preparing the reply to Boniface Edward had graciously granted a French request that a truce be conceded to the Scots to last until May 1301.[91] In the summer of 1299 Edward had patched up his quarrel with the French and at their insistence had even released King John on condition that he be kept in papal custody.[92] The French set much store upon Balliol's recent release, and yet another alteration in the guardianship reflected the change : by May 1301 there was a sole guardian, Sir John Soulis, who seems to have been nominated by Balliol.[93] A new seal of government was used : on the obverse was the name and title of King John, on the reverse the name and arms of Sir John Soulis. No longer were documents issued in the name of guardians : now they ran in the name of King John himself ; the new guardian figured modestly only as witness.[94]

In giving way to French and papal demands for the release of Balliol into papal custody, Edward had intended to exact a threefold price—Balliol's disappearance from politics, an undertaking that the pope would not meddle in Scottish affairs, and a tacit understanding that the French would also drop their interest in Scotland. On each point Edward was to be disappointed. A report made to him affirmed that Bishop Lamberton was displaying a letter under King Philip's seal, 'asserting that there will be no peace between him and the King of England unless the Scots are included. The people are putting their faith in this and in the success which they hope will be obtained by Master Baldred, their spokesman at the court of Rome.'[95]

Master Baldred Bisset, graduate of Bologna, was the most outstanding of the educated clerics—archdeacons, 'officials', deans, and the like—whose talents were employed not only in Scottish ecclesiastical affairs but in administration and diplomacy.[96] Together with two other graduates, Master William of Eaglesham and Master William Frere, archdeacon of Lothian, he was accredited to the papal court by Sir John Soulis to present a *Processus*, or legal argument, combating the English claims. Bisset affirmed that Edward 'refers to

---

[90] Stones, *Documents*, No. 30.
[91] Palgrave, *Documents*, I. pp. 247–9.
[92] Stevenson, *Documents*, II. Nos. dlxxi, dlxxiv, dlxxix, dlxxx, dlxxxvi.
[93] '*Johannes rex noster per suum custodem ibidem deputatum possidet plenarie totum regnum*' (Bisset's *Processus, Chron. Bower*, II. 218).
[94] Barrow, *Bruce*, pp. 168–9.
[95] Cited *ibid.*, pp. 167–8.   [96] *Ibid.*, pp. 166–7, 376–7.

many things but proves few things'.[97] The English historical myths
were countered by equally exotic Scottish ones : Edward, a descendant of 'William the Bastard and his accomplices', had no connection
with the ancient Britons or Trojans ; the origins of Scotland were to
be traced to Scota, daughter of Pharaoh, and 'the Egyptians may
claim more right in the kingdom of Scotland than the English'. Bisset
went on to give his own interpretation of recent times. Edward, he
claimed, had craftily taken advantage of Scottish dissensions through
'the fear which may befall even the steadfast'. He had extorted fealty
and homage from 'our king, John Balliol' and afterwards declared
that 'our king willingly confessed that he had committed treasons
and conspiracies against the King of England and . . . had thus rightfully lost his kingdom'. But, affirmed Bisset, 'surely it is not true nor
likely that such a person [Balliol] in so arduous a matter would willingly have uttered such serious and detestable confessions'. On the
contrary, Edward had forcibly taken the seal of the kingdom from
the chancellor and fabricated the letters of confession after sending
Balliol and his son to prison in England. These letters 'our king has
never ratified and never will'.[98] Bisset also appealed to wider issues
than those raised by the various precedents to which king and pope,
and society in general, then attached weight. What had happened in
the past represented no fixed and invariable pattern for subsequent
times : 'in the course of nature, which in itself cannot remain motionless, many changes have occurred'. Although this line of thought was
not pursued it was one that cut at the roots of all Edward's arguments,
based as they were on precedent, real or supposed. Moreover Bisset
asserted that by universal law (*de jure communi*) one kingdom ought
not to be subject to another, nor one king to another. In this approach
the *Processus* pointed the way to the Declaration of Arbroath.

The war of words, which was inconclusive, was followed by warfare in Scotland that was equally indecisive. In May 1301 the Anglo-
Scottish truce expired. In July Edward set out on a new campaign
in south-western and central Scotland with his son and heir, the
Prince of Wales.[99] The Scots made disconcerting moves that menaced
the English forces and harassed their attempts to set up an administration in occupied territories. Sir John Soulis was an unquestioned

[97] For the text of the *Processus* see *Chron. Bower*, II. 210–8; *Chron. Pluscarden*, I. 205–18.

[98] It is interesting that Sir Thomas Gray, an English knight, gives an account
of Edward's alleged forgery of a letter in the name of the aldermen of Ghent
(*Scalacronica*, pp. 128–9).

[99] Barrow, *Bruce*, pp. 170–71.

patriot and had the support of the Comyns. He showed himself an active leader, had the good sense to avoid a major engagement, and nonetheless kept up a constant pressure on the invaders. To add to Edward's difficulties, an English officer wrote from Edinburgh on 1 October 1301 reporting that 'the King of France's people have taken Sir John Balliol from the place where he was sent to reside by the pope to his castle of Bailleul in Picardy, and some people believe that the King of France will send him with a great force to Scotland as soon as possible.' [100] Edward hastily negotiated with the French and an Anglo-French truce, in which the Scots were to be included, was drawn up at Asnières-sur-Oise.[101] Edward had to agree that the lands, towns and castles he had lately captured in Scotland would be delivered into French custody pending negotiations for a general peace. This showed the price he was willing to pay to avert an immediate Balliol restoration.

Such a prospect was equally disquieting to at least one notable Scot. It is only by doubtful inference that Robert Bruce, Earl of Carrick, can be assumed to have taken an active part in warfare after being dropped from the guardianship in 1300 : 'the silence of the sources suggests that he was sulking'.[102] For two years he had probably contented himself with defending his earldom against all outsiders, whether English or Scots. Yet neutrality would no longer suit his purposes when it seemed that a Balliol restoration was at hand ; by February 1302 Bruce admitted that it was through evil counsel that he had risen in war against Edward and 'yielded himself to the peace and will of the king in hope of receiving his mercy'.[103]

The terms of the memorandum recording this submission are curious and have inspired controversy.[104] The word 'right' (le droit) is used with a tantalising and needless ambiguity that may have suited both Bruce and Edward. The latter held out some prospect that Bruce would be assisted to obtain, or retain, his 'right'. It has been shrewdly remarked that this 'right' was a 'rainbow of many colours', at the end

---

[100] E. L. G. Stones, 'The Submission of Robert Bruce to Edward I, c. 1301–1302', S.H.R., xxxiv. 122–34, at 132–4.

[101] Text in Palgrave, Documents, i. No. cxxii.

[102] A. A. M. Duncan, op. cit., S.H.R., xlv. 184–201, at 195.

[103] Stones, Documents, No. 32.

[104] For the text of the submission see ibid. Varying explanations of the terms and their background have been given by E. M. Barron, War of Independence, pp. 139–48; E. L. G. Stones, op. cit., S.H.R., xxxiv. 122–34; Barrow, Bruce, pp. 172–5. The best interpretation is that of A. A. M. Duncan, op. cit., S.H.R., xlv. 184–201, at 194–8.

of which Bruce hoped to find a pot of gold.[105] What is clear is that in submitting to Edward, Bruce consulted his own self-interest first and foremost. If, as has been claimed, Bruce was 'one of a number of the country's natural leaders to be inspired by the idea of the community of the realm' [106] he did not at that stage find the idea particularly inspiring.

Although the truce of Asnières brought a halt to warfare in Scotland it did not prevent Edward from consolidating what he had won south of the Forth in the campaign of 1301. The five hundred troops who served in his garrisons [107] were the basis of the military and civil administration of occupied Scotland and they obtained essential co-operation from some Scottish magnates. Had their local influence been hostile, had castles like Dunbar or Turnberry been in nationalist hands, the occupation regime could hardly have held its own. Yet collaboration was forthcoming : Alexander Balliol, a kinsman of King John, engaged to 'keep' the forest of Selkirk for King Edward with 30 men-at-arms, to be supplemented on four days warning with a further 600 footmen, and on eight days warning with 1,000 ;[108] if the occupation regime worked through Scots who possessed local influence, and if traditional forms were observed, traditional services would be forthcoming. Edward was well aware of this. If those who were 'in his peace' suffered from the exactions of his officials that was not his intention.[109] It is striking that in negotiating the truce of Asnières his envoys showed some concern lest such Scots as were 'the lowly folk of the land' (le menu pueple du pais) [110] should be troubled when (according to the treaty) a French occupation force arrived to take over the lands and castles that Edward had lately won.

No such force ever appeared. On 25 July 1302 King Philip gave feeble excuses to Edward,[111] who must have accepted them with some relief. On 11 July 1302 French military prestige—and the prestige of chivalry in general—had suffered a blow : at Courtrai French nobles had been disastrously defeated by the bourgeois Flemings who had for some time co-operated with Edward. Within a week the news was brought to a jubilant Pope Boniface, already intractably engaged in open quarrel with the French king.[112] Philip had his hands

[105] A. A. M. Duncan, op. cit., S.H.R., XLV. 184–201, at 198.
[106] Barrow, Bruce, p. xxi.
[107] Cal. Docs. Scot., II. Nos 1324, 1337.
[108] Ibid., No. 1287.
[109] See ibid., No. 1321.
[110] Palgrave, Documents, I. No. cxxi, p. 244.
[111] Ibid., No. cxxiv.   [112] T. S. R. Boase, Boniface VIII, pp. 311–12.

full. Boniface began to look on Edward with a kindly eye : 'the end of the elaborate memorials, the historical arguments, was a letter to the Scottish bishops blaming them for being the chief cause of war; the Bishop of Glasgow in especial was "a stone of offence" who had broken his oath of fealty to the well-beloved King of England'.[113] The Scots had lost the support of the pope and it looked as if they would also lose that of the French king.

To avert this, Sir John Soulis headed a strong delegation to France, leaving John Comyn of Badenoch to act as guardian.[114] Philip wanted to include his Scottish allies in a final peace with England but Edward insisted on their exclusion. Philip's dilemma was solved when King John made a last disastrous decision : in a letter written from Bailleul on 23 November 1302[115] he consented that Philip should have a completely free hand in his negotiations with the English.[116] With this letter in his hand Philip could face the Scottish ambassadors.

On 25 May 1303 Lamberton and his fellow-ambassadors reported the result in a letter from Paris to John Comyn and the community:[117]

> A final peace was made and sworn between the Kings of France and England . . . and on the same day it was ordained by the King of France and his council that solemn envoys . . . be sent forthwith to the foresaid King of England to draw him back from the war of Scotland; . . . if, however, the said King of England be so obdurate, in the manner of Pharaoh, that he will not consent to the truce . . . manfully and as one man defend yourselves . . . and if you knew how much honour has come to you throughout many regions of the globe from your last fight against the English you would greatly rejoice.

In this last remark the ambassadors were alluding to an engagement fought at Roslin on 24 February 1303. In Scotland the end of the Asnières truce on 30 November 1302 had brought fresh hostilities in which the Scots seized the offensive.[118] Their success had culminated at Roslin, where Simon Fraser and John Comyn defeated the English occupation forces under Sir John Segrave.[119]

[113] *Ibid.*, pp. 327–8.   [114] Barrow, *Bruce*, p. 177.
[115] For the date see E. L. G. Stones, *op. cit.*, *S.H.R.*, xxxiv. 122–34, at 130, n. 8.   [116] Stevenson, *Documents*, ii. No. dcxxiv.
[117] *A.P.S.*, i. 454–5. This letter seems to have been intercepted by the English, but a duplicate may have eluded the naval blockade (E. L. G. Stones, 'An Undelivered Letter from Paris to Scotland [1303]?', *E.H.R.*, lxxx, 86–8).
[118] *Cal. Docs. Scot.*, ii. Nos. 1341, 1349; iv. p. 455.
[119] *Chron. Fordun*, i. 333–5.

Hope of an armistice disappeared. Before returning home from France, Bishop Lamberton wrote to Wallace 'and besought him for love of him [the bishop] and with his blessing, that he should with all his power give aid and counsel to the community of the said land of Scotland as he had done formerly'; Lamberton's servants were instructed to back Wallace with supplies.[120] Although Wallace was to serve only as a subordinate, the fact that he was once more in the fray was striking enough to make one English chronicler believe that in 1303, as in 1297, he was the chief instigator of Scottish resistance and had been chosen by the Scots as 'their commander and captain'.[121]

The testing time was at hand. The virtual end of the Franco-Scottish alliance was the signal for Edward to begin the campaign he had long prepared. For the first time since 1294 he could tackle Scotland without having to look backwards at the French king or the pope. He had realised that campaigns south of the Forth and Clyde could bring only limited success. The north, in which no English soldier had set foot since 1298, was a sure retreat for the forces of resistance, a base from which these forces might spring back as soon as an English field army had left the occupying administration uneasily cooped up in the southern castles. To conquer Scotland it was necessary to conquer the north. Yet a crossing of the Forth was perilous, particularly so when Stirling Castle was still in Scottish hands. Lowly carpenters, busy at King's Lynn since February, held the answer to the dilemma. While Edward mustered his army at Roxburgh a fleet of thirty ships set sail conveying three prefabricated pontoon bridges from Lynn to the upper reaches of the Forth.[122] Edward's timing was perfect: he set out from Roxburgh on 30 May 1303; no sooner were the bridges in place than he was across them with some 7,000 troops.[123] By 10 June he had occupied Perth. By September he had reached Kinloss on the Moray Firth. After the north had been subdued he moved south; Dunfermline was to be his headquarters until the spring of 1304.[124]

Time-servers, as always, hastened to make their peace. Edward astutely played on the fears of those who wavered, offering lenient terms to all who would submit before 2 February 1304.[125] On 9 February 1304 English envoys held a parley with John Comyn and his council at Strathord near Perth.[126] Long and detailed personal

[120] Palgrave, *Documents*, I. 333.
[121] Rishanger's Chronicle, cited in Barrow, *Bruce*, pp. 177–8.
[122] *Cal. Docs. Scot.*, II. No. 1375.
[123] *Ibid.*, No. 1599.   [124] Itinerary in *Rot. Scot.*, I. 53.
[125] Palgrave, *Documents*, I. No. cxxviii.   [126] *Ibid.*, No. cxxxi.

terms were drawn up for Comyn and for 'those who are of his accord', who seem to have been equated with the community :[127] the most they would suffer would be exile for a year or two and some pecuniary loss. Comyn was hardly in a position to dictate conditions : all that was saved from the political wreck of Scotland was a stipulation that laws, customs and privileges be observed as in the days of Alexander III ; if any law were to be amended it was to be with the assent and advice of the responsible men of the land.[128]

Most Scottish leaders accepted these terms and the lenient personal penalties that went with them ; but Sir John Soulis preferred permanent exile in France ;[129] and Sir William Oliphant, to whom Soulis had once entrusted custody of Stirling Castle, continued to hold out. The shadowy kingship of King John, together with its practical expression in Scottish guardianship, had come to an end. To fight for an abstraction was alien to the age. Yet something impelled the garrison of Stirling to continue the fight : they were defending the castle, so they claimed, on behalf of the Lion.[130] The Scottish nation could not be seen, and King John had been lost from view, but on the royal standard above the walls of Stirling the lion rampant, symbol of Scottish kingship, could be seen by all. Not until 20 July 1304, after three months of bombardment by thirteen war engines, was the standard lowered. Even unconditional surrender was refused until Edward had bombarded the castle and its inmates for a further day with his fourteenth war engine, the newly constructed 'Warwolf'.[131] The surviving defenders were forced to beg mercy before being sent to English prisons.

In this instance, as in others, Edward showed himself gracious towards time-servers, vindictive towards staunch opponents. Early in March 1304 he had been asked whether terms should be offered to William Wallace (who may have made overtures of submission)[132] and had replied : 'Know that it is not our will that you hold out any word of peace either to him or to any of his company unless they place themselves absolutely in all things at our will, without any reservation whatsoever.'[133] In September Wallace was put to flight

---

[127] Ibid., No. cxxxiii ; Barrow, Bruce, p. 182.
[128] Palgrave, Documents, i. Nos. cxxxiii, cxxxiv.
[129] Barrow, Bruce, p. 182.
[130] Scalacronica, p. 127.
[131] Cal. Docs. Scot., ii. Nos. 1560, 1599.
[132] See J. G. Bellamy, The Law of Treason in England in the Later Middle Ages (afterwards cited as Law of Treason), 1970, p. 33.
[133] Stevenson, Documents, ii. No. dcxxxiii.

in a last skirmish on the banks of the Earn.[134] Thenceforward he was a hunted outlaw with no alternative save unconditional surrender. It was a tribute to the loyalty which he still inspired that he remained at large until 3 August 1305, when he was taken near Glasgow and handed over to the English by Sir John Stewart of Menteith.[135] On 23 August he was brought to Westminster Hall, crowned in mockery with laurel leaves. The five judges followed the procedure that Edward had introduced in treason cases : 'there was no indictment by jury ; no appeal by an individual, no accusation by the king's prosecutor but merely a statement of the crimes which the crown held Wallace to have committed, terminating with the judgement'.[136] Dragged on a hurdle to Smithfield he was hanged, cut down while still alive, and butchered ; his head was set above London bridge and parts of his dismembered body were sent north for display.

The tragic conclusion of Wallace's career left a far deeper impression than that of any of the other Scots who within the following years would suffer a similar fate. This in itself is a testimony to the unique place that Wallace had held in the hearts and minds of the Scots. Blind Harry the Minstrel was merely echoing a long-established tradition when he declaimed : 'Rycht suth it is, a martyr was Wallace.' [137]

[134] *Cal. Docs. Scot.*, IV. 477.
[135] Barrow, *Bruce*, pp. 191, 193.
[136] J. G. Bellamy, *Law of Treason*, p. 35.
[137] Blind Harry, *Wallace* (*S.T.S.*) pp. 370–2, at 372 ; *Chron. Bower*, II. 230. See also Maurice Keen, *The Outlaws of Medieval Legend* (1961), pp. 64–77.

4

KING ROBERT, CIVIL WAR
AND PATRIOTIC WAR

Although Edward had crushed the Scots he was well aware that it was beyond his resources to control Scotland forever through sheer force. It was necessary through fear or favour to obtain the collaboration of Scottish leaders and to allow them a part in some scheme of government and administration. He had begun in March 1304 by summoning them to a parliament at St Andrews,[1] and when an English parliament met at Westminster in March 1305 it was arranged that the community of 'the land'[2] of Scotland should choose ten representatives who would join twenty-one Englishmen nominated by Edward. On 15 September 1305 they met at Westminster and drafted an ordinance for the establishment of a Scottish administration.[3] Many Scottish magnates had their lands restored to them; many Scots were appointed as sheriffs and keepers of castles.[4] Yet there were indications that this latest pacification might not be trouble-free, particularly in the province of Moray:[5] the ordinance of 1305 made mention of 'removing from Scotland those by whom the peace might be disturbed'; those who served Edward were to swear to disclose information about 'disturbances and hindrances . . . to the peace and quiet of the land'; and it was announced enigmatically that 'the Earl of Carrick be ordered to put the castle of Kil-

[1] A. A. M. Duncan, *op. cit., S.H.R.*, XLV. 36–58, at 48–9; H. G. Richardson and G. O. Sayles, 'Scottish Parliaments of Edward I', *ibid.*, XXV. 300–17.

[2] Stones (*Documents*, No. 33) incomprehensibly translates the word *terre* as 'realm'.

[3] Text in *ibid.*, No. 33.

[4] *Cal. Docs. Scot.*, II. No. 1646.

[5] Barron, *War of Independence*, pp. 196–208.

drummy in the keeping of a man for whom he himself is willing to answer'.[6]

Since 1302, when he had made his peace with Edward, Robert Bruce, Earl of Carrick, had served the English king in warfare,[7] unobtrusively, but well, and seemed to have purged himself of any excessive Scottishness. After the death of his first wife, Isabella, daughter of Earl Donald of Mar, Bruce married Elizabeth, daughter of Richard de Burgh, Earl of Ulster, the most prominent of Edward's Anglo-Irish supporters. Bruce was to pay a hasty visit to England in the spring of 1304 to secure his succession to the family estates which he inherited on the death of his father, the Lord of Annandale.[8] In March 1305, when he was again in England, it was natural that he should be entrusted by Edward with an important part in the preliminary stages of the Scottish pacification. Soon he was nominated to serve on the consultative council of Edward's lieutenant of Scotland,[9] but so were a score of other Scotsmen; it became clear that Edward would not allow Bruce any special position in Scotland. It has been convincingly shown that he had fallen from Edward's favour by the autumn of 1305, and less convincingly that the change was connected with Wallace's execution.[10] A more likely reason is that Edward may have received evidence, still inconclusive, to suggest that Bruce was plotting to obtain the Scottish crown.

Whether or not Edward had learned of it, such evidence did exist: on 11 June 1304, as Stirling Castle was being bombarded, two of the bystanders, Robert Bruce and Bishop Lamberton, concluded a bond of alliance in the nearby abbey of Cambuskenneth.[11] This indenture bound each to aid the other 'against any persons whatsoever'; neither Bruce nor Lamberton would attempt any 'arduous business' without consulting the other. Subsequent events make it clear that the 'arduous business' they had in mind was an attempt to place Bruce on the Scottish throne. Since 1302 he had expected his royal pretensions, of one kind or another, to be promoted by Edward, but nothing of the sort had happened—Edward disappointed the youngest Bruce just as he had disappointed his father and grandfather. By Edward's very success, however, the pathway that might lead the Earl of Carrick to the throne had been cleared of obstacles: although John Balliol was

[6] Stones, *Documents*, No. 33.
[7] *Cal. Docs. Scot.*, II. No. 1465; Stevenson, *Documents*, II. No. dcxli.
[8] Barrow, *Bruce*, pp. 199-200, 201-3.
[9] Palgrave, *Documents*, I. No. cxxxv.
[10] See Barron, *War of Independence*, pp. 159-74.
[11] Text in Palgrave, *Documents*, I. No. cxlvi.

to survive until 1313 as an exile in France, his cause had disintegrated; Bruce's rivals, the Comyns, 'had played their game and lost';[12] the institution of guardianship, never very inspiring, had come to an end; if Scottish resistance were to revive, a new leader and a new cause would be required; and Bruce could supply both. Now thirty years old, he was no longer restrained by a conformist father: he himself was head of his family and direct representative of the Bruce claim to the throne.

The Cambuskenneth bond of 1304 had brought Bruce the alliance of the most important figure in the Scottish kirk. There can be little doubt that Bruce sought other allies and, among them, the Red Comyn. In the latter were conjoined the original Comyn claim to the throne—bypassed in 1292—and a Balliol claim: for the Red Comyn was son of King John's sister. It is possible, as tradition has it, that Bruce offered to support the Comyn claim in return for a grant of the Comyn lands, or offered to grant Comyn the Bruce lands in return for support of the Bruce claim; such a transaction would merely have been a repetition of the deal that Bruce's grandfather had made with Count Floris in 1292. But Comyn was not won over. The two had a last interview in the Greyfriars kirk of Dumfries on 10 February 1306; as they stood near the high altar Bruce lost his temper and stabbed the Red Comyn; one or more of Bruce's companions decided to 'mak siccar'.[13] In hot blood Bruce had murdered a rival, committed sacrilege, confirmed suspicions of treason. There was no escape from the consequences save by immediately putting into action whatever plans had been laid for a revolution in Scotland.

The eventual success of Bruce's bid for the throne cannot disguise the fact that it was, at the time, rash, self-willed and premature, and occurred in dismal circumstances. Automatic excommunication was a consequence of the sacrilegious murder of the Red Comyn, which was all too reminiscent of that of Henry of Almain, Edward I's cousin, thirty-five years before. Bruce seems to have petitioned the *curia* for absolution, and on 23 July 1308 the grand penitentiary issued a mandate to the Abbot of Paisley to investigate the case.[14] Whatever the outcome, excommunication was fulminated in England by the summer of 1309,[15] and frequently thereafter. More serious was

---

[12] Barron, *War of Independence*, p. 152.

[13] Although the picturesque accounts that grew up concerning the events leading to the murder, and the murder itself, must be held in some suspicion (Barrow, *Bruce*, pp. 197–9, 206–8), someone *did* 'mak siccar'.

[14] Text in *Chron. Bower*, II. 231–2.

[15] *Chron. Lanercost*, p. 213.

the inescapable blood feud with the Comyns, their kinsmen and allies, who together composed the most powerful faction in Scotland, with lands and connections scattered from Galloway to Badenoch, Buchan to Argyll. A civil war would have to be waged as well as a patriotic war; and the event that must have been thought necessary for a successful rising—the death of the sick and ageing Edward I—had not yet occurred.

But it was Bruce's opponents, not he himself, who showed confusion and uncertainty. He was resolved to 'take castles, towns and people as fast as he could'; when he crossed the Forth with sixty men-at-arms it was Scone, the traditional site of Scottish enthronements, that was his goal. It was almost incredulously reported: 'he is attempting to seize the realm of Scotland'.[16] On 25 March 1306 he was installed on some substitute ceremonial stone by Countess Isabel of Buchan, sister of the late Earl of Fife, who had arrived to claim the traditional MacDuff privilege of setting a new king on the throne.[17] Two days later Bishop Lamberton, who had 'left the council of the king of England secretly and by night', was induced to celebrate a solemn mass.[18] More enthusiastic than Lamberton, who claimed to have been bullied into support of Bruce, was Bishop Wishart of Glasgow, who was reported to have absolved him from his sins and 'made him swear that he would abide under the direction of the clergy of Scotland'.[19] Edward had good cause for the complaints that he soon addressed to the pope: the abbey of Scone was 'placed in the midst of a perverse nation' and should be removed to a 'safer' place;[20] the perjured Bishop Wishart, who had been granted timber for the steeple of Glasgow Cathedral, had used it to make engines of war that were employed against the English garrison in Kirkintilloch; Wishart had also seized the castle of Cupar and held it 'as a man of war'; David Moray, Bishop of Moray, was announcing in his sermons that it was no less meritorious to fight for Bruce against the English than to set out against the pagans and Saracens in the Holy Land.[21] The latest Scottish rising had ended Edward's policy of pacification. Behind a new policy of ruthless repression [22] was his justified belief that he had been tricked and betrayed. He watched balefully but impo-

---

[16] Stones, *Documents*, No. 34.
[17] This account of Bruce's installation has profited from the helpful advice of Professor A. A. M. Duncan.
[18] Stones, *Documents*, No. 35.
[19] *Ibid.*, Nos. 34, 35.   [20] *Foedera*, i. pt. iv, 65.
[21] Palgrave, *Documents*, i. Nos. cxlviii, cl.
[22] Barrow, *Bruce*, pp. 215–6.

tently from his sickbed in the priory of Lanercost while his subordinates dealt with Bruce.

It is remarkable that despite the handicaps that faced the new Scottish king he soon gathered considerable support. Over a hundred landholders, great and small, from virtually every part of Scotland are recorded as having rallied to his side in 1306.[23] A good number came from Annandale and Carrick where the Bruce family interest was strong; but most came from the region between the Forth and the Moray Firth, perhaps the heartland of Scottish resistance. Recruits from Lothian and the remote regions of the north and west were as yet few, though this is not necessarily to be taken as proof of a lack of patriotism in either the wholly English-speaking south-east or the wholly Gaelic-speaking north-west. Bruce was strong enough in June 1306 to approach Perth, which Aymer de Valence had occupied, but on 19 June Valence overwhelmed the unwary Scots in the wood of Methven. Many of Bruce's leading supporters were taken prisoner; the common folk lost trust in him as a leader and deserted.[24] With the Earl of Atholl and James Douglas—one of the earliest and best of his recruits—the new king sought refuge in the central Highlands. There the hardships and high courage of the fugitives in the summer months of 1306 provided romantic material for John Barbour, who, seventy years later, composed his epic poem, *The Bruce*. As Barbour takes up his tale Bruce and his companions emerge from documentary impersonality and assume flesh and blood.

It is Barbour who incidentally mentions that Bruce had a foster-brother whose death he lamented.[25] Fosterage was then, and for centuries afterwards, a feature in the upbringing of a Gaelic chief, and was associated with instruction in Gaelic language and tradition.[26] Moreover 'the society of Carrick at the end of the thirteenth century remained emphatically Celtic';[27] and, it might be added, so was the language of Carrick until long afterwards.[28] Some aspects of Bruce's future career cannot be convincingly explained unless it is constantly borne in mind that he was at home in a Gaelic setting, and unless it is likewise borne in mind that about half of the population of Scotland still spoke Gaelic. This does not mean that throughout his career

---

[23] Barron, *War of Independence*, pp. 224–35. Barron's deductions are criticised, perhaps too strongly, by Barrow (*Bruce*, pp. 216–26).

[24] Barbour, *The Bruce*, I. 46.

[25] *Ibid.*, I. 157, 160, 169–71.

[26] *Highland Papers*, I. 206; II. 35, 38; *The Black Book of Taymouth* (Bannatyne Club), pp. xvi–xxii.

[27] Barrow, *Bruce*, p. 36.   [28] See Dunlop, *Bishop Kennedy*, p. 372.

Bruce could count on mass support from the Gaelic Scots, who were then, and thereafter, divided among themselves. They were particularly divided by Bruce himself, for the Comyn blood feud had far greater repercussions in the Gaelic regions, where the Comyn interest was strongest, than in the English-speaking Lowlands. In favourable circumstances Bruce could turn his acquaintance with Gaeldom to good account, but it was a different story in the summer of 1306 when he encountered John of Lorne, son of Alexander MacDougal of Argyll and kinsman of the murdered Comyn. At Dalry, on the borders of Argyll and Perth, the new king was defeated and his remaining military force was dispersed; he had no alternative save to escape from Scotland. Yet the very fact that the MacDougals were Bruce's foes helped to make other Gaelic families his friends: Neil Campbell and the Earl of Lennox aided his escape towards Kintyre, where Angus Og, a leading figure among the MacDonalds, aided his escape by sea from Dunaverty Castle to the nearby island of Rathlin.[29]

Where Bruce spent the remaining months of 1306 is uncertain. The Dowager Queen of Norway, Isabella Bruce, was his sister, and it has been convincingly argued that he took refuge in the Norwegian islands of Orkney.[30] Another view favours his sojourning in the Hebrides and visiting Ulster.[31] The truth is probably that Bruce visited all of these places: the whole western seaboard from Ulster to Orkney was linked by rapid sea communication, and, for various reasons, he had cause to traverse the whole of it. His brothers, Thomas and Alexander, were probably sent to recruit support in Ireland. He himself obtained help from Christina, heiress of the MacRuaridh descendants of Somerled, and 'lady of many lands and islands of the west'.[32] By the end of January 1307 Edward had heard at Lanercost that Bruce and his supporters were in the southern Hebrides, and despatched ships to intercept them.[33] It was too late. By way of Rathlin and Arran Bruce slipped unseen to his own earldom of Carrick and successfully attacked the English garrison at Turnberry.[34]

Bruce's descent on Carrick had been timed to coincide with a landing by his brothers at Loch Ryan on 10 February. Thomas and Alexander Bruce had with them a certain Irish kinglet, and, no doubt, other Irishmen, as well as a chieftain of Kintyre. They were at once

[29] Barrow, *Bruce*, pp. 231–3.
[30] Barron, *War of Independence*, pp. 248–59.
[31] Barrow, *Bruce*, pp. 237–42.   [32] *Ibid.*, pp. 241–2.
[33] *Cal. Docs. Scot.*, II. Nos. 1888, 1889, 1893, 1895, 1896.
[34] Barrow, *Bruce*, pp. 240–1.

attacked and captured by Dungal MacDowell, member of a foremost Galwegian family attached to the Comyns. The two Bruce brothers were sent to Edward at Carlisle. Although Alexander was dean of Glasgow his holy orders did not save him from being hanged and beheaded alongside his brother.[35]

The execution of the two Bruce brothers was only the latest in a series of afflictions that had lately befallen the family and its adherents. After the encounter at Dalry in the summer of 1306 King Robert's queen, his daughter Marjory and other ladies, had been escorted by the Earl of Atholl and Neil Bruce, another of the king's brothers, to the supposed safety of Kildrummy Castle. In September 1306 Aymer de Valence and the Prince of Wales besieged the castle, which had to surrender when a traitor fired the grain stored in the great hall. Neil Bruce was taken prisoner. Already, however, Atholl and the royal ladies had escaped to the north, pursued by Earl William of Ross, who seized the party in the sanctuary of St Duthac at Tain. Atholl was the first earl to be executed in England for over two hundred years.[36] Neil Bruce and Christopher Seton, Bruce's brother-in-law, were also executed. In August 1306 sixteen of Bruce's supporters were summarily tried at Newcastle. On Edward's orders they were not allowed to speak in their own defence and were hanged.[37] With less cause Edward meted out punishment even to his female prisoners. Bruce's queen was to be kept in a manor house, attended by two elderly pages and two servantwomen who were 'elderly and not at all gay'. Christian Bruce was sent to a nunnery; but Mary, another sister of King Robert, was to be securely guarded in a specially-constructed 'cage'—a prison of lattice work—in Roxburgh Castle. It was at first intended that Bruce's young daughter, Marjory, would be kept in a similar construction in the Tower of London. The Countess of Buchan, who had had the effrontery to assist at Bruce's enthronement, was certainly placed in a 'cage' in one of the towers of Berwick Castle. No Scotsman or Scotswoman was to be allowed to speak to her. Four years passed before she was less rigorously confined.[38]

It was probably only on his return to Carrick that Bruce learnt the full measure of the disasters that had been inflicted upon his family and friends. If hitherto he had been merely self-seeking and

[35] *Ibid.*, pp. 240–2.   [36] *Ibid.*, pp. 227–9.
[37] *Cal. Docs., Scot.*, II. No. 1811; J. G. Bellamy, *Law of Treason*, pp. 40–2.
[38] Palgrave, *Documents*, I. No. clv; Barrow, *Bruce*, p. 230.

ambitious he was no longer so. His crown had been too dearly bought by the sacrifices of others. Ambition and chivalric adventure had ended in a tragedy that he was to redeem by identifying himself completely with the highest traditions of kingship and devotion to the cause of independence.

Hard fighting lay ahead, not only against the English but against many a Scot who had reason to hate or reject the new king. From his sickbed in Lanercost Edward mustered forces to surround him as he lurked in the wild country on the borders of Carrick and Galloway.[39] Yet against overwhelming odds Bruce was amazingly successful and inspired confidence by his personal prowess in various feats of arms. The Lanercost chronicler ruefully remarked that 'notwithstanding the heavy vengeance inflicted on the Scots who took part with Robert Bruce, the multitude of those wishing to confirm him in his kingship was increased day by day'.[40] When Aymer de Valence sent a force into the fastnesses of Glen Trool he had the worse of the encounter. In May 1307 there followed a more important engagement at Loudoun Hill in Ayrshire. After heavy losses Aymer de Valence fled.[41] Methven had been avenged. On 15 May, a few days after this episode, one of Edward's adherents wrote from Forfar with the news that Bruce

> never had the good will of . . . the people . . . so much with him as now; and it now first appears that God is openly for him. . . . And they firmly believe, by the encouragement of the false preachers who come from the host, that Sir Robert Bruce will now have his will. . . . For these preachers have told them that they have found a prophecy of Merlin, how after the death of 'le Roi Coveytous' the Scottish people and the Britons [Welsh] shall league together, and have the sovereign hand . . . and live together in accord till the end of the world.[42]

Few people then doubted the relevance of the prophecies of Merlin to contemporary politics; and Edward I could, not unreasonably, be identified as 'the covetous king' to whom the prophet had alluded. He had summoned the English host to muster at Carlisle for a summer campaign. On 7 July 1307, as he reached Burgh-on-Sands on the shores of the Solway, he breathed his last.[43] The tale spread among the Scots that an English knight saw in a vision the demons of hell tormenting the late king.[44]

[39] *Cal. Docs. Scot.*, II. Nos. 1895–913, *passim*.
[40] *Chron. Lanercost*, p. 207.   [41] Barbour, *The Bruce*, I. 181–201.
[42] *Cal. Docs. Scot.*, II. No. 1926.   [43] *Chron. Lanercost*, p. 207.
[44] *Chron. Bower*, II. 236.

The removal of the formidable figure of Edward I was an event from which King Robert's cause could draw immeasurable encouragement. The Prince of Wales, now Edward II, inherited all of his father's problems, but little of the forcefulness that alone could master them. Having led the English host as far as Cumnock in Ayrshire he withdrew to England leaving warfare to subordinates.[45] The initiative passed to Bruce ; and for some years his chief opponents were scarcely the English but rather the Comyn-Balliol partisans in Galloway, Argyll and the north-east. In September 1307 some Galwegians fled to England with their flocks and herds, while the leading men of Galloway appealed in vain to Edward II for help and were forced to pay ransom to Bruce in order to obtain a short truce.[46] This left him free to move north. In November 1307 he obtained the surrender of Inverlochy Castle and advanced up the Great Glen to confront the Earl of Ross.[47] In a letter to Edward II [48] the earl claimed to have retained three thousand men in his pay for a fortnight. Despite this force, so he claimed, Ross, Sutherland and Caithness would have been overwhelmed if he had not agreed to accept a truce until 2 June 1308. With the three northernmost earldoms neutralised, Bruce destroyed the castle of Inverness, burned the castle of Nairn and won the castle of Urquhart. He next attacked Elgin Castle but made a truce with the defenders. On his way towards the castle of Banff he fell ill and thereafter had to conduct the campaign from a litter.[49] At Slioch, near Huntly, he and his force, which the poet Barbour realistically numbers at seven hundred men,[50] were encountered on Christmas Day 1307 by the troops of John Mowbray and John Comyn, Earl of Buchan, who apparently went off to seek infantry reinforcements. On their return, a week later, Bruce made off. When he left Slioch to cross the mountains towards Mar his foes affected to believe that he was in flight ;[51] but they cautiously reinforced the castle of Coull, and some of them were already so demoralised that they moved to safer parts with their cattle ; even John Mowbray accepted inclusion

[45] *Chron. Lanercost*, p. 209.

[46] *Ibid.*, p. 210; *Cal. Docs. Scot.*, III. Nos. 14, 15.

[47] See Patricia M. Barnes and G. W. S. Barrow, 'The movements of Robert Bruce between September 1307 and May 1308', *S.H.R.*, XLIX. 46–59, at 56.

[48] The letter is undated but must have been written in November or December 1307 (Barron, *War of Independence*, pp. 283–90).

[49] Barbour, *The Bruce*, I. 212, 214.   [50] *Ibid.*, 217.

[51] Although Patricia M. Barnes and G. W. S. Barrow state that it was John Mowbray who made a 'flight across the mountains' (*op. cit.*, *S.H.R.*, XLIX. 46–59, at 52), I agree with Professor A. A. M. Duncan that the word *fugiendo* in the relevant text (*ibid.*, 58, line 13) refers to Bruce.

in a truce at the end of February 1308. Bruce, or his supporters, then attacked the castles of Mortlach (Balvenie), Tarradale and Skelbo, and renewed the siege of Elgin on 7 April. Nonetheless Mowbray, writing to Edward II on 1 May, claimed to have raised the siege and driven Bruce into retreat.[52] It is clear that up to this time no really decisive engagement had occurred.[53] At Inverurie, however, probably on the date given by the chronicler Bower (23 May 1308)[54] there was a final confrontation. The Earl of Buchan and his supporters seem to have believed that Bruce was helpless as a result of his illness. When the ailing king rose from his sickbed and appeared on horseback, supported by a man on each side, his foes lost heart and were chased all the way to Fyvie. For the Comyns the consequences of the ignominious rout of Inverurie were disastrous : Bruce advertised their ruin by the 'herschip' (ravaging) of Buchan, the centre of the Comyn power. The whole earldom was laid waste, its inhabitants slaughtered. For fifty years afterwards the herschip of Buchan was a tragedy vivid in men's minds.[55] It was clear that Bruce had the will and the power to make his foes pay dearly for their opposition.

While the king continued operations north of Tay, winning Aberdeen in June or July 1308,[56] James Douglas was active in the south-west. On Palm Sunday (7 April) 1308 he had caught off-guard the English troops who occupied his own castle of Douglas and left their slaughtered bodies to burn with the castle and its stores.[57] After this episode of 'the Douglas larder' King Robert's remaining brother, Edward Bruce, was sent with a force of Islesmen to reinforce Douglas for an attack upon Galloway, where the local truce had expired. On 29 June 1308 the leading Galwegians were defeated in a battle on the banks of the Dee (or Cree), the MacDowell stronghold on the Isle of Hestan was burnt, and more fugitives sought safety in Eng-

---

[52] Ibid., 52–3, 58–9.

[53] The documents published by Patricia M. Barnes and G. W. S. Barrow (ibid., 57–9) do not bear out their suggestion (ibid., 56) that the battle of Inverurie took place in January 1308.

[54] The chronicler Fordun simply assigns the rout of Inverurie to the year 1308 (Chron. Fordun, I. 344) which, by modern reckoning, signifies a date after 24 March. Bower's date, which is accepted by A. A. M. Duncan (Nation of Scots, p. 19), is indicated by a line of verse :

Anno milleno trecenteno dabis octo,
In festo Domini, quo scandit sidera coeli . . .

(Chron. Bower, II. 241). In 1308 Ascension Day fell on 23 May.

[55] Barbour, The Bruce, I. 219.

[56] Barrow, Bruce, p. 259.

[57] Professor A. A. M. Duncan, who has investigated the chronology of this event, has kindly allowed me to make use of his findings.

land.[58] After a herschip of Galloway much of the province was brought sullenly under King Robert's control. Although the strong castles in the region remained in the hands of the English for some time longer,[59] the latter feared in September 1308 that Bruce's partisans were about to raid England itself.[60]

Instead, King Robert confronted the MacDougals of Argyll and, after an initial campaign in August 1308, obtained the submission of their chief, Alexander of Argyll.[61] Earl William of Ross, who had delivered Bruce's queen to the English in 1306, could no longer sit on the fence after the king had proved his power by daunting Buchan, Galloway and, apparently, Argyll: on 31 October 1308 he made his peace with Bruce,[62] promised loyal service, and kept his word. The submission of Alexander of Argyll proved less trustworthy. His son, John of Lorne, was playing for time, and early in 1309 wrote to Edward II professing his loyalty.[63] Alluding to the campaign of August 1308 Lorne reported that Bruce had approached Argyll by land and sea with ten or fifteen thousand men. Against such numbers (which can hardly have existed outside the writer's imagination) Lorne could oppose only eight hundred men, of whom five hundred were continually retained in his own pay to secure his borders. He had also three castles to garrison and had to guard a loch twenty-four miles long (Loch Awe) on which he was busy building and manning galleys; the barons of Argyll would give him no aid and he was unsure of his neighbours on all sides. He had therefore concluded a truce with Bruce but was awaiting help from England.

The help never came. Some time between August and October 1309, when the truce with Lorne had either expired or been broken, King Robert, reinforced by James Douglas, conducted a second campaign in Argyll. John of Lorne lay with a flotilla of galleys on Loch Awe and had stationed men on Ben Cruachan to roll boulders on Bruce's troops as they filed through the pass of Brander that ran between the mountain and the loch. This stratagem was foiled when

[58] *Chron. Lanercost*, p. 212; *Chron. Fordun*, I. 345; Barbour, *The Bruce*, I. 228.

[59] *Rot. Scot.*, I. 80.   [60] *Ibid.*, 57.

[61] Professor Duncan has pointed out that there were two distinct campaigns in Argyll. The chronology of the following account of these campaigns is based upon his investigations, of which he has kindly allowed me to make use.

[62] *A.P.S.*, I. 477.

[63] The undated letter (*Cal. Docs. Scot.*, III. No. 80), which has been assigned by Professor Duncan to early 1309, refers to events six months earlier, since when, so Lorne claimed, he had been confined to a sick bed—perhaps by a diplomatic illness.

Douglas led a force of archers to gain the heights of Ben Cruachan and take Lorne's men in the rear.[64] The battle of the pass of Brander broke the power of the MacDougals just as Inverurie had broken that of the Comyns : within a few months John of Lorne, his father, and Bishop Andrew of Argyll, had joined the Comyns as refugees at the English court.

The chronicler Fordun saw in Bruce's victory at Inverurie the turning point in the king's career.[65] Yet it was not that sole battle but rather his extraordinary mobility and his strategy of neutralising his foes and crushing them one by one that wrought the incredible change in Bruce's fortunes. In February 1307 he had been a hunted man in the wilds of Carrick and Galloway ; by the end of 1309 he was master of more than two-thirds of Scotland. In Perth, Dundee and Banff, which could be reinforced and victualled by sea, English garrisons still held out; but so long as they were not supported by an English field army they were helpless. Bruce had won back the north, the loss of which had broken the back of Scottish resistance in 1303. The fortunes of war might fluctuate south of Forth, but the north, with its reserves of manpower and its defences of river, loch and mountain, was the hinterland that had to be secured before war against the English could be successfully waged.

Bruce's strategy and tactics, however brilliant, could hardly have won him success had he been faced by an overwhelmingly hostile population in the north. It is remarkable that a letter written from Forfar on 15 May 1307 [66] had warned the English king that the men of those parts, encouraged by 'false preachers', were ready to rise with Bruce; and if the latter moved 'towards the parts of Ross' he would find people 'all ready at his will more entirely than ever'. The sequel bore out the truth of this warning : while the northern magnates were more or less hostile to Bruce, lesser landholders, perhaps particularly those of Moray,[67] were ready to accept him as king. It has been suggested that 'the most revealing point in the new evidence about 1307–8 is the statement that the Earl of Buchan [*rectius* John Mowbray] . . . during a truce before the battle of Inverurie, had punished . . . freeholders for supporting the king', and that 'the foundation of this war was a capacity to by-pass the reluctant traditional leaders of the "community" and to appeal to and command the opinion of other social ranks in the "nation" '.[68] Their adherence must have

[64] Barbour, *The Bruce*, 1. 238–42.   [65] *Chron. Fordun*, 1. 344–5.
[66] *Cal. Docs. Scot.*, 11. No. 1926.
[67] Barron, *War of Independence, passim.*
[68] Duncan, *Nation of Scots*, pp. 20, 21.

been increasingly forthcoming as Bruce revived the traditional functions and authority of the Scottish monarchy. It was perhaps typical that when a parliament was held at Inchture in the Carse of Gowrie in April 1312 an undertaking was given that he would follow the traditional practice of dealing with the burghs through his chamberlain.[69] But if Bruce cultivated popular support he did not neglect to win the adherence of those aristocrats who were aloof, uncommitted, or hostile. One striking example was that of Sir John Stewart of Menteith who had delivered Wallace into the hands of Edward I. Although it was rumoured that Sir John plotted to double his notoriety by betraying Bruce,[70] the plot, if any, came to nothing: little by little, Sir John proved his loyalty and took high place among the king's adherents.[71] More important was the adherence (reluctant at first) of Thomas Randolph, nephew of Bruce but once a knight of Balliol.[72] By 1312 Randolph had so proved his worth that the king rewarded him with a specially created earldom of Moray.[73]

No less skilled in politics than in warfare, Bruce used his first parliament (held at St Andrews in March 1309) to mount a publicity campaign to advertise his kingship. The necessary propaganda was probably devised by Bernard of Linton, who was to hold the office of chancellor from 1308 to 1328, together with the dignity of Abbot of Arbroath to which he was appointed in 1311. On 17 March 1309 a carefully prepared declaration was issued from St Andrews in the name of the Scottish prelates and clergy.[74] This document let it be inferred that John Balliol had been only *de facto* king, wrongfully installed by the English in place of the rightful Bruce claimant. After many afflictions the Scottish people

> agreed upon the said Lord Robert, the king who now is, in whom the rights of his father and grandfather to the foresaid kingdom . . . still exist and flourish entire; and with the concurrence and consent of the said people he was chosen to be king, . . . and with him the faithful people of the kingdom will live and die, as with one who, possessing the right of blood, and endowed with the other cardinal virtues, is fitted to rule . . . since . . . he has by the sword restored the realm.

[69] Barrow, *Bruce*, p. 421.
[70] *Chron. Bower*, II. 243, n.
[71] Barrow, *Bruce*, pp. 401–2.
[72] *Foedera*, I. pt. iii, 95; Barbour, *The Bruce*, I. 236–7.
[73] Barron, *War of Independence*, pp. 397–8.
[74] Text in *A.P.S.*, I. 460. G. W. S. Barrow has shown (*Bruce*, p. 262, n. 4), that the document was initially issued at the St Andrews parliament, not (as previously thought) at a general council of the clergy held at Dundee.

A similar declaration was issued in the name of the nobles.[75] In addition to the acclamation of Bruce's kingship—ingeniously balanced on the four pillars of inheritance, virtue, election and conquest—another floridly-composed document, dated at St Andrews on 16 March,[76] answered a flattering letter which had been sent by the French king. There was to be no formal renewal of the Franco-Scottish alliance for another seventeen years; but Philip's friendly overture gave the impression that the alliance might readily be renewed in the event of future hostilities between France and England.

Nor was the French king alone in taking stock of the re-emergence of the Scottish kingdom. In vain Edward II wrote to Count Robert of Flanders in October 1309 protesting that Scottish traders and their German associates were carrying arms and victuals from the Flemish towns to Scotland :[77] the profits of warfare [78] and the seizure of some £7,000 of crusading tenths[79] gave King Robert the cash to pay the seamen and traders—Scots, German and Flemish—who from their bases in Flanders ran the English blockade to carry vital imports to Scotland, and who simultaneously waged a naval war of their own against English shipping in the North Sea.[80]

The war at sea, used by all participants as an excuse for piratical lawlessness, also extended to northern waters, where Scottish raiders captured and held to ransom the Norwegian seneschal of Orkney.[81] By this time Eric II, who had shown too ambitious an interest in Scottish affairs, had been succeeded by his brother, Haakon V. King Robert's own sister, Isabella Bruce, long outlived Eric, and, as Queen Dowager of Norway, no doubt used her influence to settle Scoto-Norwegian differences. The outcome was the conclusion of a treaty at Inverness on 29 October 1312.[82] This confirmed the annual payment of a hundred marks promised in the treaty of Perth of 1266 in return for the cession of the Western Isles.

The increasing recognition that Bruce won in Scotland and abroad reflected his success in winning the civil war and transforming it into a patriotic war. Circumstances played into his hands by giving him a powerful (though unwitting) ally in the person of Piers Gaveston. Edward II's passion for this Gascon favourite was the chief factor in the discord that existed between the English king and his magnates. The lack of co-operation between them, coupled with Edward's own

[75] Barrow, *Bruce*, p. 264.   [76] *A.P.S.*, I. 459.   [77] *Rot. Scot.*, I. 78.
[78] P. 96 below.
[79] D. E. Easson, *op. cit., Scot. Church Hist. Soc. Recs.*, XI. 63–81, at 72.
[80] *Foedera*, I. pt. iv, 177.   [81] *A.P.S.*, I. 101.   [82] *Ibid.*

inadequacy as a ruler, meant that during the crucial period of civil war in Scotland Bruce had little to fear from England. It was not until the late summer of 1310 that Edward set out from Berwick to show the flag in regions that had lately submitted to Bruce and to entice the latter into battle.[83] All the marching and counter-marching of Edward's troops was in vain: according to the Lanercost chronicler, Bruce 'in his customary manner fled and did not dare to encounter them'.[84] It would be incorrect to think that Bruce always avoided battle: the engagements at Loudoun Hill, Inverurie, and the pass of Brander, as well as others still to be fought, all prove the contrary. On the other hand he did not wage battle indiscriminately: other less chivalric methods of warfare were less risky and might be just as effective. Avoiding confrontation with the main English army, he was nonetheless active in guerrilla warfare, sending detachments of his men to harass English foragers.[85] In 1310 his strategy proved its efficacy. By December Edward was back in Berwick. Although inept he was also stubborn and was to remain there until the summer of 1311,[86] when he and his favourite returned to England to face the truculent opposition of the lords ordainers and a state of virtual civil war that lingered on even after Gaveston had been murdered on 19 June 1312.[87] Edward's departure and his domestic troubles gave King Robert the chance to carry warfare into the north of England, which had been left unharmed since Wallace's invasion in 1297. On 12 August 1311 he crossed the Solway, raided Tynedale, and returned with a great booty in the shape of cattle.[88] This cattle raid was followed on 8 September by a longer raid into Northumberland. As a result its inhabitants paid £2,000 for a truce up to 2 February 1312.[89] Thus the mere demonstration of Scottish power extracted an income almost comparable to the peacetime revenues of the Scottish crown. Nor were the extortionate truces that neutralised northern England accompanied by the disbandment of Bruce's forces: a truce in one region was merely the signal for an attack upon another; and, despite his far-reaching activities elsewhere, Bruce did not ignore the chief object of his strategy—the expulsion of the English from the strongholds they still occupied in Scotland itself.

By 1312 in the whole region north of Forth only the garrisons of Perth and Dundee remained as a symbol of English power. The fall

[83] *Cal. Docs. Scot.*, III. Nos. 166, 171; *Chron. Lanercost*, p. 214.
[84] *Chron. Lanercost*, p. 214.   [85] *Vita Edwardi*, p. 12.
[86] *Rot. Scot.*, I. 103.
[87] May McKisack, *The Fourteenth Century*, pp. 11–31.
[88] *Chron. Lanercost*, p. 216.   [89] *Ibid.*, pp. 216–7.

of Dundee in the spring of 1312 [90] gave the Scots control of the estuary of the Tay and cut off Perth from the sea. To win the town Bruce resorted to the strategem of a feigned withdrawal. For a week he and his men were not to be seen and the defenders relaxed their vigilance. Then the besiegers stole back under cover of darkness. On the night of 7–8 January 1313 the king was the first to plunge up to his neck in the icy waters of the moat and set his scaling ladder against the ramparts. These and the other fortifications were deliberately destroyed after the capture of the town.[91] The fall of Perth was followed by the last phase in the Scottish recovery of the south-west : on 7 February 1313 Sir Dungal MacDowell, the king's hardened foe, surrendered Dumfries Castle,[92] by which time the other castles of the area—Loch Doon, Lochmaben, Caerlaverock, Dalswinton, Tibbers and Buittle— seem to have fallen to the Scots.[93] King Robert could leave a thoroughly subdued Galloway when he left for his conquest of the Isle of Man in May 1313.[94] On his route from Perth to Dumfries the king seems to have detailed part of his army under Edward Bruce to lay siege to Stirling Castle.[95] The tedium of a siege that began in Lent and lasted into the summer [96] probably weighed heavily upon the king's brother, who is represented as more chivalric [97] than saga- cious. Sir Philip Mowbray, the Scottish knight to whom Edward II had entrusted the custody of Stirling, offered to surrender if an English army failed to appear within three miles of the castle by Mid- summer Day 1314. Although a similar pact (deeply resented by Edward II) seems to have put Dundee in Scottish hands,[98] Edward Bruce has been criticised for accepting Mowbray's terms and is re- ported by Barbour to have been rebuked by King Robert.[99] Since 1311 no English army had taken the field in Scotland. The year-long respite granted to the defenders of Stirling was a call to arms that even the lethargic Edward II and his discordant barons might not ignore.

While an uneasy truce settled upon Stirling, the Scottish leaders took the offensive against other English garrisons, by this time virtu- ally restricted to Lothian, the area between Forth and Tweed. In the

[90] Barron, War of Independence, pp. 388–9.
[91] Barbour, The Bruce, I. 221–6.   [92] Cal. Docs. Scot., III. No. 304.
[93] Chron. Fordun, I. 346.
[94] A. W. Moore, 'The Connexion between Scotland and Man', S.H.R., III. 393–409, at 404–6.
[95] Barron, War of Independence, p. 420.
[96] Barbour, The Bruce, I. 269–70.
[97] 'Of [his] hye vorshipe and manheid men mycht mony romanys [romances] mak' (Barbour, The Bruce, I. 227).
[98] Rot. Scot., I. 108.   [99] Barbour, The Bruce, I. 272–3.

summer of 1313, the English, or their Scottish allies, still held Linlithgow, Livingston, Edinburgh, Luffness, Dirleton, Dunbar, Yester, Berwick, Roxburgh, Jedburgh, Cavers, and perhaps Selkirk.[100] At first sight this impressive combination of mutually-supporting major and minor fortresses might well seem a unique obstacle, more formidable than any that Bruce had hitherto encountered. But the castles of Lothian straggled in a crescent-shaped formation following the coastline of the Forth and the North Sea and the valley of the Tweed; they had the advantage of easy accessibility to the sea, but the land routes that connected them were vulnerable to attack from an opposing force operating from the Lammermuirs, the uplands that projected into the concavity of the fortified crescent. Berwick, the strategic link between the maritime fortresses and those of the Tweed valley, was singled out for attack as early as 6 December 1312; the barking of a dog alarmed the sleeping town and the projected assault was abandoned.[101] The failure at Berwick was more than compensated by success at Linlithgow, Roxburgh and Edinburgh. Credit for the capture of the peel of Linlithgow in September 1313 went to William Binnock, a 'stout carle' or husbandman, who concealed armed men in his hay waggon and brought it to a halt in the entry to the peel so that the gate could not be shut nor the portcullis lowered.[102] On the night of Shrove Tuesday (19 February) 1314 James Douglas led his men, mantled in black so that they might be mistaken for cattle, up to the walls of Roxburgh. The capture of this castle by Douglas stirred Thomas Randolph to make an attempt on Edinburgh. On the night of 14 March 1314 some of the attackers diverted the garrison's attention to the gateway while Randolph and others, guided by a local man named William Francis, climbed the precipitous northern face of the castle rock. Edinburgh Castle, like Linlithgow and Roxburgh, was dismantled on Bruce's orders 'lest the English ever afterwards might lord it over the land by holding the castles'.[103]

It was not only Englishmen who had held the castles of Lothian: in contrast to the small number of Lothian gentlefolk who are known to have joined Bruce by 1312 [104] there was a much larger number who drew English pay to serve in the garrisons of Linlithgow, Roxburgh and Edinburgh. At Linlithgow it was a local landholder, Sir Archi-

---

[100] Barron, *War of Independence*, p. 414.

[101] *Chron. Lanercost*, p. 220.   [102] Barbour, *The Bruce*, I. 244-7.

[103] *Chron. Lanercost*, p. 223; *Scalacronica*, p. 140; Barbour, *The Bruce*, I. 252-67; *Chron. Fordun*, I. 346.

[104] G. W. S. Barrow (*Bruce*, p. 269) seems to lay undue emphasis on this group.

bald Livingston, who had commanded the garrison.[105] Such instances give some point to the argument that the area between Forth and Tweed, the most intensively anglicised district of Scotland, was a region apart, with little sympathy for the cause that Bruce represented.[106] Part of the explanation lies in the attitude of the chief magnate of Lothian. Patrick, Earl of March and holder of the strategically-placed castle of Dunbar, had consistently adhered to the English between 1296 and his death in 1308; his successor, another Patrick, followed his father's policy. Another influential landholder, Sir Adam Gordon, served as justiciar of Lothian on behalf of Edward II.[107] Nominally, at least, Lothian was loyal to Edward, and many of its inhabitants were therefore regarded as disloyal by King Robert. Surviving petitions [108] sent from Lothian to the English king show that the inhabitants were forced to pay blackmail to Bruce in the same fashion as those of Northumberland or Durham. By 1313, however, some men of Lothian had evidently defected to Bruce, with the result that the remainder were held in suspicion by the garrisons of the English-held castles. The garrison of Berwick raided the earldom of March and carried off thirty persons for ransom besides four thousand sheep and other livestock; finally Sir Adam Gordon was arrested and released only on giving pledges for his appearance before the English king.[109]

When Sir Adam appeared at Westminster he brought with him a petition asking Edward to provide redress for the miscellaneous grievances of 'the people of Scotland'.[110] Edward's answer on 28 November 1313 was to urge his adherents in Scotland to persevere in their loyalty towards him : by midsummer 1314 he would muster an army at Berwick for their relief.[111] The appeal from Lothian, coupled with the situation at Stirling, had persuaded Edward once more to face the insurgent Scots. By 27 May 1314 he had learned that the latter were gathering a multitude of footmen 'in strong and marshy places (where access for horses will be difficult) between us and our castle of Stirling'.[112]

Edward's military and naval preparations, which had begun in

---

[105] *Cal. Docs. Scot.*, III. 406–11.

[106] Barron, *War of Independence*, pp. 188–9, 366–8.

[107] *Cal. Docs. Scot.*, III. Nos. 211, 299, p. 403.

[108] *Ibid.*, Nos. 186, 337. G. W. S. Barrow (*Bruce*, p. 269) assigns the first of these to 1312.

[109] *Cal. Docs. Scot.*, III. No. 337.

[110] *Ibid.*, Nos. 337, 344.   [111] *Rot. Scot.*, I. 114.   [112] *Ibid.*, 126–7.

March 1314 [113] had been preceded by a superficial reconciliation with his intransigent baronial opponents.[114] An imposing army of between fifteen and seventeen thousand footmen and between two and three thousand heavy cavalry [115] set out from Berwick and Wark on 17 and 18 June, and by way of Lauderdale reached Edinburgh a day or two later.[116] Further hard marching to meet the deadline of 24 June brought the English king to within three miles of Stirling Castle with one day to spare. He was met by its commander, Sir Philip Mowbray, who affirmed that the castle was thus technically 'rescued' in accordance with the bargain made with Edward Bruce.[117] But between the castle and the rescuing army lay the army of King Robert, probably between five and ten thousand in number. The 'rescue' could be turned into a triumph if the Scots were put to flight or defeated.

Bruce had by no means committed himself to waging battle. After mustering at the Tor Wood he had fallen back to the high ground of the New Park, two miles south of Stirling Castle, and there he kept his troops in a formation that hinted at withdrawal: the vanguard under Thomas Randolph, Earl of Moray, lay beside St Ninian's kirk, nearest Stirling; it was the rearguard under the king that faced the oncoming English; between the vanguard and rearguard lay the two other Scottish battalions, one under Edward Bruce, the other nominally under the youthful Walter the Steward but actually under the command of Douglas; at some distance to the west lay the 'small folk and poverale'—ill-armed footmen and camp followers whom Bruce kept apart from his fighting troops.[118] The high and wooded ground of the New Park screened the disposition of the Scottish troops and gave them some security from the attack of cavalry and archers. As a further precaution pits were dug and calthorps (three-pronged iron spikes) were scattered [119] where the road from Falkirk crossed the Bannock burn to enter the New Park on its way to Stirling.

It was here that an engagement took place in the afternoon of 23 June 1314. An English advance party was already in sight as King

---

[113] *Ibid.*, 115–28; W. M. Mackenzie, *The Battle of Bannockburn* (1913), pp. 21–2.

[114] *Vita Edwardi*, p. 43.

[115] The numbers of the opposing forces are a matter of estimate. See Barrow, *Bruce*, pp. 293–8; J. E. Morris, *Bannockburn* (1914), p. 41; W. M. Mackenzie, *The Battle of Bannockburn*, pp. 21–32.

[116] Mackenzie, *The Battle of Bannockburn*, pp. 39–41.

[117] *Scalacronica*, p. 141.

[118] Barbour, *The Bruce*, I. 284–5, 288.

[119] *Ibid*, 286–7.

Robert rode out to supervise his frontal positions. Sir Henry de Bohun, nephew of the Earl of Hereford, spurred his charger forward hoping to win incomparable chivalric fame by killing or capturing the Scottish king. Though mounted on a palfrey and armed with only a battle-axe Bruce was too much of a knight to evade the encounter. As Bohun charged ponderously with his lance at the ready, the king sidestepped and with his axe cleft Bohun's skull. This was the signal for Bruce's battalion to drive back the dismayed English troops.[120]

Though it momentarily cast the fate of Scotland into jeopardy the king's personal feat of arms enhanced the chivalric prestige that was essential to his success. Shortly before Bruce had displayed his personal prowess the morale of his followers had already been raised when Randolph snatched victory from what might have been a reverse. Sir Robert Clifford and Sir Henry Beaumont, at the head of some three hundred horsemen, had outflanked the higher Scottish positions by riding along the Carse in the direction of Stirling. Moray was reproved by Bruce for neglecting to check this manoeuvre. It was not too late : the earl led his infantry battalion downhill to the open country. By itself, unsupported by archers, the cavalry proved helpless before the compact hedgehog formation of the Scottish schiltron. Clifford withdrew ignominiously and Moray returned in triumph to his former position.[121] The incident demonstrated that in certain circumstances footmen might attack and rout cavalry. Nonetheless, when Sir Alexander Seton, a Lothian landholder, defected to the Scottish camp that night, he found its leaders disposed to withdraw to the Lennox. They changed their minds when Seton reported the poor morale of the English and the comfortless position in which they now found themselves.[122]

During the evening and night of 23–24 June the English army had abandoned the highway and 'come out on a plain fronting the water of Forth, beyond Bannock burn, a bad, deep, marshy stream, where the said host of the English settled down'.[123] Barbour confirms this account when he represents the English as making their bivouacs on a 'hard feld' somewhere 'doune in the Kers [Carse]'.[124] It is thus clear that they spent the night on a field that lay in the triangle of low-lying ground hemmed in on one side by the loops of the wide

[120] *Ibid.*, 298–300; *Vita Edwardi*, p. 51.
[121] Barbour, *The Bruce*, I. 292–7, 302; *Chron. Lanercost*, p. 225; *Scalacronica*, p. 141.
[122] *Scalacronica*, p. 142.
[123] *Ibid.*, 141–2.
[124] Barbour, *The Bruce*, I. 313, 314.

Forth and on the other by the Bannock burn, besides being further restricted by 'sykes' (marshes) and 'pollis' (pows or streams) of which the Bannock burn (an obstacle that the English had crossed only with some difficulty) was the most notable.[125] Whatever Edward's plans in selecting such a camp site they can hardly have envisaged the possibility of a full-scale Scottish attack. From the encounter between Moray's spearmen and Clifford's cavalry Edward had learned nothing and Bruce had learned much. The confined English position— 'the gret stratnes of the plass' [126]—gave the Scots the opportunity of a narrow battlefront to deploy their inferior numbers in a repetition of Moray's tactics.

At daybreak on 24 June the three battalions commanded by Edward Bruce, Moray, Douglas and the Steward (the last two both newly knighted) [127] bore down on the cramped English position. The Earl of Gloucester lost his life leading the English vanguard in a fruitless cavalry charge against the leading Scottish schiltron,[128] that of Edward Bruce. When some of the English archers were at last put in an effective position they were taken in the flank by Sir Robert Keith's small force of light cavalry.[129] At this point King Robert threw in his own battalion. It numbered in its ranks Angus Og, all the men of Carrick, Argyll, Kintyre and the Isles, as well as a 'mekill rout' of armed men from the 'playne land' or Lowlands.[130] Doggedly the four Scottish schiltrons pushed forward like huge hedgehogs, pressing the ten English battalions into one helpless horde of horses and men. Eventually the rear ranks began to flee across the Bannock burn. In the contagious panic men fell and were trodden underfoot until the banks were bridged from side to side by the corpses. The inconspicuous stream 'that sa cummyrsum was of slyk [mud] and depnes for

---

[125] Ibid., 283, 313, 314. There has been much controversy over the nature of the surface of the Carse and the site of the English encampment, since these factors more or less determined the site of the battle. See Sir Herbert Maxwell, 'The Battle of Bannockburn', S.H.R., XI. 233–51; Thomas Miller, 'The Site of the New Park in relation to the Battle of Bannockburn', ibid., XII. 60–75; J. D. Mackie, 'The Battle of Bannockburn', ibid., XXIX. 207–10. The battlefield suggested by G. W. S. Barrow (Bruce, map 11) seems unacceptable: it includes steeply sloping ground—a circumstance not mentioned by the early writers—and is certainly not 'doune' in the Carse, however the Carse is defined. The sites favoured by W. M. Mackenzie (The Battle of Bannockburn, p. 74) and by General Sir Philip Christison ('Bannockburn—23rd and 24th June 1314. A Study in Military History', Proc. Soc. Antiq. Scot., XC. 170–79) seem more likely.

[126] Barbour, The Bruce, I. 315.
[127] Ibid., 314.
[128] Ibid., 318; Chron. Lanercost, p. 226; Vita Edwardi, pp. 53–4.
[129] Barbour, The Bruce, I. 324.   [130] Ibid., 285.

till pas', eventually gave its name to the battle for the simple reason that its existence turned the English defeat into a disaster.[131] The Scottish campfollowers added to the confusion of the stricken army by arriving on the scene to massacre and despoil the fugitives.[132] King Edward and some of the cavalry avoided the perils of the Bannock burn by escaping along the banks of the Forth to Stirling Castle. A cold welcome awaited them : Sir Philip Mowbray announced his intention of surrendering to Bruce. Edward and his entourage had to make a wide detour before fleeing eastward, pursued by Sir James Douglas. The king was chased to Dunbar where he boarded a small boat and sailed ignominiously south.[133]

[131] *Ibid.*, 335; *Scalacronica*, p. 142; *Chron. Lanercost*, p. 226; *Vita Edwardi*, pp. 53–4; G. W. S. Barrow's arguments (*Bruce*, pp. 304–9 that the battle was initially named not after the *burn* but after a *locality* 'Bannok or Bannockburn' do not provide conclusive evidence of the site of the battle.

[132] Barbour, *The Bruce*, I. 335.

[133] *Ibid.*, 336, 343–6; *Scalacronica*, p. 142; *Chron. Lanercost*, p. 227; *Vita Edwardi*, p. 54.

5

THE AFTERMATH OF BANNOCKBURN

So striking was the Scottish triumph at Bannockburn that its significance has been understandably exaggerated. The Scots can look back over a dismal vista of defeats to an unique occasion when they won the field in a full-scale pitched battle that amounted to a long-prepared duel between two incipient nations and their respective kings. Bannockburn was decisive in so far as the English, despite a supreme effort, had failed to win victory. It was indecisive in so far as they did not give up hope of subduing the Scots. Far from ending the war, Bannockburn scarcely marked the midway point. Yet the positive results of the battle were not negligible : it gave a boost to Scottish morale that survived later defeats and still influences the Scottish outlook; it gave a temporary military ascendancy that Bruce was to prolong and exploit as long as he lived.

At first the exploitation of the victory was easy enough. Save for the town and castle of Berwick all Scotland was recovered from the English. In the summer of 1314 James Douglas and Edward Bruce raided as far south as Richmond. Though Sir Thomas Gray and Sir Andrew Harclay staunchly held Norham and Carlisle, the north of England suffered from a Bannockburn complex. For a time there was talk of peace. But nothing resulted save an exchange of the captive Earl of Hereford in return for Bishop Wishart, King Robert's wife, his sister Christian, his daughter Marjory, and his nephew Donald of Mar.[1] Donald set out for Scotland but was fond of Edward II and turned back at Newcastle.

As the chances of immediate peace receded, a Scottish parliament met in Cambuskenneth Abbey, almost on the field of Bannockburn. There, on 6 November 1314, it was

[1] *Cal. Docs. Scot.*, III. Nos. 371, 372, 373, 393, 402, 403.

> agreed, finally adjudged and . . . made statute . . . that all who have died in the field . . . against the faith and peace of the said lord king [Robert Bruce] or who on the said day have not come to his faith and peace . . . . are to be disinherited forever of lands and tenements and all other *status* within the realm of Scotland. And they are to be held in future as foes of the king and kingdom, debarred forever from all claim of heritable right or of any other right whatsoever on behalf of themselves and their heirs.[2]

Despite its ostensibly immutable character this act of disinheritance was in practice an enabling statute that was not allowed to stand in the way of reconciliation. King Robert was to show himself ready to welcome back any disinherited Scot willing to serve him and him alone. He was not ready to accept those who wished to regain their Scottish lands, keep their lands in England, and serve two kings.

Now that Bruce's position within Scotland was uncontested it remained to secure the permanence of his dynasty. As yet, the king had no legitimate son. His heir presumptive was his daughter Marjory, just returned from captivity in England and still unmarried. The probability of her accession was unwelcome. In April 1315 a parliament or council met in the parish kirk of Ayr where, with the consent both of the king and his daughter, a tailzie (entail) was drawn up: if King Robert should die leaving no legitimate son the crown was to pass not to Marjory but to the king's only surviving brother, Edward Bruce, a 'vigorous man . . . highly skilled in warlike deeds'.[3]

The change in the succession was also the prelude to a change in military and political strategy. Although the spring of 1315 had brought a renewal of raids in which the Scots penetrated to the gates of York, Edward II neither continued the war nor tried to end it. An answer to the military stalemate was the opening of a second front that might force the English to accept peace. The assembly at Ayr that had just recognised Edward Bruce as heir presumptive to the Scottish crown must also have sanctioned preparations for an expedition to install him as High King of Ireland. For although the English administration at Dublin had furnished men and provisions for Edward I and Edward II in their Scottish campaigns[4] the native Irish resented English rule and might be persuaded to co-operate with the Scots. If Edward Bruce were successful there might even follow a dynastic union between Scotland and Ireland. Thus from the outset

---

[2] *A.P.S.*, I. 464.   [3] *Ibid.*
[4] J. F. Lydon, 'The Bruce Invasion of Ireland', *Historical Studies*, IV. 111–25, at 122. I am indebted to Dr. Lydon for helpful comments on this subject.

the Irish venture presented far-reaching opportunities, and these were related to the existence of two cultures, one of them Gaelic, within Scotland itself. The significance of the Gaelic regions in Bruce's career helps to explain his prolonged interest in Ireland. At some stage he addressed letters to the Irish 'kings' and clergy, asserting that Scots and Irish shared a common origin, a common language and common customs; the 'kings', prelates and inhabitants of all Ireland were asked to co-operate with Scottish envoys so that 'our people' (*nostra nacio*)—and by that Bruce seems to have meant a joint people of Scots and Irish—should be restored to its former freedom.[5]

When Edward Bruce landed in Ulster his prospects seemed bright. Having won an engagement at the Moiry Pass he sacked Dundalk on 29 June 1315 and slaughtered the burgesses.[6] Though outnumbered, the Scots profited from the dissensions among the Anglo-Irish. Richard de Burgh, the Red Earl of Ulster, spurned the help of Edmund Butler, the justiciar of Ireland. When the Red Earl was routed at Connor (or Conagher)[7] on 10 September 1315 he began to be suspected of collusion with the Scots (he was, after all, father-in-law to King Robert). On 1 February 1316 it was the turn of the justiciar to be routed at the battle of the Skerries in Kildare. The way to Dublin lay open but the Scots did not take it. Instead Edward Bruce marched back to press the siege of Carrickfergus Castle on Belfast Lough and to be invested on 2 May 1316 as High King of Ireland on the hill of Maeldon near Dundalk. Early in September 1316 Carrickfergus surrendered.[8] The stout resistance it had put up for almost a year was one reason for Edward Bruce's ultimate failure.

For the moment, however, his successes encouraged risings all over Ireland. These showed both the strength and the weakness of his position : his presence had persuaded the native Irish to rise ; but they did so not in a concerted movement, nor even in a spirit of patriotism, but rather to work off old scores now that English and Anglo-Irish authority had been weakened. To complete his conquest Edward Bruce had to make his kingship respected among the native

[5] Ranald Nicholson, 'A sequel to Edward Bruce's Invasion of Ireland', *S.H.R.*, XLII. 30–40, at 38.

[6] Barbour, *The Bruce*, II. 4–11.

[7] See R. Dunlop, 'Some Notes on Barbour's Bruce', *Essays . . . presented to Thomas Frederick Tout*, ed. A. G. Little and F. M. Powicke (1925), pp. 277–90, at 281.

[8] G. O. Sayles, 'The Siege of Carrickfergus Castle, 1315–16', *Irish Historical Studies*, x. pp. 98–9; O. Armstrong, *Edward Bruce's Invasion of Ireland* (afterwards cited as *Bruce Invasion*), pp. 92–5.

Irish. And to do this, ancient custom demanded that the High King should make a circuit of the provinces of Ulster, Meath, Leinster, Munster and Connaught.

Such a project required reinforcements from Scotland. By February 1317 King Robert had joined his brother at Carrickfergus to march 'throu all Irland fra end to othir',[9] devastating a land already suffering from famine. In Meath the Red Earl set a trap for his royal son-in-law.[10] There was bitter fighting before King Robert extricated the Scottish rearguard and forced his father-in-law to flee to Dublin. There the mayor arrested the Red Earl and warded him in the castle. This was the prelude to a night of frenzied activity in the city. On 21 February 1317 the Scots were only eight miles away and an attack was expected. In the course of chaotic attempts to fortify the city the Dubliners caused damage estimated at £10,000.[11] Had the Scots attacked, it is difficult to see how the distraught citizens could have repelled them. Yet once more, as in 1316, the Scots by-passed Dublin. Having marched through Munster to the Shannon the Bruces made no assault on the city of Limerick. Nor did they cross into Connaught. The circuit of Ireland was a failure. In May 1317 King Robert and Thomas Randolph left Edward Bruce in Carrickfergus and sailed back to Galloway with many wounded.[12]

They had returned just in time. The Scots had never held the undisputed control of the sea passage that was vital to success in Ireland. By February 1315 John of Lorne, King Robert's inveterate foe, had expelled a Scottish occupation force from the Isle of Man [13] and prevented its being used as a naval base by the Scots. For a time it looked as if they would use Anglesey: on 12 September 1315 Thomas Dun, the Scottish naval commander, sailed into Holyhead with four Flemish sea captains and captured an English ship.[14] The local population was co-operative. Indeed the Welsh were so impressed by Edward Bruce's initial successes that they asked him to be their leader:[15] old prophecies foretold that by an alliance with the Scots the Welsh would regain their freedom.[16] By July 1317, however, Sir John of Athy, the Irish admiral, had captured Dun and learnt from him of Thomas Randolph's preparations against the Isle of Man

[9] Barbour, *The Bruce*, II. 50.   [10] *Ibid.*, 50–8.
[11] O. Armstrong, *Bruce Invasion*, pp. 103–6.
[12] Barbour, *The Bruce*, II. 76; *Cal. Docs. Scot.*, III. No. 543.
[13] *Cal. Docs. Scot.*, III. Nos. 420, 421, 450, 479, 521.
[14] *Ibid.*, No. 451.
[15] *Vita Edwardi*, p. 61; *Cal. Papal Letters*, II. 138.
[16] *Chron. Bower*, II. 457–8.

and Anglesey.[17] English control of the Irish Sea made it difficult to send aid to Ireland, let alone Wales.

In Ireland there was a lull in military operations, partly on account of the efforts of the new pope, John XXII, to bring about an Anglo-Scottish truce or peace. To the Scots and the native Irish it seemed that his intervention was biased in favour of Edward II. At the end of 1317 or beginning of 1318 an Irish 'Remonstrance' was drafted and sent to the pope.[18] This document ran in the name of Donal O'Neil, the chief Ulster ally of Edward Bruce. Donal styled himself 'king of Ulster and true heir by heritable right to all Ireland'. He was willing, however, to renounce his right in favour of Edward Bruce. The Remonstrance—which may have been the work of King Robert's propaganda department [19]—alluded to Greater Scotia (Ireland) and Lesser Scotia (Scotland) and it described the kings of Lesser Scotia as having all derived their original blood from Greater Scotia, 'keeping our language and way of life to a certain extent'. Edward Bruce, according to O'Neil, was a pious, prudent and modest man of ancient Irish descent, powerful enough to redeem the Irish from the house of bondage. But on 14 October 1318 Edward Bruce fought his last battle at Faughart,[20] near Dundalk, and was slain almost on the spot where he had been invested as High King. So great was the defeat of the Scots that the escaping remnant did not even attempt to hold Carrickfergus.

A map showing the easterly routes followed by Edward Bruce in his Irish campaigns [21] bears out the claim that he had 'wasted the whole of the land occupied by the English'.[22] It has been suggested that the Scots had accomplished their main objective by depriving the English of Irish troops and provisions: 'Ireland was ruined as a source of supply, the Anglo-Irish were diverted from Scotland, and Edward II had to divide his forces and switch his attention from

---

[17] *Cal. Docs. Scot.*, III. No. 562.

[18] For the text of the Remonstrance see *Chron. Bower*, II. 259–67; *Chron. Pluscarden*, I. 243–50. The Irish background of the Remonstrance is discussed by J. Watt, in 'Negotiations between Edward II and John XXII concerning Ireland', *Irish Historical Studies*, X. 1–20; G. J. Hand, *English Law in Ireland, 1290–1324*, pp. 198–20; and J. F. Lydon, *op. cit., Historical Studies*, IV. 111–25, at 115.

[19] Ranald Nicholson, 'Magna Carta and the Declaration of Arbroath', *Edinburgh University Journal*, XXII. 140–44, at 143.

[20] J. F. Lydon, *op. cit., Historical Studies*, IV. 111–25, at 115–21; O. Armstrong, *Bruce Invasion*, pp. 116–8.

[21] See the map in O. Armstrong, *Bruce Invasion*.

[22] *Chron. Pluscarden*, I. 240.

Scotland.'[23] All this is true. Yet it is difficult to believe that it was only for ends such as these that Edward Bruce and his companions fought. A far greater issue was at stake and in this the Scots failed. They were unable to draw lasting profit from the 'special friendship' that King Robert had alluded to in his letters to the Irish. The battle of Faughart removed Ireland from King Robert's strategy for almost a decade. It was the end of any hope of replacing English authority in Ireland with a régime allied to Scotland; it was also the end of any hope of a comparable development in Wales.

The opening of a second front in Ireland had not diverted the attention of the Scots from warfare on the Marches and in the north of England. While raids into England had a political motive in so far as they might force Edward II to make peace, the more significant motive was economic : King Robert 'went oft on this maneir in Yngland for till riche his men';[24] it was typical that in May 1318 the men of Ripon offered a thousand marks to save their town from destruction.[25] The possibility of taking an English prisoner was a further inducement to serve on the Borders; when Sir Ralph Neville was captured in 1316 his ransom was set at two thousand marks.[26] Foremost in the Border warfare that followed Bannockburn was Sir James Douglas, whose exploits[27] were to be rewarded by large grants of land in the Marches.

Meanwhile the town of Berwick was under blockade by land and sea. In February 1316 the men-at-arms were eating the flesh of dying horses[28] while Flemish privateers, notably John Crabb and his nephew Crabbekyn, intercepted English supply ships.[29] And in December 1317 King Robert, newly returned from Ireland, was busy at Aldcambus, some twelve miles from Berwick, constructing siege machines.[30] They were not needed. In June 1317 Edward II had entrusted control of the town defences to the burgesses; disputes soon arose between them and the garrison,[31] and the warden of the town offended Piers of Spalding, an English burgess. At daybreak on 28

[23] J. F. Lydon, op. cit., Historical Studies, IV. 111–25, at 112–13.
[24] Barbour, The Bruce, I. 351.
[25] Chron. Lanercost, pp. 235–6; Cal. Docs. Scot., III. Nos. 707, 858.
[26] Cal. Docs. Scot., III. No. 527. See also Denys Hay, 'Booty in Border Warfare', Dumfriesshire Trans., XXXI. 145–66.
[27] Barbour, The Bruce, II. 37–47; Scalacronica, p. 143.
[28] Cal. Docs. Scot., III. Nos. 452, 470, 477.
[29] Ibid., Nos. 417, 455, 486, 511, 537.
[30] Foedera, II. pt. i, 141–2.   [31] Cal. Docs. Scot., III. Nos. 554, 555, 558.

March 1318 he betrayed the town to the Scots[32] and was rewarded by Bruce with an estate in Angus.[33] In contrast to his former policy of dismantling fortifications, the king not only preserved but strengthened those of Berwick and limited his strategy by committing himself to the defence of his new-won prize.[34]

When parliament met at Scone in December 1318 some of its enactments showed an awareness of the risk that had been taken. One statute sought to improve the arms and equipment of the common folk who did not owe feudal military service but were summoned to the king's host under the obligations of *communis exercitus* or *servitium Scoticanum*. Like their counterparts in England, who had to meet the requirements of an 'assize of arms', they were to have arms and equipment commensurate with their worldly goods : a man with goods to the value of one cow was to have a good spear or a good bow with a sheaf of two dozen arrows. After Easter each year the sheriff and the local lords were to hold 'wappinschaws' to see that the statute was observed.[35]

The military and disciplinary measures of the Scone parliament were soon put to the test for the loss of Berwick had stirred the lethargic Edward II once more to rally his disunited land in lengthy preparations for a major effort against the Scots. He achieved a reconciliation with his baronial opponents headed by Earl Thomas of Lancaster, and he tried (unsuccessfully) to persuade the authorities in Flanders to prevent Flemish traders and privateers from aiding the Scots by blockade-running.[36] Early in September 1319 he laid siege to Berwick with over eight thousand troops.[37]

The all too obvious means of countering the English threat was to march to the relief of Berwick and wage a pitched battle. But Bruce was too competent a strategist to run unnecessary risk : an attack on the entrenched English camp 'mycht weill turn to foly'.[38] Instead, King Robert sent Thomas Randolph and James Douglas on an invasion of England. One of their aims was to capture Queen Isabella, who had taken up quarters in York. She discreetly moved to Nottingham. Archbishop Melton of York tried to stop the Scottish depredations but was not destined to go down in history as a second

---

[32] *Ibid.*, No. 589; Barbour, *The Bruce*, II. 77–83.

[33] Barrow, *Bruce*, p. 395.   [34] Barbour, *The Bruce*, II. 84–7.

[35] *A.P.S.*, I. 465–6.

[36] *Cal. Docs. Scot.*, III. Nos. 639, 673, 683. For the background see W. Stanford Reid, 'The Scots and the Staple Ordinance of 1313', *Speculum*, XXXIV. 598–610, at 606–7.

[37] *Cal. Docs. Scot.*, III. No. 668.   [38] Barbour, *The Bruce*, II. 96.

Thurstan : at Myton-on-Swale near Boroughbridge his motley crew was routed on 20 September 1319 in a travesty of a battle that the Scots with grim humour styled 'the Chaptour of Mytoune'.[39] Meanwhile things had not gone well for King Edward at Berwick. He had constructed a 'sow' to undermine the walls; the Scots, under the direction of John Crabb, an engineer 'of gret subtilite', constructed a 'crane' to oppose the 'sow'. On 13 September the sow set forth for its combat with the crane and was reduced to ashes.[40] When news of the Scottish depredations in England reached the besiegers, the southerners, unaffected by the Scottish raid, pressed for continuation of the siege. The northerners were not so disinterested. King Edward's council 'fast discordit'. By 24 September most of his host had disbanded.[41] This humiliation, fresh Scottish raids into England, and renewed difficulties with his own barons, induced Edward to negotiate with the Scots. On 22 December King Robert ratified the conditions of a two-year truce.[42]

While the truce of 1319 brought a short pause to warfare it brought no slackening to a contest in which spiritual weapons were wielded. It was typical of Edward II's ambitions in this field that within a few years he petitioned the pope (in vain) that no Scot should be made a bishop within the Scottish kirk, 'for it is the prelates of Scotland who encourage all classes in their evil acts'.[43] Foremost among the bishops who from time to time opposed the English were Wishart of Glasgow, David of Moray, Lamberton of St Andrews, Sinclair of Dunkeld and Mark of the Isles. Master Baldred Bisset, Master Nicholas Balmyle and Master Walter Twynholm were representative of the important class of lesser dignitaries who supported the patriotic cause.[44] Similar support came from the friars, whose preaching 'could easily take the form of propaganda'.[45] Among monks and canons regular there was perhaps less commitment to the patriotic cause : before Bannockburn the regular clergy seem to have had 'far more frequent dealings with the English authorities in the interests of protection and privilege than the secular clergy'.[46] At the best of times the Scottish kirk was by no means a united body speak-

---

[39] *Ibid.*, 99–100; *Scalacronica*, p. 148; *Chron. Lanercost*, p. 239.
[40] Barbour, *The Bruce*, II. 100–4.
[41] *Ibid.*, 110; *Cal. Docs. Scot.*, III. No. 668.
[42] *Cal. Docs. Scot.*, III. No. 681.
[43] *Foedera*, II. pt. ii, 90.   [44] Barrow, *Bruce*, pp. 377–8.
[45] W. M. Mackenzie, *op. cit.*, *S.H.R.*, XXVII. 105–13, at 112–3.
[46] D. E. Easson, *op. cit.*, *Scot. Church Hist. Soc. Recs.*, XI. 63–81, at 66.

ing with a single voice, but rather a haphazard conglomeration of men and institutions, often at variance with one another over questions of money, privilege and prestige. Thus it has recently been questioned whether the Scottish kirk could have 'a clear policy, an opinion, an attitude distinctively its own'. It has been suggested that 'Scotsmen in clerical orders were not markedly different from Scotsmen out of them, that they were neither more nor less heroic and patriotic than their fellow-countrymen'.[47] But if the political outlook of ecclesiastics often corresponded with that of other members of the community of the realm it was not necessarily for exactly the same reasons. While ecclesiastics were part and parcel of Scottish society and were bound to be affected by the ideas current in that society they were formers of opinion rather than followers of it. And as formers of opinion they had motives which were peculiar to themselves and professional in origin, not least fears of the intrusion of English ecclesiastics into Scottish benefices.

On the whole, Clement V and John XXII aided the English policy of intrusion. Moreover, so long as the papacy withheld recognition of his title Bruce would choose to remain ignorant of its pacific initiatives.[48] The continuing Scottish raids convinced John XXII of Bruce's intransigence: in June 1318 sentence of excommunication was passed against him and his accomplices and Scotland was placed under interdict.[49] Although Bruce could prevent the promulgation of this sentence in Scotland it could hardly be hidden that it was published in England and that he, Randolph and Douglas were cursed thrice daily in every English church. The Scottish clergy were faced with the choice of obeying the king or the pope, and an English chronicle affirms that 'meny a gode preste and holy man . . . were slayn throuz al the reme of Scotland' because they 'wolde singe no masse azeynes [against] the Popes commaundement'.[50] In July 1319 Edward hopefully (but in vain) presented his own nominees to no less than seventy-nine Scottish benefices;[51] and papal letters of November 1319 cited the Bishops of St Andrews, Dunkeld, Aberdeen and Moray to appear before the pope by 1 May 1320 to give account of the state of affairs in Scotland.[52]

[47] G. W. S. Barrow, 'The Scottish Clergy in the War of Independence', *S.H.R.*, XLI. 1–22, at 3.   [48] Duncan, *Nation of Scots*, pp. 23–4.
[49] *Foedera*, II. pt. i, 151, 152.
[50] *The Brut*, or *The Chronicles of England*, ed. Friedrich W. D. Brie (1906), p. 211.
[51] *Cal. Docs. Scot.*, III. No. 653; see Nos. 655, 657, 658, 659.
[52] *Cal. Papal Letters*, II. 191.

As it turned out, the four Scottish bishops ignored the summons. The Scots hoped to avert papal wrath by sending the *apologia* that has become famous as the Declaration of Arbroath. This was a letter addressed to John XXII by the Scottish barons and dated at the monastery of Arbroath on 6 April 1320.[53] The Declaration began with allusions to the long and legendary history of the Scots ever since they had emerged from Greater Scythia. In their realm had reigned a hundred and thirteen kings of their own royal stock, no alien intervening. Although dwelling at the ends of the earth they had been singled out by God to be among the first to be brought to His holy faith—and by none other than the Apostle Andrew, brother of St Peter. They had received many favours from past popes; under such protection they had lived free and undisturbed until Edward I had taken advantage of them at a time when they themselves were guiltless of evil intent, unaccustomed to wars, and without a head. From the innumerable enormities perpetrated by him they had been delivered by King Robert, who, like a second Maccabaeus or Joshua, had cheerfully endured toil and weariness, fasting and peril. He had been made king in accordance with law and custom, rightful succession and the dutiful consent and assent of all the people. Were he to give up what he had begun, choosing to subject his people and realm to the King of the English and the English people, the Scots would strive to thrust him out and make another king, 'for so long as a hundred men remain alive we will never in any way be bowed beneath the yoke of English domination; for it is not for glory, riches or honours that we fight, but for freedom alone, that which no man of worth yields up, save with his life'.

By any standards the Declaration of Arbroath is an impressive and eloquent manifesto with a universal relevance. It is the solemn protest of a small country against the aggression of a more powerful neighbour, an appeal not only on behalf of national freedom but on behalf of a kind of personal freedom which is coupled with it. It may therefore seem cynical to question whether such language and sentiments arose spontaneously in the mouths and breasts of the eight earls and thirty-one barons in whose name it ran, or to question whether they ever met at Arbroath on 6 April 1320. Most probably

[53] See Sir James Fergusson, *The Declaration of Arbroath* (1970); Lord Cooper, 'The Declaration of Arbroath Revisited' in his *Selected Papers, 1922–1954* and in his *Supra Crepidam* (1951), pp. 48–59; A. A. M. Duncan, 'The Making of the Declaration of Arbroath' in *The Study of Medieval Records: Essays presented to Kathleen Major*; Duncan, *Nation of Scots*, pp. 25–37.

they merely complied with a royal request to bring, or send, their seals for authentication of the document.[54(a)] That the letter was an essay in propaganda can hardly be doubted. Its Latin eloquence is not of the artless and simple kind but betrays the penmanship of Bernard of Linton, Abbot of Arbroath and Chancellor of Scotland.[54(b)]

He, and the chancery clerks who no doubt helped him, set to work in an eclectic fashion, drawing ideas from the document issued by the Scottish clergy in 1309, from Sallust's *Catiline*,[55] and, most directly of all, from the Irish Remonstrance, on which it is conceivable that Abbot Bernard had previously tried his hand.[56] Unlike the Remonstrance, however, the Declaration avoids detailed representations of a juridical or legalistic nature that might weaken the impact of the rhetoric. To read into the Declaration 'a clear statement of the constitutional relationship between the king and the community' or to conclude from it that the community of Scotland was 'reaching full maturity'[57] is to mistake an emotive appeal abounding in hyperbole for a workaday constitutional treatise. The Declaration presents instead a few important ideas in cogent and sonorous phrases; and the field from which these ideas are drawn is not *legalitas* but *humanitas*. Simply because it is based on an assumption of certain universal human qualities the Declaration of Arbroath is the most impressive manifesto of nationalism that medieval Europe produced.

It is a measure of the author's skill that what he wrote has been, more often than not, taken at its face value rather than as an idealised picture of a transcendent nationalism that might beat in the breasts of some Scots, hardly in those of all. It was typical of the baronial tergiversations of the wars of independence that Sir William Oliphant, who gallantly defended Stirling Castle against Edward I in 1304, also defended the town of Perth for Edward II in 1313;[58] that Sir Lawrence Abernethy, who had come to Bannockburn to fight for Edward II, arrived late, saw the Scottish victory, and joined Douglas in chasing Edward II to Dunbar;[59] that Sir Adam Gordon, who had served for three years as Edward II's justiciar of Lothian,[60] was one of the two knights whom King Robert entrusted with the mission of

[54(a)] Barrow, *Bruce*, pp. 425–6.
[54(b)] Lord Cooper, *Supra Crepidam*, pp. 53–5.
[55] J. R. Philip, 'Sallust and the Declaration of Arbroath', *S.H.R.*, xxvi. 75–8.
[56] Ranald Nicholson, *op. cit., University of Edinburgh Journal*, xxii. 140–4, at 143.   [57] Barrow, *Bruce*, p. 428.
[58] *Cal. Docs. Scot.*, iii. 425–7; *Rot. Scot.*, i. 105.
[59] Barbour, *The Bruce*, i. 343–4.
[60] *Cal. Docs. Scot.*, iii. Nos. 181, 135, 211, 299, 403.

delivering the Declaration of Arbroath to the papal *curia*.[61] Had the wars of independence ended (as was not impossible) with a Balliol restoration in 1302, shortly after Robert Bruce had made his peace with Edward I, Bruce, the exponent of nationalism, would have figured in history as an unpatriotic Earl of Carrick, rightfully disinherited, of no more significance than the contemporary Earl of Angus who loyally served the English king. It is even more striking that within four months of the issue of the Arbroath Declaration five of the barons who sealed it—William Soulis, Roger Mowbray, David Brechin, Patrick Graham and Eustace Maxwell—were accused with others of taking part in a treasonable conspiracy against King Robert's life.

The object of the conspiracy was to kill King Robert and to put Sir William Soulis on the throne. Sir William was grand-nephew of Sir John Soulis the onetime guardian of Scotland; his father, Nicholas Soulis, had been one of the unsuccessful claimants in the Great Cause; his mother, Margaret Comyn, was the daughter of Alexander Comyn, one-time Earl of Buchan; and another daughter of Alexander, Agnes Comyn, Countess of Strathearn, was also involved in the plot.[62] One indication of the strength of a medieval king was his ability to exact the full penalty for treason. In the summer of 1320 the conspirators were rounded up and brought before a 'full parliament' that met at Scone on 4 August. An assize acquitted Sir Eustace Maxwell and four others for lack of evidence. Sir William Soulis made a confession, and with his aunt, the Countess of Strathearn, was sentenced to life imprisonment. Sir Roger Mowbray had died before his trial: his corpse was placed on a litter and brought before parliament, probably in accordance with practice under the law of arms,[63] so that his trial could proceed; it was sentenced to be drawn, hanged and beheaded; only King Robert's clemency saved it from such vilification. Sir Gilbert Malherbe, Sir John Logie, Sir David Brechin and Richard Brown were condemned to be drawn at the tail of horses through the streets of Perth and then to be hanged and beheaded.[64] Although Bruce had not gone so far as to copy the English

[61] G. Donaldson, 'The Pope's Reply to the Scottish Barons in 1320', *S.H.R.*, xxix. 119–20.

[62] *Scalacronica*, p. 144. For the background see *Scots Peerage*, vi. 135–7, viii. 241–50.

[63] See W. C. Dickinson, ' "His body shall be brought to the lists" ', *S.H.R.*, xlii. 84–6.

[64] Barbour, *The Bruce*, ii. 140–2. For other accounts of the conspiracy and its suppression see *Scalacronica*, p. 144; *Chron. Fordun*, i. 348–9.

practices of summary procedure followed by the disembowelling and quartering of the victims, the penalty he had exacted from the conspirators was, by Scottish standards, a severe one. He had demonstrated that there was no room for baronial intransigence in a kingdom that had bought unity and independence at a dear price. But contemporaries were less shocked by the treason of the Soulis conspiracy than by the severity of the 'Black Parliament' in crushing the treason.

While the Soulis conspiracy was being crushed in Scotland the Declaration of Arbroath was delivered in the *curia*, which since 1309 had been established in Avignon.[65] In a written reply dated there on 28 August 1320 [66] the pope dealt both with the Declaration and with letters that had been sent to him by King Robert. Pope John agreed to exhort the English to make peace,[67] and he also exhorted the Scots to make peace. Although he still called King Robert merely 'that illustrious man Robert, who assumes the title and position of King of Scotland' his reply can hardly be described as a 'remarkable feat of evasion'.[68]

In compliance with the pope's admonitions, negotiations for peace or truce took place between January and April 1321 at Newcastle, Berwick and Bamburgh,[69] in the presence of three envoys of the French king and two envoys of the pope. John of Brittany, Earl of Richmond, was to take with him exemplars of the record of the Great Cause so that the English delegation might 'refer to it as far as possible'.[70] If Edward thought that the Scots would take heed of documents that Baldred Bisset had rejected twenty years previously he was ludicrously mistaken. Early in January 1322, soon after the expiry of the two-year truce, the Scots were once more over the border under Randolph, Douglas and the Steward.

This Scottish attack coincided with deepening dissensions between Edward and his baronial opponents headed by the Earls of Lancaster and Hereford. The Scots concluded that they might obtain from the English baronial opposition the terms that Edward II had refused to concede. In the winter of 1321–22 there were negotiations

[65] G. Mollat, *The Popes at Avignon* (1949), p. xix.

[66] G. Donaldson, *op. cit., S.H.R.*, xxix. 119–20.

[67] For the letters he sent to England see A. Theiner, *Vetera Monumenta* (Rome, 1864), No. ccccxxx; *Cal. Papal Registers*, ii. 428.

[68] Barrow, *Bruce*, p. 426.

[69] *Cal. Docs. Scot.*, iii. Nos. 718, 720, 722, 726, 743; Stones, *Documents*, No. 38. [70] Stones, *Documents*, No. 38.

involving Douglas, Randolph, and Thomas of Lancaster, who in conspiratorial fashion adopted the pseudonym of 'King Arthur'. When open civil war broke out in England the Earls of Lancaster and Hereford retreated northwards to link up with the Scots. Before the Scots arrived, however, the two earls were intercepted by Sir Andrew Harclay. On 16 March 1322 Hereford was slain while trying to force a crossing over the Trent at Boroughbridge; Lancaster surrendered and was beheaded a few days later. Harclay received from his grateful king the new title of Earl of Carlisle.[71]

Having at long last crushed 'King Arthur', Edward II was in a mood to avenge himself on the Scots and in May 1322 began preparations for a new invasion.[72] By the time that his host crossed the Tweed in August 1322 the country in its path was stripped bare of livestock, victuals and fodder. Bruce's cautious scorched-earth strategy was justified by its results. Having reached Edinburgh without meeting opposition the English lingered for three days vainly awaiting their supply ships which were held back by contrary winds. On its withdrawal the starving army looted Holyrood and Melrose and set fire to Dryburgh.[73] The north of England was more demoralised than ever as Edward withdrew southward.[74]

As Edward found himself almost deserted Bruce was busy mustering 'all the power of Scotland, of the Isles, and of the rest of the Highlands'.[75] He crossed the Solway on 30 September and struck rapidly southward. On the evening of 13 October Edward, then at Rievaulx Abbey, was under the impression that the Scots were no nearer than Northallerton;[76] at dawn on the following day the Earl of Richmond reached the top of the escarpment between the abbeys of Byland and Rievaulx to discover that they had marched through the night and were fast approaching. In the engagement that followed, the earl was captured and Edward was chased to York,[77] where he was joined by Andrew Harclay, who found him 'confused' and returned to Carlisle ready to take an initiative of his own. On 3 January 1323 he made a private visit to King Robert at Lochmaben.[78]

[71] *Chron. Lanercost*, pp. 241–5; *Cal. Docs. Scot.*, III. Nos. 746, 749.
[72] *Cal. Docs. Scot.*, III. Nos. 751, 752, 754.
[73] *Chron. Bower*, II. 278; Barbour, *The Bruce*, II. 124–6.
[74] *Cal. Docs. Scot.*, III. Nos. 778, 790; *Scalacronica*, p. 149.
[75] *Scalacronica*, p. 149; *Chron. Lanercost*, p. 247.
[76] *Chron. Lanercost*, p. 247; *Cal. Docs. Scot.*, III. No. 790.
[77] Barbour, *The Bruce*, II, 129–35; *Chron. Lanercost*, pp. 247–8.
[78] *Chron. Lanercost*, pp. 247–8.

There Harclay negotiated 'on behalf of all those in England who wish to be spared and saved from war by Robert Bruce and all his men'. The preamble to the resulting indenture [79] affirmed that in the past the realms of England and Scotland had prospered so long as each had a king from its own nation and was maintained separately with its own laws and customs. It was to the common profit of both realms that Bruce might hold Scotland freely, entirely, and in liberty. To uphold the common profit there were to be twelve sworn commissioners, six to be chosen from King Robert's people and six to be chosen by Harclay. Within a year Edward was to consent that King Robert 'shall have his realm, free and quit, for himself and his heirs'. In return, Bruce was to make some concessions. He would pay the English forty thousand marks at the rate of four thousand a year. He would found an abbey in Scotland for the souls of those slain in the war and would endow it with five hundred marks a year. Edward would have the gratifying right to arrange the marriage of Bruce's male heir to one of Edward's own kinswomen. The final point of the proposed peace was that neither king 'shall be bound to receive in his realm a man who has been opposed to him, nor to render him the lands that he or his ancestors had in his realm if he does not wish to do it of his special grace'. Thenceforth there would be two national kingdoms, equal in status and distinct; Scots would be Scots, English would be English, and the Anglo-Scots would disappear.

It was a solution that was pragmatic, nationalist, and statesman-like. But it held no appeal for Edward II: Harclay was 'a private person to whom it in no wise pertained to ordain such things'. On 25 February 1323 he was treacherously seized in Carlisle Castle. After a summary 'trial', he was degraded from his earldom and knighthood, drawn, hanged, beheaded, disembowelled and quartered.[80]

In ridding himself of Andrew Harclay Edward had deprived England of its staunchest defender. Almost immediately he himself had to open negotiations with the Scots, first at Newcastle,[81] then at Bishopthorpe near York. One reason why the victorious Scots were willing to accept a truce was a change of affairs in Flanders, whence they had lately obtained valuable aid: in the summer of 1322 Edward feared Flemish naval attacks on the English coast and alluded

[79] Text in Stones, *Documents*, pp. 155–7.
[80] *Chron. Lanercost*, pp. 249–51; J. G. Bellamy, *Law of Treason*, p. 52.
[81] *Cal. Docs. Scot.*, III. Nos. 796, 807; *A.P.S.*, I. 479–80.

to 'these evil Flemings'.[82] His difficulties were suddenly eased with the death of the troublesome Count of Flanders in September 1322. The count's successor was a child and the regents of Flanders were prepared to co-operate with Edward: on 18 April 1323 all Scots were ordered to leave Flanders.[83] On 30 May 1323 the terms of a long truce were at last settled at Bishopthorpe.[84]

The truce was to last for thirteen years, beginning on 12 June 1323. Apart from reciprocal clauses that were intended to restore peaceful relations there was one English concession: Edward bound himself not to oppose a Scottish approach to the papacy for the release of the Scots from excommunication and interdict. Basic problems, however, were left unsettled: nothing was said of those Scots or Anglo-Scots who had been disinherited on account of their adherence to Edward; nor did the English recognise Bruce as king.[85] He was little nearer his ultimate goal.

Nonetheless the truce of Bishopthorpe brought what was at least expected to be a long cessation of hostilities. In Scotland it was possible to repair the damages of war and to undertake more intensively the social, political and economic reconstruction that had hitherto been piecemeal and intermittent. Although there are signs of conscious attempts at reconstruction somewhat earlier, notably in the Scone parliament of December 1318, which had enacted over twenty statutes in a major review of law and legal procedure,[86] it was mainly between the years 1323 and 1327 that King Robert was free to concentrate upon domestic problems.

The background to these was the effect of prolonged warfare upon the economy. There were many areas of Scotland that saw no warfare at all, or experienced it for only a short time, but the areas that suffered most from warfare were those that had hitherto been the most developed: in 1317 an English writer reported that Annandale was so utterly wasted that there was neither man nor beast left between the border and Lochmaben.[87] In many areas the productivity

---

[82] *Cal. Docs. Scot.*, III. No. 778. The background of Flemish, German and other overseas aid to the Scots is given by W. Stanford Reid in 'Trade, Traders, and Scottish Independence', *Speculum*, XXIX. 210–22, and in 'Sea-power in the Anglo-Scottish War, 1296–1328', *The Mariner's Mirror*, XLVI. 7–23.

[83] W. Stanford Reid, *op. cit.*, *Speculum*, XXXIV. 598–610, at 608.

[84] Text in *Foedera*, II. pt. ii, 73–4; *A.P.S.*, I. 479–81.

[85] Compare the Scottish ratification issued at Berwick (*A.P.S.*, I. 479–81) and the Bishopthorpe text (*Foedera*, II. pt. ii, 73–4).

[86] *A.P.S.*, I. 466. For discussion of these see *Scot. Legal Hist.*, pp. 18–24; Barrow, *Bruce*, pp. 416–8.   [87] *Cal. Docs. Scot.*, III. No. 543.

of land probably fell by as much as a half [88] and there was bound to be a disruption of the rural routine that was the basis of Scottish livelihood : only the most optimistic could persevere in the laborious agricultural cycle when their crops were destroyed year after year either by the enemy or by the Scots themselves. While growing crops could not be lifted on the approach of an English army, it was possible to drive sheep and cattle to fastnesses in the hills : a disincentive to till the soil was probably accompanied by a greater emphasis on pastoral farming and the export of wool, woolfells (fleeces) and hides. By 1327 wool exports approached five thousand sacks a year [89] (roughly one-fifth of the English figure) and this volume was scarcely ever to be surpassed throughout the Middle Ages. Hence King Robert's anxiety to keep open the vulnerable trade route to the weaving towns of the Low Countries, his attempts to encourage Netherlanders and Germans to trade with Scotland,[90] his willingness to foster the interests of the Scottish merchant burgesses by resuscitating the merchant gild of Dundee and granting a merchant gild to the burgesses of Ayr.[91] Scottish wool paid for foreign manufactures—especially munitions of war. More than that, it brought revenue to the king.

Although export duties were being levied in the reign of Alexander III [92] it is only towards the end of King Robert's reign that information about them becomes available. They were then being levied at the rate of half a mark (6s. 8d.) on the sack of wool, 3s. 4d. on each hundred woolfells, and a mark on each hundred hides.[93] Wool, woolfells, and hides could be legally shipped only on the production of an export licence sealed with the coket seal of a custumar to certify that the king's 'great new custom' had been paid.[94] While the number of baronial or ecclesiastical burghs was increased during the reign,[95] few, new or old, were granted the use of a coket.[96] Without that they could not thrive. By contrast there was no question of withholding a coket from the king's own burghs :[97] when the new

---

[88] *Ibid.*, No. 245.   [89] *E.R.*, I. 74–83.

[90] W. Stanford Reid, *op. cit., Speculum*, XXIX. 210–22, at 219–20; James W. Dilley, 'Scottish–German Diplomacy, 1297–1327', *S.H.R.*, XXXVI. 80–7.

[91] *R.M.S.*, I. 459; II. No. 3717.

[92] P. 15 above.

[93] *E.R.*, I. xcviii–xcix.

[94] *Ibid.*, c–ci; *Dunfermline Registrum*, pp. 232–3, 246, 247, 252–3; *R.M.S.*, I. 438.

[95] Pryde, *Burghs*, pp. 43–6.

[96] Lochmaben and Dunfermline were exceptions (*E.R.*, I. 99, 174, 175).

[97] For allusions to such cokets see *ibid.*, 78, 101, 175, 322.

royal burgh of Tarbert was founded a coket seal was at once made for it.[98] In an exchequer audit of 1328 the custumars of ten leading royal burghs accounted for £1,851 14s. 4¾d. About a third of this came from the great customs of Berwick; next in importance came Edinburgh, Aberdeen, Dundee and Perth.[99] The prosperity that the export trade brought to the inhabitants of the royal burghs was one from which the king might also draw additional profit in the shape of increasing burghal revenues: in 1328 the ferms of twenty-six royal burghs came to £1,133 3s. 4d.[100] In relation to the total crown revenues the burgh ferms had probably reached the peak of their importance.

This owed much to a development that immediately benefited King Robert but prevented his successors from increasing the yield of the burgh ferms. In 1319 the king granted the burgh of Aberdeen and its endowments to the community of burgesses to be held in feu-ferm. When applied to a burgh this tenure meant that all the king's revenues in the burgh (except the great customs) were transferred to the community of burgesses in perpetuity. The community held their burgh and its endowments as a collective tenant-in-chief of the crown, paying a fixed annual ferm in perpetuity. In the case of Aberdeen this was set at £213 6s. 8d.[101] In the following year Berwick, which seems to have enjoyed feu-ferm status under Alexander III, was granted a feu-ferm charter for five hundred marks (£333 6s. 8d.) a year.[102] When the turn of Edinburgh came in 1329 it was let off lightly with a mere £34 13s. 4d. a year.[103] As yet, only one or two leading royal burghs were granted the privilege of feu-ferm status. And by 1327 Berwick could not afford its high ferm; the burgh was then leased to two barons.[104] Throughout the fourteenth century, however, most of the leading royal burghs were to acquire feu-ferm status.[105]

There were important consequences within the royal burghs themselves. The earliest surviving record of the proceedings of a burgh court, that of Aberdeen in 1317,[106] shows the community of burgesses acting in a judicial capacity. After the conferment of feu-ferm status the community could also act in a fiscal capacity. It had

[98] *Ibid.*, 118, 175.　　[99] *Ibid.*, c.　　[100] *Ibid.*, lxxxviii.
[101] *A.P.S.*, I. 478.　　[102] Barrow, *Bruce*, pp. 423–4.
[103] *E.R.*, I. lxxxvii.　　[104] *Ibid.*, 63.
[105] By 1400 it was enjoyed by at least Dumfries, Haddington, Rutherglen, Lanark, Dundee, Perth, Linlithgow, Forfar, Stirling and Montrose (*E.R.*, III. 501–7), in addition to Aberdeen and Edinburgh.
[106] *Aberdeen Burgh Recs.*, pp. 1–17.

taken the final step to self-government within the burgh; for already it was recognised that the bailies and the alderman (the later provost) should be chosen 'thruch the consaile of the gud men of the toune'.[107] Whether this amounted to a 'democratic' election is uncertain: the ultimate say must have rested with the merchant burgesses. But such craftsmen as became burgesses were certainly beginning to play a part in burgh administration; and warfare and its consequences probably made the merchant burgesses not unwilling to admit to burgess-ship those social inferiors who could share their burdens both military and financial. Royal policy was, however, conservative: as the king's chamberlain began once more to hold his ayre in Berwick and other royal burghs he was to see to it that the social niceties were observed; for he was to enquire whether any fleshers who had become burgesses continued to soil their hands with the offal of animals, and whether any of the king's *nativi* were lurking in the burgh.[108]

King Robert's conservatism in such matters was at variance with the provision made in the Scone parliament of 1318 for the holding of 'wappinschaws' to ensure that each man with goods to the value of one cow should be armed with a spear or bow:[109] a husbandman who was expected to wield a sixteen-foot spear in the schiltron could no longer be expected to be content to be tied to the soil. In a society shaken up by prolonged warfare old habits and customs might be discarded. Seven entries in the register of Dunfermline Abbey, one of them as late in date as 1332, give the genealogies of men who were serfs of the monastery.[110] But even among the serfs of Dunfermline there was a new self-confidence.[111] The last recorded legal suit for the recovery of a runaway serf was to be instituted by the Bishop of Moray in 1364,[112] and a few years later David II was to issue one of the last charters setting free a serf and his descendants.[113]

The obscure, though important, changes that were taking place at the lower levels of society were accompanied by more obvious changes at the upper levels. Thanks to the wars, the Scottish baronage was less open to English influences and more likely to develop

[107] *Leges Quatuor Burgorum* (*A.P.S.*, I. 347).
[108] *De Articulis Inquirendis . . . in Itinere Camerarii* (*ibid.*, 681, 682). See also *R.M.S.*, I. 460.
[109] *A.P.S.*, I. 466.
[110] *Dunfermline Registrum*, Nos. 325–31.
[111] *Ibid.*, No. 354.
[112] *Moray Registrum*, No. 143.   [113] *R.M.S.*, I. No. 345.

characteristics of its own. Although the position of the baronage within the community of the realm had not changed, it had come to depend upon military prestige as well as upon landed wealth. Moreover, the civil war had left a legacy of feud and faction—which the king had attempted to mitigate in one of the statutes of the Scone parliament of 1318.[114] The holding of land, always a vital question, had become mixed up in politics, and any political settlement, such as the establishment of Bruce's authority, implied a settlement of contesting claims to land. King Robert's attitude to this problem has been rightly described as one of 'patient conservation and restoration . . . reluctance to overthrow ancient rights or to offend feudal susceptibilities'.[115] While vast territories fell into the king's hands as forfeitures most of these were forfeited from a small group of irreconcilables, notably Balliol and the Comyns;[116] and the land forfeited from a small group was granted out to a group almost as small. It would be wrong to suppose that Bruce's forfeitures resulted in a 'new nobility', still less in the rise of 'new men' of relatively humble origin. The transfer of land—from the crown as well as from forfeited landholders—took place within the baronial class; and the greatest prizes went to a few men who were connected to Bruce by blood or marriage or by a long period of good service.[117] Notable among these were Thomas Randolph, the king's nephew, and Sir James Douglas, the king's foremost knight, who by 1325 held Douglasdale, Jedburgh and its forest, the wardenship of the king's forest of Selkirk, and at least five baronies in southern Scotland.[118]

If the king's attitude to the quantitative distribution of land can be characterised as conservative,[119] his attitude to the qualitative distribution—the manner in which land was held—was equally so. Although in England, and Western Europe generally, there was a marked tendency away from traditional feudal military service towards contract armies made up of paid troops, King Robert was still granting land in return for the service of a knight or an archer. This in itself is perhaps unimportant : from what is known of the charters he issued he could hardly have obtained much more than the services of an additional forty knights and forty archers. But while most of King Robert's charters granted lands on terms as vague and haphazard as those of his predecessors, more than thirty of his surviving

[114] *A.P.S.*, i. 466.
[116] *Ibid.*
[118] *R.M.S.*, i. 448–50.

[115] Barrow, *Bruce*, pp. 391–2.
[117] *Ibid.*, pp. 381–96.
[119] Barrow, *Bruce*, p. 381.

charters use a novel phase : lands are granted *in liberam baroniam*, or, more fully, *in unam integram et liberam baroniam*.[120] It has been affirmed that 'the adoption of this novel standard formula was not accidental and can hardly have been a trivial matter of chancery procedure', that it was 'part of a deliberate policy of defining and stereotyping feudal rights as well as obligations'.[121] But the formula must be placed in its context : Bruce's chancery was also making grants *in liberam regalitatem, in liberam elemosinam, in liberum burgum, in liberam forestam, in liberam warennam* and *in liberum maritagium*. In these applications the word *liber*, so profusely used, means, if it means anything, 'privileged'; and there is nothing to show that a grant *in liberam baroniam* conveyed any specific privilege, or, for that matter, implied any specific obligation. It is difficult to find any lowest common denominator save the old word 'barony' that applies to these grants: some, but not all, conveyed forfeited lands; some, but not all, stipulated military service; some, but not all, stipulated suit to the court of the sheriffdom ; some, but not all, conferred a new unity upon lands that had previously been unattached to one another. Only in this does there seem to be novelty : scattered lands might become a unit with one *caput* and one payment of relief to the king; and for such increased convenience and baronial authority the holder might be expected to pay a higher relief. The significance of the grants *in liberam baroniam* (which were still being made centuries later) is not that they set up some new type of barony but that they set up more baronies of the old type and that King Robert was deliberately using the barony as an integral and important part of local government. To that extent he was re-vitalising a feudal institution that was decaying elsewhere and confirming it as a basis of local government rather than trying to supplant it by 'royal' government under the sheriffs, or, as as was the case in England, by commissions of *oyer* and *terminer* or the later justices of the peace. Thus the system of interlocking feudal and royal government that Bruce had inherited was preserved and all that was attempted was the tidying up of the feudal structure and the strengthening of the baronial basis on which local government rested.

This development was accompanied by grants that reduced royal control over local government. Malcolm, Earl of Lennox, was given heritably the sheriffships of Lennox and Clackmannan and Hugh, Earl of Ross, the sheriffship of Cromarty.[122] On 8 November 1325 the

[120] E.g. *R.M.S.*, I. No. 31.
[121] Barrow, *Bruce*, p. 410.   [122] *Ibid.*, p. 389; *Scots Peerage*, VII. 235.

king placed an emerald ring on the finger of Sir James Douglas as a token that the latter was infeft with the right to indict all robbers within his lands and that the jurisdiction of the king's justiciar was thereby diminished.[123] More extensive privileges went to those who were granted regalities. Those existing hitherto were mostly insignificant [124] and provided a precedent best forgotten; for the lord of a regality could exclude the royal officials and, to that extent, the regalities were bastions of feudal autonomy. Yet, just as he had revitalised the concept of barony Bruce also re-vitalised that of regality and thereby 'gave a fillip to the process by which the crown lost power through excessive delegation'.[125] For the time being, however, only a few grants of regality were made. Randolph was by far the most important beneficiary. By charters of 20 December 1324 his earldom of Moray and his lordship of the Isle of Man were erected into regalities and it was doubtless about the same time that his lordship of Annandale was similarly favoured.[126]

The new regality of Moray completed Bruce's settlement of the north, for Randolph now held complete civil and military control of the vast area between the river Spey and the Sound of Sleat. On the western seaboard also he was given responsibility as lord of the new regality of the Isle of Man. Elsewhere in the west the landed settlement had to take account of the three branches of the descendants of Somerled—the MacDougals, the MacDonalds and the MacRuaridhs. The first, as inveterate foes of Bruce, were forfeited and lived in exile as dependants of the English king. The MacDonald and MacRuaridh supporters of Bruce were duly rewarded: Angus Og of Islay obtained lands in the former Comyn lordship of Lochaber and was granted a charter of Morvern and Ardnamurchan.[127] On the mainland of Argyll it was the Campbells, hitherto not a particularly notable family, who received the lion's share of the spoil of the MacDougals,[128] while Sir Neil Campbell was given Bruce's sister Mary in marriage.

The landed settlement in the West Highlands and Isles had resulted in a delicate balance of power which it was probably Bruce's intention to maintain through personal supervision.[129] In 1326, with all Scotland to choose from, he went to some trouble to acquire land

[123] *R.M.S.*, I. 449.
[124] Barrow, *Bruce*, pp. 397–8.
[125] *Ibid.*, p. 398.
[126] *R.M.S.*, I. 444–7.
[127] *Ibid.*, 512.
[128] *Ibid.*, 534, 535, 554, 556.
[129] For the background see G. W. S. Barrow, 'The Highlands of Scotland in the lifetime of Robert the Bruce', *The Stewarts*, XII. 26–46.

at Cardross, near Dumbarton. There, in the Lennox, 'a strongly Gaelic district',[130] he built himself a manor-house [131] which became his home. While the king's strategy had generally led him to dismantle royal castles, and some baronial castles as well, his policy in the western approaches was different. The royal castle of Dumbarton was preserved intact and the castle of Skipness in Kintyre was repaired and victualled.[132] More strikingly, in 1325 he spent at least £450 on the construction of a large new royal castle on East Loch Tarbert where Kintyre and Knapdale met;[133] at West Loch Tarbert he constructed a smaller fortification styled a 'peel' and over the isthmus between the two—only a mile wide—he cut out a track,[134] designed probably not so much for ordinary traffic as to facilitate the haulage of galleys between the sheltered waters of the Clyde estuary and the sounds among the Western Isles. For Bruce was trying to revive the naval organisation that had existed along the western seaboard in Norse times [135] and had vessels of his own, including a 'great ship'.[136] His interest in Tarbert was not only strategic : beside the new castle rose a new royal burgh. He put the finishing touch to his western projects by enlisting the help of his most gifted cleric : Bernard of Linton gave up the abbacy of Arbroath and the chancellorship to appear in 1328 as Bishop of the Isles.[137] The king had given him £100 towards his election expenses and arranged that the abbey of Arbroath should grant him a seven-year pension.[138] He was not 'unaccountably promoted' :[139] the king's interest in the transfer suggests that Bernard's services in the Isles would be more than merely spiritual.

From the Scottish kirk as a whole, particularly from the episcopate, Bruce expected to receive political support; but though it was natural that he should bestow his benevolence upon his ecclesiastical supporters and their institutions, his benevolence was inspired less by political consideration than by spiritual remorse and a pious veneration, remarkable even by the standards of the time, for the saints, their relics and shrines. Possibly in expiation of his sacrilege in the friary kirk of Dumfries, he granted an annual rent of forty marks to

130 Barrow, *Bruce*, p. 441.   131 *E.R.*, I. cxix–cxxi.   132 *Ibid.*, 56, 57.
133 See Royal Commission on the Ancient and Historical Monuments of Scotland, *Argyll I: Kintyre* (1971), No. 316, and John G. Dunbar and A. A. M. Duncan, 'Tarbert Castle, a contribution to the history of Argyll', *S.H.R.*, L. 1–17.
134 *E.R.*, I. 52–6.   135 *R.M.S.*, I. 446, 479.
136 *E.R.*, I. 123, 126, 127, 133, 134.   137 *Ibid.*, 114.
138 *Arbroath Liber*, I. No. 358.   139 Barrow, *Bruce*, p. 378.

the Franciscans of Dumfries and another twenty marks to each of the other Franciscan houses in Scotland.[140] On 5 July 1318 he attended the consecration of the newly-completed cathedral of St Andrews and bestowed a parish kirk to be appropriated to the cathedral; the Earl of Fife added another; and the Bishop of St Andrews donated two others.[141] Much more important were the grants lavished by Bruce on the monastic houses. At a time when the prayers of monks were coming to be generally regarded as less spiritually efficacious than the masses celebrated by secular priests Bruce showed himself, somewhat conservatively, to be 'the last munificent royal benefactor of the religious houses of Scotland'; they were thereby enabled to assume 'a new lease of life ere the decadence of the fourteenth century overtook them'.[142] Melrose was a notable beneficiary: in January 1326 Bruce granted the abbey an annual rent of £100 to be used to provide each monk with a daily helping of a rare delicacy—rice made with milk of almonds—the residue of the income was to be used by the monks to clothe and feed fifteen poor men at Martinmas.[143] In March 1326 the king went further and granted the abbey, in aid of its reconstruction, £2,000 to be levied under the supervision of Sir James Douglas from the feudal casualties of Roxburghshire. Perhaps because the grant was so large an encroachment upon the royal revenues, it was expressly stated to have been made 'at the instance of our full royal power in our full parliament last held at Scone'.[144]

Generosity to the religious houses must undoubtedly have contributed to the crisis in royal finances which King Robert reported to parliament when it met in Cambuskenneth Abbey on 15 July 1326: 'the lands and rents which of old used to pertain to his crown had been so diminished by divers gifts and transfers occasioned by the war that he did not have means of maintenance befitting his station'.[145] Parliament was asked to discuss the provision of sufficient financial maintenance for the king in grateful recognition of the hardships that he and his family had borne for the recovery of the liberty of all. For some reason or other the prelates and the rest of the clergy seem to have been excused from discussing the king's request, or at least from taking direct part in the arrangement that resulted. It was the earls, barons, burgesses and 'all the rest of the freeholders of the realm' who took the remarkable step of concluding an inden-

[140] W. Moir Bryce, *The Scottish Greyfriars*, I. 204.
[141] *Chron. Bower*, II. 271–2.
[142] D. E. Easson, *op. cit.*, *Scot. Church Hist. Soc. Recs.*, XI. 63–81, at 77, 78.
[143] *Melrose Liber*, II. No. 362.
[144] *R.M.S.*, I. No. 331 and p. 430.   [145] *A.P.S.*, I. 475.

ture with the king. In this they admitted that the king's request was 'reasonable' and agreed to pay to the king during his lifetime a 'tenth penny'—one tenth of all their ferms and revenues.[146] In return for this grant the king gratefully made a concession. He had hinted that he might maintain himself by imposing an 'intolerable burden' [147] upon his people : vast quantities of victuals were being despatched by royal officials to the king's household;[148] some of these victuals were almost certainly requisitioned as 'prises' for which little or nothing might be paid. In Scotland as in England the taking of 'prises' was an ancient and unpopular royal prerogative. King Robert conceded that he would exercise this prerogative more moderately, following the customs used in the time of Alexander III.

In England parliament made its consent to taxation conditional upon redress of grievance and thereby eventually obtained a dominant position in politics. At Cambuskenneth it looked as if the Scottish parliament, or a body drawn from it, had taken the first step on the same road. But development along English lines was not, in this important respect, to continue; it was, and remained, the chief point of Scottish constitutional theory that the king should 'live of his own', and that direct taxation should be used not to finance ordinary and recurrent expenditure but only for some occasional extraordinary purpose. The grant made at Cambuskenneth, which was in any case to end on Bruce's death, was seen as an innovation that was not to be taken as a precedent.

The Cambuskenneth indenture, to which both freeholders and burgesses were parties, makes it plain that the community of the realm had by then widened to comprise social classes that had scarcely before figured in politics. Yet there is no sign of any new theory to account for a change. King Robert evidently did not regard feudal or tenurial obligation as something that defined the membership of parliament : 'in parliament the king sought to do his business, and to it he summoned those appropriate for his business'.[149] From 1318 onwards they included not only such freeholders as were tenants-in-chief but those who were not crown tenants and who approximated to the class of lesser landholders, 'lairds', rather than 'lords'. In 1326 these freeholders must have attended in sufficient numbers for their concurrence in the Cambuskenneth indenture to be regarded as binding upon all members of their class.[150] The same was true of the burgess commissioners who at Cambuskenneth made their

[146] *Ibid.*, 476. [147] *Ibid.*, 475. [148] *E.R.*, I. 196–202.
[149] A. A. M. Duncan, *op. cit., S.H.R.*, XLV. 36–58, at 55. [150] *Ibid.*

appearance in parliament, possibly for the first time : for 'the political significance of the burghs arose in Scotland as elsewhere from their taxable capacity'.[151] The widening composition of parliament was demonstrated in the summons to the parliament that was to meet at Edinburgh in February 1328 to ratify once more the Cambuskenneth indenture : the summons was a general one issued through the sheriffs, and its terms were 'social and not tenurial';[152] the sheriffs were to summon 'bishops, abbots, earls, barons, freeholders, and six competent persons from each burghal community'.[153] Burgess representation had come to stay.

In yet another respect the Cambuskenneth parliament of 1326 witnessed a significant transaction. Although the king had two surviving legitimate daughters and at least two bastard sons, his long marriage to Elizabeth de Burgh had seemed unlikely to result in a male heir. There was universal rejoicing when the queen gave birth to a son at Dunfermline on 5 March 1324. At the age of two David Bruce was brought before parliament at Cambuskenneth; oaths of fealty were sworn firstly to him and secondly to the king's ten-year-old grandson, Robert Stewart,[154] son of Marjory Bruce and Walter the Steward. In the Scone parliament of December 1318, after the death of Edward Bruce at Faughart, Robert Stewart had been recognised as the king's heir presumptive.[155] With the birth of David Bruce he lost this position, and in a new parliamentary tailzie of 15 July 1326 was recognised as successor to David only if the latter should die without an heir of his own;[156] it seemed that the Bruce dynasty was assured of continuation. Few could have supposed that the Cambuskenneth tailzie would be a live issue in politics some decades later.

Bernard of Linton had celebrated the birth of King Robert's son with Latin verses which foretold that David 'will hold warlike revels amid English gardens; or God will bring to pass a firm peace betwixt the kingdoms'.[157] In the winter of 1324 peace talks were in fact held at York, but Edward refused to contemplate 'the manifest disinheritance of our royal crown'—recognition of Bruce as independent king of an independent Scotland.[158] Thus the Scots had failed to achieve the main object that had been envisaged as following from the truce

---

[151] *Ibid.*, 51.   [152] *Ibid.*, 53.   [153] *Ibid.*, 52.
[154] *Chron. Fordun*, I. 351.   [155] *A.P.S.*, I. 465–6.
[156] The text of the tailzie, which survived till the mid-seventeenth century (*ibid.*, VI. pt. 2, 628, 664), has been lost, but the terms may be readily inferred.
[157] *Chron. Bower*, II. 279–80.   [158] Barrow, *Bruce*, p. 353.

of Bishopthorpe. And while Edward professed strict adherence to the truce he could not prevent English privateers from preying upon the vulnerable Scottish shipping route to Flanders. Piracy culminated in the seizure of the *Pelarym*, a Flemish vessel with a cargo worth £2,000. The Scots on board, including women and pilgrims, were massacred.[159] For this and other outrages Bruce demanded redress in vain.[160] Moreover although Edward had bound himself not to oppose moves for a Scottish reconciliation with the papacy he maintained his opposition.

As the prospect of peace receded, King Robert issued letters empowering Randolph and other envoys to negotiate an alliance with France. A year later, on 26 April 1326, a new Franco-Scottish alliance was concluded at Corbeil.[161] Both in peace and war French kings would aid and counsel the Scots against the English 'to the best of their power as loyal allies', while the Scots were bound 'to make war on the king of England to the utmost of their power' in the event of war between the English and the French. The renewed Franco-Scottish alliance imposed heavier commitments on the Scots than on the French, but henceforward Scotland would no longer be isolated : it had as its ally the richest and most powerful country in Europe ; if English kings attacked Scotland they would have to keep an eye on France. Bruce had set in place what was to be the keystone of Scottish diplomacy for the rest of the Middle Ages. And new cultural ties with France replaced those with England severed by long years of warfare. As early as 1313 Bishop David of Moray had projected a scheme for sending four poor scholars from his diocese to the university of Paris, and in 1325 he provided some endowment to make the scheme permanent.[162] Moreover, by 1336 Scots at the university of Orleans, the greatest law school north of the Alps, were numerous enough to comprise a distinct 'nation' (student association).[163]

Meanwhile England was racked by the dissensions that culminated in the deposition of Edward II at the hands of his wife and her paramour, Roger Mortimer, whose cruelty shocked the Scots.[164] Edward was imprisoned while Isabella and Mortimer misruled the land

[159] *Cal. Docs. Scot.*, III. Nos. 888, 889.

[160] Barbour, *The Bruce*, II. 145–6.

[161] Text in *A.P.S.*, XII. 5–6.

[162] It was not, however, until the late sixteenth century that the Scots College in Paris became a significant institution. See Violette M. Montagu, 'The Scottish College in Paris', *S.H.R.*, IV. 399–416, at 399.

[163] John Kirkpatrick, 'The Scottish "Nation" in the University of Orleans', *S.H.S. Misc. II.* 47–102, at 51.

[164] *Chron. Wyntoun*, II. 372.

in the name of the fourteen-year-old Edward III. Faithful to the last
to the imprisoned ex-king was King Robert's nephew, Donald of
Mar, who had been brought up at the English court. On the fall of
Edward II he returned to Scotland to be welcomed back and restored
to his earldom of Mar. It suited King Robert to give Donald a free
hand in his plots to raise English, Scots and Welsh for the release of
the captive Edward. When the latter's son was crowned as Edward
III on 1 February 1327 the Scots marked the event by a surprise
assault on Norham Castle.[165] Nothing would now content Bruce but
a final peace and his recognition as independent king of an independent Scotland. Even before negotiations once more broke down over
this issue Mortimer and Isabella had begun mobilisation to meet a
new Scottish invasion.[166]

The brilliant strategy that Bruce had devised for the warfare
that was renewed in 1327 was in three phases; and the first of these
opened not in England but in Ireland. It was not for nothing that
King Robert had lately paid so much attention to the western
approaches. After Easter 1327 he landed in Antrim, hoping to take
advantage of the disorders in Ulster that followed upon the recent
death of his father-in-law, the Red Earl.[167] The second phase of his
strategy came in July when the north of England was invaded by
three Scottish battalions under Randolph, Douglas, and Donald of
Mar. Hurriedly the English host arrived in Durham on 15 July to
spend some days of rain-sodden hardship in search of the Scots, who
were strongly stationed on the southern bank of the Wear near Stan-
hope. Heralds were sent in vain to invite the Scots to abandon their
position. When they did cross the river it was in a night attack led by
Sir James Douglas, who swept through the English encampment
and cut the guy-ropes of the royal tent. The young Edward was
'wonder sore afraiede' but escaped capture. Thereafter the Scots had
no difficulty in retiring from Weardale. On 7 August Edward was
told of their 'escape' and 'ful hertly wepte with his yonge eyne'. The
English host marched dejectedly back to Durham and then to York,
where it disbanded.[168] This was the signal for the third phase of King
Robert's strategy. On 12 July 1327 he had forced the Ulster seneschal to conclude a humiliating truce to last a full year from 1 August
1327.[169] As on previous occasions, the conclusion of a truce in one

[165] Nicholson, *Edward III*, pp. 13–36.   [166] *Ibid.*, pp. 15–21.
[167] Nicholson, *op. cit.*, *S.H.R.*, XLII. 30–40.
[168] Nicholson, *Edward III*, pp. 20–36.
[169] Nicholson, *op. cit.*, *S.H.R.*, XLII. 30–40.

locality was merely the prelude to Bruce's appearance in another. After the forces of Randolph, Douglas and Donald of Mar had safely returned to Scotland King Robert crossed the Tweed with a fresh Scottish army. Engines of war were erected before Norham by John Crabb and Bruce ostentatiously let it be known that his intention was to annex Northumberland and parcel it out among his followers—some charters were in fact issued.[170] While the English government could remain indifferent to raids upon the north it could not afford to ignore either the siege of Norham or the threatened annexation of Northumberland. The Weardale expedition had cost the English about £70,000.[171] It was impossible at short notice to raise a new force large enough to repel the Scots. Mortimer and Isabella had no alternative but to make peace.

In a letter dated at Berwick on 18 October 1327 King Robert dictated his terms. He was to have the realm of Scotland 'free, quit, and entire, without any kind of feudal subjection, for himself and his heirs forever'. There was to be a marriage between his son and the sister of the English king. No claim was to be presented for the restoration of those disinherited by either side. There was to be an alliance between both kings for mutual support in so far as this did not infringe the Franco-Scottish alliance. Edward was to use his good offices to persuade the pope to revoke the sentences of excommunication and interdict. The Scots would pay Edward £20,000 within three years after the confirmation of peace.[172] In some respects the six points of the Berwick letter differed from the terms of Bruce's indenture with Harclay in 1323 and showed the strengthening of the Scottish position. In other respects the characteristics of both sets of proposals remained the same: they were pragmatic and nationalist and showed Bruce's antipathy towards the disinherited Anglo-Scots.

By 1328 negotiations on the six points had gone so far that an English parliament was summoned to York to sanction the disagreeable concessions that would have to be made to the Scots. As a foretaste of what was to come, letters patent were issued on 1 March 1328 in the name of Edward III admitting that he and previous English kings had brought affliction to both realms by asserting rights of dominion, rule, or superiority over the realm of Scotland. Any such rights were now renounced. The realm of Scotland was now conceded to the 'magnificent prince, the Lord Robert, by the grace of God, King of Scots, our ally and dear friend'. Its boundaries were to be

---

170 Nicholson, *Edward III*, pp. 42–5.
171 *Ibid.*, pp. 38–40.   172 Stones, *Documents*, pp. 158–60.

those of the time of Alexander III. It was to be 'separate in all things from the kingdom of England, assured forever of its territorial integrity, to remain forever free and quit of any subjection, servitude, claim or demand.'[173] Since Bruce was thus at long last recognised by the English as king, envoys were sent north to treat with him and his parliament at Edinburgh, a parliament to which there were summoned not only the lay and ecclesiastical magnates but freeholders and burgesses. After a week's discussion of the final texts the peace treaty was concluded on 17 March 1328 in the chamber in Holyrood where King Robert lay ill. On 4 May 1328 the terms of the 'final peace' were ratified by the English parliament at Northampton.[174] The papacy lost no time in making its own peace with Scotland: on 15 October 1328 it was decided to lift the interdict and release Bruce from excommunication.[175]

The treaty of Edinburgh-Northampton,[176] the culmination of King Robert's career, was destined to have no more lasting significance than the truce of Bishopthorpe: the 'final peace' and the thirteen-year truce each brought a cessation of hostilities for only four years. Given the character of Edward III it is unlikely that any settlement achieved in 1328 would have proved enduring. It is significant, however, that the treaty of 1328 excluded only one of the six points of 1327 and that it was this excluded item that eventually led to renewed war; for the terms of the treaty said nothing of the disinherited.

The most promising clause in Bruce's letter of 1327 and in the treaty was the proposed marriage, which held out the prospect of a return to the family relationship, close, but not too close, that had existed in the thirteenth century between the Scottish and English royal houses. Edward's sister, Joan, was to be assigned an income of £2,000 in Scotland as her dower (nothing was said of a dowry). She was to be conveyed to Berwick by 15 July 1328 and a marriage was to take place 'as soon as properly can be' between her and King Robert's son and heir.[177] On 16 July 1328 David and Joan were married at Berwick; the bride was seven years old and the bridegroom four. King Robert spent almost £1,000 on the wedding celebrations.[178]

[173] *Ibid.*, pp. 161–2.
[174] E. L. G. Stones, 'The English Mission to Edinburgh in 1328', *S.H.R.*, XXVIII. 121–32.　　[175] *Cal. Papal Letters*, II. 289.
[176] Text in Stones, *Documents*, pp. 161–70.
[177] *Ibid.*, p. 165.　　[178] *E.R.*, I. 118, 119, 185.

Mortimer and Isabella had conducted Joan to Berwick, and Isabella had more on her mind than her daughter's wedding. Just as the treaty of 1328 had said nothing of the disinherited so it had said nothing of the Scottish enthronement stone or of the Black Rood of Holyrood which Edward I had seized in 1296. Isabella was entrusted with a mission to persuade the Scots to restore some of the disinherited as the price of a restoration of these relics. She had intended to take the stone northwards as a tempting bait but was forced to negotiate without it: the Londoners prevented its removal from Westminster Abbey.[179] Even so, Isabella's diplomacy had some effect: on 28 July 1328 King Robert issued a charter allowing Henry Percy to sue in Scottish courts for recovery of the Scottish lands which had pertained to his father 'by hereditary right or in any just and legitimate manner whatsoever'. Similar charters were almost certainly issued at the same time in favour of Thomas Wake, William la Zouche and Henry Beaumont. By 1330 Percy had had his Scottish claims satisfied and, in return, Sir James Douglas and Sir Henry Prendergast had recovered ancestral lands in Northumberland. Wake, Zouche and Beaumont were left disappointed.[180]

It was an ill omen that Edward III had absented himself from the marriage festivities at Berwick. Although King Robert must have looked on the wedding as the ultimate symbol of his own triumph, he too failed to attend: a point of honour made him counter Edward's disparaging absence by his own. It was given out that King Robert lay sick at Cardross.[181] But the king's infirmity did not prevent him from sailing to Ulster within a few weeks. One of the wedding guests had been William de Burgh, grandson and heir of the deceased Red Earl and full cousin of the bridegroom. There were tortuous but obscure transactions involving King Robert, Queen Isabella, William de Burgh, and Carrickfergus Castle. When Bruce landed in Ulster it was to escort William de Burgh to his heritage, perhaps also to tidy up the situation in Ulster when the local truce of 1327 expired on 1 August 1328.[182]

A year before, a hostile observer had sent news to England that Bruce would not outlive the Ulster truce: 'Sir Robert de Brus is so weak and wasted that, God willing, he will not last that time; for he could scarce move anything save his tongue.'[183] In England men

[179] E. L. G. Stones, 'An Addition to the "Rotuli Scotiae"', *S.H.R.*, xxix. 23–51, at 33, 51.
[180] Nicholson, *Edward III*, pp. 57–9.
[181] Barbour, *The Bruce*, ii. 174.
[182] Nicholson, *op. cit.*, *S.H.R.*, xlii. 30–40, at 34–8.   [183] *Ibid.*, 34.

styled his illness leprosy.[184] The king's last expedition to Ulster in the summer of 1328 was also to be the last notable enterprise of his life; in the spring of 1329 he made a slow and wearisome pilgrimage to the shrine of St Ninian at Whithorn and spent some days seeking the intercession of the saint before being carried home to die.[185] In the restrained language of Froissart,[186] or the more poignant recital of the Scottish poet Barbour, the deathbed scene at Cardross recalls the *Morte d'Arthur*. Bruce had summoned all his lords and told them of his longing to go on crusade. His body could no longer go; but he bade them choose a noble knight to bear his heart against the foes of God. With the choice of Douglas he was well content. On 7 June 1329 the king died. As the tidings spread through the land, so it was said, even knights wept bitterly, drove their fists together, and tore their clothes like madmen.[187]

[184] *Chron. Lanercost*, pp. 259, 264; *Scalacronica*, p. 159. Barbour does not describe the illness but attributes its origins to a 'fundying' or severe chill brought on by the king's early hardships (*The Bruce*, II. 174).

[185] Barrow, *Bruce*, pp. 438–9.

[186] *Chron. Froissart*, I. 67–9.

[187] Barbour, *The Bruce*, II. 177–81.

6

THE SON OF KING ROBERT AND THE SON OF KING JOHN

When the body of King Robert had been laid to rest at Dunfermline Douglas set sail from Montrose with the king's embalmed heart. Alfonso XI of Castile and León welcomed his aid in the war against the 'Saracens' of Granada. On 25 March 1330 Douglas fought his last battle. His bones were brought back for burial in Douglas Kirk, and Bruce's heart, as he had desired, was interred in Melrose.[1]

Ever since the settlement of the succession at Ayr in 1315 Thomas Randolph, Earl of Moray, had been designated to act as guardian of Scotland in the event of a royal minority. His firm rule was based on a strict enforcement of justice even in the remotest areas. Fifty criminal heads set on spikes on the ramparts of Eilean Donan Castle demonstrated his rigour in pursuing 'mysdoaris' and led the chronicler Wyntoun to exclaim:

> Wes nevyr nane in justice lyk
> Till this Erle in oure kynryk.[2]

Meanwhile the treaty of 1328 had brought peace with England, though not cordiality. So long as Mortimer and Isabella stayed in power—and they did not hesitate to murder the captive Edward II in order to do so—the Scots had nothing to fear. The situation altered on 19 October 1330 when the adolescent Edward III carried out a *coup d'état* at Nottingham, arrested and executed Mortimer, and sent Isabella into well-deserved seclusion.

[1] Barbour, *The Bruce*, II. 183–96; *Chron. Froissart*, I. 69–70.
[2] *Chron. Wyntoun*, II. 377–80; for the Highland background see W. Matheson, 'Traditions of the Mackenzies', *Trans. Gaelic Soc. Inverness*, XXXIX. 1–36.

While the keynote of Edward I's reign had been *legalitas*, that of Edward III's was to be *militia* or chivalry. Just as an outward respect for legal principles had partly concealed the egotistic ruthlessness of Edward I, so also the panache of chivalry partly concealed the aggressive ambitions of Edward III. Urbane and courteous, he nonetheless kept an eye on the main chance; more opportunist and versatile than his grandfather, he was always willing to abandon one road to his goal as soon as he encountered a tedious obstacle. He had not concealed his dislike of 'the shameful peace' of 1328 and put diplomatic pressure on the Scots to restore the disinherited Henry Beaumont and Thomas Wake. The Scots took little heed.[3] Before long Edward was to assert that he was not bound by the treaty of Edinburgh-Northampton since he had sealed it when he was under age. But he was unlikely to press matters too far until the Scots had fully paid the £20,000 promised under the treaty of 1328.

This sum was officially styled in Scotland 'the contribution for peace'. No official explanation was ever given as to why the Scots should make such a contribution, but it was popularly supposed to be reparation for the damage inflicted on the English.[4] The assessment already carried out for the raising of the 'tenth penny' granted at Cambuskenneth was also used for the levying of the peace contribution. The burgesses, however, preferred to compound for their share by paying a total of 1,500 marks in three equal instalments.[5]

By the time the last instalment of the peace contribution had been paid to the English at midsummer 1331 it had become clear that Edward's diplomacy was unlikely to secure the restoration of Wake and Beaumont. Henceforward the Scots would have to deal not with a mere segment of the disinherited but with all of them,[6] for the influential and talented Beaumont was organising an expedition in which all those with claims on Scottish lands might unite to recover those lands by force. To lend some dignity to the enterprise Beaumont conducted to England Edward Balliol, son and heir of the late King John.

For some time Edward Balliol had been living on the family estates in Picardy to which his father had retired to die in obscurity. His character was more forceful than that of his father, and by 1331 he was in the prime of life while the Bruce occupant of the throne

---

[3] Nicholson, *Edward III*, pp. 54-5, 64-5, 67-9.
[4] *Chron. Fordun*, I. 352.
[5] Nicholson, *Edward III*, pp. 59-60, 70.
[6] For the various classes of the disinherited see *ibid.*, pp. 65-7.

was a mere child. With Beaumont's help and the benevolent neutrality of Edward III Balliol was ready to make a bid for the throne that his father had too meekly vacated. Soon after the Scots had paid the last instalment of the peace contribution he returned to England and secretly did homage to Edward III for his prospective kingdom of Scotland. The English king was unwilling to allow so open a breach of the peace as an armed invasion across the border. He had no objection to a filibustering expedition by sea.[7]

Probably because of the unexpected revival of the Balliol cause Randolph hastened the first Scottish coronation. For King Robert had applied to the pope not only for the revoking of excommunication and interdict but also for the privileges of coronation and unction, which were conferred by a papal bull issued on 13 June 1329, six days after the king's death.[8] On 24 November 1331 King Robert's son was crowned and anointed in Scone Abbey by James Bennet, Bishop of St Andrews.[9] David II had succeeded not only to an independent kingdom but to a kingship from which the last hint of inferiority had been removed.

The festivities at Scone were symptomatic of a dangerous euphoria and over-confidence on the part of those who took for granted the victory that King Robert and his generation had wrested from defeat. The disinherited would face a Scotland outwardly united and secure, inwardly weakened by the recent deaths of King Robert, Sir James Douglas, Walter the Steward, Bernard of Linton, Bishop David of Moray and Bishop Lamberton of St Andrews; and Thomas Randolph was nearing his end.

The guardian was not blind to the menacing moves of the disinherited and was in the midst of military preparations south of the Forth when he died at Musselburgh on 20 July 1332. The disinherited were quick off the mark: they set sail from the Humber on 31 July and landed at Kinghorn on 6 August.[10] Their leaders included Edward Balliol, Henry Beaumont (claimant through his wife, Alice Comyn, to the earldom of Buchan), his son-in-law David of Strathbogie (claimant to the earldom of Atholl), Gilbert Umfraville (claimant to the earldom of Angus), Richard Talbot, Ralph Stafford, Henry Ferrers, Alexander and John Mowbray.[11] With them they had something like five hundred men-at-arms and a thousand footmen and archers. The Lanercost chronicler remarked: 'Oh how small a

[7] *Ibid.*, pp. 71–3, 75–8.   [8] *Nat. MSS. Scot.*, II. No. xxx.
[9] *Chron. Bower*, II. 302–3.   [10] Nicholson, *Edward III*, pp. 77–9.
[11] *Ibid.*, pp. 79–80. For their claims see *ibid.*, pp. 65–7.

number of warriors was this to invade a kingdom then all too confident of its strength !' [12]

But the moment was opportune. There was some acrimony when
the Scottish magnates assembled at Perth on 2 August to choose a
new guardian. They chose Donald of Mar, who, although a nephew
of King Robert, had nevertheless been associated with some of the
disinherited and had possibly pledged support to Edward Balliol.
Once elected, however, Mar made ready to resist the invaders. The
latter marched by way of Dunfermline towards Perth and reached
the low southern bank of the river Earn to find the high bank on the
other side—Dupplin Moor—already occupied by the forces of the
guardian.[13]

From their superior position the Scottish troops could see that
they greatly outnumbered the disinherited and spent the night in
carefree carousal. During the night the disinherited stealthily picked
their way across a ford and attacked part of the Scottish encampment. As dawn broke on the morning of 11 August 1332 they took up
a strong defensive position : the knights and men-at-arms dismounted
and formed a thin armoured line to strengthen the footmen, and
archers were posted on either flank. Mar's great host, who had looked
forward to an easy victory, were faced with a determined and well-
prepared foe. At this critical time King Robert's bastard son, Sir
Robert Bruce, accused the guardian of treachery. Mar gave him the
lie and affirmed that he would be the first to come to blows with the
enemy. There followed a confused and disorderly Scottish attack
made even more disorderly as English arrows took their toll. The
second Scottish battalion trod the first underfoot; more Scots died
by suffocation than by the edge of the sword. The mass of dying
men composed a little hill a spear's length in height. The guardian
and many another Scottish noble lay among the fallen.[14]

If God fought for the righteous cause, He had shown at Dupplin
that the righteous cause was that of Edward Balliol. After he had
occupied Perth and successfully withstood a half-hearted siege, notable Scots from the neighbouring regions hastened to assure him of
their loyalty. On 24 September 1332 Balliol was set on the throne at
Scone by the Earl of Fife and crowned by Bishop William Sinclair of Dunkeld, whom Bruce had once styled 'my own bishop'.[15]

Soon after his coronation Balliol marched south to Galloway,

[12] *Ibid.*, pp. 80–1.   [13] *Ibid.*, pp. 81–5.   [14] *Ibid.*, pp. 85–93.
[15] *Ibid.*, pp. 84–94; *Chron. Bower*, II. 259.

where Sir Eustace Maxwell of Caerlaverock had already put himself at the head of those Galwegians who had traditional loyalties to the Balliols and Comyns. After a brief stay to rally his Galwegian supporters Balliol established himself at Roxburgh. Meanwhile Sir Andrew Moray, son of Wallace's colleague and husband of Christian Bruce, King Robert's sister, had been chosen as guardian in succession to the late Donald of Mar. Not only was Sir Andrew uncle (by marriage) to the young David II but he was lord of Avoch in Ross and of Bothwell in Lanarkshire; his wide lands earned him the appellation 'le Riche'; and he was head of a family noted for its consistent patriotism.[16] When Balliol made his way to Roxburgh he was followed by Sir Andrew Moray and Sir Archibald Douglas. An attempt to capture Balliol misfired: it was Sir Andrew who was captured. With him was taken John Crabb, the Flemish military engineer and naval captain.[17] Until Sir Andrew was ransomed a year or two later the Scots were commanded by less competent military leaders.

Occasionally, however, they had their moments of success. On the capture of Sir Andrew it was Sir Archibald Douglas, youngest brother of the late Sir James, who was chosen to succeed as guardian. He seems to have concluded a truce with the unsuspecting Balliol. At Moffat Sir Archibald forgathered with Robert the Steward and John Randolph, the new Earl of Moray—both of them teenagers—and planned to take Balliol unawares. At dawn on 17 December 1332 they attacked at Annan while he and his entourage were still abed. The scantily-clad Balliol mounted an unbridled horse and rode pellmell to Carlisle,[18] whence he sent envoys to plead with Edward III.

Already, on 23 November 1332, Balliol had issued letters patent at Roxburgh which set forth the relationship that he envisaged between himself and the English king. If King John had been a vassal king his son could not expect to be independent, thus the Roxburgh letters recognised that the English king was lord superior of Scotland. It was stated that Edward Balliol had already done homage and sworn fealty to Edward III in respect of the kingdom of Scotland. Balliol bound himself and his successors to renew this bond of homage and fealty. In return, the English king would maintain Balliol and his heirs in Scotland. In recompense for aid already received Balliol granted to Edward two thousand librates—lands worth £2,000 a year—to be selected from parts of Scotland adjacent to England and definitely to include the castle, town and sheriffdom of Berwick. The

[16] Nicholson, *Edward III*, p. 92.
[17] *Ibid.*, pp. 96–7.   [18] *Ibid.*, 103–4.

two thousand librates would be separated from the kingdom of Scotland and annexed for ever to the kingdom of England.[19]

Despite this tempting bribe Edward toyed with the idea of ignoring both David Bruce and Edward Balliol and of striving to gain for himself the direct lordship of Scotland that his grandfather had once claimed. One obstacle to this inordinately ambitious policy was the obstructiveness of the English parliament. Another was Balliol's arrival as a helpless fugitive in Carlisle: the Bruce party was not, after all, so weak as Edward III had supposed; it would be necessary to follow only a moderately ambitious policy and to work with Balliol as an ally. Although the English parliament refused to accept responsibility for a renewal of the Scottish war Edward ignored it and began military preparations. In March 1333 Balliol rode over the border with a strong company of English magnates and men-at-arms and laid siege to Berwick. In May Edward arrived to direct the siege in person.[20]

In the great siege of 1319 the defenders had been notably helped by the technical skill of John Crabb. The siege of 1333 found him using his talents on behalf of the besiegers: after his capture at Roxburgh he had been forced to change sides in order to save his life and was to serve Edward III faithfully for the rest of his days.[21] So hardpressed were the defenders that they handed over hostages to obtain a truce; if not relieved by the morning of 20 July 1333 they would capitulate to the English king.

All too belatedly the Scottish guardian had begun to ravage Northumberland and to threaten Edward's queen in Bamburgh Castle, but time was now on the side of Edward III and he refused to be drawn from the siege. Sir Archibald Douglas was forced to re-cross the Tweed and march rapidly to the relief of Berwick. The Scots were now in exactly the same situation as the English on the eve of Bannockburn. By the time the Scottish host neared Berwick the English had taken up a strong defensive position on Halidon Hill, which dominated all approaches to the town, leaving the guardian, on the afternoon of 19 July 1333, with no alternative but to attack or to see Berwick surrender. The Scottish host dismounted and clambered through a bog before climbing the hill. On top, Edward had also dismounted his troops and had formed them in three battalions, each flanked by a wing of archers. As the Scots advanced they were swept by a hail of arrows. Those who came to grips with the enemy

---

[19] *Ibid.*, pp. 97–9.
[20] *Ibid.*, pp. 99–103, 105–18.
[21] *Ibid.*, pp. 120–1, 175, 188.

were forced to give way. The guardian and five Scottish earls were among the slain, and the stricken fugitives were slaughtered until night fell. Next morning the defenders of Berwick at last opened their gates to Edward.[22]

He at once took possession of Berwick and its sheriffdom as first instalment of the promised two thousand librates. Berwick was to be a useful base for English armies and fleets; with its varying hinterland it was to be the headquarters of English-occupied Scotland for more than a hundred years and symbolised the claims of successive English kings to the lordship of Scotland. Having seen to the administration of Berwick Edward III disbanded his troops and went rapidly southward. Among the Scots there remained scarcely anyone, so the English thought, who had the capacity, knowledge or desire to assemble a fighting force or to command it had it been assembled.[23]

This view seemed to be confirmed by the quiescence of the Scots in the aftermath of Halidon. Balliol was able to establish himself at Perth and to behave as if he were unquestioned King of Scotland. The disinherited were reinherited and their heritages were augmented: Henry Beaumont was to become Earl of Moray as well as of Buchan; Richard Talbot was to be Lord of Mar; David of Strathbogie, Earl of Atholl, was to be Steward of Scotland. As Strathbogie installed an English sheriff in Rothesay Castle, Robert the Steward escaped in a rowing-boat with his family charters and was welcomed in Dumbarton Castle, where David Bruce and his queen had already been sent for safety. Besides Dumbarton only the scattered strongholds of Kildrummy, Urquhart, Lochleven and Loch Doon kept alive the Bruce cause.[24] In February 1334 Balliol was able to hold a parliament at Holyrood.

The attendance at this parliament showed the strength and the weakness of Balliol's position. The Bishops of Glasgow, Aberdeen, Dunkeld, Galloway, Ross, Dunblane and Brechin had been induced to attend. The party of the disinherited was well represented. Patrick, Earl of March, temporarily in the pay of Edward III, had also come, but few other Scottish magnates made their appearance. Many must have been forfeited as traitors to Balliol; many must have been unwilling to take part in a parliament that was to receive English envoys who had come to press Balliol for a cession of the two thousand librates.

There was some delay before even this unrepresentative assembly could be induced on 12 February 1334 to issue documents ratifying

[22] *Ibid.*, pp. 123–36.   [23] *Ibid.*, pp. 137–8.   [24] *Ibid.*, pp. 138–51.

the Roxburgh letters patent. Thereafter Balliol had an interview with Edward III at Newcastle and on 12 June 1334 granted the full quota of the two thousand librates—the sheriffdoms of Berwick, Roxburgh, Selkirk, Peebles, Edinburgh and Dumfries, the constabularies of Linlithgow and Haddington, the forests of Ettrick and Jedburgh—to be annexed to the crown of England for all time to come. For what remained of his kingdom Balliol did homage to Edward a week later.[25]

Before this, however, the lull in Scottish resistance was coming to an end, and encouraging news arrived from France. Under the terms of the treaty of Corbeil the French king was not explicitly bound to make war upon the English in the event of an Anglo-Scottish war, but the French were bound to act as loyal allies of the Scots, and John Randolph, Earl of Moray, had gone to France to seek the aid of Philip VI. In the spring of 1334 Randolph returned to Dumbarton with a message inviting David II and his queen to take refuge in France. In May 1334 they landed safely in Normandy; Philip received them graciously and installed them in Château Gaillard on the Seine.[26] Edward III was to find Philip's diplomacy increasingly menacing as the war continued.

The return of Randolph with news of prospective French aid encouraged the Bruce party to take the offensive. In the summer of 1334 Randolph and the Steward, acting as joint guardians, overran most of south-west Scotland. Only in Galloway did they meet opposition: the Galwegians were divided in their allegiance, and, as the Lanercost chronicler complacently remarked, they mutually destroyed one another.[27] Next, Randolph and the Steward invaded the territories that Balliol had recently ceded to England for ever. The newly arrived English officials had to take refuge behind the walls of Berwick.[28]

They were soon joined by Edward Balliol, who was lucky to reach safety. In the face of a general Scottish uprising the disinherited had chosen to quarrel with Balliol and with one another over some Mowbray lands. Alexander and Geoffrey Mowbray joined the Bruce party. Richard Talbot and six of his knights were captured by the insurgents and held to ransom. David of Strathbogie was chased to Lochaber by John Randolph and on 27 September 1334 was forced to change sides and swear fealty to David II. Most important

[25] *Ibid.*, pp. 151–62.   [26] *E.R.*, I. 464.
[27] *Chron. Lanercost*, p. 278.
[28] Nicholson, *Edward III*, pp. 163–4, 167.

of all, Edward III had made the mistake of ransoming Sir Andrew Moray, the onetime guardian, in time to allow him a part in the Scottish rising. Sir Andrew and the turncoat Alexander Mowbray besieged Henry Beaumont in Dundarg Castle, an ancient Comyn stronghold on the Aberdeenshire coast that Beaumont had repaired. By the end of the year Dundarg had capitulated and Beaumont returned to England to find money for his ransom.[29]

Most of Scotland was lost to Edward III and to Balliol by the time the slow process of mobilising an English army was complete. Not until 14 November 1334 did Edward set out from Newcastle—winter campaigning was unpopular and he had mustered scarcely more than four thousand troops. He spent some months at Roxburgh rebuilding the castle and vainly demanding reinforcements. When the army disbanded in mid-February he had nothing to show for his efforts save a new stronghold in Roxburgh. Indiscriminate English raids in the lands between the Tweed and the Forth had alienated his chief Scottish adherent, Patrick, Earl of March, who now rejoined the Bruce party.[30] When Edward returned to England it was to face a French diplomatic offensive which resulted in an Anglo-Scottish truce to last from Easter to Midsummer 1335.

The truce suited Edward well: it allowed him time to organise English seapower for the blockade of Scotland, for the supply of his troops in the forthcoming summer campaign, and for defence of the English coast against possible French raids. In mid-July 1335 he set out from Carlisle at the head of over thirteen thousand troops; simultaneously a force under Edward Balliol set out from Berwick.[31] Although the Scottish leaders avoided the engagement that Edward was trying to provoke they did not remain inactive. The Count of Namur, cousin of Edward's queen, belatedly set out to catch up with the English army and was cornered in the ruins of Edinburgh Castle on 30 July 1335; he was forced to surrender and offer a ransom of £4,000. As John Randolph chivalrously escorted the count towards England the party was waylaid and Randolph was led off to several years of captivity in an English prison.[32]

Early in August 1335 Edward III and Balliol had reached Perth and made it their headquarters. The size of the English forces, unsurpassed in Edward's reign until the Crécy-Calais campaign of 1346, was intended to convince the Scots of the futility of resistance. David of Strathbogie hastened to make his peace with Edward and negoti-

[29] Ibid., pp. 168–72, 185–6.
[30] Ibid., pp. 174–91.
[31] Ibid., pp. 192–202.
[32] Ibid., pp. 212–4.

ated not only on his own account but on that of Robert the Steward and others. A pacification was concluded at Perth on 18 August 1335. Those who accepted its terms would be assured safety of life and limb and possession of their lands and offices; they would even be pardoned all trespasses they had committed from the creation of the world up to 18 August 1335. In addition, it was promised that the liberties of the Scottish kirk would be maintained; in the parts of Scotland directly ruled by Edward Balliol the laws of Alexander III's time would be observed. These terms amounted to little more than a face-saving formula under which David of Strathbogie could disguise the fact that he had changed allegiance for a second time.[33]

At first, Edward had high hopes of the pacification of Perth: on 22 August he rejected proposed French and papal arbitration and affirmed that by immense labours he had now established peace with the Scots. In September a fleet of fifty ships brought some 1,500 men from Ireland to attack the Steward's lands of Bute and Arran; Robert the Steward soon made his peace.[34] By mid-October both Edward and Balliol were back in Berwick. Although their vast forces had already disbanded they were confident that a short truce and some negotiation would soon bring the submission of Sir Andrew Moray and others who had not yet laid down arms. Talks were held with Sir Andrew at Bathgate but were broken off when news arrived of the activities of David of Strathbogie, whom Balliol had appointed his lieutenant in the north. Strathbogie was said to be rooting out every freeholder; he was also besieging Kildrummy Castle, which was defended by Sir Andrew's wife, Christian Bruce, sister of the late king.[35]

The threat to his wife brought Sir Andrew rapidly northward. With him he had the Earl of March and William Douglas—a Lothian landholder who was later to win notoriety as 'the Knight of Liddesdale'—and some eight hundred picked fighting men from the region south of Forth. They forded the Dee, entered the forest of Culblean which lay between them and Kildrummy, and during the night of 29 November 1335 followed a circuitous route to take Strathbogie unawares. At dawn they found him forewarned. Nonetheless a trick on the part of the crafty William Douglas provoked the enemy to break ranks in a wild onrush. As Strathbogie's men lost impetus on reaching a burn, Douglas gave a signal for his men to dash downhill with levelled spears. Strathbogie refused to yield and died fighting with his back to an oak tree.[36]

[33] *Ibid.*, pp. 207, 214–6.   [34] *Ibid.*, pp. 216, 219–22, 227.
[35] *Ibid.*, pp. 217–8, 224, 227–31.   [36] *Ibid.*, pp. 231–5.

His defeat and death in the forest of Culblean on St Andrew's Day, 1335, undid most of what Edward III had achieved in his great summer offensive. From the time of Culblean onward, claimed the chronicler Fordun, the fortune of war began to favour the Scots.[37] In vain Edward successively extended a truce up to May 1336 and received envoys from Château Gaillard at his March parliament in Westminster. It was too late to solve the Scottish question by some judicious dynastic juggling between Edward Balliol and David Bruce.[38] By February 1336 some Scots were disregarding the truce and asserting—as the defenders of Stirling had done in 1304— that they adhered to the Lion, the heraldic symbol of Scottish kingship.[39]

The victory at Culblean had confirmed the position of Sir Andrew Moray as chief leader of Scottish resistance. In the spring of 1336 a council held at Dunfermline re-appointed him as guardian of Scotland.[40] With the failure of peace talks Edward III was faced with the necessity of new campaigns in Scotland and dashed north with a small company to assume command at Perth.[41] On 12 July 1336 he rode out on an expedition that happily combined both a serious military objective and a flamboyant deed of chivalry—the rescue of Katherine Beaumont, Countess of Atholl, the widow of David of Strathbogie.

She had taken refuge in the island castle of Lochindorb and had been blockaded by Sir Andrew Moray. On 15 July Edward and his men rode twenty miles in hope of taking Sir Andrew by surprise. As the English drew near he was hearing mass in the wood of Stronkalter[42] and no one dared interrupt him. He showed remarkable coolness before withdrawing his troops at the last moment. Foiled in his hopes of bringing Sir Andrew to bay Edward pressed on to Lochindorb and had the satisfaction of rescuing Countess Katherine and 'othir ladys that ware luvely'.[43] He spent some time burning Forres and Kinloss and the neighbouring countryside, then turned southeast from Elgin (where he spared the cathedral) to take vengeance on Aberdeen, where Sir Thomas Roscelyn, a celebrated English

[37] *Ibid.*, pp. 235–6.
[38] *Rot. Scot.*, I. 384–91; *Foedera*, II. pt. iii, 142, 144; *Chron. Lanercost*, pp. 284–5.
[39] *Rot. Scot.*, I. 401.   [40] *Chron. Fordun*, I. 360.
[41] *Scalacronica*, p. 166; B.M. MS. Nero C. VIII. Wardrobe Book. ff. 242, 242v.
[42] For its location see G. W. S. Barrow, 'The Wood of Stronkalter', *S.H.R.*, XLVI. 77–9.
[43] *Chron. Wyntoun*, II. 428–30; *Original Letters*, ed. Sir H. Ellis, 3rd series, I. 35

knight, had lately met his death. On Edward's approach ten foreign vessels wisely put to sea without waiting to pay customs duties. The buildings in Aberdeen, which were among the most substantial in Scotland, were levelled to the ground.[44]

The campaign of 1336 had shown that Edward's chance of easy victory by one decisive battle had disappeared. Sir Andrew Moray had reverted to the tactics and strategy that King Robert had used so successfully. Increasingly, the English would have to rely on garrisons and fortifications to hold the Scottish territories that they hoped to control. Belatedly Edward set his military architects to work to erect in other parts of Scotland fortifications similar to those that safeguarded his control of the Borders. There, in the winter of 1334, he had repaired Roxburgh Castle. About the same time the Percies and the Bohuns, on whom he had respectively conferred Jedburgh forest and Annandale, had repaired and garrisoned the castles of Jedburgh and Lochmaben; and Eustace Maxwell, one of Edward's remaining Scottish supporters, had repaired and garrisoned his castle of Caerlaverock. Not until September 1335, however, did Edward take in hand the repair of Edinburgh Castle;[45] the summer of 1336 saw the repair and garrisoning of Dunnottar, Lauriston and Kinneff, new works in progress at St Andrews and Leuchars, and the fortification of Perth with walls and towers financed by levies on the neighbouring monasteries.[46] Balliol was to garrison Perth throughout the winter of 1336–7 while Edward retired southward. As he passed through Stirling he gave orders for the construction of a new 'peel' on the ruins of the former castle. As he passed by Bothwell he gave directions for the rebuilding of that castle.[47] After a brief visit to England to hold a parliament he came back to Bothwell and was to remain there until Christmas 1336.

The new fortifications that Edward was erecting were to serve not only as military strongpoints but as centres for his administration. In occupied Scotland his sheriffs were able to draw some revenue for the years between 1335 and 1337. But if Edward's administration was partly effective it was also intolerable. Much of the revenue was obtained from wholesale forfeitures; and from forfeited lands it was often impossible to obtain revenue since the lands were

[44] *Original Letters*, I. 35; *Chron. Fordun*, I. 360; *Chron. Wyntoun*, II. 422–3; *E.R.*, I. 449.

[45] Nicholson, *Edward III*, pp. 189, 224–6.

[46] *Chron. Bower*, II. 323.

[47] *Chron. Lanercost*, pp. 286–7; *Scalacronica*, pp. 166–7; *Cal. Docs. Scot.*, III. lvii.

waste and there was nothing left to distrain. The south of Scotland had been reduced to a desert.[48] Occupied Scotland had nothing more to lose by opposing Edward : he 'soon lost all the castles and towns that he had caused to be fortified in Scotland through default of good governance in the pursuit of his conquest'.[49]

Certainly in the months between October 1336 and May 1337 English power in Scotland suffered an overwhelming reverse. The prestige that Sir Andrew Moray had already won was increased by his remorseless attacks on the English-held strongholds. In the closing months of 1336 he captured and destroyed the fortresses of Dunnottar, Kinneff, Lauriston and Kinclaven. In February 1337, with the Earls of Fife and March and William Douglas, he was active in Fife. Only the castle of Cupar, held by Balliol's chamberlain, William Bullock, resisted the onslaught. St Andrews Castle held out for three weeks before it succumbed to a redoubtable siege machine aptly termed 'Boustour'. Each captured stronghold was destroyed. Edward looked on, apparently helplessly, from Bothwell, before leaving Scotland to spend Christmas in Newcastle. In March 1337 Sir Andrew and the 'Boustour' arrived at Bothwell and battered down the castle[50] while Edward was holding the fateful Westminster parliament that sanctioned a war more grandiose than that of Scotland.

Through his mother, sole survivor of the offspring of Philip IV, Edward could put forward a claim to the French crown. But his motive for war with Philip VI was scarcely a sudden recollection of a dynastic claim that had long remained dormant. From the dynastic issue Edward was willing to draw what profit he might—just as he had done in Scotland—but in addition warfare in itself held a lure for him and his magnates.[51] By 1337 it was clear that warfare in Scotland would bring little military glory and that expenditure upon it (£16,000 in 1336 alone)[52] far outweighed any possible return in revenue, ransom or booty. France, however, offered greater opportunities. In any case Edward had probably concluded that he could never crush Scotland until he had first disabled Scotland's ally. His efforts had been constantly hampered by fear of French naval preparations, and in 1336 the French galleys which had been assembled at Marseilles for a proposed crusade were transferred

---

[48] *Cal. Docs. Scot.*, III. 317–47, 368–93.
[49] *Scalacronica*, pp. 166–7.   [50] *Chron. Bower*, II. 323–4.
[51] May McKisack, *The Fourteenth Century*, p. 126.
[52] B.M. MS. Nero C. VIII. Wardrobe Book, ff. 244, 260, 280.

to the Channel ports. By continental warfare Edward hoped to forestall Philip's designs against England. From 1337 onwards 'both kings were engaged in feverish preparations, raising troops, ships, and supplies, cementing alliances, devising schemes of invasion.' [53]

The waning of Edward's interest in Scotland was shown in March 1337 when Thomas Beauchamp, Earl of Warwick, was appointed 'captain and leader' of the army of Scotland to 'represent the person of the lord king.' [54] Thus the organisation set up for Warwick's force 'inaugurated something in the nature of a standing Scottish command.' [55] It was not a success. In the summer months of 1337 the forces under Warwick fluctuated wildly in number but probably never exceeded 3,500 men. [56] From mid-June to mid-August the shire levies were absent. On 7 August Sir Andrew Moray seized the opportunity to raid Cumberland. At the end of September he was raiding Northumberland. In mid-October, when Warwick had only some three hundred men-at-arms, the Scots circled Carlisle and burned the nearby manor of the bishop, who had unwisely accompanied Warwick in the field. By the raids over the border Sir Andrew Moray 'enriched his army'. [57] Nonetheless much of the south of Scotland was still in English hands. At the end of the year Sir Andrew failed in an attempt on Edinburgh Castle; and an engagement at Crichton in which William Douglas distinguished himself was indecisive. There followed the 'wholesale destruction of Lothian'—apparently by both sides. [58] Meanwhile the unsuccessful Warwick was replaced by Richard Fitzalan, Earl of Arundel, and William Montagu, Earl of Salisbury, who were to be joint captains of the English forces in Scotland. [59] In contrast to the aimlessness of recent English strategy the Arundel-Salisbury expedition had a definite objective—the castle of Dunbar, rebuilt in 1333 at the expense of Edward III. [60] An attack on Dunbar, which was a thorn in the flesh of the English administration in south-east Scotland, was a sensible way of using a small field army to support the threatened English garrisons. If successful it would give the impression of a resumed English offensive.

Delayed in Northumberland by the Christmas festivities, Arundel

[53] May McKisack, *The Fourteenth Century*, p. 127.
[54] *Rot. Scot.*, I. 488; *Chron. Lanercost*, p. 289.
[55] N. B. Lewis, 'The recruitment and organisation of a contract army, May to November 1337', *B.I.H.R.*, XXXVII. 1–19, at 4–5.
[56] *Ibid.*, 16–9.
[57] *Chron. Lanercost*, pp. 291–3; *Chron. Bower*, II. 324.
[58] *Chron. Fordun*, I. 362; *Chron. Lanercost*, p. 293.
[59] *Rot. Scot.*, I. 503–10.   [60] Nicholson, *Edward III*, pp. 143–4.

and Salisbury did not begin the siege of Dunbar until 13 January 1338,[61] by which time some shire levies had already disbanded. Two Genoese galleys manned with crossbowmen had been hired to take part in a naval blockade, and engines of war had been shipped from Berwick and the Tower of London to bombard the castle. A remarkable number of sappers and military engineers—among them the talented John Crabb—set to work in the vicinity. The Earl of March had cautiously absented himself from Dunbar and left the defence in the hands of his wife, Agnes Randolph, sister of John Randolph, Earl of Moray, who had lain a prisoner in England since his capture in 1335. Countess Agnes, popularly known as Black Agnes 'be ressone scho was blak skynnit',[62] conducted the defence womanfully and with a certain flamboyance, mocking the attackers with word and gesture. When Edward III heard of her stout resistance he paid a flying visit to interview Montagu and the other magnates at Whitekirk,[63] probably in the old kirk which has survived the attacks of both English pirates and suffragettes. The king's long-postponed 'passage overseas' provided a smokescreen behind which the besiegers gracefully retired. The Dunbar expedition, which had cost almost £6,000,[64] ended with the granting of a truce to the Scots up to Michaelmas 1339.[65] An English chronicler might well remark that the outcome was 'wasteful, and neither honourable nor secure, but useful and advantageous to the Scots'.[66]

Edward III was at last ready for his 'passage overseas'. On 16 July 1338 he set sail from Orwell with 115 ships and landed at Antwerp, and with him went, sooner or later, many who had hitherto been foremost in the Scottish war, including Beaumont, who died in the Low Countries in 1340. The chronicler Wyntoun rightly affirmed that it was lucky for Scotland that Edward had embarked on the French war : if the English had concentrated on Scotland alone they would have 'skaithit it to gretly'.[67]

Good fortune was tempered with misfortune : at a time when the English threat was waning the Scots were to lose the sound leadership of Sir Andrew Moray. He had retired to his castle of Avoch in Ross, 'his own country', where he died in the spring of 1338.[68] Despite the miseries of the scorched-earth tactics he had been forced to em-

---

[61] *Chron. Fordun*, I. 363; P.R.O. Various Accounts, E. 101, 20/25.
[62] Pitscottie, *Historie*, I. 63.   [63] *Scalacronica*, p. 168.
[64] P.R.O. Various Accounts, E. 101, 20/25.
[65] *Chron. Lanercost*, p. 297; *Rot. Scot.*, I. 540.
[66] *Chron. Walsingham*, I. 200.   [67] *Chron. Wyntoun*, II. 435.
[68] *Ibid.*, 437–9; *Chron. Lanercost*, p. 296.

ploy he was remembered for his personal virtues and for the success of a strategy that had exactly copied that of King Robert: 'all the castellis he kest down'.[69] At his death the English held only two strongholds north of Forth—Cupar and Perth.

As Sir Andrew's career came to a close it was William Douglas and Alexander Ramsay of Dalhousie whose military reputations stood highest among the Scots. Each had proved himself a successful tactician. Whether either of them possessed a grasp of strategy comparable to that of Sir Andrew Moray is doubtful. In any case, neither of them had the landed authority to qualify for the post of guardian that became vacant on Sir Andrew's death. Almost inevitably the post went to Robert the Steward, now twenty-two years old and at last qualified by age to take full advantage of his position as heir presumptive to the crown. At this time, affirms the chronicler Bower, the Steward was young in years, but old in deeds, especially against the English.[70] What these deeds were it would be hard to say: although the Steward's submission to Edward III in 1335 had not lasted long there is no sign of any activity on his part for the next few years. Under the newly appointed guardian the Scottish offensive slackened. William Douglas went off to the court of Château Gaillard where the fourteen-year-old David II was beginning to be a figure to be reckoned with. It was from that quarter that a new initiative came: on 5 October 1338 French galleys burned Southampton;[71] in the following year there were similar raids along the south coast; and it was suspected that David II's court had a hand in these exploits.[72] Certainly it was with money from Château Gaillard that William Douglas hired the services of a French pirate whose five galleys blockaded the Tay [73] and cut off the English garrison in Perth from sea-borne victuals and reinforcements. Douglas also bribed William Bullock, the Scottish priest who held Cupar Castle for Balliol, to surrender the castle and join him at Perth, which was being besieged by the Earls of March and Ross and Robert the Steward.[74] Too late a relief army mustered under Balliol at the end of August:[75] Perth had capitulated on 17 August and its walls were cast down. The surrounding country had been so wasted in recent war-

---

[69] *Chron. Wyntoun*, II. 439. [70] *Chron. Bower*, II. 328.
[71] *Cal. Close 1339–41*, pp. 550–1. [72] *Ibid.*, p. 6.
[73] *E.R.*, I. 507; *Chron. Bower*, II. 330–1; *Chron. Wyntoun*, II. 451.
[74] *Chron. Lanercost*, p. 318; *Chron. Bower*, II. 330; *Chron. Wyntoun*, II. 451–4.
[75] P.R.O. Ancient Correspondence, S.C. I, vol. 42. No. 94a; *Cal. Close 1339–41*, p. 208.

fare that men died of hunger. A certain Crystyne Klek practised cannibalism.[76]

On 24 October 1339 a parliament met in Perth [77] and no doubt approved of arrangements for a siege of Stirling. Here there was no immediate success.[78] There were to be only desultory hostilities for almost two years. In the Low Countries too there was no decisive warfare; Edward established himself at Antwerp 'jousting and leading a jolly life'.[79] In diplomacy, however, he was active : Count Louis of Flanders was pro-French and, as Edward thought, had given aid and favour to the Scots as far as he could;[80] it was natural that Edward should ally himself with the bourgeois uprising against the count led by Jacques van Artevelde. The new Anglo-Flemish alliance affected the interests of Scotland as well as those of France. In 1340 David II emerged from Château Gaillard to take the field in Flanders alongside the Kings of France, Bohemia and Navarre.[81] At Lille the Earls of Salisbury and Suffolk were captured; Philip arranged that they should be exchanged for the captive Earl of Moray, and by the autumn of 1340 John Randolph was back in Scotland.[82]

He soon made up for his forced inactivity by inspiring a new Scottish offensive. He himself made a descent upon his lordship of Annandale [83] which Edward III had conferred upon the Bohuns. Meanwhile William Douglas and William Bullock devised a daring plan for the capture of Edinburgh Castle. Bullock and his men disguised themselves as English merchants and arranged to call at the castle on the morning of 16 April 1341. When the gate was opened they jammed the portcullis. A blast of a horn brought Douglas and his men from their hiding-place nearby and the townsfolk of Edinburgh rallied to their aid.[84] After winning Edinburgh the Scots could concentrate on the Borders. Randolph acted as warden of the West March, William Douglas held the Middle March, and Alexander Ramsay the East March. In the interior of the kingdom 'the land had rest' and good harvests brought an abundance of victuals.[85] The time had come to invite the king to end his seven-year exile in France.

[76] *Chron. Wyntoun*, II. 454–5.   [77] *A.P.S.*, I. 512.
[78] *Chron. Wyntoun*, II. 455–6; *Rot. Scot.*, I. 600.
[79] *Scalacronica*, p. 168.
[80] *Cal. Close 1337–39*, p. 327.   [81] *Chron. Froissart*, I. 119.
[82] *Chron. Wyntoun*, II. 462; *Cal. Close 1339–41*, p. 540.
[83] *Chron. Wyntoun*, II. 463.
[84] *Ibid.*, 457–60; *Chron. Fordun*, I. 365.
[85] *Chron. Wyntoun*, II. 463–4.

On 2 June 1341 David II and Queen Joan landed at Inverbervie from the two hired ships in which they had sailed secretly from France. The seventeen-year-old king was 'ressavyd with blythnes' by his people. He was unbridled in love; he liked jousting, dancing and gaming, and, amusing himself with such pastimes, 'rade offt blythly throw his land' [86]—which was what was expected of a young king.

David had come back to govern a land that had suffered the destruction of life and property, the clash of rival loyalties, the anarchy caused by widespread invasion. Between 1332 and 1341 the Bruce party had maintained an administration of sorts, especially in the region between the Tay and the Moray Firth. There had been occasional parliaments, justice ayres, even exchequer audits, but the surviving financial records of the period show that the difficulties of wartime administration were increased by baronial feuds and professional jealousies.[87] Not surprisingly, the chamberlain's account covering the period 1334–1340 showed an accumulated deficit of £2,881 19s. 2¼d. The only hope of recovery lay in a reconstruction of strong royal government. With the king's return the guardianship of Robert the Steward came to an end. For the next five years the king's 'dearest nephew' was to be little more than the chief lay witness to the royal charters.

Under David's personal rule there was progress toward more settled conditions of government: a chamberlain ayre was held at Inverness and the king was present when a justice ayre was held at Cupar. In September 1341 parliament assembled at Scone and sanctioned the levying of a 'contribution' from the kirk, from the communities of the sheriffdoms, and from the burghs. This was a 'second contribution', for a 'first contribution' had already been granted by a parliament held in Dundee sometime in 1340.[88] At the exchequer audit of 1342 the chamberlain's receipts from these two contributions came to about £1,205 in addition to some three hundred 'marts'. Thanks to this taxation the deficit on the chamberlain's account was a mere £1 19s. 4¼d.[89] This achievement no doubt owed something to a new rigour in royal finance and to the abilities of the new chamberlain—none other than Balliol's former chamberlain, the versatile William Bullock. Success in finance could hardly be achieved without offending vested interests; a few months after he had presented his accounts in 1342 Bullock was accused of treason,

[86] Ibid., 466; Chron. Fordun, I. 365; E.R., I. 506.
[87] E.R., I. 435–68, passim.
[88] Ibid., 511, 521, 501. [89] Ibid., clxvi, 512.

arrested by the king's command, and put in a prison where he shortly died.[90]

The contributions granted by the Dundee and Scone parliaments of 1340 and 1341 had a significance that was not only financial but constitutional : 'by September 1341 the burgesses had for the second time in about a year had their corporate part in payment of a contribution granted in parliament'.[91] Their share of the contribution was hardly a large one : of the total amount raised, about 70% came from the freeholders of the sheriffdoms, about 20% from the kirk, and less than 9%—or £100—from the burghs.[92] Yet, small though the share was, it can hardly have been made without the attendance of burgesses in the Dundee and Scone parliaments. In these two parliaments is to be found the missing link in the development of burgh representation between the end of the reign of Robert I and the later years of the reign of his son.

Burgh representation had survived a critical period, for there can be no doubt that the war had brought a severe setback to burgh life in Scotland. Aberdeen had been levelled to the ground in 1336. According to the 1342 exchequer accounts, Linlithgow and Haddington had been burnt, and Edinburgh was 'totally waste'. Perth and Inverness were 'in the hands of the king', presumably because of the dislocation of burghal administration. Yet recovery was swift : by 1341 Aberdeen had paid off its arrears to the chamberlain and was able to keep up payment of the £213 6s. 8d. that it owed each year in terms of its charter of 1319, and by 1343 Edinburgh was able to resume payment of its much smaller ferm and its export trade once more outstripped that of Aberdeen.[93]

To the Scottish kirk also, the war had brought setbacks. Some of these were a result of destruction which could be made good by renewed royal patronage—Kelso Abbey, which had probably suffered most, had its lands erected into a regality and was to have wood from the forests of Selkirk and Jedburgh for the repair of its burnt buildings.[94] But there were also setbacks in prestige and political power. There was a contrast between the part played by the Scottish kirk in the first war of independence and the part that it played in the second war of independence. In the former it had provided notable leaders and patriotic manifestoes. In the latter it provided neither :

[90] *Chron. Fordun*, I. 364-5.
[91] E. W. M. Balfour-Melville, 'Burgh Representation in Early Scottish Parliaments', *E.H.R.*, LIX. 79-87, at 86. [92] *E.R.*, I. 501-3.
[93] *Ibid.*, 470, 471, 490, 521, 529, 533. [94] *R.M.S.*, I. 483, 563, 569.

James Bennet, Bishop of St Andrews, had fled from Scotland after the disaster at Dupplin and soon died in exile in Flanders;[95] other Scottish prelates chose to leave Scotland and associate themselves, perhaps all too helplessly, with the court of Château Gaillard;[96] William Sinclair, Bishop of Dunkeld, had crowned Balliol and was present with another six bishops at Balliol's parliament in 1334; in 1335 the post of chancellor, hitherto invariably held by an ecclesiastic, went to a layman, Sir Thomas Charteris.[97]

For a time Edward III had hoped to obtain the collaboration of the Scottish kirk. He generously gave gifts of cash, wine and victuals to some religious houses,[98] but he could not resist the temptation to try to intrude Englishmen into Scottish benefices: in 1332 he had unsuccessfully informed the pope that the animosities between Scots and English would be assuaged if the treasurer of England, or, failing him, the keeper of the wardrobe, were provided to the vacant bishopric of St Andrews.[99] The policy of intrusion, coupled with the destruction of warfare, soon persuaded most of the Scottish prelates to abandon the primrose path of neutralism.

It was probably the lack of an acknowledged leader, rather than any other factor, that accounted for the merely passive resistance of the kirk to Edward III: during the nine-year vacancy in St Andrews 'the kyrk . . . ay stud in dowte and in peryle'.[100] Not until 1342 did Benedict XII come to the conclusion that the English had failed to make themselves masters of Scotland and that he might safely provide a bishop acceptable to the Scots. At the petition of David II and the King of France, William Landallis obtained the see, and was to hold it for more than forty years.[101] The Scottish kirk was on the way to recovery.

While long years of warfare had left their mark upon the burghs and the kirk they had had an even more pervasive influence upon the Scottish baronage. With some notable exceptions, such as Sir Andrew Moray, John Randolph, Earl of Moray, William Douglas and Alexander Ramsay, the Scottish barons had shown a fickle loyalty. Many had fought part of the time for Edward III and Balliol; few had fought all of the time for David Bruce; and some had fought not at all.

Among the last category was John of the Isles, son of Angus Og

[95] *Chron. Bower*, II. 307.   [96] *E.R.*, I. 450, 452, 466.
[97] *Ibid.*, 462, 468.   [98] E.g. *Cal. Close 1337–39*, pp. 223–4.
[99] Nicholson, *Edward III*, pp. 95, 110.
[100] *Chron. Wyntoun*, II. 393, 465.   [101] Dowden, *Bishops*, pp. 25–6.

and chief of the MacDonalds. In 1335 the Earl of Moray had negotiated with him at Tarbert but had failed to secure his adherence to
the nationalist cause.[102] On 12 September 1336 an indenture was concluded at Perth whereby Balliol augmented John's ancestral lands
with a grant of Kintyre and Knapdale and the Isle of Skye.[103] This
grant at least gave him a bargaining position which he could use
when the time came to make his peace with David II. On 12 June
1343 a 'final concord' was made at Ayr between the king and 'John of
Islay, our dearest kinsman'. John was confirmed in his possession of
many island and mainland territories, but Kintyre, Knapdale and
Skye were conspicuously missing.[104] A 'final concord' was simultaneously made with Ranald MacRuaridh and, probably about the same
time, charters were issued in favour of Alexander MacNaughton and
Malcolm and Torquil MacLeod.[105]

Just as the political settlement of the West Highlands and Isles
culminated in a series of land grants, similar grants were made elsewhere in Scotland to induce men to renew their allegiance to the
crown. Moreover David rewarded those who had fought for him : on
9 November 1341 a charter was issued creating the new earldom of
Wigtown to be held in regality by Malcolm Fleming, warden of
Dumbarton, who 'bore himself faithfully and laudably towards us in
both good times and bad';[106] and in the Scone parliament of 1341
David commanded the chamberlain to pay £100 as a reward to two
men who had taken part in the recent capture of Edinburgh Castle.[107]

The fall of Edinburgh Castle in April 1341, followed by the return of David II, challenged the waning English power in Scotland.
In November 1341 Edward III set out to spend Christmas at Melrose. During his stay he raided the forest of Ettrick 'in a very ill season', granted a short truce to the Scots and left for England 'half in a
melancholy with them that movid hym to that jornay'.[108] To represent English power on the Borders, Henry of Lancaster was left
behind at Berwick where he arranged a spectacular tournament with
the Scots in which Alexander Ramsay of Dalhousie distinguished
himself.[109] As Lancaster's troops disbanded at Candlemas (2 February
1342) King David went on a devastating raid through Northumberland as far as the Tyne.[110] This was followed by two notable successes

[102] Chron. Wyntoun, II. 419; Nicholson, Edward III, p. 221.
[103] Cal. Docs. Scot., III. No. 1182 (wrongly dated 1335).
[104] A.P.S., XII. 6.
[107] E.R., I. 507.
[105] Ibid., 6–8.
[108] Scalacronica, p. 299.
[106] R.M.S., I. 484–5.
[109] Chron. Wyntoun, II. 440–4.
[110] Scalacronica, p. 299.

for the Scots : at dawn on 30 March 1342 Alexander Ramsay surprised and captured Roxburgh Castle; on 10 April, after a six months' siege, the garrison of Stirling capitulated.[111] It was symptomatic of a new confidence among the Scots that they no longer destroyed the castles that fell into their hands.

Yet much of what had been achieved was jeopardised by the ambition of William Douglas. On 18 July 1341 he had been rewarded for his services with a grant of the earldom of Atholl, but Douglas's interests lay in the Borders, where he held the wardship of Liddesdale on behalf of his godson and namesake, the future Earl of Douglas. Douglas was willing to abandon his northern earldom if he could secure Liddesdale for himself. In a general council at Aberdeen in February 1342 there were tortuous manoeuvres; as a result, Robert the Steward obtained the lands of the earldom of Atholl, Douglas obtained the lordship of Liddesdale, and his godson lost his heritage.[112] Thereafter William Douglas was known not only as 'the flower of chivalry' but as 'the Knight of Liddesdale'.

One obstacle to his schemes in the Borders was Alexander Ramsay, also styled a 'flower of chivalry'.[113] The king had rewarded Ramsay with the custody of Roxburgh and the sheriffship of Teviotdale (Roxburghshire) to which Douglas conceived that he had a prior claim. When Ramsay was holding his sheriff court in the parish kirk of Hawick on 20 June 1342 he was attacked by Douglas and carried off to Hermitage Castle. He did not live long. On the intercession of Robert the Steward the king granted a remission for the murder,[114] but though the king might 'remit his rancour'—and seems to have done so sincerely—this did not end the matter. Feud persisted. The chronicler Fordun saw in Ramsay's death the end of a good fortune that the Scots had enjoyed since the engagement at Culblean; thereafter 'all things which were attempted for the good of the kingdom straightway had ill result'.[115]

A truce lingered uneasily on the Marches. At the Westminster parliament of June 1344 it was announced that 'the Scots say openly that whenever the said Adversary [the King of France] lets them know that he does not wish to keep the truces they will not keep them either, but will raid upon England and accomplish as much damage

[111] *Chron. Fordun*, I. 365; *Cal. Docs. Scot.*, III. No. 1383.
[112] *Morton Registrum*, II. Nos. 53, 61, 62, 63; *R.M.S.*, I. 588.
[113] *Chron. Pluscarden*, I. 277.
[114] *Chron. Wyntoun*, II. 466–70; *Chron. Fordun*, I. 365–6.
[115] *Chron. Fordun*, I. 366.

as they can'.[116] Thus Edward Balliol was once more put in charge of the defence of the north,[117] as he had been from time to time in previous years. In the autumn of 1344 an Anglo-French peace conference held under papal mediation at Avignon brought no result.[118] Hostilities were renewed in 1345 when the English revenged themselves upon the turncoat Sir Dougal MacDowell, who, together with the 'captains' of the clans of Galloway, had been reconciled with King David.[119] This retribution was swift: an expeditionary force set sail from Cumberland, took the 'peel' of Hestan by surprise and burned it; Sir Dougal and his household were carried off to England and sent to the Tower.[120]

Hostilities on the Borders were given a new perspective by Edward III's preparations for another campaign in France. On 12 July 1346 he disembarked in Normandy. About the same time a large Scottish force raided Cumberland and Westmorland. The banner of John Randolph waved over the expedition, but David II had also taken part.[121] In the course of this incognito visitation he probably made his own assessment of the defences of northern England which, in the circumstances of a successful and unopposed expedition, was unlikely to be a high one. There was a short lull on the Borders while both sides awaited news from France. This, when it came, was decisive enough. Edward had sacked Caen and had then won a resounding victory at Crécy on 26 August 1346. On 4 September he began his long siege of Calais.[122]

The Franco-Scottish alliance, like most alliances, was drawn up for the benefit of both parties and could not continue if the Scots did not on occasion give help to the French; and in the autumn of 1346 the French stood in need of such help. But Scottish interests also called for military intervention. It was not a question of breaking a peace or even a truce: there already was war with England; and the absence of Edward at Calais with the greatest army he ever raised undoubtedly weakened English military power at home and provided a tempting opportunity for a full-scale Scottish onslaught. King Robert's power had been based on success in war against the English; similar success might bring similar power to his son.

[116] *Rot. Parl.*, II. 147.   [117] *Ibid.*
[118] Eugène Déprez, 'La Conférence D'Avignon (1344)' in *Essays . . . presented to Thomas Frederick Tout*, ed. A. G. Little and F. M. Powicke (1925), pp. 301–20.   [119] *R.M.S.*, I. 574, 578, 580, 590.
[120] *Chron. Anonimalle*, p. 19; *Cal. Docs. Scot.*, III. No. 1462.
[121] *Chron. Lanercost*, p. 341.
[122] May McKisack, *The Fourteenth Century*, pp. 133–5.

On 6 October 1346 the Scottish host mustered at Perth. Only two notable magnates seem to have been absent—Earl Malise of Caithness and Orkney, and John of the Isles. Yet there was a contingent under Ranald MacRuaridh, 'leader of the people of the Outer Isles'. Certain lands in Kintail had given rise to enmity between him and Earl William of Ross. When MacRuaridh took up quarters in the nunnery of Elcho he was murdered at the instigation of the earl. At this ill omen men deserted 'in gret rowtis'.[123]

The king, however, held to his plans and marched south with his remaining forces. Among the English there ran wild rumours of David's intentions: he had supposedly announced that he would soon see London [124] (which he certainly did). The small Border peel of Liddell was no fit object for the attention of the Scottish host, yet at least three days were wasted in besieging it.[125] Next, the Scots exacted blackmail from Cumberland and Westmorland and quartered themselves high-handedly in the priory of Lanercost before they descended on the priory of Hexham and 'stripped it of everything'. On 16 October they encamped in Bear Park, on the outskirts of the city of Durham.[126]

At dawn on 17 October 1346, when rain and fog swept over the countryside, the Knight of Liddesdale at the head of a foraging party ran into the three battalions of an army mustered under William La Zouche, Archbishop of York, and with difficulty escaped to spread dismay through the drowsy Scottish camp. The Scots hastily advanced to Neville's Cross, dismounted, and arrayed themselves, like the enemy, in three battalions. The chronicler Wyntoun asserts that the Scots numbered only two thousand armed men, and, like any chronicler worth his salt, exaggerates the numbers of the opposing side—allegedly twenty thousand archers and abundance of men-at-arms.[127] Certainly the English had not been taken by surprise and had had ample time to make plans for mobilisation: at the constant urging of Edward III defence preparations had been going on for months.[128] The initial successes of the Scots are perhaps more surprising than the eventual outcome.

Having learnt some lessons from the battles of Dupplin, Halidon and Crécy, both sides probably wished to remain on the defensive. A hail of arrows eventually forced the Scots to advance and abandon

[123] *Chron. Lanercost*, pp. 344-5; *Chron. Wyntoun*, II. 472; *Chron. Anonimalle*, p. 23.
[124] *Chron. Lanercost*, p. 347.   [125] *Ibid.*, p. 345.
[126] *Ibid.*, pp. 346-7; Raine, *Letters*, pp. 387-91.
[127] *Chron. Wyntoun*, II. 473-4.   [128] *Rot. Scot.*, I. 668-73.

their defensive position. The first Scottish battalion under John Randolph came upon a number of 'hey dykis'. These walls broke up its
battle order and left it open to English attack. The survivors joined
up with the second battalion under the king. But this too found itself
in 'a full anoyous plas'. The discomfited troops after hard fighting
fell back on the third battalion, under Robert the Steward and the
Earl of March, stationed in a more favourable position; but the third
battalion, the largest of the three, had no stomach for fighting. The
Scottish chronicler Fordun admits that the Earl of March and the
Steward fled. The English chroniclers poke fun at the pair: 'if the
one was worth little, the other was good for nothing . . . these two,
turning tail, fought with success, for with their battalion, without any
hurt, they returned to Scotland and thus led off the dance, leaving
David to caper as he wished.' [129] The king had been gravely wounded
with an arrow in the face; on leaving the battlefield when all was lost
he was overtaken by John Coupland but refused to yield. There was
a hand-to-hand struggle in which David knocked out two of Coupland's teeth before he was overpowered.[130]

In the battle of Neville's Cross and the subsequent pursuit the
losses of the Scots had been heavy. The chronicler Fordun tersely
mentions the death of John Randolph, Earl of Moray, of Maurice
Moray, Earl of Strathearn, of the constable, marshal and chamberlain of Scotland, 'with other innumerable barons, knights, esquires,
and persons of worth.' [131] Apart from the king, the Earls of Fife, Menteith, Sutherland and Wigtown had been taken prisoner, as well as
the Knight of Liddesdale whom the monks of Durham described as
'not so much valiant as malevolent.' [132] Two of the prisoners, Fife and
Menteith, were tried for treason by Edward III; the former was
spared by reason of his kinship with Edward, but the head of John
Graham, Earl of Menteith, graced London bridge and his quarters
were hoisted on high at York, Carlisle, Newcastle and Berwick.[133]
Like Halidon, the battle of Neville's Cross had the appearance of the
elusive final victory that the English had long sought, and it might
have proved so had not the siege of Calais continued to divert the
attention of Edward III and the resources of England. Not until 13

---

[129] *Chron. Wyntoun*, II. 475–7; *Chron. Melsa*, III. 62; *Chron. Fordun*, I.
367; *Chron. Lanercost*, p. 350.
[130] *Chron. Melsa*, III. 62; Raine, *Letters*, p. 389; *Chron. Knighton*, II. 44.
[131] *Chron. Fordun*, I. 367.
[132] Raine, *Letters*, p. 389; *Chron. Wyntoun*, II. 476–7.
[133] *Rot. Scot.*, I. 687–90.

May 1347 did Edward Balliol march out of Carlisle to 'recover the realm of Scotland'. His force, no more than 3,360 in number,[134] made a foray as far as Falkirk. There was a talk of a further advance to Perth, but the Scots seem to have bought a truce until 8 September, reportedly at the enormous price of £9,000. The expedition turned homeward, commended Balliol to God, and left him on the Isle of Hestan,[135] to hold disconsolate sway in Galloway where the Balliol name still counted for something.

Belated though it was, the campaign of 1347 had wrested back from the Scots most of what they had recovered in the four years prior to Neville's Cross : only the castles of Edinburgh, Stirling and Dunbar, still in Scottish hands, had prevented an English re-occupation of the land up to the Forth and Clyde. The sheriffdoms of Berwick, Roxburgh, Peebles and Dumfries, with the forests of Jedburgh, Selkirk and Ettrick, were once more subjected to an English administration. For more than a century the Scots would have to fight to win back what had been lost in 1347.

For the time being, however, there was a lull in hostilities, not only by reason of mutual exhaustion but on account of the Black Death, an outbreak of plague, in pneumonic as well as bubonic form, that swept all Europe and appeared in England in August 1348.[136] Since there was a time-lag before it reached Scotland, the Scots assumed that they had been spared the divine wrath that had smitten more sinful nations. They called the plague 'the foul death of the English', and are represented by an English chronicler as gathering in Ettrick forest for an attack on stricken England when the plague suddenly appeared in their own midst.[137] It came to be known as 'the first pestilence' to distinguish it from the second pestilence of 1362, the third of 1379, and the fourth of 1417,[138] after which numbering was abandoned. The plague was to range through Scotland in 1349 and 1350, striking chiefly the middle and lower classes and rarely affecting the magnates.[139]

[134] *Rot. Scot.*, I. 691–2.

[135] *Chron. Anonimalle*, p. 29; *Chron. Knighton*, II. 47; *Chron. Wyntoun*, II. 478; *Chron. Lanercost*, p. 352.

[136] May McKisack, *The Fourteenth Century*, pp. 331–4. Recent works on this subject include Charles Creighton, *A History of Epidemics in Britain*, Vol. I (1965), Philip Ziegler, *The Black Death* (1969), Geoffrey Marks, *The Medieval Plague: the Black Death of the Middle Ages* (1971), and J. F. D. Shrewsbury, *A History of Bubonic Plague in the British Isles* (1970). In a review of the last work (*S.H.R.*, L. 75–8), Rosalind Mitchison stresses the importance of the pneumonic form of the disease.   [137] *Chron. Knighton*, II. 62.

[138] *Extracta*, pp. 249–50.   [139] *Chron. Bower*, II. 347.

In contrast to their English and Irish counterparts the Scottish chroniclers paid comparatively little heed to the Black Death and devoted little more space to it than an outbreak of fowl pest that had lately afflicted Scottish poultry.[140] The chronicler Bower gives a solitary statistic when he affirms that twenty-four of the canons of the priory of St Andrews—about two-thirds of the total—had perished.[141] The lack of detailed comment makes it difficult to guess the effects of the plague upon Scotland but perhaps suggests that these effects were less severe than in other lands.

The effects of military disaster were more obvious. The contemporary chronicler John of Fordun affirms that the magnates had appointed the Steward as guardian, 'deeming that as he was the most powerful of all, the general interests would be the more strongly safeguarded by him. But how as guardian he governed the realm entrusted to him his deeds make known unto all times.'[142] Nothing is said of the Steward's deeds. As heir presumptive he was well placed to advance whatever ambitions he entertained but did not enjoy unlimited authority. He was formally styled 'the king's lieutenant' rather than guardian; and it is probable that the designation of lieutenant meant that his actions were subject to review by the captive king.[143] One surviving document perhaps epitomises the Steward's position: in 1348 he wrote to the sheriff of Dumbarton instructing him to stop unwarranted exactions upon Paisley Abbey —'for our own part we beseech you, and on the part of our lord the king we firmly command and direct you, that . . . you desist from exactions of this sort'.[144]

Yet the absent king had no machinery to enforce his will. After Neville's Cross it was the Steward who appointed sheriffs and other officials [145] and it was he who ought to have supervised their behaviour. In Aberdeenshire, at any rate, where the sheriff was one of those appointed by the Steward, there was administrative chaos: the sheriff did not account for any issues of his own court and asserted that there were none; he had obtained practically nothing from various lands set to ferm; his total receipts for the year 1347–8 came to only £19 7s. 8d.—and this sum was assigned to him for his fee.[146]

Another indication of the weakness of the Steward's administration was his appointment of sub-lieutenants or sub-guardians to take

[140] *Chron. Fordun*, I. 366–7; *Chron. Wyntoun*, II. 479–80.
[141] *Chron. Bower*, II. 347.   [142] *Chron. Fordun*, I. 368.
[143] Bruce Webster, *Acts of David II, 1329–71* (duplicated handlist, 1960), pp. 21–6.   [144] *Paisley Registrum*, pp. 208–9.
[145] *Chron. Wyntoun*, II. 478.   [146] *E.R.*, I. 542–4.

charge of areas in which their landed power predominated. Thus Thomas Stewart, Earl of Angus, became his lieutenant in Angus and the Mearns. From such a decentralisation of government it was the magnates who were most likely to benefit. But the death or captivity of some fifty barons as a result of Neville's Cross left the way open for others, often simple knights, to take their place. Most striking of all was the rise of Sir Robert Erskine, who became chamberlain and was to play a leading part in politics for more than thirty years.[147]

The temporary eclipse of the baronage also led to a closer association of the clergy with government and politics. The first lay chancellor had been killed at Neville's Cross and was to be replaced by a succession of ecclesiastics, while William Landallis, Bishop of St Andrews, began his long diplomatic career as a leader of the missions to England for the release of the king. Under the influence of Landallis the Scottish kirk was to show a bold face to Edward III when he renewed the policy of ecclesiastical intrusion.[148]

Intrusion less easy to resist was forthcoming from another quarter : by the middle of the fourteenth century the pope was providing his own nominees not only to the bishoprics, but to lesser benefices as well ; by the end of the following century the practice was to be extended to insignificant benefices worth less than twenty-four florins a year. Already, too, the popes of Avignon were issuing 'expectative graces', which conferred prospective provision to benefices that were not yet vacant, and were 'reserving' the right to make a future provision to a benefice that was not yet vacant.[149] It was the benefices held by the secular clergy, rather than those held by the regular clergy, that were first affected by the various devices that emanated from the pope's plenitude of spiritual power : it caused some stir when Clement VI in 1351 made a provision to the abbey of Dunfermline.[150] Thenceforward the monasteries, as well as the institutions of the secular clergy, were to be increasingly subject to papal provision, though it is remarkable that some of the most important abbeys—Cambuskenneth, Melrose, Dryburgh and Jedburgh—do not seem to have been provided in papal consistory until the late fifteenth century.[151]

[147] Scots Peerage, v. 592–3.   [148] Cal. Docs. Scot., III. No. 1558.
[149] Cameron, Apostolic Camera, pp. lxix, xciv; G. Mollat, The Popes at Avignon, p. 336.
[150] Chron. Bower, II. 349; Cal. Papal Letters, III. 423; Coulton, Scottish Abbeys, p. 253.
[151] Cameron, Apostolic Camera, p. xxxix.

The system of reservations and provisions, resulting in direct papal appointments to benefices, rather than capitular elections or presentations by a patron, was the main feature in the centralisation of the church achieved during the residence of the papacy at Avignon (1309–1377) and 'could, from certain points of view, be of benefit to the Church'.[152] But even if the system had affected only ecclesiastics, it held ample opportunities for acrimony, litigation and downright abuse : the career of almost every prominent Scottish ecclesiastic was spattered by contests over benefices,[153] and the main motivation of the contestants, as of the papacy itself, was undoubtedly financial.[154] In the case of the greater benefices, assessed at more than a hundred florins a year,[155] provision was made in consistory, and the beneficiary paid 'common services' (usually one-third of the yearly assessment of his benefice) as well as the five customary 'little services', which were proportionate to the common services. Half of the income from consistorial provisions went to the pope and the remainder was shared among the cardinals who attended him when the provision was made. In the case of lesser benefices, assessed at between twenty-four and a hundred florins yearly, provision was not made in consistory and the 'annates' that were paid (usually half of the first year's income of the benefice) went to the pope's own revenues after they had been paid locally to a papal collector. Between 1353 and 1373 this post was held in Scotland by William Greenlaw, a noted pluralist. To enforce payment he and his successors were granted ecclesiastical powers sufficient to bring to heel any recalcitrant bishop who refused to co-operate.[156] Equally stringent methods were used to extract the common services, which had to be paid directly into the *curia*. Those who had been provided in consistory had to enter into formal obligations for payment, usually within a year in two instalments. Increasingly they had recourse to the services of the bankers who served the *curia*; and, although usury was condemned by the church, interest

[152] G. Mollat, *The Popes at Avignon*, p. 337.

[153] See, for example, the outline careers of sixty-one clerics in Burns, *Basle*.

[154] The following account is based (except where otherwise noted) upon Geoffrey Barraclough, *Papal Provisions* (1935), G. Mollat, *The Popes at Avignon*, pp. 310–44, Cameron, *Apostolic Camera*, pp. xiii–xciv, and J. Hutchison Cockburn's important article on 'Papal Collections and Collectors in Scotland in the Middle Ages', *Scot. Church Hist. Soc. Recs.*, I. 173–99. For the sake of clarity I have drawn a distinction between common services and annates (and have made other generalisations) that would be more applicable to the fifteenth century than to the fourteenth.

[155] The florin varied in value from 2s. 8d. to 3s. 7d. between 1329 and 1428 (J. Hutchison Cockburn, *op. cit.*, *Scot. Church Hist. Soc. Recs.*, I. 173–99, at 188).

[156] A. R. MacEwen, *History of the Church in Scotland*, I. 286–7.

was paid by subterfuge : 'for practical purposes canonical precepts gave way to economic necessities'.[157] By the device of 'regress' the bulls of provision were delivered to the bankers as security for the sums they advanced on behalf of their clients, and the latter obtained the bulls only after their obligations had been discharged; if the clients defaulted, the bankers could return the bulls to the *curia* (hence 'regress') and claim from it the repayment of the sums they had advanced. This intricate system (which did not, however, save the papacy from financial stringency) throve upon the supplications for benefices presented by a growing multitude of petitioners who were not slow to realise that the surest pathway to ecclesiastical preferment lay through the *curia*.[158]

The increasing traffic in benefices imposed a corresponding financial burden upon the Scottish kirk at a time when it was impoverished as a result of Anglo-Scottish warfare [159] and the lawlessness prevalent during the Steward's lieutenancy.[160] There was, however, one panacea by which the greater ecclesiastical institutions could remedy their economic ills—appropriation. And if the parsonages (*rectorie*) of the parish kirks had already been appropriated (as most had), the revenues of the vicarages might also be appropriated, and the pastoral function entrusted not to a vicar who enjoyed a 'perpetual vicarage' with rights to a share in the teinds of the parish, but to a vicar-pensioner with insecure tenure, who had only the use of the manse and its croft and was paid a usually inadequate salary by the appropriator. Ultimately more than half of the vicarages were appropriated,[161] and ultimately 'those who served the altar could not live of the altar'.[162]

The financial stringency from which the kirk as a whole seems to have suffered made the clergy cling jealously to their economic privileges, to seek new privileges, and even to assume privileges in defiance of the exclusive trading rights of the burghs. In November 1351 David II granted to the monks of Arbroath the custom to be paid on items of trade within the burgh, port and regality of Arbroath; the abbey was to have its own coket seal, which was to be as valid as the cokets of the king's own burghs. The reaction of the Dundee bur-

---

[157] Cameron, *Apostolic Camera*, p. xxxiv.

[158] See the opening entries in *Cal. Scot. Supp., 1418–1424*, pp. 1–4.

[159] *Arbroath Liber*, ii. No. 23; *Cambuskenneth Registrum*, No. 58; *Cal. Papal Petitions*, i. 250.

[160] *Paisley Registrum*, pp. 208–9; *Cal. Papal Petitions*, i. 200; Bruce Webster, *Handlist of the Acts of David II*, pp. 23, 25; *Arbroath Liber*, ii. No. 27.

[161] Ian B. Cowan, *op. cit.*, *Scot. Church Hist. Soc. Recs.*, xiii. 203–22, at 205.

[162] Ian B. Cowan, 'Vicarages and the Cure of Souls in Medieval Scotland', *ibid.*, xvi. 111–27, at 127.

gesses may be guessed from a royal mandate of March 1352 ordering
the royal officials to see that no one hindered the monks in the enjoyment of their new trading privileges.[163]

The conflict of interests between the kirk and the royal burghs did
not always go in favour of the kirk. By March 1352 the burgesses of
Montrose and Dundee, and possibly those of other royal burghs, seem
to have banded in defence of their privileges and obtained royal mandates against the Bishop of Brechin and the monks of Coupar Angus.[164] Whenever the burgesses of Dundee so desired, the justiciar and
other royal officials were to go in person to the abbey of Coupar
Angus, to the kirk of Alyth, to the townships of Kettins and Kirrie-
muir, publicly forbid trading in these places and seize the goods of the
offenders.[165]

The official support thus given to burgess communities, even
against great ecclesiastical institutions, was perhaps a sign of the increasing influence of the merchant burgesses. John Wigmer, burgess
of Edinburgh, was numbered in 1348 among the envoys who were to
go to England to treat of the king's liberation.[166] An even more notable burgess, John Mercer of Perth, had already risen in the world by
1352 when he married into the baronial family of Murray of Tulli-
bardine.[167] A long spectacular career as merchant prince lay ahead
of him. Not only were individual merchant burgesses increasingly
important in their own right but they were members of a class
capable of taking a collective initiative. There can be little doubt that
something of the sort lay behind the decisions of a council held at
Dundee on 12 November 1347,[168] where the council, acting in the
name of the king, ordered reprisals against the hostile Flemings and
ratified in advance a contract that had yet to be reached between the
merchant burgesses of Scotland and those of Middelburg in the
county of Zealand. Although the terms of this prospective contract
are unknown its substance was to be the recognition of Middelburg
as the Scottish staple port on the continent. Scottish wares were now
being carried overseas not by Germans and Flemings but by Scottish
merchants. In Middelburg they were to have their own resident
mayor [169]—later known as the conservator of the staple—who would

163 *Arbroath Liber*, II. No. 26. For a similar case in Aberdeen in 1385 see
A.P.S., II. 565.
164 *Brechin Registrum*, II. No. cccciii.
165 *R.M.S.*, II. No. 614. 166 *Rot. Scot.*, I. 718, 721.
167 W. Fraser, *The Sutherland Book* (1892), p. 16.
168 *A.P.S.*, I. 514-5. 169 *Ibid.*, 514.
E.H.S.—6*

presumably look after their interests and act as their commercial agent.[170] Although the institution of a Scottish staple in the Low Countries was to outlast the Middle Ages it was by no means permanently fixed at Middelburg: in 1348 Adam Tore and William Feth, burgesses of Edinburgh and Dundee respectively, went to Bruges to restore good relations with Flanders on behalf of the *quatre grosses villes de Escosse*.[171] This phrase undoubtedly signifies the four burghs—Edinburgh, Stirling, Roxburgh and Berwick. Since the last two were in English hands their place had possibly already been taken by other burghs: in 1369 Lanark and Linlithgow were formally appointed to fill the two vacancies.

Whether Scottish trade was centred in Middelburg or in Bruges the trading route along the English coastline was still a perilous one, even in time of truce. It was typical that when two vessels freighted in Flanders by John Wigmer and other Scottish merchants were wrecked on the Northumberland coast the cargoes, supposedly worth £4,000, were plundered.[172] In cases of this sort Edward III sought to provide redress. To Scottish merchants he was indeed to show himself remarkably favourable, perhaps for political reasons; during the lieutenancy there was the beginning of a trade between Scotland and England that was to reach impressive proportions by the end of the reign of David II. Two Scottish magnates who figured in Edward's political projects were also allowed to share in the profits of renewed Anglo-Scottish trade: in 1353, at the petition of William Douglas of Liddesdale, Edward granted safe-conducts to a number of Scottish merchants;[173] in 1357 a similar petition from John of the Isles resulted in safe-conducts for certain merchants of the Isles, who might trade in England and Ireland and the rest of Edward's dominions.[174]

This successful petition on the part of John of the Isles followed attempts on the part of the English to draw him to their side.[175] Uncommitted to either side he went his own way, striving with remarkable success to keep on good terms with the governments both of England and Scotland and meanwhile consolidating his own power. As a result of the murder of Ranald MacRuaridh on the eve of the Neville's Cross campaign the MacRuaridh inheritance had fallen to Ranald's sister Amy, the wife of John of the Isles. He thus obtained

[170] For the general background see Davidson and Gray, *Staple*, pp. 115–20, and M. P. Rooseboom, *The Scottish Staple in the Netherlands*, pp. 5–7.

[171] Rooseboom, *op. cit.*, p. 5.   [172] *Cal. Docs. Scot.*, IV. No. 10.

[173] *Rot. Scot.*, I. 758.   [174] *Cal. Docs. Scot.*, III. No. 1639.

[175] *Rot. Scot.*, I. 677; *Cal. Docs. Scot.*, III. No. 1606.

the lands of Garmoran on the mainland and Uist and other islands; probably every Hebridean island save Skye was now under his sway. Thereupon John found some pretext for annulling his marriage with Amy MacRuaridh,[176] and on 14 June 1350 a papal dispensation was issued for his marriage to Margaret Stewart, eldest daughter of Robert the Steward.[177] Thanks to this marriage, John seems to have been granted the feudal superiority of Kintyre and Knapdale.[178] The marriage was also marked by a Latin interpretation of the bridegroom's title : by Gaelic usage he could be styled *rí* (king); the Scottish government presumably regarded him as a baron; and in the papal dispensation of 1350 he was described as 'John of the Isles, Lord of the Isles of Scotland'. This style was to be passed on to his successors, together with the vast mainland and island territories that could now be described as the lordship of the Isles. John had revived the Hebridean power that his ancestor Somerled had created two centuries previously.

One potential threat to the MacDonald hegemony was the revival of the MacDougals under John of Lorne. This descendant of the John of Lorne forfeited by Robert I had by 1338 returned to Scotland in Balliol's wake [179] and was to be no mere bird of passage. But there was to be harmony rather than discord between him and MacDonald. According to an indenture of 8 September 1354 [180] John of Lorne, 'Lord of Argyll', and John of Islay, 'Lord of the Isles', would behave as brothers of one flesh.

The re-entry of the MacDougals into the society of the Gaelic west was marked by other pacts similiar to the indenture of 1354.[181] While the foremost of the Gaelic magnates were now more united than they had ever been, they were also to be increasingly associated with Robert the Steward. He had secured the Lord of the Isles as a son-in-law, and this relationship was to be further developed when Robert the Steward married for the second time. A papal dispensation of 1355 allowed him to wed John Randolph's widow, Euphemia of Ross, sister of William, Earl of Ross, who had himself married Mary, sister of John of the Isles.[182] Through the Gaelic culture of the

[176] *Highland Papers*, I. 26–7. A dispensation for the marriage had been issued on 4 June 1337 (*ibid.*, 73–5).

[177] A. Theiner, *Vetera Monumenta*, No. dlxxxviii.

[178] Landholding in Kintyre and Knapdale was complicated and obscure. Some time after 1337 lands in Kintyre had been granted, or confirmed, to the Steward and his eldest son (*R.M.S.*, I. 584).

[179] W. Fraser, *The Stirlings of Keir* (1858), p. 198, No. 2.

[180] *Highland Papers*, I. 75–8

[181] *Ibid.*, II. 142.   [182] *Scots Peerage*, V. 236–7, 239.

lands they controlled, through the intermarriages and diplomatic pacts that linked them, Robert the Steward, John of the Isles, the Earl of Ross, John of Lorne, and Gillespic Campbell, formed a sort of 'Highland Party' that David II would find troublesome when he returned to Scotland.

The fortune of war had condemned David to spend the prime of his manhood as a prisoner in England. Although his basic comfort was not neglected he was closely guarded.[183] Edward certainly hoped that he would be only too willing to escape from a wretched and hopeless position at the cost of a hefty ransom and political concessions. From 1348 onwards harsh conditions were outlined to the Scottish embassies that almost annually visited England to try to negotiate the king's release. The situation held out opportunities for Edward; it also posed problems,[184] some of which arose in unexpected quarters. When the English parliament met in March 1348 it was made a condition of a grant of taxation 'that David Bruce, William Douglas, and the other chief men of Scotland, are in no manner to be set free, either for ransom or upon their word of honour'.[185] Edward paid little heed but engaged in secret and devious diplomacy. Its character may be guessed from a memorandum of 1349[186] addressed to 'Monsieur Rauf'—almost certainly Sir Ralph Neville. He was informed that the English king's weighty affairs were greatly hindered 'because Sir E. de B. [Balliol] will not agree to good ways of establishing peace such as would seem reasonable to one side and the other'; 'Monsieur Rauf' was to acquaint Balliol with the new offers made by 'D. de B.' [David Bruce] and with the pact made between him and 'W. de D.' [Douglas of Liddesdale]. This memorandum shows that Balliol was no mere puppet of Edward, but a person determined to insist upon his own rights and thus an awkward obstacle in the way of David's ransom; it also makes it clear that David and Liddesdale were organising a party in Scotland to promote some concessions demanded by Edward as the price of their liberation.

Concessions also figure in a petition addressed by David to Pope

---

[183] See 'Papers relating to the Captivity and Release of David II', ed. E. W. M. Balfour-Melville, *S.H.S. Misc. IX,* 1–56, and the review by Ranald Nicholson, *S.H.R.*, xxxix., at p. 47, n. 5.

[184] J. Campbell, 'England, Scotland and the Hundred Years War', in *Europe in the Late Middle Ages,* ed. J. R. Hale, J. R. L. Highfield and B. Smalley (1965), pp. 196–7.

[185] *Rot. Parl.*, ii. 200–1.

[186] C. Johnston, 'Negotiations for the Ransom of David Bruce in 1349', *E.H.R.*, xxxvi. 57–8.

Clement VI. This petition, which was dealt with at Avignon on 7 August 1350, began by recalling to the pope's notice the adverse fortune that had befallen David and his fellow-prisoners.[187] The pope was asked to afford help and counsel, and to write to the King of France urging that the release of David and his fellow captives should be made a condition of any peace or long truce between the French and English. Then, without any explanatory preamble, David volunteered information on the terms that Edward III was alleged to be demanding—homage, military service against the French, attendance at English parliaments, the restoration of the disinherited, recognition of the King of England as David's heir if the latter should die childless, custody of Scottish castles as surety for fulfilment of these terms. David gave no indication whatever that he was ready to accept any of these demands, nor did he commit himself to rejecting them. The real nature of the appeal of 1350 was an attempt to put pressure on the French king to take action for David's release. Clement duly ordered that 'opportune letters' should be directed to the King of France—but to no avail.

Thus David continued to play his part in Edward's plans. In December 1350 William Douglas of Liddesdale obtained a safe-conduct from Edward to return on parole to Scotland to undertake 'certain business concerning David Bruce', to whom he was to report back before 9 February 1351.[188] The Knight of Liddesdale was to inform the Scots that David might be set free for a ransom of £40,000. As soon as the first instalment had been paid, Edward would surrender the Scottish castles and territories that he controlled. But all this was conditional on the acceptance by the Scots of one of the points outlined in the petition to the pope : if David died childless he was to be succeeded on the Scottish throne by one of Edward's younger sons.[189]

Edward's demand for this particular concession, rather than any other, was astute. Though David might be unwilling to hand over Scotland to English domination, an alteration in the Scottish succession did not, by itself, in theory at least, infringe Scottish independ-

[187] The following details are taken from the original entry in the papal register. I am indebted to the administrators of the Ross Fund of the University of Glasgow for showing me a microfilm of this important document, hitherto available only in an imperfect summary (*Cal. Papal Petitions*, I. 203) which misrepresented David's attitude. See E. W. M. Balfour-Melville, 'David II's Appeal to the Pope', *S.H.R.*, XLI. 86.

[188] *Rot. Scot.*, I. 737–8.

[189] E. W. M. Balfour-Melville, *op. cit.*, *S.H.S. Misc. IX*. 1–56, at 37.

ence. The obvious loser would be Robert the Steward, and David had little liking for the ineffective mediocrity who had deserted him at Neville's Cross. Edward had devised terms that David would undoubtedly support to the best of his ability, fortified by the hope that he would be liberated for a moderate ransom, would recover occupied territory from the English, and that in the end he might thwart Edward's dynastic policy by producing offspring of his own. Both Edward and David, having considered the imponderables of the situation, were willing to stake much on the vagaries of fortune.

By February 1352 David was in Scotland, released temporarily on parole.[190] A parliament or council that discussed the English terms seems to have been held at Scone between 28 February and 6 March 1352, when various royal charters were issued.[191] The English chronicler Knighton asserts that the Scots 'with one consent, in one voice' said they were willing to ransom their king, but not to be subject to the King of England.[192] The latter still had hopes that a favourable outcome might be reached by force, if not by negotiation. On 28 March 1352 he issued secret instructions: if it appeared that progress might be made 'in another way', and if David and Douglas of Liddesdale had ascertained that their friends would 'be of their accord', then David might be allowed to remain at large in Newcastle or Berwick until Whitsuntide 'so that one may see in the meantime what exploit he may effect'.[193] Nothing resulted. David could not, or would not, start a civil war in Scotland to force Edward's terms upon his own people. By 22 June he was once more cooling his heels in the Tower.[194]

His unsuccessful mission gave rise to rumours that he had sworn allegiance to Edward;[195] and these rumours later received spurious support thanks to the work of the fifteenth-century English forger, John Hardyng.[196] Yet despite the ambiguities of David's position in 1352 and even in later years, there is no convincing evidence that he was ever willing to acknowledge the feudal superiority of the English king.[197] The utmost that David was ready to concede was an alteration in the succession that would take effect only if he himself died childless.

[190] *Rot. Scot.*, I. 743–4, 748; *Cal. Docs. Scot.*, III. No. 1557.
[191] A. B. Webster, *Handlist of the Acts of David II*, pp. 22–3.
[192] *Chron. Knighton*, II. 356.
[193] *Rot. Scot.*, I. 748, 749, 750; *Foedera*, III. pt. i, 78.
[194] *Rot. Scot.*, I. 750, 751.   [195] *Chron. Knighton*, II. 69.
[196] Ranald Nicholson, 'David II, the historians and the chroniclers', *S.H.R.*, XLV. 59–78, at 64–5.
[197] E. W. M. Balfour-Melville, *op. cit., S.H.R.*, XLI. 86.

For a time Edward abandoned his greater ambitions in order to concentrate on more limited objectives that might be gained through Douglas of Liddesdale, with whom he concluded an indenture on 17 July 1352. Indentures of 1349 and 1350 made with other Scottish prisoners had been concluded in the presence of David II, but the indenture of 1352 was not.[198] It would seem that he and Liddesdale had parted company and that the latter's conduct was from this point onward not only dubious but treasonable. For Douglas was not only to be released, but was to be installed by Edward III in the castle of Hermitage, in the lands of Liddesdale, and in certain lands of Annandale and Moffatdale. At a month's notice Douglas would be ready to fight for Edward III and his heirs against all men. Although Douglas would not be expected to make war upon 'his own nation of Scotland'—unless it should be to his own liking to do so—he would allow English forces unmolested passage through Liddesdale and his other lands.[199]

The country to which Douglas returned was one torn by feuds and dissensions.[200] He himself, a notable instigator of feud,[201] was soon to be a victim at the hands of his own godson and namesake. This William Douglas, second son of Sir Archibald, the Scottish guardian killed at Halidon, had passed his youth in France and returned to Scotland after Neville's Cross to piece together an inheritance that included the lands of his uncle, the 'Good Sir James'.[202] William was therefore Lord of Douglas and would have been Lord of Liddesdale also but for the machinations of his godfather.[203] In August 1353 the Lord of Douglas waylaid his godfather in the forest of Ettrick. The corpse of the 'flower of chivalry' was laid to rest in Melrose.[204] Like previous assassinations, the murder of the Knight of Liddesdale brought no judicial retribution to the perpetrator, whose territorial claims were fully recognised in a Scottish royal charter of February 1354.[205] Henceforward the Lord of Douglas would control the Scottish Borders. He had laid the foundations of a power that might control the crown itself.

The murder of the Knight of Liddesdale upset Edward's latest

---

[198] Text in *Rot. Scot.*, I. 752–3. [199] *Ibid.*, 753.
[200] *Scots Peerage*, v. 595; W. Fraser, *The Red Book of Menteith* (1880), II. 29; *Chron. Wyntoun*, II. 478–9; *Chron. Bower*, II. 337.
[201] *Chron. Fordun*, I. 396; *Chron. Bower*, II. 348.
[202] *Scots Peerage*, III. 147–8. [203] P. 144 above.
[204] *Scots Peerage*, VI. 341.
[205] *R.M.S.*, I. 487–8; Fraser, *Douglas*, III. No. 292.

policy and obliged him to resurrect schemes centred upon David II.[206]
In an indenture concluded at Berwick on 13 July 1354, a draft treaty
for his release was at last achieved : David would be released in return for a ransom of 90,000 marks (£60,000), to be paid in nine instalments over the following nine years; during that period there
would be an Anglo-Scottish truce; the Scots would deliver twenty
noble hostages as surety for payment of the ransom. In October 1354,
Edward ordered that all the barons and knights of Northumberland
should gather at Newcastle to witness David's deliverance in return
for the Scottish hostages.[207] But something went wrong. Once more
David was to be bitterly disappointed.

There can be little doubt that it was the Scots who were responsible for the failure of the latest negotiations. While it is understandable that on previous occasions they had rejected a ransom treaty
which included political concessions, this objection did not apply to
the draft treaty of 1354, which was a straightforward ransom treaty.
The explanation for the Scottish action—or inaction—lay in France.
As the current Anglo-French truce drew to a close both sides were
preparing for war.[208] On 5 March 1355 King John of France ordered
the Sire de Garencières to lead fifty men-at-arms to Scotland and
to carry 40,000 *deniers d'or à l'escu*[209]—which the writer of the
Scalacronica equated with 10,000 marks.[210] This sum was 'to be
given among the prelates and barons of Scotland upon condition that
they should break their truce with the King of England and make war
upon him'.[211] Early in November 1355 Thomas Stewart, Earl of
Angus, and Patrick, Earl of March, joined with Garencières in capturing and looting the town of Berwick in a surprise nocturnal
assault,[212] after which they besieged the castle. As Edward III stepped
ashore on his return from a brief campaign in the hinterland of Calais
this startling news was brought to him, whereupon he at once began
preparations to relieve Berwick Castle.[213] When his host reached the
Tweed the Scots within the town of Berwick were too few to hold
out—Garencières had withdrawn to France and no help was forthcoming from Scotland 'by reason of the discord of the magnates'.[214]

[206] *Rot. Scot.*, I. 765–6.   [207] *Ibid.*, 768–71.
[208] J. Campbell, *op. cit., Europe in the Late Middle Ages*, p. 199.
[209] *Ibid.*   [210] *Scalacronica*, p. 303.
[211] *Ibid.*, similarly *Chron. Fordun*, I. 371.
[212] *Chron. Fordun*, I. 372; *Chron. Bower*, II. 351; *Chron. Wyntoun*, II. 482–4;
Scalacronica, p. 304; *Cal. Docs. Scot.*, IV. Nos. 3, 21.
[213] *Chron. Walsingham*, I. 280; *Scalacronica*, p. 304; *Rot. Parl.*, II. 264–5.
[214] *Chron. Fordun*, I. 373.

By 20 January 1356 Edward had recovered Berwick and arrived in Roxburgh, where, according to the Scottish chroniclers, Edward Balliol made his appearance 'like a roaring lion'.[215]

Balliol's fate had indeed been a hard one. He was by no means the incompetent puppet that some modern historians have taken him for;[216] he had been willing to fight for his rights but when supplies of men and money from England dried up he was left powerless. Latterly his pretensions were increasingly ludicrous. Despite a long rearguard action in Galloway his position had become increasingly isolated: in 1354 his ancestral castle and birthplace of Buittle seems to have fallen to his opponents.[217] Balliol had lost his last toehold in Scotland and the stage was set for the dramatic gesture at Roxburgh in which he took the crown from his head, lifted a handful of earth and stones from Scottish soil, and handed them to Edward III [218] as a symbol that he had thereby resigned his kingdom to Edward to make of it what he could.

This resignation was formally recorded in a number of documents sealed at Roxburgh on 20 January 1356 or the following days.[219] Balliol drove a hard bargain: if he was to relinquish the position of penniless king he was determined to be a wealthy pensioner; Edward III was to pay him an annuity of £2,000 for life and a gift of 5,000 marks to meet his outstanding debts.[220] Until his death in January 1364 Balliol would have a creditor's satisfaction in dunning Edward III for debts, while he paid off those of his father, the late King John, and poached in royal parks.[221]

After the transaction at Roxburgh Scotland had a new pretender in the person of the English king. Once Edward discovered that his latest diplomatic manoeuvre had failed to impress the Scots he set out on what was to be his last military expedition in Scotland. Having crossed the Lammermuirs he spent ten days at Haddington where the Franciscan friary and its kirk, 'the lamp of Lothian', were set ablaze.

[215] *Ibid.*; *Chron. Wyntoun*, II. 485; similarly *Scalacronica*, p. 304.

[216] E. W. M. Balfour-Melville, 'Edward III and David II', Hist. Assoc. Pamphlet No. G.27, p. 17.

[217] R. C. Reid, 'Edward de Balliol', *Dumfriesshire Trans.*, xxxv. 38–63; Bruce Webster, 'The English Occupations of Dumfriesshire in the Fourteenth Century', *ibid.*, xxxv. 64–80; C. A. Ralegh Radford, 'Balliol's Manor House on Hestan Island', *ibid.*, xxxv. 33–7.

[218] *Chron. Fordun*, I. 373.

[219] *Rot. Scot.*, I. 787–8; *Cal. Docs. Scot.*, III. Nos. 1591–2, 1596, 1603.

[220] *Cal. Docs. Scot.*, III. Nos. 1594–5, 1598–9, 1601.

[221] *Ibid.*, IV. Nos. 8, 11, 72; E. W. M. Balfour-Melville, 'The Death of Edward Balliol', *S.H.R.*, xxxv. 82–3.

His ships disembarked 'piratical sons of Belial' who pillaged the Virgin's shrine at Whitekirk. Thus (so the Scots believed) through the intercessions of the Virgin a wind came from the north, prevented the English fleet from entering the Forth, scattered its vessels and sank some of them.[222] Edward had perhaps hoped to march to Scone to have himself crowned, but his campaign of 1356 was to be a replica of his father's of 1322, though more devastating. The expedition, which had begun early in February, left such a trail of destruction that the Scots talked of 'The Burnt Candlemas'.[223] It did little to restrain their continuing offensive on the Borders.[224]

Although there is no sign that Edward's 1356 campaign had daunted the Scots it has been claimed that its political results place it 'amongst the most effective Edward ever launched' [225]—the supposed political results being the negotiations for the release of David II that culminated in a ransom treaty in October 1357. But the ransom treaty was hardly a result of the Burnt Candlemas: the clue to the end of Anglo-Scottish hostilities lay in France. At Poitiers on 19 September 1356 the French suffered a disaster even worse than that of Crécy:[226] King John joined David II as a prisoner of the English; under the Dauphin Charles, who acted as regent, France lapsed into chaos, and the hopes that the Scots had rested on France were dashed to the ground.

On 17 January 1357 Robert the Steward presided as lieutenant over a council at Perth, whence he issued a commission for a full-scale embassy under Bishop Landallis to treat for 'the deliverance of our lord the king and final concord between the kings and their realms'.[227] In May the ambassadors reached London and an indenture was concluded which amounted to a draft treaty for David's release in return for named hostages and a ransom.[228] Next, the Steward summoned another council which was in session at Edinburgh by 26 September 1357,[229] and no doubt discussed the draft treaty. In both this council and the preceding one the burgesses were represented along with the prelates and nobles, and no formality was neglected to ensure that responsibility for the terms of the king's release was shared by each of

[222] *Chron. Bower*, II. 354–6; *Chron. Knighton*, II. 85; *Chron. Anonimalle*, pp. 33–4.
[223] *Chron. Bower*, II. 354.
[224] *Cal. Docs. Scot.*, III. No. 1616; *Rot. Scot.*, I. 795–6.
[225] James Campbell, *op. cit.*, *Europe in the Late Middle Ages*, p. 201.
[226] May McKisack, *The Fourteenth Century*, pp. 138–40.
[227] *A.P.S.*, I. 515; *Cal. Docs. Scot.*, III. No. 1609.
[228] *Cal. Docs. Scot.*, III. No. 1629.   [229] *A.P.S.*, I. 515–8.

the three political classes of the community.[230] Six ambassadors were to carry out the final negotiations at Berwick,[231] where David arrived under escort on 28 September [232] in readiness for his release.

The resulting treaty indenture,[233] sealed on 3 October 1357, seems to have been basically the same as the draft treaty drawn up in London in May. The king was to be set free for 100,000 marks (£66,666 13s. 4d.) to be paid at the rate of 10,000 marks a year, beginning at Midsummer 1358. The full ransom was to be paid even if David died before the instalments were completed. If the instalments fell into arrears he was to return to captivity, and until the ransom was fully paid there was to be a truce, during which the territorial *status quo* was to be observed. The main guarantee for the payment of the king's ransom was the delivery of twenty noble hostages by the Scots. These were, however, regarded by the English as inadequate: David was to deliver three supplementary super-hostages to be chosen from a list comprising the Steward and other leading magnates. It was stipulated that all hostages (who might be exchanged for others from time to time) should be treated 'courteously' in England but were to live there at their own expense.[234] The good faith of the Scots was to be secured not only by hostages but by stringent conditions of a less tangible nature that included ecclesiastical sanctions. So far as ingenuity could express itself on parchment the treaty of Berwick was assured of fulfilment.

It has been claimed that Edward III might never have obtained any ransom at all from Scotland and that to that extent the treaty was something of a victory for English diplomacy.[235] But it was also, in a way, a victory for the Scots: 'David was freed on heavy terms which settled no issue but that of his release'.[236] The omission of other issues from the treaty was thus a setback to Edward's cherished ambitions; he had simply recognised that the mere possession of the person of David Bruce would no longer serve his ends. On 7 October 1357,[237] a week or so before the eleventh anniversary of his capture at Neville's Cross, King David returned to his realm as a free man.

---

[230] *Ibid.*; *Cal. Docs. Scot.*, III. Nos. 1642–8, 1650–4.

[231] *A.P.S.*, I. 518.

[232] E. W. M. Balfour-Melville, *op. cit.*, *S.H.S. Misc. IX.* 1–56, at 22.

[233] Text in *Rot. Scot.*, I. 811–4; *A.P.S.*, I. 518–21.

[234] *Rot. Scot.*, I. 810; *Chron. Wyntoun*, II. 497.

[235] J. Campbell, *op. cit.*, *Europe in the Late Middle Ages*, p. 201.

[236] *Ibid.*, p. 200.

[237] E. W. M. Balfour-Melville, *op. cit.*, *S.H.S. Misc. IX.* 1–56, at 24.

7

THE RANSOM, THE SUCCESSION
AND INTENSIVE GOVERNMENT

On 6 November 1357, a month after King David's return from captivity, a council met at Scone. There the Berwick ransom treaty was read to the assembled clergy, nobles and burgesses, and formally ratified.[1] Well aware of the burdens it had thus undertaken, the council considered how to raise money for the ransom. One expedient was to grant the king the right to requisition wool at cost price and apply the profit to the ransom.[2] Another measure was the appointment of assessors to carry out a general financial assessment (*taxatio*). They were to report the 'true value' of rents, movable goods, crops and livestock (with certain exceptions); even the names of all craftsmen were to be listed. On 14 January 1358, in little more than two months time, the assessors were to present the statistics to the king at Perth [3]—obviously in order that contributions could be levied. While making provision for the ransom, the council held fast to the one basic constitutional principle of medieval Scotland—the king should live of his own. In order to do this, David was authorised to revoke into his own possession all grants he had previously made of lands, rents or customs revenues, and what was thus revoked was not to be regranted save upon 'mature counsel'.

Although the council felt sore pressed by the burden of the ransom it showed no antagonism towards the king. His very presence seems to have inspired the enacting of ordinances designed to reform the judicial administration and restore law and order after the lax rule of the Steward :[4] 'the implication throughout is that the years of

[1] *A.P.S.*, i. 518–21.
[3] *Ibid.*

[2] *Ibid.*, 491.
[4] *Ibid.*, 492.

David's captivity were not years "of good peace" ' [5]—and that only the king could instil good peace. It was ordained that a justice ayre be held throughout the realm; the king was enjoined to preside personally over this ayre in order 'to strike terror into wrongdoers'.[6]

Just as serious as the collapse of law and order during the Steward's lieutenancy was the chaos in financial administration. The accounts of the sheriff of Fife had not been audited since 1343, and those of the sheriffs of Aberdeen and Clackmannan since 1348.[7] For some years after 1357 there was to be a laborious, and ultimately successful, attempt to catch up with arrears.[8] From 1359 almost continuously until 1376 the post of chamberlain was to be held not by a great noble but by a civil servant, Walter of Biggar, whose receipts rose year by year: at the 1362 exchequer audit they totalled £7,380 16s. 4½d. and there was a surplus of £4,544 11s. 11¾d.[9] Such figures do not give a complete picture of crown finance and their relationship to payment of the ransom is a confused one. What is clear, however, is that by Scottish standards large sums of money passed through the chamberlain's hands within a few years of the king's homecoming.

This success was partly, but not wholly, a result of the implementation of the financial measures taken by the council of November 1357. One measure, revocation, was insignificant : little was revoked. Another measure, the requisitioning of the wool crop, proved to have moderately successful results. So also did the chief measure envisaged in 1357—the levying of contributions based upon a new assessment. Although no copy survives of an assessment of 1357 the exchequer accounts show that the work of assessment was at least begun,[10] and that contributions were certainly levied[11]—the first in 1358, the second in 1359 and the third in 1360, after which they temporarily ceased. Meanwhile, in order to meet the ransom payments, one vital item of the king's ordinary revenue had to be diverted. Up to 1357 export duties had been at the rate of 6s. 8d. on a sack of wool, 6s. 8d. on each 200 woolfells and 13s. 4d. on each 'last' of hides (about 100).[12] In the spring of 1358 these duties were doubled. By Whitsuntide 1359 they were trebled.[13] Simultaneously, all the great customs were

[5] Bruce Webster, 'David II and the Government of Fourteenth Century Scotland', *T.R.H.S.* (5th series), XVI. 115–30, at 121.

[6] *A.P.S.*, I. 492.   [7] *E.R.*, I. 545–8, 559–60, 570.

[8] Bruce Webster, *op. cit., T.R.H.S.* (5th series), XVI. 115–30, at 121.

[9] *E.R.*, II. 112, 118.   [10] *Ibid.*, I. 565–81.

[11] E.g. *ibid.*, II. 46–8, 73–5.   [12] *Ibid.*, xl–xli.

[13] *Ibid.*, xl–xli. In 1368 the duties were quadrupled (p. 176 below).

'ordained to the payment of the ransom of the lord king'.[14] While it is uncertain how the first ransom instalment of 10,000 marks was paid it is clear that the great customs paid for the second. John Mercer, burgess and custumar of Perth, had been sent to Flanders as the king's agent,[15] and received from Scotland a total of £7,340 5s. 8½d.; about half came from the customs of the current year, and most of the rest came from the Scottish burgesses, who had combined to advance a loan of 5,000 marks to the king on the security of the customs.[16]

The part played by John Mercer and his fellow-burgesses demonstrates the economic basis on which the increasing political prominence of the merchant burgesses rested, and one by-product of the king's ransom was to establish the burgesses beyond doubt as one of the recognised political classes. They had been summoned to the three successive councils held in 1357—at Perth in January, at Edinburgh in September and at Scone in November—and they had been indisputably recognised as an entity whose approval had to be sought for any measure that relied upon a consensus of responsible opinion. The situation was recognised in the council of November 1357 when the phrase 'the three communities' (*tres communitates*) made its appearance.[17] This apparently new phrase, rendered in English as 'the three estates' (clergy, nobility and burgesses), was to have more reality than the vague 'community of the realm' that had hitherto been used as a catchword to convey an impression of political unanimity; the new concept gave an assured political standing as one of the 'estates' to the burgesses. The view that they were only grudgingly admitted to parliaments and councils, and that for a time they were second-rate members,[18] must be discarded.[19] Their co-operation with David II was one factor in the relative success of the reign after 1357. Burgesses such as John Mercer of Perth, Roger Hogg of Edinburgh and John Crabb of Aberdeen,[20] not only advanced short-term loans to the king,[21] they represented their estate in parliament and council and were those who profited most from the truce with England inaugurated by the ransom treaty of 1357.

The treaty had been followed by a renewal of peaceful communication with England on a scale not seen since 1296. Once more Scot-

[14] *E.R.*, II. 7.
[15] *Ibid.*, 9, 21.
[16] *Ibid.*, 10, 12, 54–6, 83.
[17] *A.P.S.*, I. 491.
[18] Rait, *Parliaments*, pp. 247–9.
[19] See A. A. M. Duncan, *op. cit.*, *S.H.R.*, XLV. 36–58, at 53, n. 1.
[20] The last must not be confused with the famous Flemish engineer of the same name: see E. W. M. Balfour-Melville, 'Two John Crabbs', *S.H.R.*, XXXIX. 31–4.
[21] *E.R.*, II. 2–3, 77, 116, 131, 167.

tish earls, barons, ecclesiastics and burgesses could go on pilgrimage to the shrine of St Thomas at Canterbury, or pass through England to the shrine of St James at Compostela.[22] Once more, Scottish scholars (among them the poet John Barbour) could safely study at the two English universities.[23] But of all the classes of Scotsmen who applied for English safe-conducts it was the merchant burgesses who were the foremost; and it was undoubtedly the new trading opportunities in England that accounted for their increasing prosperity.

There were also many interchanges of a political nature. As soon as her unfaithful husband returned to Scotland Queen Joan led the way south 'to speak with her brother the king [Edward III] and to start negotiations for a greater treaty'[24]—doubtless a final peace. In February 1359 David himself set out for London,[25] apparently in search of the elusive final peace.

When it became clear that this was not to be readily obtained David sent his trusted envoys, Sir Robert Erskine and Norman Leslie, on a mission to France. In 1359 they informed the Dauphin Charles (regent for the captured King John) that David, while a prisoner, 'was never minded to abandon the French alliance, even although, if he had done so, the king of England would have released him more easily from prison'.[26] The envoys proposed that the Scots would renew war on the English if the French would pay King David's ransom. The French were unenthusiastic: the most they could offer was 50,000 marks to be paid at Bruges on 5 April 1360 on condition that the Scots renewed the old alliance and sooner or later made war on the English.[27]

Edward III certainly feared a Scottish attack when he was on campaign in France between October 1359 and May 1360. This latest campaign made it impossible for the French to pay the 50,000 marks they had promised the Scots. On 7 May 1360, with the drafting of the treaty of Brétigny, Edward gained (on parchment at least) much of what he was fighting for in France; although the treaty also stipulated that 'the King of France will altogether abandon the alliance of those of Scotland'[28] nothing so definite resulted. The treaty of Brétigny, as modified by later negotiations at Calais, brought not an Anglo-French peace but a precarious truce that might erupt into war and tempt the Scots to intervene. Meanwhile in midsummer 1360 the

[22] *Rot. Scot.*, i. 859–60.   [23] *Ibid.*, 808–9, 815–6.
[24] *Scalacronica*, p. 176.
[25] *Cal. Docs. Scot.*, iv. No. 27; *Rot. Scot.*, i. 835.
[26] R. Delachenal, *Histoire de Charles V* (Paris, 1909–31), ii. 103–5.
[27] *Ibid.*   [28] *Scalacronica*, p. 195.

Scots stopped further payment of the ransom after belated payment of the second instalment.[29] No further payment was to be made until after a new ransom treaty had been negotiated in 1365.[30]

Whatever the reasons for the lapse in payment it was to be followed by disturbances within Scotland. For a few years after 1357 David had given signs of 'a deliberate effort to rule with circumspection and a wide measure of consent'.[31] In 1357 the Steward was granted the earldom of Strathearn, which had lapsed to the crown; in 1358 William, Lord of Douglas, already supreme on the Borders, was given added prestige by promotion to a newly-created earldom of Douglas.[32] Yet it soon became clear that the great nobles were being excluded from the king's inner counsels. David's mistress, Katherine Mortimer, seemed a fit victim for their resentment. In the summer of 1360 she was treacherously stabbed to death on the road near Soutra.[33] After Katherine's murder a new decisiveness can be seen in the king's actions: Thomas Stewart, Earl of Angus, suspected as instigator of the crime, was warded in Dumbarton Castle,[34] where he shortly died of a fresh outbreak of plague, named 'the second mortality' to distinguish it from the first of 1349. The imprisonment of Angus was followed by the king's seizure of the Earl of Mar's castle of Kildrummy in September 1362,[35] partly on account of an indenture of 24 February 1359 by which Mar had become the liege man of Edward III.[36] Having taken Kildrummy the king went farther north to spend the Christmas of 1362 at Kinloss. The royal visit was cut short in January 1363 by news of disquieting activities on the part of Robert the Steward, his sons and his allies.

It was said that the Steward and the Earls of March and Douglas had complained that money raised for the ransom was wasted 'by evil counsel' and demanded government by 'better counsel'.[37] The mention of the ransom money was a pretext that covered the self-interest and family interests of the conspirators: Douglas was brother-in-law of the disgraced Earl of Mar. The root of complaint was that the king's trusted political advisers were lesser nobles, knights and kirk-

[29] *E.R.*, II. 54–6.

[30] All future ransom negotiations take it for granted that only the first two instalments—20,000 marks—had been paid.

[31] Bruce Webster, *op. cit., T.R.H.S.* (5th series), XVI. 115–30, at 126.

[32] *Scots Peerage*, III. 150; VIII. 257–8.

[33] *Chron. Bower*, II. 365–6; *Scalacronica*, p. 196.

[34] *Chron. Bower*, II. 365; *E.R.*, II. 167–8.

[35] *Chron. Wyntoun*, II. 505; *Scalacronica*, p. 202.

[36] *Rot. Scot.*, I. 836.   [37] *Scalacronica*, pp. 202–3.

men, and that his economic advisers were burgesses. The resulting 'evil counsel' was to be displaced by the 'better counsel' that would naturally be forthcoming from the Steward, Douglas, and their like. The latter also feared the possible consequences of David's latest amorous liaison. For his relationship with Dame Margaret Logie, daughter of Sir Malcolm Drummond and widow of Sir John Logie, was potentially matrimonial.[38] Queen Joan had gone to England in 1357 and stayed there till her death in 1362. David was free to marry for the second time. Dame Margaret had borne a son to her late husband; if she were to prove a fruitful spouse to King David, the Steward's hopes of the crown would be dashed and the ambitions of his many offspring would be frustrated.

Such a prospect, coming as it did at a time when the great nobles were restive, was too much to stomach. In Fordun's words, 'a great sedition and conspiracy arose and was hatched ... by the greater and more powerful men; ... for the magnates united against their lord the king and took counsel with one another that they might bend him to their opinion upon a petition that to everyone seemed unrighteous, or else send him to exile'.[39] The unrighteous petition was probably a demand for the dismissal of the king's counsellors and Margaret Logie. The king would not give way but instead 'gathered together his lieges from the four corners of his land, offering them much money for their wages of war'.[40] David had learned from the English the advantage in discipline to be gained through the payment of wages of war; the lapse in payment of the ransom had allowed him to salt away 5,000 marks in a 'deposit' in Stirling Castle; he drew over £600 for the wages of the host that mustered at Edinburgh.[41] Moreover he could count on the steadfast loyalty of Sir Archibald Douglas, 'the Grim', Sir Robert Erskine and Sir John Danielston, lesser nobles, who had respectively been appointed as well-paid keepers of the key castles of Edinburgh, Stirling and Dumbarton.[42] The king could also take advantage of the irresolution of the opposition: there was an almost superstitious unwillingness to face the royal standard on any field of battle. Among the rebels only the Earl of Douglas showed any initiative. At length David rode rapidly from Edinburgh and caught the earl by surprise at Lanark. Although Douglas escaped, the episode marked the end of the rising: the Steward deserted his allies; Douglas and March had to submit.[43]

[38] R.M.S., i. No. 124.   [39] Chron. Fordun, i. 381.
[40] Ibid.   [41] Chron. Wyntoun, ii. 505; E.R., ii. 164.
[42] E.R., ii. 92, 114, 221.   [43] Scalacronica, p. 203.

In April 1363 the king celebrated his victory by marrying Dame Margaret Logie at Inchmurdoch, a Fife manor of the bishops of St Andrews.[44] The scene of the wedding was also the scene of the humiliation of the late rebels: on 14 May 1363 the Steward was forced to seal a document [45] announcing: 'I will be faithful for all the term of my life to . . . the Lord David, illustrious King of Scots. . . . I will aid, defend, . . . maintain and uphold my lord . . . and his officials and all those faithful to him, whomsoever they be.' The latter were at hand to act as witnesses to the Steward's submission. They included Bishop Landallis, Master Walter Wardlaw, archdeacon of Lothian and secretary to the king, Sir Robert Erskine and Sir Archibald Douglas.

The pacification of the great conspiracy was easier than the achievement of a settlement with England. There is something of an enigma in the fact that although the Scots had deliberately defaulted on the ransom payments this brought no retribution from Edward. But the outbreak of the great conspiracy had coincided with a hardening of his attitude: the situation called for a summit meeting; in November 1363 there were talks at Westminster between the Scottish and English privy councils in the presence of both kings.

The outcome of these talks was the drafting of two memoranda,[46] each listing a number of items that David was to put before the three estates as a possible basis for 'good peace and concord'. In the longer memorandum, dated 27 November 1363, it was stated that David would sound the inclinations of the estates as to whether the King of England might succeed David if the latter died without legitimate offspring. If the estates would yield that vital point Edward would make important concessions: he would forgo the residue of the ransom, release the Scottish hostages, restore Berwick and other occupied territory, compensate the remainder of the disinherited for the annulling of their claims on Scotland, grant back to the Scottish king the lands held in England by his predecessors. Homage would be required only for these English lands, not for the kingdom of Scotland. There were all-embracing and tightly-defined clauses that would take effect if the English king, by succeeding a childless David, became ruler of the two kingdoms. There would be no union of the kingdoms; the name and territorial integrity of the kingdom of Scotland would be carefully preserved and the 'King of England and Scotland' would

[44] *Chron. Wyntoun*, II. 506.   [45] *Chron. Bower*, II. 369–70.
[46] Texts in *A.P.S.*, I. 493–5; *Cal. Docs. Scot.*, IV. Nos. 91, 92.

undergo a second coronation at Scone upon the enthronement stone, which would be restored. A second and shorter memorandum was also drafted by which the succession to a childless David would go not to the English king but to one of his sons who was not heir apparent of England. Since this represented an abatement of Edward's ambitions he would make fewer concessions than those proposed in the first memorandum.

Only the first memorandum, with its carefully-defined safeguards for the preservation of a distinct Scottish identity, deserves to be considered as a possibly statesmanlike attempt to solve the troubled relationship of the two realms; it certainly invites favourable comparison with the terms of the union of 1707. The first memorandum had conceded so much to the Scots that, given English good faith—of which some Scots rightly entertained doubts—the future 'King of England and Scotland' would in Scotland have been a constitutional ruler bound by the terms of a fundamental written constitution. On the other hand, the Scots were called upon to disinherit a native-born Scot whose right of succession had been formally recognised in parliament, and to put in his place an English king whose depredations had brought misery to land and people.

On 4 March 1364 the three estates met in parliament at Scone. The texts of the Westminster memoranda were read aloud[47] and debate followed on one of the most crucial issues ever brought before a Scottish parliament. Unofficial jottings have survived of two arguments that were then presented[48] in favour of the first and second Westminster memorandum respectively. As it happened, some other argument, which eventually carried the day, must have been pressed to uphold the rights of the Steward as heir presumptive. Certainly the brief official record of the parliament states that 'it was expressly answered by the three estates . . . that they in no wise wished to grant, nor in any wise assent to, those things which were sought by the King of England and his council'.[49] The Scottish chroniclers, followed by later historians, make parliament's rejection of the English terms peremptory; and most of them represent David II as being annoyed by the decision.[50] On the contrary it may be inferred that David made no attempt to force either of the Westminster memoranda upon the estates and that both king and parliament were prepared to co-

---

[47] *Chron. Bower*, II. 369–70; *A.P.S.*, I. 492–5.
[48] Texts edited by E. W. M. Balfour-Melville, *op. cit.*, *S.H.S. Misc. IX*. 1–56.
[49] *A.P.S.*, I. 493.
[50] See Ranald Nicholson, *op. cit.*, *S.H.R.*, XLV. 59–78, at 68.

operate to meet the diplomatic crisis that was expected to follow their rejection.

For the next few years there was no specific crisis but rather a prevailing sense that one was impending. Councils or parliaments met in rapid succession to hear the reports of each embassy sent to England and to draft terms to be offered to the English in the succeeding embassy.[51] Edward's demands remained exorbitant. He would not even bind himself to a long truce. All that the Scottish envoys could obtain was an indenture of 20 May 1365 [52] which settled the ransom at £100,000, one third as great again as it had been in 1357. Previous payment of 20,000 marks was to be ignored. The £100,000 were to be paid in yearly instalments of 6,000 marks (£4,000) beginning on 2 February 1366. The truce was to last only until 2 February 1370, when either side might renew the war by giving six months notice to the other. In that case the obligation to pay £100,000 would be cancelled, but the Scots would still be obliged to pay the 80,000 marks outstanding under the treaty of Berwick.

When a council met at Perth on 24 July 1365 the four-year truce was considered inadequate. Once more, large concessions were drafted to obtain a final peace.[53] The English reaction was still unfavourable : by May 1366 they had drawn up 'four points' concerning homage, the succession, territorial cessions, and a reciprocal arrangement for military aid, and insisted that these be regarded as the basis of a final peace.[54] For the next two years one or other of the 'four points' was debated by the three estates, their envoys, and the English. Finally, when parliament met at Scone in June 1368 there was a discussion that lasted at least four days. It was then decided that 'it is not yet needful or expedient to initiate or attempt negotiation upon granting any of the said points' which had been reputed in a previous parliament as 'things unmeet, intolerable and impossible to be observed, and leading to express servitude'.[55] When parliament next met (at Perth in March 1369) [56] a renewal of the Anglo-French war was imminent,[57] and French envoys soon appeared in Scotland.[58]

Well aware of the changed diplomatic scene David accompanied a Scottish embassy to England in June 1369. It was now the turn of Edward to offer concessions, some of which concerned the Borders.

[51] A.P.S., I. 495-6.
[52] Cal. Docs. Scot., IV. No. 108; A.P.S., XII. 12-3; Rot. Scot., I. 894-5.
[53] A.P.S., I. 496-7.   [54] Ibid., 497.
[55] Ibid., 503.   [56] Ibid., 506-7.
[57] May McKisack, The Fourteenth Century, p. 144.
[58] E.R., II. 328, 348.

David had never reconciled himself to a permanent English occupation of the Scottish Marches. Ever since 1357 he had unobtrusively nibbled at the English sphere of influence; he had appointed his own sheriffs in all the Border sheriffdoms and by 1360 he even drew revenue from them all.[59] In 1360, moreover, he had personally concluded an indenture with a representative of the Earl of Hereford and Northampton by which all the revenues of Annandale were to be equally divided between the earl and the king, and disorder was to be repressed to the benefit of both parties.[60] In 1366 the Annandale settlement was again renewed.[61] One of the concessions that David extorted in June 1369 was the extension of the Annandale arrangement to the whole of the sheriffdom of Roxburgh.[62] This agreement was part and parcel of the greatest concession of all—a third ransom treaty of June 1369 [63] which ended discussion of the 'four points' and gave the Scots terms that in the previous few years would have been beyond their wildest hopes. A truce would be observed up to 2 February 1370 and would last for the ensuing fourteen years. The residue of the ransom was now fixed at 56,000 marks—in other words there was a return to the original ransom of 100,000 marks and allowance was made for the 20,000 marks paid under the treaty as well as for the four instalments of 6,000 marks already paid under the 1365 treaty. Payment of the remaining 56,000 marks was to be at the rate of 4,000 marks a year for the next fourteen years. It is incongruous that at a time when David's revenues were more flourishing than they had ever been,[64] the ransom instalment was reduced to a lower figure than ever.

To secure a peaceful Scotland in his rear Edward had paid what was for him a heavy price, for the renewal of the Anglo-French war occurred in circumstances that favoured the French rather than the English.[65] David was quite ready to fish in troubled waters. By June 1370 he was once more in London and to outward appearances on the friendliest of terms with Edward,[66] but simultaneously he sent Archibald the Grim on a mission to the French court.[67] Thus the ultimate trend of David's diplomacy remains an enigma: although he was playing off one side against the other he had not definitely committed himself to either the French or the English by the time he died.

[59] *Ibid.*, 34–43.
[60] *Cal. Docs. Scot.*, IV. No. 47.
[61] *Ibid.*, IV. Nos. **127, 128.**
[62] *Rot. Scot.*, I. 939.
[63] *Ibid.*, 933, 934–5, 938–9.
[64] P. 177 below.
[65] May McKisack, *The Fourteenth Century*, pp. 143–5.
[66] *Cal. Docs. Scot.*, IV. No. 173; *Rot. Scot.*, I. 938.
[67] *E.R.*, II. 356, **358.**

The extent to which nationalism figured in David II's diplomacy is difficult to determine. One of the charges that has been brought against him is that he was 'a lover of the gaudy chivalrous diversions of his day'.[68] Certainly David's long reign coincided with an upsurge of chivalry in Europe [69] which sometimes diverted attention from incipient nationalism. In 1365 Jean Froissart, whose chivalric chronicles and poems found a ready market wherever a French-speaking aristocracy existed, was welcomed at the Scottish court.[70] Patronage for literary works of a chivalric nature,[71] suits of tournament armour, a reported interest in the crusade, all combine to give a picture of King David as a man to whom chivalry meant much—and the current father-figure of European chivalry was none other than Edward III. Chivalry was undoubtedly the link in the special relationship that brought David and Edward together.[72] Yet it would be wrong to assume that chivalry was in either case so dominant a motive as to exclude every other. If David attended flamboyant tournaments and banquets in London he also engaged in hard bargaining. While ostensibly observing the truce he had nonetheless made inroads on English influence in the Scottish Marches, had won new and lucrative opportunities for the Scottish merchant burgesses and brought prosperity both to them and to the royal finances. Despite his chequered career he was to leave Scotland just as free and independent as it had been at his accession.

Though it is misleading to think of the later years of the reign of David II wholly in terms of Anglo-Scottish relations, the important developments that took place within Scotland itself were all influenced, directly or indirectly, by one aspect of Anglo-Scottish relations—what has melodramatically been styled 'the incubus of the ransom money'.[73] In accordance with the second ransom treaty of 1365, which had taken the place of the first ransom treaty of 1357, the Scots had not only to pay ransom instalments of 6,000 marks (£4,000) a year but had to bear in mind the possibility that the truce might nonetheless end on 2 February 1370, whereupon they would be liable to all the penalties and sanctions of the 1357 treaty unless they

[68] A. Lang, *History of Scotland*, 1. 267.

[69] For its characteristics see Arthur Bryant, *The Age of Chivalry* (1963) and E. K. Milliken, *Chivalry in the Middle Ages* (1968).

[70] See A. H. Diverres, 'Jean Froissart's Journey to Scotland', *Forum for Modern Language Studies*, 1. 54–63.

[71] *The Buik of Alexander* (S.T.S.), 1. cxcv–cc, cciii, ccviii–ccx.

[72] 'For thare wes rycht gret specialté/Betwen hym and the King Edward' (*Chron. Wyntoun*, 11. 501–2).   [73] George Burnett, *E.R.*, 11. xlv.

had meanwhile paid the total arrears under that original ransom treaty. Thus the council that met at Holyrood on 8 May 1366 [74] concerned itself not only with the matter of raising ransom instalments of 6,000 marks a year but with preparation for payment of 80,000 marks within less than four years. Just as the council of November 1357 had called for a new survey of the country's financial and economic resources so also did the Holyrood council of May 1366. There was to be a general assessment of all lands and rents within the realm, both ecclesiastical and lay.[75] When parliament met at Scone on 20 July 1366,[76] a mere seven weeks later, most of the results of the new assessment were already available.[77]

In most cases two figures were given: the first was the *Antiqua Taxatio*, an assessment of lands and rents dating from the time of Alexander III,[78] and the second was the *Verus Valor*, the 'true' or current value as determined in the recent assessment. A comparison of the *Antiqua Taxatio* and the *Verus Valor* indicates an apparent wholesale decline in landed wealth between the later years of Alexander III and those of David II. For in monetary terms landed income had been halved in a period of less than a century: according to the *Antiqua Taxatio* the assessment of the Scottish bishoprics (including all kirks) came to £15,002 16s. 0d.; by the *Verus Valor* it came to only £9,396 6s. 6d.; in the twenty-two sheriffdoms for which returns are given the *Antiqua Taxatio* amounted to £48,249 7s. 8d. and the *Verus Valor*, though not fully ascertained, came to about £23,250. It has thus been affirmed that 'evidence of the poverty of the country appears from the taxations [assessments] which the estates imposed to try to pay off the ransom'.[79] Yet although the decline was real enough in monetary terms, money is not a fixed measure. One of the causes of the general economic malaise in fourteenth-century Europe was deflation caused by the drain of gold and silver to the Orient to pay for luxury goods. The new assessment of 1366 need not necessarily be taken as proof of 'poverty' but may be taken as proof of falling prices and rents and general deflation. If there was an economic crisis it seems to have been a crisis that concerned the value of money rather than the production of real wealth in the form of goods and services. It was no easy task to adjust the coinage to deal with either inflation or deflation, especially since it was thought desirable to keep Scottish coins on a par with those of England. The parity

[74] *A.P.S.*, I. 497.
[75] *Ibid.*   [76] *Ibid.*, 498.   [77] *Ibid.*, 498–501.
[78] *Ibid.*, 499–501, 476.   [79] J. D. Mackie, *History of Scotland*, p. 88.

which had been precariously maintained was lost when a royal precept of 7 October 1367 [80] ordered that thenceforth a further tenpence
should be coined from each pound weight (Scots) of silver. In practice this meant that the Scots were minting 23.5d. from the ounce of
silver while the English minted only 22.5d. The debasement of 1367
was thus 'far from considerable',[81] though it pointed the way to subsequent drastic devaluations of the Scottish coinage in relation to that
of England.[82]

Whatever the significance of the figures of the new assessment of
1366, its importance for contemporaries was its use for the levying of
contributions. These were granted at varying rates and for only a year
at a time but came by the end of the reign to approximate to a regular
income tax. Although the contributions had crept into government
finance under the wing of the ransom it was parliament itself that
allowed them to be used for other purposes : when the Scone parliament of July 1365 ordained a large contribution of 8,000 marks it
stipulated that the money was to be used 'for the expenses of the king
and to pay his debts within the realm, and for the payment of the envoys, and for nothing more, since the great custom is ordained for
the said payment of £4,000 for the ransom'.[83] Lest the insufficiency
of the customs became the excuse for direct taxation in the shape of
contributions, the Scone parliament of 12 June 1368 re-affirmed that
the great customs should pay for the ransom and quadrupled the
export duties[84] so that they were four times the rate of 1357, 26s. 8d.
thereafter being levied on each sack of wool.

The quadrupling of the customs duties did not stop further parliamentary grants of contributions. Even although these were appropriated by parliament to some specific item of royal expenditure,
attempts to segregate them from ransom funds proved cumbersome
and unworkable. By the end of the reign all the customs were paid to
the king's chamberlain, along with contributions and other revenue,
and were used indiscriminately both for ransom payments and for
ordinary royal expenditure.[85] The king had thus won full control over
all sources of revenue, whether or not they were supposed to be set
aside for the ransom ; it was he (and succeeding kings) who benefited
from the quadrupling of the great customs. In addition another
measure increased the economic resources of the crown : the parlia-

[80] A.P.S., I. 502–3.   [81] G. Burnett, E.R., II. xcviii.
[82] By 1390 the ratio of Scottish coins to their English counterparts stood at
about 2:1; by 1451 2½:1; by 1456 3:1; by 1467 3½:1; by 1475 4:1 (R. W.
Cochran-Patrick, Records of the Coinage of Scotland, I. lxxvi).
[83] A.P.S., I. 498.   [84] Ibid., 502–4.   [85] E.R., II. lxxii.

ment which met at Scone on 27 September 1367 elected a commission representative of the three estates to consider the king's livelihood, and issued a sweeping act of revocation designed to restore to the crown all lands and revenues granted from the royal demesne ever since the death of Robert I in 1329.[86]

The measures taken in the closing years of the reign thus show King David's adroit manipulation of the constant obligation to pay the ransom, so as to increase the financial resources of the crown. The ransom itself was not always neglected : although only two payments of 10,000 marks had been made under the first ransom treaty of 1357, four payments of 6,000 marks were made under the second ransom treaty of 1365 and one payment of 4,000 marks was made under the third ransom treaty of 1369. At the exchequer audit held at Perth on 15 February 1371, a week before the king's death, the chamberlain reported that he had already set aside 4,000 marks for the next ransom instalment due at midsummer 1371, and he remarked that after that forthcoming payment the total outstanding debt on the ransom would stand at 48,000 marks.[87] The extent of David's financial triumph can be seen in his last exchequer audit covering the year from 19 January 1370 to 15 February 1371 : the chamberlain's total receipts were £15,359 14s. 9¼d.[88] The vast bulk of these receipts was forthcoming from the swelling export duties and contributions engendered by the beneficent 'incubus' of the ransom. It is doubtful if any medieval Scottish king, either before or after King David, was in so strong a financial position.

While the king's success is obvious it is less easy to determine how it affected the economic wellbeing of his subjects. The ineffective revocation of 1357 and the more effective revocation of 1367 were measures that—however unjust—became almost standard practice in succeeding reigns. The repudiation of royal debts in 1370 was also unjust; but in this respect David II was a model of financial rectitude when compared with Edward III. More fundamental was the imposition of higher export duties which might well have crippled the export trade. Yet nothing of the sort took place : the revenue from the customs increased year by year to a total of £9,521 2s. 8½d. in 1371;[88(b)] and the volume of exports did not diminish until after the king's death. In the matter of trade the interests of the king and the merchant burgesses coincided. It was typical that a royal charter of 28 March 1364[89] in favour of 'our beloved

---

[86] *A.P.S.*, I. 501–2. [87] *E.R.*, II. 355. [88] *Ibid.*

[88(b)] *Ibid.*, 351. [89] *Burghs Convention Recs.*, I. 538–41.

Scottish burgesses', assured them the right to buy and sell anywhere within the trade precinct of their own burgh, while foreign
merchants were permitted to buy and sell only from and to the merchants of the burghs, who were thus guaranteed their position as
middlemen with the attendant profits. The charter also forbade 'any
bishop, prior or other kirkman, any earl, baron or other layman,
whatsoever may be his rank, to buy or sell wool, skins, hides or other
merchandise ... save only from [or to] the merchants of the burghs
within whose liberties [trade precincts] they live'.

While the king's financial policies met with no ascertainable opposition from the burgesses they ran into undoubted opposition in an
area scarcely used to any government control, let alone taxation.
When the functions of central government were few, so also were the
political differences between Highlands and Lowlands. When under
David II these functions increased, so also did the differences between
the Lowlands, amenable to government control, and the Highlands,
which were not. The long career of John of the Isles as a virtually independent potentate illustrates the growing difficulties that faced the
crown in trying to hold Highlands and Lowlands in some sort of
unity. Although John seems to have dropped his lukewarm adherence
to Edward III he certainly resented David's attempts to extend to the
Isles the assessment of 1366 and the contributions that followed upon
it. He was not alone in his opposition to the new measures: the members of the 'Highland Party' that had formed during the Steward's
lieutenancy were frequently (with the exception of the canny Steward
himself) described as 'contumaciously absent' from parliament.[90]
When the act of revocation was passed by the Scone parliament of
September 1367[91] it became clear that it might bear heavily upon
Robert the Steward, the Earl of Ross, and especially upon John of
the Isles.[92] In fact, the act of revocation was not invariably put into
effect: it gave the king a bargaining position vis-à-vis the magnates.
John of Lorne and Gillespic Campbell made their peace with the
king and attended parliament at Perth on 6 March 1369, but John
of the Isles remained obdurate. It was ordained that the king should
force him and his sons to obedience so that they should stand to law
and undergo services and burdens as did the king's 'inland' subjects.[93]
These were no empty words. In the winter of 1369 the king led an
expedition to Inverness, where John arrived to make his submission.

[90] *A.P.S.*, I. 498–9.
[91] *Ibid.*, 499–501.
[92] *Ibid.*, 528–9.
[93] *Ibid.*, 506.

On 15 November 1369 an indenture was sealed in which he acknowledged that 'my redoubtable lord, David, by the grace of God, illustrious King of Scots, has been moved against my person by reason of certain negligences committed by me. . . .' [94] John humbly begged remission, which the king graciously conceded in return for hostages and an undertaking to obey royal officials and pay contributions. This transaction at Inverness was accompanied by another : a few months after the death of King David, William, Earl of Ross, was to present a *querimonia* [95] or complaint, on the subject of the king's conduct towards him and his brother ; Earl William had been forced to ratify a grant of lands to Sir Walter Leslie 'on account of the rigour of the same lord king and by fear of his wrath'.[96] In the last parliament of the reign, on 23 October 1370, the earl was forced to resign all his lands and to receive them back under the conditions of a tailzie [97] in favour of Sir Walter Leslie, who was eventually to succeed to the earldom of Ross.

The king's treatment of the Highland magnates was typical of his treatment of the magnates as a whole. While royal patronage went to a nobility of service, the 'stowt', and almost all who held the rank of earl, were cowed into submission. On one pretext or another, the magnates were made the victims of insecure tenure and found their way of life increasingly subject to royal surveillance : it was enacted by the Scone parliament of June 1368 that all dissensions among the magnates and nobles were to be settled by the king and by way of common justice, 'which our lord the king is bound always to administer impartially, without favour to anyone'.[98] Latterly, no noble, no matter how great, could offend the king—or the queen—with impunity : in the winter of 1368, when Robert the Steward and some of his sons did something to incur the wrath of Queen Margaret, she prevailed upon David to arrest and imprison them.[99] Although the Steward was soon released, his plumage was again ruffled in 1369 when he was deprived of his earldom of Strathearn for a few months.[100] And in 1370 the troublesome Earl of Mar was under arrest as a prisoner on the Bass Rock.[101] The traditional view that the reign marked 'the beginning of the end of medieval Scottish govern-

[94] *Ibid.*, xii. 16–7.   [95] *Aberdeen-Banff Illustrations*, ii. 387–9.
[96] *Ibid.*   [97] *A.P.S.*, i. 537–8.   [98] *Ibid.*, 503.
[99] *Chron. Bower*, ii. 379–80; *E.R.*, ii. 309, 347.
[100] *H.B.C.*, p. 489; *Morton Registrum*, ii. Nos. 96, 101. By 18 February 1370 he was once more styled Earl of Strathearn (*A.P.S.*, i. 534).
[101] *E.R.*, ii. 357.

ment' has been justifiably challenged by the affirmation that 'there was no collapse in David's reign . . . the king was not overwhelmed by the power of his barons. Any collapse, if collapse there was, came after 1371.'[102]

In his dealings with the Scottish kirk David could show the same firmness that he displayed towards the great nobles. But the firmness was tempered by a conventional piety demonstrated in pilgrimages to Canterbury, kirk-building in honour of St Monan (who miraculously extracted an arrow barb from the king's head),[103] and the grant of a specific privilege that the Scottish bishops had long sought—the right to make testaments bequeathing their goods.[104] For the Scottish episcopate included persons who were closely associated with the king : Bishop Landallis had served him year after year as a diplomatist, so also had Master Walter Wardlaw, who had been the king's secretary before he was rewarded with the bishopric of Glasgow in 1368.

The prospect of appointment to a bishopric was an inducement that must have fired the ambition of the ecclesiastics who largely staffed the king's household and administration. Ecclesiastical preferment was not, however, the only inducement; there was beginning to be a real civil service : 'from the 1360's we first hear of the king's secretary, apparently as keeper of the privy seal. . . . From 1359 comes the first surviving example of the king's signet. These are only slight signs, but they indicate a gradual development in administration.'[105] Simultaneously government and administration were becoming less haphazard, more regular. Towards the end of the reign exchequer audits, often attended by the king himself, were regularly held at Perth in January of each year. The comparatively large bulk of parliamentary, exchequer and chancery records of the period 1357–1371 indicates not only the increasing regularity of government but its increasing intensity; and these records disprove the old view that David led a life of ease and show instead that he 'was much concerned in the business of government'.[106] Indeed his handling of this business was sometimes thought *too* personal : the very intensity of government led to the growth of rules and customs of which David occasionally fell foul.[107(a)]

[102] Bruce Webster, *op. cit.*, *T.R.H.S.* (5th series), XVI. 115–30, at 130.

[103] *Chron. Pluscarden*, I. 294.

[104] *R.M.S.*, I. No. 372; *Chron. Bower*, II. 389–90; see G. Donaldson, 'The rights of the Scottish crown in episcopal vacancies', *S.H.R.*, XLV. 27–35.

[105] Bruce Webster, *op. cit.*, *T.R.H.S.* (5th series), XVI. 115–30, at 121.

[106] *Ibid.*, p. 118.   [107(a)] E.g. *E.R.*, II. 111, 361.

But there were compensations for such peccadilloes. It is striking that Wyntoun specifically commends the king for his administration of justice : [107(b)] his reference to the frequent holding of parliament, and the speedy justice to be obtained there, clearly shows that its function as a court was still looked upon as of foremost importance. Possibly for this reason councils of the three estates were upgraded soon after 1357 to the status of 'full' or 'general' councils.[108] Freed (save on rare occasions) from the burden of judicial business, they had the same composition as parliament and were equally competent to deal with all affairs of state. In parliament also there was an attempt to streamline business by making special arrangements for its judicial functions : in the Perth parliament of February 1370 the three estates elected six clerics to represent the clergy, ten knights and four esquires to represent the baronage, and seven burgesses to represent the burghs. This body was to deal with 'those matters which concern common justice, namely falsed dooms, *questiones* and other plaints which ought to be discussed, settled and determined by parliament'.[109]

The delegation of judicial powers by parliament can be traced back at least to 1341 ; delegation was a 'natural and obvious device' [110] and was not restricted to judicial matters. Committees were appointed which reported their findings or recommendations to parliament as a whole. Commissions were appointed which did not report back but were invested with the full authority of parliament to 'determine' the points referred to them. A further development took place in the Scone parliament of September 1367 when 'certain persons were elected to hold the parliament, and leave was given to others to go home on account of the harvest'.[111] Leave to go home—*licentia redeundi* or *licentia recedendi*—was to be accorded to members of parliament from time to time during the next three reigns. In such cases parliament met only to delegate its full power to a commission that was under no obligation to account for its decisions to any future parliament. In 1367, admittedly, the commission was a large one— fifteen ecclesiastics, thirteen nobles (few of them great) and thirteen burgesses. A similar procedure was adopted in the Perth parliaments of March 1369 and February 1370.[112] Lord Hailes, finding little to say in his *Annals* concerning the year 1367, had some suspicion that

[107(b)] *Chron. Wyntoun*, II. 498, 506–7.

[108] E.g. *A.P.S.*, I. 503, 526. In discussing the circumstances that inspired this change of nomenclature R. K. Hannay ('On "Parliament" and "General Council"', *S.H.R.*, XVIII. 157–70, at 161–4) makes darkness more obscure.

[109] *A.P.S.*, I. 508.

[110] Rait, *Parliaments*, p. 349.

[111] *A.P.S.*, I. 501.

[112] *Ibid.*, 506, 507–8.

the king was using this device for his own nefarious ends.[113] But it would be wrong to dismiss out of hand the reasons officially given for the grant of *licentia redeundi* : the harvest or a scarcity of provisions were matters of some consequence. Moreover the parliamentary committees and commissions fit into the broad pattern of a government that had expanded its functions, subjected them to routine and regularity, and ruled with an unexampled intensiveness.

None of this would have been possible without a forceful king. In the eleven years after Neville's Cross David had suffered, literally as well as figuratively, from the slings and arrows of outrageous fortune. He had come back to Scotland, toughened by adversity and years of painstaking political intrigue, to govern his land with 'radure' so that 'nane durst welle wythstand his will' ; all were forced to be obedient, for he would always chastise 'mysdoaris'.[114] Political offenders suffered a chastisement that was sometimes capricious; but in the last years of the reign it was never cruel or vindictive; political misdemeanours might bring the loss of lands but no political offence was punished by execution. It is thus all the more striking that David, with few assets save his own astuteness and forceful personality, made himself so completely the master of Scotland. Only in his second wife did he meet his match.

When David had married Dame Margaret Logie 'by force of love which conquers everything' [115] he had 'magnificently exalted her as queen' [116] and 'endowed her with many lands and possessions'.[117] The weakness of Queen Margaret's position was that she did not provide the king with an heir. That was hardly her fault : she had already proved her fruitfulness while David had not proved his. In an attempt to retain her influence she may have feigned pregnancy.[118] Whatever the reason—and it seems to have involved the temporary imprisonment of the Steward in the winter of 1368—Margaret fell from royal favour. By 1369 David had cast amorous eyes upon Agnes Dunbar.[119] It was assumed that 'Lady Margaret Logie, onetime queen' would content herself with a pension of £100 which the king had thoughtfully assigned to her 'after the celebration of divorce'.[120] Instead she secretly boarded a ship in the Forth and made her way to Avignon, where her no doubt considerable charms won her the kindly eye of Pope Gregory XI and his cardinals. When Dame Margaret instituted

[113] Hailes, *Annals*, II. 316.
[115] *Scalacronica*, p. 203.
[117] *Chron. Fordun*, I. 382.
[119] E.R., II. 328, 345, 357.

[114] *Chron. Wyntoun*, II. 498.
[116] *Chron. Bower*, II. 379.
[118] *Chron. Pluscarden*, I. 307.
[120] *Ibid.*, 345.

an appeal in the *curia* against her divorce there was talk of placing Scotland under an interdict until her death removed the danger in 1375.[121]

It was ironic that David II should leave a troublesome legacy to the Steward in the shape of the pertinacious Margaret Logie. When Margaret had fallen into disgrace the Steward had been admitted to something approaching royal favour. Yet, even then, David was probably reluctant to admit the inevitability of a Stewart succession. He himself was scarcely forty-seven years old and despite previous disappointments contemplated a third marriage. Agnes Dunbar had first been granted a pension of sixty marks,[122] fit enough for a royal mistress but not for a royal bride. The prospect of honourable matrimony opened before her eyes in a royal charter [123] which granted her a life pension of a thousand marks for her trousseau and adornment. Eleven days later, on 22 February 1371, King David unexpectedly died in Edinburgh. The long-suffering Steward at last secured his royal heritage.

[121] *Chron. Bower*, II. 380.   [122] *R.M.S.*, I. App. 2, No. 1652.
[123] *Ibid.*, App. 2, No. 32; *Morton Registrum*, II. No. 108.

8

THE ACCESSION OF THE STEWARTS, THE BEGINNING OF THE GREAT SCHISM AND OTHER AFFLICTIONS

If the achievements of David II are to be seen in perspective they must be viewed not only with the triumphs of Robert I in the foreground but with the failures of the first Stewart kings in the background. For almost fifty years, until the new dynasty showed some mettle in the person of James I, Scotland was to be racked by a misgovernance which proved beyond doubt that there was no substitute for a masterful king. Henceforward the threats that had to be faced were to be not external but internal: the problem of the Highlands became increasingly acute; a comparable problem arose in the Borders, an area that until the wars of independence had been among the most settled in the whole kingdom; and connected with these changes was the rise of overmighty subjects such as the Douglases and the MacDonalds of the Isles.

Robert the Steward had reached what was then the advanced age of fifty-five when he succeeded to the crown as Robert II. He was, reports the chronicler Bower, impressive in appearance, humble, mild, affable, cheerful and honourable.[1] It was the new king's humility that was the most significant of his attributes. Despite the opportunities that had presented themselves during his uncle's reign, Robert had only feebly and fruitlessly tried to elevate himself above the rest of the baronage; only two years before his accession he had been imprisoned in Lochleven.[2] Although the new king was a grandson of Robert I, the line he represented was baronial rather than royal. The contemporary poet, Barbour, is known to have written

[1] *Chron. Bower*, II. 383.　　　　　[2] P. 179 above.

upon 'The Stewartis Orygenale'[3] and to have tried to throw lustre on the new dynasty by a fabulous Trojan descent, but the errors in this timely essay in genealogy were detected by Abbot Bower;[4] and it was no secret that the Stewarts were a cadet branch of the English Fitz-alans.

Robert II's origins would have mattered little if he had shown something of the courage and vigour of his grandfather. Instead, the absence of these qualities was at once revealed when the first Earl of Douglas ominously let it be seen that he thought himself as 'royal' as any Stewart and put himself forward as a contender for the succession on the death of David II. At Linlithgow Douglas made some show of force and claimed the throne by reason of a flimsy connection with the Balliols or Comyns. He was prevailed upon to give up his unrealistic pretensions only through the forceful intervention of his stepfather, Sir Robert Erskine, George Dunbar, Earl of March, and John Dunbar, the earl's brother.[5] Thereupon the grateful new king bestowed honoraria not only upon the Erskines and Dunbars[6] but upon Douglas, who was made justiciar south of Forth and warden of the East March.[7] His son and heir, Sir James Douglas, was given an annuity of a hundred marks, the hand of the king's fourth daughter, Isabella, and a gift of £500.[8] Opposition was bought off; loyalty was not taken for granted but was richly rewarded.

On 26 March 1371, after the 'royd harsk begynnyng'[9] of the Linlithgow incident, the king was crowned and anointed at Scone by Bishop Landallis.[10] A notarial instrument was drawn up to record not only the circumstances of Robert II's coronation but also to record at much greater length the recognition of his first-born son, John, Earl of Carrick, as heir apparent to the crown. The prolixity of the language affirming him to be the king's true heir, and the fact that his right to succeed was first expounded in the privy council,[11] suggest that questions were raised, or were expected to be raised in future. In contrast to the childless David II the new king is known to have had at least twenty-one offspring, of whom only four were indisputably born in lawful wedlock.[12] John, Earl of Carrick, was not among these

[3] *Chron. Wyntoun*, II. 320. [4] *Chron. Bower*, II. 60, n.
[5] *Chron. Wyntoun*, III. 8; *Chron. Bower*, II. 382; *Chron. Pluscarden*, I. 310; Godscroft, *Douglas and Angus*, I. 99; *E.R.*, II. lxxvii; *Scots Peerage*, V. 594; Balfour-Melville, *James I*, p. 3.
[6] *E.R.*, II. 364, 366, 433, 435, 460, 672. [7] *Ibid.*, 394, 433, 435, 462.
[8] *Ibid.*, 364, 393, 433, 434, 435, 460, 501. [9] *Chron. Wyntoun*, III. 9.
[10] *Chron. Bower*, II. 386; *E.R.*, II. 393; *A.P.S.*, I. 545. [11] *A.P.S.*, I. 545-7.
[12] *Scots Peerage*, I. 15-7; *E.R.*, IV. cliii–clxx.

four. He was eldest of the 'many children of both sexes ... fair to behold' alluded to in a papal dispensation of 22 November 1347 [13] that belatedly permitted marriage between Robert the Steward and his first wife, Elizabeth Mure (or More) and declared their offspring legitimate. John had been born some ten years before the dispensation.[14] By canon law the subsequent marriage of parents made their issue legitimate; but it was questionable whether this could apply to a child born of parents who were within the 'forbidden degrees' of consanguinity.[15] Was John Stewart, technically speaking, born in incest and incapable of legitimation; and, if so, could he succeed his father on the throne? The four children of the Steward's second marriage to Euphemia of Ross were undoubtedly legitimate; one of these was Walter Stewart, Earl of Atholl, who, in a quest for the crown, would be a party to the assassination of James I, Carrick's son, in 1437. Yet it was probably not dubiety over the dispensation of 1347 but rather fear of some Douglas or English claim that caused concern over the succession: when the Franco-Scottish alliance was renewed in 1371 the possibility of a future succession dispute was envisaged;[16] in a parliament at Scone in April 1373 Robert II expressed a wish to end 'the uncertainty of the succession', and, in particular, to avoid the evils that might arise through the accession of females to the throne. Thus a tailzie was drawn up with the approval of the three estates.[17] The succession was to pass from father to son, starting with the king's first-born son, John Stewart, Earl of Carrick. If his line of descent should fail, the succession would then pass successively on the same terms to the lines of descent respectively headed by his younger brothers, Robert, Earl of Fife and Menteith, Alexander, Lord of Badenoch, David, Earl of Strathearn, and Walter, Earl of Atholl. Although the succession had passed to Robert II through a female the Scots were now imitating the French example of requiring unbroken male descent. Only on the failure of legitimate father-to-son descent in respect of the five surviving sons of Robert II's two marriages would the succession pass to heirs general.

Meanwhile the establishment of the new king's sons and daughters, legitimate or otherwise, in a landed status befitting their dignity, amounted to a large territorial settlement throughout Scot-

---

[13] *Cal. Papal Petitions*, I. 124; Dowden, *Bishops*, p. 65.
[14] *Scots Peerage*, I. 17.
[15] *Scot. Legal Hist.*, pp. 71–2, 78; *E.R.*, IV. cliv–clv; Balfour-Melville, *James I*, p. 4.
[16] Text of the treaty in *E.R.*, III. cii–ciii.
[17] *A.P.S.*, I. 549.

land.[18] Some of these progeny had been well-provided before their blood baronial was transformed into blood royal. Any deficiencies in land or title were soon made up. Most notable was the elevation of David, elder son of the king's second marriage, to the dignity of 'Earl Palatine of Strathearn and Caithness'.[19] The grant of these two earldoms in regality may well have been compensation for the precedence given to the sons of the first marriage. By 1377 seven of the existing sixteen earldoms (Carrick, Menteith, Fife, Atholl, Strathearn, Caithness and Sutherland) were in the hands of the king himself or his sons,[20] and through the marriage of his sons and daughters the new king was closely connected with the foremost noble families : the Earls of Moray and Douglas, the Lord of the Isles, the constable and the marshal, were, or soon became, sons-in-law to the king.

But the network of marriage and kinship was spread too widely to withstand strain. Nearly all the nobility of Scotland had been stewartised. Not all Stewarts were 'sib to the king', but many undoubtedly *were*, and consequently thought themselves specially privileged, or even above the law. It was to prove difficult enough for Robert II to hold patriarchal sway over his extended family circle, let alone rule Scotland. The chronicler Bower, flattering enough in his remarks concerning the king, significantly continues : 'But what shall I say concerning his sons? Some were peaceable and benign, some insolent and malign.'[21] On the whole, however, a sort of tranquillity settled upon Scotland while the new royal family digested the territorial sweetmeats that Robert II provided. The years between 1371 and 1378 had few of the stirring events that attracted the attention of chroniclers. The keynote of this first phase of Stewart rule was continuity from the days of David II.

It was in the sphere of royal finance that a change from the governmental policies bequeathed by David was to become most significant. At first, in finance, as in other respects, continuity was obvious. The chamberlain's accounts, which can be regarded as rough guides to the state of royal finances, show that no marked deterioration set in for some time. In the financial year 1373–4 the total receipts came to £14,584 9s. 9¾d. (including about £10,000 from the

[18] Grant, *Social and Economic Development*, pp. 207–8.

[19] *R.M.S.*, i. Nos. 389, 526, 666; *Morton Registrum*, ii. No. 121; Innes, *Sketches*, p. 213.

[20] *Scots Peerage, passim.*   [21] *Chron. Bower*, ii. 383.

great customs) [22] and there was a surplus of £1,878 17s. 1¼d.[23] The figures for this year were therefore almost as impressive as for the last financial year of David's reign. Moreover the receipts included the proceeds of a contribution of a shilling in the pound : [24] the sheriff-doms contributed £1,681 18s. 10d., the burghs £739 8s. 1d., and the clergy £166 9s. 5d.[25] Since these figures are incomplete no precise deductions may be made from them. More significant is a separate list of the total contributions raised in each sheriffdom.[26] Gillespic Campbell as sheriff of Argyll raised £56 2s. 4½d. From Lorne came at least £60 ; and from the lands of John of the Isles came at least £133 6s. 8d.[27] For the moment the Gaelic magnates were ready to co-operate with the new dynasty ; and the successful levying of national taxation in their lands might have effectively integrated their do-mains with the rest of Scotland. But after the contribution of 1373 no other was to be levied until 1399.[28] The practice of direct taxation, painfully evolved from David II's ransom, was allowed to lapse.

Other lapses followed. Sheriffs, and even custumars, were lax in attending the exchequer audit. In the last chamberlain's account of the reign there was no income from feudal reliefs 'because the sheriffs did not compear'.[29] In 1370–71 the chamberlain had received more than £9,000 from the great customs; in 1389–90, when the rate of duty was still the same, the total customs collected came to less than £5,000,[30] of which the chamberlain received little more than half.[31] For the gross receipts from the customs 'came to be encroached on year by year by grants of annuity, remissions of duty and the expenses of the king's family and household'.[32] In compensation, the diplo-macy of Robert II was not as costly as that of David II had been. Thus until 1382 the chamberlain's account showed falling receipts but no deficit ; and in 1380 the surplus amounted almost to £3,000.[33] But 1382, when Robert Stewart, Earl of Fife and Menteith, took over as chamberlain, brought an abrupt change : there was an immediate and lasting drop in the chamberlain's total receipts and from then until the end of the reign they ranged from little more than £3,000 to little more than £1,000. And although expenditure also tended to diminish there were occasional heavy deficits, amounting in 1385–6 to over £1,000.[34]

[22] *E.R.*, ii. 429.   [23] *Ibid.*, 428–38.   [24] *Ibid.*, 418, 430.
[25] *Ibid.*, 430–1. In the next financial year arrears of £180 16s. 8d. were received (*ibid.*, 457).
[26] *Ibid.*, 417–27.   [27] *Ibid.*, 431.   [28] P. 217 below.
[29] *E.R.*, iii. 203, 697.   [30] *Ibid.*, 202–13.   [31] *Ibid.*, 697.
[32] *Ibid.*, lix.   [33] *Ibid.*, 28–32.   [34] *Ibid.*, 679–84.

The events that had preceded the appointment of Robert Stewart to the post of chamberlain were dramatic. The previous holder of the office was John Lyon. Once the secretary of David II, he had been kept in office by Robert II, who in 1372 granted him the thanage of Glamis [35] and in 1377 made him chamberlain. Lyon made a clandestine marriage with Jean, one of the king's daughters, and by 1379 was duly recognised as the king's son-in-law and knighted. His advancement, so it was said, owed much to the good offices of Sir James Lindsay of Crawford, who, considering that his services had been insufficiently esteemed, murdered the thane of Glamis on 4 November 1382. The murderer was at the time sheriff of Lanark, and had recently been justiciar north of Forth. He was also the king's nephew.[36] Failure to punish the crime perhaps set as bad an example as the crime itself. Nor was it an isolated occurrence during the reign—the Scone parliament of March 1372 had seen danger signals in the many homicides that had recently been committed. Emergency measures were passed [37] that were to remain in force for three years, but when the three estates met in general council in Holyrood Abbey in November 1384 they asserted that 'offences and outrageous crimes have been wont to be committed against the law for no short time'.[38] A king who was neither a military leader nor a forceful personality had little chance of keeping law and order.

Robert II was only too anxious to shelve his responsibility. The first act of the Holyrood general council of 1384 was to record his desire to administer the laws of his kingdom justly and by the advice of his council. He undertook 'promptly and willingly to reform and repair any of his actions which had been negligent or contrary to law'; anyone might complain of him in his council and he would accept his council's judgment. Then it was recorded that 'because our lord the king, for certain causes, is not able to attend himself personally to the execution of justice and the law of his kingdom, he has willed ... that his first-born son and heir, the Lord Earl of Carrick, is to administer the common law everywhere throughout the kingdom.' [39] The three estates wished no ill to Robert II : there was no attempt to displace him altogether from government; instead, by a natural measure that associated the heir apparent with his father's

[35] *R.M.S.*, I. Nos. 411, 549.
[36] *Chron. Bower*, II. 395; *R.M.S.*, I. No. 679; *E.R.*, III. lii, liii, 657; *Scots Peerage*, VIII. 266-9.
[37] *A.P.S.*, I. 547-8.   [38] *Ibid.*, 550.   [39] *Ibid.*, 550.

government, Carrick was to have special and direct responsibility for one aspect of that government—the administration of justice.

There followed the enactment of a number of statutes to speed the apprehension of criminals:[40] if a suspect should withdraw himself from one sheriffdom to another, the first sheriff was to write to the second sheriff, who was to cause the fugitive to be cited by his serjeant to thole an assize. If the fugitive did not appear before the assize he was to be put to the horn as an outlaw. It was unanimously agreed that these statutes should apply even to the regalities and to the ecclesiastical franchises. Two nobles made a special reservation of their own rights under ancient law : Robert Stewart, Earl of Fife, as 'chief of the law of Clan MacDuff',[41] was willing to observe the statutes 'gratis', providing that this should not in future prejudice either himself or the law of Clan MacDuff; similarly, Archibald the Grim reserved certain points of the laws of the Galwegians, 'protesting on behalf of the privilege of his right and of the said law'.[42] The statutes of 1384, like those of 1372, were to remain valid for only three years.[43] During this period Carrick, as a new broom, might try to sweep away the lawlessness that was already bringing reproach upon the new dynasty.

The changes within Scotland that followed upon the accession of the Stewart dynasty were contemporary with important external developments. Not least of these was the outbreak of the Great Schism. Since 1309 the papal court had been established at Avignon. In 1377 Gregory XI ended this 'Babylonish Captivity' by transferring the *curia* back to Rome, where he soon died. On 8 April 1378 the cardinals elected the Archbishop of Bari as Pope Urban VI, only to be dismayed by his tyranny. Most of the cardinals gathered at Anagni to depose him on 9 August; and at Fondi on 20 September 1378 they elected Cardinal Robert of Geneva as Clement VII. Urban VI refused to consider himself deposed and held on to Rome while Clement VII set up court at Avignon.[44] Thus began the 'lang lestand scysm' ;[45] for both popes had successors. In the course of time the Avignonese popes (who did not always reside at Avignon) have come to be regarded as anti-popes and the Roman popes (who did not always re-

---

[40] *Ibid.*, 550–1.

[41] See G. Neilson, *Trial by Combat* (1890, 1909), p. 121.

[42] *A.P.S.*, I. 550.   [43] *Ibid.*

[44] Walter Ullmann, *The Origins of the Great Schism*, pp. 9–68; John Holland Smith, *The Great Schism*, pp. 116–45.

[45] *Chron. Wyntoun*, III. 61.

side at Rome) as the true popes, but while the schism lasted each side regarded its own pope as the true one, and the one pope excommunicated the other. There was 'indescribable mental confusion';[46] the seamless garment of the church was rent, and a handful of radicals denounced even the institution of the papacy. Some rulers, through caution, or for reasons of policy, were hesitant in professing obedience to either pope, or withdrew obedience after they had professed it.

It was mostly, but not entirely, international politics that at first decided the prevailing attitude in each country. By 5 November 1378 the English government had proclaimed its adherence to Urban, an Italian who could be trusted to purge French influence from the *curia*. On 16 November Charles V, with the support of the university of Paris, adhered to Clement—most of his cardinals were French, and some, like Clement himself, were kinsmen of the French king.[47] The Scots had a natural desire to follow the opposite course to that of England and believed that they were held in great affection by Clement since he was descended from the sainted wife of Malcolm Canmore. The chronicler Wyntoun was not acquainted with all the stages of this genealogy but concluded that 'Robert the Second in Scotland ... to this Clement wes cusyne.'[48] More substantial political ties with the French monarchy and intellectual ties with the university of Paris, the greatest theological school of Western Europe, brought Scotland wholeheartedly into the fold of Clement.[49]

In the past the secular states of Europe had tried to woo the favours of the papacy; now it was the turn of popes who had lost universal acceptance to woo the secular states. When a nuncio of Avignon was appointed to depose the Scottish adherents of Urban and distribute their benefices among the adherents of Clement he was furnished with various means of winning friends and gaining influence : he was empowered to grant benefices to poor clerks; he might grant dispensations to as many as two hundred persons whose illegitimate birth made them canonically ineligible to hold benefices ; he might issue twenty dispensations for marriages within certain forbidden degrees of affinity; he might grant licence to two hundred persons to have a portable altar and licences to three hundred persons to choose a confessor who might give them plenary remission on their deathbed. During the schism the Avignonese *curia* (like the Roman *curia*) was little more than a receiver and grantor of petitions.[50] Peti-

---

[46] Ullmann, *op. cit.*, p. 99.
[48] *Chron. Wyntoun*, III. 61.
[50] *Cal. Papal Letters*, IV. 240–2.

[47] *Ibid.*, pp. 54, 91, 104–6.
[49] See Ullmann, *op. cit.*, p. 96.

tions for benefices presented by a combination of academics, nepotists and pluralists induced the compliant papacy to exploit to the utmost the powers of appointment that it had already begun to acquire under the practices of provision and reservation,[51] and, in the process, to draw financial profit. Meanwhile it became usual to delegate some prominent local bishop to act as disciplinarian [52] and to crush schismatics.

It was Walter Wardlaw, Bishop of Glasgow, who was singled out for this role in Scotland: on 23 December 1383 he was created a cardinal by Clement VII;[53] and on 24 November 1384 he was appointed legate *a latere* in both Scotland and Ireland.[54] There the Archbishop of Tuam supported Avignon, and so also did an ecclesiastical assembly held at Roscommon in 1383.[55] The death of Scotland's first cardinal in September 1387 [56] ended a shrewd move that might have promoted in Ireland both the ecclesiastical interests of the Avignonese papacy and the political interests of the Scottish monarchy.

Elsewhere this conjunction of interests had important consequences. The Norwegian islands of Orkney and Shetland, subject ecclesiastically to the Archbishop of Nidaros, might have been expected to follow the Norwegian policy of allegiance to the Roman pope. But the issue was not clear-cut. About the middle of the fourteenth century a succession dispute had followed upon the death of Malise of Strathearn, who had held simultaneously the earldoms of Strathearn, Caithness and Orkney. After dispute and adjudication, a Lothian landholder, Henry Sinclair of Roslin, husband of Malise's second daughter, was invested by the Norwegian king on 2 August 1379 as Earl of Orkney.[57] It cannot have been without the support of the new earl that Clement VII provided Robert Sinclair to the bishopric of Orkney in 1384.[58] From this time onwards the bishops of Orkney were all Scotsmen.[59] In another portion of the Norwegian province of Nidaros the result of the schism was an ecclesiastical partition that corresponded to the *de facto* political partition. John Donegan, Bishop of Sodor (the Isles) adhered to the Roman pope and

---

[51] For the nature of this traffic and the procedure of the *curia* in dealing with it see the introductions to *Cal. Scot. Supp. 1418–1422*, and *Cal. Scot. Supp. 1423–28*.

[52] A. R. MacEwen, *History of the Church in Scotland*, I. 307.

[53] Dowden, *Bishops*, p. 315.   [54] *Cal. Papal Letters*, IV. 250–1.

[55] W. A. Phillips, *History of the Church of Ireland* (1934), II. 118–20.

[56] Dowden, *Bishops*, p. 315.   [57] *Scots Peerage*, II. 319–20.

[58] *H.B.C.*, p. 297; Dowden, *Bishops*, pp. 269–70.

[59] Dowden, *Bishops*, pp. 269–70.

continued in possession of the cathedral on the Isle of Man—the only part of the diocese under English control—while Michael, the unsuccessful Avignonese Archbishop of Cashel, was accepted in the rest of the diocese controlled by the Scots.[60] This division of the diocese of the Isles was accompanied by a break in the tenuous link that bound the Bishops of Galloway to their metropolitan at York. In 1378 Urban VI had provided Oswald, Prior of Glenluce, to the bishopric of Galloway. In the following year Clement VII more effectively provided Thomas Rossy, a prominent Scottish Franciscan.[61] From the outset of the schism ecclesiastical animosities had merged with Anglo-Scottish animosities. Urban VI and his Roman successors did not endear themselves to the Scots by their attempts to provide loyal Englishmen to Scottish bishoprics.[62] Thomas Rossy made 'authentic Scottish contributions to the controversies of the fourteenth century' not only in his treatise on the immaculate conception but in another treatise against the schismatic English, in which he challenged the bellicose Bishop of Norwich to single combat.[63]

The militancy shown by Rossy (and by many other Scots) in the period that began with the outbreak of the schism and the almost simultaneous death of Edward III would have been out of place earlier. Only gradually did the blows inflicted by Edward III fade from Scottish memory and allow self-confidence to revive. By itself the accession of Robert II caused no revolution in Scotland's foreign relationships. Three days after his coronation, parliament sanctioned a mission to France,[64] as a result of which Charles V issued letters patent renewing the Franco-Scottish alliance. On 28 October 1371 Robert II ratified this treaty of Vincennes; neither party would make truce or peace with the English unless the other gave its consent.[65] Certain more aggressive secret articles drafted by the French do not seem to have been ratified by Robert II. There had been no fighting with England since 1356. So far as he was concerned there would be no fighting in future. The fourteen-year truce of 1369 would not expire until February 1384, and Robert II decided to adhere to this truce, even at the cost of keeping up regular payment of the yearly

[60] *Ibid.*, pp. 287–8; *H.B.C.*, p. 254; Dunlop, *Bishop Kennedy*, p. 191.

[61] W. Moir Bryce, *Scottish Grey Friars*, I. 29–31; Dowden, *Bishops*, p. 376.

[62] Dowden, *Bishops*, pp. 45–6, 67–9, 94–6, 375–6.

[63] Hugh McEwan, ' "A Theolog Solempne", Thomas de Rossy, Bishop of Galloway', *Innes Review*, VIII. 21–9, at 28–9.

[64] *A.P.S.*, I. 559–60.   [65] Text in *E.R.*, III. xcvii–civ.

instalment of 4,000 marks on David II's ransom.[66] At midsummer 1377, however, a few days after the death of Edward III, the Scots made their last payment on the ransom of David II, leaving 24,000 marks unpaid.[67] For some years Edward had been no real threat to Scotland; but the disappearance of his name brought home to the Scots their deliverance from the threat of domination. His successor, Richard II, was a boy of ten. To the troubles of England, now occasionally raided by Franco-Castilian fleets, were added those of a royal minority. Although English kings would never forget their claims to lordship over Scotland these claims would never again be pursued so determinedly as in the days of the first three Edwards. The wars of independence were over. A war of chivalry on the Borders was about to begin.[68]

While Robert II was not eager to break the truce he could not hold back his nobles.[69] The first of a series of Border raids began with an incident at the fair of Roxburgh in 1378. At the next Roxburgh fair the Earl of March sacked and burned the town.[70] This gave rise to other incidents. In the case of some Scottish nobles, particularly the Earls of March and Douglas, one motive behind Border warfare was the recovery of territory still occupied by the English. Their motive was less national than personal: they saw no reason why they should not recover lands that were theirs by heritage. Others had motives that the current vogue of chivalry made fashionable and took part in what have been described as 'the selfish and disjointed expeditions of an aristocracy whose principal objects were plunder and military adventure'.[71]

Hostilities were not confined to land. In 1376 John Mercer, merchant burgess of Perth and financial agent of the late King David, was returning home with one of his ships when it was wrecked on the Northumberland coast. Despite the truce his merchandise was seized and he was imprisoned in Scarborough Castle.[72] The English chronicler Walsingham lamented Mercer's eventual release: it was 'to the great loss of the whole kingdom . . . for if he had been held to

---

[66] *Rot. Scot.*, I. 945, 953; *E.R.*, II. 363, 394.

[67] *Rot. Scot.*, II. 38–9. George Burnett wrongly thought that the whole ransom was eventually paid (*E.R.*, II. lxxxiii), but later realised his mistake: after 1377 no trace is to be found in the Scottish exchequer accounts of any payment of ransom instalments (*ibid.*, III. lvii–lix).

[68] The remainder of this chapter has benefited from the expert advice of Mr. Anthony Goodman of the university of Edinburgh.

[69] *Nat. MSS. Scot.*, II. No. xlvi.

[70] *Chron. Fordun*, I. 283; *Chron. Wyntoun*, III. 9–10.

[71] P. F. Tytler, *History*, I. pt. ii, 333.   [72] *Nat. MSS. Scot.*, II. No. xlv.

ransom as a prisoner of war he would have enriched the king and kingdom with his inestimable wealth'.[73] Instead, Mercer returned to Scotland to act as temporary chamberlain on the death of Walter Biggar. When Mercer arranged the last payment of the ransom instalment in midsummer 1377 he paid only half, deducting 2,000 marks as damages for his lost merchandise.[74] But this did not satisfy his son Andrew: in 1378, at the head of a squadron of French, Spanish and Scottish ships, he sacked Scarborough, where his father had been imprisoned, and swept the English seas. The prominence of merchants of both sides in warfare at sea was underlined when a London merchant named Philpott took up Andrew Mercer's challenge, raised a naval force, and captured both Andrew and his fleet.[75]

While the English generally had the better of the Scots at sea, the situation was reversed on land.[76] When John of Gaunt, Duke of Lancaster, was sent north to attend a March Day [77] on 1 October 1380 he brought a memorandum that outlined the encroachments made by the Scots since 1357 upon English-occupied lands in Berwickshire and Roxburghshire. Part of his mission was to try to persuade the Scots to respect the boundaries of 1357,[78] but despite his intimidating retinue of two thousand men [79] no general settlement was reached. Another March Day, held at Ebchester near Ayton on 18 June 1381,[80] was interrupted by news that England was in turmoil thanks to a widespread peasants' revolt. While Gaunt's palace of the Savoy went up in flames in London he himself took refuge in Holyrood Abbey as the honoured guest of the Scots nobility.[81]

Despite the duke's stay in Scotland there seems to have been little eagerness on either side for a further extension of the truce, which would expire at Candlemas (2 February) 1384. In Scotland the royal castles were made ready for war.[82] In Edinburgh Castle a certain Dietrich, presumably a German or a Netherlander, was busy constructing military machines and was paid £4 for *unum instru-*

---

[73] *Chron. Walsingham*, I. 369. The reality of his wealth is suggested by the frequent references to the wardship of his son, Andrew, which was evidently valuable (*E.R.*, III. 229, 256, 302, 329, etc.).

[74] *Ibid.*, lvii–lviii.   [75] *Chron. Walsingham*, I. 369–70.   [76] *Ibid.*, 373.

[77] This was similar to a 'Day of Trewe' (Truce Day) and amounted to a diplomatic confrontation on the Marches (Borders).

[78] *Cal. Docs. Scot.*, IV. No. 295.

[79] R. L. Storey, 'The Wardens of the Marches of England towards Scotland', *E.H.R.*, LXXII. 593–609, at 595.

[80] *Cal. Docs. Scot.*, IV. No. 297; *Rot. Scot.*, II. 38–9.

[81] *Chron. Wyntoun*, III. 16–18.

[82] *E.R.*, III. 80, 82, 87, 98, 117, 118, 660, 665, 667, 671, 672, 676.

mentum dictum 'gun'[83]—the first clear indication that the Scots were making use of firearms. Two days after the truce expired, Archibald the Grim and George Dunbar, Earl of March, secured the surrender of Lochmaben Castle, destroyed it, and thus ended the last vestiges of the English occupation of Annandale,[84] which reverted to the Earl of March. Retribution was at hand. An expedition set out under the Duke of Lancaster and encamped outside Edinburgh in March 1384. Mindful of the hospitality he had received in the town in 1381 Gaunt did not destroy it but contented himself with holding it to ransom.[85]

On 20 August 1383 Robert II had ratified an agreement whereby, in the event of Anglo-Scottish war, the French king would send to Scotland troops, money, and arms.[86] In the spring or summer of 1384 an unofficial advance party of some thirty French knights and esquires landed at Montrose, after which they joined a gathering of Scottish Borderers and raided the north of England.[87] Fear of further Franco-Scottish enterprises inspired special arrangements for the garrisoning of Berwick, Roxburgh and Carlisle at a cost of almost £10,000 to the English exchequer for the year beginning 1 August 1384.[88] The raid also showed that so far as Border warfare was concerned Robert II's authority meant nothing: Archibald the Grim did not scruple to arrange a truce of his own on 15 March 1385.[89]

While the Lord of Galloway was now peacably inclined, a general council which met in Edinburgh in April 1385 showed more warlike inclinations.[90] The French private adventurers of 1384 were followed by an official expeditionary force under Jean de Vienne, admiral of France, which landed at Dunbar and Leith at the end of May 1385. There were, so John of Fordun claimed, twenty-six bannerets, fifty knights and one thousand and fifty men-at-arms. With them they brought eighty suits of armour and eighty lances as well as a sum of fifty thousand gold francs to jingle before the noses of the Scottish king, Cardinal Wardlaw, and the more militaristic of the nobles.[91] A council of war drew up regulations in French at the be-

[83] *Ibid.*, 672. Saltpetre and sulphur, constituents of gunpowder, were also sent to various castles.   [84] *Chron. Fordun*, I. 383.

[85] *Chron. Wyntoun*, III. 20; *Chron. Bower*, II. 398; *Chron. Walsingham*, II. III.

[86] *A.P.S.*, XII. 19.   [87] *Chron. Froissart*, III. 472-6.

[88] R. L. Storey, *op. cit.*, *E.H.R.*, LXXII. 593-609, at 598.

[89] *Rot. Scot.*, II. 73; see also *Chron. Froissart*, III. 476-7.   [90] *A.P.S.*, I. 552.

[91] *Chron. Fordun*, I. 383; *Chron. Froissart*, III. 494-5; IV. 22-3. For the distribution of the subsidy see *Foedera*, III. pt. iii, 188.

ginning of July 1385 for the discipline of a joint Franco-Scottish force that would set out for the Borders.[92] Wark and two smaller strongholds in Northumberland were stormed.[93] Then came tidings that an English army headed by Richard II and the Duke of Lancaster was approaching. The French looked forward to a pitched battle in which they could win renown. To their dismay the Scots withdrew and laid waste their own land.

Jean de Vienne soon admitted that this scorched-earth strategy was the only one feasible.[94] It was the first real campaign of the young Richard II and a large army had assembled to do him honour.[95] The existence of the Great Schism removed some religious sanctions : the Scottish religious houses could now be regarded as nests of schismatics. Melrose, Dryburgh and Newbattle went up in flames. When the English army arrived in Edinburgh, the same fate befell the town and the kirk of St Giles; Holyrood was spared only through the intercession of John of Gaunt.[96] But thanks to the strategy of the Scots the invaders were soon starving and forced to return home.[97] Unable to defend the Scottish Lowlands, the Franco-Scottish troops had set out to invade the West March of England. In mid-August they plundered Cumberland on an unparalleled scale and even made a show of attacking Carlisle; in the bishoprics of Durham and Carlisle they had burned and plundered, so the French said, more than could be found in all the towns of Scotland put together.[98] When they came back to Edinburgh through lands wasted by the retreating English host, they found the countryside alive with people and cattle returning from hiding places to the primitive homes they had left to be burned by the English.[99]

In this type of warfare there was little room for French knights. The growing antagonism between them and their allies is vividly portrayed by Froissart, whose admiration for the valour of the Scots was mingled with contempt for their poverty-stricken uncouthness. When the French knights, as was their custom, sent out their pages to forage for victuals, they were attacked and some of their number

[92] *A.P.S.*, I. 554–5.
[93] *Chron. Wyntoun*, III. 24; *Chron. Bower*, II. 400–1; *Chron. Froissart*, IV. 49–51.   [94] *Chron. Froissart*, IV. 56–7.
[95] For the composition of the force and the financial background see N. B. Lewis, 'The Last Medieval Summons of the English Feudal Levy, 13 June 1385', *E.H.R.*, LXXIII. 1–26, and J. J. N. Palmer, 'The Last Summons of the Feudal Army in England', *ibid.*, LXXXIII. 771–5.
[96] *Chron. Bower*, II. 401 and n.   [97] *Chron. Walsingham*, II. 131.
[98] *Chron. Froissart*, IV. 58–63; *Chron. Wyntoun*, III. 24; *Chron. Bower*, II. 401.
[99] *Chron. Froissart*, IV. 63; *Chron. Bower*, II. 401.

slain. The French were not to be allowed to depart from Scotland until they gave satisfaction for the damages they had allegedly inflicted. The admiral had to remain behind in pawn until money was sent from Paris for his release.[100] Had the efforts of the French expeditionary force been accompanied (as was intended) by a seaborne invasion of England [101] much might have been achieved, but although the French toyed with invasion plans until 1388 the Scots appear to have been daunted by Richard II's expedition of 1385 and to have accepted a number of short truces while awaiting a favourable opportunity to renew warfare.[102]

The last of these truces was due to expire on 19 June 1388. As this critical date drew near the 'Merciless Parliament' was in session at Westminster and Richard II's authority temporarily crumbled. The Scots were tempted to take advantage of English domestic difficulties, which included rivalries between Percies and Nevilles on the Borders,[103] and seized the initiative as the truce ran out. In the summer of 1388 Robert, Earl of Fife, James, Earl of Douglas, and Archibald the Grim took a strong force across the Solway sands and spent three days raiding Cockermouth.[104] When the next expedition was planned it was decided to disconcert the English by dividing the Scottish force into two and attacking simultaneously on the east and west.[105] The larger of the two forces carried out a successful plundering raid as far as Burgh-in-Stainmore,[106] but it was the smaller force under the Earls of Douglas, March, and Moray that was to win the greater fame.

Its task was mainly to cause a diversion on the East March. There were affrays at the barriers outside the walls of Newcastle, after which the Scots withdrew. Henry Hotspur, son and heir of the Earl of Northumberland, had meanwhile discovered that the force on the West March was too strong to be attacked. He doubled back and

[100] *Chron. Froissart*, IV. 23, 24–6, 63–6.

[101] *Chron. Walsingham*, II. 129.

[102] *Cal. Docs. Scot.*, IV. No. 360; *Rot. Scot.*, II. 93. For the English background see M. V. Clarke, *Fourteenth Century Studies*, ed. L. S. Sutherland and M. McKisack (1937), pp. 36–52.

[103] Anthony Steel, *Richard II* (1941), pp. 143–61; Anthony Goodman, *The Loyal Conspiracy: the Lords Appellant under Richard II* (1971), pp. 41–9.

[104] *Chron. Wyntoun*, III. 29–30; *Chron. Bower*, II. 402–3.

[105] This is the account of Froissart, who claimed to have the facts from participants (*Chron. Froissart*, V. 210–11, 231). Wyntoun and Bower give the impression that there was no conscious division of forces but that the Earl of Douglas for some reason failed to join the Earl of Fife on the West March (*Chron. Wyntoun*, III. 34; *Chron. Bower*, II. 410).

[106] *Chron. Bower*, II. 410; *Chron. Wyntoun*, III. 34.

came upon the smaller force at Otterburn in Redesdale. Fighting began in the light of the setting sun and continued by moonlight throughout the night of 5 August 1388. Hotspur was taken prisoner by Sir John Montgomery of Eaglesham and Eglinton, who profited from an enormous ransom.[107] In the morning the body of the dead Douglas was found; no one knew who had slain him, but the victory was his. Froissart did not hesitate to narrate his last words: 'Thanked be God there hath been but a fewe of myne aunctyours that hathe dyed in ther beddes. ... I praye you rayse up agayne my baner, whiche lyeth on the grounde. ... But, sirs, shewe nother to frende nor foo in what case ye se me in, for if myne enemyes knew it they wolde rejoyse'—and thus it was that a dead man won the field.[108] Whether or not Douglas ever had the chance to make a dying speech the sentiments attributed to him were those that the age of chivalry esteemed.

Although tidings of the fight at Otterburn and the death of the second Earl of Douglas influenced the deliberations of a general council held at Linlithgow on 18 August 1388, it broke up with its business unfinished and was prorogued to Edinburgh 'by reason of the Lord Earl of Carrick':[109] it was probably during the sitting of this council that he was kicked by a horse belonging to Sir James Douglas of Dalkeith.[110] This mishap, which left the heir apparent lame, led to a constitutional revolution in so far as it gave a plausible excuse for Carrick's removal from the post of authority that he had held since 1384. Moreover his removal was to be associated with a virtual demission of office on the part of the king his father. The background to these striking political changes was Carrick's failure to maintain law and order, a failure which is reflected in a number of legal cases that figure in the records of the period.[111] It hardly helped matters when the king remitted amercements imposed by parliament upon offenders, as in the case of Sir Robert Danielston, who had been fined £160.[112] Neither the king nor his eldest son had enforced the law, nor had they won popularity by taking part in the recent warfare, nor did they strive to retain power: in a general council at Edinburgh on 1 December 1388 Robert II took the unusual step of

---

[107] *Scots Peerage*, III. 427–8; *Cal. Docs. Scot.*, IV. No. 395.

[108] *Chron. Froissart*, V. 211–31; *Chron. Bower*, II. 411; *Chron. Wyntoun*. III. 35–9.

[109] *A.P.S.*, I. 555. [110] *Chron. Bower*, II. 414.

[111] *Morton Registrum*, I. No. 10; *A.P.S.*, I. 553.

[112] *E.R.*, III. 164.

delivering a schedule under his signet which was read aloud.[113] Its purport was that he submitted himself fully to the ordinance of his general council in matters affecting the administration of justice and the defence of the realm against enemies. He wished also that his heir apparent should submit to the ordinance of the three estates. Faced with this abnegation of royal authority, the three estates issued an ordinance alluding to 'the great and many defects in the governance of the realm' which had existed for no short time by reason of the disposition of the king, as well as of his age and otherwise, and the infirmity of his first-born son (Carrick) and the tender years of the latter's son and heir. The estates agreed to choose Robert Stewart, Earl of Fife, the king's second son, as guardian of the realm. Thereupon the king commanded the chancellor that he should deliver whatsoever letters the new guardian and the council should unanimously require upon points touching the common weal and the governance and defence of the realm.[114]

The new guardian, or governor,[115] had already been notably successful in the race for landed power. He had won the earldom of Menteith in 1361 by a marriage with its heiress, and the earldom of Fife in 1371 by a bargain with the much-married and much-widowed Countess Isabella.[116] Apart from his landed influence Robert Stewart had long played a prominent part in government. And although he was to show himself more of a politician than a fighter, he had realised the importance of associating himself with the leading nobles in their warlike enterprises. Never outstanding as a military leader, he nonetheless gave the impression of sharing the fashionable chivalric outlook of the day.[117]

Despite the earl's apparent qualifications, his appointment to the new post was hedged by limitations. He was to act as guardian only so long as he behaved 'well and usefully in the aforesaid office according to the determination and declaration of the general council or parliament'. This determination and declaration was to be made each year in future in full parliament or in general council; and the king commanded that meetings of parliament or general council

---

[113] *A.P.S.*, I. 555–6.

[114] *Ibid.*, 556. For an example of a mandate issued under this arrangement in May 1389 see *Nat. MSS. Scot.*, II. No. xlvii.

[115] The Latin of the record calls him *custos*. Bower affirms that it was decided to call him governor (*Chron. Bower*, II. 414)—a title certainly applied to him in the contemporary exchequer rolls (*E.R.*, II. 698, 703); Wyntoun styles him 'wardayne'—the vernacular version of 'guardian' (*Chron. Wyntoun*, III. 40).

[116] *Scots Peerage*, IV. 14.   [117] *Chron. Wyntoun*, III. 30.

should take place before the end of each year.[118] Moreover, Fife's appointment was to hold good only until such time as the heir apparent should recover from his infirmity or 'should arrive at the ability of governing that office according to, and by, the determination of the council of the kingdom'.[119] There is some doubt as to whether this last phrase signifies the privy council or a general council of the estates. What is clear is that a conciliar authority, whether broadly or narrowly based, was to supervise the executive. Thus the general council of December 1388 had taken some steps in the same direction as the, 'Merciless Parliament' that had met in England some months previously. Though the Scots avoided the blood-letting by which the English advertised their political revolutions the constitutional changes in Scotland were nonetheless drastic.

In such circumstances it is striking that Robert Stewart, having come to power in 1388, was to keep his position almost continuously for another thirty-two years. Initially, however, he had to feel his way cautiously. When the question of the northern justiciarship was raised in a parliament at Holyrood in April 1389 he saw to it that his son and heir, Murdoch Stewart, obtained the post; but parliament guardedly made the appointment for only a year.[120] And although it decreed a salary of a thousand marks a year for the governor a condition was attached—he was not to use his office to interfere with the royal revenue.[121] This was an empty proviso, for Robert Stewart was not only governor but chamberlain. But even in this capacity he faced criticism: when his account as chamberlain was audited at Perth on 14 February 1390 the auditors mistrustfully alluded to the thousand marks 'which he claims to be due to him from the office of governor'.[122]

The rise of Robert Stewart was accompanied by that of another magnate—Archibald the Grim, protégé of the late David II. When the second Earl of Douglas died at Otterburn he left no legitimate offspring to succeed him, thus bringing into operation a tailzie of 26 May 1342 [123] of which Sir Archibald, illegitimate son of the Good Sir James Douglas and cousin of the dead Earl of Douglas, was now the sole surviving beneficiary. According to this tailzie, he would fall heir to the Douglas lands proper, including Douglasdale, Lauderdale, Eskdale, and the forest of Selkirk.[124] His succession to at least

---

[118] AP.S., I. 556. [119] Ibid. [120] Ibid., 557.
[121] Ibid. [122] E.R., II. 698, 703.
[123] Fraser, Douglas, III. 357, 359; A.P.S., I. 557–8. [124] A.P.S., I. 557–8.

one of these estates—the forest—was contested by Sir Malcolm Drummond of Strathord, brother-in-law of the dead earl, and brother of Annabella, wife of the Earl of Carrick. It was probably this royal connection which enabled Sir Malcolm to obtain letters of sasine from chancery for his infeftment in the lands of Selkirk forest. But this procedure misfired : on 2 April 1389 parliament censured the chancellor (John of Peebles, Bishop of Dunkeld) for his unjust negligence in issuing such letters.[125] Another claimant to the unentailed estates was Sir James Sandilands of Calder, son-in-law of Robert II.[126] Sir James, it seems, made common cause with Sir Malcolm and with Sir John Haliburton, for all three placed the lands they possessed, or claimed, under the protection of Richard II, who was planning (though in vain) a new invasion of Scotland. The letters of protection were dated 19 June 1389 and on the same day the three Scottish knights obtained safe-conducts to come to England with a retinue of forty men apiece.[127] Another complication centred around Margaret Stewart, Countess of Angus. She had been residing at Tantallon as the mistress of the first Earl of Douglas, who was the husband of her sister-in-law, the Countess of Mar. To the first Earl of Douglas the Countess of Angus bore a son, George Douglas, who was thus not only illegitimate but born in incest.[128] On 9 April 1389, during the Holyrood parliament, his mother resigned in his favour her earldom of Angus.[129] By 1397, moreover, James Sandilands of Calder, heir of line to the unentailed Douglas estates, had been induced by favour or fear to grant his rights to the new Earl of Angus,[130] and it was probably by reason of this grant that the Douglases of Angus became possessed of the mighty castle of Tantallon. In 1400, moreover, Angus received from his half-sister Isobel, Countess of Mar, and her husband Sir Malcolm Drummond, the lordship of Liddesdale. In the meantime Archibald the Grim had obtained possession of all the entailed Douglas estates and became third Earl of Douglas.[131]

Thus the result of the death of the second Earl of Douglas at Otterburn had been a bifurcation of the main Douglas power. Archibald the Grim, son of the Good Sir James whom the English styled 'the Black Douglas', is himself styled 'Archibald the Black' by one Scottish chronicler ;[132] certainly his descendants came to be known as

[125] *Ibid.*, 557.   [126] *Scots Peerage*, VIII. 379–80.
[127] *Cal. Docs. Scot.*, IV. No. 391; Anthony Goodman, *The Loyal Conspiracy: the Lords Appellant under Richard II* (1971), pp. 50–2.
[128] *Scots Peerage*, I. 171.   [129] *A.P.S.*, I. 565–6.
[130] *Scots Peerage*, VIII. 381.   [131] *Ibid.*, III. 159–60.
[132] *Chron. Pluscarden*, I. 339.

the 'Black' Douglases, while the Douglases of Angus became known as the 'Red' Douglases. In the circumstances in which both these territorial families originated may be found the motive for the rivalry that became apparent between them in the following century.

For the time being, the 'Black' Douglases far excelled the 'Red' Douglases in landed power. Ever since September 1369, when David II bestowed on Archibald the Grim eastern Galloway betwixt the Nith and the Cree,[133] Archibald's landed power had been increasing. In February 1372, Thomas Fleming, grandson and heir of the first Earl of Wigtown, had resigned his lands and rights in the earldom of Wigtown to him in return for a large sum of money,[134] and in October of the same year Sir Archibald obtained a royal charter confirming his possession of all the lands of the earldom, though not the title of earl, which lapsed.[135] The result of Archibald the Grim's acquisition of Wigtown was a reunification of the whole of the distinctive province of Galloway that had been split up in 1235. It now became the real basis of the power of the Black Douglases. Through his wife, Joanna Moray, Archibald had already obtained possession of the lordship and castle of Bothwell.[136] When, in addition, he obtained the entailed Douglas lands and the title of Earl of Douglas he emerged as unquestionably the most powerful magnate south of Forth. In the construction of his new tower-house of Threave, built as the centre of the lordship of Galloway, he helped to establish a new fashion in baronial architecture. In his ecclesiastical benefactions, notably the foundation of collegiate kirks at Lincluden and Bothwell, he earned the good opinion of kirkmen and helped to establish a new fashion in ecclesiastical development.[137] In warfare his prowess was unrivalled. Not only was he dexterous in acquiring lands but he was strong and just in administering them.[138]

Such a combination of qualities stood out in contrast to the futile and aimless Stewart kingship. After Robert I and David II the power and prestige of the crown had notably declined. It was already clear that nothing much was to be hoped for in the heir apparent. His younger brother, the Earl of Fife, cautiously working in co-operation with the three estates, had not yet stretched the wings of his authority when Robert II died on 19 April 1390 at the age of seventy-four in his castle of Dundonald.[139] With some justification John Major re-

133 *Scots Peerage*, IV. 144.   134 *A.P.S.*, I. 560–1.
135 *Ibid.*; *R.M.S.*, I. No. 507. 136 *Scots Peerage*, III. 612–3.
137 P. 271 below.
138 *Chron. Bower*, II. 429; *Chron. Wyntoun*, III. 77.
139 *Chron. Bower*, II. 415.

jected the eulogies of the chroniclers Wyntoun and Bower, and remarked: 'Now, whatever our writers may contend, I cannot hold this aged king, I mean this second Robert, to have been a skilful warrior or wise in counsel.'[140]

Those who had come to attend the obsequies of Robert II at Scone on 13 August 1390 remained to see John, Earl of Carrick, crowned and anointed on the following day by Walter Trail, Bishop of St Andrews. On 15 August it was the turn of the queen, Annabella Drummond, daughter of Sir John Drummond of Stobhall and niece of Margaret Logie, to be crowned by the Bishop of Dunkeld.[141] Because the name John was reckoned ill-omened (by reason of John Balliol and John II of France), the new king changed his name to Robert[142] and earned the by-name 'John Faranyeir'—'John of yester year'.[143] The change of name did not alter the omens.

At his accession Robert III was some fifty-three years old. His son and heir, named David, had been born in 1378 and was created Earl of Carrick after his father's accession to the throne. In addition to two illegitimate sons, the king's offspring eventually comprised a second legitimate son who died in infancy, a third son named James, who was finally to succeed to the throne, and four daughters, of whom one died unmarried, one was married to Archibald, fourth Earl of Douglas, another to Sir James Douglas of Dalkeith, another to George Douglas, Earl of Angus, after whose death she temporarily linked the royal family to other noble houses by a further three successive marriages.[144] Thus the stewartisation of the Scottish nobility that had begun under the first Stewart king was carried a stage further under the second. As yet, none of Robert's III's offspring was old enough to play a part in politics, and Robert himself was either too old or too incapable. He was the very person whom the three estates had discounted in 1388 as unfit to rule by reason of his infirmity; the king's younger brother, Robert Stewart, Earl of Fife and Menteith, continued for a year or two to draw his salary of a thousand marks 'for the office of guardian'.[145]

In the months that elapsed between the death of Robert II and the coronation of Robert III the perpetration of outrages unexampled in time of peace made it plain that the futility of the new king was

[140] Major, *History*, p. 329.
[142] *Ibid.*; Major, *History*, p. 331.
[144] Dunbar, *Scot. Kings*, p. 180.
[141] *Chron. Bower*, II. 418.
[143] *Highland Papers*, II. 93, 95, n. 1.
[145] *E.R.*, III. 276, 280, 312.

already recognised. At the end of May 1390 the burgh of Forres went up in flames. On 17 June so also did Elgin with its cathedral, the hospital of the Maison Dieu, the parish kirk of St Giles, and eighteen houses of the cathedral canons and chaplains.[146] According to the chronicler Wyntoun these crimes were committed by 'wyld wykkyd Heland-men'.[147] Wyntoun carefully suppressed the fact that the wild and wicked Highlanders had been led by none other than the new king's brother, Alexander Stewart, Earl of Buchan, who, until sacked by the three estates in 1388, had served as justiciar of the north and had earned the by-name of 'Wolf of Badenoch'.[148]

It was not so much Highland ferocity as feudal rapacity on the part of the Wolf that ended in the burning of Elgin. The events that led up to the outrage went back at least to August 1370, when Alexander Stewart had taken an oath that he would be the protector and defender of the lands and men of the Bishop of Moray.[149] In February 1390, however, an indenture was concluded whereby the bishop left the costly protection of Alexander Stewart, to whom he had been paying what amounted to blackmail, and instead agreed to pay a pension to Thomas Dunbar, sheriff of Inverness and son of the Earl of Moray.[150] The bishop was to be taught a salutary lesson by the burning of his cathedral. Since it was the king's brother who had planned this deed his position protected him from undue criticism,[151] which vented itself instead upon the underlings whom he had employed—the Highland caterans.

The word 'cateran' (Gaelic *cathairne*) properly signified a warrior who was lightly armed as distinct from the more substantial and heavily armed gallowglass (Gaelic *galloglaich*); to the Lowlander, however, the cateran was merely a Highland robber. The general council of April 1385 had entrusted the future Robert III (then Earl of Carrick) with the fruitless task of suppressing the caterans.[152] Their participation in the burning of Elgin drew attention to a problem that was increasingly grave—not merely the superficial problem of upholding law and order in the Highlands but the more fundamental problem of holding together in one nation the two parts of Scotland that were divergent in language and culture.

Although the poet Barbour several times alluded to the 'Erischry' of Scotland, it was the chronicler John of Fordun, writing between

146 *Moray Registrum*, Nos. 172, 303; *Chron. Wyntoun*, III. 55; *Chron. Bower*, II. 416.
147 *Chron. Wyntoun*, III. 55.
148 *Chron. Bower*, II. 416.
149 *Moray Registrum*, No. 154.
150 *Ibid.*, No. 170.
151 *E.R.*, III. lxxvi–lxxviii.
152 *A.P.S.*, I. 553.

1384 and 1387, who was the first to leave an impression of the Gaelic
Scots, their environment, and their relationship with the English-
speaking Lowlanders. 'The language and customs of the Scots,' so
he affirmed, 'vary with the diversity of their speech; for they use two
languages, namely Scottish [Gaelic] and Teutonic [English]; those
of the latter tongue possess the coastal and low-lying regions, whilst
those of the Scottish tongue inhabit the mountains and outlying
islands.' [153] Fordun thus shrewdly saw a combination of geographical
and linguistic factors as marking the limits of the two peoples. Besides
stressing the difference of language, Fordun detected other differences. The people of the seaboard were 'domesticated and cultured,
trustworthy, patient and urbane, decent in their attire, law-abiding
and peaceful, devout in religious observance, though always ready to
resist the wrong-doings of their foes'. The Highlanders and Islanders,
on the other hand, were a 'wild and untamed people, rough and
unbending, given to robbery, ease-loving, of artful and impressionable temperament, comely in form but unsightly in dress'.[154] Later
writers, such as Major and Buchanan, would elaborate this remark
when contrasting the 'domesticated', 'civilised', or 'tame' Lowlanders
with the 'wild' Scots.

It is significant that in Fordun's analysis there is to be found no
hint of a contrast between a 'clan system' in the Highlands and a
'feudal system' in the Lowlands. This does not mean that neither
clans nor feudalism existed; but it does suggest that there was in
Fordun's time no clear-cut demarcation between the two. It has been
said of the clan that 'kinship lay at its root. The members of the clan,
from its chief downwards, were supposed to be united by the common
bond of blood-relationship'.[155] But the same words could be applied
to the great baronial families of Lowland Scotland. Both in Highlands and Lowlands feudal conveyancing was general. Yet in neither
region was feudalism by itself capable of providing the secure social
grouping necessary for survival in the time of lawlessness over which
the early Stewarts presided. From the second half of the fourteenth
century onwards the clan was evolving in the Highlands as an increasingly important social, economic and military unit, and was one
of the factors in an impressive Gaelic resurgence that took place in
Scotland (and more notably in Ireland). The Gaelic word *clann*,
signifying children or offspring, acquired an extended meaning and
was applied to groups, some old, some new, that could hope to achieve

[153] *Chron. Fordun*, I. 24.   [154] *Ibid*.
[155] Mackenzie, *Highlands and Isles*, p. 83.

social, economic and political security under a patriarchal chief whose ancestry they held in reverence. In the Lowlands, when the loyalties of feudalism decayed, there was an unsuccessful attempt to maintain them by the money payments characteristic of 'bastard feudalism'.[156] But there was also a retrogression to the more primitive bonds of real or supposed kinship.[157] The development of the Highland clan was accompanied by that of Lowland families or 'kins', such as Crichtons, Livingstons, Homes and Hepburns; and family pride was expressed in tailzies to heirs male who were obliged to bear not only the heraldic arms of the family but its name as well.[158] Both in Highlands and Lowlands those who recognised a chief were expected to follow his leadership. In each region, moreover, there rose simultaneously a family that might be regarded as a 'super-kin' or 'super-clan'; for both the Douglases and the MacDonalds comprised subordinate kins or clans.

What struck the Lowlander about the Highland clan was not its social structure but its function when arrayed as a military unit. If in that function it did not differ much from the retinue of a Lowland baron, it certainly differed in appearance. According to John Major, 'the common folk . . . go out to battle with the whole body clad in a linen garment, well daubed with wax or with pitch, and with an overcoat of deerskin'.[159] When such uncouth warriors as these took advantage of the tremulous rule of the early Stewarts to descend on the braes of Angus, the Lowlanders began to think they were witnessing a new phenomenon and they linked it with the word 'clan'. The first time the word is known to have been used by a Lowland writer (the chronicler Wyntoun) was in connection with displays of Highland courage and ferocity in 1392 and 1396. Thereafter the word 'clan' was a bad word in Lowland mouths: clans did wicked things.

For the burning of Elgin was the prelude to further disorder in the north-east Highlands: in 1391 'there broke out such a struggle among the savage Scots that they troubled the whole country with their struggles, for throughout the whole county of Angus they could have no peace because of their marauding'.[160] Early in the following year there was 'hey grete discorde' when the braes of Angus were

---

[156] P. 212 below.
[157] For an indication of the significance a Lowland magnate attached to kinship see p. 218 below.
[158] See *R.M.S.*, II. Nos. 1045, 1064, 1191, 1214, 1534, 1595.
[159] Major, *History*, p. 49.   [160] *Chron. Pluscarden*, I. 253.

invaded by 'the Heyland men'.[161] At Gasklune in Stormont they held their own against a force led by Sir David Lindsay of Glenesk,[162] who was in full blossom as the latest flower of chivalry. It seemed that the armoured knight could no longer protect the Lowlands against ferocious Highland caterans. The latter soon gave another exhibition of their reckless courage : to settle discord between the feuding Clans Chattan and Kay a mortal combat was held on 28 September 1396 on the North Inch of Perth in the presence of Robert III, many of the nobility, and French and English knights ; the contestants numbered 'thre score wyld Scottis men', thirty of them under 'Cristy Johnesone', and the other thirty under 'Schir Ferqwharis sone' ; when the king cast down his baton to end the bloodletting only a dozen survived.[163]

If this clan duel had been devised to call a halt to Highland disorder, it was not very effective. New contestants were about to appear ; and they were not primitive caterans but had behind them the resources and comparatively sophisticated organisation of the lordship of the Isles. Feudalism provided some of the bonds that united it ; but although the Lord of the Isles issued Latin charters in feudal form he also issued a charter in Gaelic on 6 May 1408 [164]— surely not a solitary example—and signed it with his Gaelic patronymic—'McDomhnaill'. A homogeneous Gaelic culture contributed much to the inward strength of the lordship and made it a unique political expression of the Gaelic way of life. This was notably demonstrated in the solemn 'ceremony of proclaiming the Lord of the Isles',[165] during which he stepped into a footprint carved in a slab of stone. The inauguration was held at his manor house on an island in Loch Finlaggan on Islay.[166] A smaller island in the loch, reached by a causeway, was known as the 'Isle of Counsel'. Here, according to Archdeacon Monro's report in 1549, 'thair conveinit 14 of the Iles best Barons', together with the Bishop of the Isles and the Abbot of Iona.[167] This body was both judicial and advisory, for the Lord of the Isles occasionally issued charters 'with the consent, assent, and mature deliberation of all our council'.[168]

---

[161] *Chron. Wyntoun*, III. 58.   [162] *Ibid.*, 58–60.
[163] *Ibid.*, III. 63–4; *Chron. Bower*, II. 420–1. See also *E.R.*, III. lxxix–lxxx; Dunbar, *Scot. Kings*, pp. 173–4; George Neilson, *Trial by Combat*, pp. 251–5.
[164] *Nat. MSS. of Scotland*, II. No. lix.
[165] *Highland Papers*, I. 23–4.
[166] For a description of the site see Monro, *Western Isles*, pp. 95–100.
[167] *Ibid.*, p. 57.
[168] *Highland Papers*, I. 97. The council's composition and functions are discussed in Monro, *Western Isles*, pp. 103–10.

Such phraseology hinted at the singular status of the Lord of the Isles. It was a status that the English, at least, readily recognised, for in their eyes the house of Islay had a twofold importance : not only might it be used against the Scottish kings but it might be used in Irish affairs, or at least might be persuaded not to obstruct English interests in Ireland. On 14 July 1388, soon after the death of John of the Isles, Richard II appointed a mission to treat with his successor, Donald, son of John of the Isles and Margaret Stewart, on the subject of alliance, friendship, mutual aid and trade.[169] Simultaneously there was a worsening of relations between the MacDonalds and the Stewart monarchy. On 29 March 1389 the future Robert III (then Earl of Carrick) presented a complaint in parliament alluding to the wrongs committed against his sister, Margaret Stewart, widow of the late Lord of the Isles, by her own sons and their adherents.[170] A new source of trouble had appeared by 1394, when Thomas Dunbar, Earl of Moray, had to pay protection money to Alastair (Alexander) Carrach, Lord of Lochaber and younger brother of Donald of the Isles.[171] The depredations committed by Alastair Carrach inspired the three estates with a sense of crisis : in April 1398 it was decided that either David, Earl of Carrick, or his uncle, Robert, Earl of Fife, should lead an army in some 'crossing', presumably to the Hebrides. The submission of the rebels was not to be accepted save on condition that Donald of the Isles, his brothers Alastair and Ian, their chief councillors and other notables, together with the robbers and marauders associated with them, should compear to undergo justice at the hands of the king and council, or give notable hostages.[172] Donald appears to have obtained respite cheaply by restraining his brother Alastair —but not for long : in a council that met at Linlithgow in November 1399 it was decided that the king should send letters ordering Donald to compear before parliament to answer for having released Alastair, who was reputed a common freebooter.[173]

Donald of the Isles and those whom he harboured were by no means alone in scorning the admonitions of a distracted government. Under the year 1398 an entry in the chronicle of Moray declaimed :

In those days there was no law in Scotland, but he who was stronger oppressed him who was weaker and the whole realm was a den of

[169] *Rot. Scot.*, II. 94–5.
[171] *Moray Registrum*, No. 272.
[173] *Ibid.*, 575.
[170] *A.P.S.*, I. 557.
[172] *A.P.S.*, I. 570.

> thieves; murders, herschips and fireraising and all other misdeeds re-
> mained unpunished; and justice, as if outlawed, lay in exile outwith the
> bounds of the realm.[174]

The chronicler was merely drawing on his own experience to
confirm and elaborate the words of a statute passed in a general council held at Stirling some time in 1397. There the three estates alluded
to 'grete and horrible destruccions, heryschippis, brynyngs and
slachteris that ar sa commounly done throch al the kynrike'.[175] The
sheriffs were to be ordered to proclaim, firstly, that no one should
travel with a greater retinue than he was prepared to support at his
own cost, and secondly, that crimes of violence would be punished by
death. After making this proclamation the sheriff was to seek out
offenders, arrest them, and exact surety that they would compear at
the next justice ayre. If the offender failed to attend he was to be put
to the horn (outlawed) and those who had entered surety for him were
not only to pay the surety but pay assythment (damages) to the plaintiffs. Those offenders who could find no sureties were forthwith to be
brought before an assize; if found guilty they were to be 'condampnit
to the deid'.[176] Further provisions were modelled upon those originally enacted as temporary measures by the Holyrood general council
of November 1384. A council held at Perth in April 1398 re-affirmed
the statutes of 1397 and added other provisions. Among these was a
revolutionary ordinance: not only the sheriffs but also the bailies of
regality were to be challenged by the justiciar during his ayre to ascertain whether or not they had implemented the statutes passed at
Stirling in 1397 and at Perth in 1398.[177] All this depended upon the
holding of justice ayres. There appears to be no evidence in the
exchequer rolls of the holding of ayres between 1392 [178] and 1404,
when, or soon after, ayres were held in Cupar, Stirling and Dumbarton.[179] The absence of allusion to the ayres need not mean that they
were not held; but if they *were* held, those who presided evidently
kept the proceeds.

This was only one example of the ways in which the royal
revenues were diverted into the hands of the nobles. The remission of
customs duties, fairly frequent under Robert II, continued under
his successor.[180] Moreover, in Robert III's reign the accounts of the
expenses of the chamberlain, the custumars and the bailies of burghs

---

[174] *Moray Registrum*, p. 382.   [175] *A.P.S.*, I. 570.   [176] *Ibid.*
[177] *Ibid.*, 570–1.   [178] *E.R.*, III. 315.   [179] *Ibid.*, 643.
[180] See *ibid.*, index, under the heading 'Customs, remissions from'.

were interspersed on every page with payments of life-pensions, heritable pensions, and gifts of cash, to nobles great, middling or small. After 1397 there tended to be a deficit in the chamberlain's account. The fact that until then there was occasionally a sizable surplus is remarkable, and the explanation must be that the royal household was supported by undisclosed revenue from the crown lands, augmented as they were by the ancestral Stewart heritage. The crown had retrogressed to a primitive dependence on land, while the benefits of the more sophisticated fiscal system evolved under David II were squandered in pensions to the nobles.

Usually no reason is given in the exchequer accounts for the grant of pensions. They may be attributed to Robert III's desire to please all men, especially those of the name of Stewart. Yet one type of heritable pension stands out with sinister clarity: Robert II had begun the practice of granting heritable pensions as a retaining fee (*pro retinentia*). Thus George Dunbar, Earl of March, was to receive a heritable annual pension of £100 for his services, past and future, to Robert II, and, after his decease, to John, Earl of Carrick, his first-born son;[181] the latter, now Robert III, expanded the practice of granting pensions of retinue. By about 1394 the process was in full swing. The king's brother, Robert Stewart, Earl of Fife and Menteith, received each year two hundred marks from the great customs of Cupar and Linlithgow 'for his homage and service and for his being retained in the service of David, our first-born son'.[182] Others who were jointly retained in the service of Robert III and the heir apparent included Sir Murdoch Stewart (eldest son of the Earl of Fife), Sir Walter Stewart, Lord of Brechin (brother of the king), John Dunbar, Earl of Moray (brother-in-law of the king), Sir William Stewart of Jedburgh (a kinsman of the king), Sir David Lindsay (soon to be Earl of Crawford), Sir William Lindsay of the Byres, Sir John Montgomery of Eaglesham, Sir William Danielston and Sir John Ramorgny.[183] This list suggests the forging of a special bond of service out of the basic materials of kinship and cash. Yet all of the persons listed were probably tenants-in-chief of the crown and, on that account alone, owed homage and service to the king and his heir.

Scotland was not alone among European countries in finding that the original feudal bonds binding a vassal to his liege lord were growing insubstantial. More and more, those who held fiefs of the crown

---

[181] *Ibid.*, 203, 224. See also *ibid.*, 49, 294, 372. [182] *Ibid.*, 348.
[183] See *ibid.*, index, under the heading of 'Retinue'.

regarded them as absolute private property rather than as property held on condition of service. A heritable grant of land might bind the recipient to the crown during his own lifetime; by the time the heir succeeded to the land he regarded it as his own by right; the gratitude that his predecessor may have felt was not always transmitted to the heir, and his services might have to be bought by the crown by yet another reward. Only in times of wholesale forfeiture could the crown find at its disposal anything like a sufficiency of estates with which to reward supporters. When land was a scarce commodity for such reward it was inevitable that money should take its place. There was much to be said for this development. The great customs had brought to the crown increased financial resources. Service could be, and was, rewarded with occasional gifts; it could be rewarded, and was, with annuities limited to the lifetime of the recipient. What was disastrous was the practice that began under Robert II and became common under Robert III, of granting heritable annuities. These thus took the place of a landed fief. Often lip-service was paid to the original feudal concept: the heritable annuity was to be paid until such time as the king should infeft the recipient or his heirs in lands of the same annual value.[184] But this was a proviso that was scarcely ever implemented, and was probably regarded at the time as a mere form of words. Thus in Scotland, as in contemporary France and England, there emerged the 'money-fief'.

At the basis of the money-fief was a contract (known in Scotland as a bond or band). It was remarked by a nineteenth-century historian that the conclusion of such bonds between king and subject was 'a new feature in the feudal constitution of the country'.[185] This 'new feature' has more recently been styled 'bastard feudalism'.[186] It has been pointed out that the function of both 'true' and 'bastard' feudalism was the same: 'they differed only in the form of the reward. . . . Land ceased to be the way *par excellence* of acquiring followers; payment and sometimes mere assumption of interest supplanted it; . . . the idea of homage palled; a variety of oaths and documents were more to the taste of those who swore and those who contracted.'[187]

Among the variety of documents that were to make their appearance in Scotland bonds of alliance and bonds of manrent[188] would

---

[184] *Ibid.*, 287.   [185] P. F. Tytler, *History*, i. pt. ii, 7.
[186] See K. B. McFarlane, 'Bastard Feudalism', *B.I.H.R.*, xx. 161–80 and B. D. Lyon, *From Fief to Indenture*.
[187] P. S. Lewis, 'Decayed and Non-Feudalism in Later Medieval France', *B.I.H.R.*, xxxvii. 157.   [188] Pp. 231, 286, 358–9, 410 below.

predominate in the fifteenth century. At the close of the fourteenth century it was the bond of retinue that was most characteristic. Not only the king and the heir apparent, David, Earl of Carrick, made use of it : in 1372 the first Earl of Douglas had retained Sir James Douglas of Dalkeith to serve him with eight men-at-arms and sixteen archers against all men living, save the king; in return Sir James was to be paid six hundred marks within three years.[189] Documents of this sort, which bear a close similarity to French exemplars,[190] have mostly perished. That they were commonplace is suggested by an ordinance of the general council that met at Perth on 27 January 1399 : all the king's lieges were to support the government notwithstanding 'ony condiciouns of retenewis'.[191]

The king's brother, Robert Stewart, Earl of Fife and Menteith, was well placed to take advantage of the financial opportunities available under bastard feudalism : thanks to remissions of customs most of the wool and hides of his earldoms of Fife and Menteith were exported free ;[192] he drew annual fees of £200 as chamberlain,[193] of 200 marks as keeper of Stirling Castle,[194] and occasionally of 1,000 marks as guardian ;[195] in addition he had heritable pensions of 200 marks from the Abthania of Dull and 200 marks from the great customs of Linlithgow and Cupar.[196]

This last annuity, granted in 1394, was a pension of retinue for service to his nephew, David, Earl of Carrick, the heir apparent,[197] who was beginning to stretch his wings : at the exchequer audit of 26 May 1397 it was discovered that one of the Edinburgh custumars had paid almost £80 to the Earl of Carrick without a royal precept. At first the auditors refused to pass this item and decided to advise the king 'to inform his first-born son . . . that in future he is to receive nothing of the royal revenues from the custumars . . . without the king's written mandate . . . because the custumars do not dare, and cannot, resist him'.[198] David was evidently headstrong, and as he approached his majority it was natural that he should begin to question both the ample revenues and the ample powers that had been bestowed upon his uncle.

The reaction of Robert III to the antagonism between his brother

[189] *Morton Registrum*, II. No. 129.
[190] P. S. Lewis, *op. cit.*, Appendices Nos. 1, 2 and 3.   [191] *A.P.S.*, I. 573.
[192] *E.R.*, III. lxxxv.   [193] *Ibid.*, 644, 668.   [194] *Ibid.*, 427.
[195] This was certainly paid between 1389 and 1392 and partly paid in 1404 (*ibid.*, 238, 276, 312, 589, 610, 645).
[196] *Ibid.*, 427.   [197] *Ibid.*, 348.   [198] *Ibid.*, 407–8.

and his son was a characteristic attempt to placate both parties. In England the title of duke had existed since 1337, and on 29 September 1397 no fewer than four new dukedoms had been created.[199] It was a sign of the existing chivalric links between the Scottish and English courts that Robert III imitated the example set by Richard II : in Scone Abbey on 28 April 1398 David, Earl of Carrick, was raised to the dignity of Duke of Rothesay, and Robert Stewart, Earl of Fife and Menteith, to that of Duke of Albany. A week earlier Sir David Lindsay of Glenesk had been created Earl of Crawford and had his lands erected into a regality.[200] It was perhaps significant that while the heir apparent styled himself after the ancestral Stewart home his uncle's title hinted at the ancient kingdom of Alba (still the Gaelic term for Scotland) and pointed to pretensions that were royal rather than baronial. Certainly the new and equal dignities of the heir apparent and his uncle did nothing to reconcile them. At the exchequer on 2 May, a few days after the ceremony in Scone Abbey, the auditors called upon Albany to produce a charter under which he claimed payment in connection with a mysterious marriage contract. Nor did the auditors see eye to eye with Albany in his capacity as chamberlain; the account closed with mention of the enormous sum of £930 19s. 7d. which was in dispute between the auditors and the duke. It was probably Rothesay who was the figure behind the auditors : the dispute was to be referred to consultation between the king, Albany, Rothesay, and the council that had been 'limited' (specially assigned) to Rothesay.[201]

If this was the opening of a struggle between Rothesay and Albany, it was continued when a general council met at Perth in January 1399 [202] and resulted in a revolution that did not quite succeed. Without mincing words it was declared that 'the mysgovernance of the reaulme and the defaut of the kepyng of the common law sulde be imput to the kyng and his officeris'. Robert III had doubtless caused exasperation,[203] but it was probably not against him but against his advisers, Albany in particular, that attack was directed : the king was given the opportunity to 'excuse his defautes'; he might summon those officers whom he had appointed and 'accuse thaim in presence

[199] May McKisack, *The Fourteenth Century*, pp. 483–4.
[200] *Chron. Bower*, II. 422; *Moray Registrum*, p. 382.
[201] *E.R.*, III. 461.   [202] *A.P.S.*, I. 572.
[203] In April 1398 the council had revoked a grant which the king had made 'without the consent of the council and to the prejudice of the common weal of the realm' (*ibid.*, 571).

of his counsail'; after they had been heard the council would be ready to judge their defaults.[204]

Despite this almost open invitation to accuse Albany, Robert III seems to have preferred to bear the burden of 'mysgovernance' on his own penitent shoulders. Somewhat thwarted, the opposition had to couch its attack on the duke in the form of an attack upon the king. This, however, did not take the form of the more sophisticated and more ruthless attacks made in the English parliament upon Richard II. The three estates simply stated as a matter of common knowledge that it was obvious and well known that the lord king, by reason of personal infirmity, was unable to undertake the labour of governing the realm or restraining transgressors and rebels. Therefore it seemed to the council most 'expedient'—the very word suggests the difference between the pragmatism of the Scottish estates and the political theorising of the English parliament—that the Duke of Rothesay should be the king's lieutenant for a period of three years. Careful attention was paid to the powers that Rothesay would exercise. He was to have a commission from the king to govern the land with full royal authority, and Robert III was to oblige himself not to interfere with the lieutenant in the exercise of his functions. Finally Rothesay as lieutenant was to have the 'dispenses and costages' that had lately been granted to Albany as guardian.[205]

While it is difficult to ascertain the members of the party behind this palace revolution, it seems clear that one of its chief members, apart from Rothesay himself, was Queen Annabella. In the Scone parliament of March 1391 the three estates had settled upon her the huge annual pension of 2,500 marks for 'her adornment and other things necessary for her rank and livelihood'.[206] Now she formally complained that the chamberlain's deputies obstructed the levying of her pension. The estates decided that due payment be made 'without ony objeccioun'; also the chamberlain (Albany) was to be ordered not to hinder such payment in any manner.[207] The queen's Drummond kinsmen were probably behind her. More potent influences may be seen in Bishop Trail of St Andrews and Archibald the Grim, who were at least associated with the queen in the mind of Abbot Bower as a trio of virtuous persons.[208]

The indirect attack upon Albany was not wholly successful: he seems to have used his influence to curb the power of the new lieutenant through a 'special' council of twenty-one persons named by

[204] Ibid., 572.   [205] Ibid., 572-4.   [206] Ibid., 578; E.R., III. 252-3.
[207] A.P.S., I. 574.   [208] Pp. 220-1 below.

the three estates.[209] With the exception of Adam Forrester of Corstorphine—an active figure as auditor of exchequer, envoy, custumar and
bailie of Edinburgh, financial agent of all and sundry [210]—no burgess
figured on the special council. For what it was worth, six of the members—Albany, the Earls of Moray and Crawford, Walter Stewart,
Lord of Brechin, Sir William Stewart of Jedburgh and Sir John
Ramorgny—had been receiving annuities of retinue for their past
and future service to Robert III and Rothesay;[211] and Ramorgny—
almost as active a figure as Adam Forrester—was Rothesay's personal
chamberlain.[212] It was with this group of twenty-one 'wyse men' that
Rothesay was to consult when the three estates were not in session.
Every administrative act on the part of the lieutenant was to be recorded with the date and place and the names of those who had
counselled it so that the latter might answer to the three estates and
be punished for what the lieutenant did amiss. Rothesay was authorised to reward deserving persons with the escheats and forfeitures that
fell due during his three years of office; but those who counselled him
on such matters would have to answer for such awards to the king and
his general council. For the time being the general council seems to
have been regarded as the ultimate political authority while parliament was left with its judicial authority: it was ordained that for the
next three years the king should hold an annual parliament on 2
November so that his subjects might be 'servit of the law'.[213] All this
was on parchment admirable, but in practice there were too many
checks and balances. The Albany and Rothesay factions were probably too finely balanced for firm government; the one faction in the
'special' council could thwart administration by refusing to accept
responsibility; the other, by reason of such obstruction, might be
driven to rash measures.

The general council of January 1399 also considered the international situation. Although the Franco-Scottish alliance of 1371 had
been renewed in 1391 [214] the spirit behind it was no longer aggressive. Scotland had become a party to the international truces arranged
at Leulighem in June 1389 and a state of truce was to be prolonged
until 1399.[215] Meanwhile the chivalry-smitten armigerous classes of
both Scotland and England, deprived of more serious warfare,

[209] *A.P.S.*, I. 572.
[210] *E.R.*, III. index, *sub nomine.*
[211] P. 211 above.
[212] *E.R.*, III. 487; index, *sub nomine.*
[213] *A.P.S.*, I. 572–3.
[214] Text in *E.R.*, III. xcvii–civ.
[215] *Cal. Docs. Scot.*, IV. No. 416; *Foedera*, III. pt. iv, 39–42; *Rot. Scot.*, II.
142–3; *E.R.*, III. lxxvi.

vaunted their martial ardour in the lists. They were encouraged by
Richard II, who patronised a court of chivalry in which affairs of
honour could be settled in trials by combat. A similar court seems
occasionally to have been extemporised in Scotland.[216] The Anglo-
Scottish chivalric combats so frequent in the last decade of the four-
tenth century [217] had inspired mutual interest rather than mutual
bitterness and led to more courtly interchanges in which Queen
Annabella took a significant part.[218] There were even honest attempts
to remedy the constant breaches of truce that kept alive old enmities.
'Days of Trewe' were held fairly regularly to afford redress. It was on
these Truce Days, held with considerable formality and expensive
ostentation [219] at recognised trysting places—Reddenburn, Carham,
Hawdenstank or Clochmabenstane [220]—that there took place Anglo-
Scottish confrontations at the highest level: Rothesay, Albany and
Crawford, shortly before their elevation in rank, had met the Duke of
Lancaster and other English dignitaries at Hawdenstank in March
1398 and had arranged a prolongation of the truce until Michaelmas
1399.[221] The question of its renewal was raised in the Perth general
council of January 1399 and a commission of fourteen persons, drawn
from Rothesay's special council and headed by the new lieutenant
and Albany, was appointed to hold discussions with English envoys
at Edinburgh.[222] As soon as this commission had reached a decision
envoys were to be sent to England and a 'grete message', or embassy,
was to be sent to France.[223]

   To finance this important diplomatic activity a contribution of
£2,000 [224] was to be levied—the first evidence of direct taxation since
1373. The effect of the intervening lapse in levying such taxation was
reflected in the protestations formally recorded on the part of the kirk
and the burgesses. What had become customary and almost habitual
towards the close of the reign of David II was now regarded as unaccustomed and exceptional: the three estates united to protest that
the contribution had been granted on condition that the law would
be enforced; they also stipulated that collection of the tax was not to

---

[216] George Neilson, *Trial by Combat*, pp. 272–5.
   [217] *Chron. Bower*, II. 422–4; *Chron. Wyntoun*, III. 50; *Cal. Docs. Scot.*, IV.
Nos. 414–33, *passim*.
   [218] *Nat. MSS. Scot.*, II. No. xlix.
   [219] Rothesay was granted £800 by Robert III for his expenses on one of these
occasions in 1398 (*E.R.*, III. 473, 474).
   [220] *Cal. Docs. Scot.*, IV. No. 492.
   [221] *Rot. Scot.*, II. 142–3; *Cal. Docs. Scot.*, IV. No. 502.
   [222] *A.P.S.*, I. 573.   [223] *Ibid.*
   [224] Not £11,000 as stated by P. F. Tytler, *History*, I. pt. ii, 9.

be entrusted to the chamberlain (Albany) but to nine special receivers, three appointed by each of the estates.[225]

The outcome of the subsequent diplomacy may be seen in the commission that Richard II issued on 22 March 1399 authorising negotiation not only for a renewal of truce but for a final peace.[226] On 4 May the Scots issued a similar commission : Rothesay headed the Scottish commissioners; Albany was conspicuously absent.[227] A meeting at Hawdenstank on 14 May prolonged the truce until Michaelmas 1400.[228] Whatever chance there was of a more significant outcome was frustrated by the landing of Henry Bolingbroke in England in June 1399, the deposition of Richard II on 29 September [229] and his reported death in February 1400. The Scots, conservative in their outlook upon the political and social vicissitudes of other nations, were deeply shocked.[230] While the two countries hovered on the brink of renewing the truce the new Lancastrian king received from Scotland itself an unexpected appeal for forceful action.

It was the behaviour of the romantically fickle Duke of Rothesay that had inspired the appeal. By paying to Robert III a large sum of gold George Dunbar, Earl of March, had obtained Rothesay's betrothal to his daughter Elizabeth.[231] Archibald the Grim 'at the insinuation of the king's council' paid a larger sum than the Earl of March, whereupon the king allowed Rothesay to jilt Elizabeth Dunbar and marry Marjory Douglas. The Earl of March remonstrated with the king and requested at least the refund of the marriage payment. Robert III was evasive and March was 'more moved than he ought to have been'.[232] On 18 February 1400 he addressed to Henry IV a singular epistle [233] that wasted no time on courtly preambles but straightway announced : 'I am gretly wrangit be the Duc of Rothesay, the quhilk spousit my douchter and now . . . spouses ane other wif.' The earl reminded the king that he and Henry were within the fourth degree of kinship, 'the quhilk in alde tyme wes callit neire'. Henry, who had lately deposed his own full cousin, was now called upon as fourth cousin of the Earl of March to take part in a Scottish feud over a breach of promise.

---

[225] No record of this contribution appears in the exchequer rolls, presumably because the receivers kept their own accounts.
[226] *Cal. Docs. Scot.*, IV. No. 515.
[227] *Ibid.*, No. 519.   [228] *Ibid.*, No. 520.
[229] See E. F. Jacob, *The Fifteenth Century*, pp. 1–18.
[230] *Chron. Bower*, II. 428.   [231] *Ibid.*   [232] *Ibid.*, 421.
[233] *Nat. MSS. Scot.*, II. No. liii.

But however lightly Henry treated kinship he was not blind to political expediency; March was to be asked to swear allegiance to him and to say whether he would deliver any of his castles in return for an annuity, how many men he would require, and by what time.[234] While the Duke of Rothesay married the daughter of Archibald the Grim in the kirk of Bothwell[235] the Earl of March made his way to England and joined forces with the Percies of Northumberland in a raid upon the countryside near Haddington.[236] On 2 July 1400 an English safe-conduct was issued for Adam Forrester,[237] who came as an envoy of Robert III in a last bid to avert war. At York Henry rejected a proposal for peace based on the terms of the treaty of 1328.[238] From Newcastle on 6 August he sent off a letter to Robert III reminding him that since the days of Locrine, son of Brutus, the kings of England were lords superior of Scotland: Henry would be ready to receive Robert's homage and fealty at Edinburgh on 23 August.[239]

Henry's expedition to Edinburgh was uniquely undestructive: he was reputed to have spared the countryside out of reverence for Queen Annabella.[240] By 21 August he had arrived at Leith and announced that he had come to Scotland because he had been styled a prodigious traitor in letters, or rather libels, sent to the king of France by a certain Scottish magnate 'in the balance of whose hands the equilibrium of the kingdom has perforce to sway up and down'. Henry had appeared to see if that magnate dared to fight with him and give him the opportunity to prove his innocence.[241]

The 'certain magnate' was probably Rothesay, who shut himself up in Edinburgh Castle, which Henry assaulted in vain.[242] Once more he summoned Robert III to do homage. Robert refused to be enticed. Meanwhile Rothesay sent a defiance to Henry (whom he styled not as king but merely as his 'adversary of England') and offered combat with a few hundred nobles on either side.[243] This challenge was not quite to the liking of Henry, who by 3 September was back in Newcastle.

Peace negotiations took place in October 1401 at Kirk Yetholm, where the English recited the time-honoured rigmarole beginning

234 Balfour-Melville, *James I*, p. 17.   235 *Chron. Bower*, II.. 428.
236 *Ibid.*, 428–9; *Chron. Wyntoun*, III. 78.
237 *Cal. Docs. Scot.*, IV. No. 547.   238 Balfour-Melville, *James I*, p. 18.
239 *Chron. Bower*, II. 506–8; *Moray Registrum*, Nos. 305, 306; *Cal. Docs. Scot.*, IV. Nos. 553, 554.
240 *Chron. Pluscarden*, I. 341; *Chron. Bower*, II. 430.
241 *Chron. Bower*, II. 430; *Chron. Pluscarden*, I. 341.
242 *Chron. Bower*, II. 430; *Chron. Wyntoun*, II. 77; *Cal. Docs. Scot.*, IV. No. 562.   243 *Foedera*, III. pt. iv, 189.

with Brutus the Trojan, and the Scots uttered 'some very undiplomatic language'.[244] Then the English asked if the Scottish king would consent to arbitration over the homage question. The Bishop of Glasgow rejoined by asking whether the right of Henry IV to the English throne might also be put to arbitration. The conference broke up.

Henry IV's intervention in Scotland had interrupted the constitutional experiment that had begun in the Perth general council of January 1399 with the appointment of Rothesay as lieutenant for a period of three years. Robert III had remained as at least a figurehead and presided over a council at Linlithgow on 20 November 1399 to which the two dukes and most members of Rothesay's special council were summoned, together with some other magnates.[245] This council dealt with a complaint from Walter Lindsay, who alleged that he had been made captive by Sir John Wemyss and had been forced to enter into some obligation towards him.[246] Sir John Wemyss was a prominent knight who in 1392 had received a licence to construct on his land of Reres in Fife a castle with towers of whatever height or strength he pleased.[247] His handiwork was soon put to the test : the Duke of Rothesay besieged Reres Castle 'for the public weal', using a wooden engine especially constructed at St Andrews at a cost of £80.[248] The Reres incident certainly suggests that Rothesay did not lack forcefulness. When the three estates met in parliament at Scone on 21 February 1401 [249] they passed a statute that made it easier for the weak (ecclesiastics, widows, orphans and minors) to seek the lieutenant's good services. Such plaintiffs were no longer to be required to give pledges for prosecution of their suit.[250]

What might have brought a return to sound government came to a dramatic end. Rothesay's position was weakened with the death of the three persons who seem to have supported him. Archibald, third Earl of Douglas, died on Christmas Eve, 1400. He was, wrote Abbot Bower, 'called the grim or terrible, who in worldly prudence, courage and boldness, excelled the other Scots of his day'.[251] His soul, according to Wyntoun, sped to paradise,[252] where it was joined before

[244] Stones, *Documents*, pp. 173–82, at 180. See also E. L. G. Stones, 'The Appeal to History in Anglo-Scottish Relations between 1291 and 1401: Part II', *Archives*, IX. No. 42, 80–3.

[245] *A.P.S.*, I. 574–5.   [246] *Ibid.*, 574.
[247] *R.M.S.*, I. No. 53, p. 214.   [248] *E.R.*, III. 552, 559, 560.
[249] *A.P.S.*, I. 575–6.   [250] *Ibid.*, 576.
[251] *Chron. Bower*, II. 429; *Chron. Pluscarden*, I. 340.
[252] *Chron. Wyntoun*, III. 77.

1 July 1401 by that of Bishop Walter Trail. This 'solempne clerk' had lived 'Godlikly' and was 'the strongest pillar of the kirk, a vessel of eloquence, storehouse of knowledge, and defender of the Catholic faith'.[253] Then at harvest-time in 1401 died Queen Annabella,

> Faire, honorabil and plesand,
> Cunnand, curtas in hir efferis,
> Luvand, and large [generous] to strangeris.[254]

With the death of these three, queen, bishop and earl, it was said 'almost proverbially' that the glory of Scotland had departed, its honour had withdrawn and its decency had died.[255] From the walls of Edinburgh Castle the Duke of Rothesay watched a comet, a 'brycht stern and a clere', blaze across the skies, and took it as a baleful omen. Priestly science deemed it a sign of pestilence or the death of princes.[256]

Rothesay's three-year term of office as royal lieutenant expired in January 1402. He is reported to have spurned the advice of the special council which had been assigned to him, and it thereupon resigned.[258] He tried to draw revenue from the custumars, took £70 'violently' from a custumar of Dundee and held a custumar of Montrose captive until he disgorged £24.[259] His final act of state was an expedition to St Andrews to take over the bishop's castle and exercise the other rights that pertained to the crown during the vacancy of the see after the death of Bishop Trail.[260] The king, 'powerless and decrepit', wrote to Albany, perhaps already appointed as Rothesay's replacement, with orders to arrest the heir apparent and hold him in ward until he mended his ways. But, explains Bower, 'what the king proposed for the improvement of his son turned out to his harm'. As Rothesay was on his way to St Andrews he was arrested by his own retainer, Sir John Ramorgny, and Sir William Lindsay of Rossie (whose sister he had once jilted). Albany and the new Earl of Douglas, Archibald the Tyneman, arrived at St Andrews to convey the duke in sorry state to the manor of Falkland, where he died on 26 or 27 March 1402, of 'dysentery' or 'as others would have it, of hunger'.[261] The chronicler Wyntoun consigned him to paradise with a pleasing

[253] *Chron. Bower*, II. 430.
[255] *Chron. Bower*, II. 431.
[258] *Chron. Bower*, II. 431.
[259] *E.R.*, III. 549–50, 552, 599; compare p. 546.
[260] *Chron. Wyntoun*, III. 80; *Chron. Bower*, II. 431.
[261] *Chron. Bower*, II. 431–2; *Chron. Pluscarden*, I. 342–3.

[254] *Chron. Wyntoun*, III. 81.
[256] *Ibid.*, 432.

obituary.[262] Others were not so ready to shut their eyes and ears. When a general council met at Edinburgh on 16 May 1402 it remained in session for many days. Albany and Archibald the Tyneman were accused and interrogated; they explained that they had arrested and imprisoned Rothesay for the public weal. The reasons they gave were, by the king's instructions, omitted from the record. Rothesay was known 'to have departed this life by divine providence and not otherwise'. The king publicly declared that Albany and Douglas were innocent; he strictly commanded that no one should 'murmur against them'.[263]

The suspect circumstances in which Albany was restored to power were soon lost to sight in new Anglo-Scottish involvements. In the declining years of the fourteenth century the more or less simultaneous weakening of central government in both Scotland and England had prevented either kingdom from successfully pursuing far-reaching ambitions against the other. In 1402, however, Albany felt strong enough to ignore the blandishments by which Henry IV sought to entice him towards an extended truce or final peace.[264] Three factors inspired the Scots to a fresh and ambitious bellicosity.

One of these was the rising of Owen Glendower, who hoped to establish an independent Welsh principality.[265] Political realism inspired him to seek an alliance with the French. The prophecies of Merlin led him to believe that Wales would be freed only with the aid of the Scots and native Irish.[266] Another factor was the appearance in Scotland of a person thought to be none other than Richard II, escaped from prison.[267] By 1417 Albany claimed to have spent no less than £733 6s. 8d. on the maintenance of 'King Richard of England'.[268] Although Henry IV denounced Albany's protégé as an impostor or 'Mammet'[269] it was widely believed for many years that Richard was alive in Scotland; until the Mammet was buried with royal honours at Stirling in 1419[270] he was a figurehead for plots and risings in England. A third factor that made for war was the feud be-

---

[262] *Chron. Wyntoun*, III. 82.   [263] *A.P.S.*, I. 582–3.

[264] *Rot. Scot.*, II. 154–5.

[265] E. F. Jacob, *The Fifteenth Century*, pp. 41–2, 54–8.

[266] *Chron. Bower*, II. 452–8; Glyn Roberts, *Aspects of Welsh History* (1969), p. 314.   [267] *Chron. Wyntoun*, III. 76; *Chron. Bower*, II. 402, 427.

[268] *E.R.*, IV. 289.

[269] *Foedera*, IV. pt. i, 29–30. In a painstaking essay entitled 'Historical Remarks on the Death of Richard II', P. F. Tytler (*History*, I. pt. ii, 96–119) argued plausibly that the mysterious personage was indeed Richard II.

[270] *Chron. Bower*, II. 459.

tween the Earl of March and Archibald the Tyneman, fourth Earl of Douglas, who occupied the earldom of March and the Dunbar lordship of Annandale. When the dispossessed Earl of March raided the eastern Borders he was aided by former tenants, still loyal to 'their native lord'.[271] A retaliatory raid led by Sir Patrick Hepburn of Hailes ended at Nesbit Muir on 22 June 1402 with the capture of 'the flower of the chivalry of a great part of Lothian'.[272]

The Earls of Douglas, Angus and Moray set out to avenge this reverse and harried Northumberland to the gates of Newcastle. Returning with their booty the Scots were overtaken on 14 September 1402 by Hotspur and the Earl of March. Archibald the Tyneman cautiously stationed his troops on the summit of Homildon Hill, waiting to repel the expected English attack. All that came was a hail of English arrows. Eventually Sir John Stenton led a handful of knights to perish in a charge downhill. Others took to flight and the remainder were killed or taken prisoner. The list of captives included the Earl of Douglas, who had earned his by-name of 'the Tyneman' ('the Loser'), as well as the Earls of Moray and Angus, and Murdoch Stewart, Albany's son and heir. It was 'as if the flower of chivalry of the whole realm of Scotland was captured and held to ransom'.[273]

Homildon wiped out the English reverse at Otterburn. Hotspur was able to cross the border and obtain the surrender of a few fortalices. At one small stronghold, the tower of Cocklaws in Teviotdale, he met with staunch resistance. Instead of pressing the siege Hotspur made a truce : the tower would surrender if it were not relieved by either Robert III or Albany on 1 August 1403. Albany exclaimed, so says Bower, 'I vow to God and St Fillan that on the appointed day, if alive, I will be there, although no one bears me company save my boy Patrick'.[274] Those present marvelled at the high spirit of the duke and wept for joy. The Scottish host marched to Cocklaws to an encounter that was expected to be a second Bannockburn or a second Halidon. The sequel was ludicrous. The enemy did not turn up. Albany marched his host round the little tower while a herald explained that Hotspur had been slain at Shrewsbury.[275]

When Hotspur had besieged Cocklaws and then left it 'in suspense' he had done so either to entice the Scots to the elusive final battle or, more likely, he had used the Cocklaws affair as an excuse

---

[271] *Ibid.*, 432.   [272] *Ibid.*, 432–3.
[273] *Ibid.*, 433–5; *Chron. Wyntoun*, III. 85–6.
[274] *Chron. Bower*, II. 437.   [275] *Ibid.*, 437–8.

for gathering troops to be used against an unsuspecting Henry IV,[276] against whom the Percies had conceived grievances. One of these concerned the disposal of the ransomable prisoners captured at Homildon : the Earl of Northumberland duly delivered Albany's son, Murdoch Stewart, to Henry IV; Hotspur held on to the captured Earl of Douglas, who seems to have engaged to pay his ransom by serving him in a conspiracy against the English king. With the help of Owen Glendower the Percies would set on the throne the legitimist Mortimer claimant, descendant of Lionel, second son of Edward III.[277]

At Shrewsbury on 21 July 1403 Hotspur was slain and his rebellion crushed. Scotsmen fought on both sides : the Earl of March had abandoned the Percies when they were joined by his rival Douglas, and gave good service to Henry IV; Archibald the Tyneman, on the losing side as usual, led a force of Scots in Hotspur's vanguard and fell into Henry's hands as a prisoner.[278] Shrewsbury showed that both in Scotland and England the concept of nationalism which seemed to have taken root in the first half of the fourteenth century had been largely displaced by baronial self-interest decked in the trappings of chivalry.

Despite his victory Henry IV still had too many troubles to allow him to make war on the Scots. Negotiations resulted in a truce which seems to have been successively extended until 1406.[279] In the summer of 1403 there were abortive negotiations for the ransom and release of Archibald the Tyneman and Albany's son Murdoch.[280] Albany betrayed his anxiety over the fate of his son and heir in an obsequious letter that he addressed to Henry IV, probably in 1404 :

> I was most willing that you should keep my son Murdoch Stewart (your kinsman if it please you) with you in your honourable court . . . and have fully understood . . . how graciously you replied with regard to the release of my foresaid son. . . . And if there be any useful tasks I can conveniently undertake in these parts [Scotland] be pleased to inform me of the same . . . and I shall willingly perform them to the best of my power . . .
>
>   Your kinsman, if it please you,
>   Robert, Duke of Albany,
> Full brother of the King of Scotland and his lieutenant-general.[281]

[276] *Ibid.*, 436, 438.
[277] *Foedera*, iv. pt. i, 35–6; Balfour-Melville, *James I*, p. 25; E. F. Jacob, *The Fifteenth Century*, pp. 45–8.
[278] *Chron. Bower*, ii. 438; *Chron. Walsingham*, ii. 368–9.
[279] *Rot. Scot.*, ii. 164, 168, 173–4, 177.
[280] *Ibid.*, 167.   [281] *Nat. MSS. Scot.*, ii. No. lv.

The stalemate in Anglo-Scottish relations was interrupted by a plot of the Earl of Northumberland and Archbishop Scrope of York, who intended to muster at York with a force of Scots; the French would send an expedition to Wales to aid Owen Glendower, who was also a party to the conspiracy. The plan miscarried when Archbishop Scrope was beheaded on the orders of Henry IV. By June 1405 Northumberland was a fugitive in Scotland with his young grandson and the Welsh Bishops of Bangor and St Asaph.[282]

It was about this time that Archibald the Tyneman's younger brother, James Douglas, warden of the March (later to earn ill fame as James the Gross, seventh Earl of Douglas), took advantage of the situation by burning the town of Berwick and seizing £23 5s. 2d. from the Edinburgh custumars to cover his expenses in arranging the conflagration.[283] On 26 July 1405 he impatiently replied to the English king's reproaches in a letter that showed none of the obsequiousness of Albany and minced no words.[284] If James Douglas was representative of the outlook of the Scottish barons their mood was undoubtedly bellicose. Anglo-Scottish relations were left in topsyturvy turmoil: the Dunbars of March were honoured guests in England; the Percies of Northumberland were honoured guests in Scotland and were intriguing for French help; Albany and Henry IV, both men of the same stamp, politic, ruthless, dissimulating, seekers of cheap popularity, were plagued by domestic troubles. This was the background to an event that was soon to place the heir to the Scottish throne in the hands of Henry IV.

After the death of the Duke of Rothesay only two lives lay between Albany and the throne, those of the ailing Robert III and his surviving son, James, born at Dunfermline in 1394,[285] probably on 25 July, the feast day of the Apostle James. The existence of the heir apparent made it likely that Albany's tenure of power would not be unduly long, and some factions were perhaps already preparing themselves for the time when James would enter politics on his own account. Certainly Albany was appointed to the office of lieutenant-general not for any long or indeterminate period but for only a year or two at a time, after which the appointment was renewed (possibly after a review of his performance) by the three estates. Thus, when a

---

[282] *E.R.*, IV. xliii; *Chron. Bower*, II. 453; *Chron. Pluscarden*, I. 441.
[283] *E.R.*, IV. 44, 81; *Rot. Scot.*, II. 177.
[284] *Nat. MSS. Scot.*, II. No. liv.   [285] *Ibid.*, No. xlix.

general council met at Linlithgow on 28 April 1404,[286] Albany presided as the king's lieutenant, and the king, who was also present, ordained that the duke should be his lieutenant with full royal power for two years commencing on Whitsunday next. But while the lieutenant could, and did, summon general councils, it was assumed that only the king could hold parliaments—which he was to do each year, beginning on 3 November, primarily, no doubt, for judicial purposes, for the other enactments of this general council show a concern for the improvement of the administration of justice.[287] From the exchequer records it would appear not only that the three estates had assigned a special council to advise and perhaps control the lieutenant, but also that the auditors were capable of calling him to account. This is all the more remarkable in so far as the auditors were scarcely men of power.[288] Just as Robert III had striven to surround Rothesay with a band of pensioned retainers he now began to do the same for himself and his surviving son, carefully avoiding the selection of royal Stewarts.[289] Within a few years the young James could be expected to become more than a figurehead for opposition to Albany. On the arrival in Scotland of the fugitive Percies it had been arranged that James, together with Henry Percy, son of Hotspur, a boy of his own age, should be reared in St Andrews Castle under the learned tutelage of Bishop Wardlaw, 'a man of great expenses'.[290] Probably with some presentiment of danger the old king ended this arrangement: he would send his heir to France, ostensibly for his education, more probably for his safety.

If James was to reach France in safety much depended on the rapidity and secrecy of his crossing, for no English safe-conduct had been requested. At first all went well. The king's trusted councillor, Sir David Fleming of Biggar and Cumbernauld, escorted James swiftly to North Berwick, whence he was rowed out to the Bass Rock to wait for a ship. Then things went wrong; on his way homeward on 14 February 1406 Fleming was waylaid and slain at Langherdmanston by James Douglas, the Tyneman's brother.[291] Albany did nothing to punish the murderers. Meanwhile James had to linger for a month among the gannets of the Bass Rock, attended by Henry

---

[286] It was attended by five bishops, one prior, eight abbots, two earls, twenty-one lords, seven knights (some of whom were of higher status than some 'lords'), the commissioners of eight burghs, and other unspecified persons. The text of the proceedings is published by A. A. M. Duncan in ' "Councils General", 1404, 1423', *S.H.R.*, xxxv. 132–43.

[287] *Ibid.*, 135–6.

[288] *E.R.*, III. 608; see also 589, 610.

[289] *Ibid.*, 291, 597, 625, 627, 635.

[290] *Chron. Bower*, II. 439.

[291] *Chron. Pluscarden*, I. 347.

Sinclair, Earl of Orkney, and a Welsh bishop. Finally, after a delay long enough for news to reach England, the party embarked in the *Maryenknyght* of Danzig, bound out of Leith with a cargo of wool and hides.[292] The vessel was off Flamborough Head when it was boarded on 14 March 1406[293] by Hugh-atte-Fen and other reputable merchants and pirates of Great Yarmouth. As a truce was still in force[294] the equitable Henry IV envisaged restitution of the captured cargo. Restitution of the Scottish heir apparent was out of the question; James was lodged in the Tower. Many years later he was to write in the *Kingis Quair* of his ill-fated voyage and his capture:

> ... out of my contree,
> By thaire avise that had of me the cure,
> Be see to pas, tuke I myn aventure ...
>
> Upon the wavis weltering to and fro,
> So infortunate was us that fremyt day,
> That maugre, playnly, quhethir we wold or no,
> With strong hand, as by forse, schortly to say,
> Off inymyis takin led away
> We weren all, and broght in thaire contree.

News of his son's capture was brought to Robert III as he sat at supper in Rothesay Castle : 'his spirit forthwith left him, the strength waned from his body, his countenance grew pale, and for grief thereafter he took not food'.[295] The king, then in his sixty-ninth year, died on Palm Sunday, 4 April 1406.[296]

'In the days of this king,' wrote Abbot Bower, 'there was in the realm great fertility of victuals but the greatest discord, wrangles and strife betwixt magnates and nobles, because the king, weak in body, nowhere exercised rigour.'[297] Robert III had long laboured under a sense of personal failure. Once when Queen Annabella had inquired of him whether he would follow the example of his royal predecessors by arranging for the erection of a seemly tombstone and epitaph,

---

[292] Balfour-Melville, *James I*, pp. 30–1.

[293] For an examination of the date see *ibid.*, p. 31; *E.R.*, IV. cxcvi; *Chron. Bower*, II. 439. Two literary historians (Jean Robert Simon and Matthew P. McDiarmid) have independently concluded that stanzas 20 and 21 of *The Kingis Quair* 'fix the day of the fateful voyage as 14 March' (McDiarmid in review of *Le Livre du Roi*, *S.H.R.*, XLIX. 195–7, at 197).

[294] See the detailed examination of this question by E. W. M. Balfour-Melville (*James I*, pp. 32–3).

[295] *Chron. Bower*, II. 440.

[296] Balfour-Melville, *James I*, p. 34.   [297] *Chron. Bower*, II. 440.

he is said to have answered : 'I would prefer to be buried deep in a midden, providing that my soul be safe in the day of the Lord. Wherefore bury me, I pray, in a midden, and write for my epitaph—"Here lies the worst of kings and the most wretched of men in the whole realm." ' [298]

[298] *Ibid.*, 440–1.

9

THE ALBANY GOVERNORSHIP AND THE END OF THE GREAT SCHISM

ROBERT III was laid to rest not in a midden but in the abbey of Paisley that his ancestors had helped to found. In June 1406 the three estates met in general council at Perth to face the dire mischance of the capture of an heir apparent who had almost immediately inherited the crown.[1] Since the new king, James I, was scarcely twelve years old, and was constrained to reside in England, he could not exercise even the most nominal of royal functions. Albany, now heir presumptive, was appointed as governor of the realm and assumed more of the trappings of royalty than guardians or lieutenants had formerly possessed. Once at least, in a letter of 1410 to Henry IV, the duke styled himself governor of Scotland *Dei gracia* and wrote of his 'subjects'.[2]

Meanwhile possession of the person of the Scottish king allowed Henry IV to display a certain assurance in his dealings with the Scots. English safe-conducts were issued to Scottish knights and esquires, to Scottish pilgrims, to Scotsmen who went south to seek redress for injuries committed in time of truce, to Scottish clerics on their way to or from the continent, and, above all, to Scottish merchants and skippers, who were granted licences to trade in England on a scale not seen since the time of David II.[3] Henry's readiness to show himself obliging to a wide variety of influential Scots was a sign of his willingness to reach a settlement with Scotland. Between 1406 and the end of his reign there seem to have been almost annual meetings of commissioners, usually at Hawdenstank, to negotiate renewals of

---

[1] *Chron. Wyntoun*, III. 99; *Chron. Bower*, II. 441. No official record of this general council survives.

[2] *E.R.*, IV. xlvii–xlix.

[3] *Rot. Scot.*, II. 178–201, *passim*.

truce.[4] Occasionally, as in 1409 and 1410, the terms of reference even included discussion of a final peace.[5]

Albany's response was one of latent hostility interspersed with occasional obsequiousness. The duke entertained envoys from France and Wales;[6] and the disinherited Earl of Northumberland was allowed to use Scotland as a base from which he set out on missions to Wales, Brittany and Flanders, until finally, in February 1408, he crossed the border only to be slain in Yorkshire.[7] The unsteady relationship between Albany and Henry, who resembled one another in their deviousness, can be seen in the words with which Henry from time to time described Albany in official documents: in 1407 he was 'lately our adversary of Scotland' or 'the Duke of Albany, governor, as he asserts, of the realm of Scotland'; in 1408 he was 'our kinsman'; in July 1409 he was 'our dearest kinsman'; in November 1409 he was once more 'governor, as he asserts, of the realm of Scotland'; and in May 1411 he was once more 'our dearest kinsman'.[8]

Against this uneasy background were set various negotiations for the release of Henry's captives—Archibald the Tyneman, Albany's son Murdoch, and James I.[9] For the temporary release of the Tyneman Henry obtained a dozen noble hostages [10] and a certain written undertaking. In this document of 14 March 1407 the Earl of Douglas bound himself to serve Henry and his four sons against all men save the Scottish king.[11] Henry expected that the Tyneman, once released on parole, would act as his partisan in Scotland. It came as a shock that the earl failed to return to England when his parole expired at Easter 1409.[12]

Douglas's breach of parole was probably connected with the restoration of his rival, the disinherited Earl of March. While the Tyneman had been a captive in England, March and his family had been refugees upon whom Henry IV had heaped benefactions, including an annuity of five hundred marks.[13] Nonetheless the Dunbars were not at home in England and by 1409 were ready to abandon Henry.[14] In their return to Scotland can be traced the hand of Albany,

[4] *Ibid.*, 181–99, *passim*; *Cal. Docs. Scot.*, IV. Nos. 750, 793.
[5] *Rot. Scot.*, II. 190, 193.   [6] *E.R.*, IV. 71.
[7] Balfour-Melville, *James I*, p. 26.
[8] *Rot. Scot.*, II. 183, 190, 191, 192, 197.
[9] *E.R.*, IV. lxx–lxxi; *Rot. Scot.*, II. 178, 187, 196, 197; *Cal. Docs. Scot.*, IV No. 751.   [10] *Rot. Scot.*, II. 181–4, 186.
[11] Fraser, *Douglas*, I. 376; III. 46.   [12] Balfour-Melville, *James I*, pp. 40–1.
[13] *Cal. Docs. Scot.*, IV. Nos. 579–642, *passim*.
[14] Balfour-Melville, *James I*, p. 41.

who was probably responding to public opinion.[15] Moreover the restoration of the Earl of March would serve Albany as a check upon the power of the Earl of Douglas.

Probably in order to win the Tyneman's consent to the Dunbar restoration a bond of alliance was drawn up at Inverkeithing on 20 June 1409 [16] between the governor and Douglas, who swore to keep 'full friendschip and kindnes' the one to the other. A compromise followed: March returned, and on 2 October 1409, in the presence of a gathering of nobles at Haddington, the earl and his eldest son resigned the lordship of Annandale to Albany, who forthwith granted it to the Earl of Douglas with rights of regality.[17] This was the price of the Tyneman's consent to the restoration of March, who received back his earldom but 'not without some dismemberment of his possessions'.[18]

The restoration of the Dunbars coincided with a renewal of Anglo-Scottish warfare. In the winter of 1409 Alexander Stewart, Earl of Mar, captured the *Thomas* of London, freighted with goods belonging to the Richard Whittington of pantomime fame. Probably in retaliation Sir Robert Umfraville raided the Forth and took thirteen ships as prizes.[19] By land, however, the English were less successful: on 7 May 1409 [20] some undistinguished men of Teviotdale (*mediocres Thevidaliae*) set an example to their betters by seizing Jedburgh Castle, which was immediately destroyed on Albany's orders.[21] The renewal of warfare gave the Dunbars a chance to prove their loyalty: Patrick, son of the Earl of March, seized Fast Castle, and sometime in 1410 or 1411 Gavin, another son of the earl, co-operated with the Douglases in breaking the bridge of Roxburgh and burning the town.[22]

Henry IV could not be expected to submit tamely to the ungracious desertion of his Dunbar protégés, the absconding of the captive Douglas, and the provocative warfare that had left the English with only two Scottish strongholds—Roxburgh and Berwick. It was Douglas's conduct that irked Henry most of all. On 4 April 1410 English commissioners were instructed to secure the Tyneman's return 'by all ways possible',[23] and an envoy was sent to Albany to let drop the suggestion that fifty thousand marks would be a suitable

---

[15] See *Chron. Wyntoun*, III. 78–9; *Chron. Bower*, II. 444.
[16] *E.R.*, IV. ccix–ccxii.
[17] *R.M.S.*, I. No. 920.
[18] *Chron. Bower*, II. 444.
[19] Balfour-Melville, *James I*, pp. 43–4.
[20] *Glasgow Registrum*, II. 316.
[21] *Chron. Bower*, II. 444.
[22] *Ibid.*, 444, 447.
[23] *Rot. Scot.*, II. 194.

ransom for his son, Murdoch. On the other hand, if Douglas returned to England as a captive, Murdoch might be released 'for litel or right noght takying for his raunceon'. Douglas wisely made his peace with Henry, apparently by paying a large ransom,[24] but Murdoch was not released, and his father was soon pre-occupied by a crisis in the north.

The growth of the landed power of the multitudinous members of the royal family had occurred north of the Forth, rather than to the south, and in areas that were at least partially, if not predominantly, Gaelic-speaking. Even before the Stewart family became 'royal' its members had obtained the earldoms of Atholl in 1342, Strathearn in 1357 (though it went by marriage to a Graham before 1406) and Menteith c. 1361. Caithness followed c. 1375, Buchan c. 1382, and the MacDougal lordship of Lorne by 1390. Further Stewart expansion was to bring in Mar c. 1405 (not without scandal) and Ross c. 1415 [25] (at the cost of a national crisis).

There were four royal Stewarts who were capable of independent action in the north. One was Walter Stewart, who at the end of his life was to gain lasting notoriety. Meanwhile he made himself useful to those in power and gained the earldoms of Caithness and Atholl. Another was Alexander Stewart, Earl of Buchan and Wolf of Badenoch, who lasted until 1405 or 1406. His illegitimate son, another Alexander Stewart, was a third striking figure who was to win for himself the earldom of Mar in curious circumstances. The earldom had descended to Isabel Douglas who had married Sir Malcolm Drummond, brother of Queen Annabella.[26] In 1402 Sir Malcolm was treacherously captured and held in prison until he 'deit in hard penawns'.[27] Whoever was responsible it was Alexander Stewart who was the beneficiary. To silence malicious tongues a ceremony was carefully stage-managed at Kildrummy on 19 September 1404: Alexander Stewart stood at the gates of the castle and handed the keys and charters to the countess to do with them as she pleased; holding the keys in her hand she chose him for her husband and granted him all her lands.[28] Alexander Stewart, as Earl of Mar and the Garioch, was to be chief government agent in the Highlands until his death in 1435. Even more important, however, was a fourth figure, Albany, whose attention to Highland affairs can be seen in

[24] Balfour-Melville, *James I*, pp. 43, 44, 55; *Rot. Scot.*, II. 205.
[25] For these details see *Scots Peerage* and *H.B.C.*, *passim*.
[26] *Scots Peerage*, v. 586.   [27] *Chron. Wyntoun*, III. 87–8.
[28] *Aberdeen-Banff Illustrations*, IV. 165–73.

his construction of the new castle of Doune to guard the route into the Highlands that passed through his earldom of Menteith. It was he who headed the wholesale stewartisation of the Highlands, reduced the friction that might otherwise have divided the royal Stewarts, and gave coherence to their expansion.

At the opening of the fifteenth century only one Highland magnate remained who was powerful enough to voice discontent at the Stewart encroachments and all that they represented—Albany's nephew Donald, Lord of the Isles. The issue that led to a collision between uncle and nephew arose over the earldom of Ross. When Alexander Leslie, Earl of Ross, died in May 1402 his young daughter, Euphemia, was heiress to the earldom; she was also the grand-daughter of Albany, who assumed her wardship. The fate of other Highland earldoms suggested what the outcome was likely to be. On the other hand Donald of the Isles had contingent claims upon the earldom through his wife Margaret, sister of the erstwhile Earl of Ross. It was she who, by the terms of a tailzie of 1370, came next in the succession to the earldom if her niece, Euphemia Leslie, died without heirs or was otherwise disposed of.[29]

Probably to promote his own claim to the wardship of Euphemia, Donald let loose his younger brother, Alastair Carrach, founder of the MacDonalds of Keppoch, whose freebooting activities had been denounced in a council held at Linlithgow in 1399.[30] On 3 July 1402, some two months after the death of Alexander Leslie had opened the question of the succession to Ross, Alastair Carrach led his followers into the cathedral close of Elgin and sacked the houses of the canons; part of the burgh of Elgin was also set on fire. On 6 October 1402 Alastair returned to Elgin 'with a great army' seeking humbly to be absolved.[31] But all this did not bring the Lord of the Isles the wardship of Euphemia and her earldom : by 11 July 1405 it was Albany who was styling himself 'Lord of the ward of Ross'.[32]

Albany had thus won an initial advantage in the Ross affair. The next step in his policy came in 1406 when he conferred the earldom of Buchan upon John Stewart, his second son. According to the traditional MacDonald account, Albany, having brought up the heiress Euphemia in his own household, 'persuaded her by flattery and threats to resign her rights of the earldom of Ross to John . . . Earl of Buchan . . . much against her will. But others were of opinion

---

[29] See *Scots Peerage*, vii. 242; *A.P.S.*, i. 537–8.   [30] P. 209 above.
[31] *Moray Registrum*, pp. 382–3.   [32] *Scots Peerage*, vii. 242.

she did not resign her rights'.[33] Certainly there is no surviving evidence that Euphemia made any resignation prior to 1415, nor is there any evidence that before then Euphemia had become a nun and was therefore 'civilly dead'.[34] What seems likely is that Donald received information that some step was about to be taken that would rob his wife of her chance of inheriting Ross.

There were other complications in the affair—the relationship between Donald of the Isles and the captive James I, and the role of the MacDonalds in international politics. In August 1407 an English safe-conduct was issued to allow 'Ector Makgillane' (MacLean), nephew of the Lord of the Isles, to come to the English court 'to have colloquy with his liege lord the King of Scotland';[35] and in May 1408 English envoys were sent to negotiate peace and friendship between Henry IV and his subjects and Donald of the Isles, Iain Mor, and their 'subjects'.[36] There may have been talk of a scheme whereby Donald and James would obtain conditional English help to oust Albany and install James in Scotland. It is even possible that James sanctioned Donald's plans, of which the immediate objective was the earldom of Ross.

Within the earldom Donald seems to have been welcomed as true heir;[37] the only resistance came from the Mackays of Sutherland.[38] Having seized the royal burgh of Inverness Donald struck eastward across the Spey, apparently to win the lands that pertained to the earldom of Ross in the sheriffdoms of Banff, Aberdeen and Kincardine. But this aim was not incompatible with wider ambitions; and it was at least feared that Donald intended to loot the city of Aberdeen.[39] By 24 July 1411 his host had reached the township of Harlaw in the Garioch, near Inverurie, less than twenty miles from Aberdeen. Further advance was contested by Donald's cousin, the Earl of Mar, who had begun his career as a leader of caterans, but had latterly reformed his ways. With him Mar had the armed strength of Mar and the Garioch, Angus and the Mearns, and Buchan, as well as a troop of burgesses from Aberdeen. By Scottish standards a full-scale army had been mustered on each side.[40]

Apart from Bower's conventional picture of the one side hurling itself with wild yells against the levelled spears of the other[41] the only

[33] *Highland Papers*, I. 28.   [34] P. F. Tytler, *History*, I. pt. ii, 39.
[35] *Cal. Patent 1405-8*, p. 363.   [36] *Foedera*, IV. pt. i, 131.
[37] Boece, *History*, p. 341 v.
[38] *History of the Earldom of Sutherland*, cited in *Scots Peerage*, VII. 159.
[39] *Chron. Bower*, II. 444-5.
[40] *Ibid.*, 444-5, 500.   [41] *Ibid.*, 445.

account of the course of the ensuing battle is the MacDonald one. According to this [42] the left wing of Mar's troops under Sir Alexander Ogilvy was routed by MacLean; the central battalion under Mar was forced to give ground and was 'quite defeated'; Mar's right wing was forced back until it took refuge in a great cattle-fold, from which its residue emerged after the battle was over to take what plunder it could while Donald's troops were pursuing Mar on the way to Aberdeen.[43]

Thus, according to MacDonald tradition, it was Donald who was the victor. Abbot Bower, on the other hand, representing Lowland tradition, had no doubt that it was Mar who was victorious. But even on Bower's own showing it is clear that if Mar was the victor his victory was a Pyrrhic one.[44] Both Boece and Buchanan, writing long after the battle, somewhat cynically asserted that each side thought it had been defeated by the other.[45] John Major, more of an historian than the others, judiciously remarked:

> Though it be more generally said amongst the common people that the Wild Scots were defeated, I find the very opposite of this in the chroniclers; only the Earl [sic] of the Isles was forced to retreat; and he counted amongst his men more of slain than did the civilised Scots. Yet these men did not put Donald to open rout, though they fiercely strove, and not without success, to put a check to the audaciousness of the man.[46]

The check that Donald had received was made all the sharper by the unusually vigorous intervention of Albany. While Donald withdrew to the Isles the governor recovered Dingwall Castle in the autumn of 1411 and installed a garrison.[47] In the summer of 1412, Albany raised three armies. Although there is no account of their activities the result seems to have been the submission of Donald. He met the governor at Polgylbe, the modern Lochgilphead, handed over hostages, and took an oath to keep the peace.[48]

Despite Donald's submission there were fresh hostilities,[49] perhaps as a result of another move concerning the succession to Ross: on 12 June 1415, Euphemia was persuaded to resign her earldom, after which she appears to have entered a nunnery. By 24 May 1417 Albany's son was styling himself Earl of Buchan and Ross.[50] Whether

[42] *Highland Papers*, I. 30.   [43] *Ibid.*
[44] *Chron. Bower*, II. 445.
[45] Boece, *History*, p. 341 v.; Buchanan, *History*, II. 79.
[46] Major, *History*, p. 348.   [47] *Chron. Bower*, II. 445.
[48] *Ibid.*; *E.R.*, IV. 213.   [49] *E.R.*, IV. 265.
[50] *Scots Peerage*, VII. 242–3; *Aberdeen-Banff Illustrations*, IV. 383.

he obtained possession of Ross is another matter : Donald showed no hesitation in publicising himself as 'Lord of the foresaid Isles and of the earldom of Ross'.[51] Thus so far as the earldom was concerned the battle of Harlaw seems to have led to no definite settlement. Nor did the battle change the independent international position of the Lord of the Isles : in an Anglo-French truce arranged in 1416 by Sigismund, King of the Romans, the Lord of the Isles achieved the distinction of being named as an ally both of the English and of the French.[52]

What, then, was the significance of Harlaw? One historian regards the episode as 'really a family squabble, all the parties being related by blood or marriage'.[53] The same might be said of the Hundred Years War. Any attempt to play down the importance of the battle or to account for it on somewhat trivial grounds runs completely counter to the views held in Scotland in the fifteenth and sixteenth centuries. Harlaw was momentous because it was seen as a battle between Highlands and Lowlands. There were doubtless Highlanders who fought for Mar ; and Sir Alexander Seton—the 'Huntly' of the MacDonald account—was apparently on good terms with Donald of the Isles. But despite some blurring of the lines of demarcation each side was taken to represent one of the two cultural halves of Scotland. It was this division that one historian had in mind when he maintained that 'the battle of Harlaw (1411) ranks with the battle of Carham (1018) in its determining influence on the development of the Scottish nation . . . never since that day has Teutonic Scotland been in real danger from the Celtic race to whom it owed its being'.[54] This statement certainly requires modification : the division in Scotland was cultural rather than racial; nor was there any real danger that a decisive victory for Donald at Harlaw would have resulted in a political and cultural transformation of the whole of Scotland. Even the fearful Bower did not contemplate any such drastic revolution and thought merely that Donald intended 'to bring under his subjection the land as far as the Tay'.[55]

This was certainly a possibility : in Ireland the Gaelic resurgence of the fourteenth and fifteenth centuries drastically reduced the area of English speech subject to the Dublin administration;[56] a decisive

---

[51] *Highland Papers*, IV. 166, 169.
[52] *Foedera*, IV. pt. ii, 179; *Cal. Docs. Scot.*, IV. No. 876.
[53] Mackenzie, *Highlands and Islands*, p. 94.
[54] P. Hume Brown, *History*, I. 167.   [55] *Chron. Bower*, II. 444-5.
[56] See J. F. Lydon, 'The Problem of the Frontier in Medieval Ireland', *Topic: A Journal of the Liberal Arts*, No. 13, pp. 5-22.

victory for Donald might similarly have narrowed the cultural and political bounds of Lowland Scotland and might, in so doing, have brought other far-reaching consequences in its wake. As it was, the indecisive result at Harlaw brought no drastic change. The battle showed that the forces of the two sides were, for the time being, too finely balanced for the one to prevail against the other. But the battle also raised to a higher pitch the antagonism between Lowlander and Highlander. The time for tolerance or easy assimilation had disappeared, but the time for a wholesale attack upon Gaelic culture and upon the separatist political tendencies of Gaeldom had not yet arrived.

Harlaw was only one demonstration of the disorder that affected most aspects of Scottish life during the Albany era. The Scottish kirk was in a peculiarly vulnerable position, victim not only of Scotland's internal troubles but of the external troubles of a divided papacy. Urban VI, the Roman pope, had at least retrospectively earned his 'deposition' by his subsequent conduct: he had tortured and murdered five of his own cardinals. Nonetheless on his death in 1389 another Italian was elected to perpetuate the Roman succession. At Avignon Clement VII had revived the less respectable features of the 'Babylonish Captivity'. His successor, Pedro de Luna, an Aragonese who ruled as Benedict XIII,[57] might in happier times have done much for the church; as it was, his pontificate was a perpetual struggle, and the irregularities that had arisen during the early years of the schism were condoned rather than reprimanded.[58]

A glimpse of current conditions is given by a number of statutes passed by the synod of St Andrews c. 1400.[59] These diocesan statutes included enactments that holders of benefices should put away their concubines; priests were not to carry long knives or celebrate several masses a day for the sake of remuneration; dances, wrestling matches and other sports were not to take place in kirk yards; consistories were to be held each year in the two archdeaconries of the diocese to instruct priests in the administration of the sacraments and the cure of souls; and spiritual sanctions were to be used wholesale against a wide range of miscreants. These measures are evidence not only of irregularities but of an attempt at remedy, probably led by Walter Trail, a man of distinguished academic and ecclesiastical background

[57] John Holland Smith, *The Great Schism*, pp. 151–4.
[58] See *Cal. Papal Petitions*, I. 598, 605, 609, 610, 617.
[59] Robertson, *Concilia*, II. 64–73; Patrick, *Statutes*, pp. 68–77.

who had been provided to the bishopric of St Andrews by Clement VII in 1385.[60] Soon afterwards there were at least three meetings of the provincial council of the Scottish kirk.[61]

At the provincial council of 1388 Trail presided as conservator and upheld an appeal against an appointment made by the Bishop of Moray. It was symptomatic of the growth of secular influence over the kirk, partly as a consequence of the schism, that the Scone parliament of March 1391 reversed Trail's decision, ostensibly at the request of the clergy represented in parliament.[62] The same parliament confirmed a mortmain act forbidding the granting of property to the kirk without royal licence.[63] And when the three estates, in an act of February 1401, upheld the authority of the ecclesiastical courts, they simultaneously restricted appeals from Scotland to the *curia* : appeals against excommunication could be made to the conservator and his council, and could be taken a further stage to the provincial council 'where such matters are to be discussed so long as the schism lasts'.[64] Pragmatic as always, the three estates formulated no theory to justify this tacit denial of appeal to the papal court, but their action was a sign of secular interference in ecclesiastical matters that was to become increasingly obvious in the fifteenth century.[65]

A few months later the death of Bishop Trail left the bishopric of St Andrews vacant and thereby gave occasion for an outbreak of the unruliness typical of the period. The protagonist in this case was Master Walter Danielston, parson of Kincardine O'Neil, licentiate in arts and former student of civil law at Avignon.[66] He had already shown his talents when Sir Robert Danielston, keeper of Dumbarton Castle, had died in 1397.[67] The custody of Dumbarton, long held by the Danielstons,[68] was doubtless coveted by one or other of the royal Stewarts. Master Walter had no intention that it should slip from the grip of his own family and seized the castle,[69] where he behaved as a robber baron. Meanwhile, Archdeacon Thomas Stewart, illegitimate son of Robert II and protégé of Albany, had been elected Bishop of St Andrews but languished unconfirmed by the papacy.[70] Danielston therefore offered to exchange his castle for the bishopric. Albany met his brother Thomas at Abernethy, persuaded him to

60 Robertson, *Concilia*, II. 64–73; Dowden, *Bishops*, p. 27.
61 Robertson, *Concilia*, I. lxxvii.   62 *Ibid.*, I. lii; *A.P.S.*, I. 578.
63 *A.P.S.*, I. 577.   64 *Ibid.*, 576.
65 See, e.g. *Nat. MSS. Scot.*, II. No. lxv.
66 Dowden, *Bishops*, p. 29.   67 *E.R.*, III. 425.
68 *Ibid.*, II. 79, 80, 82.   69 *Chron. Wyntoun*, III. 76.
70 Dowden, *Bishops*, p. 29.

relinquish his claim, and in the summer of 1402 persuaded the St Andrews chapter to elect Danielston, who forthwith began to exercise episcopal authority. Probably to everyone's relief he died at Christmas.[71] Benedict XIII then provided Henry Wardlaw, chantor of Glasgow, doctor of canon law and nephew of the late Cardinal Wardlaw. The new bishop was to bring some stability by guiding the affairs of his bishopric for a further thirty-seven years.[72]

One of the problems that faced him was heresy. From the schism those of a conservative cast of mind had drawn the conclusion that the papal authority was the essence of the unity of Christendom and that an attack upon that authority was an attack upon the unity of the faith. Those less committed to tradition regarded the existing papacy as an obstacle in the way of unity. Others, such as John Wyclif in England, went further and not only attacked the papacy but 'denied current beliefs and challenged church authorities without setting forth adequate substitutes'.[73] In England Wyclif's followers, opprobriously termed 'Lollards', had been driven underground but survived until the eve of Henry VIII's breach with Rome.[74] Enough Lollard influence was felt in Scotland to alarm the lay and ecclesiastical authorities: in 1399, when Rothesay was appointed lieutenant, his oath of office pledged him to restrain heretics.[75] His successor, Albany, was singled out for praise as a defender of orthodoxy:

> He wes a constant Catholike;
> All Lollard he hatyt and heretyke.[76]

One Lollard, an English priest named James Resby, won renown by preaching in Scotland to the simple folk, but 'interspersed most dangerous conclusions in his teaching of dogma'.[77] According to Abbot Bower, Resby denied the efficacy of confession and the sacrament of penance. Perhaps more important, he held that the pope was not actually vicar of Christ and that no one could be the real pope or vicar of Christ unless he were holy. And Resby—so Bower believed—maintained forty conclusions, similar or even worse, which he had extracted from the heresies of the arch-heretic Wyclif. Such heretics, claimed Bower, were like Gog and Magog, worship-

---

[71] *Chron. Wyntoun*, III. 83–4; Watt, *Fasti*, p. 294.
[72] *Chron. Wyntoun*, III. 84–5; Dowden, *Bishops*, pp. 30–31.
[73] A. R. MacEwen, *History of the Church in Scotland*, I. 330.
[74] J. A. F. Thomson, *The Later Lollards* (1965), *passim*.
[75] *A.P.S.*, I. 573.   [76] *Chron. Wyntoun*, II. 100.
[77] *Chron. Bower*, II. 442; T. M. A. Macnab, 'The Beginnings of Lollardy in Scotland', *Scot. Church Hist. Soc. Recs.*, XI. 254–60.

pers of Antichrist, or like dragons that could fly, crawl and swim, for 'What is more heretical than to say that the actual pope is not the vicar of Christ?'[78] In 1406 or 1407 Master Laurence of Lindores, inquisitor of heretical pravity, presided over a council of the clergy which condemned Resby as a heretic. In the first known example of religious persecution in Scotland both he and his writings were reduced to ashes at Perth.[79]

It is perhaps no mere coincidence that Resby was an Englishman and that the next known exponent of radical religious views in Scotland was a certain Quintin Folkhyrde, or Folkard (Flockhart), a Scottish esquire not unknown at the English court. In August 1407 he obtained an English safe-conduct for some trip to London, whence he was to report back to Henry IV; in September he obtained another safe-conduct for a brief visit to Scotland.[80] It may be inferred that for political reasons Henry IV, like Henry VIII, was not averse to exporting religious dissent to Scotland. Folkhyrde was probably also instrumental in attracting to Scotland the interest of the Hussites of Bohemia,[81] later to be shown in the mission of Paul Crawar,[82] for it was to Prague that Folkhyrde addressed his 'News from Scotland' in 1410.

His news was embodied in four letters.[83] In the first he addressed all Christendom; the second was addressed to the Bishop of Glasgow (William Lauder) and his accomplices, and all the clergy of Scotland; the third was addressed to the secular lords and commons; and the fourth was addressed to everybody. That Folkhyrde was a zealot is obvious. The features of his seal of office, which he painstakingly described, suggest that he was a self-appointed reformer: he explained that his own surname meant herdsman of the people (*pastor populi*) and that in fear of eternal damnation and for remission of his sins he had to obey the call to denounce the evils of the clergy by 'riding through the countryside and openly publicising in the mother tongue the contents of the following letters'.[84] This mission was necessary since the temporal lords (and in his capacity as esquire he reckoned himself among them) had failed to do their duty as one of

[78] *Chron. Bower*, II. 442–3.

[79] *Ibid.*, 441–2. Duncan Shaw, in 'Laurence of Lindores', *Scot. Church Hist. Soc. Recs.*, XII. 47–62, suggests (pp. 57–60) that it was Laurence who shaped inquisitorial procedure in Scotland.   [80] *Cal. Patent 1405–8*, p. 362.

[81] T. M. A. Macnab, 'Bohemia and the Scottish Lollards', *Scot. Church Hist. Soc. Recs.*, V. 10–22.   [82] P. 300 below.

[83] Texts in *St Andrews Copiale*, pp. 230–6.   [84] *Ibid.*, p. 230.

the three estates in the Christian commonwealth. The contents of the letters are in disappointingly general terms : the luxury and other shortcomings of the clergy are condemned ; the teaching of the faith in the vernacular is urged ; so also is the obligation of clerics to sustain the poor ; questions of doctrine are left untouched. The overall tone is denunciatory rather than constructively reformative.

Although nothing more is heard of Folkhyrde the existence of a Wycliffite movement in Scotland attracted attention on the continent.[85] Heresy certainly provided one motive for Bishop Wardlaw's decision to found Scotland's first university : in a charter of 28 February 1411, addressed to the doctors, masters, bachelors and scholars of St Andrews, the bishop drew attention to the benefits of higher education 'by which the catholic faith, by an impregnable wall of doctors and masters . . . is enabled to withstand heresies and errors' ;[86] a graduation oath formulated at St Andrews in 1417 made the graduands swear to 'defend the kirk against the attack of Lollards'.[87]

The setting up of the university was more than a reaction against heresy. For more than two hundred years Scots had sought a university education, not least on account of the material rewards to which it led : towards the end of the fourteenth century Clement VII evidently found it necessary to lay down a tariff of maximum incomes (by no means stingy) for four categories of graduates; and 'at a time when ordained vicarages were still valued as low as £10 or less, the top Doctors of Theology or Law in Scotland nearly all accumulated benefices to valued totals of between £100 and £300, and the intermediate grades did for the most part attain to proportionate incomes'.[88] Nearly all the Scottish bishops were graduates, 'more than can be said of contemporary England, where the proportion was more like two-thirds'. Graduates were also common in the archdeaconries and canonries, though less so in the parishes,[89] and 'in some cases at least it appears that once a benefice was put into the hands of an ambitious university man, he would as soon as possible arrange for a curate and it would be all too likely that the parishioners (if there were any involved) would see very little of the incumbent, whose learning was not for them'.[90] Analysis of the careers of the 400 Scots who are known to have graduated in the period 1340–1410 shows that no less than half had obtained degrees in law. Hence 'it is

[85] J. A. F. Thomson, *The Later Lollards*, pp. 202–3; W. Stanford Reid, 'The Lollards in Pre-Reformation Scotland', *Church History*, XI. 3–17, at 6.

[86] *Nat. MSS. Scot.*, II. No. lxiii.   [87] *St Andrews Acta*, I. 11–12.

[88] D. E. R. Watt, *op. cit.*, *Scot. Church Hist. Soc. Recs.*, XV. 77–88, at 84.

[89] *Ibid.*, pp. 79–83.   [90] *Ibid.*, pp. 85–6.

reasonable to conclude that a very high proportion of the 400 were not primarily concerned with preparing themselves to be fit clergy to occupy benefices with cure of souls, but were rather men with careers to make, who sought professional qualifications and then looked for ecclesiastical preferment as a basis for professional advancement'.

Of the 400 there were 230 who studied at Paris, 55 at Orleans, 34 at Avignon; and 90 had been granted English safe-conducts to study at Oxford or Cambridge, but 'it is a strange mystery that only 11 of these can be shown to have done so'.[91] Bishop Wardlaw's own academic career was typical: he had graduated in arts at Paris, studied civil law at Orleans and had studied also at the papal university at Avignon; and the eight teachers who first began to give university lectures at St Andrews had all gone to French universities, as had the prior and archdeacon of St Andrews.[92] Paris was pre-eminent for its teaching and theology and philosophy; and in Orleans, 'the one great and famous law school of northern Europe',[93] the Scots had had a 'nation' (student association) of their own since 1336. In 1411 the records of the Scottish nation at Orleans alluded to the current instability[94]—possibly an indication of difficulties caused by the schism. From 1378 onwards Scottish students were liable to be treated as schismatics in England and other countries (ultimately including France) and ran the danger of having their degrees withheld.[95] The time was propitious for the foundation of a Scottish university, and it was natural, rather than exceptional, that Scotland should share in the remarkable expansion of university education that was about to take place throughout Europe.[96]

The first university lectures were delivered in St Andrews after Whitsunday 1410,[97] but as yet there was no properly constituted university. A university, or, in current phrase, a *studium generale*, could be founded only by pope or emperor; and only a *studium generale* could confer a master's licence—the *ius ubique docendi*.[98] But Bishop Wardlaw (perhaps relying on his position as papal legate) issued a charter of 28 February 1411 to the scholars of St Andrews and referred to 'your university, instituted and founded in fact by us,

[91] *Ibid.*, pp. 78–9.

[92] See J. Maitland Anderson, 'The Beginnings of St Andrews University, 1410–1418', *S.H.R.*, VIII. 225–48 and 333–60.

[93] John Kirkpatrick, *op. cit., S.H.S. Misc. II.* 47–102, at 51.

[94] *Ibid.*, 74.   [95] J. Maitland Anderson, *op. cit.*, 349.

[96] See Rashdall, *Universities*. The Scottish universities are dealt with in II. 301–24.

[97] *Chron. Bower*, II. 445.   [98] Rashdall, *Universities*, I. 8–11.

saving, however, the authority of the apostolic see'.[99] As superior of the city, and lord of the regality of St Andrews, Wardlaw conferred upon all members of the university various fiscal and judicial immunities.[100] His charter, drawn up in the form of a notarial instrument, was sent to Benedict XIII with a petition for its confirmation. The application was supported not only by the three estates but by the captive James I,[101] who probably welcomed any chance of keeping in touch with Scottish affairs. In a bull issued at Peñíscola on 28 August 1413 Benedict duly agreed 'to add the strength of apostolic confirmation' to Wardlaw's foundation.[102]

On 3 February 1414 Master Henry Ogilvy arrived in St Andrews with the papal bull, to be welcomed, so says Bower, by four hundred clerics and novices. The next day the document was publicly read. Then there was a solemn procession to the high altar of the cathedral and a chanting of the *Te Deum*. The Bishop of Ross preached a sermon. At night bonfires were kindled in the streets and there was much indulgence in wine. A few days later the celebrations began afresh. There was a procession through the city. The clergy chanted and the populace danced while bells and organs pealed out. And the bishop of Ross preached another sermon.[103]

The university that so acclaimed Benedict XIII's generosity was soon to bite the hand that fed it. The foundation of St Andrews had come just in time for it to play its part alongside the other European universities in the ending of the Great Schism and in debating the issues soon to be raised by the conciliar movement, for the universities were at the height of their influence in the ecclesiastical politics that had become international politics thanks to the schism. Paris, under its chancellor, Jean Gerson, was particularly influential and had persuaded the French in 1398 to withdraw their obedience from Benedict XIII in a vain attempt to force him to accept 'the way of cession'. The French example was not followed and in 1403 France once more acknowledged Benedict as true pope.[104] The university of Paris had also debated 'the way of council', and was behind a further move in 1409 when a general council of the church met at Pisa. This deposed both the Roman and Avignonese popes (who paid no heed) and elected a 'Pisan' pope. Then there were three popes. An advocate

99 *Nat. MSS. Scot.*, II. No. lxiii.
100 For university courts see *Scot. Legal Hist.*, pp. 405–7.
101 Balfour-Melville, *James I*, p. 54.
102 *Nat. MSS. Scot.*, II. No. lxiii.   103 *Chron. Bower*, II. 446.
104 John Holland Smith, *The Great Schism*, pp. 160–3.

of 'the way of council' ruefully remarked that 'the infamous duality had spawned an accused [accursed?] trinity'.[105] The council of Pisa also caused an international re-alignment: the Roman pope was recognised only by some Italian states; France, which in 1407 had finally withdrawn obedience from Benedict XIII, joined England and the Empire in recognising the Pisan pope; Scotland, together with the Spanish kingdoms, continued to recognise Benedict XIII, who by this time was established in the fortified town of Peñíscola on the coast of Aragon.[106] Scotland showed a touching loyalty to Benedict XIII, even at the cost of falling out of step with its ally, and Benedict was grateful. In 1414 he kindly granted, as a contribution to the prospective ransom of James I and Albany's son Murdoch, half the money due to the papacy from vacant Scottish benefices in the following five years. Benedict was moved to this gesture 'since that realm blessed by God [Scotland] has always persisted in obedience and devotion to us and the Roman church and at no time, as we believe, will depart from them'.[107] Benedict's benign attitude is typified in the preamble to a mandate that he sent from Perpignan on 5 September 1415: 'The pope is very favourable to the just desires of petitioners and treats them with due favours.' [108]

Undeterred by the fiasco at Pisa, the university of Paris co-operated with Sigismund, King of the Romans, in assembling another general council that opened at Konstanz (or Constance) on 1 November 1414 and 'continued felicitously for four years'.[109] Most of western Christendom sent official representatives, who followed university practice by acting and voting as 'nations'. In May 1415 the council deposed the Pisan pope; in July the Roman pope was persuaded to abdicate; eventually Castile, Navarre, Portugal, and even Aragon, adhered to the council.[110] In the past the drawback to the 'way of council' had been the accepted view that only a true pope could summon a general council of the church.[111] Moreover the rival colleges of cardinals, not unwilling to convert the authoritarian papal monarchy into an oligarchy under their own direction, had not been elated at the prospect of their supersession by a more representative body. Only the universal feeling that the schism had to be ended by

[105] *Ibid.*, p. 179.

[106] *Ibid.*, p. 171; A. Francis Steuart, 'Scotland and the Papacy during the Great Schism', *S.H.R.*, IV. 144–58, at 148–51.

[107] *St Andrews Copiale*, pp. 241–2.

[108] *Wigtown Charters*, No. 4; see also No. 3.   [109] *Chron. Bower*, II. 448.

[110] John Holland Smith, *The Great Schism*, pp. 191, 202–5, 208, 210–1.

[111] Walter Ullmann, *The Origins of the Great Schism*, pp. 57–8 and *passim*.

fair means or foul overcame the objections, legal or otherwise, to a general council; and the pent-up agitation of the conciliarists was by this time bound to find vent not only in a quest for a united papacy but in efforts to re-model the organisation of the church.

Although Scotland stayed aloof from the council a number of Scots, particularly those studying at Paris, had become incorporated at Constance, and the council sent Finlay of Albany, warden of the Dominicans of Ayr, on a mission to secure the adherence of Scotland.[112] When the Duke of Albany's lukewarm excuses were reported at Constance on 4 January 1417, an English doctor seems to have contrasted his behaviour with that of James I. In 1414 the university of Paris had sent to the captive king an *Epistola Consolatoria*—a letter assuring him of the university's sympathy and seeking his aid in ending Scotland's allegiance to Benedict XIII. James rightly judged that the council would succeed: Thomas Morow, Abbot of Paisley, and Thomas Myrton, canon of Brechin, probably acted at Constance as his personal representatives;[113] in ecclesiastical politics, as in other fields, James was trying to win whatever influence would facilitate his return to Scotland. When the council of Constance deposed Benedict XIII on 26 July 1417 Albany's position was an awkward one.

The council was now ready to elect a pope assured of recognition throughout all western Christendom save Scotland, the county of Armagnac, and Peñíscola. At this point difficulties arose. The council had been summoned to deal not only with the *causa unionis* (the restoration of unity) but with the *causa reformationis* (the reform of abuses). While the more radical conciliarists urged that reforms should be passed before a new pope was elected, the more conservative took the opposite view. As a compromise some moderate reforms were passed. Then on 11 November 1417 Odo Colonna was elected and styled himself Martin V.[114] A number of Scots, including James I, Archibald the Tyneman, and James Haldenstone, Prior of St Andrews, lost no time in professing obedience to Martin and asking him for favours.[115]

While Scotland wavered, it was the faculty of arts of St Andrews that seized the initiative: on 9 August 1418 it resolved that obedience should be withdrawn from Pedro de Luna 'once called Benedict'. It

112 Balfour-Melville, *James I*, pp. 69, 70–1, 121–2.

113 J. Maitland Anderson, *op. cit.*, *S.H.R.*, VIII. 333–60, at 349–51. The Abbot of Paisley became a staunch conciliarist (John Holland Smith, *The Great Schism*, p. 229).

114 John Holland Smith, *The Great Schism*, pp. 212–6.

115 Balfour-Melville, *James I*, pp. 72–4; *Cal. Scot. Supp. 1418–22*, pp. 3–14.

was agreed to announce this 'in the face of the council before the governor and the three estates of the realm . . . and in case the governor does not wish to withdraw, but wishes to persevere in the obedience of Pedro de Luna . . . then the faculty will solemnise withdrawal'.[116] Albany was not willing to give in without a struggle. He produced a spokesman—none other than an English Franciscan, Robert Harding, master of theology. After an exchange of invective 'the whole university of St Andrews rose up against him'.[117]

When the general council of the three estates met at Perth in October 1418, it was called upon to make its choice between the rival popes. Harding, upheld by the governor, presented his case *per naturas, figuras, scripturas, puncturas et alia exempla* 'which to narrate in order would engender tedium in the reader'. His illustrations included a parable involving one tree, fourteen large elephants and one small elephant. The first large elephant represented the universal church, which had fallen while leaning against the tree of papal jurisdiction. One huge elephant (Sigismund, King of the Romans) had in vain tried to uplift the fallen beast. Equally unsuccessful were another twelve large elephants (other Christian kings and princes). Then came a small elephant (the Scottish kirk) which placed itself underneath the fallen beast and so put it on its feet again. The object of this parable was to show that the council of Constance could not reunite Christendom and that only the Scottish kirk was entitled to do so.[118]

The members of St Andrews University, headed by their rector, had turned up in full force to refute Harding : his propositions contained 'scandalous and seditious conclusions, most suspect of heresy, nutritive of schisms and non-inducive of the unity of holy mother kirk'.[119] Albany resigned himself to the inevitable and sent procurators to Martin V to render him the obedience of Scotland.[120] The Great Schism was over.

The closing years of the Great Schism had coincided with new turmoils in the relationships linking England, France, Scotland and Burgundy. In these the captive Scottish king became involved and played a dubious role in the hope of purchasing his liberation. At first it had seemed to him that this could be achieved if only his uncle stirred himself. On 30 January 1412, at the age of seventeen, he wrote

[116] *St Andrews Acta*, I. 12–3.
[117] *Chron. Bower*, II. 449.
[118] *Ibid.*, 450.
[119] *Ibid.*
[120] Balfour-Melville, *James I*, p. 75.

to Albany complaining that the duke had done nothing and had even neglected to answer the letters that James had sent him in the previous year; James called upon him to work for his release 'so dowly that in yhour defaut we be nouch send to sek remede of our deliverans other qware in tyme to cum'.[121] Another four letters of the same date were addressed to a total of eighteen influential Scots in whom James reposed 'speciale traste'; he affirmed that 'the delay of our hamecome standis alanely in thaim that sowlde persue for us'[122] (presumably Albany and his faction). James's intention was to build up a party of his own to force his uncle's hand. On 3 November 1412, when Sir William Douglas of Drumlanrig visited James at Croydon, the king issued a charter in his favour 'wrate with our propre hande'; this display of James's fine penmanship[123] was to be 'selit with our grete sele in tyme to come'. On 1 December 1412 Henry issued safeconducts for 'ambassadors appointed by the general council of Scotland'.[124] Just as the release of James seemed close at hand, negotiations were broken by the death of Henry IV on 20 March 1413.[125]

The situation that faced Henry V when he succeeded his father was one of widespread discontent and lawlessness, much of it springing directly or indirectly from the deposition of Richard II.[126] In August 1414 disaffected Lollards posted bills in London affirming that Richard II was still alive in Edinburgh; and in the following year the Lollards were supposed to have offered money to the Scots if they would conduct the Mammet to England.[127] In one way or another Scotland could add to Henry's domestic difficulties. At his accession the captive Scottish king and Albany's son had been sent to the Tower to be kept securely.[128] It seemed that Henry V might ease his domestic troubles by reviving the Scottish claims of the first three Edwards. Instead he contented himself with showing coldness towards the Scots. His ambitions lay in France.

France was at this time in the midst of civil strife. Since 1392 Charles VI had been stricken with fits of insanity and became a pawn in the hands of rival princes of the blood royal,[129] in whose service

[121] *Ibid.*, p. 49.   [122] *Ibid.*

[123] Facsimile in *Nat. MSS. Scot.*, II. No. lxii.

[124] *Rot. Scot.*, II. 202.   [125] Balfour-Melville, *James I*, p. 52.

[126] E. F. Jacob, *The Fifteenth Century*, pp. 127–30.

[127] J. A. F. Thomson, *The Later Lollards*, pp. 10, 13, 16. A connection between English Lollards and Scottish nobles bent upon the release of James I is traced by W. Stanford Reid, *op. cit.*, *Church History*, XI. 3–17, at 6–8.

[128] *Cal. Docs. Scot.*, IV. Nos. 837, 838, 839.

[129] E. F. Jacob, *The Fifteenth Century*, pp. 111, 139.

some chivalrous Scots enlisted. In January 1402 David Lindsay, first Earl of Crawford and admiral of Scotland, entered the service of the Duke of Orleans,[130] who 'had specyall affectiowne all tyme to Scottis natyown'.[131] In 1408 Alexander Stewart, Earl of Mar, commanded the vanguard of the army of the Duke of Burgundy when it quelled a revolt of the citizens of Liége. As prophecy had predicted, Mar won the field and by 'gret renown thare honouryt all his natiown'.[132] In the previous year the Duke of Burgundy had confirmed the privileges that Scots traders already enjoyed in his dominions in the Low Countries and allowed them to have local commissioners to look after their interests.[133] Thus commerce, as well as a chivalric connection, was an inducement to the Scots to keep on good terms with Burgundy. In April 1413 Archibald the Tyneman made a treaty in his own name with the duke. Douglas and Henry Sinclair, Earl of Orkney, seem to have spent some months in Burgundian service.[134] By this time, however, the houses of Burgundy and Orleans were engaged in deadly feud: in 1407 the Duke of Orleans had been murdered by John the Fearless, Duke of Burgundy. The Count of Armagnac headed a faction bent upon avenging the assassination, and both parties were willing to pay a price for English aid. A new dimension was given to French troubles when Henry V claimed the crown of France as heir of Edward III.[135]

In an attempt to buy Scottish neutrality he allowed negotiations for a new truce and for the ransom of Albany's son.[136] Shortly before mid-summer 1415, as Murdoch was being conveyed northward to freedom, he was 'feloniously abducted' in Yorkshire by Lollard plotters. Although he was soon recaptured the arrangement for his ransom fell through.[137] In July 1415 the Scots broke a six-year truce concluded in 1412 and began raiding on the Borders.[138] Meanwhile, on 11 August Henry set sail from Southampton with some nine thousand troops and landed in Normandy.[139] On 25 October, he vanquished a vastly superior French army at what the Scottish chronicler Bower called 'the unhappy battle of Agincourt'.[140]

---

[130] *Scots Peerage*, III. 16.   [131] *Chron. Wyntoun*, III. 55-7.
[132] *Ibid.*, 104-16, at 115.
[133] Grant, *Social and Economic Development*, p. 330.
[134] Balfour-Melville, *James I*, pp. 51, 57; *St Andrews Copiale*, p. 238.
[135] E. F. Jacob, *The Fifteenth Century*, pp. 111, 136-42.
[136] *Rot. Scot.*, II. 213, 214.
[137] Balfour-Melville, *James I*, pp. 61-3; E. F. Jacob, *The Fifteenth Century*, p. 146.   [138] Balfour-Melville, *James I*, p. 63.
[139] E. F. Jacob, *The Fifteenth Century*, pp. 148-9.
[140] *Chron. Bower*, II. 447.

Henry's return to England was followed by fresh negotiations with the Scots. On 28 February 1416 Murdoch was released for a ransom of £10,000 and in exchange for Hotspur's son, who was restored to the earldom of Northumberland. By 1417 Murdoch had been appointed lieutenant under his father and in this capacity was brought into the work of government.[141] His release did nothing to improve Anglo-Scottish relations. In the eyes of the Scots Henry V was no hero king but 'ingenious in evil, as is clear in all his warlike deeds in France and Normandy'.[142] When Henry once more embarked for France on 23 July 1417[143] the Scots were ready to cause another diversion on the Borders. Archibald the Tyneman unsuccessfully besieged Roxburgh; Albany equally unsuccessfully besieged Berwick and 'returned home with dishonour'—it was the Scots themselves who styled this fruitless intervention 'the Foul Raid',[144] and it led to retaliation and further Border skirmishes. In 1420 some refugees from this wholly indecisive warfare sought safety in the priory kirk of Coldingham; the prior, William Drax, a monk of Durham, showed his English leanings by bringing cartloads of broom and timber so that the kirk might be set alight.[145] There were also the usual incidents at sea : as late as 1421 the canons of Inchcolm were deserting their island monastery in the summer for fear of English raids and returned only for the winter when naval activity had ceased.[146]

Such warfare brought no gains to the Scots and did little to distract English attention or resources from the war in France, where Burgundians and Armagnacs were too divided by their own quarrels to organise effective resistance. In 1418 the Burgundians proclaimed Queen Isabeau as regent while the Dauphin Charles, only surviving son of Charles VI, was recognised as regent by the Armagnacs. The hard-pressed dauphin sent ambassadors to Scotland[147] to seek aid, whereupon the three estates decided to send an expeditionary force, apparently equipped at French expense.[148] The troops were to be commanded by Albany's second son, John Stewart, Earl of Buchan and chamberlain of Scotland. Associated with him was his brother-in-

---

[141] Balfour-Melville, *James I*, pp. 65–6.
[142] *Chron. Bower*, II. 452, 453.
[143] E. F. Jacob, *The Fifteenth Century*, p. 171.
[144] *Chron. Bower*, II. 449 (mistakenly dated in 1416); *Cal. Docs. Scot.*, IV. No. 879.
[145] *Chron. Bower*, II. 459–60; *Nat. MSS. Scot.*, II. No. lxv.
[146] *Chron. Bower*, II. 467.
[147] E. F. Jacob, *The Fifteenth Century*, pp. 176–7.
[148] *Chron. Bower*, II. 458–9; *Chron. Pluscarden*, I. 353.

law, Archibald Douglas, the Tyneman's son and heir, who was given, or simply assumed, the title of Earl of Wigtown.[149] Since the aim of the Scots was to reconcile the French factions they may have pressed for a united front against the English. On 11 July 1419 an alliance was made between the dauphin and the Duke of Burgundy.[150] Already the dauphinists had made arrangements for forty Castilian vessels to transport the Scottish expeditionary force. Its numbers can hardly have amounted to the seven thousand troops mentioned by Bower,[151] but it was large enough to alter the situation in France when it disembarked at La Rochelle before the end of October 1419.[152]

The Scots had probably set sail before they heard of the disaster that was to give the English an easy predominance in France: on 10 September 1419 the Duke of Burgundy met his supposed ally the dauphin for an interview on the bridge of Montereau, and was assassinated by one of the dauphin's Armagnac followers.[153] This crime re-opened the old feud and threw the Burgundians into the arms of the English: on Christmas Day 1419 the son and heir of the murdered duke made an alliance with Henry V. King Charles and Queen Isabeau concurred: at Troyes on 21 May 1420 they concluded a great and final peace with England. Queen Isabeau let it be understood that she was an adulteress, that her son the dauphin was illegitimate, and that her daughter Catherine was therefore true heiress. On 2 June 1420 Henry married Catherine in the cathedral of Troyes.[154] One of the wedding guests was James I of Scotland.

James had been too long swung between the heights of hope and the depths of despair to refuse 'the king's command to serve him in his wars in France'.[155] On 8 December 1416, Henry V had responded to 'the frequent instances of the magnificent man James Stewart, calling himself king of Scotland', and prepared to accept hostages for his release on parole.[156] In March 1417 James had been sent to Yorkshire to hasten the coming of the hostages; but they failed to come.[157] The latest attempt to release James (though he himself was probably ignorant of it) had been an abortive scheme of a Welsh Lollard to rescue him from Windsor Castle.[158] Meanwhile the captive king was

[149] *Scots Peerage*, II. 265; III. 168.
[150] E. F. Jacob, *The Fifteenth Century*, p. 181. [151] *Chron. Bower*, II. 459.
[152] Balfour-Melville, *James I*, pp. 78–9; *Chron. Pluscarden*, I. 353.
[153] E. F. Jacob, *The Fifteenth Century*, p. 181.
[154] *Ibid.*, pp. 184–7. [155] *Cal. Docs. Scot.*, IV. No. 898.
[156] *Rot. Scot.*, II. 219. [157] Balfour-Melville, *James I*, p. 67.
[158] J. A. F. Thomson, *The Later Lollards*, p. 17.

in straitened circumstances and was dependent on the English government even for his personal expenses.[159]

The £150 James received on being summoned to France in 1420 [160] could hardly have allowed him to cut a fine figure. Yet in one respect Henry won a useful ally: the Scots in French service might be faced with the banner of their own king: when the town of Melun capitulated to Henry on 17 November 1420 the Scottish members of the garrison were hanged as traitors to King James.[161] This did not prevent the Earls of Buchan and Wigtown from undertaking a recruiting drive in Scotland and returning to France with reinforcements [162] while Henry conducted his French bride to London for her coronation. James accompanied Henry and Catherine on a state progress which was interrupted by news of a Franco-Scottish victory at Baugé in Anjou.

In this small engagement on Easter Eve (22 March 1421) the Scots, under Buchan, Wigtown, and Sir John Stewart of Darnley, successfully used tactics reminiscent of those displayed at Stirling bridge in 1297; the Duke of Clarence, heir presumptive to the English crown, was among the slain. When Pope Martin V heard the news he reputedly remarked that the Scots acted as an antidote to the English.[163] The fight at Baugé certainly demonstrated that the English were not invincible. The jubilant dauphin was said to have remarked to the detractors of the Scots: 'What think ye now of the Scottish muttoneaters and wine-bibbers?' The Earl of Buchan was made Constable of France and John Stewart of Darnley was granted the lordship of Concressault.[164]

After Baugé, there was less chance of detaching the Scots from well-rewarded service under the dauphin.[165] The most that Henry could hope for was to entice individual Scots to enter his service rather than that of the dauphin. In this policy James I still had a part to play: on St George's Day, 23 April 1421, Henry dubbed him knight and invested him with the order of the garter. On 30 May the Earl of Douglas contracted to serve Henry after the ensuing Easter with two hundred knights and esquires and two hundred mounted archers. The Tyneman had undertaken this service (against all men save the Scottish king) at the command of James, who received his reward on

[159] Balfour-Melville, *James I*, pp. 80–81.
[160] *Cal. Docs. Scot.*, IV. No. 898.   [161] *Chron. Bower*, II. 462.
[162] Balfour-Melville, *James I*, p. 85.
[163] *Chron. Pluscarden*, I. 268; *Chron. Bower*, II. 461–2.
[164] *Chron. Bower*, II. 459; Francisque-Michel, *Les Écossais en France*, I. 120–1.   [165] Balfour-Melville, *James I*, pp. 85–6.

the following day : 'through the mediation of the Lord Archibald, Earl of Douglas', he was promised release on parole soon after the forthcoming campaign in France.[166] In June 1421 James sailed to France with Henry, who received some recruits from Scotland.[167] During the siege of Meaux English troops foraged in lands dedicated to St Fiacre (or Fergus), traditionally believed to have been the son of a Scottish king, and Henry contracted a disease which his doctors reportedly described as 'the malady of St Fiacre'. Thereupon, so says Bower, the king 'with contorted countenance and wild voice responded, "Wheresoever I turn I am bearded with Scots, dead or alive" '.[168] On 31 August Henry V died at Vincennes. James accompanied the funeral *cortège* from Rouen to Westminster.[169]

The death of Henry V had been preceded by that of Albany. He had died in Stirling Castle, probably on 3 September 1420,[170] 'in a good old age, being eighty years old or more, in possession of his faculties'. In Bower's view Albany was an outstanding man, distinguished in bearing, patient, mild, communicative and affable, 'a man of great expenses and munificent to strangers'.[171] Prior Wyntoun was even more enthusiastic : if all the princes of the world were gathered together Albany would stand out as the one worthiest of renown.[172] What both Wyntoun and Bower seem to have detected as a conceivable flaw in their paragon was the fact that he did not punish powerful offenders. But even this deficiency was easily turned into a virtue : 'if any enormities perchance were committed in the realm by the powerful, he patiently temporised, knowing how to reform them prudently enough at an opportune time' ;[173] if Albany spared persons when he had good reason 'to greve thaim sare' it was only on account of his compassion.[174]

Compassion was a quality easily evoked as an excuse for avoiding controversial measures. When it was decided to destroy Jedburgh Castle after its capture in 1409, a general council held at Perth intended to finance the apparently costly operation by levying a tax of twopence on each hearth throughout the kingdom. Albany was too wary to allow the sort of unfair taxation that had led to the English

---

[166] *Foedera*, IV. pt. iv, 30–1.

[167] *Ibid.*, 31–2, 42, 44, 47, 50; *Rot. Scot.*, II. 230–1.

[168] *Chron. Bower*, II. 462.   [169] Balfour-Melville, *James I*, pp. 90–1.

[170] See *E.R.*, IV. lxxix. It was a year of epidemic 'greitar nor ony pestilence that ever was in Scotland' (*Extracta*, pp. 249–50).

[171] *Chron Bower*, II. 466.   [172] *Chron. Wyntoun*, III. 99–101.

[173] *Chron. Bower*, II. 466.   [174] *Chron. Wyntoun*, III. 99–101.

peasant rising of 1381. He sanctimoniously affirmed that during his governorship no tax had ever been levied, or ever would be levied, lest the poor folk should curse him for having introduced such an abuse. He directed that the Borderers should be paid from the great customs [175] for the destruction of the castle. Thereupon 'he acquired the innumerable blessings of the common folk'.[176]

The panegyrics of the contemporary chroniclers cannot be discounted. They show that in his day Albany was a popular ruler who displayed a flattering interest in the lower orders of society: in the second year of his governorship he was to be found with a concourse of nobles supervising the narrowing of a street in Ayr to prevent the encroachment of sand; with his own hands he fixed a stake in the ground to indicate the new width of the Sandgate.[177] Thus it is easy to see how there circulated stories that projected the image of Albany as a simple and honest man who had the interests of the people at heart. It was recounted how, during the raid of Cockermouth in 1388, a supposed charter of King Athelstan was found among the booty; Albany (then Earl of Fife) admired its simplicity and brevity; when as governor he had to listen to 'the tedious and wordy charters of our modern days' he would recall Athelstan's little charter and assert that 'there was more truth and good faith in those old times than now, when the new race of lawyers has introduced such frivolous exceptions and studied prolixity of forms'.[178]

But if Albany sanctimoniously avowed dislike of 'the new race of lawyers'—unpopular in any day or age—he was himself a master of chicanery. He could use pressure to obtain supposedly voluntary resignations, draw up tailzies that deprived others of their own well-established rights of inheritance and insert in charters nominally concerning only a landed transaction clauses that made the beneficiary his dependant or retainer; as governor he could preside over legal actions to which he himself was a party.[179] All this, it seems, was hidden from the chroniclers or was deliberately suppressed by them: Bower and the Pluscarden writer fixed their eyes on events in France; Wyntoun devoted page after page of his rhymed chronicle to the colourful exploits of Alexander Stewart, Earl of Mar, meanwhile ig-

---

[175] Two such payments were made (*E.R.*, IV. 115, 117).
[176] *Chron. Bower*, II. 444.
[177] *Ayr Burgh Charters*, Nos. 43, 44.
[178] *Chron. Bower*, II. 403; *Chron. Wyntoun*, III. 30.
[179] W. Fraser, *Memorials of the Family of Wemyss of Wemyss* (1888), II. No.

34.

noring Albany's governorship, though he was an eye-witness of it from beginning to end.

It is unfortunate that the scanty evidence of the chroniclers is accompanied by a similar lack of evidence from parliamentary records. No record of a parliament survives between 1401 and 1424; general councils were certainly held, but have left little trace. Apart from charters, only one class of evidence survives to elucidate the character of the Albany governorship—the records of the exchequer audits.

Between 1406 and 1423 these were held at Perth each year, save during the Harlaw emergency of 1411 and in 1419 when the Earl of Buchan sailed to France.[180] Buchan, second son of Albany, had become chamberlain in place of his father in 1408. Sir John Forrester acted as Buchan's chamberlain depute and probably performed the donkey work. Nonetheless the amount of money that passed through Forrester's hands was always negligible; and Albany continued to have a say in finance.[181] From the chamberlain's accounts it would seem that the royal revenues were either decaying or were being increasingly expended at source in the localities. Certainly the sums forwarded to the chamberlain were small: the audit of 27 June 1414 showed a total of £1,632 16s. 11½d.; that of 11 June 1418 showed a drop to £1,158 2s. 11d.[182] At the audit of 27 March 1408 Albany had complained that he had entertained French and Welsh envoys at his own expense 'because there was not the wherewithal from the king's revenues to pay such expenses'.[183] Usually Albany was successful in obtaining his annual fee of £1,000 as governor; by 1418, however, even this had fallen into arrears [184] and the accumulated arrears on the chamberlain's accounts came to £2,771 8s. 5d.[185]

Although much of this sum was owing to Albany and Buchan it is unlikely that they were disinterested lenders of money for the maintenance of government: their contemporary, Henry Beaufort, Bishop of Winchester, made much profit on his large loans to the English exchequer.[186] Certainly Albany and his son had methods of recouping themselves for any possible loss: in the audit of 1412 Buchan protested that 'if it befalls him to have memory of any receipts of which he has not charged himself . . . it should not be imputed to him as concealment'.[187] Two years before, a memorandum

---

[180] E.R., iv. xli.   [181] Ibid., 208–14, 306–9.   [182] Ibid.
[183] Ibid., 71.   [184] Ibid., 132, 309.   [185] Ibid., 309.
[186] E. F. Jacob, The Fifteenth Century, pp. 226–9.
[187] E.R., iv. 80.

n the exchequer records had alluded to the seamier side of govern-
nent finance : 'neither the sheriffs nor the chamberlain nor his de-
>ute rendered anything from the issues of justice ayres held south of
Forth by the Earl of Douglas, and nonetheless ayres *were* held in the
year of this account'.[188]

The chief stamping ground for financial corruption and extortion was provided by the great customs, which by 1418 were virtually
the chamberlain's only source of avowed revenue—less than £50
came from other sources.[189] Meanwhile the gross receipts from the
customs had fallen to £2,911 8s. 3½d.[190] Thanks to remissions of
customs duties,[191] and the annuities or fees paid by the custumars, the
chamberlain received little more than one third of this sum, and even
this was jeopardised. During the reign of Robert III there had been
occasional raids upon the customs,[192] but after 1406 'we are brought
into continual contact with this description of lawlessness'.[193] The
audits held between May 1409 and July 1420 inclusive showed that
Douglas had forcefully abstracted about £5,000 from the Edinburgh
custumars.[194] Usually he was good enough to give the custumars a
receipt; occasionally he even volunteered an explanation.[195] Sheltered
under his wing were others who obtained good pickings.[196] On at least
one occasion the extortioners fell out among themselves : sometime
between 1416 and 1418 the Tyneman besieged Edinburgh Castle, of
which he held custody, in order to oust his deputy keeper, Sir William
Crawford.[197] Then Douglas installed William Borthwick, whose depredations went unhindered since Albany obligingly dismissed the
Edinburgh custumars from office. The custumars, showing obstinate
zeal, continued to take notes of exported goods, whereupon Borthwick seized their records lest they be produced at an exchequer
audit.[198]

The irregularities and unruliness evident in the raids on the customs were only one aspect of a more general lawlessness that occasionally burst out in spectacular crimes : at the outset of Albany's
governorship James Kennedy was killed by his illegitimate brother ;[199]
in 1413 Patrick Graham, Earl of Strathearn through his marriage to
the heiress, Euphemia Stewart, was murdered at the instigation of

---

[188] *Ibid.*, 133.   [189] *Ibid.*, 308.   [190] *Ibid.*, 290–302.
[191] See *ibid.*, index, under 'custom, great, remitted or allowed'.
[192] *Ibid.*, III. 546, 549, 552, 567.   [193] *Ibid.*, IV. lvii.
[194] *Ibid.*, 80, 177, 201, 224, 253, 300, 322.
[195] *Ibid.*, 253.   [196] *Ibid.*, lviii–lxiv.
[197] *Chron. Bower*, II. 449.   [198] *E.R.*, IV. 321–2.
[199] *Scots Peerage*, II. 449.

Sir John Drummond of Concraig, with whom he had lately sworn a bond of perpetual alliance.[200] After he had executed the murderers of Earl Patrick, Albany sought (though in vain) to marry the widowed Countess of Strathearn to one of his grandsons.[201] Similarly he sought to draw profit from the Kennedy murder : after the crime Sir Gilbert Kennedy, father of both the murderer and his victim, tried to draw up a tailzie defining the succession to his lands and made an indenture with Albany at Stirling on 8 November 1408 ;[202] Albany undertook never to revoke the tailzie or impede it ; in return for this 'consent and gude will' Sir Gilbert was, in certain circumstances, to enter into 'speciale retenew with oure saide lorde the gouvenour and with his lauchfull ayris, in pece and in were'.

Through such indentures and bonds of alliance with individual magnates Albany did what he could to maintain his personal authority. His experience of men and affairs, acquired in a lifetime mostly spent in trying to rule Scotland, gave him a political astuteness that allowed him to hold his own. The talents which Albany possessed, and which he exercised deviously, might have shone more brightly had he not been always merely the power behind the throne. If he had been king, or even if he had been an outstanding military leader, much might have been achieved, for the international situation, on the whole, favoured Scotland.

That Albany hoped to become king is clear. His royal ambitions can be detected in the indenture which he made with the Tyneman on 20 June 1409. This was a bond of 'evin falowschip' in which Albany showed himself not as ruler of Scotland but merely as one magnate negotiating on terms of equality with another. But the governor did not forget his chances of wearing a crown : the indenture was to expire (though his friendship was to continue) 'gif it happynnis the said lorde, the Duc Albany, to grow in tyme to cum to the estate of king'.[203]

Since Albany was heir presumptive from 1406 until his death it would be captious to denounce him for hoping to become king ; whether his hopes led him to take a hand in manipulating fate is another matter. Albany was, at the least, indirectly responsible for the removal of one obstacle—Rothesay. There is no clear evidence that Albany failed to work for the release of James I ; but James certainly thought that his uncle was deliberately obstructive. When the

[200] *Chron. Bower*, ii. 447; *Chron. Pluscarden*, i. 349–50; *Scots Peerage*, viii. 260.

[201] *Scots Peerage*, viii. 260.

[202] *Nat. MSS. Scot.*, ii. No. lxi.

[203] *E.R.*, iv. ccxi; cf. p. 231 above.

duke died in 1420 James was still a prisoner, and the crown that had eluded Albany might yet be gained by his heir: Murdoch succeeded not only to the dukedom of Albany but to the position of heir presumptive and to the governorship of Scotland.

So far as outward appearances went, Duke Murdoch inherited the powers and perquisites that his father had possessed as governor. But Murdoch did not inherit his father's popularity and as governor was thought to be 'too remiss'.[204] Following in his father's footsteps he concluded an indenture[205] on 16 November 1420 with Alexander Stewart, Earl of Mar. In gratitude for 'certane gude dedis done till him' by Duke Murdoch the earl was to become 'man of speciale feale and reteneu till the forsaid Duck of Albany'. And the governor would do more good deeds; most of all he would help the earl in his schemes concerning the earldom of Mar. For Alexander Stewart held only a liferent in the earldom;[206] on his death it might pass to the rightful heir, Sir Robert Erskine. The Erskine claim, recognised by Robert III in 1391,[207] was an inconvenience to Earl Alexander, who hoped to intrude his illegitimate son, Sir Thomas Stewart, into the earldom. On certain conditions Duke Murdoch would confirm Sir Thomas's infeftment in the lands of Mar and Garioch. The main obstacle to these arrangements was none other than Duke Murdoch's son and heir, Sir Walter Stewart, who on 26 April 1421 obtained a dispensation for a marriage to Janet Erskine,[208] daughter of the rightful heir.

Sir Walter carried his defiance of his father further: he had been given custody of Dumbarton Castle, where he detained the custumars of Linlithgow until they disgorged £15 0s. 10½d.[209] In 1423 he had the audacity to issue a document from Stirling undertaking to help the dauphinists in France, to prevent his 'subjects' from helping the English, to allow no truce with England, but rather to continue the war when he should come to the throne, or at least to the governorship of the realm.[210] Through Sir Walter's behaviour and that of his younger brothers Alexander and James (likewise criticised for their insolence and lawlessness),[211] the days of Duke Murdoch's governorship were numbered: Mar was probably alienated; Douglas was aloof and extortionate.[212]

The exchequer audit of 1422[213] displayed the cumulative effect

[204] *Chron. Bower*, II. 467.
[205] Text in *Aberdeen-Banff Illustrations*, IV. 181–2.
[206] *Scots Peerage*, V. 587.   [207] *Ibid.*, 601–2; *A.P.S.*, I. 578–9.
[208] *Scots Peerage*, I. 150.   [209] *E.R.*, IV. 365.
[210] Balfour-Melville, *James I*, p. 107.   [211] *Chron. Bower*, II. 467.
[212] *E.R.*, IV. 368.   [213] *Ibid.*, 373–8.

of long years of fiscal mismanagement, corruption and extortion. Duke Murdoch was supposed to receive a total of £1,469 6s. 8d., comprising various annuities and his salary of £1,000 as governor; in fact he received £970 8s. o½d., which was assigned to meet arrears already due to him; the total arrears still owing to him came to £3,809 15s. 8d. This was the last exchequer audit held during the governorship; the finances of central government had collapsed. In this respect, as in others, Duke Murdoch had proved that he was un-equal to the task of governing Scotland. There was an increasing demand for the return of James I.

Since 1421 it was Archibald the Tyneman who had shown most interest in obtaining the king's release, probably because Douglas resented the 'simulacrum of an Albany dynasty' [214] that seemed on the way to establishment. Circumstances favoured a renewal of nego-tiations. In England the death of Henry V had brought decisive changes. The only offspring of his marriage to Catherine de Valois was a babe in arms who was to reign as Henry VI in England and, by the terms of the treaty of Troyes, was heir to Charles VI in France. In England Humphrey, Duke of Gloucester, acted as 'protector' of the realm, while his elder brother, John, Duke of Bedford, acted as regent in France. [215] There the English conquests were threatened by the dauphinist resistance that the Scots mercenaries had helped to kindle. English finances were burdened with many commitments, in-cluding the heavy cost of garrisoning the Scottish border. [216] To some English problems the release of the Scottish king might be made to provide an answer.

On 6 July 1423 the English council drew up secret instructions for its commissioners. [217] They were to ask for the 'expenses' of James's long residence in England and try to obtain at least £36,000. If there were no time to work out the terms of a final peace the commissioners were to press for as long a truce as possible, coupled with an assurance that the Scots would send no more help to France and would with-draw the troops already there. If the Scots raised the question of an English bride for James, discussions upon a marriage could proceed. If, however, the Scots did not raise this point, it would not be honour-able for the commissioners to allude to it, 'since Englishwomen, at

---

[214] Balfour-Melville, *James I*, p. 85.
[215] E. F. Jacob, *The Fifteenth Century*, pp. 211–7.
[216] *Ibid.*, p. 221.
[217] *Foedera*, IV. pt. iv, 96–7.

least noble ones, are not wont to offer themselves in marriage to men of other parts'.

James had already encountered a lady in whom he perceived 'beautee eneuch to mak a world to dote'.[218] Joan Beaufort was grand-daughter of John of Gaunt and Catherine Swynford, his mistress. It rankled in the minds of the Beauforts that they were of royal, but dubious, descent. In 1407 a charter of Henry IV had declared them legitimate but barred them from the English succession.[219] They were anxious to cast lustre upon the Beaufort name by a royal marriage and used their powerful influence to hasten the release of the poten-tial bridegroom.

The Scots were now ready to do what was necessary: on 19 August 1423 Duke Murdoch issued letters from Inverkeithing, 'with the deliberate counsel of the three estates', appointing an impressive embassy.[220] On 10 September 1423 a draft treaty was sealed at York.[221] On 4 December 1423 the final treaty for James's release was sealed at London.[222] James was to pay £40,000 (sixty thousand marks) in English coin at the rate of ten thousand marks a year to cover the 'costs and expenses' of his involuntary stay in England. But already it was assumed that ten thousand marks would be remitted as the dowry of Lady Joan Beaufort.[223] For payment of the remainder Scottish nobles were to provide surety in the shape of twenty-one hostages. Opposite the name of each noble was set down his estimated annual revenue, ranging from fifteen hundred marks in the case of Sir James Douglas of Dalkeith and Duncan Campbell, Lord of Argyll, to four hundred marks in the case of Sir Alexander Seton of Gordon.[224] The hostages were to stay in England at their own expense until James's obligations were fully met; if a hostage died he was to be replaced within three months.

On 2 February 1424 the marriage of James and Joan was solemn-ised at the church of St Mary Overy (now the cathedral of South-wark).[225] By March James and his queen were in the neighbourhood of Durham for the final formalities of his release. So far, nothing had been settled on the question of truce or final peace. Peace was in prac-tice ruled out by Henry VI's minority, and the English commissioners were instructed to accept a truce only on condition that for its dura-

[218] *Kingis Quair* (S.T.S.), p. 14.
[219] E. F. Jacob, *The Fifteenth Century*, pp. 103–5.
[220] *A.P.S.*, I. 589–90.   [221] *Foedera*, IV. pt. iv, 98–9.
[222] *Rot. Scot.*, II. 241–3.   [223] *Ibid.*, 246.
[224] *Ibid.*, 242; *Cal. Docs. Scot.*, IV. No. 952.
[225] Balfour-Melville, *James I*, pp. 99–100.

tion the Scots would not help the French.[226] This, however, was not quite what the commissioners obtained, and the credit must go to James : on 28 March he sealed an indenture at Durham providing for a truce of seven years, but professed himself unable to recall those Scots who had already set out for France ; they would not be bound to observe the truce until their return.

A concourse of Scottish nobles had come to Durham to escort James and his queen to Scotland.[227] The king was faced with the delicate task of inducing about a third of them to remain in England as his hostages. The final list of the hostages included only two earls, Moray and Crawford, but the total number was increased to twenty-seven.[228] While most of them were sent southward to the Tower the royal couple crossed the border ; by 5 April 1424 James had arrived in Melrose,[229] a free man after eighteen years of captivity.

[226] *Ibid.*, pp. 101, 104.   [227] *Rot. Scot.*, II. 244–6.
[228] See Balfour-Melville, *James I*, Appendix D, p. 293.
[229] *Cal. Docs. Scot.*, IV. No. 956.

10

SOCIETY, ECONOMY AND CULTURE IN EARLY STEWART SCOTLAND

It has been remarked that in medieval Scotland there was 'a natural affinity between the national characteristics of the people and the form of government that made the feudal system in a strange sense a truly popular one'.[1] Within at least the limits of the extended baronial families and their particular spheres of interest this was true. The Scotland of the early Stewarts saw individual acts of crime, feuds between family and family, clan and clan, and, above all, a withering of central authority; yet seldom was the general anarchy matched by a particular anarchy within the baronial or clannish communities that bounded the horizons of most of the population.

Indeed if the body politic as a whole was anarchic there was all the more need for social cohesion in each of its many component parts: 'every noble and laird in the constant struggles that went on was dependent upon the support not only of the phalanx of cadets of his house but on that of the lesser folk who formed the rank and file of his train, and these in turn were dependent on his protection'.[2] This was still the case when John Major wrote in 1521 of the relationship between the tenant farmers and their landlord: 'They keep a horse and weapons of war, and are ready to take part in his quarrel, be it just or unjust . . . if they only have a liking for him, and with him, if need be, to fight to the death.'[3] The French knights who came to Scotland in 1385 found to their surprise that the countryfolk were not a submissive peasantry. It was this very fact that prevented the accumulation of the agrarian discontent which in other lands, to the horror of

[1] Grant, *Social and Economic Development*, p. 197.
[2] *Ibid.*, p. 198.
[3] Major, *History*, p. 47.

the Scots,[4] sometimes burst out into peasant risings that were invariably followed by aristocratic repression. It would be wrong, however,
to romanticise the condition of the Scottish rural classes : the ordinary
countryman was personally free but possessed no rights upon the
land.[5]

In the earliest surviving rental of a lay landholder conditions of
tenure were certainly insecure. This rental of 1376–8,[6] compiled for
Sir James Douglas of Dalkeith, covered extensive lands in Lothian,
Dumfriesshire, Kirkcudbright, Fife, Moffatdale and Liddesdale. In
these scattered lands, brought somewhat accidentally under the
estate-management of Sir James, a uniform policy was being applied.
In each barony the various holdings, corresponding to modern farms,
were assessed, presumably in the local baron court, and were leased to
tenants, sometimes described as husbandmen,[7] on tacks that were
nearly all for only a year at a time. While it was not unusual for one
person to be granted a tack it was more common for a group of
men to combine as joint tenants. In one case a township was leased to
eight husbandmen for two years;[8] in other cases of communal cultivation the groups of joint tenants varied in number from four to ten,[9]
and paid a joint rent that averaged about £1 for each person in the
group. Each tenant, whether he shared a tack with others or undertook it alone, had to find a person as his pledge that the rent would be
paid.[10] Although rents paid in cash were now typical, they might still
be paid in the form of produce and labour. The rents that Sir James
Douglas drew each Whitsunday and Martinmas from Aberdour included four chalders of oats, sixteen bolls of barley, four sheep and
two dozen hens, in addition to £15 15s. od.[11] From each of nine
cottar-holdings in the barony of Kilbucho in Peeblesshire he drew a
rent of 6s. 8d. and four days' labour service. This service, however,
was probably not rendered directly to Sir James but to the persons to
whom he had granted tacks of his demesne in the barony—the East
and West Mains of Kilbucho.[12] If landlords still continued to farm
their demesnes on their own account they must have relied much less
upon stipulated labour services than upon labour hired on a casual
basis from among the cottars, or upon landless hired men, the *famuli*,

---

[4] *Chron. Wyntoun*, II. 499–50; III. 16–7; *Chron. Pluscarden*, I. 302; *Chron. Bower*, II. 360–1; Pitscottie, *Historie*, I. 69–71.

[5] Grant, *Social and Economic Development*, p. 252.

[6] *Morton Registrum*, I. xlvii–lxxvi.

[7] *Ibid.*, lxiv, lxv.　　　　[8] *Ibid.*, li.　　　　[9] *Ibid.*, lvi–lxi.

[10] *Ibid.*, lxii.　　　　[11] *Ibid.*, lxv.　　　　[12] *Ibid.*, xlvii–xlix.

who in the earldom of Strathearn seem to have been paid about 1d. a day in 1380.[13]

Although the agricultural classes comprised the basic categories of husbandmen, cottars and hired men, it is unlikely that these categories were closely defined or stereotyped. Within the rural community of the barony there were considerable opportunities for economic and social advancement: a man might rise above his fellows through his individual enterprise.

By contrast, burghal life showed a zest for social stratification and rigid apportionment of economic opportunities among the carefully differentiated categories of persons who lived in the burgh or used its facilities.[14] Towards the end of the fifteenth century the poet Robert Henryson, in his fable of the two mice, was to confer upon the town mouse the highest status within his community by making him 'gilt bruther and . . . ane fre burgess'.[15] The merchant burgesses, entrenched in the gild, dominated the burghal hierarchy and controlled the burgh. It was not beyond the competence of the gild court of Aberdeen to pass an ordinance in December 1401 to prevent 'Templars' (holders of former Temple tenements in the burgh) from buying flour to the detriment of the burgh market.[16] On 5 March 1406 a royal charter granted the magistrates and council of Perth the right to make burgh statutes (with the consent of the gild brethren) and to enforce them by penalties both in the court of the bailies of the burgh and in the gild court.[17]

These developments had been preceded by a concession that increased the autonomy of the burgh: on 10 April 1394 a royal charter allowed the burgesses of Perth to have their own sheriff and shrieval jurisdiction.[18] This unique privilege was a sign of the desire of the burgesses to escape from the attentions of royal officials and from the influence of the local aristocracy—in 1385 the burgesses of Ayr wished that neighbouring lands should be leased in tack to simple husbandmen and not to any 'potent lord', and in 1418 they daringly

---

[13] *E.R.*, III. 33–8. See M. M. Postan, 'The Famulus: the estate labourer in the twelfth and thirteenth centuries', *Economic History Review Supplements*, No. 2, 1–48.

[14] See the *Iter Camerarii*, a document found in the Bute MS. which has been attributed to the reign of Robert II or Robert III (*A.P.S.*, I. 695).

[15] MacQueen, *Robert Henryson*, p. 123.

[16] *Aberdeen Burgh Recs.*, pp. lxvi, cxliv.

[17] Confirmation in *R.M.S., 1593–1608*, No. 1098.

[18] Confirmation in *ibid.*, No. 1098 and *R.M.S.*, I. App. 2, No. 1720.

claimed that all the king's burgesses were exempt from distraint by a sheriff.[19]

To a greater or less extent the king's burghs were self-governing and had direct access to the king. They were the wealthiest burghs : the contribution levied in 1373 brought the chamberlain (probably after deductions) £157 16s. od. from Edinburgh, £114 4s. 5d. from Aberdeen, £74 11s. 5d. from Dundee, and only £2 os. 11d. from the bishop's burgh of Glasgow.[20] And in 1424 the four burghs—currently Edinburgh, Perth, Dundee and Aberdeen—acted as sureties for payment of James I's 'expenses' of fifty thousand marks as a condition of his release.[21] Thus the king's burghs were able to demand recognition of their own special status, perhaps as a preliminary to attempts to curb the ecclesiastical and baronial burghs which were growing in number.[22] A move of this sort may underlie the new phraseology of a royal charter of 12 January 1401 that made Rothesay a 'royal' burgh (*burgus regius* or *regalis burgus*).[23] A few months later, on 29 April 1401, another royal charter granted to Sir James Douglas of Dalkeith the erection of his town of Dalkeith as a 'free burgh of barony', with the same privileges (unspecified) as 'the rest of the barons of our realm enjoy and use most freely in their barons' burghs'.[24] Here, it seems, a distinction has crept in between the 'barons' burghs' (later to be regarded as 'unfree') and the king's burghs or 'royal' burghs (later to be regarded as virtually the only 'free' burghs).[25]

Another move towards differentiation between the two types of burgh was made when the court of the four burghs met at Stirling on 12 October 1405.[26] One of its enactments declared that no 'Templar' should buy or sell goods reserved to the members of the gild. Since the Templars were dissolved in 1309 this apparently anachronistic enactment has given the impression that the record is either spurious or misdated.[27] On the contrary the supposed anachronism concerned a contemporary issue.[28] There is thus no reason to doubt the authenticity of the important first enactment which stipulated that two or three commissioners from each of the king's burghs south of Spey should attend the 'parliament' of the four burghs each year, wherever it might be held, to treat of all things concerning the common weal

[19] *Ayr Burgh Charters*, Nos. 41, 42.

[20] *E.R.*, ii. 431.   [21] *Rot. Scot.*, ii. 243.

[22] *Kirkintilloch Burgh Court Book* (S.H.S.), pp. xxiv–xxv.

[23] *Ibid.*, pp. xxxviii–xxxix.   [24] *Morton Registrum*, ii. No. 209.

[25] *Kirkintilloch Burgh Court Book* (S.H.S.), p. xl.   [26] *A.P.S.*, i. 703–4.

[27] W. M. Mackenzie, *The Scottish Burghs*, p. 77, note 1; Theodora Pagan, *The Convention of the Royal Burghs*, p. 14.   [28] P. 263 above.

of all the king's burghs, their liberties and their court. In this context the word 'parliament' suggests that the court of the four burghs was extending its functions and that its business was now definitely deliberative as well as judicial. This 'parliament' was to be—initially at least—one that was to exclude representatives from the baronial and ecclesiastical burghs. It was a body that could formulate the common interests of the royal burghs, no doubt as a preliminary to the presentation of an agreed policy by their commissioners in the three estates; the first step had been taken towards the establishment of an institution that still survives—the convention of royal burghs.[29]

Despite such developments the importance of the burghs must not be over-emphasised: even Edinburgh, which Froissart described as the Paris of Scotland, had less than four hundred houses and could hardly be compared with provincial continental cities such as Tournai or Valenciennes;[30] yet, along with Haddington, Dunbar and North Berwick, it shared some of the export trade that had formerly passed through Berwick and accounted for between a quarter and a third of the total Scottish customs revenue. Aberdeen had temporarily fallen behind Dundee and was on much the same level as Perth and Linlithgow in exporting about one third as much as Edinburgh.[31] By contrast the few burghs situated on the west coast had scarcely any share in the export trade.

The chief Scottish exports continued to be wool and hides, but the bulk volume of wool exports was no higher in 1378 than it had been in 1327 and was to decline after 1378. There was some compensation in an increasing export of hides.[32] Even so, in 1390 the gross receipts from the great customs on wool, hides and woolfells came to less than £5,000,[33] in 1407 to £3,070 4s. 1½d.,[34] in 1416 they rose to £4,739 11s. 11d.,[35] in 1418 they slumped to £2,911 8s. 3½d.[36] In this depressing situation it was natural that miscellaneous commodities that had begun to figure among Scottish exports should be singled out for the imposition of new export duties to try to halt the drop in the most important source of royal revenue. A council held at Perth on 22 April 1398 imposed various duties, notably a charge of 2s. in the pound on the value of exported cloth.[37]

[29] See *Kirkintilloch Burgh Court Book* (S.H.S.), pp. xxxix–xl; Theodora Pagan, *The Convention of the Royal Burghs, passim.*

[30] *Chron. Froissart*, IV. 23, where, however, the number of houses in Edinburgh is wrongly given as approaching 4,000.

[31] See Appendix I, Map C; *E.R.*, II. lxxxix; III. 202–13; IV. 1–17, 240–54, 290–302. [32] *E.R.*, II. xc–xci. [33] *Ibid.*, III. 202–13. [34] *Ibid.*, IV. 1–17. [35] *Ibid.*, 240–54. [36] *Ibid.*, 290–302. [37] *A.P.S.*, I. 571.

This suggests a revival of the manufacture of cloth (probably of coarse quality). Simultaneously there was an attempt to protect this manufacture by a heavy import duty of 40d. in the pound on the value of imported English cloth 'to avoid damage thereupon ensuing to the realm'.[38] This was virtually the first import duty to be levied in Scotland[39] and was a sign of the growth of a mercantilist outlook.

While Scottish exports were still mainly raw materials, Scottish imports were still mainly manufactured articles and luxuries. The wide variety of these is demonstrated in the cargo lists of vessels captured or 'arrested' by the English on the route between Scotland and Flanders.[40] From another direction, however, the Scots were importing commodities to make up two deficiencies that were becoming apparent at home: in the more settled parts of Scotland timber was becoming scarce, and the prevalence of sheep and cattle farming was accompanied by shortages of grain. By the end of the fourteenth century there was a two-way traffic that brought Scots skippers and merchants to the furthermost Germanic ports of the Baltic in search of grain and timber.

It was chivalry that had plotted the track. The long-lasting 'crusade' led by the Teutonic Knights against the heathen Lithuanians had provided yet another field for Scottish knighthood to display its prowess,[41] and chivalric contacts soon became commercial as well. In the opening years of the fifteenth century the Teutonic Order kept resident factors in Edinburgh and Linlithgow; in 1404 it shipped to Edinburgh wheat, rye, malt and wainscoting valued at 2,800 marks.[42]

At the same period there was increasing contact between Scotland and a second, and even greater, Germanic organisation, the Hanseatic League, which included the important Baltic trading cities of Lübeck, Stralsund and Danzig. In 1423 Scottish merchants already resided in Danzig and wrote home to complain of the restrictions imposed upon their activities.[43] The restrictive policy of the Hansa was one source of friction. Another was Scottish piracy,[44] which led to retaliatory

---

[38] *Ibid.*   [39] See, however, *E.R.*, I. cxxxv and III. lxxxi–lxxxii.

[40] *Cal. Docs. Scot.*, IV. No. 462. For trade with the Low Countries see Davidson and Gray, *Staple*, pp. 120–6; J. Yair, *An Account of the Scotch Trade in The Netherlands* (London, 1776), pp. 26–62; M. P. Rooseboom, *The Scottish Staple in The Netherlands*, pp. 9–18.

[41] *Rot. Scot.*, I. 869; II. 4, 13; *Chron. Bower*, II. 416; T. A. Fischer, *The Scots in Germany*, pp. 72, 275, and *The Scots in Eastern and Western Prussia and Hinterland* (afterwards cited as *Scots in Prussia*), p. 123.

[42] T. A. Fischer, *The Scots in Germany*, p. 10. The place-name 'Lettecowe' (Linlithgow) which occurs in some records has been wrongly taken by Fischer to represent Glasgow.   [43] *Ibid.*, pp. 14–5.   [44] *Ibid.*, pp. 5–6.

seizures and trade embargoes. After an outrage committed by the Earl of Mar, a meeting of the Hanseatic diet at Luneburg prohibited importation of Scottish wool and cloth and a further diet at Elbing in 1415 imposed a total embargo. This brought protests from the Duke of Albany and a temporary settlement through Flemish mediation.[45]

The frequency of maritime disputes had already led to the appointment of a Scottish admiral, whose business was not so much naval as legal : his deputes in the more important Scottish seaports held admiralty courts to administer maritime law.[46] In 1403 David Lindsay, Earl of Crawford, was acting as admiral of Scotland,[47] and by 1423 the office was held by the pirate Earl of Mar.[48] There was nothing strange in the appointment of two earls, acknowledged leaders of Scottish chivalry, to the post of admiral. The chivalric noble, at a time when the respectable merchant believed implicitly in an economic policy of multifarious restrictions and regulations, could alone indulge with impunity in exuberant private enterprise. From the fourteenth century onwards, when Scotsmen of all classes were increasingly accustomed to travel throughout Western Europe on business that was ecclesiastical, commercial, academic or political,[49] it was the chivalric noble who led the way in revealing farther horizons to his countrymen.

Henry Sinclair, first of that family to become Earl of Orkney,[50] even disclosed a transoceanic horizon. In 1391 he had gone on a successful expedition to the Faroe Islands where he met Nicolo Zeno, a shipwrecked Venetian mariner whom he made captain of his fleet. After they had defeated and killed a rival claimant to the earldom of Orkney they listened to fishermen who told of a rich and populous land westward across the ocean. Thereupon the resourceful earl crossed the Atlantic with Antonio Zeno, brother of Nicolo, and touched at least the coast of Greenland, if not the American continent.[51] Whatever Sinclair found was evidently unrewarding. The Scots ignored the possibilities of western discovery that might have transformed their position in the world.

As it was, the resourcefulness of Scottish traders and nobles seems to have resulted in rising imports at a time when exports were falling.

[45] *Ibid.*, pp. 5–6, 13–4. [46] *Scots Legal Hist.*, pp. 396–400.
[47] *Cal. Papal Petitions*, I. 630.
[48] *Aberdeen-Banff Illustrations*, IV. 183.
[49] See A. I. Dunlop, 'Scots Abroad in the Fifteenth Century', Historical Association Pamphlet, No. 124.
[50] P. 192 above. [51] *Scots Peerage*, VI. 568–9.

The outflow of bullion, partly the result of an adverse balance of trade, partly the result of cash payments to the papal court, led to a scarcity of bullion within Scotland. One apparent remedy, applied from 1385 onwards, was to restrict its export.[52] Another, applied from 1367 onwards, was debasement of the coinage. This upset foreign exchange rates: complaints about a new Scottish coinage were made in the English parliament in November 1373; on 24 July 1374 Edward III denounced the craftiness of the Scots, who, he alleged, were passing their inferior coins in England at the face value and abstracting good English coins into Scotland; henceforth 4d. Scots was to be accepted as worth only 3d. English.[53]

This was not necessarily bad in itself: special circumstances made the English coinage the most stable in Western Europe while other areas more active in trade and manufacture, such as northern Italy, continually debased their coinage.[54] The Scottish debasement of 1373 was thus part of a general European trend; but the trend did not operate equally and simultaneously in all areas and therefore posed problems.[55] From 1373 onwards the three estates were to show their concern over the coinage and related questions. For inflation followed in the wake of debasement: in 1409 the Abbot of Dunfermline granted forty shillings a year to each of his monks to buy clothing, 'considering that all things are dearer than they were in times past', and in 1454 the Bishop of Moray would complain that 'three marks, present money, scarcely equal one mark of old money, so that formerly where six marks sufficed for the sustentation of a vicar of the choir, today ten marks scarcely suffice'.[56]

Monetary troubles did not prevent a building boom that was to last throughout the fifteenth century, stimulated partly by the shrinking of other opportunities for investment, partly by the desire to repair what had been destroyed in the wars of independence and the sporadic warfare that followed. For the bulk of the population the occasional destruction of their primitive homes in wartime was a

---

[52] *A.P.S.*, I. 554, 572.

[53] *Rot. Scot.*, I. 964; *E.R.*, II. 430.

[54] Carlo Cipolla, 'Currency Depreciation in Medieval Europe', *Change in Medieval Society*, ed. Sylvia L. Thrupp (1964), pp. 227–36.

[55] See Alison Hanham, 'A medieval Scots merchant's handbook', *S.H.R.*, L. 107–20. This ready-reckoner of *c.* 1400 shows the expertise required in dealing with the variety of weights and measures in a few leading commodities and with 'the confusion of monetary systems' in the Low Countries.

[56] *Dunfermline Registrum*, No. 399; Cameron, *Apostolic Camera*, p. lvi, n. 1.

matter soon remedied,[57] but this was hardly the case with buildings that were royal, baronial or ecclesiastical, where considerable investment was involved. At Edinburgh Castle, which became the chief royal residence towards the end of the reign of David II, repairs which had begun in 1360 [58] were succeeded by new construction: from 1367 to 1379 work was in progress on 'the new tower',[59] soon styled 'King David's Tower'.[60] This stood on the site of the present half-moon battery and was the most striking feature of the castle until its destruction in the siege of 1573. From 1360 to 1371 the total building costs at Edinburgh came to £736 13s. od.[61] The lead given by David II was followed by the first two Stewart kings, who spent a good deal on the royal castles, particularly Rothesay.[62]

The magnates were no less eager than the crown to repair the damage of war and build anew. While some of the pre-war stone castles, such as Bothwell, Kildrummy and Dirleton, were repaired, and even elaborated by the construction of new accommodation within their 'closes', they seldom served as a model for new fortifications. Instead, the most striking development in baronial architecture was the building of tower-houses. These had their counterparts in other countries and other ages but were to become distinctively Scottish. They provided a modicum of security and domesticity without the expense of constructing the thick curtain-walls of the earlier castles of *enceinte*. The lower stories of the tower usually displayed only sheer walls, a few arrow-slits, and an unobtrusive and unwelcoming doorway. This opened on to a turnpike stairway which was the sole, and easily defended, means of reaching the domestic accommodation on the upper floors.

Such was the type of residence, free-standing, rectangular in plan, massive and lofty in elevation, that was erected by Archibald the Grim at Threave [63] as the headquarters of the lordship of Galloway which he had acquired in 1369. Threave was to have its replicas, great and small, throughout Scotland. Even in the sixteenth century some tower-houses were being built which scarcely differed from it, although development had meanwhile given rise to elaborations and variations in design.

For the austere functionalism of Threave was not to the liking of

---

57 *Chron. Froissart*, IV. 23, 63. See also Aeneas Sylvius (Brown, *Early Travellers*, p. 25). 58 *E.R.*, II. 78, 79. 59 *Ibid.* See 'Guppild' in index.
60 'The greatest tower is still called David's Tower' (Boece, *History*, pp. 327–327v). 61 *E.R.*, II. cviii–cxi.
62 *Ibid.*, III. lxxiii, 313, 324, 357, 390, 463, 551, 610.
63 See W. M. Mackenzie, *The Medieval Castle in Scotland*, pp. 133–6.

all of Archibald the Grim's noble contemporaries. At Tantallon and St Andrews a curtain wall strengthened with towers guarded the landward approach to a peninsula that required little defence on the seaward sides. At Doune the castle built by the first Duke of Albany was remarkable for two features, firstly the combination of the gate-tower with the 'keep' or 'donjon' reserved for the accommodation of the lord and his personal suite, and secondly the provision of segregated living quarters for the lord's retainers, supposedly less trustworthy in the days of 'bastard feudalism' when they were mercenary troops.[64] Not every noble had the same reason to suspect treachery as had the builder of Doune, who even arranged that the castle portcullis could be raised and lowered only from a window-recess in his private hall in the gate-tower. This hall, as was usual in tower-houses, occupied almost the whole of the first floor of the tower and was a sumptuous apartment with an ornate fireplace and minstrels' gallery. Above the great hall was the 'solar' or living-room, and a small oratory. A turnpike stairway from the solar gave access to bedrooms on the third floor and to a parapet walk at the top of the tower. The pitched roof of the tower was slated and had crow-stepped gables from which tall chimneys projected. Although the gate-tower at Doune was only part of a whole complex of buildings its internal arrangements were similar to those that might be found in many tower-houses throughout Scotland.

So far as ecclesiastical buildings were concerned there was rebuilding rather than new construction; in a number of cases it was a series of fires, accidental or deliberate, that made rebuilding unavoidable, as at the cathedrals of St Andrews and Elgin and the abbeys of Arbroath, Sweetheart, Melrose, Newbattle and Dryburgh. In most cases rebuilding was accompanied by extension and elaboration and permitted the introduction of new styles of architecture. At Aberdeen Bishop Leighton followed a style that was perhaps influenced by the Teutonic architecture of the Baltic and gave his cathedral an austere and embattled appearance. There is some evidence of the presence of French masons in Scotland and the rebuilt abbey of Melrose shows some 'flamboyant' features. Although Scottish ecclesiastical architecture followed no one ideal, and individualism was so prevalent that no distinctively Scottish style emerged, the kirks of Scotland were nonetheless to 'become recognisable as belonging to nowhere else'.[65]

[64] See W. Douglas Simpson, *Doune Castle* (n.d.), p. 17.
[65] Ian Finlay, *Art in Scotland*, p. 34.

Meanwhile new ecclesiastical construction, as distinct from reconstruction, received a stimulus from a change in devotional fashion whereby votive masses were regarded as more spiritually efficacious than the prayers of monks.[66] Such masses could be conveniently arranged by payment for a stipulated number, by the hiring of a secular priest to act as chaplain, or by the endowment of a chaplainry so that a priest might perpetually celebrate mass for the soul's weal of the patron and his nominees.[67] Thus at least two chaplains served in the chapel of St Monance which David II constructed at a cost of over £600.[68] Such chapels, or even parish kirks in which a number of chaplains served, might acquire the more dignified status of collegiate kirks. These obtained their name not from any educational function (though some maintained small schools for their boy choristers)[69] but from the *collegium* (incorporation) of priests, headed by a provost or dean, whose main function was the celebration of votive masses. In other respects—the ornateness of their architecture and furnishings, the provision often made for choral music—the collegiate kirks might roughly be compared to small cathedrals. Between 1342 and 1424 about ten had been founded by wealthy landholders.[70]

One of the wealthiest of these was Sir James Douglas of Dalkeith, who in 1377–8 was receiving annual rents of about £1,000.[71] His will and testament, drawn up in 1390,[72] some thirty years before his death, gives ample evidence both of his worldly riches and his conventional piety, which manifested itself in miscellaneous benefactions throughout his career. The most obvious feature of these was his desire to obtain votive masses. In 1384 he endowed a chaplainry in the chapel of his castle of Dalkeith,[73] and in 1406 he endowed six chaplainries in the chapel of St Nicholas that he had built in his burgh of Dalkeith. The chaplains, who were all to be priests, were to contribute to the soul's weal of Sir James and his kin, of David II, Robert II, Robert III and their successors, and with Bishop Wardlaw's approval Sir James laid down further regulations 'as is the custom in similar collegiate kirks'.[74]

[66] See the remarkable encomium of the mass in *Chron. Bower*, II. 467–71.

[67] See K. L. Wood-Legh, *Perpetual Chantries in Britain* (1965).

[68] *E.R.*, II. 121, 133, 266, cvi–cviii.

[69] D. E. Easson, *op. cit.*, Scot. Church Hist. Soc. Recs., VI. 13–26, at 16–7.

[70] Easson, *Religious Houses*, pp. 173–88. See also D. E. Easson, 'The Foundation-Charter of the Collegiate Church of Dunbar, 1342', S.H.S. *Misc. VI*, 81–109.

[71] *Morton Registrum*, I. xlvii–lxxvi.

[72] *Ibid.*, II. No. 193.   [73] *Ibid.*, No. 176.   [74] *Ibid.*, No. 278.

Another of the collegiate foundations of this period was that of St John the Evangelist, established in 1419 by Robert of Montrose, canon of the chapel royal at St Andrews. St John's, the first collegiate foundation to be connected with the university of St Andrews, was headed by Master Laurence of Lindores and was to be used to foster the study of theology and arts; but it was on too small a scale to act as an important university institution.[76]

The university itself was a 'somewhat inchoate body of scholars and masters',[77] since Bishop Wardlaw's charter and Pope Benedict's bull had conferred privileges but no endowment. The accredited university teachers, or 'regent masters', thus depended on the income they obtained from running private 'pedagogies' (halls of residence) in which they offered to students both board and lodging and tuition. By 1417 competition among the regent masters to obtain student lodgers seems to have driven the charge down to 1s. 8d. a week.[78] The students who arrived at St Andrews, at the age of fifteen, or even earlier, were grammar students rather than university students. Their first task was to improve their Latin so that they could under-stand university lectures and take part in academic disputations; only after this had been achieved would they 'incorporate' or become matriculated students of the university. In theory the student had to complete eighteen months of study and to have reached the age of sixteen before his regent presented him as a 'determinant' for the bachelor's degree in arts. Having 'determined' he might study for something like a further two years to obtain his master's licence.[79] The examination for the licentiate took the form of public disputation, after which the licentiand received the master's licence which gave him, in theory, the right to teach anywhere (*ius ubique docendi*).[80] In its early days the university exacted an oath from the new masters or 'incipients' that they would teach in the university for a further two years. Before long, however, teaching was left entirely to the regents, who became a sort of professoriate that perpetuated itself through co-option, eventually excluded both students and incipients from the election of the rector, and monopolised control of the faculties.[81]

The foundation bull of Pope Benedict had permitted the setting

---

[76] *St Andrews Acta*, I. xix; *St Andrews Univ. Recs.*, p. xxi.

[77] *St Andrews Acta*, I. cxxxviii.

[78] *Ibid.*, I. 9; *St Andrews Univ. Recs.*, p. xxxii.

[79] *St Andrews Univ. Recs.*, pp. xxvi, xxxii–xxxiii; *St Andrews Acta*, I. xc.

[80] *St Andrews Acta*, I. cxvi–cxvii.

[81] *Ibid.*, cxxi, cxxvii, cxxxvii–cxxxviii.

up of five faculties—theology, canon law, civil law, medicine, and the liberal arts.[82] These faculties had varying fortunes. Until the sixteenth century medicine was studied only spasmodically at St Andrews.[83] The same was probably true of civil law, though lectures on the subject may have been given by canon lawyers who also held a degree in civil law; for 'in practice there had never been a hard and fast differentiation between canonists and civilists'.[84] To obtain a degree in canon law it was neither necessary nor usual to take as a preliminary the full arts course and obtain a degree in arts. This, however, was the normal requisite for the student of theology, which was thus the 'higher faculty': it had distinguished teachers and a small number of advanced students. In terms of numbers and influence it was, however, the faculty of arts which dominated the university.[85] From the graduation rolls of the faculty (the earliest extant in the British Isles)[86] it appears that slightly more than 4,500 arts graduates were produced between 1413 and 1579, of whom about one third obtained the master's degree.[87]

The arts curriculum comprised the three philosophies (natural, moral and metaphysical) and seven liberal arts. These were divided between the introductory *trivium* (grammar, rhetoric and logic) and the more advanced *quadrivium* (music, arithmetic, geometry and astronomy).[88] Academic controversy over the prescribed reading for the subjects of the arts curriculum was common. So also (as in most medieval universities) was controversy between 'nominalists' and 'realists'.[89] The realists held that 'universals' (concepts) have a genuine existence, being reflections of 'forms' in the mind of God; the nominalists (among them Laurence of Lindores) held that universals existed only in the human mind in so far as it 'named', and thus categorised, the data perceived through the senses.

It was mainly clerics, or prospective clerics, who sought higher education at St Andrews. But more elementary instruction in Latin was available to a wider range of students in some ecclesiastical institutions[90] and in the grammar schools that, by the fifteenth century, were to be found in most of the Scottish burghs and even in the

---

[82] *Ibid.*, clvii.   [83] *Ibid.*, clvii–clviii.   [84] *Ibid.*, clii–cliii.
[85] *Ibid.*, cxxxix, 2–3.   [86] *St Andrews Univ. Recs.*, pp. xli–xlii.
[87] *Ibid.*, p. xxv.   [88] Rashdall, *Universities*, I. 456–7.
[89] *St Andrews Acta*, I. xxi, 3, 39–41, 48.
[90] Thus Hugh Kennedy, soldier, diplomat and ecclesiastic, had been placed with the Dominican friars of Ayr to learn grammar (*Cal. Papal Letters*, VIII. 553–4). See also Innes, *Scot. Middle Ages*, pp. 169–70, 271.

coal-mining township of Tranent.[91] It is significant that Sir James Douglas of Dalkeith possessed books of grammar and logic, books of the civil law and of Scottish statutes, as well as books of 'romance'. He bequeathed these books to his sons and enjoined that the books he had lent to others should be returned to his heir, while those that he had borrowed should be restored to their owners.[92] Now, if not before, there existed, outwith the royal court and the kirk, men with the wealth, the leisure and the taste to form a reading public.

Meanwhile the English language, which for some two centuries had been little more than the common speech of the lower and middle classes in England and in Lowland Scotland, advanced rapidly up the social scale and in Scotland began to become standardised as a dialect distinct from that of northern England.[93] Even time-honoured Latin suffered somewhat through the advancement of this Lowland vernacular, while the clearest sign that French had dropped out of use in common speech, and had become a foreign language, is to be found in the famous letter that the Earl of March addressed to Henry IV on 18 February 1400 : the earl excused himself for writing in English, not because he was ignorant of French, but because 'the Englishe tongue is maire cleare to myne understanding'.[94]

Though French was in rapid decline as a spoken tongue this was not, as yet, the case with Gaelic, which persisted as the language of half of Scotland's population; no serious decline from that position was to occur until the sixteenth century. The cultural unity of Gaelic Scotland and Gaelic Ireland was also unimpaired. It was typical that the poet Muireadhach of Lissadill, when forced to exile himself from Ireland in the early thirteenth century, took refuge in the Lennox and became known as Muireadhach Albanach ('the Scot'). He was to found the MacMhuirich bardic family that held lands in return for keeping a record of the genealogy and history of the MacDonalds.[95] The MacMhuirichs, 'probably the longest-lived literary dynasty in Europe', were to function as pro-

[91] J. Grant, *History of the Burgh and Parish Schools of Scotland*, pp. 1–75. See also D. E. Easson, *op. cit.*, *Scot. Church Hist. Soc. Recs.*, VI. 13–26, at 17–22, and John Durkan, 'Education in the Century of the Reformation', *Essays on the Scottish Reformation, 1513–1625*, ed. David McRoberts, where a list of some sixty schools is given.

[92] *Morton Registrum*, II. No. 196, pp. 179, 181.

[93] Wittig, *Scottish Tradition*, p. 11.

[94] *Nat. MSS. Scot.*, II. No. liii.

[95] D. S. Thomson, 'The MacMhuirich Bardic Family', *Transactions of the Gaelic Society of Inverness* (1963), 3–31, at 4–6, 10.

fessional poets from the thirteenth century until the eighteenth.[95] They were a striking but by no means unique example of the class of professional bards who held high status under the patronage of the Gaelic lords and who composed 'classical' poetry, or poetic prose, in accordance with elaborate rules passed on from father to son or learnt after years of study in the Irish bardic schools that were probably mature institutions even in the days of St Columba.[97]

While the tradition of formal artistic composition in Gaelic was one of the earliest to develop in Europe, a literary tradition in the Lowland vernacular was one of the latest. It had its origins in the folk ballads, of which the earliest extant fragments are the poignant lines concerning the death of Alexander III :

> Quhen Alysandyr oure Kyng wes dede,
> That Scotland led in luve and le,
> Away wes sons off ale and brede,
> Off wyne and wax, off gamyn and gle;
> Oure gold wes changyd in to lede.
> Cryst, borne in to Vyrgynete,
> Succoure Scotland and remede,
> That stad is in perplexyte.[98]

When John Barbour composed *The Bruce* in 1375 the verse form that he chose was identical with that of this earliest ballad. Indeed after his prologue Barbour begins his narration by adapting the first two lines of the Alexander ballad :

> Quhen Alexander the king wes deid,
> That Scotland haid to steyr and leid . . .[99]

At a much later date the poet Robert Henryson would similarly allude to a line from the Alexander ballad in his *Taill of the Scheip and the Doig*.[100] Thus this ballad not only marked the beginning of a Lowland literary tradition but helped to shape it.

Rapid maturity was reached in Barbour's *Bruce*, a sustained work of over thirteen thousand lines.[101] Nothing is known of Barbour's career prior to 1357, when he already was archdeacon of Aberdeen.[102] By the time of his death in 1395 his literary productions

---

[96] *Ibid.*, p. 29.
[97] D. S. Thomson, 'Gaelic learned orders and literati in medieval Scotland', *Scottish Studies*, XII. 57–78.
[98] *Chron. Wyntoun*, II. 266.   [99] Barbour, *The Bruce*, I. 3.
[100] P. 581 below.   [101] *Buik of Alexander* (S.T.S.), I. civ, ccvi.
[102] For an account of his career see *ibid.*, I. clxix–ccii.

included not only imaginary romances such as the *Buik of Alexander*, a *Troy Book* or *Brut*, now lost, and the *Ballet of the Nine Nobles*, but two works that were calculated to win royal favour. One, the lost *Stewartis Orygenale*, seems to have been a romantic genealogy that flatteringly traced the new royal dynasty back to Troy.[103] The second was *The Bruce*, the work on which Barbour's reputation as a poet principally rests.

It is tempting to relate this work to the contemporary work of Chaucer and Froissart, men of much the same social standing as the archdeacon, and men whom he may have met if he made use of his various safe-conducts. Chaucer's poetic career had, however, scarcely begun before *The Bruce* was completed. Froissart, on the other hand, had composed his romance *Meliador* shortly after his Scottish trip of 1365; and this work recounted the mythical tale of rival contenders for the hand of the King of Scotland's only daughter.[104] Long before, the thirteenth-century *Roman de Fergus* had also shown how Scotland could be made the setting for a chivalric romance.[105] Such examples may have encouraged Barbour to make Scotland and Robert Bruce, its hero king, a 'matter' of romance similar to, but distinct from, the fabulous Britain over which King Arthur had once held sway. If the glorification of Bruce was calculated to win for the poet the patronage of that hero's grandson, Robert II, so also the glorification of Sir James Douglas was calculated to flatter that hero's illegitimate son, the influential Archibald the Grim.

In the prologue to the poem Barbour affirmed that stories (histories) are 'delitabill' to read, even if they are only fables; how much more pleasing they are if they are 'suthfast'. His intention was

> To put in wryt a suthfast story,
> That it lest ay furth in memory.[106]

On the whole, despite the liberties he took with some of his material, Barbour the historian triumphed at the expense of Barbour the poet. His pertinacity in recording detail makes his poem an essential historical source for the period it covers.[107] If, like his contemporaries,

[103] *Ibid.*, cxxxi, clviii, cxc, ccxiii, ccxvii, ccxx–ccxxi.

[104] See A. H. Diverres, 'Froissart's *Meliador* and Edward III's policy towards Scotland', *Mélanges offerts à Rita Lejeune*, II. 1399–1409.

[105] M. Dominica Legge, 'Sur la genèse du *Roman de Fergus*', *Mélanges de Linguistique Romane et de Philologie Médiévale offerts à M. Maurice Delbouille*, II. 399–408.   [106] Barbour, *The Bruce*, I. 1–2.

[107] A detailed examination which confirms Barbour's relative accuracy as an historian is given in *The Buik of Alexander* (S.T.S.), I. ccxxvi–ccxxviii.

Barbour regarded history as being made by great personalities, of whose success or failure warfare was the ultimate test, he at least showed personalities of flesh and blood, endowed with the moral qualities necessary for the inter-action in history of the human and the divine. Moreover, Barbour had been influenced by the patriotic propaganda of King Robert's time and his own work was to transmit its influence to posterity. The best-known lines in his poem are those in praise of freedom :

> A fredome is a noble thing!
> Fredome mayss man to haiff liking;
> Fredome all solace to man giffis :
> He levys at ess that frely levys!
> A noble hart may haiff nane ess,
> Na ellys nocht that may him pless,
> Gif fredome failyhe . . .[108]

Archdeacon Barbour's association with the cathedral of Aberdeen may have brought to his acquaintance someone lower in the ecclesiastical hierarchy, a certain John of Fordun, possibly a chantry priest who celebrated mass at one of the altars in the cathedral.[109] While Barbour represented the new developments in vernacular literature Fordun remained true to the older practice of composition in Latin. But his work was no ordinary chronicle. Displaying a wide knowledge of the Latin classics [110] he was 'a careful compiler drawing upon material not otherwise known to have been preserved'.[111] Behind his erudition lay an argumentative patriotism : the chronicle was an apologia for Scottish independence and continued the propagandist tradition that began with Baldred Bisset's *Processus* and matured in the Declaration of Arbroath and in Bernard of Linton's Latin poem that celebrated the victory at Bannockburn [112]—a poem that was to have its counterpart in the Latin verses upon the victory at Otterburn composed by Fordun's contemporary, Thomas Barry, canon of Glasgow.[113] The importance of political argument based on mythology led Fordun to devote most of his chronicle, or at least most of what he completed, to the fabulous and dark ages. Posterity

[108] Barbour, *The Bruce*, I. 10.
[109] See A. R. McEwen, *History of the Church in Scotland*, I. 298–9.
[110] For his use of Juvenal see Innes, *Sketches*, p. 47.
[111] W. W. Scott, 'Fordun's Description of the Inauguration of Alexander II', *S.H.R.*, L. 198–200, at 200.
[112] It is translated by W. M. Mackenzie in his edition of *The Bruce*, p. 497.
[113] *Chron. Bower*, II. 406–13.

might have dispensed with an account of the reign of King Constantine, son of Heth the Wing-footed,[114] if Fordun, who died *c*. 1387, had chosen to write more about the reigns of David II and Robert II.

In this respect Fordun's deficiencies were partly remedied by Walter Bower, Abbot of Inchcolm, who some fifty years later continued the earlier writer's work up to the opening years of the reign of James II. Bower's scholarly *Scotichronicon*, less austere than the annals of Fordun on which it was based, is amusingly perfervid both in its nationalism and its moral sententiousness and provides valuable indications of the outlook of fifteenth-century Scotland.[115] It concludes with an appropriate asseveration : 'Christ ! he is not a Scot to whom this book is displeasing.'[116]

A chronicler of more limited talent than Fordun or Bower was Andrew of Wyntoun, Prior of Lochleven, who composed his *Orygenale Cronykil* sometime between 1420 and 1424. In the 'Prolog' Wyntoun showed that he could write tolerable verse when not encumbered by the need to narrate historical facts. His rhyming couplets were, however, ill-suited to cope with such topics as the succession of the Pictish kings :

> 'Drwst-Gygnowre wes fywe yhere kyng.
> And aucht yhere syne Drust-Hoddrylyng.
> Syne the fyrst Drwst yheris foure.
> Sex yhere Garnat-Gygnowre'.[117]

Although Wyntoun was well-versed in the learning of the age,[118] his chronicle was neither good history nor good poetry and has been likened to a 'somewhat weary pilgrimage from the Garden of Eden to the Scotland of Robert II [*rectius* Robert III]'.[119] Few harsh realities are allowed to mar the sentimental picture of loyalty, patriotism and virtue as Wyntoun speeds his great contemporaries on the way to paradise.

The lack of depth in Wyntoun's work becomes immediately apparent when it is compared with James I's *Kingis Quair*, a work

---

[114] *Chron. Fordun*, I. 163–4.
[115] David McRoberts, 'The Scottish Church and nationalism in the Fifteenth Century', *Innes Review*, XIX. 3–14, at 5–6.
[116] *Chron. Bower*, II. 513 (*rectius* 517).
[117] *Chron. Wyntoun*, I. 402.
[118] See the 'List of Authors etc.' (*Chron. Wyntoun*, III. 179–87). This list, compiled by David Laing, also illustrates Wyntoun's knowledge of geography.
[119] *Buik of Alexander* (S.T.S.), I. cxxii.

that had the character of a spiritual odyssey based upon James's own prolonged experience of the mutability of human fortune. He had set sail in March 1406 ostensibly for the good of his education. He returned in April 1424 a better-educated man than any of his royal predecessors. For, as Abbot Bower remarked, although he had been borne into England just as Joseph had been carried away to Egypt, James had learnt much from his period of bondage.[120] It is unfortunate that Bower expatiated upon James's musical talents (of which no trace survives to posterity) and wrote only in the most general terms of James's literary talents. Bower's reticence has even contributed to the advancing of an argument that James was not the author of the *Kingis Quair*, though this argument [121] is not now generally accepted.

Apart from its literary interest the *Kingis Quair* has an historical significance : beneath the allegory and symbolism there are autobiographical allusions. Just as Robert I emerges from the pages of Barbour as a real person, so also does James I acquire a personality denied to other medieval Scottish kings whose characters can be glimpsed only fleetingly in the encomia of chroniclers or the impersonal details of contemporary records. The very language of the poem—English after the fashion of Chaucer, interspersed with a few Scotticisms [122]— reveals the effect of a Scottish childhood followed by a sojourn of eighteen years in England. For James's model was not the poetry of Barbour but that of the English poets Gower and Chaucer,

> Superlative as poetis laureate
> In moralitee and eloquence ornate.[123]

In writing the tale of his own 'aventure' James tells how in his youth fortune had been his foe and 'how I gat recure off my distresse'.[124] The poem was undoubtedly finished after James's return to Scotland, for only then did he escape from the distresses of his youth. These had once led him to question whether any underlying order existed in the universe; in recounting his personal experience James gives his mature philosophical reflections on the subject of man's earthly fate. The medieval subtlety of the poem, its symbolism, and its 'prolixitee off doubilnesse',[125] have scarcely been penetrated by some critics, who

[120] *Chron. Bower*, II. 504–6.
[121] J. T. T. Brown, *The Authorship of the Kingis Quair* (1896).
[122] *The Kingis Quair* (S.T.S.), pp. xxiv–xxvi.
[123] *Ibid*., p. 45.   [124] *Ibid*., p. 5.   [125] *Ibid*., p. 7.

have wrongly regarded it as a simple tale of courtly love.[126] In his description of his first glimpse of the lady who was to become his bride James does, admittedly, show a love that was at once courtly, warm and real. But love is merely the agency that stirs the poet from despondency to strive to escape from his fate by self-mastery. A dream-vision which occupies half the length of the poem concludes in his encounter with Dame Fortune, who sets him upon her revolving wheel of fate, bidding him to hold fast as he rises upon it.[127] On waking from this dream the poet receives a sign that its promise will be fulfilled in liberty and love—as did in fact befall when James returned to Scotland in 1424 with his bride :

> To my larges ... I am cumin agayn,
> To blisse with hir that is my sovirane.[128]

[126] See the illuminating article by John MacQueen, 'Tradition and the Interpretation of *The Kingis Quair*', *Review of English Studies* (New Series), XII. 117–31.

[127] *The Kingis Quair* (S.T.S.), p. 42.

[128] *Ibid.*, p. 44.

11

A KING UNLEASHED

While the eighteen-year captivity of James I was in some ways a misfortune for him and Scotland it was not unmitigated. He had observed at close hand the government of the country then the most intensively governed in all Europe, and had drawn from it some ideas that he was to try to apply in Scotland, one of the least intensively governed countries of Europe. It was no moonstruck poet who undertook the reconstruction of royal government. James was approaching his thirtieth year, besides his artistic and intellectual qualities he was strong, athletic,[1] and decisive. In his young manhood he had existed on pittances doled out by the English king and had possessed a royal title but not royal power; he was covetous of both wealth and power; his idealism, which could be genuine and disinterested, sometimes concealed selfishness when he assumed that his own interests were automatically the best interests of his people.

From the first days of his return to Scotland in April 1424 James showed himself to be easily aroused to wrath when the weak were oppressed by the strong, and easily aroused against the strong, guilty or otherwise, when they represented even a possible threat to his own position. Bower tells the story that when the king heard of the theft, fraud and extortion that afflicted the land, he exclaimed: 'If God grant me life and aid, even the life of a dog, throughout all the realm I will make the key keep the castle and the bracken bush the cow'.[2] On 13 May 1424, even before his coronation, James arrested Walter Stewart, eldest of Duke Murdoch's three surviving sons, as well as Malcolm Fleming of Cumbernauld, the duke's brother-in-law, and Thomas Boyd of Kilmarnock.[3] These spectacular arrests conveyed

[1] *Chron. Bower*, II. 505. [2] *Ibid.*, 511.

the first warning to the Albany Stewarts that they no longer stood above the law.

A few days after his coronation at Scone James's first parliament met at Perth on 26 May 1424. Parliament, as distinct from general council, had probably not met for about twenty years.[4] This break in continuity was emphasised when James reverted to a procedure used in 1367, 1369, 1370 and 1372, when a commission had been appointed to hold the parliament, and the remainder of the three estates had been given leave to go home (*licentia recedendi*).[5] The same procedure was used in 1424, apparently for the last time, when 'certain persons were chosen to determine the articles given in by the lord king, the rest being given leave to withdraw'.[6] Although a procedure based on 'articles' was established it had not yet taken its final form. By the sixteenth century a committee of parliament would discuss the 'articles', draft them in the form of legislation, and then submit them to a full meeting of parliament for enactment. In 1424 however this was not quite the case : the 'certain persons' did not compose a committee that had to report back to parliament but a commission to 'determine' the articles, that is to bring them to a conclusion as legislation having the full authority of parliament.

Some of the articles which were 'given in' by the king and enacted by the parliamentary commission of 1424 immediately showed the directions in which the king's mind was turning. From the first it was evident that James intended to take a strong stand against lawlessness. It was enacted that no one should 'opinly or notourly rebell aganis the kyngis persone under the payne of forfautour of lif, landis and gudis' and that 'thar be maide officiaris and ministeris of lawe throu all the realme that can and may halde the lawe to the kingis commonis'.[7] There was even a threat that those who possessed heritable jurisdictions should be responsible to the king for any defaults of justice. These admonitory measures were summed up in the optimistic announcement 'that ferme and sikkir pece be kepit and haldin throu all the realme and amangis all and sindry liegis and subjectis of our soveran lorde the kyng'. Henceforth there were to be no more private wars and warlike feuds.[8]

Another major topic dealt with in the articles of 1424 was the

[3] *Ibid.*, 481–2; *E.R.*, IV. 380, 386.

[4] The last known parliament pre-dates 1406. A list of councils held during the governorship of the dukes of Albany is given by A. A. M. Duncan, *op. cit.*, *S.H.R.*, xxxv. 132–43, at 143.

[5] *A.P.S.*, I. 501, 506, 534, 547.   [6] *Ibid.*, II. 3.
[7] *Ibid.*, 4.   [8] *Ibid.*, 3, c. 2.

question of the royal revenues, and, coupled with this, the payment of 'the fynance to be made in Inglande'. It was decided that it would be 'grevous and chargeande on the commonys to raiss the haill fynance at anyss'—in other words that the money should be raised over a period of years rather than by one crippling levy. Meanwhile an aid or tax of one shilling in the pound was to be imposed on income and movable goods throughout the whole realm, including the regalities. In many respects the arrangements were modelled upon those devised in 1357 for payment of David II's ransom; once more a Scottish Domesday Book was to be compiled in a few weeks (by 12 July 1424) and the yield of 1s. in the pound was to be forthcoming by then.[9]

Just as the ransom of David II had brought the burgesses into a new prominence and assured them a permanent place as one of the estates of the realm, James I's 'fynance' was to lead to a further advancement of the merchant burgesses, whose goodwill he henceforth cultivated. In the parliament of 1424 the burgess commissioners 'in the name of the haill merchandis of the realme' undertook to pay the whole of the first instalment of the 'fynance' amounting to 10,000 English marks (or 20,000 English 'nobles') to be repaid from the proceeds of the valuation of the whole realm. To raise the first payment the burgesses thought it would be necessary to obtain 'chevisance'—a loan—in Flanders and undertook to contribute 300 'nobles' towards the expenses of the necessary mission. For this generosity some recompense was expected : henceforth no foreign merchant was to buy any goods for export from Scotland save from a Scottish merchant.[10]

While the ransom of David II had been met in fact not through direct taxation but from the increasing proceeds of the great customs, James was determined to pay his 'fynance' from direct taxation and keep the great customs to himself.[11] Meanwhile the opportunity was taken to impose new export duties on herring, horses, sheep and certain skins.[12] There was also an announcement that those who claimed pensions from the customs were to show evidence to the king, who would answer such a claim with the advice of his council ; this

---

[9] *Ibid.*, 4, c. 10.
[10] *Ibid.*, 6, c. 27. George Burnett (*E.R.*, IV. cxxx) wrongly thought that the burgesses undertook to pay two-fifths of the king's 'fynance', amounting to 20,000 marks. A sum approximating to this was banked with the burghs (p. 290 below), and the burghs undertook to make a *loan* of 10,000 marks, but their own contribution to the 'fynance' was to be derived from the levy of 1s. in the pound on the basis of the new valuation, and its amount cannot be ascertained.
[11] *A.P.S.*, II. 4, c. 8.   [12] *Ibid.*, 6, cc. 22, 23.

hinted at a revocation of annuities payable from the customs (which was accomplished).[13] More than that, the sheriffs were to hold inquests to ascertain what lands, possessions or annualrents had belonged to the crown in the times of David II, Robert II and Robert III, and in whose hands they now were; the king might summon his tenants to produce their charters so that 'he may persave quhat pertenys to thame'[14]—and no doubt perceive what might be recovered from them.

What resulted from the financial arrangements of the 1424 parliament is not clear. The new export duties seem to have been unproductive.[15] But the proceeds of the traditional great customs showed an immediate increase: at the audit of July 1422 the gross receipts had come to £2,779 8s. 2d.;[16] at the audit of May 1425 they totalled £4,400 4s. 9½d.[17] These receipts were to rise as high as £6,912 2s. 5½d. in 1428, though the average annual yield up to the end of the reign was little more than £5,000,[18] showing a level of exports higher than during the Albany governorship but lower than in the later years of David II when the export duties were the same.

Most significant of all was the outcome of the contribution of a shilling in the pound that the 1424 parliament had granted towards the king's 'fynance'. Over a two-year period the total yield came to little less than 40,000 English 'nobles',[19] or two-fifths of the total payment due to the English. This sum was paid to the burghs, which acted as the king's bankers in this vast transaction.[20] Although a good deal had been collected, it proved impossible to continue the practice of direct taxation as in the time of David II. The long gap in direct taxation since 1373–4 had hardened the Scots in their view that it was virtually unconstitutional. According to Abbot Bower, himself one of the auditors of the contribution, James's subjects were soon complaining that they were being turned into paupers by taxation.[21] Collection of the contribution for the English 'fynance' was stopped after the second year because of the outcry against it.

Thus the financial measures of the 1424 parliament were, from the point of view of the king, only moderately successful. While he could partially restore some of the crown revenues, such as the great customs, others were unproductive, unforthcoming, or static—the fixed feu-ferms of the burghs brought in about £550 a year but half

[13] *Ibid.*, 4, c. 8; *E.R.*, IV. xciii.
[14] *A.P.S.*, II. 4, c. 9.
[15] *E.R.*, IV. cxxvi–cxxviii.
[16] *Ibid.*, 358–68.
[17] *Ibid.*, xciii.
[18] *Ibid.*, cxxv.
[19] *Ibid.*, cxxxi.
[20] *Ibid.*, 639–71.
[21] *Chron. Bower*, II. 482.

of this went in long-standing ecclesiastical pensions; by 1424 the income from the crown lands was only about £1,000 a year;[22] the king's total annual revenue can scarcely have exceeded £7,000; and from this he was expected to maintain his household, finance government, and perhaps to meet his obligations to the English. Well might Abbot Bower remark that at the king's return 'there remained too little to him of the royal revenues, lands or possessions, besides customs, wards and reliefs, to sustain his position'.[23]

By contrast some of the Scottish nobles, with far smaller obligations, had an annual revenue of as much as £1,000. This emerges from the figures given for the revenues of the hostages demanded by the English in 1423–1424: the thirty-five nobles listed had a total annual income of 21,700 marks.[24] This list by no means included all Scottish nobles, nor did it include the richest—the Albany Stewarts and the Black Douglases. A group of only four or five nobles headed by either Albany or Douglas might have economic resources superior to those of the king. If James were to rule Scotland as effectively as he wished, it was no doubt necessary either that the economic resources of the crown should be augmented—or that those of the greater nobility be diminished. The first alternative was soon shown to be difficult. James was to concentrate upon the second. There is no sign that he carried out the revocation of former crown lands that had been envisaged in the legislation of the 1424 parliament. Such a measure would have caused universal antagonism among the nobility. Instead of wholesale revocation James's policy was to be one of forfeiting individual noble families. By the end of the reign the area of the crown lands had been greatly expanded, and with the increase the crown's annual income from this source rose threefold to some £3,000.[25] James was to set a precedent that the next three kings would follow successfully, though perilously.

While there was an economic motive that influenced James's policy towards the leading nobles there were political and personal motives as well. James seems to have borne a grudge towards the Albany Stewarts for allowing him to languish in England—a grudge perhaps sharpened by the fear that an Albany Stewart might succeed to the throne. For when Queen Joan gave birth at Christmas 1424 her child was a daughter, Margaret,[26] who would be debarred from

[22] Balfour-Melville, *James I*, p. 265.   [23] *Chron. Bower*, II. 482.
[24] See *Rot. Scot.*, II. 242 and *Cal. Docs. Scot.*, IV. No. 952.
[25] Balfour-Melville, *James I*, p. 265.   [26] Dunbar, *Scot. Kings*, p. 191.

the succession by the tailzie of 1373.[27] Duke Murdoch was not only the greatest of the Scottish nobles but was heir presumptive. Besides these grounds of suspicion and jealousy there were perhaps others that harked back to the circumstances of the death of James's elder brother, the Duke of Rothesay—a theme on which the Scottish chroniclers wrote with caution. An English account was less reticent, and represented Rothesay's death as the result of a wholesale conspiracy on the part of the Scottish nobles.[28] Certainly the Rothesay affair might provide a pretext for the arrest and interrogation of almost any noble; Duke Murdoch must have been uneasy so long as his eldest son, Walter, and his brother-in-law, Malcolm Fleming, lay in royal custody. Their arrest early in 1424 was followed towards the end of the year by that of Sir Robert Graham, younger son of Sir Patrick Graham of Kincardine.[29] No one can have suspected what the ultimate result of the king's attack on Sir Robert Graham would turn out to be. It was more striking that Duncan, Earl of Lennox, the aged father-in-law of Duke Murdoch, was also arrested.[30] As James's second parliament opened at Perth on 12 March 1425 the net was beginning to tighten around the Albany Stewarts who were still at large.

In this parliament various 'articles' were proposed for 'the quiete and gud governance of the realme' [31] and were passed as legislation. James showed that he understood the dangers inherent in 'bastard feudalism' : one statute referred to the leagues and bonds [32] that allied one magnate to another in factions that promoted feud and might also promote opposition to the crown; henceforth the making of such leagues was forbidden and any already made were pronounced null and void. This significant measure was designed to break up the contemporary forms of political association among the members of the only class that could actively oppose the crown. Whatever the immediate effect it was not lasting. Some other of the statutes passed by the 1425 parliament related to the current political situation. One was a statute against 'leasing making'—the spreading of tales 'quhilk may ingener discorde betuix the king and his pepill'.[33] Another 'item' instituted an inquiry to see whether the statutes of 1424 were properly observed; if they had been broken in any point those responsible

[27] P. 186 above.
[28] See *James I, Life and Death*, pp. 48–9. This fifteenth-century narrative has much information relating to the reign of James I that is not found in any other source.
[29] *E.R.*, iv. lxxxix.
[30] *Chron. Bower*, ii. 482.
[31] *A.P.S.*, ii. 7–8.
[32] See *Scot. Legal Hist.*, pp. 285–6.
[33] *A.P.S.*, ii. 8, c. 22.

were to be punished in the manner laid down by the 1424 parliament.[34] It was possibly this item that cleared the ground for the king's sensational move on the ninth day of the parliament, when he arrested Duke Murdoch, his wife Isabella, daughter of the Earl of Lennox, and their second surviving son, Alexander, besides Sir John Montgomery, a henchman of the duke, and Alan Otterburn, the duke's secretary.[35] The youngest of Murdoch's sons, James Stewart, still remained at large; on 3 May 1425 he burned the burgh of Dumbarton and slew the king's illegitimate uncle, John, the Red Stewart of Dundonald.[36]

The Dumbarton affair must have played into the king's hands by making more plausible whatever charges were brought against the Albany Stewarts when they were tried on 24 May 1425 before an assize of twenty-one nobles during a session of parliament held at Stirling. Duke Murdoch's eldest surviving son, Walter Stewart, was convicted of *roborea*—presumably extortion—and was beheaded in front of Stirling Castle. On the following day the same fate was meted out to Duke Murdoch, his son Alexander, and the octogenarian Earl of Lennox.[37] The people mourned the fall of the Albany Stewarts, 'saying that they suppoised and ymagynd that the kyng ded . . . that vigorious execucion upon the lordes of his kyne for the covetise of thare possessions and goodes'.[38] Certainly the executions brought rewards to the king. The forfeited earldoms of Fife and Menteith were worth about £900 a year,[39] and the king also obtained the earldom of Lennox when Inchmurrin Castle surrendered on 8 June 1425.[40] James Stewart and his followers, including the Dominican friar Finlay of Albany, Bishop of Argyll, fled to Ireland to end their days in exile.[41]

By his sensational destruction of the house of Albany the king had accomplished and dramatised a royalist revolution. How he achieved this is not clear. He had presumably played upon the hopes and fears of some of the greater nobles and used them for his own ends. In addition his other allies included knights, prelates and officials of the

[34] *Ibid.*, 7, c. 4.

[35] E. W. M. Balfour-Melville has shown (*James I*, p. 120, n. 3) that the supposition that James simultaneously arrested a further score of nobles is based upon a misreading of a somewhat ambiguous passage in Bower (*Chron. Bower*, II. 482–3).

[36] *Chron. Bower*, II. 482–3.

[37] *Ibid.*, 483–4; for discussion of the procedure at the trial see Rait, *Parliaments*, p. 329.

[38] *James I, Life and Death*, p. 49.

[39] *E.R.*, VI. lxxiv *et seq.*

[40] *Chron. Bower*, II. 484.

[41] *Ibid.*, 483.

same stamp as those who had stood by David II. But James's greatest source of strength was his own powerful personality and the moral support he drew from a people that longed for firm rule; the king who showed that he could oppress the mighty could prevent the mighty from oppressing the weak.

Apart from the internal factors that had facilitated the royalist coup of 1424–25, there were also external factors that from 1424 onwards indirectly strengthened King James's position at the expense of the Scottish nobility. Unlike his predecessors, James was faced by no serious threat from England and was therefore able to devote his energies uninterruptedly to the task of governing Scotland. Moreover, James's arrival in Scotland in 1424 had coincided with the departure of nobles who might otherwise have held him in check—some went as hostages to England, others went to France, where there were dazzling prospects for Scots, particularly those—and they were many—who considered themselves well-born.

The Franco-Scottish victory at Baugé in 1421 had soon been followed by the death of Henry V and of Charles VI. While John, Duke of Bedford, governed English-occupied France in the name of the infant Henry VI, the *parlement* of Paris, which had taken refuge in Poitiers, recognised the dauphin as Charles VII. For a number of years his fortunes were precarious. On 31 July 1423 his forces had the worse of an engagement at Cravant in which the Scottish contingent suffered heavy loss.[42] To remedy this setback Archibald the Tyneman and John Stewart, Earl of Buchan, had recruited a fresh Scottish expeditionary force that landed in France at the beginning of Lent 1424; Charles VII once more showed his gratitude and rewarded the Tyneman with the duchy of Touraine and his son, the Earl of Wigtown, with the lands of Dun-le-Roi in Berry.[43] But at Verneuil on 17 August 1424 the French and their Scottish allies were vanquished. The Tyneman, who had clattered his way in history from one lost battle to another, had lost his last battle. With him fell his second son, Sir James Douglas, and his son-in-law, the Earl of Buchan.[44]

Although the heavy losses of the Scots prevented the survivors

[42] *Ibid.*, 501; A. H. Burne, *The Agincourt War* (1956), pp. 188, 193; E. F. Jacob, *The Fifteenth Century*, pp. 242–3; Balfour-Melville, *James I*, p. 104; Francisque-Michel, *Les Ecossais en France*, I. 136–42.

[43] *Scots Peerage*, III. 166; Balfour-Melville, *James I*, p. 115.

[44] Balfour-Melville, *James I*, p. 115; E. F. Jacob, *The Fifteenth Century*, p. 244; A. H. Burne, *The Agincourt War*, p. 213.

from playing a dominant part in the continuing warfare, they persevered in the service of Charles VII under Sir John Stewart of Darnley and Hugh Kennedy.[45] And in 1428 Charles VII made another attempt to obtain reinforcements from Scotland, as well as a renewal of the Franco-Scottish alliance, and a marriage between James's three-year-old daughter Margaret and Charles's almost equally young son and heir, the Dauphin Louis. In July 1428 James promised to observe the Franco-Scottish alliance, and a marriage contract was sealed : Margaret was to be sent to France in a French fleet which would also take on board six thousand Scots to enlist in the French service.[46] In November 1428 Charles VII acknowledged that the despatch of these troops might bring war between Scotland and England and endanger the Scottish hostages; he therefore granted to James and his heirs the county of Saintonge, the castellany of Rochefort-sur-Charente, and the dignity of peer of France.[47] Though French kings never implemented the grant, Scottish kings never forgot it.

Meanwhile the English had besieged Orleans. Sir John Stewart of Darnley brought short-lived encouragement to the defenders but was slain near Rouvray on 12 February 1429.[48] After this, Orleans was regarded as virtually lost and Charles VII was supposed to have been advised by the *parlement* to seek refuge in Scotland. But France was to save itself by its own exertions : 'in those days the Lord exalted the spirit of a certain wondrous maid . . . in the duchy of Lorraine'.[49] Joan of Arc brought what seemed to be supernatural intervention. On 30 April 1429 she entered Orleans at the head of a relief force. It was a Scotsman, John Carmichael or Kirkmichael, who as Bishop of Orleans welcomed Joan into the city. He was among those Scots who followed the Maid as she conducted Charles VII into Rheims on 18 July 1429 [50] for the traditional ceremony of coronation and unction that made him truly King of France.

Although the position of Charles VII became much stronger James I put obstacles in the way of sending his daughter to France for marriage to the dauphin ;[51] nor were the six thousand Scots troops stipulated in the marriage treaty forthcoming. It was not until March

[45] Balfour-Melville, *James I*, pp. 79–80, 159.
[46] *A.P.S.*, II. 26–8; *Chron. Bower*, II. 484.
[47] *Spalding Club Misc. II*, 181–6.
[48] *Chron. Bower*, II. 501; *Chron. Pluscarden*, I. 363–4.
[49] *Chron. Pluscarden*, I. 365–7.
[50] *Chron. Bower*, II. 465; John Kirkpatrick, *op. cit.*, *S.H.S. Misc. II*. 47–102, at 55; E. F. Jacob, *The Fifteenth Century*, pp. 247–8.
[51] Balfour-Melville, *James I*, pp. 213–20.

1436 that James's daughter sailed from Dumbarton. On 25 June 1436 the eleven-year-old princess was married at Tours to the thirteen-year-old Dauphin Louis, who thereafter neglected her.[52] Through this *mariage de convenance* James had attached himself closely to France at a time when the security of the Valois dynasty was at last assured. In the summer of 1435 an international congress at Arras saw the end of the Anglo-Burgundian alliance that had been essential to English success.[53] Had Margaret Stewart given birth to a future king of France the historical significance of her marriage might have been much greater.

Despite the fact that James latterly committed himself to France it was not until the end of his reign that the possibility of an alternative policy of co-operation with England became remote. James himself took advantage of access to English markets and employed two English merchants as well as a Florentine and Genoese as his factors in London. Their purchases on his behalf came to over £3,500.[54] Between 1423 and 1441 over fifty English safe-conducts were issued to persons engaged in Anglo-Scottish trade.[55] While avoiding a rupture with England so long as it suited him to do so, James also avoided full payment of his financial obligation to the English. Although some 40,000 'nobles' had been raised by taxation to help to meet the king's 'fynance' much of what had been collected remained in the hands of the burgh authorities[56] as late as 1432.[57] The king drew upon these credits as he saw fit, in payments to himself, his officials, and his commercial agents in the Netherlands.[58] Thus the total 'fynance' that the English ever received was only 9,500 marks (or 19,000 'nobles') in English coin.[59] Though the English soon resented James's failure to pay his 'fynance' they were also aware that he could not easily be forced to pay by the threat of war, which would have cost much more than what might be obtained in the way of 'fynance'. It followed that they could make use only of moral pressure and of the hostages that had been delivered in 1424 as surety for payment. But to James the hostages meant little; it probably suited him to see a

[52] *Ibid.*, pp. 225–7; Dunlop, *Bishop Kennedy*, pp. 17, 373; *E.R.*, IV. cviii; Louis A. Barbé, *Margaret of Scotland and the Dauphin Louis* (1917); R. S. Rait, *Five Stuart Princesses* (1902), pp. 1–46.
[53] E. F. Jacob, *The Fifteenth Century*, pp. 260–3.
[54] *E.R.*, IV. cxlvii–cxlviii.
[55] Grant, *Social and Economic Development*, p. 336, n. 1.
[56] P. 283 above.   [57] *E.R.*, IV. 673.   [58] *Ibid.*, cxxxii, 672–85.
[59] Balfour-Melville, *James I*, pp. 110, 146; *E.R.*, IV. cxxxii–cxxxiv.

number of potential opponents kept in England. The very arrangements that had been made in 1424 for the possible replacement of hostages probably also played into the king's hands. It was he who might arrange (or not arrange) the release of one hostage in return for the sending of a new hostage to take his place.[60] There were to be three exchanges of hostages, one in August 1425, another in October 1427, and the last in July 1432. But these exchanges were not wholesale : some of the original hostages of 1424 were left unexchanged, to die in England or to languish there for decades.[61]

In the last resort James had nothing to fear from England so long as he did not give military or political provocation, and even in these respects he might go far before his bluff was called. Thanks to James's conduct the personal reputation of Bishop Beaufort (now a cardinal) was at stake : he was held responsible for the marriage of his niece to James and the subsequent release of the Scottish king. The cardinal hoped to gain a favourable settlement in a personal interview with his nephew at Coldingham in the spring of 1429.[62] Although James avoided giving any guarantees to the cardinal the existing truce was renewed on 15 December 1430 for a further five years. This was a diplomatic triumph for James. He had evaded any commitment about the hostages or the 'fynance'. He had obtained not the general truce by land and sea that the English wanted but a general truce by sea and a limited one by land, comprising 'all the realm of Henry' north of St Michael's Mount in Cornwall and 'all the realm of James' south of the river Findhorn.[63] The 'realm of Henry' in France was still fair game for Scottish mercenaries, and James had preserved not only his alliance with France but the marriage contract that might strengthen it.

On this point the English remained touchy, and so long as his daughter remained in Scotland James was in a strong bargaining position : to forestall the French match the English were ready by the autumn of 1433 to surrender Roxburgh and Jedburgh.[64] This offer was debated in a general council at Perth in October 1433.[65] Each of the prelates welcomed the chance of a final peace on such favourable

[60] *Morton Registrum*, I. xlii.

[61] See the remarks of the Pluscarden writer (*Chron. Pluscarden*, I. 370). Full details of the hostages and the three exchanges are given in Balfour-Melville, *James I*, appendix D, pp. 293–5.

[62] Balfour-Melville, *James I*, pp. 166–9.

[63] *Cal. Docs. Scot.*, IV. No. 1043.

[64] Balfour-Melville, *James I*, p. 209.

[65] *Chron. Bower*, II. 498–9; *Chron. Pluscarden*, I. 378–9.

terms until it came to the turn of Abbot Bower of Inchcolm and the
Abbot of Scone, who dissented : the king could not make peace with
the English on account of the Franco-Scottish treaty which had been
examined by the university of Paris and confirmed by the pope. John
Fogo, master of theology and Abbot of Melrose, countered their views,
and since Fogo was the king's confessor it may be assumed that he
was acting as the king's mouthpiece. In the course of his specious
arguments, which did no credit to himself or James, Fogo questioned
the validity of the Franco-Scottish alliance, only to be menaced by
the ever watchful inquisitor, Master Laurence of Lindores, who suspected error in the theological propositions on which Fogo had based
his case. The English proposals were rejected, and subsequent negotiations for a marriage between one of James's daughters and Henry
VI were inconclusive. By May 1434 the English were making defensive preparations.[66] French envoys who arrived in Scotland in January
1435 declined James's unfulfilled offer to send six thousand troops to
France but informed him that Charles VII would be grateful for help
in the way of warfare on the Borders.[67] It was at this very time that
James chose to deprive George Dunbar of his ancestral earldom of
March.[68] The earl, who had adhered to the English along with his
father in 1400,[69] may have been thought unreliable ; certainly the forfeiture of his earldom on 11 January 1435 was calculated to make him
less reliable. In the summer of 1435 James complained that the earl's
brother, Patrick of Dunbar, 'the kingis rebell', was being maintained
by the keeper of Berwick Castle; the pair 'with grete hoste and fere
of wer' made a foray in contravention of the truce, only to be routed
at Piperden on 10 September 1435.[70] When James's daughter arrived
in France the Anglo-Scottish truce expired.

By the beginning of August 1436 the English council had heard
that James was already besieging Roxburgh.[71] After a fruitless fortnight before its walls the Scottish host broke up and withdrew 'with
the greatest shame'.[72] All the costly siege artillery that the king had
fashioned at home or imported from Flanders [73] was abandoned to the
English.[74] Since the latter had no desire to keep up a war with Scotland some sort of truce seems to have been arrived at.[75] James showed

[66] Balfour-Melville, *James I*, pp. 208–13.
[67] *Ibid.*, p. 220.   [68] P. 319 below.   [69] Pp. 218–9, 230–1 above.
[70] Balfour-Melville, *James I*, p. 221.   [71] *Rot. Scot.*, II. 294.
[72] *Chron. Pluscarden*, I. 380.   [73] *E.R.*, IV. cxlviii–cxlix, 677.
[74] *Chron. Pluscarden*, I. 376, 380; *Chron. Bower*, II. 502.
[75] Balfour-Melville, *James I*, pp. 230–1.

his frustration in a general council that met at Edinburgh on 22 October 1436 by passing a number of anti-English statutes.[76]

While much of James I's diplomacy was concerned with the triangular relationship that involved Scotland, France and England, there was another relationship—between Scotland and the papacy—that posed new diplomatic problems. If James felt the need to reassert royal authority after the lackadaisical government of the Albany Stewarts, Pope Martin V felt the need to re-assert papal authority after the disastrous divisions of the Great Schism of 1378–1418, and the spread of conciliarist ideas. Although the council of Constance had shown its adherence to doctrinal orthodoxy by making a martyr of John Hus, a Bohemian deviationist, it had also in 1415 issued the decree *Sacrosancta*, proclaiming that 'this synod legally assembled in the Holy Spirit, constituting a General Council and representing the Catholic Church, holds its power directly from Christ; every person, whatsoever his degree or his dignity, even though this latter be pontifical, is bound to obey it in everything relating to the faith and the above mentioned schism'.[77] The council had also voiced dislike of papal provisions and reservations and might have insisted on their abolition had it not been overtaken by weariness: at the critical moment 'everything that could be postponed was postponed', and Martin V, even before his coronation, 'had already been at work undoing as much as he could of the council's work for reform'.[78] His continuation and invigoration of the system of provisions was to be resented by James I, not only because of conflicts of interest between crown and papacy over the political and administrative issues involved in ecclesiastical patronage, but also because of economic issues that seemed no less important: mercantilist theories were growing in influence; in inculcating a sort of economic nationalism they corresponded to the subtle changes that were transforming feudal monarchy into national monarchy; in the long run both political and economic nationalism were to weaken the papacy, the last great bastion of medieval cosmopolitanism. James I, who fully shared the mercantilist outlook, looked askance at any outflow of bullion from his kingdom, particularly one that brought in return not an import of goods but merely a re-allocation of Scottish benefices, sometimes to the disadvantage of

[76] *A.P.S.*, II. 23–4.
[77] John Holland Smith, *The Great Schism*, pp. 196–7.
[78] *Ibid.*, pp. 216–7.

the crown. Thus James wished to control the practice whereby any cleric might go to the papal court, or send a procurator there, to 'impetrate' (petition) the grant of a benefice or of a pension from a benefice.

Like so much else in the reign the king's new policy towards the papacy was sign-posted in the 'articles' or 'items' of his first parliament in May 1424. Thus one item forbade kirkmen to go overseas or send procurators overseas without leave of the king. Another put a tax of 3s. 4d. on each pound's worth of gold or silver exported from the realm. Another forbade kirkmen 'to purchess ony pensione out of ony benefice'. This ruling was forthwith applied by the parliamentary commission of 1424 to settle 'the complaynt that Maister Nicholl of Cummock maide apone Maister Ingrem Lindissay that he purchest in the court of Rome ane pensione out of the denry [deanery] of Abirdene in dismembring of his benefice'.[79] In another dispute parliament even decided who was rightful Prior of Coldingham.[80] Though James proceeded pragmatically, and enunciated no theory or principle, he had insidiously carried much further the extension of secular control over the kirk that had begun to manifest itself in Scotland during the Great Schism. The culmination of James's programme came in the parliament of March 1428 when an act was passed which ordained that any cleric who wished to leave the realm should first approach his bishop, or the chancellor, and 'schaw to thame gude and honest cause of his passage and mak faith to thame that he do no baratry'.[81] The new offence of barratry was not defined but undoubtedly signified the purchase of benefices, or pensions from benefices, at the *curia*. Regardless of this act the barrators appear to have remained as active as ever.[82]

The development of James's attack upon papal patronage had coincided with the rise of the man who was to implement it—John Cameron, a cleric who in 1424 became the king's secretary and, shortly afterwards, keeper of the privy seal.[83] When the see of Glasgow fell vacant in 1425 the chapter bowed to the royal wishes by electing Cameron. Since the see had been 'reserved', Martin V quashed the election; as a result of royal pressure he relented and on 22 April 1426 provided Cameron to the bishopric.[84] By May 1427

[79] *A.P.S.*, II. 5, cc. 14, 15, 16; 6, c. 26.

[80] *Nat. MSS. Scot.*, II. No. lxv. [81] *A.P.S.*, II. 16, c. 9.

[82] This may be inferred from *Cal. Scot. Supp. 1428–32, passim.*

[83] Balfour-Melville, *James I*, pp. 138–9; R. K. Hannay, 'James I, Bishop Cameron and the Papacy', *S.H.R.*, xv. 190–200.

[84] Balfour-Melville, *James I*, pp. 139–40; Burns, *Basle*, pp. 16–7.

Cameron, who had previously had custody of the great seal, was formally styled chancellor.[85]

In the case of the bishopric of Glasgow the pope had given way to the king in practice, but in theory had kept rights of papal patronage intact. The tacit understanding behind this concession and others was that the king would be allowed to share papal patronage and its profits on condition that he respected the system and did not interfere with it. The understanding was jeopardised when William Croyser, archdeacon of Teviotdale, became involved in a jurisdictional dispute with Bishop Cameron.[86] By the spring of 1429 Croyser had drawn Martin V's attention to developments in Scotland, representing that it was Cameron as chancellor, rather than the king, who was the moving spirit behind the barratry legislation.[87] Croyser's tales found sympathetic ears. Two cardinals concluded that Cameron was responsible for the acts of the Scottish parliament 'against ecclesiastical liberty and the rights of the Roman church'; he was 'so guilty as to deserve deprivation'. It was none other than Croyser who was given the pleasing task of citing Cameron to the Roman court in the summer of 1429.[88]

The king did not stand idly by to see his chancellor disgraced: in the summer of 1430 an embassy reached Rome to defend Cameron and to retaliate upon Croyser by citing him to appear before the Scottish parliament. A sort of truce followed: up to the time when Martin V died in February 1431 a violent clash between king and pope had been averted.[89] Nonetheless, the papacy was under no illusion that a permanent settlement had been reached. Croyser, the self-appointed watchdog of papal interests in Scotland, was to be well rewarded to encourage his unremitting zeal: one of the last acts of Martin V was to provide him effectively—he had already been twice provided ineffectively—to the archdeaconry of Lothian, which he was to be allowed to hold in addition to his archdeaconry of Teviotdale and his other benefices. The new pope, Eugenius IV, made it even clearer that Croyser was an agent of the papacy.[90]

It was at this stage, however, that a new and uncertain factor complicated the situation. In the decree *Frequens* the council of Constance had laid down that general councils of the church should be held periodically. Shortly before his death Martin V had been in-

[85] *E.R.*, IV. 400, 428; *R.M.S.*, II. No. 89 (witness No. 74).
[86] *Glasgow Registrum*, II. 140 and No. 332.
[87] Balfour-Melville, *James I*, p. 174.   [88] *Ibid.*, p. 177.
[89] *Ibid.*, pp. 178–9; Burns, *Basle*, p. 23.   [90] Burns, *Basle*, pp. 11–2, 23.

duced to summon another council to meet at Basel (or Basle), where
the first full formal session was held on 14 November 1431. A month
later, however, Eugenius issued bulls dissolving the council and summoning a new one to meet in Bologna, where it would be more amenable to papal control.[91] The council of Basel refused to be dissolved
and re-opened old disputes by giving fresh publicity to the decree
Sacrosancta of 1415.[92]

One of the rulers of western Christendom to whom the council
appealed for support during its initial conflict with the pope was
the Scottish king. Although he did not send official representatives
Scotland was at least unofficially represented at Basel, notably by
Thomas Livingston, Abbot of Dundrennan, who soon became a
foremost member of the council [93] and was to adhere to it to the end.
Meanwhile the pope changed his mind and on 18 December 1433
revoked his dissolution of the council : 'the prolonged initial conflict
was over, and a period of comparative harmony began'.[94] It was 'to
a council for the time being at peace with the pope that James I
gave his support'.[95] At last, without incurring the reproaches of
Eugenius, James could send representatives to Basel to enlist the
council's aid in settling his dispute with the pope. But on the very day
(8 February 1434) that Bishop Cameron was incorporated in the
council so was his old foe, Archdeacon Croyser, who with no small
exaggeration denounced the Scottish king and called for justice
against him and his officials.[96] Croyser's conduct at Basel led to his
denunciation as a traitor and rebel before the Scottish parliament
(presumably the parliament that met at Perth on 10 January 1435).
Judgment was given against him in his absence and he was deprived
of his benefices and revenues; thenceforth the pope insisted on the
restoration of Croyser as well as a modification of James's policies.[97]

During this crisis, in the spring of 1435, Cameron left Basel for
the papal court to persuade the pope that the dispute might best be
resolved by sending to Scotland a legate who could reach a direct
settlement with the king.[98] Eugenius, however, remained suspicious
and for the time being refused to send a legate. By June 1435
Cameron had returned to Basel to engage in further controversy with
Croyser. Simultaneously the council promulgated decrees that attacked the whole basis of papal finance and ended 'the brief period

[91] *Ibid.*, pp. 10–1.
[92] *Chron. Bower*, II. 479.   [93] Burns, *Basle*, pp. 11–14.
[94] *Ibid.*, pp. 11–2, 13, 14–6.   [95] *Ibid.*, p. 16.
[96] *Ibid.*, pp. 25, 27.   [97] *Ibid.*, pp. 37–8.
[98] *Ibid.*, pp. 38–9; Balfour-Melville, *James I*, p. 237.

during which relations between pope and council were correct if not cordial'. Thus 'to join the council or have dealings with it after this period meant some degree of association with the anti-papal party'.[99] Yet Cameron remained at Basel and was soon joined by other Scots clerics, including two royal secretaries.[100] Meanwhile the pope wrote to seek the intervention of Nicholas Albergati, Cardinal of Santa Croce, who was presiding at the congress of Arras. As a result the cardinal sent to Scotland his secretary, Aeneas Sylvius, to restore 'a certain prelate to the king's favour'—undoubtedly Croyser.[101] Aeneas, the future Pope Pius II, compiled an unflattering account of the uncouth land where people heated themselves by burning a black stone instead of wood, where houses in the countryside were roofed with turf and those in the unwalled towns constructed without lime, where the common people were poor and destitute of all refinement, and the women fair, but not distinguished for their chastity. He concluded, shrewdly enough, that 'nothing pleases the Scots more than abuse of the English'.[102] Having acquired chronic rheumatism in Scotland he went back with no good news for the pope and the archdeacon. On 8 March 1436 Eugenius issued a bull that annulled the deprivation of Croyser and stigmatised unhelpful Scottish bishops as 'Pilates rather than prelates'.[103] Shortly afterwards he wrote directly to James demanding the restoration of Croyser and the repeal of the barratry legislation, 'which the pope, so far as is needful, himself annuls'.[104] The king can hardly have been left in doubt that he was running the risk of excommunication and interdict.

In one respect the pope's twofold demand was to be circumvented : through the mediation of the council of Basel, Croyser removed himself from the battlefield of royal and papal acrimony ; he even proved helpful to James by urging the pope to send the legatine mission that the king desired. On 2 July 1436 Antonio Altani, Bishop of Urbino, was appointed as legate. While it was no doubt envisaged that he would negotiate a concordat, it was not for this purpose alone that his presence was needed: 'the policy of securing a papal legate for Scotland had never, in James's eyes, been one of capitulation to papal demands'.[105] The terms of the legate's appointment show that it was

[99] Burns, *Basle*, pp. 39–40.   [100] *Ibid.*, pp. 43–50.

[101] Balfour-Melville, *James I*, pp. 234–5.

[102] Brown, *Early Travellers*, pp. 25–38.

[103] Balfour-Melville, *James I*, p. 237; Burns, *Basle*, p. 50.

[104] Balfour-Melville, *James I*, pp. 237–8.

[105] Burns, *Basle*, pp. 51, 52 and n., 56; see also R. K. Hannay, *op. cit.*, *S.H.R.*, xv. 190–200, at 198–9.

the reformation of the kirk that James sought; equipped with generous powers of dispensation and discipline Altani was 'to visit and
reform all churches, monasteries, etc.' and to give heed to 'the
ecclesiastical state of the realm'.[106]

To James the Scottish kirk was 'a department of national life
which he was called to reduce to order',[107] and all members of the
clergy, even those in Galloway who were still nominally dependent
on the Archbishop of York, were to enjoy 'one law and privilege and
general liberty'.[108] Despite his altercations with the papacy the king
could boast of 'the gret favouris, graciose zele and mantenaunce' that
he displayed towards the kirk and its ministers.[109] His insistence
that the ritual of public worship should incorporate prayers for the
royal family [110] sprang not only from genuine piety, but from a desire
to cast a spiritual aura around the monarchy and to publicise its
unity with the kirk, which was itself to be reformed according to
high and uniform standards. For these purposes the co-operation of
the bishops had to be forthcoming. Apart from their role in public
life, James's bishops seem to have shown in the administration of
their dioceses qualities that were diverse, but respectable.[111] Even
Cameron, despite his involvement in affairs of state, was an active
administrator of his diocese and a zealous benefactor of his cathedral.[112] But if the episcopate was, by contemporary standards, competent and well-educated, there were defects in other quarters.

It was the monasteries that chiefly aroused the king's concern.
On 17 March 1425, while the three estates were in session at Perth,
James used this public occasion to draft a letter to the abbots and
priors of the Benedictine and Augustinian orders in Scotland,[113]
warning them that 'the downhill condition and most threatening ruin
of holy religion, now declining from day to day from the original
establishment of its foundation, fill us with apprehension'. They were
to take heed 'how in our realm the decline of monastic religion, everywhere defamed and reduced to contempt, tends to destruction'. If
the abbots and priors remained negligent and idle, 'the munificence

---

[106] *Cal. Papal Letters*, VIII. 229, 288–90; Balfour-Melville, *James I*, pp. 239–
40; Burns, *Basle*, p. 52.

[107] A. R. MacEwen, *History of the Church in Scotland*, I. 336.

[108] *R.M.S.*, II. No. 164.　　　[109] *A.P.S.*, II. 10.　　　[110] *Ibid.*, 8, 10.

[111] Balfour-Melville, *James I*, pp. 274–7.

[112] *Glasgow Registrum*, pp. 323–61, *passim*; Innes, *Scot. Middle Ages*, p. 270
and appendix pp. 336–40.

[113] *A.P.S.*, II. 25. The letter is also cited, apparently with approval, by Abbot
Bower (*Chron. Bower*, II. 508–9) who as an Augustinian abbot was one of the
persons to whom it was addressed.

of kings, who formerly . . . notably endowed your monasteries . . . may repent of having erected walls of marble when it considers that you have so shamelessly abandoned your religious character'.

Yet despite James's misgivings, he led no attack on monastic endowment, rather the reverse.[114] His old-fashioned generosity towards the monasteries sprang from the conviction that all was not yet lost : the vast investment in these institutions might be redeemed if only the abbots and priors would undertake 'an ascent to the highest reaches of perfection'.[115] James was ready to point the way, even at the cost of further investment : although no sizable monastery had been founded since 1273 the king immediately followed his denunciation of the Benedictines and Augustinians with plans for the establishment of a Carthusian monastery at Perth, to be partly financed by the annexation of the parish kirk of Erroll.[116] This Charterhouse of Perth (which obtained its name not from any connection with charters but from its association with the Grande Chartreuse) seems to have preserved the unsullied reputation for which its strict order was noted, though it scarcely served James's purpose of shaming the other Scottish monastic houses into an amendment of their way of life. The Charterhouse was the last monastery to be founded in medieval Scotland and was the first to be destroyed in the reformation-rebellion of 1559.

Significantly enough, John Knox, whose sermon at Perth in May 1559 led to the attack on the Charterhouse, began his *History of the Reformation in Scotland* with an account of his forerunners who had suffered for their beliefs during the reign of James I.[117] From Abbot Bower's extraordinary list of the virtues of the mass it may be inferred that anti-sacramental heresy required confutation.[118] Its sources were England, where Lollardy still lingered, and Bohemia, which was a centre not only of Hussitism but of millenarian sects, such as the Taborites, whose excesses shocked Abbot Bower. Moreover Bower affirmed that in Scotland the views of Resby (the English Lollard burnt at Perth in 1406 or 1407) were still rife.[119] Here was a situation in which King James could display his zeal as patron and protector of the kirk by following the example of the Lollard-burning

---

[114] Balfour-Melville, *James I*, pp. 178, 270, 272.

[115] *A.P.S.*, II. 25.

[116] Balfour-Melville, *James I*, pp. 272-3; *Cal. Scot. Supp. 1428-32*, pp. 108, 113. [117] Knox, *History*, I. 1-7.

[118] J. A. F. Thomson, *The Later Lollards*, p. 204.

[119] *Chron. Bower*, II. 498; W. Stanford Reid, *op. cit.*, *Church History*, XI. 3-17, at 9-12.

Henry V. In 1425 the Scottish parliament was to pass an act against heresy that was reminiscent of the English statute of 1401 : each bishop was to hold an inquest to apprehend 'heretikis and Lollardis' and punish them as the law of holy kirk required ; the civil authorities would lend their support.[120]

Already in 1422 some heretic, possibly Quintin Folkhyrde, had been burnt in the diocese of Glasgow,[121] presumably as a result of a trial held under the bishop's authority. But it was the university of St Andrews under the leadership of Laurence of Lindores,[122] rather than the episcopate, that was most active in detecting and combating heresy. Master Laurence, who 'nowhere within the realm gave rest to heretics or Lollards',[123] had brought Resby to the stake and was to have a further resounding success in dealing with a certain Paul Crawar, a man who had studied in the universities of Paris, Montpellier and Prague and had served as physician to the king of Poland.[124] According to Abbot Bower, Crawar was a German who had been sent by the heretics of Prague with papers which testified to his medical skill, though his mission was to imbue the Scots with the Bohemian heresies. Brought to trial at St Andrews on 23 July 1433 Crawar was confuted by Master Laurence and burnt at the stake.[125]

But while James could commend the part that the university played under Lindores's guidance in suppressing heresy, there were some influences at St Andrews that were less to the king's liking. Bishop Wardlaw, chancellor of the university, and Prior Haldenstone, head of the Augustinian priory in the city and dean of the faculty of theology, had not supported the king in his stand against the papacy. James seems to have retaliated by taking sides in university politics. For 'a state of tension or at least of uneasy equipoise' prevailed between Wardlaw and Lindores, and the latter, though a theologian, had 'obviously at an early date transferred his energies and organising ability to the faculty of arts'.[126] The king's intervention tended to increase the influence of Lindores and the faculty of arts at the expense of Bishop Wardlaw and his theologian associates. At

---

[120] A.P.S., II. 7, c. 3.

[121] Knox, History, I. 1 ; T. M. A. Macnab, op. cit., Scot. Church Hist. Soc. Recs., v. 10–22, at 16.

[122] The various aspects of his career are studied by Duncan Shaw, op. cit., ibid., XII. 47–62.   [123] Chron. Bower, II. 495.

[124] T. M. A. Macnab, op. cit., Scot. Church Hist. Soc. Recs., v. 10–22, at 16–22.   [125] Chron. Bower, II. 495 ; St Andrews Acta, I. xx.

[126] St Andrews Acta, I. xvii.

first, indeed, James had more far-reaching designs and petitioned the pope that the university be transferred from St Andrews to Perth. The specious grounds of the royal petition probably concealed James's real motive, which was to remove the university from Bishop Wardlaw's influence. On the failure of this scheme the king showed his dissatisfaction by further intervention in university politics [127] and withheld a royal charter until such time as he saw the university remodelled more to his liking. James's influence may have been behind a project to set up a single 'pedagogy' for the faculty of arts: no new private pedagogies were to be established in future since they had led to a breakdown in studies and discipline. The new pedagogy seems to have been completed by 1435 and was to be put under the control of Lindores.[128] In March 1432 the king had at last conferred his favour on the university and a royal charter was issued confirming its foundation.[129] Nonetheless James still meddled in university affairs. On 13 November 1432 the faculty of arts reluctantly accepted his proposals in an *appunctuamentum* which tended to strengthen the disciplinary powers of its dean (Lindores).[130] Fortified by the *appunctuamentum* the latter kept a tight grip over the faculty.[31] The death of this spiritual and academic drill master in the summer of 1437, some months after that of his royal patron, brought a new tolerance to the university but also saw the onset of rivalries, disputes over discipline, and quarrels between the scholars and the citizens.[132]

Even before Lindores's death it is likely that there was a party in the university united in resentment of his dominance, of the king's interference in academic politics, and of the king's dealings with the papacy and the council of Basel. The dissidents no doubt saw in the visit of the pope's legate a long-awaited opportunity to voice their discontent. Shortly before Christmas 1436 the Bishop of Urbino arrived in Scotland and accompanied the court to Perth to be received in a general council that began its proceedings on 4 February 1437.[133] Up to this time thirty-seven Scottish clerics had been incorporated in the council of Basel, which was beginning to set out on the course that would shortly lead to a rupture with Eugenius. Of all the dioceses of Scotland the foremost, St Andrews, shared with poor and remote Argyll the distinction of having sent no direct representatives

[127] Balfour-Melville, *James I*, pp. 129, 181.
[128] *St Andrews Acta*, I. xix; 26–7, 28–9.
[129] *R.M.S.*, II. Nos. 199, 200.   [130] *St Andrews Acta*, I. 34–5.
[131] *Ibid.*, xx.   [132] Dunlop, *Bishop Kennedy*, pp. 269–72.
[133] *Chron. Bower*, II. 502; *Chron. Pluscarden*, I. 390.

to Basel.[134] At St Andrews, if anywhere in Scotland, Eugenius could count on support. On 21 January 1437 arrangements were being made to send a university delegation to Perth, ostensibly 'for the preservation of our privileges',[135] but it can hardly have been forgotten that it was a university delegation that had swayed opinion in a general council which met in comparable circumstances in 1418. What might have happened in a final confrontation of royal and papal authority can only be guessed: while public attention was centred on the expected settlement of ecclesiastical affairs, some of James's political enemies were planning an event that, within a few days, would throw Scotland into turmoil and make the decade-long blusterings between king and pope seem a mere storm in a tea-cup.

From James I's dealings with the papacy, as also from his activities in international politics, nothing decisive emerged. In domestic politics it was a different matter. The intensive government characteristic of David II's last years was brought back in even more intensive form. One of its characteristics was increased use of the three estates. During the Albany governorship they seem to have been convened only infrequently; between 1424 and 1436, on the other hand, there were to be at least ten parliaments and three general councils.[136]

To suit James's purposes it was necessary that these assemblies should authoritatively represent the political community, hence his concern over the attendance of the prelates and lay landholders. An act of March 1426 said nothing about the position of the burgesses, but affirmed that all prelates, earls, barons, and freeholders who were tenants-in-chief, were bound to attend the king's parliament and general council; thenceforth they were to attend in person; procurators could be employed only for 'lauchfull cause'[137]—an allusion to the recognised essoins, such as sickness, that would serve as excuse for non-appearance in a court. In the Perth parliament of July 1427 some of the tenants-in-chief who were legitimately absent were excused; the others who 'contumaciously absented themselves' were to pay an amercement of £10 each.[138] If this was an attempt to enforce the act of 1426 by pecuniary penalty it merely showed the unworkability of that act: it was feasible to expect all prelates and earls to attend; it was impossible to expect all barons and freeholders to do so. A compromise was reached in an act of March 1428: the king

---

[134] Burns, *Basle*, p. 55.
[136] Balfour-Melville, *James I*, p. 252.
[138] *Ibid.*, 13.

[135] *St Andrews Acta*, I. 44.
[137] *A.P.S.*, II. 9, c. 8.

was to issue special precepts summoning individually all the bishops, abbots, priors, dukes, earls, lords of parliament and banrents (bannerets) whom he wished to attend.[139] No longer was personal attendance to be required from 'the smal baronnis and fre tenandis'. Instead, like the burgesses, they were to be represented in parliaments and general councils by elected members : in the head court of each sheriffdom (the Michaelmas meeting of the sheriff court) 'wise men' were to be chosen as 'commissaris [commissioners] of the schire'. Moreover these commissioners were to elect 'a wise and ane expert mann callit the common spekar of the parliament', who was to act as spokesman for 'the commonis'.[140]

In these provisions there was much that was suggestive of English practice. But much was left in ambiguity : if a parliamentary peerage had been created by the act of 1428 the act said nothing about an upper house ; nor was any definition given of 'the commonis'. In any case there is no sign that any shire commissioners were ever elected under the terms of the act of 1428 and there was never to be a speaker in the three estates.[141] It is probable that barons resented being faced with the question as to whether or not they were 'small' ; and the idea of paying the expenses of commissioners can hardly have been welcome. Not until the late sixteenth century was James's scheme for shire representation successfully revived. But the immediate failure of the scheme in James's own lifetime did not mean (as one authority seems to imply)[142] the virtual disappearance from parliaments and general councils of the small barons and free tenants : during the next three reigns their attendance was significant enough to require some statutory definition.[143]

While the act of July 1428 had no ascertainable effect so far as it concerned the small barons and freeholders, it was otherwise with the prelates and greater nobles who were to be individually summoned by special precept. This provision of the act of 1428 certainly took effect. There is no indication that James intended his 'lords of parliament' to transmit to their heirs or successors a right to sit in parliaments and general councils, but gradually the amorphous Scottish nobility came to be categorised and divided.[144] Those nobles who were not 'lords'—the 'small barons' alluded to in the act of 1428— would come to be described as 'lairds'. Even so, the division between

[139] *Ibid.*, 15, c. 2. [140] *Ibid.*
[141] Rait, *Parliaments*, p. 195. [142] Balfour-Melville, *James I*, pp. 156–7.
[143] Rait, *Parliaments*, pp. 196–7.
[144] This subject is investigated by R. S. Rait (*ibid.*, pp. 178–83); see also *Highland Papers*, II. 154.

lords and lairds was not so sharp as the division of peerage and gentry in England; the small barons or lairds continued to be associated with the greater barons or lords and to sit together with them as one of the three estates. The ultimate effect of the act of 1428 was merely to increase the numbers of the greater nobles and to augment their dignity within the otherwise unchanged three estates.

The most detailed record of attendance at parliament during the reign, one compiled on 10 March 1430,[145] gives an impression of the miscellaneous turn-out even after James had made attempts at definition; in 1430 parliament comprised the chancellor (Bishop Cameron), six other bishops, six earls, the constable and the marshal, and eight 'lords' besides 'many other [unnamed] prelates, barons, nobles and commissioners of burghs'. All these personages were seated in order of precedence: on 10 March 1430, when a vote was taken, the chancellor (who evidently presided) put the question to those present 'one by one, and one after the other, as they sat in order in their seats'.[146] Their votes happened on this occasion to be unanimous, but the voting procedure certainly allowed for dissent, and James was not always able to obtain what he wanted. This was particularly the case in matters of finance: the grants of taxation made on the king's return to Scotland in 1424 were not renewed—in marked contrast to the generous grants that David II continually obtained in comparable circumstances. In 1431, when James did obtain from the three estates a contribution towards the suppression of a Highland rising, the estates not only appropriated the contribution to that particular purpose but showed their distrust of the king's conduct in financial matters by imposing stringent conditions.[147] Since the records of parliaments and general councils unfortunately continue to be records of decisions, not of debates, it is almost impossible to discover what was the process of decision-making that could occasionally result in reverses for the king. Only in regard to the English proposals of 1433 is the veil briefly lifted by the chronicler Bower, whose account of the argument between members of the clerical estate [148] is reminiscent of the account of the arguments held in the three estates in 1364, or of those held in 1418 before the renunciation of obedience to Benedict XIII. It must be concluded that, at least on great issues, there could be lively debate within the three estates before a consensus of opinion was reached, and that the consensus was not always the one desired by the king.

Nonetheless, so far as legislation was concerned, it was James who

---

[145] *A.P.S.*, II. 28, c. 6.　　　　　[146] *Ibid.*
[147] *Ibid.*, 20, c. 1.　　　　　[148] Pp. 291–2 above.

kept the initiative : the contemporary chronicler Bower styled James 'our lawmaking king' and remarked that in the parliament of 1426, (as in that of 1424) he 'proposed many things advantageous to the state'.[149] It may be assumed that it was James's own 'articles' that resulted in an output of legislation that was unprecedented in Scotland.

For none of James's predecessors or successors was so committed as he was, persistently, determinedly and emotionally, to pursuing the common weal. It was an elusive butterfly that James tried to catch in a network of ordinances. The laissez-faire of the Albany Stewarts was replaced by a sort of medieval totalitarianism that sought to regulate or re-shape many aspects of Scottish life. Nothing was too momentous or too inconsequential to escape legislation. This was demonstrated in the articles which James presented to the parliament of 1424 that initiated the new order. Incongruously intermingled with those that were to bring revolutionary political changes were others that ordered the destruction of rooks' nests and of all fish weirs in tidal waters, and prescribed a mesh of at least three inches for nets used in fresh water.[150]

One characteristic of James's miscellaneous social and economic legislation was its somewhat puritanical stress upon utility : detailed statutes of 1430 declared that no burgesses, except aldermen, bailies and councillors, might wear furs; ordinary yeomen were not to wear coloured clothes longer than knee-length ; all articles of clothing and adornment that contravened this sartorial code were to be forfeited to the king.[151] The object of such sumptuary laws (already shown to be unavailing in England) was to restrain extravagance and reduce imports at a time when the costume of fashion-conscious men and women was exuberantly rich and fantastic. In other respects also James sought to prevent his subjects from straying profitlessly along primrose paths : one statute threatened with imprisonment anyone found drinking ale in taverns beyond the hour of nine; another ordained that idle men should be forced on pain of imprisonment to find employment.[152] James not only revived wappinschaws[153] but tried to purge sport and divert it into preparation for war. Thus it was enacted that 'the king forbiddis that na man play at the fut ball' ; footballers were to be fined fourpence for persisting in their unpro-

[149] Chron. Bower, II. 482. [150] A.P.S., II. 6, cc. 12, 20.
[151] Ibid., 18, cc. 8, 9, 10; see also Scot. Legal Hist., p. 288.
[152] A.P.S., II. 11, c. 20; 24, c. 8.
[153] Ibid., 8, c. 23; 10–1, c. 17; 18, cc. 11–14.

ductive pastime. By contrast, butts were to set up near parish kirks
so that on holy days men might 'haif usage of archary'.[154] Thus James,
so far as legislation availed, sought to make the most of Scotland's
human and material resources and to replace wasteful practices with
others that were of utility to the common weal.

This policy was particularly evident in the attention paid to all
matters that directly or indirectly affected the well-being of the
country's economy. Measures were enacted for the standardisation
of weights and measures, for the observance of a close season in the
netting of wildfowl, for the extermination of wolves, for the suppression of deer-poaching, rabbit-poaching, and theft from orchards and
dove-cots; and since the Lowlands were being denuded of timber it
was made a crime to steal wood or peel the bark of growing trees.[155]
Paternalistic concern for the rural economy was coupled with concern for the welfare of even those at the lowest levels of rural society;
their lot was to be improved by better methods of husbandry, which,
it was optimistically assumed, could be inculcated by legislation.
Thus James's second parliament enacted that each 'man of sympil
estate that of resoune suld be a labourar' should either have a half
share in an ox and engage in communal tillage or else dig each day
an area at least seven feet square;[156] husbandmen who had a plough-
team of eight oxen were to sow minimum quantities of wheat, peas
and beans, besides the staple crops of bere, oats and rye; and barons
were to do likewise on their demesne lands on pain of a forty-shilling
fine.[157] One of the greatest hindrances to good husbandry—insecurity
of tenure [158]—was perhaps slightly mitigated by the king's intervention : in 1428 he won the consent of the prelates and barons to his
request that for a trial period of one year they would not evict their
husbandmen and cottars unless the lands that the latter rented were
required for the lord's own use.[159] In an attempt to remedy another
grievance of the countryfolk James tried to control the companies of
men, ranging from the retinues of nobles to bands of 'thiggers' or
sturdy beggars, who in their travels bullied husbandmen and clerics
into providing free food and lodging.[160] For law-abiding wayfarers
provision was made by another enactment which exhorted the establishment of inns within the burghs and along the main highways;[161]

[154] *Ibid.*, 5, c. 18; 6, c. 19.   [155] *Ibid.*, 7, 12, 15–6.
[156] *Ibid.*, 8.   ·   [157] *Ibid.*, 13.
[158] For the background see Grant, *Social and Economic Development*, p. 256.
[159] *A.P.S.*, II. 17; compare *ibid.*, I. 213.
[160] *Ibid.*, II. 3, 4, 8, 15.   [161] *Ibid.*, 6, 10.

and finally in 1427 the provision of inns was made a general responsibility of all the burgesses of the realm.[162]

The burgesses, with their complex society and institutions, received a fair share of James's attention. Concerned over the problems of public health and good order in their crowded communities he passed statutes restricting the entry of beggars and lepers. He also saw the need for precautions against the accidental fires that from time to time devastated the burghs—Stirling had been accidentally burnt in 1408, Linlithgow and Cupar in 1411, Aberdeen in 1423, and Linlithgow once again in 1424.[163] There was thus good reason for the detailed legislation of 1426 designed to reduce fire risks and initiate a fire-fighting service : the handling of combustible materials was to be strictly controlled; brothels, which were assumed to be particularly incendiary, were to be sited only in the outskirts of towns.[164]

Apart from such general measures there were many others that directly or indirectly affected the interests of the burgesses. The merchant burgesses in particular were subjected to the regulations by which the king tried to enforce an economic policy that was both mercantilist and nationalist. Few aspects of overseas trade were immune from regulation : it was typical that in 1425 the export of tallow and of horses less than three years old was prohibited.[165] Most important of all, however, were the statutes controlling the export of bullion.[166] These affected the interests not only of clerics but of merchants. In 1436 an act not only totally forbade all export of gold, silver and jewels but laid the merchants under an obligation that was probably unworkable—for each sack of wool and equivalent quantities of hides and salted fish that they exported they were to bring back three ounces of bullion to be coined at the royal mint. To ensure the enforcement of this statute the custumars were ordered to compile detailed lists of all export shipments 'for the serching and knowlege hereof'.[167]

But while the king could try through the three estates to regulate the economic activities of the merchants, so also could the merchants, through their gilds and their control of the burgh councils, try to regulate the economic activities of the other inhabitants of the burghs. Like the king, the merchants claimed to be promoting the common weal. Yet when they invoked the universally-accepted ideal of 'the

[162] *Ibid.*, 14.
[163] *Chron. Bower*, II. 441, 447, 463, 482; *Glasgow Registrum*, II. 316; *Chron. Pluscarden*, I. 349.   [164] *A.P.S.*, II. 12.
[165] *Ibid.*, 7.   [166] P. 294 above.   [167] *A.P.S.*, II. 23, 24.

just price' their motives were not always altruistic : in 1428 the gild
court of Ayr chose five persons to buy for the use of the gild all merchandise entering by sea.[168] It is likely that the merchants, through the
gild or the burgh council, sought to extend their price-fixing to the
goods produced by the craftsmen who were their fellow-burgesses.
The emergence of craft gilds may thus have been an attempt on the
part of the craftsmen to control not only their own standards of workmanship but their own prices and wages. The first sign of craft organisation (and of the reaction of the merchants against it) may be
seen towards the close of the fourteenth century, when the chamberlain was instructed to hold a secret inquest in the course of his ayre to
discover whether there was any 'confederacy' among any inhabitants
of the town whereby the 'neighbours' were injured.[169] In a court held
by the bailies of Aberdeen in 1398 an injunction was issued warning
the websters that 'they are not to conspire among themselves to the
prejudice of the community of Aberdeen'.[170] James was not the man
to ignore such issues, and characteristically he sought a solution in
legislation. In March 1425 it was ordained that in every town there
should be chosen a member of each craft to act as deacon of that
craft ; he was to be chosen jointly by his fellow-craftsmen and by the
town council, and was to supervise standards of workmanship to prevent fraud on the part of 'untrew men of craftis'.[171] This measure was
probably intended as a compromise ; but it said nothing on the controversial topic of regulation of prices and wage-rates, and the merchants were not content. In 1426 James yielded to their pressure : a
new statute enacted that the deacons of crafts were to remain in office
until the next parliament, but the goods of the craftsmen were to be
priced by the alderman and council in each burgh and the council
was to fix the wage-rates of such craftsmen as wrights and masons.[172]
In the following year parliament lost all sense of moderation by forbidding the election of deacons of crafts and dismissing those already
in office : they were not to hold their accustomed meetings 'which are
presumed to savour of conspiracies'.[173] The merchants had evidently
succeeded in convincing king and parliament that craft organisation
was a threat to the established social order. The passive resistance of
the craftsmen was countered by further legislation in 1428, which ordained that the council in each burgh should appoint a 'warden' for

---

[168] David Murray, *Early Burgh Organization in Scotland* (1924, 1932), II.
544–5.
[169] *Iter Camerarii*, *A.P.S.*, I. 695.　　[170] *Aberdeen Burgh Recs.*, p. 27.
[171] *A.P.S.*, II. 8.　　　　[172] *Ibid.*, 13.　　　　[173] *Ibid.*, 14.

each craft who was to examine and maintain standards of workmanship and fix prices under the threat of heavy fines; similar powers
were granted to each baron to fix prices and wage-rates within his
barony.[174] This repressive measure put the livelihood of the craftsmen
at the mercy of burgh councils controlled by the merchant oligarchy;
fortunately for the craftsmen, the act of 1428 was intended as an experiment and was to remain valid for only one year.[175]

If the social and economic legislation of James I was on an unprecedented scale, and presented some novel features, the king was
less open to the charge of innovation in dealing with legal and judicial matters for which the crown had a traditional responsibility that
had been discharged only fitfully since 1371. In James's legislative
programme there was an attempt to make up for past deficiencies:
statute after statute testified to his constant pre-occupation with law,
justice, and the preservation of order.

The sense of national identity evident in some of James's enactments came out strongly in an act of 1426 which ordained that all the
king's subjects were to be governed only by the king's laws and the
statutes of 'this realme': the laws of other countries and realms were
to be invalid in Scotland; and none of the king's subjects were to live
under 'particulare lawis na speciale prevalegis'.[176] This was an omni-
bus measure that stressed the jurisdictional independence of Scotland.
It may have been visualised by James as a counterpart of the English
statute of *praemunire* that could be used to check the encroachments
of papal jurisdiction. More obviously, however, the ordinance was
directed against distinctive local practices such as the 'laws of the
Galwegians' and the 'law of Clan MacDuff', both of which had been
specially safeguarded as recently as 1384.[177]

The announcement that only the king's laws and statutes of the
realm were to be observed was accompanied by an ambitious attempt
to revise the two legal codes chiefly used in Scotland: a parliamentary
committee of eighteen, composed of six wise men of each of the three
estates, was to 'examyn the bukis of law of this realme, that is to say
Regiam Majestatem and *Quoniam Attachiamenta*, and mend the
lawis that nedis mendment'.[178] There is no sign that much mending of
these older laws was achieved;[179] and already it was evident that it
was not enough merely to re-define the traditional law; new laws

[174] *Ibid.*, 15. [175] *Ibid.* [176] *Ibid.*, 9.
[177] P. 190 above. [178] *A.P.S.*, ii. 10.
[179] For attempts to codify Scots law in 1426, 1469 and 1487 see *Scot. Legal
Hist.*, p. 31.

were required, and James's large legislative output brought the beginnings of a real statutory law.[180] Symptomatic of its growing importance was an enactment that new laws were to be registered and
publicly proclaimed by sheriffs and bailies so that no one could plead
ignorance of them.[181] Often the new laws clarified the technicalities
of judicial procedure.[182] A whole series of such statutes was enacted
in the Perth parliament of 6 March 1430.[183]

Many other enactments demonstrated the king's desire to secure
for his subjects justice that was speedy, efficient and impartial. In an
important measure of 1425 that was to become a permanent feature
of Scottish justice he ordained that judges should assign a 'lele and a
wys advocate' to plead for 'ony pur creatur' who could not pursue his
case through lack of wealth or knowledge.[184] In practice this measure
meant the appointment of free legal counsel for the poor—a provision
that was some five hundred years in advance of English practice. The
same statute ordered that judges should do justice 'als wele to pur as
to rych' without fraud or favour; if any judges failed to observe this
statute the king would see that they were 'rygorusly punyst' as an
'ensampill til all utheris'.[185] It is clear that James's intention was to
purge the whole judicial system of corruption. Jurors who sat on
assizes were to swear that they had received neither financial rewards
nor solicitations from any litigant.[186] Another act legislated against
'maintenance' by forbidding anyone to come to court with 'multitude of folkys na with armys'.[187] The courts were not to be intimidated
and were repeatedly enjoined to act with fairness and impartiality.[188]

The fulfilment of these ideals depended on the character and
training of judges and lawyers. In Scotland there were no institutions
comparable to the English inns of court to produce a body of pro-
fessionally-trained lawyers who might hope for advancement to the
judiciary. The Scottish approach to legal training was more academic
than professional and was based upon the study of canon and civil
law at the universities, together, perhaps, with a notarial apprenticeship that taught the techniques of conveyancing. By the fifteenth
century men with such training could make their livelihood as lawyers. But, save in the ecclesiastical courts, there were no openings for
professional judges such as multiplied in England from the reign of
Henry II onwards. The Scottish judicial system as it existed in the

[180] *Ibid.*, p. 282.
[181] *A.P.S.*, II. 11; see also Rait, *Parliaments*, pp. 444–6.
[182] For procedure in civil cases see *Scot. Legal Hist.*, pp. 415–8.
[183] *A.P.S.*, II. 17–9.   [184] *Ibid.*, 8.   [185] *Ibid.*
[186] *Ibid.*, 23.   [187] *Ibid.*, 16.   [188] *Ibid.*, 9, 14, 16, 23.

reign of David I had remained virtually unaltered, and incorporated feudal elements that had long been discarded in England. Although James did not attempt to end this state of affairs, he did try to insist that the holders of heritable jurisdictions should appoint competent deputes for whose acts they would be held responsible;[189] and towards the end of the reign there were signs that the king was prepared to interfere more drastically to remedy the defects of franchisal justice.

It would be wrong to assume that the primitive Scottish judicial system was more riddled with abuses than the evolved and intricate English system (which, from fifteenth-century accounts, left much to be desired), but in Scotland the openings for bribery, intimidation, procrastination and general inefficiency were undoubtedly many. It was the king's duty as 'fountain of justice' to remedy any default of justice; and remedy could therefore be sought in any body in which the king took counsel. Hence it was that parliament and the privy council came to be burdened with 'billis of complayntis' or appeals for 'remeid of justice'.[190] The hearing of appeals, as well as miscellaneous cases of first instance, could take up much of the time of parliament or privy council at a time when both bodies were primarily concerned with state affairs rather than justice. Although judicial committees continued to be elected by parliament in James's reign,[191] and sometimes parliament as a whole dealt with lawsuits,[192] the reign saw the earliest attempt to divert elsewhere some of the mass of litigation that threatened to overwhelm king in council. First came an act of 1425 which gave parliament the option of remitting cases to the ordinary courts. A more important act of 1426 stated that the king should choose certain discreet persons of the three estates to hold 'sessiouns' thrice a year under the presidency of the chancellor. These sessions were to determine all causes and complaints that the king's council was competent to deal with. To those who served on the sessions there was offered somewhat vague hope of remuneration through the profits of justice.[193] It is clear that the sessions were not intended to displace the jurisdiction of parliament but were to exist alongside it with equal authority and competence. In this procedure can be seen the origin of the future court of session as supreme court in all civil causes.[194]

James's concern with the machinery of justice was accompanied by a campaign to make his subjects more law-abiding and to repress

[189] *Ibid.*, 3.   [190] *Ibid.*, 8.   [191] *Ibid.*, 14, 22–3, 26.
[192] *Ibid.*, 28; *R.M.S.*, II. No. 146.
[193] *A.P.S.*, II. 11.   [194] See Rait, *Parliaments*, pp. 460–7.

crime. But even if a criminal were arrested and brought before a court his lord might 'maintain' him by browbeating judge and assize; and if the crime fell within the competence of the lord's own court the criminal could be repledged to that court, where, perhaps, justice that was more lenient, or more mercenary, awaited him. There were thus obstacles in the way of an enactment of 1425 which announced that no lord or baron was to 'thole' thieves or reivers or to maintain them; if he was unable to deal with them he was to certify the king's officers.[195] The latter, however, were not always dependable. In May 1432 a semi-judicial committee of parliament issued a number of ordinances 'for stanching of the fellone slauchteres'.[196] These ordinances, which in substance merely copied those issued by the Stirling general council of 1397,[197] ended with an admonition to the sheriffs, who paid little heed. Two years later, in the parliament of March 1434, James gave vent to his wrath and threatened to take severe action against every sheriff in Scotland, whereupon the prelates besought him to mitigate his anger and obtained a pardon for the errant sheriffs, who were again warned to do justice and to enforce the acts of parliament; the lords of regality received a similar warning.[198] For James was increasingly assuming that it was his duty to see that justice was done in the regalities as well as in the 'royalty' of the sheriffdoms.[199] In the general council held at Edinburgh in October 1436 came the last and most drastic instalment of his plans for more efficient criminal justice: no lord of regality, sheriff, or baron, was to 'sell' (ransom) any thief, or agree upon a fine for the theft. The king was given certain discretionary power in enforcing this statute, which was to last during his pleasure.[200] What must have seemed even more ominous to those who enjoyed franchisal jurisdictions was an act which stated that for the next seven years the justiciars and sheriffs were not to pay too much heed to the obstructive franchises of the regalities or of the burghs: they were 'noucht to defer till regaliteis na til burghis'.[201]

Such masterfulness was to be seen also in the administrative side of government. It has been remarked that 'James, more than his immediate predecessors or successors, formulated and pursued his own policy with the aid of servants, who were little more than willing, if able, tools'.[202] Only one royal servant, Bishop Cameron, seems to have been allowed any pre-eminence. After the death of the Earl of

[195] A.P.S., II. 7–8.   [196] Ibid., 20–2.   [197] P. 210 above.
[198] A.P.S., II. 22.   [199] Ibid., 8, 21, 22, 23.   [200] Ibid., 23.
[201] Ibid., 24.   [202] Balfour-Melville, James I, p. 254.

Buchan at Verneuil his successor as chamberlain was not a great nobleman but Sir John Forrester of Corstorphine, a lesser noble of burgess origin who had acted as chamberlain depute since 1405.[203] And by 1428 the chamberlain, hitherto the chief financial officer of the crown, was receiving practically nothing from the royal revenues and 'had ceased to be a fiscal officer'.[204] While the chamberlain continued to supervise the burghs, his financial duties were entrusted to two new officials: influenced by English practice James introduced into Scotland the offices of treasurer and comptroller. Between the two there came to be recognised a division of duties, though perhaps not until the end of the century. The comptroller was to receive the rents of crown lands, the burgh ferms and the great customs; from these sources he was supposed to meet the expenses of the royal household. The treasurer, on the other hand, was to receive the crown's feudal services and casualties, the profits of justice, and any special contributions or taxes; from these sources he was to meet the expenditure of the crown in business that was not connected with the royal household.[205] The intention that underlay James's introduction of the two new financial officers was probably to exclude the great nobles from crown finance: the first appointments that he made to the posts of treasurer and comptroller were either of minor nobles or of ecclesiastics; and in this policy he set the pattern for more than a century.[206] Even so, James was not content with this re-shuffle of offices: in his reign revenues were not concentrated in the hands of either the comptroller or the treasurer; often large sums were paid directly to the clerk of the spices or to a variety of *ad hoc* financial agents, notably John Turyne, an Edinburgh merchant, John Winchester, canon of Glasgow, and Thomas Myrton, dean of Glasgow.[207] In matters of finance James evidently believed in keeping his left hand ignorant of what his right hand was doing; so far as the formulation of policy was concerned his attitude was probably similar. Lacking any personal involvement in government the faceless men who served him felt no commitment to his ideals, and some of them longed to display their own clashing individualities as soon as he was removed from the scene.

James's only apparent partner in government had been the three estates. In outward appearance at least, they had attained a higher

[203] *Ibid.*, p. 254.   [204] *Ibid.*, p. 255.
[205] See the notes on treasury administration by Athol L. Murray in *T.A.*, XII. xii–xlix.   [206] See *H.B.C.*, pp. 180–5.
[207] *E.R.*, IV. xcv; Balfour-Melville, *James I*, p. 255.

stature than ever before. Nonetheless, the impetus behind their pursuit of the 'common profit of the realm' came solely from the king. Even the admiring Abbot of Inchcolm was under no illusion about the practical results of James's programme: in the parliament of 1426 the king made divers statutes, some of them profitable enough to the realm 'if they were observed'. And Bower went on to cite Aristotle: 'to enact new laws with facility, and to change the old with facility, is marvellous damaging to good order'.[208] Despite Bower's qualms the precedents that James had set were not forgotten; and if, after his death, the three estates no longer hectically pursued the common weal, they did not altogether abandon the chase.

Throughout James's reign it was usually at Perth that the estates held their meetings, and it has been affirmed that 'the history of the reign suggests that James was trying to make Perth the capital of his kingdom'.[209] But James was at least as often at Edinburgh as at Perth, and his itinerary hardly ever deviated from the route connecting Edinburgh, Linlithgow, Stirling and Perth.[210] Perth was on the northernmost periphery of the king's regular peregrinations; it was not a centre from which his personal activity radiated equally to all parts of his realm, Highland as well as Lowland. More than any previous Scottish king James identified himself with the Lowlands.

While the legislation of his first parliament had regarded the problem of disorder as a general one and had made no distinction between Highlands and Lowlands, the second, which opened at Perth in March 1425, thought it 'spedful' that 'consideracioun salbe had of the Hieland men, the quhilkis, befor the kingis hame cumyng, commonly reft [robbed] and slew ilk ane utheris'.[211] In the parliament of September 1426 it was further ordained that lords who had lands beyond the Mounth in which there had once existed a castle, fortalice or manor-house, were to repair it and maintain it as a residence 'for the gracioss governall of ther landis'.[212] They were to set an example of 'gude polising'—efficient and 'civilised' estate management—that would induce the natives to abandon their barbarous ways. This policy, which the Dublin administration adopted in vain in medieval Ireland, was to have some gradual success in Scotland. In Campbell-dominated Argyll, at least, there existed the 'gude

---

[208] *Chron. Bower*, II. 487–8.
[209] Balfour-Melville, *James I*, pp. 129–30, 258.
[210] See James's itinerary, *ibid.*, Appendix C, pp. 285–92.
[211] *A.P.S.*, II. 8.   [212] *Ibid.*, 13.

polising' that parliament desired, together with a shrieval and
baronial administration through which the king's will could be implemented;[213] but in many Gaelic areas such administration can have
been merely nominal; and in the Isles in particular it can hardly
even have been that.

In 1423, Donald of the Isles, the protagonist at Harlaw, had
died at his castle of Ardtornish, whereupon his eldest son, Alexander,
'was proclaimed Earl of Ross and Lord of the Isles after the accustomed manner'.[214] So far as Ross was concerned[215] the king seems
to have let sleeping dogs lie.[216] A more serious issue concerned
sovereignty over the Isles: it is likely that Alexander was intriguing
with King Eric of Denmark, Norway and Sweden to bring about a
re-assertion of Norwegian suzerainty.[217] In respect of the Isles the
Scottish king was still bound to make annual payment of one hundred
marks to the Norwegians; but payment was long in arrears. At Bergen on 29 July 1426 James's envoys negotiated a settlement whereby
Eric cancelled outstanding claims and obtained a promise (apparently
disregarded) of regular payment in future.[218] This settlement was
followed in August 1428 by a striking demonstration of royal power.
According to Abbot Bower and the Pluscarden writer, James had
summoned a parliament to Inverness.[219] Although no record of such
a parliament exists, some sort of summons must have been issued,
possibly to a social gathering of the royal court; for the northern
magnates flocked to Inverness. As they appeared they were craftily
arrested, to the number of about fifty, while, so claims Bower, the
king composed jubilant Latin verse. Most of those taken at Inverness
were imprisoned in various castles until their subsequent release or
their condemnation and death as criminals; a few were tried and
executed forthwith.[220] Alexander of the Isles, who had also fallen
into the king's trap, was brought prisoner to Perth.[221] There was a
prospect that he might be allowed to enter into 'special retinue' with
the king; but this gracious attempt to turn the Lord of the Isles into
a court lap-dog failed: in a short while he absconded, burned the
burgh of Inverness and besieged the castle.[222] On 23 June 1429 the

---

213 See *Highland Papers*, II. 114–98.   214 *Ibid.*, I. 34.
215 See pp. 235–6 above.
216 *Scots Peerage*, I. 148, 264; II. 264.   217 See *Highland Papers*, I. 38.
218 *Diplomatarium Norvegicum*, xx. 764–6; see also *Chron. Bower*, II. 509.
219 *Chron. Bower*, II. 488; *Chron. Pluscarden*, I. 375. See also Balfour-
Melville, *James I*, Appendix B, p. 284, 'The Inverness Parliament'.
220 *Chron. Bower*, II. 489.   221 *Highland Papers*, II. 18.
222 *Chron. Pluscarden*, I. 375; *Chron. Bower*, II. 489.

king and his host came upon the Lord of the Isles and his men beside
a bog in Lochaber. When the royal standard was displayed Clan
Chattan and Clan Cameron deserted MacDonald.[223] On 27 August
1429 he appeared before the high altar of Holyrood in the humiliating garb of a penitent; on his knees he presented his sword, hilt foremost, to the king; the queen and the nobles pleaded with James
to show mercy. After this stage-managed spectacle, Alexander was
warded in Tantallon.[224]

His submission did not, however, mean the end of military operations. When parliament met at Perth on 6 March 1430 it was enacted that all those barons and lords whose lordships lay near the sea
'in the west and on the north partis and namely fornent the Ylis'
were to have galleys for the king's service by May 1431.[225] As a preliminary to some new expedition James seems to have intended to
seize the lands of Alexander's uncle, Alastair Carrach, to whom
Donald of the Isles had granted much of Lochaber.[226] In the summer
of 1431 Alexander Stewart, Earl of Mar, still acting as government
watchdog in the north, levied an army to take possession of the country. Alastair Carrach had taken to the hills above Inverlochy
with some two hundred archers. He was cheered by the appearance
of the galleys of Donald Balloch, a cousin of the Lord of the Isles.
This time the king was not present in person to daunt the opposition
and it was in Mar's army that the waverers were to be found : attacked in front by Donald Balloch's men they were harassed in the
flank by Alastair Carrach and his archers. The result was the rout of
Mar's force with heavy loss. After some adventures and the composition of an appropriate Gaelic couplet the earl regained the safety
of Kildrummy Castle.[227]

Following the defeat of the royal forces at Inverlochy in the
summer of 1431 the king showed his resentment and his determination to equip another expedition 'for the resisting of the kingis rebel-
louris in the northe lande'.[228] To meet the cost parliament agreed to
the levy of a contribution of a shilling in the pound. There is no surviving evidence that it was ever levied;[229] and there is conflicting
evidence as to whether there was another Highland expedition. In
any case James decided to come to terms with the captive Lord of the
Isles.

---

[223] *Highland Papers*, II. 18; *Chron. Bower*, II. 489.
[224] *Chron. Bower*, II. 490; *Chron. Pluscarden*, I. 375–6; *Highland Papers*, II.
19.
[225] *A.P.S.*, II. 19.
[226] *Highland Papers*, I. 32, 39.   [227] *Ibid.*, 40–3.
[228] *A.P.S.*, II. 20.   [229] Balfour-Melville, *James I*, p. 196.

There was another stage-managed spectacle, probably late in 1431, when the queen and the prelates and nobles interceded on behalf of MacDonald and a fellow-prisoner, none other than the Earl of Douglas, who was simultaneously released.[230] Alexander seems to have regained the lordship of the Isles unimpaired and to have avoided falling out with the king during the remainder of the reign.

According to the Pluscarden writer the king, as a result of the 'parliament' of Inverness, 'pacified the country for a long time, and it remained in peace'.[231] But this was too optimistic a view. James's all too facile trickery at Inverness had led to a strife that was wasteful and inconclusive. His Highland policy had turned out to be a complete failure : it had led to increased disorder and had widened the estrangement between Highlanders and Lowlanders.

The blatant flouting of convention shown in James I's arrest of the Highland chiefs at Inverness was not the only instance of headstrong waywardness on the part of the king.[232] The long dearth of government that had followed the death of David II had given way to an over-active government which concerned itself with every aspect of life. However good James's intentions, his rule was totalitarian and menaced vested interests that had come to be regarded as legitimate. He had established a royal autocracy that was sometimes cantankerous and vindictive, one that, lacking the resources necessary for its perpetuation, depended entirely upon the strong personality of the king and the awe in which he was held.

Apart from any dislike they felt for the general character of James's rule his subjects resented his exactions. When a contribution of 2d. in the pound was imposed in 1433 for the expenses of an embassy to France 'the people began to murmur, saying that their property was manifoldly reduced by "gelds" of this sort'. On this occasion the king saw the danger signal ahead and, according to Bower, himself one of the auditors of the tax, quickly ordered the return of all the money that had been collected.[233] On the whole, James's attempts to increase his revenue from direct or indirect taxation met with stout resistance and only limited success. He therefore resorted to other fiscal expedients, sometimes novel, sometimes archaic. Even in his first parliament he had enacted that any mines capable of producing silver worth $1\frac{1}{2}$d. from each pound of lead were

[230] Chron. Bower, II. 490; Chron. Pluscarden, I. 377.
[231] Chron. Pluscarden, I. 375.
[232] See Chron. Bower, II. 510.   [233] Ibid., 482.

to belong to the king 'as is usuale in uthir realmys'.[234] The 'recognition' of lands into the hands of the king by reason of some infringement of feudal practice became frequent.[235] Other expedients were applied in the burghs : two of them—Inverkeithing and Dundee—were heavily amerced for false judgments given in their burgh courts.[236] The chamberlain ayres were now being held in many burghs and had become a sizable source of revenue, bringing in as much as £360 13s. 4d. in 1435.[237] Heavy amercements were also levied for the old offence of forestalling—the buying and selling of goods before they had been publicly exposed for sale in a burgh market. This source of income, which brought in £342 9s. od. in 1435, affected not only the inhabitants of the burghs but their country neighbours : many landholders purchased remissions from the king for their offence.[238] While regulations that were out-of-date were strictly enforced for the king's profit 'certain poor people' of Irvine had to wait eight years for payment of victuals bought from them by the king.[239] The rich were also occasionally victimised : one of James's expedients was the collection of voluntary gifts, like the later English 'benevolences', from the most substantial persons of each of the three estates.[240] This practice 'may have been a factor in increasing the antagonism of the nobles, already uneasy at his numerous attacks upon their possessions and privileges'.[241]

The more serious of these attacks took the form of confiscation. The process began with James's questionable acquisition of the earldom of Buchan in 1424 [242] following the death of John Stewart at Verneuil. Then came a rich windfall—the earldoms of Fife, Menteith and Lennox—that fell into the royal lap in 1425 with the forfeiture of the Albany faction. In 1427 James turned his attention to the earldom of Strathearn, held by Malise Graham, son of the earl murdered in 1413.[243] On some pretext Malise was deprived of Strathearn [244] and its revenues—probably more than £300 a year;[245] by way of partial compensation he was granted the title of Earl of Menteith and some of the lands of that earldom, while other lands,

[234] *A.P.S.*, ii. 5; see also *E.R.*, iv. cxxiii.
[235] Grant, *Social and Economic Development*, p. 200; *Chron. Bower*, ii. 484.
[236] *E.R.*, iv. 669.   [237] *Ibid.*   [238] *Ibid.*, 669–71.
[239] *Ibid.*, vi. 394.   [240] *Chron. Bower*, ii. 485.
[241] Balfour-Melville, *James I*, p. 228.   [242] *Scots Peerage*, i. 148, 264; ii. 264.
[243] Pp. 255–6 above.   [244] *Scots Peerage*, vi. 142–3.
[245] In 1381 the gross revenues of the earldom amounted to £406 9s. 11½d. (*E.R.*, iii. 33–8)

together with the castle of Doune, were kept in the hands of the king.[246]

By 1433 the income from royal lands—many of them recently acquired—was at least £2,000.[247] It had been shown that of all the methods of money-raising employed by James it was confiscation that was the most profitable. It continued. George Dunbar, Earl of March, held the earldom that had been forfeited from his father in 1400 and restored by Albany in 1409.[248] James maintained that the restoration was invalid. Although the earl was given the opportunity of defending his rights in the parliament held at Perth in January 1435, judgment went against him;[249] the family of Dunbar, which for three centuries had held the earldom of March, had lost it once and for all. A few months later the king was also to acquire the earldom of Mar and the Garioch, ostensibly *ratione bastardie*—as an escheat on the death of the bastard Alexander Stewart, Earl of Mar.[250] The king's proceedings, like others before them, disregarded the prior claims of Sir Robert Erskine.[251]

To many it must have seemed that James's whole reign was one of ruthless extortion. After the execution of the Albany faction in 1425 'the comoners of his land secretly clepid [called] hym nat rightwes [righteous] bot a tirannous prynce'.[252] Even Abbot Bower, a whole-hearted admirer of the king, admits that James 'was given to the acquisition of things'.[253] Over £5,000 were spent on the rebuilding of Linlithgow Castle after it had been destroyed by an accidental fire.[254] It was to be replaced by an imposing royal residence, more palace that castle. In addition the items that the king imported from Flanders strikingly suggest the luxury of James's court: they included ostrich feathers, purple velvet, sable mantles, spices, wine, tapestry, and jewels; even stage-players or 'mimers' were hired in the Netherlands, outfitted at the king's expense, and brought to Scotland to entertain the court.[255] James's genuine concern for the poor and the oppressed had its blind spots, and the luxury of the court must have contrasted flagrantly with a chronic misery that was heightened by natural disasters: in February 1431 the plague broke out in Edin-

---

[246] *Scots Peerage*, VI. 142–3. For the king's expenditure on Doune in 1433 see *E.R.*, IV. 593.

[247] Pp. 285, 287 above. [248] Pp. 218–9, 230–1 above. [249] *A.P.S.*, II. 23.

[250] *R.M.S.*, II. No. 488; *Scots Peerage*, V. 588–9; *E.R.*, V. 55; VI. cxxi.

[251] See *A.P.S.*, I. 578; *Aberdeen-Banff Illustrations*, IV. 165; *Scots Peerage*, V. 602.

[252] *James I, Life and Death*, p. 49. [253] *Chron. Bower*, II. 486.

[254] Balfour-Melville, *James I*, p. 261. [255] *E.R.*, IV. 678, 680.

burgh; the winter of the same year was so bitterly cold that nearly all animals perished; in 1432 'the volatile pestilence' broke out at Haddington; in 1434 a bitter frost lasted more than three months so that the water-mills could not turn to grind corn; in 1435 there was great dearth in Teviotdale.[256]

In such circumstances James's apparent self-gratification, coupled with his heavy-handed acquisitiveness, was likely to make him unpopular. His various policies were strewn with victims who were bound to be resentful. The swing of the pendulum from the laissez-faire of the Albany governorship to the authoritarian totalitarianism of James's personal rule was too violent to go unchecked. But from the very outset of his personal rule James had been well aware of the risks he ran. There was an element of fatalism in his vow that began with the words: 'If God grant me life . . .'[257] He had even prepared for the worst by an act of 1428 that required oaths of fealty to be sworn to the queen, and by a similar act of 1435.[258] But while James was apprehensively aware of an undercurrent of general opposition it was only sporadically that it touched the political surface. And generally it was revealed not in the activities of the king's opponents but in the steps taken by the king to forestall them, as in 1431, when James arrested his nephews, Archibald, fifth Earl of Douglas, and Sir John Kennedy of Cassillis. Douglas, who was kept for a time in Lochleven, was released at the same time as Alexander of the Isles; Kennedy was imprisoned in Stirling till at least 1434 and finally escaped abroad.[259]

It has been surmised that the reason for Douglas's arrest sprang from his relationship with Malise Graham, erstwhile Earl of Strathearn. Shortly before the latter was deprived of Strathearn and fobbed off with a truncated earldom of Menteith Douglas had married Malise's sister, Euphemia Graham.[260] Not only did Malise lose Strathearn but he was immediately packed off to England when the second exchange of hostages took place in October 1427 and was to remain a hostage in England until 1453.[261] The king's arrest of Douglas may have been in retaliation for the earl's covert negotiations with the English, presumably intended to secure the release of Malise.[262] Another nobleman who doubtless resented the king's harsh treatment of Malise was the latter's paternal uncle, Sir Robert

---

[256] *Chron. Bower*, II. 490, 491, 495, 500, 502.
[257] P. 281 above. [258] *A.P.S.*, II. 17, 23.
[259] *Chron. Pluscarden*, I. 377; *Chron. Bower*, II. 490; *E.R.*, IV. 591.
[260] *Scots Peerage*, III. 170. [261] Balfour-Melville, *James I*, p. 294.
[262] See C. Macrae, 'The English Council and Scotland in 1430', *E.H.R.*, LIV. 415–26, at 419, 426.

Graham. In his youth he seems to have studied at Paris in the company of John Stewart, an illegitimate son of Robert II.[263] Possibly as a result of a university training Sir Robert was a man 'of grete wit and eloquence, wundir suttilye wittyd and expert yn the lawe'.[264] His opposition to the king was based not only on family grievances but on grounds of political theory, a common enough justification for rebellion in England but rare in Scotland. For some unrecorded offence Sir Robert was arrested in 1424 and imprisoned in Dunbar Castle,[265] from which he either escaped or was released. This experience did not daunt him. He is said to have shown no little indiscretion on one occasion—the date is not given—when he confronted the king in parliament : Graham

> rose upe with a grete corage, with a violent chere and countenance, sette handes upon the kyng, saying thos wordes 'I arrest you yn the name of all the Thre Astates of your reume . . .; for right as youre liege peple be bundun and sworne to obeye your majeste rialle, yn the same wise bene ye sworne and ensurid to kepe your peple . . . so that ye do hem no wronge, bot yn all right mantene and defend hem.[266]

Sir Robert rashly expected his action to be applauded, but the dumbfounded estates 'kapid silence'. Then the king, 'perceyvyng all this presumptuous rebellion', arrested Sir Robert, 'and commandid to put hym yn sure and hard prisone', after which he was banished 'and all his heritage and goodes deemed as forfaturs to the kyng'. Instead of going into exile abroad, so continues the story, Graham

> toke his way ynto the cuntreis of the Wild Scottis . . . and furthwith he renounced his legeance, and by wordes and by writyng he defied hem, seying that he had destruyd hym, his wif and his childerne, his hartages and all his other godes, by his cruell tyranny. Wherfor he said he wold slee hym with his owne handes as his mortall enmye.[267]

Whatever the truth of this tale the impression that it leaves is that Sir Robert Graham was a political idealist. Abbot Bower conveys the same impression of Graham, though the good abbot hardly shared the latter's views.

What made this ardent idealist dangerous was his eventual association with the Stewarts of Atholl. Possibly the hapless fate of the hostages helped to bring them together : David Stewart, son and heir of Walter, Earl of Atholl, had gone to England as a hostage in 1424

---

[263] *Scots Peerage*, VI. 214–15.
[265] *Chron. Bower*, II. 482.
[267] *Ibid.*, pp. 50–1.

[264] *James I, Life and Death*, p. 50.
[266] *James I, Life and Death*, p. 50.

and had died there some ten years later. Despite this the king does not seem to have suspected the Earl of Atholl (his uncle) of harbouring disaffection. Indeed it was Atholl who apparently profited from Malise's deprivation, for the king did not keep Strathearn in his own hands but on 22 July 1427 conferred it, with its palatine rights, upon Earl Walter.[269] This was, however, only a device to make James's seizure of Strathearn seem less blatant : he granted the earldom to his uncle of Atholl only in life tenure, and since the latter was then nearing his seventieth year it was not likely that James would have to wait long to secure Strathearn for himself. But this circumstance may have been of some significance to Atholl's grandson and heir, Sir Robert Stewart, son of the David Stewart who had been left to die as a hostage in England.

If the Atholl Stewarts had grounds for grievance and apprehension they also had grounds for ambitious hopes. In the eyes of the Pluscarden chronicler Earl Walter was 'that old serpent inveterate in evil days' who had craftily cleared the pathway for his own accession to the crown : acting the part of an innocent lamb he had helped to encompass the death of the Duke of Rothesay in 1402 ; he had been foremost in counselling the destruction of Duke Murdoch and his sons in 1425.[270] Whatever the truth behind these allegations it is true that the disappearance of rivals brought the Earl of Atholl closer to the throne : James's daughters were excluded by the tailzie of 1373 that barred female succession; with the last of Duke Murdoch's sons a desperate fugitive in Ireland, Earl Walter might be reckoned in terms of the tailzie of 1373 as heir presumptive to the crown until Queen Joan gave birth to twin sons at Holyrood on 16 October 1430. The publicity given to this event [271] reflected the king's joy that the problem of the succession had apparently been settled. Although the elder prince, Alexander, died in infancy, the younger, James, was established at Doune Castle, where he survived a diet of forty-eight pounds of almonds. By 1434 he had been dignified by the title of Duke of Rothesay and had his own household.[272] But the existence of an heir apparent did not end the hopes of the former heir presumptive and his grandson. Instead their hopes took more radical form : if the descendants of Robert II and Elizabeth Mure were of illegitimate descent,[273] King James was a usurper and the rightful king was

[269] Balfour-Melville, *James I*, p. 149.
[270] *Chron. Pluscarden*, I. 389; similarly *Chron. Bower*, II. 503.
[271] *Chron. Pluscarden*, I. 376; *Chron. Bower*, II. 490.
[272] *E.R.*, IV. 529, 603.   [273] See p. 186 above.

the Earl of Atholl, only surviving son of Robert II and Euphemia Ross. It was perhaps Earl Walter's heir, his grandson Sir Robert Stewart, rather than the earl himself, who coveted 'the throne usurped by the elder line',[274] but the aged earl was at least partly involved in the schemes of his grandson; and the latter had secured the adherence of Sir Robert Graham in a conspiracy based partly upon political ideals, partly upon dynastic ambitions.

Their enterprise was no doubt carefully timed to coincide with a rising tide of general disaffection. Even physically James was no longer the man who had once inspired respect : Aeneas Sylvius, who saw him in 1435, described him as 'thick-set and oppressed by much fat'.[275] The greed and ruthlessness so evident in his later years had begun to drive victims to desperation—the brother of the Earl of March had been so offended by the latter's dispossession in 1435 that he had rebelled against James and co-operated with the English.[276] James's commanding position in domestic politics had owed much to his abstinence from warfare. By taking the field at Roxburgh in August 1436 he broke the spell hitherto cast by his powerful personality : the expedition was militarily an inglorious failure. More than that, the concourse of nobles in the huge host gathered at Roxburgh bred political trouble : there was 'detestable schism and most wicked division sprung from envy'.[277] From these laconic phrases of the Pluscarden chronicler it may be deduced that in 1436, as in a better-known episode of 1482, the nobles, when arrayed for war, sensed their own power and were no longer daunted by the king. In these circumstances, when a general council met at Edinburgh in October 1436, James showed political tactlessness in passing measures that threatened the independence of baronial jurisdictions.[278]

With one opponent at least, the papacy, James was by this time ready to seek reconciliation. The Bishop of Urbino had arrived as papal legate [279] in time to join the king and his court at Perth for 'a solempne fest of the Cristynmes'.[280] At Perth, the king and queen resided in the Dominican friary while the rest of the court was dispersed in lodgings in the town. It was none other than Sir Robert Stewart, grandson of the Earl of Atholl, who was chamberlain of the royal household and in charge of its domestic arrangements. On

[274] Balfour-Melville, *James I*, pp. 4, 247.

[275] Brown, *Early Travellers*, p. 25.   [276] P. 292 above.

[277] *Chron. Pluscarden*, i. 380.   [278] P. 312 above.   [279] P. 301 above.

[280] *James I, Life and Death*, p. 52. James was certainly in Perth by 1 January 1437 (Balfour-Melville, *James I*, p. 292).

the night of 21 February 1437 he laid planks over the fosse of the friary and the conspirators entered.

There were eight of them, including Sir Robert Stewart and Sir Robert Graham. To James, who was alone with the queen and her ladies, the noise of clanking armour gave warning of the approaching danger. The door of the apartment could not be secured—Sir Robert Stewart had 'left the kynges chamburs doore opyne, and had brussed and blundird the lokes of hem yn such wise that no man myght shute hem'.[281] Using a poker the king wrenched up the planking of the floor and let himself down to the sewer that ran beneath. Its outlet had been sealed a few days previously since the king had lost so many tennis balls there. He remained hidden in this noisome tunnel while the conspirators burst into the chamber above. One of them wounded Queen Joan, who 'fledd yn hir kirtill, her mantell hongyng aboute hir; the other ladyes yn a corner of the chambur crying and wepyng all destraite.'[282] Disappointed in their quest the conspirators left the chamber only to return when one of them remembered the sewer. By the light of a torch they caught sight of the king in his hiding place. Though unarmed he fought manfully before he died by the strokes of the assassins. Too late the courtiers and townsfolk rushed with torches to the scene of the murder. Only one, Sir David Dunbar, brother of the dispossessed Earl of March,[283] managed to overtake the assassins and was wounded by them as they fled to the fastnessess of the 'Wilde Scottes'.[284]

[281] *James I, Life and Death*, pp. 52–5; *Chron. Pluscarden*, I. 389; *Chron. Bower*, II. 503.

[282] *James I, Life and Death*, p. 57.

[283] *Scots Peerage*, III. 275.

[284] *James I, Life and Death*, p. 60.

12

THE MINORITY OF JAMES II AND THE LITTLE SCHISM

When the Bishop of Urbino inspected the corpse of the murdered king he kissed its many wounds and, with tearful sighs, announced to the bystanders that James had died as a martyr for the defence of the state and the execution of justice.[1] Just as the murder of Archbishop Thomas Becket won him an adulation after his death that he had never enjoyed in his lifetime, so the melodramatic demise of James I cast a retrospective aura of good fame over the whole of his reign and dazzled the judgments of most contemporary writers [2] and of their successors. James's posthumous reputation must also have been enhanced by the undoubted contrast between his one-time masterful rule and the anarchy that followed during his son's minority. Thus there is some exaggeration in the view that 'the tragedy of James I lies in the wreck of his high purpose upon the stubborn individualism of the Scottish nobles'.[3]

In any case only a few nobles had planned the king's death. If the remainder breathed a collective sigh of relief at James's removal they at least showed a sense of propriety in disowning the removers. Sir Robert Graham was brought to trial before the justiciar at Stirling and reputedly accepted his doom with a prophetic utterance:

> Ye shalle se the daye and the tyme that ye shalle pray for my saule for the grete good that I have done to you and to alle this reaume of Scottland, that I have thus slayne and delyveryed you of so cruelle a tirant.[4]

---

[1] *Chron. Pluscarden*, I. 390.
[2] See *ibid.*, 389; *Chron. Bower*, II. 512, 514.
[3] Balfour-Melville, *James I*, p. 280.
[4] *James I, Life and Death*, pp. 62–4; *E.R.*, v. xlii, xliii.

Sentence against the Earl of Atholl and his grandson, Sir Robert Stewart, was probably passed in the parliament that met in Edinburgh on 25 March 1437.[5] The lack of sympathy for the regicides can be seen in the fiendishness of the punishments inflicted upon them, which on this unique occasion even surpassed English practice.[6]

Meanwhile on 25 March 1437 the surviving son of the dead king, a boy of six, was crowned and anointed as James II, not at Scone, near the scene of his father's murder, but in the abbey of Holyrood, to which he was conducted by the three estates 'with the greatest applause and display'.[7] It seems likely that parliament then made arrangements for the government of the realm during the minority. Although the three estates entrusted the queen mother with the custody of the young king and his sisters, and appointed a council to assist her, assigned Stirling Castle as a residence, and set her yearly allowance at four thousand marks,[8] she emerged as something less than a regent. It was the late king's nephew, Archibald Douglas, fulsomely styled 'Duke of Touraine, Earl of Douglas and Count of Longueville, Lord of Galloway and Annandale', who was to head the government as lieutenant-general.[9] The view that he had been influential during the reign of James I 'rests largely on indirect evidence'.[10] Although Earl Archibald had shunned the political limelight his self-effacement had not prevented his being temporarily arrested by James I.[11] The new lieutenant-general probably saw no reason why he should act as a drudge on behalf of the house of Stewart. It was a time of misery : a visitation of plague was followed in 1438 and 1439 by famine, 'and werraly the derth was sa gret that thar deit [died] a passing peple for hunger'.[12] To these afflictions was added the lawlessness so vividly portrayed by Abbot Bower :

> even I who am writing these things have seen and heard this very day the poor people of my own neighbourhood being stripped of their garments and inhumanly despoiled of their utensils.[13]

[5] *A.P.S.*, II. 31.

[6] *James I, Life and Death*, pp. 61–2, 64–5; *Chron. Pluscarden*, I. 390–1.

[7] *A.P.S.*, II. 31; *Chron. Bower*, II. 514.

[8] These arrangements of 1437 may be inferred from the proceedings of the general council at Stirling in September 1439 (*A.P.S.*, II. 54).

[9] *Ibid.*, 31.

[10] W. Stanford Reid, 'The Douglases at the Court of James I of Scotland', *Juridical Review*, LVI. 77–88, at 88.   [11] P. 320 above.

[12] *Chron. Auchinleck*, pp. 12, 53; *Chron. Bower*, II. 514.

[13] *Chron. Bower*, II. 474.

It was in vain that the lieutenant-general and his council, meeting in Edinburgh on 24 December 1438, passed an ordinance dealing with 'spuilzie' (spoliation).[14] Another council, which met at Stirling in March 1439, found it necessary to pass an ordinance dealing with 'rebellys or unrewlfull menne within ony castellys or fortalicis'.[15]

Among the 'unrewlfull menne' was doubtless Sir Robert Erskine, who at the outset of the minority tested the strength of the government by attempting to obtain the earldom of Mar and the Garioch that had come into the hands of James I in 1435.[16] He began by seizing control of the royal castle of Dumbarton (or, if he already held it, refused to relinquish it). On 10 August 1440 an indenture was made at Stirling 'be way of amiable composicioun' between Erskine and a committee of thirty-one representatives of the three estates specially appointed by the general council; Erskine was to have custody of Kildrummy Castle in Mar until the king came of age; as soon as he was installed in Kildrummy Castle he was to hand back Dumbarton Castle.[17] Mar was not the only earldom that inspired trouble : Sir Alan Stewart of Darnley, who had lately headed the Scots mercenaries in France, sought to make good a claim (through his mother) to the earldom of Lennox.[18] He fell foul of Boyd of Kilmarnock by reason of an old feud between the two families and was treacherously killed by Sir Thomas Boyd.[19] On 7 July 1439 the Lennox Stewarts had their revenge : 'Schir Thomas Boyd was slane be Alexander Stewart "Buktuth" and his sonnis and Mathow Stewart with his brother, and uther syndry.'[20] The result of this 'plaine battell' was that 'the heill southvest of Scotland was devydit in twa pairtis'.[21] The Lennox affair also involved Alexander, Lord of the Isles, now officially recognised as Earl of Ross.[22] His goodwill was sought by the government.[23] By 22 February 1439 he had been appointed justiciar north of Forth,[24] and he was present in the general council held at Stirling on 4 September 1439.[25] On the following day some Islesmen, whom Pitscottie styles 'notabill thevis and murtheraris', took part in

---

[14] *A.P.S.*, II. 32. [15] *Ibid.* [16] Pp. 257, 319 above.

[17] *A.P.S.*, II. 55–6; see also *Aberdeen-Banff Illustrations*, IV. 189–90.

[18] *Scots Peerage*, v. 347–8; Dunlop, *Bishop Kennedy*, p. 24, n. 3.

[19] One source (*Chron. Auchinleck*, p. 3) places the murder a few miles from Falkirk; another (Pitscottie, *Historie*, I. 23–4) places it near Glasgow.

[20] *Chron. Auchinleck*, 3, 33. Alexander was the brother of the murdered Sir Alan (Pitscottie, *Historie*, I. 24).

[21] Pitscottie, *Historie*, I. 24. [22] *H.B.C.*, 487.

[23] *E.R.*, v. 33–4, 73, 84, 86, 166.

[24] Col. Leslie, *Historical Records of the Family of Leslie* (1869), I. 87.

[25] *A.P.S.*, II. 54–5; p. 329 below.

an affray on the banks of Loch Lomond near Inchmurrin and slew John Colquhoun of Luss. Whether the Islesmen had been called in by the government or came to settle scores of their own the result was probably the same : 'the Lennox was heill ovirthrowin'.[26]

The opening disorders of the minority were accompanied by squabbles among various factions for control of government. On this subject the surviving official records are usually silent, though one record, that of the 'Appoyntement' of 4 September 1439,[27] confirms the picture of suspicion, intrigue, plotting and violence, that the narrative sources depict. These sources include the scrappy (but contemporary) *Auchinleck Chronicle* and the melodramatic *Scotorum Historiae* of Hector Boece, first published in Paris in 1527. This work gives picturesque details and set speeches but omits to supply chronology and corroboration. The same is true of the *Historie* of Robert Lindsay of Pitscottie, which, up to 1460, is basically a translation of Boece,[28] but one that, being colourfully composed in the Lowland vernacular, conveys an effect of verisimilitude that may sometimes be misleading. It is particularly unfortunate that Bower ended his chronicle just as the factions were girding their loins for political battle. Thus the politics of the minority have the character of a jigsaw puzzle from which some of the pieces are missing and in which alien pieces may have been jumbled.

What seems indisputable is the sudden rise to power of Sir William Crichton and Sir Alexander Livingston of Callendar. The former had been a trusted servant of James I, who had appointed him to the new and honourable post of master of the household, granted him the custody of Edinburgh Castle with a salary of £100, and made him sheriff of Edinburgh.[29] The baronial family of Livingston was of much the same standing as that of Crichton ; and the prolific Livingstons had a wide connection, which included the prominent conciliarist, Thomas Livingston, Abbot of Dundrennan.[30]

Thanks to the fact that the coronation of James II took place in Holyrood, Sir William Crichton was able at the very start of the minority to use his posts as sheriff of Edinburgh and keeper of its castle as a means of acquiring further influence.[31] Pitscottie relates that soon after the coronation Crichton obtained control of the young king ; the queen mother pretended to set out on a pilgrimage to White-

---

[26] Pitscottie, *Historie*, I. 29; *Chron. Auchinleck*, 3, 34.
[27] P. 329 below.   [28] Pitscottie, *Historie*, I. 12, n. 1.
[29] *Scots Peerage*, III. 52–8; *E.R.*, IV. 607.
[30] Duncan Shaw, 'Thomas Livingston, a Conciliarist', *Scot. Church Hist. Soc. Recs.*, XII. 120–35, at 123.   [31] *E.R.*, V. xlv, 63.

kirk, smuggled her son out of the castle in one of the coffers of her baggage, and instead of sailing from Leith to Dunbar sailed up the Forth to Stirling Castle, to be welcomed by Sir Alexander Livingston, who proposed to besiege Crichton in Edinburgh Castle; thereupon Crichton pointed out the hostility of Douglas towards both himself and Livingston and sought a reconciliation with the latter.[32] Although the picturesque details of this tale are suspect, its substance might account for a political change that occurred in May 1439 when Bishop Cameron was replaced as chancellor by Sir William Crichton.[33]

In the following month the Earl of Douglas died of a fever.[34] No new lieutenant-general was appointed. The queen mother ambitiously tried to fill the gap and married a minor noble, Sir James Stewart, 'the Black Knight of Lorne', who 'thocht, seing the cuntre swa devydit . . . to have had sum reull in the realme alsweill as ony utheris, be ressoun he had mariet the kingis mother'.[35] On 3 August 1439, shortly after the nuptials, Sir Alexander Livingston showed his resentment by imprisoning the queen and her new husband.[36] Since the Livingstons now had control of the boy king they could hope to dominate Scotland. At first their scheme went well: a general council of the three estates met at Stirling, and on 4 September 1439 negotiated an 'Appoyntement' for the release of the captives.[37] Queen Joan affected to believe that the Livingstons had held her in durance only through motives of zeal and loyalty towards her and her son the king. She remitted her 'griefe and displeasance', and in token of the 'traiste and hartliness' with which she now regarded the Livingstons she confided her son to their keeping until he came of age. Meanwhile she 'lent' to her son her residence of Stirling and granted to Sir Alexander Livingston the annuity of four thousand marks once assigned to her by the three estates. All the parties to the 'Appoyntement' took oath on the gospels to observe it, and it was sealed by many notables, including Chancellor Crichton. But one morning when the young king rode out with a few attendants to hunt in Stirling Park he was waylaid by the chancellor and a band of a hundred armed men, thereupon 'the king began to smylle, quhairthrow thay undirstude the king to be content of thair coming and glaid to gang

---

[32] Pitscottie, *Historie*, I. 16–23.

[33] See Dunlop, *Bishop Kennedy*, pp. 26–7.

[34] Pitscottie, *Historie*, I. 24; *Chron. Auchinleck*, pp. 4, 34.

[35] Pitscottie, *Historie*, I. 26; *Scots Peerage*, v. 2.

[36] *Chron. Auchinleck*, pp. 3, 33–4; *E.R.*, v. liii, n. 1; *R.M.S.*, II. No. 324.

[37] Text in *A.P.S.*, II. 54–5; *Chron. Auchinleck*, pp. 3, 34.

with thame, and thairfor hynt his hors be the bryddill and convoyit him to Edinburghe'.[38] This exploit stole the thunder of the Livingstons. But Crichton was prepared to be accommodating : a new reconciliation between the two factions was arranged. Livingston, it seems, was once more to have custody of the king, while Crichton continued as chancellor and was to receive a salary of seven hundred marks until the king came of age.[39] Some thought was even given to the public weal. A general council held at Stirling in August 1440 ordained that the justiciars should hold their ayres twice a year, and that the king himself should attend, or at least be nearby 'quhar his consale thinkis it maist spedful'. It was also thought 'spedfull' that the king should hastily 'ride throu oute the realme . . . quhar ony rebellione, slauchter, byrning, refe, forfalt, or thift, happynis' [40]—a tall order.

There remained one real or potential source of trouble—the young Earl of Douglas—fear of whom had probably forced Crichton and Livingston to their reconciliation. When Archibald, fifth Earl of Douglas, had died in 1439 he had been succeeded by his son William, then some fourteen or fifteen years old.[41] He was a kinsman of the young king; his father had been lieutenant-general; and it was natural that Earl William should aspire to the same post. Whatever his ambitions they were soon removed. He accepted an invitation to Edinburgh Castle and turned a deaf ear to warnings that mischief was afoot. With his brother David, and his family counsellor, Sir Malcolm Fleming, he dined in the castle on 24 November 1440. At the close of the dinner Chancellor Crichton placed a bull's head on the table, 'quhilk was ane signe and taikin of condemnatour to the death'. The two Douglas brothers were seized and put through a rigmarole of a trial before being beheaded on the castle hill.[42]

This 'Black Dinner' might have been expected to arouse a hornets' nest of Douglases thirsting for blood. Nothing of the sort happened. If Crichton and Livingston, for their own motives, good, bad, or indifferent, were eager for the demise of the Douglas brothers, there was another person, himself a Douglas, who was even more eager. This was James Douglas of Balvenie and Abercorn, whose corpulence earned him the sobriquet of 'the Gross'.[43] In his early days he had

[38] Pitscottie, *Historie*, I. 31–2. [39] *Ibid.*, 34–9; *E.R.*, v. 125.
[40] *A.P.S.*, II. 32–3. [41] *Scots Peerage*, III. 170–1.
[42] Pitscottie, *Historie*, I. 40–6; *Chron. Bower*, II. 514 (additional notes of the reign of James II). [43] Pitscottie, *Historie*, I. 46.

shown a bold spirit.[44] He was, according to Pitscottie—though the same might have been said of most of his contemporaries—'gredie to conques great rentis to his posteritie'.[45] Although James the Gross had been created Earl of Avondale a few months after the death of James I, this elevation in rank had brought him no new lands. On the other hand, James was second son of Archibald the Grim, third Earl of Douglas, and, thanks to the Douglas tailzie of 1342, it was James who came next after his grand-nephew Earl William, and the latter's brother, David, in the succession to the bulk of the Black Douglas estates.[46] Circumstantial evidence leaves little doubt that James the Gross played the part of a wicked grand-uncle and encouraged Crichton in the view that 'this realme sould be at greattar tranquilitie gif the Earle of Douglas and his brother had bene cutted of sudenlie'.[47] Earl James, at any rate, was the person who most obviously profited, for although the Douglas brothers had been executed as traitors no sentence of forfeiture was passed against them; thus James succeeded to the earldom of Douglas. By contrast, Sir Malcolm Fleming of Biggar and Cumbernauld, who shared the fate of the Douglas brothers, was sentenced to forfeiture before his execution. On 7 January 1441 his son and heir, Sir Robert Fleming, went to the mercat cross of Linlithgow and asserted, in the traditional terms of such an appeal, that the sentence was evil, false and rotten.[48] Soon Sir Robert was allowed to succeed to the forfeited lands and was given in marriage a daughter of James the Gross,[49] who thus atoned both for the slaughter of Sir Robert's grandfather in 1406 and for the judicial murder of Sir Robert's father in 1440. With the powerful James the Gross anxious to hush matters up no one stirred himself on behalf of the two dead Douglases.

Meanwhile there was some re-allocation of the Black Douglas territories. It was only to the entailed estates that James the Gross succeeded. The duchy of Touraine with the other lands in France lapsed to the French crown in default of heirs male in the direct line. For the same reason the Scottish crown received as a titbit the lordship of Annandale. The lordships of Bothwell and of Galloway (east and west) went to the young sister of the sixth earl, Margaret Douglas, 'the Fair Maid of Galloway'.[50] What had been dismembered was partly replaced by the lands that James the Gross already

[44] Pp. 225, 226 above.
[45] Pitscottie, *Historie*, I. 47.
[46] *Scots Peerage*, III. 172–3.
[47] Pitscottie, *Historie*, I. 43, 46.
[48] *E.R.*, v. lvi; P. F. Tytler, *History*, I. ii, 382–3, Notes and Illustrations, Letter K.
[49] *Scots Peerage*, VIII. 529, 533.
[50] *Ibid.*, III. 171, 176; *E.R.*, v. lvii.

held as Earl of Avondale. From his castle of Abercorn on the shores of the Forth near Linlithgow, he dominated the valley of the Avon from which he took his earlier title; he also held lands in Banffshire, Inverness-shire, Buchan and Moray,[51] and was soon exercising his mind to secure further territories for his posterity. James Dunbar, Earl of Moray, had died in 1429 leaving as co-heiresses his daughters Janet and Elizabeth. Janet, the elder daughter, had married James Crichton, son and heir of the chancellor; James the Gross arranged the marriage of her younger sister to his third son, Archibald. A tailzie of 26 April 1442 was the first move in Earl James's manoeuvres to win the earldom of Moray for his third son at the expense of Janet Dunbar and James Crichton.[52] The ingenuity required for the Moray affair was scarcely needed for a more ambitious venture—the reunification of the Black Douglas lands. By the simple expedient of a marriage between the Fair Maid of Galloway and William, son and heir of Earl James, all would be regained with the sole exception of Annandale. During Lent in 1443 or 1444 William Douglas, a youth of some eighteen years, married his cousin Margaret in the kirk of Douglas; she had not yet reached the nubile age of twelve.[53]

The acquisitiveness of the seventh Earl of Douglas (and of others) had been stimulated not only by the turmoil of political faction but also by new ecclesiastical divisions. There was a short lull before the storm of dissension, and some old divisions were healed before the new made their appearance: the barratry laws stayed unrepealed but unenforced, and Eugenius IV even showed his magnanimity on 28 December 1439 by pardoning Bishop Cameron's misdemeanours.[54] But the bishop seems to have been too closely associated with the victims of the Black Dinner: on 3 March 1441 a petition in the name of James II informed the pope that Cameron had aided 'several other lords of the king's council' in rebellion, sedition and other enormities.[55] Although Cameron kept his bishopric he was discredited and almost finished as a political figure. Just as Bishop Cameron was no longer the spokesman of the Scottish government in ecclesiastical affairs, so his old antagonist, William Croyser, was no longer the spokesman of the pope: the archdeacon had made a *volte-face* and

---

[51] *Scots Peerage*, III. 173.
[52] Dunlop, *Bishop Kennedy*, pp. 35–6 and 36, n. 1; *Scots Peerage*, VI. 306–9.
[53] Pitscottie, *Historie*, I. 47–8; *Cal. Papal Letters*, x. 130–1.
[54] Dunlop, *Bishop Kennedy*, p. 27; *Cal. Papal Letters*, VIII. 294.
[55] *St Andrews Copiale*, pp. 308–9; Burns, *Basle*, p. 70.

adhered to the council of Basel,[56] with which the pope's relationship was once more strained.[57]

In 1437 Eugenius had issued a bull transferring the council to Ferrara, whence it afterwards moved to Florence. A majority of the council of Basel refused to be either transferred or dissolved, remained doggedly in session, and on 25 June 1439 deposed Eugenius (who ignored the deposition), styling him, among other things, an incorrigible schismatic, a deviate from the faith, and a pertinacious heretic; on 5 November 1439 Amadeus, Duke of Savoy, was elected at Basel as Felix V.[58] Once more there was a schism.

While Scottish contact with the former council of Constance had been 'limited and equivocal',[59] as many as eleven Scotsmen who were bishops between 1425 and 1475 were in some way associated with the long-lasting council of Basel.[60] The most distinguished of these was Thomas Livingston, Abbot of Dundrennan,[61] who addressed the imperial diet at Mainz on 10 August 1439 and posed the rhetorical question :

> What stability would there be in the Christian polity if it could be entirely overthrown by a single sinner [the Pope] who might not, even if he persevered in his violent course, be checked by any individual or by any council or assembly? [62]

The most significant part of Livingston's career was spent on the continent. In Scotland the conciliarist influence of two other graduates of St Andrews, John Athilmer and James Ogilvie, was more direct.[63] By 1439 the pair were teaching in St Andrews. Their advent shortly followed the death of Laurence of Lindores and shortly preceded that of Bishop Wardlaw. Old influences were removed and the way was open for new. The philosophic realism of Cologne (where both Ogilvie and Athilmer had studied) won toleration alongside the nominalism of Paris.[64] More importantly, the careers of these two men, who

[56] Dunlop, *Bishop Kennedy*, p. 37; Burns, *Basle*, p. 65.

[57] For the background see John Holland Smith, *The Great Schism*, pp. 240–45.

[58] Burns, *Basle*, pp. 56, 62, 64; Dunlop, *Bishop Kennedy*, p. 37; *Chron. Bower*, II. 481.

[59] J. H. Burns, 'The Conciliarist Tradition in Scotland', *S.H.R.*, XLII. 89–104, at 90.   [60] Burns, *Basle*, p. 86.

[61] His whole career is studied by Duncan Shaw, *op. cit.*, *Scot. Church Hist. Soc. Recs.*, XII. 120–35.   [62] J. H. Burns, *op. cit.*, *S.H.R.*, XLII. 89–104, at 96–7.

[63] See *St Andrews Copiale*, pp. 204–9.

[64] J. H. Burns, *op. cit.*, *S.H.R.*, XLII. 89–104, at 91–2, 94; Burns, *Basle*, p. 77; *St Andrews Acta*, I. 48–9.

were still prominent at St Andrews a generation later, illustrate how 'something like a Scottish conciliarist tradition was created' and how conciliarist ideas were 'part of the mental equipment of educated Scots as the Reformation approached'.[65]

The controversies that drew new vigour from the contest between Eugenius and Basel were not merely intellectual and academic. Abbot Bower, who avoided taking sides, stressed the scandal caused by the schism and devoted five chapters of his *Scotichronicon* to an historical account of various schisms since 349 A.D. Despondently he remarked :

> What and how many damages accursed schisms of this sort caused in their time not only to human bodies but to souls it is not of our faculty to evaluate.

When Bower was writing, the contest between the Roman pope and the conciliar pope still continued and, so Bower says, 'still is as if *sub judice*'.[66] It was to continue until 1449. So far as Scotland was concerned the Little Schism of 1439–49 was not complicated by international rivalries ; but internal ones made it more disruptive than the Great Schism of 1378–1418 during which kirk and nation had been fairly united in their adherence to one pope. If some kirkmen stayed neutral (like Abbot Bower) others were staunch conciliarists or papalists. There was no strong figure in the government to impose a definite policy ; and in the kirk itself, after the eclipse of Cameron, there was no recognised leader on either side until Eugenius put his trust in James Kennedy.

One of the last acts of James I had been to thrust his nephew Kennedy into the bishopric of Dunkeld.[67] When Eugenius retrospectively sanctioned this Erastian appointment by a provision of 1 July 1437, he set Kennedy off on a career in which he was to show himself the most distinguished figure in the Scottish kirk of his time. In 1439 Kennedy headed those Scottish ecclesiastics who answered the pope's summons to the council of Ferrara-Florence. He must have witnessed the triumphant spectacle of the reunion of the Greek and Roman churches under Eugenius and, at what must have seemed to some contemporaries the apotheosis of the papacy, committed himself permanently as a loyal supporter of the Roman pope. Kennedy lingered at Florence and received special recognition on 23 September 1439 when Eugenius conferred upon him the abbey of Scone to be held *in*

[65] J. H. Burns, *op. cit.*, *S.H.R.*, XLII. 89–104, at 89; see also Burns, *Basle*, pp. 85–6.

[66] *Chron. Bower*, II. 475–81.   [67] Dunlop, *Bishop Kennedy*, p. 19.

commendam.[68] This early application of a practice that was to become disastrously frequent meant that Kennedy as 'commendator' did not have to perform in person the duties of an abbot, but controlled the abbey's revenues and could use them to supplement those of his bishopric of Dunkeld. Papal favour continued : on the death of Bishop Wardlaw on 9 April 1440 Kennedy was translated from Dunkeld to St Andrews; since he was unable to raise the usual 'common services' of 3,300 gold florins he automatically incurred excommunication but was graciously granted absolution and remission of half the sum.[69].

In Kennedy the papalist party now had a strong leader, and in some meeting of the three estates, probably in May 1441, it was ordained 'that no Scot may go to Basel, adhere to the council, or obey it'.[70] But no sooner had the three estates repudiated Basel and the conciliar pope than there ensued a struggle over conflicting provisions to benefices. Eugenius provided Alexander Lauder to Dunkeld, Thomas Tulloch to Ross, Ingeram Lindsay to Aberdeen, and probably 'John Hectoris' to the Isles; Felix provided Thomas Livingston (who had been deprived of his abbey of Dundrennan by Eugenius) to Dunkeld, Andrew Munro to Ross, and the sixteen-year-old James Douglas, son of James the Gross, to Aberdeen.[71] When a provincial council of the Scottish kirk met in July 1442 the bishops who had been provided by Eugenius deprived and excommunicated those who had been provided by Felix. James the Gross attended this council, probably leading with him his son (the supposed Bishop of Aberdeen) and William Croyser; they proclaimed their adherence to Basel and began to issue counter-deprivations, whereupon 'certain prelates fled by night'.[72]

On 31 August 1442 Earl James wrote to Basel to report his achievements, and in October Croyser re-appeared at Basel and joined with Thomas Livingston in persuading the council to support Douglas. On the way home, however, the archdeacon was captured by bandits and for a time was held in prison in Strassburg.[73] Earl James was thus deprived of his most useful agent. Meanwhile Eu-

[68] Burns, *Basle*, pp. 62, 64.   [69] Dunlop, *Bishop Kennedy*, pp. 39–41.

[70] See R. K. Hannay, 'A Letter to Scotland from the Council of Basel', *S.H.R.*, xx. 49–57, at 54.

[71] Dunlop, *Bishop Kennedy*, pp. 40–2; Dowden, *Bishops*, p. 289; Burns, *Basle*, p. 73.

[72] *St Andrews Copiale*, pp. 322–3.

[73] Burns, *Basle*, p. 79; Dunlop, *Bishop Kennedy*, p. 45; R. K. Hannay, *op. cit.*, *S.H.R.*, xx. 49–57, at 54.

genius tried to dispossess Croyser of his two archdeaconries and to provide two of his own nominees. In so doing the pope fell out of step with Bishop Kennedy, who collated another two nominees. One of the resulting five contestants was Patrick Home, a 'ner kynnesman' of Sir Alexander Home of Dunglass. Patrick reported that he could not visit his archdeaconry save with a mighty band of armed men.[74]

The Homes were concerned not only with the archdeaconry of Teviotdale but with the perennial problem of the priory of Coldingham. So many vested interests were involved that Coldingham was at the root of much of the trouble that occurred in south-east Scotland throughout the fifteenth century. In 1442 there were difficulties not only over the appointment of a prior,[75] but concerning the bailiary or justiciarship of Coldingham. Such an office conferred administrative control and temporal jurisdiction over the lands of a religious house and was highly coveted. Moreover, in the power vacuum left in the region by the forfeiture of the Earls of March in 1435 there was a struggle between the local baronial families of the Hepburns and Homes. Even the Homes were divided: the bailiary was coveted both by Sir Alexander Home of Dunglass and his nephew, Sir David Home of Wedderburn (supported by Sir Adam Hepburn of Hailes, who was feudal superior of both). On 20 May 1442, after an interchange of views between the Prior of Durham and the Scottish council, it was settled that Sir Alexander Home should have the bailiary for life. Then James the Gross stirred up the issue anew. As justiciar south of Forth he asserted that the decision of the king's 'partiale consale' was 'of na strenth na vertu'. With this encouragement Sir David Home seized Coldingham and drove out the prior. When the latter managed to return he confirmed Sir Alexander Home in the office of bailie, and allegedly allowed him to use the priory as a fortalice garrisoned by Border reivers who stole more than two thousand sheep from Sir David Home and Sir Adam Hepburn. The Earl of Angus mediated: Sir David was compensated for his losses by a decreet arbitral on 16 January 1444 and the two Homes were reconciled.[76]

The meddling of James the Gross in the Coldingham dispute was probably one of his last interventions in ecclesiastical politics: he is said to have died at Abercorn on 25 March 1443.[77] His son and heir,

[74] Dunlop, *Bishop Kennedy*, p. 47.   [75] *Ibid.*, pp. 49–50.
[76] *Ibid.*, pp. 51–4.
[77] *Scots Peerage*, III. 173. He 'deceissit in Abercorn the thrid zeir efter hᵉ was maid earle' (Pitscottie, *Historie*, I. 47).

William, the new eighth Earl of Douglas, rapidly concluded that the council of Basel and its pope were doomed to failure: their main support came from the universities, still conciliarist in outlook; but the secular rulers stood aloof. After May 1443 the council even discontinued its solemn sessions at Basel.[78] In Scotland it became clear that the Black Douglases could no longer be relied upon to support the conciliarists. The result was probably seen in a general council at Stirling on 4 November 1443, when it was ordained that recognition should be given only to 'actis of generale and provinciall consalys publicit and notifiit of befor and proclamit be the kingis autorite'. It was also ordained that 'ferme and fast obedieince be kepit till our haly fadir the Pape Eugenne' and that 'na persone, spirituale na temporal, change the said obedience quhil the king and the realm ordane and decrete therapone'.[79] The kirk, unable to control itself, was being controlled by the state. If the proceedings of the general council of November 1443 represented 'an ecclesiastical victory for the Bishop of St Andrews'[80] it was perhaps a hollow one; and the restoration of Eugenius's authority was scarcely complete when his death on 23 February 1447 once more raised the hopes of the adherents of Felix V. Although no time was lost in electing Nicholas V as Eugenius's successor Felix hoped to take advantage of the situation by seizing the initiative in Scotland, where Bishop Cameron had died on 24 December 1446. This reopened the possibility of manoeuvre within the Scottish episcopate. On 20 March 1447 Felix appointed the conciliarist Thomas Livingston as his legate to Scotland.[81] But the mission was in vain : Livingston speedily returned to the continent to witness the bargaining that took place as the end approached for Felix V and the council of Basel. In June 1448 the council was obliged to leave Basel and settle at Lausanne. There, on 7 April 1449, Felix V abdicated. On 18 April the council 'elected' Nicholas V and thus ended the schism.[82]

Both the council and Felix had made the most of their nuisance value and obtained generous terms from the victorious side. Livingston and the versatile William Croyser left the commends in Savoy and the Lyonnais formerly granted them by Felix, and made their way back to Scotland where 'a genuine spirit of reconciliation does seem to have prevailed'.[83] Other prominent Scottish conciliarists,

[78] John Holland Smith, *The Great Schism*, p. 246; Burns, *Basle*, p. 81.
[79] *A.P.S.*, II. 33.
[80] Dunlop, *Bishop Kennedy*, p. 307, n. 4.   [81] Burns, *Basle*, pp. 83–4.
[82] *Ibid.*, p. 84.   [83] *Ibid.*, pp. 83, 84, 85.

thanks to Bishop Kennedy, found academic openings in the university of St Andrews. With the ending of the ten-year schism the Scottish kirk was restored to as much harmony as could be expected.

The gradual restoration of order within the kirk was, however, accompanied, and sometimes interrupted, by flagrant political disorder. Through his marriage the new eighth Earl of Douglas had re-united the whole of the Black Douglas territories with the exception of Annandale and the elusive lands in France; and the earl and his kin had by no means lost hope of recovering these from the Scottish and French crown respectively.[84] Before long, Earl William was building up a party to take over the government, which was increasingly distracted by continuing lawlessness [85] and rivalry between the Crichtons and the Livingstons. Despite Pitscottie's rambling tale of repeated squabbles and reconciliations between these two factions, the members of both families had continued to figure side by side in the witness lists of royal charters until 8 February 1443, after which a gap in the records occurs.[86] Up to at least that date the two families kept up the appearance of joint participation in government. Thereafter, however, they became open foes, probably by the instigation of Earl William of Douglas, who wished to gain power by using the Livingstons against the Crichtons.

The way for a Douglas-Livingston alliance had been cleared on 16 August 1443 when Sir Alexander Livingston of Callendar purged himself by oath, in the presence of Bishop Kennedy and three other bishops, 'of having given any counsel, assistance or consent to the slaughter of Sir Malcolm Fleming' at the Black Dinner.[87] The Livingstons could now be respectably associated under Earl William in an alliance that also numbered the Flemings, the Hamiltons, and at first, the Kennedies, including the Bishop of St Andrews. Bishop Kennedy's interest in the fortunes of his family can be seen in a transaction concluded on 2 July 1444 'at Cascyllis, near the great garden thereof', when he witnessed letters of retinue by which Sir John Kennedy of Blaucharne and his son and heir 'became men for the term of ten years to Gilbert Kennedy, Lord of Dunure'; Gilbert was to pay twenty marks a year to Sir John, and a further ten marks for his homage and service; 'and because the said sum of ten marks seemed

[84] See a document of 29 October 1445 concerning Annandale cited in *Scots Peerage*, III. 172. For Touraine see Fraser, *Douglas*, I. 396–7, 462–3.

[85] *Chron. Auchinleck*, 4–5, 35; Pitscottie, *Historie*, I. 48–9; Dunlop, *Bishop Kennedy*, p. 56 and n. 3.   [86] *R.M.S.*, II. 49–62.

[87] Dunlop, *Bishop Kennedy*, p. 34, n. 3.

to be too small, the Bishop of St Andrews bound himself to pay to him two marks in addition'.[88] It can hardly be taken for granted that 'Kennedy's eyes were fixed on far horizons while the faction leaders were rending Scotland with their feuds'.[89] The advancement of Douglas, who by July 1444 seems to have been styled lieutenant-general,[90] was accompanied by the attempted demotion of Crichton. Claiming to be acting 'on behalf of the king' the two custumars of Edinburgh (one of them a Livingston) formally ordered Crichton to proceed no further with some 'process' which was being held about the lands of Castlelaw. They also cited him to answer before the king for some alleged default, and saw to it that three notarial instruments were drawn up as evidence that the inhibition and summons had been duly served.[91] Probably because Crichton did not obey this summons, the chamberlain, Sir John Forrester of Corstorphine, was instructed to proceed with distraint.[92] He required the help of Douglas, who was presumably acting as the king's lieutenant-general. On 20 August 1444 [93] the earl came with an armed host 'on the king's behalf' to the tower-house of Barnton on the outskirts of Edinburgh and called for its surrender. Barnton was the residence of Sir George Crichton, admiral of Scotland, sheriff of Linlithgow, and cousin of the chancellor, and its inmates put up some defence before capitulating. Thereupon Douglas saw to it that this Crichton stronghold was 'cassin doun to the groun'. But despite Douglas's initial success Sir William Crichton remained secure in Edinburgh Castle and was even able to take the offensive : he and his adherents ravaged the Forrester lands of Corstorphine, while Sir George Crichton attacked Earl William's lands near Linlithgow.[94] The downfall of the Crichtons was not going to be easily accomplished, even by the Black Douglas and his allies.

Their next move was to arrange the holding of a general council at Stirling at the end of October 1444 [95] to denounce the Crichtons as rebels. The intensity of political activity may be gauged from the

---

[88] *Cassillis Charters*, cited in Dunlop, *Bishop Kennedy*, p. 67.   [89] *Ibid.*

[90] Boece, *History*, p. 364. Douglas is probably the figure who appears in a joint petition of the king and lieutenant-general to the pope on 8 July 1444 (Dunlop, *Bishop Kennedy*, p. 409).

[91] *E.R.*, v. lxxxiv, 146, 147.   [92] Pitscottie, *Historie*, I. 52–3.

[93] The Auchinleck chronicler (*Chron. Auchinleck*, pp. 5, 36) gives the date as 20 August 1443. It is clear, however, that he is mistaken in the year.

[94] *Ibid.*, pp. 5–6, 36–7; Pitscottie, *Historie*, I. 53.

[95] No precise reference to this assembly is given in surviving records; and the Auchinleck chronicler has introduced a further complication by amalgamating this general council with the one that took place in Stirling exactly a year earlier (*Chron. Auchinleck*, pp. 5, 36).

number of royal charters (nearly all witnessed by the Livingstons) that
were issued at Stirling between 25 October and 4 November 1444 [96]
in an attempt to consolidate opposition against the Crichtons. The
formation of a grand coalition which included Sir Robert Erskine,
temporarily styled Earl of Mar,[97] had apparently royal sanction. For
on 16 October 1444 James II was fourteen years old and it could be
held that he was no longer under tutelage : a charter of 13 November
1444 even stated that alienations of crown rights had been revoked
by the king 'on his majority at the last general council at Stirling'.[98] If
Douglas had acted rashly in his unsuccessful attack on the Crichtons
in the summer of 1444 he had certainly learned to act more deliberately by the autumn, when the general council 'blewe out on Schir
William of Crechtoun'.[99]

But the blast of a horn and a sentence of outlawry against the
Crichtons did not bring easy victory to the Black Douglases and
Livingstons, who had meanwhile lost the support of the influential
Bishop Kennedy. Kennedy, who had hitherto been associated with
Douglas, is reputed to have been made chanccllor in place of Crichton, presumably in May or June 1444, but to have resigned within a
few weeks, after which the post certainly went to James Bruce, Bishop
of Dunkeld.[100] The growing importance of James Bruce may have
been resented by Kennedy; and it was significant that even Bishop
Cameron had been brought from retirement to serve as an auditor of
exchequer in June 1444;[101] it was becoming evident that the Douglases and Livingstons were not disposed to put all their ecclesiastical
eggs in the basket of the Bishop of St Andrews. It was even arranged
that the king should write to the pope (and persuade the King of
France to do likewise) for a revocation of Kennedy's commend of
Scone. In this case, however, Eugenius upheld Kennedy.[102] Even
before the bishop became an open foe of the Black Douglases and the
Livingstons, he reputedly joined with James Douglas, Earl of Angus,
in giving underhand aid to the Crichtons during the skirmishing

[96] *R.M.S.*, ii. Nos. 274–82.   [97] *Ibid.*, No. 279.
[98] Dunlop, *Bishop Kennedy*, p. 308, n. 1.
[99] Despite the statement of the Auchinleck chronicler (*Chron. Auchinleck*,
pp. 5, 36), it was undoubtedly this general council of 1444, not the general council
of 1443, that outlawed the Crichtons.
[100] *H.B.C.*, p. 175.   [101] *E.R.*, v. 143.
[102] Dunlop, *Bishop Kennedy*, p. 71. Later the commend of Scone was replaced by that of the priory of Pittenweem. John Major sensibly remarked :
'Two points in this man's conduct I cannot bring myself to praise—to wit, that
along with such a bishopric he should have held a benefice *in commendam*; . . .
nor do I approve the costliness of his tomb' (*History*, pp. 388–9).

that took place before the general council met at Stirling in the late autumn of 1444.[103] The Red Douglas had grievances of his own against the ruling faction.[104] So also had the queen mother, whose husband, the Black Knight of Lorne, was banished 'because he spake sumtymes raschlie that the realme was evill gydit, quhilk redounded to the defamation of the Earle of Douglas'.[105] Meanwhile the Crichtons still held Edinburgh Castle despite the sentence of outlawry passed against them in the general council. In all this there were the makings of an opposition party for Bishop Kennedy to lead. On 17 November 1444, just after the disbandment of the general council at Stirling, Kennedy and the queen mother, together with their adherents, addressed letters of inhibition to the magistrates of Aberdeen (and probably to those of other burghs) forbidding any payment of revenue 'to tha persownis that nu has the kyng in governance'. The magistrates cautiously resolved to take no action but wait and see 'qwat ordenance war made thairapon be the thre estattis'.[106]

The Black Douglases and Livingstons, who had, for their own ends, just publicised the king's 'majority' in the general council, speedily responded to the challenge offered to their authority : by 29 November 1444 they had conducted James to take part in besieging and capturing Methven Castle,[107] which was held by some member of the opposition. Then came a direct attack upon Kennedy himself. There was 'ane richt gret herschipe [ravaging] maid in Fyff be thir personis, the Erll of Crawfurd, James of Livingstoun . . ., kepar to the king and capitane of Strivling, the Ogilveis all, Robert Reach [Robertson of Struan], the lord of Kadyoch [Sir James Hamilton of Cadzow] and uthir syndry'.[108] The raiders harried 'nocht onlie the bischopis landis bot also the haill landis adjacent thairto, and brocht great pryssis of goodis out of Fyfe unto Angus'. Douglas is said to have urged his accomplices to seize Kennedy and imprison him in irons, but the bishop discreetly 'committit himself in saifgaird'— probably in St Andrews Castle—'thinkand it become him nocht to be ane fichter'.[109]

Having daunted Bishop Kennedy the ruling faction summoned

---

103 Godscroft, *Douglas and Angus*, p. 167.
104 Dunlop, *Bishop Kennedy*, p. 62.   105 Pitscottie, *Historie*, I. 57.
106 *Aberdeen Council Register*, I. 399.
107 A royal charter was dated at Methven on 29 November 1444 (*R.M.S.*, II. No. 283). For allusions to the siege and the king's presence at it see *E.R.*, v. 186, 187, 230.
108 *Chron. Auchinleck*, pp. 7–8, 38–9; *E.R.*, v. lxiii.
109 Pitscottie, *Historie*, I. 53–4.

a parliament to Perth, where it met on 14 June 1445. By 28 June, however, it was transacting business in Edinburgh, whither it had been prorogued [110] 'becaus of the sege that was liand about the castell on the kingis behalf'.[111] Sir William Crichton yielded up the castle on terms that testified to the strength of his own position : far from being disgraced he at once appeared in the king's council alongside Douglas and the Livingstons.[112] The accounts presented when the exchequer audit opened at Edinburgh on 5 July 1445 show that Crichton had his former allowance of 700 marks increased to £700, of which he received £233 6s. 8d. (350 marks) as payment for part of the year. In the following audit Crichton was paid £700 towards the total due to him for that and the previous year, amounting in all to £933 6s. 8d.[113]

It was during the session of parliament at Edinburgh that Douglas's adherents were rewarded for their patriotic services. On 28 June 1445 Sir James Hamilton of Cadzow was confirmed in all his lands, which were created a 'true, free and united lordship'—the lordship of Hamilton—while Sir James was elevated to the heritable title of lord of parliament.[114] This grant provides the first clear proof that the word 'lord', previously used loosely of any baron, was now being used as a specific and heritable title of rank, the third in the hierarchy headed by duke and earl. Among the witnesses to the grant were five other persons—Campbell, Graham, Somerville, Maxwell and Montgomery—who had previously been elevated to this new rank and were also described as lords of parliament. Moreover two new earldoms seem to have been created by charter at this parliament : Sir Alexander Seton of Gordon and Huntly, who was soon to use Gordon, rather than Seton, as his family name, was styled Earl of Huntly; at the same time Hugh Douglas appeared as Earl of Ormond, a title that took its name from a hill in the lands of Ardmannoch in the Black Isle. Another Douglas brother, Archibald, emerged at the same time as Earl of Moray in respect of his wife's lands as coheiress of the last Dunbar earl.[115] Others saw the waning of their hopes. James, Earl of Angus, failed to compear to answer for 'cryme committit til his majeste and rebellione'; on 1 July 1445 all the lands and goods of the Red Douglas were declared escheated unless he should come within a year and a day to 'undirgang the law'.[116] Simi-

[110] A.P.S., II. 33, 59. [111] Chron. Auchinleck, pp. 6–7, 37.
[112] Pitscottie, Historie, I. 57; Dunlop, Bishop Kennedy, p. 63.
[113] E.R., v. 180, 221. [114] A.P.S., II. 59.
[115] Ibid.; E.R., v. lix, lxi. [116] A.P.S., II. 59–60.

lar sentence was passed against the queen mother's husband, Sir James Stewart of Lorne.[117]

Another striking feature of the 1445 parliament was that it was presented with a sort of ultimatum on behalf of 'the prelates and clergy of all Scotland'.[118] John Winchester, Bishop of Moray, acted as their procurator and approached John Cranach, Bishop of Brechin, conservator of the privileges of the Scottish kirk, asking for an official notarial transumpt to be made of two papal bulls. An official deputation of thirty-six representatives of the three estates apparently raised no objection. The first bull, once issued by Gregory XI, gave papal approval to the charters of David II and Robert II that renounced the right to seize the movables of bishops on their death, and, by implication, granted them the right of testament.[119] In return, however, the prelates and clergy were expected to co-operate with the ruling faction. The second bull that was publicised was one of Martin V that detailed the process of deprivation against Bishop Finlay of Argyll by reason of his rebellion against James I.[120] There was no point in raking up this old affair unless there was talk of depriving some present bishop—and the obvious candidate was Bishop Kennedy, who does not seem to have attended the Edinburgh parliament and was probably licking his wounds in St Andrews Castle. There seems no ground for the view that Kennedy influenced the parliament of 1445, even by 'indirect means'.[121] If the publicity given to Martin V's bull was intended as a threat to Kennedy there were evidently powerful forces ready to back it up : the transumpt of the two bulls on 28 June 1445 was witnessed by Chancellor Bruce, Bishop of Dunkeld, three other bishops, nine abbots, eleven barons and six commissioners of the burghs—thirty in all, probably representing a majority of the deputation of thirty-six delegated by the three estates.[122] Nor is there any sign that the deputation had been 'packed' : it included no Douglas and only one Livingston, a commissioner for Edinburgh.

Since the herschip of Fife by his enemies Bishop Kennedy had 'held himself verie quyit, awaitand upoun ane better fortoune'.[123] His former political allies had deserted or disappeared. Crichton had made his peace. Angus soon followed after his barony of North Ber-

[117] Pinkerton, *History*, I. 477, appendix xiv.

[118] *Brechin Registrum*, I. 98.

[119] *Ibid.*, pp. 99–100. For the bishops' rights of testament see G. Donaldson, *op. cit.*, *S.H.R.*, XLV. 27–35.   [120] *Brechin Registrum*, I. 100–2.

[121] Dunlop, *Bishop Kennedy*, pp. 64, 609.

[122] *Brechin Registrum*, I. 103.   [123] Pitscottie, *Historie*, I. 66.

wick had been plundered.[124] The queen mother, who had taken refuge in Dunbar Castle, then in the custody of Sir Adam Hepburn of Hailes,[125] died there on 15 July 1445 while the castle was under siege.[126] Her second husband, the Black Knight of Lorne, soon applied for an English safe-conduct[127] and went into exile, while Sir Adam Hepburn surrendered Dunbar Castle. Kennedy's attempt at a *coup d'état* had completely collapsed; and he himself was left in isolation. Menaced with the same fate as the late Bishop Finlay, Kennedy escaped it by reason of a dramatic coincidence that enhanced the reputation of his spiritual powers. Some months earlier, when his lands in Fife were being harried by his foes, the bishop had summoned the Earl of Crawford before the spiritual court and there 'led upoun him ane sentance of curssing for his contemptioun of the censouris of hallie kirk'.[128] But excommunication was losing its terrors through familiarity. Thus although Kennedy 'cursit solempnitlie with myter and staf, buke and candill, contynually a yer'[129] the Earl of Crawford paid no heed. What seemed to be the obvious sequel came in the shape of a deadly conflict between the Lindsays and the Ogilvies, two great families that had hitherto been closely allied, and which, only a year previously, had jointly taken part in the raid upon Kennedy's episcopal lands.

The origin of the quarrel between the Lindsays and Ogilvies was much the same as that involving the Homes and Hepburns and the priory of Coldingham: Sir Alexander Lindsay, Master of Crawford, had been appointed bailie or justiciar of the regality of Arbroath but had been displaced by Sir Alexander Ogilvy of Inverquharity.[130] The Hamiltons supported the Lindsays; and the Earl of Huntly, a chance guest of the Ogilvies, felt constrained to fight for them until such time as the processes of digestion had rid him of obligations towards his hosts. On 23 January 1446 the armed bands of both sides marched to Arbroath. The Earl of Crawford, whose wife was an Ogilvy, heard of the impending affray and rode from Dundee to try to make peace. One of the Ogilvies mistook either the earl's identity or his inten-

[124] Fraser, *Douglas*, II. 39; III. 427; Godscroft, *Douglas and Angus*, p. 210; *E.R.*, v. 194.

[125] On the seizure of the earldom of March in 1434–35 James I had entrusted the castle to Hepburn's keeping (*E.R.*, IV. 620). In 1444 he was described as steward of the earldom (Dunlop, *Bishop Kennedy*, p. 75, n. 2).

[126] *Chron. Auchinleck*, pp. 7, 38. In an exchequer account presented at Edinburgh on 17 July 1445 she is described as 'the late queen' (*E.R.*, v. 196).

[127] *Rot. Scot.*, II. 327, 331, 347.   [128] Pitscottie, *Historie*, I. 54.

[129] *Chron. Auchinleck*, pp. 8, 39.   [130] Pitscottie, *Historie*, I. 54.

tions and speared him. The slaying of the earl made battle inevitable. The Ogilvies, who had the worse of it, suffered heavy losses and had to flee as best they could. For four days the corpse of the excommunicated Earl of Crawford lay unburied until Kennedy sent the prior of St Andrews to remove the curse.[131] The violent and dramatic death of the third Earl of Crawford seemed to demonstrate that God was on the side of Bishop Kennedy—not that this unduly daunted Sir Alexander Lindsay, the new fourth Earl of Crawford, whose long beard earned him the name of 'Earl Beardie' and whose other qualities brought him the alternative name of 'the Tiger Earl'.[132] Under his leadership the Lindsays 'held the Ogilvyis at gret subjectioun, and tuke thair gudis and distroyit thair placis'.[133] Gradually, however, royal power was reasserted and the passions of the various factions began temporarily to cool. Even the Hepburns and Homes who had quarrelled over the spoils of Coldingham sought in 1449 to settle their differences by a double marriage alliance.[134]

The last years of the decade not only saw more settled conditions in kirk and state but brief return to normal conditions in Anglo-Scottish relations—open hostility. The mutual toleration that had resulted from truces concluded in 1438 and 1444 ended, even though the latter truce was valid until 1454.[135] The reasons for a brief eruption of hostilities are obscure, though obviously connected with the internal politics of England. There the mutual harassment of Cardinal Beaufort and Humphrey, Duke of Gloucester, had terminated with the death of both in 1447. Although Henry VI had come of age he had already shown himself incapable of ruling effectively in person. By 1448 ascendancy in the English council had passed to William de la Pole, newly created Duke of Suffolk. This stimulated the growth of an opposition, as yet latent, headed by Richard, Duke of York.[136] While the two parties, with their ramifications throughout all England, jockeyed for power, military prestige was a valuable commodity, and the Percies, who held the wardenship of the English East March, and were later to prove Lancastrian, were at loggerheads with the Nevilles, who held the wardenship of the West March and were later to prove Yorkist.[137] Provocation from the Scots was

---

[131] *Ibid.*, 54–5; *Chron. Auchinleck*, pp. 7–8, 38–9.
[132] *Scots Peerage*, III. 21.   [133] *Chron. Auchinleck*, pp. 7, 38.
[134] Dunlop, *Bishop Kennedy*, p. 77.
[135] *Rot. Scot.*, II. 306; *Cal. Docs. Scot.*, IV. No. 1167.
[136] E. F. Jacob, *The Fifteenth Century*, pp. 481, 487, 489.
[137] R. L. Storey, *op. cit.*, *E.H.R.*, LXXII. 593–609, at 607.

not lacking. In reprisal an English force under the Earl of Northumberland forded the Solway, encamped by the water of Sark, and began to raid Annandale. On the following day, 23 October 1448, the invaders were routed by a Scottish force under Hugh Douglas, Earl of Ormond.[138]

In preparation for the English retaliation that was to be expected, the Earl of Douglas summoned the lords, freeholders, and 'eldest Bordouraris' to meet in a warden court at the collegiate kirk of Lincluden on 18 December 1448. There they were put on oath to testify what statutes, ordinances and customs had been used on the Marches in the days of 'Blak Archibald of Douglas' (Archibald the Grim) so that all might be recorded.[139] Among the points that Earl William approved as 'rycht speidful and proffitabil to the Bordouraris' were some which sought to maintain the cohesion and discipline of the Scottish forces, and others which arranged that ten beacon fires were to be set up on the hills of Annandale and another nine on those of Nithsdale; whenever the beacons were set ablaze all men were to assemble in a host for the defence of the countryside. These precautionary measures were soon put to the test: in the early summer of 1449 the English burned Dunbar and Dumfries and the Scots burned Alnwick and Warkworth,[140] after which a truce was concluded on 15 November.[141]

Meanwhile the Anglo-French truce had given way to renewed warfare in France. By the end of October 1449 Rouen had fallen to the French.[142] As Charles VII entered the city he was attended by the *garde écossaise*, an élite corps of Scots guardsmen which had been formed in 1445 as the senior company of the household troops of the French monarchy.[143] The days were past when huge contingents of Scotsmen fought alongside the French armies, but the Scottish guard continued to provide some openings for Scots of gentle blood who were attracted to the well-paid service of the French king. There were also individual adventurers: in the campaign of Normandy William Monypenny won his knighthood;[144] for many years thereafter he was to be employed on Franco-Scottish diplomatic missions. Apart from the many personal connections that drew France and

---

[138] *Chron. Auchinleck*, pp. 18, 40; Pitscottie, *Historie*, I. 73–6.

[139] 'The Statutis and Use of Merchis in Tym of Were' (*A.P.S.*, I. 714–6).

[140] *Chron. Auchinleck*, pp. 27, 39. Dr A. I. Dunlop points out (*Bishop Kennedy*, p. 104, n. 3) that 'the editor has assigned these events to the year 1448, but the original gives the year as 1449'. [141] *Rot. Scot.*, II. 334–6.

[142] E. F. Jacob, *The Fifteenth Century*, pp. 489, 491.

[143] W. Forbes Leith, *The Scots Men-at-Arms and Life-guards in France*, I. 58–9. [144] Francisque-Michel, *Les Ecossais en France*, I. 203.

Scotland together there remained strategic reasons for the continuance of the Auld Alliance : Charles VII desired (and achieved) the recovery of Normandy and Gascony; James II was to show himself eager to recover Berwick and Roxburgh. English troops deployed in Normandy (at a cost of £20,000 annually in time of war)[145] could not be deployed on the Borders; nor could the troops on the Borders (whose maintenance in the garrison of Berwick alone cost £5,200 in time of war)[146] be deployed in Normandy. To synchronise efforts in warfare and diplomacy against the distracted and financially embarrassed English the Franco-Scottish alliance was renewed at Tours on 31 December 1448.[147]

This was preceded and followed by intensive matrimonial diplomacy : James I had left six daughters, as well as his son and heir, all of whose marriages could be used to confirm the good will of various potentates towards Scotland and France. The process had started with the marriage of James II's sister Margaret to the dauphin in 1436. In 1442 Isabella (or Elizabeth) had married Francis, Duke of Brittany. In 1444 Mary had married Wolfaert van Borselen, son of the Lord of Campvere (or Veere) in Zealand. At the end of the same year Annabella was betrothed to Count Louis of Geneva. In 1445 the remaining two sisters, Eleanor and Joan, had been sent to France, only to find that the death of the dauphiness had coincided with their arrival. Escaping the prospect of a particularly dubious match with the dauphin, Eleanor married Sigismund, Duke of Austria, in 1449. Joan, 'the dumb lady', and Annabella, whose betrothal to the count of Geneva was eventually broken off, were to come home in 1458 to find husbands in Scotland.[148] Meanwhile, however, the marriages, or prospective marriages, of James II's sisters gave Scottish diplomacy a wider scope than it had ever before enjoyed : those who were, for the time being, friends of France, had at least a nodding acquaintance with France's poor but warlike ally.

Thus the question of the marriage of James II himself was one that aroused wide interest on the continent. The Scots, with a view to their commercial interests in the Low Countries, desired a match with a suitable princess of the house of Burgundy, Guelders or Cleves. On 6 September 1448 Philip the Good, Duke of Burgundy, was empowered by Duke Arnold of Guelders to treat of a marriage be-

---

[145] E. F. Jacob, *The Fifteenth Century*, p. 488.
[146] *Cal. Docs. Scot.*, IV. No. 1195.   [147] Dunlop, *Bishop Kennedy*, p. 94.
[148] *Ibid.*, pp. 61, 66, 84, 88–9; *E.R.*, v. lxii, lxix, lxx.

tween the latter's daughter (Philip's niece) and the Scottish king.[149] With the concurrence of Charles VII Scottish ambassadors made treaties with Burgundy and Guelders on 1 April 1449:[150] Philip of Burgundy was to be responsible for his niece's dowry of sixty thousand crowns, to be paid in two years. The clause in the treaty that provided for perpetual friendship and alliance between Scotland and Burgundy[151] was one that allowed Scottish merchants a favourable status in all the Burgundian dominions. Duke Philip had also undertaken to send his niece to Scotland at his own expense. The expected demonstration of magnificence was forthcoming: Mary of Guelders was escorted to Scotland by Netherlandish potentates in a well-armed fleet of fourteen vessels.[152] On 3 July 1449 the marriage ceremony took place in Holyrood Abbey, and the new queen was crowned shortly afterwards.[153]

The marriage of the nineteen-year-old king signalised his entry into politics. James II had been better trained to play his part than most recent Scottish kings. Unlike Robert I, Robert II or Robert III, he had grown up not in expectation of the crown but in possession of it. Unlike David II and James I he had spent the whole of his youth in Scotland and was thoroughly familiar with the prevailing conditions. A surviving portrait, commissioned by an Austrian visitor to James's court, shows, in what is probably the earliest reasonably authentic likeness of a Scottish king, a slim young man fashionably dressed in pointed shoes, long hose, large hat, and tunic with padded shoulders.[154] Although the king's expression seems innocently self-assured the artist suggests darker aspects: James's hands are on the hilt of the dagger at his waist; and in the colouring of his face there is a hint of the sinister fiery birthmark described by François Villon in his poem listing the worthies who had departed this life like the snows of yesteryear. It can hardly be taken for granted that 'subtle callousness and sustained duplicity . . . were foreign to the nature' of James II.[155]

The first to feel the weight of revived royal power were the Liv-

---

[149] J. H. Baxter, 'The Marriage of James II', *S.H.R.*, xxv. 69–72, at 71.

[150] Dunlop, *Bishop Kennedy*, p. 100.

[151] P. F. Tytler, *History*, I. pt. ii, 144.

[152] Pitscottie, *Historie*, I. 58–9; *Chron. Auchinleck*, pp. 24–5, 41.

[153] *Chron. Auchinleck*, pp. 25, 41; *Extracta*, p. 238 and n.; *Chron Bower*, II. 515; *E.R.*, v. lxxvii–lxxviii.

[154] The likeness is reproduced in Dunlop, *Bishop Kennedy*, facing p. 112.

[155] *Ibid.*, p. 106, n. 3.

ingstons. What made their faction all too vulnerable was its lack of a strong territorial base on which traditional loyalties might have been grounded : its strength was derived not from land but from crown offices. Sir Alexander Livingston of Callendar, head of the tribe, was justiciar. His eldest son and heir, James, was keeper of Stirling Castle, and, as late as May 1448, was 'keeper of the royal person'; in the summer of 1448 he also became chamberlain. A younger brother, Alexander, was captain of Methven Castle, while Robert of Callendar had custody of Dumbarton and Dunoon, and John Livingston was captain of Doune. The post of comptroller, held by Henry Livingston between 1442 and 1444, had by 1448 gone to Robert Livingston 'of Linlithgow', a cousin of Sir Alexander. Robert, who was 'probably the most considerable merchant in Linlithgow', had been a custumar of the burgh and master of works at Linlithgow Palace since the previous reign.[156] As comptroller he was intimately concerned with the very considerable finances of the royal household.[157] While it is not impossible that he engaged in peculation this can hardly be proved from surviving records; nor is it known to have been brought as a charge against him. Nonetheless the comptroller had evidently become wealthy enough to loan the king £930, which James was committed to repay on 1 April 1450 out of the instalment of the queen's dowry that was expected from the Duke of Burgundy. It must have been a tantalising consideration that forfeiture of the comptroller would save repayment of a large debt.[158]

For although there is insufficient material for an estimate of the financial position of the crown at this time, the indications are that more than the usual stringency prevailed. The customs accounts of fourteen burghs for the period July 1445–July 1446 showed gross receipts of about £4,360 but, after payments made by the custumars, there was a net deficit of about £700;[159] for the period September 1448–July 1449 there was a similar deficit of about £800.[160] And there remained the embarrassing problem of assigning the queen's dower lands for the maintenance of her own establishment: by the terms of the marriage contract James had bound himself to bestow on Mary of Guelders the enormous annual income of ten thousand French *écus* (evidently equivalent to £5,000 Scots [161]). It was probably financial desperation that led the king to attack the Livingstons,

[156] *E.R.*, v. lxxx, n. 4.
[157] See *ibid.*, 312–3, 346.
[158] Dunlop, *Bishop Kennedy*, p. 109.
[159] *E.R.*, v. 215–35.
[160] *Ibid.*, 336–48.
[161] Dunlop, *Bishop Kennedy*, p. 108, n. 4; *A.P.S.*, ii. 60–1, 66–7.

knowing full well that in some quarters their downfall would not be unwelcome.

Possibly, however, a real political issue was involved—one that connected the house of Callendar with that of the Isles. Alexander, Earl of Ross and Lord of the Isles, had died early in May 1449, leaving as his successor his son John, who was scarcely fifteen years of age.[162] The Livingstons aimed high when they arranged that the young earl should be contracted to marry Elizabeth, daughter of James Livingston, the chamberlain. If the king hoped to forestall a Livingston-MacDonald match he was too late : just before the Livingstons were arrested on 23 September 1449 the chamberlain's daughter escaped from Dumbarton to Kintyre and afterwards married the Earl of Ross.[163]

Meanwhile those who had been arrested were brought for trial before a parliament that opened in the tolbooth of Edinburgh on 19 January 1450.[164] It appears that they were accused of 'crimes committit agaynis the king or again [against] his derrest moder'.[165] The fact that James was harking back to the early days of the minority suggests that no more recent crime could reasonably be imputed to the disgraced faction. Lest impartial justice should prevail in parliament, a statute was passed which ordained that no man should rebel against the king's person or his authority; it was in this statute that mention was made of crimes committed against the king and the late queen, crimes for which those responsible were being brought to justice. The same statute gave due warning that '. . . gif it happynis ony man til assist, in rede[advice], confort, consal, or mayntenance, to thai that ar justifiit be the king in this present parliament, or sal happyn to be justifiit in tym cummyn . . . he sal be punyst in sic lik maner as the principale trespassouris'.[166] In other words, if anyone spoke in defence of the Livingstons he was to be reckoned a traitor. The opportunity was taken to pass another ordinance that extended the traditional definition of treason given in *Regiam Majestatem*.[167] On 21 January, the third day of parliament, Robert Livingston (the comptroller) and Alexander Livingston, a younger son of the Knight of Callendar, were suspended from the gallows and beheaded on the castle hill. Only two executions took place, although all the accused suffered the forfeiture of their lands and goods, and some of them, including Sir

---

[162] *E.R.*, v. xci, n. 1; xcii; *Highland Papers*, I. 47.
[163] *Chron. Auchinleck*, pp. 24–6, 41–3.
[164] *A.P.S.*, II. 33.   [165] *Ibid.*, 35, c. 3.   [166] *Ibid.*
[167] *Ibid.*, 36, c. 12; *Scot. Legal Hist.*, p. 283.

Alexander Livingston and James, his eldest son, as well as James Dundas and Robert Bruce of Clackmannan, underwent temporary imprisonment.[168]

It was at least ironic that a charter assigning the queen's dower was issued on 22 January 1450, on the day after the execution of the two Livingstons, and recorded the consent of the three estates in order to make it 'firmer and more secure'.[169] This charter, in a valiant attempt to secure for Mary of Guelders an annual income of ten thousand French écus, bestowed on her the earldoms of Atholl and Strathearn and numerous lordships and miscellaneous revenues. A further transaction took place in parliament on 24 January when the bishops knelt before the king and took up a matter that had been left unfinished in the Edinburgh parliament of June 1445 : James was persuaded to renounce the 'abusive custom' whereby the crown claimed the movables of deceased bishops and he granted the bishops the power to bequeath them by testament; it was also conceded that during an episcopal vacancy the crown would not meddle with the 'spiritual' revenues of the see, such as offerings and teinds; on the other hand, during a vacancy, the crown would still assume possession of the temporality of the bishopric and would have rights of presentation to those benefices of which the bishop held the patronage.[170]

In other respects the parliament of January 1450 was an important one. Advice was sought on eight miscellaneous statutes passed in the previous reign.[171] Furthermore, a committee of four kirkmen, four barons, and four representatives of the burghs, was chosen to examine all acts of parliament and general council that had been issued in the king's reign and in that of his father; the committee, whose findings have not survived, was to report to the next parliament or general council which of these acts 'ar gude and accordande for the tym'.[172] Apart from these indications that James II was preparing to follow in his father's footsteps, the legislation of the Edinburgh parliament is reminiscent of that of the former reign, showing a fourfold concern for justice, social order, economic stability, and royal authority. In all this there was something ominous for the remaining factions.

[168] E.R., v. lxxx and n. 3; Chron. Auchinleck, pp. 26, 43.

[169] A.P.S., II. 61; R.M.S., II. No. 306.

[170] A.P.S., II. 37–8; R.M.S., II. No. 307; G. Donaldson, op. cit., S.H.R., XLV. 27–35.

[171] A.P.S., II. 33–4; see also ibid., Chronological Table, p. 7.

[172] Ibid., 36, c. 10.

The Crichtons, if they had ever strayed from the narrow path of loyalty to the crown, had evidently read the omens successfully and were to continue to do so : Sir William Crichton was styled Lord Crichton in 1447 and by April 1448 was once more chancellor. While it is understandable that he and his kinsfolk encouraged the king to attack their old Livingston rivals it is something of an enigma that the latter were not protected by the Black Douglases. The explanation may be that an estrangement had followed upon the appointment of James Livingston to the post of chamberlain in the summer of 1448 [173] in place of Sir John Forrester of Corstorphine, whose patron was Earl William. This appointment was, moreover, only part of a new phenomenon that must have been disturbing to a faction like the Black Douglases whose view of politics was bound to be that of territorial magnates who equated land with power. For the Livingston faction was one of lairds rather than lords, indeed perhaps one of burgesses rather than lairds—even the heir of the Knight of Callendar was son-in-law of an Edinburgh burgess. It was men such as the Livingstons who would eventually break the power of the landed aristocracy in England. Well might the Black Douglases have smiled when James II wrecked a new kind of power complex instead of merely turning it to his own advantage. Politics were once more the preserve of the lay and ecclesiastical magnates, with the Crichtons—a combination of lesser lords and office-holders—being left as the faction that was least traditional in its composition. Nonetheless, if the young king had made a tactical blunder he had forcefully shown that in practice, if not in theory, his minority was effectively at an end and that, unlike his royal counterpart in England, he could wield personal authority.

[173] *H.B.C.*, p. 179.

13

THE FALL OF THE BLACK DOUGLASES
AND ITS CONSEQUENCES

After the attack on the Livingstons harmony temporarily prevailed. It was demonstrated in the loans made to the king between September 1449 and August 1450: the Earl of Douglas contributed £100, merchants of Edinburgh £131, Chancellor Crichton £500, and Bishop Kennedy £200.[1] Although the bishop seems to have played no part in the overthrow of the Livingstons and did not 're-emerge from obscurity' until the parliament of January 1450,[2] he and his kinsmen were nonetheless among those who took the place of the Livingstons at court.

The apparent formation of a new triumvirate, acting under the king and composed of Chancellor Crichton, Bishop Kennedy, and the Earl of Douglas, was interrupted by the decision of the last two to set out on pilgrimage for Rome. For Nicholas V had proclaimed 1450 a jubilee year and Rome was the centre of a celebration that marked the end of schism and the inauguration of what was wrongly expected to be a resplendent new era in the history of the church. Kennedy had reached the city by 12 January 1451, after which he obtained some favours from the pope. But Bishop Turnbull of Glasgow, who stayed at home, fared almost as well as his pilgrim colleague,[3] perhaps because Nicholas V recognised the rising political importance of this former keeper of the privy seal, who in Kennedy's absence assumed his place in the royal counsels in close co-operation with Chancellor Crichton and Admiral Crichton.[4] On the way back from Rome Kennedy took part in the procession of the Holy Blood at Bruges on 3 May 1451, after which 'a curtain falls upon his move-

<hr />

[1] *E.R.*, v. 393. [2] Dunlop, *Bishop Kennedy*, p. 106, n. 3.
[3] *Ibid.*, pp. 117-20 [4] Law's MS., cited in *E.R.*, v. lxxxv, n. 2.

ments for almost a twelve-month'.[5] His fellow-pilgrim, Earl William, had also set out from Scotland in October 1450. He had filled all Rome 'with the expectation of his coming',[6] and by reason of his display of magnificence 'was commended by the supreme pontiff above all pilgrims'.[7] Earl William had arrived in Rome at much the same time as Bishop Kennedy, and, apparently, by the same route. If their paths had hitherto crossed, or even coincided, they separated on the return journey when Kennedy made for Flanders and the earl for England. There his coming aroused almost as much interest as it had done in Rome : in February 1451 Garter king-of-arms was sent to the coast to await the earl's arrival and to conduct him to court.[8]

It was a time when the general instability in international relation-ships [9] was surpassed by the instability within England itself. In May 1450 the Duke of Suffolk was murdered at sea while on his way to exile abroad. In June rebellious peasants led by Jack Cade occupied London and murdered the treasurer. A few days later the Bishop of Salisbury was assassinated. In August, Richard, Duke of York, for whom the rebels professed a high regard, returned from Ireland, while his rival, Edmund Beaufort, Duke of Somerset, was brought back from France to counter the influence of York.[10] Meanwhile the two factions were almost equally balanced and each may have coveted the support of Douglas, while the earl may have sought English help to redress his grievances in Scotland, where his position had been jeopardised.

Before leaving Scotland Douglas had appointed one of his brothers—either the Earl of Ormond or, more probably, Lord Bal-venie—as bailie of his estates.[11] The most trustworthy account of what ensued narrates that during Douglas's absence Bishop Turnbull, Chancellor Crichton and Admiral Crichton conspired against the earl, aiming at his death :

> For by their counsel King James II besieged all the castles of the earl and slew many free tenants of the said earl, received the rest to his peace upon oath.[12]

[5] Dunlop, *Bishop Kennedy*, p. 135.
[6] Godscroft, *Douglas and Angus*, p. 181.
[7] Law's MS., cited in *E.R.*, v. lxxxv, n. 2.
[8] *Cal. Docs. Scot.*, IV. No. 1231.
[9] See Dunlop, *Bishop Kennedy*, p. 126.
[10] E. F. Jacob, *The Fifteenth Century*, pp. 492, 496–7, 499, 502–3.
[11] Pitscottie, *Historie*, I. 80; Lesley, *History*, p. 22. For an example of letters of bailiary see *R.M.S.*, II. No. 369.
[12] Law's MS., cited in *E.R.*, v. lxxxv, n. 2.

This succinct but dramatic passage is 'the only account of these proceedings on which it is possible to place any reliance'.[13] It is unfortunate that the records give little information concerning what must
be assumed to have been a major royal expedition against the lands
of the absent earl.

One clue to the king's motives is to be found in his financial
troubles. The audit of the comptroller's account on 27 August 1450
had revealed a deficit of £1,315 15s. 10½d.[14] By 1 May 1450 James
had received 20,000 écus of his wife's dowry;[15] but of the remaining
40,000 the Duke of Burgundy still owed 35,000 as late as 3 January
1452 when partial payment was ordered;[16] it is therefore possible that
the duke was delaying payment on the excuse that the question of the
queen's dower lands had not been satisfactorily settled; and the high-
sounding lordships in the central Highlands with which the queen
had been fobbed off in January 1450 [17] must speedily have revealed
their incapacity to contribute an annual income of £5,000. The king
may have found some pretext to augment the resources of his spouse
as a result of the death of his aunt,[18] Margaret Stewart, widow of the
fourth Earl of Douglas and titular Duchess of Touraine, who as
recently as 26 January 1450 had resigned her rights in Galloway to
Earl William.[19] On 25 May 1451, despite this resignation, the king
made a heritable grant of the sheriffship of Wigtown to 'his familiar
esquire, Andrew Agnew'.[20] In another charter of 20 June 1451 James
made a grant to the Prior and monastery of Whithorn, reserving to
himself 'and his successors, the Lords of Galloway', the service of the
prayers of the monks.[21] It is thus clear that by the early summer of
1451 James regarded himself as being in possession of the earldom
of Wigtown and the lordship of western Galloway. It was doubtless
his attempt to make good his incredible pretensions that had led to
resistance on the part of Earl William's representatives during the
latter's pilgrimage to Rome.

By April 1451 Douglas had arrived back in Scotland, whereupon
'the king forthwith gathered an army against the earl . . . and
approached Craig Douglas [a small Douglas stronghold on the
Yarrow] in warlike fashion, and having taken the castle, razed it to

---

[13] *Ibid.*, lxxxv. See also Fraser, *Douglas*, 1. 467.   [14] *E.R.*, v. 397.
[15] *R.M.S.*, II. No. 345.   [16] Dunlop, *Bishop Kennedy*, p. 135, n. 3.
[17] P. 351 above.
[18] Dunlop, *Bishop Kennedy*, p. 124. The exact date of her death is unknown
but seems to have taken place during Douglas's absence from Scotland (*ibid.*,
p. 131).
[19] *A.P.S.*, II. 64.   [20] *R.M.S.*, II. No. 447.   [21] *Ibid.*, No. 453.

its foundations'.[22] Something of a confrontation, resulting in a compromise between antagonistic interests, seems to have occurred after parliament opened in the tolbooth of Edinburgh on 28 June 1451. Firstly the king recounted his former promise to bestow upon the queen lands worth £5,000 yearly, and a new charter was issued on 1 July 1451 with the consent of the three estates.[23] This apparently did not rescind the grants made to the queen on 22 January 1450 but specifically confirmed some of them and added new grants of lands and revenue. Next the three estates gave their consent to other charters that concerned Earl William.[24] The earl had made a token submission by resigning his lands into the king's hands, whereupon the king restored them, 'notwithstanding any crimes committed by the said William, Earl of Douglas . . . or by occasion of forfeiture or of treason, treachery, or otherwise'.[25] Between 6 and 8 July no less than eighteen charters were issued,[26] restoring and confirming to Earl William his awesome collection of lands and offices and adding a few useful extra privileges. Neither in the charter issued in favour of the queen nor in the charters issued in favour of the earl, was there any mention of the earldom of Wigtown, which apparently remained in the hands of the king. Douglas's more or less complete restoration in the Edinburgh parliament is accurately represented by the Auchinleck chronicler :

> . . . the king resavit him till his grace at the request of the quene and the thre estatis, and grantit him all his lordschippis agane, outtane [except] the erldom of Wigtoun . . . and gaf him and all his a fre remissioun of all thingis bygane. And all gud Scottis men war rycht blyth of that accordance.[27]

But by the time another parliament assembled at Stirling in October 1451 Earl William had evidently rallied sufficient strength to force James to disgorge the ill-gotten earldom, as well as the lordship of Stewarton and Dunlop in Ayrshire, which had presumably been seized at the same time as Wigtown. The witnesses to the resulting charters of 26 October 1451 [28] seem to have been almost entirely made up of the king's supporters, who doubtless felt their humiliation keenly when Earl William now pointedly styled himself not only

[22] Law's MS., cited in *E.R.*, v. lxxxv, n. 2.
[23] *A.P.S.*, II. 66–7; *R.M.S.*, II. No. 462.
[24] *A.P.S.*, II. 67–71.   [25] *Ibid.*, 68.
[26] *R.M.S.*, II. Nos. 463–82, *passim*. Some of these are also printed in *A.P.S.*, II. 67–71.
[27] *Chron. Auchinleck*, pp. 9, 45.   [28] *A.P.S.*, II. 71–3.

Earl of Douglas and Avondale and Lord of Galloway but Earl of Wigtown,[29] a title which he had not previously used.

Thus the king's actions against Earl William in the winter of 1450–1 had brought no lasting material gain : James had led an offensive against the Black Douglas and had failed to prevail, with the result that Douglas was tempted to high-handed actions that would weaken his opponents' will to resist by proving the king's inability to protect his own adherents. The Auchinleck chronicler reports that on 21 August 1451 Sir John Sandilands of Calder, a kinsman of the king, was slain by Sir Patrick Thornton, a henchman of Douglas.[30]

A more gruesome (though less reliable) picture is painted by Boece and Pitscottie. One of their tales concerns John Herries of Terregles, 'a faithful subject to the kingis majestie at all tymes', whose lands had been harried by 'sum theiffis of Douglasdaill'. Failing to secure redress from Earl William, Herries tried to exact revenge. When his 'attempt succeidit unhappilie' he was captured in Annandale, brought before Earl William, and 'hangit schamefullie as [if] he had bene ane theif, nochtwithstanding the king commandit in the contrair'.[31] Another tale recounted by Pitscottie (though not by his predecessor Boece) concerns a certain tutor (guardian) of the laird of Bombie. This gentleman, named MacLellan, 'wald on na wayis . . . ryd with the erle of Douglas' and was imprisoned in Douglas Castle. His uncle, Patrick Gray, Lord Gray's son and heir, obtained letters under the signet asking Douglas to deliver MacLellan, and arrived at the castle, where he was courteously entertained at dinner, only to be told afterwards :

> Schir Patrick ze ar come a litill to leit; bot zondar is zour sistir sone lyand; bot he wantis [lacks] the heid; tak his bodie and do with it quhat ze will.[32]

It is likely that these stories had some factual basis, though they underwent picturesque embellishment and were invariably twisted in such a way as to cast discredit upon the Black Douglases.

---

[29] He styled himself in this way as witness to a royal charter of 13 January 1452 that confirmed some of the lands of Paisley Abbey (*R.M.S.*, II. No. 523; cf. p. 160). Mistakes have sometimes occurred (as in *ibid.*, p. 160 and *Wigtown Charters*, No. 136) by a misreading of Avondale as Annandale.

[30] *Chron. Auchinleck*, p. 45; Pitscottie, *Historie*, I. 126; *Scots Peerage*, VIII. 383.   [31] Pitscottie, *Historie*, I. 88; Boece, *History*, pp. 372–3.

[32] Pitscottie, *Historie*, I. 89–92.

It was the MacLellan incident, so Pitscottie thought, that induced the king and his privy council 'to dauntoun this wickit man'[33]—Earl William. But the clue to subsequent events is more likely to be found in another incident reported by Pitscottie—an unsuccessful attempt to waylay Chancellor Crichton. In retaliation the chancellor 'gadderit ane great companie of his freindis and assistaris, and come fordwart to Edinburgh, to be revengit upoun the Earle of Douglas . . . quho was remaning thair witht ane small number'. Thereupon Douglas was forced to flee 'to saif himself'. Well might Pitscottie remark that the 'mutuall injurieis and despytfull consaittis movit on everie syde exasperit baitht the parties . . . that the ane of thame appeirit suddenlie to bring the uther to destructioun and ruin'.[34]

The Edinburgh incident must have occurred shortly after 13 January 1452 when Earl William witnessed royal charters at Edinburgh.[35] This episode would explain why the earl, when next summoned to the royal presence at Stirling a month or so later, demanded, and obtained, a safe-conduct as a guarantee of his security.

On 21 February 1452, under the king's 'speciale assouerans and respit', Earl William arrived in Stirling Castle, then in the custody of Chancellor Crichton.[36] On the following day after supper the king broached the subject of what had come to be the outstanding issue that lay behind the current animosities—a bond that united the Black Douglases with the Earls of Crawford and Ross.[37] To these great nobles royal authority must have seemed irrelevant at the local level: it was not the business of the king to meddle in the localities which were their spheres of influence; still less was it tolerable that James should make attacks (as his father had done) upon the landed inheritance of his nobles; and to prevent such royal encroachments it might be necessary not only to band together for mutual defence but to take the offensive by encroaching upon the royal power and reducing the king to the position of ceremonial figurehead. To Douglas and his allies it must have seemed that their bond was the only security against a king who might otherwise victimise them one by one. It was James, however, who felt himself about to be victimised. Thus, (so Pitscottie reports) he told Earl William :

---

[33] Ibid., 92.   [34] Ibid., 85-7.   [35] R.M.S., II. Nos. 522, 523.
[36] Chron. Auchinleck, pp. 9-10, 46-7; E.R., v. 458, 478, 596.
[37] Pitscottie, Historie, I. 89; Chron. Auchinleck, pp. 9-10, 46-7; Boece, History, p. 373.

> It is gevin me to understand that . . . thair is sum confideratioun maid
> betuix zow and ane part of the nobillis of this realme. I pray zow thair-
> foir to braike sic bandis . . . that is nocht wount to be within ane realme
> under ane prince.[38]

The Auchinleck chronicler reports the interchange more laconically
and brusquely : when James charged Douglas to break his bond the
earl answered that 'he mycht nocht, nor wald nocht'. Thereupon
James rejoined :

> 'False traitor, sen yow will nocht, I sall!' and stert sodanly till him with
> ane knyf and strak him in the coller and doun in the bodie, and Patrick
> Gray strak him next efter the king with ane poleax on the heid and
> strak out his brains.[39]

By the time that the courtiers had finished the gory work the corpse
of the murdered earl bore twenty-six wounds.

In personally murdering Earl William on 22 February 1452
James II had perpetrated a crime comparable to Robert Bruce's
killing of Red Comyn. If the one murder was an act of sacrilege, the
other, committed in contravention of solemn obligations and the laws
of hospitality, was probably more odious in the eyes of contemporaries.
At first the Black Douglases were stunned ; but within a month they
rose in rebellion. Thanks to a number of tailzies James, Master of
Douglas, had succeeded to the title and estates of the childless eighth
earl. James had previously been marked out for a clerical career : in
1441 he had hoped to become Bishop of Aberdeen under the
auspices of Felix V ;[40] in 1443 he had matriculated as an arts student
in Cologne University ;[41] in 1447, however, an indenture had been
concluded by which he was recognised as having been born before
his twin brother, Archibald Douglas, Earl of Moray ;[42] he was therefore heir presumptive to the eighth earl of Douglas and had soon
demonstrated appropriate martial prowess by fighting a Burgundian
champion in the lists at Stirling.[43] Now, in the great crisis that had

[38] Pitscottie, *Historie*, I. 93–4. Here the date is given as 20 February. The
Auchinleck chronicler, whose authority is generally accepted, gives the date as
22 February (*Chron. Auchinleck*, pp. 10, 47).

[39] *Chron. Auchinleck*, pp. 9–10, 46–7.

[40] P. 335 above.   [41] Burns, *Basle*, p. 71.

[42] Text in a royal confirmation of 9 January 1450 (*R.M.S.*, II. No. 301); see
also Fraser, *Douglas*, I. 447.

[43] Brown, *Early Travellers*, pp. 32–8; *Chron. Bower*, II. 515; *Chron. Auchinleck*, p. 40.

befallen the Black Douglases, the new earl responded forcefully. With his brother Hugh, Earl of Ormond, and Lord Hamilton, he led some six hundred men to Stirling on 17 or 27 March 1452.[44] There, to the blast of twenty-four horns, the king and his council were denounced as forsworn and perjured. The safe-conduct issued to Earl William was put on show at the mercat cross, then, nailed to a board, it was dragged through the streets at the tail of a horse. Pitscottie reports that the Douglases and their adherents 'gaif the king uncomlie wordis, sayand they sould never obey him, nor acknowledge him againe as ane king . . . bot sould be revengit upoun his cruell tyrannie'.[45]

What seems to have taken place was a ceremony of *diffidatio*, whereby a vassal might renounce his fealty to his lord. This betrayed the conservative outlook of the king's opponents : remaining loyal to the traditions of strict feudalism they acted as injured vassals, and, at the outset of a deadly conflict that involved their lives and lands, failed to see that the struggle was one that could not be solved within a feudal context but only within a national one. Their best chance of success would have been to have declared James deposed as a per-jured tyrant and to have set up an alternative government to legiti-mise their actions. Failing to take so decisive a step they demonstrated their antiquated attitude by sacking the burgh of Stirling and setting it on fire.[46] Such an act of aristocratic arrogance was politically inept and merely made it plain that the rebels had nothing to offer save a policy of thoughtless revenge.

The king was not slow in taking advantage of the situation : 'the great bombard'—possibly Mons Meg[47]—was used to reduce the castle of Hatton in Midlothian, which belonged to one of the rebels;[48] and from March to June numerous charters were issued at Edin-burgh to woo the lairds and lesser lords.[49] Conspicuously uncom-mitted to the royal cause were members of the higher nobility, with the exception of Alexander Gordon, Earl of Huntly, William Sinclair, Earl of Orkney, and George Douglas, Earl of Angus. Two bishops—those of Glasgow and St Andrews—also rallied to the king. By 14 April 1452 Bishop Turnbull had lent James eight hundred marks from the proceeds of the jubilee indulgence recently granted by the

---

[44] *Chron. Auchinleck*, pp. 10, 47. The chronicler gives the date both as 27 March and St. Patrick's day in Lent (17 March). He probably meant the latter.

[45] Pitscottie, *Historie*, I. 95.

[46] *Chron. Auchinleck*, pp. 10, 47; Pitscottie, *Historie*, I. 95.

[47] See W. H. Finlayson, 'Mons Meg', *S.H.R.*, XXVII. 124–6, and *T.A.*, I. ccxvii.   [48] *E.R.*, v. 604–8; *R.M.S.*, II. Nos. 536, 544.

[49] *R.M.S.*, II. Nos. 537–86, *passim*.

pope to Glasgow Cathedral.[50] In return for this timely loan the bishop was for ten years to levy the crown rents of Bute, Arran and Cowal, and the customs of Ayr, Irvine and Dumbarton.[51] Shortly afterwards James received a loan of £50 from Bishop Kennedy,[52] whose mysterious year-long absence from public notice ended on 18 April 1452 when he witnessed a royal charter.[53] There were no doubts about Kennedy's loyalty, for it was to his castle of St Andrews that the pregnant queen was sent for safety. There, towards the end of May 1452, she bore a son who would later reign as James III.[54] His birth gave promise of the unbroken continuity of the royal succession and encouragement to those who, for the sake of stability, were prepared to overlook the father's crime after the initial shock had inevitably lessened.

The royalists were further encouraged by the discomfiture of Douglas's ally, the Earl of Crawford. Between him and the Earl of Huntly, the only powerful royalist north of Tay, there were animosities that dated back to the engagement at Arbroath in 1446.[55] The two once more came into conflict : Crawford had 'assembillit the haill folkis of Angus witht ane great companie of his kin and freindis' and encamped beside Brechin to intercept Huntly, who was 'command fordward witht ane great airmie for the kingis suport'. At Brechin on 18 May 1452 Huntly won the day, though not without heavy losses. And 'albeit the Earle of Crawfurde was overcome . . . he remanit in the contrie of Angus as he did of befoir, and persewit all them that was nocht of his factioun witht great cruelltie, waistand all thair landis by fyre and suord'.[56] Huntly gave up his plan of pressing south to join forces with the king, perhaps because his own country was left defenceless against Douglas's brother, Archibald, Earl of Moray, who 'enterit in the landis of Strabogie and . . . hierieit the contrie witht all utheris landis pertening to the Earle of Huntlie'. In retaliation the latter 'invaidit the landis of Murray witht greater cruelltie . . . nor was done in his boundis'.[57] Thus the royalist Earl of Huntly and the rebellious Earls of Crawford and Moray were kept busy north of Tay and none of them was free to intervene in the contest in the south.

There remained, however, another northern magnate from whom

[50] P. 387 below.   [51] *R.M.S.*, II. No. 542.
[52] *E.R.*, v. 604.   [53] *R.M.S.*, II. Nos. 544, 553, 556, 566.
[54] Thomas Dickson's theory that James III was born on 10 July 1451 (*T.A.*, I. xxxvii) has been shown to be incorrect (A. I. Dunlop, 'The Date of the Birth of James III', *S.H.R.*, xxx. 202–4; *Bishop Kennedy*, p. 136, n. 1).
[55] P. 344 above.   [56] Pitscottie, *Historie*, I. 96–9.   [57] *Ibid.*, 99–100.

Douglas hoped much—John, Earl òf Ross and Lord of the Isles. In March 1452 he openly joined the rebellion by seizing the castles of Inverness, Urquhart and Ruthven, perhaps in revenge for the ruin of his Livingston kinsfolk in 1449; for his father-in-law, James Livingston, former chamberlain, escaped from royal surveillance in Holyrood arid assumed charge of Urquhart Castle under Mac-Donald's patronage.[58] While the Earl of Ross could cause trouble in the north he could also, in his capacity as Lord of the Isles, do the same in the west. On 12 May 1452 Douglas interviewed him in Knapdale[59] and seems to have enlisted the naval forces of the Isles under the command of Donald Balloch, who had acquired by marriage the barony of the Glens of Antrim and a powerful position in the north of Ireland.[60] On 10 July 1452 his fleet of birlings raided Inverkip in Renfrew, then harried Bute, the Cumbraes and Arran, and levied blackmail.[61] This incursion was perhaps particularly designed to embarrass the rent-collecting of the royalist bishop of Glasgow.[62] Another bishop who suffered from Donald's attentions was George Lauder, who had been provided to the see of Argyll in 1427.[63] This Lowland intruder was attacked and driven into sanctuary in fear of his life.[64]

Besides the aid forthcoming from his allies in Scotland, Douglas hoped to receive aid from England. On 3 June 1452 Henry VI appointed commissioners to negotiate with 'our dearest kinsman, James, Earl of Douglas' on 'certain articles signed by the hand of our kinsman'. They were also empowered to admit Douglas to the English king's liege homage or fealty.[65] There is no evidence that at this stage Douglas did render homage to Henry VI; and in any case Earl James's intrigues had been outstripped by events in Scotland.

There, despite the widespread activities of Douglas's allies, it was the king who was left with the initiative. He had been sending out summonses to parliament, general council and exchequer, as well as letters 'for the assembly of the king's lieges to his host'.[66] Parliament

---

[58] *Chron. Auchinleck*, pp. 16, 44. See also *E.R.*, v. xciii, n. 1.

[59] *Chron. Auchinleck*, pp. 13, 54. For the date see Fraser, *Douglas*, I. 486, n. 1. A. I. Dunlop's argument (*Bishop Kennedy*, p. 151, n. 2), in favour of a date in 1454 seems less convincing.   [60] *Highland Papers*, I. 43–4.

[61] *Chron. Auchinleck*, pp. 13–4, 54–5; *E.R.*, v. 571, 577, 578.

[62] Pp. 360–1 above.

[63] He is strangely ignored by Duncan Shaw in 'The Ecclesiastical Members of the Lauder Family in the Fifteenth Century', *Scot. Church Hist. Soc. Recs.*, XI. 160–75.

[64] *Chron. Auchinleck*, pp. 14–5, 50–1.

[65] *Rot. Scot.*, II. 358.   [66] *E.R.*, v. 607.

opened at Edinburgh on 12 June 1452 and was informed that it had come to the king's notice that certain of his rivals and rebels were trying to blacken and 'blaspheme' his reputation within the realm and abroad. James required the estates to investigate the circumstances of the death of Earl William and to record their findings in an official document. This duly affirmed that, if Earl William had been under any respites and other securities on the day of his death, he had expressly renounced these 'before a multitude of barons, lords, knights and nobles'. Moreover from many letters and documents, sealed with the earl's seal, and other clear deductions and proofs, it was obvious that he had made leagues and conspiracies with certain magnates 'in oppression and offence of the most serene royal majesty', as well as frequently perpetrating rebellions with his brothers and accomplices. Nor, after 'many sweet persuasions, as well by the king as by divers barons and nobles . . . on the day of his death', had Earl William been induced to aid the king against his rebels. The earl's 'stubborn obstinacy' thus 'seems to have procured, and given, grounds for his death'.[67]

The parliament that had cleared the king's good name was one made up of his own supporters. Some who had still to obtain a reward for their co-operation were not disappointed: the Auchinleck chronicler correctly writes that 'thar was syndry landis gevin to syndry men in this parliament be the kingis secret counsall'.[68] Among the beneficiaries was Bishop Kennedy: a lengthy royal charter was issued on 14 June confirming previous grants to the bishopric of St Andrews and annexing certain lands to its regality. The charter was a grateful recognition of Kennedy's services and of the birth of the future James III in his episcopal city—something which the king did not fail to publicise as securing 'the lineal succession of our royal majesty'.[69]

The witness list to this charter suggests that James had by this time strong support from the ecclesiastical hierarchy and from the middling nobility. But only one earl (Angus) was named. An answer to the hostility or aloofness of the higher nobility was to create new earls. By 8 July Admiral Crichton had been belted Earl of Caithness. About the same time William Hay, constable of Scotland, who had a few days earlier figured as 'Lord Hay', was 'beltit Erll of Erroll'. Another new earl was James Crichton, the chancellor's son and heir,

[67] A.P.S., II. 73.
[68] Chron. Auchinleck, pp. 10–1, 48–9. See also R.M.S., II. Nos. 568–87 passim.   [69] A.P.S., II. 73–4.

husband of the elder Dunbar heiress, who was now recognised as
Earl of Moray[70] in place of Archibald Douglas, husband of the
younger heiress.

The king also turned to good account the new title of lord of
parliament, realising that its award cost the crown nothing but was
gratefully received by those who desired to rise in the world. Hence,
according to the Auchinleck chronicler, 'thar was maid VI or VII
lordis of the parliament and banrentis [bannerets]', whom he enum-
erates as the Lords Darnley, Hailes, Boyd of Kilmarnock, Fleming of
Cumbernauld, Borthwick, Lyle of Duchall, and Cathcart.[71] From
the remarkable distribution of lands, privileges and titles that had
begun in March and had culminated during the Edinburgh parliament it is clear that James had made 'an effort to win the wavering
and to build up a new party in the state'.[72]

Simultaneously there was an effort to ruin the king's opponents :
Crawford was forfeited; and Douglas and others were summoned
to compear in parliament on a certain day to underlie the law. The
contempt in which the Black Douglases held these proceedings was
shown by their behaviour : manifestoes were surreptitiously posted
up in Edinburgh declaiming that 'the king was bot ane blodie
murtherar . . . breaking of the law of hospitalietie; ane fallis ungodlie
thrister of innocent bloode witht out just quarrell or occatioun witht
money uther contumulus sayingis unworthie to rehearse'.[73]

James had rightly judged that it would take more than parliamentary action to bring his opponents to submission. Soon after 8
July, when the business of parliament was over, the host set out.
Marching by way of Peebles, Selkirk and Dumfries it 'did na gud,
bot distroyit the cuntre richt fellonly', cornfields and orchards were
laid waste, and the army in its depredations did not discriminate
overmuch between the lands of the king's foes and those of his
friends.[74] The campaign was evidently over by 26 August 1452,
when parliament once more met in Edinburgh. This was the parliament to which the Black Douglases had been summoned. But instead
of proceeding with their forfeiture it concerned itself with economic
matters and passed ordinances against hoarding of corn [75] during a
dearth that was perhaps caused by the recent depredations. Negotiations for the submission of the Black Douglases were already in

[70] *Chron. Auchinleck*, pp. 10–1, 48–9; *A.P.S.*, II. 75.

[71] *Chron. Auchinleck*, pp. 10–1, 48–9. For the holders of these new titles
see *Scots Peerage, passim*.   [72] Dunlop, *Bishop Kennedy*, p. 139.

[73] Pitscottie, *Historie*, I. 100; similarly *Chron. Auchinleck*, pp. 10–1, 48–9.

[74] *Chron. Auchinleck*, pp. 11, 49.   [75] *A.P.S.*, II. 41.

progress and resulted in an 'Appoyntement', dated at Douglas Castle on 28 August 1452,[76] which Earl James and Lord Hamilton subscribed and swore to observe. In this document Douglas and his adherents forgave those responsible for the death of Earl William. Douglas also guaranteed to revoke 'all leagues and bands, if any hes been made be me in any tyme bygane contrare to our said soverayne lord'; nor would the earl make any such leagues and bands in future; instead, being given reasonable surety for his own personal safety, he would show the king honour and worship and would defend the Borders and keep the truce.

It is striking that in the very first clause of the 'Appoyntement' Earl James bound himself not to try to obtain possession of the lands of the earldom of Wigtown until he received written permission from the queen. Similarly he undertook not to 'persew' the lands of the lordship of Stewarton until special licence had been obtained from the king. The prominence given to these provisions suggests that to king and earl the lands formerly held by the late Duchess of Touraine were still a savoury bone of contention. They figured again in a bond of manrent which Douglas concluded with the king at Lanark on 16 January 1453.[77] This document was more remarkable for the services promised by the king than for those promised by the earl. The latter bound himself to renounce all leagues against the king, swore to render him full manrent and service, and to make a declaration of this in parliament after James had fulfilled his promise of granting re-entry in the lands of Wigtown and Stewarton. Even more astonishingly James bound himself to aid the earl to consolidate his territorial power by furthering a marriage betwixt Earl James and the latter's sister-in-law, the widowed Fair Maid of Galloway, to whom, remarks Pitscottie, 'ane great part of the landis fell throw deceis of hir husband besyde the landis that apperteinit to hir in herietage quhilk he [Douglas] could be na maner of way obtein'.[78]

A papal dispensation was obviously required for such a marriage, and the king had already joined with Earl James and Countess Margaret in the petition to obtain it. It was issued on 27 February 1453 on the conventional grounds that it was intended 'to put an end to wars etc. between their respective families and friends'.[79] When Earl James 'without law or ony respect to God or goode

[76] Text in P. F. Tytler, *History of Scotland*, I. pt. ii, Notes and Illustrations, pp. 386–7. [77] Fraser, *Douglas*, I. 483–4 and n. I.
[78] Pitscottie, *Historie*, I. 101. [79] *Cal. Papal Letters*, x. 130–1.

conscience . . . tuik and marieit his brotheris wyfe'[80] he was just as much master of the whole Black Douglas territories as his late brother had been. The murder of Earl William, and all the hostilities that followed upon it, had been of no more avail in weakening the Black Douglas power than had been the attack upon the Douglas lands in the winter of 1450–51. Nor did the king make any lasting gain by the forfeiture of the Earl of Crawford in the Edinburgh parliament of June 1452. Pitscottie devotes no few pages of his *Historie*[81] to describe the heart-rending scene as Crawford humbly sought (and obtained) pardon for his misdeeds, with 'teiris brustand out aboundantlie'. The rhetoric, one may suppose, is rather that of Pitscottie himself than that of the Tiger Earl, 'a rigorous man and ane felloun', who 'held all Angus in his bandoun, and was richt inobedient to the king'.[82]

Men had rightly foreseen that the settlement of lands and titles in the Edinburgh parliament of June–July 1452 was one that 'wald nocht stand': the forfeited Earl of Crawford had been restored; Archibald Douglas was still Earl of Moray, and the other menaced leaders of the Black Douglas faction had been reconciled with the king. By contrast, for one reason or another, it was royalist adherents who had been displaced. Indeed the Crichtons, who for more than a decade had been a political family of the first rank, were suddenly relegated to obscurity: not only had Admiral Crichton, Earl of Caithness, and James Crichton, sometime Earl of Moray, died in August 1454, but they had been predeceased shortly before by Chancellor Crichton, the head of the family,[83] 'ane mane of great forsight and singular manheid and ane faithfull subject and sicker tairge [sure shield] to the commone weill'.[84] These sudden and almost simultaneous deaths broke up a faction on which the king had often relied. In September 1454 death removed another stalwart royalist, Bishop Turnbull of Glasgow, whose successor, Andrew of Durisdeer, seems scarcely to have been a man of comparable political importance. In part recompense for the singular mortality among the royalists there emerged from the debris of the former Livingston faction none other than James Livingston, father-in-law of the Earl of Ross and onetime chamberlain. His re-admission to royal service after his escapade at Urquhart in 1452[85] was no doubt symptomatic of a reconciliation between the king and the Earl of Ross. By 1 July

[80] Pitscottie, *Historie*, I. 101.   [81] *Ibid.*, 104–12.
[82] *Chron. Auchinleck*, pp. 17, 51.   [83] *E.R.*, v. cvii, cviii.
[84] Pitscottie, *Historie*, I. 127.   [85] P. 362 above.

1454 Livingston had regained his old office as chamberlain, which he was to hold until 1467.[86]

In parliament intense factionalism had, for the time being, disappeared : on 16 July 1454 the three estates re-affirmed old statutes for 'the keping and execucione of justice'; they dealt with a continuing dearth by ordaining that 'strangearis that bringis in wittalis be favorabily tretyt'; and they showed a healthy spirit of independence by limiting the king's use of purveyance to the requisitioning of 'alsmekill as will serf his houshalde'.[87]

In this Indian summer of politics, in 1453 or 1454, Richard Holland composed *The Buke of the Howlat* for the entertainment of his patrons, Archibald Douglas, Earl of Moray, and the latter's wife, Elizabeth Dunbar. While this long poem deserves consideration for its literary interest and for the light it casts upon the general social background of the time it has also some relevance to contemporary politics. Indeed the anti-hero of the poem—the howlat or owl—has been thought, partly on the basis of a mistranscribed word, to represent none other than James II.[88] But the character of the howlat was doubtless suggested by an incident at a synod held in Rome in 1411 by Pope (or Anti-pope) John XXIII, when 'a large owl . . . flew out from behind the altar . . . and fixing its eyes on the pope, sat screeching at him, until the cardinals, flapping at it, drove it away'.[89] Hence it is likely that the lugubrious howlat represents an ecclesiastic—and Bishop Kennedy, foe of the Black Douglases, is the likeliest. Much of the poem is undoubtedly a panegyric of the Douglases, 'the wer wall [bulwark]' of Scotland, whose very name

> . . . is so wonder warme, and ever yit was,
> It synkis sone in all part
> Of a trewe Scottis hart,
> Rejosand us inwart
> To heir of Dowglas.[90]

Whether all this was guileless poetry or political propaganda on the eve of renewed conflict between the Black Douglases and the crown remains uncertain.

Equally uncertain are the causes of the renewed conflict. Alluding to the settlement reached in August 1452 one historian remarks :

[86] *H.B.C.*, p. 179.   [87] *A.P.S.*, I. 41.

[88] *The Buke of the Howlat* (Bannatyne Club, 1823), p. ii.

[89] John Holland Smith, *The Great Schism*, p. 179.

[90] *The Buke of the Howlat*, stanza xxx.

'If the reconciliation was sincere on the king's part, he was to find that he had been nourishing a viper.'[91] It requires, however, some niceness of judgment to determine which side was the more viperish or the more insincere. Each side, at any rate, watched events in England to see if they could be turned to its own advantage in Scotland, and Anglo-Scottish relations afforded unexampled opportunities for political permutations in which it is difficult to recognise precisely which interests, partisan or national, were involved. On 18 April 1453 Douglas was commissioned by James II to negotiate in England for the renewal of the truce.[92] Apart from this 'national' business Douglas joined with Lord Hamilton in petitioning for the release of Malise Graham, Earl of Menteith, who had remained in England for twenty-five years as a hostage for the 'fynance' of James I.[93] By a private arrangement Douglas achieved something that the Scottish crown had disgracefully omitted to do. According to one historian, however, the 'evident motive' was 'to involve James II in trouble by a revival of the old question regarding the respective rights of the two families of Robert II'.[94] Another historian surmises that Malise's liberators 'meant to use him as a tool', though 'nothing came of their designs'.[95] At any rate the release of Malise did not figure among the offences afterwards imputed to Douglas by James. Indeed Malise was one of the earls who was to pass sentence against Douglas in the parliament of June 1455.[96] It was perhaps more significant that on 22 May 1453 Douglas and his three brothers, together with Hamilton and their usual large entourage, had obtained English safe-conducts, valid for four years, ostensibly for a journey to Rome.[97] Another safe-conduct, issued on 16 June 1454,[98] and valid for two years, entitled Douglas's mother, Countess Beatrix, his wife, Countess Margaret, and his youngest brother, John, Lord Balvenie, to travel in the English king's dominions for the sake of pilgrimage. This safe-conduct was issued when the Duke of York was at the head of the English government, having been appointed protector of the realm on 27 March 1454, when it became indisputable that Henry VI had lapsed into temporary insanity. The Yorkist accession to power was accompanied by the imprisonment of Edmund Beaufort, Duke of

[91] Dunlop, *Bishop Kennedy*, p. 145.

[92] *Cal. Docs. Scot.*, IV. Nos. 1249, 1257, 1261.

[93] P. 320 above; *Rot. Scot.*, II. 368.   [94] G. Burnett in *E.R.*, VI. xxviii.

[95] Dunlop, *Bishop Kennedy*, p. 146, n. 2.

[96] *A.P.S.*, II. 77.   [97] *Rot. Scot.*, II. 362.

[98] *Foedera*, v. pt. ii, 56. A. I. Dunlop (*Bishop Kennedy*, p. 156, n. 1), points out that the year is wrongly given as 1455 in *Rot. Scot.*, II. 374.

Somerset,[99] uncle of the Scottish king. It was in vain that James sent his stepfather, Sir James Stewart, the Black Knight of Lorne, to intercede with the English council on behalf of Somerset.[100] While James II was thus associated with the Lancastrian faction the Black Douglases had perhaps aligned themselves with the Yorkists. The surviving records merely show that in 1453 and 1454 Douglas was in touch with the English court, sometimes as an official Scottish representative. If he took the chance to engage in intrigue its purpose (as suggested by the safe-conducts issued to himself and his family) was probably precautionary.

In any case it is unlikely that the earl's transactions in England furnished the motive for the Scottish king's third attack upon the Black Douglases, though it is highly likely that events in England gave the opportunity for an attack that had long been premeditated : the Yorkists fell from power in February 1455 when Henry VI recovered his senses; Somerset was released from prison; and Queen Margaret headed a Lancastrian administration while York moved north to muster forces for the first skirmish in the Wars of the Roses.[101] Neither Lancastrians nor Yorkists were likely to be in a position to intervene in Scotland in pursuit of either factional or national advantage.

Wasting no time James seized an opportunity that might not last : at the beginning of March 1455, he suddenly besieged and 'kest doune' Douglas's castle of Inveravon.[102] He then marched to Glasgow where he was joined by his adherents from the west country and the Highlands. Near Lanark there was some skirmish with Douglas's supporters; before returning to Edinburgh the king ravaged Douglasdale, Avondale and the Hamilton lands. At Edinburgh he collected a fresh force and raided the forest of Ettrick, 'and all that wald nocht cum till him furthwith, he tuke thair gudis and brynt thair placis, and tuke faith of all the gentillis [gentry]'.[103] By the beginning of April Douglas's castle of Abercorn was being besieged by the royal forces.[104] In a letter to the French king, James reported that its towers

[99] E. F. Jacob, *The Fifteenth Century*, p. 509.

[100] Dunlop, *Bishop Kennedy*, p. 154, n. 1.

[101] E. F. Jacob, *The Fifteenth Century*, pp. 509–11.

[102] The Auchinleck chronicler's statement is borne out by an entry in *E.R.*, VI. 12, recording the purchase of equipment for the siege and demolition of the tower of Inveravon.

[103] *Chron. Auchinleck*, pp. 12, 53; *E.R.*, VI. 161.

[104] In a letter of 8 July 1455 to Charles VII (printed in Pinkerton, *History*, I. 486–8), James II stated that he laid siege to Abercorn in Easter week. In 1455 Easter Day fell on 6 April.

collapsed through the continual blows of 'machines' (*machinarum*).[105]
If these were old-fashioned engines of war they were certainly supplemented by 'the gret gun the quhilk a Frenchman schot richt
wele'.[106] Eventually, after a month's siege, so James reported to
Charles VII, the castle was taken by storm, the chief defenders were
hanged, and the lesser folk were graciously admitted to the royal
mercy. Then the fortifications were razed to the ground.[107]

It was in vain that Douglas had marched to the relief of the
castle : in a confrontation near the river Carron he advanced, only
to retire when he saw the king's host steadfastly awaiting battle. Lord
Hamilton drew his own conclusions from this indecision and 'left the
Erll of Douglas all begylit, as men said'. On the morrow Douglas
found himself deserted and fled to England with a few attendants.[108]
He left behind him, as representatives of his cause, his three brothers,
Moray, Ormond and Balvenie. At Arkinholm on the Esk near Lang-
holm they were eventually encountered by the laird of Johnstone with
a band of some two hundred men, traditionally said to have been
composed of the leading Border families. On 1 May 1455, so James
reported to the French king, there was a 'lethal conflict' in which the
Douglases were totally defeated. Lord Balvenie managed to escape
to England. The Earl of Ormond was wounded, captured, and soon
executed. Archibald Douglas had fallen in the fight, and the king
gratefully received a present of his severed head.[109]

Shortly before the fight at Arkinholm James had taken the step
that should have preceded his attack on the Black Douglases : on 24
April James Livingston, specially appointed as sheriff of Lanark
for this sole purpose,[110] summoned Douglas to answer charges of
treason. This was tantamount to a declaration of war seven weeks
after the king had opened hostilities. The deliberate delay in summoning the Black Douglases for trial had given them enough opportunity to sharpen the axe that James hoped to apply to their necks :
by the time that parliament opened at Edinburgh on 9 June 1455
allegations of 'traitorous conspiracy' and 'traitorous rebellions'[111]

---

[105] Text in Pinkerton, *History*, I. 486–8, at p. 486.
[106] *Chron. Auchinleck*, pp. 12, 54.
[107] James II–Charles VII in Pinkerton, *History*, I. 487; *E.R.*, VI. 12.
[108] Pitscottie, *Historie*, I. 119–22; *Chron. Auchinleck*, pp. 12, 53; James II–
Charles VII in Pinkerton, *History*, I. 487.
[109] Law's *Chronicle* (excerpt printed in P. F. Tytler, *History*, I. pt. ii, Notes
and Illustrations, p. 387); Pitscottie, *Historie*, I. 122–3; James II–Charles VII
in Pinkerton, *History*, I. 487.
[110] He is described as sheriff of Lanark *in ea parte* (*A.P.S.*, II. 76).
[111] *Ibid.*

could be supplemented by some specific accusations relating to incidents that had probably taken place *after* the king had begun his onslaught on his victims and had forced them to defend themselves. This point has generally been missed by historians[112] who have taken official propaganda at its face value, assuming that it was not the king but his opponents who started civil war in 1455. On the basis of this assumption the same historians have concluded that the Black Douglases would not have taken so desperate an initiative unless they were ready to claim the crown. The possibility that it was not Douglas who conspired against the king but *vice versa* has hardly been considered; nor has the absence of any evidence of a 'claim' deterred speculation.[113] Yet although the indictment of the Black Douglases was an exercise in royalist propaganda[114] it is clear that even this biased compilation stopped short of specifically accusing Douglas of aiming at the crown either for himself or on behalf of anyone else.

Whatever the pros and cons of the accumulation of charges brought against the Black Douglases it was at least clear that according to a celebrated French definition they were blameworthy—they had defended themselves when attacked. Understandably the accused did not attend to plead their cause in a parliament composed of time-servers and royalist supporters. The failure of the Black Douglases to compear could comfortably be taken as additional evidence of their guilt; on account of their contumacious absence it remained only for the crown to present its case. After discussion among the members of parliament Earl James was found guilty of treason. Similar sentences were passed against Countess Beatrix, Archibald Douglas, 'pretended Earl of Moray', John Douglas of Balvenie and four obscure adherents of the family.[115] Hugh Douglas, Earl of Ormond, had presumably been forfeited before his execution.[116] After the three estates had been committed to the forfeiture of the Black Douglases parliament was prorogued until 4 August.[117] In the intervening time its members doubtless donned their armour again: on 8 July, when James wrote to the French king, he could boast that the castles of Douglas, Strathaven and other strongholds had surrendered and had been levelled to the ground; the only Douglas stronghold that still

---

[112] Even by A. I. Dunlop (*Bishop Kennedy*, pp. 151–2), whose detailed study of the period is the best available.

[113] See G. Burnett in *E.R.*, v. civ–cv.

[114] Text in *A.P.S.*, II. 75–7.

[115] *Ibid.*, 41–2, 76–7.

[116] *E.R.*, VI. xxxvii.

[117] *A.P.S.*, II. 42.

resisted was Threave, which was under siege. Thus, so James affirmed,

> under the disposition of divine clemency, after the prosperous turn of events, we preside felicitously over our realm without any rebellion on the part of our barons or subjects, the forementioned conspirators having been wholly extirpated and expelled.[118]

The same letter alluded to another matter that revealed James's capacity for swift decision and unscrupulous behaviour: when his campaigns against the Black Douglases were drawing to a successful conclusion he had not hesitated to use his forces in a less successful venture against the English. Lancastrians and Yorkists had come to blows at the first battle of St Albans on 22 May 1455, where the Duke of Somerset and other leading Lancastrians had been slain and Henry VI had fallen into the hands of the victorious Yorkists. James had been informed by men of the Marches acquainted with conditions in English-occupied Berwick 'that if we should approach thither with our army suddenly and unexpectedly we should be able to take that town without difficulty'. Unfortunately for James his scheme was 'betrayed' by an Englishman. Notwithstanding this reverse the king still hankered after the recovery of Berwick, 'our town, long wrongfully detained by the English'.[119] Meanwhile the resentment aroused in England by James's treacherous breach of the truce was swiftly turned to advantage by the fugitive Earl of Douglas: on 15 July, in order to save Threave, he granted it to Henry VI. The latter, on the advice of his privy council (now Yorkist) paid the earl £100 'for succour, victualling, relief and rescue of the castle of Treve'.[120] On 4 August Douglas was also granted an annuity of £500 in return for services that he was expected to render to the English crown. The full amount would be paid 'till he is restored to his heritage . . . taken from him by him who calls himself King of Scots'.[121]

But Douglas's plans for a relief expedition had come too late to save Threave. Already at the sieges of Hatton and Abercorn the king's bombards had proved their worth; now at a cost of over £110 they were brought to Galloway. Among them was 'the great bombard', already mentioned in connection with the siege of Hatton. On its laborious progress towards Threave its escort was entrusted to no

[118] James II–Charles VII in Pinkerton, *History*, I. 487.
[119] *Ibid.*, 487–8.
[120] *Cal. Docs. Scot.*, IV. No. 1272.
[121] Dunlop, *Bishop Kennedy*, p. 157; *E.R.*, VI. xxxvii–xxxviii.

less a person than William Sinclair, Earl of Orkney.[122] The effect produced by the royal artillery was supplemented by a more ancient weapon—bribery : some of those who were in the castle at the time of its surrender received profitable rewards.[123]

The fall of Threave allowed the king to adhere to the timetable he had set in June, when he had prorogued parliament to 4 August 1455. On the appointed day the three estates duly assembled at Edinburgh to complete the ruin of the Black Douglases. An act, which was intended to remain in force forever, ordained that anyone who gave any aid or comfort to the survivors of the family would *ipso facto* incur the penalty of treason, and forfeiture of life, lands and goods. Not only did this act re-affirm the forfeiture of the Black Douglases that had been passed in the June session of parliament but it ordained that no descendant of those who had been forfeited would ever be permitted to succeed to, or lay claim to, any lands or possessions in Scotland.[124] This drastic measure was doubtless inspired by recent English examples :[125] the nearest Scottish precedent was probably the act of disinheritance passed at Cambuskenneth in 1314. From the other important measures passed in the parliament of August 1455 [126] it may be gathered that the civil war was regarded as ended; other issues had come to the forefront; and these were dealt with in a way which made it plain that a new era of royal supremacy had been inaugurated.

There were many factors that had contributed to the king's triumph in 1455. One of them was his grasp—unusual in that age—of the importance of heavy artillery.[127] In other respects James may reasonably be compared to Robert I. Like Bruce he had not been dispirited by early reverses but had learned from them : undeterred by failures in 1451 and 1452 he had continued to work with persistence and duplicity for the destruction of the Black Douglases. Like Bruce he was a talented military leader : he had a remarkable sense of timing and a swiftness of decision that verged upon impetuosity; he could hold his forces together and move with a rapidity that

[122] *E.R.*, VI. xxxiv, 200, 201–2, 204, 209; *T.A.*, I. ccxvii.

[123] *E.R.*, VI. xxxv, 199, 202, 204.

[124] The text of this act has been recorded in the vernacular and also (in fuller and more formal language) in Latin (*A.P.S.*, II. 42, c. 2, and 43–4, c. 14).

[125] See J. G. Bellamy, *Law of Treason*, pp. 186–7.

[126] Pp. 377–9 below.

[127] See M. Toynbee, 'King James II of Scotland : artillery and fortifications', *The Stewarts*, XI. 157–62.

must have disconcerted his opponents; he had a clear view of his objectives—the enemy castles—and, like Bruce, did not hesitate to destroy them, not only, perhaps, for military reasons, but as a sign that their former holders had been uprooted for ever. Finally, like Bruce, James had learned to neutralise one opponent while dealing with another. His task was made easier by the death of the Tiger Earl in September 1453, which deprived the Black Douglases of the valuable alliance of the Lindsays. Another mainstay of the Douglases, John, Earl of Ross, played no part in the civil war of 1455, partly as a result of timely concessions : his seizure in 1452 of the royal lands and castle of Urquhart and Glen Moriston was regularised by a royal grant allowing him to hold them for life.[128] And if MacDonald was too aloof to attend in person the decisive parliament of June 1455, he at least had the good grace to appoint procurators who acquiesced in the forfeiture of the Black Douglases.[129] It was the neutrality of Ross that allowed James a free hand in the south. In this case, as in others, the king knew the price of most men, and he was willing (like Louis XI of France) to pay it.

Bribery alone was not likely to have diverted men from loyalty to Douglas. It was rather that they came to distrust the political and military capacity of Earl James. In contrast to the decisiveness and impetuosity shown by the king the earl had acted aimlessly, and sometimes sluggishly. He did not aspire to the crown and failed to find any other objective save what was suggested by personal and territorial grievances. Nor could he dispel from the minds of his men the superstitious dread that demoralised them at the sight of the royal standard. It was an age in which, for complex reasons, the peoples of Western Europe began to put trust in monarchy rather than in aristocracy. Once James II had not only survived the consequences of his murder of Earl William but had expelled the latter's successor it was clear that in Scotland the crown could do no wrong. Despite the interruption of a long and disordered minority James II had confirmed a political trend that had first become apparent in the days of his father.

This was a triumph for the Stewart dynasty, not necessarily for the people of Scotland as a whole. Nor was the triumph achieved without cost : between 1450 and 1455 James II had instigated three outbreaks of civil war, each of which had lasted for months. These spasms of strife were fewer and less spectacular than those of the long-drawn-out Wars of the Roses in England, but were possibly

[128] *E.R.*, VI. 68, 217.   [129] *A.P.S.*, II. 77.

more destructive and had harsher consequences for the generality of the population. This is suggested not only by the verbose accounts of the civil wars in the pages of Pitscottie but also by the shorter and more telling passages of the Auchinleck chronicler, who remarks that 'subjects at this time war sa upprest [oppressed] with the weiris . . . that few travelling in the waye durst tell quhidder he wes the kings man or the Earle of Douglases'. The same writer gives another glimpse of a time of suffering when he tells how the king 'brynt all Douglasdale and all Avendale, and all the Lord Hammiltonnis landis, and heriit [despoiled] them clerlye'.[130] The accounts of the king's chamberlain of Galloway show that shortly after its conquest by the royal forces the income from some fifteen holdings of land, including the forest of Buchan, had been reduced *'propter vastitatem'*, a phrase which in this case almost certainly indicates destruction. And, so the chamberlain affirmed, certain tenants 'cannot be distrained on account of their poverty'.[131] When some of the rural population lived on the margin of subsistence it was not surprising that devastation and dislocation were followed by epidemics. Thus in 1455, so runs a laconic entry in annals of the time, 'there was a great pestilence and mortality of men through the whole kingdom of Scotland'.[132] In the autumn of 1456 the three estates adopted methods of control proposed by the clergy : there was to be no reckless burning of infected houses; those who had sufficient wealth could be quarantined in their own dwellings; the poor who were infected could be 'put forth of the town' but were not to be allowed to move freely and contaminate the countryside. Meanwhile the prelates were to 'mak generale processiounis throu out thair dyoceis twyss in the wolk for stanching of the pestilence'.[133]

During the years of civil war the king had found support in the three estates. They were evidently both serviceable and amenable; and in the years of relative stability that followed the royalist triumph of 1455 James II had no desire to ignore them. The records, which may not be complete, show that after 1455 at least one general council was held (in 1456) while parliament met about once a year. Its tenurial composition, which had always been blurred by practical considerations, was further disregarded by an act of 1458 : no tenant-in-chief who held lands of the crown less than £20 in annual value was to be constrained to come to parliament or general council

130 *Chron. Auchinleck*, pp. 12, 53.   131 *E.R.*, vi. 196–9, *passim*, 207–8.
132 *Extracta*, p. 243; *Chron. Bower*, ii. 516.   133 *A.P.S.*, ii. 46.

unless he was a baron, or unless his attendance was specially commanded by the king.[134] There can hardly have been a sinister ulterior motive :[135] it was the current political situation, rather than any constitutional change, that affected the relationship between the king and the three estates and made the latter somewhat sycophantic. If patriotism had conferred a sort of unity upon Scotland in the fourteenth century, devotion to monarchy subsumed other ideals after 1455 and became the main source of unity. God had so favoured the king, so declared the parliament of March 1458, 'that all his rebellys and brekaris of his justice ar removit out of his realme, and na maisterfull party remanande that may causs ony breking in his realme'.[136] MacDonald provided the only question-mark that could be posed against this assertion, but James's tactful treatment of the earl[137] prevented, for the time being, any large-scale eruption in the Highlands. In the Lowlands there remained no 'kin' that could by itself compete with the crown in prestige and power. Thenceforth if baronial opposition were to be successful it had not only to take the form of a coalition but had to acquire a 'royalist' character by securing a member of the royal family as a real or nominal leader.

Although the new 'lords' had supported the king against the Black Douglases, who had almost personified the higher nobility, it was not James II's intention to dispense with a higher nobility : as death or forfeiture caused gaps in its ranks they were speedily filled; above the new lords appeared new earls, and, indeed, new earldoms were erected. The Gordon earldom of Huntly dated from 1445, the Hay earldom of Erroll from 1452. In 1457 or 1458 Colin, Lord Campbell, was created Earl of Argyll, George, Lord Leslie, was created Earl of Rothes, James Douglas, Lord of Dalkeith (or Lord Dalkeith) was created Earl of Morton, and William, Lord Keith, was created Earl Marischal. Apart from the erection of these new earldoms there took place between 1455 and 1458 a re-distribution of old ones. Caithness went to William Sinclair, already Earl of Orkney, and scions of the royal house received the consideration that was to be expected : Atholl went to the king's half-brother, Sir John Stewart; March went to the king's second son, Alexander, for whom the dukedom of Albany was also revived; Moray went briefly to the king's third son, David, who died shortly afterwards; and Mar (filched from the Erskines) went to John, the king's youngest son.[138]

[134] *Ibid.*, 50.
[135] A. I. Dunlop (*Bishop Kennedy*, p. 311) is nonetheless suspicious.
[136] *A.P.S.*, II. 52.   [137] Pitscottie, *Historie*, I. 128–9; *E.R.*, VI. li.
[138] *Scots Peerage*, *passim*.

The proliferation of new titles and the re-distribution of old titles has given rise to the view that James II was 'building up a new nobility to counteract the influence of the old'.[139] It was, however, within the ranks of the ecclesiastical hierarchy or those of commerce, administration, and law, not within those of the nobility, that 'new' men of humble origin were given advancement. But if the titled nobility remained unchanged in its social origins, it did nonetheless, for the time being, lack the assurance and independence that came from hereditary succession : it was not by that, but by recent royal favour, that many nobles, however impeccable their birth, had acquired titles and even lands. Though they formed a nobility of ancestry they were also a nobility of service.

Measures designed to prevent in future the rise of any noble to the position of independent authority lately held by Douglas were taken in the very parliament of 4 August 1455 that witnessed his final forfeiture. Here a frontal attack was made on one hoary abuse— heritable tenure of office : in future no office was ever to be given in fee and heritage; any such grant issued since the death of James I was revoked.[140] Another act ordained that rights of regality should be granted only with the approval of parliament.[141] The horse had bolted before the stable door was shut. Nonetheless it was possible to bring *some* regalities to an end; for it was also ordained that 'all regaliteis that ar now in the kingis handis be anext to the rialte',[142] in other words that they should lose their distinctive jurisdictions and be merged in the royalty [143] of the sheriffdom. This was a repetition of an act first passed in the parliament of January 1450 in a more expanded form [144] that elucidated the king's motives. He intended to re-invigorate the traditional curial system of royal government, which had been debilitated by so many exemptions : the diversity of juris-dictions would gradually be reduced to uniformity in proportion to the crown's acquisition of regalities. An initial impetus to the process was certainly forthcoming with the forfeiture of so many regalities formerly held by the Black Douglases. Thereby the royal courts must have benefited from an influx of new suitors and new business. A justice ayre held at Wigtown and Kirkcudbright in 1455 or 1456

[139] Dunlop, *Bishop Kennedy*, p. 188.
[140] *A.P.S.*, II. 43. Another act of 1458 (*ibid.*, 50) sought to make holders of heritable office accountable for their misdeeds by threatening them with fines and loss of office for a year and a day.
[141] *Ibid.*, 43.   [142] *Ibid.*
[143] For the meaning of this term see p. 24 above.
[144] *A.P.S.*, II. 36.

brought in no less than £600 6s. 8d.;[145] and three ayres held at Dumfries in the next few years imposed amercements of £1,105 (though these were compounded at about half the sum).[146] The yearly profits of justice from the newly acquired lands may even have approached in value the annual rents of the lands.

The rents themselves received immediate and high-powered attention from commissioners (including Bishop Kennedy) who were appointed to make assessments.[147] From these it appears that the gross rents from East Galloway amounted to £562 3s. 4d. in 1456, and those from West Galloway to £189, besides, in both cases, large quantities of victuals. These assessments were, however, either too optimistic or too harsh: by 1460 the rental of East Galloway had fallen to £356 4s. 5½d. and that of West Galloway to £115 4s. 5d.[148] The gross rents of Ettrick for the first three terms after the forest came into the king's hands amounted to £779 10s. 0d.; afterwards the rental was fixed at £519 13s. 4d. a year.[149] Besides payments in victuals the gross rents of the earldom of Moray came to £339 18s. 8d.[150] In all, the forfeited Black Douglas lands must have brought the king gross cash rents of at least £2,000, about one-third of the total for all the crown lands.[151]

James II was anxious to see that this spectacular addition to the landed wealth of the crown, won by himself at such risk, would not be frittered away by his successors. Thus the very parliament of 4 August 1455 that disinherited the Black Douglases passed an act of annexation to endow the monarchy with an inheritance partly composed of the lands that its foes had lost forever. This act[152] ordained that in each part of the realm certain lordships and castles should be annexed to the crown; they were not to be granted in fee or freehold without the decree of the whole parliament, which was to be given only for weighty reasons.

Although the preamble to the act mentioned only lordships and castles the list of annexations was headed by 'the haill custumes of Scotland': the king was to revoke all grants from the customs that had been made since the death of James I. Next the act went on to

---

[145] E.R., VI. 195, 206.

[146] Ibid., 557-8. By contrast a justice ayre held in Aberdeen in the same period produced only £68 (ibid., 158).

[147] Ibid., 201, 203, 206, 226, 227.   [148] Ibid., cx.

[149] E.R., VI. 225, 443, 544.   [150] Ibid., cxxxix-cxl.

[151] See G. Burnett's detailed survey of the crown lands for the period 1455-60, ibid., lxxii-cxlvi.

[152] A.P.S., II. 42-3. G. Burnett provides a more accurate text in E.R., VI. cxlvii-cxlviii.

enumerate the castles and lordships that had been annexed. It may be estimated that the annexed lands which were old crown property provided gross annual rents totalling some £1,600, besides additional payments in victuals;[153] those that had formerly been Black Douglas possessions contributed some £1,450, besides payments in victuals.[154] Altogether, the whole annexed lands, plus the customs (currently bringing in some £3,000 a year, gross)[155] should have given the crown a permanent endowment that in 1455 was worth some £6,050 a year in cash. A distinction thenceforth existed between crown lands that were annexed and those that were unannexed and of which the king might freely dispose without seeking parliament's approval. The annual rents of these unannexed crown lands exceeded £3,500.[156]

The act of annexation might be regarded as a tailzie, variable only with parliament's consent, that attached lands and castles to the crown, with which, it was hoped, they were 'perpetualy to remane'.[157] One express motive was that in each part of the realm there should be lordships and castles (including Edinburgh, Stirling and Dumbarton) set aside 'for the kingis residence'. Another motive, left unexpressed, was strategic and military : for control over lands gave control over their manpower; and castles, which were not an economic asset but an economic liability, were useful not only as residences but as strongholds—in the next reign the royal castles would rightly be described as 'the keys of the kingdom'.[158] Nonetheless the chief motive behind the act of 1455 was undoubtedly an economic one, and one which was made to seem particularly attractive. For, so affirmed the preamble to the act, 'the poverte of the crowne is oftymis the causs of the poverte of the realme and mony uther inconvenientis, the quhilkis war lang to expreyme'.[159] Among the inconveniences that parliament had in mind was taxation, the need for which would be (so it was hoped) removed. Thus the act was thoroughly in accord with the Scottish constitutional tradition that the king should live of his own. Whether the act would work was another matter. Within a year its efficacy was open to question.[160]

[153] *E.R.*, VI. lxxii–lxxxv, xc–ciii, cxl–cxliii.
[154] *Ibid.*, cix–cx, cxv–cxvii, cxl–cxlii.   [155] *Ibid.*, 113–32.
[156] This would follow from a comparison of the revenues of the annexed lands, as given above, with those of the totality of crown lands, including those held by the queen in dower (*ibid.*, lxxii–cxlvi). Some of the lands held in liferent by the queen, such as the earldom of Fife and the lordship of Brechin (*A.P.S.*, II. 66–7), were among the annexed lands.
[157] *A.P.S.*, II. 42.   [158] *Ibid.*, 113.   [159] *Ibid.*
[160] As in the case of Urquhart and Glenmoriston (*E.R.*, VI. 217, 221).

The patrimony of the crown was to be better preserved by acts of revocation : on 15 November 1455 James, having attained his perfect majority of twenty-five years, revoked all previous alienations of crown property with the exception of those made in favour of the queen and his second son.[161]

The acts of annexation and revocation showed the growing importance attached to the crown lands as the main source of royal revenue. This was also indicated after 1437 in the emergence and increasing prominence of a new class of accounts in the exchequer rolls—the accounts of the *ballivi ad extra* or managers of the crown lands.[162] It was these royal bailies or receivers—who might also hold posts as local stewards, chamberlains, serjeants, mairs or crowners— who now, rather than the sheriffs, accounted in exchequer for the ferms of the crown lands.[163] It is perhaps significant that in 1455–6 every sheriff seems to have been a noble,[164] whereas the bailies of crown lands, whose financial responsibilities were often greater, were of miscellaneous social status. Some, admittedly, were nobles, but others were obscure men (presumably of proven ability) such as James Patonson, who was in charge of the ferms and grain-rents of Fife, the most valuable of all the earldoms.[165]

The bailies had to collect (and disburse) the crown rents on the basis of rentals that were the subject of frequent assessment after 1455.[166] The rents were paid by *firmarii* (fermours) of varying social status, who leased landholdings by the year, or, as tacksmen, enjoyed longer leases, perhaps for five years, renewable on payment of a grassum.[167] The tacksmen, who could sub-let the land they leased, probably made up a rural middle class, having been given some security of tenure by an act of 1450.[168] Meanwhile, however, there remained a 'variety and confusion of tenure' which comprised 'every possible combination of lease and ward and blench-ferm holding',[169] and to these might be added holdings in wadset, whereby land could be held by a beneficiary until redeemed by payment of a stipulated

[161] Dunlop, *Bishop Kennedy*, p. 176.
[162] *E.R.*, v. xxxv; vi. xxvii.   [163] *Ibid.*, vi. lxv, lxx.
[164] See the sheriffs' accounts rendered in 1455 and 1456 (*ibid.*, 83–109, 140–89). These two rolls of sheriffs' accounts are the only ones extant for the period 1437–60 (*ibid.*, v. xxxv; vi. xxvii).
[165] See *E.R.*, vi. 408–87.
[166] P. 378 above; Dunlop, *Bishop Kennedy*, p. 339, n. 5.
[167] *E.R.*, vi. lxx; Dunlop, *Bishop Kennedy*, p. 339.
[168] *A.P.S.*, ii. 35; p. 351 above; *Scot. Legal Hist.*, pp. 193–6.
[169] R. L. Jones, cited in Grant, *Social and Economic Development*, pp. 39–40.

capital sum.[170] Some standardisation was eventually to be produced by the development of holdings in feu-ferm.

The term was not new;[171] but it had undergone some definition which made it so attractive that over the course of centuries it was to become, and remain, the most prominent form of landholding in Scotland, and a form peculiar to Scotland alone. By the mid-fifteenth century the holder of a feu was not liable for certain of the customary feudal casualties; yet his tenure was heritable and secure so long as he and his heirs paid each year a fixed and unalterable feu-duty in cash. So advantageous were these terms that the feuholder was expected to pay a lump sum when he received his feu-charter; and the feu-duty might be set at a figure considerably higher than the former rent of the land. Since the early fourteenth century the crown had granted feu-ferm tenure to the communities of royal burghs, and in the mid-fifteenth century feuing sometimes retained burghal associations: in 1452 two feus of crown land were granted to the community of Cupar;[172] and on 13 July 1459 no less than twenty-three feu-charters were granted to various inhabitants of the so-called 'burgh' of Falkland[173] that had sprung up alongside the old castle that James II had begun to turn into a favourite royal residence.[174] From 1450 onwards, however, feuing was applied outside the royal burghs to the crown lands in general; and it was landholders of some standing, rather than burgesses, who were granted feu-charters.[175] The king's financial stringency doubtless prompted this new development, which was still on a small and experimental scale. In the Edinburgh parliament of March 1458 feu-ferm was included among the 'items' for discussion and enactment. It may be inferred that the king had recommended general adoption of the practice. The pointed response of 'the lordis' was that he should 'begyne and gif exempill' for others to follow, while assurance of royal approval and ratification was to be given to each 'prelate, barone or frehaldare that can accorde with his tenande apone setting of feu ferme of his awin lande'.[176]

This cautious attitude perhaps sprang from a conservative dislike of anything that savoured of a permanent alienation of land. For this reason the papacy had long tried to restrain the kirk from the experiments in feuing in which it had led the way in the fourteenth

[170] See *Wigtown Charters*, No. 146, p. 168.

[171] See p. 6 above.   [172] *R.M.S.*, ii. Nos. 580, 581.

[173] *Ibid.*, Nos. 706–28.   [174] *E.R.*, vi. lxxviii–lxxix.

[175] See *R.M.S.*, ii. Nos. 304, 305, 372, 373, 405, 406, 458, 473, 515, 528, 533, 553, 567, 572, 580, 581.   [176] *A.P.S.*, ii. 49, c. 15.

century and which had notably contributed to the definition of the new tenure.[177] Apart from a conservative dislike of alienations there were (and are) economic objections to feuing : the feu-duties, however attractive in comparison to existing rents, were perpetually fixed. But contemporaries were painfully aware that the coins in which the feu-duties were paid were by no means fixed in value or in bullion content : in 1393 44 pennies had been coined from the ounce of silver; by 1440 the number had risen to 64, by 1451 to 96, and by 1483 to 140.[178] Throughout the whole reign the three estates were constantly pre-occupied with the problem of 'the money' :[179] in the parliament of March 1458 the decision was made to cease altogether the striking of further coins until a committee of the estates had examined the question.[180] It was thus understandable that the same parliament should give only a lukewarm welcome to the king's advocacy of feu-ferm tenure : the old system of adjustable rents made it possible to compensate for changes in the value of money, even although insecure tenure hindered agricultural improvement.

Not that the 1458 parliament was blind to the desirability of agricultural improvement : a number of measures that it enacted were concerned with rural husbandry.[181] To remedy the shortage of timber, landholders were ordered to let their lands each Whitsuntide on conditions that required their tenants to plant not only woods and hedges but broom, which was used both for fuel and winter fodder. Fences were forbidden since their place was to be taken by hedges of 'lyffand wode' which might 'grow and plenyss'. Another act ordered, on pain of a ten-shilling fine payable in the baron court, that each man who worked with a plough-team of eight oxen should sow at least a firlot of wheat, half a firlot of peas, and forty beans. The barons were to do likewise on their own demesne lands on pain of the same fine to the king, and they would also be fined forty shillings if they neglected to enforce the ordinance upon their tenants. It has been pointed out that 'the introduction of the sowing of peas and beans would have been a most important innovation had the idea been to use them as a substitute for fallow'.[182] They were, however, to be sown only in small quantities in the cottar's kailyard rather than in the rigs of the open fields.

The rural legislation of 1458, to which some landholders paid

[177] Grant, *Social and Economic Development*, pp. 40, 98, 265–6.
[178] R. W. Cochran-Patrick, *Records of the Coinage of Scotland*, I. lxxv. See also *E.R.*, IX. lxi–lxviii.
[179] E.g. *A.P.S.*, II. 41, 46, 48.   [180] *Ibid.*, 48.   [181] *Ibid.*, 51–2.
[182] Grant, *Social and Economic Development*, p. 291.

heed,[183] came at a time when 'the rural communities of Scotland were by no means in a stable condition'. The subdivision of holdings was a sign of an upward trend in the population, so also, perhaps, was 'a considerable change from pastoral to arable farming'. Simultaneously however, there was beginning to be 'considerable displacement of the lesser folk', firstly through the development of the tacksman system, and, somewhat later, by the development of feuing.[184] The existence of agrarian troubles is hinted at in an act of 1458 concerning those who 'occupy maisterfully lordis landis'; at any lord's request such 'maisterfull men' were to be evicted by the local sheriff.[185] Those who were evicted doubtless swelled the ranks of miscellaneous 'sorners' who roamed the countryside as vagrants extorting hospitality.[186]

The prosecution of sorners and other vagrants could take place in baron court, burgh court, sheriff court, or even in an inquest held in the king's presence on his arrival in the head burgh of a shire.[187] This was typical of the current use of miscellaneous agencies to enforce law and order and to promote justice. What was striking was 'the fragmentary dispersal of judicial power and its corrupt inefficacy'.[188] It was presumably because of lapses in the holding of justice ayres that the parliament of March 1458 thought it 'speidfull' that they be held yearly throughout the realm 'for gude of the communys'.[189] It was probably because of the irregular sittings of the justice ayre (which alone was competent to deal with cases of robbery) that the criminal jurisdiction of the sheriffs was extended through new laws dealing with spuilzie [190] (spoliation)—a happily ambiguous term which 'was used to cover almost any action in which goods were taken *brevi manu*'.[191] In civil cases the delay of proceedings in the justice ayre was sometimes avoided by the appointment of special justiciars *in hac parte*, who were instructed to determine a certain case.[192] Despite innovations in judicial machinery the old parliamentary committee of causes and complaints was still active.[193]

[183] *Rental Book of the Cistercian Abbey of Cupar Angus* (Grampian Club), I. 141–2; Dunlop, *Bishop Kennedy*, p. 345, n. 1.
[184] Grant, *Social and Economic Development*, pp. 98, 291.
[185] *A.P.S.*, II. 51.
[186] *Ibid.*, 36, 43, 45. An act of 1458 arranged for the licensing of disabled beggars (*ibid.*, 49–50); *Scot. Legal Hist.*, p. 285.
[187] *A.P.S.*, II. 36, 43, 45, 49–50.   [188] *Scot. Legal Hist.*, p. 20.
[189] *A.P.S.*, II. 49.   [190] *Ibid.*, 34, 36.
[191] *Fife Court Bk.*, pp. 325–6.   [192] *A.P.S.*, XII. T4.
[193] *Ibid.*, II. 77–9; XII. 22–3.

Meanwhile there was further experiment with the 'sessions' that from time to time had been employed as one of the several possible types of supreme civil court, whether parliamentary or conciliar. In 1439 the work of the sessions was to be done by the lord lieutenant and the king's chosen council, who would hold two sessions a year.[194] In 1450 the king was to choose certain discreet persons of the three estates, who, together with the chancellor, would hold three sessions a year.[195] In 1456 three representatives of the clergy, three of the barons, and three of the burghs, were to hold sessions for one month, after which they would be relieved by another group of nine representatives plus the clerk of register, who after a month's service would in turn be relieved by another group of nine.[196] The parliament of March 1458 made similar arrangements for the sessions. Their jurisdiction was primarily to comprise actions of spuilzie and civil actions that did not concern fee and heritage, and from their decisions there could be no appeal to either king or parliament. This scheme was not intended to be merely a temporary expedient, but its obvious weakness was the lack of money to finance it: the three estates thought that the lords of session 'of thair awne benevolence sulde beir thair awne costis'.[197] Since there was unlikely to be much enthusiasm to undertake the unpaid work of the sessions the lords of council continued to act as an alternative supreme court.[198]

While litigants were faced with a bewildering variety of courts the operations of the courts, spiritual as well as temporal, were liable to be perverted by the practice of 'maintenance'. The parliament of March 1458 enacted that all those who attended any sort of court should come 'in sobyr and quiet maner' with no more followers than their daily household and 'familiaris'. As soon as they had taken up lodgings they were to lay aside their weapons and armour.[199] But little could be expected of this enactment when justiciars and other itinerant legal officers had themselves to be warned to reduce their retinues 'to eschew grevans and hurting of the pepill'.[200] When, despite the prevalence of maintenance, offenders were pronounced guilty, they often escaped the legal consequences by the purchase of remissions from the king. In accounts running from July 1457 to June 1458 the king's chamberlains north of Spey alluded to some two hundred remissions that had been granted.[201] There was good reason for the parliament of March 1458 to pass an act that curbed

---

[194] *Ibid.*, II. 32.   [195] *Ibid.*, 34.   [196] *Ibid.*, 46.
[197] *Ibid.*, 47–8.   [198] *Ayr Burgh Charters*, No. 49, decreet of 1460.
[199] *A.P.S.*, II. 51.   [200] *Ibid.*, 36.   [201] *E.R.*, VI. 485–6.

the judicial immunity hitherto conferred by remissions so that the rights of plaintiffs were at least partly safeguarded.[202]

At the close of this parliament, so notable for its attempts to improve justice, the three estates hinted that the king and his ministers should promote 'the quiet and commoune profett of the realme' and see that justice was 'kepit amangis his liegis'; and 'with all humilite' they exhorted the king 'to be inclynit with sik diligence to the execucioune of thir statutis . . . that God may be emplesit of him, and all his liegis . . . may pray for him to Gode, and gif thankynge to Hime that sende thame sik a prince to thair governour and defendour'.[203] It may be inferred that at least some of the judicial reforms of 1458 did not spring from royal initiative, and that they may have been unwelcome to the king. It has been affirmed that it was Bishop Kennedy who 'inspired parliament to do all that parliament could do in the way of judicial reform', and that it was he who 'tried to systematise the procedure of the lords of session as an independent court'.[204] Of this however, there is no evidence. It was perhaps the clergy in general, rather than Bishop Kennedy in particular, who inspired judicial reform; in the general council of 1456, at any rate, the clergy considered that an 'artikill belangande justice'—presumably drafted by a committee of the articles—was 'weill made', and besought the king to implement it.[205]

The obsequiousness generally shown by the clergy reflected the king's 'remarkable success in securing bishops after his own heart'.[206] Nor was the king's control of ecclesiastical appointments contested by the pope; no objection seems to have been made to an important extension of the crown's patronage *sede vacante*. In 1450 this had been limited to benefices in the bishop's gift.[207] In 1457, however, a provincial council of the clergy agreed that it extended also to major elective benefices within the diocese and even to benefices that had been reserved for papal provision, and, in 1459, in another provincial council held at Perth, the decision of 1457 was formally recorded. It was to be re-affirmed by parliament in 1462 since the king's rights allegedly sprang from a usage that was ancient, customary and laudable.[208]

Although Bishop Kennedy is not known to have actively resisted

[202] *A.P.S.*, II. 50. [203] *Ibid.*, 52.
[204] Dunlop, *Bishop Kennedy*, pp. 324, 326. [205] *A.P.S.*, II. 46.
[206] Dunlop, *Bishop Kennedy*, pp. 188–9. [207] P. 351 above.
[208] *A.P.S.*, II. 83–4.

the crown's growing influence over ecclesiastical appointments it may be surmised that he had no sympathy for developments that tended towards royal domination over the kirk. It has been pointed out that 'Kennedy's absence from the royal councils during the last years of the king's reign is both marked and significant' though it 'was not unrelieved'. Certainly there 'was no fundamental breach between the two cousins' (James II and Kennedy) and it may well have been the case that 'Kennedy's seclusion from political life was largely self-imposed in order to devote his energies to the things of education and religion'.[209] As 'ordinary' of the diocese of St Andrews he was appointed by the parliament of March 1458 to sit with the chancellor (George Shoreswood, Bishop of Brechin) on a commission of inquiry that was to investigate and reform hospitals. The most obvious result of this visitation seems to have been the annexation of the revenues of the decayed hospital of Soutra to the new Trinity College Hospital that Mary of Guelders was to found in Edinburgh shortly afterwards.[210] Kennedy was also associated with the queen in patronising the Observant Franciscans. This branch of the Franciscans had been founded by St Bernardino of Siena (d. 1444), the great mission preacher of the age. The Observants, like the earlier 'Spiritual' Franciscans, differed from the established 'Conventuals' in their eagerness to observe the original ideals of St Francis. By 1458 they were settled in a friary in Edinburgh; about the same time Kennedy established another in St Andrews; and in 1460 a third was set up in Perth.[211] The Observants were more successful than the thirteenth-century Franciscans in maintaining an ascetic tradition and 'brought a wind of spiritual revival to Scotland'.[212]

While it was to Bishop Kennedy's credit that he favoured the new evangelical movement, his contribution to higher learning—still primarily a concern of the kirk—was more significant and more personal. As Bishop of St Andrews Kennedy was also chancellor of the university. His advent came at a time when there were clashes between town and gown, chiefly over questions of the university's jurisdiction. In May 1444 Kennedy held an enquiry in the tolbooth of St Andrews and as arbiter produced a 'contract of peace'.[213] His

[209] Dunlop, *Bishop Kennedy*, pp. 192, 194.
[210] *A.P.S.*, II. 49. For the background see Dunlop, *Bishop Kennedy*, pp. 406-10; Coulton, *Scottish Abbeys*, p. 228; Easson, *Religious Houses*, p. 143.
[211] A. R. MacEwen, *History of the Church in Scotland*, I. 364-5; Easson, *Religious Houses*, pp. 109-13.
[212] Durkan, *Bishop Turnbull*, p. 58.   [213] Dunlop, *Bishop Kennedy*, p. 271.

efforts to bring the faculty of arts under the control of the university were less successful.[214] Another deep-seated problem was that of the rival pedagogies: in 1454, at Kennedy's suggestion, it was agreed that one united pedagogy should be established for a trial period of five years, later extended for a further two in the hope of repressing the quarrels of the masters and the 'dissoluteness of scholars'.[215]

Kennedy's generation was one that regarded higher education as a panacea for the ills of both kirk and kingdom. James II, who had confirmed the privileges of St Andrews University in 1445,[216] aided his staunch supporter, Bishop Turnbull, to set up a new university at Glasgow. On 7 January 1451, in response to the royal petition, Nicholas V issued a bull conferring upon the new university all the privileges and immunities enjoyed by the university of Bologna, with which he himself had been associated.[217] The Auchinleck chronicler tells how the bull 'was proclamit at the croce of Glasqu on the Trinite Sonday the XX day of June. And on the morne thar was cryit ane gret indulgence'[218]—the jubilee indulgence, from which the new university perhaps indirectly benefited. In April 1453, the king, who had erected the city and barony of Glasgow into a regality in 1450,[219] took the university under his protection, and in December the bishop, now a lord of regality, granted a charter of privileges.[220] Although Bologna had been intended as a model for the new university its first teachers, such as William Elphinstone, dean of the faculty of arts and father of the famous future Bishop of Aberdeen,[221] and Andrew of Durisdeer, who succeeded Turnbull as Bishop of Glasgow, were better acquainted with conditions in St Andrews, Louvain, Cologne and Paris. Durisdeer had been a member of the household of Cardinal d'Estouteville, who carried out a reform of the university of Paris in 1452, and this reform is reflected in the Glasgow statutes.[222]

While it may be inferred that instruction in theology and medicine was available in Glasgow it was probably the intention that the university would specialise (like Bologna) in legal studies, and that the western Scottish university would thus be 'complementary to that in the east', where theology was dominant among the higher

---

[214] *St Andrews Acta*, I. xxvi–xxix.
[215] Dunlop, *Bishop Kennedy*, pp. 289, 293–4. [216] *Ibid.*, p. 272.
[217] *Glasgow Registrum*, II. No. 361; Dunlop, *Bishop Kennedy*, p. 276; Durkan, *Bishop Turnbull*, p. 36.
[218] *Chron. Auchinleck*, pp. 16–7, 45. [219] Dunlop, *Bishop Kennedy*, p. 119.
[220] *Glasgow Registrum*, II. Nos. 353, 356.
[221] Dunlop, *Bishop Kennedy*, p. 278.
[222] Durkan, *Bishop Turnbull*, pp. 34–44. The cardinal appears to have been well known among Scottish ecclesiastics (Cameron, *Apostolic Camera*, p. xxii).

faculties. Probably through lack of sufficient post-graduate students such specialisation did not take place: 'both universities in the fifteenth century had a struggle to maintain their existence, and in both the faculty of arts was the preponderating element'.[223] At first it seemed that there would be rivalry between east and west; but initial fears in St Andrews must have been allayed when the death of Bishop Turnbull in 1454 deprived Glasgow of powerful patronage. Some encouragement was forthcoming in 1460 when Lord Hamilton granted a tenement adjacent to the Dominican friary, where the faculty of arts built a regular 'college of the faculty' or 'pedagogium'. The existence of this common hall of residence, which could practically be equated with the university, prevented the development of private pedagogies run by regent masters, so that there was 'more homogeneity in the Glasgow tradition than at St Andrews'.[224]

There, indeed, Bishop Kennedy had followed the opposite course by adding to the existing diversity, for on 27 August 1450, a few months before the foundation of Glasgow University, Kennedy had founded the college of St Salvator and endowed it from the income of four parsonages. The college was to have thirteen foundationers. Three, including the provost, were to be theologians; four were to be masters of arts in holy orders; and six were to be poor clerks studying in the university. Eventually there were also 'commoners' who were fee-paying students not on the establishment. The subordination of the new institution to the university was achieved by provision for a yearly visitation by university representatives.[225]

What made St Salvator's a 'college' in the usual fifteenth-century sense of the term was not its educational function but its corporate character and the fact that the duties of this corporation included the ministrations of the altar. For besides being an establishment for the higher education of clerics it was also one of a number of new collegiate kirks.[226] It is remarkable that none of these was instituted in the more settled years of James II's reign but that all can be dated to the troubled years of the minority and the conflicts with the Black Douglases, and it was often the leaders of faction who were the

[223] Dunlop, *Bishop Kennedy*, p. 277; Durkan, *Bishop Turnbull*, pp. 37, 53–6.

[224] Durkan, *Bishop Turnbull*, p. 58; Innes, *Sketches*, pp. 58–9.

[225] Dunlop, *Bishop Kennedy*, pp. 274–5, 279, 281; *St Andrews Acta*, I. xxii–xxv; R. G. Cant, *The College of St Salvator* (1950).

[226] Kilmun was founded in 1441, Dunglass in 1443, Dirleton in 1444, Roslin (initially and incompletely) in 1446, Crichton in 1449, Hamilton and St Salvator's in 1450, and Dumbarton in 1454 (Easson, *Religious Houses*, pp. 173–88). See also Easson's articles on 'The Collegiate Churches of Scotland' in *Scot. Church Hist. Soc. Recs.*, VI. 193–215; VII. 30–47.

founders, or would-be founders. At Roslin William Sinclair, Earl of Orkney, was busy not only enlarging his castle but building nearby what would become architecturally the most striking (though not the most pleasing) of all Scottish collegiate kirks. Not far away, Chancellor Crichton, who was also enlarging his castle, obtained collegiate status for the neighbouring parish kirk. While the foundation of collegiate kirks was largely left to the nobility the burgesses were not far behind in demonstrations of religious munificence, and the parish kirks of Edinburgh, Peebles, Stirling and Aberdeen would sooner or later receive collegiate status. Other burgh kirks were being extended or built anew. Those of St Mary at Dundee and Haddington, and St Michael at Linlithgow, scarcely differed from the collegiate foundations of the barons and even surpassed most of the latter in size, architectural distinction, and the number of their chaplainries. Together with the song schools or grammar schools that were attached to them the burgh kirks fell increasingly under the patronage of the town councils.[227] They manifested civic pride and gave some hint of relative prosperity.

This must have been derived more from domestic than from foreign trade. Of the sixty-eight burghs of barony that were created between 1450 and 1513 eleven dated from the last decade of James II's reign [228] and were doubtless authorised in response to a growing need for local markets. Confirmation of old burghal privileges, and grants of new ones, were also forthcoming from the crown,[229] though not lavishly—Aberdeen, which in 1445 hoped to obtain the right to have its own sheriff within the burgh, was to be disappointed [230] and its inhabitants felt some concern for their security. For the burghs were not immune from the less favourable characteristics of the age: Stirling and Dalkeith were sacked and burnt by the Black Douglases;[231] and internal factionalism was revealed in an act of 1458 which declared that no bands or leagues were to be made within the burghs; there was to be 'na commotioun nor rysing of commownys in hindering of the common lawe'; no inhabitant of a burgh was to

---

[227] D. E. Easson, *op. cit.*, *Scot. Church Hist. Soc. Recs.*, VI. 17–9. See also the agreement about the construction of the burgh kirk of Dundee in 1443 (*Brechin Registrum*, pp. 90–5).   [228] Pryde, *Burghs*, pp. 51–7.

[229] Grant, *Social and Economic Development*, pp. 369–70; Dunlop, *Bishop Kennedy*, p. 341; *R.M.S.*, II. Nos. 337, 431, 507.

[230] *Aberdeen Council Register*, I. 14; *Aberdeen Burgh Recs.*, p. cxl; Alexander M. Munro, *Memorials of the Aldermen, Provosts, and Lord Provosts of Aberdeen, 1272–1895* (1897), p. 44.   [231] *Chron. Auchinleck*, pp. 10, 47; *A.P.S.*, II. 77.

'be fundyn in manrent nor ride nor rowt in feir of weir witht na man bot witht the king or his officiaris or witht the lorde of the burghe'; nor was any inhabitant to 'purches ony lordschipe in oppressione of his nychtburis'.[232] Nevertheless even the greatest burghs could not ignore local lords : 'Aberdeen . . . looked to the Earl of Orkney as its defender in 1450 and to the Earl of Huntly in 1462–3, and Edinburgh came to an agreement with Logan of Restalrig in 1454–5.'[233] The king's fear of such tendencies, which threatened the crown's control of its own burghs, probably underlay the act of 1458.

In other respects the relationship between king and burghs was also uneasy. It is remarkable that in the general council of 1456 'The universale burowys of the realme' complained that the poor commons were greatly oppressed by the king's sheriffs and constables.[234] This complaint may have originated in 'the court of the parliament of the four burghs', which, according to a royal charter of 1454 that re-affirmed an ordinance of the previous reign, was to meet annually in Edinburgh.[235] The institution had presumably had a continuous existence from the time of the first known meeting of the 'parliament' of the four burghs in 1405.[236] But while the 1405 'parliament' was a representative assembly of commissioners from the burghs south of Spey, and was apparently free to discuss all matters of common concern, the act of 1454 emphasised the curial character of the assembly : the suitors of the court were to be simply the commissioners of the four burghs—Edinburgh, Stirling, Linlithgow and Lanark; and the phraseology hints at repression of discussion of matters of common concern. Thus the act of 1454, which was important enough to have a galaxy of notables as witnesses, seems to have been an attempt to prune the 'parliament' into the shape of the fourteenth-century court of the four burghs, useful to the king as a source of judicial profits. There are other signs of a self-interested antiquarianism in James II's dealings with the burghs : a chamberlain ayre held in Aberdeen on 14 February 1456 levied amercements of £25 4s. 4d. upon burgesses who offended against pristine burghal custom by dwelling outside the burgh; another chamberlain ayre in Lanark levied fifty-seven shillings for the same offence.[237] It is not surprising that in the parliament of March 1458 reference was made to chamberlain ayres 'be the quhilkis all the estatis, and specialy the pure commownis, ar

[232] *A.P.S.*, II. 50.
[233] Dunlop, *Bishop Kennedy*, p. 382; *Aberdeen Burgh Recs.*, pp. cxl–cxli.
[234] *A.P.S.*, II. 46–7, cc. 9 and 10; similarly *ibid.*, 50, c. 22.
[235] *Ibid.*, XII. 23–4.   [236] P. 264 above.   [237] *E.R.*, VI. 102, 158.

fairly grevyt'; the three estates exhorted the king to have pity on account of the many and great inconveniences caused by the ayres and to provide 'suddane remeide and reformacioune therof'.[238]

Not only did James II exploit the chamberlain ayres but in 1457 he even revived direct taxation: the burghs were stented, and, in addition, loans were exacted from merchants. There is no surviving evidence that on this occasion similar burdens were laid upon the kirk or the baronage. It was Andrew Crawford, a burgess of Edinburgh, who in 1457 accounted for 'the finance of the burghs and loans made, granted to the lord king by the burgesses and communities of burghs, as well in Flanders as in the realm'.[239] The total loans came to at least £92 16s. 8d. Flemish (almost £300 Scots) of which, according to the account, no less than £80 9s. 8d. Flemish was forthcoming from eighty-five Edinburgh merchants, who were repaid in the following year.[240]

The financial importance of the Edinburgh merchants was doubtless based on the burgh's control of virtually two-thirds of Scotland's export trade. The custumars' accounts for the period July 1455 to October 1456[241] show that the total export duties from fourteen burghs came to £3,029 1s. 7d.; Edinburgh answered for £1,908 2s. 6½d., which included the custom (£91 17s. 0d.) on 1,917 'dozens' of woollen cloth exported from Leith. But the total volume of Scottish exports was lower than it had been a generation earlier, and was only one-third as much as it had been in 1370–71.[242] Economic trends common to all Europe doubtless contributed to this situation, and as markets shrank there was a tendency for restrictions to increase, as, for example, in a statute of March 1458 'anent the estat of merchandice'. Its intent was to limit the 'multitude' of 'saylaris in merchandice'—not mariners but men who embarked with goods which they hoped to sell personally overseas—such men were to be restrained from sailing unless they were resident burgesses 'of gud fame'.[243]

The pattern of Scottish trade remained much the same as it had been at the opening of the century, though Kirkcudbright was now prospering modestly, presumably from the opening of La Rochelle and Bordeaux to Scottish trade after the expulsion of the English from France, which, with the exception of Calais, was completed by 1453. Another feature of James II's reign was the intermittent renewal of

---

[238] A.P.S., II. 50.
[240] Ibid., 306–7, 384.
[242] P. 177 above.

[239] E.R., VI. xlv–xlvi; 305.
[241] Ibid., 113–32.
[243] A.P.S., II. 49.

trade with England, 'with the quhilk this realme has part of commonyng'.[244] The 'commonyng' was mostly by sea, and there are
indications that Scottish seapower was by no means negligible. It
was 'commonly repute and haldin' that Bishop Kennedy had spent
equal amounts of money upon his tomb, the college of St Salvator,
and his 'barge', also called the *Salvator*, supposedly a 'ship the biggest
that had been seen to sail upon the ocean'.[245] The English safe-
conducts, which become more revealing in the mid-fifteenth century,
evidently deal with humbler vessels, though some were of respectable
size for their time as reckoned by the maximum tuns of wine they
could carry. They included the *Andrewe* of Scotland of forty tuns, the
Renyan (*Ninian*) of Galloway (sixty), the *George* of Leith (eighty), the
Mary and the *Cuthbert*, also of Leith (a hundred), the *Nicholas* and
Marie of Aberdeen (eighty and a hundred respectively).[246] A larger
vessel, the *Marie* of St Andrews (one hundred and sixty tuns), is recorded in more detail. In February 1453 a safe-conduct was issued for
this vessel and its cargo, together with its master, up to thirty mariners,
four merchants and their four servants.[247] Homeward bound 'with
125 tuns of wine and other lawful merchandise' the vessel was captured by English pirates and taken to Devon. By February 1456 the
Marie of St Andrews had become the *Antony* of Dartmouth and was
being used to ferry pilgrims to Compostela. James II and Bishop Kennedy, who seem both to have had a financial interest in the vessel,
had tried in vain to secure restitution, the first by diplomacy, the
second more pertinaciously, but equally fruitlessly, by litigation in the
English courts.[248]

Such incidents stirred the ground-swell of animosities that kept
Anglo-Scottish relationships stormy.[249] Pope Pius II, idealistically
organising a crusade to try to drive the Turks from Constantinople,
which they had taken in 1453, was realist enough to know that the
warlike kingdoms of Scotland and England would not take part by
reason of their mutual antagonisms.[250] Meanwhile Scottish diplomacy
was increasingly far-reaching, complex, and devious. Various factors

[244] *Ibid.*, 39.
[245] Lesley, *History*, p. 37; Boece, *History*, p. 383; Major, *History*, p. 389;
Pitscottie, *Historie*, I. 154.
[246] *Cal. Docs. Scot.*, IV. Nos. 1244, 1264; *Rot. Scot.*, II. 328, 344, 346, 358,
360.   [247] *Rot. Scot.*, II. 360.   [248] Dunlop, *Bishop Kennedy*, p. 350.
[249] *Cal. Docs. Scot.*, IV. No. 1287; *E.R.*, VI. 498.
[250] See *Memoirs of a Renaissance Pope: The Commentaries of Pius II*, ed.
Leona C. Gabel (1960).

combined to destroy the former simplicity of the triangular relationship involving France, England and Scotland. The divisions between France, Scotland's chief political ally, and Burgundy, which controlled Scotland's chief markets abroad, posed diplomatic problems, while the situation was further complicated by tentative French support for the Lancastrians and more positive Burgundian support for the Yorkists.[251] There were also issues arising in France itself that evoked James's personal interest : he claimed that his two nieces had been wrongfully excluded from the Breton succession, and hoped that Charles VII would recognise him as their guardian and let him dabble in the revenues of the duchy.[252] On 8 November 1458 he hopefully (but fruitlessly) instructed his envoys to obtain sasine of the county of Saintonge on the basis of the treaty concluded thirty years previously between his father and Charles VII.[253] Two days before, on 6 November 1458, James had also commissioned his envoys to treat, with the advice of the French king, 'about the renewal of a truce and perpetual peace' between Scotland and Denmark[254]—an initiative that would have an important sequel in the following reign. Another diplomatic initiative was also taken on 6 November 1458 when James issued a florid letter authorising his envoys to conclude an alliance with Castile.[255] In 1456 he had also tried to enlist the aid of Ludovico Sforza, Duke of Milan, perhaps also that of the King of Aragon and Naples. For, so James informed Charles VII in a letter of 28 June 1456, 'we hope confederate princes would concur with us against the English, who are the principal disturbers of the peace of all Christendom'.[256]

When parliament met at Stirling on 13 October 1455 it dealt almost exclusively with defence, and passed thirteen ordinances[257] similar to those formerly enacted in the warden courts that had been shorn of some of their powers in the previous parliament.[258] One enactment made detailed provision for defence of 'the est passage betuix Roxburghe and Berwik' : watch was to be kept at the fords, where the sentinels were to give warning of the enemy's approach by lighting beacons. Another enactment ordained that three garrisons should be maintained on the Borders : one of two hundred spearmen and two hundred archers was to be kept on the East March,

[251] Dunlop, *Bishop Kennedy*, p. 195 and n.   [252] *Ibid.*, pp. 179–81.
[253] P. 289 above; *R.M.S.*, II. No. 647; Dunlop, *Bishop Kennedy*, pp. 195–6; Balfour-Melville, *James I*, p. 163.
[254] *R.M.S.*, II. No. 642.   [255] *A.P.S.*, II. 79.
[256] Dunlop, *Bishop Kennedy*, p. 167 and n. 1.
[257] *A.P.S.*, II. 44–5.   [258] *Ibid.*, 43.

another of the same size on the Middle March, and a third, of one hundred spearmen and a hundred archers, on the West March.[259] The apprehensions evident in such measures were also voiced in instructions of 20 November 1455 that James gave to his envoys at the French court. They were to stress that the English forces which had once occupied Normandy and Aquitaine were now poised against Scotland; if Scotland were overwhelmed France would again be threatened; moreover the time was ripe for a simultaneous French attack upon Calais and a Scottish attack upon Berwick.[260]

Although Charles VII urged peace James renounced the Anglo-Scottish truce in May 1456. Early in July he invaded the Scottish lands subject to the English garrison of Roxburgh and encamped far to the south of the castle on the water of 'Calne'—the Kale, a tributary of the Teviot.[261] On 28 June 1456, a few days before this expedition, James, having dropped his former championship of Henry VI, had written to inform Charles VII that the Duke of York 'had a clear right to the throne of England'; in response to his appeals James had promised to help him to win the crown.[262] Thus it was on the basis of an understanding with the Yorkists that James appeared on the water of Kale. There, however, he was met by mysterious English envoys who induced him to abandon his enterprise.

If trickery was involved (as the Scottish writers state)[263] the king did not labour long under the deception : on 26 July 1456 a letter in the name of Henry VI was addressed to 'James, calling himself King of Scotland', rhetorically asking : '. . . have you lived so ignorant of what penalties await the rebel . . . who is so hardy as to deny his homage to his liege superior?'[264] On the basis of this ludicrous epistle the English factions appear to have achieved outward unity for a few weeks, and in response James set out on 16 August on his 'first voyage into England', reputedly passing twenty miles into Northumberland, winning and destroying seventeen towers and fortalices, and spending six days and nights on enemy soil before returning home 'with gret worschip' and no significant loss.[265] Subsequent special truces that were to last on the East and Middle Marches until 2 February 1457[266] were evidently not renewed; for in that month

[259] *Ibid.*, 44.   [260] Dunlop, *Bishop Kennedy*, p. 164.

[261] *Ibid.*, pp. 164, 166 and n. 1, 168; *E.R.*, VI. xlii, 258.

[262] Dunlop, *Bishop Kennedy*, p. 167.   [263] See *E.R.*, VI. xlii–xliii.

[264] Text in *Rot. Scot.*, II. 375–6, where, however, the year is wrongly given as 1455 (Dunlop, *Bishop Kennedy*, p. 168).

[265] *Chron. Auchinleck*, pp. 20, 56, 57; *Chron. Bower* (continuation) II. 516; *E.R.*, VI. xliii.   [266] *A.P.S.*, II. 45.

James launched another abortive attack on Berwick.[267] A new truce, concluded on 20 June 1457, was optimistically extended first to 1463, then to 1468.[268] Probably open diplomatic activity was less significant than the secret consultations that it covered :[269] 'James was plotting with Lancaster against York, while counterplotting with York against Lancaster.'[270] On 10 July 1460 the Lancastrians were defeated at Northampton and Henry VI fell into Yorkist hands. But his wife, Margaret of Anjou, a far more effective leader, was still in the field, and James rightly judged that the battle was the beginning of an English civil war rather than a final triumph for the Yorkists. England's troubles provided an opportunity, and with his characteristic rapidity of decision the king took advantage of it.

His decisiveness was not in this case an impetuous gamble : he had long waited for such a chance and had long tried to prepare his people to meet it by a revival of wappinschaws and encouragement of archery. Those over sixty years of age might meanwhile 'use uther honest gammys'—but presumably not football and golf, which were to be 'uttirly cryit doune and nocht usyt'.[271] From the proceeds of the burghal tax and loan of 1457 [272] Andrew Crawford had purchased in Flanders large quantities of war materials, including gunpowder and its ingredients and 8,800 pounds of iron, probably for the fabrication of guns in Scotland;[273] and in the general council of 1456 it was thought 'spedfull' that the king should request certain great barons to make 'cartis of weire', each of which would hold two guns of the two-chamber type, attended by 'ane cunnande man' to fire them.[274]

There was nothing that intrinsically distinguished James II's military preparations from those of his father, who had nonetheless failed dismally in his expedition of 1436.[275] There were, however, vital differences between father and son that affected their capacity in warfare : the former gave no proof of military skill while the latter, who 'gave himself with all zeal to the things of war', emerged creditably from his campaigns against the Black Douglases and the English. And though James II was 'politique in councell' he did not lack the common touch but was 'fellow to every private soldier'.[276] His passion for hunting [277]—a gregarious sport—no doubt won him popular

[267] Dunlop, *Bishop Kennedy*, p. 171.   [268] *Rot. Scot.*, II. 378–83, 393–8.
[269] *Ibid.*, pp. 390, 391; *Cal. Docs. Scot.*, IV. No. 1301; Lesley, *History*, pp. 29–30.   [270] Dunlop, *Bishop Kennedy*, p. 205.
[271] *A.P.S.*, II. 45, 48.   [272] P. 391 above.   [273] *E.R.*, VI. 309–10.
[274] *A.P.S.*, II. 49.   [275] Pp. 293, 323 above.
[276] Major, *History*, p. 386; Lesley, *History*, p. 32.   [277] *E.R.*, VII. xxxiii.

esteem, so also did his interest in tournaments.[278] Chivalry still
counted for much, as is shown in the literary work of Sir Gilbert Hay,
who, at the request of the chancellor, William Sinclair, Earl of Orkney, translated chivalric French treatises, which he rendered as *The
Buke of the Law of Armys* and *The Buke of the Ordre of Knycht-
hede*. These were compiled in Roslin Castle in 1456 and provide
the earliest extant examples of sustained literary prose in the Lowland
vernacular.[279] When enthusiastic adherence to the chivalric outlook
was still a prerequisite in Scotland for effective military leadership,
James II, 'un vaillant chevalier et homme de grant corage',[280] had
valuable attributes that were lacking in his father, a man of deeper
intellect and of severe and withdrawn temperament.

It was with a great host drawn from all Scotland that James laid
siege to Roxburgh Castle towards the end of July 1460. The unity
that he had achieved, by fair means or foul, was shown by the presence not only of staunch supporters such as the Earls of Angus and
Huntly but onetime enemies such as the Earl of Ross.[281] In the same
place, more than twenty years previously, James I had seen his force
disintegrate; but in 1460 the host would remain united even after
James II was no longer there to lead it. His objective was no easy
one : its garrison had been maintained at the cost of £1,000 a year
in time of truce and £2,000 in time of war.[282] It was a stronghold
worthy of a full-scale national effort. On Sunday, 3 August 1460,
Mary of Guelders arrived at Roxburgh to inspire enthusiasm, and
'on account of joy at the arrival of the queen'[283] the bombards were
ordered to discharge a salvo. James, 'mair curieous nor becam him
or the majestie of ane king',[284] stood nearby to watch his cherished
artillery in action. When one of the guns exploded he was struck in
the thigh by a fragment and achieved an unusual death, being 'un-
happely . . . slane with ane gun, the quhilk brak in the fyring'.[285]

[278] *Extracta*, pp. 238, 243; *Chron. Auchinleck*, pp. 19, 55.
[279] *Gilbert of the Haye's Prose Manuscript* (S.T.S.), I. 2.
[280] Cited in Dunlop, *Bishop Kennedy*, p. 208, n. 3.
[281] *Chron. Auchinleck*, pp. 20, 57; Pitscottie, *Historie*, I. 142; *Extracta*,
p. 244; Major, *History*, p. 386.
[282] Indenture of 12 February 1453, *Rot. Scot.*, II. 360–1.
[283] *Extracta*, pp. 243–4.
[284] Pitscottie, *Historie*, I. 143.
[285] *Chron. Auchinleck*, pp. 20, 57.

14

THE MINORITY OF JAMES III
AND THE ACQUISITION OF
ORKNEY AND SHETLAND

James II had died a few months before his thirtieth birthday. It was a testimony to the influence of his powerful personality that the great host which he had assembled remained united for a week or two longer. An old prophecy that a dead man would win Roxburgh Castle was fulfilled when it fell to the besieging army; the demolition of the castle—the burgh had already disappeared—marked the end of the English occupation of Teviotdale; hostilities temporarily ceased. Meanwhile there was 'gret dolour throu all Scotland',[1] not least on account of the political instability that was bound to follow upon the sudden and unexpected removal of a powerful adult king.

The surviving progeny of James II numbered five—two daughters, Mary and Margaret, and three sons, James, Alexander and John. The last, already styled Earl of Mar, was about a year old. Alexander, who had been created Duke of Albany, Earl of March, Lord of Annandale and Man, was some six years old and was absent with Bishop Kennedy in the Low Countries or France.[2] The eldest son, James, who was eight years old, was hastily crowned in Kelso Abbey on 10 August 1460, only a week after his father's death.[3] Well might the Pluscarden writer lament that 'our kings are often young'.[4] Another contemporary source laconically states : 'Death of James II.

---

[1] *Chron. Auchinleck*, pp. 21, 57–8; *Extracta*, p. 244; Pitscottie, *Historie*, I. 152–3.
[2] *H.B.C.*, pp. 57–8; Dunlop, *Bishop Kennedy*, pp. 194, 199.
[3] *Chron. Auchinleck*, pp. 21, 57–8.   [4] *Chron. Pluscarden*, I. 391.

Tumult in Edinburgh.'[5] And it has been remarked that 'the very fact that for some months there is a gap in all official records is itself evidence that chaos reigned'.[6]

When the first parliament of the new reign opened at Edinburgh on 23 February 1461 a number of nobles attended to answer complaints or to register complaints of their own. The contemporary Auchinleck chronicler asserts that 'thai did litill gud in the forsaid parliament'. What particularly annoyed him was that the magnates 'gaf the keping of the kinrik [kingdom] till a woman'[7]—Mary of Guelders, the queen dowager. Ten years later, James III, alluding to these proceedings, declared that parliament had confirmed an act of his father's reign which made it a crime of high treason to lay hands upon the sovereign without parliament's consent; parliament had also committed 'the tutory of our person to our sweetest mother . . . and to the lords of her council'.[8] These lords seem to have been Bishop Kennedy, Bishop Durisdeer of Glasgow, and the Earls of Angus, Huntly, Argyll and Orkney.[9]

While deciding that the young king 'suld ay remane with the quene', parliament had also declared that 'scho suld nocht intromit with his profettis bot allanerlie with his person'.[10] The records of the first exchequer audit of the reign, held in Edinburgh in March 1461, suggest that the king's revenues were controlled by the lords of the regency council and that the queen's revenues were delivered to her own officials.[11] Though Mary of Guelders was not allowed to dabble in the crown revenues she had ample of her own to allow her to play a leading part in politics. As a widow she had full control over her dower. When she held an exchequer audit of her own at Edinburgh in July 1463 her officials accounted for almost £4,000 forthcoming from her dower lands, besides large quantities of victuals.[12] Her total annual income may well have amounted to the enormous total of £5,000 formerly granted to her.[13] Certainly she was wealthy enough

---

[5] *Brief Latin Chronicle*, cited in Dunlop, *Bishop Kennedy*, p. 213.   [6] *Ibid.*

[7] *Chron. Auchinleck*, pp. 22, 59.

[8] C. A. J. Armstrong, 'A Letter of James III to the Duke of Burgundy', *S.H.S. Misc. VIII.* 19–32.   [9] Lesley, *History*, pp. 33–4.

[10] *Chron. Auchinleck*, pp. 23, 60. George Burnett (*E.R.*, vii. xlvi–xlvii) without justification assigned this decision to July 1462. The entry in the chronicle is linked to the arrival of the 'lord of Curthous' (Louis de Bruges, Lord of Gruythuse) who came to Scotland as a Burgundian envoy at the close of 1460 (Dunlop, *Bishop Kennedy*, pp. 214–7, 222; p. 403 below).

[11] *E.R.*, vii. 2, 4, 28, 29, 31, 35.

[12] *Ibid.*, 161–200. The rents of the earldom of Strathearn were for three terms, those of the earldom of March, presumably administered on behalf of the Duke of Albany, were for one term.   [13] *Ibid.*, xlix.

to improve the amenities in her dower-houses (Stirling Castle and the manor of Falkland) and to spend over £600 on the construction of a new castle, Ravenscraig, on the south coast of Fife,[14] 'probably the earliest structure in Scotland designed specifically for use with guns'.[15] She also spent some £1,100 on her foundation of Trinity College in Edinburgh, which comprised a collegiate kirk served by a provost, eight prebendaries and two choristers, and a hospital for the maintenance of thirteen poor persons.[16]

The widowed queen 'had apparently come to occupy a position similar to that enjoyed by Joan Beaufort after the death of James I, and in that time of faction the result was equally unsatisfactory'.[17] So at least believed Bishop Kennedy, who, on his return to Scotland, probably early in 1461, reported to Charles VII that the kingdom was menaced with perdition. He had 'found a great division in the said country caused by the queen, whom God pardon, from which there resulted a great dissension between the said queen and me, and great likelihood of slaughter between the kinsmen and friends of either party'.[18] One of the queen's partisans is noted by the Auchinleck chronicler, who remarks that after the death of James II she 'tuke Master James Lyndesay for principale counsallour, and gart him kepe the preve sele'.[19] Lindsay, who had formerly been keeper of the privy seal, was already provost of the collegiate kirk of Lincluden and was to acquire the chantorship of Moray and the deanery of Glasgow.[20] Soon the regency council was divided into two factions—the 'young lords', headed by the queen, and, perhaps, by Colin Campbell, Earl of Argyll, and the 'old lords', headed by Bishop Kennedy and George Douglas, Earl of Angus.[21] Foreign policy helped to define the two factions, for while Kennedy was at first consistently pro-Lancastrian, Mary of Guelders followed a more wayward course.

The vicissitudes of Scottish domestic politics were a storm in a tea cup when compared to those of England. As a result of the battle of Northampton on 10 July 1460 the Yorkists came to power; and in October 1460 the Duke of York was recognised as Henry VI's

---

[14] *Ibid.*, xlix–lii.

[15] E. M. Jope in review of Stewart Cruden's *The Scottish Castle*, *S.H.R.*, XLII. 148–54, at 153.

[16] *E.R.*, VII. lii–liv.   [17] Dunlop, *Bishop Kennedy*, p. 219.

[18] Waurin, *Anchiennes Cronicques*, cited in Dunlop, *Bishop Kennedy*, pp. 211, 219.   [19] *Chron. Auchinleck*, pp. 22, 59.

[20] *H.B.C.*, p. 181; *Cal. Docs. Scot.*, IV. Nos. 1310, 1366, 1382.

[21] Dunlop, *Bishop Kennedy*, p. 233; *E.R.*, VII. xlvii, where, however, Kennedy is wrongly regarded as one of the 'young' lords.

heir while the latter's young son, Edward, Prince of Wales, was disinherited. Margaret of Anjou was by no means content with this
settlement and came to Dumfries with her son to beg 'help and suple
aganis the Duke of Yorke'. In the nearby collegiate kirk of Lincluden,
where the provost, James Lindsay, doubtless acted as host, the English
queen was welcomed by the Scottish queen. According to the Auchinleck chronicler 'thai remanit thar togidder x or xii days. And thai
said thai war spekand of mariage betuix the forsaid prince [of Wales]
and King James the thridis sister [Mary] and sum said that thai war
accordit on baith the sydis'.[22] It was probably in December 1460 that
the Lincluden conference took place.[23] It was interrupted by cheer-
ing news of a great Lancastrian victory at Wakefield on 30 December
and of the death of Richard, Duke of York. Margaret of Anjou
thereupon hurried south with a 'great army of Scots, Welsh and other
strangers and Northmen'.[24] Despite a victory at the second battle of
St Albans on 17 February 1461 she was out-matched by Duke
Richard's son, Edward, who on 4 March proclaimed himself king as
Edward IV. When he defeated the Lancastrians at Towton on 29
March 1461 his authority was, for the time being, incontestable. By
April Queen Margaret was back in Scotland as a fugitive with the
deposed Henry VI, Prince Edward, the Dukes of Somerset and
Exeter, and other notable Lancastrians.[25]

In return for hospitality and the prospect of Scottish military
support the exiles paid a high price: on 25 April 1461 they surrendered Berwick.[26] The burgh, which had been in English hands
almost continuously since 1333, was sufficiently re-assimilated by
1465 to send its custumars to account at the Scottish exchequer; but
since the customs, great and small, amounted to only £31 5s. 1½d.[27]
it is clear that there had been a catastrophic decline from the prosperity that had existed before the English occupation. Strategically,
however, the recovery of Berwick was important for the Scots and
gave them hope of security on the East March. The exiled Lancastrians had not only restored Scotland to its traditional bounds
but had also promised to cede Carlisle, which they and the Scots
soon besieged, only to be repulsed in May 1461.[28]

[22] *Chron. Auchinleck*, pp. 21, 58; *E.R.*, vii. 8.
[23] For this dating see Dunlop, *Bishop Kennedy*, p. 215, n. 6.
[24] *Chron. Auchinleck*, pp. 21, 58; *Three Fifteenth-Century Chronicles*, cited
in Dunlop, *Bishop Kennedy*, p. 220.
[25] Dunlop, *Bishop Kennedy*, pp. 220–1; *E.R.*, vii. xxxvi–xxxvii.
[26] *Rot. Parl.*, v. 478; *E.R.*, vii. xxxvii–xxxviii.   [27] *E.R.*, vii. 364.
[28] *Rot. Parl.*, v. 478; *Paston Letters*, cited in *E.R.*, vii. xxxviii.

It was now the turn of Edward IV to try to stir up trouble in Scotland. He found a ready agent in the disinherited Earl of Douglas, who on 22 June was appointed to head a mission to negotiate with the Earl of Ross and Donald Balloch.[29] Already disorders were rampant in the Highlands and Isles. After the death of James II 'the first slauchter' occurred on Kerrera, when Colin Campbell, Earl of Argyll, descended on the island and rescued his kinsman, John Stewart of Lorne, who was being kept in durance by Alan of Lorne, his brother or half-brother, described as sister's son of Donald Balloch,[30] the kinsman and close associate of the Earl of Ross. The latter was specially summoned by Marchmont herald to compear as a defendant at the first parliament of the new reign in February 1461.[31] When he arrived he was attended by 'all the lardis of the Ilis'[32] and apparently remained undaunted, for at the end of June 1461 Bishop Kennedy and Bishop Durisdeer of Glasgow interviewed him in Bute in an attempt to reach an understanding 'by treaty or otherwise'.[33]

But it was to Yorkist overtures that Ross paid heed. According to an indenture concluded at London on 13 February 1462[34] he, Donald Balloch, and the latter's son and heir, John, together with their 'subgettez', were at Whitsuntide 1463 to become the liegemen of King Edward, after which, to their 'uttermest myght and power' they would aid him in his wars in Scotland and Ireland. From Whitsuntide 1462 the earl was, during his lifetime, to receive from the English king a hundred marks yearly in time of peace and £200 in time of war; Donald Balloch would receive £20 in peacetime and £40 in wartime; and his son would receive £10 in peacetime and £20 in wartime. They were also entertained with the hope of sharing with the Earl of Douglas in certain territorial spoils. For

> if it so be that hereafter the said reaume of Scotlande or the more part thereof be conquered, subdued, and brough to the obeissaunce of the said most high and Christien prince [Edward IV] . . . the same erles [Ross and Douglas] and Donald shall have . . . all the possessions of the seide reaume beyonde Scottish See [the Forth].

These lands were to be divided equally among them as vassals of the English king, while Douglas was also to 'have, enjoie and inherite

---

[29] *Rot. Scot.*, II. 402; *Cal. Docs. Scot.*, IV. No. 1317.
[30] *Chron. Auchinleck*, pp. 21–2, 58–9; *Scots Peerage*, v. 3.
[31] *E.R.*, VII. xxxix–xl, 20.   [32] *Chron. Auchinleck*, pp. 22, 59.
[33] Dunlop, *Bishop Kennedy*, p. 223; *R.M.S.*, II. No. 1196.
[34] Text in *Rot. Scot.*, II. 405–7.

all his own possessions, landes and enheritaunce on this syde the seid Scotysshe See'.

The Earl of Ross now acted more boldly than ever : according to the Auchinleck chronicler he 'past till Inverness and tuke the kingis fermes and all vittalis of the kingis, and proclamit all the gudis and the landis of the kingis intill his handis and gaf remissionis and respittis'.[35] Although the government was long unaware of Ross's secret league with the Yorkists, it was soon aware of the earl's activities at Inverness, which James III afterwards styled a 'treasonable usurpation upon our royal authority and royal crown'.[36] Earl John was summoned 'under pane of forfalt' to answer charges in parliament. The earl, however, 'comperit nocht', whereupon the three estates adjourned the case until 24 June 1462 and 'continewit the forsaid parliament till that day, to be haldin in Aberdene'.[37] There was presumably no parliament since the king 'did not come'.[38] Soon after January 1463 MacDonald, having doubtless met opposition to his rent-collecting in some of the crown lands near Inverness, laid them waste by fire.[39]

Thus the treaty of London had results serious enough, but hardly comparable to those envisaged in its terms : before it was concluded Ross had already behaved in boisterous fashion, and afterwards he merely behaved in a more exaggerated fashion. His outlook may be compared to that of Charles the Bold : if the latter had no liking for the evolution of a unitary state under a new monarchy in France, the former had no liking for similar developments in Scotland; and the domains of the Earl of Ross had a cultural homogeneity that made them potentially better material for home-rule than the rich hotchpotch of French and Netherlandish territories conglomerated since 1433 under the house of Burgundy.[40] It has been affirmed that 'there can be no doubt that Ross was steeped in duplicity',[41] and that through him Edward IV could 'stab Scotland in the back with the Celtic dirk'.[42] But the Lowland Douglas was equally obliging with a Sassenach poniard, and in his duplicity MacDonald did not differ overmuch from many of his contemporaries. The Scottish government, despite its official welcome to the Lancastrians, seems to have

---

[35] *Chron. Auchinleck*, pp. 23, 60.   [36] *A.P.S.*, II. 108–9.
[37] *Chron. Auchinleck*, pp. 23, 60.   [38] *E.R.*, VII. 143.
[39] *propter vastitatem terrarum . . . per incendium comitis de Roos* (*E.R.*, VII. 347, 357).
[40] See M. P. Rooseboom, *The Scottish Staple in The Netherlands*, pp. 15–16.
[41] Dunlop, *Bishop Kennedy*, p. 223.
[42] A. Lang, *History of Scotland* (1900), I. 336.

sent Lord Hamilton on an exploratory mission to Edward IV in April 1461.[43] And a few months later Edward was not only initiating his scheme for a dismemberment of Scotland with the complicity of the Earl of Ross but was commissioning the Earl of Warwick, his chief general and diplomatist, to negotiate a truce with the ambassadors of his 'dearest kinsman', James, King of Scots. In September and November 1461 Edward issued safe-conducts for imposing Scottish embassies, whose members, after talks on the subject of a truce, seem to have been escorted home by Windsor herald.[44]

The ambassadors, who included Master James Lindsay, were probably despatched on the initiative of the 'young lords' attached to Mary of Guelders, who to Kennedy's annoyance toyed with the idea of reaching an accommodation with the Yorkists. Bishop Kennedy, at any rate, professed to have met with obstruction from Queen Mary, while 'all the great lords of the realm' allegedly complained that Scotland was threatened with perdition to please the King of France, whose 'exhortation and charge' Kennedy was avowedly trying to implement in fostering a Scottish-Lancastrian alliance.[45] On the other hand the French king's disaffected vassal, Duke Philip of Burgundy, whose niece was Mary of Guelders, hoped that the Scots would support the Yorkists, and at the close of 1460 had sent the Lord of Gruythuse as an envoy to Scotland to advocate their cause.[46] Moreover the queen's policy was perhaps not uninfluenced by personal factors. For it was rumoured that she had had a love affair with the refugee Lancastrian Duke of Somerset, that he had spread abroad the news of his amorous conquest, and that Mary, finding herself scorned, had in a fit of repugnance urged Patrick Hepburn, Lord Hailes, to try to slay the duke.[47] If he tried he failed, but his son, Adam Hepburn, was to replace the duke in the queen's affections.

Adam, the Master of Hailes, was seeking a divorce from his wife, and the queen's relationship with him 'caussit hir to be lichtliet [scorned] witht the haill nobilietie of Scottland'.[48] After a brief and penitential reconciliation with Bishop Kennedy during Lent in 1462,[49] Mary ensconced herself in Dunbar Castle, of which her lover's father, Lord Hailes, was keeper,[50] and was doubtless the source of

[43] *Rot. Scot.*, II. 402.   [44] *Ibid.*, 402–4; *Cal. Docs. Scot.*, IV. No. 1326.
[45] Kennedy's despatch, cited in Dunlop, *Bishop Kennedy*, pp. 215, 216.
[46] *Ibid.*, pp. 214–7, 222.   [47] *Ibid.*, p. 227.
[48] Pitscottie, *Historie*, I. 158; Major, *History*, p. 388; *Scots Peerage*, II. 148.
[49] Dunlop, *Bishop Kennedy*, p. 227, n. 5; *E.R.*, VII. 78–80.
[50] *Chron. Auchinleck*, pp. 22, 59.

the 'evil and peril' and 'great division' of which Bishop Kennedy complained.[51]

The queen certainly continued to act independently. On 17 March 1462 she had advanced a total of £290 to Margaret of Anjou,[52] doubtless to finance the English queen's voyage from Kirkcudbright to Brittany, which she reached on 16 April 1462 on her way to plead her cause before the new French king, Louis XI.[53] Having bid farewell to her guest, Queen Mary immediately received the Earl of Warwick at Dumfries. There, in April 1462, they talked of 'a long truce, double alliances and friendship', to be cemented by royal marriages, including, so it was rumoured, a match between the queen herself and Edward IV. In May 1462 Warwick sent a report of 'good news from the Scots', who, in a parliament held at Stirling, were to have appointed envoys to follow up the talks at Dumfries. Because of Kennedy's opposition, however, no envoys were appointed. Nonetheless, at the end of June 1462 Queen Mary and her 'young lords' went to Carlisle to negotiate with Warwick. Whatever 'appoyntements' were made at Carlisle, they were reported in England as having been made 'by the yong lords of Scotland, but not by the old'; the former were believed to have dealt fraudulently, 'as was afterwards plainly evident'.[54] Indeed despite Kennedy's fears of Queen Mary's supposed Yorkist proclivities, it is possible that she, no less devious than others, was merely driving time until the result was known of Queen Margaret's mission to France.

There in June 1462 Margaret made a treaty with Louis XI and in October sailed back to Scotland with Sir William Monypenny and Pierre de Brézé, seneschal of Normandy. Having collected Henry VI and Somerset they disembarked in Northumberland and installed garrisons in the castles of Alnwick, Bamburgh and Dunstanburgh.[55] In retaliation, Edward IV allowed the disinherited Earl of Douglas to harry the Borders[56] and sent Warwick to beleaguer the Lancastrian garrisons in Northumberland. Margaret of Anjou, Henry VI and De Brézé, most of whose ships were wrecked, made a stormy escape by sea to Berwick.[57] Soon the garrisons of Dunstanburgh and Bamburgh capitulated, and Somerset temporarily made his peace with Edward IV. The Scots had, however, engaged their honour to rescue

[51] Kennedy's despatch, cited in Dunlop, *Bishop Kennedy*, pp. 238, 256.
[52] *E.R.*, VII. 80.   [53] Dunlop, *Bishop Kennedy*, p. 227.
[54] *Ibid.*, pp. 227–30.   [55] *Ibid.*, p. 231.
[56] *Cal. Docs. Scot.*, IV. Nos. 1332, 1333; *Rot. Scot.*, II. 404.
[57] Dunlop, *Bishop Kennedy*, p. 231; Pitscottie, *Historie*, I. 156.

the garrison of Alnwick; and the Earl of Angus had further inducement since on 22 November 1462 Henry VI had promised him an
English dukedom if he would pass 'with hym into his reaume of
England ageyns his rebelles and traitours, for the recoverynge of
the saide reaume and the destruccioun of the same rebelles'.[58] On
5 January 1463 a relief expedition under Angus and De Brézé successfully brought the garrison of Alnwick to safety despite Warwick
and his men. No sooner had Warwick left Northumberland than
Margaret of Anjou once more placed garrisons in Bamburgh, Dunstanburgh and Alnwick. To follow up this success she bargained for
full-scale Scottish intervention. It was rumoured in England that she
had promised Kennedy the archbishopric of Canterbury, and had
tempted the Scottish king with the prospective cession of seven English 'sherifwicks' as well as a marriage between his sister Mary and
Prince Edward. Early in July 1463 Henry VI, Queen Margaret,
Queen Mary, and the young James III set out with a Scottish army
and 'great ordnance' to besiege Norham Castle. At the approach of
Warwick they ignominiously retreated; and it was reported that they
would regret their enterprise until the Judgment Day on account of
a devastating retaliatory invasion of the Scottish Borders.[59] In this
emergency [60] Bishop Kennedy had prepared to take the field in person
alongside the young king. Eventually, so reported Kennedy, 'the
enterprise of the said King Edward was broken, and the said traitor
[Douglas] repulsed, and justice taken on his brother'.[61] The latter,
Lord Balvenie, had been captured and was executed at Edinburgh,
while his captors shared prize money of 1,200 marks.[62] Queen Margaret realised that after the fiasco at Norham nothing was to be
gained by remaining in Scotland. She left Henry VI housed under
Kennedy's care at St Andrews while she herself sailed from Bamburgh
with her son and De Brézé to beg succour from none other than her
adversary the Duke of Burgundy.[63]

The departure of Queen Margaret reduced Bishop Kennedy's
obligations to the Lancastrians; and the death of George Douglas,

---

[58] Fraser, *Douglas*, III. 92–3.   [59] Dunlop, *Bishop Kennedy*, pp. 232, 236–7.

[60] See the fragmentary undated record described as 'Minutes of Parliament'
(*A.P.S.*, XII. 30–1, at p. 31). This record has been assigned to the close of 1464
by A. I. Dunlop (*Bishop Kennedy*, pp. 322–3) but must surely be dated in the
opening months of that year, probably in mid-January 1464, when Lord Kilmaurs
presented a complaint in some otherwise unrecorded parliament (*A.P.S.*, XII.
29–30).

[61] Kennedy's despatch, cited in Dunlop, *Bishop Kennedy*, p. 237.

[62] W. Fraser, *The Scotts of Buccleuch* (1878), II. 63–4.

[63] Dunlop, *Bishop Kennedy*, p. 237.

Earl of Angus, in March 1463, followed by that of Queen Mary in December,[64] left him to dominate the political stage : in some meeting of the three estates, presumably early in 1464, he obtained custody of the young king.[65] The situation was critical : on 8 October 1463 the commissioners of Louis XI and Edward IV had agreed to an abstinence of war, and Louis had omitted to include Scotland. Not surprisingly, as Kennedy pointed out, 'the whole of the said realm was much dismayed'.[66] The bishop, hitherto committed to a Franco-Scottish alliance, soon demonstrated that he, like others, could change his mind, and that he did not regard the French as indispensable allies. Negotiations with the Yorkists culminated at York on 1 June 1464 with the conclusion of a truce to last for fifteen years.[67] Edward IV took the precaution of paying annual pensions, totalling £366, to Bishop Kennedy and Bishop Spens of Aberdeen,[68] whose behaviour in accepting such funds was not altogether irreproachable even by the standards of the time. Edward evidently suspected that Henry VI might again be allowed to use Scotland as a base. The capture of the deposed king in Lancashire on 13 July 1465[69] removed a major source of friction, and an indenture concluded at Newcastle on 12 December 1465 even prolonged the existing fifteen-year truce until 1519.[70] This was carrying optimism too far; but for over a decade Anglo-Scottish relations were to subside into an abnormal state of relative tranquillity.

Bishop Kennedy, who may be credited with beginning the settlement of Scotland's external problems, was no less successful in dealing with the country's internal problems, of which the most pressing were those posed by the activities of the Earl of Ross. Trouble had again flared up on the western seaboard, where Alan McCoule had slain John Stewart, Lord Lorne and Innermeath, probably in pursuance of the earlier feud in which the Earl of Argyll had intervened.[71] A parliament that met early in 1464 ordained that the culprit be put to the horn and that 'nochtwithstanding the lettres written of befor to the Erle of Ross . . . new lettres be writtine baith be autorite of the king

[64] E.R., vii. liv–lv; Pitscottie, Historie, i. 157–8.
[65] Dunlop, Bishop Kennedy, p. 241 and n. 6.
[66] Kennedy's despatch, cited in Dunlop, Bishop Kennedy, p. 238.
[67] Rot. Scot., ii. 410–2; Cal. Docs. Scot., iv. No. 1341.
[68] Cal. Docs. Scot., iv. No. 1360. On 13 July 1467 Bishop Spens was paid a further £133 6s. 8d. (ibid., No. 1371).
[69] Dunlop, Bishop Kennedy, p. 248 and n. 5.
[70] Cal. Docs. Scot., iv. Nos. 1362, 1363; Rot. Scot., ii. 418–20.
[71] P. 401 above.

and of parliament chargeing hym that he nothir supple nor resett the saide Alane in the saide dedis'.[72] By August 1464 Kennedy had arrived in Inverness, where the Earl of Ross was confronted with the lords of council and, in the course of a reconciliation, had to confess his seizure of £74 12s. 3d. from the burgh customs.[73] Although Ross did not attend a 'congregation' of lords spiritual and temporal that assembled in Edinburgh on 11 October 1464, he at least took the trouble to appoint procurators, a formality that he was also to observe when parliament met in 1467 and 1471.[74]

The 'congregation' seems to have been an afforced privy council, composed of five bishops, three abbots, five earls, the procurators of another three earls, a score of lords, and, reportedly, many other un-named nobles, as well as a few officials.[75] It is remarkable that this assembly, which did not include burgesses,[76] dealt with business that ought more properly to have been brought before the three estates in parliament or general council. It has been supposed that after 1456 general councils were no longer held.[77] On the other hand it has been conjectured that 'a register of the proceedings of general councils in the reign of James IV and possibly in that of James III has been lost'; and there exist stray references to general councils that met in 1473, 1497, 1511 and 1512.[78] It therefore seems likely that there was con-tinuity between the general councils of the fifteenth century and the 'conventions' of the sixteenth century.[79] Nonetheless general councils may have altered in character: for 'a tendency to omit the summons of burgesses marked the development of general council into conven-tion until the active reign of Queen Mary'.[80] This tendency is certainly apparent in the composition of the 'congregation' that Bishop Ken-nedy had summoned.

Part of its business concerned the working of the act of August 1455 that had annexed certain lands to the crown:[81] it was agreed that the annexed crown lands alienated by James II should be re-sumed by the crown without legal process.[82] Although the surviving record tells only of the act of resumption the assembly had also been summoned 'for the peace and tranquillity of the realm and doing

[72] 'Minutes of Parliament', A.P.S., XII. 31.   [73] E.R., VII. 296-7.
[74] A.P.S., II. 84, 87, 98.   [75] Ibid., 84.
[76] R. K. Hannay (op. cit., S.H.R., XVIII. 157-70, at 167) wrongly writes of 'a considerable assembly of representatives of the estates'.
[77] Dunlop, Bishop Kennedy, p. 315.   [78] Rait, Parliaments, p. 139.
[79] R. K. Hannay (op. cit., S.H.R., XVIII. 157-70, at 167-8). For the nature of these conventions see A.P.S., II. 594, 598, 606.
[80] Rait, Parliaments, p. 139.   [81] Pp. 378-9 above.   [82] A.P.S., II. 84.

justice'.[83] A parliament that had met some months earlier had thought it 'speidfull' that three sessions be held each year, one in Edinburgh, another in Perth, and another in Aberdeen, to deal with civil cases which had arisen since 'the cessing of the last sessionis',[84] presumably those which, according to the Auchinleck chronicler, the first parliament of the reign had 'ordanit . . . to sit' at Aberdeen, Perth and Edinburgh.[85]

While Bishop Kennedy could wholeheartedly promote justice by trying to revive the sessions, and could likewise show zeal in securing the crown's landed patrimony by the act of resumption, his attitude towards the crown's control of ecclesiastical patronage was ambiguous. At the Edinburgh parliament of October 1462, which he must have attended,[86] he did not lend his name to a re-assertion of the extended rights of the crown during episcopal vacancies that had been won by James II towards the close of his reign.[87] Perhaps Kennedy saw a man after his own heart in his nephew, Patrick Graham, to whom he lent his support when the bishopric of Brechin became vacant : Graham, who had 'academic qualifications and a local family influence', but apparently no previous experience in royal service, was provided to Brechin on 28 March 1463.[88] When Kennedy died on 24 May 1465 it was Patrick Graham who was to succeed him as Bishop of St Andrews.

With the possible exception of the advancement of Patrick Graham, Bishop Kennedy's achievements in the last year and a half of his life, the only period when he was undisputed head of government, support the testimony of Pitscottie that he was 'maist abill of ony lord . . . to gif ane wyse consall or ane ansuer . . . and spetiallie in the tyme of parliament . . . [in dealing with] trubillis that appeirit [in] the realm, and spetiallie contrair the leisemajestie'.[89] Certainly the minority of James III, despite squabbles and disaffection, had not lapsed into the anarchy that had marked the minority of James II when Kennedy's influence was more circumscribed. At his death the crown was outwardly strong, not least, perhaps, on account of the recovery of the late queen's dower lands : in 1462 the bailies of the crown lands had accounted for money rents of slightly less than

---

[83] *Ibid.*   [84] 'Minutes of Parliament' (*ibid.*, XII. 31).

[85] *Chron. Auchinleck*, pp. 22, 59.

[86] Kennedy was in Edinburgh at the time (see his itinerary, Dunlop, *Bishop Kennedy*, p. 435).

[87] *A.P.S.*, II. 83–4. Nor had Kennedy witnessed the act of the provincial council of 1459 on which the 1462 act was based (p. 385 above).

[88] Dunlop, *Bishop Kennedy*, pp. 251–2.   [89] Pitscottie, *Historie*, I. 160.

£3,000 a year;[90] in 1465 the crown rents, exclusive of victuals, though inclusive of heavy arrears,[91] were yielding over £7,500 a year.[92]

There were tempting pickings for those who remained to share power when the successive deaths of Angus, Queen Mary, and Bishop Kennedy left the thirteen-year-old king at the mercy of lesser politicians. If outward respectability was maintained it was thanks to the continuity supplied by professional civil servants: Andrew Stewart, Lord Avondale, an illegitimate descendant of Duke Murdoch of Albany, served as chancellor from 1460 to 1482; Archibald Whitelaw, archdeacon of Lothian, was secretary from 1462 to 1493.[93] Other steadying influences were provided by the Abbot of Holyrood and Colin Campbell, Earl of Argyll, master of the royal household since 1464,[94] both of whom were fairly active in government and served as auditors of exchequer.[95] Lord Livingston, chamberlain from 1454 to 1467,[96] was a former leader of faction who had not altogether mended his ways; and more volatile politicians were to be found among the Kennedies and Boyds, who took advantage of the aloofness of the earls in order to emulate the example set by the Livingstons and Crichtons during the minority of the previous reign.

Robert, Lord Boyd, son of the Sir Thomas Boyd slain by Alexander Stewart in 1439, and himself probably the slayer of Sir James Stewart at Drumglass in 1445, held a territorial power centred on Kilmarnock.[97] In 1463 and 1464 he had been a member of Scottish embassies to England alongside his more prominent younger brother, Sir Alexander Boyd of Drumcoll,[98] who by June 1466 was evidently one of the lords of council and was serving for the second time as one of the auditors at exchequer.[99] In 1464, moreover, Sir Alexander had been appointed captain of Edinburgh Castle with an annual fee of two hundred marks.[100] He seems also to have been appointed to instruct the young king in chivalric exercises[101] and was certainly by March 1466 chamberlain of the royal household.[102] Thus he had

[90] The total was about £4,300; but all save one of the accounts ran for three terms, thus the yearly income was about £2,800 (*E.R.*, VII. 107–36).

[91] The arrears of Galloway alone were £729 8s. 6½d. (*ibid.*, 308).

[92] *Ibid.*, 308–61. In this estimate allowance has been made for the fact that some of the accounts run for more than two terms.

[93] *H.B.C.*, pp. 175, 186. [94] *Cal. Docs. Scot.*, IV. No. 1341.

[95] *E.R.*, VII. 107, 302, 308, 380, 520. [96] *H.B.C.*, p. 179.

[97] *Scots Peerage*, VI. 141–2; p. 327 above.

[98] *Cal. Docs. Scot.*, IV. No. 1341; *Rot. Scot.*, II. 409.

[99] *E.R.*, VII. 302, 380, 424. [100] *Ibid.*, 284, 362, 422.

[101] *Ibid.*, lvii. [102] *R.M.S.*, II. No. 867; see p. 365, No. 40.

control of the chief stronghold in the kingdom and easy access to the king.

The implications of this potentially dangerous situation do not seem to have been realised by Bishop Kennedy, who throughout his career had by no means neglected to promote the interests of his own elder brother, Gilbert, Lord Kennedy, and the other members of his prolific kin. Lord Kennedy, who in 1463 had been granted the custody of Stirling Castle with an annual fee of £80,[103] began to figure in 1465 as a frequent witness to royal charters.[104] There was every reason to suppose that, reinforced by his numerous and well-placed kinsmen and by his royal descent, he would step into the shoes of his younger brother the late bishop. Nor were the Boyds expected to oppose such a move : Sir Alexander Boyd had married a certain Janet Kennedy; and Lord Boyd's son and heir, Thomas, was contracted on 20 January 1465 to marry the youngest daughter of Lord Kennedy.[105]

An indenture sealed at Stirling on 10 February 1466[106] gives a revealing picture of contemporary politics and shows that the dominant Kennedies and Boyds had momentarily to share power with Lord Fleming. It made mention of other bonds that were to be respected by the various parties : Lord Fleming had made earlier 'bandis' with Lord Livingston and Lord Hamilton; Lord Kennedy and Sir Alexander Boyd had made bonds with the Earl of Crawford, Lord Montgomery, Lord Maxwell, Lord Boyd, Lord Livingston, Lord Hamilton and Lord Cathcart, as well as with Patrick Graham, the new Bishop of St Andrews. Other records show that the last-named, on 30 June 1466, used a marriage contract as a vehicle for an indenture of alliance between himself and the Earl of Morton,[107] who in turn would receive from Hugh Douglas of Borg in 1474 a bond of manrent promising service in peace and war against all persons save the king.[108] It is perhaps no mere accident of survival that from about 1460 onwards there is increasing evidence of the bonds of alliance and manrent by which men of rank sought in shifting times to achieve, at the least, security, and, at the most, political power and the prizes that went with it.

In the indenture of 10 February 1466 that bound Lord Kennedy and Sir Alexander Boyd in an alliance with Lord Fleming, it was agreed that these three nobles and their 'kyn, friendis and men' would

---

[103] *E.R.*, vii. 346, 392.
[104] *R.M.S.*, ii. Nos. 832–75, *passim*; see also p. 365, No. 20.
[105] *Scots Peerage*, v. 142, 148.
[106] Text in Tytler, *History*, i. pt. ii, 387–8, Notes and Illustrations, Letter O.
[107] *Morton Registrum*, ii. No. 222.   [108] *Ibid.*, No. 227; see also No. 236.

stand together during their respective lifetimes 'in all thair caussis and querell, leifull and honest . . . aganis al maner of persones . . . thair allegiance til our soveran lord alanerly outan [excepted]'.[109] The addition of the last phrase shows that this particular bond was not one that directly menaced the monarchy but one designed to turn the royal minority to good account by sharing the spoils of political power. It was agreed that Lord Fleming should be 'of special service and of cunsail to the kyng' as long as Lord Kennedy and Sir Alexander Boyd were in the king's council. Fleming undertook that he would not 'tak away the kyngis person fra the saidis Lord Kennedy and Sir Alexander', nor would he aid anyone else to do so but would warn them of any such plot. He would also advise the king 'to be hertly and kyndly to the foirsaidis Lord Kenedy and Sir Alexander, to thair barnis [children] and friendis'. In return, if some suitable royal office should happen to fall vacant, Fleming was to be 'furderit thairto for his reward', while in preference to anyone else he was to have wards, reliefs, marriages or offices for a reasonable composition. The parties to the indenture thereupon gave their oaths to observe its terms without fraud or guile, having sealed it and touched the gospels.[110]

The upshot came a few months later while the exchequer audit was being held at Linlithgow.[111] According to Buchanan, the earliest writer to describe the incident, the young king was taken from the exchequer on a hunting party; when Lord Kennedy suspected that all was not well he was felled by a blow struck by Sir Alexander Boyd, who rode off with the king and installed him in Edinburgh Castle, where Sir Alexander held sway.[112] Parliamentary records show that the abduction took place on 9 July 1466 and that those responsible were Lord Boyd, Sir Alexander Boyd, Lord Somerville, Adam Hepburn, son and heir of Patrick, Lord Hailes, and Andrew Kerr, son and heir of Andrew Kerr of Cessfurd.[113] All these, with the curious exception of Sir Alexander Boyd, were soon to receive a royal remission for their action. For on 13 October 1466, a few days after parliament had opened in the tolbooth of Edinburgh, Lord Boyd knelt before the throne in the presence of the three estates and asked whether his majesty had conceived any indignation against him and his companions for 'riding with him after the exchequer from his palace of Linlithgow to Edinburgh', whereupon the king, ripely advised, announced that Boyd had acted by royal command and that

[109] P. F. Tytler, *History*, I. pt ii, 388.   [110] *Ibid.*
[111] *E.R.*, VII. 380.   [112] Buchanan, *History*, cited in *E.R.*, VII. lix.
[113] *A.P.S.*, II. 185–6.

no rancour was held against him and his companions—a declaration that Boyd cautiously asked should be recorded among the acts of parliament and issued under the great seal.[114]

In the same parliament the king announced that it was his pleasure that his kinsman, Lord Boyd, should have governance of the royal person, the king's brothers and the royal castles, as well as execution of the royal authority and justice, until he himself had reached the age of twenty-one.[115] Parliament also appointed 'certane lordis', presumably of the Boyd faction, to have the full power of parliament until 1 February 1467 to deal with a number of matters, notably the marriages of the king, his brother and sister. This commission was also 'to sit and juge the persouns that haldis [withholds] fra oure soverane lorde the king, or fra my lorde of Albany, thare castellis'.[116]

The intended victims of this last provision were Gilbert Kennedy of Kirkmichael, who held Dunbar Castle (the property of Albany by reason of his subsidiary title as Earl of March) and Lord Kennedy, who held the royal castle of Stirling. Before long, Archibald Boyd had replaced Gilbert Kennedy as captain of Dunbar,[117] and by 25 October 1466 the court was at Stirling, where letters under the great seal were issued re-affirming the remission granted to Lord Boyd and his appointment as keeper of the royal person and exerciser of the royal authority.[118] Lord Kennedy did not resist : he was held under arrest for a few months in Stirling Castle, custody of which was transferred from him to Chancellor Avondale.[119] It seems highly unlikely that Lord Kennedy had connived at the abduction of the king from Linlithgow, making merely 'a feint of opposition' and submitting to 'a brief imprisonment . . . for appearance sake'.[120] After the Linlithgow episode Kennedy ceased to be a frequent witness to royal charters. There can be no doubt that he and his kin, on the point of establishing a hegemony of their own, had been foiled by the Boyds, while Lord Fleming was by-passed as insignificant. The Kennedies were lucky to escape with relatively small loss while the Boyds battened on the spoils of their *coup d'état*. What is remarkable is that a further *coup* appears to have taken place within the Boyd faction: after the seizure of the king, Lord Boyd became a frequent witness to royal charters;[121] but his younger brother, Sir Alexander, appears as

[114] *Ibid.*, 185.　　　　　[115] *Ibid.*
[116] *Ibid.*　　　　　[117] *E.R.*, VII. 494.
[118] *A.P.S.*, II. 185; *R.M.S.*, II. Nos. 891, 892.
[119] *E.R.*, VII. 441, 443, 458, 522, 601.　　[120] G. Burnett, *ibid.*, lix.
[121] See *R.M.S.*, II. Nos. 881–983, *passim*, and p. 365, No. 8.

a witness virtually for the last time in August 1466.[122] Soon afterwards he was supplanted by Lord Boyd in the well-paid custody of Edinburgh Castle [123] and retired into obscurity for a year or two until he was made to pay for the misdeeds of his more successful brother and nephew. The latter, Lord Boyd's son and heir, Thomas, had not hitherto figured on the political scene, but was intended by his father to be the real beneficiary of the family's daring bid for power. The king's sister, the Lady Mary, might have been a useful (though costly) asset in international diplomacy. James wept for shame when she was bestowed in marriage upon Thomas Boyd.[124] In prospective cash she brought a poor dowry of only a thousand marks to her husband;[125] but he was created Earl of Arran, and, with his wife, received a considerable territorial settlement based upon that new earldom.[126]

The marriage of Thomas Boyd to the king's sister had doubtless been arranged by the commission of lords appointed by parliament in October 1466, whose powers were to expire on 1 February 1467 :[127] Thomas Boyd had been created Earl of Arran at least as early as 22 February 1467,[128] which suggests that the marriage had by then taken place. No doubt it could be explained away—the report which the commission was to receive from 'certaine lordis now beande in Inglande' probably made it clear that the Yorkists were for the present, unable, or unwilling, to offer suitable matrimonial terms to the Scottish royal family. Hence, perhaps, a decision to marry off the Lady Mary cheaply within Scotland, to keep the king's brothers in reserve, and to seek a continental match for the king. One possible match was already contemplated : for the parliament of October 1466 had significantly empowered the commission of lords to deal not only with royal marriages but 'the annuale of Norway';[129] and this, together with other grounds for animosity between the crowns of Scotland and Denmark-Norway, had formerly led Charles VII of France to propose a marriage settlement on the eve of a meeting of Scottish and Danish envoys at Bourges in 1460. There, shortly after the death of James II,[130] the Scots had proposed incredible conditions for a marriage settlement : all arrears of the Norway annual, which

122 He witnessed a royal charter at Lochmaben on 13 August 1466 (*ibid.*, No. 884 and p. 365 No. 15).   123 *E.R.*, VII. 500, 591, 663.
124 C. A. J. Armstrong, *op. cit., S.H.S. Misc. VIII.* 19–32, at 30.
125 *E.R.*, VII. 463.   126 *R.M.S.*, II. Nos. 912–5.
127 *A.P.S.*, II. 85.   128 *Cal. Docs. Scot.*, IV. No. 1368.
129 *A.P.S.*, II. 85; pp. 46, 82, 315 above.
130 K. Hørby, 'Christian I and the pawning of Orkney', *S.H.R.*, XLVIII. 54–63, at p. 56.

the Scots had not paid since 1426 and only rarely before, were to be remitted; the bride was to bring a dowry of 100,000 écus for her 'adornments'; and the crown of Denmark-Norway was to surrender to that of Scotland its rights to Orkney and Shetland.[131] The first condition was statesmanlike but the remaining two were exorbitant. It is not surprising that Christian I, who in 1460 'was probably at the peak of his power',[132] far from negotiating on these terms, took a closer interest in the islands that the Scots openly coveted.

There the authority of the Danish crown had been weakened by a remarkable 'scotticisation', that had gone far in Orkney, though less so in Shetland. This had taken place through two agencies—the kirk and the house of Sinclair.[133] Although the bishopric of Orkney was still subject to the metropolitan authority of Nidaros, the Bishops of Orkney and many of the clergy had long been Scottish,[134] so that 'by 1450 it is thought that there was not a single Norse or native ecclesiastic in Orkney'.[135] Scottish ecclesiastical influence was supplemented by that of the Sinclair earls.[136] In 1434 Earl William of Orkney had done homage to an earlier Danish king but he had not renewed his homage to King Christian, whereas, by contrast, the earl's contacts with the Scottish monarchy had been close. On 8 December 1461 he was summoned to do homage to the Danish king, but although he had recently protested his loyalty he does not seem to have obeyed the summons: in the next few years prior to 1468 'there is evidence that the earl's attitude hardened into outright hostility'. By 1466 Christian was trying to use Bishop William Tulloch and the lawman of Orkney to maintain his authority, with the result that in 1467 the bishop was temporarily imprisoned by the earl's eldest son.[137] Christian (who was faced with rebellion in Sweden and opposition in Denmark)[138] may have realised that the maintenance of Danish authority in Orkney was, for the time, impracticable, and that a solution of some problems might be reached by way of a marriage alliance. Thus a commission of the three estates, which met at Stirling on 12 January 1468 with the full power of parliament, decided 'anent the mariage of our soverane lord' that 'thar be send ane ambassate in all gudely hast betuix this and the monethis of Marche or Aprile next

---

[131] Barbara Crawford, 'The pawning of Orkney and Shetland', S.H.R., XLVIII. 35–53, at pp. 36, 39.

[132] K. Hørby, op. cit., p. 57.   [133] Barbara Crawford, op. cit., 40.

[134] P. 192 above.   [135] Barbara Crawford, op. cit., 40.

[136] For an outline of their history and genealogy see E.R., VIII. xxxv–xxxix, lxxiv–lxxvii.   [137] Barbara Crawford, op. cit., 41, 42, 44 and n. 3.

[138] K. Hørby, op. cit., 61–2.

tocum in Denmark and uther placis'; and this embassy was also to
receive from the king and his council instructions 'anent the mater of
Noroway'. The embassy was to be financed by a levy of £3,000
granted by the commission 'throu vertu of the powere commitit to
thaim in the last parliament'. To make up this sum each of the estates
was to contribute £1,000.[139] Possibly delays in raising the contribution hindered the appointment of the embassy : it was not in March
or April but on 28 July 1468 that its members were named in letters
issued at Edinburgh under the great seal. Most notable among the
eight ambassadors were Chancellor Avondale, Thomas Boyd, Earl
of Arran, Andrew Durisdeer, Bishop of Glasgow, and William Tulloch, Bishop of Orkney,[140] who although he had no official position
in Scotland, and was a subject of the Danish king, was doubtless
valuable as an interpreter and mediator—he was on good terms with
King Christian both before and after the negotiations.[141]

The resulting treaty, ratified by Christian on 8 September 1468,
settled that his only daughter, Margaret, would marry the Scottish
king. The latter would bestow upon her in dower the palace of
Linlithgow and the castle of Doune, together with one-third of the
royal revenues—the maximum permitted under an ordinance passed
by the Scottish parliament in October 1466.[142] It was also agreed that
thenceforth each king and his successors would be obliged to render
aid to the other against all parties save existing allies. If the Scottish
alliance brought Christian little hope of effective help it at least removed one party from the list of his potential enemies. Moreover the
main source of past animosities was neatly removed : for the dowry
that Margaret of Denmark was to bring to her husband included the
ending of the Norway annual and a quitclaim for all arrears and
damages. The rest of the dowry was to consist of 60,000 Rhenish
florins. Ten thousand were to be paid before the Scottish ambassadors
left Denmark; until the remainder was fully paid, the Scottish king
was to have all the lands, rights and revenues pertaining to the
Norwegian crown in the Orkney Isles.

This impignoration, which in Scottish terms was neither more nor
less than a wadset, was to prove by far the most significant feature of
the treaty. There has been some discussion as to whether Christian

---

[139] *A.P.S.*, II. 90–91.

[140] Their commission is recorded in the resulting marriage treaty, the text of
which is printed in *E.R.*, VIII. lxxvii–lxxxvii, and (with translation) in *Royal
Charters and Records of the City of Kirkwall* (ed. John Mooney, 1950), pp.
96–109.

[141] Barbara Crawford, *op. cit.*, 43, 49.   [142] *A.P.S.*, II. 85.

ever intended that he or his successors might redeem by payment what he had surrendered, or whether he merely intended to disguise a permanent cession of a troublesome liability. The latter view is, however, questionable : there was nothing unusual in the Orkney wadset since Denmark itself 'was largely pawned already' and 'mortgaging parts of the kingdom was . . . a common transaction both within and without Scandinavia'. Nor was there anything in the treaty to suggest that the arrangement was meant to be permanent.[143] Moreover in one contingency the treaty made specific provision for the ending of the wadset : if Margaret were to outlive her husband she would have the option, within three years of his death, of leaving Scotland, providing that she undertook not to marry the King of England or any of his subjects; on leaving Scotland she would lose her dower of the third part of the royal revenues, but would in compensation receive from the Scots the sum of 120,000 Rhenish florins, less 50,000 florins, which would be deducted as payment of the residue of her dowry; thereupon the rights of the Norwegian crown in Orkney would be redeemed and the lands would be restored. Since the previous two Scottish queens had outlived their husbands the possibility that Margaret might be able to take advantage of this complex provision was, to contemporaries, a very real one; and the provision (which has not been noted in recent studies) received additional Scottish ratification on 13 May 1471.[144]

There is thus no evidence that Christian intended to cut the link between Orkney and Norway; and his wadset of the islands must be regarded as primarily a financial expedient. Indeed his resources were so straitened that he could pay only two thousand of the ten thousand florins that were due before the departure of the Scottish ambassadors. The outcome was another financial expedient : on 28 May 1469 he issued letters granting to the Scottish king a wadset of the royal lands, rights and revenues in the Shetland Isles until such time as the deficit of eight thousand florins was paid.[145] In this case no mention was made of the contingency that Margaret might leave Scotland as a widow, and, indirectly, redeem the wadset.

After the twelve-year-old Margaret of Denmark had been wed to the eighteen-year-old James III in Holyrood Abbey on 10 July 1469 [146] the Scots were free to make the most of the concessions they had won from King Christian. They had gone remarkably far to-

---

[143] Barbara Crawford, *op. cit.*, 45–51. [144] *A.P.S.*, II. 187–8.
[145] The text of this document is printed as an appendix in Barbara Crawford, *op. cit.*, 52–3. [146] Lesley, *History*, pp. 37–8; *T.A.*, I. xliv.

wards attaining the terms they had proposed at Bourges in 1460; and James was soon to show some ingenuity in consolidating his newly acquired rights in the Northern Isles, thereby making the Danish concessions even more valuable than at first they appeared to be. Seven royal charters, issued on 17 September 1470,[147] show that William Sinclair, Earl of Orkney and Caithness, had resigned the first of those titles, and, as Earl of Caithness and Lord Sinclair, received compensation from the king in return for conveying to him the castle of Kirkwall and the earldom of Orkney, presumably with its dependency of Shetland.[148] The compensation included the castle of Ravenscraig (newly built by Queen Mary), certain adjacent lands in Fife, a life pension of fifty marks (soon increased to four hundred) from the great customs of Edinburgh,[149] and a variety of miscellaneous privileges.[150] On the whole James had paid a fair price for his new acquisitions and there is no need to suppose that Sinclair had been forced to resign his rights.[151]

The result of James's bargain was that the Scottish crown now possessed permanently all the comital rights in Orkney and Shetland. When parliament on 20 February 1472 annexed the earldom of Orkney and lordship of Shetland to the crown, 'nocht to be gevin away . . . except anerly to ane the kingis sonis of lauchfull bed',[152] it can have been only these comital rights that were annexed. Nonetheless the king, by reason of the treaties of 1468 and 1469, also held a wadset of the royal rights in the Northern Isles and was thus completely their master.

In August 1472 Bishop Tulloch, already appointed keeper of the privy seal,[153] was granted a tack of the Northern Isles, which apparently included custody of Kirkwall Castle and certain profitable rights,[154] in return for a yearly rent of £466 13s. 4d., of which £120 were to be paid in cash and the remainder in barley and salted marts which were sent to Leith.[155] By 1476, however, assessment in terms of

---

[147] *R.M.S.*, II. Nos. 996–1002.   [148] But see the following footnote.

[149] The question of this annual pension involves some difficulties : the grant of 17 September 1470 was of fifty marks (*R.M.S.*, II. No. 998); a confirmation of 11 May 1471 puts it at four hundred marks (*A.P.S.*, II. 101)—which the earl actually received annually during his lifetime (*E.R.*, VIII. 120, 190, 191, 253, 312, 390, 466, 546). Perhaps the pension was increased from fifty to four hundred marks as a result of some unknown transaction conveying the lordship of Shetland to the king.

[150] *R.M.S.*, II. Nos. 997, 999, 1001, 1002; *A.P.S.*, II. 101. See also *E.R.*, VIII. xlvii, n. 2.   [151] As stated by G. Burnett in *E.R.*, VII. lii, n. 1.

[152] *A.P.S.*, II. 102.   [153] *H.B.C.*, p. 296.

[154] See *R.M.S.*, II. No. 1376.   [155] *E.R.*, VIII. 224–5.

barley had been reduced, making the total annual rent worth only £366 13s. 4d.[156] Two years later, by which time Tulloch had been advantageously translated to the see of Moray, the tack was granted, during the king's pleasure, to Andrew Painter, Tulloch's successor as Bishop of Orkney.[157] By 1485, when Painter was still tacksman, the arrears of rent stood at £374 8s. 6d.; part of this sum was remitted and the bishop's previous factor was arrested.[158] Meanwhile disregard for Norse custom was shown by a decision of the auditors of exchequer in 1476 that the fee of the lawman of Orkney should no longer be paid save by a special mandate from the king.[159] And if control by the Scottish crown brought an end to depredations by the Hebrideans, the inhabitants of Shetland were by 1484 being plundered 'by the lords of Norway and their agents'.[160]

When the vessels that had brought James III's bride to Scotland anchored in the Forth, the ship of the Earl of Arran had been boarded by the Lady Mary, who bore her husband such tidings of her brother the king that Arran hoisted sail and sped back to Denmark with his wife.[161] His precaution was well justified: when parliament met in Edinburgh in November 1469 its members not only witnessed the queen's coronation but heard charges of treason against the Boyds.[162]

The usually garrulous Pitscottie surprisingly says nothing of the attack on the Boyds. Nor does the evidence of royal charters, which is remarkably sparse between February 1469 and April 1470,[163] give any clue as to the formation of a faction antagonistic to the Boyds. By May 1468 the latter had even strengthened their position by a marriage between Lord Boyd's daughter, Elizabeth, and Archibald, Earl of Angus, head of the Red Douglases.[164] If an opposing faction had arisen it may have included the king's uncles—John and James Stewart, half-brothers of his father, who both rose to some prominence on the fall of the Boyds.[165] John Stewart was already Earl of Atholl; his brother, James Stewart of Auchterhouse, was created Earl of Buchan sometime between April and September 1470, and, in the only significant change of office that accompanied the fall of the Boyds, supplanted Lord Boyd as chamberlain.[166] Since the other offi-

[156] *Ibid.*, 363, 453, 483, 614.   [157] *R.M.S.*, II. No. 1376.
[158] *E.R.*, IX. 306-7.   [159] *Ibid.*, VIII. 364.
[160] *Ibid.*, xlix.   [161] Lesley, *History*, pp. 37-8.
[162] *A.P.S.*, II. 93-8, 186-7.   [163] *R.M.S.*, II. 203-4.
[164] *Ibid.*, No. 945; *Scots Peerage*, I. 182-3.
[165] Both are thereafter fairly frequent witnesses to royal charters (*ibid.*, *passim*).   [166] *H.B.C.*, pp. 179, 471.

cials remained in office they certainly acquiesced in the attack on the Boyds and may have co-operated in it. The leader of the attack was, however, undoubtedly the king himself; and the attendance of no less than ten earls in the parliament of November 1469,[167] as compared with the less imposing comital attendance at the parliaments of October 1467 and January 1468,[168] shows that the greater nobles were ready to associate themselves with James as soon as he had made his intentions clear by formally summoning the Boyds.

The summons, which must have been issued at least forty days before the opening of parliament, was duly executed at Kilmarnock and the mercat cross of Ayr : Lord Boyd and his eldest son, Thomas (no longer described as Earl of Arran) were called upon to compear on 22 November 1469 to answer for having traitorously abducted the king from Linlithgow on 9 July 1466, as well as for 'the traitorous vituperation and degradation of our royal authority and majesty, in treasonably taking upon themselves the rule and governance of our person and our brothers; and for many other treasonable actions, rebellions, crimes and transgressions'.[169] Lord Boyd realised that in the circumstances his royal remission [170] was worthless : just as his son had fled to Denmark so he fled to England.[171] It was therefore an easy task for David Guthrie, clerk of the rolls and register, who acted as royal 'proloquutor', to produce 'many reasons, allegations, laws, acts and statutes of parliament' to demonstrate the guilt of the two accused. Thereupon the clergy removed themselves, and the dempster of parliament delivered sentence of forfeiture of life, lands, rents, possessions, offices and goods.[172] Sir Alexander Boyd, lately spurned by his brother and nephew, was nonetheless involved in their fall. He too had been summoned, and, unlike his kinsmen, did not escape. On 22 November 1469, when he was brought before parliament, he vigorously denied his guilt and submitted himself to the verdict of an assize of fifteen barons, headed by the Earls of Crawford and Morton. Since Sir Alexander had obtained no specific royal remission for the abduction of 1466 he was particularly vulnerable; he was beheaded on the castle hill of Edinburgh and his property was forfeited.[173]

Meanwhile in Denmark the forfeited Earl of Arran and his wife seem to have received a cold welcome : by February 1470 the pair had arrived in Bruges, where they were lodged in the Hôtel de Jerusalem, the residence of Sir Anselm Adournes. It was probably under

[167] A.P.S., II. 93. [168] Ibid., 87, 88, 89, [169] Ibid., 186.
[170] Pp. 411-2 above. [171] Pp. 476, 479, 491 below. [172] A.P.S., II. 186.
[173] Ibid., 186-7.

the auspices of the Boyds that this Flemish patrician had been knighted, for his connection with Scotland, which was to be a long one, had begun in 1468, when he had been sent there as an envoy of Bruges.[174] Soon after receiving Arran, who seems to have been joined by his father, Lord Boyd, Sir Anselm chivalrously set forth on a pilgrimage to the east. In his absence Arran sought the patronage of Charles the Bold, Duke of Burgundy, a kinsman of the earl's wife : the Duchess of Burgundy (Margaret of York) acted as godmother to Arran's son. Another temporary resident in Bruges was none other than the duchess's brother, Edward IV, who had been driven from England in October 1470 and was to return victoriously in March 1471. It is conceivable that Edward and his brother-in-law of Burgundy 'saw in the Boyds a means of weakening the Franco-Scottish alliance'.[175] When Sir Anselm returned from his eastern travels he set out from Calais on 4 October 1471 in the company of the Boyds. On their arrival in England, where Edward IV was now happily restored as king, Arran undertook a mission to the court on behalf of the Duke of Burgundy and remained safely in England with his father while the Lady Mary went on with Adournes to Scotland to try to soften the heart of her brother.[176] Their efforts were unavailing. Sir Anselm was to be consoled by a grant of the liferent of Cortachy, and in 1472 the king even granted him some of the lands forfeited from Lord Boyd.[177] Whether by compulsion or complaisance Mary married Lord Hamilton. On 12 July 1474 the king issued a charter in favour of his sister and her new husband.[178] It was not until 1476, by which time two children had been born of this match, that a papal dispensation was obtained to remove the impediment of blood relationship.[179] Mary had also borne two children, James and Margaret, to her first husband.[180] It is uncertain whether her marriage to him had been ended by divorce or by his death.[181] Arran was survived by his father, Lord Boyd, who joined the disinherited Douglas as a pensioner of Edward IV.[182]

Apart from any personal rancour that James III may have felt towards Arran, the disposal of the Boyd lands must have put an obstacle in the way of the restoration of the earl and his father. For the for-

---

[174] C. A. J. Armstrong, op. cit., S.H.S. Misc. VIII. 19–32; W. H. Finlayson, 'The Boyds in Bruges', S.H.R., xxviii. 195–6, at 195.
[175] W. H. Finlayson, op. cit., p. 195.   [176] Ibid., p. 196.
[177] R.M.S., ii. Nos. 1060, 1123.   [178] Ibid., No. 1177; see also No. 1178.
[179] E.R., viii. lii–liii. Hamilton's first wife, Euphemia Graham, was divorced before his second marriage.   [180] T.A., i. xlii; p. 512 below.
[181] E.R., viii. l–lii.   [182] Pp. 476, 491 below.

feiture of the three leading Boyds had characteristically inspired a landed settlement in favour of the royal family. On 27 November 1469 some morsels of forfeited property were included among the annexed crown lands, but most of the forfeitures, including Arran, Stewarton and Kilmarnock, were added to Bute, Cowal and Renfrew to be annexed to the 'principality' of Scotland as a patrimony for the first-born son of each Scottish king, so that none of these annexed lands was to be alienated without the consent of parliament.[183] This did not prevent James from granting the queen a liferent of the barony of Kilmarnock. This grant of 25 June 1470 was to pay for her gowns and 'the ornaments of her head' and was a token of James's 'great affection and love'.[184] It was not part of the queen's dower, which seems to have been cautiously withheld until after she bore a child. On 17 March 1473 Margaret presented James with a son and heir, the future James IV, who within a few months was styled Duke of Rothesay, Earl of Carrick and Lord of Cunningham.[185] Probably in thanksgiving, Queen Margaret, whose piety was marked, went on pilgrimage to the shrine of St Ninian at Whithorn.[186] In March 1476 Margaret was to bear a second son, also named James, so that if his elder brother died without legitimate offspring there might yet be a King James. A third son, John, was born in December 1479.[187] Meanwhile on 11 October 1473 certain lands and revenues were at length assigned as the queen's dower with the consent of the three estates.[188] Queen Margaret's acquisitions were not to prove so troubling in politics as those of her predecessor. In practice her revenues were collected by the king's officials,[189] and her expenses were met by the king's treasurer, who in 1473-4 disbursed no less than £757 9s. 10d. for her clothes and a few miscellaneous items.[190]

[183] *R.M.S.*, II. No. 992.   [184] *Ibid.*, Nos. 992, 1340.
[185] *T.A.*, I. xlv; *R.M.S.*, II. No. 1127.   [186] *E.R.*, VIII. 215; *T.A.*, I. 44.
[187] *H.B.C.*, p. 58.   [188] *A.P.S.*, II. 188-9; *R.M.S.*, II. Nos. 1144, 1365.
[189] *E.R.*, VIII and IX, *passim*.   [190] *T.A.*, I. 29-39.

15

PARLIAMENT AND ITS BUSINESS, 1469–1488

The events of 1469 conformed to what was to be the cyclical pattern during the reigns of most of the Scottish monarchs of the fifteenth and sixteenth centuries—a royal minority, or its equivalent in the case of James 1, was followed by an attack led by the king upon those who had hitherto ruled in his name. Within this broad pattern there was a particular similarity between the events of 1449 and 1469: just as the marriage of James II and Mary of Guelders had marked the king's entry into politics, being followed by the downfall of the Livingstons, so also the marriage of James III and Margaret of Denmark marked the virtual end of the royal minority and the king's personal political career was initiated by the downfall of the Boyds. Although James's subsequent career was clouded by a grave crisis in 1482 and ended tempestuously, it was also interspersed with what were, from the viewpoint of the crown, a number of bright successes of the type already won through the forcefulness of his father and grandfather. A study of parliament and its preoccupations is therefore not one that reveals an uninterrupted progress towards a sorry end; but it does reveal some of the mistakes and mischances that beset the king.

During the reign parliament met almost invariably once a year at Edinburgh;[1] and in some years, notably 1478, more than one session of parliament was held. General councils were also held, though their records have not survived.[2] Those of parliament, on the

[1] See *A.P.S.*, II. Chronological Table, pp. 10–8.
[2] Rait, *Parliaments*, pp. 138–9; *A.D.C.P.*, p. v; p. 407 above.

other hand, are available after 1466 in the extant parliamentary register,[3] which relates proceedings in somewhat fuller form than in the earlier lawyers' collections. One apparently new feature was the recording, from 1468 onwards, of the names of those who attended parliament. Thus, virtually for the first time, it is possible to check the actual attendance against the theoretical attendance. The latter remained unaltered, and a general reference in 1471 to the compearance of 'all those who ought, and wished, appropriately to be present'[4] may have been intended to cover the inclusion of those whose right to attend was not particularly apparent. In the parliament of June 1478, for example, the king's secretary, the clerk register, and the 'officials' of Glasgow, Dunkeld and Lothian attended, the first two being listed under the heading of 'abbots and prelates' and the three 'officials' forming a separate group by themselves, to which no description was attached.[5] In the parliament of March 1479 the exceptionally large attendance was made up of eight bishops, the Prior of St Andrews (who took precedence over the fifteen abbots with whom he was grouped) eleven earls, twenty-one lords of parliament (including Chancellor Avondale), twenty barons and the commissioners of twenty-eight burghs,[6] some burghs probably sending more than one commissioner. Generally, however, there seems to have been difficulty in securing adequate attendance. In October 1474 couriers were sent with letters 'to the lordis that come nocht to the parliament.'[7] On 24 February 1484 there was concern over 'the estatis and lordis that ar nocht cumin to this parliament to gif ther consale.' It was agreed that they 'suld be blamyt' by the king, for by this time absenteeism was a sign of political disaffection.[8]

The practice of continuing (proroguing) parliament, which was common in the later fifteenth century, was partly connected with the difficulty of obtaining adequate attendance, though other reasons also operated.[9] Continuations publicised a forthcoming session of parliament and elicited the attendance of those present at the original

---

[3] Rait, *Parliaments*, p. 138.   [4] *A.P.S.*, II. 98.
[5] *Ibid.*, 116.   [6] *Ibid.*, 120–1.
[7] *T.A.*, I. 53.   [8] *A.P.S.*, II. 165; pp. 520–3 below.
[9] An act of November 1469 (*A.P.S.*, II. 97 c. 14) which stated that the continuation of courts (including parliament) was not essential for judicial purposes, does not seem to have settled the question. See in general Rait, *Parliaments*, pp. 329–34. On one occasion in 1475 or 1476 parliament was continued to avoid an outbreak of plague (Lesley, *History*, p. 41). This continuation is not mentioned in extant records, though the exchequer rolls show that there was a plague during 1475–6 and that 70 marts were sent from Orkney to support the infected, who had been isolated on Inchkeith (*E.R.*, VIII. 364).

session. Often the existing parliament was continued to some future date and a commission representative of the three estates was appointed to have the full power of parliament and to meet as parliament on the specified day. Thus on 6 May 1471 parliament was continued to 2 August, when it was to be held by the Duke of Albany and a commission of eight clerics, six earls, ten lords, and nine burgh commissioners. This commission, which was given powers of co-option, was to conclude business unfinished in the May session of parliament and deal with other matters 'for the commone gud of the realme'.[10]

There must always have been a temptation to 'pack' commissions (and committees as well), and this was obviously suspected in 1488,[11] but the commissions seem to have been fairly large bodies, varying in number from twenty-four to over fifty, and always representing, more or less on equal numerical basis, each of the three estates; such bodies were scarcely more, or less, amenable to royal or factional pressure than was parliament itself. Since the aim of James III, particularly in the troubled conditions towards the end of his reign, was to secure a large attendance at parliament, there is no reason to doubt that the explanation of the use of commissions was simply that put forward by the three estates in June 1478 : 'for sparinge of lauboure and travale of thaim self'.[12]

The commissions differed only in their unlimited power from the committees that were also frequently appointed in parliament. The record of the session of June 1478 gives a picture of the organisation of parliament in its fullest form.[13] Not only was a•commission of eight members of each estate appointed to meet in the coming October,[14] but to cope with the work of the existing session three committees were appointed : one committee *ad causas* to deal with causes and complaints, the miscellaneous suits brought before parliament as a court of first instance ; a second committee *ad decisionem judicii* to deal with falsed dooms ; and a third committee *pro articulis advisandis* to discuss and draft 'articles' for enactment by the three estates. Each of these three committees was composed of nine members—three from each estate—the committee of the articles being composed, in the main, of the more consequential members of parliament. In addition the clerk register was to be *ex officio* a voting member of each committee ; with this exception no member of one committee was a member of another. Thus from a total attendance

[10] *A.P.S.*, II. 100–1.   [11] P. 525 below.   [12] *A.P.S.*, II. 119.
[13] *Ibid.*, 116–7.   [14] *Ibid.*, 119.

in parliament of perhaps sixty no fewer than twenty-eight were engaged in committee work. About half of these were also appointed to the commission of twenty-four that was to meet in October, the other half of the commission being mostly made up of members of parliament not appointed to one or other of the committees. Thus, in all, about two-thirds of the members of parliament were engaged on one or other of the four bodies it appointed. It was provided that no committee member should be allowed to absent himself save for reason of sickness, his personal involvement in a matter under discussion, or his exclusion at the request of a litigant. These arrangements (or some of them) were intended to serve as a model 'to be kepit . . . in all tymes tocum'.[15] While the records do not show that it was the invariable practice to appoint three committees in every parliament there is enough evidence to show that each type of committee was fairly frequently employed.

Least frequently employed was the committee to deal with falsed dooms, which seems to have been appointed on only five occasions between 1467 and 1485.[16] In a few instances the decisions of the committee were recorded along with the proceedings of parliament : in 1469 the auditors rejected an appeal against a judgment given in a sheriff court and justice ayre held at Dumfries and amerced the appellants;[17] in 1478 an appeal against a judgment given in a justice ayre at Cupar was upheld and the suitors amerced. In this instance the judgment of the auditors, uttered by the mouth of the dempster of parliament, was also 'affirmed' by the king, 'sitting in the place of judgment in royal state'.[18]

A committee for causes and complaints was appointed on at least fourteen occasions during the reign, usually being made up of nine members, three from each estate.[19] From the cases recorded as being brought before the auditors in April 1481 it appears that it was not only persons of consequence, such as Patrick, Lord Hailes, but obscure persons as well, who sought its services—one case concerned the disputed ownership of a certain brown horse.[20]

The committee of the articles, the history of which may go back to the reign of James I,[21] was certainly prominent in the parliaments of James III. On one occasion the king seems to have presented articles of his own (as James I had done in 1424), for in July 1473 the estates furnished 'avisment' on 'the articlis opinnit be our

[15] *Ibid.*, 117.   [16] *Ibid.*, 88, 93, 114, 117, 169.
[17] *Ibid.*, 93.   [18] *Ibid.*, 117.   [19] E.g. *ibid.*, 124.
[20] *Ibid.*, 134. See also *A.D.A.*, *passim*.   [21] Pp. 282, 286, 305 above.

soverane lorde in this instant parliament'.[22] Generally, however, it was left to a committee to draft and present articles for enactment. Such a committee was appointed on at least fourteen occasions between 1467 and 1485. Its membership varied between nine and sixteen, and each estate was always represented, more or less equally.[23] No indication is given of the method of appointment or election to this committee (or to other committees or commissions). Usually the work of the committee was begun and finished during one session of parliament. Thus on 9 May 1485 parliament was opened in Edinburgh; on the following day the committee of the articles, fifteen in number (about one-quarter of the membership of this parliament), was appointed; on 26 May the report of the committee, comprising seventeen items, was approved by the king and the three estates.[24] It was exceptional that in the parliament of November 1469 a committee was appointed to advise upon certain specific matters, and, in general, 'uppone all uthir articulis that salbe thocht spedfull', and to refer their recommendations 'to the next parliament or generale consail'; since this committee of twelve was to remain in session for two months its members were to have their expenses paid by their respective estates.[25] It was probably the matter of expenses that prevented the repetition of this experiment.

The same reason inhibited the holding of judicial sessions: in a parliament of 1468 it was thought 'speidfull' that a session be held at Edinburgh for one month, and another at Perth for five weeks; three clerics, three barons and three burgh commissioners were named to hold these sessions. But a reference in the parliamentary record to 'the expensis of thaim' was deleted, and the nine lords of session were evidently to be financed unsatisfactorily from the 'unlawes' that they levied in their court.[26] For the rest of the reign there is no other reference to the holding of judicial sessions, nor was there any other move towards the creation of a salaried and professional judiciary.[27]

Instead, the place of the lords of session was taken by the lords of council: it was settled in October 1467 that all cases left undecided in parliament should be referred to their decision.[28] What they lacked in payment for their judicial services was doubtless partly compensated by their access to political power; they were the king's

---

[22] *A.P.S.*, II. 103.   [23] E.g. *ibid.*, 121.   [24] *Ibid.*, 168–73.
[25] *Ibid.*, 97.   [26] *Ibid.*, 92.
[27] Dunlop, *Bishop Kennedy*, p. 324.   [28] *A.P.S.*, II. 88.

nominees, and since they were not appointed in parliament there was no need to include representatives of the third estate.[29] It would seem that they dealt with the same types of litigation as the auditors of causes and complaints, with the exception of actions involving fee and heritage;[30] and the immediate popularity of their court may be seen not only in the hundreds of cases brought before it but in attempts to reduce the flood of litigants. An act of November 1469 (re-affirmed in November 1475)[31] stipulated that litigants in civil actions should first take their suits before the judges ordinary (justiciars, sheriffs, stewards, bailies, barons, provosts or bailies of burghs). Only if the judge ordinary refused justice, or administered partial justice, was complaint to be made to king and council, who would do justice and punish the culpable judge with suspension from office. In May 1474 the judges ordinary were exhorted to give justice so that plaintiffs 'vex nocht our soverane lorde nor his consale with no complayntis bot gif it be on officiaris that will nocht do justice'.[32] In October 1487 there was a further attempt to limit recourse to the lords of council : all civil cases were to go to the judges ordinary, save for certain categories—those pertaining to the king, complaints made by kirkmen, widows, orphans, minors and foreigners, and complaints made against officials. A few months later, in January 1488, this act was repealed on the grounds that 'it wer deferring of justice to mony partiis that couthe nocht get law ministerit to thame before ther ordinaris'.[33] It must be inferred that the ordinary courts were inefficient or corrupt. In November 1469 parliament took it for granted that there were judges ordinary 'quhilkis wil nocht execut thare office and ministir justice to the pure pepil' ;[34] an act of October 1487 arranged that on the last day of each justice ayre an assize should be held to inquire whether sheriffs and crowners had performed their duties properly; if not, they were to be punished.[35]

It was the justice ayres in particular that were concerned with the punishment of serious crime. An act of November 1475 ordained the holding of the ayres twice a year through all the realm to deal with criminal cases; and this was only one of seven acts passed between 1458 and 1488 that enjoined the holding of the ayres.[36] From this it would seem that against the general background of curial ineptitude the ayres stood out as being worthy of respect.

---

[29] This is evident from the sederunts (*A.D.C.*, I. 3–79).
[30] *Ibid.*, 4.
[31] *A.P.S.*, II. 94, c. 2; 111, c. 3.
[32] *Ibid.*, 107, c. 11.
[33] *Ibid.*, 177–8, c. 10; 183, c. 17.
[34] *Ibid.*, 94, c. 2.
[35] *Ibid.*, 177, c. 8.
[36] *Ibid.*, 111, c. 2; *Scot. Legal Hist.*, p. 19.

The trouble was that they were not frequent enough. An act of
November 1475 complained that sheriffs, stewards, bailies and other
officers, had been holding 'courtis of guerra'—a resort to judicial
duel under the laws of arms. Possibly this was, at best, an expedient
to counter the infrequency of the ayres; but it was held that 'justice
aris . . . ar spylt [spoiled] be the said guerra courtis', which were believed to lead to 'grete hereschip and skathe' and were no longer to
be held by anyone; whoever disregarded this prohibition would
be considered guilty of manslaughter and usurpation of royal
authority.[37] It may be assumed that the holding of justice ayres
remained infrequent, for an act of May 1485 ordained that 'for the
encres of justice and tranquilite' they should be held twice a year (in
spring and autumn) 'unto the tyme that the realme were brocht to
gude rewle'. In October 1487 there was again an admonition that
justice ayres should be arranged 'in al gudely haist in al partis of
the realme'.[38] Part of the difficulty in arranging ayres may have been
finding suitable persons of 'wisedome' who were minded to execute
justice and who had 'powere and strenthe of ther aune' and required
only slight support from the crown. In 1487 and the following year
it was evidently decided to acknowledge the accomplishments of
such ideal justiciars by styling them 'justices general' or 'gret
justices'.[39] In October 1487 the three estates had also undertaken
that lords of regalities and other franchise holders would not exercise
partial justice or make fines with transgressors.[40] This was the only
enactment of the reign that directly dealt with the regality courts,
hitherto a common target of legislative criticism. It may be suspected
that they were no longer criticised not because they had improved
but because the government had enough to do in trying to deal with
defects in the royal courts.

The obvious weaknesses in the administration of justice during
the reign derived not only from the lack of a professional judicial
bench but from other causes—the attitude of the king, contempt for
law and order in a society where 'maintenance' was taken for
granted, and the confusion of the law itself. In November 1469 a
parliamentary commission was instructed to consider 'the reductione
of the kingis lawis, Regiam Majestatem, actis, statutis and uther
bukes'; the intention was that these diverse legal sources 'be put in
a volum and to be autorizat, and the laif [rest] to be distroyit'.[41] In

---

[37] *A.P.S.*, II. 112, c. 11.   [38] *Ibid.*, 170, c. 4; 176, c. 2.
[39] *Ibid.*, 176. c. 2; 182, cc. 5, 6. See also p. 523 below.
[40] *A.P.S.*, II. 176, c. 3.   [41] *Ibid.*, 97, c. 20.

July 1473 parliament was again concerned with 'the mending of the lawis for the declaracioun of diverss obscure materis.' The barons besought the king to take two wise persons of each estate 'to fynd gude invenciouns . . . for to declare the daily materis that cumys befor the kingis hienes that as yit thare is na law for the decisioune of thame'. Their findings were to be shown to the next parliament for ratification so that 'at that tyme thare be a buke maid contenand al the lawis of this realme that sall remain at a place quhare the lafe may have copy and nane uther bukis be usit, for the gret diverssite now fundin in diverss bukis put in be diverss persouns that ar callit men of law'.[42] But James III was no latter-day Justinian. Nothing was done to produce a digest of Scottish law; and the only 'mending' of the law that took place was piecemeal and on a small scale.[43]

What vitiated the work of the courts was not so much the state of the law as the general disregard for the law. In May 1474 it was necessary to legislate against the 'gret derisione ande skorne of justice' shown by persons who preferred to pay 'ane litill unlaw of silver' rather than answer charges in the justice ayre.[44] Perjury was evidently common, leading to 'falss inquestis and assisses'[45] that must have disheartened the law-abiding. In October 1487 an act guarded against 'maintenance' by re-affirming a former statute which enjoined litigants to come to court unarmed 'in sobre and quiet wise'; if a sheriff heard that 'ony partiis makis convocacioun and gadering of armis to cum to the courtis' he was to order the illicit gathering to disperse; if it did not, he was to dissolve the court and inform the king, so that the disobedient might be warded for a year.[46] The list of feuds brought to the notice of a parliamentary commission in March 1479[47] shows the background whence 'maintenance' sprang.

Great as were the problems of lawlessness and disorder they might nonetheless have been partly overcome (as they were to be in the next reign) if the king had shown constant determination. At first it had seemed that he would apply himself to the task. The acts of the parliament of November 1469 suggested that a strong royal initiative would be forthcoming; and in May 1471 proclamation was ordered that those complaining of acts of slaughter since the previous parliament should present their complaints to the king, who would afford them impartial justice.[48] By July 1473, however,

[42] *Ibid.*, 105, c. 14.
[43] E.g. *ibid.*, 94–5, c. 3; 95, c. 4; 96, c. 12; 106–7, c. 6; 107, cc. 8–10; 112, c. 8.   [44] *Ibid.*, 107, c. 14.
[45] *Ibid.*, 97, c. 20; 100, c. 9; 111–2, c. 4.
[46] *Ibid.*, 177, c. 9.   [47] *Ibid.*, 122.   [48] *Ibid.*, 99, c. 3.

it was evident that the king's interests lay elsewhere; the prelates exhorted him

> to tak part of labour apone his
> persone and travel throw his
> realme and put sic justice and
> polycy in his awne realme that the
> brute [renown] and the fame of
> him mycht pas in utheris contreis;

the realm would be easy to rule if James would

> mak bot esy travel in his
> awne persone in the execucioune
> of justice.[49]

In March 1479 it was affirmed that the king

> is of gud mynd and dispositioune
> to the putting furthe of justice ...
> and sall, God willing, in tyme
> tocum, with the aviss of the lordis
> of his counesale, attend
> deligently tharto be setting and
> halding of his justice aieris in
> all partis, and utherwais as
> accordis and salbe thocht
> expedient and proffitable.[50]

Three years later it was announced that the king, being grateful for the 'hertfull lufe' of his lieges

> has now schewin and declarit
> his mynde opinly ... [to] ger
> justice be evinly ministerit ...
> and apply him to the puttin
> of gude reull in all partis
> of his realme.[51]

The inference to be drawn from these pronouncements is that James was, at best, only intermittently zealous in the execution of justice, though the situation was to change at the end of his reign, when treason was the most prominent of crimes.

It may also be gathered that by his undue grants of respite and

---

[49] *Ibid.*, 104, cc. 6, 7.   [50] *Ibid.*, 122.   [51] *Ibid.*, 139, c. 3.

remission the king himself set up one of the stumbling-blocks in the way of improvement. In July 1473 the three estates besought him 'that he walde closs his handis for al remissiounis and respettis for slauchter . . . for a certane tyme'.[52] In June 1478 the reason that slaughter, treason, robbery and theft were 'sa commoun throuout the hale realme' was imputed to grants of remission and respite, whereupon the king 'at the gret instant request of the lordis of the thre estatis' agreed to stop such grants for three years to come in respect of manslaughter committed since his twenty-fifth birthday, so that 'in the meyntyme the cuntre may be put in pece'.[53]

Parliament's preoccupation with the problem of law and order was matched by its preoccupation with the problems of the currency and the shortage of bullion: an act of May 1471 affirmed that 'the mater is gret and tuechis the hail body of the realme in gret nernes'; one act of July 1473 described the king's lieges as being 'bare of money', and another deplored the 'skantnes of bullioune that is in the realme'.[54]

It is difficult to reconcile these statements with the evidence of the accounts of the moneyers: for in the thirteen years from 1437 to 1450, when no great outcry was raised, they coined 48 pounds of gold and 611 pounds of silver; in the nine years between 1460 and 1469 by which time concern was apparent, they coined 21 pounds of gold and 900 pounds of silver.[55] The two accounts that survive for the rest of the reign show an improvement: in one, covering the period March 1473 to July 1476, the amount of gold coined was given as 13 pounds 5 ounces, and the silver as 421 pounds 13 ounces;[56] the other apparently covering the period October 1486[57] to August 1487 shows the amount of gold coined as 8 pounds 1 ounce, and of silver as 181 pounds, from which the king's profits in seigniorage were £30 11s. 8d.[58] It must be admitted, however, that the coinage was not solely the result of the smelting of newly acquired bullion but of the re-coining of money of earlier date. Even so, it would seem that currency shortage was not occasioned so much by a reduction in the supply of bullion as by an increase in the demand for it. Possibly this arose from the import trade, for which there are no

[52] *Ibid.*, 104, c. 7.

[53] *Ibid.*, 118, c. 2.

[54] *Ibid.*, 100, c. 8; 105, cc. 12, 15.

[55] *E.R.*, IX. lxii, lxiv.

[56] *Ibid.*, VIII. 392.

[57] Mistakenly given as 1487 in the record (*ibid.*, IX. 549).   [58] *Ibid.*, 548–9.

statistics of consequence;[59] but since the export of coin or bullion was restricted (by statute at least) this seems questionable. More probably the growing demand for currency arose through an expanding domestic market : an increasing volume of business transactions required an increased monetary circulation. To contemporaries, however, this was not apparent and the whole problem was seen as the result of a shortage of bullion. Certainly it was one that could have been solved had supplies of bullion been forthcoming to meet the demand for an increased volume of currency.

It is curious that measures were not devised to bring existing stocks of bullion into circulation : though parliament was aware that 'there is mekil bullioune put in diverss werkis' there was no attempt to restrict the conversion of bullion into plate; parliament's concern was rather to see that the work of goldsmiths (who were held in suspicion) should be supervised by a warden and deacon of the craft, who would examine and stamp the works produced.[60] In other respects, however, legislation showed an awareness of possible solutions to monetary difficulties : measures were adopted which were somewhat similar to those used by modern governments.

A number of statutes concerned the 'in halding' (conservation) of bullion. Early in 1464 it was decided that searchers should be appointed at all ports to see that no one carried out more bullion than would suffice for his expenses as far as the Low Countries.[61] In October 1466 the 'moderate expenss' allowed to those travelling overseas was set at one English 'noble' (then worth about 25s. Scots) and this regulation was to apply to clerics as well as laymen.[62] In July 1473 parliament advised the appointment of 'sercheouris and inquisitouris' to stop illicit export of bullion. It also intended to appoint a commission of three clerics, three barons and three burgesses 'ffor the serching of the money'.[63] By February 1484 attention was turned to the 'grete skaith and damage' caused through the export of money by prelates and clerks 'for promociouns and pleis in the court of Rome'. In an act reminiscent of the barratry legislation of James I it was ordained that whoever had business at the papal court should be permitted only the stipulated travelling expenses and should come to the auditors of exchequer to 'mak knawin his finance made in merchandiss of the realme to the avale of the some that he spendis in the court of Rome'.[64] The intention, which was sensible enough,

---

[59] Import duties (mostly on goods from England) remained negligible (ibid., lxxv).   [60] A.P.S., II. 105–6, c. 17; 172, c. 15.   [61] Ibid., XII. 30–1.
[62] Ibid., II. 86, c. 12.   [63] Ibid., 105, cc. 11, 16.   [64] Ibid., 166, c. 11.

was that trafficking at Rome should be financed by the export of
Scottish products rather than cash or bullion. Conservation was also
to be fostered by restriction of certain imports. In May 1471 it was
on account of 'the gret poverte of the realme' that the wearing of silk
(a luxury import) was limited to knights, minstrels, heralds, and those
with landed rents of at least £100 a year.[65] In July 1473 parliament
also re-affirmed a statute of James II which forbade the import of
English cloth : it was not to be received in return for the export of
salmon and other fish; instead the exporters were to bring back gold
and silver.[66]

For together with the policy of 'in halding' of bullion went one
of 'in bringing' of bullion. Early in 1464, in an act that conflated
previous measures, it was provided that both Scottish and foreign
merchants were to bring in four ounces of silver for each serplar (half
a sack) of staple wares that they exported. The intention was to
secure a favourable balance of trade by ensuring that the proceeds
of export were not entirely spent upon financing imports. The silver
thus imported by the merchants was to be taken to the master of the
mint, who would give coins to the value of 8s. 9d. for each ounce;
and this procedure would be supervised by the exchequer.[67] Similar
measures were approved by parliament in October 1466, May 1474,
November 1475, February 1484 and May 1485; the amount of silver
to be compulsorily imported varied from two ounces to four ounces
for the export of each serplar of wool, last of hides, last of salmon, or
four hundred pieces of cloth; the price paid by the mint for each
ounce of silver rose from 8s. 9d. in 1464 to 9s. 2d. in October 1466,
to 12s. od. in November 1475 and May 1485.[68] In addition, in 1468
and 1473 parliament re-affirmed in general terms all previous acts
concerning the conservation and import of bullion, as a result of
which it trusted that 'thare sulde sudanly cum bullioune in the realme
in gret quantite'.[69]

Another means to the same goal was to alter rates of exchange.
This was a more complex business than it would be today, for there
were two distinct but inter-related rates of exchange—the domestic
and the foreign. The domestic rate was that between Scottish coins
and the pounds, marks, shillings and pennies, which were not coins
but merely units of account. On this basis there were 12 nominal
pennies in the nominal shilling, 160 in the nominal mark, and 240

---

[65] *Ibid.*, 100, c. 7.   [66] *Ibid.*, 105, c. 15.   [67] *Ibid.*, XII. 30–1.
[68] *Ibid.*, II. 86, c. 11; 106, c. 4; 112, c. 6; 166, c. 10; 172, c. 16.
[69] *Ibid.*, 105, c. 11; 90, c. 8; 92, c. 1.

in the nominal pound. But in addition there were actual coins called pennies, which might be 'black' (composed mainly of copper) or 'white' (composed mainly of silver) and even pennies of gold.[70] Thus a rate had to be fixed between the actual black, white and gold pennies and the unit of reckoning known as a penny; similarly with other Scottish coins such as the groat, the demy and the lion. When the three estates complained in October 1467 that the whole realm was 'gretumly hurt and skathit' since the money of the realm had 'lawer courss than uther realmis about us has' they meant that actual Scottish coins were undervalued in terms of the nominal units of account and that this was the reason why 'the mone of this realme is borne out in gret quantite'.[71] Ostensibly in order to conform with rates in Flanders, the Scottish coins were therefore revalued upwards in terms of units of account—the demy and the lion, each formerly valued at 10s., were raised to 12s.[72] But at the same time foreign coins which circulated freely in Scotland were also revalued upwards, and proportionately more so than Scottish coins. Thus, for example, the English rose noble, which stood at 25s. in October 1466, was now raised to 32s.[73] In fact the Scottish revaluation of 1467 concealed a devaluation in terms of foreign exchange—a natural response to a situation in which it was desirable to attract foreign currency into Scotland.

Tampering with the domestic rate of exchange was bound to cause trouble. Nor was this unforeseen, for in the parliament of October 1467 it was recognised that the upward valuation of coins in terms of units of account would have serious repercussions, since it was in these units, not in actual coin, that all payments were expressed. Thus it was pointed out that 'ilk estate sulde be gretly hurt and skathyt in the changing and heing [raising] of the courss of the mone . . . bath in dettis paying and contractis, bigane annuellis, wedsettis and landis set for long termes, custumis and procurass of prelatis and all uther dettis'. It was therefore ordained that 'payment be maide in the samyn substance and valour'. Nonetheless Archibald Whitelaw, king's secretary and dean of Dunbar, and Richard of Kintore, burgess of Aberdeen, in the name of the clergy and the burghs respectively, requested with some foresight that the interests of their estates be safeguarded if the king 'proclamis his mone to lawer price'.[74] By 1468 there was 'grete romour . . . because of diversiteis

---

[70] *Ibid.*, 88–9, c. 1; 90, c. 5; 166, c. 10.   [71] *Ibid.*, 88, c. 1.
[72] Compare *ibid.*, 88, c. 1 and 92, c. 1.   [73] *Ibid.*, 86, c. 12; 88, c. 1.
[74] *Ibid.*, 89, cc. 2, 4.

of payment within the realme throu the takking in of the rentis be
the auld payment and gevis it oute agane be a derrar price'. There
had also been inflation, since 'the penny worthis ar rysin with the
penny and mekle derrar than thai war wont to be'. Therefore 'to
content the commons' it was ordained that 'the mone have fra hine-
furth universaly a [one] cours throw out the realme'. And that
'cours', or rate, was to be the one that prevailed before the revaluation
of October 1467. Thus the revaluation was rescinded : the lion and
the demy, set at 12s. in October 1467, were to return to the previous
rate of 10s.[75] But foreign currency was not quite reduced to the pre-
1467 rates, for the intention was 'to draw it within the cuntre';[76] thus
the English rose noble, which had been set at 32s. in October 1467,
dropped only to 28s. instead of to the 25s. at which it stood in October
1466.[77] In November 1475, when there was 'gret scantnes and want
of gold . . . throw having out the samyn becauss it stands here at
lawere price than in uther cuntreis', foreign gold coins would again
be revalued upwards in terms of units of account and the rose noble
would be set at 35s. Simultaneously parliament made provision 'to
remove discorde . . . betuix creditouris and thare dettouris' resulting
from 'variacione of the courss of gold and silver'.[78]

Apart from the variations inspired by the hope of attracting an
influx of foreign currency there were others caused by the unsettled
state of the Scottish currency : as new coins were minted, with higher
or lower bullion content than preceding coins of similar type, domestic rates of exchange had to be modified. In May 1474 it was recommended that the three estates should appoint a commission not
only to fix rates of exchange but to devise new money.[79] In the following year the coiner was to be instructed to mint twelve groats from
the ounce of silver, having the same fineness as the new English
groat.[80] This coinage was to be minted not by smelting existing coins
but from the quota of silver that merchants were obliged to import,
for parliament believed that the practice of re-minting existing coins
resulted in a loss of bullion through 'the translacione be the fire'. It
was therefore ordained that thenceforth no currency, whether Scottish or foreign, should be smelted either by the king's coiners or by
goldsmiths, unless by the king's special command.[81] This enactment
was evidently ignored by the king, for in June 1478 parliament complained that the realm was 'wastit of money' since most of the old

[75] *Ibid.*, 92, c. 1.   [76] *Ibid.*
[77] *Ibid.*, 86, c. 12; 88, c. 1; 92, c. 1.   [78] *Ibid.*, 112, cc. 9, 10.
[79] *Ibid.*, 106, c. 4.   [80] *Ibid.*, 112, c. 6.   [81] *Ibid.*, 112, c. 7.

gold and silver coinages, both Scottish and foreign, had been 'translatit and put to fyre'. Because of this complaint the king agreed to cease further minting until the realm was 'stuffit of bulzeone that it may be sene and knawin quhareof that new money may be strikin'; he was to take the minting irons from the coiners and put them in sure keeping 'sua that ther cum na mare hurt to the realme throu the stryking of moneye in tyme cumming'.[82]

If the minting of gold and silver coins led to criticism there was even more discontent as a result of the minting of copper coins. In October 1466 parliament had enacted that 'for the eiss and sustentatioune of the kingis liegis and almous deide to pure folk' there should be issued £3,000 worth of copper coins, four to the penny, to be used for the purchase of common necessities such as bread and ale. Since there was some question whether 'white' pennies should have 'hale courss',[83] in other words be acceptable in unlimited quantity as full legal tender, it is not surprising that the 'black' pennies were to be only limited legal tender—in the purchase of 'grete merchiandice' they were to be accepted only to the extent of 12d. in the pound. From the resulting coinage the king made a profit of £650 in seigniorage.[84]

For some unstated reason this experiment soon lost favour and the moneyer responsible won notoriety as 'Wille Goldsmyth called Halfpeny man'—for the black money had been issued as halfpennies, not farthings as parliament had directed.[85] In October 1467 parliament announced that the coining of 'the blak pennyis' was to be stopped, so that 'thar be nane strikyn in tyme to cum under the payne of dede'.[86] Nonetheless there were evidently further issues of pennies and 'plakkis' which contained some silver but aroused suspicion : in July 1473, it was ordered that, pending an investigation, 'the striking of thame be cessit'.[87] This was a pious hope : in a signet letter of 23 July 1483 the king ordered payment of £180 16s. od. 'to the werkmen that wrocht the blac money of oure command'.[88] Since their expenses were so considerable it may be assumed that the quantity of black money they had produced was not small. It was doubtless this money that had contributed to the political crisis of 1482.[89] After the episode at Lauder brig there was a 'crying down' (*declamatio*) of the placks with which the name of Cochrane, the king's familiar, was

[82] *Ibid.*, 118, c. 3.
[84] *Ibid.*, 86, c. 12; *E.R.*, ix. lxv.
[86] *A.P.S.*, ii. 88–9, c. 1.
[88] *E.R.*, ix. 218–9.
[83] *Ibid.*, 90, c. 5.
[85] *E.R.*, ix. lxv.
[87] *Ibid.*, 105, c. 12.
[89] Pp. 499–500 below.

associated. Nor was the process achieved without considerable inconvenience : in May 1483 the hammermen of Edinburgh complained that they were 'rycht havely [heavily] hurt and put to greit poverty throw the doun cumming of the blak money'.[90] The devalued placks continued to be regarded with suspicion : in the parliament of May 1485 the king commanded that 'nane of his liegis refuse thaim . . . nor rase ther penny worthis hear [higher] na thai wald sell for uther money, gold or silver, under payne of dede and eschete of all ther gudis'.[91] Shortly afterwards it was announced that dearth and inflation had resulted from 'greit quantities of fals counterfatit money plakkis strikin in cunze of lait'. These counterfeit coins, produced both inside and outside the realm, were made 'sa subtellie' that it was 'unpossible to decerne and knaw the trew fra the fals'. Hence in response to the request of the three estates the king had given orders 'to ceiss the courss and passage of all the new plakkis last cunzeit and gar put the samyne to the fire'. From the bullion obtained by their smelting a new penny of fine silver was to be produced 'like the xiiijd. grote'; one of the groats would be given for seven placks, true or counterfeit, if the latter were delivered to special receivers by a certain date.[92]

By this time an ambitious scheme, first mooted in February 1484 and confirmed in May 1485, had been devised for the minting of a new coinage. A 'fyne penny of gold' was to be struck of the same weight and fineness as the English rose noble. There were also to be new silver pennies or groats equal in fineness to the old English groat. Ten of these silver pennies were to be coined from the ounce of silver and each was to be rated at fourteen pence in units of account. The new gold penny would be worth thirty of these silver pennies (or groats). There were also to be gold coins worth twenty groats and ten groats, and it was stipulated that all other money should be 'conformit therfor'.[93] Silver groats and gold pennies called 'unicornys' were certainly being coined by 1487.[94]

The enactments of February 1484 and May 1485 that gave details of the new coinage also declared that the king should appoint a wise man 'that has knaulage in the money' to be warden of the mint and to examine and assay the quality of the coins.[95] This moderate measure seems to have been ignored by the king : in

90 *Edinburgh Burgh Recs.*, I. 47; see also *E.R.*, IX. lxvii.
91 *A.P.S.*, II. 172, c. 16.   92 *Ibid.*, 174, c. 1.
93 *Ibid.*, 166, c. 10; 172, c. 16.   94 *E.R.*, IX. 548–9.
95 *A.P.S.*, II. 166, c. 10; 172, c. 16.

January 1488 parliament made more detailed provisions for the organisation of the mint and stipulated that its officials be supervised by the exchequer. For in an indictment of previous practice it was asserted that the whole realm was suffering not only from the activities of counterfeiters but 'throw making of fals money that nowther kepis wecht nor fynace efter the forme of the act of the kingis parliament'; and it was evidently the royal mint that was producing this false money.[96]

An act of May 1474 had somewhat despairingly affirmed that 'the mater of the mone is rycht subtile'.[97] James III can hardly be blamed if he failed to pick his way adroitly through the morass of subtlety. Nonetheless the evidence suggests that in currency matters he added a subtlety of his own and became suspect to parliament by reason of his minting operations. And, just as he seems to have failed to execute the acts for the reformation of law and order, so also he seems to have failed to execute the fairly sensible acts for the conservation and augmentation of stocks of bullion. As early as November 1475 parliament complained of 'the pretermitting [postponement] and sleuth [sloth] that has bene in the execucioune of the actis maid for the in bringing of bulzone . . . and alsa the serching and kepin of the money fra passin furth of the realme'. The king was enjoined to see the acts 'scharply put to execucioune' and to 'deput true and abill serchers'.[98] In June 1478 it was announced that the king 'has grantit now to mak the actis of his parliament . . . be observit and kepit, and . . . be put to scharp execucioune'. In December 1482 the same acts were to be 'put to execucioune'. In February 1484 they were to be 'scharply put to execucioune'. In January 1488 the act regarding 'searching' was re-issued in an extended form that made the illicit export of money by Scotsmen or foreigners a crime punishable in the justice ayre. Once again 'sharp execucioune' was enjoined.[99] There can be little doubt that in this matter, as well as in that of law enforcement, James III constantly failed to fulfil the expectations of his parliaments.

The problem of bullion supplies, and hence of the currency, might not have existed if Scottish exports had been flourishing. Customs duties still remained at the later fourteenth-century level: two marks

[96] *Ibid.*, 182, c. 9. See also c. 10. For details of the mint and the coins it produced see *E.R.*, v. 67; vII. 368–9; IX. lxi–lxviii; and the comprehensive works of I. H. Stewart and R. W. Cochran-Patrick.

[97] *A.P.S.*, II. 106, c. 4.   [98] *Ibid.*, 112, c. 6.

[99] *Ibid.*, 118, c. 3; 144, c. 8; 166, c. 11; 182, c. 11; 183, c. 13.

(26s. 8d.) on the sack of wool, one mark on the great hundred (120) of woolfells, and four marks on the last (200–240) of hides. In addition a few new duties had been levied, of which the more important were those on the export of woollen cloth and salmon. Cloth, as in the reign of James I, paid an *ad valorem* duty of 2s. in the pound, and an *ad valorem* duty on salmon of 2s. 6d. in the pound was raised in 1466 to 3s., and in 1480 to 4s.[100] During the reign the gross proceeds from the customs perhaps averaged £3,300 a year,[101] but in 1486–7 they were only £2,781 6s. 5½d.,[102] less than one-third of what they had been in 1371. In 1478–9 a high-point was reached when the great customs from over twenty burghs came to £3,887 18s. 2½d. (gross). Almost half of the total was forthcoming from Edinburgh; about one-sixth came from Aberdeen, which was followed in order by Dundee, Berwick, Haddington and Perth.[103] Berwick had apparently regained a modicum of its former prosperity by specialising in the export of salmon, in which it rivalled Aberdeen.[104] A mysterious fishy migration that brought shoals of herring from the Baltic to the Scottish coasts provided a new item of trade: Irvine, the port at which duty was collected on the export of salted herring from the west coast, accounted for thirty-three lasts and duty of £9 18s 0d.[105] The growing importance of the off-shore fisheries was recognised by an act of May 1471 which encouraged the burghs and the lords spiritual and temporal to construct or acquire ships and boats 'witht nettis . . . for fyschinge', so that there might result 'gret encress of riches to be brocht within the realme of uther cuntreis'.[106] Another commodity—salt—was also beginning to figure among Scottish exports. In 1478–9, 243 chalders of salt were exported from Dysart and 145 from Preston, probably Prestonpans. By 1486 the exports from Dysart doubled, though those from Preston remained about the same.[107] Meanwhile the former staples of Scottish exports—wool, woolfells and hides—had dropped in importance, presumably because of lessened demand abroad. These staple wares were no longer exported in quantity from many burghs, and Edinburgh was unique in continuing to specialise in them: in 1478–9

---

[100] *E.R.*, IX. lxx, lxxii–lxxiii.   [101] *Ibid.*, lxxv.

[102] *Ibid.*, 536–48.   [103] *Ibid.*, VIII. 620–32.

[104] Berwick exported 80 lasts and 11 barrels, Aberdeen 102 lasts and 10½ barrels (*ibid.*, 620, 631–2). There were twelve barrels in each last; the barrels were of Hamburg measure, each containing 14 gallons (*ibid.*, IX. lxxii–lxxiii). For the salmon trade see Grant, *Social and Economic Development*, p. 316.

[105] *E.R.*, VIII. 621–2.   [106] *A.P.S.*, II. 100, c. 10.

[107] *E.R.*, VIII. 627, 631; IX. lxxiv.

wool, hides, woolfells, and similar natural products brought in £1,625 14s. 5½d. (about 90%) of the Edinburgh customs.[108] Most of the remainder was made up from the export of 2,326 dozen pieces of woollen cloth, which paid £139 6s. od. in custom. Dundee, which paid duty £36 16s. od., came next in this line of business, followed by Kirkcudbright (export duties £23 15s. od.), Haddington (£21 17s. 6d.) and Wigtown (£17 10s. od.)[109] The ports of the south-west, long the Cinderellas of trade (or the scarlet women of smuggling) thereby acquired some significance,[110] and it must be presumed that the weaving of cloth had become an important home industry in Galloway. Nonetheless, since most burghs, with the exception of those north of Aberdeen, exported at least some cloth, it would seem that this relatively new development had begun to affect most of Lowland Scotland, though its importance should not be exaggerated.[111] The overall picture of the export trade was one of concentration in Edinburgh, increased diversification in the products exported, but a low general level of exports.

Another aspect was the increased interest in trade shown by the barons and the king. A diplomatic interchange of 1475 shows that Sir John Colquhoun of Luss possessed a ship of his own, and a safe-conduct of 1485 suggests that Lord Lyle was about to embark as trader in a ship of fifty tuns.[112] The Edinburgh customs returns for 1486–7 show that Lord Seton was exporting salt, and Lady Hamilton, the king's sister, was exporting hides. By 1473 her husband was reclaiming land from the tidal reaches of the Forth near his new castle of Craiglyoune; he had already five saltpans in operation and intended to construct others.[113] James himself, whatever his other failings, was not unmindful of his own economic interests : it is significant that the accounts of the treasurer, audited in December 1474, were not only signed by the auditors but bore the king's signature, rapidly scrawled by a hand well used to holding a pen.[114] Not only did the king import luxuries from the Low Countries through Scottish merchants like John Dalrymple,[115] but in 1476 he tried to establish a direct connection with Italy by granting a three-

[108] *Ibid.*, VIII. 629.   [109] *Ibid.*, 623, 624, 625–6, 630.

[110] See A. L. Murray, 'The Customs Accounts of Kirkcudbright, Wigtown and Dumfries, 1434–1560', *Dumfriesshire Trans.*, XL. 136–62.

[111] *E.R.*, IX. lxxi, lxxii–lxxiii.

[112] *Cal. Docs. Scot.*, IV. No. 1429; *Rot. Scot.*, II. 464.

[113] *E.R.*, IX. 547; *R.M.S.*, II. Nos. 1140, 1178.

[114] See the facsimile in *T.A.*, I. 75.

[115] *E.R.*, VII. 31–2; Dunlop, *Bishop Kennedy*, p. 357; Grant, *Social and Economic Development*, pp. 321–2.

year safe-conduct so that Jacob Dini and his associates, merchants of Florence, might be unimpeded by acts of parliament in selling their goods to the lords of council and the king's 'familiars'.[116] James also engaged in trade on his own account: 'the king's hides were sent to France and Flanders for wine, his ships sent to France and Denmark, his woollen cloth exported for saltpetre and for wine, and his merchandise sent to France', while 'the armed merchantmen belonging to the king were employed by turn in trade, in war, and in missions to foreign states'.[117] The barley owed to the king as rent from Orkney was in 1475–6 shipped to Leith, converted into malt, and delivered to the king's ships, presumably for export.[118] In 1475 John Barton, senior member of a seafaring family of Leith, was serving as captain of the king's carvel, probably the famous *Yellow Carvel*;[119] and as early as 1477 James recognised the services of another Leith skipper, Andrew Wood, by giving him a nineteen-year tack of the lands and town of Largo.[120] By 1488 Captain Wood was 'principall servand to the king . . . haveand wages of him, and furnist him and his schipis oftymes to pase quhair he pleissit'.[121] If the economic interests of burgesses, barons and king had once been distinct they were no longer so in the reign of James III.

One consequence was the increased involvement of king and parliament in commercial diplomacy. A breach in trade with Flanders was serious enough to receive the attention of a parliamentary commission in January 1467. The causes can hardly be described as 'more obvious than is usual in this period of obscurity'.[122] For they are not to be explained by Franco-Burgundian animosities and the desire of the Scots to show their loyalty to the French alliance. A letter of James III,[123] which has been tentatively ascribed to 1474, but which more probably refers to the breach in 1467, gives only vague reasons for dissatisfaction with Bruges and other Flemish towns, though it is obvious from the acts of the parliamentary commission in 1467 that the sense of grievance of the Scots was acute. It was enacted that from 1 August 1467 no ships or goods should be sent to the Flemish towns of the Swyn, the Sluys, the Damme, or Bruges, and that all Scots should remove themselves and their goods from these places on pain of banishment from Scotland. Meanwhile the king, on the advice of his council, granted

[116] *R.M.S.*, II. No. 1266. [117] *E.R.*, VIII. lix.
[118] *Ibid.*, 364. [119] *Ibid.*, lx.
[120] *Ibid.*, 450; *R.M.S.*, II. Nos. 1563, 1720. [121] Pitscottie, *Historie*, I. 214.
[122] Davidson and Gray, *Staple*, p. 132.
[123] Reproduced in facsimile, *ibid.*, facing p. 136.

'tollerance and sufferance' to Scottish merchants to trade with Mid-delburg, though 'nocht to remane thar as at a stapele' until the king should see 'quhat fredomes and priviliegis thai sal haf in tym to cum at the place quhar thai sal be staplit'. A mission was to be sent 'in al gudly haste and to bring ansuere agane thar apone'.[124] This mission seems to have been undertaken by Thomas Folkert (Flock-hart), former dean of gild of Edinburgh, and Alexander Napier, former and future provost of the burgh, who had recently been knighted.[125] They were appointed by the king on 24 April to nego-tiate with the magistrates of Middelburg.[126] Presumably until the result was known it was ordained that 'al stapele gudis [were] to remane and to stapele and pas to na merkatis', which seems to mean that an embargo was placed on the export of staple wares. Mean-while the parliamentary commission also ordained that merchants might continue to trade with La Rochelle, Bordeaux, France and Norway.[127] It is curious that no mention was made of the Baltic or German trade. In the Baltic regions there is certainly evidence of increasing Scottish interest : a German chronicle affirms that twenty-four Scottish ships entered Danzig between 1474 and 1476; by 1475 the Scots maintained an altar in the church of the Benedictines in the city.[128]

The disruption of trade with Flanders in 1467 was not long-lasting. In 1469 the ancient privileges of the Scots were confirmed, and on 31 May 1472 the king ordered Scottish merchants to take their goods to Bruges and not elsewhere.[129] A few days later James issued a commission to Sir Anselm Adournes as conservator of the privileges granted to Scottish merchants by the Dukes of Burgundy. Though settled in Bruges (of which he became burgomaster in 1475)[130] Sir Anselm was of Genoese extraction and had been sent on missions as far as Persia, in the course of which, so James believed, he had reflected credit on Scotland and its king, not only at the papal court and in Christian lands, but among the barbarous nations of Saracens and Turks.[131] An account of these journeys was dedicated to James,[132] who had diverted himself in his youth with Sir John

---

[124] *A.P.S.*, II. 87, cc. 6, 7.

[125] *Edinburgh Burgh Recs.*, I. 258-61. Napier was described as a knight in a charter of February 1467 (*R.M.S.*, II. No. 908).

[126] Facsimile letter of James III, Davidson and Gray, *Staple*, facing p. 136.

[127] *A.P.S.*, II. 87, c. 8.   [128] T. A. Fischer, *Scots in Prussia*, pp. 8-11.

[129] Davidson and Gray, *Staple*, pp. 134 and n. 1, 139.

[130] W. H. Finlayson, *op. cit., S.H.R.*, XXVIII. 195-6, at 196; pp. 419-20 above.

[131] Davidson and Gray, *Staple*, p. 134 and n. 2.

[132] W. H. Finlayson, *op. cit.*, 196.

Mandeville's fanciful book of travels.[133] The king doubtless esteemed someone who had traversed strange lands and was ready to overlook Sir Anselm's championship of the fallen Boyds.[134] The commission granted to him as conservator gave him some jurisdiction (in conjunction with resident Scottish burgesses) over Scottish subjects in the Burgundian dominions, and allowed him as salary a tax on staple wares which 'the provosts, bailies, town councillors and merchants of our realm . . . granted to him with unanimous consent and assent in our parliament by their letters under the common seals of the said burghs of our realm'.[135] This grant, made before the king had reached years of discretion, was revoked in 1476, partly because Sir Anselm was an alien, whereupon the king appointed his familiar esquire, Andrew Woodman, as conservator.[136] In 1483, however, the post was said to be vacant by the death of Sir Anselm (who may have recovered the office in the course of the visit to Scotland that ended in his death) whereupon the conservatorship was bestowed by the king upon Thomas Swift, his familiar servant.[137]

The changes in the conservatorship were accompanied by changes in the site of the staple : by 1477 it had returned from Bruges to Middelburg,[138] possibly as a consequence of the troubles that beset Flanders during and after the over-strenuous career of Charles the Bold, who was killed by the Swiss in January 1477.[139] His successor was Maximilian of Hapsburg, husband of Charles's daughter and heiress. Maximilian was soon to be King of the Romans, and, after 1493, emperor. On assuming control of the Burgundian territories he hastened to reach an understanding with the Scots. In June 1478 parliament was told that letters which were 'rycht hertfull, thankfull and honourable' had arrived from the Duke of Burgundy 'for the keeping of fredome of merchiandis of this realme in time tocum and reformacioune of the scathis that thai haf sustenit in tyme bigaine'. An embassy, to be financed by 'the hale burowis', was to be sent to the duke to renew and confirm the old alliance and 'to purchess uther grettare privilegis gif thai can be gottin in favoure of the merchandis'.[140] The parliamentary commission appointed in

[133] E.R., VII. 500.   [134] Pp. 419–20 above.
[135] Estaple de Bruges, cited in Davidson and Gray, Staple, p. 134, n. 3.
[136] R.M.S., II. No. 1234.   [137] P. 514 below; R.M.S., II. No. 1548.
[138] Davidson and Gray, Staple, p. 135.
[139] It is significant that after 1477 Sir Anselm Adournes was exiled from Bruges as a result of these troubles (W. H. Finlayson, op. cit., S.H.R., XXVIII. 195–6, at 196).   [140] A.P.S., II. 118, c. 4.

March 1479 was again to consider 'the gud of merchandice ande sending to the Duk of Burgunze'.[141] The latter was engaged in warfare with France until the death of his wife in 1482, when he made peace. In the following year Bruges made a successful attempt to woo the Scots away from Middelburg.[142] Nonetheless new causes of friction arose through Maximilian's issue of a letter of marque. This was a rough and ready method of securing redress for some commercial injury : it allowed plunder of the ships and goods of all countrymen of the perpetrator until the original loss had been recovered—a procedure that was all too likely to lead to counter-reprisals. The letter issued by Maximilian had resulted from a sentènce given by the lords of council, who, with the courts of the seaport burghs, and those of the admiral and his deputes, shared jurisdiction over maritime cases.[143] The burgh commissioners hoped that a sealed copy of the transactions of the lords of council would suffice as 'verificacioune of justice' in demonstration that Maximilian's subjects had no cause for complaint, 'quhilk may be distruccioune of the said letter of marque'. This was apparently having serious repercussions on Scottish trade, since to achieve its 'doune putting' parliament decided to send an embassy of one clerk and two burgesses to the King of the Romans. Their expenses were to be paid by 'the hale merchandis of borowis' and the burgh officials were 'to speid the inbringing of the said expenss' on pain of imprisonment.[144]

This was only one example of concerted action initiated by, or imposed upon, the burghs. The parliamentary commission appointed in October 1466 had been given power to 'autorize, ratify and apprufe, or til annull as thai think expedient and profitable, al actis and statutis avisit and commonit in the sessiouns of burowis for the gude of merchiandice'.[145] These 'sessiouns of burowis' were perhaps burgh representatives meeting under the form of the court or 'parliament' of the four burghs. The last allusion to a meeting of this body

---

[141] *Ibid.*, 122.   [142] Davidson and Gray, *Staple*, p. 135.

[143] See *Scot. Legal Hist.*, pp. 398-9. For maritime cases brought before the lords of council see *A.D.C.*, I. 93, 274-5. The record of a dispute of 1461 involving merchants of Amsterdam and Danzig which was brought before Alexander Napier of Merchiston as admiral-depute of Alexander, Duke of Albany, is given in T. A. Fischer, *Scots in Germany*, pp. 239-41.

[144] *A.P.S.*, II. 178, c. 11. The affair was still unsettled in 1491 and the expenses to which it gave rise were still the subject of dispute in 1496 (Theodora Pagan, *Convention of Royal Burghs*, pp. 18-9).

[145] *A.P.S.*, II. 85, c. 2.

is found in 1507,[146] and the last record of its transactions in 1500. On 10 November in that year the 'court of the parliament of the four burghs' met in the tolbooth of Edinburgh under the presidency of the chamberlain, Lord Home, and issued enactments in favour of the merchants' trade monopoly.[147] Thus if the judicial functions of the court were becoming less necessary or desirable it was none-theless able to acquire new functions in dealing with topics close to the hearts of the merchants. It is therefore strange that the closing years of the fifteenth century saw a quest for some other type of assembly that would replace, or at least supplement, the ancient one, and also, perhaps, the chamberlain ayre, which fell into desuetude after 1517.[148] In March 1484 a tax payable by seventeen burghs north of Forth was 'modifiit be the commissaris of burghis the tyme of the parliament haldin at Edinburgh'.[149] In the parlia-ment of October 1487 'the haill commissaris of burrowis' also acted jointly in presenting 'actis and statutis' which they desired to have 'ratyfyit and apprevit in this present parliament and to be put to execucioun for . . . the weilfar of merchandis'.[150] Among the statutes which were thereupon ratified by the three estates was one which ordained that

> zerely in tyme tocum certane commissaris of all borowis, baith southe and north, convene . . . anis in ilk zere in the burghe of Inverkethin on the morne efter Sanct James day [26 July] . . . to comoune and trete apoune the welefare of merchandis, the gude rewll and statutis for the commoune proffit of borowis and to provide for remede apoune the scaith and iniuris sustenit within burowis.[151]

It is tempting to regard this act as the foundation charter of the convention of royal burghs (only recently dissolved). But 'no record of any meeting in Inverkeithing is now extant, and the practice of holding annual conventions there, if such a practice ever existed, seems to have been speedily discontinued'. It was not until the mid-sixteenth century that the convention of royal burghs definitely emerged. Meanwhile it remained uncertain what form extra-

---

[146] Theodora Pagan, *Convention of Royal Burghs*, p. 13.
[147] *Edinburgh Burgh Recs.*, I. 86–7.
[148] Athol Murray, 'The Last Chamberlain Ayre', *S.H.R.*, xxxix. 85.
[149] *Burghs Convention Recs.*, I. 543. The stent roll that was then produced, the earliest extant record of the apportionment of taxation by the burghs, shows that Aberdeen and Dundee were each to pay £26 13s. 4d. They were followed by Perth (£22 4s. 6d.) then by St Andrews and Inverness (each £10 os. od.).
[150] *A.P.S.*, II. 178.   [151] *Ibid.*, 179, c. 17.

parliamentary meetings of burgh commissioners would finally take, and meetings of various types continued to be held.[152]

There was, however, little doubt as to the policies that such meetings were intended to foster, and parliament, which usually met in the tolbooth of Edinburgh, surrounded by the booths of the merchants,[153] could confidently be expected to ratify what had been devised for the welfare of mercantile interests. In 1438, and again in 1499, the magistrates of Edinburgh showed their anxiety to regulate the freighting of ships in the interests of merchants.[154] Thus the parliamentary commission of 1467 passed an act requiring the completion of charter-parties (written contracts between skippers and merchants) which would assure the latter of the safety and careful handling of the goods that they shipped. This act was re-affirmed at the request of 'the haill commissaris of burrowis' in the parliament of October 1487.[155]

More significant, however, was an act of 1467 which ordained that no craftsman should 'use merchandise' unless he renounced his craft.[156] This act was also re-affirmed in October 1487, when provision was made for its execution through 'searchers', who would confiscate to the use of the king the merchandise of the over-ambitious craftsman.[157] When the court of the parliament of the four burghs was held in Edinburgh on 10 November 1500 these acts were re-affirmed and it was ordained that only merchants who were resident burgesses should pass with merchandise to France or Flanders.[158] In 1467 it had also been ordained by parliament that only those who were 'famous and worschipfull' and possessed of at least half a last of goods should be allowed to take their goods abroad for sale.[159] Part of the explanation for this act may have been that in Germany there were so many itinerant Scots of small means that they brought disrepute upon themselves and their nation : passing as pedlars or pilgrims they acted like vagabonds.[160] But the main reason for the acts that were designed to keep craftsmen out of trade was the desire of the established merchants to guard their own

---

[152] *Burghs Convention Recs.*, I. vii; see also Theodora Pagan, *Convention of Royal Burghs*, pp. 24–5.   [153] *Edinburgh Burgh Recs.*, I. 39.

[154] *Ibid.*, 5–6, 78–9.   [155] *A.P.S.*, II. 87, c. 4; 178, c. 15.

[156] *Ibid.*, 86, c. 2.   [157] *Ibid.*, 178, c. 14.

[158] *Edinburgh Burgh Recs.*, I. 86–7. Copies of this ordinance were to be extracted from 'the book of the acts of the court of the parliament of the four burghs' by each burgh.

[159] *A.P.S.*, II. 87, c. 3.

[160] T. A. Fischer, *Scots in Germany*, pp. 241–2; *Scots in Prussia*, pp. 4–6 and c., n. I.

monopoly and ward off competition at a time when trade was in decline.

In other respects too, the merchant oligarchy that controlled the burghs showed a desire to curb the craftsmen. An act of parliament of November 1469 curtailed the holidays of masons, wrights and other craftsmen. Henceforth they were to abstain from work only on 'gret solempnit festis'; if they showed undue religiosity in abstaining from work they were, somewhat incongruously, to be punished by excommunication.[161] Another more important act of the same parliament complained that in the yearly choosing of alderman (provost), bailies and other burgh officials there was 'gret truble and contensione' caused 'throw multitud and clamor of commonis sympil personis'[162]—who undoubtedly comprised the craftsmen. The latter, it may be assumed, were claiming a share in burgh administration, or at least in burgh elections.

The earliest account of a burgh election is to be found in the surviving burgh records of Aberdeen, which open in 1398 with a notice of the election in the Michaelmas head court of various officials—the alderman, four bailies, four serjeants, and thirteen appraisers of flesh, wine and beer, whose pleasing duty was to test the quality of these commodities. This election is recorded as being made 'with the consent and assent of the whole community'. But it would be rash to assume that this was a 'democratic' election. It must be asked, 'whether, indeed, the "community" of the burgh is not . . . the merchant gild'. Certainly when the records of the Aberdeen gild court book commence in 1441 they show that the burgh council 'was elected by the gild, in the gild, at its regular meeting on the Friday following the Michaelmas head court'.[163] It is at least clear that elections were held each year, as laid down in the old *Leges Burgorum*—in a charter of 1391 there is an allusion to the alderman of Dundee and 'twelve good men of his council chosen yearly'.[164] It is also clear that the burgh court held by the bailies was never displaced by the gild court. But the latter, over which the alderman or provost might preside alongside the dean of gild, was not limited to the regulation of trade and strictly gild business: it might receive accounts and have control over the admission of new burgesses; often the gild and burgh records were kept in the same book by the same clerk, and the officials of the gild were officials of

---

[161] *A.P.S.*, II. 97, c. 15.   [162] *Ibid.*, 95, c. 5.
[163] *Aberdeen Burgh Recs.*, pp. 21, ciii–civ.   [164] *A.P.S.*, I. 577.

the burgh. In Edinburgh there existed not only an ordinary town council, perhaps elected in the burgh court, but a supplementary body called the 'dusane', a body not of twelve but of thirty-two, or even forty-five, which seems in 1453 and 1458 to have been elected, together with provost, dean of gild and treasurer, by the gild brethren in the Michaelmas gild court.[165] In 1463 the dusane was of the usual number of thirty-two, 'quhairof', affirms an early transcriber of the records, 'everie ane stylit be his craft'.[166]

If the dusane was made up on this occasion entirely of craftsmen the circumstance is startling, for those who had been elected to it ten years previously had included merchants of note and consequence such as Adam Cant and John Lamb, respectively former and future dean of gild.[167] Moreover it was the dusane which drew up leets for the election of the burgh officers, as was revealed in an investigation held by the chamberlain and certain lords of council on 6 October 1456. This procedure had, however, been broken by the choice of a bailie whose name had not appeared on the leet.[168] The fact that this led to the intervention of the chamberlain and lords of council indicates that high feelings had been aroused. Thus there are some grounds for supposing that in Edinburgh—which by itself encompassed half the burghal life of Scotland—there had been the 'contensione' in elections of which the act of 1469 complained.

The remedy devised by the act was a subtle one. It was 'thocht expedient' to continue the practice of yearly elections laid down in the *Leges Burgorum*, but the electorate was to be a limited one : the retiring burgh council was to choose the new council; the retiring council, together with the incoming council and with a representative of each craft, was to elect the burgh officers, including the alderman (provost), bailies and dean of gild. This procedure was modified by a further act of May 1474 which stipulated that four 'worthy persounis' of the retiring council should be chosen to sit on the incoming council.[169]

The acts of 1469 and 1474 seem at first to have been observed only in Edinburgh, which probably inspired them : in 1590 the magistrates of Aberdeen would defend their exclusion of craftsmen from the town council by affirming that

---

[165] *Edinburgh Burgh Recs.*, I. 1, 18. The entry under 3 October 1403 (p. 1) should be dated 1453 : the names of those elected coincide with those of the officials of 1454 (*ibid.*, 258).

[166] *Ibid.*, 20.

[167] Compare *ibid.*, 1–2 and 256–8.

[168] *Ibid.*, 15.

[169] *A.P.S.*, II. 95, c. 5; 107, c. 12.

thair is nocht ane uniforme ordour . . . observit amang the haill burrowes . . . anent the chesing and electing of thair magistratis and offi-
cieris, bot dyvers burrowes hes dyvers customes . . . nather yit is the
actis of parliament anent the chesing and electing of magistratis uni-
versalye observit amangis the haill burrowes.[170]

But sooner or later this legislation did have an influence on most
Scottish burghs. Among the acts ratified at the behest of the burgh
commissioners in the parliament of October 1487 was one that re-
affirmed the measure of 1469 and required that it be 'put to execucioun in tym to com', so that the burgh officers should be chosen
from 'the best and worthiest induellaris of the toun' (resident merchants?) and not 'be parcialite nor masterschip, quhilk is undoing
of the borowis'.[171] Yet the acts that had been passed tended to
aggravate the very abuses that were feared: the act of 1474 could
even be interpreted as meaning that *at least* four of the old council
should be seated on the new: in theory there was nothing to prevent
the old council from re-electing itself *en bloc* as the new. In 1567
the inhabitants of Cupar would complain that

> the auld counsale, having alwayis facultie to elect the new, thay cheis
> men of thair factioun and swa haldis the publict officis and counsale
> amangis a certane of particular men fra hand to hand, usand and
> disponand the common gude of the said burgh at thair plesour.[172]

Such 'parcialite' could be combined with 'masterschip'. For even
the greatest burghs looked to the baronage for leadership. Patrick
Charteris was provost of Perth in 1447, Andrew Charteris between
1465 and 1473, John Charteris in 1507.[173] In Aberdeen Gilbert
Menzies was provost by 1506 and had initiated the thraldom of the
burgh to the 'raice of Menzeissis'.[174] In Edinburgh Sir Alexander
Napier of Merchiston was frequently provost until at least 1471
and John Napier of Merchiston was provost in 1484.[175] A decision
of the burgh council in 1478 that for the 'honour and worschip of
the towne' the provost should have a yearly fee of £20 [176] doubtless
made the post more attractive and showed the desire of the burgh to
have as its head someone who would keep up appearances. On 8

[170] *Burghs Convention Recs.*, I. 325–6.   [171] *A.P.S.*, II. 178, c. 14.
[172] *R.P.C.*, I. 582. For a similar complaint of the community of Aberdeen in
1590 see *Burghs Convention Recs.*, I. 312–5.
[173] *R.M.S.*, II. Nos. 400, 896, 1122, 1648, 3107.
[174] *R.P.C.*, IV. 533; *Burghs Convention Recs.*, I. 313; *R.S.S.*, I. No. 1738.
[175] *Edinburgh Burgh Recs.*, I. 258–61, 265.   [176] *Ibid.*, 37.

August 1487 Patrick Hepburn, Lord Hailes, was chosen as provost and appointed James Crichton of Felde (Philde in Perthshire) as his depute 'because the haill towne committit power to his lordschip to cheise his deputes . . . as aft as he sall think expedient'. In 1513, after Flodden, no less a person than Archibald Douglas, Earl of Angus, would be provost.[177]

Whatever the ultimate consequences of the act of 1469 regulating burgh elections the feature that may well have seemed most novel and important was that it allowed each craft to choose one of its members to have a vote in the election of the burgh officers: thus in eschewing the participation of a 'multitud' of 'commonis sympil personis' the measure gave some recognition to the claims of crafts-men and may well have been intended as a concession that would reduce friction within the burghs. This seems, at any rate, to have been the effect in Edinburgh during the rest of the century. Nor is it likely that this was accidental: for the act of 1469 had assumed the distinctiveness of each craft; it had transformed an amorphous multitude, which might have taken the form of a union of *all* crafts-men, comparable to the merchant gild, into a number of separate organisations that were necessarily small and likely to develop sectional interests.

It is striking that such individual craft organisations, which attracted suspicion in the reign of James I,[178] acquired respectability in the second half of the fifteenth century. It came to be recognised that those who exercised a particular craft might pursue certain activities in common, and to some of these activities the burgh authorities could not in decency refuse approval. Thus on 12 January 1451 seventeen skinners of Edinburgh bound themselves to contribute to the upkeep of a chaplainry which they had founded in St Giles Kirk and also of the altar of St Christopher at which the chaplain was to celebrate. At the request of the skinners this obliga-tion was registered 'in the common book of gild of the same burgh'. Thus indirectly the authorities recognised an organisation uniting the skinners, since the upkeep of their religious benefaction re-quired stipulated contributions and an organisation to enforce them. It was also ordained that if any discord should arise among the skinners it was to be submitted to the determination of their brethren 'and to the decreet of the council and dusane of the burgh'.[179] On 13 September 1456 the question of support of an altar

[177] *Ibid.*, 52, 277.   [178] Pp. 308–9 above.   [179] *Edinburgh Burgh Recs.*, I. 9–11.

also figured in a concession made by the provost, bailies and council in favour of 'the haill craft of the baxteris', so that no baker was to be made a freeman or burgess 'without the avys and consent of the maist pairt of the worthiest of the craft'.[180] It was not, however, until after the act of 1469 had regulated burgh elections that the development and recognition of craft associations—the 'incorporated trades' of modern time—gained momentum. On 18 February 1473 ten Edinburgh hat-makers compeared in the tolbooth before the provost, bailies and council 'in judgement sittand' and presented a 'bill of supplicatioun', requesting that they might choose 'ane deacon amanges thame for conserveing of the said craft and all guid rewlles and ordinances'. The magistrates granted this supplication as being 'reasonabill and profitabill' and ratified a number of ordinances that were thereupon presented. These controlled terms of apprenticeship and entry to the craft, ostensibly in the interests of maintaining standards. The stipulation that 'nane of the said craft purches ony lordschipe incontrair ony pointtis of the said craft' was one that the magistrates, fearful of the intervention of powerful outsiders, must have welcomed. Thus the burgh's seal of cause (the seal of the burgh court) was attached to the documents recording the supplication and ordinances.[181] In this semi-judicial fashion the hat-makers secured powers of organisation and discipline. Further incorporations by seal of cause soon followed—the skinners in 1474, the masons and wrights in 1475, the websters (weavers) in 1476, the hammermen (blacksmiths, goldsmiths, lorimers, cutlers, buckle-makers and armourers) in 1483, the fleshers (butchers) in 1488, the coopers in 1489.[182] And the process would continue, for, as the cordiners (leather workers) explained in a supplication for incorporation in 1510, 'multitude but [without] reull makis confusioun'.[183] Thus by permitting organisation within each individual craft the merchant oligarchy turned the radicalism of the multitude into the conservatism of the few. By 1490 at least twelve crafts were so respectably organised that their deacons were associated with the burgh council in letting the burgh muir.[184]

Whatever the social and economic discords within Edinburgh its inhabitants were united against the outside world and showed an aggressive community spirit. From at least 1436 onwards the magistrates often tried, for the 'common proffitt', to purchase in bulk all

[180] *Ibid.*, 14.   [181] *Ibid.*, 26–8.
[182] *Ibid.*, 28–30, 30–2, 33–4, 47–9, 54–6, 57–8.
[183] *Ibid.*, 127.   [184] *Ibid.*, 58.

cargoes of victual, and sometimes timber, that were landed at Leith. Thereafter all inhabitants of the burgh might buy at a favourable price whatever they required from the bulk purchase, on the understanding that what they bought was not to be re-sold.[185] In 1462 it was ordained that the whole community should enter into a mutually profitable conspiracy so that 'na nychtbour . . . tak upon hand to warne ony strangaris of the price of vittuallis in the cuntrey'.[186] Unscrupulous community spirit was particularly aroused in exploiting the rights over the port of Leith which the burgh had obtained from Sir Robert Logan of Restalrig in 1398.[187] In 1428 Edinburgh has also been granted by James I the right to exact tolls upon ships, boats and cargoes for the 'fabrik and reparatioun of the port or herberie of Leith'—a grant which was thereafter several times renewed and confirmed.[188] Edinburgh's stranglehold over its unfortunate port was shown by an ordinance at the close of the century which arranged that 'all nichtbouris and all deikynis with thair craftismen' should be ready to descend upon Leith with the provost and bailies to hold a court 'for reforming of injuries done aganis thair fredome [privilege]' and by another ordinance which in 1482 prohibited the holding of any market in Leith.[189] On 16 November in the same year a royal charter confirmed Edinburgh's control over the port, and another charter of the same date increased the autonomy of the burgh by permitting the provost to be sheriff within its bounds, so that the inhabitants would no longer be subject to the jurisdiction of the 'landward' sheriff.[190]

Despite the pugnacious self-reliance of the Edinburgh burgesses, they, and the other burgesses of the realm, were hard pressed to maintain their status as one of the three estates. While individual burgesses continued to advance themselves, their estate as a whole suffered from the depression in international trade that perhaps left its mark in the 'voide placis' in Edinburgh to which allusion was made in royal letters patent of October 1477.[191] The growing attention that the burgesses paid to collective action perhaps betrayed their unease. It was ominous that they had been omitted from the 'congregation' of lords spiritual and temporal held by Bishop Ken-

---

[185] *Ibid.*, 4-5, 6, 19-20, 59.   [186] *Ibid.*, 19-20.
[187] *Edinburgh City Charters*, No. xx.
[188] *Edinburgh Burgh Recs.*, I. 3-4, 7-8, 14, 25, 43-7; see also pp. 23-4.
[189] *Ibid.*, 46, 50, 59.
[190] *R.M.S.*, II. Nos. 1525, 1526. The burgesses were to show their gratitude by celebrating a mass each year for the soul of James II.
[191] *Edinburgh Burgh Recs.*, I. 34-6.

nedy in 1464.[192] And though no attempt was made to unseat them from the estates they were tolerated rather than respected, and underwent various snubs. While burgesses were naturally employed in negotiations concerning trade, they were not represented on the 1468 marriage embassy to Denmark [193] nor on the embassy of 1471 that was to mediate between France and Burgundy. This was all the more striking in the latter case since the lords, 'considering the estatis', thought that the embassy should consist of one bishop, one earl, one lord, one knight, one clerk, and one herald.[194] Yet the burgesses contributed one-third of the £3,000 allotted to the expenses of the marriage embassy and one-third of the 3,000 crowns granted for the embassy of mediation.[195] Thereafter they seem to have been unable to pay their way on equal terms with the other two estates, a fact which was all the more obvious since attempts to levy taxation on the basis of a general assessment had been given up : in parliament each estate granted a specific proportion of a tax and made its own arrangements for its collection.[196] In February 1472, when parliament granted £5,000 to the king to send an expedition to Brittany, the clergy and barons were each to pay two-fifths of the contribution and the burghs the remaining one-fifth. When a contribution of 20,000 marks was granted in the parliament of March 1479 for the marriage of the king's younger sister, and when another was granted in the parliament of April 1481 for the victualling of Berwick, the clergy and barons again offered two-fifths each and the burghs the remaining one-fifth. [197]

Taxation was rare and was granted, as shown above, only for extraordinary expenditures on royal marriages, diplomacy, or military preparations. Moreover it may be questioned whether the grants were in every case followed by actual payment to the king : he did not send an expedition to Brittany and his younger sister ended her days in blighted spinsterhood.[198] Taxation may therefore be ignored in any examination of the royal revenues. Their approximate composition *c*. 1486 has been estimated (too generously) as follows :

---

[192] P. 407 above.   [193] See *E.R.*, VIII. lxxix–lxxx.
[194] *A.P.S.*, II. 99, c. 2.   [195] *Ibid.*, 90, c. 1 ; 99, c. 2.
[196] Rait, *Parliaments*, p. 491. The clergy had valuation rolls for each diocese and apportioned taxation on a diocesan basis (*A.P.S.*, II. 102–3). In 1468 the barons paid their share of the tax for the marriage embassy on the basis of inquests held by lairds in the sheriffdoms (*ibid.*, 90–1). By 1484 the burghs had their stent roll (p. 445 above).
[197] *A.P.S.*, II. 102, 122, 134.   [198] Pp. 488–9 below.

from crown lands	£10,600 (gross receipts)
from sheriffs	£1,720 (gross receipts)
from customs	£3,300 (gross receipts)
from burgh ferms	£760 (gross receipts)

£16,380 [199]

Even in monetary terms, as well as in purchasing power, the revenues of James III cannot have surpassed those of the crown in the last year of David II's reign. Their composition, as can be seen, had radically altered: the bulk of David's income was provided by the great customs and direct taxation; the bulk of James's income was forthcoming from the crown lands.

The change is explained by the vast additions made to the crown lands since 1424, a process of accretion which by no means abated in the reign of James III. Besides minor or temporary acquisitions he secured the lands of the Boyds, Orkney and Shetland, and the earldom of Ross, and recovered the earldoms of March and Mar by the forfeiture of his brothers.[200]

What the king inherited or acquired he tried to keep; and if his patrimony was depleted from time to time by generous grants it was well understood that these could be revoked, more or less plausibly, if they had been made before he had reached his 'perfect age' of twenty-five years.[201] Thus John Stewart, Lord Darnley, who was recognised as Earl of Lennox in 1473, had his title revoked on 12 January 1476, though it was not until 10 July 1476 that the king proclaimed in parliament a 'general revocation' of all grants prejudicial to the crown.[202] Revocation, whether particular or general, seems the likeliest explanation for many resignations and re-grants of land. Sir William Monypenny, Lord Avondale, Lord Lindsay of the Byres, Sir John Colquhoun of Luss and Archibald Douglas, Earl of Angus, were among those who resigned lands; and it was the king's 'familiars' who sooner or later received grants of these lands.[203] Thus acts of revocation seem to have led to a game of musical chairs

---

[199] *E.R.*, IX. lxxvi. The figures are criticised by Athol Murray in 'The Comptroller 1425–1488', *S.H.R.*, LII. 1–29.

[200] See *E.R.*, IX, lxix; pp. 480, 485, 516 below.

[201] Prior to 1474 there was some revocation from which a certain apothecary in receipt of an annual fee of £20 was exempted (*E.R.*, VIII. 253).

[202] *H.B.C.*, p. 480; *A.P.S.*, II. 113.

[203] *R.M.S.*, II. Nos. 1202 (Colquhoun); 1213 (Angus); 1264, 1299, 1587, 1627 (Monypenny); 1613, 1632 (Avondale); 1657, 1693 (Lindsay).

between nobles and 'familiars' in which the ultimate losers included some nobles of consequence.

Besides revocation there was another mainstay of the royal patrimony- –annexation. In the parliament of November 1469 the Boyd lands had been annexed to serve as an endowment for royal heirs apparent. In the parliament of February 1472 the earldom of Orkney and the lordship of Shetland were annexed to the crown and were not to be given away save, perhaps, to a legitimate son of the king. In July 1476 a similar arrangement was made regarding the earldom of Ross, and in October 1487 the earldom of March and lordship of Annandale were annexed to the crown.[204]

It was conservation and extension of the crown lands, rather than increases in their value, that led to any rise in the royal revenues from this source, for, on the whole, landed rents seem to have remained more or less unchanged throughout the reign.[205] Alterations seem to have been made not so much in the rents themselves as in the rate and frequency of 'grassums' (usually equal to a year's rent) or in the varying exaction of a similar payment known as 'introitus' on the renewal of a tack.[206] When these payments are taken into consideration there appears a slight downward trend in the cash returns from land : in 1470–71 the chamberlain of Fife accounted for money rents of £598 15s. 10½d. and grassums of £393 8s. 4d.; in 1486–7 the rents had somewhat increased to £632 12s. 1½d. but the grassums were only £190 17s. 6d.[207] Such a trend seems to have been general. Moreover by 1479 the account of the chamberlain of Fife showed arrears of £28 17s. 4d. and by 1487 his arrears had increased to £954 3s. 4d.[208] At the same audit the arrears of Strathearn were given as £486 11s. 2d. and those of Galloway as £236 4s. 6½d.[209] Already in the parliament of February 1484 such arrears had caused concern. It was asserted that 'the kingis malis, rentis and fermez . . . ar haldin fra his hienes, apoune the quhilk his estait and houshald suld be sustenit'. The proposed remedy was that the master of the household (then the Earl of Crawford) and the comptroller (then Thomas Simson of Knockhill, chamberlain of Fife) should investigate the withholding of rents and,

[204] *A.P.S.*, II. 102, 113, 146, 179–80, 187.

[205] G. G. Coulton (*Scottish Abbeys*, p. 138) cites the rental of Coupar Abbey as showing that the rise in rents kept no pace with the fall in money value, and that in some cases there was no rise in rent at all.

[206] *E.R.*, IX. xxxiii–xxxiv.   [207] *Ibid.*, VIII. 92; IX. 509.

[208] *Ibid.*, VIII. 568; IX. 505.   [209] *Ibid.*, IX. 460, 491.

with lords of council, should 'pas and distrenze the officiaris in thai partis'.[210] At least one negligent rent collector was arrested.[211]

With the exception of laxity in rent-collecting towards the end of the reign it would seem that there was careful attention given to the exploitation of the royal lands. The accounts of the *ballivi ad extra*—the bailies, chamberlains and receivers who administered the crown lands—survive in large number and are supplemented towards the end of the reign by detailed rentals periodically drawn up by commissions of assessment appointed by letters under the privy seal.[212] Thus in 1484 the king appointed a commission of twelve persons, headed by the Earl of Argyll and Lord Avondale. A minimum of three of these persons might act, providing that they included the comptroller, who was the key figure in all such commissions since he had general oversight of the king's landed revenues. The commissioners were instructed to set the rents of the royal lands 'that beis fundin richtwisly vaikand, and to prolong and continew takkis of thaim for the space of fyve yeris or within, as salbe sene speidfull to them'.[213] Tacks for five years were generally granted in Galloway, but elsewhere three-year tacks were usual; only exceptionally were longer tacks granted. In Bute and a few other areas there were 'kindly tenants' who did not require to obtain tacks or pay grassums but paid a customary rent.[214]

Grants in feu-ferm seem to have been comparatively rare, though not so rare as has been generally supposed:[215] James III, besides granting a number of tenements in Berwick in feu-ferm to encourage the re-population of the burgh,[216] made at least seventeen other grants[217] and confirmed at least thirteen grants of feu-ferm made by others.[218] Just as significant as feuing in its repercussions upon landholding was the development of an open market in land by the 'new inventiouns of selling of landis be chartir' that were noted by parliament in November 1469.[219] Besides the voluntary sales that resulted there were also compulsory sales under the terms of another act of the same parliament that authorised the apprising

---

[210] *A.P.S.*, II. 165, c. 6.　　　　[211] *E.R.*, IX. 306–7.

[212] *Ibid.*, xxxiii.　　　[213] *E.R.*, IX. 603.　　　[214] *Ibid.*, xxxiv–xxxv.

[215] See Dunlop, *Bishop Kennedy*, p. 344; Grant, *Social and Economic Development*, p. 268.

[216] *R.M.S.*, II. Nos. 1165, 1275, 1280, 1285, 1293.

[217] *Ibid.*, Nos. 1058, 1074, 1141, 1148, 1150, 1152, 1159, 1334, 1387, 1421, 1518, 1545, 1563, 1568, 1718, 1727; *T.A.*, I. 11.

[218] *R.M.S.*, II. Nos. 1029, 1040, 1081, 1204, 1313, 1384, 1393, 1463, 1502, 1508, 1560, 1574, 1688.　　　[219] *A.P.S.*, II. 94–5, c. 3.

and sale of lands to recover debts.[220(a)] From the combined evidence of the voluntary and compulsory sales of land it would seem that transfers of land took place mainly within the baronial class, partly to the disadvantage of the lords, partly to the advantage of a small group of ecclesiastics, partly to that of some burgesses, for whom an investment in land was a stepping-stone to gentility, very greatly to the advantage of the king and his 'familiars'.[220(b)]

Thus, thanks to various developments, land was no longer a concern only of the barons, trade no longer a concern only of the burgesses; all were consciously engaged in money-making; and the crown, while continuing to act (with or without parliament) as the ultimate regulator of all enterprise, was itself preoccupied with the administration of its own vast landholdings and was engaged in other miscellaneous undertakings. The position of the majority of the population who worked on the land is less clear. It was they, doubtless, who in 1468 spread the 'grete romour' about landlords who used the change in money values as an excuse for raising rents; and it was 'to content the commons' that there was a return to the *status quo*.[221] The evidence that during the reign rents did not rise suggests that a relative shortage of labour prevented rack-renting and allowed the rural population a standard of living high enough to encourage the domestic market.

By change in custom, or by legal enactment, there existed new opportunities for all classes, even for craftsmen. Nonetheless these opportunities became available at a time when the export trade was languishing, the returns from land were not improving, and the variations in the currency were generally exasperating. In such a situation those who fared badly, or hoped to fare better, might well turn their attention to politics, seeking preferment under the crown, or advancement through an opposition that might be rewarding. The church too offered tempting spoil, for it gave few signs of enterprise of its own, and its vast wealth—demonstrated by its ability to pay two-fifths of taxation—made it a possible victim of the enterprise of others.

This was particularly demonstrated in the case of the Benedictine priory of Coldingham, which 'remained one of the richest of

220(a) *Ibid.*, 96, c. 12.
220(b) Ranald Nicholson, 'Feudal Developments in late Medieval Scotland' *Juridical Review*, April 1973, pt, i. 1–21, at 9–16.
221 *A.P.S.*, II. 92, c. 1; pp. 434–5 above.

border prizes'.[222] Its position as a dependency of the English priory of Durham had been often threatened since at least 1378 : the priory was coveted by the late Bishop Kennedy, and also, more persistently, by the Benedictines of Dunfermline (whose claims were given lively publicity in Abbot Bower's influential *Scotichronicon*),[223] while the local baronial family of the Homes (sometimes engaged in rivalry among themselves) had vested interests that they were determined to maintain. In Scotland, however, there was at least growing agreement that the connection between Coldingham and Durham had to be broken. The occasion came with the onset of warfare with the Yorkists at the opening of James III's reign : 'by mid-May 1462 the last English monks north of the Tweed had been ejected from Scotland for ever',[224] and in the parliament of October 1466 it was pointedly ordained 'that na Inglis man have na benefice, seculare nor religouss, within the realme'.[225] It was in vain that the Durham monks sought until 1478 to recover their lost priory by litigation in the *curia* : they were by no means alone in finding papal justice more expensive than effective. Meanwhile it seemed that the beneficiary of their failure would be Master Patrick Home, archdeacon of Teviotdale, who in 1461 sought to obtain the priory of Coldingham *in commendam*.[226] In 1464, however, Sir Alexander Home of that Ilk, bailie of Coldingham since 1442, successfully sought the appointment of his son John as prior so that he (Sir Alexander) 'could continue to exploit the very real wealth of the priory in the interests of his own determination to play an aggressive and ambitious role in Scottish and border politics'.[227] This aim was countered in April 1472 when James III successfully petitioned the pope that the priory be suppressed and its revenues united to the royal chapel of St Mary at St Andrews. For over a decade there was stalemate : 'although . . . James never . . . abandoned the plan to exploit Coldingham in his own interests, the Homes proved formidable and eventually successful antagonists'.[228]

In 1472, the year when he staked a claim to Coldingham, James also intervened in the appointment of an Abbot of Dunfermline : although the monks had elected one of their number, the king 'promovit Henry Creychtoun [Crichton], Abbat of Paislay, therto, quha wes preferrit be the paip, through the kingis supplicationis, to the

[222] R. B. Dobson, 'The last English monks on Scottish soil', *S.H.R.*, XLVI. 1–25, at 3.

[223] *Ibid.*; *Chron Bower*, II. 163–5.   [224] R. B. Dobson, *op cit.*, 8.

[225] *A.P.S.*, II. 86, c. 9.   [226] R. B. Dobson, *op. cit.*, 6–7, 25.

[227] *Ibid.*, pp. 13–5.   [228] *Ibid.*, pp. 20–1 ; pp. 523–4 below.

saide abbacye'.[229] This left vacant the abbey of Paisley, to which James secured the appointment of Master Robert Shaw, parson of Minto. Writing a century later, Bishop Lesley singled out the king's intervention at Dunfermline and Paisley as the beginning of the degradation of Scottish monastic life :

> . . . the godlie electiones war frustrate and dekayde, becaus that the court of Rome admittit the princis supplicationis, the rather that thay gat greyt proffeit and sowmes of money thairby; quhairfore the bischoppis durst not conferme thame that wes chosin be the convent, nor thay quha wer electit durst not persew thair own ryght: and sua the abbayis come to secular abussis; the abbottis and pryouris being promovit furth of the court, quha levit courtlyk, secularlye, and voluptuoslye.[230]

Lesley's analysis is open to criticism : there had been lapses in monastic life before the crown's supposedly decisive intervention in 1472—it was not altogether unusual that in 1466 the Prior of Whithorn had been accused of grave charges, including fornication, and had been forced to resign ;[231] and as early as 1425 James I had uttered strictures against the Benedictines and Augustinians.[232] Nor was Lesley correct in assuming that prior to 1472 'godlie electiones' had been common, for rights of election had long been frustrated by papal reservations, provisions, and grants *in commendam,* and it was often as the upholder of 'godlie electiones' (which he could manipulate) that James III tried to extend his control of appointments (already considerable in the case of secular benefices) to the monastic benefices as well.

In view of the existing contentions over appointments to these, of which Coldingham provided a notable example, such a development might have proved salutary; but much depended on the use to which the crown put its extended powers of patronage. In the reign of James III the object seems to have been to use the heads of monastic houses in royal administration; it was somewhat novel, though hardly scandalous, that Archibald Crawford, Abbot of Holyrood, and David Lichtoun (or Leighton), Abbot of Arbroath, served successively as treasurer, and that the latter, together with the Abbots of Cambuskenneth and Paisley and the Prior of Pittenweem, were commissioned to assess crown lands.[233]

[229] Lesley, *History,* pp. 39–40.
[230] *Ibid.*
[231] *Wigtown Charters,* pp. 9–10.
[232] Pp. 298–9 above.
[233] *H.B.C.,* p. 181; *E.R.,* IX. 631, 649.

Not without a struggle did the crown wrest a share of ecclesiastical patronage from a reluctant papacy. The contest had begun in October 1466 during the dominance of Lord Boyd, who could count on some popular support in legislating against the malpractices of the *curia*. Patrick Graham, Bishop of St Andrews, was vulnerable since the papacy had granted him the abbey of Paisley *in commendam* after the existing abbot had been deprived for failure to pay a pension to one of the cardinals.[234] Thus the parliament of October 1466 passed (in vague terms) an act against pensions and a more explicit act which threatened any holder of a commend with the loss of his temporality and the penalties of rebellion.[235] When Graham thereupon resigned his commend of Paisley[236] the pope tempted fortune by granting him on 28 April 1467 a commend of the priory of Pittenweem.[237] In the parliament of November 1469 it appeared that James III intended to pursue the ecclesiastical policy of Lord Boyd and to use the Bishop of St Andrews to that end. An act was passed which alluded to an indult (privilege) granted by Nicholas V to the late Bishop Kennedy, whereby the Bishop of St Andrews was permitted to confirm elections in the monastic houses in his diocese. These were named, and included Coldingham and Dunfermline as well as another ten abbeys and three priories. Since this indult was 'to the comoune proffit of the realme' it was to be 'observit and kepit' under pain of treason. The same act also forbade any of the king's lieges to purchase (by papal provision) any benefice to which presentation or confirmation customarily pertained within the realm.[238] It was therefore James's intention to limit papal provisions by insisting upon the right of Scotsmen to nominate to benefices of which they held the patronage, and the right of Scottish monastic chapters to proceed with the 'godlie electiones' esteemed by Bishop Lesley. Thanks to the St Andrews indult local nominations and elections could be locally confirmed and papal patronage could be largely excluded from the most important Scottish diocese.

Much, however, depended upon the attitude of the papacy and upon that of the Bishop of St Andrews, who was thrust willy-nilly into the position of upholder of royal patronage. Paul II responded by announcing that the St Andrews indult had been revoked.[239] In the

---

[234] R. K. Hannay, *The Scottish Crown and the Papacy*, p. 6.

[235] *A.P.S.*, II. 85, cc. 4 and 5.

[236] R. K. Hannay, *The Scottish Crown and the Papacy*, p. 8.

[237] Leslie J. Macfarlane, 'The Primacy of the Scottish Church, 1472–1521', *Innes Review*, xx. 111–29, at 113.   [238] *A.P.S.*, II. 98, c. 21.

[239] R. K. Hannay, *The Scottish Crown and the Papacy*, p. 8.

parliament of May 1471 no reference was made to the indult but the right of 'fre eleccioune' was re-asserted; no papal collector was to levy taxes on the clergy higher than those customary in the past; there were to be no annexations or unions of benefices, unless for the endowment of collegiate kirks (now the most favoured of ecclesiastical institutions); other annexations and unions made since the king's accession were to be annulled. The restriction upon such appropriations came two centuries too late to have any effect on the structure of the Scottish kirk but was notable as tacitly assuming that parliament could undo what the pope had sanctioned in an area hitherto regarded as fully within his jurisdiction. Cumulatively the measures of May 1471 (which were to be observed on pain of treason) were intended to remedy 'the gret dampnage and skaith dayli donne to al the realme' by resort to the *curia*, 'considering the innowmerable riches that is had out of the realme thar throw'.[240] Using different methods, James III had gone at least as far as James I in challenging papal authority, particularly since the parliament of May 1471 also renewed restrictions on the export of money. He had established a bargaining position which it was doubtless the task of the Abbot of Cambuskenneth to exploit when he was appointed in the following month as the king's procurator and plenipotentiary on a mission to Paul II and the *curia*.[241]

But it was the Bishop of St Andrews who was to win the attention of the *curia*. Graham had business of his own to transact in Rome : he owed at least 3,100 gold florins for his various bulls of provision, and it was doubtless his financial troubles that had brought him into controversy with the monks of his erstwhile commend of Paisley and the dean and chapter of his former bishopric of Brechin, and induced him to contest the bequests made by the late Bishop Kennedy, proceedings which were not likely to endear him either to his colleagues or to the university of St Andrews.[242] Moreover it seems that Graham had gone to seek papal support for a policy that was at variance with that of the crown.[243]

His arrival at Rome must have occurred shortly after the death of Paul II and the election of Sixtus IV, who saw in the presence of the foremost Scottish bishop an opportunity to devise a new policy towards Scotland. Its features showed that Sixtus was either unaware of Scottish conditions or was misled by Graham : on 13 August

[240] *A.P.S.*, II. 99, c. 4.   [241] *R.M.S.*, II. No. 1034.
[242] Leslie J. Macfarlane, *op. cit.*, 113–4; Dunlop, *Bishop Kennedy*, p. 296.
[243] J. Herkless and R. K. Hannay, *Archbishops of St Andrews*, I. 42–3.

1472 a bull was issued erecting the bishopric of St Andrews into an archbishopric with metropolitan authority; henceforth the Bishops of Glasgow, Dunkeld, Aberdeen, Moray, Brechin, Dunblane, Ross, Caithness, Galloway, Argyll, the Isles, and Orkney were to be suffragans who owed obedience to the new archbishop, to whom they were enjoined to show reverence and honour.[244] Sixtus's bull was couched in courteous terms flattering to the Scots, and it took note of current criticisms of undue recourse to the *curia* by hinting that the existence of a metropolitan would reduce the number of appeals to Rome. The bull also recognised political realities by including in the metropolitan's province three bishoprics that had hitherto been technically outside the Scottish kirk : Galloway was removed from the shadowy jurisdiction of the Archbishop of York; the Isles and Orkney from that of the Archbishop of Nidaros, and, so far as Orkney was concerned, this was yet another move that tacitly assumed permanent Scottish control of the Northern Isles.[245] It was perhaps less pleasing that the bull hinted that the Scottish ordinaries (the bishops) had been wont to overstep their power and required to be disciplined by a metropolitan, and also that ecclesiastical cases 'are drawn to a forbidden court [*e.g.* parliament] and dealt with there'. Nothing in the bull alluded to the leading cause of controversy—the disputed control of ecclesiastical patronage—and although the new metropolitan would have powers of confirming elections this had not in other countries proved any obstacle to the exercise of papal control over appointments. Three centuries earlier the erection of St Andrews to archiepiscopal dignity would have been welcomed in Scotland and would have solved obvious problems; by 1472 it was a move that only disturbed vested interests. In the promotion of Patrick Graham the Scottish bishops saw their own demotion, and James III, who does not seem to have been consulted, saw a challenge to the authority over the kirk that he was exerting himself to acquire. News of the outcry in Scotland must have reached Graham, who tactfully remained on the continent until at least September 1473.[246] By that time the pope had injudiciously appointed him legate *a latere* and collector of a tithe to be imposed on the kirk, and had in other ways augmented his powers and privileges, mostly in order that he might raise money in Scotland for a crusade against the Turks. Moreover,

---

[244] Robertson, *Concilia*, I. cx.

[245] It is significant that a few months previously the bishops who granted a tax to James III included those of Orkney and Galloway (*A.P.S.*, II. 102–3).

[246] Leslie J. Macfarlane, *op. cit., Innes Review*, xx. 111–29, at 114.

in direct contradiction of the recent act against unions and annexations, the revenues of the priory of Pittenweem (lately recognised by royal charter as pertaining to the Prior and chapter of St Andrews)[247] together with those of seven parish kirks (including one that was a benefice of John Laing, the treasurer) were granted for the maintenance of the archbishop's household; and Graham was empowered to visit and reform all monasteries, even those of Kelso and Holyrood (the latter held by Archibald Crawford, frequent auditor of exchequer and soon to be treasurer) which had been exempt from such visitations.[248] Finally Graham was granted the abbey of Arbroath *in commendam* for a period of five years.[249]

The opposition to the absent archbishop gathered momentum. In August 1473 the king sent to St Andrews for a chaplain who could divulge 'certane materez anent the bishop', and orders were issued to put an embargo on 'schippis that suld have past to the Bischop of Sanctandros'.[250] In October or November a summons was issued for a 'generale consale twiching the archbischop'.[251] Mention in May 1474 of 'the inbringing of the kingis last taxt grantit be the clergy' may support Bishop Lesley's statement that the bishops had offered the king twelve thousand marks for his help against the archbishop.[252] By February 1474 James had recognosced the temporalities of St Andrews and had sent a notary there to publish an appeal, presumably to the pope, against Graham.[253] After his return to Scotland Graham does not seem to have attended parliament or to have witnessed royal charters. He was evidently in deep disgrace and was not recognised as archbishop.

There is little to support the view that Graham was 'a prelate of singular and primitive virtue' bent upon reform.[253(b)] It was as a great-grandson of Robert III and a nephew of Bishop Kennedy rather than by any personal qualifications that he had obtained the bishopric of St Andrews in 1465 when scarcely thirty years old, despite the fact that there were at that time at least five bishops of greater experience.[254] Although 'there is no evidence to suggest that

---

[247] *R.M.S.*, II. No. 1039.

[248] J. A. F. Thomson, 'Some New Light on the Elevation of Patrick Graham', *S.H.R.*, XL. 83–8, at 84, 86.

[249] R. K. Hannay, *The Scottish Crown and the Papacy*, pp. 8–9.

[250] *T.A.*, I. 43, 67.   [251] *Ibid.*, 46.

[252] Lesley, *History*, p. 41; *T.A.*, I. 50. The 'taxt' may however have been that of £2,000 offered by the clergy in the parliament of February 1472 to dissuade the king from a personal expedition to Brittany (*A.P.S.*, II. 102–3).

[253] *T.A.*, I. 49; *E.R.*, VIII. 318–9.   [253(b)] Tytler, *History*, I. pt. ii, 206.

[254] Leslie J. Macfarlane, *op. cit.*, *Innes Review*, XX. 111–29, at 113.

he was other than a conscientious and hard-working bishop'[255] Graham played no outstanding part in public administration. At a critical juncture in the relationship between crown and papacy he had associated himself with the latter. But if this sprang from a sincere dislike of James III's growing mastery over the kirk Graham did not demonstrate his opposition straightforwardly, and his stance was weakened by the prolonged pursuit of benefices and privileges that culminated in his appointment as archbishop and legate. Latterly he had alienated both the king and the prelates and was left deserted. He was therefore valueless to the *curia*, and, unable to pay his debts, incurred excommunication in 1475, after which his troubles seem to have brought on a mental breakdown. By September 1476 the pope had been informed that Graham had lost his reason, and in December a papal commission of inquiry was set up under John Huseman, a German canon lawyer. It found that Graham was a 'heretic, schismatic, falsifier, simoniac, person of irregular life, blasphemer and excommunicate', who asserted that he himself was a pope chosen by God for the reformation of the kirk.[256] Graham was therefore deprived of his archbishopric on 9 January 1478, after which he was imprisoned in Inchcolm and Dunfermline, and finally in Lochleven, where he died.[257]

James III (albeit with the support of the prelates) had broken Scotland's first archbishop. The papacy, which had promoted Graham, was further discredited by his fall, and the king was left demonstrably master of the kirk. It now suited James's purposes to recognise the institution of the archbishopric, providing that it would not be bestowed upon anyone who might acquire delusions of grandeur, or upon anyone sufficiently reputable to use it as a possible leader of clerical intransigence. Thus experienced bishops, such as Thomas Spens of Aberdeen, Ninian Spot of Galloway and William Tulloch of Moray, were bypassed, together with John Laing, a civil servant recently promoted to Glasgow. James had detected a 'safe' man in William Scheves, who 'started under the double handicap of illegitimacy and non-baronial parentage'.[258] He had been installed in the archdeaconry of St Andrews by Patrick Graham in 1472, and in 1474 secured papal provision. He was also provost of the collegiate kirk of Crichton, and in 1474 was provided (unsuccessfully) to the

[255] *Ibid.*, p. 114.
[256] J. A. F. Thomson, *op. cit.*, *S.H.R.*, XL. 83–8, at 87–8; *T.A.*, I. li and lii, n. 2.   [257] Lesley, *History*, pp. 42–3.
[258] Leslie J. Macfarlane, *op. cit.*, *Innes Review*, XX. 111–29, at 115.

archdeaconry of Dunblane, and in 1474 (successfully) to the deanery of Dunkeld.[259] He had graduated at St Andrews in 1456 and had worked for another four years in that university before studying medicine and astronomy at Louvain under a teacher of repute.[260] These advanced studies seem to have led to preferment at court. Astronomy included astrology, which was both respectable and fashionable. Whether or not Scheves was court astrologer, he certainly received an annual fee of £20 between 1471 and 1474 for his services as royal physician.[261] In 1474 he was to be found making payments on behalf of the king for the purchase of green ginger, 'certane potigariis' (medicines), velvet, Holland cloth, seventy pair of 'patynnis' (clogs), and the sewing of the royal shirts. It would therefore seem that he had been given some official post, perhaps in the wardrobe alongside a certain Rob Scheves.[262] From 1475 onwards he also acted as auditor of exchequer.[263] It was undoubtedly Scheves's connection with the court rather than his academic and ecclesiastical attainments that won him the archbishopric. Six weeks before Graham's deprivation it had already been settled in the *curia* that Scheves was to be his successor; on 11 February 1478, two days after the deprivation, Scheves was provided to the archbishopric.[264] If the papacy had any doubts about his qualifications they were perhaps put to rest by a bargain whereby Prosper Camogli de' Medici was provided to the bishopric of Caithness in May 1478. The first (and last) Italian to obtain possession of a Scottish bishopric was admitted to the temporalities in 1481 but resigned three years later.[265]

Scheves was consecrated in Holyrood in the spring of 1479 in the presence of the king and nobility and was to hold the archbishopric of St Andrews until his death in 1497.[266] He was never able to win much co-operation from his suffragan bishops, and resentment at the existence of a metropolitan seems to have prevented the holding of a provincial council for several decades.[267] But Scheves acted as a loyal servant of the crown, participating in routine public business in parliament, hearing civil cases as a lord of council, serving as auditor of exchequer, commissioner of crown lands, and latterly as ambas-

[259] Watt, *Fasti*, pp. 89, 105, 307, 350; Leslie J. Macfarlane, *op. cit.*, *Innes Review*, xx. 111–29, at 115, 116.
[260] *Ibid.*, p. 115.   [261] *E.R.*, VIII. 120, 190, 253.
[262] *T.A.*, I. xlviii, 18, 21, 23, 28.   [263]ᵃ *E.R.*, VIII. 266, 326, 401.
[264] J. A. F. Thomson, *op. cit.*, *S.H.R.*, XL. 83–8, at 88; Leslie J. Macfarlane. *op. cit.*, *Innes Review*, xx. 111–29, at 116; Watt, *Fasti*, p. 295.
[265] See Cameron, *Apostolic Camera*, pp. xlvii–xlix.
[266] Watt, *Fasti*, p. 295; Lesley, *History*, p. 43.
[267] D. E. Easson, *Gavin Dunbar ... Archbishop of Glasgow* (1947), p. 59.

sador. Nor did he bring discredit upon his ecclesiastical office, but proved himself 'a cultured and learned man with a genuine love of his country and its history, a conscientious archbishop who late in life turned to theology, a generous benefactor of the university of St Andrews'.[268]

Co-operation between Scheves and James III formed part of a resumed campaign to extend crown control over ecclesiastical patronage. In the parliament of October 1479 all grants and privileges previously bestowed upon the bishopric of St Andrews were confirmed in favour of the new archbishop and his successors. This measure (in an obvious reversal of former policy) particularly included all 'uniounes and annexaciounis of any benefice maid be oure hali faider the pape'.[269] Two charters were issued which formally detailed the privileges that had just been confirmed in parliament.[270] One of these reissued the Golden Charter once granted to Bishop Kennedy.[271] The other professed the king's devotion to St Andrew, patron saint of the realm, and James's singular favour towards Archbishop Scheves; it confirmed a variety of privileges, especially the indult granted to Bishop Kennedy by Nicholas V. This was perhaps the main object of the exercise, for already in the parliament of March 1479 the act of November 1469 ordering the observance of the St Andrews indult had been presented for ratification and confirmation.[272] In the parliament of March 1482, when this indult was again re-affirmed, its provisions were extended to other dioceses 'that hes been in use, consuetude, or possessioune, of confirmatioune of electionis'; and in May 1485 the same matter was again raised.[273] Until 1487, when its function was taken over by a more advantageous indult, the St Andrews indult was one of the twin pillars of the king's ecclesiastical policy.

‾ The other was the claim to rights of patronage *sede vacante*. This claim was re-affirmed in the parliaments of April 1481, March 1482, and also in that of February 1484, when it was decided that the chancellor should write to the pope 'for the defence of our souverane lordis patronage'.[274] Meanwhile, in the parliament of December 1482

---

[268] Leslie J. Macfarlane, *op. cit., Innes Review*, xx. 111–29, at 118. The archbishop's interests may be traced in the surviving books that once belonged to his large collection. See John Durkan and Anthony Ross, *Early Scottish Libraries*, pp. 47–9; John Durkan, 'The Beginnings of Humanism in Scotland', *Innes Review*, IV. 5–24, at 5, 17–9; *T.A.*, I. liii, n. I.

[269] *A.P.S.*, II. 128–9. [270] *Ibid.*, 193–6.

[271] P. 363 above. [272] *A.P.S.*, II. 123.

[273] *Ibid.*, 140–1, c. 15; 171–2, cc. 10, 12, 14.

[274] *Ibid.*, 133, c. 7; 141, cc. 16 and 17; 166, c. 9.

it was ordained that the acts against the purchasing of pensions from benefices should be 'put to execucioune'.[275]

To the papacy all this posed a renewed menace. In some notable instances Sixtus IV resisted : in 1483 the Glasgow chapter had elected George Carmichael and the Dunkeld chapter had elected Alexander Inglis, the clerk register, whose archdeaconry of St Andrews was intended to go to the king's 'traist counsallour', Master John Ireland, professor of theology.[276] These proceedings vindicated the right of election which James (for his own purposes) championed. In each case, however, Sixtus IV vindicated the right of papal provision : he annulled the elections, provided George Brown to Dunkeld and translated Robert Blackadder from Aberdeen to Glasgow. This move allowed the pope to translate William Elphinstone from Ross to Aberdeen and to make a provision to Ross.[277] About the same time John Hepburn was provided to the priory of St Andrews.

In the parliament of May 1485 reference was made to these appointments, and while it was announced (in vain) that the king would 'nocht suffre Maister George Broune, nor nane utheris that has presumyt to be promovit to the saide bischopric of Dunkelde contrare our souveran lordis mynde', it was also conceded that Blackadder, Elphinstone and Hepburn were 'thankfull personis to our souverane lord, and of his speciale consale, and . . . admittit be his hienes to ther temperaliteis'.[278] The new pope, Innocent VIII, did not fail to take the hint that there would be no more royal championship of free elections and that papal provisions would be accepted by the king so long as they were made in favour of 'thankfull personis'.

At the outset of his pontificate Innocent was evidently anxious to achieve a settlement with the Scottish crown : by April 1485 James, Bishop of Imola, had arrived in Scotland as legate *a latere*.[279] The king showed his esteem for the legate 'with royal gifts', taking him with him wherever he went.[280] Imola probably witnessed the proceedings in the parliament of May 1485, where the king publicised his objectives in readiness for a diplomatic confrontation with the papacy. The occasion was provided by preparations to send the customary embassy to Rome to tender Scotland's obedience to the new pope. According to the instructions drawn up in parliament the embassy was to inform Innocent of Scottish grievances and seek a

[275] *Ibid.*, 144, c. 9.   [276] *Ibid.*, 171, c. 8.
[277] Watt, *Fasti*, pp. 3, 98, 149, 269.   [278] *A.P.S.*, II. 171, c. 8.
[279] J. A. F. Thomson, 'Innocent VIII and the Scottish Church', *Innes Review*, XIX. 23-31, at 25, n. 17.   [280] Boece, *Vitae*, p. 52.

multitude of privileges,[281] in particular that the pope concede to the king and his successors a six-month delay before any papal disposition of prelacies or elective benefices so that 'our souverane lordis writing and supplicacioun may be sende for the promocioun of sic personis as is thankful to his hienes . . . sen'[since] all the prelatis of his realme has the first vote in his parlment and of his secrete counsale'.[282] Meanwhile the legate had evidently sent reports that induced the pope to act benignly towards James III, who in the spring of 1486 was presented with the golden rose, a traditional token of special papal regard which had been forwarded from Rome.[283]

It was not until December 1486 that the Scottish embassy, accompanied by the legate and headed by Archbishop Scheves and Bishop Blackadder of Glasgow, arrived in Rome. Despite an altercation on 2 February 1487, when to their disgust the orator of the King of Hungary was given precedence over them,[284] the ambassadors acquired valuable privileges for themselves and their king. It was probably as a result of James's desire to reward Scheves that the pope augmented the latter's dignity on 27 March 1487 by making St Andrews a primatial see with the same rights as Canterbury. As primate of Scotland and *legatus natus* the archbishop was now beyond dispute at the head of the Scottish hierarchy.[285] Much more important was an indult of 20 April 1487 whereby Innocent conceded that he would delay making appointments to cathedral kirks and monasteries with annual revenues exceeding two hundred gold florins until they had remained vacant for eight months; during this period he would await the 'humble supplications' of the king and his successors, 'so that . . . we may the better be able to proceed to these provisions as we shall think expedient, urging our successors that in such provisions they take equal care to observe our practice'.[286]

In one respect—by granting a delay of eight months instead of only six—Innocent had granted more than the parliament of May 1485 had desired; and the advantage to the crown was correspondingly increased since bishoprics and abbacies could be kept vacant somewhat longer while the king drew the revenues of the temporali-

---

[281] *A.P.S.*, II. 170–2, cc. 5, 6–12, 14.   [282] *Ibid.*, 171, cc. 7, 9.

[283] J. A. F. Thomson, *op. cit.*, *Innes Review*, XIX. 23–31, at 26; Charles Burns, 'Papal Gifts to Scottish Monarchs: the Golden Rose and the Blessed Sword', *Innes Review*, XX. 150–94.   [284] J. A. F. Thomson, *op. cit.*, 26.

[285] Leslie J. Macfarlane, *op. cit.*, *Innes Review*, XX. 111–29, at 116; J. A. F. Thomson, *op. cit.*, 27.

[286] Text in J. Herkless and R. K. Hannay, *Archbishops of St Andrews*, I. 257–8.

ties, exercised the ecclesiastical patronage *sede vacante* that he per-tinaciously claimed, and negotiated to obtain provision of an acceptable new bishop or abbot. But the pope did not bind himself to accept the nominations presented in the king's 'humble supplications'. The efficacy of the indult therefore depended on the current relation-ship between crown and papacy.

This relationship was soon soured: thanks to the troubles that ended in James's downfall the king was suspicious of everyone, in-cluding the pope. In the parliament of January 1488 there were more fulminations about 'impetrations at the court of Rome of bishopricks, abbacyis and uthir beneficis'; the crown's rights *sede vacante* were again re-affirmed, and could be applied, so parliament asserted, in the bishopric of Aberdeen, which was still technically vacant since Bishop Elphinstone's bulls of appointment had not been delivered.[287]

Just as James's position was weakened through political troubles so also for different reasons was that of his protégé, the archbishop, whose 'relationship with his hierarchy, never an easy one, rapidly deteriorated after his primatial appointment'.[288] In February 1474 Thomas Spens, Bishop of Aberdeen, had set a precedent by obtaining exemption from the jurisdiction of Archbishop Graham.[289] In May and June 1488 Bishop Blackadder of Glasgow and Andrew Stewart, Bishop of Moray, respectively obtained bulls exempting them from the primate's jurisdiction.[290] At the end of the reign both primate and king were under attack and the kirk was divided.

While it is evident that the erection of St Andrews to metropolitan and primatial status introduced a new element of discord within the Scottish kirk, this was the result, originally at least, of the initiative of the papacy, not that of the crown. What resulted from James's own forceful intervention in the affairs of the kirk is harder to assess. His acquisition of the indult of 1487 was one that subsequent kings would exploit, and the example that they set was not necessarily one that he himself would have followed. If in his time scandal existed in ecclesiastical high places it was probably no greater than in previous reigns, and in most cases arose from the bitter struggle for benefices, aggravated by the vacillating and mercenary practices of the *curia*. And these it was James's ambition to circumvent. His influence over ecclesiastical appointments was used to promote serviceable men,

[287] *A.P.S.*, II. 183–4, cc. 12, 19.
[288] Leslie J. Macfarlane, *op. cit.*, *Innes Review*, xx. 111–29, at 117.
[289] *Ibid.*, 114.   [290] *Ibid.*, 117.

mostly with administrative experience. Despite his underhand methods in securing appointments those who were appointed had respectable qualifications, or, as in the case of Scheves, proved themselves not unfit for office. It was James, rather than the pope, who furthered the career of William Elphinstone, drawing him from academic life (he was rector of Glasgow University in 1474) to onerous responsibility as 'official' of Lothian, auditor of exchequer and of the parliamentary committee of causes and complaints, and probably securing his provision to the bishopric of Ross. If it was through the initiative of the papacy that Elphinstone was further promoted, its treatment of the best Scottish bishop of the time also illustrates 'how legalistic and inflexible the legitimate processes of the Apostolic Camera could sometimes be . . . to the prejudice of good sense, and vexation of the faithful'. For Elphinstone's difficulties in paying the 'common services' due to the *camera* for his promotion to Aberdeen meant that his bulls of provision were not released for five years, during which he remained unconsecrated bishop of that diocese.[291]

Elphinstone was apparently on familiar terms with the king, who, thanks to the bishop's admonitions (so affirms Boece) displayed an edifying piety in almsgiving, generous gifts to kirks, and personal devotion; for whenever James beheld an image of Christ or the Virgin he would burst into tears and prayer.[292] The king certainly showed favour to a wide variety of ecclesiastical institutions. He confirmed grants made to the Franciscan Observants (now established in seven leading burghs),[293] and bestowed an annuity of twenty-four marks upon the Dominicans of Edinburgh on condition that they celebrated a daily mass for the soul of Queen Margaret.[294] His interest in St Salvator's was shown by his acquisition of the patronage of the college from Lord Kennedy and his kin, who were compensated (perhaps inadequately) in Galloway.[295] It was with royal encouragement that the collegiate kirk of St Duthac was established at Tain.[296] Apart from Tain and the abortive erection of Coldingham as a collegiate kirk, the reign saw the establishment of new collegiate kirks at Guthrie and Restalrig, as well as a 'new erection' at Dalkeith, to which some parish kirks were appropriated.[297] Beside the new kirk of Restalrig James

[291] Leslie J. Macfarlane, 'William Elphinstone, Founder of the University of Aberdeen', *Aberdeen University Review*, XXXIX. 1-18, at pp. 6-8.

[292] Boece, *Vitae*, p. 52.   [293] Easson, *Religious Houses*, pp. 109-13.

[294] *R.M.S.*, II. Nos. 1164, 1434.   [295] *Ibid.*, No. 1128.

[296] *Ibid.*, No. 1694. See also John Durkan, 'The Sanctuary and College of Tain', *Innes Review*, XIII. 147-56.

[297] Easson, *Religious Houses*, pp. 173-88; *Morton Registrum*, II. No. 230.

built a handsome octagonal chapel to enshrine the relics of St Triduana.[298] In Edinburgh Queen Mary's foundation of Trinity College was followed by the raising of St Giles to collegiate status and its munificent endowment by the burgesses—its provost was to receive the enormous annual pension of 220 marks from the magistrates.[299] Elsewhere the foundation of chaplainries went on apace, particularly in the burgh kirks.[300]

The burgesses devoutly invested not only in the votive masses celebrated by chaplains but also, with more worldly motives, in the exploitation of ecclesiastical revenues. Thus the prominent Edinburgh burgesses Walter Bertram and Patrick Barron each founded a chaplainry in St Giles and each obtained tacks or feus from Henry Crichton, the Abbot of Dunfermline intruded by the king in 1472.[301] Nor was it only the temporalities of the religious houses that were involved in such transactions : Abbot Crichton was following a common practice when, a few months after his appointment, and possibly to help to pay for it, he obtained £450 by granting to a burgess of Linlithgow a nineteen-year tack of the teinds of the parsonage of Stirling.[302] Heavy burgess investment in the mass, coupled with investment in the kirk's spiritualities and temporalities, was an explosive mixture liable to ignite as soon as John Knox pronounced that the mass was idolatry.

[298] David McRoberts, op. cit., Innes Review, XIX. 3–14, at 13.

[299] R.M.S., II. No. 1397.

[300] Ibid., Nos. 1157, 1238, 1320, 1328, 1333, 1339, 1392, 1400, 1469, 1544, 1586, 1596, 1628, 1655, 1672, 1692.

[301] Ibid., Nos. 1392, 1544; Dunfermline Registrum, Nos. 479, 480, 488.

[302] Dunfermline Registrum, Nos. 476, 481; Coulton, Scottish Abbeys, pp. 93–4.

16

DOMESTIC AND INTERNATIONAL
POLITICS, 1469–1488

The complexity of James III's reign after 1469, sufficiently illustrated in the surviving records, is hardly made simpler by the surviving narrative sources. John Major, perhaps significantly, ended his consideration of Scottish affairs in 1469, while Hector Boece's *Scotorum Historiae* terminates in 1460. The continuation by the Piedmontese Giovanni Ferreri (Johannes Ferrerius), who from 1531 to 1545 taught in the abbey of Kinloss,[1] is of a later generation and, like the other sixteenth-century writers, Robert Lindsay of Pitscottie, Bishop John Lesley, and George Buchanan, Ferrerius seems uncritically (though not necessarily wrongly) to have accepted popular traditions. Buchanan's work, the least trustworthy of the lot, has even been styled 'little else than a classical romance'.[2] In addition there survives an anonymous chronicle that is useful but all too short. The narrators are thus poor guides through the fields of domestic and international politics where James's attempts to gain his ends met sometimes with success, sometimes with failure, and at length with disaster.

On the whole the international situation favoured Scotland : with the recovery of Berwick the Scots had no further ambitions to be satisfied at the expense of recurrent enmity with England. If peace or an effective truce could be achieved James would be free to assert himself both at home and on the continent, where he hoped to cut a fine figure, particularly by intervening in the disputes between Charles the Bold of Burgundy and Louis XI of France. In the parliament of

[1] John Durkan, *op cit., Innes Review*, IV. 5–24, at 14–6.
[2] Tytler, *History*, I. pt. ii, Notes and Illustrations, p. 388.

May 1471 certain articles concerning France, England and Burgundy were presented, as a result of which it was proposed to send an embassy to 'labour delygently for trety and concorde' betwixt the King of France and the Duke of Burgundy, to both of whom Scotland was bound by 'tender alyans'. The ambassadors, who were to be financed by a grant of 3,000 crowns from the three estates, were to seek 'a convenient place for the mariage of my young lady, our soverane lordis sistir'.[3] What parliament intended was that the king's younger sister, Margaret, should be married in such a way as to reconcile the courts of France and Burgundy. The aim of Louis XI, however, was to attach James to his side by beguiling him with hopes of acquiring the duchy of Brittany, with which James had a tenuous connection through Duchess Isabella, his aunt.[4] This manoeuvre looked likely to succeed: when parliament met in February 1472 there was support for James's project of a 'passage utouthe [outwith] his realm for the recoveryng of his richt of Bertane [Brittany]'. Towards the furnishing of an expedition of six thousand men the three estates made a grant of £5,000, 'of the quhilk the king was content'.[5] But the clergy had some forebodings. They pointed out that the king was still 'in tender age' and as yet had no offspring to maintain the royal succession; if James left the realm it would be 'opyn be apperance to his ald ennemyis of Ingland'; they therefore professed their 'grete tender lufe' for the king to 'induce him to remain at hame' and tried to make their grant towards the proposed expedition conditional upon the king's non-participation.[6]

The argument of the clergy lost some force after the birth of a royal son and heir on 17 March 1473. In the parliament of July in that year James presented a number of articles, the last of which concerned 'the passing of the king'.[7] Probably to enlist support for this scheme James showed favour to a number of nobles before, and during, this parliament,[8] and Sir Alexander Home was made a lord of parliament.[9] But despite James's timely favours the lords announced that they could 'nocht in na wiss gif thare counsale to his passage'. They took it for granted, however, that they could impose no veto if the king were 'uterly determyt to pas'. At any rate he could not do so 'in this sesone' since no preparations had been made.[10] If, nonetheless, the king were 'determit', he should recall a letter which had been sent

---

[3] *A.P.S.*, II. 99, c. 2. [4] P. 347 above. [5] *A.P.S.*, II. 102.
[6] *Ibid.*, 102-3. [7] *Ibid.*, 103, c. 2.
[8] *R.M.S.*, II. Nos. 1111, 1117, 1120, 1126, 1133, 1136, 1147.
[9] *A.P.S.*, II. 103. [10] *Ibid.*, 103, c. 2.

to the King of France (probably one that accepted the latter's terms for a conquest of Brittany) since 'na mater can be convoyit to the honour, worschip and profit of his hienes without cessing of the said letter'.[11]

If parliament failed to dissuade the king from his 'passage' it had an alternative scheme—to convert the 'passage' from a military expedition into one that was diplomatic. It was asserted that the only honourable and acceptable cause for the king's personal intervention overseas was mediation between France and Burgundy, since 'throw the contencioune being betuix the said princis the grettast part of Cristindome is trublit'. Successful mediation would aid resistance to 'the gret ennemy of Cristin faithe', the Great Turk, and would be pleasing to God; it would redound to James's honour and might 'bring him therthrow to his richt, nocht alanerly to the counte of Zanctone bot als of the duchery of Gillire'.[12] Thus James's cupidity was diverted from Brittany both to the French county of Saintonge (in regard to which James I had once received an undertaking from the French)[13] and to the duchy of Guelders, where the duke's son had imprisoned his father, so that, it was confidently asserted, 'the duchery of Gillir be naturall successioune of law and resone pertenis to our soverain lorde',[14] presumably since James had reversionary rights through his mother.

It would be difficult to guess which of the three claims, to Brittany, Saintonge or Guelders, was the most illusory; but the last two were at least the less dangerous and could be raised, so it was thought, in the course of mediation. For, once the letter to Louis XI had been recalled, so parliament advised, James should send an embassy to Burgundy and France to announce his readiness to mediate. If the ambassadors found that Louis refused to deliver Saintonge they were to report this 'injustice and unkyndlyness' to the allied Dukes of Burgundy and Brittany and seek their aid in obtaining Saintonge; the Duke of Burgundy was also to be exhorted to help James secure Guelders. If, however, both Charles and Louis were *each* willing to gratify James (all too naïve a supposition) then the ambassadors should try to have James accepted not merely as mediator but as arbiter.[15]

The prelates craftily pointed out that James's success in this ambitious plan might be furthered if he 'war now in the meyntime to . . . travel throw his realme and put sic justice and polycy in his awn

---

[11] *Ibid.*, 103, c. 4.   [12] *Ibid.*, 103, c. 3.   [13] Pp. 289, 393 above.
[14] *A.P.S.*, II. 104, c. 5.   [15] *Ibid.*

realme that the brute [renown] and the fame of him mycht pas in utheris contreis'. Thus James was flatteringly enticed to attend more diligently to the governance of his own kingdom. Thereby, so the prelates continued, 'he mycht be grace of God be callit to gretare thingis than is zit expremit'.[16] This was doubtless a hint that James might eventually be elected emperor. When parliament met in May 1474 it was thought expedient that the king should send an embassy to his father-in-law of Denmark 'to mak and bynde confideracione and alliance with the emperour [Frederick III]'.[17] Thus thanks to the extraordinary wiliness of the lords and prelates in the parliament of July 1473 James's proposed 'passage' was transformed, if not into a diligent pursuit of justice, at least into harmless and inconclusive diplomacy. It was Charles the Bold who won the duchy of Guelders.[18]

Parliament had not only hinted that the king should pay more attention to the execution of justice but had reminded him that continental ambitions could not safely be pursued when the attitude of England was uncertain. That country was recovering from new political troubles. A series of remarkable vicissitudes had begun in August 1469, when Edward IV had become the virtual prisoner of the Earl of Warwick (the Kingmaker). After the king secured his liberty Warwick sailed to France, allied himself with Margaret of Anjou, and invaded England in September 1470. Edward IV fled to the Burgundian dominions. There followed the release and 'readeption' of Henry VI under Warwick's tutelage. The game of musical chairs continued when Edward returned in March 1471 to defeat Warwick and the Lancastrians at Barnet on 13 April and Tewkesbury on 4 May. After the death of Warwick and of Henry's heir, Edward, the capture of Margaret of Anjou, and the murder of Henry, Edward IV resumed his reign.[19]

A few Lancastrian refugees, including the Earl of Oxford and Lords Lovel and Latimer, received Scottish safe-conducts.[20] In May 1471 the Scottish parliament, fearful of a Yorkist invasion, undertook military preparations : it was agreed that prelates and barons should make 'cartis of weir'; it was ordained that the length of spears should be standardised at six ells, and each yeoman who 'can nocht deil witht the bow' was to have 'a gud ax and a targe of leddyr to resist the schot of Ingland'; wappinschaws were to be held; football and golf were to be abandoned.[21] By July 1473, however, the 'cartis of were' were evidently not forthcoming, and the barons undertook to 'mak thaim incontinent'.[22] By May 1474 they were still not forthcoming.[23] Since 1471, however, fears of Yorkist hostility had gradually abated. The readeption of Henry VI had been too short-lived for the Scots to have committed themselves to the Warwickian Lancastrians,[24] and the restoration of Edward IV was followed for almost a decade by repeated interchanges of ambassadors, commissioners, envoys and heralds,[25] though their business was not always amicable. In the spring of 1473 Charles the Bold had even intervened to induce the Scottish and English kings to guarantee for at least two years their existing truce, which was supposed to last to 1519.[26]

There followed polite but somewhat cold exchanges of view. On 13 July 1473 James replied to a message of the Earl of Northumberland.[27] The English warden had complained of 'gret attemptatis committit be oure liegis of Liddalisdale uppoun Inglismen aganis the forme of the trewis'. James rejoined by asserting that 'in likwiss oure liegis ar richt complaintewss of Inglismen duelland within Tindaile and Riddisdaile, quhilkis daili makis depredacionis and herschippis upoun oure liegis'. Northumberland's pursuivant had also remonstrated 'twiching the resaving of the Erle of Oxinfurde within oure realme'. James admitted that Oxford 'of lang tyme passit had oure saufe conduct'—which was still unexpired—but complained that 'oure rebell and tratoure, Robert Boid, is resett within your toune of Anwik'.[28] Lord Boyd was in fact receiving a yearly pension of two hundred marks from Edward IV;[29] and the forfeited Earl of Douglas, whose annuity had been confirmed during Henry VI's readeption,[30]

[21] *A.P.S.*, II. 99–100, cc. 5, 6.   [22] *Ibid.*, 105, c. 13.
[23] *Ibid.*, 106, c. 5.
[24] Only one Scottish mission, for which safe-conducts were issued on 13 November 1470 (*Rot. Scot.*, II. 425–6) seems to have been sent during the readeption.
[25] *Cal. Docs. Scot.*, IV. Nos. 1394, 1395, 1397, 1398, 1408, 1409, 1413, 1460; *Rot. Scot.*, II. 429, 430–4, 436–8, 444, 454.
[26] *Cal. Docs. Scot.*, IV. No. 1405; *Rot. Scot.*, II. 436.
[27] *Cal. Docs. Scot.*, IV. No. 1430 (Appendix 1. No. 24). The editor has assigned this document to 1475, but its reference to Oxford, who in 1475 was in prison (E. F. Jacob, *Fifteenth Century*, p. 572), indicates an earlier date. There can be little doubt that James's letter was written shortly before the meeting of commissioners at Alnwick on 28 September 1473, where the activities of Oxford were again discussed (p. 477 below).
[28] *Cal. Docs. Scot.*, IV. No. 1430 (Appendix 1, No. 24).
[29] *Ibid.*, Nos. 1413, 1415, 1440, 1441.   [30] *Ibid.*, No. 1392.

again had it confirmed by Edward IV a few years later, when it was said to amount to £390.[31]

The Scottish parliament of July 1473 was somewhat suspicious of Edward's intentions and noted that he had failed through 'ignorance, reklesnes or malice' to deliver safe-conducts so that Scottish commissioners might come to Alnwick for redress of breaches of the truce.[32] But the safe-conducts had at least been enrolled, if not issued, on 21 April, and English commissioners had been named.[33] When the English and Scottish commissioners at length met at Alnwick on 28 September 1473 they made remarkable progress in approving a schedule for the holding of March Days at a number of places in the Borders and in dealing with outstanding problems. The English again complained of 'the resetting of th'Erle of Oxfurd',[34] who was hovering off the English shores and would soon seize St Michael's Mount in Cornwall.[35] The Scots answered that they had not aided the earl and that his existing safe-conduct, which would expire at Michaelmas, had not been renewed. The siege of St Michael's Mount and the submission of the earl in January 1474[36] removed this cause of dispute. A claim presented by a number of Scottish merchants was the subject of adjudication by the English commissioners at Alnwick, after which full satisfaction was forthcoming from Edward IV, who presented the merchants with silk and woollen cloth to the value of £200 English or £911 8s. 0d. Scots.[37]

A more serious claim concerned a Scottish vessel described as 'the barge of St Andrews', but more precisely identified as the famous *Salvator* constructed by Bishop Kennedy. Sometime before August 1472 it had been wrecked and plundered near Bamburgh.[38] In the meeting at Alnwick the Scottish claim was referred to the admirals of both kingdoms, though without result, since the parliament of May 1474 arranged that a forthcoming embassy should raise the subject of 'the barge'.[39] By 3 February 1475 the affair was settled when Edward

---

[31] *Ibid.*, No. 1423. [32] *A.P.S.*, II. 104–5, c. 10.
[33] *Rot. Scot.*, II. 436–7.
[34] *Cal. Docs. Scot.*, IV. No. 1431 (Appendix 1. No. 25). The editor has mistakenly assigned this document to 1475, but it was signed by the same notables as those who acted as Scottish commissioners at Alnwick in September 1473 (compare *ibid.*, No. 1409). Its contents obviously refer to the conditions of 1473, not those of 1475.
[35] E. F. Jacob, *The Fifteenth Century*, pp. 571–2; *Cal. Docs. Scot.*, IV. Nos. 1406, 1412, 1413.
[36] E. F. Jacob, *The Fifteenth Century*, pp. 571–2.
[37] *Cal. Docs. Scot.*, IV. No. 1412 (Appendix 1, No. 23).
[38] *Rot. Scot.*, II. 434–5; Lesley, *History*, p. 39.
[39] *Cal. Docs. Scot.*, IV. No. 1409; *A.P.S.*, II. 106, c. 2; Lesley, *History*, p. 40.

paid compensation of five hundred marks, English, and received letters of acquittance that James had issued in readiness on 25 October 1474.[40]

The behaviour of the English king in the wake of the Alnwick meeting must have stimulated the confidence of Scots merchants, who obtained English safe-conducts for themselves and their vessels both during the readeption of Henry VI and the restoration of Edward IV; a few licences were also issued to allow English merchants to export goods to Scotland.[41] Thus, at least after the meeting of the commissioners at Alnwick on 28 September 1473, Edward had proved by his actions that he was willing to allow the truce to become a reality. The Scots responded. The parliament of May 1474 thought it expedient to send 'ane honorable ambassat in Ingland' to work for 'gud materis of frendschep and amitie . . . and keping of the pece in tym to cum'.[42]

What parliament had in mind was a marriage alliance. For on 15 June James empowered the ambassadors to propose a match between the king's son and heir and Cecily, Edward's youngest daughter.[43] On 29 July 1474 Edward appointed commissioners to discuss this proposal.[44] The preliminaries were settled, in almost unseemly haste, by indentures drawn up on the following day.[45] Thereafter the business proceeded with suspicious speed. English ambassadors even came to Edinburgh, where they concluded an indenture on 26 October 1474.[46] Its preamble stated that :

> Forasmuche as this noble isle called Grete Britaigne canne not be kepte and mainteigned better in welthe and prosperite than such things to be practized and concluded betwene the kyngs of both reames, England and Scotland, wherby thaye and thair subgetts might be assured to lyve in peas . . . hit hath be agreed . . . that, considered the longe continued troubles betwene the both reames, with grete and mortell werre that hath followed theruppone, for the appesyng . . . of the same . . . a more especiall wey is to be found . . . than only the truste of the trewe . . . that is now, or any other trewe that couthe be devysed betwixt both partees.

The 'more especiall wey' was to be a marriage between James, Duke of Rothesay, and the Lady Cecily. For

[40] Cal. Docs. Scot., IV. Nos. 1414, 1416, 1424; Rot. Scot., II. 445.
[41] Cal. Docs. Scot., IV. Nos. 1389, 1407, 1411, 1433, 1439, 1457; Rot. Scot., II. 426, 427, 432, 438, 440, 443–4, 452, 455.   [42] A.P.S., II. 106, c. 2.
[43] Rot. Scot., II. 443.   [44] Ibid; Cal Docs. Scot., IV. No. 1414.
[45] Rot. Scot., II. 444, 446.   [46] Ibid., 446–50.

the said marriage is thouthe to be the very rote and establisshment of all the love, favour and assistence that the one partie shalle owe to the other.

Thus a formal betrothal was solemnised in the Blackfriars of Edinburgh. The prospective bride and groom did not take part, she being five years of age and he not having reached his second birthday.[47] It was the Earl of Crawford and Lord Scrope who, as proxies, joined hands and plighted troth.[48]

It was stipulated in the indenture of 26 October that the marriage was to follow as soon as the couple were of fit age. Cecily's dower was specified, and her dowry was set at 20,000 marks, English. A first instalment of 2,000 marks was to be paid to James III within three months, and a further two yearly payments of the same amount were to be made, after which the remaining 14,000 marks were to be paid at the rate of 1,000 a year. All instalments above the sum of 2,500 marks were to be returned if the royal marriage for any reason did not take place.[49] This proviso, together with the scheme of extended payments of the dowry, was intended to keep the Scots peaceable. As a further guarantee both kings were to re-affirm the existing truce (to last till 1519) and neither side would aid the traitors and rebels of the other.[50] On 3 November 1474 James ratified the marriage treaty and truce,[51] and on the same day Edward ordered proclamation of the truce to be made throughout England.[52] On 3 February 1475 James acknowledged receipt of the first instalment of 2,000 marks towards the dowry.[53] For a small outlay Edward had neutralised Scotland.

Since at least 1474 the English king had planned an invasion of France, and in July 1474 had allied himself with Duke Charles of Burgundy. Thus 'the new marriage treaty was, next to his own treaty with Charles, the most important advantage which Edward had yet gained over Louis, and the most necessary to the success of an English invasion of France'.[54] James, piqued by his disappointments over Brittany and Saintonge, paid no heed when Edward crossed to France in July 1475 with a large army, which included the Earl of Douglas and Lord Boyd, each of whom led a retinue and received wages of war.[55] Since no effective Burgundian help was forthcoming Edward

[47] *H.B.C.*, pp. 38, 58.
[48] *Foedera*, v. pt. iii, 47–8; *Cal. Docs. Scot.*, iv. No. 1417.
[49] See *Cal. Docs. Scot.*, iv. No. 1420. [50] *Rot. Scot.*, ii. 447.
[51] *Cal. Docs. Scot.*, iv. No. 1418. [52] *Ibid.*, No. 1419.
[53] *Ibid.*, No. 1425. [54] E. F. Jacob, *The Fifteenth Century*, p. 575.
[55] *Cal. Docs. Scot.*, iv. No. 1428.

allowed himself to be bought off by Louis XI. At Picquigny on 29 August 1475 an Anglo-French truce was concluded to last for seven years, and Edward was to receive from Louis an annual pension of 50,000 crowns.[56]

It seems likely that on the eve of his departure for France Edward let slip some information regarding the treaty of London that he had concluded with Earl John of Ross in 1462.[57] Such a move could be represented as evidence of Edward's good faith in implementing the provisions of the marriage treaty of 1474 that bound the English and Scottish kings to aid one another against rebels; more to the point, the information was likely to distract James's attention from France by arousing his ire against MacDonald. On 16 October 1475 Unicorn pursuivant appeared with letters of peremptory summons at the earl's castle of Dingwall (to which he was denied entry) and at the gates cited the earl to compear in parliament at Edinburgh on 1 December to answer for 'tresonable ligis and bandis mad be him with Edvarde, King of Yngland', and other miscellaneous treasons and crimes.[58] When parliament met on 1 December the earl was not there, where-upon Chancellor Avondale presented the case against him, the three estates unanimously adjudged him guilty and the dempster pro-nounced that the earl had forfeited to the king his life, lands, rents, superiorities and offices.[59] As a result MacDonald 'humyllit himself and come to the kingis will apoun certaine condiciones'.[60]

These were revealed in a parliament at Edinburgh in July 1476. MacDonald, who appeared in person, resigned to the crown the earl-dom of Ross, the lands of Knapdale and Kintyre, and the sheriffships of Inverness and Nairn. Thereupon the earldom of Ross was at once, with the assent of the three estates, annexed to the crown. The new status of the former earl was clarified when the king created 'John of Islay' a baron, banneret, and lord of parliament, with the title of 'Lord of the Isles', and ordered the heralds to proclaim him as such.[61]

A fuller account of these transactions is given in a charter of 15 July 1476 which was witnessed by many notables.[62] In the same charter MacDonald's remaining territories, presumably at his own request, were entailed to any future legitimate male offspring, failing whom, they were to pass to his illegitimate son, Angus of Islay, and

[56] E. F. Jacob, *The Fifteenth Century*, pp. 575–8.
[57] Pp. 401–2 above.   [58] *A.P.S.*, II. 109–10.
[59] *Ibid.*, III.   [60] Lesley, *History*, p. 41.
[61] *A.P.S.*, II. 113.   [62] *Ibid.*, 189–90.

the latter's legitimate heirs male. From his remaining lands, which were still considerable, the Lord of the Isles was to render due rights and services to the crown, and, together with his tenants and the inhabitants of his lands, he was to cause to be observed the laws and customs of the realm like other barons, freeholders and lieges of the realm—a tall order.[63] Macdonald's fateful decision to submit upon such terms prevented a civil war in which, aided by geography and can loyalty, he might conceivably have held his own, for James III was no inspiring military leader. But neither, so it would appear, was Macdonald. His submission opened the far north and west to the Lowland influences that were bound to follow, sooner or later, in the wake of crown control.

The events of 1476 had imposed a strain upon the MacDonald hegemony that fatally disrupted its unity and, in the process, led to more disorder. The house of Islay was itself torn with dissension : by March 1478 Elizabeth Livingston, MacDonald's estranged spouse, had informed the pope that her husband was trying to poison her.[64] More important was the attitude of MacDonald's illegitimate son and heir, Angus,[65] who chafed at the truncation of his patrimony and at his father's generous grants to the MacLean, MacLeod and MacNeill vassals of the MacDonalds. And 'when the MacDonalds and heads of their family saw that their chief and family was to be sunk they began to look up to Angus Ogg, the young lord'. A clan seannachie recounts how Angus hounded his father from his lodging, forcing him to spend the night in the shelter of an upturned boat. On the morrow the Lord of the Isles formally laid a curse upon his son.[66]

It was probably the latter who was responsible for raids upon Arran, which was 'laid waste by the Islesmen' in 1477 and 1478.[67] It was Angus's father who had to answer to the government. By 7 April 1478 the Lord of the Isles had been summoned before the king in parliament for harbouring troublemakers.[68] But by December 1478 James had been led to believe in the innocence of the Lord of the Isles and renewed the grant of his lands (with the previous exceptions of Ross, Kintyre and Knapdale).[69] It was probably about this time, and certainly as a result of the quarrel between Angus Og and his

[63] Ibid., 190; R.M.S., II. No. 1246; Highland Papers, I. 123.
[64] Highland Papers, IV. 206–9.
[65] His career is imaginatively recounted by I. F. Grant in Angus Og of the Isles.
[66] Highland Papers, I. 47–50; Gregory, Western Highlands, p. 51.
[67] E.R., VIII. 487–8; Highland Papers, I. 51.
[68] A.P.S., II. 115.   [69] R.M.S., II. No. 1410.

father, that the latter appeared unexpectedly at Inveraray with a small retinue and humbly sought the good services of Argyll,[70] whose daughter was wife of Angus Og.[71] The result seems to have been an interview on the Sound of Mull, where father and son had assembled in their galleys with the chief men of the Isles and the Earls of Argyll and Atholl.[72] Instead of pacification both sides resolved to fight. At 'the Bloody Bay' near Tobermory, probably sometime in 1481, the galleys of Angus Og prevailed against those of his father, the Mac-Leods of Lewis and Harris, MacLean of Duart and MacNeill of Barra.[73] Henceforth it was Angus Og who was the effective head of the MacDonalds, and his father became a mere protégé of the crown.

The Earl of Argyll, who would soon be made chancellor, was at least the indirect beneficiary of the troubles that beset the Mac-Donalds after 1475. Nor did he omit to secure his own interests : after the battle of 'the Bloody Bay' the Earl of Atholl 'being provided with boats by Argyle crossed over privately to Isla, where Angus Ogg's lady, daughter of Argyle, was, and apprehended Donald Du, . . . a child of three years of age, and committed him prisoner to Inch Chonnil . . . where he remained in custody until his hair got grey'.[74] Donald, the son of Angus and therefore, under the tailzie of 15 July 1476, the potential heir to the lordship, was to cause no small trouble when he escaped from Campbell custody.[75]

The feuds that had broken out among the MacDonalds and their vassals in the aftermath of the king's forfeiture of the earldom of Ross were by no means unique : the parliament of March 1479 included 'the gret trubill that is in Ross, Cathness and Suthirlande' as only one feature of 'the gret brek that is now, and apperand to be, in diverss partis of the realme' : Angus was disturbed by feud between the Earl of Buchan and the Earl of Erroll, between the Master of Crawford and Lord Glamis; a feud between Lord Maxwell of Caerlaverock and the laird of Drumlanrig threatened peace in Nithsdale and Annan-dale; Teviotdale was the scene of factious contention between the Rutherfords and Turnbulls, between the sheriff and his uncles and the laird of Cranston.[76] Even more serious than baronial feuds was the estrangement between the king and his brothers, Alexander, Duke of Albany, and John, Earl of Mar. These two, according to Pitscottie,

[70] *Highland Papers*, I. 48.   [71] *Ibid.*, 50; *Scots Peerage*, v. 47.
[72] *Highland Papers*, I. 49.
[73] *Ibid.*, 49–50; Gregory, *Western Highlands*, pp. 52–4; I. F. Grant, *Angus Og of the Isles*, pp. 133–5.   [74] *Highland Papers*, I. 50.
[75] P. 545 below.   [76] *A.P.S.*, II. 122.

presented the stirring figures expected of men of their rank, while the king was thought to be 'ane that lovit sollitarnes and desyrit never to heir of weiris nor the fame thairof, but delytit mair in musik and polliecie of beging [architecture] nor he did in the goverment of his realme; for he was wondrous covettous in conquissing of money rather than the heartis of his barrouns, for he delyttit mair in singing and playing upoun instrumentis nor he did in defence of the Bordouris or the ministratioun of justice'.[77]

It is by no means certain that James had no interest in Border defence and wars: although over £750 were paid to the masters of works in 1473, probably for building operations at the royal residences, this sum included expenditure on artillery.[78] Nor did the king altogether neglect fashionable country sports: he collected greyhounds and hawks.[79] But the records certainly have entries that indicate his liking for music: John Broune, lute player, was paid £5 so that he might go overseas to learn his craft; he, or some other luteplayer, went to Bruges and received a solicitous gift of a barrel of salmon from the king.[80] Ferrerius gives the impression that James was something of a dilettante who ignored class boundaries in his patronage not only of scholars but of skilled craftsmen.[81] Pitscottie's allusion to the king's 'conquissing of money' seems to have been well founded: Bishop Elphinstone was reputed to have urged him to eschew avarice;[82] at James's death it was found that his notorious 'blak kist' and other receptacles contained enough treasure to stuff Aladdin's cave, much of it in the form of jewels and ornaments that were doubtless works of art.[83] In addition the king's outlay on clothes and personal accoutrements was surpassed only by that of the queen, and amounted in 1473–4 to £639 os. 5d.[84] An extravagant court ill suited 'a barane land . . . fertile of folk, with great scantnes of fude'[85] that was racked by famine, inflation and feud.

Together with an expensive court went a high-flown view of royal authority. One significant act of 1469 affirmed that James possessed 'ful jurisdictioune and fre impire within his realme' and that he might therefore create notaries public (hitherto the prerogative of the pope and the emperor); henceforth notaries created by the emperor were to

[77] Pitscottie, *Historie*, I. 162–3. [78] *T.A.*, I. 74; see also *ibid.*, ccci.
[79] *Ibid.*, 43, 44, 45, 46.
[80] *Ibid.*, 43, 59, 60, 67; see also *E.R.*, IX. xliv, n. 1.
[81] Ferrerius, *Continuatio*, p. 391. [82] Boece, *Vitae*, p. 51.
[83] P. 531 below. [84] *T.A.*, I. 13–28.
[85] *The Harp* (printed in *Chron. Pluscarden*, I. 392–400).

have no authority within Scotland.[86] In the parliament of April 1478 a clerk was accused of 'tresonable usurpacioune' for having legitimated a bastard 'in the name and authorite of the emperoure, contrare to oure souverain lordis croune and majeste riale'.[87] The implication was that the Scottish king was to be regarded as the equal of the emperor. Nor was he beneath the king of France in dignity; for an ineffective act of 1472 ordained that the royal arms should no longer bear the double tressure of fleurs de lys [88] which might heraldically be construed as evidence of a subordinate relationship to the crown of France. Evidently touchy on questions of his dignity and authority, James was described by Polydore Vergil as 'impatient of criticism, quick to make a foolish decision and slow to revoke it'.[89] Already the king had shown his political capriciousness in his attack upon the Boyds in 1469; a decade later he was to give another demonstration in an attack upon his two brothers, whose conventional tastes and extrovert character doubtless won them a popularity that the king resented.

Hitherto Albany and Mar seem to have tactfully avoided the political limelight or to have been deliberately excluded from government. In contrast to the king's uncles, Atholl and Buchan, his brothers seldom attended parliament and hardly ever were mentioned as witnesses to royal charters. Nonetheless, as admiral of Scotland and warden of the East and West March,[90] Albany had important official duties. His lands in Annandale (a den of thieves according to Pitscottie) probably demanded close attention; so also did his lands of the earldom of March where (so Pitscottie avers) the duke manfully resisted the encroachments of the rapacious Lord Home. Finding himself thwarted by Albany (who appears to have maintained a gang of desperadoes that included some renegade Homes),[91] Lord Home concluded a bond with the Hepburns and sought the good services of 'ane new courteour start upe [upstart] callit Couchren, quho had at that tyme great preheminence . . . and credence witht the king'.[92] It was through Cochrane's machinations, so Pitscottie asserts, that a witch (with some accuracy) prophesied to the king that he would be slain by one of the nearest of his kin, whom he took to mean his brothers.[93] In England a member of the Duke of Clarence's household had lately been executed for necromancy and practising with magic

---

[86] *A.P.S.*, II. 95, c. 6.
[87] *Ibid.*, 115.
[88] *Ibid.*, 102.
[89] Mackie, *James IV*, p. 12.
[90] *R.M.S.*, II. No. 1428.
[91] *A.P.S.*, I. 128.
[92] Pitscottie, *Historie*, I. 163–5.
[93] *Ibid.*, 166–7.

arts against Edward IV's life; Clarence himself was then accused by his brother the king of 'unnatural and loathly treason', sentenced to death by an act of attainder, and drowned on 18 February 1478 either in a bath or a butt of malmsey wine.[94] Necromancy and fraternal treason were in the air; and James probably heeded the prognostication of a more professional adept of the occult sciences than a mere witch—Dr Andreas, who had appeared in the Scottish court by 1471, had acquired some repute by correctly prophesying the death of Charles the Bold.[95]

Thus in the spring of 1479 Albany was imprisoned in Edinburgh Castle. He escaped to his own castle of Dunbar, which he garrisoned and munitioned before fleeing to the French court.[96] Probably in December 1479, after Dunbar had fallen, the king's remaining brother, the Earl of Mar, 'wes takin in the nicht in his awin house, had to Cragmillar, and kepit thair at the kings commaund, and wes convict of ane conspiracie be witchecrafte aganis the king; . . . thair wes also mony and divers witches and sorceraris, alsueill men as wemen, suspect of that cryme, convict and burnit for the same at Edinburghe'.[97] A short contemporary chronicle gives a similar account: 'that yer [1479] was mony weches and warlois [warlocks] brint on Crag Gayt; and Jhone, the Erle of Mar, the king's brother, was slayne becaus thai said he favoryt the weches and warlois'.[98] The earl appears to have lost his life, either by accident or design, in a house in the Canongate, while seated in a bath after undergoing the fashionable medical treatment of bleeding: Lesley succinctly remarks that 'they cuttit ane of his vanes and causit him bleid to dead'.[99] Since a charter of July 1480 makes it clear that the earldom of Mar had been forfeited to the crown[100] some sentence must have been passed against the earl; and since there is no surviving record of proceedings against him in parliament this sentence may have been awarded in some extempore court of the royal household of the type that had done to death the sixth Earl of Douglas in 1440.

[94] E. F. Jacob, *The Fifteenth Century*, pp. 579–81.   [95] *E.R.*, VIII. lxviii, n. 2.

[96] Lesley, *History*, p. 43; *E.R.*, VIII. lxx–lxxii; Ferrerius, *Continuatio*, p. 393 v.; short contemporary chronicle appended to the B.M. Royal MSS. 17 DXX of Wyntoun, printed in Pinkerton's *History*, I. 502–4, at 503. Pitscottie's colourful account of the duke's escape from Edinburgh Castle (*Historie*, I. 185–8) may have some factual basis but is inserted out of context.

[97] Lesley, *History*, pp. 43–4. The date of Mar's arrest is given as December 1480 by Lesley but the previous year is much more likely.

[98] B.M. Royal MSS. 17 DXX in Pinkerton, *History*, I. 503.

[99] Lesley, *History*, p. 43; *Pitscottie, Historie*, I. 167–8; Ferrerius, *Continuatio*, p. 393 v.   [100] *R.M.S.*, II. No. 1446.

It was possibly news that he was about to be 'justified' by such a court that had prompted Albany to make his escape.[101] Since he was no longer in royal custody, and was unlikely to compear to defend himself, it was safe to institute a public prosecution in parliament. It was apparently in the parliament of October 1479 that the charges against Albany and his partisans were first heard. As was to be expected, none of the accused compeared. In what seems to have been a test case the king obtained a sentence of forfeiture of life, lands, possessions and goods against John Ellem of Buttirdene, captain of Dunbar, and his twenty associates.[102] By contrast the process against Albany was continued until 17 January 1480 with the consent of the three estates 'and at the gret raquest, instance and supplicacioune of thame'. A similar continuation was granted in respect of Patrick Home of Polwarth and other accomplices of Albany.[103] The parliament that was to have been held on 17 January 1480 was continued by special royal precept until 13 March, when it was held by a commission. The commissioners duly summoned Albany, Patrick Home of Polwarth, and twenty others (none of whom compeared) and then continued the processes against them until 4 May. The same procedure was successively followed by another fourteen parliamentary commissions, the last continuation being until 11 March 1482.[104] Since parliament did not meet until a week after that date [105] it would seem that these processes against Albany and his accomplices were deliberately allowed to lapse; at any rate nothing more was heard of them.

What lay behind the repeated adjournments is uncertain. It is possible that the case was kept open as a means of putting pressure upon the fugitive Albany to make a voluntary submission. On the other hand in the case of Ellem of Buttirdene and his accomplices the king had asked for the 'sensment' of parliament, which was willing to condemn those who had held Dunbar against the king. So far as Albany and the others were concerned the 'sensment' of parliament was evidently different and its 'supplicacioune' led to the first adjournment. Afraid to demand sentence, which might have been in favour of Albany, James stubbornly kept the case open for month after month, hoping perhaps for some shift in opinion against the duke. Already, it would seem, James could not count on easy compliance with his wishes and the Albany affair demonstrated the existence of a rift between king and barons.

[101] Pitscottie, *Historie,* I. 185.   [102] *A.P.S.,* II. 125-8.
[103] *Ibid.,* 128.   [104] *Ibid.,* 129-36.   [105] *Ibid.,* 136-7.

Meanwhile Albany had received a polite welcome at the French court. On 9 March 1478 the duke had obtained from the 'official' of Lothian a divorce from Catherine Sinclair, daughter of the Earl of Caithness,[106] and on 19 January 1480 he married Anne de la Tour, daughter of the Count of Auvergne and Bouillon—their son, John, would become governor of Scotland in 1515.[107] Louis XI, who may have resented the Scottish king's pretensions to act as mediator between France and Burgundy, probably took sardonic pleasure in sending the scholarly Dr Ireland on an embassy to Scotland to try to achieve a reconciliation between James and Albany. James was also to be induced 'to move weir contrar King Edward of Ingland'.[108] This French request was probably stimulated by a pact of friendship that Edward IV had concluded in August 1480 with Mary and Maximilian of Burgundy; but since Louis XI did not himself wage war against Edward, and continued to pay him the pension of 50,000 crowns promised in the treaty of Picquigny,[109] it would have been impertinent to suggest that the Scots should start a war with England had not warfare already broken out.

For the betrothal of the Scottish heir apparent to Edward's daughter Cecily in October 1474 [110] had not led to a lasting improvement in Anglo-Scottish relations. It would be wrong to give the impression tha+ there was 'haggling over the payment of the . . . dowry' :[111] up to the spring of 1479 Edward had paid (with occasional slight delay)[112] all that was due; but he was no longer eager to cultivate Scottish friendship after he had extorted the Picquigny settlement from the French.[113] In contrast, James's eagerness for friendship with England increased, as was shown in the somewhat obsequious language of his letters to 'the richt excellent, hie and michty prince, oure derrest cousing and bruthir, the King of Inglande'.[114] Under the impression that he had reached a firm settlement with England James planned to win prestige on the continent by a pilgrimage to St John's shrine at Amiens. Since he feared that a long sea passage would be detrimental to his health he obtained a safe-conduct on 15 May 1476 to pass through England with a train of up to four hundred

106 *Ibid.*, 283.   107 *Scots Peerage*, I. 153–4.
108 Lesley, *History*, p. 44.
109 E. F. Jacob, *The Fifteenth Century*, pp. 583–4; p. 480 above.
110 Pp. 478–9 above.   111 Mackie, *James IV*, p. 9.
112 See *Cal. Docs. Scot.*, IV. No. 1452, and Appendix 1, Nos. 29, 30.
113 P. 480 above.
114 *Cal. Docs. Scot.*, IV. Appendix 1. Nos. 29, 30.

attendants.[115] The application for such a safe-conduct was a hint that he expected to be invited to the English court; and there can be little doubt that James hoped also to add to his own renown by intervening personally in Franco-Burgundian disputes. For some reason the projected pilgrimage was delayed and a second English safe-conduct was issued on 17 March 1478, this time allowing James to travel with as many as a thousand attendants.[116] By this time also, James was deeply engrossed in plans to enhance Anglo-Scottish friendship by further matrimonial alliances. In the parliament of November 1475 the three estates encouraged the king to make arrangements for the marriage of his younger sister, Margaret, and offered help in defraying the expenses.[117] Her marriage was one of the matters to be dealt with by a parliamentary commission appointed in July 1476.[118] By the following year approaches had been made to Edward IV not only for a marriage between James's sister and the Duke of Clarence, but also another between the Duke of Albany (at that time uncontaminated by treason) and Edward's sister, the newly-widowed Duchess of Burgundy. Edward instructed his ambassador, Master Legh, to explain that 'aftre the old usaige of this our royalme, noon estat ne person honnorable communeth of mariage within the yere of their doole [mourning]'[119]—a point of etiquette that affected the Duchess of Burgundy, but hardly the Duke of Clarence. Despite Edward's coldness James persevered with his matrimonial schemes: in June 1478 another parliamentary commission was to discuss the marriage of his sister (who had lately left the Cistercian nunnery of Haddington to make her début at court)[120] after an embassy to be sent to England 'in all gudly haist' had reported back with 'hasti ansuere'.[121] Edward condescended to negotiate for the marriage of his brother-in-law, Anthony Woodville, Earl Rivers.[122] By 2 February 1479 the terms of a marriage contract had been worked out: Margaret was to bring to Earl Rivers a dowry of 4,000 marks (English) but this sum was to be deducted from forthcoming instalments of the dowry that Edward owed James in respect of the marriage planned between Cecily and the Scottish heir apparent.[123] On 23 January 1479 an

---

[115] *Rot. Scot.*, II. 453.
[116] *Ibid.*, 455.
[117] *A.P.S.*, II. 112, c. 5.
[118] *Ibid.*, 114.
[119] Edward IV—Master Legh, 1477 (B. M. Cotton MSS. Vespasian C. xvi. f. 121, in Pinkerton, *History*, I. 501).
[120] *T.A.*, I. cclxxxvi.
[121] *A.P.S.*, II. 119, c. 12.
[122] *Rot. Scot.*, II. 456. T. Dickson (*T.A.*, I. cclxxxvii) was misled in believing that these negotiations were authorised on 14 December 1482, the date wrongly given in *Foedera*, v. pt. iii, 126–7.
[123] *R.M.S.*, II. No. 1417.

English safe-conduct was issued so that Margaret might come to England with up to three hundred attendants for her marriage to Earl Rivers.[124] In the parliament of March 1479 the three estates granted the king a contribution of 20,000 marks (Scots) for the marriage expenses : this sum was to be raised in three equal annual instalments, beginning at midsummer 1479, the clergy and barons each paying a total of 8,000 marks and the burgesses the remaining 4,000.[125] Up to this time there was some point in the sardonic criticism of James's pro-English policy voiced by the author of *The Wallace* : 'till honour ennymis is our haile entent'.[126]

Blind Harry (or whoever wrote in his name) was soon justified in his forebodings. For although James's sister was supposed to be conducted south for her marriage by 16 May 1479 [127] she did not set out. On 22 August another safe-conduct was issued so that she might come to the English court for her marriage in November;[128] and on 23 November another safe-conduct was issued so that James might go on his deferred pilgrimage to Amiens.[129] But neither safe-conduct was to be used : it was doubtless about this time that it could no longer be hidden that Margaret was pregnant.

The father of her child (a daughter also named Margaret) was William, third Lord Crichton.[130] He appears to have sought the sanctuary of St Duthac at Tain : despite an intervening pardon for many past 'traitorous actions' he was certainly skulking there on 30 December 1483 when he was cited to answer for new treasons.[131] His affair with the Lady Margaret must have wrecked the pro-English policy that James had patiently pursued for five years just at the time when (in his eyes) it was about to be triumphantly vindicated. Edward's behaviour towards Scotland had since 1474 been correct, though not enthusiastic, and though his reaction to the news of the misconduct of Earl Rivers's betrothed may in private have been one

---

[124] *Cal. Docs. Scot.*, IV. No. 1455.   [125] *A.P.S.*, II. 122.

[126] See Matthew P. McDiarmid, 'The Date of the *Wallace*', *S.H.R.*, XXXIV. 26–31, at 30.   [127] *Cal. Docs. Scot.*, IV. No. 1455.

[128] G. Burnett and T. Dickson (*E.R.*, VIII. lxiii and *T.A.*, I. cclxxxvii) were misled in believing this safe-conduct was issued on 22 August 1482, the date under which it is wrongly recorded in *Foedera*, v. pt. iii, 123. The correct date is given in *Rot. Scot.*, II. 457.   [129] *Rot. Scot.* II. 457.

[130] Full details of the life of James's sister and her daughter are given in *T.A.*, I. Appendix 1. cclxxxvi–ccxcii. Since Crichton attended the parliament of October 1479 (*A.P.S.*, II. 124), his liaison with the Lady Margaret cannot at that time have been apparent.   [131] *A.P.S.*, II. 159.

of amusement it must in public have been that of outraged honour. He had ample occasion to make a break with James, whose desire for sincere cordiality was in Edward's view unfashionable and un-rewarding. Edward was now plotting with Louis XI against Maximilian of Burgundy, and with Maximilian against Louis,[132] who in return would send Dr Ireland to Scotland to stir up James against Edward.

Dr Ireland, who must have arrived in the spring or early summer of 1480,[133] probably found James smarting under Edward's re-criminations over the Lady Margaret. They were evidently sufficiently serious to cause Bishop Spens of Aberdeen, who had always urged peace upon the rulers of Scotland, France, England and Burgundy, to die 'of malancolie' on 15 April 1480.[134] Some fifty Scotsmen resident in England obtained letters of denization between February and September 1480 [135] to avoid the misfortune of some of their compatriots whose property was confiscated.[136] The anonymous author of a short contemporary Scottish chronicle laconically re-marks that in 1480 'raise ane gret wer betwix Ingland and Scotland; and that yer the Erle of Anguys with gret power of Scotts passyt in Ingland, and brynt Balmburgh, and lay thre nytis and thre dais in Ingland'.[137] In retaliation the Duke of Gloucester, who since 1470 had been warden of the English West March,[138] led a raid into Scotland, and at a meeting of the English council in November 1480 it was decided that Edward himself would lead an expedition against the Scots, though he was in fact to leave this business in other hands.[139]

From October 1480 to March 1481 there were intensive prepara-tions in England for the coming campaign : a fleet was assembled, Lord John Howard was appointed king's lieutenant and captain of a force of 3,000 men who were engaged to serve for sixteen weeks; the disinherited Douglas was resuscitated and given 200 marks; shortly

---

[132] E. F. Jacob, *The Fifteenth Century*, pp. 582–4.

[133] He served as one of the lords of council in civil causes for the first time on 15 July 1480 (*A.D.C.*, I. 78).

[134] Lesley, *History*, p. 44; Boece, *Vitae*, pp. 36, 37. As recently as 1477 Spens had been sent on embassy to England (*Rot. Scot.*, II. 454).

[135] *Cal. Docs. Scot.*, IV. Nos. 1462, 1465. The latter entries from the patent roll of 20 Edward IV refer to the year 4 March 1480–3 March 1481, not 1479–80. Somewhat later another score of Scots obtained letters of denization (*ibid.*, Nos. 1468, 1471, 1473).   [136] *Ibid.*, Nos. 1467, 1485.

[137] B.M. Royal MSS. 17 DXX, in Pinkerton, *History*, I. 503.

[138] *Rot. Scot.*, II. 423–4.

[139] E. F. Jacob, *The Fifteenth Century*, pp. 584–5.

afterwards the disinherited Lord Boyd received a gift of £20.[140] While these preparations were being undertaken in the winter of 1480 or the early spring of 1481 Edward issued instructions to his ambassador, Master Legh, that amounted to an ultimatum to the Scottish king : 'upon grete groundes and urgent causes', especially on account of Scottish breaches of the truce, Edward was determined 'to make ayeinst the said Scottes rigorous and cruel werre'. Master Legh (if he saw fit) was to announce that James was illegally occupying Berwick, Coldingham and Roxburgh, 'having no right nor title unto thaym'; that he had neglected to do homage; that Edward 'as soverain of Scotland' intended to see the wronged Douglas restored to his possessions; and that the Prince of Scotland (the Duke of Rothesay) was to be delivered to England by the end of May 'for th' accomplisshement of his said promised mariage'. If all four demands could not at once be met by the Scots Edward would content himself with the delivery of Berwick and the prince to avoid 'th'effusion of Christen blode'. Finally, Master Legh was to accumulate evidence to refute charges in a letter brought by Ross herald in which blame for breach of truce was laid upon the English Borderers.[141]

It was this mission of Ross herald that James had in mind in March 1482 when he gave his own retrospective version of the events that had led to war : he had sent 'his writing' (doubtless the letter to which Edward IV alluded) with a herald and pursuivant to offer redress of breaches of truce on a reciprocal basis, but the herald and pursuivant were 'lang haldin and taryit in Ingland be the revare [robber] Edward, calland him[self] King of Ingland', after which they had been dismissed without answer in word or writing, as an affront to James, whose only desire was to have peace and keep the truce.[142] Bishop Lesley adds that the Scottish envoys were deliberately detained until Edward had despatched 'ane navye of schippis' to the Forth, where they appeared off Leith, Kinghorn and Pittenweem and 'invaidit all the schippis that wes in the Firth, and tuik awaye with thame aucht [eight] greit schippis, bot wes not sufferit to land in ony parte, saffing at Blacknes, quhair they brint the toun and ane greit barge schip wes lyand besyd'.[143] Whether or not the Scottish heralds were purposely detained, Edward's instructions to Master

<hr>

[140] These entries (*Cal. Docs. Scot.*, IV. Nos. 1463, 1466), wrongly ascribed by Joseph Bain to 1479, were made during the exchequer year 30 September 1480— 29 September 1481.

[141] *Ibid.*, No. 1436 (Appendix 1, No. 28). This document has been wrongly ascribed by the editor to 1475–6.

[142] *A.P.S.*, II. 138.   [143] Lesley, *History*, p. 44.

Legh certainly show that it was not his intention that James's plea for peace should go unanswered. The absence of any reference to Edward's insulting demands in any surviving Scottish source shows either that they were never delivered, or, what is perhaps more likely, that James, who had an overweening sense of his own dignity, was so chagrined that he kept silent about them.

The English naval attack, however, made it clear that war had broken out, and induced James to summon parliament, which seems to have met since October 1479 only in the form of the parliamentary commissions that went through the rigmarole of summoning Albany. When the three estates met in April 1481 they adopted some defensive measures: the acts concerning wappinschaws were to be 'put to dew execucioune' and some attempt was made to standardise the arms used by the host—spears were to be at least five ells in length; and prototype shields in leather and wood were to be sent to each sheriffdom so that they could be copied by those armed with axes rather than with spears or bows; the host was to be called out on eight days warning, and those who assembled were warned not to despoil the countryside; it was announced that the king would repair 'his' castles of Dunbar and Lochmaben and 'stuff' them with victuals and artillery, and all lords with castles on the Borders or on the coast were enjoined to follow the king's example.[144] Special provision was made for the defence of Berwick, which was likely to be the main English objective: the three estates 'for the plesance of the kingis hienes' granted a contribution of 7,000 marks to victual the town; two-fifths would be paid by the beneficed clergy, another two-fifths by 'landit men' (except those who served in person in Berwick) and the remaining one-fifth by the burghs; it was noted that the burgh commissioners (except those of Montrose) had already committed themselves to uphold Berwick.[145] No provision had been made for prolonged warfare—Berwick was to be victualled for only forty days, and the host for only twenty, whereas Lord Howard's three thousand troops were to serve for sixteen weeks.

As it happened, the host had no sooner been assembled in the campaigning season of 1481 than it was dismissed, having accomplished nothing. For, as James angrily explained in the parliament of March 1482, he had assembled 'the hale grete powere of Scotland ... for the resistence and invasioune of oure ennemyis of Ingland' but had been shown certain papal bulls and monitions and had disbanded his troops in the belief that the English would be similarly

[144] *A.P.S.*, II. 132–3, cc. 1–6.   [145] *Ibid.*, 134.

obedient to papal demands—which they were not, but inflicted upon Scotland 'grete byrnyngis, hereschip and distructioune'.[146] A somewhat fuller picture is given by Lesley, who states that when the Scots host was about to invade England there arrived a messenger of King Edward, sent from a cardinal legate in England;[147] by apostolic authority James was ordered to cease the war on pain of interdict, so that Christian princes might prepare an army against the Turks; James thereupon disbanded his host, but Edward once more sent his fleet to the Forth, where it lay off Inchkeith, though its attacks on the coast were repulsed by local resistance; thereafter the Scottish Borderers raided the English Marches 'and tuik away mony praies of guidis, and distroyit mony townis, and led mony presonouris in Scotland, so that greit trubles and invasiones was betuix the tua realmes all that yeir'.[148]

When a well-attended parliament met in Edinburgh in March 1482 it proceeded with ordinary judicial business[149] and made some enactments dealing with ecclesiastical affairs,[150] but its preoccupation was with the war. James professed his own desire for peace and fulsomely denounced the duplicity, perjury and aggressiveness of the 'Revare Edwarde', who 'throu birnand averice and for fals reif [robbery] and conqueist . . . is aluterly set to continew in this were that he has movit and begunnyne, and be all his powere tendis and schapis to invaid and distroye and . . . to conquest this realme'. This declamation, which was not wholly unfounded, elicited from the three estates a profession of their loyal determination to resist : they would 'remane and abide at the command of his hienes with thare persouns and all thare substance of landis and gudis in the defence of his maste noble persoune, his successioune, realme, and liegis, as thai and thare forbearis has of all tymes done of before'[151]—a profession that was soon to be dramatically belied.

Meanwhile the king and the three estates made preparations for a full-scale war and showed that they had learnt some lessons from the fighting of the previous year. It was thought desirable to win early information (probably by spies) of English invasion plans. Wappinschaws were to be held every fortnight and the host was to be ready to assemble as soon as warned. The royal couriers, whose duty was to convey warning, were accused of slothfulness in the past, and a

---

[146] *Ibid.*, 138.

[147] The envoy was probably 'Gelicane, the papis messinger', to whom James paid £20 (*E.R.*, IX. 218 n.).

[148] Lesley, *History*, p. 45.

[149] *A.P.S.*, II. 137; 140, c. 14; 141.

[150] *Ibid.*, 140–1, cc. 15, 16, 17.

[151] *Ibid.*, 138–9, cc. 1 and 2.

speedier service was to be organised. Over each stretch of coastline six miles long, and the country up to one mile inland, a captain was to be appointed to lead a *levée en masse* 'for the resisting and inpugnacioune' of English attacks. If the English king sent forces headed by wardens they were to be resisted by the Scottish wardens with corresponding forces; if he led an invasion in person he was to be resisted by the Scottish king in person, at the head of 'the hale body of the realme, to leyf and dee with his hienes in his defence'.[152] At long last the necessity for large-scale payment of troops was recognised : the king offered to maintain at his own expense a garrison of five hundred in Berwick. To this the estates agreed to add a further six hundred troops stationed in Border strongholds. The Berwick garrison was to be in place on 1 June, and the Border garrisons, commanded by six captains, on 1 May. Each captain was to recruit his hundred men by his own choice and was to appoint two deputy captains. He was also to receive wages and disburse them at the daily rate of 2s. 6d. for each spearman and 2s. for each archer. It was stipulated that half of the 'wageouris' should consist of spearmen and the other half of archers.[153] Thus, apart from the Berwick garrison, for which the king paid, the three estates committed themselves to providing £67 10s. od. a day, which, over a three-month period, would come to more than £6,000. This heavy expenditure was to be apportioned 'eftir the forme of the ald use and consuetude', the clergy and barons each being responsible for two-fifths, and the burghs for the remaining one-fifth.[154] This apportionment, hardly an old one, thus suddenly acquired venerability.

Despite these intensive preparations for defence there were grounds for unease. It was decided that an embassy from the king and the three estates should be sent to Louis XI and the *parlement* of Paris to seek aid. Whatever part Louis had played in fomenting Anglo-Scottish war it was significant that James's earlier appeals for aid had 'gottin nane answer'.[155] Nor was the relationship between the king and the three estates quite so harmonious as on the surface appeared : in the parliamentary record the profession of loyalty of the three estates was immediately followed by the king's recognition of their 'grete affectioune and hertfull lufe' and his undertaking that with 'gude and trew consale of his prelatis, lordis, and wise discrete persouns', he would cause justice to be impartially administered and apply himself to 'the puttin of gude reull in all partis of his realme

[152] *Ibid.*, 139, cc. 4, 5.   [153] *Ibid.*, 139–40, cc. 7–10.
[154] *Ibid.*, 139–40, c. 7.   [155] *Ibid.*, 140, c. 13.

... to the grete disconfort and confounding of his ennemyis and of all fals tratouris and untrew hertis'.[156] The prominent place given to this undertaking, and its wording, suggest that there had been accusations that the king did not follow the counsel of 'wise discrete persouns', that justice and government in general were defective, and that there existed 'untrew hertis' who saw opportunities in the king's resulting unpopularity. Moreover it would seem that the king, perhaps by some rash words, had antagonised his uncles, the Earls of Atholl and Buchan, by raising the question of their 'takin and intrometting ... of the castel of Edinburgh' sometime during the royal minority.[157] On 18 March James seems to have tried to conciliate Atholl by granting him in flattering terms a tailzie of his earldom in favour of heirs male.[158] Four days later, however, Atholl and Buchan obtained from the king in parliament a formal exoneration for their assumption of the custody of the castle.[159] Between the king and his uncles suspicion obviously existed. Already, too, Edward was tampering with the loyalties of various Scots : on 22 June 1481 he had authorised the mayor of Carrickfergus and Patrick Haliburton (a Scots chaplain in his service) to conclude an alliance with two prominent MacDonalds—John, Lord of the Glens of Antrim, and Donald Gorm.[160] To counter this move James seems to have encouraged the ever-restive native Irish : he paid £10 'to ane Ireland man',[161] and he equipped a ship at Ayr to be sent to the Lord of the Isles (who had loyally attended the abortive assembly of the king's host in 1481)[162] for the capture of the traitorous Master Patrick Haliburton.[163] Much more serious was a commission that Edward issued on 22 August 1481 empowering the Duke of Gloucester and the disinherited Douglas to promise lands, lordships and gifts to all Scotsmen who would collaborate with the English.[164] In the parliament of March 1482 Lord Lyle was accused of treasonable correspondence with Douglas but was acquitted by an assize of sixteen barons headed by the Earls of Atholl and Morton,[165] which was doubtless a setback for the king. James was, however, able to rally some support against 'the tratour James of Douglace quhilk is now cummyng to the Bordouris' : proclamation was to be made that anyone who slew Douglas

---

[156] *Ibid.*, 139, c. 3.   [157] *Ibid.*, 138.
[158] *R.M.S.*, II. No. 1503.   [159] *A.P.S.*, II. 138.
[160] *Cal Docs. Scot.*, IV. No. 1469. George Burnett mistakenly confused the Lord of the Glens with the Lord of the Isles (*E.R.*, IX. xl).   [161] *E.R.*, IX. 219 n.
[162] Lesley, *History*, p. 45.   [163] *E.R.*, IX. 211.
[164] *Cal. Docs. Scot.*, IV. No. 1470.   [165] *A.P.S.*, II. 137–8.

or delivered him alive should be infeft heritably in lands worth a hundred marks a year and have a cash reward of a thousand marks and assurance of the king's 'lufe and tendernes'. Proportionate rewards were offered for the slaying or capture of Douglas's underlings. At the same time his accomplices, with the exception of Alexander Jardine, Master Patrick Haliburton and Sir Richard Holland (author of *The Buke of the Howlat*) were given twenty-four days' grace to obtain remission and forgiveness for past misdeeds; if they neglected this opportunity they would 'never be ressavit to favouris nor grace'. Probably lest desperation should drive criminals to consort with the enemy a general respite and remission was offered to all (particularly the Borderers) who had committed treason or trespass in the past.[166] So that the wardens might root out the 'untrew persounis' who favoured Douglas, the king revoked all exemptions from the jurisdiction of the warden courts, except in respect of persons in the town and castle of Berwick.[167]

Before long, Scottish malcontents could seek encouragement from a more illustrious patron than Douglas: at the end of April 1482 a Scottish carvel brought the Duke of Albany from France to Southampton, whence he was conducted to London to be installed in the 'Hospice de Erber' at Edward's expense.[168] Disappointed at the failure of Louis XI to secure his restoration Albany was ready to seek the good services of Edward at the price of notable treason: at Fotheringhay Castle on 10 June 1482 the duke, rather prematurely styling himself 'Alexander, King of Scotland', promised that after he had acquired his realm he would do homage to the English king, break the alliance with France, and surrender Berwick within a fortnight of his arrival in Edinburgh.[169] In an indenture of the following day Edward bound himself to aid Albany to obtain the Scottish crown and made it clear that he wanted not only Berwick but much of the Scottish Borders as well. Edward also undertook to grant his daughter Cecily in marriage to 'Alexander, King of Scotland'—if the latter 'can mak hym self clere fra all othir women . . . withyn ane yere next ensuyng'.[170] Although Albany's royal pretensions were, for the time being, to remain secret, he joined Gloucester, who on 12 January had been appointed Edward's lieutenant-general in charge of an expedition against his 'capital enemy', the Scottish king.[171]

---

[166] *Ibid.*, 139, c. 6.   [167] *Ibid.*, 140, c. 12.
[168] *Cal. Docs. Scot.*, IV. No. 1474. E. F. Jacob wrongly states that Albany had arrived in England in April 1481 (*The Fifteenth Century*, p. 585).
[169] *Cal. Docs. Scot.*, IV. No. 1475.   [170] *Ibid.*, No. 1476.
[171] *Rot. Scot.*, II. 458; *Cal. Docs. Scot.*, IV. No. 1474.

Gloucester's initial objective was Berwick. James had tried with some success to restore both the town's prosperity and its Scottish character by granting waste tenements to Scottish clerics and burgesses,[172] and after the outbreak of war he had incurred 'grete cost and expenss . . . in the fortifying, strenthing and biggin [construction] of the wallis . . . and reperacioune of the castell and stuffing thareof be artilzery'.[173] Throughout the winter of 1481–2 Berwick had been besieged by land and sea; but apart from destroying the newly-built encircling wall the besiegers had hitherto had no success.[174] It was doubtless the renewed threat to Berwick caused by the approach of Gloucester and Albany with a full-scale army that induced James to call out the Scottish host in July 1482 and to lead it in person.

The host assembled on the Burgh Muir of Edinburgh, marched to Soutra, and on the following day to the village of Lauder.[175] A number of lords now had the opportunity for which, according to Pitscottie, they had long planned : discontented with James's methods of government they had realised that 'thay could do nathing mair in this matter quhil [until] they war togither upoun the feildis in campt or battell'—it was when the magnates were gathered in arms and surrounded by their retainers that they stood least in awe of the monarch. Pitscottie even suggests that for this reason the malcontent nobles had deliberately broken the Anglo-Scottish truce so as to bring on war and cause the king to call out the host ;[176] it was certainly the Earl of Angus who had burned Bamburgh,[177] and when the magnates gathered in the kirk of Lauder and chose twenty-four of their number to concert measures against the king it was he who was 'principall of the consall'.[178] The others included the Earls of Huntly, Buchan and Lennox (*rectius* Lord Darnley) and Lords Gray and Lyle.[179] The boldness of their subsequent proceedings can be explained only on the assumption that for one reason or another James had alienated the majority of his nobles.

That the king's alleged lack of interest in military matters was involved may be discounted : his conduct of war measures was not lax; he was commended by parliament for his heavy personal expenditure in the defence of Berwick;[180] he seems to have had an

[172] *R.M.S.*, II. Nos. 1165, 1275, 1280–2, 1293; p. 298, n. 1.
[173] *A.P.S.*, II. 139, c. 7.   [174] Lesley, *History*, p. 45.
[175] Pitscottie, *Historie*, I. 172–3.   [176] *Ibid.*, 171.
[177] P. 490 above.   [178] Pitscottie, *Historie*, I. 173.
[179] These are the names given by Lesley (*History*, p. 48). Pitscottie's list seems unreliable.   [180] *A.P.S.*, II. 139, c. 7.

interest in artillery and during the current warfare spent over £200 on the purchase of iron for the fabrication of bombards and 'serpentines';[181] during the same period he showed concern for naval defence by spending over £300 on the construction of two 'roll bargis' (galleys);[182] finally the fact that James headed his army in person (which according to a recent measure he was not obliged to do, since he was not opposed by Edward in person) disposes of any suggestion of pusillanimity.

It was rather the inadequacies of James's administration that inspired disaffection: a sixteenth-century writer summed up what seems to have been the general opinion when he affirmed that he was not remarkable for his energy as a ruler.[183] In this respect some qualifications are required, for James did not altogether neglect government: the civil service was expanded, and holders of the new posts of director of chancery and receiver-general of the household augmented the civil servant element at exchequer audits, which followed their normal course even during the warfare and baronial disaffection of the summer of 1482.[184] Over government finance James seems to have kept a keen watch, and it was probably in order to prevent the growth of any vested interest in the key office of the comptroller that its holders (invariably clerics or lairds) were changed no less than twelve times between 1470 and 1488, while during most of this period the post of treasurer was held by the Abbots of Holyrood and Arbroath.[185] It is also clear that in some aspects of government, particularly in his contest with the papacy, James pursued his ends pertinaciously. He evidently had a liking for diplomacy and high politics, and, in the royal interest, notably developed the concept of treason and announced that by the common law of the realm the successors to traitors could not inherit their possessions save by royal grace.[186] In the more humdrum affairs of government that most nearly concerned his subjects he was less interested—it is perhaps significant that a note for the purchase of velvet lining for a riding gown was jotted down during parliament.[187]

Although parliament itself probably met as frequently as in previous reigns, the three estates and the king must have experienced some mutual disillusionment, largely because the problems in which they were involved were so intractable. In stubbornly ignoring

---

[181] T.A., I. ccci.
[183] Ferrerius, Continuatio, p. 391.
[185] H.B.C., pp. 181, 183–4.
[187] T.A., I. 24.

[182] E.R., IX. 218 n.
[184] E.R., IX. 163–209.
[186] R.M.S., II. No. 1203.

remonstrations on the subject of remissions [188] the king forfeited the goodwill of his subjects. The sale of remissions was not new, but it was unpopular. In *The Harp* [189] one anonymous poet obviously had James II or James III in mind when he declared :

> Bot of a [one] thing all gude men mervalis mair:
> Quhen grete counsale, with thine awn consent,
> Has ordanit strate justice na man to spair,
> Within schort tym thou changis thine entent,
> Sendand a contrair lettir incontinent,
> Chargeand that of that mater mair be nocht;
> Than al the warld murmuris that thou are bocht.

In *The Thre Prestis of Peblis* another anonymous poet satirised James's pliant and mercenary attitude towards justice,[190] and not without cause : between August 1473 and December 1474 the king drew almost £550 as the price of remissions and compositions granted to over sixty persons in respect of offences ranging from the receiving of outlaws to murder.[191] It was typical of the complexity of James's character, and of the consequent complexity of the reign, that the maladministration of justice sprang not only from greed but from clemency.[192] More serious in the immediate context of 1482 was the debasement of the coinage by the issue of the 'black money',[193] a copper coinage, so declared Bishop Lesley, 'unmeit to have course or passage in ony realme, quhairwith the pepill grudgeit, and sua wes the caus of greyt darthe and hunger throuchout all the cuntrey'.[194] It was not debasement that caused a shortage of food but rather 'gret distructioun throw the weris . . . of corne and catell',[195] coupled with an English naval blockade which stopped trade ; hence an act of the parliament of March 1482 to attract foreign merchants 'and specially to gar [cause] vittalis be brocht in, sen [since] thar is now skantnes therof'.[196] The issue of a debased coinage was itself an inflationary measure ; it coincided with a time of scarcity when prices would naturally be high ; the combined effect was doubtless a sudden and extraordinary rise in the price of necessities. Thus a contemporary chronicler narrates that in 1482 'thar was ane gret hungyr and deid in Scotland, for the boll of meill was for four punds ; for thar was

[188] Pp. 430-1 above.   [189] *Chron. Pluscarden*, i. 392-400.
[190] *The Thre Prestis of Peblis* (S.T.S.), pp. 31-8.
[191] *T.A.*, i. 2-12.   [192] See Boece, *Vitae*, pp. 52-3.
[193] Pp. 436-7 above.   [194] Lesley, *History*, p. 48.
[195] B.M. Royal MSS. 17 DXX in Pinkerton, *History*, i. 503.
[196] *A.P.S.*, ii. 141, c. 18.

blak cunye in the realm, strikkin and ordinyt be King James the
thred, half-pennys, and three-penny pennys, innumerabill, of coppir
. . . and mony pur folk deit of hungar'.[197] It was not only the poor
who were affected : the Franciscan friars of Dundee had to pawn
their books and ecclesiastical furnishings 'to sustain a miserable
life' ;[198] one laird on 10 May 1482 entered into manrent with the
Earl of Morton for money in his necessity.[199] According to the Pluscarden chronicler reformation of the coinage was one of the marks
of a good ruler ;[200] deformation of the coinage was doubtless the mark
of a bad one ; and by the summer of 1482 the resulting exasperation
with James must have been wholesale and led to popular condemnation of all aspects of his government. There can be no doubt that it
was James III to whom the poet Robert Henryson alluded in his
fable of *The Lion and the Mouse* as a king who

> . . . takis no laubour
> To rewll nor steir the land nor justice keip,
> Bot lyis still in lustis, slewth and sleip.[201]

In the same poem the reason why the hunters (the nobility) snare the
lion (James) is conveyed in the lines

> The lyone yeid to hunt
> For he had nocht, bot levit on his pray,
> And slew baith tame and wyld as he wes wunt,
> And in the cuntre maid a grit dirray.[202]

A comparison of these two passages shows their incongruity : in the
first the king is represented as slothful, in the second as energetically
preying upon his tame (Lowland) and wild (Highland) subjects ;[203]
yet it is true that James could display energy as well as indolence and
that some of the nobility had suffered at the hands of a government
that in certain respects, particularly in transactions relating to land,
was active enough. A sixteenth-century manuscript [204] relates the
story that James with his own hands tore up the Earl of Morton's
charter and was forced by the nobles to sew it up again. Although

---

[197] B.M. Royal MSS. 17 DXX in Pinkerton, *History*, I. 503.
[198] W. Moir Bryce, *The Scottish Grey Friars*, II. 129–33.
[199] *Morton Registrum*, II. No. 236.   [200] *Chron. Pluscarden*, II. 65.
[201] MacQueen, *Robert Henryson*, pp. 152–3, 170.   [202] *Ibid.*, 171–2.
[203] This was a neat allusion to such events as the forfeiture of the Boyds and
the king's acquisition of the earldom of Ross.
[204] Printed in Pinkerton, *History*, II. 501.

this tale is apocryphal it at least symbolises the fear and resentment aroused by the king's tendency to regard the title to land not as indefeasible but subject to constant review and confirmation. There was probably also resentment that advancement to lands and offices, both lay and ecclesiastical, was no longer the natural perquisite of the nobility but had to be earned by drudgery in administration (as in the case of the Earl of Argyll and Lord Avondale) whereas it was forthcoming for others whose origins and talents seemed alike obscure.

These were the men whom Pitscottie styled the king's 'secreit servandis or cubecularis',[205] whom Lesley thought were the 'unworthye vyle persouns' who were the king's 'counsallouris',[206] and whom modern historians have pejoratively designated as 'favourites'.[207] A short contemporary chronicle, with more reticence, described them as members of the king's household;[208] James himself usually called them his 'familiars'. Up to the summer of 1482 this term was applied in official records to over twenty persons, of whom most, including William Roger, were styled familiar esquires,[209] some, including James Hommyl, as familiar servants,[210] and some as familiar clerks,[211] while the group included a number of physicians and apothecaries[212] whom the hypochondriac king retained, besides Thomas Cochrane and Thomas Preston (not styled familiars in the few references made to them in extant records).[213] It has been remarked that 'the names of Cochrane, Leonard, Torphichen, and Roger, . . . conspicuous in the pages of the late sixteenth-century historians, do not appear at all in the lists of witnesses in the Register of the Great Seal; nor do they figure in the sederunts of the Lords of Council'.[214] Certainly none of the familiars, with the exception of John Ross of Montgrenan, prominent as a lord of council in civil

---

[205] Pitscottie, *Historie*, I. 176.   [206] Lesley, *History*, pp. 48–9.
[207] Mackie, *James IV*, p. 19.
[208] B.M. Royal MSS. 17 DXX in Pinkerton, *History*, I. 503.
[209] *R.M.S.*, II. No. 1418. See also Nos. 1116, 1119, 1141, 1454, 1475; *E.R.*, IX. 494 n.
[210] *E.R.*, IX. 93–4. See also *R.M.S.*, II. Nos. 1150, 1285, 1341.
[211] *R.M.S.*, II. Nos. 1280, 1357, 1468.
[212] Dr Andrews (*T.A.*, I. 69); Master Conrad (*R.M.S.*, II. No. 1343); Master Thomas Smith (*ibid.*, No. 1357).
[213] R. L. Mackie (*James IV*, p. 15), wrongly follows some narrative sources which give Cochrane's first name as Robert. Lesley (*History*, p. 48) names him Thomas, and there can be no doubt that the Thomas Cochrane alluded to in proceedings before the lords of council (*A.D.C.*, I. 49, 82), was the Cochrane who became notorious. For Preston see *E.R.*, IX. 218.
[214] Mackie, *James IV*, p. 16.

causes [215] and Sir John Colquhoun of Luss, familiar chamberlain of the household, who was killed at the siege of Dunbar in 1479, held any position in government. Torphichen (a fencing-master) and Leonard (a shoemaker) are not even mentioned in any extant record, though it should be borne in mind that the records of the household, as distinct from 'state' records, are no longer extant, and that for James's reign the accounts of the treasurer, full of intimate detail, survive for only 1473–4. Most of the familiars probably had official duties in the royal household, and these are occasionally mentioned : one familiar esquire was a member of the royal guard,[216] William Roger was probably clerk of the spices,[217] and one familiar clerk nicknamed 'Stobo' (perhaps the author of *The Thre Prestis of Peblis*)[218] was a scribe employed in writing letters to the pope and foreign potentates.[219]

The favour in which the king held his familiars was displayed in the grants he bestowed upon them, sometimes to the detriment of the nobility. It was out of reverence for the king (which may mean under royal pressure) that Lord Hamilton granted lands in Lanarkshire to his kinsman, David Hamilton, a familiar esquire.[220] By 1473 another familiar esquire, David Crichton, had supplanted the Earl of Argyll in the custody of Edinburgh Castle, worth two hundred marks a year ;[221] he soon obtained lands resigned by the Earl of Angus, by Robert Lauder of the Bass, and by Sir John Colquhoun of Luss,[222] and had his lands erected as a free barony.[223] In 1473 a quarter of the earldom of Lennox was bestowed in heritage upon another familiar esquire, John Haldane of Rusky, 'as first and principal of the same'.[224] Although this grant reserved the liferent of the whole earldom, which had been conferred in 1471 upon Chancellor Avondale,[225] the latter can hardly have relished Haldane's advancement. Still less can it have pleased Lord Darnley, who was officially recognised as Earl of Lennox in 1473 only to have his title revoked in 1476.[226] James Hommyl, the king's tailor, described more flatteringly as 'familiar servitur and werkman for oure persoun', received miscellaneous small grants from 1473 onwards, and by letters under the privy seal

[215] E.g. *A.D.C.*, I. 19, 29, 79.   [216] *R.M.S.*, II. No. 1283.
[217] *E.R.*, VIII. 190.
[218] This is plausibly argued by T. D. Robb in the S.T.S. edition of the poem, pp. xiv–xix.
[219] *R.M.S.*, II. No. 1341.   [220] *Ibid.*, No. 1284.
[221] *E.R.*, VIII. 190, 253.   [222] *R.M.S.*, II. Nos. 1202, 1213, 1299.
[223] *Ibid.*, No. 1356.   [224] *Ibid.*, No. 1116.
[225] *Ibid.*, No. 1018.   [226] *H.B.C.*, p. 480.

was awarded in 1478 a yearly pension of £20 for life.[227] William Roger, a talented musician whose pupils were held in esteem long after his own death,[228] had accompanied an English embassy to Scotland and then entered James's service as a familiar esquire, being rewarded with no less a grant than the barony of Traquair. Aristocratic resentment probably caused this grant to be revoked in 1476, after which Traquair was bestowed in more conventional fashion upon the king's uncle, the Earl of Buchan.[229]

It was Thomas Cochrane, however, whose advancement seems to have been most bitterly resented. Originally an apprentice to a mason, he 'become verie ingeneous into that craft, and bigit [built] money stain house'.[230] Thanks to his skill he was appointed the king's master mason, and in this capacity was probably the architect of the great hall of Stirling Castle. In 1480 he was granted a total of £60 due to the king as a result of litigation before the lords of council, and he was the tenant of lands in Cousland probably conferred by the king and worth £20 a year.[231] Much more striking is the fact that Lesley and Pitscottie state that Cochrane was made Earl of Mar after the death of the king's brother—an event for which Pitscottie held Cochrane responsible.[232] It at least seems that 'the revenues of the earldom were out of the crown's hands during the period when Cochrane is said to have been earl'.[233] If Cochrane was indeed made Earl of Mar, or given its revenues, or even a post of responsibility in administering the earldom, such a step was injudicious in the extreme. For while the talents of James's familiars would be mostly recognised as respectable by modern standards they were not the sort that by fifteenth-century standards were expected to be notably rewarded.

Apart from the disturbance to aristocratic vested interests implied in the advancement of some of James's familiars, a constitutional issue was involved : it was believed, and possibly correctly, that the king's policies and behaviour were influenced by the secret whisperings of his low-born familiars; following counsel that was 'young', not 'wise',[234] he 'keipit him self quietlie, leveing voluptuouslie, and had lychtlyit [scorned] his awin nobill quene, and intertanit ane howir [whore] callit the Daesie, in her place; and . . . causit slay

[227] *E.R.*, ix. xlv, 93–4.
[228] Ferrerius, *Continuatio*, p. 395.
[229] *R.M.S.*, ii. No. 1418.
[230] Pitscottie, *Historie*, i. 176.
[231] *A.D.C.*, i. 49, 82.
[232] Lesley, *History*, p. 48; Pitscottie, *Historie*, i. 166–8.
[233] *E.R.*, ix. xliii–xliv.
[234] See *The Thre Prestis of Peblis* (S.T.S.), pp. 31, 38.

his awin brodir, the Erle of Mar, and banisd his uther brodir the Duik of Albany',[235] Moreover direct responsibility for the latest disastrous debasement of the coinage was attributed to Cochrane.[236] According to Pitscottie the latter 'grew sa familiear witht . . . the kingis grace that . . . all men that wald have had thair bussienes drest [expedited] . . . come to Couchrin, and maid him forspeiker for them and gaif him large money'.[237] To the anonymous eighteenth-century author of *The Life of Sir Robert* [sic] *Cochran, Prime Minister to King James III of Scotland*,[238] such a situation was natural enough, and the purpose of his fanciful treatise was to satirise Sir Robert Walpole. But to the fifteenth-century Scottish nobility, the situation was novel and unnatural : the court had become the place in which policy was formulated, parliament and council merely the places in which it was publicised; the great lords and officers of state, the king's official councillors, were no longer his real counsellors but had become mere administrators, relegated to such tedious tasks as assessing royal lands, auditing accounts, hearing literally hundreds of cases as auditors of causes and complaints or as lords of council,[239] while the king 'wrocht mair the consaell of his housald, at war bot sympill, na he did of thame that war lordds'.[240] The new breed of courtier had displaced the feudal baron and, thanks to the personal interests of James III, good birth was not by itself a qualification for a place as courtier : 'be this way the kingis grace tint [lost] money of the harttis of the

---

[235] Lesley, *History*, p. 48. The Daesie, together with Lesley's later reference to James as 'taking his plesour of wemen' (*ibid.*, p. 55), would seem to dispose of a recently expressed view (A. J. Stewart, *Falcon: The Autobiography of His Grace James the 4 King of Scots*, pp. 19–20), that the attachment between James and his familiars was homosexual and that this explains what took place at Lauder. There are several allusions to James's lust : in Robert Henryson's fable of *The Lion and the Mouse* it is linked with the vice of sloth (p. 500 above); according to Boece (*Vitae*, p. 51), Bishop Elphinstone urged the king to eschew lust and content himself with Queen Margaret, 'the chastest of women', as 'the consort of a genial couch'; Buchanan, whose veracity may be questioned, relates that James seduced the wife of Lord Crichton and that it was as an act of revenge that Crichton seduced the king's sister. (See P. F. Tytler, *History*, 1. pt. ii, Notes and Illustrations, pp. 388–9). In *The Thre Prestis of Peblis* (S.T.S., pp. 39–44), an apocryphal tale of the attempted seduction of a burgess's daughter seems to allude to the amours of James III.

[236] Lesley, *History*, p. 48; Pitscottie, *Historie*, 1. 169.

[237] Pitscottie, *Historie*, 1. 168–9; Ferrerius, *Continuatio*, p. 395; Lesley, *History*, p. 48.

[238] Published (2nd edn.) in London in 1734.

[239] The sederunts of the lords of council in civil causes (*A.D.C.*, 1. 3–79), disprove the view that the nobles were not pulling their weight in the administration of justice.

[240] B.M. Royal MSS. 17 DXX in Pinkerton, *History*, 1. 504.

lordis . . . and allso of thair souns and brether that faine wald have
servit the kingis grace bot thai could gett na place for this Couchrin
and his companie'.[241] Thus in the kirk of Lauder an attack upon the
courtiers was planned.

According to a seventeenth-century source some difficulty arose
as to who was to initiate the attack : the mice would fain hang a bell
around the cat that preyed upon them, but which mouse was to bell
the cat? The Earl of Angus, who may not have forgiven the king's
attack upon the Boyd kinsfolk of his wife,[242] is traditionally believed
to have volunteered and thereby became known as Archibald Bell-
the-Cat.[243] Pitscottie gives a colourful account of what followed :
Cochrane, whose accoutrements and campaigning outfit were
ostentatiously impressive, was arrested by Angus and Sir Robert
Douglas, laird of Lochleven ; it may well be believed that the former
snatched the gold chain from the doomed courtier's neck while the
latter grasped the ornate hunting horn that he carried;[244] certainly
one of the baronial underlings took the opportunity at Lauder to
purloin £146 from one of the Edinburgh custumars.[245] The lynching party probably extemporised a court of some sort : Cochrane and
Thomas Preston were afterwards deemed to have been sentenced to
forfeiture.[246] They, William Roger, and other courtiers, were hanged
from Lauder brig and 'the blak silver' (the coinage attributed to
Cochrane) was 'cryit downe' or devalued. Not all of the courtiers
perished, for the lords 'slew ane part of the king's housald, and other
part thai banysyt'. Among the latter were James Hommyl the tailor,
and John Ramsay, a young courtier of good birth who was spared
at the 'ernist supplicatione' of the king. James himself was taken
back to Edinburgh and on 22 July 1482 was warded in the castle in
the keeping of his uncle of Atholl.[247]

Had the ringleaders of the Lauder conspiracy marched forward
to relieve Berwick their conduct would have been less questionable
and their capacity for leadership more obvious. Instead they allowed
the host to disband and left the country without government and

---

[241] Pitscottie, *Historie*, I. 170.   [242] Pp. 418–9 above.

[243] See Mackie, *James IV*, p. 19.   [244] Pitscottie, *Historie*, I. 175.

[245] *E.R.*, IX. 219 n.

[246] *A.D.C.*, I. 82; *R.M.S.*, II. No. 1533. Lesley (*History*, p. 49), states that the
victims were 'convict'.

[247] Pitscottie, *Historie*, I. 175–6; B.M. Royal MSS. 17 DXX in Pinkerton,
History, I. 503; Ferrerius, *Continuatio*, pp. 394v–395v. Lesley (*History*, p. 49)
wrongly states that Hommyl was hanged.

without defence. The opportunity was immediately seized by the Dukes of Gloucester and Albany: leaving the siege of Berwick they marched unopposed upon Edinburgh and encamped outside the town at the beginning of August. It was fortunate for the townsfolk that the mission of the English army was political rather than military: Albany was well placed to turn recent events to his own advantage and to emerge as Alexander IV, vassal of the Yorkists; hence Gloucester's aim was not to defeat the Scots (they had already defeated themselves) but to exact the political rewards of victory. This meant that there had to be negotiations with the Scottish leaders —whoever they were. On 2 August they appeared, not in the form of Bell-the-Cat and his henchmen but in that of Archbishop Scheves, James Livingston, Bishop of Dunkeld, the Earl of Argyll and Chancellor Avondale,[248] who crawled bravely from the wreck of government as a group of moderate royalists. They were hardly the audience to whom Albany had hoped to propound his royal pretensions; nor, without the participation of James III (which could have been obtained only by a siege of the castle) were they capable of ceding the territories that Edward coveted. Thus Albany seems to have decided to conceal the full scope of his schemes in the hope that he could construct a government that would countenance them: like Henry Bolingbroke in 1399 and Edward of York in 1471 he had ostensibly come back merely to secure his own inheritance.

This was something which Scheves and his party were hardly in a position to withhold, particularly since there was obviously widespread sympathy for the dispossessed duke, and the process of forfeiture against him had not culminated in a sentence. Thus on 2 August 1482 the archbishop and his three colleagues sealed an obligation in which they undertook to obtain remission and restoration for Albany and his adherents if the duke would observe his allegiance to James III.[249] This last provision demonstrated the political acumen of Scheves and his party: if it were broken they were no longer committed to supporting the duke; nor could Albany refuse to accept this condition without immediately publicising his own designs upon the throne, for which the time was not yet ripe. Gloucester, the watchdog over Yorkist interests, understood Albany's dilemma and contented himself with a written assurance that despite any agreements the latter had made, or might make, with Scottish lords, he would remain true to the treaty of Fotheringhay[250]—a stipulation that explains,

---

[248] Lesley, *History*, p. 49; *Cal. Docs. Scot.*, IV. No. 1479.
[249] *Cal. Docs. Scot.*, IV. No. 1479.   [250] Mackie, *James IV*, p. 22.

though hardly excuses, Albany's subsequent conduct. In another respect Gloucester showed commendable moderation : instead of sacking and burning Edinburgh he accepted 'only such presentes as the merchantis gentelly offered him and his capitaynes' ;[251] and on 4 August he obtained from Provost Walter Bertram and 'the hale fallowschip of merchandis, burgesses and communite' a bond that committed them to refund the advance instalments of Cecily's dowry if Edward signified his intention to break off the match between his daughter and the Duke of Rothesay.[252] On 27 October Edward duly intimated through Garter king-of-arms that this was his intention.[253]

A truce might have been expected to follow these arrangements, but it suited Albany that the English should continue their efforts to capture Berwick rather than that he should immediately blight his prospects by incurring the odium of yielding the town. Thus Gloucester marched back to resume the siege of Berwick while Albany went through the farcical motion of leading a force as far as the Lammermuirs, supposedly to raise the siege. The defenders of Berwick, who had acquitted themselves well against the English, saw that they had been either betrayed or deserted : the town (though not the castle) seems already to have been lost by 24 August 1482 when they capitulated and 'partit thairfra with bagg and baggages'.[254] By November Edward was making arrangements to provision the town and castle, and in February 1483 he graciously confirmed the charters of the burgesses.[255]

Meanwhile, shortly after his assumption of government, Albany had gone with the archbishop, Chancellor Avondale and the Earl of Argyll, to hold consultation at Stirling with Queen Margaret and the nine-year-old Duke of Rothesay. Probably the suggestion was made that the Queen should use her good offices to induce James III to abdicate in favour of the heir apparent, and that Albany be recognised as governor. The queen's advice was that James must first be set at liberty. It can hardly have been on account of Albany's implementation of this proposal (as Lesley suggests) that Scheves, Argyll and Avondale 'throw gret feir fled into thair awin cuntreyis'.[256] What is more likely is that the duke had disclosed his own hopes of attaining the crown and that this had lost him the support of the influential trio. Thus Albany had to seek other allies.

[251] *Ibid.*, p. 21.   [252] *Cal. Docs. Scot.*, IV. No. 1480.
[253] *Ibid.*, Nos. 1481, 1482, 1483, 1484.
[254] Lesley, *History*, pp. 49–50; *E.R.*, IX. xlii and n. 1.
[255] *Rot. Scot.*, II. 458–60.   [256] Lesley, *History*, p. 50.

Their identity is revealed in the witness list of a charter dated at Edinburgh on 25 August 1482.[257] Avondale had been replaced as chancellor by John Laing, Bishop of Glasgow. Other witnesses, including James Livingston, Bishop of Dunkeld, were probably associated with the new administration less by inclination than by a desire to preserve government. Three witnesses, however—the Earls of Atholl and Buchan and their brother, Andrew Stewart, Bishop elect of Moray (now keeper of the privy seal), formed a special group : they were the king's uncles and one of them, Atholl, had custody of Edinburgh Castle and the imprisoned king. The price of their support for Albany was that Andrew Stewart should be made Archbishop of St Andrews. Probably the king was induced to write to persuade the loyal Scheves to go through the motions of appointing procurators to resign the archbishopric.[258] By 8 November the Edinburgh burgesses had also been induced to pledge their already strained credit to furnish 6,000 gold ducats to finance the promotion of Andrew Stewart at the *curia*, receiving in return a promise of repayment from him, his brothers, and three of their associates.[259] Meanwhile the king was to be released, which meant that he was to be delivered to Albany. This, however, could not be arranged without stratagem since Atholl was under some commitment to the ringleaders of the Lauder conspiracy : although he was a witness to the charter issued by the new administration on 25 August, and to its next recorded charter on 10 October,[260] his honour had to be saved in the interim by a 'siege' of the castle that lasted until Michaelmas (29 September)[261] when, so affirms the credulous Bishop Lesley, its defenders capitulated 'for want of victuallis'.[262]

James, well aware of the part he was expected to play, accompanied his brother in a triumphal procession from the castle to the abbey of Holyrood,[263] 'quhair they remainit ane quhyle in great mirienes'. To publicise Albany's faithful service to the king who had once injured him, two charters were issued on 16 November granting

[257] *R.M.S.*, ii. No. 1517.

[258] P. 513 below; Lesley, *History*, p. 50; Ferrerius, *Continuatio*, p. 396v. J. Herkless and R. K. Hannay (*Archbishops of St Andrews*, i. 109), criticise Scheves for failing to behave like a second Anselm or Becket; they seem unaware that times had changed and that the issues were different.

[259] *Edinburgh City Charters*, No. liii.

[260] *R.M.S.*, ii. Nos. 1517, 1518.

[261] B.M. Royal MSS. 17 DXX, in Pinkerton, *History*, i. 504.

[262] Lesley, *History*, p. 50; Ferrerius, *Continuatio*, p. 396v.

[263] Pitscottie, whose account of this period is hopelessly confused, is probably correct in this detail (*Historie*, i. 182).

to the magistrates of Edinburgh the office of sheriffship within the burgh and strengthening the burgh's control over the vassal town of Leith;[264] these favours were rewards for the support the burgesses had given to the king's 'dearest brother', even exposing their lives to danger, in besieging Edinburgh Castle and restoring James to complete liberty. For the same reason (and to compensate for the losses he had incurred on the king's behalf) Walter Bertram was granted an annual pension of £40 payable during the lifetime of himself and his wife.[265] Albany's exercise in propaganda was not in vain : the heroism of the Edinburgh burgesses was commemorated by Robert Henryson in the fable of *The Lion and the Mouse*; the mice who free the lion (James) trapped by the hunters (the nobility) are the Edinburgh burgesses, and the leading mouse is doubtless Bertram.[266]

Albany's own heroic services had been recognised in a 'great council' in which he was granted the earldom of Mar and the Garioch and was styled in a manner that indicated not only his restoration to all his former lands and offices but his assumption of the post of king's lieutenant-general.[267] To consolidate his position the duke summoned a parliament to meet at Edinburgh. When it assembled on 2 December 1482 Scheves, Argyll and Avondale were notable absentees. It is also striking that in contrast to the previous parliament of March 1482 there was a complete absence of lairds. That these were reckoned to be supporters of the king may be deduced from the announcement continuing parliament to 1 March 1483 but excusing from attendance all persons with an income of less than £100.[268] In other respects, however, the composition of the parliament of December 1482 was perfectly normal, and the attendance much the same as in the parliament that James had held in April 1478.[269] The crucial question that was to be decided by parliament was whether Albany should be recognised as lieutenant-general. The method devised to achieve this goal proceeded from a review of the existing war with England. It was ordained that 'pece be takin with Ingland gif it can be had with honour' : a herald was to be sent to announce the willingness of the Scots to renew the truce

[264] *Edinburgh City Charters*, Nos, liv, lv; p. 452 above.

[265] *E.R.*, ix. 219–20; *R.M.S.*, ii. No. 1829.

[266] Equating the mouse with 'the ordinary people of Scotland', John Mac-Queen (*Robert Henryson*, pp. 170–3), does not detect the more precise allegory.

[267] *R.M.S.*, ii. No. 1541. Although the charter is inserted in a position that would indicate a date between 18 and 20 January 1483 the editor rightly states in a footnote that it was probably issued between 29 September and 10 October 1482 (as the witness list suggests).

[268] *A.P.S.*, ii. 145.

[269] Compare *ibid.*, 115, 136–7, 142.

and (all too optimistically) the marriage contract between Rothesay and Cecily. If, however, the English were determined to wage war, James professed his readiness to 'defend his realme in honour and freedom'. Next it was announced that 'it accordis nocht to the honoure of his hienes [James] to put his nobile persone daily to dangere'; he should therefore 'speke to his bruther, the Duke of Albany, to tak apone him to be lieutenent generale of the realme . . . and to avise how he sal be supportit to bere the grete charge and costis of the saide office etc.' A further act ordained that the warden courts should be held frequently to punish 'baith tratouris and theyfis', and since Albany was warden of the East and West Marches this measure would have given him the power to suppress whomsoever he deemed to be traitors.[270]

Despite his apparent victory Albany could make no headway in the cross currents of Scottish politics. Those who attended parliament were not all supporters of the duke rather than of the king : the more worldly-wise were aware that James was not a free agent and they had come to fish in troubled waters; the less worldly-wise, deluded by Albany's own propaganda, believed that James was really free, and expected to see him wielding his former authority. Thus Albany had to take his place in parliament as merely foremost of the barons,[271] while, it may be supposed, James sat in state, and, to at least a limited extent, had the chance to influence the proceedings and revive old loyalties. In July exasperation with the king and his familiars was wholesale, but it must have varied greatly in intensity; it is unlikely that every magnate approved of the exploits of Bell-the-Cat; and some may have been shocked into a new loyalty towards James as recollection of his former conduct was replaced by sympathy for his humiliation, and as the months of famine were replaced by better times; for after the king's release 'the victall grew better chaip, for the boll that was for four pounds was than for xxii s. of quhyt silver'.[272] It was a sign of the reviving of James's authority that no outright appointment of Albany as lieutenant-general was made in parliament but that the three estates assumed that it was the king who had to make the appointment. Whether or not the king did, Albany's power was already waning. He appeared for the last time as witness to a royal charter on 25 December;[273] it was Bishop Livingston of Dunkeld, a former associate of Scheves, Argyll and Avondale,

[270] *Ibid.*, pp. 143–4, cc. 1–2, 4.   [271] *Ibid.*, 142.
[272] B.M. Royal MSS. 17 DXX, in Pinkerton, *History*, I. 504.
[273] *R.M.S.*, II. No. 1533.

who became chancellor when Bishop Laing of Glasgow died on 11 January 1483;[274] on the following day Albany issued letters from Dunbar empowering the Earl of Angus, Lord Gray, and Sir James Liddell of Halkerston to go on a mission to Edward IV.[275]

Liddell had already been employed by Albany on a similar mission in the autumn of 1482,[276] but the association of Angus and Gray with the duke was new and must have been formed after the December parliament which Angus attended.[277] Until then, he had been sulking in Tantallon,[278] a residence calculated to inspire any owner with delusions of unique grandeur. In August, when news of Lauder was fresh, when Gloucester's army was at the gates of Edinburgh, and when James was a prisoner, an alliance between Albany and Bell-the-Cat might have been overpowering, and such an alliance must have seemed almost inevitable. But it is clear that the conspiracies of Albany and Bell-the-Cat had been entirely distinct and in no way co-ordinated. Apart from any feeling that Albany had stolen his thunder, Angus must have suspected that the duke had promised Edward to restore the disinherited Douglas. The latter too was a natural ally of Albany, but his restoration would mean not only that Angus would lose the headship of the Douglas 'name' to the senior branch, but would lose the lordship of Douglasdale granted to his father by James II.[279] Thus Albany had either to choose between Angus and Douglas or arrange a settlement between them. This was the belated object of the mission to the English court. On 11 February 1483 Angus, Gray and Liddell signed and sealed a treaty at Westminster with the Earl of Northumberland and other English commissioners. The terms resembled those formerly agreed upon at Fotheringhay and, in addition, bound Albany to assist the restoration of Douglas in accordance with a convention arranged between the latter and Angus; in return Edward would help Albany to acquire the Scottish crown by conquest. On the following day arrangements were made to send Douglas to Scotland.[280]

It was too late. James III's restoration to power may be traced by the appearance as witnesses to his charters of Scheves in January, Argyll in February, and Avondale in March,[281] and the corresponding

---

[274] *H.B.C.*, p. 175.
[275] *Cal. Docs. Scot.*, IV. No. 1486.
[276] *Ibid.*, No. 1478.
[277] *A.P.S.*, II. 142.
[278] In contrast to Buchan and Atholl he witnessed no royal charters in this period. On 28 September he was in Tantallon (*R.M.S.*, II. No. 1619).
[279] See *ibid.*, No. 774.
[280] *Cal. Docs. Scot.*, IV. Nos. 1489, 1490; *Rot. Scot.*, II. 458.
[281] *R.M.S.*, II. Nos. 1544, 1555, 1563.

disappearance of the king's three uncles. Only one of these, Buchan, dared to join Albany in Dunbar, and a charter issued there by the duke on 21 February [282] suggests that his following had dwindled to a handful of desperate men, including Lord Crichton and James, 'Lord' Boyd, son of the first marriage of the king's sister with the forfeited Earl of Arran, nephew of Angus's wife, Elizabeth Boyd, and grandson and heir of Robert, Lord Boyd, who seems to have died shortly before.[283] By this time also, those who were beneficiaries under charters issued by Angus and his predecessors were obtaining royal confirmations,[284] which suggests that the earl's intrigues in England had become known and were expected to lead to his forfeiture.

The parliament of December 1482 had been continued until 1 March 1483 and duly assembled on that date, when Scheves, Argyll and Avondale were appointed to the committee of the articles. Since James was not yet ready to crush Albany there were successive continuations until 27 June.[285] In the meantime the duke was forced to accept the humiliating terms of an indenture drawn up at Edinburgh on 16 March 1483 and signed and sealed by him at Dunbar three days later.[286] Albany was 'nocht in tyme tocum' to 'use . . . the office of lieutenend generale . . . bot discharge hyme therof now incontinent'. He was to produce to parliament a letter under his seal refuting 'a sclandir and murmur rising in the cuntre' that he had been poisoned while at court.[287] He was to swear never in future to make treasonable leagues with the English king, renounce those that he had already made, deliver letters to this effect that could be displayed to Edward, and use his influence to obtain peace and the marriage alliance. The duke was also to deliver to James letters of manrent promising lifelong loyalty, renounce all bonds that he had made in Scotland, especially those binding him to the king's three uncles, the Earl of Angus, Lords Crichton and Gray, Sir John Douglas (Master of Morton), Alexander Home (nephew of Lord Home), and James Liddell of Halkerston, discharge all of them from their undertakings to Edward, and 'nocht hauld thame in daily houshauld in tyme tocum'. None of these persons, nor the duke himself, was to approach within six miles of the king without special leave. In addition some of Albany's supporters were to be further humiliated : the Master of Morton was to surrender the sheriffship of Edinburgh ; Angus was to surrender his offices as justiciar south of Forth, as steward of Kirk-

[282] *Ibid.*, No. 1573.

[283] *Scots Peerage*, v. 145.

[284] *R.M.S.*, II. Nos. 1550, 1560.

[285] *A.P.S.*, II. 145.

[286] Text in *A.P.S.*, XII. 31–3.

[287] See Lesley, *History*, pp. 50–1.

cudbright, and as sheriff of Lanark, as well as his custody of Threave
Castle and a lucrative wardship; Buchan was to surrender the cham-
berlainship (now given to the Earl of Crawford),[288] the wardenship of
the Middle March and the custody of Newark Castle; together with
Crichton and Liddell, he was also to 'devoid the realme of Scotland
and the realme of Ingland' for three years. His brother, Andrew
Stewart, Bishop elect of Moray, saw the waning of his hopes of sup-
planting Scheves in the archbishopric by means of 'the pretendit
procuratouris of resignacioune therof that he [Scheves] wes throw
force, aw, and dreid, compellit to constitut and mak, as is notourly
knawin': instead of supporting Andrew Stewart's ecclesiastical
schemes Albany was obliged to bestow his 'hertly favouris and
tendirness' upon Scheves.

In return for all the king's demands upon Albany and his followers they received few concessions: the king undertook to regard
his brother with 'hertly lufe, favore and tendirnes in tyme tocum'
and to grant remissions to him and all adherents whom he named;
the names were to be forwarded to the chancellor within twenty
days, and Albany was to 'mak faith that thai personis tuke part with
him, and that he sal ask remissioune to nane uthir bot to thame that
tuke part with hyme'. In these few words, perhaps, may be seen the
whole object of the lengthy indenture: for if such a list were ever
delivered by Albany it would have given James a chart by which to
map his future political course. Nor was the indenture likely to prove
any obstacle: the signed and sealed letters of security to be given to
Albany depended upon his 'kepand his lauty . . . to oure soverane
lord'; and the loyalty of Albany, if not also the good faith of James,
proved as lasting as snow in summer. On 17 May 1483 Rothesay
herald summoned the duke and Liddell of Halkerston to compear in
parliament on 27 June to answer charges of treason.[289] Shortly after
this summons, having collected his Whitsuntide rents, Albany fled
by sea to England and arranged that an English garrison should be
admitted to his castle of Dunbar.[290] The 'parliament' of 27 June was
in fact a continuation of that of 1 March and was held by Crawford
and Argyll, acting as the king's justiciars. Their duty was simply to
continue the processes against Albany and Liddell from day to day
until 8 July when the king and the three estates assembled. After
the summonses and charges had been rehearsed, John Ross of Mont-

[288] H.B.C., p. 179. [289] A.P.S., II. 151, 152.
[290] E.R., IX. 427. Lesley's account (History, p. 51), wrongly states that the
duke sailed to France.

grenan, the king's advocate, obtained the expected verdict of forfeiture against Albany and Liddell of Halkerston, who tactfully
failed to compear.[291]

Within a year of the twofold threat to his crown that stemmed
from the bitter humiliation of Lauder and Albany's bid for power
James had adroitly mastered his opponents. It may well be believed
that it had been a year when 'thair wes greit thift, reiff and slauchter
in divers partis of the realme, quhilk come be the occasioun of the
diversitye betuix the king and his nobles'.[292] It was probably typical
that Sir Anselm Adournes, one of the more exotic of the king's
familiars, was involved in the faction-fighting (he destroyed the
east mill of Linlithgow)[293] and that he was slain by Alexander Jardine, a henchman of Douglas,[294] while Albany's attempt to restore the
Boyds by granting their former lands in liferent to Lady Hamilton
and in fee to her son by her first marriage, led to the slaying of the
latter by Hugh Montgomery of Eglinton.[295]

For the royalists, at least, there was some reparation of past misfortunes: as a result of litigation before the lords of council Archibald Preston, probably a kinsman of the deceased Thomas Preston,
was installed in the lands of Cousland formerly occupied by the luck-
less Cochrane; and as a result of litigation before the lords auditors
of causes and complaints the widow of Thomas Preston was awarded
substantial sums of money.[296] Of the survivors of the attacks upon the
king's familiars John Haldane had his lands erected into the free
barony of Gleneagles,[297] John Ross of Montgrenan sat once more
as a lord of council in civil causes,[298] James Hommyl resumed his
well-paid sewing of the royal garments,[299] and the young John Ram-

---

[291] *A.P.S.*, II. 145–52.   [292] Lesley, *History*, p. 50.
[293] *E.R.*, IX. 400, 460. Adournes held lands near Linlithgow (*R.M.S.*, II. No.
1735).
[294] Adournes was dead by 29 January 1483 (*R.M.S.*, II. No. 1548). Flemish
sources describe his slayer as 'Sander Gardin', whom W. H. Finlayson took to be
the marquis (sic) of Huntly, and whom a critical correspondent took to be Alexander, third son of the first Earl of Huntly (*op. cit.*, *S.H.R.*, XXVIII. 195–6, at 196;
XXIX. 120). There can be little doubt, however, that 'Sander Gardin' was 'Alexander Jarding', a diehard Douglas follower who was excluded from a general
remission offered in the parliament of March 1482 (*A.P.S.*, II. 139, c. 6; p. 496
above).
[295] See *Scots Peerage*, V. 149–50, where, however, the view that James III
sanctioned the restoration of James Boyd is based upon a misunderstanding of a
royal confirmation (*R.M.S.*, II. No. 1573).
[296] *A.D.C.*, I. 82; *A.D.A.*, pp. 115, 116, 120.   [297] *R.M.S.*, II. No. 1546.
[298] *A.D.C.*, I. 81–118.   [299] *E.R.*, IX. 249.

say, who had had a narrow escape at Lauder, was well rewarded for the risk he had run. Described as a 'familiar esquire of the chamber' he was granted some titbits of land in September 1483.[300] Then on 25 February 1484, with the approval of parliament, he was granted the lordship of Bothwell (revoked from Lord Monypenny) and to this grant some representatives of each estate attached their seals. On the same day they also sealed a grant whereby Ramsay and his mother, Janet Napier (now wife of an Edinburgh burgess),[301] were confirmed as tenants of lands recently awarded to them by the lords of council at the expense of Lord Crichton.[302] After attaining his majority the new Lord Bothwell would figure as ambassador, witness to royal charters, and commissioner for the assessment of crown lands.[303]

Even before the forfeiture of Albany the king had begun to fill the gaps among his familiars, and by the end of the reign their number probably exceeded forty. From the Lauder episode he had at least learnt to exclude the exotic, and to give some heed to good birth. Thus Oliver Sinclair, son of the Earl of Caithness, appeared as a 'familiar knight', as did Sir Patrick Hepburn of Dunsyre who had lately held Berwick Castle against the English;[304] and Alexander Kennedy, son of Lord Kennedy, became an usher of the chamber.[305] In addition, as was pompously announced in a charter of 1484,[306] James was prepared to reward services to the state of a type that the nobility could understand—victory in warfare was particularly mentioned. Already John Dundas of that Ilk, described as 'familiar esquire of the chamber', had obtained the lands of the barony of Bothkennar for helping in the release of the king from Edinburgh Castle,[307] and James, having considered the trusty deeds of his familiar servant, Andrew Wood, both on land and sea, especially his exploits against the English, had rewarded him 'in the time of parliament' by converting his nineteen-year tack of the township of Largo into a grant in feu-ferm.[308]

Further opportunity for the bestowal of rewards and familiarity was forthcoming through the forfeiture of Albany. If the date of a royal charter is to be believed, the Earl of Argyll had already, on 29

---

[300] *R.M.S.*, II. No. 1565. [301] *Ibid.*, No. 1591.
[302] *A.P.S.*, II. 153–4; *R.M.S.*, II. No. 1577. Crichton also lost lands through a decreet of the lords auditors of causes and complaints (*ibid.*, No. 1575).
[303] *R.M.S.*, II. Nos. 1666–1722, *passim*; *E.R.*, IX. 631, 639, 649.
[304] *E.R.*, IX. xlii and n. 1.
[305] *R.M.S.*, II. Nos. 1552, 1665, 1718. [306] *Ibid.*, No. 1590.
[307] *Ibid.*, No. 1539. [308] *Ibid.*, No. 1563.

April 1483, been granted certain lands forfeited from 'Alexander, onetime Duke of Albany',[309] some two months before sentence of forfeiture was passed on 8 July. Thereafter parliament had appointed a commission of twenty-three ecclesiastics, twenty-three barons, and the representatives of ten burghs, to have power to annex to the crown the lands forfeited from the duke and Liddell of Halkerston, 'sa that thereafter our soveran lord may be avisit how he wil dispone the remanent to the rewarding of his trew liegis that has in tymes bigain done, and sal in tyme tocum do, his hienes gude and trew service'.[310] Portions of Albany's lands were eventually bestowed upon the Earl of Crawford, John Home, familiar esquire of the chamber, the familiar Alexander Home of that Ilk (Master of Home, grandson and heir of Lord Home) and Alexander Bruce, familiar esquire.[311]

Meanwhile the political eccentricities of Scotland had been surpassed by those of England : Edward IV had died on 9 April 1483 ; his son, the young Edward V, was deposed on 25 June and subsequently perished with his brother in the Tower; the Duke of Gloucester acceded as Richard III on 26 June ; and, in the course of the blood-letting that accompanied and followed these events, Lord Hastings was executed on 13 June, Earl Rivers on 23 June, and the Duke of Buckingham on 2 November, while from the spring of 1484 onwards Richard III was expecting an invasion led by Henry Tudor, Earl of Richmond, who was raising forces in France.[312] Thus when Albany reached England after his flight from Dunbar at Whitsuntide 1483 the times were not propitious for a major expedition to reinstate him in Scotland. Instead Douglas was granted an annuity of £200 on 12 February 1484 [313] and was probably given a free hand to co-operate with Albany. The pair descended upon Lochmaben when a fair was being held on 22 July 1484.[314] It had not been forgotten that in the parliament of March 1482 a reward in cash and land had been proffered to anyone who killed or captured Douglas.[315] Inspired by self-interest, if not patriotism, the Borderers rallied. Robert and Edward Crichton, members of the Sanquhar branch of that family, were afterwards favoured with charters for their part in the engagement, while Alexander Kirkpatrick, an old retainer of Douglas, took the earl prisoner and was duly rewarded with lands worth £100

[309] *Ibid.*, No. 1564.   [310] *A.P.S.*, II. 146.
[311] *R.M.S.*, II. Nos. 1571, 1572, 1599, 1638; *E.R.*, x. xl.
[312] E. F. Jacob, *The Fifteenth Century*, pp. 610–28, 639.
[313] *Cal. Docs. Scot.*, IV. Nos. 1494, 1496, 1497.
[314] Lesley, *History*, p. 47; Godscroft, *Douglas and Angus*, pp. 205–6; *E.R.*, IX. 519; *A.P.S.*, II. 173.   [315] *A.P.S.*, II. 139, c. 6.

a year 'to instigate others . . . to perform such services in future times'.[316] James displayed his clemency by sentencing Douglas to no worse fate than confinement in the abbey of Lindores. Albany escaped to France, where in 1485 he jousted in a tournament with the Duke of Orleans (afterwards Louis XII) and was mortally wounded by the splinter of a lance.[317] The last episode in the Anglo-Scottish hostilities that had begun in 1481 was enacted at Dunbar, where the castle was held by the English garrison installed by Albany.[318] Siege operations were conducted ineffectively from time to time, and the defenders had the benefit of some months respite under the terms of the Anglo-Scottish truce of September 1484 [319] before the crown recovered the castle, apparently on 6 December 1485. By 30 June in the following year Lord Bothwell had been granted its custody with an annual fee of £100.[320]

The episode at Lochmaben and the prolonged siege of Dunbar did not prevent Scottish attempts to end the war : Bishop Elphinstone of Aberdeen, who headed Scottish peace missions, was granted safe-conducts by Richard III in November 1483, March, April and August 1484.[321] On 12 September 1484 the bishop, Master Archibald Whitelaw, and another six Scottish envoys were formally received in Nottingham Castle,[322] where they concluded indentures for a three-year truce and a marriage between Rothesay and Anne de la Pole, daughter of the Duke of Suffolk and niece of the English king.[323] Peaceful plotting and counter-plotting could now take the place of open war.

Although the Franco-Scottish alliance was assumed to be in existence during the reign of Louis XI, it does not seem to have been formally renewed, possibly because James was aware of Louis's notorious double-dealing. Latterly there had even been signs of strained relations between France and Scotland : in the Albany-dominated parliament of December 1482 complaint had been made that the goods of Scottish merchants were being requisitioned in France 'be command of the [French] king, as is allegit . . . contrare to the aliance and band betuix the realmes'; Walter Bertram was to

---

[316] *R.M.S.*, II. Nos. 1594, 1597, 1603; *E.R.*, IX. 519.
[317] Lesley, *History*, pp. 47, 51; *Scots Peerage*, I. 152; *E.R.*, X. lxvii.
[318] Lesley, *History*, p. 51.
[319] *A.P.S.*, II. 146, 165, c. 2; *E.R.*, IX. 288, 432, 434.
[320] *E.R.*, IX. 433, 523.   [321] *Rot. Scot.*, II. 461–2, 464.
[322] See 'Negotiations of the Scottish Commissioners at Nottingham', *Bannatyne Misc. II*, 32–48.
[323] *Cal. Docs. Scot.*, IV. No. 1504; *Foedera*, v. pt. iii, 149–55.

be sent to France to remonstrate. Opposite this entry in the record is a marginal entry: 'this grant contenit in this writing is fulfillit be our soverain lordis lettres direct of before';[324] James evidently recognised the futility of remonstrances. The situation seems to have changed with the accession of Charles VIII, who in March 1484 sent to Scotland Bernard Stewart, Sieur d'Aubigny, for a renewal of the Auld Alliance.[325] Its ratification by the two kings was probably accompanied by the enlisting of Scots mercenaries and discussion of their possible employment by Charles to further the fortunes of Henry Tudor, Earl of Richmond.[326] If James had outwardly reconciled himself with Richard III he had also secretly ingratiated himself with the man who would displace the Yorkist from his shaky throne. Although accounts vary as to the number of troops who accompanied Henry on his invasion of England in August 1485 there can be no doubt that they included Frenchmen under the Sieur d'Aubigny and Scots under Alexander Bruce of Earlshall.[327] This 'familiar esquire' would be rewarded by James in February 1486 for the good service he had performed not only within the realm but outside it.[328]

The defeat and death of Richard III at Bosworth on 21 August 1485 brought Henry Tudor to the throne as Henry VII. His coronation was attended by a Scottish delegation that included Bishop Elphinstone and Lord Bothwell. Thereafter 'negotiations between Henry VII and James III were in fact almost continuous'.[329] A remarkable stability existed since neither monarch was by nature aggressive and the internal disaffection that faced each was of comparable dimensions: Henry would soon be troubled by the first Yorkist pretender of his reign—Lambert Simnel—and James by the opposition of the Border barons. Thus Henry made no attempt to hinder James's recovery of Dunbar Castle, and with the conclusion of a three-year truce at London in July 1486[330] amicable counterplotting gave way to an amity that was intended to cover Western Europe. In addition one clause showed that James's hopes of dynastic alliances with England had blossomed afresh: there were to be negotiations for the marriage of his second son, James, Marquess of Ormond,[331] and the Lady Katherine, third daughter of Edward IV

---

[324] *A.P.S.*, II. 144–5, cc. 6, 11.   [325] Mackie, *James IV*, p. 26.
[326] Conway, *Henry VII*, pp. 5–7.
[327] *Ibid.*, pp. 5–7; Mackie, *James IV*, pp. 27–8.   [328] *R.M.S.*, II. No. 1638.
[329] Conway, *Henry VII*, p. 10.   [330] Text in *Rot. Scot.*, II. 473–7.
[331] It is wrongly stated in *H.B.C.*, p. 486, that the creation of this marquessate dated from 29 January 1488: the title had been bestowed on the king's second son by 23 January 1481 (*R.M.S.*, II. Nos. 1457, 1470).

and sister of Henry's own queen.[332] In the following year English ambassadors came to Edinburgh and concluded an indenture on 28 November 1487.[333] This alluded to 'the grete tendur lufe and kindnes' that the two kings had hitherto displayed to one another, and revealed the sprouting of two additional matrimonial schemes 'for the incressing of mare love and amite' : James himself had been widowed by the death of Queen Margaret in the summer of 1486; having paid respect to her memory by trying to have her canonised [334] he was free to seek the hand of Elizabeth Woodville, widow of Edward IV; and it was thought that the Duke of Rothesay might marry one or other of Edward IV's brood of daughters.

One stumbling-block to Anglo-Scottish understanding might thereby be removed : the question of Berwick had caused difficulties in the negotiations for the truce of July 1486,[335] and in November 1487 James, who had won Orkney and Shetland through marriage, made it clear that he expected the proposed marriages to bring 'the finall appeasing and cause of cesing all sic debaitis and controversies as in tyme past has bene for the castell and town of Berwik . . . of the quhilk castell and town . . . the said King of Scottis desiris alwais deliverance at the finale appeasing of the said mariagis or any of thame'. This weighty matter was probably to be discussed, together with 'uthir gretir intelligencis for the incressing of mare lufe, amyte and tenderness' at a conference to be held by the two kings in person in July 1488 'at sic a place as canne be betwix thame agreit'.[336] For the first time in two hundred years the Scottish and English kings were sincere and like-minded in a desire for peace.

The desire was not shared by some Scottish nobles, particularly those who were powerful on the Borders. They had not rallied to the defence of Berwick when it was in Scottish hands, but now that it was occupied by the English it was fair game for plunder. Hence regardless of truces and the general trend of James's diplomacy they made menacing moves against the town in September 1485, September 1487, and January 1488.[337] The Borderers, so long inured to warfare, sensed that their peculiar power would be shattered if real peace were established : for almost two centuries they had been the bulwark of Scotland and they assumed (as the ballad hero Johnnie Armstrong

---

[332] *Rot. Scot.*, II. 475.   [333] *Ibid.*, 480–2.
[334] Mackie, *James IV*, p. 34, n. 5.   [335] *Rot. Scot.*, II. 475.
[336] *Ibid.*, 480–1.   [337] Conway, *Henry VII*, pp. 8–9, 10, 11.

still did in 1530) [338] that their military services atoned for their lawless insubordination; if military service was no longer in demand the Borderers could no longer be a law unto themselves and their unemployed chiefs would be disregarded. To this consideration the Red Douglas cannot have been blind. He had hastened to win the good graces of the king in March 1484 by founding a chaplainry in St Bride's Kirk for the soul's weal of, among others, James and his queen.[339] This gesture perhaps earned his appointment to the wardenships of the Middle and Eastern (or Southern) Marches.[340] But it did not prevent a decreet of the lords of council on 7 December 1485 as a result of which a few of the titles to annualrents held by Angus were apprised to raise a sum of about £50.[341] Nor did the earl figure as a witness to royal charters.[342] In the background hovered the spectres of the victims of the Lauder lynching : 'no truce could efface the memory of such a deed on either side',[343] especially on that of James III, whose similitude, the lion of Henryson's fable, proudly announced :

> I lat you wit my mycht is merceabill
> And steris [disturbs] none that ar to me prostrat.

Angus and his accomplices were not disposed to prostrate themselves. It was in vain that the poet hoped

> That tressone of this cuntre be exyled
> And Justice ring [reign] and lordes keip thair fey [fealty]

Equally in vain Henryson addressed James in the lines :

> Without mercy Justice is creweltie
> . . . .
> Quhen rigour sittis in the tribunall,
> The equety of law quha may sustene? [344]

Treason, and its punishment, hung heavily over the land.

Lord Crichton provided the first manifestation. In the parliament of October 1483 a decreet of the auditors of causes and com-

---

[338] G. Donaldson, *Scotland: James V to James VII* (1965), p. 50.

[339] *R.M.S.*, II. No. 1586.

[340] In the truce treaty of July 1486 (*Rot. Scot.*, II. 476), Angus is named as warden of the Middle and Southern Marches, Lord Maxwell as warden of the West March.   [341] *R.M.S.*, II. No. 1664.

[342] See p. 527 below.   [343] Conway, *Henry VII*, p. 3.

[344] MacQueen, *Robert Henryson*, pp. 151, 171, 173.

plaints ordered that some of his lands be apprised to satisfy damages of over 540 marks as a result of a spuilzie he had committed upon Lord Borthwick.[345] By decreet of the lords of council on 12 February 1484 more of Crichton's lands were apprised in compensation for £800 in gold and a gold chain obtained by spuilzie committed upon John Ramsay of Bothwell, his mother, Janet Napier, and her burgess husband.[346] Already Crichton had been summoned to answer charges of treason on account of his complicity with Albany. He did not compear when process was led against him in parliament on 19 February 1484; on 24 February he was sentenced, along with forty more obscure persons, to forfeit life, lands, goods, offices and possessions.[347]

One enactment of this parliament urged that before the end of the session the king should receive the great lords and 'put thaim in freindschip and concord or [before] thai depart fra his presens' and that the justiciars should do likewise with 'smallar personis . . . sa that our souverane lordis liegis stand in peax . . . and be obedient to oure souverane lordis autorite'.[348] But the troubles of the last few years made it almost impossible to distinguish between feuds and crimes that were 'ordinary' and those that were political. Some misgiving must have been caused by the advice of the lords of the articles that justice ayres and warden courts should set to work, and that the king should obtain the co-operation of 'certane lordis and hedismenn of the Bordouris . . . for the apprehending . . . of the masterfull trespassouris that ar fugitive fra his lawis'.[349] In the past the king's lavish grants of remission had been unpopular; the members of parliament must have had mixed feelings when it was announced on 24 February that for three years the king would issue no remissions in respect of treason, slaughter, and certain other crimes.[350] The motive was divulged in another act in which the king was urged to cause diligent inquisition to be made to detect those who had partaken in Albany's treason 'and to mak thame be punyst . . . in exemple of all utheris in tym tocum to comytt sa odious crime and offence aganis his majeste'.[351] In the next parliament, in May 1485, James Gifford of Sheriffhall was sentenced for treason for his deliverance of Dunbar Castle to the English,[352] and it was thought expedient that the king should summon lords and 'hedismen' from all parts of the realm to act as a sort of grand jury of presentment that would denounce

[345] *R.M.S.*, II. No. 1575. [346] *Ibid.*, No. 1577.
[347] *A.P.S.*, II. 154–64. [348] *Ibid.*, 165, c. 8. [349] *Ibid.*, 165, c. 3.
[350] *Ibid.*, 165, c. 8. [351] *Ibid.*, 165, c. 3. [352] *Ibid.*, 172–4.

'notour trespassouris', who should be 'takin and justifiit without remissioune'.[353]

It was significant that the following parliament of October 1487, in which the lairds outnumbered the earls and lords,[354] showed obvious deference to the king, who had 'benignly grauntit to thaim all ther desiris and requestis'.[355] At the opening of proceedings James acknowledged that the realm was 'greitlie brokin' through treason and other crimes and through 'default of scharpe execcutioune of justice and ouer commoun granting of grace and remissiounis'; for the following seven years there would be no more remissions and the guilty would be 'punist extremely'.[356] Thereupon the members of each estate undertook to take oath that they would not support any 'manifest tratouris' or other criminals but would help to 'inquere and gett knaulage of the said trespassouris' and bring them to justice.[357] Thus, according to Bishop Lesley, 'the king begouth to use sharp executione of justice in all partis, quhilk mony culd nocht abyde'.[358]

Their discomfort was increased by spiritual means. For at royal request Sixtus IV issued a bull in May 1484 ordering obedience to the king.[359] This did not mean that James was panic-stricken and abjectly invoking papal support : requests for papal intervention were simply attempts on his part to grasp all available weapons with which to coerce the opposition; far from being cowed he was in aggressive mood, and his approaches to the papacy for support were part and parcel of his general attitude of expecting the papacy to comply with all his wishes. The guarded attitude of the papacy towards James's protests over provisions was diplomatically balanced by its readiness to give political backing. Thus in August 1485 Innocent VIII took note of the recent disputes over ecclesiastical appointments and, more fulsomely, accepted the king's interpretation of recent political troubles : certain nobles had not blushed to stick out their necks against the king, whereupon evils innumerable had ensued ; James was exhorted not to withdraw the pardon he had extended to the offenders ; excommunication and interdict would be pronounced against all individuals and communities who flouted the royal authority; copies of this admonitory letter were to be posted in every cathedral. Thereupon the Bishop of Imola, the papal legate then in Scotland, fulminated no few excommunications and interdicts.[360] It was perhaps a misfortune for James that the co-

---

[353] *Ibid.*, 170, c. 4.   [354] *Ibid.*, 175.   [355] *Ibid.*, 176, c. 2.
[356] *Ibid.*, 176, c. 3.   [357] *Ibid.*   [358] Lesley, *History*, p. 55.
[359] Mackie, *James IV*, p. 30.   [360] *Ibid.*, pp. 31–2.

operative legate left Scotland to accompany Archbishop Scheves on the mission to Rome that resulted in the indult of 1487.[361]

Another consequence of the mission was even more ill-fated for the king : in the parliament of May 1485 it had been decided that the envoys should petition for 'ane ereccioun of Coldingahame to our souverane lordis chapel' [362]—in other words that the revenues of that Home-ridden establishment, now of uncertain status, be used for the foundation of a collegiate kirk at Coldingham which would be an additional royal chapel. This petition, granted by the pope in April 1487,[363] earned the king the enmity of the Homes, who had lately been his familiars.[364] By October 1487 their opposition was obviously so strong that parliament declared that anyone who obstructed the king's plans for Coldingham would be punished as a traitor.[365]

When parliament was prorogued to 11 January 1488 the announcement of the agenda for the next session summed up all that the malcontent nobles found most distasteful : the proposed dynastic alliances with England, the Coldingham business, and 'the process of forfatur of the laird of Drumelzier and Edward Hunter'. Warning was given that any prelate or lord absent from the forthcoming session (and the Homes were notably absent from the current session) would incur the king's 'indignacioun and displesance'.[366]

The Homes were nonetheless absent (and so also was Lord Hailes, their Hepburn associate) when parliament re-assembled on 11 January 1488. And even more obviously than in the previous session the lords were outnumbered by the lairds. The loyalty of the latter was recognised at the close of parliament on 29 January when four of them were created lords and one was knighted along with the heirs of Lords Kennedy and Carlyle. On the same day the king's second son, James, Marquess of Ormond, was created Duke of Ross.[367]

The proceedings of this parliament showed that the king had not relaxed his intention of using judicial machinery to crush political opponents : it was thought expedient that he should choose two 'gret justices' from a short leet of four (Lords Bothwell, Lyle, Glamis and Drummond). Those chosen would act south of Forth, while their northern counterparts would be the Earls of Huntly and Crawford. It was also suggested that, once ayres had been arranged, the king

[361] Lesley, *History*, p. 54.
[363] Watt, *Fasti*, p. 347.
[365] *A.P.S.*, II. 179, c. 19.
[362] *A.P.S.*, II. 171, c. 7.
[364] P. 516 above.
[366] *Ibid.*, 180.   [367] *Ibid.*, 180–81.

should send wise lords and persons of his council to act as assessors and counsellors to the justices. Whatever the intrinsic merits of this scheme it was one that entrusted criminal jurisdiction to prominent political figures who had axes to grind. The ordinance was significantly accompanied by an announcement that it was expedient that the ayres previously arranged should be 'dissolvit' and new ones proclaimed in spring.[368] To the king's opponents this change must have seemed ominous. Parliament also went ahead with the agenda formerly arranged. Preparations were made to finance an embassy to England to treat of the proposed royal marriages. It was nothing new that the condition was made that these could not go forward unless the castle and town of Berwick were delivered to the Scots or destroyed :[369] James had stipulated the same condition in the negotiations with the English ambassadors the previous November.[370] Even if the marriages were not agreed upon, the king and his council were empowered to make truces at their discretion; and the Borderers can hardly have relished an enactment that truce-breakers should be punished so 'extremely' that 'throw the terroure and exempill therof sic like trespasses may be forborne in tyme tocum'.[371] Notice was also taken of those persons who had treasonably contravened the act of the previous session regarding Coldingham : the clerical offenders were to be summoned to answer in the church courts and the laymen to be summoned before a parliament to be held in May. Since it was reckoned 'hevy to travale the hale estatis to the said parliament' it was decided that a commission of the estates be appointed 'to have the powere of the hale parliament to procede in the said mater'.[372] Finally, when parliament was continued to 5 May, seventeen ecclesiastics, eighteen barons, three civil servants, and the representatives of twelve burghs were named to sit upon this commission.[373]

It never met. The herald sent to summon the Homes at their stronghold of Fast Castle was 'evill intreitit',[374] and on 2 February James Schaw of Sauchie, keeper of Stirling Castle, whose wife was a Home, released the heir apparent into the hands of the king's opponents.[375]

There can be little doubt that they found it easy to turn the

[368] *Ibid.*, 182, cc. 5, 6, 7. [369] *Ibid.*, 181–2, cc. 2, 3.
[370] P. 519 above. [371] *A.P.S.*, II. 182–3, cc. 4, 14.
[372] *Ibid.*, 182, c. 8. [373] *Ibid.*, 184. [374] Pitscottie, *Historie*, I. 201.
[375] *Ibid.*, 203; Ferrerius, *Continuatio*, p. 399 v.; *A.P.S.*, II. 223; *R.M.S.*, II. No. 3011.

prince's head. The death of Queen Margaret, who in 1478 had been entrusted with his custody,[376] removed an influence that might have prevented his association with his father's adversaries. Whether or not the association already existed, the king suspected that it did; although the Duke of Rothesay was close to fifteen years of age he was apparently kept away from parliament, and it would seem that he was held in Stirling virtually as a prisoner. The elevation of his younger brother (another James) as Duke of Ross was an event that hinted that the Duke of Rothesay was not irreplaceable; and the heir apparent's new associates doubtless did not hesitate to assure him that his father purposed his demotion from the succession—if not worse.[377]

In this crisis the king did not panic but took various steps to secure his position and to show his moderation. Bishop Elphinstone, an admirable choice as mediator, was made chancellor on 18 February 1488 in place of Argyll, whose loyalties may already have been wavering. By the advice of his council the king proclaimed on 21 February that for 'certane ressonable and gret causs' the parliamentary commission that was to sit on 5 May had been dissolved and that a new 'generale parliament' was to be held in its place on 12 May: general precepts of summons would be issued and, in addition, special letters under the signet would be issued to all the prelates and great lords 'to schew and declare to thame the causs of the settin of his said parliament' [378]—an opportunity for the king to publicise his own interpretation of recent events.

For some months both the king and the opposition had doubtless engaged in a quest for support from the papacy and other powers. In the parliament of January 1488 it had been thought expedient that no papal legate or messenger should be allowed entry to Scotland until his business had been ascertained.[379] James probably suspected (though wrongly) that the legate who was on his way (but arrived too late) [380] would co-operate with the opposition rather than with himself. More important was the attitude of England. It has been thought that Henry VII had been alienated from James by the demand for the delivery of Berwick, but this was not necessarily the case: Henry, who paid remarkable attention to finance, had by 1486 'enormously reduced the regular annual cost of keeping the

[376] R.M.S., II. No. 1361.   [377] Pitscottie, Historie, I. 203-4.
[378] A.P.S., II. 184.   [379] Ibid., 183-4, c. 16.
[380] Lesley, History, p. 57; Conway, Henry VII, p. 19.

Marches'[381] and may well have thought that the savings resulting from a stabilised frontier more than balanced the empty prestige of holding Berwick. Elphinstone and Lord Bothwell, James's supporters, had been among those involved in recent negotiations with England, and James's uncle, the Earl of Buchan (now loyal to the king) had visited the English court in December 1487 and returned to Scotland in the following spring having received marks of favour from Henry.[382] His efforts to win English support were seconded by those of Lord Bothwell, who was present at Windsor for the celebration of the feast of St George (23 April).[383] Both Buchan and Bothwell would later be accused of having tried to persuade Henry to invade Scotland in person, and Bothwell was held responsible, with the Bishop of Moray, Lord Forbes, Ross of Montgrenan, and three other royal familiars (including Hommyl the tailor) for the fabrication of a commission empowering the English to break the truce.[384] The supporters of the prince, on the other hand, had not neglected to try to present their case to Henry: they had applied for English safe-conducts for Bishop Blackadder of Glasgow, Bishop Brown of Dunkeld, the Earl of Argyll, Lord Hailes, Lord Lyle, the Master of Darnley and the Master of Home.[385] Since Argyll was evidently styled chancellor in this application it must have been forwarded prior to 21 February 1488 when he was replaced as chancellor by Bishop Elphinstone. Not until early May, when there was a lull in hostilities in Scotland, did Henry issue these safe-conducts, and it is unlikely that they were used. For by then ambassadors had arrived in Scotland to denounce the baronial rising and to declare that the Kings of France and England 'thoucht the same as ane commoun injurie done unto thame selves, and the exampill to be verraye wickit and pernicious'.[386] Thanks to the commission conveyed by Bothwell to the Earl of Northumberland—so it was later alleged—the English had proclaimed war upon the prince's party, some of whom had been plundered and even slain.[387] But this English intervention, possibly on the part of the garrison of Berwick, was on too small a scale to affect the outcome of the insurrection.

It was not until March 1488 that it became indisputable that there *was* an insurrection. Hitherto, it would appear, the prince merely remained at Linlithgow issuing manifestoes[388] with some of

[381] R. L. Storey, *op. cit.*, *E.H.R.*, LXXII. 593–609, at 608.
[382] Conway, *Henry VII*, pp. 16–7.
[383] *Ibid.*, p. 18.
[384] *A.P.S.*, II. 201, 202.
[385] *Rot. Scot.*, II. 485–6.
[386] Lesley, *History*, p. 57.
[387] *A.P.S.*, II. 201.
[388] Pitscottie, *Historie*, I. 203–4.

his new friends, while others frequented the court at Edinburgh and strove for a compromise. Angus even appeared briefly as a witness to royal charters until 7 March, and Argyll remained as a witness until 23 March,[389] when he too left court. This was also the last appearance of the elder statesman Avondale, who seems to have died shortly afterwards.[390] By this time James was virtually beleaguered in Edinburgh Castle, and his efforts at mediation brought only the haughty demand that he abdicate in favour of the prince.[391] A break in the entries in the great seal register after 23 March [392] shows that the king had given up the attempt to carry on normal government from Edinburgh. Leaving his isolated position in the castle he boarded one of Andrew Wood's ships that was ready to sail to Flanders. He was chased on the way to Leith and some of his baggage fell into the hands of his assailants, who used the treasure to hire troops.[393]

It was not in Flanders but in Fife that James disembarked. With the exception of the Campbell territories and those of Lord Gray in Angus and Lord Drummond in Strathearn all of Scotland north of Forth was ready to rally to his side. As he rode towards Aberdeen, the seat of loyal Bishop Elphinstone, he ordered the sheriffs to call out the host.[394] James also visited Lindores to seek the aid of its tragic recluse, the disinherited Douglas. The latter had already, it would seem, rebuffed the advances of the prince's party and is reported to have told James: 'Sir, you have kept me and your black coffer in Stirling too long; neither of us can do you any good'.[395] At Aberdeen, however, powerful royalist supporters were assembling, as is shown in the witness list to a charter issued there on 16 April.[396] With the backing of 'all the Northt of Scotland' the king took the field.[397] His objective was the rebel headquarters in Linlithgow, and the position that he occupied at Blackness was one that would enable him to receive supplies and reinforcements shipped in by Andrew Wood.

At Blackness skirmishes were interspersed with negotiations for a peaceful settlement. James commissioned Bishop Elphinstone, Huntly, Erroll, Marischal, Glamis and Alexander Lindsay to treat

---

[389] *R.M.S.*, II. Nos. 1708, 1709, 1717, 1722. The part played by Angus is discussed in Fraser, *Douglas*, II. 82.　　　[390] *Scots Peerage*, V, 349.

[391] Lesley, *History*, pp. 56–7.　　　[392] *R.M.S.*, II. 362.

[393] Pitscottie, *Historie*, I. 202, 204; Ferrerius, *Continuatio*, p. 399v.

[394] Pitscottie, *Historie*, I. 202.

[395] Godscroft, *Douglas and Angus*, p. 206; Ferrerius, *Continuatio*, p. 399v.; Lesley, *History*, p. 58.

[396] *Moray Registrum*, p. 234; Conway, *Henry VII*, p. 15.

[397] Ferrerius, *Continuatio*, p. 400; Pitscottie, *Historie*, I. 204.

with the commissioners of the other side—Bishop Blackadder, Angus, Argyll, Hailes and Lyle. They at least agreed upon the points that had to be settled.[398] It was to be arranged 'that the kingis hie honour . . . be exaltit', that he should enjoy honour, security and freedom, and that 'thar be prelatis, erlis, lordis and baronis and utheris persouns of wisdome . . . unsuspect to his hienes . . . dayly about his nobill persoune to the gud giding of his realme and liegis'—a provision which to the minds of the opposition doubtless meant the dismissal of the king's existing councillors. The remaining items mostly concerned the safeguards and favours expected by the prince and his party. He too was to be surrounded daily by 'wiss lordis and honerabill persouns'. He was to receive from the king 'honerabill sustentaccioune'. He would 'tak in hertlie favoris all . . . that has bene with the kingis hienes in consale or uthir service now in this tym of truble'. His own supporters who had in the past 'done displessur to his hienes' would 'mak honerabile and aggreabile amendis . . . thar liffis, heretage and honouris except', and they would have the king's 'favoriis and grace . . . and hertly forgevinnys'. It was hoped that the personal dissension between lords of each side, especially that between the Earl of Buchan and Lord Lyle, would be set at rest, and consideration was to be given as to 'how my lord prince sall in all tymes tocum be obedient to his faider the king, and how that faiderly luff and tendernes sall at all tymes be had beteux thame etc.'. But although these articles were subscribed by the king he was tempted to repudiate them : 'the saidis articulis wes diverss times grantit to and broken be the perverst counsale of diverss persouns . . . quhilkis counsalit and assistit to him in the inbringing of Inglissmen and to the perpetuale subjeccione of the realm'. Shocked by the king's behaviour (so it was later alleged) Huntly, Erroll, Marischal and Glamis left him and, according to one official version, returned home ; another official version, anxious to put the best face upon their action, stated that they adhered to the prince 'and his trew opynzoune for the commoune gud of the realme'.[399]

Neither James's shilly-shallying nor his skirmishing did him any good : he had lost valuable supporters and was forced to hand over Buchan, Ruthven and two others as sureties for his observance of the original terms of the pacification.[400] After this he returned to Edinburgh Castle. A resumption of sparse entries in the great seal register from 18 May onwards indicates a partial restoration of

[398] *A.P.S.*, II. 210; *R.M.S.*, II. Nos. 2529, 2530.
[399] *A.P.S.*, II. 201, 202, 210–1.   [400] *Ibid.*, 201.

government.[401] But the character of the entries shows that the situation was far from settled : James was evidently buying support in readiness for a renewed struggle. The most prominent of those favoured was Crawford, whose devoted and heroic service at Blackness was rewarded on 18 May by a grant of the burgh of Montrose and his creation as Duke of Montrose.[402] Ten days later Alexander Cunningham, Lord Kilmaurs, was created Earl of Glencairn. In the case of two other beneficiaries the favours that were bestowed were made conditional upon continuing loyalty[403]—a sad indication that by this time James believed that he could trust no one. In his distraught uncertainty he was persuaded, allegedly by Lord Bothwell, to leave Edinburgh and to make a final attempt to crush the opposition.[404] The ships of Andrew Wood that commanded the Forth allowed him to cross once more to Fife to link up with his northern supporters. A muster took place in Perth, where Lord Lindsay of the Byres presented the king with a great grey charger that could outdistance any horse in Scotland. Once more the whole north rallied to James's support.[405]

On 11 June 1488 the royalist army had passed through Stirling on its way towards the rebel headquarters at Linlithgow when it found that the prince's army had reached the Carron and was advancing to the encounter. The two armies were arrayed for battle on or near the field of Bannockburn,[406] and it was ironic that James had brought with him the sword of Robert Bruce.[407] He had placed himself in the centre battalion of his troops 'witht all the burrowis and commons of Scotland', flanked on one side by the men of Fife and Angus, and on the other by those of Strathearn and Stormont. The rearguard was composed of men from Stirling and the west; and the vanguard consisted of Highlanders under the Earls of Atholl and Huntly. On the opposing side were the men of the Merse, Teviotdale, East Lothian, Liddesdale, Annandale, and parts of Galloway; and the Homes and Hepburns led the vanguard.[408] It was a confrontation between north and south; and, by a curious reversal of the usual state of affairs, the Highlanders were conspicuous among the king's supporters.[409] Even more striking was the opposition of king and prince. The tragedy of the situation is caught in the lines cited in Pitscottie :

[401] *R.M.S.*, II. Nos. 1723–36.
[402] *Ibid.*, No. 1725.
[403] *Ibid.*, Nos. 1727, 1730.
[404] *A.P.S.*, II. 202, 204.
[405] Pitscottie, *Historie*, I. 204–5, 206.
[406] *Ibid.*, 205–6; Lesley, *History*, p. 57.
[407] *E.R.*, X. xxxix; *T.A.*, I. lxxiii.
[408] Pitscottie, *Historie*, I. 206–7.
[409] See *Highland Papers*, II. 26–7.

> The civill weir, the battell intestine,
> Nou that the sone with baner bred displayit
> Aganis the fader in battell come arreyit.[410]

The banner that the prince displayed was the royal standard.[411] This audacious assertion of his own kingship demonstrated his determination to unseat his father and was calculated to inspire the insurgents and dismay the royalists.

It certainly had that effect upon the king himself. Perhaps he was 'never hardie nor yeit constant in battell'; perhaps he remembered the old prophesies that he would fall by the hand of his nearest of kin. At any rate he was urged (allegedly by Ross of Montgrenan) to leave the field.[412] Hard fighting at once commenced beside the little Sauchie burn (now the Sauchinford burn) that would eventually give its name to the battle.[413] At length the royalists were forced back to the Tor Wood and as darkness fell took to flight.[414] Some were evidently pursued across Stirling bridge by the prince, who in turn was put to flight and chased by a counter-attack led by Ross of Montgrenan.[415]

In the confusion no one had thought to provide an escort for the king, who fled distractedly on his great grey charger, possibly making for Andrew Wood's ship lying in the Forth. All that was officially known of what afterwards occurred was that he left the field at the beginning of the battle, 'fell into the hands of vile persons and was slain'.[416] Pitscottie, whose great-uncle, David, Lord Lindsay of the Byres, fought for the king at Sauchieburn, is the only writer to give a circumstantial account of the king's death. According to his story the king fell from his charger when it leapt across the Bannock burn. Carried senseless into the nearby mill he regained consciousness and asked for a priest. The miller's wife found a mysterious stranger— 'sum sayis he was the Lord Grayis servand'—who said, 'Heir ame I, ane preist, quhair is the king?' After a few words with the king the supposed priest drew a sword and stabbed him in the heart.[417]

---

[410] Pitscottie, *Historie*, I. 212.   [411] *Ibid.*, 207.   [412] *Ibid.*; *A.P.S.*, II. 204.
[413] Mackie, *James IV*, p. 43, n. 4. The site is discussed by Angus Graham in 'The Battle of Sauchieburn', *S.H.R.*, XXXIX. 89–97.
[414] Pitscottie, *Historie*, I. 208.   [415] *A.P.S.*, II. 204.
[416] *Ibid.*   [417] Pitscottie, *Historie*, I. 209.

17

NEW MONARCHY TRIUMPHANT

It was reported that as a penance for his part in the events that led to the death of his father the new king, James IV, wore an iron belt around his waist.[1] Whatever his remorse it came late rather than early : in October 1488 he endowed masses for his mother alone; not until 1496 did he begin to provide for the weal of his father's soul.[2] For some days, so Pitscottie narrates, it was believed that James III had escaped to Captain Wood's ship. But even before the captain had denied this with 'dispytfull ansueris'[3] the victorious faction had assumed government : on 12 June 1488, the day after Sauchieburn, the new king's peace was proclaimed and a great seal charter was issued in his name.[4] Five days later six of his leading supporters were appointed to take an inventory of his father's treasure in Edinburgh Castle. This hoard, which included not only cash but such venerable relics as the shirt of Robert Bruce, probably yielded the large sum of £24,517 10s. od. mentioned in the first accounts of the new treasurer.[5] Even so, it was believed that this was only a 'small litle parte' of the late king's savings, and in February 1492 secret inquests were ordained in the hope of unearthing the remainder.[6]

The notables appointed to rummage through the late king's treasure were also among those who had been appointed on 15 June to grant tacks of all vacant crown lands. Under the guise of a commission of assessment they were to enjoy unusually far-reaching

---

[1] Pitscottie, *Historie*, I. 217–8; Lesley, *History*, p. 59.
[2] *R.M.S.*, II. Nos. 1783, 2306; *A.P.S.*, XII. 34; *Wigtown Charters*, No. 15; *R.S.S.*, I. No. 2040.
[3] Pitscottie, *Historie*, I. 213–5.
[4] *A.P.S.*, II. 207, c. 4; *R.M.S.*, II. No. 1731.
[5] *T.A.*, I. 79–87, 97, 166–7; *E.R.*, x. 82; *R.M.S.*, II. No. 1820.
[6] *A.P.S.*, II. 230, c. 2. At least one prosecution resulted (*T.A.*, I. lxxi, n. 6).

powers.[7] The intention was probably to make life miserable for members of the defeated party. The commission also gives the earliest indication of the composition of the new government: Colin Campbell, Earl of Argyll, had replaced Bishop Elphinstone as chancellor; Sir William Knollis, Preceptor of the headquarters of the Knights of St John at Torphichen, had replaced the Abbot of Arbroath as treasurer; Patrick Hepburn, Lord Hailes, was master of the household, John Hepburn, Prior of St Andrews, was keeper of the privy seal, and Master William Hepburn was clerk register. Before long, Alexander, Master of Home, who was to succeed his grandfather as second Lord Home in 1490, appeared as chamberlain; he died in 1506 leaving a son who, as third Lord Home, was almost as influential.[8] No official post was given to Angus, probably because it was recognised that his talents were more destructive than constructive. Although he was to remain influential until the end of the reign, Bell-the-Cat was no politician. It was the Hepburns and the Homes upon whom the new king relied, and to whom he always remained grateful.

The coronation appears to have been sparsely attended,[9] and although an exchequer audit was begun on 7 July,[10] and the lords of council resumed the hearing of civil actions on 12 July,[11] the holding of a parliament was delayed for a few months until the new regime had consolidated its power. Captain Wood was among the majority who, however much they detested the manner of James IV's accession, were at least willing to support him after it had taken place: on 28 July a confirmation was issued of the captain's feu of Largo formerly granted by James III.[12] Some irreconcilables, notably John Ramsay, Lord Bothwell, and Sir John Ross of Montgrenan, had fled to the English court. The danger that they might provoke the intervention of Henry VII was partly allayed by negotiations which culminated in a three-year truce drawn up at Coldstream on 5 October 1488.[13] On the following day the first parliament of the reign opened at Edinburgh.

The attendance demonstrated that the new government had won general acceptance: among the thirty-four ecclesiastical representatives were eight bishops, including such associates of the previous king as Archbishop Scheves and Bishop Elphinstone; the thirty-five

[7] E.R., x. 629–30.

[8] Ibid., xli; xiii. clx–clxii.

[9] Pitscottie, Historie, i. 216–7.

[10] E.R., x. 1–73.

[11] A.D.C., i. 121.

[12] R.M.S., ii. No. 1758.

[13] Conway, Henry VII, pp. 22–6; Rot. Scot., ii. 488–90.

barons included ten earls, headed by Argyll and Angus; and sixteen burghs sent commissioners.[14] On 8 October there was a debate upon the 'causs of the feild of Stervilin in the quhilk umquhile James, King of Scotlande . . . happinnit to be slane'. It was satisfactorily agreed that this mischance was the fault of the defeated party and the 'perverst consale' which had led them astray; the new king and his supporters were completely innocent.[15] More attention seems to have been paid to the punishment of prominent supporters of the late king.[16] Buchan, and possibly some others, came to terms and obtained a royal remission. Bothwell and Montgrenan (still in England) were condemned.[17] In addition some of the statutes passed by parliament inflicted penalties, direct or indirect, upon the defeated party, against whose members the king had conceived 'gret and hie displessur'. All who held heritable office were to lose it for three years; those who held office for life or for a shorter term were to be 'secludit aluterly fra the saidis officis'.[18] It was also ordained that all grants of lands, including those in feu-ferm or blench-ferm, of tailzies, and of offices and dignities, which had been made by James III after 2 February 1488 should be annulled if they were considered prejudicial to the crown.[19] The victorious faction was in no repentant mood, and hardly showed 'statesmanlike moderation',[20] though it did make some concessions, usually in vague terms. It would seem that all lands and houses that had been seized during the civil war were to be restored to the original occupants, while the 'pure unlandit folkis' whose goods had been plundered were to receive recompense from the great men of the defeated party. It was also enacted that the rights of inheritance of the heirs of those who had fallen at Sauchieburn fighting *against* the present king should be safeguarded, while the heirs of those who had fought *for* the present king had their inheritances augmented by a general cancellation of all alienations made by their predecessors.[21] The complex and often imprecise terms of the settlement of 1488 provided ample scope for litigation, though it rarely reached the lords auditors or the lords of council.[22]

It was the business of the parliament of October 1488 not only to settle the conflicts of the past but to outline policy for the future. The perennial problem of justice was to be tackled by securing the

---

[14] *A.P.S.*, II. 199–200. [15] *Ibid.*, 210–1, c. 15; 269–70.
[16] *T.A.*, I. 92, 93. [17] *A.P.S.*, II. 201–6. [18] *Ibid.*, 207, c. 6.
[19] *Ibid.*, 211, c. 19. A similar act was also passed in February 1490 (*ibid.*, 222–3, c. 25).
[20] Mackie, *James IV*, p. 46; Rait, *Parliaments*, pp. 36–9.
[21] *A.P.S.*, II. 207, cc. 4, 5; 211, c. 20. [22] See, however, *A.D.A.*, I. 130.

involvement of king and magnates: James was to attend the ayres accompanied by the justiciar; a number of lords took oath to search for criminals and 'justify' them, and were to compel 'small' lairds to take the same oath; the Earl of Angus was to enforce this act in five sheriffdoms, and similar spheres of influence that covered all Scotland (with the notable exception of the Isles) were mapped out for other magnates. This act, which virtually turned the magnates into local justiciars, was to remain in force until the king was twenty-one.[23] Another act announced that James, now over fifteen years old, was 'of perfitt age to complett the haly band of matrimonze'; an embassy was to be sent abroad to seek as bride 'a nobill prenciss borne and discendit of ane worchepfull houss'. The prospect of an imminent royal marriage was designed not only to titillate loyalty towards the new king but to serve as excuse for a tax to cover the expenses of the matrimonial embassy. In accordance with recent practice one-fifth of the tax was to be raised by the burghs; the clergy would provide two-fifths, so also would the barons and free tenants; the 'commoune pepill' were to be exempt. The total contribution of £5,000 was to be paid before 15 January 1489,[24] by which time parliament, which had been continued to 14 January, would have re-assembled.

The very brief and incomplete record of the parliament of January 1489 reveals two contentious matters. One was an act that the see of Glasgow should become an archbishopric with the same privileges as that of York.[25] This initiative, which was ultimately successful,[26] was a reward for Bishop Blackadder of Glasgow, who from the first had associated himself with the new government,[27] and a spiteful insult to Archbishop Scheves of St Andrews, who had been too closely associated with the old government. A second contentious issue is hinted at in an allusion to the 'displessere' which the Earl of Buchan had aroused in the new king.[28] At this point the record peters out, leaving the nature of Buchan's offence undisclosed. It may have been connected with a surety of 10,000 marks which Buchan, along with Lords Gray and Erskine, had apparently pledged to the king. They were prosecuted for payment on 17 January 1489 before the parliamentary auditors of causes and a decreet was issued for the distraint of their lands.[29] The penalty might have been more

[23] *A.P.S.*, ii. 208, cc. 8, 9.
[24] *Ibid.*, 207, c. 2.
[25] *Ibid.*, 212–3, c. 2.
[26] Pp. 557–8 below.
[27] See *R.M.S.*, ii. No. 1915.
[28] *A.P.S.*, ii. 213, c. 5.
[29] *A.D.A.*, i. 120.

severe had the government been aware of the contents of a letter written at Edinburgh on 8 January by Alexander Gordon, Master of Huntly: he reminded Henry VII of the 'threasonable ande cruel slauthir of my soverane lorde and kyng [James III] falsely slayne be a part of his fals and untrew legis', and announced that Buchan would be sent to England to seek help, presumably to overthrow the new government.[30]

It is likely that this plot had been provoked by the government's unwillingness to let bygones be bygones: not content with the settlement of October 1488 it seems to have summoned many supporters of James III to answer charges in a subsequent parliament, probably that of January 1489. This may be inferred from Pitscottie's circumstantial account of the trial (and acquittal) of his great-uncle, David, Lord Lindsay of the Byres.[31] Assuming the 'statesmanlike moderation' of the new government, historians have tried in vain to fit Pitscottie's tale into the context of the parliament of October 1488,[32] even although Lord Lindsay, far from being prosecuted, was then nominated to 'justify' criminals in Fife.[33] A renewed and untimely threat to the supporters of the former king was likely to make them desperate, while some supporters of the new king were equally likely to be driven into disaffection by the way in which rewards were distributed. In January 1490 the custody of Stirling and the keeping of the king's younger brother, John, Earl of Mar, would be entrusted to Alexander Home, the chamberlain.[34] During the first two years of the reign the latter, together with other Homes, profited from twenty-two great seal charters while the Hepburns were the beneficiaries of nine,[35] containing great prizes: John, Prior of St Andrews, became keeper of Falkland; Patrick, Lord Hailes, was granted custody of Edinburgh Castle, the sheriffship of Edinburgh, and the keeping of the heir presumptive, the Duke of Ross; by 10 September 1488, even before the forfeiture of John Ramsay, Lord Bothwell, Hailes had not only been appointed admiral of Scotland but styled Earl of Bothwell.[36] The situation was clarified in the parliament of October 1488 when the lordships of Bothwell and

[30] Text in Pinkerton, *History*, II. 437 (though wrongly assigned to 1491); Conway, *Henry VII*, p. 26.

[31] The 1814 Dalyell edition of Pitscottie (I. 239), gives the date as 10 January 1489, the S.T.S. edition (I. 226), as 10 May 1489. There is no record of a parliament in May, though one did open in Edinburgh on 14 January.

[32] See Mackie, *James IV*, p. 48, n. 3.   [33] *A.P.S.*, II. 208.

[34] *Ibid.*, 211, c. 18; *E.R.*, x. xlviii; *R.M.S.*, II. Nos. 1919, 1946.

[35] *T.A.*, I. lxx, n. 1.

[36] *R.M.S.*, II. Nos. 1732, 1741, 1742, 1774; *A.P.S.*, II. 211, c. 17.

Crichton were erected into the earldom of Bothwell and the new earl was belted.[37] In the following month he was appointed steward of Kirkcudbright and granted the custody of Threave.[38] There was a tendency to forget the vital part played in the drama of 1488 by those who were not Hepburns or Homes; Lord Lyle and the Lennox Stewarts were envious 'that the king wes mare governit be utheris of the factione nor be thame'.[39]

As 'great justiciar of Scotland' Lord Lyle had presided over the treason trials of October 1488.[40] Sir John Stewart of Darnley, who since 1473 had maintained pretensions to the earldom of Lennox,[41] had been recognised as earl in October 1488, and, with his son Matthew, had been granted custody of Dumbarton Castle.[42] Only intense disenchantment with the government could have driven such adherents into open disaffection. In April 1489 heralds were sent to Dumbarton and to Lyle's castle of Duchal, presumably with summonses to answer charges in the parliament that would be held on 26 June. They did not compear but garrisoned their castles and were forfeited along with William, onetime Lord Crichton,[43] already forfeited in the previous reign, whose lands had lately been conferred upon the new Earl of Bothwell. Parliament also put a price on the head of the leading rebels and concerted the military preparations that had been begun at the end of April:[44] the king, with a host levied from south of Forth, was to set siege to Duchal and Lennox's castle of Crookston on 19 July; simultaneously Argyll would besiege Dumbarton with three forces from north of Forth, which would relieve one another at intervals of twenty days.[45] On 10 July 'Mons', the great bombard, was carted from Edinburgh Castle and other guns were hastened westward. By 4 August they were being trundled homeward;[46] Duchal and Crookston had surrendered, though Dumbarton still held out.

While the parliament of June 1489 had supported the king against the rebels it had also sought to reduce the dominance of the Hepburns and Homes by defining the composition of the council in an act that was to remain in force until the next parliament. The council was to be broadly based, although the inclusion of burgesses does not seem to have been contemplated. At least six of the coun-

---

[37] *A.P.S.*, II. 205, 206.
[38] *R.M.S.*, II. No. 1799.
[39] Lesley, *History*, p. 59.
[40] *A.P.S.*, II. 199.
[41] *E.R.*, x. xlvi.
[42] *R.M.S.*, II. No. 1794.
[43] *A.P.S.*, II. 213; 215, c. 11.
[44] *Ibid.*, 215, c. 11; *T.A.*, I. 109, 110, 111, 112, 144, 163.
[45] *A.P.S.*, II. 214, c. 7.
[46] *T.A.*, I. 117, 123.

cillors were to be in continual attendance upon the king. It was also stipulated that the Earls of Huntly and Crawford should join the council 'quhen thai cum', and that the same applied to all prelates and great barons.[47] This re-modelled council met at Stirling as a 'great council' on 18 September 1489 and restored David Lindsay, Earl of Crawford, to the dukedom of Montrose[48] which he had lost through the act of 1488 that cancelled grants made by James III after 2 February. This restoration was a timely concession to meet a new threat: on 12 September the government was denounced at Aberdeen on the grounds that 'no punishment had been imposed on the treasonable vile persons who put their hands violently on the king's [James III's] most noble person'.[49]

The ringleader of the rising in the north was Lord Forbes. It had been arranged in the parliament of June 1489 that he and the Earl Marischal should join the government forces at Dumbarton in mid-September.[50] Instead they joined the Master of Huntly, adopted as their banner the 'bludy serk' (blood-stained shirt) of James III, and, so the new king announced, made 'certane ligs and bands' with the defenders of Dumbarton.[51] As a result the latter sallied from the castle, burned the town, and drove off the besiegers. Lennox then led a force to join up with the northern insurgents. On the night of 11–12 October he and his men were intercepted and routed by the king and Lord Drummond at Gartalunane near Aberfoyle.[52] A week later the king set out to supervise operations against Dumbarton.[53] Even so, the insurgents were undaunted: despite their rout at 'the feild of the Mos' they sent a manifesto to James denouncing Bishop Blackadder and the Hepburn-Home partisans, who were allegedly exploiting the royal authority and treasure and trying to destroy the king, his brothers, Archbishop Scheves, and 'the haile barownis and nobles of this realme'.[54] The royalist forces in their camp at Dunglass Castle, three miles from Dumbarton, had by this time to be held together by wages contributed by the clergy. It was not until mid-December 1489 that the defenders of Dumbarton capitulated.[55]

The favourable conditions on which they did so were demonstrated when parliament met in February 1490: the Earl of Lennox, his son Matthew, and Lord Lyle, presented a 'lamentable complaint'

---

[47] *A.P.S.*, II. 215, c. 8.   [48] *Ibid.*, 215–6; *R.M.S.*, II. No. 1895; p. 573 below.
[49] *Aberdeen Council Register*, p. 45.   [50] *A.P.S.*, II. 213; 214–5, c. 7.
[51] *T.A.*, I. lxxxviii, n. 4; Lesley, *History*, p. 59.
[52] *T.A.*, I. xcv, 122; Lesley, *History*, pp. 59–60.
[53] *T.A.*, I. 142.   [54] Sir William Fraser, *Lennox Book* (1874), II. 128–31.
[55] *T.A.*, I. xcv–xcvi.

to the king, alleging that the parliament of June 1489 had not
observed 'just and gudely ordoure according to the commoune law'
when it had sentenced them to death and forfeiture; the sentence
was accordingly annulled and the clerk register was ordered to destroy
all record of the process so that 'it be never sene in tyme tocum';
pardon was granted to all persons south of Forth who had been
involved in the rising and to over 130 persons who had held Dumbarton Castle against the king and burned the town; all forfeited
lands, whether or not they had been granted away by the king, were
to be restored.[56]

Although Lord Gordon, Master of Huntly, had taken the field
near Dunkeld against royalist forces,[57] the government seems to have
overlooked the affair of the 'bludy serk', which simply petered out.
An atmosphere of reconciliation seems at last to have prevailed. In
January 1489 Henry VII had sought the pope's intervention on
behalf of Ross of Montgrenan.[58] By a charter issued at Dunglass in
October 1489 he was restored to some of his forfeited lands; by
November 1490 he was a royal familiar and received back the lands
of Montgrenan which Patrick Home of Fast Castle was induced to
resign.[59] Similar consideration was shown towards Sir John Ramsay,
onetime Lord Bothwell, who, together with Sir Adam Forman and
John Liddell (son of the Laird of Halkerston once forfeited for supporting Albany),[60] had been surreptitiously sent by Henry VII with
a boatload of munitions to reinforce the rebels in Dumbarton.[61] Long
before he obtained a remission and life pension in 1497 Sir John
Ramsay was active about court; he too became a familiar and by
1499 was serving once more on commissions of assessment; in 1510
he would be granted the barony of Balmain.[62] In this case James's
clemency was misplaced: Ramsay acted as Henry VII's spy in collaboration with the Earl of Buchan, who proved himself 'a remarkably competent traitor'.[63] By April 1491 the two were privy to an
abortive plot to deliver James IV and the Duke of Ross into the
hands of Henry VII.[64] Possibly the Earl of Angus was involved. At
any rate he alone became an object of suspicion: on 29 July 1491
Lyon king-of-arms was sent to order the earl to ward himself in his

[56] *A.P.S.*, II. 213–4, 217–8, 223, c. 26; XII. 33–4; *R.M.S.*, II. No. 1956.
[57] *R.S.S.*, I. Nos. 14, 32.   [58] *T.A.*, I. lxxxii; Conway, *Henry VII*, p. 25.
[59] *R.M.S.*, II. Nos. 1785, 1904, 1989, 2049; see, however, No. 2262.
[60] P. 516 above.   [61] Conway, *Henry VII*, pp. 28–30.
[62] *R.M.S.*, II. Nos. 2348, 2349, 2412, 2453, 2554, 3460; *E.R.*, XI. 432.
[63] Conway, *Henry VII*, pp. 27, 36–7.
[64] *Ibid.*, pp. 36–7; *E.R.*, X. liv and n. 1.

own castle of Tantallon; by October Tantallon was being besieged, blockaded and bombarded. At the end of the year Angus and his son, George Douglas, entered into a pact with Henry VII : they would try to induce James IV to keep the peace with England; if war broke out Henry was not to make peace unless Angus were included; meanwhile if the earl and his son were 'put to that extremytie that they may not, by the eyde and supportacion of the kinges highnes of England, broke or joyse [enjoy] theyr landes and revenues within the roialme of Scotland, ne make their partie good', they would deliver Hermitage Castle to Henry in return for compensation in England.[65] On the same day (29 December 1491) that the envoys of Bell-the-Cat made this agreement in England a complex settlement was initiated in Scotland : as a result of multiple exchanges of lands the Red Douglas lost his hold upon the Borders.[66] Already in 1489 the wardenships of the East and West Marches which he had held had been transferred with the castle of Lochmaben to the Earl of Bothwell for a period of seven years. Thereafter the three wardenships, together with other offices on or near the Borders, seem to have been allotted at the king's pleasure among Hepburns, Homes and Kerrs.[67] And although Angus was appointed chancellor early in 1493 he was replaced by Huntly in 1497.

The king's firm, but moderate, treatment of Bell-the-Cat, the evil genius of his father's reign, epitomises the re-establishment of a monarchy in which the sovereign held undisputed sway. For almost twenty years, at a time when Europe was racked by strife between monarchy and aristocracy, James III had promoted the royal supremacy, and only twice had his authority been overthrown. Unlike Henry Tudor, James IV was not starting a new dynasty which had to make its way in the world but was continuing an ancient one that had already mapped its course. The natural hiatus in personal monarchical rule caused by the new king's minority lasted for only a year or two. The last attempt to hold him in tutelage occurred in the parliament of February 1490, which revoked the exemptions he had granted from the matrimonial tax, hinted that he should not exploit for his own use the revenues of his two brothers, appointed auditors to oversee the accounts of officials, nominated the lords who were to serve on the privy council, and gave them effective powers : it was

[65] Fraser, *Douglas*, II. 91; Conway, *Henry VII*, p. 38 and n. 5.

[66] *R.M.S.*, II. Nos. 2072–4, 2092, 2106; *E.R.*, x. lv, n. 3.

[67] *A.P.S.*, II. 214, c. 6; *R.M.S.*, II. Nos. 1874, 1875, 1893, 1921, 2027, 2092, 3406; *R.S.S.*, I. No. 291.

declared that the king had humbled himself to promise that he would be guided by their advice until the next parliament.[68] But these measures had no prolonged effect, the last tremors of Sauchieburn subsided when the parliament of February 1492, in an act 'for the eschewing and cessing of the hevy murmour and voce of the peple', belatedly, and fruitlessly, offered a reward for detection of the slayers of James III.[69] It was the latter's concept of monarchy, not the medieval constitutionalism of the magnates, that James IV would pursue.

A reconstructed court party enhanced his self-assurance. His familiars, eventually more than fifty in number, included six or seven who had served under his father. There were no exotics, though the king's naval interests were revealed in the presence of two sea-dogs— Robert Barton of Over Barnton and Andrew Wood of Largo (who must be carefully distinguished from another familiar, Andrew Wood of Blairton and Fettercairn).[70] Mostly the new familiars were aristocratic, linking the court not only with baronial families but with the ecclesiastical hierarchy. Some of them held office in the royal household.[71] Others acquired administrative responsibilities: George Parklee, Andrew Wood of Largo, and Sir Alexander Mc-Culloch of Myreton, held respectively the custody of Linlithgow, Dunbar and Stirling.[72] On the other hand the list of over a hundred witnesses to great seal charters shows a heavy preponderance of lay and ecclesiastical magnates and a marked absence of familiars.[73] Freed from governmental anxieties and from the more tedious types of administration the familiars were, above all, courtiers and boon companions of the king: James would send a puncheon of wine to the house of John Tyrie, provost of the collegiate kirk of Methven, when he intended to lodge there:[74] he would buy 'daunsing gere' for Thomas Boswell and Patrick Sinclair;[75] he would play 'at the tables' with Robert Colville,[76] and the happy-go-lucky Sir Alexander Mc-Culloch was in constant attendance.[77] Wholly dependent upon royal favour, such men gave social expression to the new monarchy. Although they were rewarded all too generously for their parasitical services they were too conventional to be suspected of malign influence and aroused no controversy.

[68] A.P.S., II. 218, c. 4; 219, c. 8; 220–1, cc. 10–2; Rait, Parliaments, p. 485.
[69] A.P.S., II. 230, c. 3.   [70] T.A., I. lxxvi, n.
[71] R.S.S., I. No. 459; see also E.R., XI. 246; XIII. lxxvi–lxxxiv.
[72] R.M.S., II. Nos. 1735, 1743; R.S.S., I. Nos. 672, 978; E.R., XIII. xciii.
[73] R.M.S., II. pp. 848–50.
[74] T.A., I. cii.   [75] Ibid., II. 413.   [76] R.S.S., I. No. 415.

Not only did James avoid the type of favouritism that had brought disrepute upon his father but he also managed to avoid the discredit his father had endured over currency problems. During the reign of James IV the 'inbringing' and 'inhalding' of bullion, together with a new coinage and its defects, drew the attention of the three estates [78] but had no political repercussions. By 26 June 1493, when the king's tutelage was symbolically ended by a sweeping act of revocation that preceded his twenty-first birthday by some nine months,[79] the troubles of James's accession were over and he himself, rather than a coterie of nobles, controlled government. No fresh political troubles had as yet appeared. Only the old troubles of the north and west stood between James and complete mastery of his kingdom. It was natural that he should resume the aggressive attitude of his predecessors towards the tradition of Gaelic autonomy represented by the MacDonalds of Islay.

A foreign observer reported that James IV spoke 'the language of the savages who live in some parts of Scotland and on the islands'.[80] Nor did James despise the music and poetry of the 'savages': he rewarded players of the clarshach and even Highland bards. In addition his hunts in Glenartney and Glenfinglas,[81] together with many other expeditions, military, devotional and amorous, made him more closely acquainted than his predecessors with many regions of the Highlands and Isles. Yet the Gaelic regions were more than ever regarded as the abode of outlandish folk [82] whose restlessness offended the majesty of the new monarchy. Almost simultaneously, though by no means in co-operation, Henry VII undertook the subjugation of Ireland [83] and James IV began the daunting of the Isles.

In the previous reign the partial forfeiture of John of the Isles had led not to royal supremacy in the Gaelic regions but to increased turmoil. After the battle of the Bloody Bay it was John's illegitimate son, Angus Og, who flouted the government by striving to recover Ross, feuding against the MacKenzies of Kintail, and impoverishing Inverness, where in 1490 he was assassinated by an Irish harper.[84]

[77] *Ibid.*, No. 2430.

[78] *A.P.S.*, II. 208–9, c. 11; 213, c. 1; 215, cc. 9, 10; 221–2, cc. 14, 18; 226, c. 12; 233, c. 10; 234, c. 12; 238, c. 4; 250–1, c. 12; 254, cc. 43, 44; *A.D.C.P.*, p. lx.   [79] *A.P.S.*, II. 236–7, c. 22.

[80] Pedro de Ayala, cited in Brown, *Early Travellers*, p. 38.   [81] *E.R.*, x. lxi.

[82] Major, *History*, pp. 47–50.   [83] Conway, *Henry VII*, ch. III.

[84] *E.R.*, x. lxii, n. 2; Gregory, *Western Highlands*, pp. 52–4; Derick S. Thomson, *op. cit.*, *Trans. Gaelic Soc. of Inverness* (1963), 3–31, at 14; *Highland Papers*, I. 51–2.

Angus's place as ringleader of the insurgent MacDonalds was taken by Alexander of Lochalsh, son of Celestine, half-brother of the Lord of the Isles. Alexander's ally, Farquhar Mackintosh, son of the captain of Clan Chattan, captured and destroyed Inverness Castle and raided Cromarty. The marauders were defeated in 1491 at the battle of Blairnepark by the rival MacKenzies, who now began their rise to prominence, believing that their valuable services to the crown purchased immunity for their own excesses.[85] Eventually both Farquhar Mackintosh and MacKenzie of Kintail were warded in Edinburgh Castle.[86]

In the eyes of the government the root of disorder stretched back to the Isles: the parliamentary commission appointed in May 1491 had been instructed to discuss 'the mater of the Ilis . . . and to provide sua that the kingis lyegis may lif in quiete and peax'.[87] John of the Isles, far from conforming to the eulogistic portrayal composed by his MacMhuirich bard,[88] was either unable or unwilling to control his kinsmen and nominal followers and was merely an obstacle to the forceful policy that the young king intended to initiate. Probably in the parliament of May 1493 the Lord of the Isles was forfeited and his domains were annexed to the crown. John meekly accepted his fate and became a pensioner at court until he died in obscurity.[89]

To assert control over his new acquisitions the king visited Dunstaffnage, and probably the neighbouring Isles, in the late summer of 1493,[90] and in autumn toured the regions around Inverness that had lately been the scene of disorder.[91] Alexander MacDonald of Lochalsh and John MacDonald of Dunivaig and the Glens (*alias* 'of the Isles' or 'of Islay'), grandson of Donald Balloch and head of the MacDonalds of the south, appear to have been knighted,[92] and the former, some time before he was killed by MacIan of Ardnamurchan, received a promise from the king that all the freeholders of the lordship of the Isles would be infeft in their lands.[93] James

---

[85] Gregory, *Western Highlands*, pp. 56–7, 82; Grant, *Social and Economic Development*, pp. 192–3; *Highland Papers*, II. 24, 30; *E.R.*, x. lvii–lviii.

[86] Gregory, *Western Highlands*, p. 91; *A.D.C.*, II. 94–5.   [87] *A.P.S.*, II. 228.

[88] 'The Red Book of Clanranald', in *Reliquiae Celticae*, II. 259–64.

[89] *E.R.*, x. lix; *T.A.*, I. cxiii, cxviii; Gregory, *Western Highlands*, p. 58. The evidence in *A.D.A.*, I. 177, which has been interpreted as signifying that the Lord of the Isles was *not* forfeited in May 1493 (*Highland Papers*, I. 50, n. 2) is irrelevant since it refers to a transaction of 1490 (*R.M.S.*, II. No. 1969). Some doubt remains, however, whether John of the Isles died at Paisley (*Highland Papers*, I. 50–1) or at Dundee (*T.A.*, II. 354, 357).   [90] *R.M.S.*, II. No. 2171; *E.R.*, XI. 145.

[91] *E.R.*, x. lx–lxi.   [92] *Ibid.*

[93] *R.M.S.*, II. No. 2438; Gregory, *Western Highlands*, pp. 92–3.

was evidently in no hurry to fulfil this undertaking. Although he paid a second visit to the Isles in May 1494 [94] the result does not seem to have been reassuring : on 5 July the lords of the 'Westland', 'South-land', and 'Estland' were summoned to attend the king at Tarbert. The old castle once constructed by Robert I was victualled and gar-risoned, and the expense of its renovation was partly met by a tax paid by the prelates.[95] Once more it became a royalist base for mili-tary and naval operations in the Isles. Once more, as in the days of Bruce, the crown sought to establish a naval force in the Clyde estuary.[96] The immediate objective of the forces that gathered at Tarbert in July 1494 appears to have been Sir John MacDonald's castle of Dunaverty in south Kintyre.[97] No sooner had a royal garri-son been installed than the castle was recaptured and the governor was hanged, reputedly in sight of the royal ships.[98] MacIan of Ardnamurchan probably made his peace with the government by delivering up Sir John MacDonald and some of his sons, who, to the horror of the Ulster annalist, were eventually hanged in Edinburgh.[99]

After Christmas, 1494, there was talk of 'the kingis passing in the Ilis', but the project was delayed until May 1495, when he embarked on the Clyde with the lords of the 'Westland', 'Estland', and 'South-land', and a force of gunners.[100] Captain Andrew Wood had by this time been knighted and commanded the king's ship, the *Flower*. Provisions were sent from many parts of Scotland for the support of the host, which by 18 May appears to have been established at Mingary Castle in Ardnamurchan.[101] The expedition secured the submission of a number of chiefs, who obtained confirmations of their charters between July 1495 and October 1496.[102] In addition James took control of Islay and Tiree, where the comptroller was sent on a commission of assessment.[103] The expenses of the expedition and of the measures undertaken by the king's subordinates after his departure appear to have been met by a heavy 'taxt of the Ilis'.[104] Possibly one of the results was the construction of a new castle at Loch Kilkerran (the present Campbeltown),[105] which became a base

[94] *E.R.*, XI. 181.   [95] *T.A.*, I. 215, 237; *E.R.*, x. 407, 451, 478.
[96] *E.R.*, x. 477; *T.A.*, I. 245–54; *R.M.S.*, II. No. 2420; *R.S.S.*, I. No. 448.
[97] *T.A.*, I. 244.   [98] Gregory, *Western Highlands*, p. 89.
[99] *Ibid.*, pp. 89–90; E. Curtis, *Medieval Ireland*, p. 355; Conway, *Henry VII*, p. 96; *T.A.*, I. 238, 239.   [100] *T.A.*, I. 240–2.
[101] *E.R.*, x. 473, 474, 478, 486, 494, 513, 515, 569, 571; *R.M.S.*, II. No. 2253.
[102] *R.M.S.*, II. Nos. 2264, 2281, 2286, 2287, 2327, 2329; *Highland Papers*, I. 242.   [103] *E.R.*, x. 550.   [104] *T.A.*, I. 312, 315.
[105] Gregory, *Western Highlands*, p. 93.

for the king's next three hurried expeditions to the Isles in March, May and August 1498.[106] These were probably occasioned by the utter unworkability of an act of council of 3 October 1496 which declared that any summons issued upon any inhabitant of the lordship of the Isles before 26 April 1497 was to be executed by the chief of his clan. If the latter failed to perform this invidious task he himself was to be proceeded against as if he were the principal defendant in the case. In the summer of 1498 the submission of Alexander MacLeod of Dunvegan, Torquil MacLeod of Lewis, Ranald MacAllan of Uist and Eigg, and Angus 'Rewochsoun Makranald' of Eigg, Arisaig and Morar, was marked by the issue of charters granting them the lands they held within the lordship of the Isles.[107]

These last charters, at least, were not affected by the general revocation that the king enacted at Duchal Castle on 16 March 1498, the day before he attained his 'perfect age' of twenty-five.[108] It was presumably to make clear that previous charters were now invalid that letters were entrusted on 20 March to a servant of Lord Gordon 'that passit in Ilis to all the hedis men of the cuntree with the kingis writingis'.[109] To the cowed nobility of the Lowlands the repeated extortion of blackmail for the renewal of charters after a revocation had become common practice. To the chiefs of the Isles it was a novel and insulting infringement of their rights. Most must have been unwilling, if not also unable, to pay the compositions that were expected, and therefore, in the view of the government, became mere tenants-at-will.[110] Nor did the king, pursuing a wild goose chase in quest of international renown, resume his personal intervention in Hebridean affairs. His replacement by the Earl of Argyll was initiated in August 1499 when the latter was granted custody of Tarbert Castle. Much more ominous was the issue on 22 April 1500 of a commission of assessment, of which Argyll was to be an essential member, to grant three-year tacks of all the lands of the lordship of the Isles with the exception of Islay and Kintyre. In all the lands subject to this commission Argyll was to be the king's lieutenant-general with virtually limitless powers for a period of three years.[111] On 11 August 1501 comparable powers were bestowed upon Lord Gordon, who had lately succeeded his father as third Earl of Huntly : he could compel the 'erlis, lordis, baronis and hed kinnysmen' north of the

[106] T.A., I. clxiv–clxv, clxvi–clxvii.
[107] R.M.S., II. Nos. 2420, 2424, 2438, 2439.
[108] T.A., I. cxlv, 383; E.R., x. lxvi--lxvii.   [109] T.A., I. 383.
[110] See Gregory, Western Highlands, p. 94.   [111] R.S.S., I. Nos. 413, 513, 520.

Mounth to give 'bandis and oblissingis' to keep the peace, and was to enforce payment of the king's rents in Lochaber.[112] Some months before, the king had granted to Duncan Stewart of Appin certain lands in Glencoe.[113] This may have inspired the MacIans of Glencoe to release Donald Dubh from Argyll's custody in Inchconnel Castle and to convey him to the protection of Torquil MacLeod of Lewis.[114]

Donald Dubh was the son of Angus Og by a daughter of Argyll.[115] Although Angus was an illegitimate son of John, the last Lord of the Isles, he had been recognised in a tailzie of 1476 as the rightful heir; and although Donald Dubh was in turn regarded by the government, rightly or wrongly, as an illegitimate son of Angus, he was the representative of the direct line of the Lords of the Isles now that the humiliated John of the Isles had died. It came as a shock to the government to learn that Donald was now in the unreliable hands of Torquil MacLeod, who was summoned before the lords of council in November 1501 but did not compear.[116] To make matters worse, MacKenzie of Kintail and Farquhar Mackintosh contrived to escape from prison. The first, however, was soon slain and Mackintosh (to James's great relief) was soon retaken.[117] Nonetheless, within the next two years it was evident that there was a widespread movement to revive the lordship of the Isles on behalf of Donald Dubh; in the parliament of March 1504 Lauchlan MacLean of Duart was forfeited for the treasonable maintenance of 'Donald, bastard and unlauchtfull sonne of umquhile Anguss of the Ylis, bastard sonne to umquhile Johne of the Ilis . . . for the causatioune of oure soverane lordis liegis to obey to the saide Donalde as Lord of Ylis . . . usurpand oure soverane lordis autorite'.[118] Thereafter summonses for treason proliferated.[119] Nor were royalist forces inactive: in the parliament of March 1504 Huntly undertook to besiege, capture and garrison the castles of Eilean Donan in Loch Alsh and Strome on Loch Carron, 'quhilkis ar rycht necessar for the danting of the Ilis', providing that the king sent a ship with artillery to aid in the sieges. At the same time an incomplete record suggests that separate commands covering the whole of the Highlands and Isles were entrusted

---

[112] *Ibid.*, Nos. 722, 723.   [113] *R.M.S.*, II. No. 2565.

[114] *E.R.*, XII. lvii; Gregory, *Western Highlands*, p. 100.

[115] He is not to be confused with the Donald Owre mentioned in William Dunbar's poem and the *Treasurer's Accounts*. See J. D. Mackie's review of R. L. Mackie's *King James IV* (*S.H.R.*, XXXVIII. 133–6, at 135).

[116] Mackie, *James IV*, pp. 190–1; *R.S.S.*, I. No. 792 .

[117] *T.A.*, II. xcii.   [118] *A.P.S.*, II. 241, 247–8.

[119] *Ibid.*, 256–66, *passim*.

to Huntly, Crawford, the Earl Marischal and Lord Lovat.[120] Huntly was also to be consulted about the re-building of Inverlochy Castle, and Argyll was to look after the masons at work at Dunaverty and Loch Kilkerran. Finally an inventory was to be taken of the king's artillery in all parts of the realm.[121] Some, at least, was placed on board the ships which the king inspected at Dumbarton in April 1504. The flotilla, fitted out by Sir Andrew Wood, accompanied by Hans Gunnare and Robert Barton, and commanded by James Hamilton, the new Earl of Arran, set sail in May 1504 and seems to have bombarded the almost inaccessible castle of Cairn-na-Burgh in the Treshnish Isles until it was taken and entrusted to Argyll, who for its custody in the next four years was paid over £400.[122] The novel demonstration of the powers inherent in naval artillery seems to have resulted in the submission of MacIan of Ardnamurchan, who was graciously received at court in November 1504.[123] In May 1505 Lauchlan MacLean of Duart was among the chiefs who received a five-year respite for their part in supporting Donald Dubh;[124] and in June 1506 commissioners of assessment met at Dunadd to compose the feuds of the Isles.[125] The last stronghold of the insurgents was Torquil MacLeod's castle of Stornoway, which was attacked by Huntly in the summer of 1506 with a naval squadron based upon Dumbarton and equipped with guns brought from Edinburgh Castle.[126] By October 1506 Stornoway had evidently fallen and by August 1507 Donald Dubh was safely warded in Stirling Castle.[127]

The rising of Donald Dubh had elicited from the parliament of March 1504 an unwonted show of concern for the betterment of government in the Highlands and Isles, where 'the pepill ar almaist gane wilde'. Their misbehaviour was imputed to the 'greit abusioune of justice' which resulted from the absence of justice ayres, justices and sheriffs. In future the North Isles were to be served by a justice and a sheriff based (all too cautiously) at Inverness or Dingwall. Another justice and sheriff were to serve the South Isles from Tarbert or Loch Kilkerran (Campbeltown). New sheriffs were also to be established in Ross and Caithness. These arrangements were based on the reasoning that the sheriffdom of Inverness was 'oure greit' and required to be divided so that officers were on hand 'to put gude reule

[120] A.P.S., II. 240.   [121] Ibid., 248.
[122] T.A., II. 428, 429, 431, 433, 434, 435, 442, 446, 448; E.R., XIII. 224.
[123] T.A., III. 103; R.M.S., II. No. 2895.
[124] R.S.S., I. Nos. 1083, 1163, 1174, 1197, 1203, 1208.
[125] E.R., XII. 709–10.   [126] T.A., III. 200, 338, 340, 350.
[127] Ibid., lxxxii, 349.

amang the pepill'. Thus, as Bishop Lesley approvingly remarked, 'it was certanely knowen quhair and in quhat place justice shuld be ministrated in the justice arys and shiriff courtis'.[128] In addition the troubled regions were to be purged of the remnants of ancient Celtic law and be ruled by the king's laws and by 'nane othir lawis'.[129]

The resources of the kirk were to be used to further such ends. During the episcopate of John Campbell, Bishop of the Isles between 1487 and 1510, there was an attempt to turn the ancient abbey of Iona, formerly under the patronage of the MacDonalds, into a bishop's seat that would replace the cathedral on the Isle of Man lost to the English. Nothing definite resulted. But in 1510, when Campbell, a man with local connections, was succeeded by the king's treasurer, George Hepburn, member of that favoured Lowland kin, the king successfully petitioned the pope that the new bishop might hold Arbroath and Iona *in commendam*, so that 'his authority and nobility of race may bind that uncivilised people in devotion to the church'.[130] Similarly there was an attempt, ultimately successful, to suppress the abbey of Saddell, long associated with the MacDonalds, so that its revenues might be diverted to the bishopric of Argyll.[131] In Argyll also, a bishop with local connections (Robert Colquhoun) was succeeded in 1497 by a Lowlander, David Hamilton; since he served among 'wild people' he received royal grants to strengthen his hand, including a grant of ferms in Kintyre to maintain the episcopal castle that had been built there, as well as another grant of the judicial profits of justice ayres and sheriff courts in Argyll, Lorne, Knapdale, Kintyre and Cowal.[132]

From 1507 until the end of the reign an illusory peace settled upon the Highlands and Isles, and, in Bishop Lesley's estimation, they had been thoroughly daunted by the king's firmness.[133] The MacDonalds of the Isles, like the Black Douglases before them, had disappeared as overmighty subjects. But whenever the crown, in the language of James VI, managed to 'beate downe the hornes of proude oppressours',[134] a power vacuum was created that the crown was usually unable to fill. That did not mean that there was no one

[128] *A.P.S.*, II. 241–2, cc. 3, 4, 5; 249, cc. 3, 5; Lesley, *History*, p. 73.

[129] *A.P.S.*, II. 247, c. 27; 252, c. 24.

[130] Watt, *Fasti*, pp. 207–8; Mackie, *James IV*, p. 158; *Highland Papers*, IV. 185; *R.S.S.*, I. No. 184; *R.M.S.*, II. No. 3784.

[131] A. L. Brown, 'The Cistercian Abbey of Saddell, Kintyre', *Innes Review*, XX. 130–7.   [132] *R.S.S.*, I. Nos. 1196, 2369, 3208.

[133] *E.R.*, XIII. xxviii–xxxix; Gregory, *Western Highlands*, pp. 104–5; Lesley, *History*, p. 73.

[134] *The Basilicon Doron of King James VI* (S.T.S.), I. 69.

else who yearned to fill it. Many barons or chiefs who were under-mighty but ambitious began to raise their horns and strive for mastery among themselves. Thus, so the MacMhuirich seannachies recorded, 'there was a great struggle among the Gael for power'.[135]

The struggle took three forms. One of these was shown in the attempts to restore the lordship of the Isles until the death of Donald Dubh in 1545. Another was shown in the ambition of the heads of cadet branches of the MacDonalds to achieve some of the pre-eminence that had formerly belonged to the eldest branch. A third was shown in the strivings of other clans to increase their power and possessions at the expense of all the MacDonalds. Thus the result of the forfeiture of the Lords of the Isles was unusual chaos in the West Highlands and Isles throughout the sixteenth century whenever (and it was more usual than unusual) the crown was afflicted by minorities or other distractions.

Those who came off best in the threefold struggle were not the surviving MacDonalds but the Campbells, the Gordons, and, eventu-ally, the MacKenzies. In so far as they kept on good terms with the Edinburgh government their aggressions at the expense of weaker neighbours were unrestrained; and the latter, dispossessed of their lands, swelled the number of 'broken' clans, notably the MacGregors, whose resentful depredations caused further disorder. The accumula-tion of land and power by the Campbells was particularly spectacu-lar. Sir Duncan Forrester, a Lowland intruder, found it expedient to resign his barony of Skipinch to the Earl of Argyll in 1502.[136] Further territorial expansion was achieved when one Campbell married the heiress of the last Stewart Lord of Lorne[137] and another married the heiress of the Thane of Cawdor.[138] Similar advancement was achieved by Alexander Gordon, third Earl of Huntly. Like Argyll, he received sweeping powers as a commissioner for the assessment of lands,[139] he was granted custody of the castles of Inver-lochy and Inverness,[140] and was generally regarded as the king's chief agent in the northern Highlands and northern Hebrides.[141] In addi-tion the Gordons profited from the afflictions of John, Earl of Suther-land, upon whom a brieve of idiotry had been served in 1494; in 1514 they eventually won the earldom of Sutherland through mar-

---

[135] 'The Red Book of Clanranald', in *Reliquiae Celticae*, ed. Alexander Mac-Bain and John Kennedy, II. 163. [136] *R.M.S.*, II. Nos. 2669, 2670.
[137] Gregory, *Western Highlands*, p. 83. [138] *Highland Papers*, I. 125-7.
[139] E.g. *R.S.S.*, I. No. 1579. [140] *R.M.S.*, II. Nos. 2950, 3379.
[141] *R.S.S.*, I. No. 1690; Gregory, *Western Highlands*, pp. 105-6.

riage.[142] Thus James IV's intervention in the Highlands and Isles scarcely reduced disorder but made the Campbells and Gordons the crown's indispensable agents in controlling continuing disorder.

This situation might have been avoided had James not been distracted by diplomacy. From the outset of the reign a succession of truces [143] had not concealed the surreptitious hostility that existed between him and Henry VII.[144] Nor did the truces prevent unofficial warfare at sea : in 1489 and 1490 Andrew Wood, commanding the *Yellow Carvel* and the *Flower*, repelled English marauders at the estuaries of the Forth and Tay; a charter of May 1491 allowed him to use English prisoners in building a fortalice at Largo 'to resist and expel those pirates and raiders who have often attacked from the sea';[145] and another charter of 1504 alluded to his good service when, on some past occasion, an English fleet and army had tried to capture Dunbar.[146] Injuries inflicted by the English on land and sea were evidently substantial enough for Henry VII to pay a thousand marks and fifty pounds in compensation.[147] The sparse official references to such warfare are supplemented by Pitscottie's circumstantial account of a naval encounter 'verie terrabill to sie', when, in the summer of 1490, Captain Wood captured three English vessels commanded by a certain Stephen Bull.[148]

Anglo-Scottish animosity was a factor that was not ignored when European diplomacy took a new turn after 1494 thanks to the invasions of Italy by Charles VIII and Louis XII of France. Italy became the battleground of Europe, where the new monarchies of France and Spain contended for mastery, while the papacy strove to protect and expand its own territories. In the parliament of May 1491 it had been decided that Scotland's traditional alliance with France should be renewed,[149] and an embassy, which included the seasick poet, William Dunbar, set sail. The result was a ratification on 4 March 1492 of a Franco-Scottish treaty directed against England.[150] It was the aim of the Spanish monarchs, Ferdinand and Isabella, to disrupt the Franco-Scottish alliance and to align Scotland, as well as England, alongside Spain, or at least to prevent the

---

[142] *T.A.*, I. 238, 239; *A.D.C.*, I. 378, 379; *E.R.*, XIII. cxxxvi.

[143] E.g. *Rot. Scot.*, II. 488, 503–5; *Cal. Docs. Scot.*, IV. Nos. 1545, 1592; *A.P.S.*, II. 220, c. 9; 226, c. 14. [144] Conway, *Henry VII*, p. 32.

[145] *R.M.S.*, II. No. 2040; *A.P.S.*, II. 227. [146] *R.M.S.*, II. No. 2775.

[147] *Cal. Docs. Scot.*, IV. No. 1597; Conway, *Henry VII*, pp. 40–1.

[148] Pitscottie, *Historie*, I. 226–30. [149] *A.P.S.*, II. 224, c. 2.

[150] *T.A.*, I. cix–cx.

Scots from threatening England, so that it had a free hand to engage in their continental schemes. In June 1489 parliament had advised delaying the conclusion of an alliance with France until Spanish envoys arrived in Scotland (with alternative offers).[151] When a Spanish embassy was received at Linlithgow in August 1489 its offers were tantalising enough to win the envoys a 'reward' of six hundred crowns, tactfully secreted in six pairs of gloves. Although some kind of indenture was concluded the ambassadors appear to have exceeded their powers by offering James the hand of an infanta of Spain, while all that the Catholic Monarchs were prepared to offer was an illegitimate daughter of Ferdinand. They reproached their envoys for deluding the Scots, but somewhat inconsistently thought it wise to put off James with false hopes lest he drew closer to the French king.[152]

Whether or not the Scots were deluded, they remained antagonistic towards Henry VII, even after he had reached an understanding with France in the treaty of Étaples of 3 November 1492.[153] It was not apparent to contemporaries that the Wars of the Roses had ended; if English internal dissensions could be revived the Scots might profit, particularly by a recovery of Berwick. Thus Scotland played a part in the schemes of Margaret of York, Dowager Duchess of Burgundy and sister of the late Edward IV. In 1489 and 1490 her emissaries visited the Scottish court, which had already issued safe-conducts to Lord Lovel and all other Englishmen who adopted his Yorkist 'opinion'.[154] James's domestic preoccupations, particularly in the Highlands and Isles, prevented any immediate attachment to the cause of the white rose. But by 1495 this was represented by a likely pretender: Perkin Warbeck, a Flemish impostor,[155] was recognised by Duchess Margaret, and temporarily by Maximilian, King of the Romans, as Richard, Duke of York, the younger of the two sons of Edward IV who had been imprisoned in the Tower by Richard III. In the summer of 1495 the pretender stirred up support in Ireland, and, having failed there,[156] made his way to Scotland. The Scots had already committed themselves to his cause: in July 1495 Bishop Elphinstone and other envoys had asked Maximilian (now emperor designate) to join in an alliance against England; Maximilian's daughter, so they vainly hoped, might marry James, and, in return

[151] *A.P.S.*, II. 214, c. 3.   [152] *T.A.*, I. xci–xciii.

[153] Mackie, *James IV*, pp. 67, 78, 81.

[154] *T.A.*, I. 99, 120, 130; *R.M.S.*, II. Nos. 1738, 1798; Conway, *Henry VII*, pp. 31, 48.

[155] For his origins and early career see *T.A.*, I. cxxiv–cxxvi.

[156] E. Curtis, *Medieval Ireland*, pp. 354–5.

for supporting the 'Duke of York', the Scots might regain Berwick.[157] In November 1495 preparations were being made to receive 'Prince Richard of England' at Stirling.[158]

Whether or not James took Perkin's pretensions seriously it suited his policy to appear to do so. Perkin was married with great pomp to Lady Catherine Gordon, daughter of the Earl of Huntly. A special contribution was levied to provide the pretender with a yearly allowance of £1,200, and a 'tax of spears' or 'spear silver'—doubtless similar to the old feudal scutage—was exacted to finance military preparations.[159] There was a flurry of diplomatic interchanges as James made ready to invade England, and the courts of England and Spain sought to induce him to change his policy. Robert Blackadder, Archbishop of Glasgow, was twice sent to win concessions (and an infanta) from Ferdinand and Isabella, who at least urged the pope (though in vain) to make Blackadder a cardinal.[160] They also sent Don Pedro de Ayala on an embassy to Scotland in the summer of 1496. Although this likable hidalgo failed to alter James's policy he lingered amiably at court for more than a year, and in his reports to Spain gave an account sometimes shrewd, sometimes flattering, of Scotland and its king.[161] Less flattering accounts of James, together with proposals for the kidnapping of Perkin, were sent to the English court by Sir John Ramsay. He furnished precise details of James's preparations to break the truce and invade England on behalf of the pretender, who had promised to cede Berwick and pay the Scots fifty thousand marks.[162] While Ayala exaggerated Scottish military power Ramsay assessed it more critically and pointed out all too prophetically (though prematurely) how James's 'young adventurousness' could be duly curbed if his invading army were intercepted on its passage back to Scotland.[163]

On 19 September 1496 the host set out from Ellem, crossed the Tweed, and ravaged the valley of the Till. No Englishman would rally to Perkin. James tired of the expedition in a few days. In the following month he went hawking in Perthshire.[164] Early in June 1497 it was the turn of the English to make a foray as far as Duns,[165]

[157] Mackie, *James IV*, pp. 78–9; Conway, *Henry VII*, p. 99.
[158] *T.A.*, I. cxxii–cxxiii.
[159] *Ibid.*, cxxvii; *R.S.S.*, I. No. 405; Lesley, *History*, pp. 63–5.
[160] Mackie, *James IV*, pp. 81–2.
[161] *T.A.*, I. cxxxv; *E.R.*, XI. lviii; Brown, *Early Travellers*, pp. 39–55.
[162] Pinkerton, *History*, II. 437; Conway, *Henry VII*, pp. 99–102.
[163] *T.A.*, I. cxxxvii–cxxxix.   [164] *Ibid.*, cxxxix–cxliii; *E.R.*, XI. lix–lx.
[165] *T.A.*, I. 341; *R.M.S.*, II. Nos. 2362, 2365.

after which James led another brief raid across the Tweed.[166] Perkin was now a nuisance rather than an asset and was allowed to depart with his wife in a Breton ship aptly named the *Cuckoo*. Having sailed from Ayr with Robert Barton in July 1497 he landed first at Cork, then in Cornwall. By October he was Henry's prisoner, and two years later he was executed.[167]

Perkin's departure did not hold back James's preparations for 'the great raid', for which more 'spear silver' was exacted, as well as private contributions from various notables, particularly the abbots. Minstrels played as Mons Meg was trundled from Edinburgh Castle (until its carriage collapsed). The host mustered at Upsetlington on 5 August and vainly assaulted Norham Castle for a week. Only a rebellion that had broken out in Cornwall in May 1497 had prevented an overwhelming concentration of English forces. When Thomas Howard, Earl of Surrey, marched north, James was prepared to fight, but only on chivalric terms : possession of Berwick was to be settled either by a general engagement between the two armies or by a hand-to-hand combat between the two commanders. When Surrey announced that he was not authorised to hazard the town on such terms James 'ffled shamefully and sodeynly with all his company'. To the disappointment of Henry VII five days of foul weather sufficed to disperse Surrey's troops before the Scots could be sufficiently chastised. Thanks to the mediation of Don Pedro, who had helped to amuse James at cards during the siege of Norham, a seven-year truce (later extended) was concluded at Ayton on 30 September 1497.[168]

James was lucky to have been extricated from campaigning so lightly. His preparations had been costly, the results minimal; and service in the host was unpopular.[169] But his personal valour, which aroused the admiration of Don Pedro, left the king with an undiminished conceit of his qualities as a general. A moderate defeat might have given him a grasp of military realities : it was reported to the Spanish court that James had seen 'the ears of the wolf';[170] but he had not seen its jaws. The eagerness of Henry VII to reach a settle-

---

[166] *T.A.*, I. cl–cli.
[167] Conway, *Henry VII*, pp. 109–11; *A.D.C.P.*, p. lx; *T.A.*, I. cli–cliv; *E.R.*, XI. lxi–lxii; Lesley, *History*, pp. 66–7.
[168] Conway, *Henry VII*, pp. 109–14; Mackie, *James IV*, pp. 86–9; *T.A.*, I. cliv–clviii; *E.R.*, XI. lxii–lxiv; Lesley, *History*, pp. 65–6.
[169] A number of remissions were subsequently granted to those who were absent from the host at Ayton (*R.S.S.*, I. Nos. 1956–8, 1961, 1962, 2095, 2100, 2189, 2330).   [170] Mackie, *James IV*, p. 90.

ment left the impression that Scotland's military might was held in awe.

At last, however, James was willing to reach a settlement with Henry, who assuaged the Scottish king's rankled pride when the latest truce was jeopardised by an affray at Norham in the summer of 1498. In November Bishop Fox of Durham was received in private audience at Melrose in his dual capacity as custodian of Norham and close adviser of Henry VII. James made it plain that his prior condition for peace and friendship with England was a marriage between himself and Henry's elder daughter, Margaret, then nine years old.[171]

From the very outset of his reign James had used his own marriage prospects as an asset in internal politics and international diplomacy.[172] He, who quested the hand of an infanta of Spain or an emperor's daughter, can only have been insulted in 1493 when Henry offered him the daughter of the Countess of Wiltshire.[173] Although James pursued his matrimonial quest assiduously he did so with no sense of haste : he had two younger brothers, James, Duke of Ross, and John, Earl of Mar, to assure the succession while he himself dallied with mistresses in a court graced by his aunt, Lady Margaret Stewart, onetime mistress of Lord Crichton. The king's first mistress was Marion Boyd. Their son, Alexander Stewart, born in 1493, was to become Archbishop of St Andrews.[174] The second royal mistress, adopted in 1496, was Margaret Drummond, daughter of Lord Drummond. She and two sisters died suddenly in 1502 after a suspect breakfast.[175] The generosity that James had displayed towards Margaret and her kinsfolk [176] was surpassed by that shown to her rival and successor, Janet Kennedy, daughter of Lord Kennedy. In 1498, it would appear, she was about to be married to Bell-the-Cat, who, having prematurely granted her his lordship of Bothwell, had to content himself with Katherine Stirling.[177] In 1499 the new Lady Bothwell bore a son to the king, who expressed his thankfulness for Janet's 'services' by granting her first the lordship of Menteith, and then, in June 1501, the castle and lands of Darnaway, conveniently

[171] *Ibid.*, pp. 90–2.
[172] E.g. *A.P.S.*, II. 207, c. 2 ; 224, c. 3 ; 230, c. 1 ; 233–4, c. 11.
[173] *Cal. Docs. Scot.*, IV. No. 1588.
[174] Mackie, *James IV*, p. 81 ; *T.A.*, I. cxxxii–cxxxiii ; *E.R.*, XII. xl–xlix.
[175] Mackie, *James IV*, pp. 80–81,. 100–101 ; *T.A.*, I. cxxxii–cxxxiii ; II. 358–451, *passim* ; Tytler, *History*, I. pt. ii, 394.
[176] *R.M.S.*, II. Nos. 2299, 2311 ; *R.S.S.*, I. No. 326.
[177] *R.M.S.*, II. Nos. 2434, 2457, 2539 ; *R.S.S.*, I. No. 258.

sited on the route to St Duthac's shrine. A few days later their son,
James Stewart, was created Earl of Moray.[178]

Meanwhile the project discussed at Melrose in November 1498
had been followed by lengthy negotiations that encountered no insuperable obstacle. Henry VII was aware that by marrying his
daughter to the Scottish king he might make it possible for James, or
his issue, to succeed to the English throne. In such an event, however,
so Henry informed his councillors, the greater would draw the less—
a Scottish king might win England but he would inevitably make it
the predominant partner in a Greater Britain. On 24 January 1502,
soon after the bride had attained the nubile age of twelve, the marriage treaty was concluded in London: Margaret Tudor was to receive a dower of lands and castles in Scotland worth £2,000 sterling
or £6,000 Scots a year; James was to receive a dowry of £10,000
sterling or £30,000 Scots.[179] The marriage treaty was accompanied
by another—the first since 1328—of perpetual peace between Scotland and England.

In the entourage of Bishop Andrew Forman, one of the Scottish
negotiators, was the poet William Dunbar, who acknowledged his
hospitable reception in the Guildhall by a poem in praise of London,
'the floure of cities all'. In the summer of 1503 he was ready with
another poem to celebrate the marriage of 'The Thrissil and the
Rose'.[180] Costly preparations had been made in both countries for
the northward progress of the royal bride, who was received at Lamberton Kirk by the Archbishop of Glasgow, the Earl of Bothwell and
other notables. At Dunbar the guns of the newly rebuilt castle gave a
royal salute. At Dalkeith Castle the king, magnificently arrayed in
velvet and cloth of gold, first met his bride. Four days later they
made their state entry into Edinburgh amid an ostentatious display
of religious and secular pageantry. On 8 August the marriage was
solemnised in the abbey of Holyrood and there followed five days of
festivities in the new palace of Holyroodhouse, where the king belted
forty-one knights and created three new earls—Arran, Montrose and
Glencairn. Despite James's incredible expenses—each of his two
gowns cost more than £600 and the wine bill exceeded £2,000—
some of the English guests were not impressed; the new queen wrote
tearfully to her father; and James paid a discreet visit to St Duthac's

[178] R.S.S., I. Nos. 495, 730; R.M.S., II. No. 2585; Lesley, History, p. 81.
[179] Cal. Docs. Scot., IV. No. 1680; R.M.S., II. Nos. 2602–4, 2624; E.R., XII.
xlix–liv.
[180] Mackie, James IV, pp. 95–6.

shrine (and Darnaway).[181] In July 1505 he received from Henry the final payment of the queen's dowry.[182] Until Henry's death in 1509 the relationship between Scotland and England was one of friendship and co-operation,[183] and neither country was seriously engaged in continental warfare.

That did not mean that there was any slackening in James's diplomacy, which was addressed not only towards France, Spain, England and the papacy but towards lesser powers with which James had a connection through kinship, commerce, or chivalric ambition. Kinship accounted for James's protective interest in the duchy of Guelders.[184] Both kinship and commerce explained his dealings with Veere and its Van Borselen lords,[185] as well as his support for his uncle, King Hans, who held uneasy sway over Denmark, Norway, and sometimes Sweden.[186] In August 1488 Junker Gerhard, uncle of King Hans and grand-uncle of James, had visited Scotland, possibly as a belated mediator whose mission was rendered unnecessary by Sauchieburn.[187] The parliaments of June 1489, February 1490 and May 1491 approved the sending of an embassy to renew the alliance with Denmark.[188] The successful mission of Sir James Ogilvy of Airlie in 1492 was followed by two return visits of the Danish chancellor,[189] and in 1499 France became a party to the alliance. Thus 'Danish-Scottish relations began to assume an importance in general European politics'.[190] Soon afterwards the troubles of King Hans became so acute that Bishop Lesley wrongly believed that he came in person to Scotland to seek aid.[191] The aid was certainly forthcoming : a tax was levied and in May 1502 there were preparations for 'the

---

[181] *Ibid.*, pp. 102–12; Pitscottie, *Historie*, I. 238–40; Lesley, *History*, pp. 72, 73.

[182] *R.S.S.*, I. No. 1117. [183] Lesley, *History*, pp. 72, 79.

[184] *Ibid.*, p. 74; *James IV, Letters*, Nos. 71–3, 226, 233, 283, 297; Mackie, *James IV*, pp. 113, 212, 213.

[185] Lesley, *History*, p. 75; *R.M.S.*, II. No. 3165; *James IV, Letters*, Nos. 130, 186, 208, 225.

[186] For the background see the section on Scotland and Denmark in *James IV, Letters*, pp. xxxix–xliii; W. Stanford Reid, 'The Place of Denmark in Scottish Foreign Policy, 1470–1540', *Juridical Review*, LVIII. 183–200; James Dow, 'Skotter in sixteenth-century Scania', *S.H.R.*, XLIV. 34–51; Thorkild L. Christensen, 'Scoto-Danish relations in the sixteenth century', *ibid.*, XLVIII. 80–97, and 'Scots in Denmark in the sixteenth century', *ibid.*, XLIX. 125–45.

[187] He was to pay a second visit in 1497 (*T.A.*, I. lxxvi, cxliv).

[188] *A.P.S.*, II. 214, c. 4; 219, c. 6; 224, c. 4; Mackie, *James IV*, p. 54.

[189] Lesley, *History*, p. 62; *T.A.*, I. cxii, cxviii, and n. 5.

[190] W. Stanford Reid, *op. cit.*, *Juridical Review*, LVIII. 186; *R.S.S.*, I. No. 391.

[191] Lesley, *History*, pp. 72–3.

furnising furth of our soverane lordis armey to pas to Denmark'.[192]
An expeditionary force of a few ships and some two thousand men
eventually returned, having failed to forestall the fall of Stockholm
and the capture of Queen Christina by the insurgent Swedes.[193]
Their alliance with Lübeck was likely to maintain a Hanseatic
stranglehold upon Baltic trade, to the disadvantage of both Denmark
and Scotland. Although James sent no further troops to his uncle's
aid his diplomacy helped to achieve the acceptance of a truce by
Lübeck in 1507. It scarcely lasted a year. In 1508 James sent one of
his new ships, the *Margaret*, commanded by Andrew Barton, to assist
King Hans, and in the following year Andrew and his brother Robert
were busy in the Baltic.[194] Indirectly both this naval activity and
occasional attempts to strengthen the tripartite alliance of Scotland,
Denmark and France, would contribute to crisis a few years later.[195]
Meanwhile, however, James's far-reaching diplomacy, the growing
prestige of his sea-captains, and his own role as peace-maker, combined to give Scotland increasing weight in European politics. The
marriage alliance with England had caused no breach with France.[196]
From the time of James's marriage until the death of his father-in-
law, Scotland had no serious foreign foe and many apparent friends.
This favourable situation was recognised by Pope Julius II, who
presented James with the golden rose and the sword of state still to
be seen in Edinburgh Castle.[197]

James's attitude towards the papacy was the normal one of the
age : he was 'quick to exploit, ready to enlist the aid of parliament
when necessary, scrupulous about procedures, cautious, but grateful
too'.[198] Not only had the papacy failed to learn any lessons from the
conciliarist movement but it had altered for the worse since the death
of Innocent VIII in 1492. His successor, Roderigo Borgia, who
reigned as Alexander VI from 1492 to 1503, was debauched and
sinister; and Julius II (1503–1513) was a warrior pope who in 1508
formed the league of Cambrai to despoil the Venetians.[199] The decline in the prestige of the papacy made it less able to resist the chal-

[192] *A.D.C.P.*, p. lix; *E.R.*, XII. xxxvii.   [193] See *James IV, Letters*, No. 37.

[194] W. Stanford Reid, *op. cit., Juridical Review*, LVIII. 189–90, and 'Seapower in the Foreign Policy of James IV of Scotland', *Medievalia et Humanistica*,
XV. 97–107, at 99, 102–3.   [195] Pp. 595–6 below.

[196] Mackie, *James IV*, pp. 100, 101; Lesley, *History*, pp. 74, 76, 77–8.

[197] Lesley, *History*, pp. 63, 75; Charles Burns, *op. cit., Innes Review*, XX.
150–94.

[198] Leslie J. Macfarlane, *op. cit., Innes Review*, XX. 111–29, at 128–9.

[199] Mackie, *James IV*, p. 202.

lenge of new monarchy. Although Innocent VIII's successors were not bound to observe the terms of the indult granted to James III in 1487 the crown regarded it as a perpetual privilege, and the parliament of June 1493 was prompted to ordain that the king should cause it to 'be observit and kepit, and suffer na promotionis to gang throw in the contrare'.[200] It was nothing new that appointments to the greater benefices were made by papal provision, but this was now set in motion by the crown : 'the really effective transaction . . . came to be the royal nomination with advice of council'.[201] Ever resourceful in legal devices the papacy encouraged the practice of resignation *in favorem*, whereby an incumbent resigned his benefice to a successor, thus avoiding a vacancy in which the king might intervene.[202] But there was nothing to prevent the king from inspiring such a resignation to suit his own purposes. Moreover the parliaments of October 1488, June 1493 and July 1496 saw a wholesale revival of the barratry legislation of James I and of all the legislation of James III that had been designed to safeguard and increase the crown's ecclesiastical patronage, reduce the flow of bullion to the *curia*, and control individual recourse to Rome, the intent being that the crown should enjoy a monopoly of trafficking with the papacy.[203] So long as the latter received the traditional common services and annates it cared little how the traffic was handled : James was even conceded the right to nominate to thirty benefices.[204] The register of the privy seal shows that throughout the reign he made over two hundred nominations or presentations ;[205] and William Dunbar, the poet, was not alone in being granted a pension while waiting until the king provided him with a benefice.[206]

Not only did the crown control many ecclesiastical appointments but it was responsible for a major change in ecclesiastical organisation : the demand for a second archbishopric was motivated partly by a desire for a parity with England, mostly by politics. Although Archbishop Scheves stubbornly opposed the erection of Glasgow as a second archiepiscopal see, the papacy was reluctantly induced to comply : on 9 January 1492 Robert Blackadder was created Archbishop of Glasgow and assigned control as metropolitan, primate and

[200] *A.P.S.*, II. 232, c. 4.
[201] R. K. Hannay, *The Scottish Crown and the Papacy*, p. 10.
[202] See *Wigtown Charters*, Nos. 147 and 197.
[203] *A.P.S.*, II. 209–10, cc. 13, 14; 232–3, cc. 2–9; 237–8, c. 2; R. K. Hannay, *The Scottish Crown and the Papacy*, p. 10.
[204] *R.S.S.*, I. No. 1596.   [205] *Ibid.*, *passim*.
[206] *Ibid.*, Nos. 2018, 2079, 2144, 2119, 2199, 2269, 2302, 2412, 2423.

legatus natus over the sees of Galloway and Argyll and (initially) Dunkeld and Dunblane as well. Wasteful controversy between the two archbishops ensued (to the annoyance of parliament) and the leadership that might have been forthcoming from an effective primacy of St Andrews was undermined.[207]

The sequel to the death of Archbishop Scheves in 1497 demonstrated the trend of affairs. To pursue a cynical scheme of financial chicanery the king secured the appointment of his brother, James, Duke of Ross (about twenty years of age) as the next Archbishop of St Andrews, obtaining in exchange the valuable ducal lands. Whatever the merits of the duke-archbishop he was too young to be consecrated. At his death in 1504 the king stimulated the practice of using the kirk as an employment bureau for the illegitimate sons of the crown and nobility by bestowing the archbishopric upon his eleven-year-old bastard son, Alexander Stewart, which in effect meant that the archbishopric was administered by the crown.[208] The boy-archbishop, like his predecessor, was also nominally made chancellor and was granted one or two rich commendatorships; he (or the crown) thus controlled the abbey of Dunfermline and the priory of Coldingham. These scandalous and demoralising appointments made it clear that the kirk had become a department of state: 'the papacy has been criticised, with some justification, for its failure to resist such abuses, but the role of secular power, which sought them, deserves no less severe criticism'.[209]

When bishops and abbots were increasingly nominated for worldly reasons their spiritual function was bound to suffer. It may be admitted that Bishop Elphinstone presented an unique example of devotion not only to the crown but to the kirk: if he spent three months in Edinburgh on judicial business he passed at least six months a year in his diocese and used royal favour and the profits of government office to promote its welfare.[210] But even Elphinstone could resort to legal chicanery to attain his laudable ends.[211] In his eyes, as in those of James Beaton, second Archbishop of Glasgow, and George Brown, Bishop of Dunkeld, nepotism within the kirk was to

---

[207] J. A. F. Thomson, *op. cit.*, *Innes Review*, XIX. 23–31, at 30–1; Leslie J. Macfarlane, *op. cit.*, *ibid.*, XX. 111–29, at 117–8.

[208] See *James IV, Letters*, Nos. 20, 21, 24.

[209] J. A. F. Thomson, *op. cit.*, *Innes Review*, XIX. 23–31, at 31. See also Leslie J. Macfarlane, *op. cit.*, *ibid.*, XX. 111–29, at 118–22, 127; *E.R.*, XII. xxxii, xli–xlii; XIII. lxxxvi–xcii.

[210] Leslie J. Macfarlane, *op. cit.*, *Aberdeen University Review*, XXXIX. 1–18, at 9–13; *E.R.*, XI. xxxv–xxxvi; XIII. clix–clx.

[211] See the case of Sir David Lindsay (*A.D.A.*, I. 141).

be accounted a virtue rather than a vice;[212] and it was doubtless thanks to Elphinstone's patronage that his lay kinsfolk received advancement—one presided over the royal nursery, three were royal familiars, and one of these was created a lord of parliament and was expected to lead a hundred spearmen in time of war.[213] More aspersions might be cast against Andrew Forman, Bishop of Moray, apostolic protonotary, commendator of Kelso and Dryburgh, tacksman of Dunbar Mains, keeper of Darnaway, chamberlain of Moray, custumar north of Spey. This talented diplomatist was a Scottish Wolsey 'whose contribution to the wellbeing of the Scottish church can only be considered marginal'.[214] A similar picture is presented by Andrew Stewart, Bishop of Caithness, commendator of Kelso and Fearn, chamberlain of Ross and Ardmannoch, keeper of Dingwall and Redcastle, who served for a time as treasurer and comptroller and dabbled deviously in government finance.[215]

The examples of the duke-archbishop and boy-archbishop of St Andrews, of Bishop Hepburn of the Isles, of Bishop Forman and Bishop Stewart show how ecclesiastics who enjoyed royal favour could expect to be rewarded by the grant of abbeys *in commendam*. This growing practice was a major factor in the decline of monastic life, though the decline was not yet wholesale : while the lords of council were concerned that the abbey of Jedburgh was 'ruinos and hable to failze and fall doune',[216] the priory of Whithorn benefited from royal pilgrimages and in 1508 was at its most flourishing with a complement of twenty-four canons.[217] The interest in gardening shown by one Abbot of Kinloss was counterbalanced by his indulgence in fleshly pleasures ; but his successor, Thomas Crystall, was a model of minor virtues.[218] Like the bishops the abbots were increasingly drawn into royal administration : those of Cambuskenneth, Paisley, Dunfermline and Arbroath, together with the commendator of Glenluce, each served as treasurer. The Abbots of Jedburgh, Holyrood, Cambuskenneth, Glenluce, Scone and Dunfermline served alongside the Bishops of Caithness, Dunblane, Argyll, the Isles, Aberdeen, Ross and Moray on commissions for the assessment of crown

[212] Mackie, *James IV*, p. 156; *E.R.*, XIII. clviii–clix; *R.M.S.*, II. Nos. 3667, 3795; Watt, *Fasti*, ad indices.

[213] *R.M.S.*, II. Nos. 2468, 2662, 3128, 3204, 3251, 3875; *R.S.S.*, I. Nos. 388, 799; *E.R.*, XIII. lxxxv.

[214] Leslie J. Macfarlane, *op. cit.*, *Innes Review*, XX. 111–29, at 126; *E.R.*, XIII. clii–clviii. [215] *E.R.*, XIII. cxlvi–clii; *R.S.S.*, I. No. 1351; *R.M.S.*, II. No. 3758.

[216] *A.D.C.P.*, p. lx. [217] *Wigtown Charters*, pp. 17, 90–1; *R.M.S.*, II. No. 2075.

[218] See Coulton, *Scottish Abbeys*, pp. 120, 148–9, 212.

lands.[219] The Abbot of Lindores was keeper of Linlithgow palace,[220] and Patrick Paniter, the king's chief secretary, obtained the abbey of Cambuskenneth in 1513, as well as a dispensation from assuming canonical garb for a further two years.[221] A hierarchy so closely associated with the crown was ready to comply with the royal wishes even in the matter of taxation, and special contributions levied upon the clergy became increasingly frequent.[222]

One by-product of the close association of kirk and state was an outburst of liturgical and devotional nationalism. Hitherto the Scottish liturgy had closely followed the English 'use of Sarum', and Scottish saints had been neglected. A new spirit was apparent in 1490 when Archbishop Scheves searched at Fordoun for the relics of St Palladius; and Bishop Elphinstone's Aberdeen Breviary of 1509–10, with its list of seventy Scottish saints, the climax to an emphasis on the bygone glories of Scottish Christianity, provided a distinctively national liturgy.[223] It was also typical of the age that the king's exploitation of the kirk was accompanied by religious idealism and assiduous personal devotions. During Lent James was to be found with the zealous Observant Franciscans at Stirling, where he had helped them to establish a house. From the antagonisms of the more worldly Conventuals the Observants were protected by the king : 'Theirs', so he informed the pope, 'is the popular religion ; by their care the salvation of souls here is most diligently advanced, the negligence of others most fully remedied, the sacraments administered, and the word of God spread abroad by the lips of the faithful'.[224]

James's regard for the small band of ascetic evangelists implied no criticism of the more dominant features of contemporary religious life.[225] He made offerings 'to the reliques' at St Andrews and presented a cross enshrined in silver to the altar of St Duthac, who 'divided his reverent regards with . . . the saint of Galloway'.[226] In the course of his frequent pilgrimages to Tain and Whithorn he not only bestowed alms but paid for a 'trental' of masses (thirty) at a time.[227] During the reign the great seal register records confirmations

---

[219] *E.R.*, x. 663, 710, 711; xi. 388, 395–6, 451; xii. 660, 686, 694, 698, 704; xiii. 593. [220] *R.S.S.*, i. No. 296.
[221] Mackie, *James IV*, pp. 157–8. [222] E.g. *T.A.*, iv. 391–3.
[223] David McRoberts, *op. cit.*, *Innes Review*, xix. 3–14.
[224] A. R. MacEwen, *History of the Church in Scotland*, i. 364–6; *James IV, Letters*, Nos. 76, 77; Coulton, *Scottish Abbeys*, p. 230.
[225] See A. I. Dunlop, *op. cit.*, *Scot. Church Hist. Soc. Recs.*, xv. 153–67, at 167. [226] *T.A.*, i. cxiv–cxv, cxlvi, clxii. [227] *Ibid.*, cxlviii–cxlix, clxi.

of the endowment of more than a hundred chaplainries (some of them founded by the king himself),[228] representing an annual outlay of about £1,000 on the salaries of chaplains whose chief duty was a somewhat mechanical celebration of the mass. The new collegiate kirks of Seton (1492), Semple (1504) and St Mary of the Fields, Edinburgh (1512), were surpassed by the King's foundation at Stirling (1501), where James fulfilled his father's fateful ambition of erecting a chapel royal. Its staff, modelled on that of a cathedral, was headed by the Bishop of Galloway and included a chantor, chancellor, treasurer, subdean, sub-chantor, archdeacon and 'official'.[229]

George Vaus, the first 'Bishop of Galloway and the chapel royal' had fathered a son.[230] Although letters of legitimation under the privy seal do not always give the name of the father, there are frequent indications of clerical paternity: one legitimation was issued for the son of a canon of Holyrood, another for the son of a parson of Maybole; chaplains were particularly prolific.[231] Clerical incontinence was nothing new; but the scurrility it aroused [232] was more perilous when the kirk was demoralised, leaderless, beset with incongruities, and worldly. In Paris the scholastic theologian John Major, conciliarist in outlook, expressed misgivings in measured academic language.[233] Lollardy had not been forgotten and may have been reinforced by 'Flemish spirituality' inspired by the Brethren of the Common Life.[234] In 'The Flyting of Dunbar and Kennedie' the poet Walter Kennedy humorously calumniated his opponent with the vituperative terms of 'Lollard laureate' and 'lamp lollardorum'. William Dunbar, far from being a heretic, wrote more seriously that

> The schip of faith tempestuous wind and rane
> Dryvis in the see of Lollerdry that blawis.[235]

Even more striking is John Knox's circumstantial account of a trial held in 1494 when Archbishop Blackadder summoned thirty persons,

---

[228] *R.M.S.*, II. Nos. 2536, 2549, 2681, 2796, 2903, 3774; *A.P.S.*, II. 267, c. 8.
[229] Watt, *Fasti*, pp. 335–41; *E.R.*, XII. xxxviii; *A.P.S.*, II. 240, 274; *R.M.S.*, II. Nos. 2760, 3002–3; *R.S.S.*, I. Nos. 1789, 2207; *James IV, Letters*, Nos. 52, 53.
[230] *Wigtown Charters*, No. 201.
[231] *R.S.S.*, I. Nos. 1610, 1708, 1946, 2254, 2258, 2335, 2336, 2422.
[232] In his *Tabile of Confession* William Dunbar wrote of 'Sic pryd of prelattis, hant of harlottis'.
[233] Major, *History*, p. 136; J. H. Burns, *op. cit.*, *S.H.R.*, XLII. 89–104, at 100.
[234] Durkan, *Bishop Turnbull*, pp. 40, 44.
[235] William Dunbar, *The Praise of Aige*.

mostly members of genteel Ayrshire families, to be interrogated
before king and council upon thirty-four heretical opinions. These
included a denial of transubstantiation, of the Petrine doctrine, of
the efficacy of masses, papal indulgences, and adoration of images,
as well as an assertion that 'thei which ar called principallis in the
church ar thevis and robbaris'. Whether or not the 'Lollards of Kyle'
held all these opinions it is clear that their bold spokesman, Adam
Reid of Barskimming, questioned the traditional number of the
sacraments and had no respect for 'proud prelates'. His witty and
cunning ripostes at the expense of the archbishop deprived the proceedings of the gravity necessary for dire punishment, and, so reports
Knox, 'the bischop and his band war so dashed out of countenance
that the greattest part of the accusatioun was turned to lawchter'.[236]
Laurence of Lindores must have turned in his grave.

While most of the changes that affected the kirk were clearly
adverse, those that influenced burgh life are more difficult to evaluate.
There was a striking increase in the number of burghs.[237] The Earls
of Buchan, Huntly, Argyll and Bothwell, Lords Home and Glamis,
were each allowed to establish a 'free burgh in barony',[238] and among
the score of lairds who obtained the same privilege was Sir Andrew
Wood of Largo.[239] Seven monasteries were similarly favoured,[240] and
Bishop Elphinstone was responsible for the erection of no less than
four baronial burghs.[241] Although some of the new burghs of barony,
which were mostly rural, had only a shadowy existence (if any),[242]
the attempts to found them testify to a real, or potential, increase in
internal trade, from which the feudal superiors hoped to profit. But
the new foundations impinged upon the ancient monopolies of the
royal burghs: the conflicting privileges claimed both by the old
royal burgh of Wigtown and the newly-recognised 'free burgh'
of Whithorn (one of the few non-royal burghs whose situation allowed
it to participate in overseas trade) led to prolonged recriminations
and litigation.[243]

Recriminations also flourished within the burghs, where mer-

---

[236] Knox, *History*, I. 1–2; D. E. Easson, 'The Lollards of Kyle', *Juridical
Review*, XLVIII. 123–8; W. Stanford Reid, *op. cit.*, *Church History*, XI. 3–17, at
14–17.   [237] See Pryde, *Burghs*, pp. 52–7.
[238] *R.S.S.*, I. Nos. 154, 478; *R.M.S.*, II. Nos. 1864, 1993, 2013, 2064.
[239] *R.M.S.*, II. No. 3880.
[240] *Ibid.*, Nos. 1767, 1944, 2115, 2292, 2336, 2350, 2574.
[241] *Ibid.*, Nos. 2132, 2443, 2492, 2588.
[242] *Wigtown Charters*, p. 6.   [243] *Ibid.*, pp. 137–9; Nos. 109–20, *passim.*

chants and craftsmen continued their disputes. There can be no doubt with which side the government sympathised. William Dunbar, in his satire upon Edinburgh, was probably expressing court opinion when he wrote :

> Tailyouris, soutaris and craftis vile
> The fairest of your streets dois fyle.

Fear of tumultuous craftsmen probably underlay the act of May 1491 that forbade bonds or convocations within the burghs, and further acts of June 1493 rejected the fairly liberal policy of the previous reign by resuscitating the punitive legislation of James I : the appointment of deacons by the craftsmen was 'rycht dangerous' and might cause 'greit troubill . . . and convocatioun and rysing of the kingis liegis'; the craftsmen made statutes of their own for their own profit, which deserved great punishment; masons and wrights convened to make rules of work, claiming payment on holy days as well as working days, 'or els they sall nocht laubour nor wirk'; if a craftsman began a job and then, at his own pleasure, left it, no other craftsman would continue the work; thus all those guilty of devising such rules should be indicted as oppressors of the king's lieges; meanwhile the craftsmen were not to levy contributions among themselves; their deacons were to lose office for a year and thereafter confine themselves to criticising the work of their fellow-craftsmen. Another act of June 1496 blamed the craftsmen for rising prices.[244] The merchants consolidated their position both through the court of the four burghs, which in 1500 forbade craftsmen to 'use merchandise or sail in merchandise',[245] and in the parliament of March 1504, where it was enacted that all officers exercising jurisdiction within burghs were to be merchants; the consent not only of the town council but of the merchant gild was to be required for the admission of new burgesses; both craftsmen and gentlemen burgesses (lairds enrolled as burgesses) were to be prevented from making leagues to usurp the authority of the magistrates.[246] But despite attempts to hold down the craftsmen they continued to organise themselves : in Edinburgh the waulkers and tailors each obtained incorporation under the seal of cause in 1500 ; the surgeons and barbers followed in 1505 (thus initiating the still-flourishing Royal College of

[244] *A.P.S.*, II. 226–7, c. 17 ; 234, cc. 13, 14 ; 238, c. 5.
[245] *Burghs Convention Recs.*, I. 505 ; *Edinburgh Burgh Recs.*, I. 88–9.
[246] *A.P.S.*, II. 252, cc. 25, 29, 31, 32, 35.

Surgeons of Edinburgh), and the cordiners followed in 1510.[247] Nor were the Edinburgh craftsmen content with their share in burgh government: in 1508 they approached the town council, which already included 'ane pairt of the craftismen of the toun', to ask that six or eight craftsmen should sit on the 'daylie counsale of the toun'. As a result this issue was to be referred to parliament.[248]

It was nothing new that parliament concerned itself with the affairs of the burghs, but it was typical of the new monarchy that offences such as regrating and forestalling now became the concern of the privy council, which hoped to prevent the cornering of the market by monopolistic practices and thus avoid a dearth of food supplies.[249] In general the burghs lost something of their independence. In October 1488 they were denied the right to repledge accused burgesses to their own courts (though some burghs subsequently had the privilege confirmed and Stirling even acquired the rare distinction of possessing its own sheriff within the burgh).[250] In the parliament of March 1504, which saw a wholesale reassertion of ancient burghal practices, it was ordained that the commissioners of burghs should be warned to compear when contributions were to be levied so that they might vote as one of the three estates.[251] It may be inferred from this astonishing enactment that taxation had recently been imposed without burghal consent and that the continued existence of a third estate was in jeopardy.

For the burghs were hardly in a flourishing condition. From 1498 onwards they were ravaged by recurring visitations of plague that stilled the clamour of busy markets and made mockery of the naïve pageantry and buffoonery that enlivened their holy days.[252] In 1497 a new pestilence, the 'grandgore'—venereal disease brought to Europe in the ships of Columbus—had also made its appearance: the magistrates of Aberdeen 'for eschewing of the infirmity come out of France and strange partes' ordered the closure of brothels and piously hoped that their sinful inmates would turn to honest work.[253] New financial demands also came with warfare and an exacting government: in 1497 Dundee was stented for 450 crowns to pur-

[247] *Edinburgh Burgh Recs.*, I. 80–1, 82–3, 101–4, 127–9.
[248] *Ibid.*, 118.
[249] *A.D.C.P.*, p. lxiii; *R.S.S.*, I. No. 1568.
[250] *A.P.S.*, II. 208, c. 10; *R.M.S.*, II. Nos. 2259, 2605, 3608.
[251] *A.P.S.*, II. 252, c. 30.
[252] *Edinburgh Burgh Recs.*, I. 72–143, *passim*; Mackie, *James IV*, pp. 150–2.
[253] *Edinburgh Burgh Recs.*, I. 71; *Aberdeen Burgh Recs.*, I. 425. See also R. S. Morton, 'Some aspects of the early history of syphilis in Scotland', *British Journal of Venereal Diseases*, XXXVIII. 175–80.

chase exemption from conscription; some years later its whole community was accused of contempt of royal officials and had to purchase a remission, while in 1511 its burgesses were to be distrained for misdemeanours.[254] Above all, the leading burghs suffered from the continuing trade recession. William Dunbar, full of praise for London, poured scorn upon the poor wares of Edinburgh.

In the backwater of Veere, rather than in the declining city of Bruges or the rising city of Antwerp, Andrew Halyburton, conservator of the staple, carried on small-scale transactions in the traditional commodities of the Netherland trade.[255] The greater enterprise shown in the Baltic had meanwhile spilled over into the interior of Germany, where Scottish traders settled in sizable numbers. They doubtless showed their patriotism by aiding Scottish monks to win control of the Schottenklöster—monasteries founded by Irish monks in the early Middle Ages at a time when the Irish unwarily styled themselves Scots. In 1515 a Scotsman was appointed Abbot of Ratisbon, and by then a score of Scottish traders had settled in that Bavarian city.[256] But their trade can hardly have been with Scotland : it was presumably the lack of opportunity and lucrative wares at home that had induced them to emigrate to a remote land where their expertise was more profitable than in Scotland. Even in depressing times some Scottish merchants enjoyed affluence, but if foreign trade was the life-blood of the burghs the blood was thin.

This is clearly shown in the accounts of the custumars. No new commodities figured in the export trade, and the export of fish, cloth and salt, which had increased during the previous reign, now subsided into stagnation along with that of wool, woolfells and hides. Although the customs duties on these last three products were still levied at the rates introduced by David II, and duties on additional products had meanwhile been imposed, the gross receipts from the great customs during James's reign scarcely averaged £3,000 a year, one-third as much as in 1371 ; Edinburgh scarcely accounted for £2,000, Aberdeen, its nearest rival, for £500. In the troubled conditions of the last year of the reign the total customs receipts were not

[254] R.S.S., I. Nos. 112, 1647; R.M.S., II. No. 3663.
[255] See The Ledger of Andrew Halyburton, ed. C. Innes, pp. lxv–lxvi, lxxii; Davidson and Gray, Staple, pp. 128–9; R.S.S., I. Nos. 550, 1583; A.P.S., II. 252, cc. 26, 27.
[256] M. Dilworth, 'The First Scottish Monks in Ratisbon', Innes Review, XVI. 180–98; T. A. Fischer, Scots in Germany, pp. 141–2, 153–4, and Scots in Prussia, pp. 235–6.

much more than £2,000.[257] Admittedly some allowance has to be made for a number of grants of exemption from customs duty : it was by this means that the king paid the dowry of his bastard cousin, Margaret Crichton, when she married the Edinburgh merchant, William Todrik.[258] Allowance has also to be made for maladministration in the collection of the customs.[259] With a view to improving returns there were experiments in granting tacks of the right to collect the customs.[260] In October 1510 this practice culminated in a three-year tack whereby Andrew Stewart, Bishop of Caithness, and Thomas Dickson, parson of Turriff, became custumars-general and were to collect the customs of the whole realm for their own profit in return for payment of £4,000 a year into the exchequer.[261] By March 1511 this over-optimistic scheme had to be revised.[262]

In his report on the king's annual revenues Pedro de Ayala had ludicrously estimated the customs receipts at 25,000 ducats (about £20,000), and most of his other estimates were scarcely less exaggerated. Nonetheless he was probably not far off the mark when he affirmed that the king 'is in want of nothing, judging from the manner in which he lives, but he is not able to put money into his strong boxes'.[263] James could not be accused of parsimony in the distribution of his revenues, but perhaps of extortion in their acquisition : save for the difference in the value of money, which raised an artisan's daily wage from the 4d. of the fourteenth century to the princely sum of 12d. in debased coin, it would appear that he had far surpassed the financial achievements of David II. Certainly the sums that the treasurer accounted for were unprecedented : between June 1488 and February 1492 the total (in round figures) came to £31,857; between February 1501 and September 1502 it was £20,709; between September 1502 and February 1505 it was no less than £70,345.[264] The chief contribution to this vast sum was forthcoming from instalments of the queen's dowry amounting to £23,333 6s. 8d. Apart from this non-recurring payment the other

[257] *E.R.*, XI. xxviii–xxix, liii. In 1488–9 the customs, including arrears, amounted (in round figures) to £2,890 (*ibid.*, x. 131–45); in 1491–2 they came to £2,464 (*ibid.*, 352–64); in 1494–5 to £2,345 (*ibid.*, 528–39); in 1507–8 to £3,317 (*ibid.*, XIII. 84–96); in 1512–13 to £2,161 (*ibid.*, 569–79).
[258] P. 489 above; *R.S.S.*, I. No. 1219; *T.A.*, I. ccxc; *E.R.*, XII, xxxi–xxxii, 465. For other exemptions see *R.S.S.*, I. Nos. 436, 490, 1335, 1436, 1466, 1494, 2089.   [259] See *A.P.S.*, II. 234, c. 12; 235, c. 17; *R.S.S.*, I. Nos. 159, 190.
[260] *E.R.*, XII. xxxi; *R.S.S.*, I. No. 1129.
[261] *R.S.S.*, I. No. 2140.   [262] *Ibid.*, No. 2223.
[263] Brown, *Early Travellers*, p. 43.   [264] *T.A.*, I. 166–8; II. 19, 196.

main sources of income during the two-and-a-half-year period were as follows.[265]

from prelates	£10,546
	and £320 Flemish
from feudal profits	£7,056
from the sheriffs	£6,944
from judicial profits	£6,083
from compositions for charters	£4,113
from compositions for tacks and feus	£586
from the fees of the great seal	£534

Little information exists as to the revenues forthcoming from the sheriffs, though most was probably derived from their collection of fines imposed in the justice ayres and listed in the rolls of 'estreits' (extracts).[266] The large sums drawn from the prelates [267] must, in part at least, have resulted from taxation. During the reign this was fairly frequently levied for extraordinary purposes; but only the compliant prelates could be relied upon to pay up.[268] On the other hand the sum that the king received from feudal profits (wardships, marriages, reliefs and non-entries) can have represented only the tip of an iceberg: one wardship and marriage was valued at 700 marks in 1501, another at £1,000 in 1511.[269] But the exaction of the crown's feudal rights was chaotic: 'it is evident that both the king and the ward received little . . . and it may be conjectured that the real gainers were the receiver himself, or persons to whom the king gave charges upon the ward estate; in some cases . . . the whole revenue was gifted to a royal favourite'.[270] Indeed this was the normal way in which the crown's vast potential income from wardships, reliefs, non-entries and escheats was disposed of,[271] without ever being subjected to account.

Similarly the profits of justice that the treasurer received in the form of compositions and fines must also have represented the mere tip of an iceberg. For the king acquired immense reward, both in popularity and cash, by responding to the insatiable longing of the three estates for more and better justice. The longing was expressed in repeated enactments dealing with the technicalities of the law and

---

[265] See *ibid.*, II. 163–96.
[266] See *ibid.* I. lxxix.
[267] *Ibid.*, II. 191–2.
[268] See Mackie, *James IV*, p. 59.
[269] *R.S.S.*, I. No. 661; *R.M.S.*, II. No. 3612.
[270] *E.R.*, XIII. cviii–cxi.
[271] *R.S.S.*, I. *passim.*

its administration,[272] in confused experimentation (hardly successful until the next reign) with the central administration of civil justice in the overlapping supreme courts of lords of council, session and causes,[273] in injunctions that the king should attend the justice ayres, which were to be held in spring and autumn in all parts of the realm,[274] and in another injunction that he should help to compose feuds.[275]

These feuds were the roots of crime, disorder and injustice. Often one magnate and his 'surname' had to be exempted from the jurisdiction of a sheriff or steward who was his rival and with whom he was engaged in 'variance' or 'dedly inimyte'.[276] Surety of £1,000 had to be demanded to keep the peace between Lords Ruthven and Oliphant.[277] In 1508 the rivalry between Crichtons and Maxwells erupted into a spectacular riot at Dumfries.[278] Most deadly of all was the feud which led in 1490 to the burning of six score Murrays in the kirk of Monzievaird by their Drummond foes. James's execution of the Master of Drummond (brother of his future mistress) demonstrated that he was capable of exacting full punishment without respect of rank.[279]

The Borders, where there was 'greit misreule', were the scene of further demonstrations of judicial severity. In August 1504 the king went on 'the raid of Eskdale' in the company of Lord Dacre, warden of the English March, and passed a few weeks in hawking and hanging.[280] Some years later James set off in dead of night for a judicial raid upon Teviotdale and carried out 'Jeddart justice' by bringing his prisoners to the tolbooth of Jedburgh with nooses already hanging around their necks.[281] About the same time the Hepburns, who had been given the task of daunting the ill-disposed Armstrongs, were furnished with letters of fire and sword permitting the wholesale butchery of the malefactors.[282]

---

[272] *A.P.S.*, II. 224, c. 5; 225–6, cc. 8, 9, 11; 227, c. 18; 230, c. 4; 234–5, c. 16; 238–9, c. 6; 250–4, cc. 8–11, 13, 22, 40, 41, 46; *R.S.S.*, I. Nos. 801, 802; *Scot. Legal History*, pp. 21–2; *A.D.C.P.*, pp. xxvii–xxviii.

[273] *A.P.S.*, II. 223, c. 27; 226, c. 16; 248–9, 256–7; *A.D.C.P.*, pp. xxviii–xxxii, lxi; R. K. Hannay, *The College of Justice*, p. 22, and 'On the Foundation of the College of Justice', *S.H.R.* xv. 30–46.

[274] *A.P.S.*, II. 208, c. 8; 218, c. 2; 225, c. 10.   [275] *Ibid.*, 218, c. 3.

[276] *R.S.S.*, I. Nos. 95, 97, 228, 1723, 2307, 2430.   [277] *A.D.A.*, I. 141.

[278] *R.S.S.*, I. Nos. 1745, 1750, 1791; Lesley, *History*, p. 79.

[279] Pitscottie, *Historie*, I. 237; *T.A.*, I. cii–civ; *E.R.*, x. l–lii; *A.D.A.*, I. 150, 151; *R.S.S.*, I. No. 613.

[280] Lesley, *History*, p. 85; *E.R.*, XI. xliii–l; XII. lix; *T.A.*, II. 452–5.

[281] Lesley, *History*, p. 81; *T.A.*, IV. xxiii.

[282] *R.S.S.*, I. Nos. 587, 700, 701, 2165.

But unrestrained severity was exceptional. A more constructive treatment of disorder was to be seen in the 'bands' of the South and Middle Borders (pacts for mutual security) enforced in the parliament of March 1504,[283] and a remunerative treatment of disorder took the form of making compositions and selling respites and remissions. It was for this purpose that the king so often graced the justice ayres, reminding the guilty by his daunting presence that, if need be, the full rigour of the law might be unleashed—as it sometimes was.[284] Also in attendance were the 'lords componitors'—often the Bishops of Aberdeen and Caithness—whose function was to bargain with the guilty and allow them to atone for offences by payment of a composition. Treason against the king's person, arson and rape were, however, generally beyond composition.[285]

The sums involved were considerable: the composition for one remission might well cost £50;[286] as a result of proceedings in a justice ayre at Perth, Lord Drummond owed the king £1,695, which were compounded for 500 marks;[287] in 1511 £1,200 were expected as the remainder of the 'estreats' of three justice ayres of Berwickshire and Lauderdale.[288] The occasional severity of the king not only made offenders all the more eager to purchase remissions but allayed the criticism that his father had incurred by trafficking in them. A proclamation made at Inverness in 1501 announced that the king and his lords had at divers times come north and compounded with all applicants for remissions; many, however, presumed upon the king's clemency; after the forthcoming ayre he would no longer compound for 'commone gret crimes'.[289] This warning was probably intended to stimulate demand and certainly brought no interruption to the profitable traffic: during the reign the privy seal register shows 522 grants of remission. The main categories of crime for which these were granted were manslaughter (182 cases), forthocht felony (88 cases), support of rebels and outlaws (71 cases), theft (69 cases) and oppression (31 cases). General remission was forthcoming for all the inhabitants of Argyll, Bute and the Cumbraes. Specific remissions were granted to many nobles accused of a variety of crimes.

A somewhat different picture emerges in the case of the 168 respites that were purchased to delay legal proceedings for any period ranging from a few weeks to nineteen years. More than one third

---

[283] *A.P.S.*, II. 248.   [284] *T.A.*, I. lxxix, clxiii; Lesley, *History*, pp. 73-4.

[285] *R.S.S.*, I. Nos. 2154, 2314. The procedure of the justice ayres is outlined in *T.A.*, I. lxxviii–lxxix.

[286] *R.M.S.*, II. No. 3757.   [287] *R.S.S.*, I. No. 1807.

[288] *R.M.S.*, II. No. 3645.   [289] *A.D.C.P.*, p. lix.

of these were granted to persons who wished to go overseas. Study in France accounted for three respites.[290] Pilgrimages to Rome, Compostela and Amiens accounted respectively for the issue of four respites, five respites and eight respites;[291] and a bailie of Peebles hopefully obtained a respite to cover a trip to Jerusalem.[292] Robert Barton significantly obtained five respites to safeguard his interests during his absence on overseas ventures.[293] So far as he was concerned it may be suspected that the real motive was to evade justice. This was the evident motive in some hundred cases where absence overseas could not be pleaded as an excuse.

While the dubious traffic in respites and remissions doubtless furnished a large proportion of the receipts of the treasurer it was the income from crown lands that was the chief source of funds for the second great financial officer, the comptroller. An act of February 1490 sought to protect the king's poor tenants against the oppression of neighbouring lords,[294] but nothing could protect them against commissioners of assessment who imposed unrealistic rents. It was either this or incredible maladministration that resulted in the accumulation of heavy arrears : by 1507 one bailie owed £1,114, and by 1509 Lord Maxwell, steward of Annandale, owed £3,745, which were remitted for a composition of £1,000.[295] Nonetheless, despite arrears, revenues rose in monetary terms, if not in real value : in 1457 the net rents of the lordship of Galloway were £431 ; in 1505 they were £1,026.[296] Ettrick forest, richest jewel in the royal patrimony, provided over £2,500 a year.[297] Altogether, the crown lands furnished the comptroller with more than three times as much as he received from the customs : in the period from September 1508 to August 1509 the total receipts of Sir Duncan Forrester were (in round figures) £13,245, of which £2,412 came from the custumars and £8,993 from the administrators of the crown lands.[298] The gross receipts from these (including arrears) rose from about £8,300 a year in the period from 1488 to 1502 to about £12,300 a year in the period from 1502 to 1513.[299]

Feuing of the crown lands was partly responsible for the in-

[290] *R.S.S.*, I. Nos. 384, 712, 1998.

[291] *Ibid.*, Nos. 212, 221, 485, 1794; 641, 670, 1057, 1424, 1441; 1251, 1257, 1425, 1523, 1545, 1653, 1684, 1840.   [292] *Ibid.*, No. 1821.

[293] *Ibid.*, Nos. 642, 767, 2071, 2371, 2455.

[294] *A.P.S.*, II. 222, c. 22.   [295] *E.R.*, XII. 488; *R.S.S.*, I. No. 1834.

[296] Athol Murray, 'The Crown lands in Galloway, 1455–1543', *Dumfriesshire Trans.*, XXXVII. 9–25, at 22.   [297] *E.R.*, XII. 34, 535; XIII. 524.

[298] *Ibid.*, XIII. 253–4; see also *ibid.*, 115–9.

[299] Compare *ibid.*, X. 249–94; XII. 1–75, 483–589; XIII. 502–64.

creased returns. Up to 1504 James seems to have granted feus on much the same scale as his father. Rapid development was initiated by an act of the parliament of March 1504 which made it clear that the king might grant feus, even from the lands annexed to the crown, providing that there was no diminution in rental, grassums and other duties, and that all freeholders were allowed to do likewise.[300] Often it was stated that a new feu-duty exceeded the old rent (sometimes being twice as much). After 1504 a 'general process set in of converting the royal tenants into feuars; ... feu-ferm became the almost universal tenure of small parcels of lands and a very usual tenure even of larger estates granted by the crown'.[301] The process is clearly seen in the case of the lands of the old earldom of Fife. Until 1508 they were almost always rented on three-year tacks either to individual tacksmen or to joint tenants practising communal farming on the run-rig system. In the rental of March 1510 nearly all the lands were granted in feu.[302] The forest of Ettrick was feued in April 1510, the lordship of Methven in the following month, and the lordship of Stirlingshire in April 1511.[303] Between 1488 and 1513 the great seal register contains scarcely thirty confirmations of feus granted by the king's subjects, but no less than 117 grants of feu by the king, one third of them in favour of familiars. By 1513 the feu-duties accruing to the king from grants recorded in the great seal register amounted to over £3,300 annually, besides large quantities of victuals. It was not yet apparent that the crown's immediate gains would be outweighed by losses when the feu-duties remained unalterable in time of inflation and rising rents.

In many cases the new feu-holders were obliged by the terms of their feu charters to undertake various improvements: one of them was supposed to build a residence of stone and lime, with granary, stable and dove-cot, to plant orchards, gardens and oak trees, to set up beehives and construct bridges.[304] It was improvements such as these that John Major had in mind when he advocated feuing.[305] But if feuing led to improvement it was at the cost of some hardship: 'many tenants could with difficulty pay their rents, still less could they pay the increased feu-duty and had to allow others to take their holdings'.[306] The resulting plight of the poorer rural classes is well illustrated by the poets of the period. Those who were forced off the

---

[300] *A.P.S.*, II. 244, cc. 30, 31; 253, cc. 36, 37.
[301] Aeneas J. G. Mackay, *E.R.*, XIII. cxix–cxx.   [302] *Ibid.*, cxxi–cxxv.
[303] *Ibid.*, 626–8, 642–3, 649.   [304] *R.M.S.*, II. No. 3643.
[305] Major, *History*, p. 31.   [306] Aeneas J. G. Mackay, *E.R.*, XIII. cxxv, cxxviii.

land could expect no sympathy if they turned to begging (as many seem to have done): in March 1504 parliament revived James I's punitive legislation against mendicancy.[307]

Another act of March 1504 allowed those with an income of less than a hundred marks to absent themselves from parliament unless specially summoned; they were, however, to appoint barons of the shire or 'the maist famouss personis' to act as their procurators and 'to ansuer for thame'.[308]

This act seems to have aggravated the problem of securing adequate attendance. After the first parliament of the reign [309] attendance regularly dwindled, even in the course of a particular parliament: on 3 February 1506 the sederunt comprised seventeen ecclesiastics, twenty barons, and the commissioners of six burghs; by 16 February there were only eleven ecclesiastics, eleven barons, and two men who represented the burghs.[310] In the brief record of the parliament of May 1509 no sederunt is given, and, apart from the time-honoured affirmation of the privileges of the kirk, the only business done appears to have been the issue of one or two charters and a rescinding of a scheme for division of sheriffdoms.[311] Throughout the reign parliament had become progressively, and farcically, unrepresentative of the political classes. To that extent its authority was bound to be less impressive: in 1504 Logan of Restalrig protested that whatever was concluded by acts or statutes of parliament should not redound to his prejudice.[312] No parliament seems to have been held by James IV after 1509.

The place vacated by parliament was presumably partly filled by the privy council. Although its existing records are copious they take the form of 'a register of judicial decisions in session of council', and since there is 'a remarkable absence of minutes regarding action in public policy' it has been conjectured that a council register devoted to affairs of state has been lost.[313] At any rate there is little information concerning the political activities of the council. The composition of this body was, after 1490, left to the discretion of the king: it was an instrument of his authority, not of the authority of parliament, and could be used as he desired. Ayala reports that James 'lends a willing ear to his counsellors, and decides nothing without

---

[307] *A.P.S.*, II. 251, c. 14.

[308] *Ibid.*, 244, c. 26; 252, c. 23.

[309] Pp. 532–3 above.

[310] *A.P.S.*, II. 262–3, 266.

[311] *Ibid.*, 267–8, 274–7.

[312] *Ibid.*, 248.

[313] R. K. Hannay, *A.D.C.P.*, pp. vi–vii. A short list of entries concerning public affairs between 1501 and 1513 is given on pp. lix–lxvii.

asking them; but in great matters he acts according to his own judgment'.[314] Nor is it likely that the privy council was consulted on the multitude of small grants made by the king; in these cases all that was required was an expression of his intentions to the appropriate official.

Here lay the importance of the court, which also partly filled the place vacated by parliament. The familiars, the courtiers most regularly in attendance upon the king, were those who could most readily catch the king's ear. It is a testimony to their assiduity and influence that James did not, like his father, garner the resources that he acquired, but distributed them lavishly in gifts of lands, wardships, marriages, reliefs, escheats and life annuities.[315] There was no outcry against this spoils system simply because royal liberality was regarded as a virtue and the circle of beneficiaries was wide : James was indirectly taxing the landholding classes in order to display his generosity to the members of the same classes who were in favour at court.

Certainly the spoils system was not intended to abase the higher nobility, some of whom now decorated the court and pursued 'policy' as well as feuds. The traditional dignity of earl was bestowed more frequently than in the past : Patrick Hepburn had been made Earl of Bothwell in 1488; in 1503 James Hamilton was made Earl of Arran, William Graham was made Earl of Montrose, and Cuthbert Cunningham, grandson of the first Earl of Glencairn who had been killed at Sauchieburn, was restored to that title; in 1507 Hugh Montgomery was made Earl of Eglinton; and in 1509 David Kennedy was made Earl of Cassillis. The less traditional title of duke, however, was evidently to be reserved for members of the royal family: in 1489 David Lindsay had been restored to the dukedom of Montrose, but only for his own lifetime; following his death James blocked the ducal pretensions of the Lindsays by erecting an earldom of Montrose for the Grahams. A regard for ancient nobility and a desire to let bygones be bygones was displayed in the grant of a pension of £200 to the onetime ninth Earl of Douglas until his death in 1491.[316] The only vindictiveness that James showed towards the higher nobility was reserved for George Leslie, second Earl of Rothes, who was outlawed.[317] Yet in 1513, when William Leslie succeeded to the earldom, he was granted back the residue of what the king had seized from his elder brother 'be ressone of recognitioun, alienatioun, fore-

---

[314] Brown, *Early Travellers*, p. 41.
[315] See *R.S.S.*, I. *passim*.   [316] *E.R.*, x. lxii, lxvii.
[317] See Ranald Nicholson, *op. cit.*, *Juridical Review*, April 1973, pt. i. 1–21.

fatour, non-entres of airis or ony uther wais'.[318] Although the power
of the greater nobles had been subordinated to the pre-eminence of
the king they kept their dignity. The deep-seated rancours of the
previous reign had been pacified, and James presided over a dazzling
court that in its pageantry and liberality provided the populace with
the equivalent of bread and circuses.

Even so, there were jarring anomalies between court and country: when evicted peasants were starving James could afford to
devote the customs and burgh maills of Peebles to the 'keping and
feding of herons',[319] to gamble (and lose) £70 in one night on a game
of cards,[320] and to keep his mistresses in a style that was extravagantly
ostentatious. Had his interests been confined solely to a courtly milieu
disaffection might easily have arisen. But this was not the case. In his
devotion to Venus, James did not neglect Mars. Pitscottie approvingly reports his patronage of chivalry. Bishop Lesley tells of one
tournament 'with counterfuting of the round tabill of King Arthour'
when 'ane quha callit himself the wyld knycht' held the field against
French contestants. 'This wyld knycht,' he adds, 'wes the king himself, quha wes vaileyaunt in armeis, and could very well exerce the
same.'[321] Ayala reported in 1498 that James 'loves war so much that
I fear . . . the peace will not last long'.[322] The king also appeared to
love justice; his personal activity in its administration blinded his
subjects to its mercenary character and convinced them of the seriousness of his vocation as a ruler.[323] His conventional piety and his
occasional retreats into religious seclusion concealed his misuse of the
kirk and gave the impression of high-minded conscientiousness. His
boundless energy, perhaps a sign of psychological insecurity, sent him
galloping over the countryside: Lesley reports (somewhat incredibly)
that in one day he rode alone from Stirling to Elgin *via* Perth and
Aberdeen, and on the following morning continued to St Duthac's
shrine.[324] No Scottish king knew his country so well; never can the
Scottish people have known a king so intimately. And, as the
treasurer's accounts show, in all the king's progresses there was continual distribution of largesse on a scale appropriate to the status of
the recipients—drink-silver to masons; alms to priests and friars, the
poor, the sick, the deformed, the deranged; gratuities to messengers,
hostesses, huntsmen, ferrymen, fiddlers, falconers, fools, singers (in-

---

[318] *R.S.S.*, I. No. 2501.   [319] *Ibid.*, No. 1937.   [320] *T.A.*, II. 132.
[321] Pitscottie, *Historie*, I. 231–2; Lesley, *History*, p. 78.
[322] Brown, *Early Travellers*, p. 41.
[323] Lesley, *History*, pp. 63, 96. For instances of James's meddling with the
course of justice see *R.S.S.*, I. Nos. 813, 1733.   [324] Lesley, *History*, pp. 75–6.

cluding the maidens of Forres), luters, harpers, guisers, jugglers, and Highland bards.

Thus James acquired, and kept, an easy popularity. Only Sir John Ramsay, shrewd and traitorous, denounced the wilfulness of the king [325] as he moved farther than ever towards the absolutism that had become a possibility since the first stirrings of the new monarchy under James I. The king told Ayala that 'his subjects serve him with their persons and goods . . . exactly as he likes', and, so Ayala thought, James esteemed himself 'as much as though he were lord of the world'.[326] The king's pride was shared by his people; it was doubtless the common opinion of the Scots that Ayala was reporting when he remarked that 'on land they think themselves the most powerful kingdom that exists'.[327] Until 1509 no cloud darkened the horizon.

[325] Conway, *Henry VII*, p. 107.
[326] Brown, *Early Travellers*, pp. 40, 41.   [327] *Ibid.*, p. 48.

18

THE AUREATE AGE AND ITS END

Although Pedro de Ayala noted that the Scots were poor, spending their time in warfare (often among themselves) rather than in profitable work, his account was much more favourable than that of Froissart or Aeneas Sylvius. He affirmed that 'there is as great a difference between the Scotland of old time and the Scotland of today as there is between bad and good',[1] and hinted that James IV was responsible for this advancement. Whether or not, as Ayala claimed, James could speak Latin, French, German, Flemish and Spanish, he was certainly aware of the multifarious changes taking place in Western Europe and was anxious to emulate other rulers in whatever brought renown and prestige. To this end he employed royal patronage with more flamboyance and less discrimination than his father. At court, errant knights, Moorish dancers, a French alchemist and a French dog-fancier, musicians from Italy and from Schleswig, Flemings imported to work in the mint or to cast artillery, rubbed shoulders with William Dunbar, master of the new aureate poetry, John Ireland, the grave theologian, Bishop Elphinstone, intent upon his new university, guisers, tellers of gestes, players of the clarshach, jugglers, tight-rope dancers, and the king's fool; pageantry and buffoonery went hand in hand, and novelty reached its apotheosis in the mock tournament of which a negress was the prize. There was an intermingling and jostling of native and medieval traditions with new importations from a continent swept by cultural and political change and technological innovation.

All the changes of the time are hardly comprised in the term 'renaissance', long battered and misused. For change had not

[1] Brown, *Early Travellers*, pp. 43, 49.

occurred in a void : much was merely the result of development that had been continuous throughout the Middle Ages ; even classical learning was not 're-born' but was increasingly viewed through the eyes of Cicero rather than through those of Aquinas and the subsequent scholastics. By studying the unvarnished Greek and Roman originals, so it was thought, man would best develop his higher faculties and perfect himself. The cult of the classical past was a humane study that at best might provide fresh inspiration ; at worst the humanist often contented himself with insubstantial imitation. It was this period of continuity, of fusions and juxtapositions, sometimes brilliantly successful, sometimes incongruous, that produced in the groat issued by James III in 1485 'the earliest renaissance coin portrait outside Italy'.[2] But although the coin also depicted the pretensions of James III to imperial authority the idea was conveyed not with the laurel wreath or fillet of a Roman emperor but with the arched crown associated with the medieval emperors.

In architecture, sculpture, painting and the minor arts the continuity of medieval tradition was more obvious than novelty. If the great hall of Stirling Castle, thought to have been designed by Cochrane, was 'the first large-scale building in the whole of Great Britain to display the influences of the renaissance'[3] the influences were to be seen in the application of Italianate motifs rather than in structural innovations. Not even Italianate motifs decorated the large additions made by James IV at Linlithgow : their sober design was in the native 'vernacular' tradition, and the turrets of Holyrood and Falkland, which might well have been mirrored in the Loire,[4] probably date from the succeeding reign.

It was the construction of a *palatium* (a great hall) that made these royal residences 'places' or 'palaces'. In the greater baronial and ecclesiastical establishments there was a similar stress upon halls and comfort rather than upon towers and defence.[5] But the 'policy' sometimes advocated in building licences[6] was still usually expressed by a tower as austere as the landscape. So essential a classical concept as symmetry was avoided in buildings great and small.

Close commercial ties with the Netherlands helped to reinforce an attitude towards the visual arts that was realistic rather than idealistic, as in the beautifully illuminated liturgical books, the finest

[2] David McRoberts, 'Notes on Scoto-Flemish Artistic Contacts', *Innes Review*, x. 91–6, at 92, n. 6.   [3] *Ibid.*

[4] *E.R.*, XII. xxxvii–xxxviii; XIII. xciii–xcvii.

[5] Mackie, *James IV*, pp. 114–6; W. M. Mackenzie, *The Medieval Castle in Scotland*, p. 149.   [6] *R.M.S.*, II. No. 3336.

of which were imported from Flanders.[7] Idealism is certainly to be found in the panels which Hugo van der Goes was commissioned to paint for Trinity College, but the idealism is not the classical, pagan and humane of fifteenth-century Italy but something Gothic, Christian and brooding; religious mysticism is combined with a secular mysticism which depicts the majesty of the new monarchy in the dominance given to the flowing robes and ermine capes of James III, his queen, and the lesser royal figure (often taken to be the youthful James IV but more probably his uncle, the Duke of Albany).[8]

While warfare and iconoclasm have left only vestiges of the art and architecture of the period, neglect has resulted in the loss of much of the literature of the age. Gaelic poetry, dependent upon oral transmission, was particularly perishable. The collection compiled between 1512 and 1526 in the *Book of the Dean of Lismore*[9] probably represents only a small part of the output of the professional bards but shows the variety of their repertoire—Ossianic ballads, elegies, satires, incitements to battle, 'flytings', some moral and didactic verse.[10] Thanks to the political changes initiated by James III and James IV there would be less patronage for the bards in future. Well might the contemporary MacMhuirich declaim :

> Tyrants [the kings] suffered a strong blast from the wise, strong tribe [the MacDonalds], though now they are unhonoured; there is no joy without Clan Donald.[11]

One consequence of declining patronage was the new prominence of Gaelic folk-poetry, the work of amateurs, often talented, but not trained in the bardic tradition.[12]

---

[7] Leslie J. Macfarlane, 'The Book of Hours of James IV and Margaret Tudor', *Innes Review*, XI. 3–21; David McRoberts, 'Dean Brown's Book of Hours', *ibid.*, XIX. 144–67; David McRoberts, *Catalogue of Scottish Medieval Liturgical Books and Fragments* (1953).

[8] David McRoberts, *op. cit.*, *Innes Review*, x. 91–6; David Laing, 'Historical Description of the [Trinity College] Altar-piece . . .', *Proc. Soc. Antiq. Scot.*, III. 8–22, and 'Supplemental Notice', x. 310–24; Conway, *Henry VII*, p. 2.

[9] Published and translated in *Reliquiae Celticae*, ed. Alexander MacBain and John Kennedy, I. 1–109.

[10] Wittig, *Scottish Tradition*, pp. 185–6.

[11] Derick S. Thomson, *op. cit.*, *Transactions of the Gaelic Society of Inverness* (1963), 3–31, at 15.

[12] Derick S. Thomson, 'Scottish Gaelic Folk-Poetry Ante 1650', *Scottish Gaelic Studies*, VIII. 1–17; John MacInnes, 'Gaelic Songs of Mary Macleod', *ibid.*, XI. 3–25.

By contrast the Lowland poets, never professionals, not only developed the folk-poetry that had originated in the ballads but made it a poetry of art, more courtly both in theme and diction. Here too, much has perished : some of the makars (poets) whose deaths were lamented by William Dunbar are nothing more than names, while some works which do survive are of arguable date and authorship : the 'gud gentill Stobo', whose name certainly occurs in official records,[13] cannot with certainty be credited with *The Thre Prestis of Peebles*; and only recently has 'Blind Harry', author of the *Wallace*, acquired verisimilitude.[14] In any case these works, together with Myll's *Spectakle of Luf*, are of minor account [15] in comparison with those of the great trio of makars—Robert Henryson (*floruit* 1480–1490), William Dunbar (*c.* 1460–*c.* 1521) and Gavin Douglas (*c.* 1474–1522), whose achievements have at last begun to attract the attention they deserve.[16] Their themes were not solely native or chivalric but were sometimes inspired by works of classical origin. Their range of expression was extended by their introduction of 'aureate' polysyllabic words of French or Latin origin. New subtleties were discovered in the contrast of homely vernacular words that bespoke byre, broom and heather, with others that evoked a Mediterranean landscape of porticoes, laurels and 'the palm triumphale'.[17]

Many words 'of a decidedly humanistic appearance' were first introduced into the English language by Robert Henryson, who in 1462 was teaching law in Glasgow University and prior to his death was schoolmaster at Dunfermline. But Henryson's humanism (like that of his fellow poets, William Dunbar and Gavin Douglas) was not Italianate : 'he heralds the Northern Renaissance whose continuity with the Middle Ages extended even into the late seventeenth and early eighteenth century—there was no decisive break with the past'.[18] For although Henryson adopted classical motifs he also made impressive use of the ancient technique of alliteration ; in his sonorous Chaucerian stanzas 'gude moralitee' and 'seriositee' were 'hid under

---

[13] *T.A.*, I. xcix–ci; *E.R.*, XI. xxix–xxx.

[14] See Matthew P. McDiarmid's introduction to *Harry's Wallace* (S.T.S.).

[15] See Wittig, *Scottish Tradition*, pp. 103–30.

[16] R. L. Mackie gives an interesting summary of the makars in *James IV*, pp. 171–87. For more specialised works see the Bibliography, pp. 633–4 below.

[17] Wittig, *Scottish Tradition*, pp. 62–3, 78–9.

[18] MacQueen, *Robert Henryson*, pp. 20–2; *Works of Robert Henryson* (S.T.S.), I. xc. See also John MacQueen, 'Some aspects of the early renaissance in Scotland', *Forum for Modern Language Studies*, III. 201–22, and L. B. Hall, 'An aspect of the renaissance in Gavin Douglas' *Eneados*', *Studies in the Renaissance*, VII. 184–92.

the cloke of poesie'; and the influence of Boethius, so apparent in *The Kingis Quair*, re-emerges in *Orpheus and Eurydice*, a Gordian knot of intricate medieval allegory. Similarly in the satirical *Morall Fabillis* an explicit *moralitas* (often blatantly naïve) is directed at the reader who is not versed in allegorical tradition; for those who are skilled, subtleties abound.

In Henryson's finest poem, *The Testament of Cresseid*, there are also 'two levels of meaning, the literal and the allegorical . . . but . . . the figurative sense is solidly based on the literal', for the leprosy with which the gods have punished Cresseid for her desertion of Troilus and her subsequent harlotry is 'the visual representation of Cresseid's invisible sin'.[19] The concluding description of 'the woeful end of this lusty Cresseid', when her former lover rides past and fails to recognise her among the lepers is 'one of the most moving things in literature'[20] and shows the poet's taut control of pathos :

> Than upon him scho kest up baith her ene,
> And with ane blenk it come into his thocht
> That he sumtime hir face befoir had sene
> Bot scho was in sic plye he knew hir nocht,
> Yit than hir luik into his mynd it brocht
> The sweit visage and amorous blenking
> Of fair Cresseid, sumtyme his awin darling.

Although Henryson skilfully used humorous irony it is his seriousness, his depth of thought, that is most characteristic. Summing up the best of medieval morality, but seldom dull or morbid, his work has a timeless quality. His greatness as a poet—and he ought surely to be esteemed the greatest of Scottish poets—is seen in his technical mastery of great themes. Wrestling with the problems of soul and body, good and evil, he depicts the struggle with conciseness, realism, directness, and apparent simplicity, sometimes with humour, sometimes with restrained pathos, as in his poignant *Prayer for the Pest* (Plague) :

> Use derth, O Lord, or seiknes and hungir soir
> And slak thy plaig that is so penetryfe.
> The pepill ar perreist; quha ma remeid thairfor
> Bot thow, O Lord, that for thame lost thy lyfe?

The seeming indifference of the deity to human wretchedness is also indicated in *The Taill of the Scheip and the Doig*, when the

---

[19] MacQueen, *Robert Henryson*, pp. 64, 91.   [20] *Ibid.*, pp. 88–9.

sheep, representing the 'pure commounis that daylie ar opprest', directs to God the reproachful and unanswered question :

> Seis Thow not this warld owerturnit is,
> As quha wald change gude gold in leid or tyn? [21]

Henryson visualised a benevolent deity :

> . . . we may have knawlegeing
> Off God Almychtie be his creatouris
> That he is gude, ffair, wyis and bening.

Like Lorenzo Valla, however, he believed that God's ways are beyond human understanding :

> Nane suld presume be ressoun naturall
> To seirche the secreitis off the Trinitie,
> Bot trow fermelie, and lat all ressoun be.[22]

Coupled with the sensitive observation of time, place and circumstance, and the realism that convincingly transformed countryfolk, burgesses, lawyers and clerks into the likenesses of beasts, went an equally accurate assessment of contemporary wrongs and injustices.[23] Anger inspired by these is veiled in irony, compassion is muted into resignation :

> The sweitest lyfe, thairfor, in this cuntrie
> Is sickernes [security] with small possessioun.[24]

This lesson was not learned by William Dunbar. In his poem *Of Covetyce* he could join in the fashionable practice of decrying extortionate landlords ; in another poem on the even more fashionable theme of the fickleness of fortune he could lament that

> Nane heir bot rich men hes renown
> And pure men ar plukit doun.

But Dunbar himself hankered after lands and riches. Failing to win them he suffered the pangs of a disappointed careerist. In *To the*

[21] *Ibid.*, 127–31.
[22] *The Preiching of the Swallow, ibid.*, pp. 153–65.
[23] See M. E. Rowlands, 'Robert Henryson and the Scottish Courts of Law', *Aberdeen University Review*, XXXIX. 219–26.
[24] *The Taill of the Uponlandis Mous and the Burges Mous*, MacQueen, *Robert Henryson*, pp. 121–7.

King he pathetically contrasts the high expectations of childhood with the (allegedly) unrewarding outcome of his pursuit of royal patronage :

> I wes in youthe, on nureice kne,
> Cald dandillie, 'bischop', dandillie,
> And quhone that age now dois me greif
> A sempill vicar I can not be.
> . . . .
> How suld I leif and I not landit,
> Nor yit withe benefice am blandit?

This poem may be compared with the lament *Quhen he wes sek* (often misleadingly styled *The Lament for the Makaris*), where the procession of doomed mortals is somehow subordinated to the 'me' that ends the sombre Latin refrain :

> On to the ded gois all estatis,
> Princis, prelotis and potestatis,
> Baith riche and pur of al degre;
>   Timor mortis conturbat me.

The 'egocentric attitude' that has been detected in Dunbar [25] is less likable than the broad humanitarian outlook of Henryson but is largely compensated for by versatility in diction, technique and theme. Moreover Dunbar's subjectiveness and his touches of self-revelation, rivalled only by those of François Villon, were something new in literature. For in much medieval writing, even in personal correspondence, there was a reticence and repression of personality which contrasted strongly with the unrepressed public display of emotions by both small and great. In Dunbar there is at least a hint of the humanistic stress upon individual man rather than upon mankind. Yet, unlike most humanists, he had a concept of the individual man that was earthbound rather than sublime; he eschewed the flattery in which most of them indulged; and even although he was dependent upon the king for a generous pension of £80 [26] he was not subservient. As a lifelong courtier, however, Dunbar had little empathy with those engaged in the humdrum affairs of simple life and was not loth to expose merchants, craftsmen and peasants to the caustic amusement of the well-bred. Not that he neglected to poke fun at the seamier side of court life, as in *Of the Ladyis Solis-*

[25] Wittig, *Scottish Tradition*, p. 55.   [26] *E.R.*, XIII. cii–cvii.

taris at Court. Moreover the varying moods of the court elicited not only ceremonial pieces such as *The Thrissil and the Rose*, and conventional devotional works such as *Ane Ballat of Our Lady*, but also the whimsical oddities of *The Devillis Inquest* and the scurrility of *The Flyting of Dunbar and Kennedy*, unsurpassed in 'metrical ease, in masterly alliteration, in sumptuousness of ribaldry, in variety of ridicule or in impetuosity of invective'.[27] Thus 'of all the makars, Dunbar is the most accomplished virtuoso, and flits most easily from one plane to another'. He is also 'a virtuoso whose command of an almost inexhaustible variety of metrical forms is such as no English poet possessed until the nineteenth century',[28] while his work 'contains the best examples of a volatile and bizarre fancy controlled by art'.[29] All this provides showy entertainment; but seldom (in contrast to Henryson's compositions) is much demand made upon the reader's intellect or sensibilities.

The subjectivity apparent in Dunbar's work is also a striking feature in that of Gavin Douglas, though it was hardly inspired by disappointed ambition : this third son of Bell-the-Cat obtained the lucrative provostship of St Giles in Edinburgh in 1503 and left it in 1515 only to become Bishop of Dunkeld.[30] It was rather humanistic emulation, a savant's pride of achievement, that led to self-assertion. Sometimes Douglas harangues the reader, sometimes he carries on a dialogue with him, sometimes he loses patience with his supposed literary adversaries, wishes that he could pull their ears, and expostulates : 'O hald your pece, ye verray goddis apis!'[31]

The rather laboured allegorical poem *The Palice of Honour* harks back to the tradition of the *Kingis Quair* but is not uninfluenced by contemporary humanism and has 'Spenser-like passages of impressionistic description'.[32] Douglas's fame, however, rests on *The Eneados*, not only 'one of the great renaissance translations' but 'the most sustained work in Scots poetry, and, considering the scale, the most consistent'.[33] In translating Virgil's *Aeneid* Douglas sought academic precision and adopted high standards of literary criticism : pouring scorn upon the version of Caxton he even found fault with

---

[27] T. F. Henderson, *Scottish Vernacular Literature*, p. 144.
[28] Wittig, *Scottish Tradition*, p. 58.
[29] Douglas Young, 'William Dunbar', *S.H.R.*, xxxviii. 10–9, at 19.
[30] Watt, *Fasti*, p. 357.   [31] Wittig, *Scottish Tradition*, p. 83.
[32] Matthew P. MacDiarmid in review (*S.H.R.*, xlviii. 180–1) of *The Shorter Poems of Gavin Douglas* (S.T.S.). This review also argues that Douglas was not the author of *King Hart*.
[33] Wittig, *Scottish Tradition*, pp. 77, 78.

Chaucer, the idol of the makars.[34] But despite the fidelity of his own version he could not resist the temptation to render specific what Virgil had left in general terms : sometimes the result is cumbrous, sometimes there is increased vigour and colour—one modern poet has daringly affirmed that the translation is better than the original.[35]

It was a translation into a language that Douglas, alone among the makars, called 'Scots' rather than 'Inglis'.[36] The language of the *Eneados* shows the Lowland vernacular at its best, ranging from the rough and guttural suited to rustic themes to the aureate of the more elevated—'the ryall style, clepyt heroycall . . . observand bewte, sentens, and gravite'.[37] In the prologues which he prefaced to each book of the poem Douglas was not tied to an original and was free to unloose his rich vocabulary on whatever themes took his fancy (with some passing reference to the book that was to follow). In these prologues he could expound his views on the Christian symbolism of Roman mythology, discuss the morality of warfare, utter wise saws and pithy proverbs, and, above all, describe the passing seasons not in stilted terms but in 'great nature poems, the first in Scots or English in which landscape is depicted solely for its own sake'. There are no conventional medieval May mornings but 'sharply-defined sense images drawn from a multiple awareness of nature that was to remain unrivalled until the eighteenth century'.[38] The bleakness of a Scottish winter is impressionistically conveyed in the line :

> The wynd maid wayfe the reid weyd on the dyk.

The rare summer days teem with insect life and close with a fiery sunset :

> All byrnand reid gan walxin the evin sky,
> The son enfyrit haill . . .[39]

The combination of scholarly aim, self-assertiveness, diction both rough and mellifluous, and a voluptuous sensitivity to nature, makes Douglas unique.

---

[34] *Ibid.*, p. 77.   [35] *Ibid.*, pp. 79–80.
[36] *Ibid.*, p. 85. Douglas was hardly the first (as Wittig supposed) to think of the Lowland vernacular as a language distinct from English : the *Lament for the Dauphiness* was translated from *lingua Gallicana* into *lingua Scoticana* (*Chron. Pluscarden*, I. 382), and Ayala reported that there was as much difference in the speech of Scots and English as in that of Aragonese and Castilians (Hume Brown, *Early Travellers*, p. 39).   [37] Wittig, *Scottish Tradition*, p. 79.
[38] *Ibid.*, pp. 85–6.   [39] *Ibid.*, pp. 85–90.

The trio of great makars of the aureate age was matched by another of notable scholars—John Ireland (*c.* 1440–*c.* 1496), John Major (*c.* 1469–1550) and Hector Boece (1465–1536).[40] Ireland, a theologian in the conciliarist tradition,[41] had been a prominent teacher at Paris before he entered the service of James III.[42] Besides his theological works in Latin three were composed in the Lowland vernacular; of these the only extant one is *The Meroure of Wyssedome*, presented to James IV in 1490. Ireland apologised (though somewhat vauntingly) that he wrote this work in English rather than in 'the tounge that I knaw better, that is Latin', and claimed that he was ignorant of 'the gret eloquens of Chauceir, na colouris that men uses in this Inglis metir that gret clerkis makis na counte of'.[43] The *Meroure*, which expounds the principles of the Christian faith and offers godly admonitions, is of interest as being the earliest extant sustained composition in Scots prose that is an original work as distinct from translation. It 'achieves an admirably clear expository method that our modern theologians might well emulate'.[44]

The achievements of John Major were more distinguished than those of Ireland. Despite his humble origin as son of an East Lothian countryman he made his way *via* Cambridge to Paris, where in 1493 he began a long and brilliant career in the university. It was a time when Paris attracted a throng of Scottish students, among them Hector Boece, Patrick Paniter and Gavin Douglas. In 1509, at the instance of the influential Douglas, an effort was made (though in vain) to tempt Major back to Scotland with the offer of the treasurership of the Chapel Royal. When he did return in 1518 it was to take up an appointment as principal regent in Glasgow University, after which he moved to St Andrews. There, according to John Knox, possibly one of his students, he was 'a man whose word was reckoned an oracle in matters of religion'.[45]

Major was 'among the last of the schoolmen, the teachers of the

[40] Their works, and those of lesser scholars, are listed by W. Forbes Leith in *Pre-Reformation Scholars in Scotland in the Sixteenth Century* (1915).

[41] J. H. Burns, *op. cit., S.H.R.*, XLII. 89–104.

[42] For his career see the notes to the edition of *The Meroure of Wyssdome* by C. Macpherson and F. Quinn (S.T.S., vol. I, 1926, vol. II, 1965), and review of vol. II by Matthew P. McDiarmid in *S.H.R.*, XLVIII. 179–80.

[43] *Gilbert of the Haye's Prose Manuscript* (S.T.S.), I. lvi.

[44] Matthew P. McDiarmid, *op. cit., S.H.R.*, XLVIII. 179–80, at 179. See also B. Miner, 'John Ireland and the Immaculate Conception', *Innes Review*, XVII. 24–39, and Brother Bonaventure, 'The popular theology of John Ireland', *ibid.*, XLI. 1–22.

[45] See Watt, *Fasti, ad indices*, and the 'Life of the Author', by Aeneas J. G. Mackay, prefixed to the S.H.S. edition of Major's *History*, pp. lxvii–lxviii.

old learning by the rigid scholastic discipline and methods'.[46] His old-fashioned Latin style was decried as 'Sorbonnic' by the humanists, and Melancthon declaimed: 'What waggon-loads of trifles! What pages he fills with dispute whether horsemanship requires a horse, whether the sea was salt when God made it.'[47] But the old learning was capable of application to new themes. Even in Major's theological works, and particularly in the commentary on Book IV of Peter Lombard's *Sentences*, which he published in 1509, there were digressions which showed that the professional academic and one time rustic had a deep interest in the folklore of Scotland and in its social and economic life.[48] As early as 1509 he was a staunch advocate of feuing. By 1521, when he published his *History of Greater Britain*, he had also become an advocate of union between Scotland and England. Like Guicciardini's *History of Italy*, Major's *History* was based on the assumption that a geographical unit, whether peninsula or island, should be treated as an historical unit. Hence for the first time, possibly for the last time, the inter-related histories of Scotland and England were compared, in equal detail, with surprising lack of bias, and with balanced comment. Major showed 'a wonderfully sound historical instinct, distinguishing truth from the fables with which Scottish annals were then encrusted'.[49] To the consternation of his friend, Gavin Douglas, he even rejected the story that the Scottish kings were descended from Scota. Had his *History* become more widely known, European historiography might have jumped forward two hundred years. In that humanistic age Major was damned by his unfashionable Latin style.

Hector Boece of Dundee shared (though naïvely) Major's interest in geography but had an eye for marvels rather than for economics and sociology. His *Lives of the Bishops of Mortlach and Aberdeen* was ingenuous and eulogistic. In his *Histories of the Scots from the Origin of the Race*, published in 1527, he adopted the approach of Livy—colourful narration rather than analysis and interpretation—and a suitably Augustan Latin style. This influential work (a model for that of George Buchanan) wiped out the historiographical advance made by Major.

Like Major, Boece was to have an influence upon university life in Scotland. In 1497 he was summoned from Paris to become regent

---

[46] Major, *History*, p. xlvi.   [47] *Ibid.*, p. lx.
[48] James Burns, 'The Scotland of John Major', *Innes Review*, II. 65–76.
[49] Aeneas J. G. Mackay, Major's *History*, p. lxxxiv.

master in arts, and eventually principal, of the new university of Aberdeen. This was the brain-child of Bishop Elphinstone, who, with the backing of the king, obtained the necessary papal bull on 10 February 1495. The new university was ostensibly intended to cater for those parts of the kingdom 'separated from the rest . . . by arms of the sea and very high mountains, in which dwell men rude and ignorant of letters, and almost barbarous'.[50] The foundation bull also specifically provided for the instruction of laymen as well as clerics. This novel feature[51] recognised the increased interest of the laity in higher education. A second novelty, which was symptomatic of increasing government intervention in every aspect of national life, was the addition of two of the king's councillors to those masters and scholars, who, under the bishop as ex-officio chancellor, were to formulate the university's constitution.[52] A third novelty was that the faculties at Aberdeen were to include not only arts, theology, canon law and civil law, but medicine. Hitherto this subject had not been altogether neglected in the English and Scottish universities; but Aberdeen was the first of them to aspire to a separate faculty. The king's interest was enlisted and moderate endowment was provided for a doctor of medicine who could be a layman. His precepts were probably less efficacious than those of the craft of surgeons and barbers of Edinburgh, who had a monopoly in the burgh of the sale of the newly invented *aqua vitae* (whisky)—one of the more reliable medicines—as well as the yearly gift of a criminal's corpse 'to mak antomell of, quhairthraw we may haif experience'.[53] By contrast the 'mediciner' of Aberdeen was expected to give instruction after the fashion of Paris—deduction from fanciful theories rather than from practical experience.[54] The courses in theology, arts and canon law were also to be modelled on those of Paris, but an exception was made for civil law, which was to follow the course of Orleans, 'the true source of the great influence exerted by Roman law upon the law of Scotland'.[55] The problems that Elphinstone faced, and surmounted, in providing for the teaching of civil law suggest that he hoped (though in vain) that Aberdeen would develop a strong law school.[56]

[50] *Nat. MSS. Scot.*, III. No. viii. See also Boece, *Vitae*, p. 57.

[51] Leslie J. Macfarlane, *op. cit.*, *Aberdeen University Review*, xxxix. 1–18, at 11.   [52] *Ibid.*, 14; Rashdall, *Universities*, II. 320.

[53] *Edinburgh Burgh Recs.*, I. 101–4.

[54] *Aberdeen Fasti*, No. 46; *R.M.S.*, II. No. 2358.

[55] John Kirkpatrick, *op. cit.*, *S.H.S. Misc.*, II. 47–102, at 56, 57.

[56] Leslie J. Macfarlane, *op. cit.*, *Aberdeen University Review*, xxxix. 1–18, at 16; Rashdall, *Universities*, II. 319.

It was some time before the papal bull of 1495 could be fully implemented. For ten years Elphinstone was busy cajoling endowments,[57] while not far from St Machar's Cathedral, where the central tower was nearing completion, rose the crowned tower and chapel of his new college, dedicated to the Virgin, but soon known as King's College. In 1505, when the essential buildings were almost ready for occupation, the constitution of the new establishment was published. As in the case of St Salvator's a collegiate kirk was the nucleus of an academic community. The total foundation of thirty-six members, later augmented to forty-two, can hardly have been as great as the staff of the cathedral, where there were no less than twenty vicars-choral, one of them the eminent musician, John Malison. Initially at least, some of the learned cathedral canons gave instruction in the university,[58] which doubtless also attracted some students who had no bursaries and were not on the foundation. 'From the university of Aberdeen', so Boece could affirm, 'there went out in a short time many men trained in theology, canon law and civil, and very many trained in philosophy'.[59]

Though Scotland now had one more university than England it was a pity that the funds and talents so carefully garnered for Aberdeen had not gone instead to sustain one or other of the two older universities. James III had renewed his father's grant of privileges to Glasgow;[60] Archbishop Blackadder had shown some interest; and reform had been attempted in 1492; but John Major, who disapproved of a 'multitude of universities', opined that Glasgow was 'poorly endowed, and not rich in scholars'.[61] In St Andrews the position was somewhat better. A sort of co-optative professoriate had emerged, and uniform competence, if not specialised brilliance, probably resulted from the 'regenting' system whereby each regent master conducted a group of students through the whole of the arts curriculum.[62] A major source of dispute within the university had been appeased in 1470, when St Salvator's College was induced to renounce the privilege (lately conferred by papal bull) of granting degrees independently of the university.[63] Another source of trouble had been eliminated by the long-delayed suppression of private pedagogies: all save the poorest students or the sons of the local

[57] See *R.M.S.*, II. Nos. 2442, 2570, 3598, 3733; *Aberdeen Fasti*, pp. 9–52.

[58] Leslie J. Macfarlane, *op. cit.*, *Aberdeen University Review*, XXXIX. 1–18, at 11–7; *Aberdeen Fasti*, pp. 53–64, 80–108.

[59] Boece, *Vitae*, p. 91.   [60] *R.M.S.*, II. No. 1095.

[61] Major, *History*, pp. 28–9; *St Andrews Acta*, I. xxxviii.

[62] *St Andrews Acta*, I. cxxi–cxxv.   [63] *Ibid.*, xxix–xxxii.

townsfolk were now obliged to reside either in St Salvator's or in the less flourishing Pedagogy. Alexander Stewart, the boy-archbishop, had thoughts of re-modelling the latter, but in 1512 chose to convert a hospital for elderly women into the new college of St Leonard's for the maintenance of twenty poor clerks, students of arts, and six students of theology.[64] Thus during the reign the university continued to fulfil a modest role : it could number William Dunbar and Gavin Douglas among its graduates, though Douglas was by no means the only graduate who regarded his St Andrews career as a preparation for finer things in the French universities.

The traditional higher education was not the one selected for Alexander Stewart: in 1508 the boy-archbishop was sent to Padua and spent some months at Siena, where he was taught Greek and rhetoric under the tutorship of Erasmus, the leading humanist of the age.[65] Humanism was beginning to affect Scotland. Its possible sources were 'study in Italy, especially at the highly humanist papal court ; contact in the Low Countries ; and Italian influence coming to Scotland through France'.[66] It is remarkable that as early as 1433 the library at Glasgow Cathedral held a copy of Petrarch's *De Vita Solitaria*.[67] Though such a work was hardly commonplace in fifteenth-century Scottish libraries, where the more traditional scholastic fare abounded,[68] there were personal book collections which hinted at the humanist inclinations of the owners, as in the case of Archibald Whitelaw, tutor of James III and chief secretary between 1462 and 1493. An example of his Ciceronian Latinity survives in the record of negotiations at Nottingham in 1484, when he 'purposyd a oracyon' using no little hyperbole in his flattery of Richard III and going out of his way to explain the meaning of a Greek word.[69] Patrick Paniter, who became chief secretary in 1505 and tutored Alexander Stewart before his trip to Italy,[70] was cast in the same mould. In a Latin of 'Corinthian glitter' he could 'turn a grace-

---

[64] *R.M.S.*, II. No. 3812; *St Andrews Acta*, I. xliii–xliv; J. Herkless and R. K. Hannay, *The College of St Leonard* (1905).

[65] Lesley, *History*, p. 80; Leslie J. Macfarlane, *op. cit.*, *Innes Review*, xx. 111–29, at 121–2.

[66] Durkan, *Bishop Turnbull*, p. 36.

[67] *Ibid.*, p. 45.

[68] See John Durkan and Anthony Ross, *Early Scottish Libraries, passim*, and Anthony Ross, 'Libraries of the Scottish Blackfriars : 1481–1560', *Innes Review*, xx. 3–36.

[69] 'Negotiations of the Scottish Commissioners at Nottingham', *Bannatyne Misc., II.* 41–8; see also Durkan, *Bishop Turnbull*, pp. 43, 56–7, and MacQueen, *Robert Henryson*, pp. 13–5.

[70] Leslie J. Macfarlane, *op. cit.*, *Innes Review*, xx. 111–29, at 121.

ful compliment to a foreign princess, put off the demands of an importunate ally with expressions of deep affection which, seeming to promise everything, promised nothing, throw the cloak of piety over some peculiarly twisted simoniacal transaction, or recite the grievances of merchant or mariner, unaccountably thrust into prison in some foreign port. Sometimes, as when he pleads with the pope to establish peace and concord in Christendom, he reaches real eloquence'.[71] Had his pupil, Alexander Stewart, lived longer, St Andrews, like Cambridge, might have reluctantly given an early welcome to the new learning.

Even in Italy the universities at first resisted the humanist movement. Yet 'it was bound to influence the grammar schools where students received their preliminary training, and in due course infiltrate into university teaching itself'.[72] Little can be certainly known (though much may be inferred) about the condition of the Scottish grammar schools.[73] According to the so-called 'Education Act' issued by the parliament of June 1496[74] they were at least expected to equip their pupils with 'perfyte Latyne'. The act itself was a statement of educational aspirations: all barons and substantial freeholders, on pain of a £20 fine, were to send their eldest sons and heirs to grammar school from the age of eight or nine; after they had mastered Latin they were to spend three years studying arts or law in the universities. The effectiveness of the act, or the extent to which it corresponded to prevailing conditions, is hard to estimate. In 1501, however, the son and heir of Patrick Home of Fast Castle would obtain leave 'to pas to Parisch to the skulis to lere . . . vertuis and sience'—and to take his wife with him.[75] Several examples may also be found of laymen who had obtained a master's degree;[76] and Henry, Lord Sinclair, can hardly have been altogether unschooled when he besought Gavin Douglas to undertake a translation of Virgil or Homer.[77]

But it was not the aim of the 1496 act to produce aristocratic dilettanti. Its purpose was to inculcate 'knawlege and understanding of the lawis . . . sua that thai that ar schireffis or jugeis ordinaris . . . may have knawlege to do justice'. Thus, it was hoped, 'justice may reigne universalie throw all the realme', and 'the pure pepill sulde

[71] R. L. Mackie in *James IV, Letters*, p. xxxiii.

[72] Durkan, *Bishop Turnbull*, p. 34.

[73] See MacQueen, *Robert Henryson*, pp. 4–12, 15.

[74] *A.P.S.*, II. 238, c. 3. See also Lesley, *History*, p. 63; *St Andrews Acta*, I. xxxix–xl; D. E. Easson, *op. cit.*, *Scot. Church Hist. Soc. Recs.*, VI. 13–26, at 23–4.

[75] *R.S.S.*, I. No. 712.

[76] E.g. *ibid.*, No. 2196.   [77] Mackie, *James IV*, p. 169.

have na neid to seik our soverane lordis principale auditouris for ilk small injure'. The pragmatic attitude towards education was further illustrated by the attitude of the Abbot of Arbroath, who in 1497 was sending some of his monks to university so that 'having learned legal remedies they may frustrate the attacks of certain folk and the sinister machinations which impend against our abbey'.[78]

A practical and utilitarian spirit also inspired the experimentation that the king encouraged. It was probably an apocryphal story that he placed two infants on Inchkeith in the charge of a dumb woman to determine what tongue nature would inspire them to speak.[79] Better attested is the king's patronage of medicine and surgery. One pharmacist, William Fowler, was given exemption from service on inquests and from payment of taxes.[80] John Damian de Falcusis, the 'French leech', fared much better. His vain experiments at Stirling in 1503 in search of the *quinta essencia*—the fifth 'essence' that might transmute base metals into goid—were subsidised by the king,[81] who also made him Abbot of Tongland. The failure of Damian's experiment in flying from the battlements of Stirling inspired one of William Dunbar's satires :

> The air was dirkit with the fowlis
> That come with yawmeris and with yowlis
> With skyrking, skrymming and with scowlis
> To tak him in the tyde.[82]

Bishop Lesley more soberly recounts Damian's explanation that 'thair was sum hen fedderis in the wingis, quhilk . . . covet the mydding and not the skyis'.[83]

In technological advancement the king showed a persistent interest. At his 'instance and request' and for 'the honour and proffit of the realm' a notable initiative was taken by Walter Chepman and Andrew Millar, the first of whom was both a clerk in the secretary's office and a prominent Edinburgh merchant. In 1507 the pair undertook to 'bring hame ane prent . . . and expert men to use the samyne'.[84] Since books printed on the continent were already making their way into Scotland the investment of Chepman and Millar was

---

[78] Coulton, *Scottish Abbeys*, p. 309.   [79] Pitscottie, *Historie*, I. 237.
[80] *R.S.S.*, I. No. 899; see also No. 1343.
[81] *T.A.*, II. 138, 359-62, 374, 402, 422; see also *James IV, Letters*, No. 32.
[82] *The fenyeit Freir of Tungland* (Wittig, *Scottish Tradition*, p. 68).
[83] Lesley, *History*, p. 76.
[84] *R.S.S.*, I. No. 1546; *T.A.*, I. ci; *E.R.*, XI. xxix.

to be safeguarded by prohibiting the export of manuscripts for print-ting abroad. Meanwhile, it was optimistically hoped, the new printing press in Edinburgh would be kept busy publishing 'bukis of our lawis, actis of parliament, croniclis, mess bukis and portuus [brevi-aries]'. Here, as in much else, there was a utilitarian and nationalist aim : knowledge of the laws would be disseminated; chronicles (prob-ably Bower's *Scotichronicon* was intended) would inculcate patriot-ism; so also would the liturgical works. For the press was to be used to popularise the developing Scottishness of the kirk :[85] Chepman and Millar were to print not legends of the saints in general but 'legendis of Scottis sanctis' as composed by Bishop Elphinstone; and the liturgical works were to be 'eftir our awin Scottis use', replacing those modelled upon the English 'use of Sarum'—no 'bukis of Salus-bery use' were to be 'brocht to be sauld within our realm in tyme cuming'.[86] Not all of this ambitious publishing programme was carried out. In 1509 and 1510 appeared the two fine volumes of Elphinstone's *Aberdeen Breviary*; but tales of chivalry and romance, Blind Harry's *Wallace*, some of the poems of William Dunbar and Robert Henryson, provided more profitable printing than acts of parliament.[87]

Even more obviously than in the case of the printing press royal and national prestige could be enhanced by technological advance in the manufacture of artillery and the construction of ships. In Edinburgh Castle Robert Borthwick, probably aided by Hans Gun-nare, George van Erisling and French artificers, was kept busy casting guns, among them the famous 'Seven Sisters'.[88] Artillery had begun to revolutionise naval warfare : after a lapse of centuries the warship, as distinct from the converted merchantman, was beginning to re-appear; improved facilities for construction and repair were required; a new breed of mariners was beginning to vie for renown alongside the military élite. Sir Andrew Wood, a mere inhabitant of Leith, had by-passed burgess-ship in his social rise, was the king's 'familiar knight' by 1495, and by 1513 was just as concerned as any noble that his surname and arms be preserved to posterity. In all the typical developments of the age—feuing, tower-building, the erection of burghs of barony, the foundation of chaplainries, remissions and respites—he was to be found involved.[89] The three Barton brothers,

[85] See p. 560 above.   [86] *R.S.S.*, I. No. 1546.
[87] Mackie, *James IV*, pp. 170–1.
[88] Pitscottie, *Historie*, I. 259–60; Lesley, *History*, p. 81; *R.M.S.*, II. No. 3546; *R.S.S.*, I. Nos. 916, 2033; *E.R.*, XIII. clxvii–clxxi; *T.A.*, IV. 276–8.
[89] *R.M.S.*, II. Nos. 2231, 2825, 3880; *E.R.*, XIII. clxxix–clxxxi.

John, Robert and Andrew, bid fair to profit by Wood's example.[90] The need for such men had been demonstrated at the outset of the reign when the depredations of foreign pirates, even in the waters of the Forth, made parliament willingly approve a licence for the fortification of Inchgarvie Isle by John Dundas.[91] King and parliament were also well aware of the potentialities of the new off-shore herring fisheries. These not only increased the kingdom's natural resources[92] but gave employment to men and small vessels that could be pressed into royal service in time of war : both economic and strategic motives lay behind the acts of June 1492 and March 1504 that exhorted burghs and nobles to build fishing boats of at least twenty tuns burthen.[93] In 1505 the king acquired Newhaven (then undeveloped) from Holyrood Abbey, built a pier and dockyard, and in 1511 granted the new port to Edinburgh.[94] In shipbuilding James gave a lead to his subjects. He had inherited a few royal ships from his father ; one or two vessels were purchased, a few others were ordered in the shipyards of Flanders and Brittany; even more significantly timber, tackle and shipwrights were imported from Normandy.[95] The woods of Darnaway were felled for shipbuilding at Leith[96] and those of Fife for the construction of the *Michael* at Newhaven. This vessel, which the French king thought the greatest in Christendom,[97] was reputed to have cost £30,000. Although this, and some other details given by Pitscottie,[98] may be discounted, he was very near the mark in reporting that the crew numbered three hundred.[99]

In 1506 James had informed Louis XII that the creation of a fleet for the protection of Scottish shores was a project of long standing that was close to his heart ; both he and the fleet, so he unctuously affirmed, would be ready to do the bidding of the French king.[100] James showed no intention of using his ships to compete with those of Portugal and Spain in winning the spices of the Indies, the slaves of Africa, the silver of the Americas. Apart from protecting Scotland

[90] See W. Stanford Reid, *Skipper from Leith, passim*; *E.R.*, xiii. clxxxi.

[91] *A.P.S.*, ii. 270; *R.M.S.*, ii. No. 2038.

[92] See *A.P.S.*, ii. 183, c. 15; 209, c. 12; 237, c. 24; *E.R.*, x. 638; *R.S.S.*, i. Nos. 286, 709, 710.

[93] *A.P.S.*, ii. 235, c. 20; 251, c. 15.   [94] *R.M.S.*, ii. Nos. 2864, 3551.

[95] W. Stanford Reid, *op. cit.*, *Medievalia et Humanistica*, xv. 97–107, at 99–101; *E.R.*, xiii. clxxxiv–clxxxvi; *R.S.S.*, i. No. 323; Lesley, *History*, p. 62.

[96] *E.R.*, xiii. clxvi.   [97] *Flodden Papers*, p. 70.

[98] Pitscottie, *Historie*, i. 251–2.

[99] 295 'mariners of the great ship' were paid by the treasurer, mostly at the rate of 35s. a month (*T.A.*, iv. 502–5); see also *E.R.*, xii. xxxv and n.

[100] *James IV, Letters*, No. 42.

the new and costly fleet had four functions : it was an asset in James's complex diplomacy;[101] it proved its worth in the daunting of the Isles; it was used to suppress foreign piracy in the North Sea—in 1506 Andrew Barton, captain of the *Margaret*, sent the king a barrel stuffed with the heads of Dutch freebooters;[102] finally, it could improve James's chances of being accepted as commander of a grand crusade against the Ottoman Turks.

This project, thanks to its long medieval antecedents, had overtones that were quixotic, and the problems it involved were possibly insurmountable. Yet never before did Western Europe stand in greater need of a grand crusade. For while the far corners of the globe were being brought into the service of Europe and Christianity, Christian Europe was itself shrinking : the galleys of Islam swept the Mediterranean; Hungary would soon be lost; and Vienna, besieged in 1529, would not be freed of the Turkish menace until its deliverance by Sobieski in 1683.

The anxiety that James seems to have felt about the Ottoman advance was possibly stimulated by Archbishop Blackadder, who died at Jaffa in 1508 during a pilgrimage to the Holy Land.[103] First-hand information was also forthcoming from two Greek nobles who visited Scotland, as well as from the laird of Fast Castle, who in 1509 came home after a period in Turkish service in Cairo.[104] In 1510 James outlined to the Marquis of Mantua his hope that 'one army drawn from all nations may be turned against the enemies of Christ'. Alone among the rulers of Europe the Scottish king was prepared to act in the interests of Europe as a whole.[105]

He was not, as has been asserted, a 'moonstruck romantic'.[106] Never blind to his own interests, he had a longer experience of statecraft than most rulers and could rival all of them in deviousness. Yet, having achieved some stability in the relationships that now linked Scotland on honourable terms with France and England, James had no desire to see that stability upset by bickerings in Italian vineyards. The crusading scheme, together with the missions of mediation entrusted to Bishop Forman, might end the international power struggle that became increasingly obnoxious after 1509.

---

[101] W. Stanford Reid, *op. cit.*, *Medievalia et Humanistica*, xv. 97–107.
[102] Lesley, *History*, p. 74.
[103] See David McRoberts, 'Scottish Pilgrims to the Holy Land', *Innes Review*, xx. 80–106.   [104] *T.A.*, II. xxvii; Lesley, *History*, p. 80.
[105] Mackie, *James IV*, p. 205; *James IV, Letters*, Nos. 307, 308, 332, 353, 356, 386, 422, 503, 516.   [106] Mackie, *James IV*, p. 201.

In that year James's astute and pacific father-in-law was succeeded by Henry VIII, an egocentric teenager whose tantrums and petulance bespoke an inferiority complex. Although he confirmed the treaty of perpetual peace with Scotland, and in May 1510 made a treaty with France,[107] Henry was restive and pugnacious. So also was Julius II. Lately he had humbled Venice with the help of the French; in 1509 he became implacably committed to expelling them from Italy, and in October 1511 he concluded a 'Holy League' with Venice and Ferdinand of Aragon. Henry's adherence to this anti-French coalition was soon bought when Ferdinand duped him with the promise of aid towards the recovery of Aquitaine for the English crown. Meanwhile the question of the royal succession in both England and Scotland must have contributed to the nervousness of their rulers.[108] James's queen vied with Henry's (Catherine of Aragon) in natal misfortunes, and the unexpected deaths of James's two brothers —Mar in 1503 and the duke-archbishop in 1504—brought the Earl of Arran and the Duke of Albany, absentee and half French, closer to the throne. But from 1509 until 1516 James's queen was Henry's heir presumptive. It was hardly tactful that her second son, Arthur (born in 1509 only to die in 1510) was given the name once borne by Henry VIII's elder brother, a name that was 'British' rather than Scottish or English. On 10 April 1512 James's confidence, and Henry's irritation, must have been increased when Queen Margaret at last gave birth to a son [109] (the future James V) who escaped infant mortality to inherit his mother's potential claim to the English crown. Henry's pettiness was displayed in his refusal to transmit to his sister the bequests made to her by their father.[110]

The two courts had also become estranged over incidents at sea. The uses to which James intended to put Scottish seapower were not necessarily those of the naval captains on whom he depended. The Bartons were pirates whose activities he abetted, particularly by renewing letters of marque granted to them by James III.[111] Foreigners who complained to the lords of council were met by judicial procrastination and unhelpfulness. In the spring of 1511 James again re-issued the letters of marque and Andrew Barton set sail, finding it difficult to tell the difference between the intended victims (the Portuguese) and the English. In June he was encountered in the

---

[107] *Ibid.*, p. 200.   [108] *James IV, Letters*, pp. xxxiv–xxxv.
[109] *Ibid.*, Nos. 443, 444.   [110] *Ibid.*, No. 543.
[111] *Edinburgh Burgh Recs.*, I. 119–20; W. Stanford Reid, *Skipper from Leith*, p. 35.

Downs by the English admiral, Sir Edward Howard, and his brother, Lord Thomas Howard. The *Lion* and the *Jenny Pirwin* were captured and Andrew Barton fell in the engagement. In vain James heatedly demanded that Sir Edward Howard should be arraigned in the warden court for breach of the peace treaty and the death of Andrew Barton. Henry replied with a taunt that it did not become one prince to accuse another of infraction of a treaty merely because justice had been done on a thief or pirate.[112] It was ironic that, independent of the continental power struggle, warfare almost ensued between Scotland and England in 1511 and that Louis XII on 8 November, five days before England entered the Holy League, strove to reconcile James and Henry.[113]

Soon Louis realised his mistake. He had already denounced Julius II as a traitor to Christendom and summoned a general council of the church to meet at Pisa. Louis had no wish to be distracted from the Italian conflict by an English menace to France and hoped to distract the English with a Scottish menace to England. In January 1512 he promised James that vast French assistance for the crusade would be at his disposal a year after the pope should agree to peace with France. In April James was told that Louis would support him in any rightful claim to the English crown. In July James renewed the Franco-Scottish alliance: if either partner were at war with England the other would at once make full-scale war upon the English.[114] It mattered little that the renewed Franco-Scottish alliance was incompatible with the Anglo-Scottish peace treaty that had been renewed in 1509.[115] It was a time when treaties represented little more than wishful thinking: although an English expeditionary force appeared in Guienne in the summer of 1512 and the coasts of Brittany were raided by Sir Edward Howard's fleet, James did not break with England; and at Bayonne the English waited in vain for the aid promised by Ferdinand, who merely used them to distract the French while he seized Navarre and then made a one-year truce. But Ferdinand's temporary defection from the Holy League was counterbalanced by the adherence of Emperor Maximilian, lately the ally of France; and the costly failure in Guienne stung Henry's pride.[116] The expedition planned for the summer of 1513 was one that he meant to command in person.

---

[112] Mackie, *James IV*, pp. 207–11; *James IV, Letters*, pp. lii–liv.
[113] *Flodden Papers*, No. iv, p. 13.
[114] *James IV, Letters*, pp. liv–lxi; Mackie, *James IV*, pp. 202–7, 213–9.
[115] For a comparison of the terms see Mackie, *James IV*, pp. 98–9, 216–9.
[116] *Ibid.*, pp. 214–25.

What James would do if Henry landed in France was doubtful. In Scotland there had been not only protracted preparations for war but lengthy deliberation on all aspects of the power struggle. In 1511 and 1512 councils had been summoned to discuss relations with France and the pope.[117] James did not commit himself to sending representatives to the Gallican council of Pisa but continued to regard a reconciliation of France and the papacy as his chief diplomatic objective, partly, perhaps, because it might lead to the pope's releasing him from the excommunication he would incur by breaking the peace treaty with England. Meanwhile, it was hoped, Denmark might be aligned with France and Scotland. King Hans would not commit himself to France, responded evasively to the anxious solicitations of his nephew, and eventually sent him some munitions,[118] but not the Danish ships that James hoped to add to his own fleet.[119]

Whilst most of Europe feverishly prepared for a new campaigning season, fresh uncertainties, and hopes, were aroused by the death of Pope Julius. The first tidings of his demise were brought to Scotland by John Barton, whose ship, laden with munitions from France, reached the Forth on 20 March 1513. Eleven days later it sailed back carrying Bishop Forman on a mission to the French and papal courts.[120] Shortly before Forman departed, an English ambassador, Nicholas West, arrived at the Scottish court, where he was to spend an acrimonious and unrewarding three weeks, passing his spare time spying upon the fleet. He strove to obtain a guarantee of Scottish neutrality, even, if possible, a loan of the *Michael*. In return he had nothing to offer. James gave him details of the French king's promise of help for the crusade and explained, 'now you see wherefore I favour the French king and wherefore I am loth to lose him, for if I do I shall never be able to perform my journey'. On 13 April West had to leave for Berwick, having failed to extort from James any definite answer as to whether he would, or would not, remain neutral if Henry invaded France.[121]

Forman would be equally unsuccessful at Rome. The new pope, Leo X, did not offer him the cardinal's hat that Julius II had once hinted at bestowing, but in other respects adhered to the policies of his predecessor and provided the English with letters permitting the excommunication of James if he broke the peace treaty.[122] On the

---

[117] *A.D.C.P.*, pp. vi–vii. [118] Lesley, *History*, pp. 85–6.
[119] W. Stanford Reid, *op. cit.*, *Juridical Review*, LVIII. 183–200, at 191–3.
[120] Mackie, *James IV*, pp. 230–2. [121] *Ibid.*, pp. 230–7.
[122] *Ibid.*, pp. 232–3, 236.

way to Rome, however, Forman had transacted important business at the French court, where he presented James's request that Louis should send to Scotland troops, guns, ships and money. Louis was reminded that if Scotland joined in the war France was not to make peace until James had obtained the English crown.[123] James ambitiously hoped to draw the French from their Italian adventures in order to further his own dynastic schemes. If these were successful Scotland and England would be united and he would be free to lead the grand crusade. Louis tactfully twisted James's inordinate requests to his own advantage. In counter-proposals that reached Scotland at the beginning of June he suggested that the Scottish fleet be sent to France, where it would be fully equipped and victualled and a subsidy of 50,000 francs would be paid, then (at some indefinite time) the vessels would be sent back to Scotland with seven French galleys to be used at James's discretion; if James were to invade England as soon as Henry invaded France he would best advance his claim to the English crown.[124] Similar proposals, together with a special request for the *Michael*, had already been put forward by Jehan de la Motte, who in May 1513 acted for the third time as Louis's ambassador at the Scottish court.[125] But James remained uncommitted: on 24 May he wrote to Henry, his 'dearest brothir', to suggest that both Scotland and England become parties to the truce already concluded between France and Aragon; although James also expressed regret that Henry's admiral, Sir Edward Howard, had recently been killed in a naval engagement with the French, he pointedly alluded to the crusade by affirming that the valiant knight's services would have been put to better use in warfare upon the enemies of Christ.[126] Since this appeal had no effect upon Henry, James concluded that he must at least make some moves to disconcert the English and satisfy the French: in June the vessels in the Forth were made ready for war and a mobilisation of sailors was ordered for July.[127]

Early in that month news must have reached Scotland, almost simultaneously, that the French army in Italy had met disaster at Novara on 6 June and that Henry VIII had sailed on 30 June to begin his invasion of France by laying siege to Thérouanne in Artois.[128] Possibly also there arrived a ring from Queen Anne of France and an appeal to James to advance three feet into England for her sake. James's own queen counselled peace. So also did Bishop Elphin-

[123] *Flodden Papers*, No. xvi. [124] *Ibid.*, No. xvii.
[125] Mackie, *James IV*, pp. 217–9, 237–9. [126] *James IV, Letters*, No. 550.
[127] *T.A.*, iv. 413–4, 480, 481, 483. [128] Mackie, *James IV*, p. 240.

stone, who was shouted down in the council (so Boece asserts) 'because, like a mad old man, he had spoken stupidly and thoughtlessly against the commonweal, against their sacred treaty and ancient league'.[129] The ancient league with France meant much to Bishop Forman : in June Louis XII had begun to put pressure on the chapter of Bourges to accept him as archbishop; Forman eventually obtained this French archbishopric as a reward for persuading James to go to war.[130]

But even at the last moment James played for time : on 24 July the host was summoned to muster at Ellem in Berwickshire;[131] yet when Lyon king-of-arms was despatched to Henry on 26 July he carried a sort of ultimatum, not an outright declaration of war;[132] and although another herald left for Paris on 27 July with the news that the fleet had sailed, the *Michael* and its attendant vessels, nine or eleven in all,[133] had emerged from the Forth to head north, rather than south.

It is inconceivable that the commander of the fleet, the Earl of Arran, no Medina Sidonia but a man formerly entrusted with naval operations in the Hebrides, had disobeyed orders. In 1495, when James was bent upon doing mischief to Henry VII, he had accepted the homage and co-operation of Hugh O'Donnel of Tyrconnel,[134] one of the two great Gaelic chiefs of Ulster. A second Hugh, son and heir of the first, had visited the Scottish court to conclude an offensive and defensive alliance with the king on 25 June 1513. The 'greit Odinle of Ireland', whom James recognised as prince and kinsman, was promised assistance in ships and men. In mid-July he left Edinburgh with a great cannon, another piece of artillery, ammunition, workmen, and eight quarriers 'for undirmynding of wallis'.[135] The *Michael*, which carried at least fourteen gunners, could be used for the same purpose and could disembark a vast complement of troops to enter the breaches in enemy strongholds. Having rounded Cape Wrath and shown the flag in the Hebrides it battered Carrickfergus, the chief English stronghold in Ulster.[136] When the spoil of Carrick-

[129] Boece, *Vitae*, pp. 104–5; Pitscottie, *Historie*, I. 256, 261.

[130] Mackie, *James IV*, p. 277.   [131] *T.A.*, IV. 416–7.

[132] *James IV, Letters*, No. 560; Lesley, *History*, pp. 87–91.

[133] Mackie, *James IV*, pp. 242–3.

[134] *R.M.S.*, II. No. 3856; *T.A.*, I. 242; Conway, *Henry VII*, pp. 85–6.

[135] *R.M.S.*, II. No. 3856; *T.A.*, IV. 415–6, 434–5, 527; Lesley, *History*, p. 86; *James IV, Letters*, Nos. 89, 104–6. For the Irish background see E. Curtis, *Medieval Ireland*, p. 362.   [136] Pitscottie, *Historie*, I. 256–7.

fergus was carried to Ayr there was still an opportunity to recall the fleet. It sailed on to France. Eventually most of the vessels would come back. But a Scottish fleet would never be re-fashioned: the *Michael*, sold to the French king for 40,000 francs, was left to rot.[137]

Meanwhile, so claims Pitscottie, as James sat in St Michael's Kirk in Linlithgow, 'verie sad and dollarous', a strange man warned him to desist from his projected enterprise then 'vanischit away . . . as he had bene ane blink of the sone or ane quhipe of the whirle wind'.[138] But the king's mind remained unaltered. Despite his ambitions he had laboured for three years in the cause of peace. Had Henry VIII shown some signs of goodwill there would have been no war; so long as there was little likelihood of real friendship with England it seemed better to stand by France. Nothing could be farther from the truth than to suppose that this decision was rash and precipitate.

Early in August James had sent his warden, Lord Home, to raid Northumberland. On their withdrawal the booty-laden Scots were ambushed at Milfield between the slopes of Flodden Hill and the river Till, and lost heavily from the fire of English archers concealed among the bracken and thickets. The warden extricated himself with heavy loss, leaving his banner behind him. The humiliation of this 'Ill Raid'[139] probably stimulated the king in his warlike preparations. While contingents of the Scottish army made their way across the bleak Lammermuir hills to muster in the valley of the Whiteadder, preparations were made to send the artillery southwards. On 17 August it made its cumbrous way from Edinburgh Castle. There were seventeen guns in all, 'as goodly guns as have been seen in any realm'.[140] They were drawn on their way by four hundred oxen, and attended by a gang of forty workmen, a crane, powder-carts, and pack animals carrying gunstones.[141] The king, having returned from a devout pilgrimage to the shrine of St Duthac[142] in Ross, set out from Edinburgh on 19 August, probably with the provost and some local contingents that had been mustered on the Burgh Muir.[143] A presage of disaster had occurred on the previous night when some unexplained summons was issued from the Mercat Cross calling on members of the expedition to compear within forty days in the nether

[137] *A.D.C.P.*, pp. 39–40; W. Stanford Reid, *op. cit.*, *Medievalia et Humanistica*, xv. 97–107, at 106–7.

[138] Pitscottie, *Historie*, I. 258–9.

[139] Mackie, *James IV*, p. 246.

[140] 'Trewe Encountre', p. 146.

[141] Mackie, *James IV*, pp. 247–8.

[142] *T.A.*, IV. 419.

[143] Mackie, *James IV*, pp. 247–8.

world.[144] The plague had probably reached Edinburgh,[145] and must have been carried to the host as it mustered at Ellem.

On 22 August the Scots forded the Tweed and confronted Norham Castle. On the same day Thérouanne surrendered to Henry VIII. Had the news ever reached James it would have confirmed him in his belief that the threat to France was not to be lightly dismissed. The governor of Norham had boasted that he would hold it against the Scots until Henry came back from France. He held out for only six days.[146] After the capture of Norham the Scots advanced a few miles southward into the valley of the Till. A week was spent in subduing the castles of Etal and Wark. By 4 September, Lady Heron, whose supposed romantic connection with James[147] is probably apocryphal, had surrendered Ford Castle.

At Twizelhaugh on 24 August James had been persuaded to issue an ordinance of a type that seems to have been traditional before some dire engagement : the heirs of any member of the host who might be slain, or die of wounds or disease, would be exempt from payment of the usual feudal casualties.[148] But it was by no means certain that any dire engagement would take place. It may be inferred from James's leisurely proceedings that his strategy was not an ambitious one, that he had no mind to attack Berwick[149] or penetrate deeply into England but was merely engaged in a military demonstration, enough to preserve his credit with the French king but not enough to earn the undying hostility of Henry VIII and render peace-making unduly difficult.

It was not the intention of Thomas Howard, Earl of Surrey, that James should escape so lightly. Before sailing for Calais Henry had entrusted the defence of northern England to the septuagenarian earl.[150] He had worsted James in 1497, escorted his bride to Scotland in 1503, and could well assess the psychology of his opponent. Surrey's well-laid plans for the mobilisation of the northern counties worked well. Despite the downpour of rain that hindered the passage of an army over sodden tracks, he had marched rapidly northward from his base at Pontefract. The English fleet had weathered a storm and arrived in the Tyne in time to land a thousand soldiers and mariners and a number of ships' guns. By 4 September this contingent, led by Surrey's son, Thomas Howard, the new English admiral,

---

144 Pitscottie, *Historie*, I. 260–1. 145 *Edinburgh Burgh Recs.*, I. 141.

146 Mackie, *James IV*, pp. 249, 256. 147 Pitscottie, *Historie*, I. 262–4.

148 *A.P.S.*, II. 278; cf. *R.S.S.*, VII. viii.

149 See, however, J. D. Mackie, 'The English Army at Flodden', *S.H.S. Misc.* *VIII*. 35–85, at 37–8. 150 Mackie, *James IV*, pp. 240–1.

had reached Alnwick.[151] While the English forces were arrayed there, Surrey engaged in diplomatic exchanges with James, possibly in the belief that he might elude him by slipping back to Scotland only to return when the English army had dispersed; and dispersal was imminent, for if Surrey did not lack men he was certainly short of supplies, notably beer.[152] Thus Rougecroix pursuivant was despatched to inform James that the earl would be prepared to wage battle with him on 9 September. Lest James should pay no heed to this challenge the English admiral added a jibe alluding to his part in the death of Andrew Barton : Howard 'was nowe come in hys awne proper person too be in the vauntgarde of the felde to justifié the death of the said Andrewe'. On 6 September a reply came by Islay herald to say that James would wait to do battle until noon on 9 September.[153]

For the last few days James had been at Ford Castle, but on 5 September he set fire to it and crossed to the western bank of the Till. The new Scottish encampment was placed between three hills, and the obvious approach, a narrow gulley, was defended by an entrenchment behind which the Scottish artillery was placed.[154] For the Scots to station themselves in a strong fortified camp was a novel practice, which may have owed something to French military advisers and recent experience in the Italian wars.[155] It showed a foresight that displeased the English : the Scots had placed themselves on ground 'like a fortresse or campe' rather than accepting the site of battle thought appropriate by Surrey.[156] But James was not impressed by this chivalric objection. In 1497 he had once challenged Surrey to hand-to-hand combat and the earl had avoided the encounter by chiding the king for his condescension in being willing to fight a mere earl.[157] Now James denied Rougecroix an interview but sent him a message to inform Surrey that 'it beseemeth him not, being an earl, so largely to attempt a great prince'; James would 'take and hold his ground at his own pleasure, and not at the assigning of the Earl of Surrey'.[158]

Diplomacy having failed, Surrey marched alongside the eastern bank of the Till out of range of the Scottish guns and camped for the night. On the morning of 9 September the English once more marched northwards on the eastern side of the Till. As yet, the Scots

[151] *Ibid.*, pp. 250–1.   [152] 'Trewe Encountre', p. 147.
[153] *James IV, Letters*, No. 566; Mackie, *James IV*, p. 253.
[154] 'Trewe Encountre', p. 146. See the map in Mackie, *James IV*, p. 258.
[155] Mackenzie, *Flodden*, pp. 72–3.   [156] *James IV, Letters*, No. 566.
[157] M. J. Tucker, *The Life of Thomas Howard, Earl of Surrey* (1964), p. 67.
[158] 'Trewe Encountre', p. 146.

saw no reason to leave their own well-defended camp. Suddenly the Earl of Surrey with the English rearguard began to ford the river at Heton, while his son, the admiral, took the vanguard and the artillery over Twizel bridge, five miles north of the Scottish position and out of range of the Scottish guns.[159] If the Scots had been watchful there would probably have been time to contest the passage of the Till. Had they attacked when the English rearguard and vanguard were not only divided, but engaged in crossing the river, the English could hardly have avoided disaster. Why the Scots did not attack at this point is an enigma. Part of the explanation may be that James had announced that he would wait to do battle at noon on 9 September; when noon came and the English forces were seen apparently making for Berwick, he may have rashly assumed that Surrey was ignominiously declining the prescribed encounter.[160] All too late the Scots discovered that the enemy had crossed the river and lay between them and Scotland. Thus the Scots were compelled to make an unexpected volte-face. James hastily moved to the edge of Branxton Hill near Flodden to deny the high ground to the English.[161] Even this new position was potentially a strong one. But the Scots had no time to take much advantage of it. Surrey realised that to make the most of the initiative he had already won he must make an immediate advance upon the outwitted and flurried Scots. The situation was one that was calculated to bring out all that was most impetuous in the character of the Scottish king. Don Pedro de Ayala had made one serious criticism of James: 'he is not a good captain because he begins to fight before he has given his orders'.[162] The time had come for coolness and well-considered orders, but James was not the man to give them. A council of nobles, under the urging of Patrick, Lord Lindsay, is said to have enjoined him not to venture his own person in fighting the arthritic Surrey, 'ane old cruikit cairll liand in ane charieot'. James was infuriated and was not to be dissuaded from winning knightly renown in the midst of his troops.[163] Sharing the risks of his men he risked the fortunes of his kingdom.

Personal daring could not make up what had been lost through carelessness. In face of the enemy the Scots were left with few advantages. Their numbers were reduced through desertion to perhaps

159 J. D. Mackie, *op. cit., S.H.S. Misc. VIII.* 35–85, at 36, 39–40.
160 *Ibid.*, p. 37; Mackenzie, *Flodden*, p. 37.
161 Mackie, *James IV*, pp. 259–60.
162 Brown, *Early Travellers*, p. 40.   163 Pitscottie, *Historie*, I. 267–9.

little more than the English total of twenty thousand.[164] Although James had a fine train of artillery, this comprised siege guns of heavy calibre that had battered the walls of Norham, and it is questionable whether all seventeen heavy guns could have been moved to the new position in time.[165] Moreover the skilled foreign gunners had been sent with the fleet to France, leaving in charge the king's secretary, Patrick Paniter.[166] By contrast, the English had guns from their fleet, of smaller calibre than the Scottish culverins, but more numerous and more easily manoeuvred; and they had expert German gunners to use them.[167]

There began an artillery duel that was probably the first in history significantly to affect the outcome of a battle. Although the Scottish artillery made a great noise that at once drove some impressionable English levies to headlong flight,[168] it failed to find the correct range: the heavy gunstones went flying overhead while the opposing artillery quickly found the range of the Scots, killed their master-gunner and silenced their guns.[169] In the past it had been the task of the English archers to goad the Scots into leaving a defensive position; at Flodden strong wind and a heavy shower of rain hindered archery [170] and it was the well-handled English artillery that forced the Scots to attack. Besides, as the Scottish government affirmed some months later, James was 'impatient at the sight of them' [the English] and, 'keeping no order among his men', left his advantageous ground to engage the enemy.[171]

About four in the afternoon of 9 September, on a blustery day of alternate rain and sun, the Scots began to advance. Although at first favoured by the lie of the land they could not gain much impetus. Both sides fought on foot and the wet and slippery ground must have prevented the tightly-packed Scottish battalions from making a headlong charge. Below Branxton Hill the ground levelled out or even rose on the English side. Moreover the Scots relied on their long spears or pikes. In 1481 an act of parliament had attempted to standardise the length of these at seventeen feet six inches. A number had been imported from Veere just before the outbreak of war, and the Scots had probably been trained by French military advisers to use their pikes

---

[164] For estimates of the numbers of the opposing armies see J. D. Mackie, *op. cit.*, *S.H.S. Misc. VIII.* 35–85, at 47–69; Mackenzie, *Flodden*, pp. 45–9; Mackie, *James IV*, pp. 251–2.

[165] J. D. Mackie, *op. cit.*, *S.H.S. Misc. VIII.* 35–85, at 40–1, 42.

[166] *James IV, Letters*, p. xxxi.   [167] Mackie, *James IV*, pp. 263–4, 274–5.

[168] Mackenzie, *Flodden*, p. 77.   [169] Lesley, *History*, pp. 94–5.

[170] 'Trewe Encountre', p. 150.   [171] Mackenzie, *Flodden*, p. 21.

in 'the manner of the Almayns',[172] forming phalanxes comparable to the traditional Scottish schiltrons. Such phalanxes could be irresistible so long as they were not brought to a halt and broken up. But at Flodden the ground was irregular and soft underfoot, and in places even marshy. When it came to hand-to-hand fighting the Scots found their long pikes far less useful than the nine-foot English halberds or bills, which combined an axe-head and spear-head. The pikes were meant for intact formations and were too unwieldy for individual use. As secondary weapons the Scots carried long swords : 'it was finally as swordsmen, not as spearmen, that the Scottish army made its dour disastrous stand at Flodden'.[173] But even the swords were no match for the deadly English bills. The English remarked upon the fine quality of the Scottish armour, against which arrows had been much less effective than usual. But in long-drawn-out fighting heavy armour and heavy swords were cumbersome.

On the Scottish left, the battalion under Lord Home and the Earl of Huntly had soon dispersed the opposing battalion. Further advance was halted by English reinforcements. Thereafter Home and the Scottish Borderers took no further part in the fighting and eventually escaped over the Cheviots with less loss than the other Scottish contingents.[174] On the Scottish right, the Highlanders under the Earls of Lennox and Argyll broke array and were routed by an English attack on the flank and rear. The king, in command of the centre battalion, came within a spear length of the Earl of Surrey only to fall among the slain.[175] This 'shows how desperate the fighting really was and how close James came to victory ; . . . for if Surrey were in the rear directing his men, then James very nearly penetrated the entire depth of the English line'.[176] Even after many of the Scots had taken to flight, others remained fighting till nightfall. Long before then, the Scots had been driven from the ground where their king's dead body lay; and the prolongation of the fight merely made the disaster all the worse. The Scottish losses were far greater than the English not only in number but in the rank of the slain. Beside the king fell his illegitimate son, the young Archbishop of St Andrews, whose death led Erasmus to lament : 'What hadst thou to do with fierce Mars . . . thou that wert destined for the Muses and for Christ ?' [177] Also among the slain were George Hepburn, Bishop of

---

[172] *Ibid.*, pp. 71–3.
[173] *Ibid.*, p. 93.
[174] *Ibid.*, pp. 8, 81–2.
[175] *Ibid.*, pp. 84–5.
[176] M. J. Tucker, *The Life of Thomas Howard, Earl of Surrey*, p. 114.
[177] Erasmus, *Adages*, cited in J. Herkless and R. K. Hannay, *The Archbishops of St Andrews*, I. 262.

the Isles, and eight of Scotland's twenty-two earls. Few Scots were admitted to quarter. Once James's pierced body had been recognised it was honourably conveyed to Berwick, finally to Richmond, where it lay in a leaden casket but was never accorded the state funeral that Henry VIII at one time planned for it.[178]

In July 1512 an Edinburgh student at the university of Orleans had written in an elegiac poem :

> Love James the Fourth, O Scotland, with whose aid
> Auspicious Fame will thee to heaven exalt.[179]

Flodden saw the end both of James IV and heavenly exaltation. Sometimes in the past the Scots had suffered a reverse as great as that of 1513 and had quickly recovered ; they did not regard Flodden as an irretrievable disaster ;[180] but the disaster was not retrieved.

[178] *James IV, Letters*, No. 568.
[179] John Kirkpatrick, *op. cit., S.H.S. Misc. II.* 47–102, at 97.
[180] Gordon Donaldson, *Scotland: James V to James VII* (1965), p. 17.

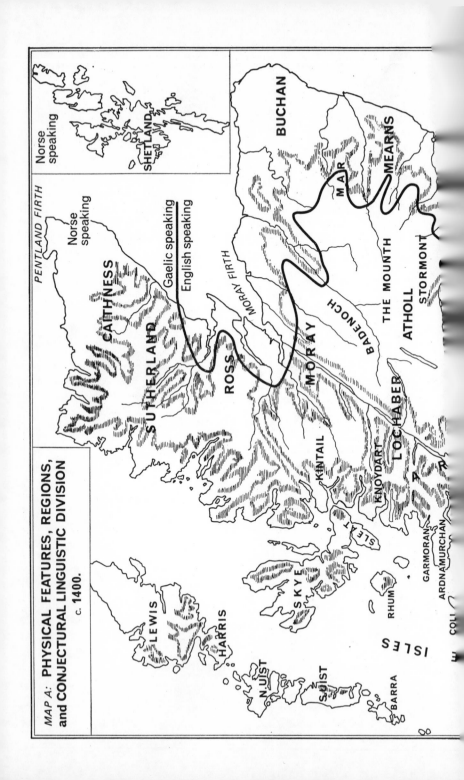

MAP A: **PHYSICAL FEATURES, REGIONS, and CONJECTURAL LINGUISTIC DIVISION**
c. 1400.

Norse speaking

SHETLAND

PENTLAND FIRTH

Norse speaking

Gaelic speaking
English speaking

CAITHNESS

SUTHERLAND

ROSS

MORAY FIRTH

MORAY

BUCHAN

MAR

MEARNS

BADENOCH

THE MOUNTH

ATHOLL

STORMONT

LOCHABER

KINTAIL

KNOYDART

SLEAT

GARMORAN

ARDNAMURCHAN

LEWIS

HARRIS

SKYE

RHUM

N. UIST

S. UIST

BARRA

ISLES

COLL

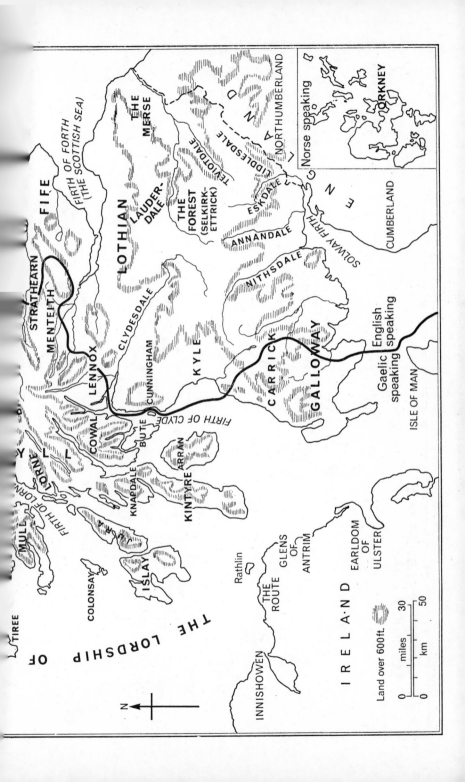

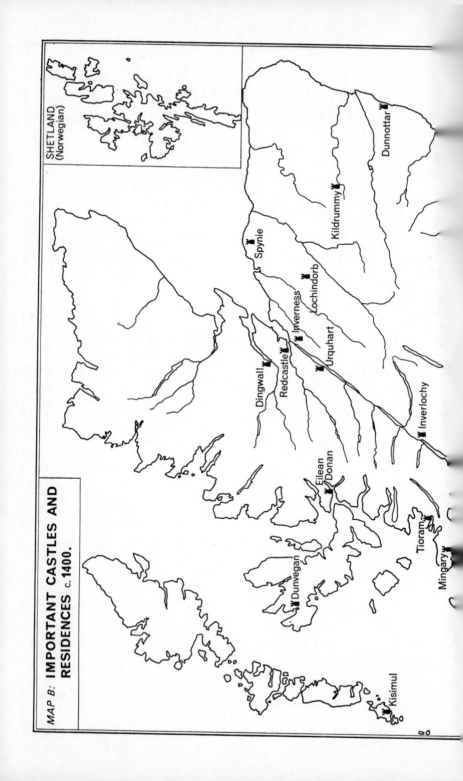

MAP B: **IMPORTANT CASTLES AND RESIDENCES** c. 1400.

SHETLAND (Norwegian)

Dunnottar

Kildrummy

Spynie

Lochindorb

Inverness

Redcastle

Urquhart

Dingwall

Inverlochy

Eilean Donan

Dunvegan

Tioram

Mingary

Kisimul

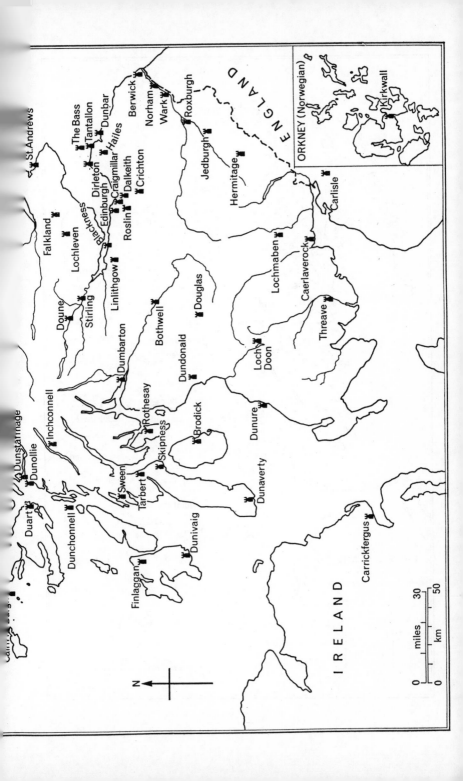

IRELAND

ENGLAND

Inverness

Elgin   Banff

Aberdeen

Brechin
Forfar   Montrose
Dunkeld   Arbroath
Perth   Dundee
Cupar   St. Andrews
Dunfermline   Crail
Stirling   Kinghorn
Inverkeithing   N. Berwick
Dumbarton   Linlithgow   Dunbar
Rothesay   Glasgow   Edinburgh   Haddington
Rutherglen
Irvine   Peebles   Berwick
Lanark   (English
Ayr   occupied)

Dumfries
Wigtown   Kirkcudbright

N

0   miles   50
0   km   100

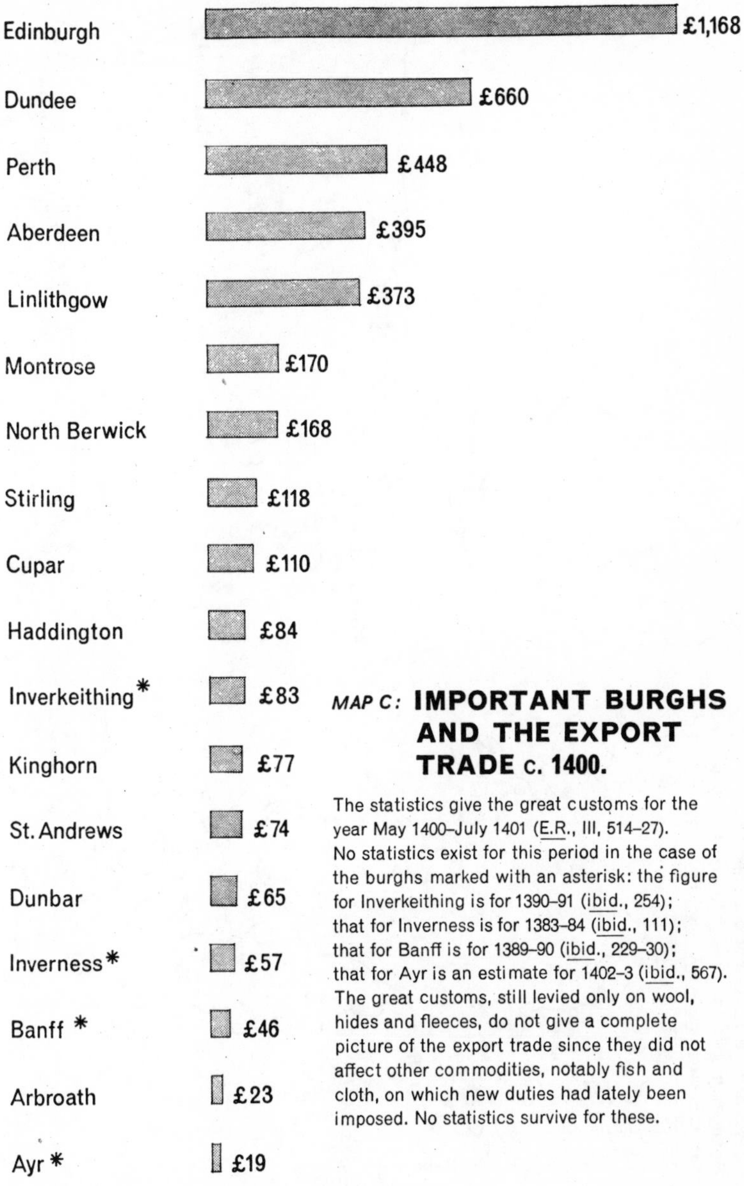

Burgh	Amount
Edinburgh	£1,168
Dundee	£660
Perth	£448
Aberdeen	£395
Linlithgow	£373
Montrose	£170
North Berwick	£168
Stirling	£118
Cupar	£110
Haddington	£84
Inverkeithing *	£83
Kinghorn	£77
St. Andrews	£74
Dunbar	£65
Inverness *	£57
Banff *	£46
Arbroath	£23
Ayr *	£19

MAP C: **IMPORTANT BURGHS AND THE EXPORT TRADE c. 1400.**

The statistics give the great customs for the year May 1400–July 1401 (E.R., III, 514–27). No statistics exist for this period in the case of the burghs marked with an asterisk: the figure for Inverkeithing is for 1390–91 (ibid., 254); that for Inverness is for 1383–84 (ibid., 111); that for Banff is for 1389–90 (ibid., 229–30); that for Ayr is an estimate for 1402–3 (ibid., 567). The great customs, still levied only on wool, hides and fleeces, do not give a complete picture of the export trade since they did not affect other commodities, notably fish and cloth, on which new duties had lately been imposed. No statistics survive for these.

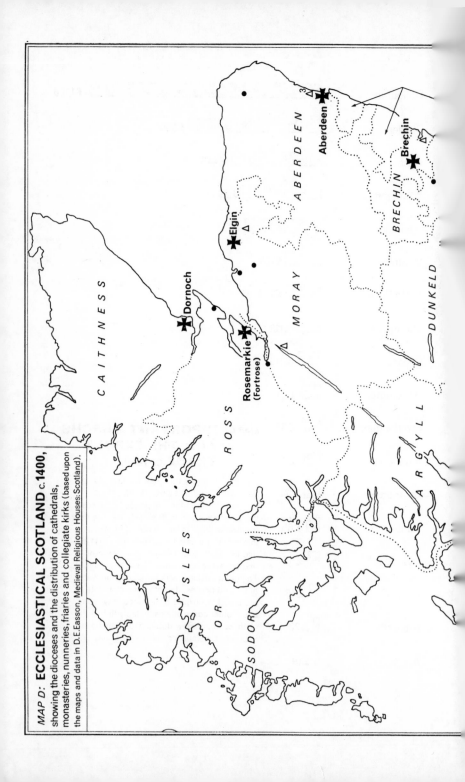

MAP D: **ECCLESIASTICAL SCOTLAND** c.1400, showing the dioceses and the distribution of cathedrals, monasteries, nunneries, friaries and collegiate kirks (based upon the maps and data in D.E.Easson, *Medieval Religious Houses: Scotland*).

CAITHNESS

Dornoch

ROSS

Rosemarkie (Fortrose)

Elgin

MORAY

ABERDEEN

Aberdeen

BRECHIN

Brechin

DUNKELD

ARGYLL

ISLES

OR

SODOR

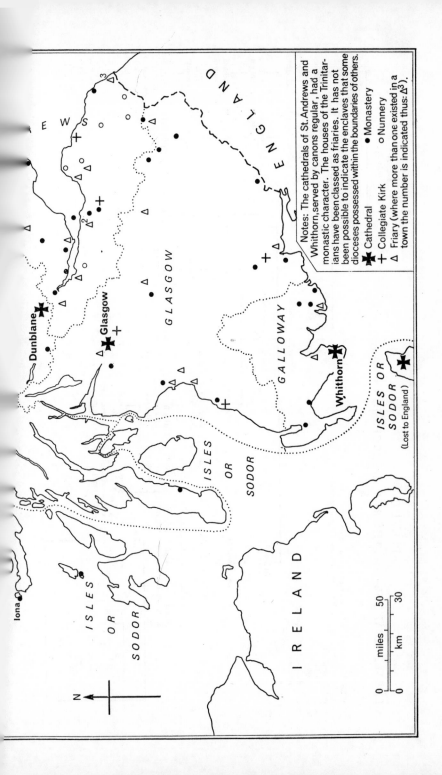

Notes: The cathedrals of St. Andrews and Whithorn, served by canons regular, had a monastic character. The houses of the Trinitarians have been classed as friaries. It has not been possible to indicate the enclaves that some dioceses possessed within the boundaries of others.

✳ Cathedral
● Monastery
○ Nunnery
✚ Collegiate Kirk
△ Friary (where more than one existed in a town the number is indicated thus: $\triangle^3$).

APPENDIX 2

GENEALOGICAL TABLE A: THE ROYAL SUCCESSION 1286–1329

NOTES: Names in capital letters are those of persons who figured
in the Great Cause, 1291–92. Persons and dates of minor relevance
have been omitted.

E.   Earl
d.   died
o.s.p.   died without offspring
=   married

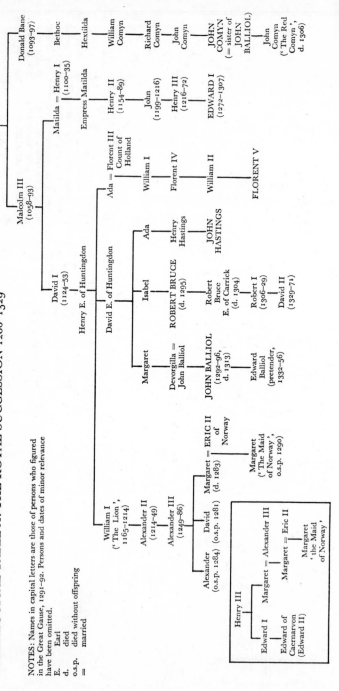

APPENDIX 2

GENEALOGICAL TABLE B: THE ROYAL HOUSE 1329–1437

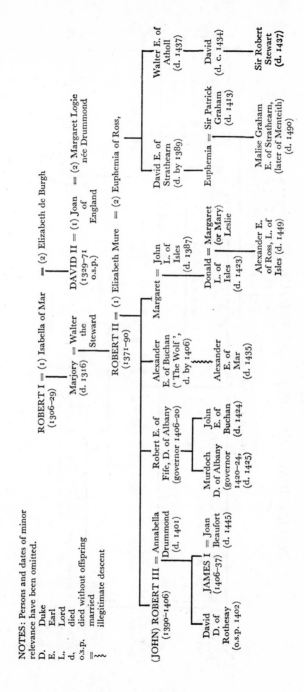

NOTES: Persons and dates of minor relevance have been omitted.

D. Duke
E. Earl
L. Lord
d, died
o.s.p. died without offspring
= married
~ illegitimate descent

APPENDIX 2

GENEALOGICAL TABLE C: THE ROYAL HOUSE 1437–1513

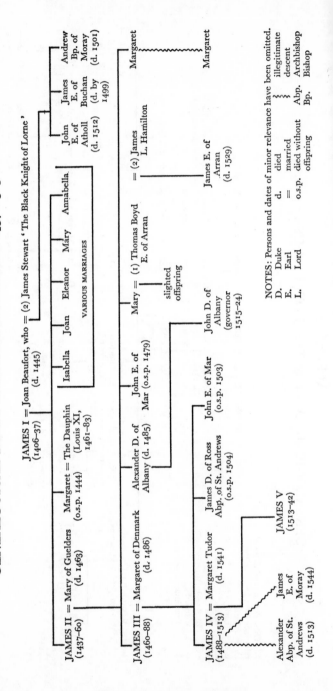

NOTES: Persons and dates of minor relevance have been omitted.

D.	Duke
E.	Earl
L.	Lord

d. died
= married
o.s.p. died without offspring

〈 illegitimate descent

Abp. Archbishop
Bp. Bishop

APPENDIX 2

GENEALOGICAL TABLE D: THE HOUSES OF DOUGLAS AND ANGUS 1298–1513

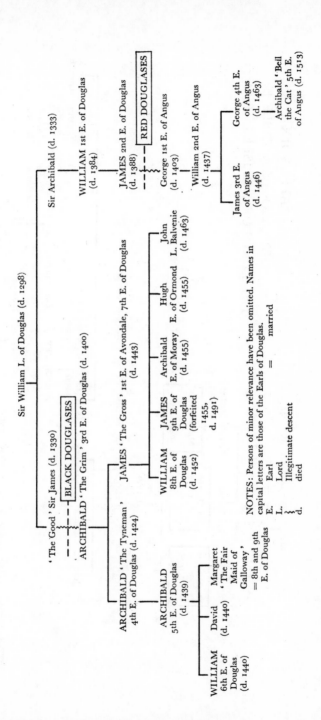

NOTES: Persons of minor relevance have been omitted. Names in capital letters are those of the Earls of Douglas.

E.   Earl
L.   Lord
〰〰   Illegitimate descent
d.   died
=   married

APPENDIX 2

GENEALOGICAL TABLE E:
THE LORDS OF THE ISLES 1164–1545

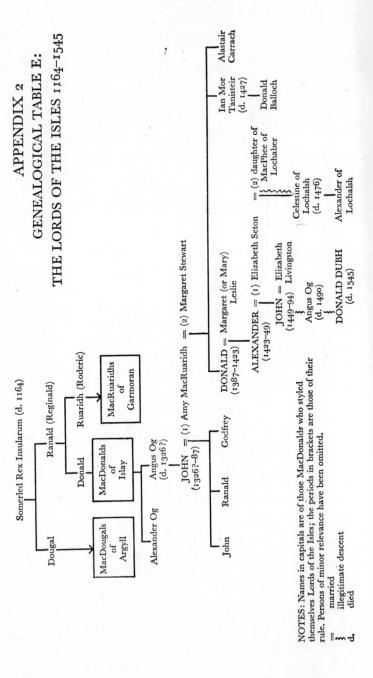

NOTES: Names in capitals are of those MacDonalds who styled themselves Lords of the Isles; the periods in brackets are those of their rule. Persons of minor relevance have been omitted.

= married
〰 illegitimate descent
d. died

BIBLIOGRAPHY

The more specialised books and articles cited in footnotes are in general omitted from the Bibliography. The place of publication is not given except for older and rarer books. Neither date nor place is given for publications of clubs and societies. A list of the abbreviations used in this volume is printed on pp. ix–xvi.

1. Guides and Works of Reference

(a) Guides to Sources

Thanks to the historiographical prominence of Scottish clubs and societies, C. S. Terry, *Catalogue of the Publications of Scottish Historical and kindred Clubs and Societies . . . 1780–1908* (1909) and its continuation to 1927 by C. Matheson (1928) are indispensable. They are supplemented by the *Handlist of Scottish and Welsh Record Publications* by P. Gouldesbrough, A. P. Kup and I. Lewis (Brit. Records Assoc., 1954) and by the official list of government publications in *British National Archives* (H.M.S.O.). M. Livingstone, *A Guide to the Public Records of Scotland* (1905), lists the original records in H.M. Register House, Edinburgh. These are described by J. M. Thomson, *The Public Records of Scotland* (1922). Lists of accessions to the Register House since 1905 are in *S.H.R.* from VOL. XXVI. As a key to the valuable material in the *Historical MSS. Commission Reports*, C. S. Terry, *An Index to the Papers Relating to Scotland* (1908), is no substitute for the indexes to the individual reports. The fullest lists of books are to be found in A. Mitchell and C. G. Cash, *Contribution to the Bibliography of Scottish Topography* (S.H.S.), of which VOL. I is arranged topographically and VOL. II topically; there is a continuation in P. Hancock, *A Bibliography of Books on Scotland, 1916–50* (1960).

Among specialised guides, *Sources and Literature of Scots Law* (Stair Soc.) has much wider scope than its title suggests. Scottish cartularies, with one or two notable exceptions, are listed in G. R. C. Davis, *Medieval Cartularies of Great Britain* (1958). W. R. Scott, *Scottish Economic Literature to 1800* (1911), is continued and supplemented in three articles on the bibliography of Scottish economic history by W. H. Marwick in *Econ. Hist. Rev.*, III. 117–37, 2nd Ser., IV. 376–82 and XVI. 147–54. A related field is covered by G. Donaldson, 'Sources for Scottish agrarian history before the eighteenth century', *Agricultural Hist. Rev.*, VIII. 82–90. H. R. G. Inglis, J. Matheson and C. B. B. Watson provide a guide to *The Early Maps of Scotland* (2nd edn., 1936).

(b) Aids to Study (Biographical)

Scottish biographical information is well represented in the *Dictionary of National Biography*, ed. Sir Leslie Stephen and Sir Sidney Lee (2nd edn., 22 vols., 1959–60), but use should also be made of Robert Chambers, *Biographical Dictionary of Eminent Scotsmen* (3 vols., 1868–70, and other edns.). *The Handbook of British Chronology* (Royal Hist. Soc., 2nd edn.) gives lists of kings, officers of state, bishops, dukes, marquesses and earls. Fuller details of the royal family, together with short notes upon the more dramatic events in each reign, are given in A. H. Dunbar, *Scottish Kings: A Revised Chronology of Scottish History* (2nd edn., 1906). The *Scots Peerage* by J. Balfour Paul (9 vols., 1904–14) deals similarly with the noble families and is replete with genealogical data. It may be supplemented with the help of Margaret Stuart, *Scottish Family History: A Guide to Works of Reference on the History and Genealogy of Scottish Families* (1930); the slighter, but more up-to-date *Scottish Family Histories* (1960) of J. P. S. Ferguson; and George F. Black, *The Surnames of Scotland* (1946). The holders of specific offices are dealt with in G. W. T. Omond, *The Lord Advocates of Scotland* (2 vols., 1883); S. Cowan, *The Lord Chancellors of Scotland* (2 vols., 1911); and J. Herkless and R. K. Hannay, *The Archbishops of St Andrews* (5 vols., 1907–1915). Details of the episcopate as a whole are given in J. Dowden, *The Bishops of Scotland* (1912). The bishops, together with other ecclesiastical dignitaries (but not, save incidentally, members of the monastic and mendicant orders) are conveniently listed in D. E. R. Watt, *Fasti Ecclesiae Scoticanae Medii Aevi* (1969), an invaluable reference work. Lists of the graduates of the three medieval universities are given in *The Early Records of the University of St Andrews* (S.H.S.); *Munimenta Alme Universitatis Glasguensis* (Maitland Club); and *Officers and Graduates of the University and King's College, Aberdeen* (New Spalding Club). Merchants and craftsmen are represented in the *Roll of Edinburgh Burgesses and Guild Brethren, 1406–1700* (Scot. Rec. Soc.).

(c) Aids to Study (Topographical)

The most useful topographical guide is F. H. Groome, *Ordnance Gazetteer of Scotland* (1882–85 and later edns.). Several important works on various subjects are arranged topographically, notably the *Reports* of the Royal Commission on Ancient and Historical Monuments and Constructions of Scotland, which not only give plans of the major medieval buildings but indications of their history. Ian B. Cowan in his outstanding *Parishes of Medieval Scotland* (Scot. Rec. Soc.) lists each parish in alphabetical order and summarises its ecclesiastical history. A useful appendix shows the pattern of appropriation. Lists of burghs of the king, burghs not dependent on the king, and burghs of barony and regality, together with short notes on changes of status, are compiled in G. S. Pryde, *The Burghs of Scotland: A Critical List* (1965). Statistics relating to the establishment, organisation, and relative wealth, of houses of monks, canons, friars, collegiate kirks and hospitals, are arranged in D. E. Easson, *Medieval Religious Houses: Scotland* (1957). This valuable and impressive pioneer work may shortly be replaced by a revised version compiled by Ian B. Cowan. Archdeacon Monro's description of the Western Isles in

1549 has been so well edited by R. W. Munro in *Monro's Western Isles of Scotland and Genealogies of the Clans* (1961) as to become an indispensable guide to the topography and antiquities of the Hebrides.

(d) Aids to Study (Linguistic)

John Jamieson, *An Etymological Dictionary of the Scottish Language*, ed. John Longmuir (5 vols., 1879–87), will be superseded by W. A. Craigie, *A Dictionary of the Older Scottish Tongue* (1931–), of which the first four volumes have appeared.

(e) Aids to Study (Chronological)

A. H. Dunbar, *Scottish Kings* (p. 622 above) deals specifically with the chronology of Scottish history, but the *Handbook of Dates for Students of English History* (Royal Hist. Soc.) has a relevance that extends north of Tweed.

(f) Aids to Study (Sigillography, Heraldry and Numismatics)

These fields are dealt with in the following works: H. Laing, *Descriptive Catalogue of Impressions of Ancient Scottish Seals* (Bannatyne Club) and *Supplemental Catalogue* (1866); J. H. Stevenson and M. Wood, *Scottish Heraldic Seals* (1940); A. Nisbet, *A System of Heraldry* (1816); R. W. Cochran-Patrick, *Records of the Coinage . . . to the Union* (2 vols., 1876); E. Burns, *The Coinage of Scotland* (3 vols., 1887); I. H. Stewart, *The Scottish Coinage* (2nd edn., 1967) and 'Scottish Mints' in *Mints, Dies, and Currency*, ed. R. A. G. Carson (1971), pp. 165–289, which is particularly valuable for the period 1280–1357.

II. PRIMARY SOURCES: RECORDS

(a) Government Records

For practically the whole period the activities of central government are represented in a number of volumes in three essential compendious works: *The Acts of the Parliaments of Scotland*, ed. T. Thomson and C. Innes (12 vols., 1814–75); *Registrum Magni Sigilli Regum Scotorum: the Register of the Great Seal of Scotland*, ed. J. M. Thomson and others (11 vols., 1882–1914); *Rotuli scaccarii regum Scotorum: the Exchequer Rolls of Scotland*, ed. J. Stuart and others (23 vols., 1878–1908). The period does not yet figure in the volumes of the *Regesta Regum Scottorum, 1153–1424*, though those dealing with the *acta* of Robert I and David II may shortly appear. The above works are supplemented for the later fifteenth and early sixteenth century by *Compota thesaurariorum regum Scotorum: Accounts of the Lord High Treasurer of Scotland*, ed. T. Dickson and Sir J. Balfour Paul (1877–); *Registrum secreti sigilli regum Scotorum: the Register of the Privy Seal of Scotland*, ed. M. Livingstone and others (1908–); *The Acts of the Lords of Council in Public Affairs, 1501–1554: Selections from Acta Dominorum Concilii*, ed. R. K. Hannay (1932). Some entries in *The Register of the Privy Council*, ed. J. H. Burton and others (1877–), retrospectively refer to the period prior to 1513.

Civil justice (often involving cases with criminal overtones) is illustrated in *The Acts of the Lords Auditors of Causes and Complaints, 1466–94*, ed. T. Thomson (1839); *The Acts of the Lords of Council in Civil Causes*, ed. T. Thomson and others (1839 and 1918–); and *Acta Dominorum Concilii, 1501–3* (Stair Soc.). Records of criminal justice are printed in R. Pitcairn, *Ancient Criminal Trials in Scotland* [1488–1624] (3 vols., Bannatyne and Maitland Clubs).

Scotland's relationships with other powers are recorded, *passim*, in T. Rymer's *Foedera, Conventiones, Literae etc.* (London, 1704–35; The Hague, 1737–45; London, 1816–69). Relevant records in French archives are printed in A. Teulet, *Inventaire chronologique des documents relatifs à l'histoire de l'Ecosse conservés aux archives du royaume à Paris* (Abbotsford Club). Similar material concerning relations with Norway and Denmark is to be found in *Diplomatarium Norvegicum* (20 vols., Kristiania, 1849–1919). Records of Anglo-Scottish relations are mostly those of the English government. A basic source for practically the whole period is *Rotuli Scotiae*, ed. D. Macpherson and others (2 vols., London, 1814–19). This enrolment is the medieval equivalent of a file upon Scottish affairs maintained by the English government. A similar span of time is also covered by the collection of miscellaneous records summarised and translated in the *Calendar of Documents relating to Scotland*, ed. J. Bain (4 vols., 1881–88). This valuable work, which contains some inaccuracies, is now being revised under the supervision of the Scottish Record Office. In addition the many volumes of *Calendars* of the patent and close rolls preserved in the Public Record Office (H.M.S.O.) include miscellaneous entries relating to Scotland. An indication of the classes of record in the P.R.O. and British Museum in which unprinted material may be found is given in Ranald Nicholson, *Edward III and the Scots* (1965), pp. 258–9.

Anglo-Scottish relations during the wars of independence are particularly illustrated in the following collections: *Documents Illustrative of the History of Scotland 1286–1306*, ed. J. Stevenson (2 vols., 1870); *Documents Illustrative of Sir William Wallace* (Maitland Club); *Documents and Records Illustrating the History of Scotland*, ed. F. Palgrave (London, 1837); *Scotland in 1298*, ed. H. Gough (1888); and E. L. G. Stones, *Anglo-Scottish Relations, 1174–1328* (reprint 1970), which presents the most important documents both in the original language and in translation.

Records of the intensive diplomatic activity during the reign of James IV may be studied in *Flodden Papers* (S.H.S.), *The Letters of James IV* (S.H.S.), and *Letters and Papers, Foreign and Domestic, of the Reign of Henry VIII*, I., ed. J. S. Brewer and R. H. Brodie (1864, 1920).

(b) Ecclesiastical Records

There are no extant Scottish records precisely corresponding to the English episcopal registers: various compilations pertaining to bishoprics, religious houses or collegiate kirks are mainly collections of charters, often under the title of *Liber* or *Registrum*. Most of these have been printed by the Bannatyne Club, others by the Maitland, Abbotsford and Grampian Clubs, S.H.S. and S.B.R.S. The *Copiale Prioratus Sanctiandree*, ed. J. H. Baxter (1930), is a letter-book of Prior Haldenstone of St Andrews and contains valuable material relating to ecclesiastical and political affairs in the late fourteenth and early fifteenth century. A variety of information of judicial, liturgical, social, political and economic significance may be obtained from the following ecclesiastical records: the *St Andrews Formulare* (Stair Soc.); the *Liber Officialis Sancti Andree* (Abbotsford Club); the *Rentale Sancti Andree* (S.H.S.); the *Rentale Dunkeldense* (S.H.S.); the rental books of the diocese of Glasgow and of the abbey of Coupar-Angus (Grampian Club); the *Correspondence, Inventories, Account Rolls and Law Proceedings of the Priory of Coldingham* (Surtees Soc.); the *Breviarium Aberdonense* (Bannatyne Club) and the *Epistolare in Usum Ecclesiae Cathedralis Aberdonensis*, ed. B. McEwen (1924).

Relations between Scotland and the papacy are illustrated in the following collections of records: *Vetera Monumenta Hibernorum et Scotorum Historiam Illustrantia*, ed. A. Theiner (Rome, 1864); the *Calendar of Scottish Supplications to Rome* (3 vols., S.H.S.); the *Calendar of Entries in the Papal Registers relating to Great Britain and Ireland*, ed. W. H. Bliss and others (1893–). In addition microfilmed copies of records in the Vatican Archives (and other continental archives) are held by the Department of Scottish History, the University of Glasgow.

The extant statutes of diocesan synods and provincial councils are collected in *Concilia Scotiae: Ecclesiae Scoticanae Statuta* (Bannatyne Club), translated by David Patrick in *Statutes of the Scottish Church* (S.H.S.).

University records are represented in the following works: *Early Records of the University of St Andrews* (S.H.S.); *Acta Facultatis Artium Universitatis S. Andree, 1413–1588* (S.H.S.); *Munimenta Alme Universitatis Glasguensis* (Maitland Club); and *Fasti Aberdonenses* (Spalding Club).

(c) Burgh Records

Records of burghal law and administration are collected in *Ancient Laws and Customs of the Burghs of Scotland, 1124–1424* and *1424–1707* (S.B.R.S.) and in *Extracts from the Records of the Convention of the Royal Burghs of Scotland*, ed. J. D. Marwick (1870–90). Notable collections of burgh muniments are printed by the Spalding Club and S.H.S. (Aberdeen); by the Ayr and Wigtown Archaeological Assoc. (Ayr); by S.B.R.S. (Edinburgh, Glasgow and Peebles). In addition there are the following useful works: *Charters and Other Writs Illustrating the History of the Royal Burgh of Aberdeen*, ed. P. J. Anderson (1890); *Charters, Writs and Public Documents of the Royal Burgh of Dundee*, ed. W. Hay (1880); *Extracts from the Records of the Royal Burgh of Stirling*, ed. R. Renwick (1884).

(d) Private Muniments

Contents of private charter chests figure largely in the many family histories produced by Sir William Fraser, of which the most important is the *Douglas Book* (4 vols., 1885). Private archives are also represented in the *Reports* of the Royal Commission on Historical Manuscripts (1870–), in the publications of the Spalding and Maitland Clubs and S.R.S. The *Registrum Honoris de Morton* (Bannatyne Club) is of particular significance, as is the *Ledger of Andrew Halyburton*, ed. C. Innes (1867), which records the commercial transactions of a Scottish merchant based in the Netherlands from 1492 to 1503.

Many private collections have in recent years been deposited in the Register House (see lists of accessions in *S.H.R.*), and the National Register of Archives (Scotland) has reports on many which still remain in private custody.

(e) Miscellaneous Records

Some clubs and societies have produced collections of primary sources (both record and narrative) of miscellaneous provenance, as in the case of *Highland Papers* and *Wigtownshire Charters* (S.H.S.) and *Collections for a History of the Shires of Aberdeen and Banff* (Spalding Club). There are also occasional *Miscellany* volumes with no unifying theme, notably those of the Bannatyne Club and S.H.S. Miscellaneous records figure in the *Calendar of the Laing Charters*, ed. J. Anderson (1899). Others are reproduced in facsimile (and transcription) in *Facsimiles of the National Manuscripts of Scotland* (1867–73). The student and general reader will find comprehensive and well-chosen collections from a variety of sources in the *Source Book of Scottish History*, ed. W. Croft Dickinson, Gordon Donaldson and Isabel A. Milne (2nd edn., 3 vols., 1958, reprinted 1963), and in *Scottish Historical Documents*, ed. Gordon Donaldson (1970).

A few protocol books recording deeds drawn up by notaries public are extant for the period prior to 1513. They include those of James Darow, 1469–84 (*Scottish Antiquary*, x–xi); James Young, 1485–1515 (S.R.S.); Cuthbert Simon, 1499–1513 (Grampian Club); John Foular, 1501–28, and Gavin Ros, 1512–32 (S.R.S.).

III. Primary Sources: Narrative

(a) Chronicles

These are the chief narrative sources for the period up to the mid-fifteenth century. The few, but essential, Scottish examples are: the chronicles of John of Fordun, ed. and trans. W. F. Skene (1871–72)—discussed on pp. 277–8 above; Andrew of Wyntoun, ed. D. Laing (1872–79)—discussed on p. 278 above; Walter Bower, ed. W. Goodall (Edinburgh, 1759)—discussed on p. 278 above; and the *Auchinleck Chronicle*, ed. T. Thomson (Edinburgh, 1819, 1877)—discussed on p. 328 above. The part played by Scotland in the age of chivalry is illustrated in the works of Froissart (various edns.). Most English chronicles at least touch upon Scottish affairs. Of special importance are the *Vita Edwardi Secundi*, ed. N. Denholm-Young (1957); Thomas Walsingham's *Historia Anglicana*, ed. H. T. Riley (1863); and, above all, two northern works —the *Chronicon de Lanercost* (Maitland Club) and Sir Thomas Gray's *Scalacronica* (Maitland Club).

(b) Poetry

An essential source for the reign of Robert I is Barbour's epic poem *The Bruce* (S.T.S. and various edns.)—discussed on pp. 275–7 above. Wyntoun's *Cronykil* (already mentioned) is poetry of a sort. Blind Harry's *Wallace* (S.T.S.) presents a misleading version of the hero's career but is a pointer to opinion in the time of James III, as is also *The Thre Prestis of Peblis* (S.T.S.). Other poetical works (mostly in S.T.S. edns.) have at least some incidental value as historical sources, particularly in the case of the *Kingis Quair* and the poems of Robert Henryson and William Dunbar.

(c) Early Histories

These, though generally of dubious reliability, often contain material not found elsewhere. The anonymous *Life and Death of King James the First* (Maitland Club)—discussed on p. 286 above—presents a view of James I which differs from that of the chroniclers. John Major's remarkably shrewd *History of Greater Britain* (S.H.S.)—discussed on p. 586 above—is particularly to be valued for its sociological observations. Hector Boece's *Scotorum Historiae* (Paris, 1527), its continuation by John Ferrerius (Paris, 1574)—discussed on pp. 472, 586 above—and George Buchanan's *History of Scotland* (ed. J. Aikman, 1827–30) are humanist works: fact and fancy are artfully and inextricably intermingled; James III almost emerges as a second Tiberius. Bishop Lesley's *History* (Bannatyne Club) is more down-to-earth and makes commendable use of parliamentary records. Robert Lindsay of Pitscottie's highly-coloured and long-winded *Historie* (S.T.S.)—discussed on p. 328 above—does most to fill the gap left by the chroniclers. John Knox's *History of the Reformation* (various edns.) is a source for the history of heresy in the fifteenth century. Traditional histories of the MacDonalds (together with other miscellaneous items relating to the Highlands) are in *Highland Papers* (S.H.S.) and *Reliquiae Celticae*, ed. Alexander MacBain and John Kennedy (1892, 1894).

(d) Travellers' Tales

The impressions of Scotland recorded by foreign visitors are presented entertainingly in P. Hume Brown, *Early Travellers in Scotland* (1891). The report of Pedro de Ayala is an essential source for the reign of James IV.

IV. SECONDARY WORKS

(a) General Histories of Scotland

The histories of J. H. Burton, P. Hume Brown and Andrew Lang have served at least two generations and ought to be laid in honourable rest. P. F. Tytler's *History* (9 vols., 1828–43 and later edns.) and J. Pinkerton's *History . . . from the Accession of the House of Stuart to that of Mary* (London, 1797) have appendixes of original documents, some of which are not printed elsewhere. The collections of essays by R. W. Cochran-Patrick—*Mediaeval Scotland* (1892)—and by Cosmo Innes—*Scotland in the Middle Ages* (1860) and *Sketches of Early Scotch History* (1861)—contain interesting oddities. Of the same character, though of greater calibre, is Lord Cooper's *Selected Papers, 1922–1954* (1957). In *The Scottish Nation* (B.B.C. Publications, 1972) the period is covered in four essays by notable medievalists. This useful work has appeared too recently to have influenced the present volume. Treatment of the late medieval period in Rosalind Mitchison, *History of Scotland* (1970), and T. C. Smout, *History of the Scottish People, 1560–1830* (1969), has the merits and defects of impressionist painting; the vignettes in Gordon Donaldson, *Scottish Kings* (1967), are less eye-catching but have more exactitude. Probably the only considerable general history recently written by someone whose main interest and expertise lay in medieval studies is W. Croft Dickinson, *New History of Scotland* (VOL. I, 1961). Partly topical and partly chronological in format its treatment of political and economic history is less commendable than its careful exposition of legal and constitutional developments and its lively appraisal of medieval society, particularly that of the burghs.

Modern Scottish historical scholarship is seen at its best not in works of synthesis but in the articles on a wide range of late medieval topics that appear in the learned periodicals, notably the *S.H.R.* (1903–28, 1947–). Thanks to the absence of up-to-date and large-scale general histories the neglected prefaces of the *Exchequer Rolls* and *Treasurer's Accounts* have a special importance: usually the editors follow the accepted historical view; often, when it conflicts with the records, they introduce necessary modifications.

(b) Political, Military and Diplomatic History

Among the following works those of G. W. S. Barrow, E. W. M. Balfour-Melville, G. Donaldson, A. I. Dunlop, R. L. Mackie, G. Gregory Smith and W. Stanford Reid, as well as *The Scottish Nation*, though primarily devoted to political, military and diplomatic history, also illustrate other branches of history in their respective periods.

1. *1286–1357.* The period of the wars of independence has inspired a number of works which need not be taken too seriously. One exception is E. M. Barron, *The Scottish War of Independence, A Critical Study* (2nd edn., 1934). Designedly contentious it deals in detail with the years from 1295 to 1314 and argues that the struggle for independence was maintained by 'Celtic' Scotland (somewhat loosely defined). Reaction against Celtic romanticism seems to be carried too far in G. W. S. Barrow, *Robert Bruce and the Community of the Realm of Scotland* (1965), where the importance of Lothian appears to be exaggerated, and where a new romanticism centred upon the concept of the community of the realm is certainly inspired in many readers, even if it can hardly be supposed to exist in the austere mind of the author himself. In the half of the book that covers the years between 1286 and 1306 the best possible interpretation is placed upon the sometimes dubious conduct of the future Robert I. Thanks to the recent discovery of a valuable document (see *S.H.R.*, XLIX. 46–59) the dating of the campaigns of 1307 and 1308 is subject to revision. Despite the scholarly ingenuity shown in discussions of the location of Bannockburn the conclusions seem unconvincing. The comparatively thin treatment of the years between 1314 and 1329 is emphasised by omission of a study of the Bruce invasion of Ireland, even although that event permanently affected the balance of power in medieval Britain by turning the English colony in Ireland from an asset to a liability. Nonetheless Professor Barrow's work is undoubtedly outstanding, and hence deserves the application of rigorous standards of criticism: it ought to be read in conjunction with the penetrating review article by A. A. M. Duncan (*S.H.R.*, XLV. 184–201), which, although eulogistic, suggests important modifications of interpretation.

A further few years of the wars of independence (1327–35) are covered in

Ranald Nicholson, *Edward III and the Scots* (1965), a blow-by-blow study of warfare and diplomacy. The remaining years of the wars of independence figure in J. Campbell's essay on 'England, Scotland and the Hundred Years War' in *Europe in the Late Middle Ages*, ed. J. R. Hale and others (1965). The treatment of Anglo-Scottish relations in F. M. Powicke's volume of the Oxford History of England—*The Thirteenth Century 1216–1307* (1953)— is conscientious, though the hero is neither Balliol, Wallace nor Bruce. In the subsequent volume—*The Fourteenth Century 1307–1399* (1959)—May Mc-Kisack seldom lingers north of Tweed. J. Bain, *The Edwards in Scotland, 1296–1377* (1901) may deservedly be neglected.

The importance of the relationship between Scotland and Ireland is shown in G. H. Orpen, *Ireland under the Normans*, VOL. IV (1920), in E. Curtis, *Medieval Ireland* (1938), and in Olive Armstrong, *Edward Bruce's Invasion of Ireland* (1923). J. F. Lydon in his essay in *Historical Studies IV*, ed. G. A. Hayes-McCoy (1963), and in his *Lordship of Ireland in the Later Middle Ages* (1972) stresses exploitation of Ireland as a source of troops and supplies for the campaigns of Edward I and Edward II against the Scots.

The background of the Franco-Scottish alliance of 1295 (and of the last Norwegian interventions in Scottish affairs) is outlined by Ranald Nicholson in *S.H.R.*, XXXVIII. 114–32. In *Les Préliminaires de la Guerre de Cent Ans, 1328–42*, E. Déprez pays some attention to Franco-Scottish relations.

Specialised studies include detailed works on the battle of Bannockburn (see the footnotes to pp. 87–9 above), while the recent 650th anniversary of the Declaration of Arbroath has evoked a number of publications of which the most important are Sir James Fergusson, *The Declaration of Arbroath* (1970), and an essay by A. A. M. Duncan, *The Nation of Scots and the Declaration of Arbroath* (1970), which is particularly valuable because of its sociological approach.

2. *1357–1437*. The later years of the reign of David II are the subject of articles by Bruce Webster ('David II and the Government of Fourteenth-Century Scotland', *T.R.H.S.*, 5th series, XVI. 115–30) and Ranald Nicholson ('David II, the historians and the chroniclers', *S.H.R.*, XLV. 59–78). Both attack the hitherto accepted view that David was an incompetent king under whom there was a decline in government. No detailed modern study exists of politics under Robert II and Robert III, although E. W. M. Balfour-Melville casts backward glances in *James I, King of Scots* (1936). This thorough examination of the reign of the first forceful Stewart king is arranged all too chronologically (though its attention to chronological detail is of value). It is a serviceable factual study founded upon meticulous scholarship rather than a work of interpretation. Anglo-Scottish relations are treated in a similar, though less scholarly, manner in so far as they figure in Sir James Ramsay's *Genesis of Lancaster*, 1307–99 (2 vols., 1913), and his *Lancaster and York* (2 vols., 1892). E. F. Jacob's volume in the Oxford History—*The Fifteenth Century 1399– 1485* (1961)—provides (with no few slips and omissions) a background to devious Anglo-Scottish diplomacy and to the increasing interest in France shown by the Scots. This is also outlined in Francisque-Michel, *Les Ecossais en France, les Français en Ecosse* (1862), which may be supplemented by W. Forbes Leith, *The Scots Men-at-arms and Lifeguards in France* (2 vols., 1882), and Louis A. Barbé, *Margaret of Scotland and the Dauphin Louis* (1917).

3. *1437–1488*. Apart from the relevant chapters in *The Scottish Nation* and G. Donaldson, *Scottish Kings*, this period, characterised by strife between new monarchy and old baronage, has elicited only one notable work: Annie I. Dunlop, *The Life and Times of James Kennedy, Bishop of St Andrews* (1950). Despite the clerical character of the hero this book devotes at least as much attention to the politics of the years between 1437 and 1465 as to ecclesiastical affairs. If the author is perhaps mistaken in believing that her bishop moved unsullied through the political morass she has at least shown remarkable skill in describing each feature of the morass and the ways in which its victims were engulfed. Her understanding of fifteenth-century Scotland is unsurpassed, and her work, though not well arranged, and hardly easy reading, reaches the heights of scholarship and will long remain indispensable.

The growing importance of connections between Scotland and Denmark is shown in a number of recent articles (see notes to pp. 413–4, 555 above). Agnes Conway in *Henry VII's Relations with Scotland and Ireland, 1485–1498* (1932) provides an extremely helpful monograph on the particularly complex diplomacy that accompanied the fall of James III and the rise of James IV.

4. *1488–1513*. The accounts of the reign of James IV given by Eric Stair-Kerr and I. A. Taylor are superseded by R. L. Mackie in *King James IV of Scotland* (1958). This vivid and eminently readable work displays a thorough scholarship, sparingly employed, however, in those fields of legal, constitutional and economic history, which, if too assiduously cultivated, bring diminishing returns in readability. Perhaps as a result the interpretation of the personality of James IV seems to lack depth. The view that the king wanted war in 1513 is particularly open to question. James IV's hard-headed exploitation of developments affecting landholding is studied by Ranald Nicholson in 'Feudal Developments in Late Medieval Scotland', *Juridical Review*, April 1973, pt. i 1–21. G. Gregory Smith in *The Days of James IV* (1890) uses extracts from a variety of sources to illustrate the reign. Extra-sensory perception is employed by A. J. Stewart in *Falcon: The Autobiography of His Grace James the 4 King of Scots* (1971).

The account of Anglo-Scottish relations in the Oxford History by J. D. Mackie—*The Earlier Tudors, 1485–1558* (1952)—benefits from the expertise of a scholar well acquainted with the Scottish background who has also contributed to studies of the Flodden campaign. A likely explanation of the disaster is given by W. M. Mackenzie in *The Secret of Flodden* (1931). The naval activity of the period is illustrated in W. Stanford Reid, *Skipper from Leith: the History of Robert Barton of Over Barnton* (1962).

(c) Legal and Constitutional History

James Mackinnon's *Constitutional History of Scotland from Early Times to the Reformation* (1924)—a clear and sensible work which, however, says remarkably little concerning parliament—had the misfortune to be overshadowed by the virtually simultaneous publication of R. S. Rait's *Parliaments of Scotland* (1924). The latter work gives a thorough treatment of all aspects of parliament and related assemblies. Topical in arrangement it fails to convey an overall impression of development—save perhaps that the Scottish parliament was somehow doomed to an inglorious end. It is extremely valuable as a factual study, less so as a work of interpretation. Some of Rait's misconceptions are corrected in A. A. M. Duncan, 'The early parliaments of Scotland', *S.H.R.*, XLV. 36–58.

Studies of the evolution of Scots law and the multiplicity of courts are conveniently summarised in the *Introduction to Scottish Legal History* (Stair Soc.). W. Croft Dickinson's indispensable trilogy—*The Sheriff Court Book of Fife* (S.H.S.), *The Court Book of the Barony of Carnwath* (S.H.S.), and *Early Records of the Burgh of Aberdeen* (S.H.S.)—has earned distinction not so much on account of the records edited but rather by reason of the introductions, which thoroughly describe the courts through which local government was conducted.

More specialised studies include Ian D. Willock, *Origins and Development of the Jury in Scotland* (Stair Soc.); R. K. Hannay, *The College of Justice* (1933); George Neilson, *Trial by Combat* (1890); *The Register of Brieves* (Stair Soc.); A. A. M. Duncan, 'Regiam Majestatem: a reconsideration', *Juridical Review*, N.S., VI. 199–217; and Ranald Nicholson, *op. cit.*, *ibid.*, April 1973, pt. i. 1–21.

The type of law which may be presumed to have existed in the Isles is briefly examined in Mackinnon's *Constitutional History*, and, at greater length, in John Cameron, *Celtic Law* (1937).

(d) Social History

The fullest general survey is C. Rogers, *Social Life in Scotland from Early to Recent Times* (3 vols., Grampian Club). I. F. Grant, *The Social and Economic Development of Scotland before 1603* (1930), shows insight into the characteristics of Scottish society in its rural and clannish setting. James Mackinnon's curiously named *Social and Industrial History of Scotland* (1920) is little more than a brief general history.

Specialised studies include John Warrack, *Domestic Life in Scotland, 1488–1688: A Sketch of the Development of Furniture and Household Usage* (1920); S. Maxwell and R. Hutchison, *Scottish Costume* (1958) and J. T. Dunbar, *History of Highland Dress* (1962).

(e) Economic History

I. F. Grant's work (see above) is less commendable for its treatment of economic history than for its treatment of social history. In the absence of an authoritative general survey the economic history of the period is best learnt from the prefaces to the *Exchequer Rolls* and *Treasurer's Accounts*. One aspect, agrarian history, receives terse treatment in T. B. Franklin, *A History of Scottish Farming* (1952). Another, the organisation of overseas trade through the staple, has mysteriously elicited two impressive works—J. Davidson and A. Gray, *The Scottish Staple at Veere* (1909) and M. P. Rooseboom, *The Scottish Staple in the Netherlands* (1910). Trading connections and Scottish settlement in Germany and the Baltic region are less impressively described by T. A. Fischer in *The Scots in Germany* (1902), The *Scots in Eastern and Western Prussia and Hinterland* (1903), and *The Scots in Sweden* (1907).

(f) Burgh History

A useful general history of this subject is given in W. M. Mackenzie, *The Scottish Burghs* (1949), which may be supplemented by W. Croft Dickinson's introduction to *Early Records of the Burgh of Aberdeen* (S.H.S.). In the introduction to the *Court Book of the Burgh of Kirkintilloch* (S.H.S.), G. S. Pryde discusses the characteristics of burghs of barony in the medieval period. The representative assemblies of the burghs are treated in Theodora Pagan, *The Convention of the Royal Burghs* (1926) and, together with the role of the burgesses in parliament, in J. D. Mackie and G. S. Pryde, *The Estate of Burgesses in the Scots Parliament and its relation to the Convention of the Royal Burghs* (1923).

Among the many works dealing with the history of particular burghs some which deserve mention are A. M. Munro, *Memorials of the . . . Aldermen, Provosts and Lord Provosts of Aberdeen, 1272–1895* (1897); Samuel Cowan, *The Ancient Capital of Scotland* [Perth] (2 vols., 1904); Robert Renwick and Sir John Lindsay, *History of Glasgow* (VOL. I, 1921); and David Robertson and Marguerite Wood, *Castle and Town: Chapters in the History of the Royal Burgh of Edinburgh* (1928). Aspects of the history of Edinburgh are also treated in the publications of the Old Edinburgh Club (1908–).

(g) Ecclesiastical History

Ian B. Cowan's *Parishes* (p. 622 above), D. E. Easson's *Religious Houses* (p. 622 above), D. E. R. Watt's *Fasti* (p. 622 above) and John Dowden's *Bishops* (p. 622 above) conveniently provide essential data.

The general history of the medieval kirk is dealt with at length in A. Bellesheim, *History of the Catholic Church in Scotland* (4 vols., 1887–90); John Cunningham, *The Church History of Scotland* (2 vols., 1882); A. R. MacEwen, *A History of the Church in Scotland* (2 vols., 1913, 1918); and John Dowden, *The Mediaeval Church in Scotland* (1910).

Important aspects of developments on the continent figure in T. S. R. Boase, *Boniface VIII* (1933); G. Mollat, *The Popes at Avignon* (English translation, 1949); Walter Ullmann, *The Origins of the Great Schism* (1948); and John Holland Smith, *The Great Schism* (1970). 'The Conciliarist Tradition in Scotland' is traced by J. H. Burns in *S.H.R.*, XLII. 89–104 and in *Scottish Churchmen and the Council of Basle* (1962), which lists some sixty Scots who were associated with the council. Financial relationships with the papacy are authoritatively explained in the introduction to *The Apostolic Camera and Scottish Benefices*, ed. A. I. Cameron (1934), and their political effects are summarised in R. K. Hannay's essay on 'The Scottish Crown and the Papacy' (Hist. Assoc. of Scotland).

Works on the episcopate include the turgid *Archbishops of St Andrews* of J. Herkless and R. K. Hannay (5 vols., 1907–15); Annie I. Dunlop's *James Kennedy* (see p. 630 above); John Durkan's succinct, but illuminating, *William Turnbull, Bishop of Glasgow* (1951); and Leslie J. Macfarlane, 'William Elphinstone, Founder of the University of Aberdeen' (*Aberdeen University Review*, XXXIX. 1–18)—the forerunner to a substantial biography which may shortly appear.

Various aspects of monastic life are somewhat critically surveyed in G. G. Coulton, *Scottish Abbeys and Social Life* (1933). One of the mendicant orders is well represented in W. Moir Bryce, *The Scottish Greyfriars* (2 vols., 1909).

Articles of special importance are: Ian B. Cowan, 'The development of the parochial system in medieval Scotland' in *S.H.R.*, XL. 43–55 and 'Some Aspects of the Appropriation of Parish Churches in Medieval Scotland' in *Scot. Church Hist. Soc. Recs.*, XIII. 203–22; D. E. Easson, 'The Collegiate Churches of Scotland' (*ibid.*, VI. 193–215; VII. 30–47); A. I. Dunlop, 'Remissions and Indulgences in Fifteenth-Century Scotland' (*ibid.*, XV. 153–67); and Donald E. R. Watt, 'University Graduates in Scottish Benefices before 1410' (*ibid.*, XV. 77–88).

Two notable periodicals—the *Records of the Scottish Church History Society* (1923–) and the *Innes Review* (1950–)—are mainly devoted to ecclesiastical history.

(h) Cultural and Intellectual History

There are two works of a general nature: W. G. Blaikie Murdoch, *The Royal Stuarts in their Connection with Art and Letters* (1908); and, more important, John Durkan, 'The Cultural Background in Sixteenth-Century Scotland' in *Innes Review*, x. 382–439.

1. *Art.* Ian Finlay has produced useful studies in *Art in Scotland* (1948), *Scottish Crafts* (1948), and *Scottish Gold and Silver Work* (1956). These may be supplemented by James S. Richardson, *The Medieval Stone Carver in Scotland* (1964), and David McRoberts, 'Notes on Scoto-Flemish Artistic Contacts', *Innes Review*, x. 91–6.

2. *Architecture.* The standard works are D. MacGibbon and T. Ross, *Castellated and Domestic Architecture of Scotland* (5 vols., 1887–92), and *Ecclesiastical Architecture of Scotland* (3 vols., 1896–97). Two expert modern works are Stewart Cruden, *The Scottish Castle* (1960), and John G. Dunbar, *The Historic Architecture of Scotland* (1966). Nigel Tranter, *The Fortified House in Scotland* (5 vols., 1962–70), is more popular in character. In W. M. Mackenzie, *The Mediaeval Castle in Scotland* (1927), the stress is less architectural than social. The *Reports* and *Inventories*, county by county, published by the Royal Commission on Ancient and Historical Monuments are authoritative.

3. *Music.* The standard work is H. G. Farmer, *A History of Music in Scotland* (1947).

4. *Literature.* Useful accounts of Scottish Lowland Literature are to be found in the volumes of the *Oxford History of English Literature*. A lively but hardly comprehensive survey is given in Kurt Wittig, *The Scottish Tradition in Literature* (1958); more restrained accounts are to be found in T. F. Henderson, *Scottish Vernacular Literature* (1898), J. H. Millar, *A Literary History of Scotland* (1903), and A. M. Kinghorn, *The Middle Scots Poets* (1970). R. L. Mackie provides an interesting summary of the makars in his *James IV* (1958), pp. 171–87. Studies of individual authors (mainly poets) will be found in the introductions to the numerous S.T.S. editions. Two important works are J. W. Baxter, *William Dunbar: A Biographical Study* (1952), and John MacQueen, *Robert Henryson: A Study of the Major Narrative Poems* (1967), which has

a wider cultural and historical relevance than the title suggests. J. H. Delargy in his review (*S.H.R.*, XLI. 144–8) of John G. McKay's *More West Highland Tales* (1960) gives a guide to works on Gaelic prose narratives. General surveys of Gaelic literature include N. MacNeill, *The Literature of the Highlanders* (1892, 1929); M. Maclean, *The Literature of the Celts* (1902, 1926) and *The Literature of the Highlands* (1904, 1925).

5. *Libraries and Printing*. The standard works are John Durkan and Anthony Ross, *Early Scottish Libraries* (1961), and H. G. Aldis, *A List of Books printed in Scotland before 1700* (reprint, 1971).

6. *Scholarship*. A. Fleming, *The Medieval Scots Scholar in France* (1952), is hardly an impressive work; and W. Forbes Leith, *Pre-Reformation Scholars in Scotland in the Sixteenth Century* (1915), is little more than a catalogue. Duns Scotus is prominent enough to figure in many works on the history of philosophy. John Major and John Ireland are treated in a number of articles (see notes to pp. 585–6 above). Gaelic scholarship is outlined by D. S. Thomson in 'Gaelic learned orders and literati in medieval Scotland' in *Scottish Studies* XII., 57–78. In a seminal article John Durkan examines 'The Beginnings of Humanism in Scotland' (*Innes Review*, IV. 5–24).

7. *Education*. The standard work on schools, J. Grant, *History of the Burgh and Parish Schools of Scotland* (1876), requires to be supplemented by D. E. Easson's 'The Medieval Church in Scotland and Education' in *Scot. Church Hist. Soc. Recs.* VI. 13–26 and John Durkan's 'Education in the Century of the Reformation' in *Essays on the Scottish Reformation, 1513–1625*, ed. David MacRoberts (1962).

Hastings Rashdall's standard work, *The Universities of Europe in the Middle Ages* (3 vols., 1964), gives due place to the Scottish universities. The three medieval universities are also the subject of the following works: J. M. Anderson, *The University of St Andrews* (1878, 1883); R. G. Cant, *The University of St Andrews* (1946)—both of which may be supplemented by Annie I. Dunlop's helpful introduction to *Acta Facultatis Artium Universitatis S. Andree, 1413–1588* (2 vols., S.H.S.); J. D. Mackie, *The University of Glasgow, 1451–1951* (1954); and R. S. Rait, *The Universities of Aberdeen* (1895).

(i) Regional and Local History

A pertinent study of this branch of history is B. C. Skinner, 'Local history in Scotland: a comment on its status and some recent writing' in *S.H.R.*, XLVII. 160–7. Works dealing with local history are too numerous to mention. The best are usually produced under the auspices of a publishing society, such as the Dumfriesshire and Galloway Natural History and Antiquarian Society (1862–) or the East Lothian Antiquarian and Field Naturalists' Society (1924–). Detailed information is available in the works of A. Mitchell and C. G. Cash, P. Hancock, C. S. Terry, and C. Matheson (see p. 621 above). The following two regions, however, require special mention:

1. *The Borders*. George Ridpath's *Border-history of England and Scotland* (1776) has hardly been superseded. A more readable work is W. R. Kermack, *The Scottish Borders (with Galloway) to 1603* (1967). Thomas I. Rae's excellent *Administration of the Scottish Frontier, 1513–1603* (1966) casts consider-

able light on the earlier period. Denys Hay examines 'Booty in Border Warfare' in *Dumfriesshire Trans.*, xxxi. 145–66.

2. *The Highlands and Isles.* There are few books which deal with this important area other than by way of clan or family histories. Notable exceptions are: W. R. Kermack, *The Scottish Highlands* (1957)—invaluable but all too concise; W. C. Mackenzie, *The Highlands and Isles of Scotland* (1949)—of great value for the sixteenth century, less so for the Middle Ages; and Donald Gregory's rather outmoded *History of the Western Highlands and Isles* (2nd edn., 1881). The introduction, appendices and notes to *Monro's Western Isles of Scotland and Genealogies of the Clans, 1549,* ed. R. W. Munro (1961) comprise an indispensable study of the lordship of the Isles, the downfall of which is portrayed in I. F. Grant, *Angus Og of the Isles* (1969), a work in which facts are supplemented by imaginative improvisations. The relationship between Highlanders and Lowlanders is outlined in Ranald Nicholson, 'Medieval Scotland: One State, Two Cultures' in *Studies in Medieval Culture* iv. (to appear shortly).

(j) Clan and Family Histories

Thanks to the remarkable Scottish propensity for genealogical exhibitionism such works dominate Scottish historiography in number, if not in quality. Guides to this extensive literature are given by J. Balfour Paul, J. P. S. Ferguson, Margaret Stuart and George F. Black (p. 622 above). Some of the best works are those produced by Sir William Fraser, which comprise both edited family records and narrative history. One classic work is still of value—David Hume of Godscroft, *The History of the Houses of Douglas and Angus* (Edinburgh, 1644).

INDEX

Carrick (*continued*)
 Stewart, John (later Robert III), *and* David (later Duke of Rothesay).
Carrickfergus, 93–5, 121, 599–600.
Carthusians, 11, 299.
Cashel, Archbishop of, *see* Michael.
Cassillis, Earl of, *see* Kennedy, David.
Castile, Castilians, 123, 244, 250, 393, 584n.
Castlelaw, 339.
Castles, 14, 18, 25–6, 37, 134, 144, 157, 195, 314, 374, 378–9, 412, 492; custody of, demanded by Edward I (1290), 34.
Casualties, 7, 313, 567, 601; *see also* Escheats, Marriage, Non-entries, Reliefs, Wardships.
Caterans, 205, 208, 234.
Cathcart, Sir Alan, 1st Lord, 364, 410.
Cathedrals, 2, 11–13, 522.
Catherine of Aragon, Queen of Henry VIII, 595.
 de Valois, Queen of Henry V, 250, 251, 258.
Causes and Complaints, auditors and committee of, *see* Parliament, Committees of.
Cavers Castle, 85.
Cawdor, Thane of, 548.
Cecily, daughter of Edward IV, betrothed to Duke of Rothesay, 478–9, 487, 488, 491, 507; offered to Duke of Albany, 496.
Chamberlain of Scotland, 17, 22, 81, 109, 143, 147, 165, 176, 213, 214–15, 218, 249, 255, 308, 312–13, 339, 445, 448, 513; his accounts and receipts, 22, 140 (1334–40 *and* 1342), 165 (1362), 177 (1371), 187–8 (1374), 188, 201 (1390), 210–11 (generally under Robert III), 254 (during Albany governorship); his ayres, 17, 109, 140, 308, 318, 390–1, 445; his deputes, 215, 313.
Chamberlains of crown lands, 380, 384, 456.
Chancellor of Scotland, 22, 142, 150, 200, 294, 295, 304, 311, 330, 384.

Chancery (the king's chapel), 19, 22, 111, 202; director of, 498; records of (1357–71), 180.
Chapel Royal, *see* Coldingham, St Andrews, Stirling.
Chapels, Chaplainries, Chaplains, 26, 271, 389, 450, 471, 520, 561, 592.
Chapters (monastic and cathedral), 9, 460.
Charles, the Bold, Duke of Burgundy, 402, 420, 443, 472–3, 475, 476, 479, 485.
 Dauphin of France (later Charles V), 162, 167.
 Dauphin of France (later Charles VII), 249, 250, 288; rewards Scots after battle of Baugé (1421), 251.
 V, King of France, renews Franco-Scottish alliance (1371), 193; recognises Clement VII (1378), 191.
 VI, King of France, 219, 249, 288; concludes peace of Troyes (1420), 250, 258.
 VII, King of France, 289, 292, 340, 346–8, 369–71 *and n*, 393, 399, 403, 413; renews Franco-Scottish alliance and makes marriage contract (1428), 289.
 VIII, King of France, 518, 526, 549.
Charterhouse, of Perth, 299.
Charteris, Andrew, 449.
 John, 449.
 Patrick, 449.
 Sir Thomas, chancellor, 142.
Château Gaillard, 130, 133, 138, 142.
Chaucer, Geoffrey, 276, 279, 583–4, 585.
Chepman, Walter, printer, 591–2.
Chene, Henry le, Bishop of Aberdeen, 99.
Chiefs, 7, 73, 207, 317, 543, 544.
Chisholm, James, Bishop of Dunblane, 559.
Chivalry, 83, 84, 88, 124, 133, 144, 159, 194, 199, 200, 208, 214, 216–17, 223, 266–7, 396, 409, 552, 555, 574, 579, 592, 602; patronised by David II, 174; its connection with

PRAISE FOR *SOLOVYOV AND LARIONOV*

'[A] wry and whimsically humorous historical detective story.'
Times Literary Supplement

'Vodolazkin has produced a romanticized hero's quest that affirms the "indivisibility and harmony" of history and personal fate.'
Wall Street Journal

'Third-person narration, circular structure, and archetypal characters lend this beautifully written literary mystery the feel of a modern fable.'
Booklist

'More than a beautifully written coming-of-age story...one of the finest novels I have read in years.'
World Literature Today

'There is sprightly, funny satire here and, beneath it, a surprising vein of poignancy.'
Kirkus

'Absorbing, darkly witty, history-soaked pages for literary and historical fiction fans.'
Library Journal

'A very unique blend of literary genres... I became captivated by this Russian tale with all of its stories within a story. This is a true Russian novel with all the complications that Russian novels entail.'
Marjorie's World of Books

'An ambitious first novel. It is to Vodolazkin's credit that he pulls it off, creating a substantial, beguiling work that engages the reader on several levels, encompassing a detective story, historical events and even a little romance.'
The Herald

PRAISE FOR *LAURUS*

'Stylistically ornate and compulsively readable…delivered with great aplomb and narrative charm.' *Times Literary Supplement*

'A remarkable novel… Russia's answer to *The Name of the Rose*.' **Atticus Lish, author of *Preparation for the Next Life***

'Impressive… *Laurus* cannot be faulted for its ambition or for its poignant humanity. It is a profound, sometimes challenging, meditation on faith, love and life's mysteries.'
Financial Times

'In *Laurus*, Vodolazkin aims directly at the heart of the Russian religious experience and perhaps even at that maddeningly elusive concept that is cherished to the point of cliché: the Russian soul.' *The New Yorker*

'Vodolazkin explores multifaceted questions of "Russianness" and concludes, like the 19th-century poet Fyodor Tyutchev, that Russia cannot be rationally understood. This is what leads him, with a gradual, but unstoppable momentum, to place faith and the transcendent human spirit at the centre of his powerful worldview.' *Washington Post*

'A treasure house of Russian medieval lore and customs…a very clever, self-aware contemporary novel…a quirky, ambitious book.' *Los Angeles Review of Books*

'Love, faith and a quest for atonement are the driving themes of [this] epic, prize-winning Russian novel… With flavours of Umberto Eco and *The Canterbury Tales*, this affecting, idiosyncratic novel…is an impressive achievement.' *Kirkus*

Solovyov

and

Larionov

Eugene Vodolazkin

*Translated from the Russian
by Lisa C. Hayden*

ONEWORLD

A Oneworld Book

First published in North America, Great Britain and Australia
by Oneworld Publications 2018
This paperback edition first published 2019
Originally published in Russian as *Соловьев и Ларионов*
by AST, Eleny Shubinoi imprint
The publication of the book was negotiated through Banke,
Goumen & Smirnova Literary Agency (www.bgs-agency.com)

ISBN 978-1-78607-609-0
ISBN 978-1-78607-036-4 (ebook)

This publication was effected under the auspices of the Mikhail Prokhorov Foundation
TRANSCRIPT Programme to Support Translations of Russian Literature

Published with the support of the Institute for Literary Translation (Russia)

ИНСТИТУТ ПЕРЕВОДА

AD VERBUM

Typeset by Palimpsest Book Production Limited, Falkirk, Stirlingshire
Printed and bound in Great Britain by Clays Ltd, Elcograf S.p.A.

Oneworld Publications
10 Bloomsbury Street
London WC1B 3SR
England

In memory of my great-grandfather

1

He was born by the train station bearing the unprepossessing name *Kilometer 715*. The station was not very big, despite the three-digit numeral. There was no movie theater, no post office, not even a school. Nothing but six wooden houses stood along the railroad bed. He left that station shortly after his sixteenth birthday. He went to Petersburg, was accepted at the university, and began studying history. This was to be expected, considering the surname—Solovyov, just like the famous historian—with which he had been born.

Solovyov's advisor at the university, Professor Nikolsky, called Solovyov a typical *self-made man*, who had come to the capital with a string of sledges bearing fish, but of course that was a joke. Petersburg had ceased being the capital long before Solovyov's arrival in 1991, and no fish was ever to be found at *Kilometer 715*. To the adolescent Solovyov's great regret, there was neither a river nor even a pond there. Reading one book after another about maritime journeys, the future historian cursed his landlocked existence and decided to spend the remainder of his days—a rather considerable number at the time—at the place where land and sea met. The attraction of large bodies of water, along with his thirst for knowledge, settled his choice in favor of Petersburg. In other words, the comment about the fish sledges would have remained a joke if not for its emphasis on overcoming one's initial circumstances; something elegantly stated in the English expression. Say what you will, but the historian Solovyov was a most genuine *self-made man*.

General Larionov (1882–1976) was another matter. He came into the world in Petersburg, in a family where being a military officer was hereditary. All of his relatives were officers, with the exception of the future general's father, who served as the director of the railroad department. As a child, Larionov even had the good fortune to know his great-grandfather (there was a penchant for longevity in the family), who was, naturally, a general, too. He was a tall, straight-backed old man who had lost his leg back in the Battle of Borodino.

In the eyes of the young Larionov, every movement his great-grandfather made, even the very knock of his peg leg on the parquet floor, was filled with a special dignity. When nobody was watching, the child loved to lift his right foot up, traverse the room on his left leg, and recline on the sofa with a deep sigh, resting his arms on the back of the sofa like great-grandfather Larionov. Larionov's grandfather and his lush-mustached uncles were not really any worse than his great-grandfather, but neither their gallant officer's appearance nor their talent for eloquence (his great-grandfather was not a talker) could even begin to compete with the absence of a leg.

All that reconciled the child to his two-legged relatives was their abundance of medals. He liked a medal one of his uncles had received, *For the suppression of the Polish rebellion*, more than anything. The melody of the word combination fascinated the boy, who did not have the faintest idea about Poles. In light of the child's obvious affinity for the medal, his uncle finally gave it to him. The boy wore this medal—along with the medal *For the conquest of Shipka*, which he received from another uncle—right up until the age of seven. The word *Shipka* certainly lost out to the word *rebellion* in terms of sonority but the beauty of the medal itself made up for its phonetic shortcomings. The child's happiest moments were spent sitting among his officer relatives with the two medals on his chest.

These were still Russian officers of a bygone time. They knew how to use cutlery (including the fish knife, now forgotten), effortlessly kissed ladies' hands, and performed numerous other courtesies unimaginable for officers of a later epoch. General Larionov had no need to overcome his circumstances. Quite the opposite: he needed only to absorb the qualities of his environs, to brim with them. Which is, in fact, what he did.

His inclination to become a general manifested itself in early childhood, when he began lining up wooden hussars in even rows on the floor before he had fully learned to walk. Seeing him engaged in this pursuit, those present uttered the only possible combination of words, 'General Larionov.' Ponder the naturalness of the union of those two words: they were made for one another, they were pronounced without a pause and became a united whole, flowing from one to the other, just as a rider and his horse become a united whole in battle. General Larionov. This was his first and only name among the family, and he became accustomed to it immediately and forever. General Larionov. Whenever the child heard that form of address, he stood and silently saluted. He did not learn to speak until he was three and a half years old.

What, one might ask, unites two such dissimilar individuals as the historian Solovyov and the General Larionov, if of course it is permissible to speak of uniting a budding young researcher and a battle-weary commander who, furthermore, is no longer of this earth? The answer lies at the surface: historian Solovyov was studying General Larionov's activity. After graduating from St. Petersburg University, Solovyov began his graduate studies at the Institute of Russian History, where General Larionov became his dissertation topic. Based on entries in reference books, there is no reason to doubt that by 1996—that being the time under discussion—General Larionov already belonged wholly to Russian history.

Needless to say, Solovyov was not the first to devote himself to studying the famous general's biography. Over the years, a couple of dozen scholarly articles had appeared at various times. They were devoted to various stages of Larionov's life and, above all, the mysteries associated with him that have yet to be unraveled. Although the number of works appears considerable at first glance, it seems completely insufficient if compared to the interest that General Larionov has always inspired, both in Russia and overseas. The fact that the number of scholarly research works is significantly fewer than the number of novels, films, plays, etcetera, in which the general appears—either as a figure or as a prototype for a character—does not appear to be accidental. This state of affairs symbolizes, as it were, the predominance of mythology over positive knowledge in everything concerning the deceased.

Beyond that, critical analysis by French researcher Amélie Dupont has shown that the mythology has even penetrated various scholarly articles about the commander. Which explains why the topic of research becomes a minefield, to a certain extent, for anyone just beginning work on the subject. However, even those articles (and Dupont writes about this, too) in which the truth comes across, thanks to all the splendor of scholarly argumentation, shed light on such narrow problems and episodes, that the significance of the extracted and argued truth is reduced to nearly nothing. It is remarkable that Dupont's work (*The Enigma of the Russian General*, a book published in French and Russian) is still the sole monographic research dedicated to General Larionov. This circumstance emphasizes, yet again, the dearth of sources on the subject. The fact that the French researcher managed to collect material for a monograph is due exclusively to her selflessness and particular treatment of her topic, which she has called the topic of her life.

In reality, it is no exaggeration to say that Dupont was born to research the Russian commander. In her case, this was not a matter of the historian's external features, something the scholarly community permits itself to mock, due to her height (187 centimeters) and the emergence of a mustache after the age of forty. It is known, after all, that barbs and jokes behind a prominent specialist's back (Dupont is called *mon general* in certain narrow circles) are usually nothing more than a form of envy. Consequently, mentioning Dupont's destiny for her designated topic is, above all, a reference to her unusual persistence, something without which it would essentially have been impossible to discover the tremendously important sources she subsequently published. And, truly, those who surmise that the emergence of the mustache that caused the inappropriate reaction in scholarly circles could be attributed, first and foremost, to the researcher's fascination with her topic, were not far from the truth. For the sake of objectivity, however, it must be noted that General Larionov himself did not have a mustache.

In all the preserved photographs (see the insets in Dupont's book), there appears before us a carefully shaven person with his hair cut short and parted. The part is so even and the quality of the shaving so flawless that one unwittingly detects the scent of eau du toilette when contemplating the photographs. With regard to his appearance, General Larionov made the only possible valid decision, just as he did in most other situations. Thinking that his ideally proportioned facial features needed no framing, he did not style himself after Alexander III, as did the officers around him. What is interesting is that his face did not look handsome, despite its proportions. His face became livelier at a mature age, particularly in elderliness. It is not uncommon to contemplate a photograph of a person in his youth, marveling at its blatant insufficiencies and almost embryonic look when compared to what came later. In cases of this sort, one experiences regret regarding the existence of that stage in the life of the person portrayed. Needless to say, feelings of this sort are very highly ahistorical. As far as the general goes, his face looked more chiseled thanks to wrinkles that appeared, with age, under his eyes, and the bump that emerged on his nose. During one period of his life, between the ages of thirty-five and forty, his appearance was reminiscent of Cardinal Richelieu because of his facial expression and that bump, though not because of all his features. The peak of the general's activity—as well as the mysteries connected with him—dates back to this period. Perhaps his resemblance to Richelieu was the resemblance of people possessing mysteries? Whatever the reason, that resemblance departed with time, too.

Even a fleeting glance at Dupont's illustrative material attests to the undeniable prevalence of photographs from the final period of General Larionov's life. The old man never made a point of having his picture taken but he also never put on airs by turning away from any cameras that greeted him: he regarded them with utmost indifference. That regard gave portraits of the general a naturalness rare for the genre. Perhaps the triumph of two photographic portraits of the general in international competitions at various times should be ascribed, above all, to that natural-ness?

There is no doubt that even those who are not at all familiar with the general's activity and have not heard his name would recall the black-and-white photograph of the old man sitting on a folding chair at the very edge of a jetty (Yalta, 1964). It became a classic of world photography, rather like the locomotive falling out the window of a Paris train station, rather like the lighthouse among raging waves, etcetera. Despite the summer heat, the old man is dressed in a white service jacket. He is sitting under a partially transparent awning, his legs crossed. The toe of a light-colored shoe is stretched before him, parallel to the ground, and almost blends in with the jetty, making it seem as if the lighthouse standing close by is balanced on the toe of that elegant shoe. The old man's gaze is directed into the distance and filled with the particular attention of one not interested in anything closer than the horizon. That old man is General Larionov. One cannot deny that all previous photographs pale in comparison with that shot of the general, that they have grown to feel inexpressive and, to some extent, unworthy of this outstanding person. That the general remained in his descendants' memory in his most, so to speak, mature form, could be considered his indisputable success. However, the biggest success of his life was, most likely, simply that he was not shot at the conclusion of the Civil War. This has always been considered inexplicable.

What is consequential, though, is that historian Solovyov decided to concentrate on that very enigma. Here, one might foresee objections of the sort that question whether historian Solovyov is, say, a figure capable of untangling this very complex historical snarl. And is it even worth placing hope on a very recent graduate who is, moreover, a *self-made man*? These objections do not seem well founded. It is sufficient to point out—and Dupont was the first to establish this fact—that Arkady Gaidar was commanding a regiment at the age of sixteen and a half. As far as *self-made man* goes, well, under a broad understanding of the term, anyone who has ever succeeded at accomplishing anything in life should be considered one.

It is sufficient to mention just one detail with regard to Solovyov's work on self-improvement: he was able to change his Southern Russian pronunciation to aristocratic Petersburg pronunciation. Needless to say, there is nothing about the Southern Russian pronunciation, in and of itself, that is shameful or belittles the dignity of its speakers (just as, say, deficient Moscow speech is incapable of discrediting residents of the capital). Mikhail Gorbachev, after all, led perestroika in Russia using Southern Russian pronunciation. Unlike Solovyov, Gorbachev was not a historian—he himself made history without taking particular care about the orthoepic side of matters, a tendency that continued even after he left his post and retired. As far as Solovyov goes, when he murmured Russian tongue twisters in the dormitory kitchen, he was working on something that went beyond simply training himself in pronunciation: he was, as he characterized it, eliminating the provincialism within himself.

Solovyov's thesis advisor, the eminent Professor Nikolsky, played an important role in Solovyov's development. After reading his student's first important paper, which was devoted to Russia's conquest of the Far East, the professor invited Solovyov to his office, where he said nothing for a long time, blowing on the paper tube of a *Belomorkanal* cigarette all the while (he had taken a liking to those cigarettes while working at the forced labor site bearing the same name).

'My friend,' said the professor after lighting the cigarette, 'scholarship is dull. If you don't get used to that notion, it will not be easy for you to pursue it.'

The professor requested that Solovyov delete from his paper the words *great*, *triumphant*, and *only possible*. He also asked his student if he was familiar with the theory according to which Russians squandered the energy granted to them by conquering expanses of inhuman dimensions. His student was not. Prior to acquainting Solovyov with this theory, Prof. Nikolsky requested that he delete the phrase *phenomenon indicating progress*, too. The author of the paper was asked to pay special attention to the formatting of biblio-graphical and persuasive footnotes. A careful look at this aspect of the paper revealed that the only properly formatted footnote was 'Ibid., 12.'

To be utterly candid, the majority of what Prof. Nikolsky said seemed like nitpicking to Solovyov, yet it was this very discussion that formed the basis of a friendship between professor and student. The professor was at that age when his quibbles could no longer be offensive to the young man and Solovyov's own history, which was anything but simple, did its part in forcing his advisor to show more leniency toward his student.

Prof. Nikolsky never tired of repeating to his mentee that, as a rule, pretty phrases in scholarship are misguided, and the beauty of those phrases is based on their alleged univer-sality and an absence of exceptions. But—and here the cigarette in the professor's hand would trace a smoky ellipsis—that absence is spurious. No exhaustive truths exist (hardly any exist, the professor corrected himself, bringing the statement into accord with his own theory). For each *a* there is always a *b* and a *c* to be found, as well as something that no letters can convey. An honest researcher takes all that into account, but his pronouncements cease being beau-tiful. Thus spoke Prof. Nikolsky.

At some point, Solovyov's blue-eyed romanticism gave way to a pronounced inclination toward precision, so this was a time when he discovered a particular beauty: the beauty of reliable knowledge. This was a time when the young man's papers started to be mottled with enormous quantities of exhaustive and meticulously formatted foot-notes. Footnotes became for him more than an occasion to express respect for his predecessors. They revealed to him that there was no one realm of knowledge where he, Solovyov, would be first, and that scholarship is, to the highest degree, a process that is bequeathed. They were representatives of great, all-encompassing knowledge. They watched after Solovyov and educated him, forcing him to rid himself of approximate and uncertain assertions. They blew open his smooth school-based exposition, because a text, just like existence itself, cannot exist without conditions.

Solovyov inserted footnote after footnote, marveling that he had managed to get by without them at the beginning of his scholarly career. When footnotes began accompanying nearly every word he wrote, Prof. Nikolsky was forced to stop him. He announced to Solovyov, in passing, that scholars usually get by without footnotes at the end of their careers, too. The young researcher felt disheartened.

Despite Solovyov's expectations, the Pacific Ocean—to which he fought his way in his first important paper—did not become his primary topic. Prof. Nikolsky was able to convince his student that the most important part of history takes place on a continent. Only a strong familiarity with that part of history gives a researcher the right to leave dry land from time to time. After a wrenching internal struggle, Solovyov decided to postpone setting sail.

Solovyov came to appreciate Petersburg fully during his five university years. He began wearing high-quality but unostentatious clothing (clothing becomes more colorful when advancing south, and not only in Russia), referenced the powers that be with the short word *they*, and took a liking to evening strolls on Vasilevsky Island. His habit of taking strolls continued later, after renting an apartment on

the Petrograd Side (Zhdanovskaya Embankment, No. 11).
He would walk home after finishing his work at the library.
Sadovaya Street. Summer Garden. Troitsky Bridge. In the
winter, when the Summer Garden was closed (in accordance
with its name) and its statues were boarded up in boxes,
Solovyov would choose another route. He would reach the
Neva River via Griboedov Canal and then turn on to
Dvortsovy Bridge, after walking past the Winter Palace
(which was open year-round, unlike the Summer Garden).
At home, he would place his soaked boots on the radiator.
By morning they would turn white, from the salt scattered
by the yard workers.

Solovyov came to love the Public Library's special winter
coziness: Catherine the Great's figure in a half-frosted window,
pre-war lamps on the tables, and the barely audible whispering
of those sitting behind him. He liked the indescribable library
scent. That scent united the aromas of books, oak shelves,
and worn runner rugs. All libraries smell that way. The
snow-covered, one-story village library where the young
Solovyov had borrowed books smelled that way. It was an
hour and a half's walk from the *Kilometer 715* station; Solovyov
stopped by the library after school before heading back to his
station. He would sit, half-facing the elderly librarian Nadezhda
Nikiforovna's desk, while she searched for his books somewhere behind the cabinets. As he awaited Nadezhda
Nikiforovna's return, Solovyov would examine his violet
fingers, which he sank into his rabbit-fur hat. Her voice would
emerge from behind the cabinets from time to time.

'Captain Blood: His Odyssey?'
'Already read it.'
He read everything. The village library became his first

true revelation and Nadezhda Nikiforovna was his first love. Unlike the houses by the railroad, the library was very quiet and did not smell of railroad ties. Mixed in with the fabulous library potion was the smell of *Red Moscow* perfume. This was Nadezhda Nikiforovna's perfume. If there was anything Solovyov felt was missing later, in his Petersburg life, it was likely *Red Moscow*.

'In Search of the Castaways?'

Her quiet voice made goosebumps slowly descend down Solovyov's spine. After licking a fingertip, Nadezhda Nikiforovna would pull his library card out of the drawer and enter the necessary notation. Fascinated, Solovyov followed the movement of her large fingers, with their dulled nails. A cameo glistened on her ring finger. When she placed a book on a shelf, Nadezhda Nikiforovna's ring grazed the wood and the cameo produced a muffled plastic sound. That sound took on an extraordinary elegance, almost an elite quality, in Solovyov's ears because it was so unlike the clanging of train carriage couplers. Later, he would qualify it as world culture's first bashful knock at the door of his soul.

More often than not, Solovyov did not come to the library alone: he was with a girl named Leeza, who lived in the house next door. Leeza was not allowed to walk home by herself and was ordered to wait for Solovyov at the library. She would sit some distance away, silently observing the book exchange process. Sometimes she would borrow something Solovyov had already read. Solovyov immediately forgot about Leeza after coming home. He would recollect all the details of his visit to the library, indulging himself in dreams of married life with Nadezhda Nikiforovna.

It should be emphasized that he was eight years old then

and his dreams were fully virtuous. Remote as he was from civilization's hotbeds (and based on Nadezhda Nikiforovna's expression, from those hotbeds' settled ashes, too), Solovyov vaguely imagined the tasks of marriage, as well as the ways it takes its course. As it happened, that village library was his sole link to the outside world, ruling out the availability not only of erotic publications but of suggestive illustrations in periodicals as well. Nadezhda Nikiforovna censored new acquisitions in her free time, ruthlessly cutting those items out.

There is nothing surprising in the fact that five years later, when their instincts were awakening, Solovyov and Leeza were deprived of all manner of guidance in *that* sphere and progressed by groping along, in the literal sense of the word. Nevertheless, when the adolescent Solovyov engaged in sex in later years, he did not consider himself unfaithful to Nadezhda Nikiforovna. The idea of marriage, which had so warmed his heart as a child, lost no attraction for him then, either. The change took place only upon recognizing that certain things should not be demanded of Nadezhda Nikiforovna.

Leeza's surname—Larionova—does not lack interest in this present narrative. This present narrative is inclined to accentuate various resemblances and coincidences because there is meaning in any similarity: similarity opens up another dimension and alludes to a true perspective, without which one's view would certainly hit a wall. In taking on research into General Larionov's life and work, Solovyov bore in mind his own previous familiarity with that same surname. He placed significance on such things. Needless to say, the young researcher could not yet explain the role of the Larionovs in his life, though even then he felt the role would not be secondary.

As happens more often than not with events that are intended to occur, Solovyov's research topic came to him by chance. Another graduate student, Kalyuzhny, had worked on the topic before Solovyov. Yes, this pleasant fellow lacked all manner of scholarly energy and, really, most likely any energy whatsoever. His efforts were sufficient for him to make his way to some academic beer joint and settle in there for the entire remainder of the day. Kalyuzhny regarded the general sympathetically and experienced an undeniable curiosity regarding his fate. The primary thing he did not understand was that (and here Kalyuzhny's index finger slid along a glass) the general had remained alive. Over the course of several years, Kalyuzhny retold Dupont's classic research to everyone who sat down at his table. This long retelling obviously wore him out in a real way because he did not write a single line during those years of unending narration. Gathering his last strength, graduate student Kalyuzhny unexpectedly did what the general had not brought himself to do in his day: he left the country. Kalyuzhny's further fate is unknown.

Solovyov's fate is known, however, and, according to the unanimous opinion of his colleagues, it was up to him to replace his drop-out associate. Only a few months after entering graduate school, Solovyov delivered a paper at a conference: 'Studying the Life and Activity of General Larionov: Conclusions and Outlooks.'

The conclusions that Solovyov drew and the outlooks he summarized made a most favorable impression on the scholarly public. The paper testified not only to the young researcher's well-organized mind but also, in equal measure, to his deep insight into the topic. The climax of the paper, which evoked extraordinary animation in the hall, was his introduction of corrections to data in Dupont's monograph that had been considered unshakable until that day.

And so, it turned out that there were only 469 soldiers on record in the 34th Infantry Division of the 136th Taganrog Regiment, not the 483 soldiers Dupont asserted. It also emerged that the French researcher had, on the other hand, reduced the number of soldiers in the 2nd Native Division of the Combined Cavalier Brigade to 720 (the true number was 778). Dupont did not shed full light on the role of Colonel Yakov Noga (1878–?) in the Crimean campaign; however, the officer's level of education had clearly been overstated: the French researcher mistakenly indicated that Noga graduated from the Vladimir and Kiev cadet corps, though he graduated only from the Vladimir (named for Saint Vladimir) Kiev Cadet Corps. Solovyov set forth a series of more minor quibbles with the French monograph, but in this case one must think it permissible to limit discussion to the examples cited above. Even they are enough to characterize the quality of the young scholar's work and his unwillingness to blindly trust his predecessors' authority.

This was Solovyov's finest hour. Dupont hid behind a marble column in the conference hall as she listened to Solovyov's paper. According to the accounts of those who saw her at that moment, the French historian's eyes were brimming with tears. A person less dedicated to scholarship might have been offended by all the corrections that Solovyov introduced. That person might have become embittered or, who knows, shrugged their shoulders and snorted with disdain. Or said, let us suppose, that the specified clarifications held an extremely relative value in explaining the Crimean events of 1920. But Dupont was not that sort of person. At Solovyov's 'Thank you for your attention,' she ran out from behind the column and embraced the presenter. Was that ardent scholarly embrace—which combined sobbing and smudged mascara and a prickly mustache—not a triumph of sincere values and evidence of the sanctity of the great international solidarity of researchers?

Standing behind the lectern, her faced streaked with mascara, Dupont recalled everyone who had devoted themselves to researching the post-revolutionary period at various times. She referred, with particular emotion, to Ieronim A. Ratsimor, who had conceived of, but not managed to complete, the monumental *Encyclopedia of the Civil War*.

'He died on the letter *K*,' Dupont said of the deceased, 'but if he could have held on for just one more letter, our level of knowledge about General Larionov would have been different, completely different. But now we see,' and with these words the researcher once again drew Solovyov to herself, 'our worthy successor. Now we can feel calm about leaving.'

The polite Solovyov initially wanted to object to what Dupont had said, to ask that henceforth she continue engaging in the work that was so important to everyone, but she would not allow it. With a sweep of her huge hand, she seemed to conjure out of thin air her monograph about the general, which she then forcefully pressed to Solovyov's chest. After kissing him again in parting, she marched across

...nference hall and vanished into the duskiness of a corridor.

She called him from Paris. Positively everything about the young researcher interested her: his views on history overall, his biases in terms of methodology, and even—this was completely unexpected—his material standing. Unlike all the other areas, Solovyov found no intelligible answer to her question about the matter. Dupont herself deduced the reality of the Russian scholar's material standing: it was simply lacking.

Stunned by that circumstance, Dupont delved into the reasons for such a somber state of affairs. Standing firm on determinist positions, the representative of French historical scholarship lined up a long cause-and-effect chain. There is no point in citing it in full: the events Dupont referred to are well known to any Russian schoolchild, though perhaps it is worth dwelling on several fundamental principles that are characteristic of this chain.

According to Dupont, several factors determined our society's advancement, with key roles played by an insufficient propensity for labor, an inclination for appropriating another's property, and a heightened sense of justice. The cause-and-effect chain that had formed within the French researcher's head finally coiled into a circle that she recognized, on second thought, as vicious.

The state of affairs she depicted did not, in fact, seem rosy: appropriation of another's property intensified—to an extreme—a sense of justice within society, which in turn sharply reduced the society's propensity for labor. Needless to say, the latter circumstance could not help but stimulate an inclination for appropriating another's property and that automatically led to an even more heightened sense of justice and even less propensity for labor. It was within this context that Dupont examined the destructive Russian revolutions, the many-year rule of Communists (no less destructive, according to her assessment), and a whole series of other events.

That combination of factors was combustible on its own ('*Molotoff cocktail!*' Dupont sighed), and was aggravated by a personal factor. A series of figures proceeding along Russian history's teetering stage had managed to push the contradictions to extremes. In the French scholar's view, president Boris Yeltsin occupied a special place among them and had obviously misused his skills as an orchestra conductor. The success of his Berlin performance made him so giddy that he thought of nothing but the conductor's baton from then on. Under that baton's light stroke, the appropriation of another's property finally reached the point where the sense of justice was no longer intensifying and the propensity for labor was no longer decreasing. As far as Yeltsin's decisive manner for problem-solving went, Dupont characterized it in her article 'The Headless Horseman', published in *Sobriety and Culture* in 1999, as a typical cavalry charge.

There is no doubt that Dupont became entangled in a whole series of questions while forming her chain of cause-and-effect. For example, she demonstrated an overt exaggeration of the role of the individual in history (it probably comes as no surprise that Dupont's political views were staunchly de Gaullist), most likely brought on because the history she herself was working on was the history of a general. Beyond that, the dialectic of the necessary and the accidental—which is so important for a correct assessment of historical events—became a stumbling block for her. She simply could not figure that out by using Russian history. At some point, she began to see that necessity was accidental in our country to a certain degree. In other words, she could not manage to distinctly formulate the reason behind Solovyov's squalid existence. And so Dupont transferred all her irrepressible energy to something more consequential. She replaced her search for answers to Russia's accursed questions with a search for funds for the young scholar's needs.

After brief reflection, the French researcher made an appeal to the All-Russian Scientific Foundation, with the vague hope that this particular institution was counterbalancing the government's shortchanging of its scholars. After a short conversation in Moscow—people in the know had advised her to get in touch with the fund's employees only in person—the foundation's experts regarded the proposed research topic as insufficiently all-Russian. In saying their goodbyes, ('There was a shadow of something left unsaid at our meeting!' Dupont complained afterwards), they recommended their guest approach the Russian Foundation for Scientific Workers.

They heard out Dupont more favorably at the Foundation for Scientific Workers, and even fed her tea with biscuits of the *Stolichnye* brand. Along the way, they asked if she was an employee or at least an expert at any kind of French foundation. Upon learning that Dupont had nothing to do with French foundations, they inquired of the researcher who exactly at the All-Russian Scientific Foundation had recommended she approach the Foundation for Scientific Workers, and asked what that person had said. Surprised

by the question and, above all, the questioner's unusual
tone, Dupont choked and they pounded her on the back
until an ill-fated shard of one of the *Stolichnye* biscuits
emerged from the Parisienne's throat. They asked no further
questions after that, helped her on with her coat, and
gallantly kissed her hand. In Moscow, by the way, they do
that no worse than in Paris.

Dupont undertook a further attempt to help the
Petersburg graduate student: she got in touch with the S.M.
Solovyov Foundation by telephone. In Dupont's mind, a
foundation named for the great Russian historian could not
refuse to support another historian, one who was both still
young and bore the same surname. Oddly enough, in this
case it was precisely the surname that became the stumbling
block. Afraid of being accused of nepotism, there was a
refusal on the other end of the line to even review an appeal
of this sort. Astonished at the scrupulousness of Russian
foundations, a pensive Dupont hung up the receiver.

Finally, at the suggestion of colleagues, she appealed to
some famous entrepreneur or other, allegedly a man of
contradictions who mixed market speculation with philanthropic activity. It is entirely possible that the contradictions
were exaggerated since, according to information that
reached her later, philanthropic activity inexplicably turned
out to be one of the most profitable income items of his
entrepreneurship. Whatever the case, Dupont approached
him with a long letter, in which she noted the thoroughness
of the scholar's work and enumerated, among other things,
the corrections the latter had entered with regard to
manpower in the subunits.

To the addressee's credit, he did not force Dupont to wait

long for an answer. His letter offered the highest appraisal of Solovyov's industriousness and attention to detail. The philanthropist then went on to point out that data for 1920 offered no relevance for him since he was predominantly interested in information about armies currently in operation.

Needless to say, even such a gallant rejection could not suit a person whose colleagues had nicknamed her *mon general*. Dupont set off on another attack and wrote the patron a far more voluminous letter. This letter examined, in the most detailed fashion, the essence of each of the adjustments Solovyov had entered, with historical parallels and brief statistics regarding comparable subunits of European armies. As for the relevance of the data, the enterprising philanthropist was introduced to an extremely ancient point of view, according to which all history repeats itself. After subjecting the designated theory to constructive criticism, Dupont nonetheless stipulated that she certainly did not exclude the possibility of certain recurrences. The only point with which the French researcher categorically refused to agree was the possibility (even theoretical) that a second General Larionov could appear on the peninsula. In concluding her letter, so there would be no omissions, she even specified that people of the general's sort are born only once every thousand years.

It is unknown what had the greater effect here—the digression into the territory of the philosophy of history, the French researcher's resoluteness in standing up for her position, or the actual volume of the letter—but the entrepreneur-philanthropist answered with approval. He even joked agreeably in his response that the researcher's observation regarding a general of Larionov's sort might exclude the possibility of such a general appearing in the near future but it instilled certain hopes for the period following the year 2882. In expectation of that blessed epoch, he was designating that Solovyov receive, throughout his graduate studies (i.e. for three years), a stipend that was small but adequate for a modest life. This was a genuine victory.

Solovyov was stunned by the news of the stipend. He knew nothing of the efforts being made by the French woman on his behalf and felt genuinely happy when he heard about the gift. The phrase saying the stipend was designed for a modest life could not cloud his joy. On the one hand, Solovyov's life had always been modest, but on the other, he supposed, justifiably, that his notions of modesty differed mightily from his benefactors' notions. As informed as they were, they could not even guess the extent of the modesty of a scholar's life in Russia.

'You should go to Yalta,' Dupont told the scholarship recipient. 'I've looked high and low at everything in the capitals, but I've never made it all the way to Crimea. If there's something new to be found anywhere, it'll be in Yalta.'

She said that at the beginning of July. Solovyov spent about three weeks systematizing his papers. During that process, it emerged that there would be a conference (that, by some strange coincidence, was supposed to be funded by the S.M. Solovyov Foundation) in Kerch in August— *General Larionov as Text*—and so, despite the event's quirky title, Solovyov sent in his topic for a paper.

Feeling prepared for work under Crimean conditions, Solovyov appealed to the director of the institute for permission to travel for his work. Judging by the director's pensive chewing at the temple of his eyeglasses, Solovyov grasped that such work-related travel was not being granted to him uncontested. And here the young scholar began feeling awkward when he remembered, for the first time in three weeks, that Yalta was a resort city. Solovyov began explaining his motives for the trip with a vehemence unusual for an academic institution (in his agitation, he even forgot to mention the conference) but the director relaxed his toothy grip on his glasses and waved them in the air in agreement. After all, in recent years, work-related travel had been unfinanced due to lack of funds and involved nothing more than permission to be absent from the institute. Solovyov received that permission.

He left the institute's ostentatious building and headed, unhurried, in the direction of Tuchkov Embankment. On a whim, he turned down a side street, and ended up in a café. Solovyov could not remember when he had last been in a café and ascertained, with some surprise, that his life was becoming less modest. Solovyov viewed the dinner he ordered for himself that evening as a farewell meal. He already had a train ticket and could feel it (not without pleasure) when he put his hand into his jacket pocket. Without a doubt, August was the most apt month for work-related travel to Yalta.

2

Solovyov traveled south the very next day, on a train from St. Petersburg to Simferopol. Needless to say, trains were not the young historian's usual means of transportation. His life had taken shape in such a way that anyone capable of reading palms would have seen a railroad line parallel to Solovyov's lifeline. The trains that streaked past the small station called *Kilometer 715* were the first to reveal to him the existence of a large and fancy world beyond the station's limits.

Solovyov's first recollections of smells and sounds were attached to the railroad. Locomotive whistles woke him up in the mornings and the rhythmic clacking of wheels lulled him to sleep at night. His bed vibrated slightly when trains went by and his ceiling was streaked with the reflections of the lights in the compartments. As he dropped off to sleep, he stopped distinguishing exactly where that smooth but loud movement was coming from—here or outside. The iron knobs at the head of his bed jingled rhythmically and the bed slowly gathered speed, carrying Solovyov off to cheerful childhood dreams.

Solovyov learned to read using the placards on long-distance trains. It is worth noting that it was the trains' swiftness that brought about his speed-reading skills, which later eased his perusal of publications about the general: those publications were just as numerous as they were fantastic. It was from those same placards that Solovyov first learned of the existence of a series of cities to which the rails under his own windows ran, leading due north on one side and due south on the other. The station called *Kilometer 715* lay in the middle of the world.

Solovyov watched the trains with Leeza Larionova. After walking up the steps to the platform, they would sit down on a bench that had lost its color long ago and begin their observations. They loved it when the long-distance trains reduced their speed near the station. Then they could discern not only the placards but also rolled-up mattresses on bunks, tea glasses in special metal holders, and—most important of all—passengers who represented the mysterious world from which the train had come. It was not that they were glad for the trains because they were longing for a world unfamiliar to them; more likely, the very idea of 'long-distance' captivated them.

Their regard for the electric local trains and freight trains that occasionally streaked past the station was calmer. The people on the locals were more or less familiar to them, but as far as the freight trains went, well, there were no people on them at all. These were the longest and dullest of trains. They consisted of tank cars filled with oil, flatcars burdened with lumber, or just closed-up boxcars.

By a very early age, Solovyov knew the schedule for all the trains that went by the station. This information, which some might think capable of becoming a useless burden, played a considerable role in the future historian's life. For one thing, Solovyov was inculcated with a taste for valid knowledge—this may be why the young historian's regard for the mythology surrounding General Larionov was subsequently so unforgiving—from the very beginning of his conscious life. For another, a faultless mastery of the schedule cultivated in Solovyov a heightened perception of time, a real necessity for a genuine historian. The schedule used numbers that were never round. Nowhere in those figures were there approximate denotations such as *after lunch*, *in the first half of the day*, or *around midnight*. There were only 13:31, 14:09, 15:27. These unkempt fringes of time were as tousled as existence itself and possessed a very specific sort of beauty: the beauty of verity.

Solovyov's mastery of the schedule was not accidental. His mother worked as a controller at a crossing adjacent to the station. And though there was not much of anything to control there (the crossing could go unintersected by cars or trucks for days), Solovyov's mother would lower the crossing gate three minutes before any train appeared, put on her uniform jacket, and step out onto the control booth's little balcony. There was something captain-like in her unnaturally straight figure, her motionlessness, and her stern facial features. Sometimes the din of a train would wake Solovyov up in the middle of the night and he would look out the window at his mother. Her resolute standing, baton raised, held him spellbound. It was like that, in profile, that she imprinted herself upon his memory, amidst the train's rumbling and its flickering lights. When Solovyov read later about churches in abandoned northern villages and how a priest in that area ministered to an empty church, he thought that referred to his mother, too. Her selfless service, without any visible goal, continued, unvarying, like the sunrise. Regardless of changes in government, time of day, or weather conditions.

It was weather conditions, however, that turned out to be fatal for her. One frosty winter night, she was chilled to the bone and contracted pneumonia. She initially treated it with vodka and honey. From time to time, her mother, granny Solovyova, would take the baton and head out to substitute for her daughter at the crossing. Some time later, when the patient became worse, the old woman massaged her back and chest, spreading the suffocating smell of turpentine through the house. A few days later, Solovyov's mother announced unexpectedly that she was dying. Exaggeration was not the norm in his family, so the old woman grew worried. There was no point in sending to the nearest village, since there was nobody there but a drunken doctor's assistant. The old woman ran to the control booth to stop a train. Solovyov's mother died, but the old woman kept on waving her daughter's baton. Not one train stopped.

The trains almost never stopped anyway. Only rarely, predominantly in the summer, when the tracks were over-loaded, did trains pull up to the station, sighing heavily. The carriage attendants would step out onto the pock-marked slabs of the platform as if they owned the place. Behind them were fat men in T-shirts and women in tight-fitting exercise pants. And more rarely, children. Children were usually allowed no further than the vestibule, where they burst from their pensive grandmothers' hands. Adults smoked, drank beer straight from the bottle, and crushed mosquitoes with resounding slaps. When the children managed to make it to the platform, little Solovyov would run off, but continue to follow the proceedings from the bushes. During those moments, he was not the only one keeping an eye on the train that had arrived: the six houses surrounding the station were all eyes and ears, too. The residents pressed themselves against windows, stood in doorways, or cast quick glances at the arrivals as they pretended to dig in their kitchen gardens. It was not the done thing to walk up to the platform.

Only Solovyov's mother—when she was alive—was within sight of the passengers. The passengers, whose appearance seemed even more idle when compared with the railway worker's focused, solemn standing, made no attempt to call out to her. It was obvious right away that this motionlessness was of a specific type. Paying no attention to the passengers, Solovyov's mother gazed at the point where the rails met, as if watching for the arrival of her impending death. When reading later about the elderly general's famous gaze, Solovyov imagined it without the slightest effort. He remembered the way his mother had looked into the distance.

Solovyov's grandmother did not watch in that same way. Gazes into the distance were not really characteristic of her. Most often, she would sit, propping up her cheek with the palm of her hand and looking straight ahead. She outlived her daughter by several years and died not long before Solovyov graduated from high school. Her death pushed him to move to Petersburg. It was in Petersburg that he first heard about General Larionov.

Broadly speaking, it was not accidental that both Solovyov and Larionov were children of railroad workers. Perhaps it was exactly this that determined certain similar characteristics, despite all their external differences. Railroad workers in Russia have a special mission because the role of the railroad in our country is not the same as in other places. The time that we spend traveling is measured in days. That time is enough not only for a good conversation but—in successful cases—even for making marriage plans. What marriage could be planned on the *Munich–Berlin* express in seats lined up one after the other, with radio jacks in the armrests? Most likely, none.

People who are somehow involved with the railroad are all predominantly even-tempered and unhurried. They know about conquering an expanse. These people know how to listen to the sound of the even clatter of wheels and will never start rushing around: they understand that they still have time. This is why the most serious of foreigners also choose a week or two, once a year, to take a ride on the Trans-Siberian Railway. There is little need to mention that these people resolutely prefer a train to an airplane, other than for transatlantic situations, at any rate. The Americans leave them no choice at all.

General Larionov's father had no choice, either. Airplanes were simply not flying at the time he decided to associate his life with the railroad. Strictly speaking, at that time, even the railroad itself had not yet become a truly day-to-day matter. Using it demanded of passengers not only a certain degree of courage but also a progressive mindset. Possessing these qualities in full measure, Larionov, director of the railroad department, spent half of his on-duty hours on wheels. He was entitled to use a special first-class lounge carriage that was hitched to the end of the train. It was in that carriage that he would set off to Crimea, for his vacation. As a scrupulous person, the department director paid for his family's passage in that carriage, notwithstanding the persuasion of railroad employees who considered that his privileges should extend to his family. The governess rode in second class on the same train and the servants in third. This latter circumstance served later as cause for various forms of speculation and even conclusions regarding the openly undemocratic character of relationships within the Larionov household.

In answer to accusations of that sort, one might cite the opinion of Ieronim A. Ratsimor, who pointed out in his 1992 article 'Sprouts of Democracy in the Russian Military Environment from the Late 19th to Early 20th Centuries', that, for a number of reasons, class ideology prevailed over democratic ideology at the end of the nineteenth century. Ratsimor also put forth the supposition that democracy is not a universal concept and is generally not obligatory for characterizing all times and peoples. When established in countries not prepared for it, democracy is capable of bearing the saddest of fruits. According to the historian's convictions, the distinctness of Russia's class divide regulated social relationships far more effectively than democratic procedures. Using material from the general's biography, he convincingly demonstrated that, while still a pupil and junior cadet, Larionov was obligated to ride second class but after becoming a senior cadet, he could only ride third since senior cadets were already considered to have attained a low army rank and were not admitted into the two other classes.

Less radical points of view were also expressed with

regard to democracy in the Larionov family. The graduate student Kalyuzhny surmised, verbally, that the defining traits of the seating arrangements of those riding south were determined not so much by the opinion of Larionov, department director, as by the presence at the station of the elder General Larionov, who was allegedly incapable of coming to terms with scorn for Russia's class divide. The latter man was, to be sure, known for his conservatism, which he expressed in part through a disdainful regard for the railroad. To him, the realm of the railroad seemed unworthy of their family line—in the veteran's watery eyes, it presented something akin to a circus attraction. Only the post of department director brought a certain seriousness to his grandson's work and partially reconciled the old man with this odd choice of profession. And though the hero of the Battle of Borodino considered train travel inappropriate for himself, he invariably came to the train station at Tsarskoe Selo to see his family off on their travels. As he made his way along the row of carriages on his peg leg, he would stop by the locomotive with unexpected timidity and spend a long while watching the steam bursting out of the boilers. Then he would shrug his shoulders for effect, hurriedly make the sign of the cross over his family members, and resolutely hobble toward the exit, an echo resonating under the station's metal arches. One might suppose the last thing on his mind at those moments was the passengers' seating arrangements.

Those trips were preserved in the future general's memory as one of the brightest pages of his childhood. In *Notes for an Autobiography*, which Dupont found and published, General Larionov describes in detail the railroad journeys of his childhood. The carriage itself evoked the greatest delight for him; with brass handles polished to a shine, oak paneling, and—most importantly—a glass rear wall that displayed the entire expanse of road already traveled. To the juvenile Larionov, it seemed as if the carriage at their disposal was a giant spider capable of producing two steel threads that ran out from under it at high speed and converged on the horizon.

The child was particularly keen on watching sunsets that lent enchanting colors to the forest on both sides of the railroad bed. The colors dimmed with every minute and the trees darkened, approaching the railroad bed ever closer. For the future general, who had first-hand familiarity with Russian folk tales, the train's motion was reminiscent of an escape from a spellbound forest. Clutching at the nickel handle on the bunk, he anxiously observed the rocking of fir crowns, from which, to his mind, it would be most opportune for an unseen adversary to attack. Only after some time had passed, when it was completely dark and the small glass wall had begun reflecting the carriage's cozy luxury, would the child calm down, unclench his numbed fingers, and let go of the nickel handle. General Larionov caught himself making that motion later, when he let go of a handle on the hatch of an armored train one summer evening in 1920. The scent of wormwood wafted from a stilled field. Sudden silence had replaced the sounds of battle, with the only exception being the brooding metallic noises that carried from somewhere below, deep underneath the carriage and inaccessible to the eye.

His Crimean battles ended just as abruptly as they had begun. These battles took place while traveling and were just as unpredictable as the movements of the general's armored train around Crimea. Larionov was often reproached—justifiably so, one must deem, albeit with a certain qualification—for excessive use of railroad transportation. The qualification is the fact that the railroad network in Crimea is not overly developed to this day. As is common knowledge, central Crimea is linked to only three cities on the coast: Kerch, Sevastopol, and Yevpatoria. It thus follows that the general's excessiveness, even in the worst case, could have had only an extremely limited character.

There did exist, however, a positive side to the general's predilection. Constrained by the lack of railroad track, General Larionov actively worked toward its construction. Even in his pre-Crimean period, he put together a narrow-gauge railroad in the forest near Kiev, as a test. He entered Crimea's railway history first and foremost as the person who built a fully fledged railroad bed from Dzhankoy to Yushun.

The general's childhood impressions turned out to be so strong that he even chose an armored carriage as his place of residence in Crimea. A host of legends has formed about that carriage, but all that is known and confirmed documentarily is that it was home to four birds (a crane, a crow, a raven, and a starling) and that Alexander Vertinsky visited the hospitable carriage and sang the well-known anti-war song 'I Don't Know Who Needs That And Why' for the general. According to Alexei Ravenov's *In the Blue Train Carriage*, those present said General Larionov's distinctive, unearthly gaze was noticeable even then; it was reflected, in particular, in the photograph from 1964 that reminded historian Solovyov of his deceased mother's gaze.

Solovyov thought back to that gaze yet again as he was speeding past railroad crossings, booths, and controllers with batons. He was standing by an open train window, the curtain flittering to his right like a bird that had been shot. Sunlight illuminated waves of fine hair along his arm, which felt the window frame's metallic coolness. Solovyov thought the hairs were coarsening in the sweltering August wind, that their bright glistening was a sign of a gradual transformation to copper. He pressed his lips to the hairs for a minute, as if to assess their wiriness, but they turned out to be surprisingly soft.

Solovyov was a most genuine passenger of long-distance trains. He drank tea from a glass in a metal holder without pulling out the spoon, went to the lavatory with a towel on his shoulder, and sauntered around stations in a Petersburg University T-shirt. But the important thing was that he was riding in a compartment carriage for the first time in his life. After closing the compartment door for the night, he took a passing, admiring glance at his reflection in the mirror. The bulbs from the light in the lower bunk were reflected behind his back, too, as were some bottles with little plastic cups on them, a taciturn gentleman in a tracksuit, and two young female students. In short, there was everything that created the railroad's aching coziness; a brief unity before parting forever. As he lay down in his upper bunk, Solovyov enjoyed listening to the students' whispers. He did not even notice himself falling asleep.

He was awoken by light falling across his face. The train was standing still. Solovyov's window was under a station streetlamp. Slowly, so as not to awaken the sleepers, he lowered the snug-fitting window and a warm, night breeze

wafted into the compartment. A central Russian breeze, it
abstractly occurred to Solovyov, who did not know where
the train had stopped. The name of the deserted station
was hidden in the darkness: apparently, it was a lone streetlamp burning in the window. But the lack of people in that
expanse was illusory. In the depths of the station, where
window glass meekly gleamed against the building's dark
contours, a quiet conversation was taking its course between
two people. After sliding into the shaded part of his bunk,
Solovyov discerned their unmoving figures on a bench,
facing one another. He saw, in their bentness and in their
chins that rested on their hands, something extraordinarily
familiar that he could not, however, call to mind.

They were having a conversation that was utterly connected
to the place in which the train was standing. The people they
were naming were undoubtedly known only here and the
details mentioned were also not likely to be understood
without the preliminaries of living here a long time, but even
so, Solovyov was unable to shake off an agonizing sense of
déjà vu. In an attempt to determine where he had seen these
same figures, Solovyov recalled all the stations and substations
he had ever traveled through, but nothing similar came to
mind. It turned out that situations varied at each of the
stations he had seen. There were completely different people
sitting everywhere (and even, perhaps, at the very same time),
and it followed from that, in turn, that if the train were to
stop at one hundred stations during the night, he would hear
one hundred different stories. The diversity of existence made
his head spin.

Meanwhile, the talkers fell silent. The one sitting on the
right took out cigarettes, which he shared with his conver-

sation partner. Two small fires appeared in the dark, one after the other, bringing to mind the lights at a crossing.

'That's all crap,' said the one sitting on the left.

Solovyov suddenly recalled where he'd seen figures like these. They were chimeras from Notre-Dame Cathedral, on the cover of a history textbook.

The train arrived in Simferopol at three o'clock the following afternoon. It was raining in the Crimean capital. The rain had most likely just begun—steam was still rising from the hot pavement. Solovyov purchased a trolleybus ticket to Yalta after a short wait at the ticket window. He decided to travel between the two cities using this unusual trolleybus connection, perhaps the only one in the world. The route from Simferopol to Yalta had surprised even General Larionov in his time: he lived to see the launch of the trolleybus route, and, by then, nothing had surprised him in a long time. His fantasies, which were historically limited to the railroad, had never hinted at the possibility of an intercity connection of this sort.

The general remembered carriage connections (the office was located on the first floor of the Oreanda Hotel) perfectly, just as he remembered carriages with rubber tires and the changing of horses in Alushta. He did not immediately grasp why the trolleybus had become a replacement for all that. He was soberly aware that, unlike the railroad, a trolleybus line was not suitable for transferring heavy armaments or any significant number of troops. Even so, despite the absence of strategic significance for the trolleybus line, the general began regarding the innovation fairly positively after all and rode the trolleybus to Gurzuf one spring.

After the trolleybus had driven up, Solovyov settled into

a window seat in the back row, in keeping with the ticket he had purchased. Passengers entered through the front door and heaped their luggage up on the back platform, resting it against a door that was not open for boarding. The passengers on the trollybus were almost entirely vacationers. They reclined noisily in their seats and wiped away sweat with the edges of their T-shirts. The only exception, by all indications, was a workingman with a girl who was about ten. They sat near Solovyov and had almost no belongings.

Despite the rain, the stuffiness had not subsided. It eased only when the trolleybus left the city and worked up a speed that was unexpected for such a vehicle. As if on command, the florid nylon curtains were pulled out the windows and knocked against the glass from the other side. This synchronized flapping lent the trolleybus a festive, somehow even nuptial, look. As the trolleybus climbed Chongarsky Pass, the workingman's daughter began feeling nauseous. Her father took a match out of a box and suggested she put it in her mouth. This folk remedy proved ineffective. The little girl looked at the match, then at the calloused fingers extracting it from the box, and vomited.

The weather changed completely after Chongarsky Pass. The rain clouds remained beyond the northern side of the ridge and the sun beat through the windshield of the trolleybus as it began its careful descent along the winding mountain road. Nature did everything it could to stun Solovyov that day. The sun, which replaced the rain so suddenly, was not simply shining in a flawlessly blue sky. Both the sun and the sky were reflected, mirror-like, somewhere far below, like an unending mosaic that shimmered through the cypress trees floating in the windows. That was how Solovyov saw the sea for the first time.

Needless to say, General Larionov's childhood reminiscences—which were found in an émigré's archives and published by the very same Dupont—were already known to Solovyov by this time. Despite the fragmentariness of the text and the author's stated intention to touch on his more mature years—this was the basis for Dupont's confidence that the subsequent chapters which had been lost still existed—it is here that a description of the general's first encounter with the sea is preserved. It follows from that description that the future commander's family also traveled from Simferopol, although even then the opportunity existed to arrive in Sevastopol by rail and ride from there along the coast to Yalta.

Five-year-old Larionov managed to remember that his family was traveling in carriages with two springs. He remembered the word *springs* very well because he repeated it the whole way (as has been noted already, the child did not speak until he was three and a half years old, but he vigorously made up for lost time afterwards). The younger Larionov's carriage was driven by an elderly Tatar, a handsome, smartly dressed man whose mastery of Russian was, without exception, inferior to all his passengers. Being sociable by nature, he reacted animatedly to the word *springs* and leaned on the coach box each time, showing the location of the spring with his whip handle. The coachman remained like that in the memoirist's consciousness: inclined to the side with fine drops of sweat on his forehead and a benevolent smile.

Like Solovyov, the future general was surprised by the

sharp change in the weather at Chongarsky Pass. The published notes also reference flecks of sunlight playing on the waves and viewed through the slow motion of cypresses. Special mention was given to the freshness of a wind, blowing not from dusty roadside groves but from that chilly turquoise expanse where the sky imperceptibly came together with the water. His mother's light dress, locks of his English governess's fair hair, and multicolored ribbons braided into the horse's mane fluttered in the wind.

The general's associative memory also forces him to speak of a piercing wind on Chongarsky Pass on November 1, 1920, when Crimea's remaining defenders retreated to the ports, worn out after one-sided battles. According to Dupont's supposition, a more detailed description of the evacuation was located in the part of the reminiscences that has not reached us. A faint hint cast by the general in passing, which may be seen as an intention to return to a theme he had broached superficially, speaks in favor of that. The general touches on those November events only because when watching from blizzardy Chongar as the White Army retreated (it was whiter than ever at that moment), by Larionov's own admission he saw nothing but two landaus descending, in a leisurely fashion, toward the sea.

The trolleybus turned along the shore. Now the passengers not only saw the sea but sensed its briny freshness, too. At the request of the police, all cars on the highway stopped twice to let government motorcades through. The preoccupied faces of those government ministers were more likely guessed at than seen in cars rushing past at vast speeds. They were riding to their holidays and thinking about the significant decline of the peninsula's funding. This manifested itself most of all in the condition of the palaces of the Russian aristocracy. The condition of the roads was no better, though. The summer sun and winter rain, coupled with the process of erosion, had produced a multitude of ruts and cracks in the Crimean roads. If the cracks had been patched up anywhere, it was on the government highway, though even that repair was only partial, or so Solovyov surmised, jolting in his seat every now and then.

The sun was already hiding behind Mount Ai-Petri when they pulled in to Yalta. A cloud had drifted across the mountain's peak, where it was mingling with rays that shone so unusually straight that they appeared to be beams from a spotlight. Mountains clustered around the station from three sides, leaving open only a boulevard that ran toward the sea. An evening freshness was already beginning to make itself felt in Yalta, along with a restlessness that touched Solovyov's heart. A sense of light alarm. The ancient feeling of a person about to spend the night in an unfamiliar place.

Solovyov stepped off the trolleybus and found himself surrounded by women. They vied with one another to offer him lodging and there were so many possibilities that the young historian felt lost. He could choose between a bed, a private room, or a cottage. He was invited to stay near the Spartacus movie theater, by the Chekhov museum, and even on Leningrad Street. Solovyov did not know the city. Pressured by the agitated landladies, he agonized over the location of his future lodging. The Petersburg graduate student's soul leaned toward being Chekhov's neighbor, but that offer was for an entire cottage that even his whole stipend would not cover. 'Leningrad Street' sounded unacceptable given that the city's original name had been returned. After some wavering, he settled on the Spartacus movie theater: the proposed apartment was right next door, on Palmiro Togliatti Street.

Solovyov remembered how Nadezhda Nikiforovna had solemnly taken Giovagnoli's novel *Spartacus* from a shelf that her cameo ring had touched and presented the book to him. In the course of subsequent discussion of the book, it emerged that Nadezhda Nikiforovna—like the adolescent Solovyov—had shed tears over make-believe, too, and turned out to sympathize with the gladiator very much. This had decisively strengthened Solovyov's decision to enter into marriage with her. As far as Palmiro Togliatti went, Solovyov appreciated his lovely name despite suspecting him of communist ties.

Solovyov and the woman rode to the Spartacus by trolley-bus. They crossed the road and ended up on Togliatti Street, which was narrow, quiet, and green. Solovyov liked the courtyard where his lodging was located. Just like the street name, everything about it was Italian: the terraces that had been added on and the intricate stairs that led up to them, the clotheslines hanging between the windows, and the branchy plane tree that was over everything. This, at any rate, was how Solovyov imagined Italy to be.

As he walked up a steep wooden staircase behind his hostess, he examined her unshaven legs. Those legs (like Solovyov's legs, too) elicited from the steps a knocking, creaking, and squeaking of unbelievable force. The deafening stairs spawned in the young man's mind the image of a huge out-of-tune instrument. After walking along a terrace covered with flower pots, Solovyov and his guide ended up in a dusky hallway. Once Solovyov's eyes had adjusted to the darkness, he discerned several gas burners and thought he had landed in a communal apartment. It truly had once been a communal apartment but it had managed to separate itself from Solovyov's lodgings through complex architectural solutions. The entry was hidden behind a small ledge in the wall, making it invisible at first glance. The woman took a key from her purse, winked at Solovyov, and opened the door.

The apartment consisted of two connected rooms and a glassed-in veranda. The door to the far room turned out to be locked. Solovyov was told there were things in there that the owners did not intend for lodgers to use. The first room, which led to the veranda, was at his full disposal. The veranda was also the kitchen, with a stove, counter, and cabinet containing dishes. In the far corner of the veranda was a structure reminiscent of a telephone booth covered with plywood.

'It's the bathroom,' said his escort, flushing the water to prove her point.

She wrote down Solovyov's passport information, took money for two weeks in advance, and disappeared through the door, winking just as enigmatically as she had earlier. When her clomping footsteps had faded, Solovyov flicked the door lock from the inside and began unpacking his things. He took his swimsuit out of his travel bag right away and put it on. Then he pulled out a towel and neatly placed it in a small rucksack. He shoved the key he had received into his shorts pocket and looked around. He was completely prepared for his first encounter with the sea.

3

As we know, Crimea was transferred from Russia to Ukraine in 1954, under an order from Nikita Khrushchev. It should be noted that this circumstance drew General Larionov's attention in its day. The unexpected addition to Ukraine made no less of an impression on him than the launch of the trolleybus line. And yet the aged general was not at all inclined to dramatize this circumstance.

'Russians, do not regret Crimea,' he announced, sitting on the jetty one May day in 1955.

Public statements were a great rarity for the general and a crowd quickly gathered around him. Flashing his erudition, the general reminded the listeners that Crimea had belonged to the Greeks, Genovese, Tatars, Turks, etcetera, at various times. And though their dominion was fleeting in historical terms, they had all left their own cultural traces here. In touching on Russia's traces, the general sketched out, in brief energetic strokes, an impressive panorama, from elegant parks and palaces to the lady with the lapdog. His speech concluded with military clarity: 'As a person who has defended these places, I am telling you: it is impossible to hold your ground here. For anyone. That is characteristic of the peninsula.'

The general knew what he was talking about. He had needed to hold the line in Crimea twice in 1920, in January and November. The events of October and November ended up being the final collapse of the White Movement. He was unable to hold on to Crimea.

Even so, the first defense (which nobody considered possible at the time) in January ended up being successful. It was this defense that held off the Reds' capture of the peninsula for nearly a year. Researchers assess the situation that took shape toward the beginning of 1920 more or less identically. The decline of the White Movement was becoming more obvious at this time.

'After all, we're not going to the fair, we're coming back from the fair,' is what General Larionov whispered in his horse's ear one sunny January morning.

For everyone observing that scene, the general's words took the form of a small cloud of steam. In the absence of witnesses, it remains a mystery how that phrase could have reached the public domain. There is no denying the multiple references in the historical literature to the trusting, nearly human relationship between the horse and General Larionov, who called the animal *my friend* and addressed lines specifically to the horse. And yet it would be ridiculous to imagine that the horse could respond to the general in kind, even more so that the horse was chatting right and left about what had been whispered in her ear.

The general, however, addressed the exact same words to a British envoy in November of that same year. The text arrived by telegraph because the general himself was securing his army's evacuation from Crimea and heading up the last line of defense. Needless to say, in the telegram to the British envoy (it has been preserved) there is not a word about the phrase not being addressed to him alone. Be that as it may, in scholarship—as, for example, in Vitaly Romanchuk's *In Decline*—the text in question is quoted with a reference to January. What is more, it is quoted fairly frequently in scholarship, yielding in popularity only to the well-known explanation of the reasons for the Whites' defeat. This explanation, which the general formulated with disheartening directness, is in the introduction to the reminiscences that Dupont discovered. It reads, 'A clod of dung, of medium size, began rolling through Russia. It grew with incredible speed due to the adherence of similar material, of which, alas, there turned out to be very much in Russia. We were crushed by that clod.'

And so the situation that had taken shape by January 1920 was anything but simple. The lethal clod depicted so elegantly by the general was rolling through Northern Taurida, which was the threshold to Crimea, and no one envisioned a force capable of impeding it. In fact, the supreme command of the White Army did not intend to defend Crimea. The Whites' primary forces were retreating and there were battles in those two directions, the Caucasus and Odessa, from where a counterattack was subsequently planned, after respite and regrouping of forces. If events developed favorably, they intended to force the Reds from Crimea with the return of troops that were encircling the peninsula in two streams rushing north. But that was a matter for the future. In January 1920, Crimea was tacitly destined for surrender. The limited forces sent to defend it shattered everyone's last doubts about that. Everyone's but General Larionov's.

As we know, Dupont's article, 'Leonidas and His Children', presents a rigorous enumeration of troops at the general's disposal during the defense of Crimea. So as not to force the reader to chase down this work, which is generally difficult to find, we will reiterate, in brief, the data cited in the article:

13th Infantry Division	800 bayonets
34th Infantry Division	1,200 bayonets
1st Caucasus Rifle Regiment	100 bayonets
Slavic Regiment	100 bayonets
Chechen Regiment	200 sabers
Don River Cavalry Brigade	1,000 sabers
Headquarters Convoy Corps	100 sabers

The troops enumerated had twenty-four light and eight horse-drawn weapons at their disposal. In the course of organizing the defense, General Larionov also succeeded in procuring six tanks (three heavy and three light) as well as eight armored trains. Despite all the armored trains turning out to be defective, they became a big source of moral support for the son of the railroad department's director.

For anyone with even the slightest knowledge of military matters, the above enumeration leaves no doubt: the White Army had decided, at the highest level of command, to relinquish Crimea. Only 3,500 fighters were sent to protect the front, which stretched for 400 versts. The general was aware that it was impossible to defend Crimea in Northern Taurida. And so he did not even begin to do so.

Without a doubt, General Larionov was inspired by a brilliant idea from Spartan king Leonidas, who decided to fend off the Persians in a narrow gorge. As we know, Leonidas's military contingent was extremely limited (a tenth of what General Larionov had at his disposal, not to mention the complete absence of armored trains), but that did not prevent him from fighting in the worthiest manner. This battle was analyzed in depth during tactical lessons at the Second Cadet Corps, where the future general studied back in the day. King Leonidas's feat made an indelible impression on cadet Larionov.

As life would have it, the general took part in battles that unfolded on emphatically open terrain. These were flood plains, boundless rye fields, or steppes that were parched until they cracked. During World War One, Larionov happened to fight in the mountains for a time, but those mountains turned out to be the Carpathians, which by 1914 had become thoroughly weathered and were not at all suitable with respect to defense. General Larionov mentally thanked fate that it was not the Persians opposing him in these tactically unsuitable circumstances. Only in January 1920 did he sense that his hour had come. Like the renowned Spartan, the Russian general was visited by the abrupt realization that the only chance for a successful defense was to narrow the front. He decided against defending Northern Taurida and moved his troops toward Perekop.

The Perekop Isthmus was probably the most joyless place in Russia's south. It was difficult to breathe there in the summer heat because of fumes from the dead waters of the Sivash, lagoons often referred to as the Putrid Sea. A wind would come up from time to time, rolling dried-out seaweed along salt-splotched soil but bringing no feeling of freshness. The wind became an utter disaster in the winter.

It drove stinging drifting snow over an uninhabited icy expanse where there were not even any shrubs to stop it. The wind carried away all hope of warming up. It crept behind the lapels of army overcoats and froze fingers to gun barrels, extinguished campfires made from cart debris and strewed Perekop's lunar landscape with ash. It is not surprising that territory of this sort made a most unfavorable impression on General Larionov. And so he decided not to defend it.

After familiarizing himself with the history of the defense of Northern Crimea, the military commander noticed that a common mistake of defenders each time was their absolute determination to stand firm on the Perekop rampart. Meanwhile, in light of the climatic conditions already described, simply being on the Perekop Isthmus sapped a huge amount of strength, resources, and morale because there is nothing more ruinous for an army than sitting in trenches in the bitter cold. The road to Crimea was opened after defenders were thrown from the Perekop ramparts. The resourceful general acted differently so as not to repeat his predecessors' mistakes. He decided to grant his adversary this expanse drifted with snow and deprived of any form of habitation. They did not wait for the Reds on the Perekop Peninsula; only a small outpost was left there and its role boiled down to informing the main forces of an attack. They waited for the Reds at the exit from the isthmus.

The Red Army lived up to the general's expectations. Their cavalry, reinforced by the infantry, was drawn onto the isthmus immediately after the White Army's troops abandoned it. The Red Army soldiers began feeling anxious at sunset, after walking along the icy desert the entire day and not encountering an enemy with which to do serious battle. Advancing so late at night seemed dangerous to them. They thought they were choosing the lesser evil by deciding to spend the night on the frozen steppe.

Many researchers consider that as early as January 1920 the commander of Red troops in the Crimean zone was Dmitry Zhloba (1887–1938), the son of a peasant and a graduate of the Moscow Aviation School (1917). There is an opposing opinion, too, according to which, by January 1920, Dmitry Zhloba was still continuing his training because of his failure to complete his flight hours under the school's program.

Everyone familiar with this aviator's story, of course, also knows of the vexed relations that developed between him and the other students at the aviation school. On the whole, they were far younger than Zhloba and indulged themselves in mocking the peculiarities of his appearance (the nearly complete absence of a forehead plus the presence of two extra upper teeth) and kept him away from the flying machines however they could. Bullied by his younger comrades, the aviation school pupil only had the opportunity to fly at night, thus restricting his qualification. Night flights were not scored as flying time for Zhloba. As a result, it was recommended he fly the required number of hours again—now in the daytime—something he undertook with varying success until 1920. In the end, he was appointed commander of the First Cavalry Corps and ceased his dangerous experiments in aerial expanses.

Zhloba the cavalryman turned out to be more fortunate than Zhloba the aviator. He was able to exert his influence over the personnel of his corps, particularly the horses. The animals unquestioningly obeyed the peasant's son's booming voice, which was intolerable at close range, and rushed to attack at his first shout. As he charged to attack the enemy with his unsheathed saber, Dmitry Zhloba imagined that it was his former fellow pupils from the Moscow Aviation School before him. The frenzy he displayed in battle did not just make an impression on the adversary; after a certain point in time, it even began causing apprehension within the corps subordinate to him.

Nobody objected when Zhloba announced they would spend the night on Perekop. Even if another, more acceptable plan had existed, it is unlikely that anyone would have dared contradict the commander. There was no such plan, though, and there could not have been. Everything that happened with Zhloba's troops after that hour was helping to realize General Larionov's strategy. The Red forces spent the night under a chilly Perekop sky. And then another night. Their overwhelming numerical superiority went untapped. Without the opportunity to fully deploy their battle formations, they could not resolve to attack the Whites first. The longed-for battle seemed to have evaded Dmitry Zhloba.

After spending a third night on Perekop, half the corps' personnel were sick and the aviation school alumnus realized he risked losing his troops without a battle. He decided to act. At dawn on the fourth day, the Reds moved toward the exit from the Perekop Isthmus and came under brutal fire to their flank, from the Yushun side. Their attack ended with a messy escape and the capture of prisoners. It should be noted that prisoners were the primary source of replenishment troops for the White Army. Those taken prisoner were placed on active duty again and began moving in the exact opposite direction. They fought with just the same inflexibility as before captivity. Such was this war.

Dmitry Zhloba left in order to return. After gathering his forces, he once again attempted to burst into Crimea but—just like the first time—did not succeed in moving further than Perekop. The White general had built lines of defense that seemed insurmountable. Larionov, however, knew that they, too, were vulnerable. According to the Russian battle captain, General Winter had rendered an invaluable natural service by freezing the Red attack but was now threatening to switch to the enemy side. The winter of 1920 was so harsh that something unexpected happened. The Sivash, which is as briny as a barrel of salted cucumbers, began to freeze. On the days when Dmitry Zhloba was stubbornly hitting at the isthmus's stopped-up exit, General Larionov was sending men to the Sivash to monitor the formation of ice.

Initially, thin glass-like layers covered the gulf's water in the mornings. The general grew anxious when it stopped thawing under the daytime sun. Only a few days later, the ice was so solid it could hold a lightly armed infantryman. The general began sending loaded carts to the Sivash to test the firmness of the ice at night, so as not to give away the object of his apprehensions. The general's Thermopylae plan would crumble in an instant if the ice were to freeze a little more firmly, because the infantry and cavalry and all the Reds' available heavy weaponry could cross over the Sivash's ice. In fact, it appeared to have been frozen for several days but Dmitry Zhloba, distracted by yet another storm of the Perekop Isthmus, was paying no attention whatsoever.

The panic that began mounting in Crimea after the Reds' occupation of the isthmus gradually subsided. Institutions unpacked the paperwork they had hastily tossed into plywood crates. Everything was prepared for evacuation in those days. Thousands of refugees from central Russia, who had broken free of the Bolsheviks and were deathly afraid of landing back there, were planning to evacuate with the army. 'Deathly' is what they said, and they were not far from the truth. Only a very few of those who were not able to join the evacuation to Constantinople survived.

It is interesting that the establishment of Soviet power in Crimea was the topic that Prof. Nikolsky assigned to Solovyov in his fourth year of study. Solovyov did not know then that he would study the general's fate, but from then on, the topics he cultivated grew ever closer to what would become the main focus of his research in the future. Solovyov approached his work with all possible meticulousness and found several unpublished reminiscences in the archives, which would serve as the basis for a paper at the end of his fourth year.

It concerned primarily Sevastopol, which turned out to be a harbinger of the Communist spring. Solovyov described how notices were hung up in the city, inviting all *formers* to gather at the city's circus for job placement. Despite his efforts, the researcher was unsuccessful in clarifying why the circus had been chosen. Whether that would become a portent of prevailing absurdity, whether the gathering place hinted at ancient tearing to shreds by wild animals, or whether the circus was simply the only hall the Bolsheviks knew . . . none of the *formers* sensed a ploy. These were noncombatant *formers*; those who had been in combat were already in Constantinople. *Former* accountants, secretaries, and governesses all arrived obediently at the square in front of the circus. When the square was filled, troops encircled it and strung up barbed wire. So many people had come that they could not even sit down. Several thousand *formers* stood in the square for two days. On the third day they were taken outside the city and shot.

And that was only the beginning. After collecting data for all Crimea's cities, Solovyov reached the conclusion that around 120,000 people were put to death on the peninsula during the first months of Soviet power. This exceeded the data cited in Ratsimor's *Encyclopedia of the Civil War* by 15,000. The data on the elderly, women, children, and injured who were killed by firing squad diverged seriously and needed to be increased.

The paper was written very capably, using abundant factual material attested to by 102 footnotes. Prof. Nikolsky saw the paper's narrative style—which seemed excessively emotional to him—as a minus. He requested that Solovyov remove rhetorical questions as well as passages that expressed the researcher's attitude toward the Reds' actions. From the professor's point of view, the figures were the most eloquent part of the paper. In the final reckoning, they needed no detailed commentary.

In his fifth year of study, Solovyov wrote his diploma thesis on 'The Role of Latvian Riflemen in the October Coup and Latvia's Loss of Independence in 1939'. In his account, the two events reflected in the title turned out to have both a cause-and-effect relationship as well as, even more so, a moral and ethical relationship. According to Solovyov, by fighting on the coup plotters' side, the Latvian riflemen were supporting a regime that also subsequently devoured Latvia, its independence, and the riflemen themselves. This time, his paper was not accompanied by rhetorical questions. There was minimal commentary.

Despite the young historian's paradoxical thinking (or perhaps, actually, thanks to it), Prof. Nikolsky published the paper in the journal *Past and Present* in 1996. Several months later, a brief but forceful review of Solovyov's article, signed by 'The Council of Veterans', appeared in *Der Kampf*, a popular Riga publication. Its authors saw no connection between the specified events and, for their part, discussed the possibility of an alternative course of history in 1939. They saw Latvia's hypothetical future in the rosiest of hues.

Prof. Nikolsky considered it essential to stand up for his student under the circumstances and so published his own 'Response to the Riga Veterans' in *Past and Present*. He began with a theoretical introduction that validated the importance of the moral factor in history. In the scholar's opinion, moral inferiority deprived states of the energy they needed for a trouble-free existence. The professor showed how this ravaged them from within, transforming them into empty shells flattened by the very first wind. Within this context, he examined the fall of the great empires of the ancient world and the modern age.

True to his theory regarding the absence of all-encompassing scholarly truths, the professor also indicated that it is only possible to speak of tendencies, not of rules. By way of exception, he offered the example of the English and Americans, who conducted separate talks with the Bolsheviks behind General Larionov's back during that same year, 1920, and did not suffer in the least as a result. In the Petersburg professor's opinion, distance, and the fact that both Anglo-Saxon states were surrounded by water, turned out to be the decisive factors in the matter's happy outcome. The geographical factor also allowed those states to bide their time entering World War Two, until the circumstances had been clarified to some extent. Water played a deciding role in these cases; Nikolsky met Solovyov halfway here.

In making his conclusions, however, the professor admitted that his view of things might be excessively gloomy and Latvia's big future really had been taken away from it. From Prof. Nikolsky's point of view, his skepticism could be explained by the fact that historians deal primarily with the deceased and so are, for the most part, pessimists. The Russian professor concluded his essay unexpectedly, saying history is the science of the dead and there is little room there for the living.

Needless to say, the aphoristic form of that statement was intended, first and foremost, to underscore the necessity of maintaining a certain distance from the material under study. Even so, Solovyov's advisor's remark made an indelible impression on Solovyov. He was in a rather dejected condition when he entered the graduate program at the Institute of Russian History. The marble in the Large Conference Room, where he took his entrance exams, reminded him of an anatomical theater. Solovyov was able to come to terms with the historical figures awaiting his study only because they were still alive during the period of their activity.

Graduate student Kalyuzhny's departure definitively saved Solovyov from a crisis in his worldview. Solovyov inherited from the general's melancholic admirer not only a scholarly topic, but also one single bibliographical card and a fundamental research question: why did the general remain alive? The card contained—but of course!—data on Dupont's book. Solovyov read the book and found the topic interesting and little-studied. On top of all that, General Larionov was absolutely dead and was, thus, a lawful object for scholarly research. Even under the strictest of historical measures, it was already possible to work with him.

But the general was not simply dead. Unlike many historical figures, even when he was alive, he had considered death to be an unavoidable fact of life.

'Look at them,' he would say about those figures, 'they're acting as if they don't know that death awaits them.'

The general knew death awaited him. He was preparing for it as he marched in the foothills of the Carpathians and checked posts on the Perekop Isthmus. And afterwards, whenever someone knocked on his door late at night, the thought flashed through his mind, every time, that it was death knocking. And, yes, of course he was expecting death when he was an old man sitting on the jetty in his folding chair. He was surprised that it hadn't come sooner, though he never regretted that.

The general was once photographed in a coffin. He stopped by a funeral home, bringing a photographer with him, and requested permission to use a coffin for a short time. They could not refuse him. The general smoothed the fold lines on his creased uniform, lay down in the coffin, crossed his arms on his chest, and closed his eyes. A photographer took several shots amidst the undertakers' uneasy silence. The most successful shot is almost as renowned as the famous photo on the jetty. It accompanies the majority of publications about the general. Few people know the shot was taken during this prominent person's life. Without suspecting the level of their own astuteness, some researchers have noted the absence of signs of death in the shot. Moreover, employing a figurativeness traditional for these purposes, they expressed opinions to the effect that it looked as if the general was sleeping. In reality, the general was not sleeping. Looking out from under his squinting eyelids, he was observing the reaction of those gathered and imagining what they might have said about him in the event of his actual death.

It is possible he was sorry that he would not see his own funeral and had thus decided to arrange a sort of rehearsal. It cannot be ruled out that this sort of conduct was an attempt to either deceive death (I died long ago, why bother looking for me?) or to hide from it. The general did not hide from death in his younger years, but people do change in old age . . .

Another explanation—one originating from the general's long-standing and almost intimate relationship with death—appears more pertinent. Was what happened a way to flirt with death or—this is entirely possible, too—a manifestation of a particular elderly coquetry? It is impossible to answer these questions accurately now, just as it is impossible to reason in any reliable way about how life and death come together in someone's fate. All that can be ascertained is that in the end the general met with his death. It found him without any particular effort when the time came.

In pondering the topic of death in General Larionov's story, Solovyov sought to understand the psychology of a person for whom a preparedness to die is the first and primary requirement of their profession. Solovyov was attempting to get a feel for the state of a person on the eve of battle, when any action, thought, or recollection might be his last. Was it possible to grow accustomed to that? It is known that on the evenings before battle, the general gazed at himself for a long time in a pocket mirror as if he were attempting to memorize himself at the very end. He slowly turned his hand, as if he were imagining it lying in the next trench. The inseparability of the human body's limbs seemed overstated to him on those evenings.

Did a person have a right to attachments under those circumstances? War-time friendship is piercing, just as war-time love is piercing: everything is as if for the last time. This is grounds for experiencing those attachments with the utmost keenness or, conversely, for renouncing them completely. What did the general choose at the time?

He chose reminiscences. In the event of the possible absence of a future, he extended his life by experiencing his past multiple times. The general sensed, almost physically, a living room with silk wallpaper, along which his shoulder glided when he was escaping the attention of guests after— obviously at his parents' order—one of the servants had abruptly brought him here, into a kingdom of dozens of candles, clinking dishes, cigars, and huge ceiling-high windows that were recklessly thrown open in Petersburg's Christmas twilight. The general firmly remembered that the windows were open, against the usual winter rules; he remembered because for a long time he continued considering Christmas the day when warmth set in. Remembering that, he knew he had been mistaken.

But the general had a certain something else to recall on his evenings before battle: his first visit to the Yalta beach. It is described in detail in the portion of the general's memoirs published by Dupont, which permits stopping at key moments of that event while omitting a series of details. What affected the child more than anything else was the sea's calm force and the power of a frothy, ragged wave that knocked him from his feet and carried him away during his first approach to the water. Unlike the other members of his household, he was not afraid. As he leapt on shore, he was purposely falling on the very brim of the surf, allowing the elements to roll his small, rosy body. Overcome by all the sensations, he jumped, shouted, and even urinated slightly, observing as a trickle that nobody noticed disappeared into a descending wave, vintage 1887.

The beach occupied a special place in the child's life from that point on. Even in the 1890s, when circumstances did not always permit him to appear there naked, the joy of the future military commander's encounter with the beach was not diminished. As before, he encountered the waves with a victorious cry, though he still did not allow those excited behaviors that marked his first meeting with the watery element.

Despite the ceremoniousness of the nineteenth century, this period had its own obvious distractions. In those years, when dresses had just barely risen above the ankle and no one was even dreaming of uncovered knees, fully undressing was, in a certain sense, simpler than now. Nude swimming among peasant men and women and, what is more, the landed gentry, was not something out of the ordinary in the Russian village and was by no means seen as an orgy.

This simplicity of values concerned the beach at times, too. Prince Peter Ouroussoff's *Reminiscences of a Vanished Age* notes that visitors to private beaches in the early twentieth century could even bathe naked.

Even so, the beach had arrived as a Western European phenomenon, bringing its own series of rules. One needed to dress for the beach, albeit in a particular way: not in usual undergarments but in a special style of tricot that was striped and clung to the figure in an interesting way. The short-coming of a beach outfit, however, was the same shortcoming of other clothes from that time: it left hardly any parts of the bather's body uncovered.

When fighting in continental Europe, the general invariably recalled the beach: the damp salinity of the wind, the barely discernible smell of cornel cherry bushes, and the rhythmic swaying of seaweed on oceanside rocks. With the ebb of a wave, the seaweed obediently replicated the stones' forms, just as a diver's hair settles on his head like a bathing cap that gleams with the water that flows from it. The general remembered the smell of blistering hot pebbles after the first drops of rain fell on them and heard the special beach sounds: muted and somehow distant, consisting of children's shouts, kicks at a ball, and the rustling roll of waves on the shore.

For the general, the beach was a place for life's triumph, perhaps in the same sense that the battlefield is a place for death's triumph. It is not out of the question that his many years sitting on the jetty were brought on by the possibility of surveying (albeit from afar) the beach, legs crossed, in his trusty folding chair under a quivering cream-colored umbrella. He only looked at the beach from time to time, his body half-turned, but that gave him indescribable pleasure. Only two circumstances clouded the general's joy.

The first of those was the presentiment of winter, when a beach drifted with snow transformed into the embodiment of orphandom, becoming something contrary to its initial intended designation. The second circumstance was that everyone he had ever happened to be with at the beach was long dead. Hypnotized by the beach's life-affirming aura at the time, the general had not allowed even the possibility that death would come for those alongside whom he was sitting on a chaise longue, opening a soft drink, or moving chess pieces. To the general's great disappointment, none of them remained among the living. No, they had not died at the beach (and that partially excused them) but still they had died. The general shook his head, distressed at the thought. Now, after the passage of time, it can be established that he has died, too.

4

Historian Solovyov appeared on the Yalta beach twenty years after General Larionov's death. Solovyov's first encounter with the sea did not proceed at all like the future military commander's. Solovyov came to the sea as an adult, so carefree rolling around in the waves seemed indecorous to him. The researcher had also had the chance to familiarize himself with the corresponding part of the general's memoirs before making his appearance at the beach and the very fact of that reading would not have permitted him to do—as if for the first time—everything the young Larionov had permitted himself. Undoubtedly, contrivance and even a certain derivativeness would have shone through any attempt of the sort. As Prof. Nikolsky's student, Solovyov essentially thought that no events whatsoever repeat themselves because the totality of conditions that led to them in the first instance never repeats. It should come as no surprise that attempts to mechanically copy some past action or other usually evoked protestation in the researcher and struck him as cheap simulations.

Solovyov's behavior differed strikingly from Larionov's. The young historian took a towel from his rucksack and spread it on the warm evening pebbles. After taking off his shorts and T-shirt, he laid them neatly on the towel, stood up straight, and was immediately acutely aware of his own undressedness. Each hair on Solovyov's skin—which was untanned and visible to all—sensed a caressing Yalta breeze. Solovyov knew this was exactly how people went around on the beach but he did not know what to do with himself. He pressed his arms instinctively to his torso, his shoulders slouched, and his feet sunk conspicuously into the pebbles. Solovyov had not just come to visit the sea for the first time: he had never in his life been on any sort of beach, either.

Making a concerted effort, he headed stiffly toward the water. The pebbles, which the waves had polished to shining, became surprisingly hard and sharp under the soles of Solovyov's bare feet. He tottered, shifting from one half-bent foot to another as he balanced his arms in the air and desperately bit his lower lip. This helped him reach the spot where the waves were already rolling in. This sparkling area only seldom remained dry, during the brief instant between ebbing and incoming waves. Even in that instant, though, he could see that it was covered with small, fine stones that were turning to sand, which the sea carried away. Standing here was thoroughly enjoyable.

Solovyov went still when he felt the water's milk-warm touch. This was comparable to his experience the first time Leeza Larionova's lips touched him. Standing in water up to his ankles, Solovyov no longer knew which of those touches made a greater impression on him. He felt dizzy when he looked at the two light swirls of water by his feet. Solovyov took several steps forward so he could stay on his feet. Now he was standing in water up to his knees. The waves around him were no longer seething, they were shifting instead with unfathomable motions akin, perhaps, to the play of muscles under skin. Here—a few steps from the surf where the sea was beating itself into froth and spray behind his back—there was not even a trace of that hysteria. The sea was greeting Solovyov with a powerful rhythm of rising and dropping, and with the calm inquisitiveness of its depths. Solovyov stopped when the water reached his chest. He did not know how to swim.

As has already been noted, there were no bodies of water at *Kilometer 715*. The adolescent's imagination was fed by books about nautical adventures and by radio shows (an old wall radio was the only form of mass media in the Solovyov home). Station *Kilometer 715*'s strictly continental location only stoked that imagination. Why did Solovyov not become a sailor? He himself could not have given a precise answer. Yes, his love for the sea and everything connected with the sea was infinite, but even so . . . We could approach the explanation from another angle. There exist people who possess the gift of contemplation. They are not inclined to interfere with the course life takes and do not create new events, because they believe there are already enough events in the world. They see their role as comprehending what has already taken place. Might that attitude toward the world be what begets genuine historians?

Oddly enough, contemplativeness was characteristic of General Larionov to a certain degree, too. This manifested itself, perhaps, in a special way, and not all at once, but let us ask ourselves the question: are there many generals who are known to be contemplative? Basically, no, there are not many. In essence, a general's task is contrary to contemplation. But seeing the commander's fogged-over eyes and seeing how, in the middle of a seething battle, his gaze hardens at the most distant point of the landscape—that place where you can no longer track down even the enemy's rear guard—well, anyone seeing a general like that would think that he was a contemplative person.

That is what those who accompanied General Larionov on the Crimean campaign in 1920 thought, too. The abrupt pensiveness that seized him, both during the breaks between battles and during the course of battles, was noticed not just by his brothers in arms: it often became a topic for discussion, too. Needless to say, these discussions carried the highest degree of confidentiality and were told only in the discussants' memoirs (the general was not the sort of person to permit himself to be discussed so unceremoniously), but they existed, which means there was a reason the conversations came about.

For many who had the opportunity to observe the general in 1920, Larionov made the impression of someone who was pensive and even slightly aloof. That impression was all the more unexpected since nothing of the sort had been noticed about him during his previous campaigns. To the contrary: he embodied action and decisiveness. In fact, those were the very qualities that had made him a general.

In fairness, it should be pointed out that not everyone noticed, to an equal degree, the change that took place with the general in 1920. Numerous memoirists thus seem to rely on later impressions and when they underscore the general's aloofness, they are obviously exaggerating the degree of his condition in 1920. Some agree, a bit uncertainly, with the descriptions, almost out of politeness, saying that the facts could not be denied in 1920, either, in light of the general's later mentality. By reconciling various testimony, as Vladimir Blagoi does in his article 'Pensiveness: His Special Friend,' all that can be established with veracity is that General Larionov had revealed a certain contemplativeness by 1920. This quality developed as the years passed, eventually leading to the general's utter engrossment with the sea.

What ended General Larionov's activity became the beginning of historian Solovyov's activity. A contemplative relationship with the sea did not permit the latter to master one single maritime profession. He was afraid that if his relationship with the sea was too close, that could lead to disappointment and force him to fall out of love with the watery element. Standing up to his chest in water, the young researcher experienced doubts (in view of his unstable position, this could also be called wavering) as to whether he and the object of his love were engaged in relations that were too intimate.

Apart from this wavering, which was completely new to him, the Petersburg graduate student asked himself yet again about the correctness of his chosen research topic; though in some sense the topic had been chosen for him. He had asked Prof. Nikolsky this same question at one time, when Nikolsky first proposed he work on land-based topics.

'No matter what a person studies, above all he is studying himself,' the professor said enigmatically. 'Keep in mind, young man, that accidental topics do not exist.'

The words left the professor's lips in a shell of cigarette smoke. The words' very tangible appearance, coupled with his teacher's wisdom, played their role because Solovyov decided not to insist on a nautical topic and threw all his passion into researching continental events. After the suggestion to conduct his graduate work on the fate of General Larionov, Solovyov went to see Prof. Nikolsky again and asked him the old question about the choice of topic. The old man no longer smoked because his doctor had forbidden it. Otherwise, though, his answer was the same as several years before.

Was Solovyov studying himself by studying General Larionov's fate? This was yet another difficult question the historian posed to himself. Sensing that he was beginning to freeze in the water, he knew he lacked the time to resolve the question now. Beyond that, the bather's motionless standing in the water had already attracted the attention of the few people remaining on the beach. Solovyov decided to leave the question open; he began slowly moving toward shore.

The researcher's body had taken on a cyanotic tinge and was covered with goosebumps because he had stayed in the water so long. His awkward inhibitedness before bathing had given way to something altogether mechanical that had no relation to walking. Not one of Solovyov's joints would bend, and only by force of will did the young man move his body in the direction of his towel. Solovyov felt much better after drying off. Neither the sea nor the air were cold that evening. Motionlessness (it occurred to Solovyov) is very unhealthy for a person.

The sun was no longer on the beach. Yalta's beaches are surrounded by mountains from the west, so the sun disappears fairly early. It sets beyond the mountain ranges, but for a long time its diffused light still streams over the quieting sea, the stalls for changing clothes, and seagulls pecking at watermelon rinds. The city beach after six in the evening is a peculiar beach. Its colors are dim, shot through with the yellowness of a vanishing sun, just as it shoots through black-and-white photographs of beaches in bygone years. Maybe, Solovyov asked himself, the Yalta beach in evening is actually a remnant of what the young Larionov saw? Or perhaps this was the beach the juvenile Larionov saw, only now, years later, through the depths, as it were, of decades?

Solovyov had forgotten to bring dry underwear with him so he had to put on his shorts right over his wet swimsuit. He was, after all, a person without the slightest bit of beach experience. After Solovyov sat down to buckle his sandals, the contour of his swimsuit developed on the back of his shorts, as if on wrinkled photographic paper. He, however, was unable to see that. He picked up his rucksack and pensively headed in the direction of the embankment.

As he walked along the waterline, Solovyov looked up and slowed his pace in surprise. Someone was sitting at the very end of the jetty in a chair that closely resembled the one he had seen in the photograph. That someone was a lady. And though the distance did not allow Solovyov to make out all the details, it was obvious that the lady was getting on in years. She was sitting motionless, like Larionov, with her legs crossed, and the breeze was lightly stirring the hem of her long dress. This woman undeniably knew the value of effective poses.

Solovyov was initially moved to approach the woman, but he did not make that move. He could not imagine what he could ask her or how to begin speaking with her. He did not even have a notion of how one should approach ladies like her. Should one immediately kiss her hand or was it enough to bow slightly? It was entirely possible that this case called for a smart clicking of the heels along with a simple tilt of the head. Solovyov might have decided to draw nearer to the unknown woman but when he wiped his sweaty hands on his shorts, he discovered that they, for their part, were wet, too. By now, the trace of the swimsuit had also managed to make its mark distinctly in the front. His clothing, frivolous in the first place and now dampened besides, excluded any possibility of introducing himself to her. After wavering for an instant, Solovyov dashed home to change his clothes.

The stairs were so surprised as he flew up that they managed not to produce a sound, whereas the key, slipping along the plate nailed around the keyhole, produced an inconceivable scrape. After managing to unlock the door, Solovyov flung his rucksack into the corner, tossed off his shorts and swimsuit, and left the house a second later wearing white, completely dry, pants.

He had hurried in vain. Even from the embankment, it was obvious that the jetty was deserted. Continuing to walk by force of inertia, Solovyov was puzzled that an older lady in such a long dress could have slipped away in such a short time. And with a chair, too. Now he was not even certain he had seen her. Solovyov stopped. Today was August 2, the day on which General Larionov had died. The date had arisen just as suddenly as the unknown woman on the jetty. Had she truly been sitting there? In a certain sense, it would have been simpler for Solovyov to regard her appearance as an optical illusion. At least that would have been less upsetting. Considering the date of the incident, Solovyov preferred in the end to give it a metaphysical explanation.

He resolved to consider what he had seen to be the general's spirit visiting the jetty.

Solovyov decided to stroll along the famous Yalta embankment before returning home. Twilight was falling and the first lights were burning on the embankment. These were old-fashioned streetlamps, in the spirit of the thirties through the fifties, with domed globes sprouting from sprawling cast-iron branches. Though not an admirer of the fanciful Soviet Empire style, Solovyov nevertheless had an interest in it, almost a fondness for it. Buildings in that style, which simultaneously resembled nothing but were reminiscent of everything on Earth, had outlived their empire. From time to time, guesthouses, camps for Young Pioneers, and centers for artists gazed out of the coastline's greenery, looking like elders who had lost their way. These were the last structures initiated into the secrets of labor union leisure, and they alone remembered steelmakers' placid benders, procedure nurses' hale and hearty voices, and party activists' laborious orgasms. The full complement of people who had filled those walls had departed for nonexistence, just as everyone who had made their way into the aging General Larionov's peripheral vision—policemen wearing white shirts secured with belts, medal-wearers in defiantly wide pants, sellers of hot spiced honey drinks, Pioneer-camp counselors, hip dressers, and ex-cons—had departed from the Yalta embankment, heading in the same direction.

When he looked at objects characteristic of the epoch, Solovyov often yearned for times he had not seen; this surprised even him. He did not aspire to live in those times and he did not consider them either gentle or even interesting, but still he felt a yearning. There was not, however, any reason for this feeling to surprise the young man; this was a yearning over *something other*, a burning desire to make it his own, because that *something other* was now forever deprived of those who had known it at one time as their own. Unaware of this, Solovyov experienced the paternal feeling of the historian who has adopted another time.

As he walked along the embankment, Solovyov observed its reflection in the meek sea. Neon signs, amusement rides, and streetlamps quivered in the evening's ripples, and were occasionally severed by boats, with the penetrating sounds of karaoke in the background. Awaiting him under fabric awnings were vendors of ice cream, popcorn, and glowing bracelets. Photographers with apathetic monkeys on leashes waved to him from beneath palm trees. Waitresses in black skirts and see-through snow-white blouses greeted him at every restaurant. Solovyov certainly liked the south but he was a reserved young man. He did not visit one single restaurant or purchase one single glowing bracelet.

Solovyov stopped at the Central Grocery and bought a stick of cured sausage. After some thought, he also bought bread, cheese, butter, olives, and two bottles of beer. Instead of walking home along the embankment, he took a quiet parallel street: Chekhov Street. Past the Lutheran church. Past an unusual building in the Mauritanian style. Past an adult store covered over in red paper. Being an adult, Solovyov wavered by the store but quickly pulled himself together and walked on by. Visiting that sort of establishment was a pursuit he considered unworthy of a historian.

Back at home, Solovyov first washed his hands. After the stuffy, hot street air, the water felt unexpectedly cold. It flowed from the tap with a pressure surprising for the south, as if it were the Uchan-su Waterfall, which was unknown to Solovyov, though while on the embankment he had received several invitations for excursions to see it. After drying his hands with a holey but clean towel, he got down to eating.

Solovyov's dip in the sea and walk had given him a healthy appetite. He ate up one little sandwich after another, washing them down with unrefrigerated local beer. The radio he'd switched on was broadcasting local advertisements. It hung on the wall like a black formless box and offered (*rototillers for sale, reasonable prices*) large non-resort objects rather like itself. It spoke in an aging female voice with a barely detectable southern Russian accent. The radio in Solovyov's house at the *Kilometer 715* station had spoken in roughly the same voice. Only occasionally (when leading morning exercises and reading the national news) did it shift to shameless Moscow tones. It even looked roughly the same: ebony and clumsy; sometimes speaking, sometimes singing. The main thing was that it was never silent.

Solovyov began the next morning with a visit to Yalta's Executive Committee. He set off for No. 1 Soviet Square with his graduate student identification. A calm, plump woman with a large bust met him at the Cultural Department. She sat in front of Solovyov, positioning her bust on her arms and her arms on the table. The firmness of her position, apparently reflecting the positions culture had conquered in Yalta, was pacifying. Solovyov forgot all his prepared phrases and stated the aim of his visit in an informal manner. The plump woman did not interrupt. After some thought, he told the story about his studies of the general and—surprising himself—even about graduate student Kalyuzhny, whose dreamy inaction had cleared the way to these studies for Solovyov.

The woman in charge of culture in Yalta knew how to listen. She took in all Solovyov's stories, remaining both kindly and impassive. A restrained smile never left her face. When her guest's eloquence finally ran dry, she responded with a full speech that, as became clear right away, had arrived too late.

From her explanations, it followed that Nina Fedorovna Akinfeeva—the woman who helped Larionov in the last years of his life—came to Yalta once a year, for the anniversary of the general's death. Nina Fedorovna came to the jetty (the functionary released one of her gelatinous arms and pointed toward the window) and sat there for a few hours in honor of the general. She then disappeared for points unknown and returned to Yalta again the next year.

'Yesterday was the day the general died,' said the woman.

Her breasts hung for a short moment, then froze in place again on her arm, as if in compensation for Akinfeeva's traveling nature. Solovyov was upset. He told his conversation partner that he had been a few dozen meters from Nina Fedorovna (how simple were the names of secrets!) but had not risked approaching her with wet splotches on his shorts and so had run off to change his clothes and then . . . The young man punched his knee in annoyance and apologized right then and there. The punch and the apology were both accepted with identical degrees of good will.

After allowing the Petersburger to vent his emotions completely, the representative of culture in Yalta announced the following important fact. Despite her unestablished place of residence, Nina Fedorovna Akinfeeva had not refused housing space (26.2 square meters) in Yalta but had registered her daughter there: Zoya Ivanovna Akinfeeva, born in 1976, unmarried, and a correspondence student at the Simferopol Pedagogical Institute.

'Ivanovna is an invented patronymic,' smiled the plump woman. 'Nobody has seen that Ivan.'

Judging from the girl's dark complexion, it might just happen that he was not an Ivan at all. Making up for her own long silence, the senior employee gave an account of the Akinfeev family's history.

In the early 1970s, a new resident, Nina F. Akinfeeva, moved into the communal apartment where General Larionov lived (how can that be? he lived in a communal apartment?!) Authorization for the room was issued from the city's housing stock and allotted through the Anton Chekhov Museum, where Akinfeeva, who needed housing, was employed. By the time the new resident moved in, the general had long been a widower. Here, the storyteller tactfully fell silent.

Solovyov knew from Dupont's book about the death of the general's wife in the mid-sixties. Lacking specific information about this woman, the French researcher had alluded to her rather briefly. The general's son was discussed even more briefly; the scholarly lady had not managed to trace his fate after he came of age. The Yalta civil servant had managed to trace his fate, though, if only partially. After resting her unblinking gaze on Solovyov, she announced that the general's only son had taken to drinking and left home. She just could not remember if the son had taken to drinking first and then left home or vice versa, meaning taken to drinking after leaving home. Even in the absence of chronological clarity, however, both facts were at hand and both induced the storyteller's agitation. She stopped smiling, leaned back in her chair, and mechanically adjusted the straps of her brassiere under her blouse. Solovyov began to think he was watching some sort of old movie, though he could not remember how the movie ended.

In the early 1970s, Nina Fedorovna Akinfeeva was around forty and she, like the general, was completely alone. After moving into the communal apartment, Nina Fedorovna unexpectedly acquired a reason to exist. The general became the object of her reverence and care, occupying all her thoughts, energies, and time. She took to reading books about the anti-Communist White Movement. They power-fully crowded out the Chekhov studies that had once occupied an exceptional position in her consciousness. Little by little, Nina Fedorovna's museum colleagues began to notice, alarmed, that Anton P. Chekhov was no longer at the center of her interests.

It is difficult to say what, exactly, served as the reason for the museum employee's spiritual regeneration. Did her vanity play a role here (residence in the same communal apartment as a great person), or was it the opposite, meaning pity (residence of a great person in a communal apartment)? Was this the influence of the magnetic qualities of the general himself, a person who at one time commanded armies and was most likely capable of subordinating a lonely museum worker to his will? And, finally, was there, behind everything that happened, a banal communal apartment dalliance, as some of the employees at the Chekhov Museum were inclined to think (this opinion was reinforced by hints of their colleague's unpredictable temperament)? This, however, should be qualified by saying that other museum workers categorically rejected the possibility of a dubious relationship with the elderly general. In the course of discussions that arose spontaneously, the supposition was expressed that Nina Fedorovna might just as successfully have developed a similar relationship with Anton Chekhov.

The following notable fact testifies, circumstantially, to the bond between these two lonely people being purely platonic. One fine morning (after numerous years of selfless service to the general), Nina Fedorovna embraced the object of her reverence and ran out of the house without saying a word. She returned about three weeks later in an unrecognizable condition. Her face was all scratched and her clothing was torn. The fugitive was breathing heavily. She brought with her the scent of the forest and cheap cigarettes, and a devastated bankbook. The general welcomed her without a single question. Several weeks later she burst into sobs and confessed to the general that she was pregnant. The general, sitting in his chair, lifted his head. Nina Fedorovna placed her trembling fingers into his extended hand, and he silently squeezed them.

Nobody, including the museum and the cultural department that administers it, ever learned what thickets had attracted Nina Fedorovna during her days of flight. Innate energy that had awakened within the museum worker drove her toward continuing the human race and threw her into the embrace of something age-old, savage, and natural. The museum's management saw this particular case as unprecedented as well as unworthy of imitation. Considering, however, that Nina Fedorovna had become pregnant on the very brink of the conclusion of her child-bearing years (it was emphasized in the trade union's character reference that this was the last chance for the member of the museum's collective) material assistance in the amount of seventy-five rubles was allocated to her. The fallen employee was also presented with *The Stone Foot*, a poetry collection by Grigory V. Ursulyak, the museum's director. The museum did not regret the assistance afterwards. Years later, when Akinfeeva left Yalta for points unknown, her daughter replaced her in that institution of enlightenment.

Life did not change a bit in the communal apartment after that. Nina Fedorovna returned to the responsibilities that she had previously chosen to take upon herself. Every day (in the early morning, and sometimes in the evening) she accompanied the general to the jetty, carrying his folding chair and awning behind him. The time after the onset of darkness was devoted to preparing his memoirs. The general had previously written them himself but was forced to set them aside after the age of eighty, when his hand took on a mind of its own. New opportunities opened up for the general when a helper appeared in his life. He began dictating his recollections.

Just before giving birth, Nina Fedorovna asked the general what she should name the child.

'Name her Zoya,' said the general.

It remained unknown whether he was emphasizing the life-affirming meaning of what had happened—in keeping with the name, Zoya—or was simply oriented to the church calendar, with its saints' days. The woman was only asking what to name the baby if it was a boy but the general replied that it would be a girl.

She was taken to the maternity hospital a few days later.

After ordering that a small icon of Saint Panteleimon be removed from the windowsill, the head doctor—in light of the arriving patient's age—made the decision to perform a caesarean section. During the entire nine months of her pregnancy Nina Fedorovna had feared childbirth complications and her anxieties, sadly, were warranted.

The complications were brought on by forceps that were forgotten in the birthing mother's belly during the operation. The doctors must, however, be given credit. When they heard complaints of sharp pain in the abdominal cavity, they flawlessly chose, from an abundance of possibilities, (the nurse who forgot the forceps made the diagnosis), the correct reason, which essentially ensured the success of the second operation, too.

Nina Fedorovna left the hospital about twenty days later. When she crossed the apartment threshold with Zoya, who was wearing a pink ribbon, the general was already gone. He had died.

Solovyov looked into the cultural worker's bottomless eyes. A deep knowledge of the city's cultural life and a willingness to share that knowledge were discernible there. Sympathy for the fate of General Larionov and those around him was also apparent. At the same time—Solovyov's conversation partner expressed this with a deep sigh—the Yalta City Executive Committee's influence on human fates had it limitations.

5

After lunch, Solovyov headed to the Chekhov Museum. He climbed up a long, winding lane, crossing from one sidewalk to the other, seeking out the shade. The ascent reminded him of scholarly work, which—as he had already managed to comprehend—never moves in a straight line. Its trajectory is unpredictable and describing the research requires inserting a hundred vignettes. Any research is like the motion of a dog following a scent. The motion is chaotic (outwardly) and sometimes reminiscent of spinning in place, but it is the only possible path to a result. It is essential for research to check its own rhythm against the rhythm of the material under study. If they resonate with one another and if their pulses beat in time, then research is ending and fate is beginning. Thus spoke Prof. Nikolsky.

Finally, Solovyov saw what he was looking for. Before him lay a small square that—amidst all Yalta's development—reminded him of a crater after an explosion. A group of hideous bronze figures was arranged along its perimeter, depicting, according to the sculptor, Chekhov's most famous characters. The sculptures, however, did not seem to insist on having any direct relationship with Chekhov. Seemingly too shy to walk right up to the writer's house, they huddled forlornly by the trees that framed the square.

The museum itself consisted of a concrete administrative building and an elegant cottage from the beginning of the century (this was Chekhov's house). Inside the concrete structure, Solovyov asked for Zoya Ivanovna. They looked at him with curiosity and made a telephone call. Solovyov stepped outside for some air while he waited for Zoya Ivanovna. A few minutes later, the Chekhov garden's little gate clanged and a young woman appeared. The honey-colored tone of her skin and dark hair left no doubt: this was Zoya Ivanovna. It was her patronymic that had been called into question at Yalta's city hall. There was something multi-ethnic about her, of the carnival in Rio—most definitely not Chekhovian. Her face was imperturbable.

She was wearing a gauzy, nearly immaterial dress, flustering the young researcher. Distracted, he began telling her about his study of General Larionov, for some reason alluding, again, to graduate student Kalyuzhny. Angry with himself, he switched abruptly to an analysis of mistakes in Dupont's book and unexpectedly finished with Prof. Nikolsky's response to the Latvian veterans.

'Would you like me to show you the museum?' Zoya asked sternly.

'I'd like that,' said Solovyov.

He followed Zoya ('just don't call me Ivanovna!'), mechanically copying her light, feline gait. How could her father have been an 'Ivan' . . .

It was cool inside the Chekhov house. Solovyov mentally thanked Russian literature as he went inside, out of the Yalta heat. It occurred to him that the coolness inside the house reflected something invigorating, some sort of well-spring source of the country's literature. He liked that phrase and so uttered it for Zoya.

'Unfortunately,' and here she touched the wall with her palm, 'it wasn't only cool here in the summer.'

Zoya told him the house was also impossible to heat properly in winter. It was put up by a Moscow architect who was unfamiliar with Yalta's climactic peculiarities and so was, consequently, incapable of building anything satisfactory here. Zoya's slender fingers slid prettily along the wallpaper's rhombuses. The portrayal of a boundless Russia systematically ruined by Moscow served as the backdrop to her story. She had a grateful listener in the Petersburger Solovyov.

The tour turned out to be very detailed. The museum guest visited all the rooms in the Chekhov house, even the ones not usually intended for visits. He was permitted to lift the telephone receiver in which Lev Tolstoy's voice was once heard, calling Chekhov from Gaspra. In the bedroom, he touched bed linens embroidered with the laundry's mark *ACh*. With the look of an illusionist pulling the final and most beautiful dove out of a hat, Zoya sat him down next to her on the writer's bed. Solovyov forgot about Chekhov entirely while sitting on the museum exhibit. His tour guide's dark body, which shone through the whiteness of her dress, commanded his attention.

Then they went out to the garden (out to the garden, Solovyov whispered). Walking past bamboo planted by Chekhov, Zoya led her visitor to two benches that formed a right angle in the very corner of the garden. At Zoya's suggestion (a restrained presidential gesture), they each sat on a bench, as if they were in negotiations. Solovyov explained again the aim of his stay in Yalta, this time more calmly and lucidly.

Zoya listened to him, almost leaning against the back of the bench but not quite resting against it. Solovyov recalled that in the cadet corps this was customarily done to improve one's posture. He reported on his trip to Yalta's City Hall, too, though he kept quiet about the details relating to Zoya personally. At the story about Nina Fedorovna's return from the maternity hospital, Zoya interrupted him, 'His room was completely ransacked when my mother and I came home. The new resident greeted us wearing the general's slippers.'

Zoya turned out to be very observant for a person who was wearing a newborn's pink ribbon when she arrived.

The Kozachenko family had moved into the general's room. They were not Yaltans. The Kozachenkos had landed themselves in the *Russian Riviera* from some remote place or other; they were from around either Ternopol or Lvov. On its own, life in the middle of nowhere was probably incapable of prying them from that spot: that life did not burden them. As it happened, Petr Terentyevich Kozachenko, a civil defense specialist, had taken ill with tuberculosis, an uncharacteristic illness for specialists like him; it was even a bit bohemian.

While undergoing treatment in Alupka, Petr Terentyevich managed to determine that the Magarach Wine Institute in Yalta had an urgent need for a specialist of his type. He was accepted quickly after offering his services and returned to his historical motherland as an employee of the wine institute. Petr Terentyevich's new employment turned out to be completely unexpected for his family. His wife, Galina Artemovna, was astounded at her husband's abuse of power and flat-out refused to move. In the family scene that followed, she inserted their son, Taras, between herself and Petr Terentyevich. Pointing at Taras, she accused Petr Terentyevich of irresponsibility. Ten-year-old Taras looked off to the side, plentiful soundless tears rolling down his cheeks.

It is possible that Petr Terentyevich might have backed down (meaning he very likely would have backed down) under different circumstances, but the struggle over the move seemed like an unexpected struggle for his very life. He exhibited an inflexibility that did not really typify his relationship with his wife. He had his name removed from government registries (for which his wife cursed him, daily), resigned from his previous job, and anxiously groped at the lymph nodes around his armpits.

Galina Artemovna, who had already mourned her husband mentally, even before his Crimean trip (she regarded his illness in all seriousness), was perplexed by Petr Terentyevich's obstinacy. The hope of maintaining the housing that was provided to him as a civil defense representative (and, according to rumors, an employee of certain other government agencies), reconciled her to her husband's possible death. Frightened by his feverishness to move, she stealthily clarified her right to their aforementioned living space and bitterly established that in the event of her husband's death or departure, the real estate would automatically return to the government. Galina Artemovna's stance softened as a result. She preferred departure to death.

The Kozachenko family initially received only a room in

a dormitory through the Magarach Wine Institute. Vexed, Petr Terentyevich began seeking out support from other government agencies and even offered to compile reports regarding intellectual ferment within the establishment that had hired him. Those government agencies reacted fairly listlessly. According to information from senior employees who had contact with Petr Terentyevich, all that was fermenting at the Magarach Institute was young Massandra wine. The intellects at the institute resided in a state of complete serenity. In and of itself, however, Petr Terentyevich's vigilance was acknowledged as laudable and so, as a form of incentive, he was assigned a room that had freed up in a communal apartment.

'And they moved in with us,' sighed Zoya.

She straightened her sheer dress and Solovyov's gaze settled unwittingly on her knees. The first evening breeze touched the crown of the Chekhov cypresses.

The Kozachenkos had packed light for their move. They sold their furniture in their native Ternopol before heading into the unknown. All they carried into the general's spacious room was three folding beds, several basins of various sizes, and a ficus purchased at a Yalta flea market. They hung a portrait of Ukrainian poet Taras G. Shevchenko (1814–1861) in the corner furthest from the window, underneath Ukrainian towels embroidered in traditional red and draped on the wall. A great deal of empty space remained.

The sense of expanse was enhanced because their neighbor Ivan Mikhailovich Kolpakov had removed all items from the general's room the day before the Kozachenko family moved in. This operation for seizing the deceased's property was conducted with military rapidity. One night,

Ivan Mikhailovich unglued from the general's door the strip of paper bearing an official seal and, with his wife, Yekaterina Ivanovna Kolpakov, aiding and abetting, transferred everything into their room, right down to the general's glasses and Grigory V. Ursulyak's book *The Stone Foot*. Back in the day, the general had agreed to browse through the book, at Nina Fedorovna's request.

An oak cabinet with carved two-headed eagles presented particular complications: the couple found themselves unable to lift it. After an hour and a half of fruitless efforts (a blow was inflicted upon Yekaterina Ivanovna's back, for her lowly lifting capacity), they managed to drag out the fairly mutilated cabinet after placing plastic lids under it. Yekaterina Ivanovna meticulously swept the floor in the general's room.

Needless to say, the actions undertaken by the couple ended up being too naïve not to be disclosed. However, they ended up being disclosed, at the very least, because of the cabinet's magnitude: the door to the Kolpakovs' small room would not close. The newly visible area contained stacked beds and bundles of books, which the Kolpakovs never read. Yekaterina Ivanovna's concluding attempt to cover their tracks certainly could not have deluded anyone.

The civil defense worker's inquisitive mind imagined what had happened in detail. After accusing the Kolpakovs of appropriating property that had been transferred to the state, he announced that he intended to inform the state of the loss inflicted. The undiplomatic Kolpakov immediately inflicted a blow upon Petr Terentyevich's face. The boy, Taras, who was standing in the doorway of the allocated room, began to cry. Infliction of serious bodily harm was added to appropriation of government property.

Ivan Kolpakov felt cornered and drank himself into a
stupor. And, oh, was he amazed when Petr Terentyevich
himself woke him up in the morning, a glass of beer in his
hand. Kolpakov might possibly have considered his neighbor
an *extraterrestrial* when he looked at the iridescent bruise
around his eye. At first, Ivan Mikhailovich even deflected
the hand holding the glass. Only after drinking the beer and
coming to grips with his initial agitation did he prove capable
of hearing out Kozachenko.

Petr Terentyevich let it be known too that there were
potential options in the matter. The deceased's items that
were crammed into the Kolpakovs' room—Kozachenko's
hand soared over the alienated belongings—should be divided
evenly among the conflicting parties. As a prominent item,
the cabinet should be given to the state, to avoid a scandal.
In addition (and here Kozachenko's voice took on a prosecu-
torial tone), the general's books were being transferred from
the Kolpakovs' portion to the Kozachenko family, as compensation for the maiming that had been inflicted.

Kolpakov approved Petr Terentyevich's draft treaty
unconditionally. The items were divided in half, the
Kozachenkos took full possession of the books (with the
exception of *The Stone Foot*, whose title had intrigued
Kolpakov), and the cabinet was offered to the state.

The state initially displayed interest in the cabinet but
was forced to refuse it in the end. The cabinet had been
brought in before the apartment was renovated to accom-
modate more residents and now the cabinet simply was not
fit for removal. It turned out that the entrance to the apartment had diminished during the elapsed decades of the
Soviet regime. Kolpakov refused to keep an item that

hindered closing the door, and it was reinstalled in its
previous territory after Petr Terentyevich's lengthy doubts
concerning the presence of the two-headed eagles.

The fate of the trophy literature proved more complex.
After determining that there was not one single edition of
Taras Shevchenko among the general's books, Petr
Terentyevich lost interest in them and furtively brought
them to a second-hand bookstore. He kept sulkily silent
afterwards, when Nina Fedorovna returned and persistently
questioned the neighbors about the general's books. When
the truth came out later, Nina Fedorovna rushed off to the
bookstore, to at least buy up what was left. Unfortunately,
not very much remained.

As for *The Stone Foot*, Ivan Kolpakov attempted to begin
reading it but was quickly disenchanted. Being unfamiliar
with the basics of versification, he could not comprehend
why the texts inside were arranged in columns. Ursulyak's
imagery turned out to be equally unfamiliar to him: it was,
as a matter of fact, pretty unadorned. Finally, he could not
ascertain why the publication that had found its way to him
had been given its name. Without making any arrangements
with Petr Terentyevich, he brought the book to the second-
hand bookstore where, it would seem, its story came to an
end, but *habent sua fata libelli*.*

One fine day, Ursulyak stopped by the second-hand bookstore, saw *The Stone Foot* on the shelf, and read the personalized
inscription written in his own hand. Poet and director Ursulyak
purchased his own book and gave it to Nina Fedorovna once
again, pronouncing that every person should have something

---

* Books have their own destinies (Latin).

that cannot be sold. This was not, in fact, the first incident of the sort in his poetic practice: at second-hand bookstores, he sometimes bought up books he had once inscribed, returning them to their remiss owners with the notation *Reissued*. He developed a knack for determining the presence of *The Stone Foot* as soon as he stepped inside. Sales clerks knew that and readily took *The Stone Foot* on consignment.

'Zoya, we're closing,' came a shout from somewhere beyond the garden.

'We're closing,' Zoya corroborated sadly.

After opening the gate, she waited for her Petersburg guest to exit, then closed it with a clang already familiar to Solovyov. She entered the administrative building without saying a word. Solovyov huddled sheepishly by the gate. He had not been invited to enter the building, but nobody had said goodbye.

He did not want to be pushy. He did not want to ask if he could see Zoya home, though of course he wanted to see her home. On the other hand, it would have been strange and even disagreeable if Zoya herself had asked for that.

'You're still here?' Zoya asked, though she did not look at all surprised.

Solovyov nodded and they made their way out. Zoya was not headed toward the stairs, down which Solovyov had walked from the square to the museum. After going around the corner of the administrative building, they walked out toward another gate. From that gate, a path looped between the buildings of a sanatorium and led them out.

'And what happened to the memoirs the general dictated to Nina Fedorovna?' Solovyov asked. 'Were they in the general's room, too?'

The young woman shrugged absent-mindedly. 'Probably . . . it was such a mess then.'

They went down to the Uchan-su River, walked along it for about fifty meters, and ended up on a stone bridge. Leaning her elbows on the railing, Zoya observed the Uchan-su tirelessly fighting its way toward the sea, through cobblestones and chunks of wood. She looked calmly at Solovyov.

'Are those memoirs very important to you?'

'Yes.'

There was a small bazaar on the other shore. At Zoya's suggestion, they bought a watermelon and took it to a nearby park. After settling on a bench, Zoya took a Swiss pocket knife from her purse. This woman always carried the essential items.

After cutting the watermelon in half, Solovyov placed one half aside, on a plastic bag. From the second half, he cut thin, neat semicircles, divided them into smaller segments, and spread them out on the same bag. There was something primordially masculine in his handling of the knife, something that was undeniably expressed in Zoya's gaze, which was following his hands. Solovyov himself could see that he had been very deft; it surprised him a little. The watermelon was truly sweet.

'Your mother didn't lay claim to the general's property?'

'She didn't have any official rights.'

'But how did she keep living with the people who . . .'

'. . . Who robbed her? It was fine. That's life.'

Life dealt worse things, too. Nina Fedorovna found it challenging not only to lay claim to the property but even to express the offense she had felt. One could do that if seeing the offenders in court or perhaps only meeting them every now and then on the street. But having them alongside oneself every day, using a communal toilet with them, and leaving a pot of soup in a shared kitchen—that was utterly impossible. Most likely, the hurt that Nina Fedorovna felt did not so much pass as dull. The sight of the general's various small items (many of which she had given to him) popping up with one of the couples, reignited that feeling, though, overall, it was deemed to have faded.

Moreover, oddly enough, Petr Terentyevich began striking up conversations with her in his time away from his medical procedures. After half-sitting on a kitchen table that had been handed down to him, he told Nina Fedorovna about constructing a respirator under home conditions and applying splints to bone fractures, about antibacterial injections and the effect of chlorine vapors on the upper airways. Despite having never given a gift to anyone in his life, he suddenly gave her the evacuation map for a factory that manufactured reinforced concrete as well as a model of the ventilating opening of an emergency exit that he made himself. He even wanted to give his collection of toxic agents to Nina Fedorovna for her birthday, but Galina Artemovna opposed that adamantly when, by chance, she learned of her husband's intention. She quickly made a mental note of her husband's contact with their female neighbor. Galina Artemovna looked upon that ironically but did not speak up at all. Sometimes she even gave the impression that this state of things suited her.

In actuality, the work-related topics that so agitated Petr Terentyevich had always left Galina Artemovna indifferent. Neither highly detailed classifications of nerve agents, which he had mastered to perfection, nor his ability to determine the type and size of a gas mask with his eyes closed made any sort of impression on her. It is possible that he turned to Nina Fedorovna—who heard him out politely—to see out what the specialist lacked in his own family. Most likely, Petr Terentyevich's sympathy for Nina Fedorovna's late motherhood played a role, reminding him that he and Galina Artemovna, too, had been able to have a child when they were nearly forty.

There were some pronounced changes with respect to the Kozachenko pair. This might have been characterized as estrangement, if, of course, they had been close before. But they had not been close. Definitively caught up in his illness (which was not, by all indications, as scary as the couple initially thought), Petr Terentyevich made the rounds of Yalta's pharmacies after work. He compared medicine costs, attempting each time to ascertain their wholesale prices.

On one of those evenings, Ivan Kolpakov subjected Petr Terentyevich's wife to an unexpected sexual advance: in his state of drunkenness, he had thought she was his own wife. Galina Artemovna's lack of resistance confirmed his delusion and he did with his neighbor all that his modest fantasies directed. Kolpakov's mistakes began repeating regularly after that, with the only difference being that now it was Galina Artemovna herself who prompted him with regard to little novelties she had never seen from her civil defense specialist.

Petr Terentyevich, who suspected nothing, continued his platonic relations with Nina Fedorovna. At Petr Terentyevich's request, he was retold the play *The Cherry Orchard*, which vividly reminded him of his favorite Taras Shevchenko poem, 'The Cherry Orchard by the House.' Once he even asked Nina Fedorovna to show him the Chekhov Museum because he'd heard so much about him (Chekhov). His wife was copulating with Uncle Vanya (Kolpakov) as Petr Terentyevich stood in Chekhov's study with a group of museum visitors. Tears in his eyes, he hearkened to the story of Chekhov's deadly skirmish with the very same disease he had, feeling himself to be a bit like Chekhov at that moment. It is possible that in the depths of his soul, Petr Terentyevich also wanted to tell a German doctor, 'Doktor, ich sterbe,'* but there were no German doctors in his life and could not have been.

After thinking about death at the Chekhov Museum, he decided to order himself a funeral with music. This was the only thing from the realm of the beautiful that he could permit himself. In the will he had prepared, five hundred Soviet rubles from an unshared bank book was allocated specifically for that purpose. That sum seemed to him like more than enough for a performance of Chopin in the open air. And though he was not really planning to die, the instructions he had made brought a certain tragedy and loftiness into his life.

His life did not end in a Chekhovian manner. When he returned home one day at an inopportune hour, he found an *abominable love scene* in his very own bed. That was the description that escaped from Petr Terentyevich. Beside himself with rage, he rushed at Ivan Kolpakov and proceeded to pepper him with punches. Being under the influence of

* 'Doctor, I am dying.' (German)

alcohol, Kolpakov initially took the blows fairly meekly. In the end, he lost his temper and, cursing, flung Kozachenko away from him. As Petr Terentyevich fell, he hit the back of his head on one of the heads of the double-headed eagle carved on the cabinet and lost consciousness.

The ambulance doctor who arrived roughly an hour and a half after the call ascertained that the trauma to Petr Terentyevich was not consistent with enabling survival. Unable to figure out that wording, Ivan Kolpakov grabbed the doctor by the collar and demanded an answer to a simple question: is Kozachenko dead or alive?

'Dead,' the doctor answered curtly and left without saying goodbye.

Endeavoring to anticipate police questioning, Ivan Mikhailovich decisively enticed Galina Artemovna to his room. He persuaded her not to mention the true cause of her husband's death. Strictly speaking, there was no real need to persuade her anyway. She had already long been experiencing doubts about Petr Terentyevich's longevity so it was now only the mode of his death, rather than its fact, that could make much of an impression on her. The sobered-up Kolpakov displayed unexpected oratorical abilities. The first words he uttered ending up hitting the bull's eye: he promised to marry the widow.

She complied with his requests, without wavering or even displaying any particular coyness. When the police came, they were told that Petr Terentyevich had been weak from illness and grown dizzy. Waving her arms around, Galina Artemovna showed how unfortunately her spouse had fallen. They sat the inconsolable widow on the bed (it was already made up with three plumped pillows, one on top of the other) and ordered the neighbors to give her enough valerian so she'd feel better. Taras, who was fourteen at the time, stood in the corner of the room, holding the broken-off eagle head in his hands. Big, slow tears dropped from his eyes.

Petr Terentyevich was not buried as he had dreamed. Galina Artemovna was extremely indignant to discover her husband's unaccounted-for five hundred rubles; she buried him without music. In addition to Taras and Galina Artemovna, those walking behind the coffin were Ivan Mikhailovich, Nina Fedorovna and the little Zoya, and a representative of a certain organization (he mysteriously placed a finger to his lips at all questions) with which, it emerged, Petr Terentyevich's entire conscious life had been linked.

It was this very organization that took care that the event was fittingly solemn. Taking into account that the deceased had been housed in the room of a White Guard general, Petr Terentyevich's death from a two-headed eagle was assessed as almost heroic and, in the highest degree, anti-monarchical. The unknown person installed an aluminum tripod with a star and a pointed Red Army hat on Kozachenko's grave. For some reason, no representatives from the deceased's primary place of work were in attendance. Even so, the Magarach Institute allocated fifteen liters of wine for the wake, but, in light of Galina Artemovna's cancellation of the wake, Ivan Kolpakov, who was secretly engaged to her, drank all fifteen liters.

As for Kolpakov, he was in no hurry whatsoever for what had been secret to become evident. Either he thought the danger of unmasking had been overcome or the cost of the issue itself seemed too high to him, but he simply stopped mentioning the promise he had made to the widow. Moreover, even the small bed-based joys that had bonded him with Galina Artemovna ceased shortly thereafter. Their contact was reduced to Kolpakov's brief visits, for treating morning hangovers with Petr Terentyevich's leftover medicinal alcohol.

Another *abominable scene* took place one morning and, in many ways, hastened a denouement. As she waited for Ivan Mikhailovich to vacate the washbasin (he was washing at great length, gargling, grunting, and clearing out phlegm), the widow remarked, reproachful, that other people needed to wash, too. Exclaiming, 'Then wash!' Ivan Mikhailovich Kolpakov splashed her in the face with water from a large tin mug that was nearby. The water was cold but clean.

Galina Artemovna felt insulted and demanded an explanation. She pointed out to the boor that actions of this sort were inadmissible, reminding him at the same time of his promise to enter into marriage with her. With his characteristic harshness, Ivan Mikhailovich led the wetted woman to the mirror and suggested she remember how old she really was. The breaker of the marriage promise recommended she think not about a wedding but about a funeral. In response to the threat of telling the police the whole truth, Ivan Kolpakov burst into Homeric laughter.

He underestimated Galina Artemovna. She did not, in fact, go to the police; after all, what could she have said there after her own eloquent statements? Ivan Mikhailovich's line about a funeral sent her mind in an unexpected direction, though. After brief deliberations, she decided to die on the same day as her betrothed. Galina Artemovna waited for yet another visit aimed at hangover treatment (there was not much of a wait) and then dissolved her husband's collection of toxic agents into his alcohol and handed the solution to Ivan Kolpakov. Several minutes later, Ivan Mikhailovich passed away in the arms of Yekaterina Ivanovna, his lawful wife, whom he just managed to reach. Convinced of the preparation's efficacy, Galina Artemovna drank all that remained.

'They were buried in separate graves,' said Zoya, finishing her sorrowful story. 'And Taras was left all by himself. He's still living in our apartment.'

The watermelon rinds stretched into a short but even wedge on the bench. Solovyov neatly collected them and carried them to a nearby trash bin (a pack of tissues, so he could wipe his hands, immediately appeared out of Zoya's purse). Exactly half the watermelon, that which had been placed on the plastic bag, remained.

They left the park and headed toward the sea. In the evening's duskiness, signals from a lighthouse took on the ever-more distinct form of a broadening beam of light. The rhythm of its blinking attracted attention, forcing one to wait for another flash and involuntarily count out the seconds until it appeared. In the slight twilight breeze, it was finally obvious how very hot the day had been.

'I have the day off tomorrow,' said Zoya. 'Want to go to the beach?'

'I don't know how to swim.'

Solovyov uttered that almost as if he were doomed. Just as men announce their lack of experience when in bed with a lady who has seen everything.

'I'll teach you,' Zoya promised after a pause. 'It's not complicated at all.'

It was completely dark when they approached Zoya's building on Botkinskaya Street: it was a two-story building with high gothic windows. So, it occurred to Solovyov, this is where the general lived. A figure that had initially gone unnoticed moved away from the building's walls, which were overgrown with grapevines.

'Good evening, Zoya Ivanovna. I was walking by and saw there wasn't any light in the windows so decided to wait.'

Solovyov examined the unknown man in the light of the streetlamp. Before him stood a man of more than sixty, wearing a light-colored shirt in a quasi-military style. His appearance—from the carefully ironed trousers to the combed-back hair—was an example of a special old-fashioned luster as it appeared in the polished *Studebakers* and *Hispano-Suizas* that surfaced now and again in Yalta's flow of automobiles.

'Everything's fine,' said Zoya, unsurprised.

She took a few steps toward the front door and added, without looking at anyone, 'Good night.'

6

The beach was already packed with people when Solovyov and Zoya arrived at around ten in the morning. They stepped carefully over extended arms, glued-on paper nose protectors, and jelly-like rear ends glistening with lotion. It was body parts that drew the eye in this crowded festival of flesh. Forcing himself to regain his focus, Solovyov noticed an empty spot by a stand with a life ring. There was just enough space for two towels. Solovyov considered it an undeniable stroke of luck that this spot was located by a ring. The means of rescue was right at hand if he found himself in a critical situation.

The life ring turned out to be unnecessary. Solovyov was surprised to discover that Zoya was a born swimming instructor. As she walked into the water with him, she ordered him to lie, stomach-down, on the sea's surface. When Solovyov's body—which was unaccustomed to water—slowly began sinking, Zoya lightly but confidently supported him with both arms. He felt a bit shy about being in such a strange, baby-like position in a young woman's arms, though he could not help but admit that the training turned out to be a pleasant business.

They carefully made their way to their towels after coming out of the water. Zoya lay on her back, extending one arm along her body, and using the other to shade her eyes from the sun. Solovyov sat with his chin resting on his knees. This embryonic pose seemed ideal for an observer. The morning beach was something unprecedented for Solovyov and it evoked his curiosity.

Solovyov was very taken with the Tatar women peddling baklava and strings of nut candies on trays. They crouched next to buyers, pulling a plastic bag out from under a sash and putting a hand inside as if it were a glove, then taking their Eastern goods from a tray. Large beads of sweat glistened on their faces. The Tatar women settled up with baklava lovers, stood easily with no signs of tiredness, and continued their journey over the scorching pebbles. Their shouts, slightly muted by the tide, sounded along the entire expanse of the beach, mingling with the shouts of sellers of kvass, cola, beer, dried bream, and kebabs made of smoked whelks.

Solovyov examined the human bodies. Liberated from their clothing, almost nothing bound them and they felt no boundaries with anyone. He saw muscular types whose skin had been tanned by the sun, a result of a constant presence at the beach. Even tattoos that had been applied long, long ago, before they began to frequent the beach, were lost. These men moved toward the water with a special gait. This was the gait of the *kings of the beach*: torso swaying, holding their arms slightly away from their sides. When they came back onto dry land, their swimsuits clung to their bodies, clearly outlining their genitalia. Aware of this effect, the kings of the beach pulled at the waistbands of their

swimsuits with two fingers, releasing them with a businesslike snap. The swim trunks immediately lost their excessive
anatomism. With their merits obvious to everyone, the kings
of the beach needed no additional advertising.

Alongside them—and herein lay the great equality of the
beach—there hovered the possessors of flabby breasts that
had been bravely liberated from swimsuits, one-size-fits-all
bellies, and old women's shapeless, ropy legs stitched with
the violet threads of veins. Everything that would have given
rise to protest in any other situation turned out to be permissible at the beach and, for the most part, evoked no
indignation.

Solovyov leaned back and rested on his elbows. He began
watching Zoya when he was certain her arm was firmly
covering her eyes. His gaze slid from Zoya's shaved armpits
to her thighs, above which ran the thin line of her bikini.
Solovyov lost himself admiring the barely perceptible and
somehow placid movement of her belly. When he raised
his eyes, he met Zoya's gaze and smiled from the unexpectedness.

When they went back into the water, Zoya ordered
Solovyov to turn on his stomach and try to make the froglike
motions that she had demonstrated first. Zoya's strong hands
supported Solovyov in his froglike motion and slid along
the trainee's neck, chest, and belly, touching—anything is
possible deep under water—his body's most sensitive points
from time to time. When Solovyov's motion seemed insufficiently froglike to Zoya, she swam under him and
synchronized the rhythm of their two bodies to show him
how this actually looked. People standing on shore followed
the lesson with undisguised interest.

Zoya's nontraditional and perhaps even somewhat eccentric methods could not help but yield fruit. The result of their mutual efforts was that Solovyov swam several meters, experiencing the fabulous sensation of *the first time*.

He had experienced this sensation only twice in his life. The first incident occurred at about the age of seven, when he suddenly rode away after an exhausting lesson in riding a two-wheel bicycle: his grandmother let go of the seat by accident when she grew tired of running after him. Solovyov registered, forever, his abrupt acquisition of balance. The smooth motion while coasting, akin to soaring; the crunch of pine cones under the wheels.

He experienced the second sensation of this type at the end of the second seven-year period in his life. It concerned a realm unconnected with grandmotherly help, something of a far more delicate nature and not at all bicycle-related. Out of necessity, Nadezhda Nikiforovna's censorship concerned only printed sources, but prohibited information had verbal distribution channels, too. Classmates supplied Solovyov with certain details about relations between the sexes, though that was all presented in the crudest, most mechanistic ways. Solovyov's education in that regard progressed so one-dimensionally and chaotically that by the time he had a notion of the essence of the sexual act, he was somehow still unaware that children appeared as the result of those same actions.

The connection between those two phenomena ended up being thoroughly unexpected for him, even unpleasantly so. Solovyov did not much want to connect a joyous and anticipated event such as the appearance of a child with the disgusting rhythmic motions that his classmates showed him while laughing. It cannot be ruled out that, deep down in his soul, the boy platonically in love with Nadezhda Nikiforovna simply did not want to believe it. A sober look at things hinted to schoolboy Solovyov that he and Nadezhda Nikiforovna were not fated to have children in this fashion.

Solovyov was shaken by that revelation, and during a school gathering he imagined, in turn, all the parents in attendance during production of his classmates. Taking that further, he imagined the schoolteachers in the same mode, up to and including the principal (*Bigfoot* was her nickname), a bulky, unsmiling woman with braids folded on her head. Based on the existence of all their children, Solovyov came to the indisputable conclusion that each of them had done *that* at least once in their lives. Including the principal, difficult though it was to believe. Copulation scenes more or less emerged for the rest of the teaching staff, but Solovyov's fantasy turned out to be powerless when applied to the principal. In the end, the adolescent managed to imagine her, too, but the spectacle turned out to be ghastly. Peace of mind came only with the thought that the dreadful phenomenon had taken place one single time and would never be repeated.

After exhausting all available possibilities, Solovyov moved on to examining other people in his immediate surroundings. Now, the portraits that had been looking at him from the classroom walls for so many years captured his attention. Solovyov was a child of the late Soviet period, so there was not a broad selection at his disposal. The central, largest portrait in the classroom belonged to Vladimir Ilyich Ulyanov (Lenin). It was he who attracted the adolescent's attention most of all.

Solovyov had to turn his head constantly to unite Lenin with his wife, Nadezhda Krupskaya, who occupied a modest spot in the classroom pantheon between Anatoly Lunacharsky and Anton Makarenko. The concluding picture turned out to be far more imaginable than that of the principal: either Solovyov's fantasy had managed to get some rest or this was an optical effect from the convergence of distant images.

'Did Lenin have children?' Solovyov once asked during a biology lesson.

'He did not,' said the teacher. 'But is that really a question on the subject of *amphibians*?'

'Yes,' said Solovyov.

Krupskaya's Graves-disease profile, along with her partner's small, spiteful motions lent the pair a defiantly amphibious look. Well, then, needless to say, they did not have children; they just made each other nauseous.

Karl Marx turned out to be the concluding entity in this portrait-driven period. No matter how Solovyov struggled, in his imagination, Marx only ever united with Friedrich Engels. Not yet suspecting the possibilities of this kind of alliance, Solovyov left the founding fathers in peace.

Solovyov acquired his own first experience of this sort in the vicinity of the *Kilometer 715* station. Looking back on the circumstances of his life, that hardly seems very unexpected. The majority of what happened during Solovyov's adolescence was tied to the station in some way or other, with the only exceptions being Solovyov's relationship with Nadezhda Nikiforovna and his study at school, both of which took place an hour and a half's walk from his place of residence. Needless to say, the tender experience under discussion could not have been acquired either at school or,

even more so, at Nadezhda Nikiforovna's. It was acquired
in Solovyov's home.

The house was a fairly dilapidated structure. It consisted
of an entryway, a kitchen, and two small rooms adjoining
the kitchen. The windows looked out on a railroad embankment that was not high but was overgrown with grass. After
his mother's death, Solovyov, who had previously been
housed in the same room as his grandmother, moved into
his deceased's mother's room. He did that from an instinc-
tive striving to fill the emptiness that had arisen after his
mother's departure. When he entered that emptied room,
he creaked the cracked floorboards and slept on his mother's
bed, making her departure seem less irrevocable to him. In
the end, the room's emptiness was partially filled because
someone else, in addition to Solovyov and his grandmother,
also began spending time there: Leeza Larionova.

Leeza had been at the Solovyovs' before. She was
Solovyov's only peer in the whole area around *Kilometer 715*;
in fact, she was the only child there besides him. When she
came back from school with Solovyov she would go home
to eat but would show up an hour later at the Solovyov
home, where the two of them would sit down to do their
homework. Leeza listened attentively to Solovyov's reasoning
when solving math problems, hardly ever contradicting him.
And when Solovyov struggled, she would prompt him,
timidly and often in question form, about the correct way
to solve them. Sometimes it seemed to Solovyov that even
in cases when he was incorrect, she wrote the same things
in her notebook so as not to offend him. There was no
doubt that verity was not an end, in and of itself, for Leeza.

Leeza could have been what was defined, in previous

times, as the head of the class. She had a clear mind but lacked the key thing for a career as head of the class (or, admittedly, for any career): ambition.

Their shared walks to and from school were a manifestation of nothing more than ordinary neighborly relations. At least in the beginning. They had walked together since first grade. This sort of travel seemed safer to their household members. In families that lacked men (Leeza lived with her mother) the word 'safety' possessed special weight.

Little Solovyov was embarrassed about walking to school with Leeza. The most distressing thing about those circumstances was that he and Leeza were labeled *bride and groom*. This common taunt for cases like theirs was all the more hurtful for Solovyov because, of course, he secretly considered Nadezhda Nikiforovna to be his bride. The moment they neared the school, Solovyov demonstrated in every way possible that an immense distance stretched between these two people who were apparently arriving together. The future historian turned away, lagged behind, made faces behind Leeza's back and, in brief, reached extraordinarily, extraordinarily high levels of detachment that nevertheless still allowed their shared return home.

His treatment of Leeza was especially harsh in the presence of Nadezhda Nikiforovna. True, there was nothing there that might have been deemed as not *comme il faut*: Solovyov knew his chosen one tolerated no brattiness. At the library, Leeza's lot was to receive icy gazes and short answers in a scratchy voice. To Solovyov's annoyance, Nadezhda Nikiforovna did not understand that he was making these efforts, under the circumstances, for her sake. From time to time, she herself addressed Leeza when she was waiting for Solovyov. Oddly enough, the little girl was one of Nadezhda Nikiforovna's frequent visitors, too. Although the selection of books was not conducted as ceremoniously for Leeza as for Solovyov, Leeza read a lot. Perhaps even a little more than Solovyov himself.

By the time she was fourteen, Leeza had evolved into a nice-looking, slender young woman. She did not go to the head of the class and she had not become a beauty, either. The appearance that nature had given her—well-balanced, subtle facial features, wheat-colored hair, and gray eyes—presented vast opportunities for choosing a style. If Leeza had decided to become a beauty, a restrained drawing of her facial features would have imparted her appearance with a light impressionistic shading that striking faces lack. But that did not happen.

It would be incorrect to say that Leeza did not want to be a beauty. That would imply a certain purposeful will, a conscious position she had taken regarding the issue of beauty. Leeza conducted herself as if that realm did not exist for her. Knowing Leeza's poverty, others offered to let her use their cosmetics, but she politely declined. Unlike other girls, who shimmered with all the colors available in the Russian provinces, Leeza was not the object of her classmates' attention at school parties. The boys in her class preferred girls who had a look that was more mysterious and—considering the violet splotches around their eyes—slightly extraterrestrial. It was with these girls that they shared exhausting slow dances.

The thought of those dances flashed through Solovyov's mind one time after finishing some homework (perhaps not the most arousing thing to do), when he felt a burning-hot erection and unexpectedly found himself pressing his whole body against Leeza. The unexpectedness had come about not because Solovyov had never imagined this sort of possibility. He had, in fact, imagined it: whenever his grandmother's snoring began resounding in the next room at night, his fantasy painted this event in full detail. He distinctly sensed the touch of his own hands as if they were Leeza's and fell still on the damp sheet after experiencing a blend of delight and shame as ancient as growing up. No, the unexpectedness was in the fact that his fantasy had never envisioned—as something real—everything he had just undertaken with Leeza. But now that had happened. Could Solovyov handle his arousal? Under certain circumstances, yes. For example, if his grandmother had been at home. But she was not there at that moment.

Sensing that he was shaking, Solovyov took Leeza's hand and pressed it to his bulging sweatpants. He nearly lost consciousness from the forbiddenness of what was happening and from the union of such contradictory inclinations (it seemed to him that the highest degree of contradiction also begat the highest degree of the forbidden). In the remnants of his consciousness that had not yet been lost, there pulsated the thought of Leeza touching the most secret thing on earth. Never afterward did the differences between genders excite him so much: this sort of union of contradictions turned out to be an ordinary matter in adult life and it was unavoidable, too, if approached dialectically. What had once seemed so hidden and inaccessible to him turned out, on closer inspection, to be almost the most sought-after object. In presenting it so insistently to Leeza, the future scholar did not yet know about its role in the history of culture or even history as a whole. He was acting without looking back at his predecessors.

Standing right up against Solovyov, Leeza looked at him with a calm and slightly surprised gaze. As was the case with homework, it seemed that only she knew the correct solution. She truly did know it. Leeza lightly touched her lips to his and lay her head on his shoulder. Emboldened, he thrust his hand under her blouse. He touched her back, her belly, and what was below.

He was unable to undo a single one of the hooks hidden under her blouse. Leeza did this herself. Leeza also took off the rest of her clothes and obediently lay on the bed, where Solovyov had led her by the hand. He did not utter a word for the rest of that scene. Solovyov quivered for real and from just his convulsive movements (all he had managed to finish doing completely was undress), Leeza was always able to guess what was expected of her. All in all, not very much guesswork was required here.

Accompanied by the wretched squeaking of springs (that squeaking communicated the condition of his body rather precisely), he somehow perched himself on Leeza and froze. Unable to unite their two bodies from the start, he no longer understood what, exactly, to do next. Here, Leeza took matters into her own hands again. He felt himself being directed and, with the indefatigability of an athlete, began making the same motions his classmates had so repulsively shown him. He experienced an orgasm several moments later. This was his *first time* with a woman. And it was far more intense than riding a bicycle.

The absence of blood surprised Solovyov. When he examined the spots on the sheet after Leeza left, he was unable to find anything resembling blood. He could not even allow the thought that Leeza had already become a woman before their relationship. Solovyov knew, down to the minute, how Leeza spent her time. Leeza's social circle was also well known to him. Properly speaking, he was that circle.

Everyone at *Kilometer 715* knew there should be blood. Even Nadezhda Nikiforovna—who excised any mentions of a sex life—would leave, untouched, information about the blood that resulted on a wedding night. Perhaps her stern hand was stopped by the thought that the presence of blood could serve as an important restraining factor for anyone intending to enter into a sexual relationship. Under a worst-case development of events, meaning entering into said relationship, according to Nadezhda Nikiforovna's reckoning, the possible absence of blood would disillusion the male entering into the relationship and deter him from repeated attempts.

As comfort for the bloodthirsty Solovyov, the sheet turned crimson during one of their subsequent lovemaking sessions, the third or fourth of their encounters when his grandmother was not at home. The previous times—Solovyov obviously did not understand this because of his lack of experience—their contact had been too convulsive and chaotic. When the unavoidable finally happened, there was so much blood that the sheet had to be washed immediately. Solovyov fetched icy water from the well and Leeza laundered the sheet, periodically blowing on her numbed fingers; there had been no time to heat the water. There was also no opportunity to legitimately dry the sheet, so it had to be put on the bed again after laundering. Only at night, after his grandmother had begun to snore, did Solovyov hang the sheet on two chairs and sleep on top of the blanket, covered by a jacket.

Their romps became regular. His grandmother's trips out were fairly rare, so every now and then they had to switch to Leeza's house when, needless to say, it was empty. The complication here was that Leeza's mother, a railroad track inspector, could show up at any time. The length of an inspection was surprisingly varied and depended on her degree of tiredness, her mood, and some higher industrial considerations, the essence of which were familiar only to those in the know regarding protocols for railroad track inspectors. Neither Leeza nor Solovyov, even more so, belonged to those ranks and so several times their undertakings nearly failed. More than once they were saved by the clang of an empty pail they had inconspicuously placed by the garden gate, but it was impossible to count on such an unreliable and, even more importantly, attention-attracting method. And so they returned to Solovyov's house.

As children of railroad workers, Solovyov and Leeza decided to make the fullest use of the railroad's possibilities, something that is, by the way, often underrated in contemporary life. With impeccable mastery of the schedules for passenger and freight trains, they effortlessly discovered that train traffic through *Kilometer 715* was nearly uninterrupted several times a day. In the most fortuitous cases, the unceasing running of trains in both directions took ten to twelve minutes. That was plenty for brief but torrid love. The din of the trains drowned out any sounds capable of arising under this sort of circumstance. First and foremost, the screeching of bedsprings. Solovyov's grandmother was not in the habit of entering his room during their endeavors, but in crucial situations, the participants briefly used the hook on the door.

Regarding the issue of noises. Solovyov's awareness of the female component of sex was not limited to *blood*. Prior to entering into sexual activity, he also already had a notion of *moaning*. As performed by his classmates, moaning turned out to be even less attractive than the motions they demonstrated. Be that as it may, under the sexual roles that Solovyov had adopted and delegated, Leeza was not responding to his masculine movement with feminine moaning. Having been convinced by his classmates at some point that one thing was guaranteed to evoke the other, Solovyov's unease was no joke. After sharing his doubts with Leeza, she faintly began moaning a little. Insecurely listening to her moans, Solovyov did not find them convincing, which distressed him even more. Sometimes it even seemed to him that Leeza was moaning out of a sense of duty rather than on account of a physiological necessity to moan.

Furthermore. At times it occurred to Solovyov that Leeza was experiencing far less need than he in these forbidden and, at the very least, premature relations they had entered into. This was not just because it was never she who initiated their little madnesses (that could be written off to female shyness) but that her attitude toward coitus was passionless in some sense. Leeza never had to be persuaded and she yielded right away but she *yielded*: calmly, benevolently, and without Solovyov's impatience and trembling. It seemed that in this realm, as in many others, she did not want to distress him. Generally speaking, Leeza's conformity seemed boundless. At times, when Solovyov was especially impatient and there was no opportunity for seclusion in the offing, they made love without preparation or undressing. Leeza agreed to that, too.

Later, when he remembered these hectic relations, which were for all intents and purposes childlike, despite their adult content, Solovyov never stopped feeling surprised that Leeza did not become pregnant. All they knew about the realm of precautions was that there were safe and unsafe days in terms of conception. Leeza had won math meets so she calculated the days. As far as birth control devices went, there was no opportunity at all for young people to buy them in a place where everyone knew them. Solovyov went several times to the regional capital, where he bought condoms, sweating profusely from embarrassment. The condoms were quickly gone and a trip to the city required an entire day. The only birth control device they always had in abundance was the ability to break their embraces at the right moment. This required no small force of will and malfunctioned several times. Solovyov regarded the absence of consequences as their exceptional luck since it would have been catastrophic for both of them at *Kilometer 715* if Leeza had become pregnant.

There is no doubt that the adolescents' luck truly was exceptional. They made love constantly, not just inside but also in the open air. Sometimes Solovyov and Leeza stepped into the woods on their way home from school to indulge themselves in love, on the mosses and lichens they had just finished studying in biology. The contours of those florae were imprinted on Leeza's pink bottom when she got up from the ground and brushed herself off. They did *that* more than once in the snow, too, spreading out Solovyov's skimpy coat and melting the snow's crust with their hot fingers. Even so, Solovyov's room was the primary spot for their intimate relations. The association of their encounters with the train schedule not only brought about a degree of order that was rare in cases like this but also lent them an unexpected Pavlovian nuance: trains passing through the station evoked an involuntary erection for Solovyov.

Now, he sensed an erection unassociated with any railroad effect. When Solovyov opened his eyes, he knew he had just woken up. The first thing he saw was Zoya's unblinking gaze directed at him. Solovyov turned over on his stomach. With a crocodile-like motion, he raked hot pebbles toward himself and squinted again. He realized that this time he had woken up as a person able to swim. He certainly did like Zoya.

Zoya invited Solovyov to her place that evening. He arrived with a bouquet of flowers but knew right away that what he had presumed would happen was not to be. There, in Zoya's room, in addition to Solovyov, was the old-fashioned gentleman he had seen the day before, as well as a thin old woman. She was wearing a black hat with the veil folded back and black mesh gloves. A few minutes later, the doorbell rang and a man with the look of a mighty warrior entered. He appeared to be over sixty. Despite his age, biceps of significant size revealed themselves under an untucked, cotton, pensioner's sort of shirt. Solovyov thought the group seemed worthy of a painting. At first, he just could not grasp what, exactly, had gathered such dissimilar people.

General Larionov had gathered them. This became clear when Zoya introduced the attendees to one another. At first, Solovyov thought he had misheard. The old woman turned out to be Princess Meshcherskaya, although—and here, a tinge of apology could be heard in Zoya's voice—she was not born until after the revolution.

'That never prevented me from being a princess,' the old woman said, before offering her hand to Solovyov.

He bent over her extended hand and felt the mesh texture of her glove on his lips. He was kissing a princess's hand (admittedly, *any* lady's hand) for the first time in his life. As was the case with the beach, no such opportunity had presented itself either in Petersburg or (even more so) near station *Kilometer 715*.

The two gentlemen in attendance were the children of White Guardsmen that the general had somehow saved from death. This circumstance permitted them, as they expressed it, to not only deeply revere the general but also to have been born in the first place. Based on several phrases these people uttered, Solovyov concluded that they had transferred their love for and devotion to the general on to Zoya, who was a sort of adopted daughter to the deceased, even though he had never seen her. This apparently comforting circumstance made Solovyov wary. He grew definitively upset upon remembering yesterday's encounter with Shulgin (that turned out to be his name). Given the terms of his guardianship, something obviously taken very seriously, the chances of developing a relationship with Zoya seemed slim.

Zoya asked Solovyov to help her as she was preparing to serve tea. They went to the kitchen, where there stood a balding man, five to seven years older than Solovyov. He could not be called a fat man in the strictest sense; he was more likely flabby. Slackened. Threatening to either collapse or deflate. Somehow, he was not completely standing, but slanted, resting against a firm support behind his back. Zoya nodded at him, barely noticeably, and turned on the gas under the teakettle. Solovyov greeted him to avoid awkwardness. Answering 'hi' (it was quiet and perhaps even shy), the unknown man disappeared into his own room. Though they had never met, Solovyov recognized him immediately: this was Taras Kozachenko.

As they waited for the teakettle to boil, the curious Solovyov examined the spacious kitchen where the legendary general had put in an appearance every day over the course of more than half a century.

'This was *his* table.'

Zoya pointed at the oilcloth-covered wooden structure that Taras had been leaning against. The oilcloth had been finely hacked up (vegetables were chopped there) and stained red from a dried sauce. Next to a glass containing wilted dill there lay a whetstone of implausible size, and behind it—as if to illustrate its capabilities—were two knives with unevenly sharpened blades. At the very corner of the table, wrapped in gauze, stood a jar of kombucha with the fungus. This was *his* table.

Solovyov cautiously bent back the sticky oilcloth and touched the surface of the table. He attempted to imagine the general wiping this table with a rag. And regulating the flame on a primus stove with fried eggs crackling.

'The general hardly ever cooked,' Zoya announced.

According to Zoya, Varvara Petrovna Nezhdanova, who was assigned housing in the general's apartment in 1922, helped him with all his household matters. She was a quiet, terse young woman who came to Yalta from Moscow and then stayed in Yalta. After finding a job at city hall as a typist, she was given a room in the general's building.

'I can cook for you,' Varvara Petrovna said one day.

'Then cook,' said the general.

They married two years later.

Over tea, Zoya told those in attendance about Solovyov. It turned out that Shulgin's friend, whose surname was Nesterenko, already knew of Solovyov. When in Petersburg on business, he had gone to a conference at the Institute of Russian History and heard Solovyov's paper that had made such a strong impression on everyone: 'Studying the Life and Activity of General Larionov: Conclusions and Outlooks.' Nesterenko himself had initially been upset that the young researcher's conclusions had turned out to be far fewer than the general's true venerators wanted. The abundance of outlooks envisioned in the paper, however, compensated for the disappointing situation in the realm of conclusions. In the final reckoning, this permitted Nesterenko to return home feeling almost uplifted.

In speaking about scholarly topics, they also recalled that the conference 'General Larionov as Text' was scheduled to begin a few days later, in Kerch. Neither Shulgin nor Nesterenko understood why the conference was being held in Kerch rather than Yalta. They listed, at length, grounds for why a conference devoted to the general could only be held in Yalta. Displaying unexpectedly practical thinking for a princess, Meshcherskaya suggested that hotel prices were significantly lower in Kerch. At the same time (and here the princess's erudition in the field of semiotics manifested itself), she was distressed to acknowledge that, unlike Yalta, Kerch was not a *signifying* (semiotically speaking) place in the general's life history. In the end, it was the princess who spoke in defense of the conference's title, parrying attacks from Shulgin and Nesterenko, who bluntly refused to imagine General Larionov in text form.

The conversation livened up even more when the

attendees learned that Solovyov planned to speak at the conference. Since not everyone (notably Zoya) was able to leave Yalta during the days of the conference, they asked Solovyov to read his paper in this house. Of course, Solovyov—who pushed his cup so abruptly that a bit of tea spilled on the tablecloth—did not mind. He considered it an honor to read a paper in this company and (here was the main thing), in *this* house. Since he did not have the text of the paper with him at that moment (and it would have been strange if he had, confirmed the attendees), they agreed the reading would take place within the next few days. It would be difficult to dream of a reading in a more *signifying* place.

As for Solovyov's potential listeners, they had things to tell, too. With the exception of Zoya, they had all known the general personally and well. The atmosphere Zoya was raised in, however, had furnished her with information about the general to such a degree that during their subsequent reminiscing about the general over tea, she permitted herself to supplement and even correct the guests' statements. The Chekhov Museum employee's wonderful memory made up for her absence of personal experience. Based on the stories told by the figures gathered in the general's home that August evening, his post-revolutionary fate unfolded in the following way.

The general greeted the Reds' arrival within the walls of his own Yalta dacha (Princess Meshcherskaya made a circular motion with her hand, indicating these very walls). This was where he lived when he did not need to stay on the armored train. The general not only avoided death in a surprising way but had not even been evicted from his home.

The general was subjected to *having additional residents moved into the premises.*

A local Komsomol cell was stationed on the first floor of his dacha. In previous times, nobody could have thought this space capable of housing such a number of figures wearing pointy, woolen Red Army hats. They straightened their uniform shirts and saluted each other when they met by the front stoop. On the second floor, one room was assigned to the aforementioned Varvara Petrovna, another was given to the revolutionary sailor Kuzma Seregin, and a third went to the general. Since the second floor had no kitchen, a large room there was modified for the purpose.

The Larionov family built this house with gothic windows in the nineteenth century, during the mid-nineties. Despite the family's deep army connections, the dacha was built using the labor of civilian workers who were paid, further-more, out of the Larionovs' own money. Like the majority of Yalta dachas, it had only two stories but each was high. When the future general stepped over the threshold, he was already at an age when the magical words *art nouveau*, which his mother uttered in the foyer, were not empty sounds for him. Those two French words had resounded repeatedly in Petersburg, too. They accompanied the home's entire construction and his parents uttered them with a special sort of progressive facial expression. When showing the house to Yaltan neighbors, the general's parents comported themselves a little like Columbus and, strictly speaking, they had a right to do so: the style was still almost undiscovered, in Yalta as well as the capital.

The style was unfamiliar to Kuzma Seregin, too, when he moved into the general's house in 1921. Art nouveau turned out to make a dispiriting impression on this representative of the navy. For the first two days of Seregin's stay in the house he dropped everything (he was a member of the Red Navy's firing squad) and worked on modifying the room that had been handed down to him. After rejecting the intricate moldings on the ceiling as bourgeois excess, he chiseled them off the ceiling. He painted the oak paneling with gooey green paint and went over the oak parquet with it, too, after finding the color interesting. The general observed the clashing styles but kept calm, never once rebuking the master of firing squad matters. By comparison with changes across Russia, events in Larionov's own house could no longer genuinely disturb him.

Being rowdy by nature, though, Seregin was a bit afraid of the general. For him, the general was a phenomenon no less alien (and perhaps even more alien) in nature than art nouveau, but he could not proceed with the general as he had with the ceiling moldings. Despite his revolutionary consciousness and propensity for cocaine, the sailor saw his neighbor first and foremost as a general.

The Red Navyman's servile reflex was also reinforced one time after he initiated hand-to-hand combat with the general and was quickly knocked off his feet, dragged to the front steps, and dunked in a rain barrel. For some time, he tried to take it out on Varvara Petrovna, who had witnessed the event, but he dropped that, too, after seeing the general's benevolence toward her. He did not calm down for good until he quietly enquired at his place of employment as to the prospect of the general becoming an object for the firing squad. So as not to burden his comrades with extra work, he offered to do the work independently, as a house call, so to say. He was genuinely surprised when he received a categorical refusal; he then began respecting the general even more. It was Seregin, incidentally, who was the first to ask the key question of the general's biography: why was he not shot?

Seregin lived in the general's house for seven years. Once caught in the vortex of the revolution, he simply could not return to a tranquil life. His revolutionary consciousness and increased consumption of cocaine pushed him toward actions and words (and words are also actions, as Lev B. Umansky, a member of the Joint State Political Directorate troika, said) that were unacceptable to the young Soviet system of political power. Seregin's very own firing squad executed the troika's verdict for Seregin. According to his comrades' recollections, that was Seregin's only consolation.

Umansky, whom the general recognized as the person who commanded the Red Armymen during Seregin's arrest, moved into Seregin's room. As the Red Armymen tied up the resistant tenant, Umansky checked the condition of the window frames and doors, and confirmed the exact measurements of the vacated room with Varvara Petrovna. It later emerged that Umansky, who did not yet have housing in Yalta, did this whenever he conducted an arrest. Seregin was shot on very short notice, so there is no reason to doubt that the accommodations suited him.

Umansky differed, favorably, from Seregin because he did not engage in nighttime debauchery. If he brought ladies home now and then, he made them take off their shoes and handed out slippers he had readied specially. The women were initially from the Komsomol, spirited away from the cell on the first floor. Those who slept with him thought that (as an honest person) Umansky should marry them. Without involving himself in discussion of his own honesty, he rationally announced that he simply could not marry everyone at once, despite his desire to do so.

Regular scandalous scenes on the second floor caught the attention of the cell's leadership and they began investigating the issue of *amoral behavior*. Umansky, who had thoroughly chickened out, was forced to go to the cell and explain, in the presence of the Komsomol's core membership, why marriage should be considered an obsolete phenomenon. His speech made a fairly good impression on the core membership, which was largely composed of males. The female portion of the group regarded it with more restraint but could not resolve itself to object openly.

From that day forward, the Komsomol women did not set foot in Umansky's room. On the one hand, the young women in the cell were too offended to go up to the second floor again. On the other, upon reflection, Umansky himself decided to get by with ladies from the embankment: they may have been more distant ideologically, but they were preferable in terms of their mastery of sexual techniques. Unlike the Komsomol women, whose inflexibility thoroughly irritated Umansky, Marxist worldviews did not prevent them from kneeling when necessary.

In fact, out of everyone the general had occasion to see in a communal living situation, Umansky was not the worst neighbor. During the years Umansky was a flatmate, the potent smell of urine (which had appeared when Seregin settled into the apartment) disappeared from the bathroom. Umansky (usually in the person of one of the ladies who visited him) invariably took his turn washing the floors in the kitchen and other common areas. From the general's point of view, Umansky's striving for outer cleanliness and orderliness compensated, to some degree, for his inner impurity.

The general considered Umansky a scoundrel and did not particularly hide that. At the same time, there was also a sort of sentimental shading in his attitude toward Umansky. This manifested itself in full measure later, when the general expressed regret that the room next door had been freed up prematurely. As far as Umansky went, it was flattering for him to live in the same apartment as someone so famous. Although he was once tempted to expand his living space by arresting the general and his wife, to the Political Directorate employee's credit, his taste for good company prevailed in his soul over strictly mercenary interests.

It emerged years later, though, that before Umansky's best feelings triumphed over his worst feelings, he had, in fact, made a move to free up the apartment. A certain mysterious power, however, had hindered an arrest of the general that time, too. Moreover, during the course of his attempt, Umansky also determined that Larionov, whom he had thought to be unemployed, was on the books at the Museum of City History as a consultant and was even receiving a salary.

Knowing better than anyone that the general hardly left the apartment (his strolls along the jetty were the exception), Umansky made quick work of sending an inquiry to the Museum of City History regarding the former general's employment activities and the nature of his consultations. Unexpectedly, the answer came from Umansky's own department and, judging from the tone, it assumed no further questions. Umansky stopped there: he was a pragmatist and essentially it was not his calling to be a spiteful person. He decided that in the long run he could find another apartment elsewhere but would not be able to find another general.

Motivated by those considerations, he even attempted to gain the general's favor. It is interesting that the general, who had narrowed his social circle to an absolute minimum, also conversed with Umansky from time to time. Being people of polar opposite temperaments and convictions, there is no doubt they interested one another. They discussed tactics for close combat and the admissibility of the Brest peace, the expediency of women serving in the army and the work of field kitchens during the autumn-winter period, and, in moments when the general was in a philosophical mood, the moral problematics of *Dead Souls*, which Nikolai Gogol called a poem.

Life close to the general seemed so edifying for Umansky that it distracted him from the apartment question for a while. The Political Directorate employee even initially had doubts when the opportunity came up, by chance, to move into his own well-appointed apartment. After his superior, Grigory G. Piskun, announced to him that everyone housed on an entire floor had been shot to improve conditions for his subordinate, Umansky thought it awkward not to move into the vacated apartment. After receiving the housing assignment, he arranged a farewell banquet at his former place of residence and did not begrudge the Political Directorate's stupendous special supplies.

The banquet exceeded all expectations, both in terms of the quantity of refreshments and, so to say, its degree of farewell-ness. There was an unexpected ring at the door as the event was coming to a close, and the apartment filled with operatives in their leather jackets. Recognizing the arrivals as his co-workers, the man of the hour felt touched, thinking this was an ingenious form of congratulations that befitted the department; he offered drinks to the arrivals. When he was knocked to the floor and held face down, he remarked to those in attendance that the joke had gone too far, but nobody laughed in response. Contrary to Umansky's expectations, his removal from the apartment was not accompanied by merriment, nor was his shooting, which was carried out in a most serious manner a week after his arrest.

It later became known that the direct reason for Umansky's arrest turned out to be the ladies he brought home from the embankment. The vigilant Komsomol women—who had been rejected by the person under investigation—sent signals regarding those visits. After the very first face-to-face questioning with some of the ladies (as well as with the Komsomol women), Umansky admitted that his sexual liaisons were indiscriminate and repented sincerely. His statement that—despite an abundance of casual relations—the Political Directorate was the only organ that he, Umansky, was genuinely dedicated to, was also entered into the record of his interrogation.

The problem, however, was not with the ladies from the embankment. It lay in the fact that during a rare visit of foreign vessels to Yalta, those ladies had managed to converse with a crew that had come ashore and allegedly conveyed information of state importance overseas. It was also established that the indiscriminate sexual liaisons were shams, intended in the capacity of cover, and the female citizens who visited Umansky were actually nothing more than intermediaries between him and eleven foreign spies (investigators determined that eleven people had visited Umansky).

Umansky began by objecting that his liaisons were indiscriminate but not shams (this, by the way, was confirmed by all eleven females involved) and that the only thing that had reached him via an intermediary turned out to be gonorrhea (medical documentation was presented), but that was no help. Crushed by the gravity of the evidence, the suspect confessed in short order to everything he was being incriminated of and, to the pleasant surprise of the investigation, even added several hitherto unknown episodes.

In those days, General Larionov and Varvara Petrovna awaited arrest, too: in the eyes of the investigators, the fact that the general was Umansky's neighbor should, in and of itself, have become one of the most important proofs of Umansky's guilt. But that did not happen. This is all explained by the fact that Umansky's superior, Piskun—who had initially favored him and even vacated a large, well-appointed apartment for him—had been severely criticized by his own wife at one time. She had pointed out the fact that the living conditions of his subordinate, Umansky, now surpassed Piskun's own. Shaken by that fact, Piskun began seeking a way out of the situation that had arisen. Their establishment's code of honor did not assume the direct reallocation of living space, so Piskun decided to execute Umansky. Only after that—in light of the uselessness of so much living space for a man who had been shot—did Piskun consider it possible to move into the apartment given to Umansky. Under those conditions, neither the room belonging to the general nor the general himself was of interest to Piskun.

Umansky's mother came to Yalta not long after he was shot; oddly enough, she had come from the city of Uman. She packed her son's things into three canvas cases then piled everything that would not fit on a huge velvet table-cloth and knotted its corners together in pairs. The general helped her to the bus station. Carrying one case in his hand, he pushed the neighbors' pram, with the velvety bundle on top. Umansky's mother carried the other two (lighter) cases. Poplar leaves showered down on them as they walked along Moscow Street on that sunny October morning in 1934. Umansky's mother set the cases on the ground from time to time and caught her breath. During one of those rests, the woman said she had never approved of her son belonging to the Political Directorate and tenderly recalled the time when he had been a well-known card shark in Uman. That sort of activity seemed more lucrative and not as dangerous, despite regular beatings.

In the early 1970s, that autumn farewell merged in the general's memory with another, which was also autumnal, but occurred much later and became a typical case of déjà vu (which is, essentially, what permitted those events to blend). Surprisingly, the general could name 1958 as the year for this farewell but could not recollect the circum-stances attending it. He even cited the name of the lady he was seeing off: her name was Sofia Christoforovna Pospolitaki. The general was carrying a suitcase and pushing a pram then, too, but there was a child this time. Contrasting with the child's complete silence, the pram's springs produced a piercing, almost hysterical, screech. Sofia Christoforovna was embarrassed about this unpleasant sound, even though she was not producing it. She shrank her head into her shoulders with a confused smile. Contrary to the chronology, the general sometimes thought he was accompanying Umansky's mother again on this second occasion, when she was taking her small son, who had not yet been shot, away from Yalta and out of harm's way.

Whose child was this? According to the general's recollections, the child could not have belonged to Sofia Christoforovna, due to her age. All the general could assert with veracity was that the child was not his. Poplar leaves fell on them on Moscow Street, too. A gust of wind blew several leaves under the collar of Sofia Christoforovna's between-season coat. The general stopped and extracted the leaves out from under her collar and Sofia Christoforovna thanked him, with unexpected duration and warmth. The general found it difficult to say who this lady was and why, exactly, he was seeing her off.

This circumstance prompted him to think that the majority of events in his long life had managed to repeat themselves. And not just once. In order that they not merge completely, the general decided to return to the work he had abandoned as a historian.

'That,' said Zoya, 'was precisely when he began dictating a continuation of his memoirs to my mother.'

Umansky's room sat unoccupied after he was shot. Piskun's actions with regard to his colleague had been so rapid that there had just not been enough time to take the latter off the housing registry. Responsible tenant Larionov's payments had shielded the housing office workers from seeing the bloody, truly Shakespearean drama that had played out between the two Chekists. The housing office simply had not learned about the death of the man from the city of Uman. Now, by a strange confluence of circumstances, the executed Umansky, who had been a big fan of Nikolai Gogol during his lifetime, had turned into a *dead soul* himself, freeing the general from the threat of someone else being moved in. Umansky's silent otherness in the housing office's lists went on for an entire twelve years— right up until the post-war housing audit in 1946, which is when the person who later became Ivan Kolpakov's father moved into the apartment.

The general's son was born in an apartment lacking flatmates. It will evidently never be known now if it was the fact of the apartment freeing up that inspired the general to have a child or circumstances of a more personal character (according to rumor, Varvara Petrovna was infertile until she was thirty). Princess Meshcherskaya was of the opinion that the general had simply not wanted to have a child previously because of his uncertainty about remaining alive. The thought of possible arrest sat so firmly in his head that even after marrying Varvara Petrovna in 1924 (this was done secretly) the general did not consider registering their relationship officially with the Soviet authorities, so as not to subject her to danger. On the other hand—and here Shulgin practically refuted the princess's point of view—why should the general's perspective on his future have changed at that particular time, in the mid-thirties? An unbiased analysis of the sociopolitical situation did not give even the slightest grounds for that.

Whatever the case, the child appeared. When the general greeted Varvara Petrovna in the lobby at the maternity hospital, he examined the dirty-yellow floor tiles with disgust. Each little square of tile, along with the smell of bleach, came laden with something unbearably Soviet and devoid of human qualities. The general attempted to remember the smells in the military hospitals he had seen— of course bleach had been used to clean there, too, what else did they have for cleaning?—but for some reason the smell was not as oppressive. Sisters of mercy, their hair gathered under white kerchiefs with a red cross in the middle, walked inaudibly from bed to bed.

Glass doors that had lost their transparency (from haphazard whitewash smudges) opened. The first to exit was a fat nurse with a parcel tied in blue ribbon. Varvara Petrovna looked bashfully out at her husband from behind the nurse's back. The general took the parcel from the nurse and peered at it. He looked long and hard, as if attempting to read the infant's future fate in his wrinkled and almost hideous face.

'He looks like you,' said the nurse, interpreting his gaze in her own way. 'Couldn't resemble you more.'

The general silently held out fifty rubles for her. He had been told the day before that medical personnel should be properly thanked: fifty rubles for a boy, thirty for a girl. Talk of equal rights was still out of the question back in 1936.

No, the boy did not resemble him. More specifically, his features—the form of his nose, line of his lips, and shape of his eyes—thoroughly reflected the general's, but this outward likeness only emphasized the full degree of their overall dissimilarity. This was how wax figures of the greats have nothing in common with their originals precisely because they do not convey what is most important: their enormous force field. The general showed no interest what- soever when his wax figure was put on display at Madame

Tussaud's museum years later. After absentmindedly glancing at the photograph they sent him, the general placed it in some book or other and forgot about it forever. The wax copy could not surprise him. He saw it in his own son for many years.

They named the boy Filipp. He was born during a time when, in the general's opinion, it would be better not to be born a man. In the grand scheme of things, it was better not to be born at all.

'A time of servitude,' the general defined it in brief, pushing Filipp's pram uphill, along Botkinskaya Street.

This was the very same pram, the neighbors', in which Umansky's things had been delivered to the bus station. The neighbors had handed over the pram to the general's family for good, in commemoration of the arrival of the general's firstborn. By the time of the handover, the pram had a thoroughly museum look but, then again, the general was already a museum consultant at the time. Given the state of things, the general found no reason to refuse the gift.

The general neatly cut four narrow strips from his military map case and used them to replace worn-out straps in the pram's inner workings. He sewed a new canopy from a duffel bag of the thinnest calfskin and attached its edges to the pram's metal frame.

'That's not a pram,' Tsilya Borisovna Prozument, an employee at the milk kitchen, would repeat. 'It's a masterpiece of applied art.'

They respected the general at the milk kitchen. They gave him the very best milk, called him *papochka* and Varvara Petrovna *mamochka*, and the general liked that. For their part, the employees at the milk kitchen liked that a genuine combat general was doing such civilian things. In that they saw the symbol of something they themselves were unable to express thoroughly, getting by (and what would you say about a general like that?) with only rhetorical questions and interjections.

Unlike his father, Filipp began talking at an early age. Even so, almost nothing that Filipp said when he was very small (admittedly, just like later) lingered in witnesses' memories. By contrast, the general's spirited silence was more eloquent. Out of fairness, it is worth noting that Filipp was also not very eager to use his ability to speak, despite having acquired it early. Filipp's speech primarily boiled down to naming objects he needed but since his requirements were always surprisingly few, his sentences came out sounding correspondingly spare.

Filipp was not a stupid child. When necessary, he dealt with the complexest of tasks, in both school and nonschool contexts. The main difference between him and his father was that there were very few tasks on this Earth that he recognized as necessities. Everything the general did during his life was a necessity for him—he simply had no other reasons for his activeness. What (as Dupont asked in her day) transformed *can* into *must* in the general's life, what forged that life into a continuous chain of necessities? A sense of duty? Ambition? A thirst for activity? All those qualities taken together, defined as a life force? This (asserted Dupont) was in the general. And this was not (asserted Zoya) in Filipp.

After some consideration, Filipp's mother signed up the ten-year-old for a stamp collecting club. The little boy was taught to pick up stamps with tweezers but no interest in stamp collecting sprang up in him.

'It develops a child,' Varvara Petrovna loved to repeat.

'It envelops a child,' the general once said.

To the general, collecting stamps seemed like a wretched matter. Filipp stopped going to the stamp collecting club.

At his mother's insistence, Filipp enrolled in the correspondence program at the Institute of Light Industry after he graduated from high school. Light industry was not Filipp's calling and had never been an area of interest for him. (It remains unknown if there was ever an area of interest for him.) At the same time, Filipp had never displayed any particular dislike of light industry (he heard an airiness in the very definition of light industry) and he was not against taking courses at the institute.

Filipp worked as a laboratory technician at the Magarach Institute when he was a correspondence student. After finishing his higher education, he became a senior laboratory technician. Although Filipp's career growth stopped there, he had acquired a genuine passion for the first time in his life: the degustation of wine. Those who explain this passion as an elemental inclination toward alcoholism are not completely correct. In a certain sense, this point of view is based on a statement from the general himself, who once suggested that alcoholism is the lot of low-energy people. This was said in another regard, without specific explanations of what ought to be understood as energy, but the phrase was used concerning the general's son after some time had passed.

In actuality, Filipp's initial passion truly was degustation. After several years working at Magarach, he could effortlessly not only determine, by taste, any brand of Crimean wine and its harvest year, but also name the exact place where the vine was located on the mountain's incline. His degustation sessions were imprinted on the memory of Magarach Institute employees. As one memoir reported, he would swirl the wine with a light wrist motion and observe its slow, thick flow along the sides of the glass while telling of the variety's characteristics.

It was he who was invited to the most crucial Crimean degustations. Filipp's soft-spokenness and his long, melancholic fingers made an indelible impression on the Party elite. And though the high-placed guests also asked to have a bottle or two of Stolichnaya (out of foresight, these were kept in the refrigerator, along with brined cucumbers) set out for when they heard stories about the Golitsyn wine cellars, that did not diminish their respectful regard for the taster's knowledge.

Filipp truly did take to the bottle. Needless to say, that did not happen instantaneously, as some individual employees of the Magarach Institute were inclined to assert. These assertions are explainable because they were fundamentally an attempt to separate the concepts of degustation and alcoholism and, thus, defend the uniform's honor. By naming 1965 as the date of the senior laboratory technician's slide into alcoholism, they turn a blind eye to the fact that his consumption of alcohol had, wrote one insider, obviously gone beyond the boundaries of degustation even before 1965. It is another matter entirely that this particular year turned out to be a fateful year in the history of Filipp's fall: Varvara Petrovna died in 1965. She was the only person who had been restraining Filipp at the precipice that had long loomed.

His relationship toward his father was respectful but could not be called love. Meaning, perhaps, that it was love, but a love that preferred not to meet with its object, inasmuch as possible. Filipp avoided contact with his father from a very early age. The general had never been rough with his son and had not even raised his voice at him, but that fact had not made their relationship any warmer.

Freud played no part here. If Filipp was jealous of his father's attachment to anyone, it was most likely to fate, which distributes such unequal gifts to people close to one another. He felt like a shadow of his father, and that annoyed him. Abstracting oneself from Filipp's personal defining traits, it is appropriate to ask: was it possible at all to love a person like the general? Varvara Petrovna considered it possible.

In the end, things even worked out that the general spent his nights in one room and Varvara Petrovna and her son in another. From the perspective of housing permits, this division seemed impeccable. The Kolpakov family lived in one room, the general in another, and in the third were Varvara Petrovna and Filipp, whose father was never officially determined. Nevertheless, even an official determination of paternity would never have canceled out the striking dissimilarity between the general and his son.

Varvara Petrovna's death caused yet more estrangement between them. Now, they almost never communicated. Filipp locked himself in his room when he came home from work. One could gauge what happened in the room only by his departures for the bathroom during the night: there was paralytic shuffling of feet and spasmodic groping at the whitewashed walls in the hallway. Nothing was known, either, about what happened when he was at work, though his early returns home on cold days evoked constant and unvarying questions from the Kolpakov family. From time to time, acquaintances told the general that his son had been sitting for long periods on benches at the former Tsar's Garden. That he was standing on the little bridge over the Uchan-su River, leaning heavily on the railing, or simply dozing at the bus station snack bar. The general would nod silently in reply. When he ran into his son on the embankment during daytime hours, he realized Filipp was no longer working anywhere. Filipp refused the help (including money) that the general offered. Eventually, he disappeared.

What was later called a disappearance was most likely an unexpected departure. During the general's usual outing to the jetty (everyone knew very well what time that was), Filipp showed up at the apartment with a large suitcase. According to Kolpakov, who had recently finished his army service, it was a typical demob suitcase, with aluminum stars fastened to it, a decal of an unknown beauty (made in the GDR), and sweeping letters that indicated the air force. According to Kolpakov, Filipp was absolutely sober. He spent no more than a half-hour in the room then left with his own suitcase (purchased, in Kolpakov's opinion, at the Yalta flea market), locking the door of his room with a key and saying nothing. Nobody saw him after that.

'No, people saw him,' Zoya corrected herself after pausing. 'He came over soon after the general's death. They looked at him like he was from Mars.'

Filipp's room was vacant for several years, until his absence was officially determined. The general had no rights to the room: his marriage to Varvara Petrovna was not registered and Filipp had not even used his name. According to a decision at Yalta's city hall, the vacant room was given to Nina Fedorovna. The housing commission that came to assume the room used the word *emptied*. When they forced open the door Filipp had locked, the meaning of the word became apparent to its full extent. It turned out that behind the door there were no books, no furniture, not even any flower pots. There was nothing at all in the room.

8

Solovyov's doorbell rang at eight o'clock the next morning. It was Zoya.

'It's Saturday,' she said. 'I'm going to the beach. Want to come with me?'

Solovyov could not wake up at all. It seemed like he kept having a strange, perhaps not completely seemly, dream, in which either Zoya or Leeza Larionova was waking him up early in the morning . . .

'Yes, I do.'

Leeza Larionova really had woken him up when he was young, and he had liked that. She would appear soundlessly, like the first snow, which betrayed its own arrival by imparting a certain glow to a room and an improbable whiteness to the ceiling. She would close the door behind her and look at him silently. He would wake up from that gaze.

'Of course I do.'

He was planning to invite Zoya to have some breakfast and was about to put on the teakettle but Zoya said they could have breakfast at the beach. She even refused to sit down and half-smiled as she observed Solovyov hastily tucking his shirt into his shorts.

At the beach they bought a few hot savory pastries—
chebureki—and two bottles of cola. They settled on their
towels and began their breakfast. The *chebureki* turned out
to be so hot—and greasy, too—that Solovyov froze in a
position of bewildered expectation, his back straightened,
and making a helpless gesture. The fatty liquid oozed
through his fingers and disappeared into the pebbles,
steaming. Zoya took some tissues out of her bag and wiped
Solovyov's hands, one finger at a time, unhurried, then
showed him how to hold a *cheburek* properly. She was never
at a loss, this Chekhov Museum employee, even in the most
complex of situations.

But the cola was cold, very cold. And not fatty. Solovyov
placed the neck of the bottle to his mouth and observed the
cola's vortex-like motion inside the bottle. What seethed right
in front of Solovyov's own eyes blended with the surf, even
seeming larger and more significant than the surf, and it
entered his parched throat as if it were the Black Sea's most
festive wave. He drank the whole bottle without stopping.

After breakfast, there was swimming. As they approached
the water (Zoya took Solovyov by the hand), they took
several steps in the foam of a departing wave and walked
into the approaching wave. The feeling of *the first time* did
not leave Solovyov. Surprised at his own recklessness, he
followed Zoya into the deep water. His froggish flailing was
no match for the rhythmic smoothness of Zoya's motions,
but he was swimming even so, and he was swimming
without anyone's help.

Zoya's obvious superiority did not dishearten Solovyov;
on the contrary, it probably attracted him. It might even
have aroused him a little. In the end, superiority in the

watery element really indicates nothing; everything could take a completely different turn on solid ground anyway. But every bar set higher than his own gave rise to Solovyov's competitive interest, and that interest (as he pondered the matter in hindsight) had been lacking in his relationship with Leeza. Why had Leeza been embarrassed about her merits?

The sun was no longer a morning sun and it stood, unmoving, somewhere over the central part of the beach, burning full blast. Zoya took out some thin lotion that squeezed out on Solovyov's scorching back with a snorting sound. An instant later, he sensed it spreading concentrically along his neck, shoulder blades, and lower back. The lotion's cool freshness was becoming a quality of Zoya's fingers.

'You know, I keep thinking about what the general dictated to my mother. You must want to find that?'

She had switched to the informal *you*. And so naturally.

'Yes, I do.'

Zoya's fingers were massaging Solovyov's thighs. He felt his legs shuddering, involuntarily, in time with Zoya's motions. It felt to him as if the whole beach was enviously following along with his pleasure, not allowing him to receive that pleasure to its full extent.

'Those sheets of paper couldn't have just vanished without a trace. This doesn't hurt?' He sensed the rhythm of Zoya's hands somewhere a little below his knee. 'I think I even know where they could be.'

Zoya held her pause. Solovyov turned, grasping that a continuation would not follow in the same breath.

'Where?'

'At Kozachenko's. Those dung beetles were digging up

everything they could while my mother was busy having me at the maternity hospital.'

The Kozachenko couple rolling a ball of manure popped up in Solovyov's consciousness: sheets of the general's memoirs, stuck to the sides of the ball, flashed through his mind. Zoya thought the younger Kozachenko would not give up those sheets very easily. Not because he needed them (what, after all, could he have done with them?) but because of the unshakable inherited rule not to let out of one's hands anything that had ever fallen into them.

Now Zoya—they had left the beach and were walking slowly along Botkinskaya Street—had a plan. Solovyov looked from time to time at the museum employee's jet-black hair, which was tangled after swimming; he was discovering her for himself all over again. Absolutely nothing Chekhovian remained in what she was proposing. Zoya thought the only chance of obtaining the manuscript from Taras Kozachenko was to conduct a secret search of his, Taras's, room. Zoya leaned on Solovyov's shoulder as she shook beach pebbles out of her sandal.

'But maybe,' Solovyov was awkwardly supporting Zoya by the waist, '. . . maybe we should start by actually asking Taras?'

'No way. Then he'll bury that manuscript once and for all and we'll never see it again. Our strength is in him not knowing *what*, exactly, we're going to look for.'

Solovyov looked at Zoya with doubt; his gaze did not escape her.

'This was dreamt up for your sake, after all . . .'

Solovyov felt that in full. Lagging a half-step behind Zoya, his shoulders grazed against willow branches that drooped almost to the sidewalk and he thought about the unpredictability of a historian's work.

When they reached her house, she asked him to come inside. All the residents were present on Saturday. Besides Taras, Yekaterina Ivanovna Kolpakova was standing in the kitchen: Solovyov had only heard about her up until now. Despite Galina Artemovna (Taras's mother) poisoning Yekaterina Ivanovna's husband; despite his cheating on Yekaterina Ivanovna with that very same Kozachenko woman and his murder of Petr Terentyevich, Taras's father; and despite, finally, Galina Artemovna ending her life as a result of all those events . . . The relationships among those still alive were completely calm. Their relationships could even be called amicable, to that certain degree possible under communal apartment conditions.

Among Russian people, a vendetta ceases just as suddenly, and without motivation, as it begins. Hostility fades in a chain of uninteresting events, just as an echo fades in a sultry Crimean pine forest and just as graves fade in the tall weeds of Russian cemeteries. Yekaterina and Taras frequently went to Yalta's cemetery together, which was notable, even by Russian standards. This was not so much a triumph of reconciliation as a matter of something being convenient and perhaps even mutually beneficial for both of them. Yekaterina Ivanovna bought inexpensive begonias for the three graves and Taras brought a cart with a twenty-liter canister of water, something that was in catastrophically short supply at the cemetery. While visiting their relatives (*landsmen*, as Yekaterina Ivanovna sometimes jokingly called them), they divided the begonias and the water evenly amongst the graves.

Zoya and Solovyov stayed in the kitchen after greeting the neighbors. To Solovyov's surprise, his companion not only entered into conversation with the others but also asked him to tell them about the Hermitage—you know, what you were telling me today—after which she went to her room anyway, leaving Solovyov in the middle of the kitchen with his strange story. Taras and Yekaterina Ivanovna stood in the corner, leaning against the general's cabinet, and were, ludicrously enough, truly prepared to take in Solovyov's narrative. After stating that the Hermitage, along with the Louvre, is one of the leading museums in the world, Solovyov noted, unseen by his listeners, that Zoya had left her room with a finger to her lips. As Solovyov told of the number of exhibits at the Hermitage (to Yekaterina Ivanovna's restrained moan), Zoya flattened herself against the wall and sidestepped her way to Taras's door. Solovyov faltered from the unexpectedness. Zoya made a scary face and—making her hand into a sort of bird's beak—gestured to the storyteller that he should not stop speaking.

If one were to stand next to each exhibit for thirty seconds (Zoya disappeared into Taras's room) and be at the Hermitage every day from morning until evening, one would need eight years to see *all* the exhibits.

'Eight?' Yekaterina Ivanovna asked for clarification.

Zoya appeared in Taras's doorway, noiselessly tossed up her hands, and disappeared into the depths of the room once again.

'No fewer than eight,' Solovyov reiterated.

Taras took a bottle of kefir from the refrigerator, shook it, and poured some into a tea bowl with chipped edges. He chose an unscathed section and pressed his puffy lips to it.

Taras asked nothing about the Hermitage. He listened silently to Solovyov, licking away his broad white mustache from time to time. And Solovyov, who would never have agreed of his own free will to infiltrate Taras's room, felt like a genuine plotter, if only because he had to conspire a story with a plot for those standing before him. His descriptions grew more emotional, evoking in his listeners interest mixed with light surprise. The surprise increased when the story suddenly cut off (Zoya had silently closed the door behind her and slipped into her room) and Solovyov vanished to Zoya's room, saying goodbye along the way. Those who remained, standing, had the sense of something left unsaid.

'I didn't find the manuscript,' said Zoya after Solovyov closed the door behind him. 'But this turned up in a drawer.'

She twirled a ring of keys on her finger.

'I'm sure he has the manuscript. We'll have time to look at everything carefully on Monday, when he goes to work.'

'Zoya . . .'

This turned out to be the only objection Solovyov was allowed to utter. Zoya placed her finger with the keys to his lips and peered into the hallway. Once she was certain nobody was left in the kitchen, she stole toward the front door on tiptoe and beckoned to Solovyov. Involuntarily copying Zoya's motions, he took several steps toward the exit. He stopped between Zoya and the door. Her hand touched the massive hook hanging on an eye, attached to the side of the door that did not open. The hook readily began swinging as it slid along an indentation that had formed over the years.

'Foucault's pendulum,' she whispered right into his ear. 'I'll take Monday off.'

Solovyov spent Sunday morning in church. This was the Alexander Nevsky Cathedral, which was elegant, its five cupolas towering over Kirov Street (formerly Autskaya Street). As Solovyov ascended the stone staircase, he imagined the general entering the church.

The general came here often during his trips to Yalta. In the winter of 1920, he flew up this staircase like a large bird of prey; the flaps of his military overcoat extended over the steps, his entourage dispersed at his sides. He walked a little more slowly in the summer, as if he were watching a military formation on the platz, but he saw messy columns of paupers who had flowed there from all of boundless Russia, as they did in those days. A military orderly walking a half-step behind him tossed coins to them.

It was stuffy in the church during the summer. Neither an open side door nor a flung-open window lent any coolness. Through them poured Yalta's damp, sweltering heat, scented with acacias and the sea, and vaguely trembling over the candles' unmoving flame. Streaks of sunlight pierced the duskiness inside the church, illuminating the large drops of sweat that flew off the priest's nose and chin with his every movement. Even the general, who usually hardly perspired, kept wiping his forehead and neck with a silk handkerchief. In those services, which were anything but simple, Larionov saw a special southern charm that consisted of the fact that, for one thing, at the end of the liturgy he would take a hundred-meter walk along Morskaya Street and find himself on an embankment that glistened in the surf and he would breathe, full-chested, after unfastening the top buttons of his service jacket.

He came here as a very elderly man, too. With a cane,

and wearing a canvas jacket with a pocket stretched by a
massive case for his glasses. People recognized him, as in
days past. As in days past, they stepped aside, making way
for him, and took deep bows for the coins he gave them.
He walked with the special firmness of one striving to
maintain his balance (occasionally he swayed anyway). At
times he would stop, place both his hands on his cypress
cane, and inspect the toes of his shoes. Sometimes he would
sit on a bench in the yard and observe from the shadows,
businesslike, as people carried infants into the church,
straightening lacy bonnets along the way. Observe how, in
the far corner of the church grounds, water from a hose
moistened dust and the first drops that fell on the asphalt
turned to steam. In those moments, his face lacked all expression and seemed to be falling away. It brought to mind a
mask that had been removed, and came to life only with
the old man's barely noticeable chewing.

Looking at the general, it was difficult to grasp whether
he noticed everything happening around him or if, according
to the words of a poet unfamiliar to him, his eyes were
addressing other days. Those who observed the general in
those moments (including in the line of duty), confirmed
afterwards that they did not consider his gaze to have halted,
despite the motionlessness of his face. That gaze might be
categorized as unlifelike, unlit, or unearthly, but not at all
halted.

Yes, General Larionov's eyes were addressing other days.
Even so, nothing escaped their attention. Through the para-
military guise of paupers, vintage 1920, wearing uniform
tunics with holes instead of epaulets and through carts that
delivered barrels of water to the church (they were rolled

from the carts onto the earth along twenty-inch boards),
the general's eyes undeniably saw trolleybuses that drove
noiselessly along the former Autskaya Street behind the
church fence, carrying 1970s female worshippers, and saw
women taking neatly folded headscarves from their bags in
front of the church and hurriedly tying them. They used
their thumbs to tuck in strands of hair that came out. Why
were there hardly any men there?

When Solovyov showed up at Zoya's on Monday morning,
none of the others were in the apartment. After closing the
front door behind him, Zoya lowered the huge hook with
a clang. 'That's just in case,' she said.

Solovyov remembered the pail he and Leeza used to set
out as a signal but did not mention this memory. He was
experiencing excitement of a completely different kind now.

With a calm motion that was somehow even expert, Zoya
turned the key in Kozachenko's door, opened it, and
gestured to Solovyov, inviting him inside. Solovyov initially
wanted to make the same gesture but then he crossed the
threshold after realizing that gallantry was out of place in
this situation.

The first thing he saw in the room was the oak cabinet
with the two-headed eagles. The elder Kozachenko had
knocked his head on one of those heads. The double bed
was the center of the drama that had played out. And so
Kozachenko the younger had not thrown away the furniture.
In the corner, displayed below a decorative Ukrainian towel,
was a cross-stitched portrait of poet Taras Shevchenko. To
the right of the portrait (and how about that—Solovyov did
not even grasp this at first) were two photographs of Zoya.
Zoya in the kitchen at the general's table with a vase of

chrysanthemums in the background. Zoya at the beach. The bottom of her bathing suit slightly slipping off a bone covered with taut skin. Solovyov thought the life of a bachelor in the company of photographs like that could not be easy. Even under Shevchenko's supervision.

'Is he in love with you?'

Zoya shrugged. Standing at the bureau desk, she pulled out drawer after drawer, looking through the contents. Zoya's calm in conducting this quiet search surprised Solovyov, who was, at the very least, extraordinarily agitated, even though he was not shaking. Her thumb inspected stacks of paper (blank, as a rule), sliding along the edge of the sheets. The sheets generated a light fan-like sound at the motion, reminiscent of the rustling of a deck of cards being shuffled before a deal. Sometimes there was jingling, sometimes there was clicking. Zoya would lay items on the desk then put them away after she had finished looking through yet another drawer.

Solovyov confined himself to examining Taras's scanty book selection. The majority of them were devoted to the city of Alupka and the Vorontsov Palace. It was emerging that Taras had a one-track mind. The only book unrelated to the palace was a publication describing various alarm systems.

'What does he do for work?'

'He's a guard at the Vorontsov Palace.'

Zoya looked through piles of linens, plunging her hand deep under each sheet. The linens were shabby. There were holes and frayed spots even on the folds. It inopportunely occurred to Solovyov that they could even be the result of Kolpakov's activeness. Objects frequently outlive those who

have used them. Bed linens with Chekhov's embroidered
initials had been preserved, too. The bed in the museum
was still made with them. Although . . . Maybe these holes
were the consequence of the love-struck Taras's insomnia?
Solovyov cast another glance at the photographs.

'I found it.'

Zoya said that with the same calm that she had been
searching, but Solovyov flinched. Was that really possible?
Contrary to Solovyov's absolute lack of faith in success (and
he himself did not understand why he had gotten mixed
up in all this) there were yellowed sheets of paper, with fine
writing, between two flowery duvet covers.

'It's my mother's handwriting.'

Solovyov lifted the top part of the linen pile and Zoya
pulled the papers out of the cabinet with a magician's
gesture. This was a victory. Despite the dubious method of
achieving it, it remained a victory, and what a victory! In
the end, Taras had no rights whatsoever to the manuscript.
In the end, his parents had simply stolen this manuscript
. . . Researcher Solovyov's brief history, which had unfolded
primarily in libraries and archives, had made an obvious
salto mortale and transformed into a detective story. Never
before had the search for scholarly truth seemed so gripping
to him. The dramatism of research, something unknown
to the world, took on visible forms when it came out into
the open. Solovyov stood by the window and held the sheets
of paper on his outstretched hand. He was not reading
them. He simply inspected Zoya's mother's minute handwriting, sensing Zoya's breathing at his temple. From time
to time, little bird-like figures appeared over the handwriting,
introducing additions and edits in another hand, one very

familiar to Solovyov. Meaning the general had worked on the dictated manuscript later . . . From somewhere in the very depths of those lines—and Zoya's hand was squeezing his elbow—Yekaterina Ivanovna's sad eyes slowly surfaced. Yekaterina Ivanovna was standing on a little metal bridge that had been built to reach the terrace of the next house (a bed's headboard served as its railing); she held a grocery bag and was wordlessly watching Solovyov through the window glass.

They left Kozachenko's room. Zoya locked it with the key and hurried to unhook the front door. Pressing her back to the door of her own room, she listened to Yekaterina Ivanovna's heavy steps in the entryway, reminding Solovyov in some sense of Princess Tarakanova in her dungeon. Zoya quietly let Solovyov out of the apartment after Yekaterina Ivanovna entered her own room.

Walking downhill along Botkinskaya, the uneasy Solovyov wondered what would happen to Zoya now. His unease was momentary, though, and without it, Solovyov, a person with scruples, could not have surrendered himself to the joy of possessing the manuscript. The small packet of sheets, which were inscribed with a compact, precise script, belonged only to him. It fluttered with each swing of an arm that was beginning to tan, and (this was unbelievable) the packet evoked not the slightest interest among pedestrians.

Solovyov did not feel like going home. It was tough to be alone with his happiness, just as it is tough when someone's relationship is condemned, illegitimate, and, perhaps, even criminal. People put that out in the open. They rush out in public with it, visiting receptions, clubs, and shows

. . . Solovyov went to the embankment. As he stepped down
from its upper sections, he saw a row of seats like those
that line stadiums. These grandstands for spectators faced
the best show on earth: the sea.

Solovyov delighted in the motion of the waves and
himself felt a little like the general. Like the inveterate
smoker who lingers before lighting a cigarette (a special
type of voluptuousness), Solovyov was in no hurry to begin
reading. Rejoicing in his spoils by feel, he stroked the slightly
limp edge of the sheets and knocked the packet against his
knees to give it an ideally correct appearance.

The general's memoirs began like this, 'At the age of ten,
my parents sent me to the Second Cadet Corps.' Ten years
old. The description of everything that happened before
that had been published by Dupont, who, as we know,
assumed that a continuation existed. And so the French
researcher's scholarly intuition permitted her to predict this
sweet moment Solovyov was experiencing on the embankment in Yalta. He read sheet after sheet, placing what he
had read at the end of the packet. Distancing himself from
the first sheet even as he inexorably neared it. Tearing
himself away from Akinfeeva's close lines from time to time,
he scanned the horizon and thought about how his reading
process was akin to a round-the-world journey whose goal
is to return to the starting point.

9

The general's parents sent him to the Second Cadet Corps at the age of ten. We will acknowledge the anachronism of the previous sentence and leave it at that. In some sense, he was already a general as a ten-year-old because strictly (although nonhistorically) speaking, he was always a general. Who could have dared imagine him as anything other than a general? Dupont had already posed that question in her day. And—in the article 'This Is Not Today's Tribe'—she answered in her characteristically uncompromising manner: nobody.

In dictating to Nina Fedorovna his recollections of the years of his life at the Second Corps, the general emphasized that the gold stitching on the black uniforms at that educational institution was somewhat thinner than in other corps (the First, the Nikolaevsky, and even the Alexandersky, for example), not to mention that the trousers for the Second Corps' cadets, unlike those for many other corps, were dark blue, not black. The general also pointed out that later, when weapons handling was introduced in the combatant companies, the Second Corps was given the right to carry dragoon sabers on sword belts as the guards did.

They rose early, at six in the morning. To a horn. That was fine in summer, during the white nights, but it was intolerable in winter. In summer, the future general rose a half hour before reveille so he could greet the horn fully conscious, in order not to let it horn in on his sweetest morning dreams. That did not work out in winter. He could not bear to leave a bed warmed during the night and plunge into the bedroom's penetrating cold. The temperature never rose above ten degrees there, that was the rule. In the late nineteenth century, it was not recommended that young men sleep in warm quarters.

They washed in cold water to the waist and that was a little worse than the horn. They went out on the platz in just woolen jackets. In any weather. It is possible that this Spartan training drew cadet Larionov's attention to King Leonidas's feat. The opposite, however, cannot be ruled out, either: that the Spartan king's feat reconciled Larionov to such a harsh routine. What does remain a fact is that both the Spartan training, and the cadet's extensive familiarity with the course of battle, came in very, very handy for him during his mature years.

When he walked outside for morning formations, Larionov would try not to notice the snowflakes melting underneath his collar. He thought about how the Spartans— who, generally speaking, were connoisseurs of difficulty—did not have a problem like the Russian cold. Larionov would lift his head from time to time and look at his classmates huddled in the darkness of the December platz. They were small, not awake, and covered in bits of ice. In the glint of the gaslights, only the insignias on their hats, polished to glimmering, and their red noses, were visible. Their eyes watered from the prickly morning wind and from sleep that had not passed. The difficulties did not break them. On the contrary, they nourished them, tempering body and spirit. They grew into strong fellows and genuine officers. 'They have all died,' the general wrote over one line.

Cadet Lanskoy had a special place in the general's life at that time. The general obviously singled out this handsome and, judging from the description, arrogant boy in his reminiscences. Cadets Larionov and Lanskoy stuck together for several years. Their relations were not friendship in the usual sense. Lanskoy did absolutely nothing to bring about or, later, strengthen those relations. His contribution to the friendship was that he permitted himself to be admired.

In some certain way, Lanskoy was worth admiring. He was possibly the best student of all, without making visible efforts. He pronounced his answers softly and even, somehow, condescendingly. This annoyed the teachers, but there was nothing to find fault in. His audacity was reckless. On a dare, he swam under the ice of the Zhdanovka River, from one hole in the ice to another. Despite very strict rules, he sometimes left the corps' billeting before bedtime and returned toward morning, through the window.

One time, cadet Larionov escaped with him. After changing into civilian clothes, they rambled around snow-covered Petersburg for half the night. Larionov felt absolutely wretched about it. Violating discipline felt like genuine betrayal to him. He himself would have been hard pressed to say *what*, exactly, he had betrayed, but he had no doubt that betrayal had come to pass. Around 2:30, the cadets dropped in at a tavern and ordered a half-glass of vodka each. They managed to return unnoticed that night but in the morning Larionov, who had never before been sick, got sick. His temperature rose. He was hit with the chills. Tears streamed from his eyes. They were tears of repentance but nobody knew that. Nobody but Lanskoy. He visited Larionov at the infirmary on the third day and said, 'Larionov, you're a decent person. You're sick from violating the routine. You shouldn't have escaped with me.'

Cadet Larionov expected his friend to visit him again but that did not happen. After Larionov's release from the infirmary, Lanskoy greeted him from afar. Larionov nodded and did not even approach him. They fell out of touch after graduating from the corps.

The majority of subjects (other than languages) were taught at the corps by military men. Cadets were supposed to have six lessons a day, followed by horseback riding and drill training. At first, riding devoured almost all Larionov's attention. It is likely that this is the age that should be considered the beginning of the general's long conversations with horses, something referred to in the literature (such as cavalry commander Semyon Budyonny's *A Good Attitude Toward Horses*) multiple times.

After familiarizing himself with the events at Thermopylae, tactics became another of the boy's favorite subjects. When he read those lines, Solovyov recalled a pencil sketch of a battle map that he had discovered in a Petersburg archive. By comparing the document with analogous sketches—at least eighteen battle maps of Thermopylae are attributed to cadet Larionov—it was possible to prove, without a doubt, that it belonged to the future general. The particular interest of that discovery consisted not only in the drawing being the earliest of those known but also that Leonidas himself was depicted in the upper right-hand corner of the sheet, in a general's epaulets and with a two-headed eagle on his chest.

Among non-military subjects, Larionov liked dance. Considering the child's overall mentality, this passion might appear somewhat unexpected, but that was only at first glance. Unlike their successors, in those days Russian officers loved to dance and did so capably. The Russian officers' corps was very refined. Their well-balanced development—this was exactly what the cadets of the Second Corps were striving for—supposed more than manliness. It supposed elegance, too.

On top of all that, the cadet's attitude toward dance was affected by a statement from the corps' charter that had been framed and placed in the dance hall. According to Gurkovsky's *The Cadet Corps of the Russian Empire*, the note held that the system for teaching dance was developed by a French dance school and took into consideration grace and beauty as well as the human body's possibilities for expressing itself, both when resting and when moving. This text was the first to direct Larionov's attention to the human figure's plentiful possibilities.

The child also had a weakness for extracurricular reading. A housefather conducted this, reading classic Russian literature aloud to his charges. After noting Larionov's interest in reading—as well as the cadet's exemplary pronunciation—the housefather often instructed the boy to read aloud. The elderly soldier would sit in a corner of the classroom, cover his eyes with his hand, and listen to his pupil's reading. He would bob his head approvingly in time with the reading, which would have given the impression of absorbed attention had the bobbing not been implausibly rhythmic. Sometimes a faint whistle would sound from his inflated nostrils, through a brush of coarse hair. They read Pushkin's *Poltava*, Lermonotov's *Borodino*, and Gogol's *Taras Bulba*, but everyone especially liked *Singer in the Camp of Russian Warriors*.

The whistling would cease at the first lines of the Zhukovsky. Absolute silence, though, came with a later stanza: 'Our Figner, dressed as an old man, enters / The enemy camp in the dead of night; / Steals like a shadow among their tents, / Sees everything there with his sharp eyes . . .' Over all, just 'Our Figner, dressed as an old man' would have been enough, on its own, to attract attention, pronounced as it was almost as one word. And he was stealing in, too, among tents . . .

In 1894, Larionov allegedly read aloud the short story 'Surgery', which his father had brought for him. Accustomed to Russian classics, the housefather woke up but did not interrupt the cadet. The housefather liked the story, thanks to his own experience in dentistry. Upon learning that Chekhov was the author of the work, he wrote a letter to Lev Tolstoy, asking him if Anton Chekhov was a classic. Tolstoy did not answer. It should be concluded from this that in 1894 Chekhov was not yet a classic. Construction had not even begun on his Yalta home.

The reading repertoire for the wards of the Second Cadet Corps was not limited to the aforementioned works, however. Under their mattresses, hiding from their house-father's eyes, were novels by Madame Genlis, verses from

Mister Barkov, and Nikolai Chernyshevsky's *What Is to Be Done?*—all copied out in the cadets' distinct hands. When the elderly general recalled those years, he expressed admiration in the fact of copying Chernyshevsky's novel. It was not just the copying but also the very reading of that thing that seemed like some sort of feat to him. From the memoirist's point of view, Russian letters had never generated a more helpless text.

The old housefather discovered those books during an inspection of the cadets' bedroom. After lengthy convincing by his students, he left them Madame de Genlis. In the end, he even agreed to turn a blind eye to Barkov. But he simply could not reconcile himself with Nikolai Chernyshevsky's work: the very mention of that surname sent him into a fit of rage. He threatened to expel from the corps and court martial the boy who had copied the novel. His identity could not be established then (it is possible that nobody wanted to), but the general knew it well. He considered it possible to mention only eight decades later, when there was no longer any threat to the copyist. He was cadet Lanskoy.

The housefather's reaction was explainable. The Second Cadet Corps felt a share of responsibility in everything concerning Chernyshevsky. He had entered the corps as a tutor in 1853, while preparing his master's dissertation. It is unlikely that this particular circumstance served as the beginning of all his troubles, but speaking purely chronologically—there is no getting around this—that circumstance preceded his troubles. Temporal as well as spatial patterns were later established, too.

Colonel Pazukhin, the ballistics instructor, drew widespread attention to the fact that the key points in the city for this writer and democrat fell along a single straight line. The

Second Cadet Corps (place of work) ➔ No. 7, Zhdanovskaya Embankment (place of residence) ➔ Peter and Paul Fortress (place of imprisonment) ➔ Mytinskaya Square (place of mock civil execution). In becoming familiar with these patterns, cadet Larionov could not have known that, by virtue of the connectedness of everything on earth, historian Solovyov—a researcher studying General Larionov's battles with the consequences of Nikolai Chernyshevsky's work— would rent a room on that very same straight line (No. 11, Zhdanovskaya Embankment). This method for structuring thoughts, which was far from simple, forced Solovyov to tear himself away from the text and look at the sail of a distant yacht. A moment later he was reading again.

Entering the corps did not at all signify that the future general was isolated from the outside world. After passing an exam for his ability to salute and stand at attention, he was granted the right to go outside. Like cadets of other corps, the wards of the Second Corps had but one limitation: they were prohibited from walking on the sunny side of Nevsky Prospekt. It is possible that this prohibition was seen as a part of their Spartan education, as a necessary measure for acquainting the cadets with the shady side of life.

Sometimes the cadets were taken to the theater. These outings were a real holiday for them. Their time did not yet possess contemporary entertainment opportunities. Theater, which has now receded into the realm of the elite, was at the vanguard of the nineteenth century's *entertainment industry*. As a means for education, theater was considered a mixed blessing or—depending upon the type of show—even dangerous. The theater was closed for Great Lent.

At the cadet corps, the preferred theater was the Alexandrinsky and the preferred show was Alexander Ostrovsky's *The Storm*. According to the future general's calculations, the cadets went to see *The Storm* sixteen times during his years of schooling. Such an obvious preference for one play over all others was explained by the housefather's personal biases. His sympathy for Katerina manifested itself so visibly at the theater that those around him would begin to turn to look at him. From the very first line of the show, the aging soldier would sit, grasping at the armrests of his seat. Indignant at Boris's spinelessness, he would crumple his peaked army cap and hit himself on the knee with it. During Kabanikha's monologues, he would lift his own huge fist and, slowly, with a despairing grimace, sink it into the loge's raspberry-colored velvet. When Katerina said, 'Why is it that people can't fly!' the housemaster's facial features would collapse immediately and he would cover his face with his hands, then begin sobbing as loudly as if he were baying. The civilian audience, who had already long been looking into the hall rather than the stage, would fall silent in respect. They were shaken by the Russian Army's sentimentality.

Larionov returned home during school vacations. Oddly enough, his parents' attempts to spoil the child brought him no joy whatsoever. He visited sweet shops primarily out of filial obedience and, to the surprise of those around him, did not exhibit his previous enjoyment when washing down airy éclairs with orangeade. It seemed to him (and this was the whole point) that with conduct such as this, he was betraying the Spartan ideals he had adopted, that each outing to an establishment of this sort nullified his months of drill

training, washing with ice-cold water, and wakeups before
the morning horn. All that reconciled the cadet with visits
to the sweet shop was that, generally speaking, the food at
the corps was pretty good. According to those in command,
food limitations were not part of a Spartan-style education.
Future officers needed to eat well.

Larionov's parents' non-military conversations seemed
strange to the boy. He heard vagary and something unconvincing in the tone of their conversations, though the
topics under discussion agitated him very much at the
time, despite (or perhaps because of?) their civilian nature.
And so the cadet recalled discussions of the life philosophy
of their distant relative Baroness von Kruger, who had
entered into marriage four times. They had talked about
the baroness in the family before, too, but this grew more
frequent when she entered into new marriages. At the
same time, the elder Larionovs, who held dear their reputation as liberals, allowed no direct condemnation of the
baroness and when in public even remarked along the lines
that what was happening with the baroness only emphasized her exactitude and maximalism.

The fact that Baroness von Kruger gathered all four
husbands together and had dinner with them at a restaurant
called The Bear became a critical point in the Larionovs'
relationship with their relative. Larionov's mother burst into
tears upon learning that news and said she would not allow
the baroness in their home. At the meek objections of
Larionov's father, who held that such a meeting could not
make their relative's quadruple-marriage situation any
worse, Larionov's mother shouted, 'How can you not under-

stand that this is absolutely, simply shockingly unseemly?!'
The cadet, who had witnessed the scene, mentally swore
to himself not to do anything of the kind. For many years,
the notion of shocking actions was, for Larionov, linked to
that very incident.

'To that very inci—' is, if one is absolutely precise, the
end of the manuscript that reached Solovyov. The page to
which '. . . dent' was carried was missing and thus, in some
sense, the full word was reconstructed. Solovyov looked
through all the pages again. There was no doubt: the manuscript was incomplete. He thought about how it held a huge
value even though it was incomplete, since any publication
of new information about the general's childhood years . . .

Even so, his primary feeling was disappointment. During
the time he was reading the manuscript, Solovyov had
managed to get used to its completeness, rather he had not
allowed the possibility that it was incomplete. With its
sudden cut-off, it was as if Solovyov had slipped from the
height of happiness where he had initially found himself.
'There it is,' thought the historian as he stood, 'ingratitude.'
His legs had fallen asleep from sitting still and he had difficulty negotiating the several steps that led to the top of the
embankment.

Solovyov bought a plastic folder at a kiosk, placed the
manuscript inside, and set off aimlessly along the embankment. He skirted the Oreanda Hotel and ended up by the
monument to Maxim Gorky. He could not remember
anything the general had said about Gorky, though he
certainly had said something about him . . . Gorky was
standing in his peasant shirt and tar-blackened boots. The

road behind him divided in two: an upper road and a lower road. Not a word on the marble pedestal indicated what awaited the traveler. Along which road, one might ask, would Gorky himself have traveled? After choosing the lower, Solovyov remembered, word for word, the general's statement about the writer: 'He is walking along a downward path' (1930). This was truly a Yaltan image. Other than the embankment, all the city's paths led downward.

There was a café at the end of the lower, tree-lined path (interwoven acacia branches, a thick shadow). They served cold kvass soup as a first course and rice pilaf as the second. The pilaf was nothing special but the soup was wonderful. Solovyov ordered another serving of soup instead of dessert and ate it slowly. Very slowly, the way one eats something that cannot go cold. He was sitting on a covered veranda, watching the tablecloth and a mysterious potted plant flutter in a refreshing wind. Solovyov ate the soup; his free hand rested on a cool metal railing. Beyond the railing—with no transition whatsoever—there began the huge blue sea.

He did not return home until after dark. The doorbell rang about fifteen minutes after his arrival. Solovyov was not expecting anyone. Knowing that one should exercise caution in southern cities in the evenings, he asked, 'Who's there?'

'Zoya.'

Solovyov could not have confused that voice with any other. Zoya truly was standing outside the door. She had changed out of the gauzy, sheer dresses he had seen on her all these days and into blue jeans and a light-colored T-shirt. A gym bag hung on her shoulder. Solovyov stepped aside and Zoya came in, unhurried. There was something in her new guise that made her look like a camper, but there was no doubt that it became her. She even sat down as people sit at a train station, placing the bag on her knees and pulling her crossed feet under the chair.

'How's the manuscript?' Zoya asked. 'Were your hopes justified?'

'It turned out to be incomplete . . . it cuts off in the middle of a word, can you believe it?'

'Is that right?'

Zoya unzipped the bag with a slow, somehow even sleepy motion.

'That manuscript's still very important,' said Solovyov, checking himself. 'I couldn't have dreamt of a stroke of luck like that.'

'Well then, we'll look more,' said Zoya, extracting a huge bunch of grapes. 'We need to find it in its entirety.'

'Need to? But where?'

'We have to think.'

A two-liter plastic bottle appeared on the table right after the grapes. Contrary to the inscription on the label, it was certainly not Pepsi-Cola sloshing inside. The dense, wavy flow along the bottle's walls attested to the nobleness of the beverage. Just as a person's breeding can be sensed by a very first motion.

'It's Massandra wine, Nesterenko brought it,' said Zoya, nodding at the bottle. 'His sister works at the winery.'

There were no wine glasses to be found in the apartment so Solovyov brought two faceted glasses from the kitchen. He held the massive bottle with both hands as he poured the wine. The wine came out in irregular glugs, yielding from time to time to air that wanted to enter. The bottle seemed like a living being to Solovyov. It grunted, as if offended, when it inhaled. Its plastic sides trembled spasmodically under the young man's hands. He set the bottle on the floor after pouring half a glass each for himself and Zoya. The vessel turned out to be disproportionally large for the table where they were sitting, and even the faceted glasses lacked the power to ease that contrast.

'To the success of our searches,' said Zoya.

The wine's unusual properties stunned Solovyov. Its full body and bouquet reminded him of a liqueur, but still it remained wine. After drinking some, Solovyov imagined what the contents of amphorae had been like. He sensed the flavor of a nectar he had read about when studying ancient sources. The young historian had no doubt that the ancients had extolled this very liquid. It was this very liquid the Greek gods had tasted during their rare forays into the Northern Black Sea Region.

Zoya saw that he liked the wine. She herself was drinking it in small swallows, first as a lady, and, second, as a person spoiled by a divine beverage. Plucking off the grapes, Zoya brought them to her mouth without hurrying, then placed them between her front teeth. The grapes held that position for a few moments, offering a demonstration of both the elegant form of Zoya's teeth and their whiteness. Then the grapes disappeared in her mouth and rolled around behind her cheeks for a while. The Petersburg researcher found this transfer of grapes erotic but could not bring himself to say anything aloud. Solovyov's helper was, without a doubt, a connoisseur of the grape.

'Taras knows we were in his room today.' Zoya did not

change her pose or stop eating grapes as she announced this. 'Yekaterina Ivanovna told him everything.'

Solovyov leaned against the back of the chair. The old-fashioned lampshade was stratifying in their faceted glasses, blending its dark-pink light with the wine's burgundy color.

'How will you . . .' Solovyov took hold of his glass (the colors disconnected again). 'How will you go home now?'

Zoya shrugged. 'Who the hell knows what that Taras will do? You can never guess what to expect from someone timid like that.' Zoya plucked yet another grape. 'They told me he was beside himself.'

'You can't go home today. Stay with me.'

The grape in her teeth stayed there longer than usual and Solovyov knew Zoya was smiling.

'I think that would look strange. No. I'll crash at the train station today and tomorrow the whole thing will be forgotten. Everything gets forgotten in the end.'

'You're spending tonight at my place.'

Zoya fell silent. She took a sip of wine and used an easy football-like motion to roll a stray grape along the table. They could hear nocturnal cars driving past outside the window, on the former Autskaya Street. The shaven-headed Crimean elite was racing around at high speed in imported cars with blinding headlights. The baleful sighs of a trolleybus were occasionally audible when silence set in. The trolleybus would slow down, its crossbars clicking somewhere up among the junctions of the overhead wires, and then the vehicle would gather speed again. Cafeteria workers—tired and untalkative, with bulging shopping bags at their feet—were riding the dimly lighted trolleybus. Young

Yaltan ladies, their faces made up, were riding. Veterans of various wars, intoxicated by alcohol, were riding; they had put on their medals beforehand so the police would not beat them. The veterans swayed along when the trolleybus turned and their decorations produced a quiet, melodic jingle.

Zoya went to bed on the couch, Solovyov on a folding cot. The only sheets (the same ones Solovyov had been sleeping on) were given to her. Zoya herself expressed readiness to accept them. The guest also assigned sleeping spots. Solovyov was fairly happy that everything was resolving itself without his involvement. Even so, when Zoya flicked the light switch, it was not without sadness that he acknowledged he had assumed events might develop differently. But it turned out this assumption of his was unacceptable for the girl from the Chekhov Museum.

'Good night.' There was the sound of a T-shirt being pulled off.

'Good night.'

Lying in the dark, Solovyov listened, futilely, for Zoya's breathing. The silence in the room felt unnatural to him. He thought that perhaps Zoya was purposely not moving because she was listening for him. He was afraid even to inhale loudly: the fold-out bed let out a savage screech at the slightest motion. He did not know what time it was, though all he would have to do to find out was turn toward the lighted electronic clock. But Solovyov did not turn. He was afraid even to open his eyes.

When he opened them, the room turned out to be less dark. Meaning not absolutely dark. Whether it was the moon or the coming dawn, the outlines of objects could be seen fairly clearly. The bottle's silhouette on the table. An uneaten bunch of grapes resembling Mount Ayu-Dag. The glisten of Zoya's belt buckle on the chair. Solovyov caught his breath: that glisten intensified his feelings to their limit, just as the motion of a train had in another time. Perhaps even more strongly. He tried to figure out if Zoya was sleeping. Her head was dark on the white spot of a pillow; her arms were behind the back of her head. Nobody sleeps like that . . . The fold-out bed squeaked as Solovyov touched the bottom of his belly and sensed moisture. Whether Zoya was sleeping or not—for some reason, Solovyov did not doubt this—she was lying there completely naked.

Cool air was beginning to waft through the open window. That meant it really was dawn.

'I'm cold,' Zoya said, as calmly as if she were continuing a conversation.

'I can close the window,' said Solovyov, not moving.

'I'm cold.'

In that repetition there was no apparent point and there was no intonation—there was nothing there but rhythm. Solovyov recognized that rhythm flawlessly. With a feline motion, he leapt off the fold-out bed without a single squeak. He went over to Zoya's bed and pressed his legs into her. He felt Zoya's hair on his damp skin. A moment later he was lying next to her.

'Hold on . . .'

As if out of nowhere, she took a condom and placed it in Solovyov's hot hand. As he put on the condom, Solovyov had no time to be properly surprised that it had appeared. A second later, Zoya's legs had entwined behind his back with unexpected strength. This was no comparison for Leeza's bashful love. There had never before been such energy, flexibility, and passion in his life. Never before had Solovyov felt such powerlessness over his body. Never before had the image of a boat amid waves been so close for him. That image was the last thing that flashed through Solovyov's mind before his final plunge into the abyss. A hurricane had been hiding behind the museum employee's outward phlegmatism.

10

The next morning (which began late), they realized that this was the day Solovyov had promised to read his paper about General Larionov. The reading was to be held at Zoya's house. Despite recent events, Zoya thought the reading was appropriate; this puzzled even the lecturer himself. He was even more surprised that evening when he was coming into the entryway of the communal apartment and ran straight into Taras. Taras was absolutely calm, even courteous. He was the first to greet the guest, after which he backed away, toward the kitchen, and continued standing there, leaning against the general's cabinet. He was not invited to hear the paper.

The attendees were the same as the first time: the princess plus Shulgin and Nesterenko. It occurred to Solovyov that the fact of the powerful Nesterenko's presence might also be restraining Taras from repeating yesterday's hysterics. In any case (Taras's face expressed its usual shyness), Zoya's neighbor was fully able to calm down naturally. Solovyov himself gradually calmed down, too. Coming here was not nearly as simple for him as he had led Zoya to believe that morning.

Solovyov felt a sudden awkwardness as he took the text of his prepared paper from the folder; this time, the feeling was not related to Taras. What Solovyov wanted to report could not appear either important or even worthy of attention for the group that had gathered. All his findings and corrections regarding the Crimean operations seemed like utter pointlessness by comparison with what they knew about the general. But it was too late to retreat. So Solovyov began his reading.

Strictly speaking, this was not even a reading. When he sensed that method of delivering the material was out of place here, the young historian switched to telling a story; this was close to the text of his paper but did not lack for improvisation. This was happening for the first time in his scholarly life. It was not that he could not render his previous papers without reading aloud—every phrase of what he had written was just right and he knew the texts by heart. The academic honor code mandated speaking from a prepared text. The folder of papers lying on a lectern was the first, albeit most approximate, attestation of a report's scholarliness. It was as if all further qualities of what was pronounced did not exist without the written text. Solovyov knew of only one exception: a paper that Prof. Nikolsky had read at a conference lectern, in a monotone, sentence after sentence, from sheets containing nothing but caricatures sketched with a ballpoint pen. It was Prof. Nikolsky who had forbidden Solovyov from speaking without a written text.

Solovyov did not even glance down as he turned page after page of his paper. A feeling of flight had seized him, almost the same as that first ride on a bicycle. He recalled the dates of battles, the strength of subunits on both sides, and the military ranks of all the senior officers taking part in combat.

The topic of Solovyov's paper was 'General Larionov's Rout of Zhloba's Cavalry Corps.' It concerned a key operation in 1920 that allowed the Whites to hold on to Crimea until late autumn. Solovyov began by briefly touching on the composition of the troops positioned on the front line in Northern Taurida. Here he could not help but speak of General Kalinin's Second Cavalry Division (1,500 sabers + 1,000 bayonets) and about General Guselshchikov's Third Cavalry Division (3,500 sabers + 400 bayonets from general Abramov's Don Corps): these troops were positioned from the Azov Sea to the village of Chernigovka. Naturally, he did not forget about the Drozdov Division, either (it was located by the village of Mikhailovka) or about General Morozov's Second Cavalry Division. In speaking about the line of the front to the west of Mikhailovka, Solovyov mentioned General Babiev's Kuban Cavalry Division and the Native Division positioned to its left along the front. Finally, the Markov and Kornilov Divisions were located in the region of Kakhovka, while General Barbovich's division was positioned closest to the Dnieper Estuary.

Opposing those forces were divisions of the Reds' Thirteenth Army, including the First and Second Cavalry Divisions of Dmitry Zhloba's Combined Corps. The numbers for just that one corps—including the troops attached to it—reached 7,500. After some wavering, Solovyov decided not to dwell on the numerical data of other divisions that supported Zhloba (for example the Latvian and the 52nd Rifle Division, which were in the area of Beryslav).

After casting a glance at his listeners, the researcher felt that an overabundance of figures might dull their attention.

In speaking about the Reds' plans, Solovyov began by limiting himself to pointing out Zhloba's corps' intention of attacking the Don Corps and taking Melitopol. After grasping, however, that this picture would be incomplete, the speaker nevertheless elaborated that four divisions were mobilized from Fedko's group in the area from Zherebets to Pologi at the same time as the 52nd and Latvian Divisions were already moving out of the area from the region of Berislavl to Aleshki. Zhloba placed particular hopes on Fedko's group, something that raised no doubts among the attendees. Fedko, however, did not warrant those hopes.

Did General Larionov know about the Reds' plans? Sources available to researchers (Solovyov carefully evened out the file of papers lying in front of him) gave no answer to that question. The general acted as if he was familiar with the enemy's plans in full detail. He had always been a half-step ahead of the Reds before, but those half-steps invariably determined the outcome of the fighting. Zhloba's most cunning schemes broke down against the measures the White commander had taken, regardless of whether they were the result of reconnaissance activity or the general's ingenious foresight. Solovyov preferred to think the latter.

After the general had studied his opponent's way of thinking (this happened fairly quickly), he flawlessly guessed all the operations Zhloba had conceived. In Solovyov's opinion, the general's strength consisted of an absolutely precise assessment of Zhloba's strategic potential. It was not overly high (which was natural) but was not lower than average, either. As General Larionov himself once said, flight school is capable of raising anyone—Dmitry Zhloba among them—to an average level. Then again, it was the hand of fate that threw Zhloba into the cavalry before he had the chance to take wing as he should have. This merging of the earthly and the heavenly in his fate (along with unfavorable genetics, according to some data) significantly twisted the Red commander's brains. To General Larionov's credit, he was able to sort through those intricacies.

Early in the morning, he ordered that strong coffee be served; he would drink it in small sips, sitting on the steps of his armored train car. After the coffee, he smoked his first cigarette. When the weather was not windy, he blew smoke rings, observing their melancholy motion toward the sky. When there was wind, the general released the smoke in a thin stream, unconcerned about its further fate. It is usually thought that it was during those moments that he formed the plans that ended up ruining Red commander Dmitry Petrovich Zhloba's career.

The steppe's drowsy breathing, which moved in barely perceptible waves, and the scent of grass that was still fresh, instilled calm and joy in the general. The sun rose quickly over the horizon, as if it were in a speeded-up film, and the steppe changed its colors. The steppe appeared to the general in the form of a kaleidoscope that had been hurriedly deployed around the armored train. It was unlimited in its capabilities, boundless, and strewn with the ash of his cigarette.

Sometimes General Larionov would lie down in the grass and observe the life of its inhabitants. In his eyes, this life appeared just as petty as human life. Perhaps not as brutal.

The grass's businesslike residents ate each other but they did so out of necessity, conforming to biology's ancient laws. They did not experience mutual hatred. Encouraged by the general's motionlessness, these creatures ran along his splayed fingers, between which something was already sprouting, springing up, and maturing. One could maintain that more than a dozen or two ants, grasshoppers, aphids, beetles, and numerous other creations he would have had difficulty giving names to had passed through his hands. Located in a region of embittered battles between the Red and White Armies, they maintained strict neutrality. Their ability not to notice social cataclysms achieved an absolute, evoking the general's admiration.

There was something posthumous in the general's fingers when they were plunged into the grass. If this was connected with life, then it was in some sort of broad, age-old sense of converting human bodies into grasses and trees. Pressing his face to the crushed stalks, the general imagined himself dead on that field. Arms outstretched. Head sprinkled with earth. This is how he saw his soldiers again and again after battle.

The general remembered how one time, when he was still a cadet, he had gone to military summer camp. During field exercises, he had to dig trenches while being timed. There was a hot spell. He was digging a trench for the first time and became horribly tired. Nausea rose in his throat and his legs began to shake. He was soaked in sweat. After digging the trench, cadet Larionov lay down in it and closed his eyes. A fabulous coolness replaced the scorching sun. The shouts of officers, clanging of shovels, and clatter of horses on the road still carried to Larionov, muted, as if from hundreds of versts away, but none of that was with him any longer. Maybe it was in another world.

'A blissful coolness,' he whispered, imagining he was lying in a grave.

'It's not the time to rest up, cadet!'

An officer was looking at him from somewhere above, almost as if from the clouds that were sailing past, over the trench.

'I'm *deathly* tired,' said the boy.

The officer walked away without saying anything. The expanse he had vacated was immediately covered over by a celestial curtain speckled with white clouds.

'Thank you,' the cadet uttered soundlessly. He did not rule out that this had been an angel.

The general continued to lie there. He already sensed a powerful call from below. He was experiencing the soothing sense of growing into the earth that, as it seemed to him, was familiar to everyone killed in battle. The killed understood that everything was over for them and they could enjoy the repose that had arrived. The general's immobility was almost otherworldly. Only the cautious glance of the sentries—the general knew they were observing him, for security reasons—prevented him from giving himself over, completely, to merging with the earth.

In speaking about the essence of what happened during the summer of 1920, Solovyov could not help but quote from Mikhail A. Kritsky's famous characterization in *The Kornilov Shock Regiment*, which discusses how, over the course of multiple battles, the Russian Army surrounded Zhloba's cavalry, squeezing the troops into a dead-end situation and severely reducing their maneuverability.

Because of the natural crowding that came about, Zhloba's group lost a significant degree of the cavalry's most important qualities: movement and maneuverability.'

The natural crowding into which Zhloba cast the troops entrusted to him was the result of General Larionov's considered and protracted actions. Like an experienced chess player, the general offered a sacrifice to his adversary: a few pawns at the center of the board that Zhloba swallowed very readily. After winning a series of localized battles, the Higher Aviation School graduate did not notice that the places he was victorious were located on a defined axis and had a precisely delineated direction. The victories ceased when the general was of the opinion that Zhloba had moved far enough in that direction. Zhloba continued to attack out of inertia, but this time the adversary was not thinking of retreat. And although the general's army did not counter-attack, all the Reds' attempts to move further were crushed on that very first line of trenches that, it turned out, had been dug more than a week earlier.

Only after familiarizing himself with how solidly the defense had been prepared in this spot did Zhloba begin to understand that his own victorious march had done nothing more than enable the Whites to occupy previously arranged positions. That understanding became complete for him the morning the Whites' first lines appeared at the rear of the troops he headed. General Larionov had personally led them into battle, leaving his habitable armored train for the occasion. The general was not one to take a risk for the sake of risk. He simply knew that sometimes one must lead the troops oneself. He sensed those moments flawlessly.

After warning his listeners that he was going to depart

from the Zhloba theme for a while, Solovyov reminded them of the famous breach in Kakhovka. He had in mind an episode of the war when part of General Larionov's army ended up surrounded. Discussions began about surrendering as prisoners.

The general formed his troops and lit a cigarette. He released several smoke rings and those who had gathered watched, entranced, as they soared.

'This is the sort of question I do not wish to decide for you,' said the general. 'Whoever wants to may go ahead and surrender.'

The general began heading toward his horse but stopped halfway. The smoke rings he'd released were still hanging in the air, like doleful zeroes. The general's horse was stamping its hoof. Several dozen people broke ranks and gloomily wandered toward the front line. The general did not utter a word. He looked at them without judgment, most likely surprised. He himself could not explain his certainty that death awaited them. He knew cases when the Reds had shot only officers and then mobilized the rest. Everyone watched, silent, as those who were leaving moved toward the grove: it was a red grove. With clouds gathering over it. They choked up when they saw those people moving under that leaden sky. And felt better after they had finally disappeared behind the trees.

This is how strange the war was—Russians against Russians—when soldiers taken prisoner could fight the very next day for the other side. They did so just as selflessly as before. There were quite a few people for whom shifts of this sort became a habit. For some, it was the only possible work under war conditions. For some, it was a way of life at a time when, by and large, people were indifferent about who they fought for. *L'existence* for civilians did not give them the thrill they needed. Or that intoxicating military brotherhood that is available only in the face of death. As a rule, it was a bullet that stopped those shifts. Or a saber. Essentially, there were not many choices.

Lightning flashed beyond the grove where the departed had disappeared. It was still very far away: the thunder only caught up a minute after. Another minute later, several bursts of machine gun fire sounded from the grove. Both the general and his soldiers remained silent. It is possible there were more bursts of fire but they were no longer audible through the drumming of the rain pounding at their tents, helmets, and field kitchens. It was the drumming before marching out. They began a prayer service under pouring rain.

The general did not lead them toward the grove. They moved along the steppe, southwesterly, to where the thunderstorm was slowly heading and where—according to the general's notions—the encirclement was less dense. They walked for a long time. Water flowed from their soaked clothing into their boots, squishing loudly. Larionov formed his soldiers into a hollow square a few hundred meters from the Red positions. The cavalry was placed up front, at the head, with the general. What alcohol remained was distributed to his personnel.

The general broke into a trot, as did his horse cavalry. The general drew his saber and the cavalrymen galloped off, their sabers drawn, too. He felt the cold drenching rain snaking down his back and it was pleasant. They rode into the adversary's position—this happened on its own—as lightning struck. The celestial electricity glinted threaten-

ingly on the general's saber. Along the way, he remembered
'Our Figner, dressed as an old man . . .' Our Figner . . .
Lightning flashed three times in a row, illuminating listless
shadows by the tents. Three brief flashes did not pinpoint
any movement among the defenders, though they were not
really defending anyway. Forlornly pressing into whatever
was closest to them, these people first let in the general,
then the cavalry and then, of course, the infantry, too. This
all happened without a single shot.

In Solovyov's opinion, the history of the Kakhovka breach
was the complete opposite of what happened near Melitopol.
Since an oppositeness in substance implies a particular
resemblance in form (Prof. Nikolsky called this 'historical
circumstances'), the young historian did not consider it
possible to examine these two cases of encirclement in
isolation. After showing a map of the Kahkovka breach with
bright red arrows, Solovyov took a map of Zhloba's encirclement from his folder, too. The sheets were held up briefly
and then handed around. The princess held them longest
of all. She drew her index finger along the arrows and looked
pensively at the lecturer from time to time.

Zhloba began racing around after (as Kritsky so aptly put
it) falling into the cul-de-sac. At first, Zhloba tried to get
away from the general's cavalry that had overtaken him,
but he ran into intense machine gun fire. This is where
Zhloba finally grasped that he was surrounded. He again
turned his troops to meet the cavalry but that could no
longer improve matters. The appearance of the legendary
general heading up the attackers made a stunning impression
on the Reds. They began surrendering.

Zhloba successfully boarded his armored train and began

rolling north, fighting battles along the way. The armored train, accompanied by a detachment of about two hundred men, managed to leave the encirclement. This was all that remained of a cavalry corps of many thousands. Lacking troops, weapons, the armored train (which eventually had to be abandoned during the retreat), and, most importantly, horses, Zhloba fell into severe depression. All that remained at his disposal was an old airplane that he had never used in battle, for reasons of principle. Forgotten by everyone, the machine was collecting dust in a hangar outside the combat zone.

Zhloba remembered the plane. After reaching the sought-after hanger, he rolled it outside with the help of local peasants. The women hurriedly wiped down the fuselage. Someone applied strength to turn the propeller, and, to everyone's astonishment, the motor started. The propeller rotated fitfully at first, as if it were gathering strength for each new movement of its blades. Little by little, the rotation grew uniform and the two propeller blades transformed into a large, translucent circular area. The machine jounced and snorted for several minutes but would not budge.

'The motor's warming up,' the peasant men nodded knowingly.

They puffed on hand-rolled cigarettes to reconcile what was happening with their own agitated consciousness. And to attach an everyday quality to the nearness of flying technology. Using an expert motion, the aviator turned some sort of lever and the machine jerked sharply, then stopped as if it were rooted to the ground.

'Get away!' Zhloba yelled, almost flying out of his seat. He placed in that shout all his hatred for his former flying classmates. All the pain of the insults he had suffered at various times. All the bitterness of the defeat that had come to him. The peasants, who were already on edge, scattered. The airplane began moving and rolled along the steppe, shuddering on the potholes. A minute later, it took off.

After circling over the disheartened witnesses to the takeoff, the plane set a southerly course, to where General Larionov's units were finishing disarming the Red Armymen they had taken prisoner. Everything was proceeding peacefully, even somehow routinely. The regimental clerk was compiling a list of the prisoners, also indicating the types of weapon confiscated and the names of the horses. The former Red Armymen stood in a long, joyless line, waiting for the clerk to record them. After registration, they were led off in groups for lunch.

Some who were standing there lifted their heads when they heard the airplane's motor. They all knew the general had eleven such machines in his equipment, so this must have been one of them. Nobody was concerned. The clerk dipped his pen into a spill-proof inkwell and stretched, satisfied, lacing his hands together in front of himself. Indifferently and near-sightedly, he observed the dot growing in the sky. The mere fact of flying technology no longer attracted attention in 1920.

There was something unusual in the airplane's movement. Observed from below, its flight lacked that grand tranquility that usually accompanies large flying objects (organisms) in the air—from balloons and dirigibles to eagles and seagulls. More and more heads turned toward it. The airplane turned somersaults in the air. It resembled a fly, an angered bumblebee, or perhaps even a hummingbird.

This was not the height of aerobatics: Zhloba was extraordinarily far from even the thought of executing Nesterov's 'dead loop.' This was not even a manifestation of the aviator himself being so extremely wound up, either, though the abruptness of his motions, needless to say, could not have been conducive to fluidity in flight. The reason for what occurred lay in the cables for the steering rod: they were not in working order because the machine had been in the damp hanger for so long. Need it be said that Zhloba's affective state had not allowed him to verify their tension?

Whether it was that a wind rose or the energy of desperation that had carried Zhloba toward his flight destination, well, at some point he actually ended up over the Whites' positions. When he saw below him the scene of his disgrace, he threw his arms on the fuselage and hung down. The airplane finally stopped jerking after losing its steering and began flying over the steppe at low altitude. Hanging over his adversary's positions—as if he were leaning on a window-sill and conversing with someone on the street—Zhloba floated over the field kitchens, lines of prisoners, and the herds of horses they had lost. His fluttering hair and pale, unshaven face were very visible from below. Tears from the head wind glistened in his eyes. He was an ideal target. Each person standing below understood that the aeronaut was seeking death. And nobody shot at him.

On Prof. Nikolsky's advice, Solovyov saved one of his important findings for the conclusion of his paper. During his work on the topic 'General Larionov's Rout of Zhloba's Cavalry Corps,' the young historian had decided to compile a maximally precise, inasmuch as was possible, hourly account of the activity of both commanders during the month of June 1920.

Many of Solovyov's colleagues regarded that work as deliberately unachievable so suggested that for starters he write down his own hourly life in June (during the previous year, for example) and then later set his sights on events seventy-six years in the past. The hidden irony in that advice touched on not only the possibility of searches of this sort but also their practicability. To his colleagues, these searches seemed, to some extent, like scholarly pedantry or (this sounded more offensive) scholarly poseury. It turned out that Prof. Nikolsky was the only person who approved of the graduate student's plans, without reservations. And that was enough.

Solovyov disagreed with his colleagues' irony and actually did compile his own life story for June of the previous year. This proved to be completely straightforward. He spent the entire time of his final examination period—that was what fell in June—sitting in the Public Library. All his remaining actions were associated with exams. Their times were calculated easily, according to the schedule of exams and other tests he had kept. From his course on source study, the young man had internalized the idea that any piece of paper, even one of little significance, could later become an important historical source. He knew the value of documents and never threw them away.

As far as June 1920 went, that task did turn out to be more complex, though it was not at all unachievable. Solovyov first pieced together the texts from all the memoirs regarding that stretch of time. After ascertaining the basic character of General Larionov and Zhloba's actions, the scholar moved on to highly focused archival searches. He looked through thousands of written orders, telegrams, and telephonograms from that time (frequently they specified not only the date but also the hour and minute of sending) and compiled—in spite of his colleagues' doubts—a fairly detailed listing of what happened during the month of June. The result turned out to be stupendous.

It emerged that on the night of June 13 into 14, e.g. before the start of active military operations, General Larionov and Zhloba's armored trains stood facing one another. This occurred on territory that was neutral at the time, namely near Gnadenfeld, a settlement of German colonists. Aided by telegrams sent by both sides, the historian managed to establish that Zhloba's armored train arrived at 23:30 on the first track, stood there until 04:45, then headed north. The sources Solovyov used allowed him to calculate the arrival time of the general's armored train as 23:55. It departed at 03:35, in a southerly direction. And though the number of the track where the second armored train stood is not indicated in the documents, the process of elimination managed to determine that, too: it was track No. 2. There were only two tracks at the Gnadenfeld station.

Prof. Nikolsky was very satisfied with his former student (and are any students 'former'?). More than anything, he approved of the result from the point of view that Solovyov had been on the right track with his methods. Despite all his love for brave deductions, the professor considered empirical research the only possible basis for any scholarly work. On top of that, he emphasized that any work, even if it looks pointless at first glance, will certainly bear fruit if the work has a source. In this regard, by the way, he did not rate the future Crimean conference very highly. He called the majority of its participants 'inspired blowhards' but did not talk Solovyov out of going.

'You need to see that, too,' he told the graduate student in parting. 'Once, at any rate.'

The second circumstance that evoked the professor's interest in Solovyov's finding was its significance for the history of the war itself. Until now, no documents had existed that directly or circumstantially confirmed a personal meeting of the two adversaries. Even so, conjecture about the possibility of such a meeting had been expressed in the émigré press back in 1930. Lacking any factual confirmation for his conjecture, in *Ten Years Later*, author Yuri Krivich permitted himself to go even further. He posed the question of whether the hypothetical meeting was the general's attempt to arrange a secret connection with the Reds. Since the question was posed in an accusatory tone, the essence of the general's betrayal remained unclear. How did it come about that he prevailed over the Reds in one of his most convincing victories as a result of a deal with them? And, consequently, why did the Reds need that sort of deal? The only thing the author could produce to support the theory was the unchanging question: why did the general remain alive at the end of the war?

It is interesting that the Red side later also expressed a supposition regarding the general's meeting with Zhloba. Moreover, this mention of a deal—this time, naturally, in favor of the Whites—no longer sounded like a hint. The deal was announced as if it were a verified, albeit unconfirmed, fact. Since Zhloba had already been shot by that time—under a decision of the 'troika' of the People's

Commissariat for Internal Affairs—in his article 'At the Last Boundary', Sergei Drel expressed restrained satisfaction that justice had triumphed after all with regard to the traitor, albeit slightly in advance of the determination of his guilt. Solovyov concluded his talk with this sarcastic phrase, which he thought was not lacking for effect.

Princess Meshcherskaya nodded silently but genially. Zoya watched as Shulgin finished constructing some sort of complex, albeit two-dimensional, figure out of matches. Since the table shook constantly, he had thought it pointless to create a figure with volume. Nesterenko was sleeping.

11

Zoya spent the night at Solovyov's again. This time there was none of the uncertainty that had tormented them both, and so they made love without hesitation after a light dinner with wine. There was no tension at all. Unhurried and even with a certain flirtatiousness, Solovyov undressed and waited for Zoya under the sheet. She took off her clothes, standing half-facing him. Solovyov delighted in how she moved: Zoya knew how to undress.

She removed her attire calmly and elegantly, with a subtle portion of the resignation any Russian woman simply felt obliged to display for her possessor. After taking off her jeans, she glanced at them in her hand and tossed them onto a chair, with a quick jingle of the belt buckle. She extracted a pair of panties out from under a long shirt with a man's cut and carefully, using her index finger and thumb, placed them on her jeans. She touched her shirt collar with both hands, slowing down. She undid the long row of buttons as if she were in doubt. The shirt slid from her shoulders but its edge remained in Zoya's small fist. Set against the background of her dark skin, the bright linen of her shirt fell to the floor casually, folding into an unusual flower scented with deodorant. A bikini tan line flashed on Zoya's supple bottom.

She was different that night. After revealing her spiritedness the night before, today Zoya demonstrated technique that was no less outstanding. To Solovyov's surprise, the museum employee's knowledge of this non-Chekhovian realm was boundless. The image of a boat amongst waves that had entered the researcher's thoughts yesterday had faded. There was now something else that did not lend itself to instantaneous definition. Solovyov had no time at all for deliberation, though.

The morning was fabulous. Relaxed, quiet, and contented. There was complete calm, like after a visit to the bathhouse. The body's absolute lack of inhibition, delight emanating from each of its cells. Or even the feeling a day after playing football. A pleasant ache in the leg and pelvic muscles, an unwillingness to get up. Combined with a feeling of deep satisfaction: Solovyov thought he was genuinely experiencing this phrase for the first time.

Zoya sat on top of him and began giving him a massage. She started with his hair. She gathered it in waves, clasping her hands together on top of his head. She kneaded his neck and back. At first she touched him, just barely, with the very tips of her fingers, as if she were injecting through them a mysterious electricity that made goosebumps cover Solovyov. Then her palms made powerful grasping movements. They turned Solovyov's back to gelatin, to clay, removing the crystalline current it had received and instead pouring in a muscle-stretching energy. From time to time, when Zoya's movements were particularly vigorous, Solovyov felt the touch of her intimate hair in the small of his back. Then—

after Zoya resettled on his legs—she massaged the lower back itself, then his behind (what an apt name that is, anyway). That turned out to be especially pleasant; its softness was made for massages. Zoya sank her palms into the stillness of his strongest muscles. The pulsing of her palms repeated the rhythm of those very same muscles, imitating their ancient movement. She moved on to his legs. She achieved their full relaxation by rubbing them on both sides. This was how footballers going in as substitutes were handled, too. Soles of the feet. Heels, with a rubbing, circular motion. Each toe thoroughly. The apotheosis of the corporeal. A fresh morning breeze with a juniper aroma rushed through the open window and blended with the smell of their bodies.

After breakfast, they headed for the embankment. Solovyov took the opportunity to check his height and weight along the way. He thought medical scales were something one would no longer run into on Petersburg's streets: splotchy white after having been repainted, the quiet clanging of the hanging weights. Where had they disappeared to? Where had the machines selling carbonated water gone? What about the barrels of kvass and beer? It occurred to Solovyov that not one history book had noted their departure, just as not one history book had said anything about their arrival. But they truly had existed. They had defined a way of life, making it more bearable, if only, needless to say, to the limited degree they could.

An elderly man wearing glasses weighed Solovyov. The lenses of his glasses were large and bulging. His eyes seemed to be, too, as he monitored the markings on the scale. Strictly speaking, he was not monitoring the markings. He could determine anyone's weight from a distance. There was a rubber band instead of a right temple on his glasses.

'Sixty-eight and a half kilos. Would you like your height, too?'

'I would,' said Solovyov.

He stood at the height measurer and the moving part of the apparatus lowered onto his head with an unexpected knock.

'One meter seventy-nine. You need another half kilo for full harmony.'

Solovyov tossed up his hands and paid. He felt Zoya's cool palm under his T-shirt.

'I'll feed you,' Zoya promised in a whisper. Her lips touched Solovyov's ear. 'For full harmony.'

Despite the bright sun, it was refreshing on the embankment. A strong wind was blowing off the sea. Splashes rose over the concrete ledge by the water and settled somewhere far away, on the second tier of the embankment. A small, neat rainbow accompanied their flight. The splashes evaporated with improbable speed after shining one final time under the pedestrians' feet.

Zoya took off her sandals, picked them up, and began walking barefoot. Based on her glowing face, Solovyov knew she expected the same of him. Hiding his inner unwillingness, he took off his sandals and carried them in his hands, too. The asphalt turned out to be incredibly hot, so walking on it was almost torture. The squeamish Solovyov experienced no less suffering from the assumption that he was most likely walking over someone else's gobs of spit, dried though they might be. He understood Zoya's line of thinking, though. This was an essential shot for a romantic movie. Except that shoeless walks in the movies usually included rain. Nobody burned the soles of their feet in those situations, and besides, everything generally looked more hygienic.

It was hot for Zoya, too. She bounded all the way to the steps leading to the lower embankment, then turned. Everything was different on the lower embankment. The water had not had a chance to flow back into the sea and it quivered on the concrete in huge warm puddles. The surf sloshed over, splashing them from time to time, but that was pleasant.

Near the pier, they went back to the upper level; this was a remnant of the former embankment. The one Chekhov knew, with two-story brick houses, curlicue railings on little balconies, and palms in huge pots. From afar, a cupola of the St. John Chrysostom Church shone golden, rising over Yalta's greenery. Zoya's hand directed Solovyov into a gap between buildings and they found themselves by a chairlift. Seats for two swung around with a metallic growl, returning from somewhere up high. They approached the platform with jerky, paralytic motions and received passengers without stopping. After letting Zoya go first, Solovyov managed to sit at the last moment. He plopped down hard on the seat, and the whole structure began to rock. Of course Zoya noticed his agitation, but she didn't acknowledge it.

The surface slowly slid out from under their feet. The wooden platform ended, and next came bushes and a tree with a rubber sandal on top. Roofs and yards. Flying over the yards was most interesting of all: people were hanging out laundry, playing dominos, and punishing children. They were repairing a car, a tiny Zaporozhets that stood on wooden trestles. Carefully, finger by finger, wiping their hands with rags, walking off to the side, and pensively looking at the car. Life was showing itself in all its diversity.

Solovyov took Zoya's hand and experienced a persistent sense of déjà vu. At one time he had loved recognizing the past in the present. He saw that almost as a historian's destiny. Later, influenced by Prof. Nikolsky, he rid himself of that unidirectional view of things after learning to recognize the present in the past, too. 'Contrary to popular notions,' wrote Prof. Nikolsky, 'time is a two-way street. It is also possible that there is no traffic at all. One should not think tha . . .' Solovyov looked again at the roofs below. Chagall, well, of course. His painting reflected them.

As they floated over what was formerly Autskaya Street, Zoya swung her feet (this, it belatedly struck Solovyov, was how sandals ended up in trees). There was something child-like in the smoothness of the skin on her legs. But they were adult, purely feminine, and arousing at the same time. Trolleybus rods slid along wires right under their seat. The trolleybus roof proved to be unexpectedly large and peeling. Not resembling something intended to be streamlined. Some things are not usually seen from above.

Solovyov felt some inner nervousness when he jumped down, but he did not lose face. A view of a strange structure with columns unfolded at the spot where they touched down. It might have been considered a cult building if not for its particular resort-area monumentalism, something that is an integral part of southern Soviet cities. It is possible this was a Soviet cult: Solovyov imagined himself and his

traveling companion as Komsomol members. Elder
comrades were bringing two young creatures to mysterious
communist spirits in sacrifice. Against the backdrop of the
sea. The hair of those in attendance flopped dramatically
in the wind. Solovyov wanted to have Zoya amid these
columns, but made no signal. It was enough for him to
acknowledge that she would have agreed, without a second
thought.

The peak where they now found themselves was no
longer truly Yalta. Solovyov walked along a path in the
woods, lagging a little behind Zoya. He liked watching her.
Zoya knew this and made no attempt to slow her pace. He
repeated to himself for the hundredth time that this lithe
young woman was his, and for the hundredth time this gave
him a feeling of delight.

The forest grew thicker, but they were not alone there.
Branches cracked here and there, multicolored T-shirts
flashed, and people called out to one another. Not being
alone gave Solovyov particular pleasure, too. Those accompanying them (they had gathered from throughout the
area, purposely) saw Zoya's litheness. Perhaps they sensed
her spiritedness. But only he (only he!) truly knew her
liana-like qualities that drove one insane. Even the first
sensations he had experienced with Leeza (Solovyov
compared everything that happened afterwards with those
sensations) now seemed adolescent and silly to him. It felt
awkward to even recall Leeza now. Awkward not because
of Leeza (her chances were minimal by comparison with
Zoya) but because of himself, who had drawn her into
such an unfavorable comparison. He tried to push Leeza
out of his consciousness, as one might gently push away

a grandmother who had wandered into a party raging in the living room. A minute later, he truly had forgotten about her.

They crossed a paved road during their walk downhill. They walked past small yards overgrown with grape vines. These yards were even smaller than the one where Solovyov was housed. They were enclosed by headboards, steam heat radiators, prams, and even the doors of a microbus—a Playboy bunny blushed saucily on one of those doors. Judging from the inscription below it, the car had some connection to St. Pauli, Hamburg's entertainment quarter. Solovyov thought about how objects' fates are sometimes more interesting than humans'. What had that bunny seen in its previous life? A light Hamburg rain? Street musicians, asphalt glistening with lights from strip bars, pushy barkers, prostitutes in uniform orange overalls (that arouses), paupers with dogs, and English sailors waddling along the whole breadth of the street? Who had the bunny driven around St. Pauli? That, in essence, was not important. The bunny's innocence had been returned to it here, in the quarter where the door now resided. Children were playing in a sandbox. It was just a bunny to the new family. Nobody was interested in its past.

The enclosure, which was entwined with vines, acquired an artistic unity. And the aesthetic of a poor but honest seaside existence that gratefully accepted everything, saved everything, and did not permit itself to squander head-boards. Solovyov peered into one of the little yards. He saw a family lunching under an awning. A woman dishing boiled potatoes onto plates. A man with a lucid face who had already dispensed the 150 grams of vodka he was ready to swallow. A child on a tricycle. A southern bird unknown to Solovyov that was swinging on a cypress branch and singing, non-stop.

Zoya stood at a distance and waited patiently. Her friend was absorbed by the same romanticism that had become the essence of her everyday life, even as a child, something for which she had another word: poverty. Zoya was thinking she knew a seamy side of that romanticism but Solovyov did not. That was not the case. Solovyov pictured life in these small worlds very well. He himself had grown up in one of them. He was not seeking unfamiliar sensations. He saw in those small yards a reflection of his childhood.

They came home (to Solovyov's) toward evening. At Zoya's insistence, they stopped at the market on the way back and bought some meat and vegetables. Now Zoya was sautéing meat. Solovyov inhaled its aroma and thought about how long it had been since he had eaten home-cooked food. Pressing against Zoya from behind and resting his chin on her shoulder, he watched as neat pieces of pork browned all over, sizzling and spattering grease. Zoya had intended to fix something else after cutting vegetables for salad, but Solovyov took the tireless young woman in his arms and carried her into the other room. The young man feared he would not survive yet another of her merits.

They washed down the meat with wine diluted with cold mineral water. It tasted delicious. The wine had ceased being nectar and its thick crimson color turned a bright pink, but the wine's flavor now felt more refined. Then Zoya made coffee. She said that they needed to be in excellent form tonight.

'Why?' asked Solovyov.

'Because today we're going to search for the end of the general's memoirs. I know where it might be.'

Solovyov looked closely at Zoya. She knew. A wasp flew in the window and flew right back out after uncertainly circling over the table. Solovyov did not break the extended silence and did not ask where they were going. That would only have consolidated the strange hegemony that Zoya had begun to establish over him. Let her say it herself if she wanted.

Zoya washed the dishes and then began getting ready. She opened the bag she had brought over the day before; something inside clanged like it meant business.

'Here, you carry this.'

Performing the search in the evening did not trouble her in any obvious way. Though (Solovyov cast a glance at the mysterious bag) what time could be considered 'natural' for this sort of search?

They left the house at around eight. They took a trolleybus to the bus station then transferred to a small shuttle van. It scrambled up a winding mountain road with a roar that was unexpected for a small vehicle, then ended up on a highway running parallel to the sea. An evening coolness was already apparent here. One of the passengers slammed shut a roof hatch. The only open window was next to Solovyov but he had no intention of closing it. He stuck his elbow out, enjoying the cooling Crimean breeze.

The vehicle stopped at settlements and guest houses. The passengers lowered their heads exaggeratedly as they got out so as not to hit them on the door frame. Nobody boarded. When the vehicle stopped in the forest, there was nobody left but Zoya and Solovyov.

'Alupka Park,' said the driver. 'Last stop.' As he watched the couple make their way along the little road and stretch their numbed legs, he added, 'Last van's at 10:30.'

'Thanks,' Zoya said, turning. 'We'll be leaving on the other side.'

The vehicle turned around right there, on the park's tree-lined alley. A minute later its engine fell silent behind the trees. In the engine's slow, dying sound there rang something of farewell and additionally, perhaps, something alarming. What Solovyov was experiencing was not fear in the usual sense. It was the uneasy feeling of one who turns out to have bought a one-way ticket. To a huge, drowsy park. With an eccentric traveling companion. With a heavy bag holding unknown contents.

'Count Vorontsov's Hungarian lover lived with him.'

A pause. Solovyov was already starting to get used to Zoya's habit of omitting all manner of prefatory discussion. Zoya thought it was up to her conversation partner to connect the links of the chain that led her to make some statement or other. More accurately put, she did not think about this. She had not even contemplated it.

'Vorontsov was old and she acquired yet another lover. A young cornet . . . This Lebanese cedar.' Zoya walked over to a sprawling tree and stroked its unembraceable trunk. 'Everything here was planted at Vorontsov's order.'

The Lebanese cedar tree's bark consisted of what looked like large tiles that had just recently been glued on. Ants that were just as large ran along them. A squirrel sat about two meters from Zoya's hand. Its reddish-brown coat blended with the tree trunk, making the squirrel almost undetectable. Its arched tail quivered now and then. The squirrel did not run away, staying in place by force of will.

'One time Vorontsov caught them in bed together,' said Zoya, now addressing only the squirrel. 'When the cornet ran out of the bedroom, covered in a sheet . . .'

Zoya ripped her hand from the tree trunk and the squirrel jumped right off, onto the grass. It sat there for an instant, as if deliberating on what it had heard. Solovyov beckoned to it, motioning with his fingers.

'Have you noticed that squirrels are twitchy?'

He drew a little closer but the animal hid behind the nearest cedar, following the cornet's example.

'The Hungarian woman thought Vorontsov would shoot her right then,' said Zoya, her gaze taking on a rigidity. 'She knew his temperament. But he rang the bell and told the servant, "Wash madam and change the linens."'

Zoya walked right up to Solovyov and hissed into his lips, 'She de-tes-ted him from that day on.'

Zoya stood so close that it was impossible not to kiss her. It was a long, exhausting kiss, filled with gratitude for the information about Vorontsov.

Walking past a pond with swans, they ended up at *Big Chaos*, a majestic heap of stones brought here at Vorontsov's order. Zoya began jumping from boulder to boulder, climbing higher and higher. Solovyov reluctantly followed her. He painstakingly assessed each jump but his foot slipped several times. Stubborn, he did not ask Zoya about today's plans. Her silence and this ridiculous moving around on the rocks was beginning to irritate him. Zoya stopped when the gently sloping ascent ended. Continuing to climb up would have been insanity. It even seemed so to Zoya.

They sat down on one of the rocks. The sun had disappeared behind the trees long ago but the rock was warm, almost hot. There was not a soul around. Sitting on the rock in such a strange place, set against the thickening dusk, Solovyov felt like he had gone astray. Having a girlfriend had not made things easier. More likely the opposite.

It was almost dark when they began climbing down. Zoya took a flashlight from the bag she had handed to Solovyov and directed its light at the closest boulders. Solovyov, whose eyes had already begun to grow accustomed to the dark, finally lost his orientation. The flashlight distorted the form of the rocks. The angle of the light made barely noticeable indentations seem to be huge hollows, but Zoya's beam completely ignored real crevices between the rocks. Fantastical shadow play intensified all that: Zoya waved the flashlight from time to time as she showed Solovyov the way. Solovyov held on to the bag, which was swinging on his shoulder; he did not much believe they could descend safely. He was completely wet when they finally made it down.

The flashlight proved far more useful below. It revealed trees that had sprouted up suddenly (they had not been there an hour ago), roots snaking along the paths, as well as boulders the tireless Vorontsov had scattered here and there. Zoya's flashlight accentuated a bronze plaque on one of the boulders, drawing it out of the dark. The boulder was a memorial stone for Vorontsov's dog. A minute later they saw its ghost. An indeterminate four-legged creature stood about ten meters away, where the flashlight just barely reached. Its infernal gaze reflected the remnants of Zoya's light. Judging from its height, the animal might even have been a cat.

Solovyov had figured out long ago where they were going. Maybe he had already figured it out when Zoya first mentioned continuing the search. In reality, there was not much need for imagination here since they had examined everything thoroughly in Taras's room. If there was anything more to search for, to add to what they had found (where, other than at home, might this kind of person store something?), then only his workplace remained. Lighted by the moon that had risen, Taras's workplace revealed itself in all its oriental majesty. It was the Vorontsov Palace, seen from below.

The seekers of the manuscript climbed over a fence and ascended toward the centaur-like palace. They turned a corner and found themselves in the English part of the grounds, which Solovyov particularly liked. He had never been here, ever, but even at night he found his bearings with ease on this small street leading toward the main entrance. A good half of Soviet historical films had been shot on this narrow expanse. Solovyov felt a little like d'Artagnan. As a person with a European way of thinking, he would have preferred to come into the palace from this side.

Zoya saw matters differently. After showing Solovyov the palace from all sides (as the museum employee saw things, there should be a tour even if there would be a break-in), she led him to a Moorish façade that looked out on the sea. A wire stretched along a wall to the left of a mosaic arch that gleamed in the moonlight. Zoya took a penknife from her pocket and cut it.

'Alarm system?' Solovyov whispered.

Zoya nodded silently. They walked several meters along the western wing and stopped by a glass door, where Zoya asked Solovyov to take off the bag. Solovyov suddenly felt completely calm; his initial fear had subsided. These goings-on had obviously stepped outside the bounds of reality. Using the flashlight, Zoya took out two objects, only one of which Solovyov recognized: a glass cutter. Zoya did not begin with that, though. She took the second object (three rubber circles, arranged in a triangle), placed it against the glass, pulled some sort of lever, and the contraption remained, hanging on the window. It had suction cups.

Then came the glass cutter's turn. Zoya used it to trace an oval around the suction cups stuck to the glass. As Solovyov observed the Chekhov specialist's dexterousness in wielding the glass cutter, it occurred to him that in the event of their capture, the clause about break-ins with previous concert would not apply to them: there was no previous concert between him and Zoya. She had not uttered a word about her plans. And he had not asked her anything.

Zoya used the handle of the glass cutter to knock lightly on the glass a few times. Then, grabbing the suction cups, she noiselessly removed the oval traced on the glass and handed it to Solovyov. Thrusting her hand into the opening that had formed, she flicked a latch from inside. The door opened.

Zoya took the suction cup device from Solovyov's hands, placed it on the ground, and unstuck it from the glass oval. The suction cups were returned to the bag with a clang. Of everything that had happened, what struck Solovyov most was probably Zoya's composure. She was first to enter Vorontsov's kingdom.

Zoya found her bearings flawlessly in the deceased count's

palace, even with the flashlight switched off. She took Solovyov's hand and led him through several rooms where all he could see (this was a strange tour) were several gleaming vases and the fire alarm system's lifeless flashing. Darkness intensified the sound: the creak of a floor, the squeak of door hinges, and even—this was right by Solovyov's ear—the bag chafing on his shoulder.

They ended up in the staff area. Solovyov figured that out from the size of the rooms and, most importantly, the windows. They stopped in one of the rooms. Zoya squeezed Solovyov's hand and froze. The light came on suddenly. After his eyes adjusted to the light, Solovyov saw they were standing by a wall. Zoya's free hand was lying on the switch. She was smiling.

'This is Taras's room.'

The space was tiny. A window covered in metal shutters. Shelf hanging on the wall, heaped with some sort of electronic odds and ends. Chair. Desk. Zoya's photograph on the desk.

'I'm sure he's in love with you.'

A steamship's whistle sounded from somewhere far away, as if from another world.

'He loves me.' Zoya turned the photograph upside down. 'Is it really possible not to love me?'

She turned the chair and sat, straddling it, then pulled out the desk's side drawers, one after another. They were all empty. They were all noisily sent back. The desk's middle drawer turned out to be filled with papers. Zoya pulled out an armload, carelessly dumping them on the floor. Taras's papers slid into a formless mass, surrounding a chair leg. Solovyov crouched beside it. Zoya plucked a plastic folder out of the papers before he'd managed to examine what was lying there.

'That's it!'

Zoya's mother's hand, familiar to Solovyov, was visible through the transparent folder. Zoya offered her cheek and tapped it with her finger.

'Clever girl,' said Solovyov, kissing Zoya.

They crammed the other papers into the drawer. At first it would not close, so Solovyov had to pull the papers back out and stack them in a compact bundle on the table. Zoya seemed to ponder something before turning out the light.

'Want to make love in Vorontsov's bedroom?'

The light went out. Depth and resonance had been restored to the silence. Solovyov felt Zoya's hand on his belt.

'Are you sure you want that?'

The hand pulled lightly at his belt. It was a gesture of disappointment. The selfless female accomplice's terse *oh, you*. And Solovyov understood that. But he truly *did not feel like it*. A sense of danger suppressed other instincts in him. Unlike in Zoya. She was constructed the exact opposite way.

They walked through several rooms without turning on the flashlight (Solovyov thought they were not walking the same way as when they arrived), then stopped in one of the rooms. Solovyov's knee bumped into something soft. A bed. A canopy hung over it like a formless blot.

'Are you planning to screw me here or not?'

The echo of Zoya's question resounded through all the palace's chambers and returned to the bedroom, where it flung Solovyov on the bed with a quick push to the shoulder. He froze as he sank into Vorontsov's feather bed. Zoya descended upon him the next second. Despite his light shock, Solovyov noted that she had managed to undress. She was so worked up that she had not managed to pull off his clothes (come on, why are you acting like a corpse!?) All that remained for Solovyov was to give in. His jeans were lowered. Zoya was convinced that the corpse comparison was unjustified.

Solovyov had never experienced anything like this before. Even yesterday night, which had seemed so absolutely stupendous, faded. He felt the silk of the palace bedspread with his buttocks as he saw Zoya's profile dancing against the background of the enormous canopy. Maybe it was actually the canopy, not Zoya, that lent his senses a keenness he had not known before. Such intimate relations with the past aroused him as a researcher. At that instant, he did not feel like history's guest. He was a small but integral part of it. His merging with Zoya seemed to him like a merging with the past. Which had become accessible and discernible and had undressed before him. This was the orgasm of a true historian.

Zoya was lying on Vorontsov's vast bed with her arms spread wide. Her breathing was almost back to normal but her heart (Solovyov laid his head on her chest) was still pounding rapidly and resonantly. Creaking floorboards sounded in the doorway.

'Did you hear that?' whispered Solovyov.

She did not stir. The creak repeated and Solovyov squeezed Zoya's hand.

'I think it's Vorontsov's ghost,' Zoya said without lowering her voice. 'No big deal. Anyway, we did his favorite thing.'

She lurched and sat up on the bed.

'It's time.'

Solovyov heard the slapping of bare feet and the rustle of clothing being donned. He fastened his belt and stood, too. He was experiencing a pleasant weakness and a lack of desire to move. The task of leaving unnoticed, which is important for any burglar in his right mind, now seemed of little significance to him.

'It's too early to relax,' said Zoya.

She noticed his apathy. Zoya handed him the bag and again led him through the dark rooms. How did she know this palace so well? They ended up in the same place they had entered. From here they could see the sea and the moon's path on the water. Little lights of different colors were blinking in the corner of the room.

'That's strange,' Zoya muttered, 'I shut off the alarm system. Why is it lit here?'

'The door's open anyway. We can leave.'

'We can, of course . . .'

Without saying a word, Zoya approached the blinking panel and tugged a long switch.

In the first seconds, Solovyov did not even realize it was a siren. The noise was deafening. It came out of nowhere, out of utter quiet. In terms of strength, this noise could only be compared with silence. This noise was the converse of quiet: like all opposites, they possessed common characteristics. Crimea's entire southern coast was being notified of the trespassers at the palace.

Zoya grabbed him by the hand and they set off running. Solovyov turned by one of the famous Vorontsov lions. Inside the palace, lights went on one after another, almost like in the movies. There was nothing Solovyov wanted more at that moment than to turn into a stone lion and greet, calmly dignified (his paw on a sphere), the police, dogs, and volunteers who would come running. To greet everyone who would set off to defend the deceased count's property. Following Zoya, he leaped lightly onto a metal fence. His foot caught on something as he was jumping down and he rolled below, along the incline. Stones dug at him, roots caught at him. Zoya's bag with the break-in tools and the general's manuscript hit his face and chest. He stopped in some kind of bushes. Which, to top things off, scratched him very painfully.

'Still in one piece?' asked Zoya.

Zoya's silhouette was still spinning but the alarm was no longer sounding. Why had she turned it on? Why had they run below where there was nothing but the sea, where they would be much easier to catch? It would have been better to make their way upward, to the highway. At least they could have hailed a car there. Solovyov was jogtrotting obediently behind Zoya. She was in high spirits despite the circumstances. Pointing out, in a chipper voice, where to turn. She jumped off the parapets with a happy whoop. Why was she so elated?

They made their way to an open patch of ground over the sea. There was a strong wind blowing here that had not been noticeable in the park. Waves were rolling over huge boulders that formed something like a bay. Tatters of foam looked rather sinister in the moonlight.

'It's Vorontsov's bathing area,' Zoya said, gesturing below. 'There should be a boat somewhere among those rocks.'

They went down some steps and began walking to the left, along the rocks. There really was a boat between two boulders. Ten meters from the boat, waves slapped heavily at the rocks from the outside of the barrier, slipping off them with an offended grunt. Back in his adolescence, Solovyov had learned from books that landing is the most dangerous thing for shipwreck survivors. Or casting off, like now. A wave tosses a lifeboat against the crags and smashes it to bits. The end.

Solovyov left the bag on shore and jumped onto the boulder nearest the boat. He still vaguely hoped there would be no oars in the boat. No, they lay on the bottom. Solovyov caught the mooring clamp and leaned over the water.

'The boat's on a chain,' he said, almost festively, 'with a lock.'

Zoya took a hammer and chisel out of the bag and silently extended them to Solovyov. His companion's power of foresight astounded Solovyov almost more than the surf. He dragged part of the chain onto the rock, chose one of the links, and struck it with all the power of his desperation. He wound up and struck again. His strikes at the chain brought sparks from the rock but moved him no closer to his goal. The goods were solid. One time, Solovyov missed the chisel with the hammer and struck himself very painfully on the knuckle. He bit his lip and tolerated the pain in silence, but Zoya, who was sitting alongside him, apparently saw it all. It even looked to him like she was smiling. A piece of the chain finally fell from the rock with a jingle. They could (could!) set sail.

After sitting at the oars, Solovyov held out his hand to Zoya but she jumped into the boat herself. The boat swayed and floated away from the rock it had been chained to. Zoya sat at the stern. Solovyov meekly rowed toward a supposed exit from the bathing area.

'Not there!'

Zoya showed him two small crags. There was no longer any water between them, only foam. But this was where the boat passed through. The water had no set direction in that spot. There were no dangers hiding underwater here. Solovyov was able to row out of the bathing area and get a safe distance away. Only then did he dare raise his head. The shore they had left was calm and no visible signs of pursuit could be observed. The open ground that loomed over the bathing area was empty. The Vorontsov palace stood out on the mountain like a gleaming rectangle.

Solovyov relaxed too early. He realized when he saw the boat's stern in the air that they were on the crest of a wave.

'Head into the wave!' Zoya commanded 'Row right! Right again!'

The boat handled poorly. It seemed cumbersome and unwieldy to Solovyov, and too big for one rower (why had Zoya not once offered to row with him?). On the other hand, he sensed all the boat's fragility and insignificance in comparison with the night waves. After adapting to this, he began rowing more evenly. Solovyov's motions were no longer spasmodic, and the oars rowed ever less frequently at the air. They went along the shore, roughly one hundred meters away. They met the waves head-first. They aligned the boat on its primary course.

About an hour and a half later, Solovyov felt like he had rowed his hands raw. Zoya gave him her handkerchief and he wrapped one hand with it. He used his own T-shirt for the other hand. Solovyov was tired, too. He had used a lot of unnecessary motion in the beginning but now that his rowing might be considered exemplary, he had very little strength left. He tried to alternate, rowing two different ways. Moving the oars with only his arms allowed him to rest his back. And, conversely, he could leave his arms motionless and push the boat forward by moving his back. This helped, but not significantly.

Solovyov rested during the intervals between large waves. He had started to feel nauseous from exhaustion and rocking. He felt like lying down in the bottom of the boat—just as cadet Larionov had once felt like lying down in the bottom of a trench—and enjoying the repose. He was so worn out that the sea's choppiness no longer evoked his fear. Zoya's presence was all that prevented him from lying down.

'I have no more strength,' Solovyov finally said.

They landed on some sort of beach. Even after the front of the boat had knocked into the pebbles, Solovyov still could not believe this was the end of their sail. He sat, bent, with his hands on the oars, and could not find the strength within to go ashore. With Zoya's help—he was no longer shy of his condition—he jumped heavily over the side and took a few strides through the surf.

Zoya attempted to push the boat away from the shore but it came right back. She took the boat by the remnants of the chain and led it to the breakwater. The current was different there. Rocking forlornly by the concrete wall, the boat began slowly drifting toward the open sea.

There were lounge chairs visible under a beach awning. Without saying a word, Solovyov wandered to the closest chair. He was out like a light before he had a chance to collapse onto it.

The beach caretaker woke them up in the morning. He

shook Solovyov by the shoulder and told someone (Zoya?) that vacationers would be coming here after breakfast at the guesthouse.

'What guesthouse?' Solovyov asked in a silent whisper.

He pulled his T-shirt, with brown spots from his bloody palms, out from under his head.

'Blue Wave,' said the caretaker.

Zoya was sitting on the next lounge chair, hugging her knees. Solovyov went to the water and rinsed off.

About fifteen minutes later, they were already on the highway, where they boarded a shuttle van to Yalta. Solovyov fell asleep right away when he got home and slept until evening. When he woke up, he could not believe what had happened during the night. On his first attempt to get out of bed, he realized it was all true. He got up on the second attempt.

His primary thought was about the text. Which had been procured with such difficulty and which he had never even glanced at. From the bag with the break-in tools he extracted a crumpled plastic folder, pierced in ten places. The papers inside were in a lamentable state.

That was not his primary source of distress, though. There were only three sheets of paper. They contained a detailed explanation of what comprised the unseemly behavior of Baroness von Kruger, who had dinner at The Bear restaurant with her four former husbands. All the baroness's husbands turned out to be officers. The general's relative was uncommonly consistent in her passions. Detailed descriptions were made of the husbands, down to their military ranks and places of service. In the general's final edits to the text, there were notes in the margin with the years of death and places of interment (they were buried in various locations) for each of the participants at the infamous luncheon. In touching briefly on the menu, the general highlighted in particular that there were oysters and—naturally—oyster knives on the table. 'Do officers of today's army,' the general asked rhetorically, 'know what an oyster knife is?' The general offered no answer in the initial text, but gave one in the margins of the final version: 'No.'

The text they had discovered said nothing about other events. There was no need to assume a possible continuation of the memoirs. The text ended in the middle of the page, under which there was a date (13/07/74) and the laconic 'Dictated by me. Gen. Larionov.' What had compelled Taras to keep these three particular sheets of paper at work? Perhaps that was the most enigmatic aspect of the whole matter.

12

Solovyov headed to the conference the next morning. Zoya saw him off at the bus station. She went to the museum after putting Solovyov on the Simferopol trolleybus. They had called Zoya the night before and insistently requested she show up at work. They had few employees and some were on vacation, so there was nobody to tell visitors about Chekhov.

The trip to Kerch was not short. Crimea, which had formerly seemed small to Solovyov, was revealing previously unaccounted for expanses that required time to cross. Discoveries of this sort, thought the drowsy Solovyov, were what distinguished field research from office work. He fell asleep somewhere near the Nikitsky Botanical Garden. The trolleybus was already driving through Simferopol when he opened his eyes.

Solovyov had a snack in Simferopol. He bought a smoked chicken leg at the station and ate it without bread, washing it down with cold beer. It was delicious, if unrefined. He wiped his hands and mouth with a napkin. He tossed the bone to a dog that came to him; there are lots of stray dogs in southern cities. He took his unfinished beer bottle and headed for the platform. There was about an hour until the next local train to Kerch.

There were already people on the platform. Two women with children. Wearing cotton dresses that had wilted in the heat. One wearing a bucket hat, the other a straw hat that had slid back. Both with suitcases. Solovyov sat down on a bench, took a swig from the bottle, and set it alongside his foot. A peasant man with a sack on his shoulder. It was immediately obvious he was a peasant. A woman collecting bottles. A plastic bag in one hand, a stick in the other, to check the rubbish bins. Dark blue eyelids. Crimson lips. The tanned skin of a person who spent all her time outside.

'May I have the bottle?'

Solovyov nodded. The lady swished what was left at the bottom of the bottle and pressed it to her mouth. She sat down on Solovyov's bench (the bottle was sent into the bag with a clink). Leaned against the back. Pulled a cigarette butt out of the bin and lit it with delight.

A piglet hopped out of the peasant's sack, squealed, and began running around the platform. It was afraid to jump down. The peasant (they are capable of this) caught the piglet without losing his dignity. Put it in the sack and tied it. Lit a cigarette.

'And that's the end of democracy,' said the bottle collector. She was not addressing anyone in particular.

The local train somehow pulled up almost unnoticed. It was old, its paint had peeled in the sun, and there was plywood where the glass had been smashed. Everybody boarded except the bottle collector. She continued sitting on the bench; this platform was her workplace. Maybe her home, too. The carriage began to move and she disappeared. Forever, thought Solovyov, as he fell sleep. Forever . . .

He woke up about an hour later and fell back to sleep. He

thought he would never catch up on his sleep after the night in Alupka. That night, he had borrowed his own strength from the coming month and was now slowly paying it back. The palms of his hands (Zoya had smeared them with sea buckthorn oil the night before) hurt as before. And Zoya could not come with him. He caught himself thinking he was glad about that.

The owner of the piglet was sitting across from Solovyov. Solovyov observed as the sack squirmed despondently on the floor; he sympathized with the piglet. The peasant was looking out the window, lost in thought (or not thinking about anything?) There was something wood-like, cracked, in the peasant's face. It radiated motionlessness. The age-old motionlessness of the Russian peasantry, decided the young historian. That was what made the gaze so sustained, intent, and absent.

Solovyov was housed in the Hotel Crimea. The hotel's gray granite exterior presented a restrained solemnity from the late 1950s. This was apparently the city's main hotel. And the first hotel in Solovyov's life. He received his key from a sleepy woman at the reception desk ('a porter,' Solovyov whispered, since this was how he wanted to picture things).

'Close the window at night,' said the woman. 'Cats jump into the rooms.'

'Cats?'

After crossing the lobby, he turned and said, 'I love cats.'

But the woman was no longer there.

Solovyov went up to the second floor. The keyring was weighted down by a vaguely pear-shaped wooden fob, making it difficult to turn the key in the lock. Within the lock, Solovyov overcame (pressing firmly into the door) some sort of impediments invisible to the world. Dull scraping and the pear thudding against the door accompanied whatever happened inside the lock.

The door opened anyway. Solovyov looked around after entering the small rectangular room. The window faced what was not quite a garden: it was an ambiguous green environment where all the objects (bed frames, bar counters, tires) served as plant stands. There really were cats strolling along a wall overgrown with ivy.

Solovyov left his things in the room and went out into the city. He enjoyed taking a deep breath of Kerch's evening air. The sea in Kerch was not Yalta's resort sea. The sea was regarded completely differently here. It even smelled different. It had an ancient port aroma that included a light tinge of decay: seaweed on the breakwaters, fish in crates, and fruit crushed during shipment.

Solovyov walked along Kerch's main street and liked it. 'Le . . . Street,' he read on a half-faded sign. Some sort of French continuation might have followed that, and the street itself did seem a bit French to him. The crowns of old acacias had intertwined over the street's three-story houses, giving it the look of an endless gazebo. It was cool in the thick shadow that was turning to darkness. Le . . . Street. Solovyov could guess the street's full name.

He bought himself some yellow bird cherries. When he saw a pump in a courtyard, he stopped there to wash them. To do so, he had to make several motions with the pump handle (it was cast iron with a lion on the grip) and then quickly run over to the spout and put the plastic bag of cherries underneath. Solovyov filled the bag with water, turned it upside-down, and released the water. The water disappeared through a blackened metal grate. Several cherries rolled down there, too.

The cherries turned out to be delicious: ripe, but firm. Solovyov took them in pairs, by their fused stalks, and gently—one after another—removed them from their stalks with his lips. He rolled the cherries in his mouth. Delighted in their form. Carefully bit into them, sensing the cherries' special (yellow) sweetness. The flesh came away from the pits easily and the pits moved toward his lips, as if on their own, casually jumping down into Solovyov's palm.

It was already dark when he returned to the hotel. Solovyov noticed some sort of motion even before turning on the light in his room. When he flicked the switch, he saw a cat on the windowsill. The cat neither hid nor ran. He walked away calmly, even seeming to hesitate. If Solovyov had addressed him, he would have stayed. His smoke-colored tail quivered. A clump of fur, also smoke-colored, hung on the zipper of Solovyov's bag.

'So you were digging around in my bag?' Solovyov asked and then remembered, with shame, how he himself had dug around in Taras's things.

The cat looked out the window with affected indifference. He was observing Solovyov with his peripheral vision and attempting to understand what might follow this sort of tone. Anything at all could follow. When Solovyov took a step toward the window, the cat jumped down from the windowsill to the ledge.

Feeling tired after his day of travel, Solovyov decided to go to bed. He fell asleep immediately and slept dreamlessly. A heavy slapping on the floor woke him up at dawn. He opened one eye halfway and saw two cats next to his bed.

Solovyov waved his arm drowsily and the cats left, in a dignified manner. Solovyov thought that he ought to close the window after all, but fell straight back to sleep.

Participant registration for the 'General Larionov as Text' conference began at nine that morning. It took place at the Pushkin Theater, a stately building with a hint of classicism, on Kerch's central square. The city was offering the best it had for studying General Larionov as text.

Solovyov saw the registration table when he entered the theater's cool lobby. A young woman with red hair was sitting on a swiveling barstool beside the table. Her nose ring sparkled dimly.

'Solovyov, Petersburg,' said Solovyov. He thought the woman was no younger than thirty.

'Wow!' She made a full turn on the swiveling stool and was once again face-to-face with Solovyov. 'Dunya, Moscow. I'll register you, Solovyov.'

Dunya jumped down from the stool (Solovyov noticed the same kind of stools at the bar at the other end of the lobby), marked something in her papers, and held out a conference folder with the program. Solovyov opened the program and walked slowly toward the auditorium.

'Your badge,' Dunya bleated after him.

Solovyov turned. Dunya was sitting on her stool again and holding a nametag with his surname.

'Mizter, you forgot your badge,' she said, beckoning to him. 'I'll pin it on for you.'

Without getting up from her stool, Dunya pinned the nametag to Solovyov's shirt, breathed on its plastic glossiness, and wiped it with her skirt hem. Solovyov examined Dunya's untanned legs for several seconds.

'Thank you.'

He started walking away but Dunya politely took him by the elbow.

'What about your folder?'

He really had left it on the table.

'Another absent-minded professor,' said Dunya, shaking her head. 'Your type needs looking after.'

Several people were already standing behind Solovyov and he rushed to get out of their way. He glanced at the program as he walked. His paper was set for the conference's second—and final—day.

About forty minutes remained until the beginning of the morning session, so Solovyov decided to go for a walk. During that time, he managed to have a look at the Lenin monument, the post office, and the Chaika department store. When he returned to the theater, he saw Dunya by the columns. She was smoking.

'Is it time?' Solovyov politely asked.

'It's time to get out of here. The opening's the most insipid part. That's right, young man.' Dunya put out her cigarette on the column's rough surface. 'You'd be better off treating a lady to coffee. I know a place nearby.'

A Volga sedan pulled up to the theater. A fat man in a light-brown suit got out and headed toward the entrance, tucking his shirt into his pants as he walked.

'Local boss,' said Dunya. 'With a story about the cannery that's sponsoring us. You interested?'

Solovyov shrugged. Dunya made such a face at the word 'cannery' that it would have been awkward to take an interest.

As Solovyov followed the energetic Dunya, he was angry with himself for his indecisiveness. In the first place, he did want to see the conference opening. In the second place (Solovyov suddenly realized this in all its clarity), more than anything, he felt tired of Zoya. This was the start of the second reel of some strange film he did not even seem to have agreed to be involved in.

They walked half a block and ended up in a dark vaulted basement. A chandelier shaped like a steering wheel hung from an enormous hook where the basement's vaulted ceiling came together.

'This little joint reminds me of "Gambrinus",' said Dunya. 'I discovered it yesterday.'

Solovyov ordered two coffees with Chartreuse. The liqueur was served in faceted vodka glasses. Dunya poured half her shot into her coffee and drank the other half in one swallow.

'When will academician Grunsky speak?' asked Solovyov.

'I think it's actually right now. Alas, neither academician Likhachev nor academician Sakharov will be here today. So you can relax.' Dunya lit a cigarette and the smoke began rising prettily toward the steering wheel. 'I'd advise you not to get caught up in the academicians, the title has depreciated a lot. And Grunsky's just plain stupid.'

'Then how'd he get to be an academician?'

'He had enough maneuverability. Connections.' She blew out smoke in a thin stream. 'Well, and he was brownnosing everybody in charge at the Academy.'

Dunya's attitude seemed too categorical to Solovyov but he kept quiet. He refused to imagine a stupid academician.

The break was ending when they returned. The theater was crowded and the attendees' muted buzz reminded him of an intermission at an operetta. Scenery of a medieval castle in the mountains intensified that impression. The

gothic scene swaying in a draft might not have fit the conference theme but the organizers thought it created a pacifying,
romantic backdrop.

Solovyov could see a small fat man on the stage, to the
left of the castle wall. The man stood at the chairman's
table, half-facing the auditorium, with one hand thrust in
his pocket (not a flattering pose for the short-legged). Using
his free hand, he carefully piled hair on his bald spot. The
name card on the table said, 'Acad. P.P. Grunsky.' Nothing
that Dunya had reported was mentioned on the card.

There was something unnatural—in the sense of theat-
rical—about even the conference attendees' appearances.
Despite the hot spell, they were strolling around in suits
and running their hands along the lapels of their outmoded
jackets again and again. This wasn't even because of the
hot spell; the suits were blatantly out of character for their
owners. And for their faces, which were rough and devoid
of expression. These people pressed their arms to their
torsos as they walked timidly around the theater. Looked
at themselves in the mirror in the foyer. Dampened their
combs in the little fountain outside the theater and fixed
their hair. These were cannery employees, sent by their
bosses to lend the event a more mass scale. According to
the conference organizers, very broad swaths of the population should hear papers about the general.

Two cannery employees approached Grunsky and asked
for his autograph. This was audible thanks to the numerous
microphones that equipped the stage. They were all over
the place, dangling from somewhere above, like motionless
black lianas. Grunsky led the requestors to the table and
wearily, but with visible pleasure, signed the two programs

they held out to him. This was the first time in his life he had been asked for his autograph.

Solovyov and Dunya took seats in the parterre. Solovyov removed the program from his folder. Leaning toward his shoulder, Dunya ran her fingernail along the second surname listed after the break.

'Tarabukin's a terrible pain but he gets a lot done. One of the few who'll say anything relevant here. He's sitting to my right.'

Solovyov slowly turned his head. The left-handed Tarabukin was nervously noting something in a folder of papers lying on his knees. His gnarled fingers and their countless knuckles might have made an even bigger impression than his left-handedness. Tarabukin was chewing the fingernails on his right hand and kept examining them pensively.

'Before lunch . . .' Grunsky tapped his fingernail on the microphone and the hall shook with a deep, drumming sound. '. . . we have one more paper before lunch, so I ask you to focus. The floor goes to Professor Tarakubin with the paper "Larionov and Zhloba: a Textological Collision".'

'Tarabukin, if you will,' protested Tarabukin, but his voice was drowned out by the general noise.

Dunya shook with silent laughter. Meanwhile, Tarabukin was already energetically making his way to the stage. He gestured as he walked and his entire appearance expressed indignation, either from the incorrect pronunciation of his surname or the impossibility of making his way to where he was to speak.

'Quiet, please,' Grunsky tapped at the microphone again. 'One more paper before lunch. The speaker prepared *handouts*, they'll be distributed now.'

Tarabukin clambered up the little stairs onto the stage, continuing to gesture, and walked under the hanging microphones.

'. . . ucking smarty pants, what are you talking about, *handouts*? In Russian . . .'

Tarabukin stopped short when he heard he was on the air. Now he silently crossed the stage—small and rumpled—without a shadow of regret about what he had said. After Tarabukin had taken his place behind the lectern (at his height, he truly proved to be *behind* it), a heavyset woman with braids arranged on her head started making her way toward the stage. She moved slowly, placing her feet heavily on the steps, and reminding Solovyov of his high school principal, a woman nicknamed Bigfoot. Judging from the hand she extended in Grunsky's direction, she was saying something to him, but her words were inaudible.

'Who's the co-chair?' Grunsky asked again, into the microphone. 'You're the co-chair? Where were you before?'

The women answered him again after conquering the final stairs. The academician shrugged and glanced at the program.

'Nobody said anything to me about co-chairing.'

The woman who had come up on stage turned to the audience and pointed out someone on the parterre for Grunsky. Despite her gait, she certainly was not Solovyov's high school principal.

'So, may I begin?' Tarabukin asked sarcastically, but nobody was paying attention to him.

'She's corresponding member Baikalova,' said Dunya. Her face expressed delight. 'Fiesta with a bullfight.'

'There's not even a second chair here,' said Grunsky,

slightly lifting his chair by its back to illustrate. 'I don't know where you'll sit.'

'One of us should prove to be chivalrous, Petr Petrovich,' said Baikalova.

She was already within range of the microphones. Grunsky threw up his hands, 'Well, that's a fine how-do-you-do!'

Baikalova bowed low, from the waist, to Grunsky and turned to face the audience. Tarabukin, suffering, rolled his eyes. The cannery workers smiled shyly.

Grunsky approached the edge of the stage and signaled to someone to bring a second chair. A man in a pensioner's shirt with patch pockets jumped out of his seat and shook it, demonstrating to Grunsky that they were fastened not only to the neighboring seats (everyone sitting in that row shook) but also to the floor. Grunsky gestured his understanding and returned to the table.

Two men in overalls hurried up the steps to the stage. They disappeared behind the curtains but reappeared a minute later, dragging a massive throne with a scraping sound. They pulled it up to the table and explained something to Grunsky, who was grasping the back of his own chair as a precaution. Grunsky nodded and showed Baikalova the throne with a gallant gesture. She sized up Grunsky with a malicious gaze and moved heavily across the stage.

Baikalova had to ascend to the throne—which did not look out of place by the castle—in a literal sense. She first climbed onto a step attached to its base and then, holding the lion heads on the armrests, clambered up to the seat, which required some effort. Since the throne was not an item envisaged for use by someone sitting at a table, it turned out to be rather high. Baikalova's legs did not reach the floor, swinging slightly instead, like shapeless sausages, under the thin tabletop. Further beneath the tabletop—this was visible to the audience, too—the academician's feet were moving chop-chop, as if he were in the homestretch. There was no question he had won this little competition.

'Please, go ahead, colleague,' said Grunsky, turning to Tarabukin.

'Yes, do,' said Baikalova, looking down on Grunsky.

'Thank you very much,' Tarabukin responded. After thinking, he uttered it in pieces. 'Thank you. Very much.'

Leaning against the armrest furthest from Grunsky, Baikalova rested her cheek on her hand. Her lips stretched apart, forming a raspberry-colored diagonal line along her face.

Tarabukin huffily began his paper. He uttered the introductory phrases—which in and of themselves contained nothing nasty, offering a listing of sources he had used—with a bitter, almost denouncing, intonation. It was they, his sources, who took the blame for the scholar's disrespectful treatment of the scholar. It was they who answered for his mangled surname, for his ridiculous waiting on the stage, for everything that had thrown the scholar utterly off balance. Even in this difficult frame of mind, though, the presenter spoke in particular about two sources he had studied.

The first of them was General Larionov's *Notes for an Autobiography*, in Dupont's edition. Only when turning to that did Tarabukin forget the offenses committed against him. In characterizing Dupont's publication (and speaking of it with the highest praise) the speaker switched to an unusual tone, as if he were anticipating an important statement. Which is how things turned out. What Tarabukin was thinking about was the second source he had used: a heretofore unknown report by Dmitry Zhloba about his troops' entry into Yalta in November 1920. Tarabukin himself had found this source in the Archive of the Ministry of Defense.

But the researcher's revelations did not just consist of that happy finding; there was more. Propelled by a sixth sense (without which, as we know, no discoveries are made), he revealed unbelievable things by juxtaposing Zhloba's report with General Larionov's childhood remembrances.

A first glance at Tarabukin's materials for distribution made it obvious that the two texts were very closely connected. The texts had been created by utterly dissimilar people and they described completely different times. That is what made their resemblance so striking. An astonished buzz ran through the slightly hushed hall.

The most vivid coinciding occurrences in Zhloba's report and the general's recollections were in the printouts (not wishing to utter the borrowed English, *handouts*, he called them *handgrips*) that the speaker offered. Enjoying the impression he had made, Tarabukin slowly read off the first of the coinciding spots:

Fragment No. 1

Gen. Larionov	D.P. Zhloba
Notes for an Autobiography	*Report Regarding Entry into the City of Yalta*
A group of young Tatars greeted us as we entered the city. They were all on horseback, all dressed up.	. . . when we reached the city limits, a brigade on horseback greeted us. Tatars everywhere, attire:

Upon seeing our carriages, they shot into the air and shouted something in Tatar. *Maman* and my governess, *Dolly*, were very frightened but *Papa* explained to them that the Tatars were just welcoming us. *Maman* waved her hand to them. One of them rode over to the ladies' carriage, unfastened something from his saddle, and handed it to the stunned *Dolly*. 'It's kumys,' smiled the Tatar. 'Drink to your health.' *Maman* wanted to pay for it but the Tatar only flapped his arms. They shot a little more and galloped off into the mountains, going about their Tatar business. 'Charming,' said *Dolly*.

national. They began firing into the air upon seeing our armored vehicle. They didn't understand Russian. I felt uneasy but our commissar, comrade Rozaliya S. Zemlyachka, explained that this was their way of greeting. Meaning, firing weapons. I saluted them. One of them rode over to comrade Zemlyachka and handed her a canister. 'It's kumys,' said the Tatar. 'Drink to your health.' Comrade Zemlyachka signaled to him that we would receive the kumys free of charge. The Tatar flapped his arms. They turned around and galloped into the mountains. 'Very nice comrades,' said comrade Zemlyachka.

Corresponding member Baikalova, who had not received one of Tarabukin's *handgrips*, was leaning heavily on the armrest closest to Grunsky and ostentatiously squinting to peer at the papers on the table. With exaggerated amiability, the academician pushed them in Baikalova's direction but they remained in place. Glancing at the audience, Baikalova threw up her hands.

'You're sitting up too high,' Grunsky said, also to the audience. 'And therein lies your misfortune.'

There was absolute silence in the hall when Tarabukin moved on to read the second excerpt.

<u>Fragment No. 2</u>

Gen. Larionov *Notes for an* *Autobiography*	**D.P. Zhloba** *Report Regarding Entry into* *the City of Yalta*
Many paupers gathered at the corner of Autskaya and Morskaya Streets, by the Alexander Nevsky Cathedral. This was a strange and varied public. Alongside old women wrapped in black there sat young women with children, tradesmen who had succumbed to drink, and *the barefoot tramps* whom Gorky would describe later. I would not be surprised if Gorky himself had been sitting there . . . They all crossed themselves devoutly. When leaving the service, *Maman* gave something to all of them, without	We found a lumpen element by the church at the corners of Autskaya and Morskaya Streets. Predominantly of male gender. Everyone who sat there was engaged in panhandling. The appearance of one of the aforementioned persons reminded me of the proletarian writer A.M. Gorky. I will not allow the thought that this was comrade Gorky, given his location on the isle of Capri. Everyone crossed themselves. Comrade Bela Kun warned them strictly with regard to crossing themselves and seized change from their hats

exception. Her favorite was a tall, one-legged old man. He would sit, displaying his peg leg for all to view. When we walked down the stairs, out of the cathedral, he waved welcomingly with his crutch. Sometimes he bowed. Smiled at us toothlessly. And one-leggedly.

One time *Maman* forgot money and was very upset. When the old man realized that, he approached her unnoticed and gave her everything he had: a ruble and a half in change. He didn't want her to leave distressed. 'Well, isn't that just lovely?' *Maman* said, giving the money out to the paupers.

as unearned income. A one-legged old man particularly attracted comrade Kun's attention. He smiled at our comrades and waved to them with his crutch. Comrade Kun suspected him of being two-legged and ordered him to stand and produce his missing leg for inspection. When the one-legged man began to refuse, Kun kicked him in the face and forced him to empty his pockets, where there happened to be more change, beyond what had been taken away earlier. 'What was I telling you?' comrade Kun asked those present and everyone agreed with him.

Snoring became audible in the hall when Tarabukin paused. The sounds were muted, like distant thunder, but that did not make them less apparent. Academician Grunsky put his hand to his forehead and peered out from under it at his neighbor sitting at the table. Sometimes he covered his eyes with his hand and shook his head as if lamenting the co-chair he had received. It truly was Baikalova snoring. The corresponding member had fallen asleep quickly and easily while squinting at the texts that had been distributed, and now the microphone that hung over her head was broadcasting her snoring for the audience. This was first-class snoring, with a rumble on the inhale and a whistle on the exhale. With rolling and modulation, complaints and threats, sincere sighs and mockery. Unfortunately for Baikalova, Tarabukin could not find the example he needed and was feverishly flipping sheet after sheet. The ruthless academician took the table microphone, walked around the table on tiptoe, and brought it right to his co-chair's nose. The hall shook with a thundering peal. The snorer awoke and looked, crazed, at the microphone the academician was extending.

'We have a schedule to keep,' said Baikalova in a husky voice.

With an emcee's gesture, Grunsky pointed at Baikalova and returned to his place.

'What a jerk,' said Dunya, beginning to laugh.

'I won't . . .' Tarabukin was still shifting his papers around. 'I won't, because of the lack of time, read all the examples, I have twenty-three of them . . . But excerpt No. 19 . . . uh-huh, there it is . . . I'll still cite this one.'

Fragment No. 19

Gen. Larionov	**D.P. Zhloba**
Notes for an Autobiography	*Report Regarding Entry into the City of Yalta*
One time I *vanished*. I was around six years old. I left our house without saying anything to anybody and	They'd already reported to me that the general hadn't evacuated. We'd searched the whole city for him. I rode to

wandered aimlessly. Why did I do that? I don't know. I didn't have any set goals, I remember that. I walked downhill, along Botkinskaya, examining my surroundings. Laborers were placing a huge carved cabinet on a cart and the carthorse was pawing at the ground, its flanks trembling. Both the cart and even the horse seemed small compared to the cabinet. The cart began moving heavily up the hill and the laborers supported the cabinet from both sides. This contraption moved jerkily, in time with the horse's steps. With a sad creaking. I stared after them, until they disappeared around the corner. And even then they continued creaking, unseen, for a time.

Later, I ended up on the embankment. I stood, leaning against the fence at the Tsar's Garden, and watched street musicians. Cello, two violins, and a

the general's house at the head of the advance party but he wasn't there. 'Vanished, did he?' shouted comrade B. Kun. 'Vanished,' confirmed the maid. 'He went out an hour ago. Didn't say anything.' Comrade Zemlyachka jabbed her in the thigh with a pen knife and we galloped downhill, along Botkinskaya Street. A group of laborers was loading a cabinet with a two-headed eagle onto a cart. 'Have you seen the general?' I asked the laborers. 'We saw him,' said the laborers. 'He walked by here in 1888. And it's 1920 now.'

'Ah, so that's it!' I shouted. 'That's your idea of a joke? Well, here's mine.' I lashed their mare with my whip and she dashed off. The cabinet fell on the roadway but didn't break. A sturdy item. The laborers silently went after the cart. I ordered that the cabinet be brought into the general's house.

flute. They played there for many more years, I saw them on each of our trips to Yalta. My back could feel the cool rhombuses of the fence. I admired their ancient Jewish faces, nubby fingers with fine hair on the phalanges, and dusty black clothing. Their leader was an old violinist. The wind brought his long gray hair to his lips, flattening it there. He would blow the hair away or toss it by nodding his head. He made horrible grimaces as he played, and I watched him, unable to tear myself away. Everybody knew this was an expression of devotion to the music. Nobody laughed. The musicians played music by request or for no particular reason. Copper coins scattered into the open violin case. There was nothing they couldn't play. To this day, I think most of them when I hear the word *music*. I listened to those

We saw some musicians by the Tsar's Garden. I halted the squad and listened, spellbound. They were playing on two little violins and one big one. Plus a wind instrument flute. 'The soldiers' hearts have coarsened from war,' I told the musicians. 'Play something touching for them.'

A violinist stepped forward and said, 'Soldiers, have a listen to Oginsky's *Polonaise*.' He swung his bow and the musicians simultaneously began playing. The first violinist's face changed as he played.

'He's full of emotion,' comrade Kun told those present, a large tear flowing down his own cheek. As I listened to the heartfelt music of the *Polonaise*, I thought we'd missed the general after all. He couldn't, in his right mind, stay in the city of Yalta.

We stayed there a fairly long time. Several privates dismounted and sat on the ground, listening to the

musicians for a long time—
the entire time they played
there. I didn't budge, even
when they were taking their
ceremonial bows. Only
when their instruments
ended up in their cases was
the magic gone. I knew then
that not another sound
would be heard.

I continued my journey
along the embankment.
The embankment was
narrow then, not like it is
now. I walked right next to
the cast-iron railings; the
sea's edge was just on the
other side. My hand slid
over the lower crosspiece
of the railing: it was black
with silvery, hanging
drops. I collected those
drops in my hand and they
ran along my arm, flowing
up my sleeve. That was
nice.

I turned on Morskaya
Street and ended up by a
pharmacy I knew. It was
cool inside the pharmacy. It
smelled of oak cabinets and

music. I didn't prevent them.
And didn't say anything. And
comrade Kun didn't say
anything, either, though he
wanted to in the beginning.
That's how it seemed to me.
And the horses stood still
and didn't stomp their feet
because an animal
understands everything,
even music. It's a medical
fact. Horses have never failed
me, that's a fact, too. But
people have failed me more
than once. I place little hope
in them.

Then we went to ride
along the embankment. It's
narrow so we re-formed into
columns of two as we rode.
A horse loves that formation.
I rode silently. Generally I'm
quiet when I'm on the move,
so I don't get distracted from
my thoughts. And I look at
the horse's mane if I'm not in
battle. I finger the mane with
my hand. Now and then you
burrow your face in the
mane, too. The mane has a
special smell.

medicines. 'What can I do for you?' the pharmacist asked and patted me on the head. The tip of his nose was bulbous. I was proud to have come here by myself. I was quiet because I didn't need anything at that time. After showing me a chair, the pharmacist disappeared into the next room. The chair was huge, with leathery folds. It reminded me of an old bulldog. I have not seen such a good chair since. The pharmacist brought me a cough drop. I popped it in my mouth and went outside.

Finally, I ended up at the jetty. I stepped onto it because that, it seemed, was where my road lay. When I reached the end of the jetty, I saw that the sea surrounded me on three sides. I didn't grasp that when I was walking. But I saw it after stopping. Wet green stones rocked from

From the embankment, we turned on Morskaya Street and went to the pharmacy. Comrade Gusin and I. He needed a new bandage because the old one was soaked with blood. Comrade Zemlyachka had licked away the blood that soaked through. 'What can I do for you?' asked the pharmacist. It seemed I'd seen this person with the weather-beaten face somewhere.

'Change his dressings,' I told the pharmacist and pointed at Gusin. While the pharmacist bandaged Gusin, I sat in a soft chair. It was cool and calm. I could have stayed there forever.

'Try not to lose blood, comrade,' the pharmacist told Gusin in parting. 'A person only has six liters.'

'Two three-liter jars,' joked comrade Zemlyachka.

We set off along the embankment again. Where comrade Kun touched me on the waves, the wind droned somewhere at the top of the lighthouse but—and this was most important—there was no more road. I stood, pressing my back against the lighthouse, and I was scared. I thought the jetty had pulled away and started moving out from under my feet. I froze with horror when I sensed the pitching. I got down on all fours, pressed into the warm, rough wall, and crawled to the opposite side of the lighthouse. Only there did I dare rise to my feet and slowly, step by step, head toward the other end of the jetty. When I raised my head, I saw my father: his anxious face, his arms open wide for an embrace. I knew that those arms would not allow me to perish now. I ran the rest of the distance. I ran to my father and cried. I threw myself into his arms.

the leg—there!—with the crop. Lightly. And pointed at the jetty with that same crop. I looked around and couldn't believe my eyes: the general. In the flesh. Just standing, at the edge, arms on his chest. The general!

Our sailors were already keeping watch at the jetty. That's why we were in no hurry. The general already had nowhere to go but into the water. Comrade Kun proposed tying up the general along with two critically wounded Whites and tossing them into the sea, but comrade Zemlyachka condemned that method as ultra-liberal and bloodless. Comrade Kun was offended and later drowned all the critically wounded without consulting comrade Zemlyachka. They galloped on to the jetty and I stayed on the embankment. The general walked slowly toward them.

Tarabukin poured himself some water from a pitcher as he finished excerpt No. 19. He drank thirstily and with a light moan, like a person who still has a lot left to say. Grunsky sensed the speaker's frame of mind and stood up from his chair: this was an eloquent appeal to finish up. These gestures were inaccessible for Baikalova, who was lodged in her throne and limited to ostentatious glances at her watch. Tarabukin had been standing half-facing the co-chairs but now quickly turned in the opposite direction, toward the second-tier loge (left side), and began expounding on the results of his intertextual analysis.

And those results—paradoxical to the highest degree!— consisted of the following.

First. The events described by the general (1888) preceded, chronologically, what Zhloba (1920) recounted. That said, however, the time when Zhloba prepared his report preceded the time when the general created his memoirs (presumably the late 1950s to the early 1960s).

Second. Notwithstanding the obvious resemblance of the chosen compositions, textual borrowing from either author could not be ascertained. Further. From the scholar's point of view, there was not even a hint of one author being familiar with the other's text.

Third. Both texts were also impossible to trace back to a common source because, despite their closeness, they recount (and here the speaker pounded his fist on the lectern) different events.

Tarabukin poured from the pitcher again. Standing as before, with his back to the co-chairs and his side to the audience, he proceeded with the second glass. The noise of Tarabukin's deep swallows rang from the hall's loudspeakers, sounding like a gigantic metronome. Grunsky, who had just sat down, stood again and tapped at the microphone.

'We have a schedule to keep,' said Baikalova, in order not to yield the initiative to the academician.

Powerless to ignore what was happening, Tarabukin turned sharply toward the co-chairs and grazed the pitcher with his elbow. After a slow-motion, almost infinite moment of flight, the pitcher shattered to smithereens on the stage.

'I understand,' said Tarabukin, quietly but tragically, 'that standing between a person and his lunch is a thankless matter but I still have a fourth point. And I ask that it be heard out.'

Grunsky and Baikalova stared wordlessly at the same point in the distance, as if they were in the finale of some sort of play. The falling pitcher had drawn them together a little. Both they and the audience members understood it was best to hear everything the speaker had to say. Grunsky sat down, in a clear expression of submissiveness.

Tarabukin's fourth point turned out to be his longest. By developing the ideas of Alexander Veselovsky on historical poetics and Vladimir Propp on the morphology of the folk-tale—while polemicizing with them at the same time—the researcher transferred conversation about the resemblance of the general's and Zhloba's texts into the realm of the correlation of motifs. To Tarabukin's misfortune (and, admittedly, the attendees', too), he got bogged down in clarifying the reasons he agreed and disagreed with his predecessors. Tarabukin understood well that these details were unnecessary but drifted further and further away from the topic of common motifs, even as he strove with all his might to return to it.

The speaker's—and the audience's—anxiety increased with every minute. With bated breath, the whole audience followed his tragic floundering in the maelstrom of scholarly thought, but there was no life ring. They did not want to throw it from the presidium; it could not be thrown from the audience. The cannery workers (the portion of the audience sympathizing most with Tarabukin) were ready to applaud, but the speaker needed to stop or at least pause for them to do so. He did not stop. Shrinking his head into his shoulders, he spoke ever faster and less distinctly, as if he hoped to find in his flow of speech some magic word that would crush his opponents for good.

When Tarabukin looked up from the lectern, he saw Grunsky's all-forgiving eyes. Baikalova was pensively examining her fingernails. This was the final blow for the speaker and he burst into tears. Thunderous applause rang out in the hall. Everyone headed off for lunch.

13

The cannery director headed up the column of people exiting the theater. After chasing off the factory employees who had begun attaching themselves to the column, he led the researchers to Cafeteria No. 8 on Lenin Street, where lunch had been set for the conference's participants and guests. Grunsky walked to the director's right, Baikalova to his left. The director's arms were flung half-open, as if welcoming a speedy oncoming wind; this kept making the edges of his jacket flap against the co-chairs, who were trying not to fall behind him. The column's leading edge was moving through the middle of Lenin Street, a pedestrian area, splitting the oncoming walkers into two even groups that flowed around the column. Everyone in the city knew the cannery director. Even from afar, pedestrians yielded the road to him and his scholars, regardless of their attitude toward his wares, which spawned controversy.

Inside the cafeteria, there was a smell of bleach and unappetizing food that had been eating into the establishment's walls for decades. Spray cans of air freshener that were used at the factory director's request (the cafeteria workers pointed them at the artificial flowers on the table) only worsened the situation. They added a sickening, sweetish undertone without removing the old smell.

The positioning of the rectangular tables reminded Solovyov of his old school cafeteria. A paper tablecloth covered each table, which seated four. Solovyov had already started sitting down at one but then, at the last minute, he noticed Dunya waving to him from the other end of the room. She was standing by a big oak table that was unlike the others. Solovyov hesitated for a moment then walked toward her. As a member of the conference's organizing committee, Dunya had been seated at the same table as the cannery director, Grunsky, Grunsky's secretary, Baikalova, and a man with crossed eyes. Dunya had decided to invite her new acquaintance.

Tarabukin was the last to enter the cafeteria. After finishing his presentation, he had initially entertained no thoughts of food. Tarabukin had categorically refused to go to the cafeteria with everyone. He walked down to the parterre, collapsed in a fourth-row seat, and sat there motionless for a few minutes. But he began to feel hungry after calming down a little so, after some hesitation, decided to go to the cafeteria anyway.

Right from the start, it looked to him as if there were no empty places; Tarabukin felt like nobody was expecting him. His tortuous decision to come to lunch had suddenly turned out to have unwelcome results for everyone, effectively rendering it ridiculous. His tragic figure in the doorway made everyone fall silent.

'As might have been expected, there aren't any places,' Tarabukin said quietly.

It turned out, however, there were still empty places at

three tables. As Tarabukin (who was a little flustered) was choosing where to sit, the cannery director rose a little and—pressing his necktie to his stomach—loudly invited the latecomer to his table. The invitation was accepted. Tarabukin proudly straightened his shoulders and began shuffling over to the director's table.

Women from the cannery helped the cafeteria workers carry lunches to the tables. They built pyramids of dishes on flowered plastic trays, lifted them in one sharp motion, and, weighted down, transported them through the dining hall. They placed them on the corner of a table and neatly unloaded them with help from those sitting at the table. The soup and main course were served in identical dishes inscribed *SocNutr*. The dessert was in cups with the same inscription; the handles were broken to stave off theft. The handles of the aluminum spoons had been twisted into spirals for the same reason. The fork handles had no spirals since they had been brought from the cannery for the conference (forks were not used in Cafeteria No. 8). As it happened, there were no knives, even at the cannery.

Despite the uniform crockery, the meal service was not identical for all attendees. Solovyov noticed that at his table (unlike at the others), some olives stuffed with shrimp had appeared and there was black caviar gleaming bashfully from a *SocNutr* salad dish with chipped edges. Dunya caught Solovyov's gaze and, barely perceptibly, mimed a sigh. As someone clued-in, she knew there was no equality in the world.

'I'd like to introduce you to Valery Leonidovich,' said Grunsky, turning to the cannery director. 'He's one of the managers at the Solovyov Foundation.'

The director stopped spreading caviar on his bread and looked at Valery Leonidovich.

'And I'd like to introduce Solovyov himself,' said Dunya, with a smile.

'At such a young age . . .' began the director, but then he suddenly went silent and finished spreading his bread with caviar.

'Why was the conference moved from Yalta to Kerch, anyway?' Baikalova asked Valery Leonidovich. 'After all, Yalta is the general's city.'

Grunsky rolled his eyes, unnoticed by Baikalova. The same expression flashed across his secretary's face; he was a young man with dark hair parted down the middle.

'What, don't you like it here?' asked the director, making a showy gesture at the table.

'I'll answer your question about why it was moved,' said Tarabukin. 'The Fund simply didn't have enough money for Yalta.'

Valery Leonidovich rubbed the end of his nose. He seemed to think it unnecessary to comment on Tarabukin's statement. One of his eyes was directed at Baikalova, the other at the cannery director. It felt to Tarabukin as if they were not even looking at him. The reality of things was rather different.

'Really, where, as a matter of fact, can that money come from?' Tarabukin went on, his fury growing. 'Where, I ask you, can it come from, if the Foundation's renting half a palace in the center of Petersburg? If the salaries for people who *help scholarship* are the sort even a Nobel laureate wouldn't dream of? Mind you, I'm only speaking right now about the legal side of their activities . . .'

Tarabukin had switched to an impassioned whisper and everyone sitting at the table stopped eating at once.

'Forgive me, what's your name?' Valery Leonidovich asked Tarabukin. Baikalova and the cannery director simultaneously introduced themselves by name and patronymic.

Grunsky's secretary giggled.

'Valery Leonidovich asked for Nikandr Petrovich's name and patronymic,' said Dunya, unperturbed.

'Nikandr Petrovich,' said Valery Leonidovich, 'do me a favor: never count someone else's money. Never. That can end badly.'

'Are you threatening me?' Tarabukin asked slowly.

Those sitting at the neighboring tables began turning around. Valery Leonidovich's eyes diverged to opposite ends of the room. Grunsky's secretary sighed and served himself more shrimp-stuffed olives.

'A young person's body needs shrimp,' said Grunsky.

'Are you really Solovyov?' asked the cannery director.

'I really am,' said Solovyov.

He felt Dunya step on his foot under the table. The director pulled a business card out of his pocket and handed it to Solovyov.

'You don't regret that the conference is taking place in Kerch?'

'No,' said Solovyov, 'I don't regret it.'

There was still an hour and a half of free time remaining after lunch. Dunya suggested to Solovyov that they go to Mount Mithridat. Dunya thought it should be interesting for him, as a historian. Solovyov nodded pensively.

They walked up the mountain along dusty little streets that had a slummy look. A foot could slip easily on the roadway's loose cobblestones, and Dunya nearly fell once. She linked her arm through Solovyov's after that. The trees ended with the last buildings, the cobblestones underfoot changed to crushed limestone, and, gradually, the road turned into a path. Solovyov thought they were wading in a sea of wormwood that hung over the road. A petrified, motionless sea. There was something biblical in that image that did not correspond to post-lunch strolls, and he tried to free himself from Dunya's arm without being noticed. Dunya, however, noticed, but didn't let on to Solovyov.

Dunya was talking about the city of Pantikapaion and King Mithridates. She was unexpectedly fervent in describing Pantikapaion's vexed relationship with the superpower of his time. They approached the ruins of Mithridates's palace. A large lizard was sitting on a chunk of a column.

'After his own son betrayed him, Mithridates ordered a slave to stab him with a sword.'

Dunya made a dramatic stabbing lunge and the displeased lizard crawled down onto the ground. It did not like the sharp motions.

Solovyov sat down on one of the chunks of the ruins. It was hot. Warmed air was rising, visibly, over other chunks. It seemed to Solovyov that those hazy-transparent streams were ancient history that had lingered in some inconceivable way until his arrival but were now evaporating from the remnants of rock, under the heat of the sun. Might Mithridates have placed his palm on this column? In the evening, when the sea was already blowing cool air and the column was still warm? After ordering everyone to leave— concubines, bathhouse attendants, and bodyguards—did it really matter who? And then he himself would place his palm on this column and stand there? And sense its porous surface? And admire the fading strait? Looking out at where the sun turns into the sea, not tearing himself away until his eyes began to smart? Of course he might have. How, then, does his history differ from the general's history? Both fought in Crimea. Neither could hold on to Crimea. Everyone falls into exactly the same traps.

The evening session bore a very promising title: 'The Other General.' Grunsky and Baikalova co-chaired again, this time sitting side-by-side in identical chairs. The throne and the previous scenery were gone from the stage. Instead of a medieval castle, a tavern on the Lithuanian border now swayed slightly behind the co-chairs' backs. The cannery director thought this backdrop acclimated the audience to the session's informal character.

As he announced the first paper, academician Grunsky expressed the hope that the post-lunch presentations would offer a fresh view of the question and that *generaliana* might possibly become a new word. The academician likened blind following of a source to splitting hairs and pledged his support to everyone unafraid of breaking with tradition. In passing, he recalled Prof. Nikolsky's (Solovyov winced) proposed classification of researchers—offered in his *Archivists and Orators*—and declared Nikolsky's approach methodologically unsound. After condemning tradition-alism as a phenomenon, the chair turned over the floor to a presenter with the surname Kvasha. As Kvasha was coming on stage, Baikalova said she endorsed her colleague's remarks and expressed certainty that the vener-able scholar's nontraditional orientation might be a good stimulus for many young people dedicating themselves to science. The audience looked spontaneously at Grunsky's secretary.

'That's in revenge for the throne,' Dunya whispered to Solovyov.

Kvasha was already standing at the lectern. He had dark skin and closely cut hair; he was fairly gloomy. After asking to be forgiven for playing with words, he began by saying that his innovation—the paper was called 'General Larionov as Holy Fool'—had its own tradition. Needless to say, he was referring to Alexander Ya. Petrov-Pokhabnik's article, 'The General's Holy Foolishness', published back in 1932 in *The Phenomenology of Holy Foolishness*.

This article listed some of the general's traits and actions that did not fit with the usual accepted notions of army life overall, or with the officer corps' upper echelon, in particular. Among other things, there were references to the general's recurrent conversations with horses, his pathological (in the author's opinion) passion for railroad transport, and also the four birds (crane, raven, swallow, and starling) that lived in the general's train car, something witnesses had confirmed; some were cited in Alexei Ravenov's article 'The Blue Train Carriage.' Beyond those facts, there were also veiled allusions regarding certain allegedly strange orders from the general immediately before the Reds captured Yalta. Nothing concrete was said about these orders except that Larionov's subordinates were extraordinarily surprised to hear them. It was apparently at this time that the term 'holy fool' was first applied to the general.

Kvasha began his criticism of Petrov-Pokhabnik's work by offering details from the author's biography. Kvasha had

managed to ascertain that before Petrov-Pokhabnik evacuated from Crimea, he had been registered as holding the
position of stableman (Kvasha was of the opinion that this
may explain Petrov-Pokhabnik's jealousy toward the general's conversations with horses, as well as his obvious distaste
for railroad transport) in the army entrusted to the general,
after which, following his move from Constantinople to
Prague, he made a living writing out clean copies of works
by the Prague Linguistic Circle. Having grown accustomed
to the process of making copies, Petrov-Pokhabnik himself
did not even realize he was writing his first paper on the
informational structure of sentences, evoking Roman
Jakobson's unfeigned amazement. Petrov-Pokhabnik was
forced to leave the circle in the early 1930s as a result of his
openly Saussurean understanding of the problems of
synchrony and diachrony. Members of the circle were
prepared to forgive him anything at all, just not following
Ferdinand de Saussure.

It was during that same period—while making a clean
copy of a collection of articles, *The Phenomenology of Holy
Foolishness*—that the former stableman would prepare and
submit his piece about the general for the collection. As a
person who gave his all to his material, Petrov-Pokhabnik
himself began holyfooling it a bit, too. He would walk
Prague's streets barefoot in any season—something people
there still recall—and shock passers-by with announcements
about how there had simply not been any truly scientific
studies of holy foolishness until his. Sometimes he tossed
stones at the windows of the Prague Linguistic Circle.

Oddly enough, Kvasha's primary grievance with his predecessor was that he did not understand *the phenomenology of*

holy foolishness. His predecessor's infatuation with holy fools' external attributes (this infatuation manifested itself, among other things, in the curses Petrov-Pokhabnik addressed to his opponents) meant he could not gain genuine insight into holy foolishness as an occurrence. From Kvasha's point of view, by focusing on the eccentric side of the matter, Petrov-Pokhabnik did not discern the foremost aspect of holy foolishness: the spiritual sense.

Alongside this was the Prague researcher's misunderstanding of several Church Slavonic texts. After all, noted the unrelenting Kvasha, Petrov-Pokhabnik's previous line of work did not assume his familiarity with Church Slavonic. Kvasha himself knew the language perfectly, which allowed him to not only quote Church Slavonic texts with ease but also to fully understand them. After briefly touching upon the history of the study of holy foolishness as a whole, referencing myriad articles from around the world, Kvasha appealed for the most important points to be stressed, and then moved on to examine an issue related to the general.

Kvasha did not deny elements of holy foolishness in the general's behavior. Beyond that, he showed—basing his discussion on research into the hagiography of holy fools—that the general's contemporaries' recollections about him were often rooted in ancient Russian examples. For the presenter, one of the key points of this juxtaposition was the description of holy foolishness as being *dead for the world*. '"The hagiographical hero",' Kvasha read, bringing his glasses to his eyes to read from Tatyana Rudi's 'On the Topic of the Hagiography of Holy Fools', 'withdraws from the everyday situation, from life in his "native" society, and shifts into another society or—from the point of view of that previous society—into an "alien" one, as if he has ceased to exist for it (the previous society) and has thus shifted within it to the status of "dead".' After finishing the quotation from Rudi's article, the researcher offered eloquent examples of how the general left his society.

First and foremost, he addressed statements about the birds staying in the train car with the general and mentioned, as a parallel, a story (from the Kiev Caves Patericon) about Isaac of the Kiev Caves, in which an incident with a raven served to push Isaac into becoming a holy fool. The presenter, however, answered in the negative regarding whether the general's holy foolishness began with the appearance of the aforementioned birds in the train car.

Continuing the avian theme, Kvasha also recalled parallels that were closer to the general, both in terms of time and line of work. He had in mind facts from the biography of Russian Field Marshal Alexander Suvorov, who did not consider it disgraceful to crow like a rooster in cases of objective necessity. And so, after announcing for all to hear that he would attack the Poles under Kościuszko's command at the first rooster's crowing, he misled them (the Poles). In fact, the field marshal himself cock-a-doodle-doo'd that evening, without waiting for the morning roosters. He also flapped his arms against his sides, striving for an external resemblance to a bird. His troops marched out at twilight and thoroughly routed the enemy. Under more tranquil circumstances, the great commander was known to wake his soldiers with a cock-a-doodle-doo.

Beyond that—and this was the closest parallel to the general's behavior—at Great Lent, Suvorov ordered that one room in his house be strewn with sand, then he arranged potted firs and pines there and let in birds. The birds were released into the wild after Easter, upon the arrival of warm weather.

Needless to say, the presenter mentioned the general's infamous conversations with horses, something Petrov-Pokhabnik had examined in his day, too. Kvasha considered his predecessor's coverage of this topic detailed but tendentious.

Kvasha also acknowledged that the general's ride on a cart with a load of sand along the frozen Sivash was not exactly traditional for the upper echelons of the officer corps. Despite the ride being explainable—to verify the ice's strength—the method itself could not but provoke questions.

In working with materials from the Crimean Agricultural Archive, Kvasha was also able to discover a statement about how the general ordered soldiers and officers to help peasants plow the land in their free time away from battle. As grounds for this order, he cited the expropriation of the peasants' horses for the cavalry, which obliged the army to at least help them (the peasants), if only in this way. Irritated by having to fulfill functions not appropriate for them, according to the discovered document, the officers 'indulged in grumbling.' All that reconciled them with the strange order was that the general personally harnessed himself up and pulled a plow, accompanied by a tiller of the land who smiled, bewildered. In analyzing the fact that he had cited, the presenter cautioned attendees against considering this a complex form of Tolstoyism. Despite the special places in Lev Tolstoy's writings for both the horse theme (*Strider, The Story of a Horse*) and the railroad theme (*Anna Karenina*), the writer's position on religious issues was not close to the general's. It is well known, too, that Lev Tolstoy's tilling of the land did not mean he foresaw the human being replacing the horse.

Amidst the extensive material that drew Kvasha's scrutiny, there was a special place for the famous instance when the general was being photographed in a coffin. Going against long-standing research traditions, the presenter was not inclined to explain that action simply with the general's eccentricity. From Kvasha's point of view, in this instance, the general's striving for the *dead world* received one of its most visible expressions. The presenter also reminded his listeners that some saints chose a coffin as their permanent residence.

In Kvasha's opinion, this intense attention to the theme of death was a distinguishing feature for the general. As a component of his profession, death, it seemed, needed to become a customary thing for him ('Although can one grow accustomed to death?' Kvasha asked, taking his gaze away from the lectern for a moment) and, in some sense, workaday. That is likely how things were during the general's service in the active army. His—if it could be expressed this way—liveliest interest in death began manifesting itself after the Civil War, and only grew over the years.

The general gathered information about the lives but, even more meticulously, the deaths of his fellow pupils, brothers-in-arms, and even enemies, at least those who did not leave him indifferent. He even created two folders, accordingly labeling them *Living* and *Dead*. One of the folders—the choice depended on the state of the person of interest to the general—held a sheet with basic information about each person's life or death. The *Living* folder was initially unbelievably plump, while the *Dead* folder seemed nearly weightless. The situation changed over time. The general was forced, ever more frequently, to transfer sheets from one folder to the other. This continued until only one lone sheet remained in the *Living* folder. That was the sheet titled *General Larionov*.

And then the general began to doubt the accuracy of the records he had kept. He lost faith that he was the only one alive and all the others had died. This appeared illogical. 'Why,' noted the general on the sole remaining sheet, 'am I, who should have been shot back in 1920, alive, but those whom nobody had planned to shoot are dead?' The situation seemed so provocative to him that he transferred all the sheets from the *Dead* folder into the *Living* folder. After a pause, he put his own sheet in the *Dead* folder. Only that way—Kvasha raised his gaze to the audience again—was it possible not to allow the living and the dead to mix.

The researcher also examined, apart from the other proceedings, two oral stories about the general taken down by a folklore expedition in the Crimean village of *Izobil'noe*. The first told how, allegedly, the general took Perekop without the permission of Anton Denikin, Commander-in-Chief of the White Army, and sent Denikin a telegram with the following content: 'Glory to God, glory to us, Perekop's captured, it's here with us.' The second story described a Christmas dinner that took place in the commander-in-chief's Sevastopol headquarters. In answer to Denikin's question about why General Larionov, who was sitting at the table, was not eating, the general replied, 'It's Lent, dear father, one mustn't eat before the first star.' Purportedly, Denikin ordered right then and there that the general be awarded a star.

Kvasha's paper subjected the stories to criticism, both from a factological perspective and for the handling of information sources. In brief, that boiled down to the following:

1) the commander-in-chief during the period under examination was no longer Anton Denikin but Baron Petr Wrangel;

2) General Larionov had not taken Perekop but had, rather, defended it; and

3) stories about Alexander Suvorov were precursor texts for both accounts.

In the initial story about the dispatch in verse form, it was not Perekop under discussion but the Turkish fortress Turtukai; additionally, the letter was addressed to none other than Field Marshal Petr Rumyantsev. In the story about the star being awarded, Suvorov was addressing not Petr Wrangel (and certainly not Anton Denikin) but Catherine the Great, accordingly calling her 'dear mother'. For Kvasha, the most interesting aspect in both folkloric pieces seemed to be that folk art made no distinctions whatsoever between Generalissimo Suvorov and General Larionov. The researcher called that circumstance 'symptomatic'.

In concluding his paper, Kvasha lamented that, other than Petrov-Pokhabnik's vague allusions, there was nothing known about the general's strange actions during the time Yalta was surrendered. The presenter called on his colleagues to make every effort to ascertain what actions might have been under discussion. From his point of view, clarifying those circumstances would not only add color to the portrait of the general, but might also shed light on the question that still remained unanswered: how, as a matter of fact, had the general remained alive?

Kvasha appeared to want to add something but Grunsky was tapping on the microphone. Kvasha tossed up his hands, put his papers in a folder, and calmly (by comparison with Tarabukin, at any rate) descended from the stage. Kvasha's conflict-free departure heartened Grunsky, who announced the next paper and called on the presenter to stick to the schedule. Everyone understood that the moderator's stern tone referred to the previous presenter.

Solovyov listened inattentively to this paper and the next. His head had begun to ache. Likely from an abundance of impressions that day, he thought. Or was it from the outing to the scorching Mount Mithridates (sun stroke)? Striving to grasp what exactly the presenter wanted to say increased the ache, extended it, and forced him to feel every brain cell.

'The operation's name was *signifying*,' said the presenter, Kholin.

The presenter's exceedingly soft voice and inability to speak directly into the microphone did not encourage focus. The discussion concerned operation *Foxhole*, something Solovyov himself had studied a little. Kholin quoted the operation's English-language name, the one Larionov used with western envoys. Before the Reds' decisive storm of Perekop, the general had ordered two additional rows of trenches be dug, as if the quantity might still change something.

'So these trenches replace the fighting spirit that I need, but my army has lost!' the general shouted to the shovelers.

He was walking along the defensive lines and earth was

scattering out from under his boots into the freshly dug trenches.

'I want to lie down in your trench, so everyone will leave me in peace!' the general shouted in another place.

The shovelers did not know that was the general's old dream. They silently went about their work, puzzled as to why he needed such a big trench in this case.

'The name of the operation was *signifying*,' Kholin repeated. 'If you divide the word *Foxhole* in two, you'll understand what the general wanted to say.'

Kholin observed, not without pleasure, as the whispers of everyone reading at once ran through the audience.

'It was as if,' said the presenter, waving his hands but still speaking quietly, away from the microphone, 'the general was saying goodbye with that word, that he would survive.'

The audience absorbed this for an inadmissibly long time.

'The key word is *whole*,' said a smiling Kholin. 'He was saying that he was a sly fox and would escape *whole*.'

The whispering gradually transformed into a buzz. With a bob of his head, the presenter returned some unruly hair to its place. Baikalova wrote something on a piece of paper and showed it to Grunsky. Grunsky read what she had written, moving his index finger from one word to another. Twice. He shrugged.

'But the second part of the word,' the concerned Baikalova said into the microphone, 'I mean, in "foxhole", it would be "hole", with just an "h", which means a pit. So it's not "whole" with the "w" for entire . . . I did study English . . .'

Kholin leaned on the lectern and his head twitched toward

his shoulder. His face expressed nothing but fatigue. He smoothed his hair and slowly began shifting his papers on the lectern. Baikalova rose from her place and looked questioningly at the presenter.

After a silence, Kholin said, almost as silently, 'I will verify your information.'

Solovyov felt like getting some fresh air. To do that, he would have to give an excuse to Dunya but did not know what to say. In any case, he had missed the transition to a new presenter and now it would be awkward to leave. Solovyov was annoyed at his own indecision. Alex Schwartz, a gender studies specialist from Boston, was speaking. She spoke Russian in a pleasant masculine baritone. She selected her words carefully, preferring infinitive verb forms and nouns in the nominative case. Solovyov's headache kept worsening.

Schwartz began her report on the general with a detailed story about famous 'cavalry maiden', Nadezhda Andreevna Durova (1783–1866). The American researcher reminded attendees that it was not easy for women to make their way into the Russian Army at the turn of the nineteenth century. A woman's lot was considered to be needlework (Schwartz demonstrated several motions for embroidery). The kitchen (cutting imaginary vegetables). Bed (motions of horseback riding).

But. Young Nadezhda had trouble with needlework. Lace. To tear (miming). To ruin (miming). To tangle (miming). Schwartz read a quotation from Durova's book *The Cavalry Maiden*: "'These two so very contradictory feelings,'" Schwartz quoted Durova, "'love for one's father and repugnance for one's sex—perturbed my soul with identical force and so,

with a firmness and constancy very uncommon for someone
my age, I devoted myself to contemplating a plan for leaving
the realm to which nature and customs assigned the female
sex."'

For her upbringing, the girl was sent to flank hussar
Astakhov. He taught her to wield a saber (miming). To shoot
(miming, with onomatopoeia). To ride horses (miming,
same as bed). Noticing that Baikalova had stood up, the
presenter addressed her with a calming gesture: 'Are you
interested in how this all ties in with the general?'

'I am,' said Baikalova.

Schwartz came out from behind the lectern, approached
Baikalova, and half-embraced her. 'It's just the general was
a woman. Like Nadezhda Andreevna. Like you and me. You
not know?'

Baikalova preferred to keep silent. She was, after all, still
in Schwartz's embrace.

'Why Zhloba not shoot him?'

'Why?' Grunsky asked, cautious.

'He knew general's secret. Loved him.'

Solovyov got up and began making his way to the exit,
not looking at anyone. Only when he was out in the fresh
evening breeze did he sense that his shirt was wet with
sweat. He undid two or three buttons and unstuck his shirt
from his chest. Dunya came up behind him and placed her
chin on his shoulder, 'Shall we go?'

Solovyov moved his shoulder, barely noticeably, 'I have a
headache.'

'I have aspirin in my room,' she rubbed her nose against
his neck.

Solovyov was looking at the Chaika department store, staring. 'My head aches because of you.'

Dunya did not say a word. She turned and vanished behind the theater's columns. Solovyov headed slowly toward his hotel.

14

The next morning did not portend scandal. The surface of the sea looked polished, without ripples. The wind that had been blowing in the evening had been replaced by conciliatory airy waves. Those waves blended a morning coolness with a barely discernible smell of fish, and Solovyov liked that mix very much. But scandal did come to pass.

Kvasha and Schwartz led the morning session. More precisely, Schwartz led it and Kvasha sat next to her. She took the microphone at the very beginning and then did not let it out of her hands. Kvasha did not protest. Initially, he contemplated the crystal chandeliers in the hall, but then he began quickly writing something on the papers lying in front of him.

Just before the first presenter came on, a rather short man wearing a tracksuit appeared on the stage. Swaying slightly, he walked to the moderators' table and leaned his hand on it. He stood motionless for a while, gazing at the floor.

'Who are you?' the good-natured Schwartz asked him in her choppy, accented Russian.

'Me?' The man paused. 'Well, let's say I'm the lighting technician.'

He crouched and placed his elbows on the table.

'You look very tired,' said Schwartz.

The man calling himself the lighting technician nodded. He reached for the pitcher, poured himself some water, and drank.

'I'm just a little tired.'

He rose to his feet and slowly walked away. Moscow researcher Papitsa was already standing below, by the stairs, waiting for the stage to free up. The small Papitsa cast a contemptuous glance at the lighting technician then flew up the stairs. He was wearing a tuxedo and his bow tie peered out only occasionally from underneath a long beard that seemed to be the wrong size. His icicle-like mustache scattered threateningly in various directions. This made him look simultaneously like Don Quixote, Salvador Dali, and Felix Dzerzhinsky. Taken individually, those figures had nothing in common with Papitsa. The presenter's beard, tuxedo, and abrupt motions reminded Solovyov of the puppet show that came to his school before each New Year holiday.

He'd loved those performances for the puppets' spiffy costumes, the spangles on the curtains, the aroma of a holiday tree that had already been placed in the corner of the assembly room but was not yet decorated, and the thought of an upcoming vacation. He loved those performances even in high school, when completely different things interested him, when he stealthily squeezed Leeza's hand while they were in the assembly room and thought about how they were sitting at a children's show but were connected by a relationship that was not childlike; that made him unbelievably turned on.

Solovyov cautiously turned his head and scanned the room for Dunya. She was sitting two rows away from him. She was sitting very straight, and not taking her eyes off the stage. That, thought Solovyov, must be how an outcast woman sits. For the first time, he felt something like sympathy for her.

The audience awaited Papitsa's paper with impatience. This was not related to the researcher having some sort of high standing in historical science. Papitsa did not have high standing. This was not even connected with Papitsa's beard, which made his oral presentations far more attractive than the written ones. The reason for the interest lay in general-iana's fundamental question, which was expressed in his paper's title: 'Why Did the General Remain Alive?'

There was movement in the lighting balcony, just as Papitsa began his paper. The face of the man who had gone onstage came into sight behind the balcony's steel structure; a moment later, spotlights began shining, one after another. Backlighting was coming only from the right balcony, causing sinister black shadows to form onstage. Two colored beams—green and dark blue—were directed at the co-chairs.

Papitsa read with an energetic delivery, gesturing and stamping his feet as he stood. He was reading in the literal sense, without taking his eyes from the text. His gnarled fingers slid along the edge of the lectern, sometimes coming away from it, sometimes falling still. Papitsa leaned on the microphone from time to time, deafening the audience with the crackling of his beard. Then he would push himself sharply away from the lectern so his body would stretch up perfectly straight, inclining and then freezing at that unnatural angle.

Papitsa painstakingly enumerated the reasons why the general should have been shot. There were, in the researcher's assessment, twenty-seven reasons. At the same time, there were only two alternatives for avoiding execution. The general did not use either; implied were escape to Constantinople or going underground. From this, there followed the existence of a third alternative, hitherto unknown. This alternative for escaping the firing squad was—and here the presenter straightened up and looked into the audience—collaboration with the Reds.

The researcher's argumentation was not new. Papitsa repeated conjecture about the general meeting with Dmitry Zhloba, things that had been stated back in the day, both in the émigré and the Soviet press, in Krivich's *Ten Years Later* as well as Drel's *At the Front Line*, but he did not draw in any additional evidence. Papitsa did not know the results of Solovyov's work, showing that on the night of June 13–14, 1920, from 23:55 until 03:35, Zhloba's and General Larionov's armored trains stood facing each other at the station in Gnadenfeld. Going further than his predecessors, Papitsa also surmised that Dzerzhinsky (at this moment, the presenter looked, extraordinarily, like Dali) had recruited Larionov back in 1918 and that Larionov fulfilled all the Cheka's assignments to the letter from then on. The researcher explained the general's resounding victories as tactical considerations. He surmised that they were launched with the goal of deflecting attention from the decisive battle in the autumn of 1920 at Perekop, which the general allegedly lost under an agreement. Papitsa called all the battles waged before that 'staged' and appealed for them not to be taken seriously.

'General Larionov was a Cheka agent for the entire Civil War, from beginning to end,' concluded the presenter. 'And there's your answer to the question of why he was not executed.'

'He's lying,' rang out a female voice in the auditorium.

A lady was moving toward the stage along the center aisle of the parterre. A click sounded in the lighting balcony and Papitsa found himself in the center of a red beam.

'If I may,' said Kvasha, moderating, 'The general had better alternatives for helping the Reds, though. Why, then, one might ask, would he wait around until November 1920 . . .?'

The lady walking through the hall went up on the stage and approached the presenter. Solovyov recognized her when she turned toward the audience. She was Nina Fedorovna Akinfeeva.

'He's lying,' Nina Fedorovna repeated into the microphone.

She was exactly a head taller than the speaker. Papitsa ran a hand along his red beard, 'I'm open to counterarguments. Prove to me that I'm wrong.'

Without saying a word, Nina Fedorovna took him by the beard and led him out from behind the lectern. Papitsa did not resist. As they walked through the parterre, another spotlight came on and followed them right to the exit. Nina Fedorovna's face expressed rage. Papitsa's face (it was turned upward) was devoid of expression. Once the two of them had disappeared behind the velvet drape at the exit, Alex Schwartz announced Solovyov's paper. The emancipation of Russian women had exceeded all her expectations.

Solovyov felt close to desperation. This was the second

time he had seen Nina Fedorovna Akinfeeva and the second time she had eluded him. Even as he began his paper, he kept glancing at the velvet drape, hoping Nina Fedorovna would return after all. But she did not come back.

Solovyov handled himself calmly behind the lectern. He had read this paper for the small Yalta circle so felt no anxiety now. He did not even glance at the text. As he was presenting, he noticed everything taking place in the audience and on the stage. The cannery director nodded sympathetically from the first row of the parterre as Solovyov spoke. Schwartz occasionally said something to Kvasha, who shrugged in reply. The lighting technician's face flashed again somewhere among the spotlights and then, drawn by some outside force, disappeared from the balcony forever. Papitsa, who had returned to the room unnoticed, was sitting in the back row. Only Nina Fedorovna was missing.

Solovyov looked around again after finishing his paper. He had always been interested in how actors feel onstage. Do they hear chairs creaking? A cough? Whispering in the parterre? Now he knew: they hear it. They see when someone is leaving the hall, half bent over. That is annoying. At Kvasha's nod, Solovyov left the podium. Deliberately and with dignity, as a person not in a hurry.

Solovyov heard the next presenter begin as he walked past the first half of the rows of the parterre. He thought he should stay in the auditorium a few more minutes, if only as a courtesy. He thought that but did not stop. He felt fatigue. Without slowing his pace, Solovyov walked to the end of the parterre and exited the hall. Nina Fedorovna was smoking nervously by one of the columns. She was watching the door intently, obviously believing Papitsa had gotten out of this too easily. Deliberating whether or not to repeat her impressive performance with the researcher.

Solovyov felt unrestrained by gravity. It seemed as if he would be carried away by the very first gust of a sea breeze and his meeting with Nina Fedorovna would, again, not take place. But he was not carried off. After sensing solid ground under his feet, Solovyov took a step toward the elderly woman. He touched her arm with the gesture of someone capturing the Firebird. He knew she would not escape now.

'That was great . . . how you got him.' Solovyov smiled, lost. He had waited a long time for this conversation but had not imagined it would begin like this.

'Uh-huh.'

Surprise replaced indignation. Nina Fedorovna took a deep drag on the cigarette.

'I'm writing my dissertation about the general . . . I need your help.'

Solovyov began speaking quickly and muddledly, as if he were afraid Nina Fedorovna would refuse. He told her about what he had already accomplished in Petersburg and even named most of the corrections he had made to Dupont's data. Nina Fedorovna listened to him sympathetically, though a bit absently, too. Clearly, she could not keep up with the abundance of figures Solovyov cited. Nina Fedorovna went to the waste bin (Solovyov went with her), put out her cigarette butt on its concrete edge, and shot it into the urn's maw like a catapult, with two fingers. Nina Fedorovna lit another cigarette when Solovyov began telling her about his Yalta investigations. She livened up noticeably during the story about his searches with

Zoya. After some hesitation, Solovyov decided to describe it all.

After hearing him out to the very end, Nina Fedorovna said, 'But the general's memoirs about his childhood were with us, at home. Why did you have to get into Kozachenko's?'

Solovyov looked closely at Nina Fedorovna. She was not joking.

'It's just that Zoya said . . .'

'Zoya's a difficult girl.' Nina Fedorovna smiled. 'I was the same. You don't believe me?'

Solovyov did not answer. After a pause, he said, 'So that means none of the general's memoirs are lost?'

'What the general dictated to *me* was kept . . .' Nina Fedorovna went silent. Her tone assumed further questioning.

'So then what has been lost?'

'Not long after the general's death, his son came to visit. He asked what of his father's was left. I gave him a notebook the general himself wrote.' Nina Fedorovna leaned against the column and closed her eyes. The corners of her lips turned up.

'And where's his son now?'

'I don't know.'

Solovyov leaned against the column opposite her. Atlantis and a caryatid. His fatigue had returned.

'I remember. He went to some little settlement. He left an address.' As before, Nina Fedorovna kept her eyes closed. 'Not even a settlement, a railroad station. A platform.'

Solovyov felt the column begin wobbling behind his back.

'And what . . .' he was already listening to himself from a distance, 'what was the station called?'

'I don't remember. Some woman there took pity on him so he stayed.' Nina Fedorovna opened her eyes and her face grew serious. 'She simply took pity on him.'

'Maybe it was *Kilometer 715*?'

A street-cleaning truck emerged out from behind a bed of nasturtiums. A rainbow began developing in the droplets that hung over the flowers.

'Maybe . . . May well be. That's where he went.'

Solovyov went back into the hall. He listened inattentively to the other papers. The presenters and the conference and Crimea itself had suddenly lost his interest. He was thinking about the only spot on earth where everything that had been significant to him at varying times in his life had come together: the general's manuscript, Leeza Larionova (Leeza *Larionova*!) and, finally, his own home. He was thinking about *Kilometer 715*.

Solovyov understood that this coincidence was not accidental. It was no longer a coincidence but a coalescence. The more unbelievable the joining seemed, the more non-accidental it became. This non-accident proved the correctness of the direction that had opened up for the searching, but its importance—the sudden realization of Leeza's importance in his life made him shudder—was the main proof. On top of everything else (Solovyov remembered this in the final moment and felt drops of sweat on his brow) Leeza's patronymic was *Filippovna*. This final proof was already unnecessary—it was superfluous—but Solovyov accepted it gratefully, too. He did not understand why he had not written to Leeza once in all those years. That was inexplicable.

No matter what a person studies, he is studying himself. Thus spoke Prof. Nikolsky. It fascinated Solovyov that the direction of his search was approaching, closer and closer, the line of his own life. He was stunned by the interweaving of material from his research and his own fate, and by their indivisibility and harmony. If he had ever genuinely loved Leeza, then that was what was happening at this very moment.

Stroking the armrest of his seat on the bus every now and then, Solovyov imagined her hand. He remembered the freshness of her lips as his temple sensed the coolness of the window glass. He thought only of Leeza the whole way to Yalta. He wanted her as never before. Wanted her as the general's granddaughter. As the one to transform him into a relative of her important grandfather. And, of course, as Leeza, his first woman. The scholar's coalescence with his material had reached its apogee.

What did he know about Leeza's parents? Her mother was a railroad track inspector. A weary woman with hair as coarse as wire that was always coming out from under her headscarf. Melting snowflakes glistened on it when Leeza's mother came in from the cold. Leeza had different hair. Very soft. Smelling of sweet smoke because she dried it over the woodstove. Leeza's mother smelled of fuel oil. She did her rounds of the tracks depending on her mood. She could be out for the whole day. Or an hour. It was impossible to guess in advance how long she would be absent. It was he who had thought to place the pail by the garden gate as a signal. It could not be used all the time; it would have raised suspicion.

Her father . . . Solovyov remembered him vaguely.

Remembered he was tall. Unshaven. He began all his sentences with *well*. Well, hello. Well, a blizzard. Not an especially distinguishing feature; nobody would have noticed it, if not for Solovyov's grandmother. You don't have to say 'well' all the time (she would say). He would smile. Ask for three rubles until payday. Don't worry, everything will turn out well anyway (said Solovyov's grandmother). She would give him three rubles. Moistening her fingers with saliva as she counted out each ruble. Rarely did she give just one bill, a three-note. Banknotes over one ruble made her leery. Sometimes change popped out of her fingers and he would gather it off the floor. Occasionally, he would ask permission to sit for a while on the bench. Well, I'll rest a bit, okay? He smelled of alcohol. Solovyov did not yet know it was alcohol. It was the smell of Leeza's father. Leeza's father would not go home. He would sit down on the bench, not taking off his coat. His rabbit-fur hat would slide down his face. He would sleep and be calm. Finally, he disappeared somewhere. Completely disappeared.

Solovyov arrived in Yalta late that evening. It began to rain as he was standing at the trolleybus stop. It was raining even though there did not seem to be clouds in the star-strewn sky. Solovyov decided against waiting for the trolleybus and headed home on foot. The rain was nice after the afternoon heat. It was not a heavy rain; its fine drops reminded him of a thickly condensed fog. By the city market, Solovyov turned on Kirov Street, formerly Autskaya Street. Music carried from the embankment and every so often a spotlight beam appeared somewhere overhead. The beam slid along the tops of the cypress trees and the wet cupolas of the Alexander Nevsky Cathedral.

Everything on Palmiro Togliatti Street was just as it had been two days ago. The creaky staircase, the dim bulb under the canopy over the door. It occurred to Solovyov that this resembled a homecoming. After many years. Coming home as another person. He lingered as he was turning on the light in the room, as if he feared seeing something unexpected there. No, everything was the same. Everything.

Solovyov took the bag off his shoulder. It was heavy. The cannery director had handed him some examples of their products when they said their goodbyes. He had called Solovyov 'the very same Solovyov' again and said he was proud to know him. Neither the director nor Solovyov clarified the meaning of 'the very same.' Solovyov was, for himself, always 'the very same.' He had taken the cans so as not to offend the director. Now he decided to sample them.

Solovyov pulled out one of the cans at random and opened it. The right-angled can with the lid flying up over it reminded him of a grand piano. It was goby fish in tomato sauce.

Someone rang the doorbell.

It rang again. Solovyov continued looking, focused, at the fish. Their understated tomatoed existence seemed like the height of orderliness. It did not allow even the thought of having chaos in one's life. But chaos existed. It had raced into Solovyov's life and carried him away, into its vortex. Flinging him into the Kozachenko apartment, into the Vorontsov Museum, and into the insane nighttime rowing amidst raging waves. That chaos was Zoya. Solovyov had no doubt it was Zoya ringing. He stood and looked at his reflection in the china cabinet. Went to the door. After one more ring, he moved the bolt aside. Taras stood in the doorway, 'I knew you were home. I've been watching the windows.'

Solovyov silently invited him in. Taras moved toward the center of the room fitfully, as if he were sidestepping. He set his hands on the back of a chair. He stood crookedly, his head bent toward his shoulder.

'I have a favor to ask you,' said Taras. 'Leave.'

Solovyov remained silent. Somewhere outside, a door opened, spilling out the sounds of clattering dishes, music, and guests' cries. A moment later, everything went quiet.

'Leave. She's impossible to handle. You'll be done for with her.'

'What about you?'

Taras kept silent.

'Did you know about the searches in your room?' asked Solovyov.

'I put the papers there myself, where she said to.'

Taras lowered himself slowly onto the chair. For a moment, Solovyov was afraid Taras was losing consciousness, but he was not.

'Did you know we'd go to the Vorontsov Palace, too?'

'Of course. I was there that night.'

Taras looked Solovyov in the eye for the first time. There was nothing in that gaze but sadness. Solovyov turned away, 'So why did you agree to it?'

'That's what she wanted.' Taras's fingers touched the fish can. They slid along the rim of the lid, as if symbolizing Taras's own rather difficult journey. Solovyov felt like he had become a witness to some sort of drama that he did not quite understand but that was undoubtedly a drama, and he started to feel sorry for the man sitting before him.

'Do you want some tea?'

'I got you a ticket for tomorrow, to Petersburg.'

Taras said this without taking his gaze from the fish in tomato sauce—Taras himself (it occurred to Solovyov) was essentially one of those fish. Why was he suffering like this with Zoya? Why was he enduring all these passions? Taras hesitated, then took the ticket from his breast pocket and placed it in front of Solovyov. It was curled. Not wanting to flatten out.

'I'm not going to Petersburg,' said Solovyov, sticking the ticket back in Taras's pocket. 'But I am leaving. Tomorrow. And I'll try not to see Zoya.'

Taras silently offered his hand. It was limp and damp. Of course, with hands like those Taras could not count on Zoya's love.

Solovyov left the house early in the morning. He truly was going. He did not feel that he owed anything since he had paid for more days than he had stayed. He left the key to the room with the neighbors.

Solovyov turned onto Chekhov Street instead of going to the trolleybus. Despite the weight of his bag, he felt like walking part of his route to the bus station. He was saying goodbye to Yalta. Without knowing it himself, Solovyov was walking along the same route as General Larionov walked one evening in August, around the 24th, in 1938. He was walking around in military-style trousers, albeit without stripes. And a tunic. The general did not stand out in the crowd wearing that clothing. Many people dressed like soldiers during the thirties. The military style was fashionable in that epoch.

The general was walking around without stripes on his

trousers, but of course it was obvious to everyone that this was a general. His army bearing could be sensed in how he held his head, the way his shoulders turned, and the confidence with which he treaded, from his heel to his toes. A military man through and through. Upper echelon of the officer corps. His arms moved in time with his gait: lightly, confidently, but not swinging. The general displayed restraint in his every action.

At the corner of Botkinskaya and Chekhova Streets, he stopped at a kiosk selling carbonated water. Water cost ten kopecks without syrup, thirty with syrup. The general asked for water with syrup. He took the glass, which sweated instantly, and observed the swirling bubbles for a few seconds. The foam on the surface was exploding with thousands of the very finest droplets; they could just barely be felt when the glass came close to the cheek. The general delighted in how little bubbles rose behind the thick glass, after springing up within each of the glass's facets. Oleander blossoms pinkened through the bubbles as if they were in a magic lantern. Pedestrians slipped past. A bicyclist rode past. A cart with milk canisters. The sharp smell of a horse.

It was hot in Yalta despite the evening hour. The general delighted in drinking his carbonated water. His Adam's apple moved in time with his swallows. He took a handkerchief from his tunic pocket and wiped his sweaty brow. Noiselessly placed the glass on the wooden counter. Elongated contours of growth rings retained remnants of paint. Wasps crawled along round syrupy spots. The general lifted his glass again, slowly turned it over, and covered one of the wasps. Both he and the water saleswoman observed the insect's behavior. The wasp slowly took flight, made several circles under the glass, and touched the top with a buzz. Fell. Clambered up again, climbing along the side, and went still. The general turned the glass over (the gesture of someone releasing doves), allowing the wasp to fly out. The wasp was in no hurry. Moving in a spiral, it reached the edge of the glass. Flew off, dignified. The drinking glasses jingled finely when a truck drove by. The water saleswoman wiped her hands on her apron.

'Another glass?'

The general looked pensively at the saleswoman. The carelessly styled hair, the starched headpiece. He was looking through the saleswoman.

'No,' the general said. Focus returned to his gaze. 'There's no need.'

Yes, this was August 24. There was no doubt. 1938. Judging from the stuffiness of the evening, there would be a thunderstorm during the night. The first clouds were gathering over the Oreanda Hotel. The sun was shedding its final rays on the St. John Chrysostom Church. The general was walking along Chekhov Street. He watched holidaymakers with beach bags, parasols, and towels on their shoulders. Some were wearing pajamas.

The tango. So light, as if from afar. Swelling. A high male voice soared over an orchestra. A band stage revealed itself behind wrinkled acacia trunks. Woodwinds glinted. And a banjo glinted. Musicians in white suits and Latin American hats just as white. A trumpeter soloed. He gave all his air to the trumpet, barely able to inhale on time. The embodiment of exhalation. His cheeks were like a caricature but his lips were refined and sensual.

People were dancing by the band stage. Little by little,

they made way, yielding the space to one couple. He. A predator with hair the color of a raven's wing. A belligerently straight part. A roomy, pleated shirt that hung over narrow trousers. A wet stripe on the back. She. A dove in a white dress. When he spun her, her head tilted back slightly. Weak-willed to some extent. All of her in his arms. His leg sank into the froth of her dress. She still managed to elude him.

From Chekhov Street, the general went to Morskaya Street. To his left, a two-wheeled cart turned with a clatter. Its wheels skidded slightly on the polished cobblestones. Grass was breaking its way through a stone drain gutter. The street led to the sea and the general's heart filled with joy. Even as a child he had loved streets leading to the sea. He saw grounds for hope with the sudden appearance of blueness between two rows of houses.

The general walked up to a pharmacy. It occupied the first level of a squat two-story building. Oak door, copper doorknob, little bell. Art nouveau style. A spring pulled the heavy door back with a creak. The pharmacy seemed cool after the street. And quiet. The general appreciated coolness and quiet. He waited until the pharmacist, Kologrivov, came out after hearing the bell. There were small test tubes, little boxes, and vials behind the cabinets' thick glass. The smell of liquid medicines and *Extra* tooth powder. The general wanted to have a talk with the pharmacist about causes of death. About death overall.

Kologrivov welcomed the general. He was a quiet, gray-haired man with a fleshy nose—the end of his nose looked bulbous. Blue eyes. The general came here to relax because he found Kologrivov's calm pleasant. The general usually sat in the chair behind the dressing screen and listened as

Kologrivov sold medicines. Those who came to the pharmacy required iodine, Vishnevsky ointment, diarrhea remedies, cotton wool, bandages, dried chamomile, condoms, and Condy's crystals. Rarer: castor oil and fish oil. They required advice. Pharmacist Kologrivov gave it in a soft voice (he never raised his voice). This gave General Larionov a sense of coziness. He felt as he had in childhood when he would hide among the coats and furs in the entryway, listening to the servants' leisurely discussions. Sometimes he would fall asleep. Sometimes the general fell asleep and Kologrivov would speak with clients in a half-whisper, so as not to wake Larionov.

It was nine in the evening. Kologrivov locked the pharmacy and invited the general into the adjoining room. There were educational posters hanging there, depicting the human body at various ages. Michelangelo's David divided the ages up to thirty and the ages after thirty. Separate visual aids there highlighted the circulatory system, digestive system, nervous system, and male skeleton (front view). With pointer in hand, pharmacist Kologrivov intended to talk about each of the systems but began his story with the skeleton.

The skeleton, which supports everything, is composed of 206 bones. The skull—which had always seemed, to the general, to be something seamless—has 29 (for a total of 235, the general mechanically noted). As Larionov attempted to imagine himself as a skeleton, he groped at his eye socket with a finger. This was far from the first time he had acted this way, something the pharmacist was aware of.

The general interrupted Kologrivov, 'People say the skull's contours show through on a person's face before his death.'

'That happens when death sets in by natural means.'

The general nodded and looked pensively at the skeleton. 'And what if death sets in by unnatural means?'

'Then the skull's contours show through only after death.'

It was darkening outside. Kologrivov spoke of blood circulation. In front of him was a yellowed diagram of lesser and greater blood circulation. Arteries were denoted in red, veins in blue. The general liked this combination of colors. He unbuttoned one of his tunic sleeves and examined his blue veins. This did not escape the pharmacist's gaze. He continued his story about blood: a person has an average of five or six liters. It is pumped by the heart, (weight: around 300 grams), which consists of two halves, left and right. Each half has an atrium and a ventricle. Kologrivov circled them with the pointer. The atrium received blood, the ventricle pushed it out.

'Cold metal pierces my living heart . . .' the general softly declaimed.

'The most perfect pump in the world.'

'Piercing something so well thought-out,' said the general, choosing his words, 'a creation so refined and vital, is that not a crime?'

'Instant unnatural death.'

'What could be more unnatural . . .'

The general fell silent. He discovered there was a double 'n' in the last word he had uttered.

Pharmacist Kologrivov explained briefly about the digestive system and the nervous system. At the general's request, he moved on to examine natural death. Now there were posters in the foreground depicting the body at various ages. After hesitating slightly, Kologrivov took out a depiction of

a person's development in the womb and hung that alongside the others. He scratched the back of his head.

'I don't see the one about conception,' said Kologrivov.

'You want to say that conception is the beginning of
natural death?'

'Perhaps. I suspect our delivery boy took that one.'

Kologrivov talked about conception without the poster.
Addressing the time in the womb, he showed the embryo's
position. This pose was familiar to the general. His soldiers
sat this way in Perekop during autumn 1920. The general
ordered them to use their last supplies of kindling wood to
light fires. He forced the soldiers to jump over them. He
raced around that icy desert like a madman, saving the
remnants of his army. He attempted to rouse his soldiers,
prodded them under the ribs, pounded their cheeks . . .

Could an embryo be roused? As he listened to pharmacist
Kologrivov, the general felt an understanding coming to him
in hindsight. His soldiers had no longer thirsted for victory.
They were not dreaming of women. Or money. They were
not even dreaming of warmth. Their exhaustion was deeper
than wishes like those. More than anything on earth, his
soldiers wanted to return to their mothers' wombs.

The transformation of a pink, wrinkled creature into a
child. Adolescent age. Pubic hair growing in, enlargement
of the member (for men), change of voice. Awakening of
sexual instincts.

'That was the age I suddenly realized I would die, too,'
said the general. 'This was the time of first nocturnal emis-
sions.'

'Immortality leaves along with innocence,' said the pharmacist. He moved the pointer again from the *Adolescent*

poster to the *Child* poster. 'Children don't believe they'll die.'

Complete rebuilding of the body. Intense growth of the skeleton and muscle mass. Changes in the hormonal realm, the metabolism, etcetera. The body begins having a smell, especially the soles of the feet. Socks have to be changed as frequently as possible. Pimples. Under no circumstances should they be squeezed with dirty hands. A child's soft features sharpen, cheekbones become prominent. A beard and mustache begin growing (primarily for men). The human body develops—Kologrivov approached the image of David—until around the age of thirty.

'And then?' asked the general, admiring.

'It develops then, too, but in the opposite direction.'

Kologrivov sighed and pointed to the poster *Person at age 40–50 years (Male. Frontal View)*. The fat layer under the skin thickens. The skin stretches. The face becomes flabby and bloated. The body accumulates stores of fat, particularly in the stomach and hips. The torso seems disproportionally large, even caricature-like, compared to the legs. Round fatty lumps begin forming on the legs and arms. On other parts of the body, too. They distort the former rigor of its lines and speak of metabolic troubles. Increased growth of hair on the back, chest, brow ridge, and in/on the ears and nose.

It goes from bad to worse. Hair grays. The smell of an old person's bitter sweat appears. The skin withers and bunches up in wrinkles. The body's aging is accompanied by sclerotic thickening of the arteries. They become tight and fragile, and threaten to rupture. The teeth gradually fall out. This can be partially rectified with false teeth (if made carelessly, they make pronunciation whistle slightly) but even a measure such as this is not capable of breaking the general negative tendency. Discs flatten between vertebrae, the spine loses its elasticity and settles. The person shrinks in height. The organs become impossibly worn out. The brain starts to contain excess amounts of water, making its work more difficult. In the end, it becomes hard for the person to live. He dies.

The horns of the evening's last boats sounded outside the window.

'Does that mean,' asked the general, 'that life is the fundamental reason for a person's death?'

Pharmacist Kologrivov sat on a chair and looked calmly at the general. 'One might, Your Excellency, say just that.'

15

Solovyov arrived in the regional capital early in the morning. They told him he would be unable to reach the *Kilometer 715* station by rail. Even local trains no longer stopped there. Solovyov took a bus.

The bus was old, just like in his childhood. Solovyov had not even seen vehicles like this in Petersburg. When the bus went over potholes, it shook for a long time, convulsively, as if it had an asthmatic cough. When the doors opened at the stops, the bus made a sound like glass being pressed. Solovyov got out at the village where his school was. He would need to go the rest of the way on foot.

Solovyov began heading along the familiar road but then he stopped, turned, and walked briskly toward the school. A padlock hung on the front door. Summer vacation, Solovyov remembered. It was vacation. He walked up to one of the windows and pressed his forehead to the glass. The Russian literature room developed, hazily, behind poplars reflected in the glass. The seats were flipped up. Any answer began with those seats clattering; it ended with clattering, too.

'Why is the military trilogy titled *The Living and the Dead*?

So . . .' and the teacher's finger would search the list in the grade book, 'Solovyov!'

Solovyov's seat flipped up. In actuality, the general had only two folders. When he learned that everyone he had attended school with had died, he transferred them from the *Dead* folder to the *Living* folder. And that was that. Would Solovyov himself have done the same? That was another question entirely. But his classmates' absence behind the desks gaped. It was like death. Worse than death because in their distinct absence, his classmates were simulating their existence somewhere (most likely not far away). Their shadows were visiting the glass factory. Or a cowshed penetrated by drafts. Maybe the tractor-repair station that served local collective farms.

'Whose side is the author of *And Quiet Flows the Don* on? Does anyone have any thoughts in that regard?'

Nobody did. They did not know for certain whose side the author was on. Or who, basically, the author was. The grade books and textbooks were on the teacher's desk. There were fat folders on the *Materials for Distribution* shelf. Were there any *Living* and *Dead* folders there? Did the school maintain records like that?

Without even realizing it himself, Solovyov had walked to the library. He stood on the front steps for a few minutes. What could he even begin talking about with Nadezhda Nikiforovna? He could tell her about what happened yesterday. Or maybe a week ago. It was impossible to tell a life. Several years in Petersburg had changed him a lot but to her he was his previous self. *Previous*. Solovyov felt awkward remembering his childhood dreams. He decided not to go in.

He went in anyway. A young woman was sitting in Nadezhda Nikiforovna's place. Solovyov did not know her.

'Would you like to register?' she asked.

'I'm already registered.'

The woman nodded, unsure, and Solovyov realized she had not been here long. There was no cameo ring on her hand. There was a small ring with an emerald. It would not make a good sound when touching a shelf. Just a quiet plasticky sound.

'What are you interested in?'

Solovyov was interested in where Nadezhda Nikiforovna was, but he did not say that.

'Do you have *Captain Blood: His Odyssey*?'

Solovyov waited for her to vanish behind the cabinets before he left the library on tiptoe. He was afraid the new employee would announce Nadezhda Nikiforovna's death to him as she handed him the book.

He walked toward the forest; the *Kilometer 715* station lay beyond it. In the woods, he was surprised that the formerly two-lane road was in disrepair and had narrowed, transforming into a path. The ferns beside the road, which always used to be trampled and stunted, had grown tall. They swayed in a warm breeze that carried the smell of the collective farm. Solovyov and Leeza had walked to school along this road. Very few people walked along it now, that was obvious.

Solovyov could walk here with his eyes closed. He could easily repeat all the words he and Leeza had said in this forest. He remembered precisely, down to every fir tree he saw, what had been said where. Or rather he had forgotten, but he remembered when he saw the trees. It seemed to him that at one time he had left those words to hang here, and now he was simply gathering them from the fluffy boughs as he walked along.

Solovyov was thinking about what Leeza would say when they met. He sensed his own guilt for his silence but his feeling for her was so complete that he was experiencing no fear at all before their meeting. The ardor that was rising in waves within Solovyov's chest was capable of—he had no doubt of this—melting away both his guilt and her possible feeling of offense. Possible. Deep down, Solovyov did not even think that Leeza might be offended at him.

The forest became sparser and Solovyov saw the first houses: his and Leeza's houses. The road led to them. In another minute or two, four more houses came into view on the right, and the station platform was on the left. Solovyov noticed there was no longer a *Kilometer 715* sign on the platform. None of the passengers on long-distance trains could now learn exactly what station they were riding through.

Solovyov began walking more slowly as he left the woods. The path disappeared completely right at his house. Tall grass wound around his legs and caught in the buckles on his sandals. It was attempting to hold him there. To prevent his unexpected return. What awaited him beyond the tightly drawn, sun-faded curtains? He stopped and looked at his house. He had not been here for six years.

The little gate would not open; Solovyov had to climb over it. When he found himself on the other side of the gate, he began pulling up the grass and thistle that had grown between the bricks in the path. Solovyov stomped on the thistle then took the broken stalks with two fingers and carefully tossed them aside.

Once he was able to open the gate, Solovyov dragged his bag into the yard. The yard had turned into a jungle. The plants stood as motionlessly as if they were in a photograph, and even the freight train passing by (his feet sensed the earth's trembling) did not disturb their peace. Solovyov remembered a children's book, *The Land of the Dense Grasses*. He had read it on the recommendation of Nadezhda Nikiforovna, who might also have turned to grass. Solovyov trampled tall, fragile August stems as he made his way to the front steps. The dandelions' white parachutes flew out from under his feet.

Wild cherry was growing on the front steps. It had fought its way through separated boards and had already spread its branches to the railing. Solovyov touched the sapling's trunk, drawing his index finger along it. The trunk was soft and smooth, as if it had been polished. Quiet set in after the train left. This was full, absolute quiet; anything further would be non-existence. Solovyov sensed himself growing into nature. His house and yard had already become nature. His turn was coming now. Solovyov pulled out the sapling with one tug and felt like a killer. He understood he had no other option.

Solovyov fumbled behind the door jamb and took out a key. He did this before he remembered this was where the key lay. His hand remembered this motion. The key worked. At first it spun emptily, unable to handle the lock's rusted mechanism, but then a familiar click sounded on the second rotation and the door creaked open.

He entered a chilly dimness. Everything remained the same as on the day he left. Everything but this: the ideal cleanliness found only in abandoned houses. Solovyov had left hastily six years ago. He was going to take his entrance exams and packed up a suitcase, just tossing aside unnecessary things. Leeza stopped him when he began stuffing everything into cabinets. She said she would tidy it all up. She looked at him, half-sitting on the windowsill. Solovyov remembered the motion of her fingers, touching the boards on the windowsill one by one, as if they were playing a piece nobody could hear.

He walked into the room and drew open the drapes. There were neither spiders nor cobwebs in the corners of the ceiling (they had been swept away by a twig broom wrapped in gauze). Because there were no flies. Solovyov realized that when a fly flew in from outside, buzzing. It was the only living being he had encountered thus far at *Kilometer 715*. The fly flitted uncertainly around spots on the tablecloth that had not come out in the laundry and then flew over to the doorknob.

A sturdy rag looped around the knobs on both sides of the door: Solovyov's grandmother had tied rags on the doors so they closed firmly and would not blow open in a draft. She had placed cardboard under wobbling table legs. Glued strips of newspaper to cracks in the glass. This was the inventiveness of old age. The resourcefulness of debility. Of an overall debility, of an inability to change anything in life. When Solovyov left the house after his grandmother's death, he was leaving that inescapability, too. He was afraid he would inherit it, too, along with the house.

There was a sound of shuffling shoes on the front steps. They were purposely loud, striving to attract attention. That was superfluous in the ongoing quiet. Solovyov turned slowly, 'Yegorovna!'

'You came back, my dear one . . .'

Taking tiny steps, Yegorovna walked into the room and pressed herself against Solovyov. Awkwardly, without bending, he caught her with his arm and felt an old person's cool tears running down his neck.

'How's life treating you, Yegorovna?'

'Life?' she pulled away, puzzled and almost offended. 'We're living it out! Yevdokia Firsova and I. Remember Yevdokia?' Her chin, fuzzy with little gray hairs, began trembling. 'We're the two waiting for death. Just two at the whole station.'

'Yegorovna, but where's Leeza'?

'Leeza . . .' Yegorovna stopped crying, and that was even more frightening for Solovyov. 'So, Leeza left. Her mother died and then she left. What, you didn't know?'

'Where'd she go?'

'God only knows, probably went to college, like you. A year ago. Maybe more than a year.'

Yegorovna took a rag out of her pocket and blew her nose, 'Leeza's mother was very sick so she took care of her. Then when her mother died, I wanted to bathe the deceased for her but Leeza did it herself. Bathed her herself. Buried her here with us. And then Leeza packed up and left . . .'

Yegorovna was making her way out. She went down the front steps, moving her hands along the railings, but her monotone still sounded. From somewhere far away, tailing off, Yegorovna continued telling Solovyov about Leeza, whom he seemed to have lost forever. Solovyov lowered himself onto his grandmother's bed and his head sank into a huge feather pillow. It was too much.

The room went dark abruptly after the sky darkened. A

vine on the window frame began fluttering and a weightless flower that had been lying by an icon floated down, right onto Solovyov. A lightning bolt struck somewhere far away, beyond the forest. Thunder merged with the sound of a passing train. After the train was gone, he could hear heavy raindrops drumming on the canopy over the front steps.

Solovyov no longer understood if he was watching a thunderstorm as he had done in his childhood or if he was dreaming a thunderstorm while lying on his grandmother's bed. Or if he was actually in his childhood, lying on his grandmother's bed and watching a thunderstorm. Bolts of lightning flashed outside the window, in the gap between the half-closed drapes. An oil lamp's jittery flame was reflected on the ceiling. His grandmother was bowing in prayer, touching the floor. Leeza was standing in the doorway and smiling. She placed a finger to her lips. Water streamed down her hair. This was not a dream. Leeza truly had come. She had drawn closer to Solovyov and was holding his hand.

Solovyov opened his eyes. Yegorovna was sitting on the edge of the bed.

'It's potatoes and mushrooms. Eat it while it's hot.'

She held out a tin dish for him.

'Thank you.'

He sat up on the bed, looking senselessly at Yegorovna's back. Leeza was not here. He had woken up with that sense and now could not get used to it. Leeza was not here.

'It'll get cold,' said Yegorovna. She was already at the door.

Solovyov nodded and took the spoon Yegorovna had brought. He had not eaten potatoes with a spoon for a long time so it initially seemed as though the dream was continuing. But the dream had gone.

After his nap, he felt like washing. He went to the well, lowered a pail on the well sweep, and attempted to collect some water. The bottom fell out of the pail when Solovyov raised it, disappearing into the depths with a matte gleam. He found another pail in the shed and fastened it to the well sweep with wire. He collected some water, washed, and tasted the water. The water was just as fresh as when he was a child.

The sun peeked out again and Solovyov was surprised at the length of this day. Its length and variety. It was a quiet summer evening, the kind when he and Leeza would often sit on the front steps. Sometimes go for walks. They could walk on the only street, on the platform, in the forest, or in the cemetery. There were no other places for walks at *Kilometer 715*. Solovyov put on a fresh T-shirt. He went over to the cabinet with the mirror and combed his hair. He was ready to leave the house.

The street greeted him with absolute quiet. Even these six houses comprising the street had lived their own lives at one time. Their life had not been turbulent, it had simply been life, with shouting over fences, dogs barking, roosters crowing, and the sounds of transistor radios. Now, though, there was nothing but the sound of leaves. The rustle of grass. This was life after a nuclear explosion.

Solovyov stopped next to the platform. In the tall grass, the steps leading to the platform could be divined by their railing. A young rowan tree was growing in the controller's booth, where his mother had once stood. Groping for the steps with his foot, Solovyov clambered onto the platform.

The grass was a little lower there, growing in intricate patterns that stretched along cracks in the asphalt. Solovyov walked over to a bench. In the strictest sense of the word, this was only a halfbench. One of its three cast-iron sections was lying on its side, covered with broken slats. He sat down cautiously on the part that remained standing. Leaned against the back. Closed his eyes.

If he imagined it was his mother in the controller's booth instead of the rowan tree (the rails had quietly begun humming) and if he imagined the bench was whole and Leeza was sitting on it (he was still not opening his eyes), then what was happening might be declared a quiet summer evening from his childhood. The rumbling of the rails was inaccessible to the untrained ear. This was not yet a rumbling, it was the soundless tension of metal prepared to carry a train that was still far away. But Solovyov heard it. He even knew which train it was. The 20:32. Moscow–Sochi.

Oddly enough, it truly was the Moscow–Sochi train. Despite all the changes in schedules and in the country in general, it passed through the station at exactly 20:32. In actuality, Solovyov was not surprised. Even if attempts had been made to tinker with the schedule, there would have been an obvious need to revert to 20:32. There was no better time to transit through the *Kilometer 715* station.

Freshness blew from the woods surrounding the station. Mowed grass on the railroad bed gave off a refined, slightly sharp aroma. That blended with the smell of railroad ties warmed by the sun. With the whisper of a weeping willow over the platform. This tree had grown as if out of nowhere; nobody saw where it began. Its roots were lost below, in the tall grass. Maybe it had no roots at all. It did not even have a trunk: there was only a crown over the platform.

Leeza announced the trains that passed through. She announced them by placing her palms together like a little boat and pressing them against the sides of her nose: it came out like a microphone, only quieter. They had heard announcements like this in the regional capital; nothing was announced at the *Kilometer 715* station. Solovyov gave permission for the trains to proceed through the station. Copying his mother's motion, he lifted the baton with his right hand. He looked through the train just as tiredly. After some time, he achieved the same kind of look from Leeza. Everybody passing through should know this work was just a routine for them.

Solovyov was still sitting with his eyes closed at 20:32. As the train approached, he thought that Leeza had managed to announce it after all. He was sure she was sitting next to him on the bench at 20:32. That his mother was standing in the controller's booth. She could not help but be there at that time.

They all needed to pull themselves together. To exhale and not move. This instant would remain if they did not frighten it away. Just as there was a moment when it is important for someone wounded in battle not to die. After prevailing over those critical seconds, the body accustoms itself to life once again. That was what the person who turned out to be Leeza's grandfather had said. If Solovyov behaved himself properly here, on the platform, life would again find its past. Catch hold of it. What had seemed dead would suddenly discover its own pulse and the three of them would return home together: Solovyov, his mother, and Leeza. Everything happening later—the deaths of his mother and grandmother, his departure, studying at the university—would turn out to be a misunderstanding, an impetuous departure from this evening's coziness.

They would return home. His mother (the clang of the valve on the gas tank) would put on the teakettle. Pour water into a basin and make him rinse off his feet. On the bottom there would be a triangular spot where the enamel was chipped. He would put a cork sailboat in the basin. His grandmother would read aloud from *Robinson Crusoe*. Leeza would take her cup in both hands. He would slowly move the water around the basin with his feet. The sailboat would begin rocking on the waves. A diesel locomotive whistle would sound somewhere in the distance. No, of course they would not return. Not Leeza. Solovyov raised his eyes toward the controller's booth. And especially not his mother. The wind from a passing locomotive engulfed him. The 21:47, St. Petersburg–Kislovodsk. The train had gone through unannounced.

Only after turning on the light in the entryway did Solovyov realize it was already dark. He boiled the vermicelli he had brought with him and opened yet another can of food. It was goby fish in tomato sauce again. It seemed almost absurd that they were here. The gobies looked at Solovyov with sadness, making him feel even more unhappy. Moths were beating against the kitchen window. Their wings never stopped working as they clutched convulsively at the frame, rose along the glass, and slid down again.

Solovyov went into his own room, the one he had occupied after his mother's death. Compared with the overall order in the house, his room constituted an exception. It was not exactly untidy, it was closer to 'untouched'. something that immediately caught the eye. A Russian language textbook lay open by a bed leg. The cover faced upwards, just as he had left it on the morning of his departure. Solovyov crouched and picked up the book. Tried to close it. It would not close; it could only be pressed shut. With difficulty. With the unyield-ingness of a stiffened body. He laid the book on the desk and it opened to the previous page again. The use of 'not' with verbs was what had interested him that morning. Always written as two words. What an idiot, thought Solovyov; he slowly stretched out on the bed. The bed squeaked, as usual. He pulled off his T-shirt and jeans, and threw them on the floor. He clasped the pillow with both arms and buried his face in it. Ceasing to exist.

Solovyov awoke from the jingling of bed knobs at the head of the bed. An endless freight train was passing through outside his window. It went slowly, waiting for the far signal to change. Wearily sat for a bit on the railroad tracks. Solovyov's whole body sensed its vibration. His arms were still embracing the pillow. He was curled around a balled-up blanket. One freight train replaced the other, heading in the opposite direction; this one went noticeably faster. It continued accelerating, drawing the rhythm of its wheels to the boundaries of the possible. A long time ago, Solovyov and Leeza had listened to that rhythm together. The rumble broke off at its upper limit. The sound of the departing train seemed like an echo in the sudden quiet. Solovyov settled in on his back. He felt a sticky dampness when he pulled the blanket out from under himself.

Solovyov headed for the cemetery early the next morning. On his shoulder he carried a small hoe that he had found

in the shed. In his hand was an inexplicably persistent gladiolus that had sprouted in what used to be the flowerbed.
The cemetery was in the forest, about twenty minutes from
home. It was difficult to divine the road that led there.

Solovyov remembered the first funeral he had seen. He
was surprised that people scattered flowers in front of
the coffin the whole way. He had seen the men from the
station who were carrying the coffin step on crimson aster
heads; he thought he could hear them crunch. He had
stopped and watched as the procession moved further
away. Leeza stayed and stood alongside him. Once
everyone had disappeared into the forest, he and Leeza
began picking up the flowers. Many of the flowers turned
out to be intact. Some did not even have road dust on
them. Solovyov's grandmother would not allow them to
keep the flowers in the house; that bouquet upset her
very much then.

Solovyov and Leeza went to the cemetery often, especially
in summer. They would sit on narrow memorial benches
and on stone pedestals warmed by the diffused forest sun.
Sometimes (balancing) on metal fences painted to look like
silver. Leeza's white legs would be crisscrossed with pink
streaks after sitting on the metal fences.

Crosses stood on the graves; sometimes there were iron
obelisks with stars. Monuments were a rarity at the cemetery. They were trucked in from other places, carefully
carried around the graves, and set in mortar, with a trowel
tapping from all sides. This installation method evoked
respect. There was something real and kindred in the name
of that action itself, in the trowel tapping or in driving a
cigarette butt into crumbly clay. And they were not installed

immediately after the funeral but later on, after a year or two, once the ground had settled.

One time a monument with a poetry inscription was installed at the cemetery. It was on the grave of a station chief who had fallen under the Moscow–Sevastopol express train. Solovyov liked the text very much:

> *Don't tell me he has died, for he still lives!*
> *Although the altar's smashed, its flame still leaps,*
> *Although the rose is plucked, it's still in bloom,*
> *Although the harp is cracked, its strings still weep.*

> *We mourn.*
> *The management of the N railroad hub.*

Because of the collective signature under the text, Solovyov thought for a long time that the management of the railroad hub had written the beautiful poetry. As was clarified later, however, out of everything that was carved into that slab, the only words belonging to the railroad workers (other than the signature) were 'We mourn'. While studying in Petersburg, Solovyov learned that poet Semyon Nadson (1862–1887) was the author of those lines that had remained in his memory. Be that as it may, the day the monument was installed, Solovyov told Leeza that in the event of death he would want to have the same kind of monument, with poetry carved into it, installed at his grave. Solovyov said: *in the event of death*. In the depths of his childish soul, he did not allow such an event.

Solovyov did not like the obelisks. They quickly became ramshackle: the paint peeled off and the iron rusted. Little by little, their fastening pins were exposed and the obelisks began listing, expressing their hollow essence. They produced an unattractive tinny sound when touched.

Wooden crosses were another matter. Solovyov regarded those differently. Crosses were not set in mortar. They were dug into neat round pits and the earth around them was stamped on for a long time; there was no waiting for it to settle. Little Solovyov saw in that motion—which was un-cemetery-like and even similar to a dance—a lightness that partially reconciled him with life beyond the grave. Finally, he even told Leeza that he would like to lie beneath a cross rather than beneath a heavy monument. Leeza agreed. She did add, though, that a person feels nothing in the grave. But she agreed.

Solovyov remembered how his mother had been buried. How she had been lowered into a frozen wintery grave. How they could not pull out the ropes, which got caught under the coffin, and how people looked at them, with regret, from a clay heap. Nobody wanted to crawl into a grave at *Kilometer 715* for the ropes. They simply tossed in the ends, which hit the coffin like sonorous gray icicles.

When they returned from the cemetery, Solovyov told Leeza that while they were warm his mother was in an icy grave. Leeza responded again that dead people feel nothing in graves, but that did not reassure Solovyov. He could not fall asleep. Leeza sat at the head of his bed all night while he thought about how his mother must be cold in the grave. Especially considering her high temperature during her last days.

That was the day he grasped the true essence of the cemetery. He began fearing that his grandmother might be carried off there on a morning just as cold and that the cemetery would accept her with the very same hospitality. He was frightened because his world was unraveling. Slipping away, like sand through his fingers, and nothing could be done about it. Even so, he still did not consider himself mortal at that time.

The realization that he would die came to him one summer day. After making love in the forest, he and Leeza went to the cemetery. Their feet stepped lightly on moss, where pine cones crunched from time to time. They sat on one of the metal fences and Solovyov asked, 'Do you understand that we'll die in the end, too?'

Leeza looked at him in surprise. She nodded.

'Well, I just figured it out now.'

'After we did . . . *that*?'

'I don't know . . . we do *that* all the time but it occurred to me now.'

Why had they gone to the cemetery after *that*?

Solovyov stood at the graves of his mother and grandmother. They were essentially one grave, inside the same metal fence, under the same cross. The two small mounds had even merged into one during the years that had passed. Solovyov placed the gladiolus right by the cross and made a few cautious motions with the hoe. The grass at the cemetery pulled out more easily than the grass in the yard at his house. This grass had grown in the shade and did not have resilience or an abundance of sun. Clump after clump fell under Solovyov's hoe with a short, rich sound. The graves were revealed little by little: their joining turned out to be imagined. The mound on his mother's grave was slightly higher because soil had been added at various times.

Solovyov often went to his mother's grave during the first year after her death. Whispering, he would tell her about everything that had happened that day and ask for advice. He had done that during her life, too, after his mother had stopped speaking with him, as punishment for bad behavior. She would keep silent until the moment he asked her advice. Agonized, Solovyov thought up questions and asked them with a serious look. Not sensing a ploy (or perhaps sensing a ploy), his mother would answer. But only while she was alive. She did not answer a single one of his questions after her death.

Although Solovyov continued telling her about everything, over time it worked out that he went to see her ever less frequently, and there were ever more events in his life. He gasped for breath, both from the abundance of events and because they remained unspoken. Feeling indebted to his mother, he attempted to at least tell her the essential things, but here, too, his debt grew with unbelievable speed. He realized he was hopelessly behind.

'You can't tell a life, Mama,' he whispered to her once and burst into tears.

He told her nothing after that. He consoled himself with the thought that she knew everything anyway.

The year his mother died, Solovyov attempted to imagine her in the grave. When spring came, he thought ground water had permeated her coffin and his mother was lying in a cold bath. In the summer, he was already certain her skin had turned black and her eyes had fallen in. He tried— but failed—not to think about the short white worms he had seen on animal corpses. A year and a half later, after the earth on the grave mound had abruptly settled, he guessed that the coffin's lid had rotted and fallen in. Several years later, Solovyov began to feel better when, according to his notions, only a skeleton remained in the grave.

The Solovyov who was tossing weeded grass over the fence did not yet know that it lay ahead for him to find General Larionov's notebook, in which all the stages of the human body's decomposition were listed in detail—from cyanotic spots to a fully bared skeleton. Some of the listings came about as a result of the general's note-taking on specialized literature regarding exhumation and postmortems. Most of the notes were based on his personal experience and reflected what he saw on his rounds of the battlefield. Since the battles did not cease for days, sometimes not even for weeks, the corpses turned out to have decomposed to varying degrees before the burial team's arrival. This significantly increased the general's research base.

Solovyov recited a prayer for the repose of the soul. In his memory, he always heard the prayer as recited by his grandmother, so it was strange for him to hear his own voice now. The wind stirred in the crowns of the pine trees. The grave by which Solovyov was standing was the only one in the cemetery that was cared for.

When he came home, he put the hoe in the shed but then he stopped in the doorway. He went back, took the hoe, and left the yard. He walked along the fence and stopped by the neighboring gate. This was Leeza's yard. It was difficult to open the gate: Leeza's yard was just as overgrown as Solovyov's, though she had left only a little over a year ago. Solovyov fought his way to her front steps with no less frenzy than he had come to his own on the first day, though this time he was armed with a tool.

The key to Leeza's house was hidden in the same place as the key to his house, behind the door jamb. Solovyov sensed an unlived-in smell in the house as soon as he entered. More accurately, the absence of a smell. That had never happened in this house. It always smelled of something here, most often of food. Leeza's mother had loved to cook. She made beef stroganoff, turkey in cream sauce and French-style meat, things that nobody else made around here. People at *Kilometer 715* ate filling meals but they lacked delicacies.

There was always a special smell in Leeza's house at Easter. It was the smell of sacredness and celebration, joy and gifts. It joined the aromas of farmer's cheese, fresh dough, and—for some reason—incense. There was no church near the station so to Solovyov, Leeza's house seemed like a place of worship at Easter. Remembering the smell, Solovyov thought that the general's son might just have shown up at the station at Easter. That would definitely explain why he had stayed here.

Solovyov went into Leeza's room. He extended his hand to the shelf over the desk and pulled out a book at random. It was the previous year's directory for college applicants. Solovyov sat on the bed and leafed through it carefully. There were no indications in the directory about which institution Leeza planned to attend. There was not one dog-eared page or one checkmark in the margins to be found. To Solovyov's chagrin, Leeza was very neat.

He found a packet of small notebooks in one of the desk drawers. These were his own school notebooks from various years, from the very first, with large handwriting that still lacked a slant, to his sloppy ones just before graduating.

Solovyov lowered himself onto the chair and began examining Leeza's collection sheet by sheet. After suddenly going still over a fifth-grade essay, he observed a wet drop spread on the rough paper and absorb the blueness of the ink.

Solovyov himself did not know why he was continuing these searches. He had already been sitting in Leeza's house for more than three hours but had not run across anything that might give him an idea about where to find her. Solovyov had realized long ago that he would learn nothing new here about either Leeza or her father. He was simply going through Leeza's papers and touching her books, and that calmed him.

He discovered a folder of paper airplanes in the bookcase. They were airplane notes he had sent to her over the fence. In a past life. Early in the mornings: the lines were blurry in places from dew. Of course he could have said everything over the fence but he preferred airmail. He liked to write and liked to watch his words soar up into the air. And she had saved all that. Where should he look for her now?

Solovyov caught himself thinking that Filipp Larionov interested him less as the general's son than as Leeza's father. He would have liked to see him again, place him alongside Leeza, delight in their kinship, and be amazed at how Leeza, who was infinitely loved and essential to him, had come out of the ancient Larionov line.

Leeza had not come out of the Larionov line. More accurately, she was from the Larionov line, but from a different one. Larionov's line had no connection to her. That realization came about with no transition whatsoever, all at once, like distant lightning. Filipp, the general's son, was not Larionov. The information written down in Zoya's apartment resurfaced in Solovyov's memory in all its obviousness. General Larionov and Varvara Petrovna Nezhdanova had not officially registered their marriage. Filipp, their son together, was Nezhdanov.

Solovyov left for Petersburg the next day. As he closed up his house, he thought that he was closing it forever. He tried not to look back. He took the rest of the Kerch canned goods to Yegorovna. She cried again. Solovyov cried, too, because this parting with Yegorovna was also forever. As he went outside, without the canned goods, he recognized the burden he had been carrying in his bag. And he smiled.

What had dawned on him belatedly in Leeza's house did not drive him to despondency. Oddly enough, it was even a relief. Leeza's ties to the general's line—and Solovyov felt this ever more distinctly with each minute—had carried a heavy weight. That connection had been lending Leeza a certain excess worth that she did not need. She was his love, his forgotten and rediscovered joy. He knew he had to search for her.

16

When Solovyov arrived in Petersburg, he realized autumn had set in. Autumn was reflected in the windows at the Tsarskoye Selo train station, it called out here and there in the porters' voices, and drifted along a platform in the form of a forgotten newspaper. The coming of autumn would not have been so obvious if there had been rain. But a feeble and irrevocably autumnal sun was shining. No doubt remained that summer was already over here.

The joy of return enveloped Solovyov. He inhaled the biting Petersburg air and sensed it was exactly what he had been lacking. He walked along Gorokhovaya Street to the Fontanka River and turned right. Cold air wafted off the dark water. Ripples coated the river. Solovyov noticed he was the only person wearing a short-sleeved shirt.

Solovyov lived on the city's Petrograd Side. As already stated, he rented a room on Zhdanovskaya Embankment that Prof. Nikolsky had found for him through acquaintances. The professor had explained that the embankment had nothing to do with Soviet politician Andrei Zhdanov. It received its name from the Zhdanovka River, which immortalized clerks by the name of Zhdanov, former owners of these lands. For its part, the surname Zhdanov dates back to the word *zhdan*, denoting a long-awaited child. With the addition of the negative particle *ne*, the word *nezhdan* denoted (correspondingly) an unawaited child. By all indications, a distant ancestor of Filipp Nezhdanov was such a child. Solovyov was thinking about that as he entered the archway of house No. 11 on Zhdanovskaya Embankment.

House No. 11 was special. This was manifested not only in the grandiose Stalin-era Empire style of its architecture: the workshop for engineer Mstislav Sergeyevich Los, a character in Alexei Tolstoy's (1882–1945) novel *Aelita*, was located in the building's courtyard. Los, who planned to fly to Mars, was seeking a travel companion. Tolstoy had lived right here, too, on Zhdanovskaya Embankment, in house No. 3. He had taken up residence near author Fyodor Sologub (1863–1927) and was not planning to fly anywhere, having recently returned from abroad.

House No. 11 was constructed in 1954. It stood on the same spot as the building and courtyard that Tolstoy described. Thus (Solovyov reasoned as he walked up the stairs) the fantasy writer's work took into consideration the actual particularities of the previous building No. 11. Given Alexei Tolstoy's death in 1945, the book did not take into consideration the peculiarities of the current No. 11. In that sense, the fictional make-believe in *Aelita* corresponded to actual life in the 1920s more than to the objective reality of the 1990s. Solovyov's next conclusion: the border between make-believe and reality disappears when time is taken out of the equation. He wiped his feet on the mat and shut the door behind him.

Solovyov lived in a two-room apartment. This was a happy version of a communal apartment: given its small population, it had not been reduced to a complete wreck. Additional happiness lay in the fact that Solovyov's flatmate hardly lived here. Once every two or three months he would arrive suddenly from somewhere like Murmansk or Syktyvkar and then leave just as suddenly a few days later. His girlfriends came to see him on those days, though Solovyov saw them only in passing, too, when they ran from the next room to the shower late at night, wrapped in towels.

The apartment had windows on both sides of the building: they looked out over the courtyard (including part of Ofitsersky Lane) and the embankment. The windows in the kitchen and his flatmate's room looked into the courtyard. Solovyov's room (and this was its amazing quality) had a view of the Zhdanovka River, a small chunk of Petrovsky Island with the Petrovsky Stadium, and, further, beyond the trees on the island, the Malaya Neva River. In Solovyov's opinion, the stadium spoiled the picture a lot, but nothing could be done about that.

The stadium did not just ruin the view. It complicated life. Existence near the stadium had its own shadowy and (in many of the courtyard's secluded corners) damp sides, because fans of the Zenith football team urinated with reckless abandon. They urinated under the archway, in the entryways, and by the fences; they urinated during matches, whether the main team or the reserves were playing; and before and after matches. They urinated as if Zenith were the champion although the team was not even in the top three at the time.

Fans left behind heaps of rubbish: beer cans, chip bags, dried fish heads, corn cobs, and newspaper cones, flattened on the asphalt. All this was thickly strewn with sunflower seed hulls. The hulls swirled in light little tornados that blew off the river and rose over the roofs of building No. 11, Zhdanovskaya Embankment, Ofitsersky Lane, and the entire Petrograd side.

Solovyov had arrived on a match day. He was not a fan and he regarded football matches with irritation. At the same time, there was something about how they took place that appealed to him. The roar of many thousands of fans at the stadium excited him: that roar was sometimes indistinct, like a distant waterfall, and sometimes explosive (after a goal). But it was always powerful.

Solovyov sat on the windowsill and watched spectators disperse after the match. They flowed across the wide bridge over the Zhdanovka River like a viscous mass that could not come apart: that bridge was directly under Solovyov's window. To Solovyov, the slow procession that was devoid of anything personal and the continuous, indistinct rumble seemed to be the embodiment of history's gait. Majestic and pointless, like any concerted movement.

Looking out the window at the motley crowd, he remembered the black-and-white crowds in revolutionary newsreels. The spasmodic motions of people walking. The comical rocking of those standing; in modern filming, you did not notice that those standing are also moving. Little clouds of steam. They came up suddenly, as if they had been added in. Disappeared suddenly. The same with cigarette smoke. People were now walking that same way past the Second

Cadet Corps (now the Military Space Academy), where the general once studied.

Football fans wearing Zenith caps were walking past the Second Cadet Corps. Thousands of dark blue caps. Thousands of dark blue scarves. They irritated Solovyov tremendously. And they did not know that a general had studied here. Solovyov began to feel lonely because of the abundance of people.

This feeling was new for him. He had never yet felt lonely in Petersburg. Even in the absence of friends, this city—with its strange aura and a people unlike in the rest of Russia—had sated him. He had not felt abandoned before when he was all by himself. He felt that now, though. It crossed his mind that Leeza had abandoned him, though in actuality it was the opposite. Solovyov picked up Tolstoy's *Aelita* and peered out the window.

Beyond the gate, a wasteland reached to the embankment of the Zhdanovka River. Beyond the river there stood the vague contours of trees on Petrovsky Island. Beyond them, there faded a doleful sunset that could not fade away. Its light touched at the edges of long clouds that seemed like islands reaching into the sky's green waters. Above them was green sky where a few stars had begun shining. It was quiet on the old Earth. That was the only spot in the book that Solovyov genuinely liked even though it twice referred to the sky's green color, for no reason. Sometimes it even seemed to him that there was no need to continue.

Solovyov went outside after the sunset had faded. Interesting, where had the wasteland been, anyway? Or was it a fantasy of Tolstoy's, who wrote his novel while still in Germany? Solovyov's foot grazed a beer can and it rolled off the sidewalk with a clink. Had Nikolai Chernyshevsky seen that wasteland? If he had seen it, that would affirm that cadet Larionov must have seen it, too.

Solovyov went to the institute the next day. Even as he was approaching the famous building with its columns, he caught a glimpse of academician Temriukovich. Temriukovich was walking along, dressed in a Mackintosh raincoat with a fifties cut: it had roomy sleeves (one of them was smudged with whitewash) and its shoulders, which had once been angular, were now sagging and rumpled. The end of its untied belt dragged along the ground. Solovyov did not want to catch up to Temriukovich. Elementary courtesy would have demanded pointing out the smudged sleeve and dragging belt to the academician, but something hinted to the graduate student that there was no point in doing so. Solovyov slowed his pace and followed the academician.

Solovyov regarded Temriukovich with respect and there was a special reason for that. It was through Temriukovich's efforts that the complete collected works of Sergei M. Solovyov were published during the Soviet era. Despite not being a relative of Sergei Solovyov, graduate student Solovyov believed in their spiritual kinship and felt favorable toward everyone who was somehow connected to the great man with whom he shared a surname.

As a scholar, Temriukovich was not one to reach for the stars, but there was no need in his case anyway. The necessities for the edition he had conceived were painstakingness and diligence in the task, and, to some extent, fortitude. An edition of Sergei Solovyov was not something that was taken for granted in the Soviet Union. As a reward for successful completion of the work, Temriukovich was nominated to become an academician. Nobody counted on his being elected. Above all, candidate Temriukovich.

'Neither Bakhtin nor Lotman were academicians,' he had consoled himself, 'they weren't even corresponding members.'

But Temriukovich's situation turned out differently from Mikhail Bakhtin's and Yuri Lotman's. Destiny was favorable to Temriukovich, unlike Bakhtin and Lotman. This manifested itself on one occasion, when the members of the Academy of Sciences had not come to any agreement about a candidacy. The generally foolproof mechanism—which had made academicians out of institute directors, members of the government, oligarchs, and people who were simply respected—went haywire. By not agreeing amongst themselves, the academicians intuitively voted for someone who, to their thinking, had no chance whatsoever of making it. They voted almost unanimously for Temriukovich.

There was widespread surprise at the moderate joy displayed by the newly elected academician. A much more enthusiastic reaction was shown by those who had worked toward this goal, spending years cultivating Academy members and trotting from floor to floor of the Academy's tall Presidium building with its strange-looking golden top stories that inspired the popular nickname *The Cologne Bottle*. Yes, Temriukovich accepted congratulations politely and expressed satisfaction with the academicians' vote but—as noted by corresponding member Pogosyan, who was in attendance when the results were announced—Temriukovich's thoughts were far away.

And that was the simple truth. The new academician's colleagues suddenly recalled the *overt aloofness* that had accompanied Temriukovich for the last few years. If his condition might initially have been described as *deep pensiveness*, nothing but *overt aloofness* could describe the current state of affairs. That, however, was still not the worst of it. Temriukovich's coworkers began noticing that he was talking to himself. The first to take notice was Igor Murat, a candidate of historical sciences.

'Let's have a look, see what kind of book this is,' Temriukovich said one day, as he approached a bookcase, 'probably rubbish.'

The publication that interested the academician was Igor Murat's book, *The Revolutionary-Democratic Movement in Left-Bank Ukraine During 1861–1891*. The author was standing on the other side of the bookcase, unnoticed by Temriukovich. Murat had just plunged an immersion heater into a glass of water and was preparing to have tea. Murat froze when he peered through the shelves and watched the academician pick up *The Revolutionary-Democratic Movement in Left-Bank Ukraine During 1861–1891*. Murat turned his gaze to the heater. It was now impossible to turn it off soundlessly. Murat listened, speechless, as the academician moistened his index finger and paged through the book.

'Shit,' said Temriukovich with a sigh as he put the book back. 'Premium quality shit.'

The water had begun boiling noisily in the glass and Temriukovich peered around the bookcase. He saw the pale Murat there.

'I heard what you were saying about my book,' whispered Murat.

'I didn't say anything,' said the unruffled Temriukovich, 'all I did was think about it.'

That calmed Murat slightly.

The academician's oddities continued, though. At first, he still showed consideration for his coworkers and only ventured to make sharp remarks when he believed he was alone. Later, he did not exactly stop noticing those around him but, as Pavel Grebeshkov, the institute's deputy director of scholarly affairs expressed it, he had crossed the line between internal and external speech. When addressing listeners, Temriukovich spoke expressively and intelligibly. He addressed himself in soft, rapid speech, just as theater actors utter texts with the stage direction 'aside.'

That was the format in which he accused administrative manager Vladlen Maslo of dishonesty in carrying out multi-year renovations on the institute's building. When he tripped over some scaffolding one day, the academician assumed, in an undertone, that Maslo was a thief, which was allegedly why the renovations were so grueling and unsuccessful. This occurred in the presence of witnesses. Unlike Murat, Maslo appealed to the director immediately, demanding that Temriukovich be fired from the institute due to his, Temriukovich's, mental incompetence. The thought that Maslo could appropriate government funds seemed insane to the director, too. To the latter's credit, he did not fire Temriukovich.

'Temriukovich is a full member of the Russian Academy of Sciences,' said the director, 'and under formal reasoning, I have no grounds for doubting his mental competence.'

And so membership in the Academy of Sciences helped Temriukovich avoid being fired. He continued coming to the institute only on required days, as he had been doing for the last forty years.

After entering the building, Temriukovich headed for the

coat check. The man at the coat check bent across the counter to take the academician's raincoat.

'Where'd you lean against something, Mikhail Sergeevich?' the attendant asked.

Temriukovich looked at the smudged sleeve and did not answer. Addressing himself on the stairs, he said, 'Can't a person ever hear anything nice?'

After Temriukovich had disappeared around a corner, Solovyov went up to the second floor. He went to the director to inform him that he was back from his trip. Strictly speaking, there was no real necessity to do so; a written report would have sufficed. But the fact that the trip had taken place in August and in Yalta gave Solovyov no peace. He remembered the director's look in parting and he thought the gaze was ironic. Solovyov wanted to tell the director personally about his findings, and, first and foremost, the text he had found. The plastic folder with the general's memoirs was melting in his hands and growing slippery; it had nearly fallen on the floor twice. Solovyov wanted rehabilitation. Maybe even encouragement.

The director's office door was ajar. The director himself was not visible but his voice was audible. He was telling someone off: 'Of all possible feelings, the only thing you have is a grasping reflex.'

After thinking, the director repeated it, syllable by syllable, 'A gras-ping re-flex.'

A listless objection was heard in response. The words were indiscernible (what could they be in a case like this?) and all that remained was intonation. Simultaneously ingratiating and tedious. A woman was speaking. She calmed the director a little.

'You can't live on reflexes alone,' he said conciliatorily. 'Forgive me, but you can't be such a reptile.'

This turned out to be an inopportune moment to visit. Solovyov had wearied instantaneously. He realized he was not even interested in finding out who, exactly, the director was addressing. Solovyov walked slowly toward the Twentieth-Century History Department, his department. Who could be called a reptile? At the end of the corridor, he turned to look back anyway. Tina Zhuk, a graduate student, was coming out of the director's office. She had a very loud voice and Solovyov was surprised she had just been speaking so softly. It turned out that Tina could do so when she tried. Temriukovich was her research advisor. The academician did not like his graduate student and everyone at the institute knew it. Nobody liked her.

In the Twentieth-Century History Department, Solovyov donated one hundred rubles for a gift for a coworker, Baksheeva. Baksheeva, a candidate of historical sciences, had just had a baby and they were giving her an electric teakettle. The trade union committee chair decided to show Solovyov the electric teakettle after she'd accepted his money. She placed a finger to her lips, opened the cardboard box, and took out the gift. She, Novoseltseva, had invested her own personal money, at least temporarily, until she had recovered the sum for the teakettle. She showed Solovyov the list of donors: it was always a big risk to collect money for an item that had already been purchased. Solovyov flicked the teakettle with his fingernail. The sound turned out to be unexpectedly low and muted. The department office was empty. Lots of people were still on vacation.

Solovyov saw Temriukovich again on the second floor:

he was headed toward the administrative offices. Tina Zhuk was walking slightly behind him. When she saw Solovyov, she pointed at Temriukovich and touched her temple with her finger.

'He called me a snake in the grass,' she whispered to Solovyov. 'Can you imagine? He's already completely lost it.'

Solovyov observed as Zhuk's nose began moving in time with her lips. He had not noticed this before. It was possible this could be explained by her anxiety. Administrative manager Maslo popped out of the closest door.

'Solovyov,' he said, without a hello. 'We're going to start taking down the scaffolding in an hour. We'll need your help.'

Solovyov nodded to Tina. Temriukovich turned around as if he had remembered something and began walking in the opposite direction. Maslo disappeared behind the door as soon as he saw that.

'Stole a pile and now hides,' Temriukovich mumbled, looking at the floor. 'Vacations on Majorca. And I, a full member of the Academy of Sciences, vacation in the city of Zelenogorsk. One might ask why!'

'Because he's greedy,' Tina Zhuk answered after the academician had moved further away. 'He's just a glutton. And senile.'

Solovyov went outside and headed off toward the University, the famous Twelve Colleges, a long red building that stood perpendicular to the Neva River. Solovyov hoped to find out something about Leeza in that building. Based on what Yegorovna had said, Leeza had left more than a year ago. If Leeza left to go to college, she should be in her second year now. Solovyov realized he did not know what department Leeza might have entered. Furthermore, there was no evidence she had entered a university in Petersburg. Strictly speaking, there was not even any certainty that Leeza had entered a university anywhere at all.

He was greeted with surprise at the administrative office. They had no obligation to provide student information to him.

'This is very important to me,' said Solovyov.

When all was said and done, Solovyov was a recent student himself, so they accommodated him. There turned out to be three Larionovas at the university. Not one of them was Yelizaveta. One was studying in the geography department, the second was in Solovyov's very own history department, and the third was in journalism. Solovyov decided to meet all three just in case there was an error in the rolls.

He did not have to leave the Twelve Colleges building to go to the geography department. By checking the schedule, he learned where the second-year students had classes and went into the classroom during the break. A map of mineral resources in Siberia, speckled with red spots, hung on the wall. There were many resources. A great many.

Solovyov approached the first table and asked where he might find Larionova. They showed him. Even from afar, he knew it was not Leeza and thought about leaving without going up to her. He began taking a step but for some reason looked again at Larionova; her face was dotted with acne. It recalled the map of Siberia. This was probably what prevented him from making a fast exit. If he acted that way, reasoned the young historian, Larionova's classmates would decide her appearance had driven him away. He did not want to cause Larionova—even if she was not Leeza—additional distress.

He walked over to her and wanted to explain what, exactly, had happened but Larionova did not let him say a word. She took him by the elbow and walked out of the classroom with him. Larionova continued holding Solovyov by the elbow in the hallway but did not look up. She had a sweet face, despite the acne.

'I'm looking for a young woman whose surname is Larionova,' said Solovyov, 'but it turns out it's not you.'

Larionova nodded. That was how things always worked out in her life.

Solovyov searched out the second Larionova the next day. She was writing a term paper on ancient battle tactics but knew nothing about the prominent general who shared her surname. That surprised Solovyov. In the first instant, the thought even flashed through his mind to tell her about the general and his Thermopylae passions. The history department's Larionova was tall and broad-shouldered. Of all the Larionovas Solovyov had seen, basically, she deserved to be the general's granddaughter more than the rest. Despite that circumstance (or perhaps precisely because of it), Larionova the second did not inspire Solovyov. He did not even consider telling her about anything and kept the conversation to a bare minimum.

There turned out to be the most hassle with Larionova number three. They told Solovyov at the journalism department that Larionova was sick, so he went to see her at the dormitory. There was no immediate answer when he knocked at Larionova's room. Judging from the noise beyond the door, they were celebrating something in the room. Solovyov had lived in a dormitory for several years so he knew dorm sounds and smells so well that, based on the specifics of how they were combined, he could determine to a high degree of accuracy the reason behind the festivities. Most frequently, people celebrated birthdays, weddings, and passing exams in dorms. Sometimes they just drank vodka but there were no good smells for that. In those cases, they made do with bread, sausage, and marinated cucumbers.

It was not exam time. They were not celebrating a wedding (Solovyov cracked the door open). Birthday was left.

'Come in,' several guests shouted at once.

Solovyov went in. About ten people were sitting at two desks that had been pushed together. Two of them were on chairs, one was on a nightstand, and the rest were on two beds. One of the beds had needed to be pulled a little toward the table. A portrait of Fidel Castro hung on the entire wall over the bed that had not been moved.

Solovyov had not expected to recognize the television news host Makhalov as one of those sitting (as it happened) on the bed under Fidel. Makhalov, who was slightly drunk, rocked pensively and placed his head on a dark-haired young woman's shoulder. When Solovyov stated the reason he had put in an appearance, it emerged that she was Larionova. Her name was Yekaterina.

Yekaterina was celebrating her birthday. There was a glass bowl of Olivier salad in the middle of the table. A dish of olives right next to the salad. For beverages there was predominantly vodka, which they were drinking out of little plastic cups. Solovyov wanted to leave but they convinced him to stay and drink to Yekaterina. They convinced him loudly and spiritedly. Then they forgot about him.

Every now and then Makhalov kissed Yekaterina on the lips and each time there was a sound like quiet chewing. That—as well as the salad on their lips—gave their kisses a piquant gastronomical flavor. Makhalov called her by her full name—Yekaterina—and the others followed suit, calling her that, too, even those who, by all appearances, had long known her well.

Solovyov was sitting on the bed next to Makhalov. Oddly enough, he did not feel like leaving. Not because he liked it here (it is not very likely he could have said that) but because he did not know where he should go now. He felt enervated after determining that not one of these Larionovas had anything to do with Leeza. He realized that his searches could be endless. Why, really, was he looking for Leeza only at the University? And why only in Petersburg?

One of the guests was describing how he and his girlfriend had made love on a beach one night in Gurzuf. After a while, it felt to them as if a whole group of people was watching. They stopped what they were doing and approached the observers. Much to their surprise, they discovered it was rocks. Then they made love on those rocks. The girlfriend turned out to be Yekaterina.

Makhalov said that, as a rule, television news was a lie. Moreover, the problem was not the content itself (he drank, and inhaled through his nostrils, pursing his lips) but how it was presented: how much, the order, vocabulary choices, etcetera.

They poured vodka for Solovyov yet again. His little

plastic cup ended up filled to the brim. To his own surprise, Solovyov drank it all in one gulp and chased it with olives. Applause rang out. When Solovyov glanced at his little cup, he saw it was full again. Solovyov was no longer sure he had actually drunk the previous one.

'Sad though it is, you have to sleep with someone to get on television,' said Makhalov.

'I don't believe it,' shouted Yekaterina.

'Imagine,' Makhalov sighed, and Solovyov felt Malakhov's hand on his knee.

Then a person arrived with a bottle of Metaxa brandy. Solovyov no longer felt like drinking but they all began persuading him that he definitely had to try the Metaxa. Solovyov tried the Metaxa.

Unexpectedly, Makhalov farted loudly and several people began giggling.

'We'll make it through the winter,' said Makhalov.

Yekaterina nodded with an expression of calm certainty. The guests drank again. Their motions were growing ever more chaotic and at some point they themselves disintegrated into their component parts: eyes, arms, mouths, and little plastic cups. Solovyov unintentionally leaned back and hit his head on the wall. Fidel was the last person he saw before his head struck.

Solovyov came to late at night. He guessed that it was late at night from the darkness in the room and the absence of guests. Once his eyes had grown accustomed to the murkiness, he realized there were at least two people in the room other than him. There was a light disturbance on the next bed.

Solovyov discerned two silhouettes there: one lying, the

other sitting. The sitting one was unsuccessfully attempting to revive the lying one by shaking the person's head and whispering something in the person's ear, but the lying person only defended himself limply. The lying person spoke in a constricted, unintelligible whisper, but from the general tone of the answers, it followed that the person wanted to sleep. Based on a series of indirect indicators, Solovyov guessed that the attacking side was the birthday girl. This was confirmed when Yekaterina lost her patience and suddenly said loudly, in a bitter voice, 'If you don't want to love me, others will.'

Solovyov tensed up, anticipating something unpleasant. He hoped the lying person would not allow things to develop under that scenario. In answer, though, the voice resounded just as loudly, 'Good luck.'

It was Makhalov's voice. There was not a speck of jealousy in it.

The aspiring journalist jumped noisily over to Solovyov's bed. Solovyov squeezed his eyes shut with all his might. Yekaterina shook him by the shoulder but he did not wake up. An instant later, he felt her fingers on the zipper of his jeans. Solovyov could pretend not to wake up but he had no prerogative to resist if he was asleep.

'Objectively speaking,' said Yekaterina, 'he's already prepared to make love to me and that's despite being sound asleep. Unlike you, who's awake.'

There were sounds of someone flushing in a bathroom and, flipflops tapping, returning to their room.

'Don't flatter yourself,' Makhalov muttered. 'That has nothing to do with you. He's dreaming of another Larionova.'

17

Solovyov worked intensively in the archives throughout September and October. After finishing a section about events during the first half of 1920, he turned to the second half of that same year. On October 1, the young historian reached the October period of the Civil War; that seemed like a good sign to him. He and his material were beginning to resonate with one another.

October (one of Russia's most unfortunate months) turned out to be unlucky for the White Movement in Crimea, too. The White Army was retreating. After suffering defeat near Kakhovka, the army left Northern Taurida, fighting. The army's path lay toward Perekop, for which General Larionov had specific plans.

Solovyov estimated the White Army's numbers taking part in defensive battles at approximately 25–27,000 (by comparison, Dupont's *The Enigma of the Russian General* raises them for no reason, speaking of 33–35,000). In Solovyov's opinion, the Reds' forces totaled around 130,000 (Dupont writes of 135–140,000). These figures, however, did not fully take into account the losses the Whites incurred in defending Northern Taurida, something Solovyov particularly noted. He emphasized that only statistics for certain army units could be vouched for with any degree of certainty:

Consolidated Guard Regiment	400 bayonets and sabers, 3 heavy weapons
13th Infantry Division	1,530 bayonets and sabers, 20 heavy weapons
34th Infantry Division	750 bayonets and sabers, 25 heavy weapons
Kornilov Division	1,860 bayonets and sabers, 23 heavy weapons
Drozdov Division	3,260 bayonets and sabers, 36 heavy weapons
Markov Division	100 bayonets and sabers, 21 heavy weapons

Solovyov explained the Reds' four- or five-fold superiority over the Whites by the separate peace treaty that the Reds and Poles had concluded behind the general's back. The agreement untied the Reds' hands: after withdrawing their large forces from the western front, they moved them south, against the White Army. The Whites' position was becoming critical.

All that remained for the White Army of the entire, huge country was a patch of land surrounded by sea. It was connected to the mainland by the narrow isthmus for which the retreating army was striving. The White Army's fate depended on who reached the isthmus first: if cut off from Crimea, the White Army would not have the slightest chance of being saved. This did not just affect the army, though. The downfall of the White troops would subject to mortal danger thousands of others who had retreated to Crimea with those troops. They would not have time to evacuate.

The general was in a hurry. He had a slight time advantage that he was afraid of losing. After the battles near Kakhovka, he moved his troops southeast through Northern Taurida without giving them respite. He was still not giving up. As he reviewed episodes of the Kakhovka combat in his mind, he was still relying on the power of his soldiers' desperation and the special courage of the doomed. After that strange forced march began, however, the general sensed the beginning of the end for the first time.

This was not an army advancing toward Perekop, it was an unorganized column of sleepwalkers traveling along the ice-bound expanse of Northern Taurida. Leaning from his saddle, the general peered into his soldiers' faces and saw an expression of *mortal exhaustion* on those faces. He knew this expression. He had seen it on the faces of those who froze in snow banks. Of those who stood up straight and walked into machine gun fire. But never before had he seen this expression on every face. The general was beginning to understand that he had lost more than just an individual, if very important, battle. It was becoming clearer to him with every minute that the war, as a whole, had been lost.

His army could no longer fight. The reason was not the poor uniforms (though they truly were poor) and not the lack of ammunition (which was, indeed, lacking). This was not even about the army's demoralization: the general had managed to restore his soldiers' fighting spirit even after worse defeats. The reason was that the army had *depleted its entire reservoir*. It was this very expression that the general used in the telegram he sent to foreign envoys when he was halfway to Perekop. In their response, the envoys requested an urgent meeting. They needed the general's explanations. But what was the point of a meeting like that? What, in actuality, could he explain to them?

After dropping the reins, the general took a sheet of paper and a pencil from his map case. His horse slowed to a walk. He thought a bit and wrote to the envoys that there was no more rage in his soldiers' eyes. There was no joy. There was no fear. There was not even suffering. There was nothing there but an endless wish for repose. How does it happen, the general asked, that an object suddenly loses its qualities? Why does a magnet demagnetize? Why does salt stop being saline? After reading what he had written, the general folded the sheet in neat quarters and ripped it to pieces. They fell behind his back like large snowflakes.

The soldiers could not warm up. They stuffed straw under the thin broadcloth of their military overcoats but it did not help. Sometimes the soldiers burned tumbleweeds so they could at least hold their numbed fingers over them for a minute. Gusts of wind carried off the tumbleweeds; small fiery balls scattered along the steppe when dusk was falling. That wind flung prickly bits of ice into the marchers' faces and the wind got under their overcoats, removing the last bit of warmth radiated from the soldiers' fatigued bodies.

The soldiers wanted to sleep. After two days of uninterrupted battle, some fell asleep on their feet. Lulled by the column's even pace, they closed their eyes involuntarily and continued walking in their sleep. The artillerymen began sitting on the gun carriages but the general forbade that. As they drifted into sleep, they fell from the gun carriages and under the wheels.

The general did not allow them to lie down on the carts. He pulled from the carts those wounded but still capable of traveling and forced them to walk. Cursing the general and his orders, they walked. They held the sides of the carts and left a bloody trail in the snow, but they walked. Their bandages trailed behind them. And they remained alive. The gravely wounded, unable to move, could not warm up. They shouted that they were freezing. Someone covered them with coats, mattresses, and rags, but still they could not warm up. The majority of them had frozen by the end of the march.

As the general straightened an overcoat that dangled from one of the carts, he touched the firm, oblong object that was holding the overcoat. It was a frozen soldier's arm. It held the overcoat in a death grip. The general rode off abruptly and observed the overcoat trailing behind the cart for a while.

The field kitchens had no provisions. The general ordered that what little still remained be given to the wounded. But only thin soup remained. This soup could not satiate the wounded; it could not even warm them. They looked upward incessantly as they lay on the carts, feeling nothing but the cold. This was a cosmic cold, emanating from distant, indifferent stars.

It was the kind of cold that made the soldiers think they would never warm up now. Not warm up and not get a good sleep. Many wanted to die and the general knew that. He forbade his soldiers to daydream about death.

'Whoever of you dies,' said the general, 'will end up in the grave unwarmed.'

There was no answer.

'He will freeze eternally,' said the general.

The soldiers walked in complete silence. They were afraid that their last remnants of warmth would leave, along with the words they uttered. All that sounded were the even clatter of horse hoofs, the creak of carts, and the crunch of frost under the gun carriages' wheels. And the groans of the wounded. A while later (their sense of time was dulled, too) a quiet glass-like sound blended in with those other noises. The general rode off to the side and saw ice chafing against rocks by the water. They had retreated to the Sivash. The salt-water lake was covered with a thin icy crust.

An explosion rang out somewhere in the distance. And then closer. Again in the distance. This was the Reds' artillery shelling. It created the impression that the Reds were shooting at random. The retreating troops did not slow their pace. Sometimes the shells landed a few dozen meters from the column. They raised pillars of water in the sea that flashed briefly and gloomily in the moonlight. At times they exploded with a deafening dry bang; the general understood then that the Sivash had frozen solid in places. This discovery made him feel uneasy.

'General Winter,' whispered General Larionov. 'He's made his appearance a month earlier than usual.'

They saw distant campfires at around two in the morning. This did not bode well at all for those retreating and the general knew it. Those campfires meant that isolated Red units had managed to go around his army from the east and enter the isthmus first. It was also possible that the

Sivash had frozen so much in places that the Reds could cross from the side of the village of Stroganovka. Now they awaited the general's troops along their retreat route. Movement continued, though those campfires meant death.

The general did not dismiss the idea that events could develop that way, though he considered it improbable. He surmised that the Reds would want to intercept him, but here he was counting on the Sivash, which did not usually freeze. His calculation did not hold true. He was left hoping that only the Reds' vanguard had managed to cross.

The general could not imagine that the cavalry—particularly the artillery weapons—could have crossed the first thin ice. He could not imagine that much of any significant enemy force could have made its way here during the time the Whites were on their inhuman forced march. Even so—regardless of how many of them there were—the Reds had arrived on the isthmus first. Despite the cold. And the barely frozen Sivash. The general's army was like a worn-out horse. He had worn it out in hopes of saving it. It was the first time in his life that the general had subjected soldiers to an ordeal like this. It was the first time in his life that he felt the inevitability of defeat.

He scrutinized the soldiers' faces yet again, as if searching for clues. The cold had smoothed the features of those faces, depriving them of expression. Frost lay on their mustaches and eyebrows. There was nothing in his soldiers' eyes but the campfires burning up ahead. Did they surmise what those campfires meant? Even if they did, the pull of that flame was so strong that it was already impossible to stop their motion toward it.

And the general did not even try. Stopping here would

have been tantamount to death. On this bare and completely unprotected plain, his troops would be swept away by the Reds' superior forces. Occupying positions on the well-fortified Perekop remained their only chance of salvation. For that, they now needed the impossible: an attack.

'Prepare for battle,' said the general, his words drowning in the beginnings of a blizzard.

The general said it loudly and nobody heard him. He knew it was useless to repeat. He spurred his horse and galloped off to the leading column.

Why had the Reds lit the campfires? Why did they not continue moving toward Perekop? Were they unable to? Had they made a quick stop to warm up? This will remain one of the war's enigmas. In Solovyov's opinion, the Reds also did not suppose the enemy was capable of ending up in this sector so early. According to all their mental calculations, the general and his army could not have turned up here until at least the next morning. It is possible the Reds did not expect the general to accomplish the unthinkable, so had calmly lit their campfires. Even if they had not lit them calmly, though, they simply could not have survived on a night like that without fires.

Solovyov attributed the Reds' mind-boggling carelessness to their being completely frozen. To the narrowing of blood vessels in the brain as a result of hypothermia. This was how the historian explained the fact that the Reds did not even have an outpost. They glimpsed the White Army only when the figure of a horseman emerged in front of them, out of the blizzard, which was finally running wild.

'Who goes there?' they asked by a campfire.

'Friend,' answered the general.

He slowly rode up to the nearest campfire, where those sitting recognized him. It was impossible not to recognize him. Even in 1920, in the absence of television and glossy magazines, the general was one of several faces everyone knew. When seen from below, he seemed huge. He looked like a monument.

Nobody stirred by the fire. People hold their breath like this when lightning balls appear: they feign nonexistence, hoping it will disappear. But the general was not disappearing. He and his horse grew each time the fire blazed. The Red commander emerged from the darkness. Stood still. His hand extended on its own to salute.

'Your Excellency . . .'

'At ease,' said the general.

The general's army was passing by behind his back but he was watching those seated at the campfires. For their part, they were still sitting motionlessly, watching the general. How his horse stamped its feet, how its flanks occasionally trembled. The bay horse was turning white before their eyes. The general was turning white: his military overcoat, his hood, and the reins in his hands. His face was also white. Never before had they seen such a white general. The cavalry was slowly floating past their very eyes in the drifting snow, as if it were surmounting sediment at the bottom of the sea. The infantry passed by. The heavy weaponry rode by. This went on for a long time, but nobody could grasp how long. Time had stopped. When the last infantryman had passed, the general nodded silently and vanished in the darkness.

They approached Perekop at dawn. The general ordered they demolish all remaining structures there and build campfires with them. A train with foodstuffs and firewood was already on its way from Dzhankoy. The general checked the condition of the fortifications and ordered they stretch barbed wire where there were breaks. At first he wanted to set up camp with tents but he knew that was already impossible. He commanded only that nobody lie in the snow. An instant later, everyone was sleeping but the posted sentinels. The sentinels needed to be relieved every hour. People simply had no strength for more.

The foreign envoys awaited the general in Dzhankoy. The general felt nothing but contempt for the envoys. He placed no great hopes in his meeting with them but decided to go anyway. The thought of evacuating the army had made his decision. He headed for Dzhankoy after leaving General Shatalov in his place.

The general rode his armored train car along the tracks he had laid. The warmth in the car and the clacking of the wheels made his head spin. The general felt something he had felt only in childhood. This was a feeling of joy and immortality.

'Joy and immortality,' he uttered.

This feeling had come to him several times recently, so the general thought he would most likely die soon. That was the last thing he had time to think before falling asleep.

A locomotive's drawn-out whistle awakened the general. It came from a passing train. They had stopped at a station.

'Dzhankoy?' the general asked the valet.

'Dzhankoy,' replied the valet.

He was holding a soap dish in one hand, a towel in the other.

The general went over to the washstand. For some reason,

the water was cold even in the warm train car, and the general remembered how he had doused himself with water every morning in the cadet corps. How his body and his comrades' bodies had been covered in goosebumps. He had a different body then. He took the towel from the valet and used it to rub his face until it was red. It was completely different.

The foreign diplomatic mission employees had gathered in a small chamber at the city council. They were sitting on bentwood chairs along both sides of a threadbare runner rug. The rug began at the doorway and led to a long oak table. Everyone rose when the general appeared, accompanied by an escort. The escort remained by the doorway and the general walked through the chamber, without glancing at anyone. He unbuttoned his military overcoat and half-sat on a chair.

'We are leaving Crimea,' the general said, in a silent whisper. 'We will hold Perekop as long as required to evacuate everyone.'

The diplomatic mission employees looked at the general, expressionless.

'I need to save my army,' the general went on. 'I need your help.'

'How splendid that you take your decisions without consulting your allies,' said the British envoy.

The general took a cigarette case from his pocket and opened it with a melodic sound.

'I appealed to your king, asking how many people he would accept in the event of our evacuation.'

Seeing the general had taken out the cigarette, an orderly brought him a match.

'He did not even respond to me,' the general's words blended with the cigarette smoke, sounding indistinct.

The British envoy wanted to object but the general raised his hand as if to save him the trouble.

'I'm appealing to all of you: accept my soldiers. *The comrades* will not spare anyone's life,' the general crushed the cigarette in a massive marble ashtray. 'Not anyone's. I shall take my leave.'

He walked slowly along the runner rug but stopped just short of the door.

'Half a year ago, England prevented me from planting minefields in Odessa's water zone. Why?'

He was standing, with his head lowered. He did not turn.

'I do not know,' said the British envoy.

'Well, I do know. British transports are now exporting grain from there, purchased for nothing from the Bolsheviks. That grain is soaked in Russian peasants' blood.'

The general returned to Perekop late that evening. The reconnaissance chief reported to him that the enemy had managed to move significant forces toward Perekop during the day. The general nodded. He already felt the Reds' pace and expected their offensive in the morning.

The general gave the wake-up signal an hour before dawn. He did not announce formation after they played reveille. He ordered only that the fires be stoked to blazing.

'Jump over the fires!' the general shouted and his voice came back to him in the regiment commanders' shouts, like a weak echo.

'Jump over the fires!' he shouted again in the quiet that had set in.

Several people hinted at slight movement then immediately dissolved into the overall motionlessness. The army had fallen into lethargy in an obvious way. The general rushed to the closest fire and began shaking those who were sitting there. One after the other they stood and looked at him with vacant, weepy eyes. Never before had he seen his army *like this*. The general was genuinely frightened for the first time in his life.

He tore around among the campfires, attempting to bring his army back to life. Pounded soldiers on the face and in the gut. Shouted that they would be slaughtered like pigs.

Larionov distributed a half-glass of vodka to each but it had only a sedative effect. He ordered that a march be played, but the musicians' fingers would not move in the cold. He buried his face in his hands and disappeared into the commander-in-chief's tent.

When the other generals approached him in the tent, he said, 'This army has died. And will never rise from the dead.'

A distant thundering sounded as he spoke. The Red artillery was beginning to shell. The Reds shelled often but poorly. Their shells fell either in front of the fortifications or far behind them. The lack of clustering in their shelling showed the Red grenadiers' complete failure. If there was anything the general needed to watch out for, it was only a rogue shell.

The general calmed down once the battle had begun. It was as if he had forgotten his momentary outburst: he led using calculations from the artillerymen, who had determined the direction for a counterstrike. Their only reliable reference point was the Reds' heavy weaponry. Using that reference point to the fullest, the Red artillery was suppressed twenty minutes later.

In the quiet that set in, the general again walked along the fortifications and made certain that his order to repair them had been carried out. In some spots, they had dug out broken stakes. In their places they had installed intact ones that had just been brought from Armyansk. They had not bothered to remove the cut barbed wire: they just unwound new wire alongside it.

'Everything is ready for hosting *the comrades*,' said the general.

The comrades did not make them wait. Their first wave arose in the distance as if it had coagulated out of drifting snow; it began nearing the line of defense. The Whites did not shoot. Nor did the Reds. They walked, stooped, like someone still incapable of straightening up early in the morning. On a cold, early morning by a putrid gulf. This is how they would have walked to the factory in their previous life. Their ashen sleep-deprived faces were already visible. (As before, nobody was shooting.) Some had pliers in their belts for cutting barbed wire; this gave the approaching men even more resemblance to a crowd of workmen. But they were not workmen.

Behind the first wave was a second and a third and a fourth after that . . . The general lost count. It seemed those waves were moving from the horizon itself. They were creeping in with the indifference of volcanic lava. With the indivisibility of a locust swarm. This was a solid, unified force. The revolutionary masses in their highest manifestation. They were being created somewhere in the depths of a large country and had been pressed forward, to this narrow isthmus. The general knew these masses were enough for ten White Armies and, in the end, would engulf both his barbed wire and his machine guns.

He felt the defenders' gazes and their expectation of his command. He even seemed to think his troops had perked up a little, in light of the mortal danger. The machine gunners had already sat down by their Maxim guns. They were straightening the ammunition belts and stroking the barrels. There was no tension in their movements: on the contrary, there was something proprietary, and that irritated the general. He looked at his watch but could not figure out what time it was. That was not actually important anyway.

The machine guns could hit from two thousand paces and the Reds were already much closer. They were walking with an uncoordinated, hobbled gait, staring at the frozen grass. The soldiers were trying to deceive death, which had already taken up its position beyond the barriers. So as not to attract its attention, they were not looking it in the eye, just as one does not look into the eyes of the possessed. Death awaited the young and, thus, seemed insane to those soldiers. They saw it and deflected their gazes. The barrels of their rifles were half-lowered. They were not fighting, they were here for something else. They simply walked, bobbing on the hillocks. From north to south.

The general knew this wave was doomed. He wanted to give these soldiers an extra minute. Wanted to see them alive one last time. Could not look at them enough. Or enjoy, enough, observing their awkward forward motion. Their motion was a sign of life. Even their wooden strides and even the spasmodic waving of their arms differentiated life from death. That would be taken away from them in a minute. Replaced with the full repose that differentiates death from life.

Everything would happen upon his order. Several dozen waves destined for the passage from life to death were following behind the first. The speed of their passage depended on the speed of the shooting from his Maxim guns. Which were stilled in readiness. Everything would happen even without his order. These armies could no longer exist without one another.

The general feverishly tried to remember which side he was fighting on. He knew this was a useless trick of the consciousness and a withdrawal from another question—the most important one—but he just could not remember. Those around him watched with surprise crossing into alarm. The cavalry and infantry were watching. The artillerymen were watching. Only the wind could be heard.

'Fire,' whispered the general.

His command was just a cloud of steam. It contained no voice. The next second, though, machine guns hit the Reds' forward waves. The artillery began working on the rear guard. It seemed strange to the general that these consequences could be reached with one brief word. That they had not even heard. That they had uttered to themselves. He saw how deftly the machine gunners handled the ammunition belts. How the servicemen brought crates of ammunition with a calm, almost ant-like, focus. Volley followed volley. It was not uplifting for him. There was no more joy of battle in him. He knew (volley) that he already had another army now. Or maybe (volley) it was he who was different. Maybe his own (volley) sense of devastation had spread to the army and the army had ceased to exist. Died.

Everyone in the first wave fell in his own way. Some flapped their arms. Others grasped their bellies. Writhed on the ground with inhuman shouts. Some stopped moving then fell to the ground silently after standing in an already unearthly calm. Other people entered the gaping chasms that had formed. It had been a long time since this first wave had been the first. The machine guns became ever more precise as another wave approached, mowing down an entire wave at once. A new, live wave arrived where the first had perished; to the general's mind this was a very strange celebration of life.

Some broke ranks and ran over to the barbed wire. They attempted to get their pliers so they could at least sever one strand of barbed wire before dying. They did not manage to do so. They were killed by shots aimed from several rifles at once. Those who shot nodded approvingly to one another. They understood these dead were heroes.

The machine gunners' faces were sweaty and stern. Angels of death must have faces like that, thought the general. The machine gunners played first violin in this dreadful orchestra. They poured water into the cooling tanks of their Maxim guns, dipper after dipper, but the water was not fast enough to cool the metal. They could sense its temperature even through their gloves.

The Reds had many men—they did not need to count their losses. Never before had the general seen commanders sacrifice their own soldiers with such calm. The Reds had been carrying out a frontal attack for several hours already. From a military science perspective, the attack was pointless. What could they accomplish? Take all the bullets themselves? Cover all the barbed wire with their bodies? From

the perspective of dreadful reality, this attack was indisputable. An attack like this could not be countered forever.

The Reds, who had set out for unprecedented sacrifices,
knew this. The general, who would never allow himself to
have victims of that sort, knew this. He saw that a new
reality constructed on other fundamentals was arriving,
along with the Reds. He already had trouble understanding
it and thus rejected it with ever greater passion. And
continued resisting it.

The Reds' attack ceased with the early autumn twilight.
It dissolved in the semi-darkness. It subsided like water
during ebb tide. Unnoticed. Soundlessly. Revealing everything
preserved on the ocean floor. Bodies lay everywhere the
Red waves had been, as far as one could see in the
approaching darkness. Each lay alone. They lay on top of
one other. They hung on wires. Some were stirring. The
general sent a medical team to gather the living. He left
burying the dead to the Reds. The general was preparing
to hand over Perekop.

Solovyov made a very detailed description of the general's preparation for his final military operation. The
operation consisted of securing the troops' retreat to the
port. In this case, the issue no longer concerned organizing
a brilliant victory, as before. The general was working to
save his soldiers' lives. According to historian Solovyov, this
was about organizing a defeat with the fewest losses: a defeat
no less brilliant, in its own way, than the previous victories.

The general first dictated a special instruction turning
over to the White Army the entire fleet of ships assigned
to Crimean ports. He also designated five ports from which
the evacuation would be implemented. They were Sevastopol,

Yalta, Yevpatoria, Feodosia, and Kerch. But the main order, which stunned everyone, concerned the White Infantry's southerly march.

They had to act rapidly, without making too much noise, without extinguishing the fires, and taking a minimum of uniforms. The main and less maneuverable part of the army headed toward the ports in secret and began loading onto transports. The cavalry, machine gun detachments, and some artillery remained. They covered the departure of the White Army's infantry regiments. Perekop's defenders would need to abandon their positions and rush off, at a trot, to the ports at the very moment the last regiment reached the port. That was the general's plan. He set it out for those close to him and nobody objected. They never objected to what he said.

The general walked slowly along the line of defense and peered into the faces of those left hanging on the wires. Suffering was still present on those faces. The general knew this expression would leave them in a few days. Any expression would leave them. Especially if the weather warmed.

This was a strange inspection and a strange formation. The formation had been disrupted at each step. Those being inspected stood, their knees bent back, heels not aligned, and arms cast on the wire. They stood however they could and there was no reason to demand more from them. To the general, these people did not seem quite dead yet. Decomposition had not yet touched them. He still hoped to detect in their facial features at least a shadow of what separates life from death.

The general stopped next to a cadet who had been killed, a boy of around sixteen. The collar of his military overcoat had caught on the wire's barb, not allowing him to fall. The general straightened the cadet's collar as if this were a real inspection. The collar looked almost natural now: it was raised all around. The cadet's cheek and chin had been torn off: he had fallen on the wire face-first before being suspended by his collar. He continued pressing the pliers in his right hand.

The general immediately recognized the person standing beside the cadet. He could not help but recognize him, despite not having seen him in decades. He remembered his voice as deliberately quiet and remembered his gaze as condescending. That gaze was now more likely one of surprise. It was a one-eyed gaze because this man had no second eye. A bloody hollow gaped in its place. The general remembered the winter Petersburg night, the vodka in the tavern. The sense of weightlessness, the coziness of people who had escaped everyone. The intense unity of co-conspirators. The unbearable shame of one who had neglected his duty. Before him stood Lanskoy.

Lanskoy stood, his head pressed to a post. Both his arms were cast upon the wire. The general thought they hung with genuine lifelessness. There was something reminiscent of a puppet theater. Of a puppet conversing with a spectator. The comparison appeared to the general to be improper but precise.

What could Lanskoy tell the public? That he was a hero? That he despised death and threw himself on the wire? But that would be an untruth . . . Lanskoy despised life and threw himself on the wire. That was probably the reason he had gone to the Reds. The general walked right up to Lanskoy and attempted to close his only eye. His eyelashes fell with a barely audible crunch but the eye would not close. The general embraced Lanskoy. He pressed himself to his intact cheek. A tear ran down Lanskoy's cheek and froze in place. It was the general's tear.

'Bury him,' ordered the general.

His troops left almost soundlessly. The squeak of boots, muffled by gusts of wind. A farewell symphony, it occurred to the general. The only difference being, he thought, that his people were not extinguishing the fires: the number of campfires needed to remain the same, unlike in Joseph Haydn's version. A reduction in the number of performers should not be revealed to the viewer too early. That was the essence of the general's composition.

He approached one of the fires. Kologrivov, a captain in the medical services, was maintaining the fire. The captain was one of those who was staying on Perekop until the end.

'Good day, Your Excellency,' said Kologrivov, standing at attention before the general.

'At ease, Captain.'

He sat across from Kologrivov. He pushed a log that had burned through on one side closer to the center of the fire.

'The transition from life to death interests me,' said the general.

'It is, Your Excellency, inevitable.'

Patches of light from the fire changed the color and contours of Kologrivov's face.

'I do know that. How does it happen?'

'There are two ways: natural and unnatural. Natural . . .'

'Natural isn't a threat to us now,' the general interrupted. 'Tell me about the second way. Let's go.'

He took Kologrivov by the elbow and led him to the wire. As they walked past the staff tent, the general took the kerosene lantern that hung there. A broad but dim circle now preceded their motion.

The attackers had managed to upend one of the supports at the part of the barrier they had reached. It hung on the wire, almost touching the ground. Three bodies hung alongside it. They belonged to Red cadets (no longer belonged, thought the general). The bodies of several more cadets lay on the ground. Things had come to single combat in this defense sector.

The general cast light on one of the bodies on the wire. Somehow, this body was hanging particularly inconsolably: arms spread, head nearly touching the ground. Kologrivov took the dead man's shoulder and turned him on his back. With a squeak, the two other bodies began swaying.

'Aorta chopped in two,' Kologrivov said, showing it on the corpse. 'More than one liter of blood flowed out.'

'More than one? How much is that?' asked the general. 'Three? Five? Ten?'

'A person has only five or six liters of blood. At least two and a half flowed out of him.'

The general directed the lantern at the ground underneath the wire. It was crimson. The blood had frozen as it flowed out. In concentric circles. Like lava. It was still warm in the body but had frozen on the ground.

'Blood is a special liquid tissue,' said Kologrivov. 'It moves through the circulatory vessels of the living body.'

'What does this body lack for being alive?' asked the general.

'Blood, I suppose. Approximately two and a half liters.

I'll use this opportunity to point out that one-thirteenth of the weight of the human body is blood.'

'One can come to understand the combined action of the organs, but for me that still doesn't add up to life,' said the general. He outlined a circle with the lantern. 'Life as such.'

'And one hundred grams of blood contains approximately seventeen grams of hemoglobin.'

'But even if you gave that cadet two and a half liters of blood, he still wouldn't come back to life.'

'He wouldn't come back to life,' said Kologrivov. He crouched in front of one of those lying on the ground. 'And this person was struck on the skull by a saber. Shine the light, Your Excellency . . . As I thought, the right temporal lobe is cut in two.'

'You've explained the causes of their deaths but I still have no clarity,' agonized the general, seeking the right words. 'Maybe the whole trouble is that you haven't explained the causes of their life to me.'

'A person's life is inexplicable. Only death is explicable,' said Kologrivov. He stroked the dead man's hair, which stood like wire. 'The saber entered about five centimeters into the temporal lobe. In my view, he had no chance. It's interesting that the right temporal lobe is responsible for libido, sense of humor, and memory of events, sounds, and images.'

'Does that mean that when the soldier was dying he no longer remembered events, sounds, or images?'

'He did not even have a sense of humor. And his libido was missing. This death belongs in the "unnatural" category.'

A cannon struck somewhere in the distance; indistinctly, as if groggy. Its echo rolled through the sky and went quiet.

'Come to think of it,' said the general, 'who among us knows what's natural and what's not?'

'I'll note, *à propos*, that the human brain weighs an average of 1,470 grams.'

'Maybe death is natural if it comes to a person in the prime of his life?'

'And has a volume of 1,456 cubic centimeters.'

'Maybe there's a certain logic to death at that highest point?'

'And it consists of eighty percent water. That's just for your information.'

'Then why bother to wait for the point when the body's becoming decrepit and almost disintegrated?'

The captain stood up.

'Because, Your Excellency, by then nobody begrudges the loss of the body, when it's like that.'

The general looked closely at Kologrivov. He walked over to him and embraced his shoulders.

'Well, of course: death comes only to a person's body. I'd simply forgotten the most important part.'

18

Solovyov continued searching for Leeza. The unexpected complications he ran into at the university had not stopped him, although they had made him more cautious. The scholar realized that direct contact with women possessing a surname dear to him harbored its own dangers. He had already made paper-based correspondence a top priority in his appeals to other educational institutions because he was able to analyze the responses carefully and keep personal communications with the Larionovas to a minimum.

Since Solovyov did not know which university city Leeza might have gone to, he decided to try his luck in Moscow, too. To some extent, using postal communication methods also disposed him favorably toward Moscow. Considering his challenging experience with the search, the postal method struck the young historian as the safest way to go.

Solovyov wrote a long letter to the rector of Moscow State University, asking that his request be treated sympathetically. He composed the letter with an informal air, even telling of his childhood friendship with a person he had (regretably, largely due to his own fault!) lost. To sound more convincing, Solovyov also referred to the readers' triangle consisting of himself, Nadezhda Nikiforovna, and Yelizaveta, the person being sought. Not wishing to create the impression he was a simpleminded person, Solovyov did not let slip a single word about his designs on Nadezhda Nikiforovna.

For some reason, Solovyov was counting a great deal on his appeal to MSU so waited impatiently for a response. He did not know exactly how long it took for letters to travel from Petersburg to Moscow but figured they should not take very long. He still remembered, from a university course on Russian literature, that Dostoevsky's letters from Germany took four or five days. Considering that fact—as well as the technological revolution that had taken place— Solovyov allocated about two days for letters to travel from Petersburg to Moscow. He assumed the same for the return journey. Solovyov allotted about three or four days for the Moscow rector to check into his question.

To his surprise, no answer had arrived ten days later. Nor did one arrive twenty days or even a month later. Solovyov wanted to send another letter to Moscow but feared being pushy. So as not to lose time, he decided to look for Leeza in other Petersburg educational institutions. Solovyov was flabbergasted when he opened a directory for college applicants. The number of educational institutions was beyond the bounds of reason.

Solovyov appealed first to the Herzen State Pedagogical University, which had still been called an institute not long before. This establishment—where opportunities had broadened after the renaming—not only found a Yelizaveta Larionova among its ranks but also allowed Solovyov to take a look at her personal records.

Solovyov heard his heart beating as he entered the dean's office at the philology department. It reverberated out from under the ceiling, where two workers nailing up a cable seemed to be echoing his heart. Solovyov was asked to wait a little. In case they checked biographical data, he had the years Leeza had started and graduated from high school. They were the same as his years. What else could be in the document? He crossed his arms over his chest to muffle his heartbeats. The sad-faced workers slowed their pace, too, as they drew a green cable along a pink wall. A woman from the dean's office brought a thin folder and extended it to Solovyov.

'Is this her?'

There was a photograph glued to a left-hand corner of the form so Solovyov did not need the biographical data. The photo was not very large, but nothing larger was required for full clarity.

'No.'

Solovyov did not give up. He appealed to all institutions, even the very unlikeliest. Sometimes they gave him information over the telephone, sometimes they required a visit. They hung up rather frequently, suggesting he not pester them. In those cases, Solovyov beseeched. Insisted. Several times he bought candy for female employees in rectors' offices. One of them jokingly asked Solovyov how much she might be able to replace Leeza for him. It felt as if the list of educational institutions would never end.

Another two weeks later, a student named Yelizaveta Larionova turned up at the Lesgaft Institute of Physical Education. When Solovyov learned of this by telephone, he caught a taxi and went to the institute. He simply had no time to consider Leeza's association with sports.

An older, broad-shouldered woman, obviously a former athlete, greeted him in the administrative offices. She sized up Solovyov and asked his height.

'One meter, seventy-nine,' said Solovyov.

During his time searching for Leeza, he had grown out of the habit of being surprised.

'Our Yelizaveta is two meters, four,' said the woman. After a silence, she added, 'So you're not an athlete?'

Solovyov could tell from her face that she was not making fun of him.

'I'm a historian,' he said. 'Peter the Great was two meters, four. Yelizaveta has a promising future.'

'She's a nice girl. She's on the city basketball team.'

She straightened a lamp on the desk. Her face was serious, as before.

Notification of a registered letter from Moscow arrived at the very end of October. Solovyov discovered it in his mailbox when he returned from the library. He was invited to bring his passport to the post office to receive the letter. As he closed the box, Solovyov thought this kind of solemnity must mean something in and of itself; there would be no point in sending a negative answer by registered mail.

He was at the post office ten minutes before it opened. Addressee Solovyov's heart was beating as never before. After signing for the letter, he tore open the envelope right there at the window and proceeded to read it. It was signed by the vice rector for general affairs (the surname was feminine) and reported that a Yelizaveta Filippovna Larionova truly was studying at MSU. Following that, however, was the supposition—and here the letter's tone became less formal—that this was not the same Yelizaveta the Petersburg historian was seeking. This Moscow Yelizaveta was 39 years old and working toward her second degree. At the end of the letter, the vice rector wished Solovyov success in his search and expressed the hope that he would certainly find his Yelizaveta. Judging from the date on the letter, she had expressed that wish exactly a month ago.

Solovyov started to leave but then returned and demanded to see the post office manager. When that person appeared, Solovyov silently showed him the postmark. The manager took his glasses out of his uniform smock and carefully studied the postmark.

'A month,' he said. 'Sometimes it's longer. Sometimes they don't arrive at all.'

Solovyov looked over the manager's head. He felt his hatred boiling. Hatred and despair: the hand on the wall clock was leading them around in a circle.

'Dostoevsky's letters from Germany took five days,' Solovyov informed the man.

'Dostoevsky was a genius,' retorted the manager.

A few days later, Solovyov resorted to yet another option. He published brief appeals to Leeza in Moscow and Petersburg newspapers, with a request to telephone (a number was given). There were quite a few calls in the days following the publication. Four Leezas telephoned, two of them were Larionovas. A Taisia Larionova telephoned, saying she was prepared to answer to *Leeza* if necessary. A woman who did not give her name telephoned. She offered a discounted portion of Herbalife. The calls ceased roughly a week later.

Solovyov directed all the force of his striving for Leeza and all the resentment that had accumulated during his fruitless searches into his dissertation research about the general. Never before had he worked so much or so passionately. He found document after document but they brought him no closer to Leeza. After catching himself in that thought, Solovyov realized he subconsciously hoped they would help him close in. Why?

One day he ran into Temriukovich in the corridor at the institute.

'You're studying General Larionov, if I'm not mistaken?' said Temriukovich.

'I am,' said Solovyov.

He took a few steps toward Temriukovich.

'I read a folkloric text way back when,' said Temriukovich, 'and a strange thought occurred to me: might it be connected with the general?'

Temriukovich fell silent. Solovyov could neither confirm nor even deny the academician's thought. He could only nod respectfully. Temriukovich approached him, right up close, and Solovyov smelled his rotten breath.

'How do you regard strange thoughts?' asked Temriukovich.

'Well . . .' Solovyov backed away slightly. 'Do you happen to remember where you saw that text?'

'Where I saw it?' Temriukovich suddenly burst out laughing. 'Do I remember? Well, of course I remember: *Full Russian Folklore Collection. Entries for 1982.* Part two of that year's volume. Starting on approximately page 95.'

Temriukovich's face fell. He turned slowly and walked off down the hall.

Solovyov heard him say, 'Maybe my suggestion will help that young man.'

Despite the academician's hunch, the young man doubted the utility of the information he had acquired. He remembered it, though, when he happened to be at the public library, so decided to have a look at the *Full Russian Folklore Collection*. Much to his surprise, he really did discover the text Temriukovich had referred to, in the second of two volumes of entries from 1982. It began, in complete accordance with the citation, on page 95 and ended on page 104. It had been recorded by participants of a folklore expedition, from the words of 89-year-old Timofei Zhzhenka, a resident of the village of Berezovaya Gat in the Chernigov Oblast's Novgorod-Seversky region.

Timofei Zhzhenka told the folklore expedition's participants about events of some long-ago war. Commentaries to the text spoke of the impossibility (as commonly happens in folklore) of clarifying what war was actually involved. The publishers were inclined to regard its time of action as the epic period, though they also pointed out, in all honesty, that there was a definite obstacle to that sort of conclusion.

They had in mind the mention of the railroad, something that, as a rule, was not in epic texts. Futhermore, the narrative opened by referencing a railroad station—Gnadenfeld, where the events described unfold—something uncharacteristic of folklore. Just that name made Solovyov grab hold of the embossed cover of *Full Russian Folklore Collection* with both hands.

Timofei Zhzhenka used ornate dialectical expressions to describe a summer night when two armored trains stopped, almost simultaneously, at the aforementioned station. Two generals emerged from the two armored trains; this looked fully folkloric. Each of them presumed the station was in his troops' hands and pensively (*they had things to think about*, explained Timofei Zhzhenka) took a walk next to his armored train. Suddenly, one general (*the general that was ours*, according to Timofei's scant definition) recognized the other in the light of a station streetlamp. Without emerging from the darkness, he signaled to his valet, who was with him, and they crossed under the carriage to the second armored train.

Meanwhile, the second general put out his cigarette with the toe of his boot and began going up into his own train carriage. When he was standing on the carriage's platform, he gave the guards permission to go to bed. They did not need to be told twice; they disappeared into the next carriage. The guarded man went to his quarters. A minute later, there was knocking at the second general's door.

'What do you want?' He opened the door abruptly and was pushed inside.

'So we meet after all,' said the one who entered.

He placed the barrel of a Nagan revolver to the forehead of the carriage's master and commanded the valet take the other's weapon.

'I'm not afraid of you,' uttered the man who had been disarmed.

'Sit,' said the one who had entered, nodding at a chair that stood by a small round table. Several sheets of paper lay on it, under a spill-proof inkwell. For some reason, there was no pen. The carriage's master awkwardly (*uncomfortably*, Timofei characterized it) slid down the back of the chair to its seat. Perched on the edge, he laid his hands on the sheets.

'You won't dare shoot.'

'Why?'

'Because my guards will come running if there's a shot.'
Beads of sweat covered his forehead.

'I don't think so,' said the one who had entered. He took
a watch from his breast pocket and opened it with a barely
audible clink. 'A train with our wounded will pass through
this station very soon. It's a very long train . . .'

'I don't give a shit about you.'

'Nobody will hear a thing.'

The watch returned to the pocket with a click. A light
tremor could already be sensed under their feet.

'You feel that? That's our wounded coming. Of course
many are deceased, too.'

The sound swelled. The eyes of the one at the table froze
on the inkwell. The medical train reached the station and
the station was drowning in its rumbling. The inkwell began
coming into resonance with the train and set off on an
unhurried journey across the table. It began trembling hard.
It turned on its axis and advanced inexorably toward the
edge. The man at the table grabbed the inkwell and hurled
it at the wall with all his strength when it was about to fall
off.

'Damn it, why the hell aren't you shooting?'

Shards scattered in all directions. The inkwell shattered to
the floor in thousands of little glass pieces. It had cracked
through the unbearable noise. The last carriage of the
medical train rumbled past outside. In the absolute silence
that followed, the general answered the question that had
been posed, 'Because death is incapable of teaching anything.'

He let his valet go ahead and followed him. He closed
the door behind himself without a sound.

When Solovyov went outside, he felt like he was over-flowing with new knowledge. He was afraid of spilling it. He thought he seemed too fragile for this knowledge and could easily smash, like the inkwell.

When recording folklore, a text like this truly could be taken as folkloric: everything depended on the force of expectation. The narration was conducted in a good vernacular language. It took on a rhythm through its multiple repetitions. And what could have been recorded in the village of Berezovaya Gat but folklore, anyway?

That was the reasoning of those who published the text. In a commentary to the publication, they called upon the reader not to worry about certain details from modern history that were undoubtedly present in the story. The researchers determined its plot to be ancient to the highest degree. In elaborating on their point, they indicated that in this case they regarded the narration of the judge Ehud's murder of Moab king Eglon as a precursor.

Despite the bloodless finish to Zhzhenka's narration, the commentary's authors took notice of its high degree of resemblance to the biblical narration in the Book of Judges. As examples, they offered the high status of the characters, intrusion into their apartments, and the complete nonparticipation of their guards. It would have been naïve to suppose, pointed out the commentary's authors, that such an ancient text would not undergo any changes when reproduced.

A line of reasoning like that was legitimate. It could, seemingly, satisfy the most demanding researchers, not to mention numerous specialists in the field of textual deconstruction. It did not satisfy Solovyov. The historian knew something the folklorists who wrote the commentaries did not know: Timofei Zhzhenka was General Larionov's valet in 1920.

Solovyov decided to walk home. He was deliberating over whether a folkloric text could be considered a historical document. And, strictly speaking, was that text folkloric? Posing the question that way automatically ranked folklore in the realm of make-believe. After stopping on Palace Square, Solovyov asked himself to what degree history itself was make-believe. That question seemed completely natural on the main square of an empire.

It was a warm evening for the beginning of November. Warm and damp, in Petersburg's way. An angel's lowered head was looking at the gleaming cobblestones. Solovyov looked at the angel. A silvery haze shimmered in the beams of spotlights directed at the column. That Timofei Zhzhenka did not, prudently, give his characters names still did not render his story make-believe. Maybe he was not so simple, this Timofei. Who in Soviet Russia would have published the general's valet's memoirs? (Did the valet write his memoirs? Did he write at all?) Timofei Zhzhenka had seemingly found a witty way to tell future generations about what he had seen. Having no doubt that the general's life would be studied one day. Solovyov smiled at his thoughts as he opened his umbrella. *Sapienti sat.** That was about what Timofei might have thought.

The rain intensified as Solovyov approached his building. It was draining from somewhere above in long, cold streams, drumming on the tin of the ledges and bursting with a roar from rainspouts plastered in adverts. His umbrella saved

* Enough for the wise (Lat.).

him only partially. It did not shelter him from the water-saturated wind. The wind swooped down out of nowhere and the gusts stung Solovyov as if he had been hit by a wet rag. The wind twisted the arm holding the umbrella, bending its spokes and exposing the fabric's inner and defiantly dry side. Solovyov had to close the umbrella when it nearly flew away at the corner of Zhdanovskaya Embankment and Bolshoy Avenue. He felt cold rivulets under his shirt and could hear a repulsive squishing in his shoes, even through the sound of the downpour. The only thing left for him to do was run.

At home, Solovyov undressed and got into the shower. Water manifested itself completely differently now: its flows were hot and friendly here, its embraces ticklish and tender. There was something of Leeza's touch in that, which made him feel her absence even more acutely. Leeza did not know of the discovery he had made today. And it was so important to him to tell someone about it.

When Solovyov came out of the bathroom, he threw on his robe and dialed Prof. Nikolsky's number. Nobody came to the phone at the other end of the line. Solovyov dialed the number again and waited a little longer. He almost heard the crackling old apparatus in the professor's hallway. The professor would hurry for the second call after being too late for the first. That happened with old people. Old people asked that callers wait as long as possible before hanging up. The professor was making his way through a cluttered hallway. Losing his slippers as he went. Holding glasses that were slipping from his nose. (Solovyov felt uncomfortable but did not put the phone down.) The professor's sleeve caught on a door knob. On a nail sticking out of a bookshelf.

His foot grazed a pile of journals on the floor. The pile scattered into a fan that would refresh nobody.

In the end, the professor did not answer. Solovyov wanted to call someone else but there was nobody else to call. He realized that when the tones inside the phone changed, as if they had tired. He kept listening to them, not wanting to put the receiver down; they sounded like signals from Mars might sound. That sort of connection was, essentially, organic at house No. 11 on Zhdanovskaya Embankment. Contact with Planet Earth was ruled out for that evening.

Prof. Nikolsky's absence troubled Solovyov. He headed to the university in the morning and learned there that the professor was in the hospital. The dean's office employee was reluctant to answer his question about what had happened to the professor. It was not customary to give out this sort of information.

'Something about his lungs . . . They're doing tests.'

The hospital where Prof. Nikolsky was undergoing tests was in the northern part of the city. Solovyov bought some oranges along the way. Upon reflection, he also bought some German cookies. His thought was that these foodstuffs were incapable of harming the professor's lungs.

Solovyov had no trouble finding the pulmonary department. There was no sense of the usual stench of Russian hospitals there. Perhaps lung disease did not assume a smell. The nurse on duty was sitting in the corner of the hallway. She was noting down something in a journal, slowly tracing out letter after letter. Solovyov asked which room the professor was in. The nurse answered without raising her head. Her knitting lay next to the journal. Based on her reverie, it was clear she had only just set it aside.

'What happened to Professor Nikolsky?' Solovyov asked.

Her pen was moving with the placidity of a knitting needle.

'Nothing good.'

Prof. Nikolsky had a small but private room. Nobody answered when Solovyov knocked. He pressed the door handle and cautiously opened the door a little. Prof. Nikolsky was half-lying on the bed. This was the same unusual pose the professor himself had talked about at one time, during lectures about the Petrine period. At the time, this—half-sitting (half-lying?)—was considered healthful for sleeping, so blood would not rush to the head. Prof. Nikolsky was half-lying (half-sitting?) like that in his room. His eyes were closed.

Solovyov's purposeful gaze proved more efficacious than his knock. The professor opened his eyes. It is possible he was not even sleeping. Most likely (Solovyov grasped this from the professor's tranquility) he had heard the knock. Solovyov greeted him before crossing the threshold.

'Come in, my friend.'

The professor gestured, barely noticeably, pointing to a chair beside the bed. There was a whiff of his usual good-will in that gesture, but there was something more now, too. What Solovyov initially took for tranquility was undoubtedly something else that customary words did not fit.

'So, I brought . . . here.'

Solovyov took the oranges out of the bag. When he was on his way here, he had intended to ask the professor about his health but now he could not do so. He remembered the cookies and pulled those out.

'And these . . .'

Disheartened by his own eloquence, Solovyov held out the packages for the professor.

'Thank you.'

He put the packages on the blanket. Now the packages and the blanket moved, barely noticeably, in time with Nikolsky's breathing. His breathing—so it seemed to Solovyov, anyway—was rapid and irregular. The professor's pale, hairless chest was visible behind baggy pajamas; a small aluminum cross shone on his chest. Solovyov thought that he had never seen the professor's body: he did not remember seeing him without a necktie. Nikolsky took Solovyov's hand.

'How's the dissertation?'

'I'm almost finished.'

'Good work. Bring it to me, all right?'

Solovyov's dissertation lay in his bag. He nodded.

'How are you feeling?'

'Not so great . . . But even so, better than your general.' The professor was trying to sit up more and the oranges slid down to the edge of the bed. 'Did you manage to find the end of his memoirs?'

'Not yet. But I found something else.'

And Solovyov told of yesterday's discovery. Nikolsky heard him out without interrupting.

'The truth is more wonderful than make-believe.'

A nurse came in and held out a plastic lid with several pills for the professor. He tossed all the pills into his mouth at once with a familiar motion that even had a devil-may-care feel, then drank them down with water. This made no impression whatsoever on the nurse.

'You know,' said Solovyov after waiting for the door to close behind the nurse, 'with everything almost done, right now a sort of unusual feeling has come up. Maybe it's dissatisfaction. It's hard for me to express . . .'

'Dissatisfaction is a *usual* feeling. Especially when finishing work.'

Nikolsky said that somewhat sluggishly and Solovyov wondered if there had been a sedative among the tablets.

'I had something else in mind. Dissatisfaction . . . with the general's life. Maybe with life overall. Anyway, that's pretty heavy material . . .'

'No, go on.'

The professor's hands were folded on the blanket.

'So, imagine: there's this general. Clever. Hero. Living legend. Then, it's as if his fate short circuits. Darkness after a bright light. A squalid Soviet pension. A communal toilet. Somehow, it's even silly.'

'Why?'

Solovyov shrugged.

'It's a strange thought: maybe for him it would have been better to be shot?'

The nurse came in again, this time with a syringe on a tray.

'Turn around.'

The professor slowly turned on his side and lowered his pajama bottoms a little. Solovyov went over to the window. The street was barely visible in the November dusk. The poorly washed glass reflected only the nurse and the professor. But the professor did not know that.

'Relax. Don't squeeze your buttocks.'

Nikolsky began coughing uncontrollably. Something

glassy clinked on the tray and the nurse left the room. Nikolsky wiped the tears that had formed in his eyes from coughing.

'I could say that I should have died a little earlier, in some more pleasant kind of place. And not be living out my last days here . . .'

Solovyov wanted to object, but the professor threatened him with an index finger.

'But I'm not going to say that. Not because I like what's happening. It's just that the meaning of life is not in reaching a peak. Life's meaning is most likely in its entirety.' He pressed his palms into the mattress and returned to a half-sitting position. 'What does your general write about most?'

'I don't know. Probably about his childhood.'

'So there you go. That's very distant from all his victories but it's the most important thing for him. After all, he gauged everything later based on his childhood . . .' Nikolsky looked up at to Solovyov. 'Does that seem far-fetched to you?'

Solovyov abruptly walked over to the window and sat on the window sill.

'No, damn it . . . Pardon me. I suddenly realized why the two descriptions coincide . . . The general's childhood reminiscences and Zhloba's report about entering Yalta; imagine, they coincide right down to the details! I heard this during the summer, at the conference . . . I'll need to check it all, but it seems like I understand . . .'

Nikolsky was sitting with his head tilted toward his shoulder. It seemed to Solovyov that the professor's attention was dissipating. That impression went away when Nikolsky raised his head.

'I was just thinking about the peak in the general's life. Of course that's what you found yesterday.' (The professor had begun muttering.) 'It works out that he lived more than half a century after that. After or as a result of that? It's a good question. It's probably both things . . .'

Solovyov saw the nurse through the door, which was ajar. She was looking sternly at him, even shaking her head. Solovyov nodded that he understood everything. He turned toward the professor to say goodbye but the professor was asleep. He was dreaming of the article, 'Regarding a Christian Understanding of History', that he had begun writing before ending up in the hospital. Despite the fact that the article opened with a minutely detailed examination of the category of progress, the scholar did not perceive substantial signs of progress in history. The majority of nations had periods of ascent but as a rule achieved those a) at the expense of other peoples and b) for an extremely limited time. The interaction of those rises and falls was the sum of the vectors that absorbed one another and constituted the essence of world history. It had no common vector. With this state of things, it remained unclear what historical progress, which is now taken as an axiom, was composed of. Was it in the ability—the professor dreamt of a rhetorical question—to destroy ever larger numbers of people with each century? He did not consider it necessary to answer that question, but even in his sleep he did not forget to cite studies, such as Nikolai Berdyaev's *The Meaning of History*, on similar problematic issues. With this state of affairs, Prof. Nikolsky refused to assess events in world history according to their degree of progressiveness. He allowed only one single criterion for their assessment: the moral criterion. Declaring the notion of progress a fiction, the sleeping historian noted that the structure of a nation's life is very much reminiscent of the life of an individual and that it ends in the exact same nonprogressive way: in death. This gave him grounds to move on to the problem of the correlation of history and the individual. Prof. Nikolsky preferred the question of how history allows the individual to play a role over the traditional exploration of the role the individual plays in history. In the scholar's treatment, history, when compared with the individual, appeared as something derivative and, in a certain sense, ancillary. To him, history looked like a frame—sometimes meager, sometimes sumptuous—where the individual placed his portrait. The scholar did not propose another intended goal for history. His fingers slid, barely noticeably, along the blanket's creases as if he were attempting to fumble for that frame. As he moved on to the next point in his article, the professor dreamt that he would very likely never finish writing it.

19

A quiet whistling began sounding at dawn. Solovyov opened his eyes a little, just the tiniest bit, so as not to let his dream slip away. He did not exclude the possibility that the whistling had been in his dream. The dream was pleasant. The dream attempted to hold on to Solovyov's flickering eyelashes even as it receded. Solovyov could not have retold the dream; he could not remember, even roughly, what the dream had been about, though he continued to feel its mood. The mood was all that remained of the dream and Solovyov realized he had woken up. Despite the early morning hour, it was not dark in the room. Solovyov knew this light. It was the light of the first snow. The freshness of the first snow was drifting through a small open window in the kitchen.

The whistle was sounding in his waking life. It was a quiet, cautious whistling, more of an intermittent whistle. Solovyov raised himself up on his elbow and looked around. The whistling disappeared. There was nothing unusual in the room. Solovyov lay down again and the whistling resumed. He slid his feet into his slippers and went to the kitchen. He stopped in the kitchen doorway. A great titmouse was sitting on the cupboard door.

The bird was obviously watching him, though for some reason it was not facing Solovyov. Only one of its eyes was visible, lending the bird an inappropriately coquettish appearance. The bird had flown in through the high ventilation window, which had been opened for the night. Why had it not flown out through the window? Unable to find it? Or did it not want to? Solovyov thought that they might live together. He took a step toward the bird, who fluttered to the ceiling light fixture. The sound of wings was unexpectedly loud in the quiet of the kitchen. The thought even flashed through his mind that the word *fluttered* was onomatopoeic. This was exactly how bird wings sounded.

Solovyov shrugged and walked over to the window. A drum beat was streaming through the little window along with the frosty air. Initially it was pure rhythm, barely discernible and almost lacking sound. This rhythm was resounding from Ofitsersky Lane, just in front of the Military Space Academy. It was located in the buildings of the former Second Cadet Corps.

Solovyov stood with his forehead pressed to the glass, surprised at the unusualness of his current place of residence. Its markedly military-space orientation. He watched as a column of cadets moved, implausibly slowly, toward the archway of his building. They probably wanted to salute the spot where engineer Los's workshop had stood. After all, they must want very much to go to Mars if they had entered the Military Space Academy.

Despite their outward unhurriedness (and in this lies the monumentalness of how the masses move), the forward column had managed to cover a significant distance in the murky snow. Solovyov had already discerned several drummers leading the column. A man with a banner was marching ahead of the drummers. His legs rose to waist-level and with each step that imprinted itself in the snow, a tassel on the banner's peak flew up recklessly. Perhaps he wanted to go to Mars more than the rest.

A whistling sounded behind Solovyov's back. The bird was sitting on the cabinet again. This time the bird was not looking at him sideways. His bright yellow breast faced Solovyov. Solovyov stood on tiptoe and opened the window wider. Out of uncertainty, he spoke to the bird at full volume, 'If you don't want to stay, then fly.'

He walked away from the window for effect and pointed at the small ventilation window with his hand. Both the gesture and his intonation felt utterly false. The bird preferred not to move and if Solovyov were the bird, he would not have flown away, either. When Solovyov attempted to come closer to the cabinet, approaching from the other side, the bird flew up toward the lower window and hit the glass several times with a ringing thud. The bird fell to the floor, flew up, and struck the glass again. Solovyov rushed to the window and the bird flew off into the other room, tracing a semi-circle around the kitchen.

Solovyov followed the bird slowly into the other room. The bird was sitting on a bookshelf, prepared for a further encounter with the glass. Its eyes shone with the determination of a kamikaze. Solovyov stopped at the threshold, leaning against the doorjamb. He pitied the bird. He pitied the glass that might not withstand it. But the sound of the bird striking the window was genuinely unbearable for him. A prolonged, throbbing sound. The sound of live clashing with unlive.

'Now listen, bird . . .'

Solovyov thought this was a voice for addressing someone standing on a ledge. Someone who had strapped on explosives. It was an unnaturally calm voice. A voice for difficult situations.

'The big window's taped up for winter. But I'll open it so you can fly away . . .'

The bird was listening. Solovyov slowly moved along the opposite wall. After reaching the window, he forcefully slid the latch and pulled the window handle. The frame gave way with a dry crackling. Shreds of loosened cotton wool began fluttering in the wind. Holding his breath, Solovyov stole back to the doorway. Steam came out of his mouth when he finally exhaled. The surprised bird observed snowflakes melting on the parquet floor. The first column of cadets had managed to come through the archway and was now drumming from the side of the house with the open window.

'Are you going to fly?'

The bird hesitated a little and flew over to the windowsill. Solovyov took several cautious strides toward the window. The bird could not stride. After starting to jump around the windowsill, it moved closer to the open window. Sat on the window frame as if it were a picture frame. Froze like a tiny yellow paintbrush stroke. In the mix of air currents behind the bird, there quivered towers of light and, under them, the stadium's pseudo-classical columns. Down below, right by the window frame, the cadets were flowing like jelly over the bridge that led to the stadium. Ignoring the laws of physics—and the danger threatening them—they continued their drumming and collective marching on the bridge. The surprised bird turned its head several times. It flew away, without waiting for the bridge to collapse from the force of all those marching feet coming down at once.

When Solovyov arrived at the Institute, they told him that some woman or other from Moscow had been asking for him. She was now sitting in the institute library. Solovyov started off for the library but ran into Temriukovich along the way.

'Listen, Solovyov . . .' said Temriukovich, but then Tina Zhuk came up behind him and interrupted.

'Not bothering you, am I? I just wanted to say . . .'

Temriukovich's hand unexpectedly landed on Tina Zhuk's lips.

'Just for your information: you have a very loud voice. Intolerably loud for an academic establishment.'

Temriukovich turned and began shuffling down the corridor. Zhuk made a ghastly grimace and dashed off after Temriukovich.

'Loud and unpleasant,' Temriukovich sighed to himself. 'With a voice like that, it's better to keep quiet.'

'I wanted to say that the academic secretary was looking for you,' Zhuk uttered defiantly.

But the academic secretary himself was already approaching Temriukovich. He took the academician by the elbow and whispered something fiercely in his ear. Temriukovich continued moving, ferociously looking over the academic secretary's head every now and then. They stopped by the library door.

'Did you hear about how our senile one caused a stir at Cinema House?' Tina Zhuk asked Solovyov.

She was not even trying to speak quietly.

'Fine, what do you need from me this time?' Temriukovich asked the academic secretary with irritation, freeing his elbow.

The academic secretary walked around the academician from the opposite side and took him by the other elbow. He was speaking to Temriukovich in an emphatically patient way. Solovyov gathered that he would not be able to get into the library so was now looking for an opportunity to get rid of Tina.

'He barged in on a closed screening at Cinema House where they were only letting in people with membership cards . . .' Zhuk rolled her eyes.

When they reached the men's room, Solovyov excused himself and went in. Tina Zhuk did not come in. Oddly enough, thought Solovyov. Oddly enough. He stopped at a sink and turned on the water. He looked at his reflection in the mirror and wet his hands. Swept the hair off his forehead. Temriukovich raced in as Solovyov was about to leave. Temriukovich rushed for a stall without noticing Solovyov, slamming the door behind himself with a bang.

'The only place at the institute where it's easy to breathe,' carried from the stall.

The end of the sentence was accompanied by furious watery burbling.

Solovyov left the men's room and headed for the institute library. Other than the elderly librarian (how very little she resembled Nadezhda Nikiforovna!), only Murat was sitting in the reading room. He lifted his head when Solovyov appeared and Solovyov greeted him.

'You looking for someone?' asked Murat.

After hesitating, Solovyov told him about the researcher from Moscow.

'There was someone,' confirmed Murat.

The door to the reading room opened and Temriukovich came into sight. He froze silently on the threshold, not letting go of the door handle. The librarian smiled. Temriukovich went out, leaving the door open.

'I heard a good story about him,' said Murat. He took a box of mints out of his pocket. 'Want one?'

'No, thanks.'

'So there was a premiere at Cinema House. Something of a crush at the entrance. Everybody's showing their membership cards and invitations . . . Sure you don't want one?'

Solovyov shook his head. Murat scooped out a few mints with three fat fingers and popped them in his mouth.

'And then, all of a sudden, out of nowhere . . . Anyway, long story short, Temriukovich turns up. Gets in without any explanations whatsoever. "Member at Cinema House?" they ask him as he goes by and he says, "No, I have it with me" . . .'

Solovyov glanced at the librarian—she was laughing. There sure were all kinds of librarians.

'Do you happen to know where that researcher might have gone?' Solovyov asked them both.

Murat shrugged.

'Most likely for lunch,' said the librarian. 'She left her bag here.'

Solovyov stopped as he was nearing the institute café and heard Tina Zhuk's voice. Ultimately, he was not sure he needed to meet with the Moscow researcher. But he went in anyway.

Solovyov saw Tina first. She was sitting and telling a story

at a table with an institute guard and two women who
worked in the modern history department. The women
were laughing hard. Judging from their faces, the history
was extremely modern. The guard was sitting half-facing
Tina and listening with dignity, as befit a strong person.
Every now and then, he brushed crumbs off his camouflage
uniform.

The Moscow researcher was drinking tea at the next
table. She was the only person in the café that Solovyov did
not know. She was around fifty. Wearing a sleeveless jacket.
There was an unmotivated bow on her head. When Solovyov
approached her table, she herself asked if he was Solovyov.
Solovyov confirmed it. The researcher gave her name as
Olga Leonidovna (an invitation to sit down) and said she
worked at the Rumyantsev Library. She had brought him
some materials about the Civil War.

'I left them in the reading room,' Olga Leonidovna smiled.
'I'll just finish my tea, okay?'

'No rush.'

Solovyov smiled, too. Essentially, the bow suited her.

'Leeza Larionova sent them for you. As I understand it,
you must know her.'

A chair pulled away from the next table and Solovyov felt
like the chair's motion was floating in his eyes now.

'And I have mine with me, too, by the way,' said the
guard, standing up.

He straightened his pants and winked at everyone there.
Tina Zhuk's other two neighbors got ready to go after him.
A window floated slowly along the wall.

'You saw Leeza in Moscow?'

'She and I work in the same department at the library.'

'And . . . how is she?'

'She applied to the philology department last year but didn't get in. She was working at some factory . . .'

'They say it costs eight thousand *green ones* to get into college in Moscow,' said Tina Zhuk. 'Minimum.'

Olga Leonidovna looked at Tina with surprise.

'She obviously didn't have eight thousand.'

'Obviously,' said Tina, putting on lipstick in front of a little mirror, then standing up. 'Greetings, everybody.'

The reading room was empty but Olga Leonidovna switched to a whisper.

'This year Leeza was accepted at the correspondence course division and got a job with us. She sorts through the new acquisitions in the Manuscript Department.' She pulled a plump folder out of a plastic bag and extended it to Solovyov. 'It's a photocopy. A certain something that arrived recently for the collection.'

'Thank you.'

Leeza had held this folder in her hands. Leeza.

Solovyov left the institute and went to the train station. He boarded a trolleybus but then got out at the very first stop and returned to the institute. In the clerical office, he requested a referral letter for the Rumyantsev Library. Just in case. When he got to the station, he learned that the earliest train was leaving in three hours; he bought a ticket. This was a very early train that arrived in Moscow at 4:30 in the morning; the library opened at nine. But Solovyov preferred waiting in Moscow to waiting in Petersburg. Inactivity felt intolerable to him now. On top of that, waiting in Moscow was waiting near Leeza.

At home, Solovyov tossed the most necessary items into

a bag. He thought for a moment, then also put in the folder he had received: he had not even had a chance to open it yet. In memory of his trip to Crimea, he took a can of food. Meat he had bought at a nearby store. For an instant, he had the feeling he was leaving forever. Solovyov looked around. He had everything he needed. He shut the door hard and turned the key in the lock twice. It sounded like two distant gunshots in the echoing stairwell. Like an echo of Solovyov's decisive actions. The clanking of the key had its own significance, even a point of no return, inasmuch, needless to say, as that descriptor could be attached to a key. Solovyov caught a taxi outside. He rode up to the station a half-hour before the train's departure.

He went into the entrance hall and bought a newspaper. As he left the entrance hall, he put it in a trash bin. He took the can from his bag and gave it to a pauper. Went out to the platform. Under bright spotlights, pipes on the carriages were belching smoke. Or steam. Most likely steam: it disappeared instantly over the carriages' roofs, which glistened with ice. Conductors wearing black felt boots stood by the carriage doors. They blew into their mittens from time to time, pressing their lips to their wrists. Sometimes knocking one felt boot against another with a muffled sound. Solovyov showed his ticket and went to his compartment. He greeted the three women who were already sitting there. They answered in chorus. It was nice for him that they were women, not men. The train began moving.

Only after Solovyov had climbed up to the top bunk did he remember the folder. He went back down, got the folder, and crawled back up with it. He turned on the lamp over his head. After getting used to the dim lighting, he opened the folder. He was flabbergasted.

After everything he had heard during the day, he had found something now that was capable of stunning him. There, in the poorly lighted bunk, Solovyov held in his hands the end of the general's memoirs. He could recognize that handwriting in any lighting. Yes, he was stunned. But not surprised.

In the folder was a photocopy of the notebook Filipp had taken at one time and which had suddenly surfaced in the form of *a new acquisition* for the library. It remained unclear if it had been *acquired* from Filipp, where Filipp himself was, and whether he was still on the face of the Earth at all. There were no library markings on the manuscript at all other than the call number.

It was a thick notebook with graph paper. It was too large to copy with facing pages, so each page was copied individually, making for many sheets. Strictly speaking, the notebook could have fit the copier with the pages facing, albeit without the margins: from time to time, the general had made markings in the margins (which he had neatly ruled in pencil). Judging from the various shades of ink, the markings were made at different times. The general had obviously reread his writings more than once and left remarks and additions. 'Dead.' Or: 'Still alive.' Or (facing the words 'It was cold'): 'It was not so much cold as damp.'

It was not so much cold as damp when the remnants of the White Army rolled off toward Chongar. The bulk of the troops had already left Perekop a few days before and were now being loaded onto transports in the ports. The cavalry that remained on the Perekop Peninsula had covered their retreat. The cavalry then held on there until the general received a report one night that his troops were already in the ports. The cavalry soundlessly left Perekop that same night.

The heavy weapons had been disabled. They had removed the locks and left them in position. They had not extinguished their campfires, which Captain Kologrivov's detachment was to watch over until morning. These 150 volunteers had offered to remain until morning. They covered the retreat of Perekop's last defenders.

They led the horses by their bridles for the first several hundred meters. They saddled them before reaching Armyansk and the cavalry moved off at a trot. In the vicinity of Dzhelishay, a small number of the troops turned toward Yevpatoria and the rest continued on toward Yalta and Sevastopol. As he ascended Chongarsky Pass, the general was thinking of those who remained on Perekop. In his mind he asked their forgiveness.

A snowstorm came up on the pass. The huge, wet snow-flakes did not drop to the ground. They got caught in the wind and drifted, on a low-altitude flight. Where the pass began to dip, the snowflakes soared upward, as if the hanging, murky clouds were already waiting for them to come back. It slowly grew light.

Sitting motionless in the saddle, the general observed as the remnants of his army laboriously descended from the pass. The horses began slipping on the icy road, scrabbling to keep their balance, sometimes sitting on their haunches. Some fell, trapping their riders beneath them and pinning them to the frozen mud. Shouts and foul language hung over the pass. Many dismounted and carefully led the horses down, holding them by the reins. 'Motion along an inclined plane,' was the general's notation in the margin.

When they arrived in Yalta, the general gave everyone several hours to rest. He headed for evacuation headquarters, stationed in the Oreanda Hotel. The general carefully familiarized himself with the list of evacuated personnel and inventory of vessels. He assigned the transportable wounded to the steamship *Tsesarevich Georgy*. (Bela Kun would shoot the untransportable wounded two days later.) The steamship *Kronshtadt*, on which the Sevastopol Navy Hospital and the Mine and Artillery School were evacuating, took numerous wounded. The rest were loaded on ships with their own troop units.

There were not enough vessels. At the last minute, the transports *Siam*, *Sedzhet*, *Rion*, *Yakut*, and *Almaz* were added to the available tonnage. Under the general's order, everything in the Crimean ports that was capable of staying afloat, including old barges, was made available for the needs of the evacuation. It worked out to 126 large and small vessels. The majority of them were already prepared to sail and stood at outer anchorage.

After noon, a launch was sent directly to the Oreanda and the general, accompanied by his deputy, Admiral Kutepov, headed to the anchorage. The launch went past steamships packed with people. Past barges so laden that their sides nearly dipped into the water. It was frightening to let them set sail. But it was even more frightening to keep them here.

The general climbed up a rope ladder to the cruiser *General Kornilov*. The crowd on deck was so dense that it was almost unable to part when the general made his appearance. As he crossed the deck, he could barely elbow his way behind the Cossacks clearing a path for him. The exact same sort of crowd languished in the hold. At least it was warmer there than on deck, but there was already a palpable stench: there was only one toilet for the entire hold. The hold's largest compartment turned out to be under lock and key.

'What's in there?' asked the general.

'The chief quartermaster's cabin,' said Admiral Kutepov.

'Open it.'

The chief quartermaster held the key but it was already impossible to find him in the crowd. The general nodded to the Cossacks and they peppered the door, hitting it with their rifles' butt ends. A minute later, the lock and the lower hinge had been broken off. The door swung on its upper hinge with a pitiful screech and dropped. The quartermaster's compartment was completely stuffed with expensive furniture. Mahogany cabinets stood pressed against one another. The sides of the cabinets faced those entering, but they were astoundingly beautiful even from the side, gleaming in the porthole's scant light. This light was reflected in several Venetian mirrors arranged along the walls. There were large crates neatly stacked in the corner of the cabin; baled tablecloths lay on them, right under the ceiling.

'Overboard,' said the general.

He came back on deck after finishing his inspection of the cabin. The first of the cabinets had already been delivered there. The sailors rocked the item and tossed it on the count of 'three.' It fell into the water with a fountain of spray and stayed afloat for a time. Then it began heavily sinking, to applause on deck. As it departed for the deep, the cabinet released bubbles as if it were a live being. As the general was making his way down to the launch, two sailors dragged the quartermaster out of the hold.

'Does this one go overboard, too?'

'Let him live,' said the general.

He went ashore after visiting several more ships. He asked about those who had remained on Perekop, but nobody had seen them here yet. Dusk was falling. The general dismissed the Cossacks by the entrance to the Oreanda Hotel. He went up to his room and looked out the window at the sea. He sat at the table, poured himself some cognac from a decanter, and drank it. There was a knock at the door. He had no strength to answer.

'May I?'

Admiral Kutepov entered the room. He laid a hand on the general's shoulder.

'You need to get some rest. We're sailing in the morning.'

'The ones coming from Perekop . . . They still haven't arrived,' said the general.

'The Red artillery will smash us to smithereens if we don't cast off tomorrow . . . May I?' The admiral took the decanter and poured himself some cognac. 'Besides, the ones you're speaking of . . .'

'Yes?'

'I think nothing threatens them any longer.'

The admiral emptied his glass in one gulp and was now thoroughly savoring the drink. Pursing his lips. Closing his eyes. The general drank, too. And also closed his eyes.

When he opened them, Captain Kologrivov was standing before him. The general knew he was dreaming of Kologrivov; he saw in that nothing good for Kologrivov's fate.

'Well, how are you doing out there?' the general asked, looking away.

'Nothing threatens us any longer,' said Kologrivov. He poured himself some cognac without asking permission. 'It's a pity you weren't there. This was the only chance for you to get a genuine feel for Thermopylae after all.'

'But there were only 150 of you.'

'And you aren't Leonidas, either, isn't that right? And so here, you know, it's one thing after another.'

The general woke up shortly before dawn. What he had thought was a firm pillow turned out to be the cuff of his sleeve. He could feel the table's velvet covering under his hand. Lights were flashing to one another in the black motionless sea outside the window; the ships at anchor were ready to sail. The general looked at his watch. A farewell prayer service was to begin on the embankment in an hour.

The commanders of the forces sailing from Yalta came for the prayer. The embankment was packed with people. At the first sounds of the service, the general sank to his knees and all the officers followed suit. The entire huge crowd also knelt. A damp sea wind whipped at the priests' stoles and snapped the tricolored banner against the flagpole. The general attempted to understand each word of the service but was distracted, without realizing it himself. He was thinking that the evacuation could certainly have taken place even without him.

The prayer service was ending. Bestowing his blessing, the bishop sprinkled the general with holy water and several drops fell behind his collar. There was no doubt this had already happened in his life. He had happened to experience so very many unforgettable things. Raindrops running under his tunic. Standing drowsily on the bank of the Zhdanovka River. Semi-darkness. A wind just as wet. Could that water, then, be considered holy? It had fallen straight from the sky. The general fingered a pencil in his overcoat pocket. It would have been better for him to have stayed on Perekop after all. Maybe he had stayed there, though.

The general slowly rose from his knees. From the faces of those standing, he understood they had been waiting only for him.

'Do deign to say a parting word,' Kutepov appealed to the general.

The general watched as the bishop's gray hair whipped in the wind. His hair lashed at his eyes and got into lips opened from shortness of breath, but he made no attempt to remove it. This had happened in the general's life, too. The same elderly bishop and the same gray hair whipping. But he could not remember where. Life had begun repeating itself. The bishop did not look at anyone individually and the pause did not weigh upon him. His face expressed no impatience. The general remembered: it was the violinist from his childhood. He had played right here, by the fence at the Tsar's Garden.

'I have nothing to say.'

Admiral Kutepov smoothed his hair and took several steps toward the crowd. He cleared his throat. A horse began neighing behind those standing.

'We did all that we could . . .'

Kutepov glanced at the general, as if searching for new words. But the general was silent. Kutepov thought a bit, then asked everyone's forgiveness. The general nodded; he found that appropriate. Kutepov cast a look around the crowd, breathed some air into his lungs, and shouted, 'Farewell!'

'Farewell,' the general said to Kutepov. 'My mission has ended.'

'The launch is waiting for us,' said Kutepov, nodding in the direction of the sea.

'I commanded ground operations and now the naval operation is beginning. You're the admiral, not I.'

The admiral looked at his watch.

'We can't linger any longer.' Still acting as if he did not understand, Kutepov took a folder with a two-headed eagle from the general's hands.

'You'll need that in Constantinople,' said the general.

'There's no sense in waiting for them.'

'Including a final statement of the treasury and correspondence about providing asylum.'

'They perished on Perekop and you know it.'

'This is not, really, about them.'

'General, the Reds will not simply kill you, they'll slice you to pieces.'

'It's not worth spending time bickering. There are 145,000 people waiting for you. And that's just according to the lists. I think there are many more of them in reality.'

Admiral Kutepov shifted the folder from his right hand to his left, then put his hand to his peaked cap. He did that so slowly that he had time to inadvertently twist his finger at his temple. Or perhaps it only seemed that way to the general.

The embankment emptied out fairly quickly. There were only horses that had been abandoned during evacuation. Not all their saddles had even been removed. Horses nobody needed dispersed along the neighboring streets. They neighed from hunger. They were returning to the embankment again in expectation of their masters; they rubbed against icy streetlamps. The horses interpreted their abandonment as a misunderstanding.

The wind was flattening flyers against the fence at the Tsar's Garden; they had been scattered around several days ago. The general picked one up. In the flyer, comrade Frunze called upon Yaltans not to put up resistance. He guaranteed universal amnesty for the city's residents. The general unclenched his fingers and the scrap of paper flew off into the empty expanse of the embankment. The city's residents had no intention of putting up resistance.

Yalta was preparing for the Reds' entry in a different way, though. Shop windows were being boarded up. Provisions and table silver were being hidden in houses. The measures were warranted but, as it later turned out, insufficient. When the city froze from horror a day later, both the stores and the table silver seemed like mere details. Yaltans did not even remember those amidst the terror that broke out, just as nobody among the Reds remembered comrade Frunze's flyers.

Captain Kologrivov's detachment entered the city after the smoke of the last steamship had disappeared beyond the horizon. Retreating under the Reds' fire, Kologrivov had managed to save most of his detachment. They were saved that day at dawn by a very strong snowstorm that suddenly came down over Perekop. The blizzard allowed the detachment to leave and disoriented their pursuers. It accompanied the detachment for half the day, hiding it in a solid snowy shroud. Kologrivov's detachment had not perished. They had lost their way.

In the thick snow, the detachment took a mistaken course from the start—to the peninsula's eastern extremity—rather than the Yalta direction that General Larionov had instructed. They did not figure out their mistake until the dead of night, at the Vladislavovka junction railway station. Instead of moving toward the nearest port, Feodosia, and getting on a ship there, the detachment stayed true to the order and turned back, to the west. In order to get to Yalta, they headed along the road they had already traveled, toward the center of the peninsula, not turning south until then. Only toward the evening of the next day did Captain Kologrivov's detachment turn up in Yalta.

When he welcomed the detachment, the general did not consider accommodating them in barracks. He housed them in homes that (according to his information) had been vacated during the evacuation. Rest was a vital necessity for the soldiers after their grueling passage. Burning their military uniforms was just as necessary for them. The general ordered that they begin with that.

He himself went to the city theater. After a brief meeting in the wardrobe room, they brought him all their Tatar costumes (around two dozen) and craftsman costumes (eight). Everything was fine with the Tatar clothing but the craftsman costumes had an ineradicably foreign air to them (they had been sewn in Italy). Furthermore, they were tidy in a nonlocal way. After some thought, the general refused them, instead requesting tuxedoes with top hats; the props for *The Merry Widow* were checked, as well, while searching for those. Several chimneysweeper costumes were found, too, along with ethereal prop-room ladders that the general preferred to refuse: he said he was not encouraging superfluous theatricality. He also asked if the theater had any costumes for paupers but all they found were tatters for a holy fool (*Boris Godunov*); this was unacceptably light-weight for the month of November. The general took individual pieces from the theater's wardrobe—including a dozen sashes and hats—to have in reserve. He ordered that everything he set aside be loaded on a cart and brought to the Oreanda Hotel. Written in the notebook's margin in the general's hand, opposite the story of visiting the theater, was 'a good idea.'

Not everyone, however, thought it was a good idea. That became obvious when the tardy detachment formed up by the Oreanda Hotel at dawn. The soldiers heard out the general's explanations and glumly confirmed their readiness to submit to his orders. These were essentially neither explanations nor orders. The general did not explain anything and, even more so, did not order anything. He simply spoke about what, in his opinion, would be best to do at the given moment. The soldiers understood little of what was happening and one can only guess exactly what thoughts were slinking around in their heads regarding their military commander's condition. Their sullenness was, as the saying goes, written all over their faces, but the inertia of their esteem for the general kept them from insubordination. In the end, they, too, lacked plans for how to save themselves.

The general headed toward the Yalta city limits with a group of horsemen dressed in Tatar costumes. The horsemen swayed beautifully in their saddles, as befits those who grew accustomed to horses in childhood. The general reminisced about how, many years ago, a horse had pawed at the ground, bringing down a rain of pebbles in a gorge.

He then noticed one of his cavalrymen making his horse paw at the ground and he nodded approvingly. He recognized the Petersburg dressage school. Pebbles bounced off ledges in the gorge and flew even better than in the general's childhood. The other horsemen kept to a steady trot and the general listened carefully to their hoofbeats. Resonant clopping on the stony road blended with dull thudding on ivy growing over the road. The rhythm should not betray any anxiety. It was the rhythm of people far from war. Someone needed to fetch kumys from the nearest Tatar village. The general said he wanted them to ride with kumys. He thought he had made provisions for everything, down to the smallest details. They looked at him with undisguised surprise. After the general had ridden off, Captain Kologrivov explained to the soldiers: 'What has occurred once before carries a seal of approval. Do as he orders.'

'One cannot step into the same river twice,' objected warrant officer Sviridov.

He had left his third year of philosophy studies to go to war.

'It doesn't matter what river we're stepping into,' said Captain Kologrivov. 'The main thing now is to not drown.'

Spurring his horse, he galloped off after the general. They had much to accomplish in the day ahead. To begin with, they placed some brand-new shoeshine booths on the corners of several streets (the ones that had stood there previously had been dismantled for firewood by residents during a cold spell). The general ordered that the booth on Morskaya Street be moved fifty meters away from the corner since it had stood on that very spot during his childhood.

Housed in the booths were shoe shiners who mastered

their profession in short order. Remembering his cadet training, the general personally showed them how to shine shoes properly. He urged them not to misapply the polish since too much polish would not allow you to attain the necessary shine. It should be taken from the jar with the very edge of the brush. The general demonstrated to the trainees the proper methods for brush-handling and for rubbing a cleaned shoe with velvet. They shined shoes pretty decently for people who had held nothing but rifles in their hands for two years.

The general placed a group of men on Autskaya Street to repair the roadway. At his request, city officials sent two cartloads of cobblestones to Autskaya (across from the St. Theodor Tiron Church). The general asked that they not send round and rough cobblestones (the kind called *cats' heads*). He ordered the highest quality paving stones: cut granite blocks.

At the city council, they attempted to draw the general's attention to the fact that the roadway in the area around the St. Theodor Tiron Church had recently been repaired; they proposed repairing a lower, thoroughly worn, part of Autskaya Street. The general's childhood memories, however, pointed to his chosen spot, which essentially did not permit him to agree with the city officials' arguments. He recommended pulling up the old stones to install the new ones.

The general also reopened two stores abandoned by their owners: a shoe store and a sweet shop. All told, ten people were dispatched to staff them. Thanks to the breakdown of shoe and sweets production, there was nothing to sell in those stores. Strictly speaking, there was nothing to sell them for, either, since money was swiftly becoming simply paper. In a brief parting address, the general emphasized that the absence of wares was a temporary phenomenon since both sweets and shoes were in demand under any regime. He did not know if there would be money under the new regime. In honor of opening the sweet shop, they gave the general a lollipop that appeared, upon close examination, to be in the shape of a rooster. It was the only ware they discovered in the store. The rooster smelled of burnt sugar and had no color. When the general went outside, he gave it to a newspaper delivery boy.

A barbershop opened up after noon. In giving brief instructions to the future barbers, the general announced to them that under no circumstances should they stop making cutting motions, even when they were lifting the scissors over the client's hair. According to the general's observations, it was customary among genuine barbers to cut air, too. He sharpened a razor on a leather strop and neatly wiped the blade on a towel while shaving one of the trainees. In so doing, he showed several characteristic gestures he had noticed as a child—barbering mastery is judged based upon their accuracy. He cautioned against approximating a barber's actions, saying that every little bit counts in this field. He advised taking a cigarette out of an ashtray with the ring and little fingers because only those fingers remain free of lather. The top of the head should be scratched, if necessary, with those same fingers. He recommended discussing city news during haircuts and shaving, because that is the usual practice in barbershops. He depended on their intuition for everything else.

The general lodged soldiers Shulgin and Nesterenko in

a vacant two-apartment house. He was concerned the soldiers' bachelor life might provoke inquiry into their past and ordered that two women who agreed to simulate marriage be brought to them. On top of all that, the general vaguely recalled that two families truly had lived in a house like this. The families were friends for many years. It was already impossible to decide if it was this house or not because the general remembered nothing but the front stoop.

He and his father had walked up a stoop like this to go into a house at one time. Two men were playing chess in the living room. They represented families on friendly terms. One of them held a knight (the future general could never have mistaken that figure for anything else) in his hands, touching it to his lower lip from time to time. The knight's ears rode fully into the chess player's puffy lip. The other man repeated some phrase, in a reverie. He had uttered the phrase many times but the general could not remember it, try as he might. Had they played here?

The general warned the reestablished families (he was certain of the resemblance between the present and past families) about the emphatic need to be friends. It was noted in the margin across from this statement that friendship did occur, as was to be expected, and eventually both couples had children as a result of simulating marriage. Boys: Shulgin junior and Nesterenko junior.

The general gathered both families in the living room of one of the apartments and proposed that the men play chess. He sat Shulgin and Nesterenko on chairs opposite one another. A chessboard was placed on a stool between them. Shulgin crossed his arms on his chest and Nesterenko was requested to press his hands into his knees. This lent a naturalness to the game that had begun. They played briskly but were not in much of a hurry. Sometimes the women would appear behind the players' backs and cast contented gazes at the board, not understanding anything. The general advised the women to wipe their hands on their aprons during those moments. Or wrap themselves in a shawl, as if chilled. Crockery clinked ever so slightly in the sideboard when the women trod on the plank floors. The general delighted in the coziness that had come about.

'Someone should say,' he requested of the players, '"We're bringing in the minor pieces."' That's what they say in similar situations.'

'Is that obligatory?' Shulgin was curious.

The general thought and answered, 'No, it's not obligatory. You can just press the knight to your lower lip and say something of your own. The main thing is to utter it pensively. Several times.'

Then they left for the church, where the general seated paupers in the necessary order. One of them very much resembled Maxim Gorky, which was a definite plus in this particular situation. The similarity was so great that this person later even posed for Yalta's monument to the proletarian writer. Another pauper, who did not resemble Gorky, was ordered to simulate not having a leg. Only this, in the general's opinion, could ensure him certain immunity when the Red Armymen appeared.

The general instructed five musicians by the fence at the Tsar's Garden. One of them could not play any instrument at all but had, so it seemed to the general, a good ear. His task during performances of musical compositions was to listen carefully, conveying the essence of the performance through facial expressions when possible. This musician had long gray bangs that he should toss from his eyes with a sharp head motion. He was also given a violin and asked to draw the bow near the strings. But not to touch them.

Toward the end of the day, the general ordered that a cabinet be taken out of his house. A big oak cabinet with a two-headed eagle. The general ordered a cart be brought and he positioned loaders to look after it. The loaders had just returned from Perekop and did not quite imagine how they ought to handle such a heavy item. Furthermore, they still did not understand where or why it should be moved. Recalling a famous social-democratic slogan, the general announced to them that the ultimate aim is nothing, but movement is everything. The cabinet's aimless motion did not contradict the new ideology, making this pursuit relatively safe. As he was walking away, the general advised the loaders not to be shy about using coarse language; when in contact with the Reds this could create an atmosphere of similarity in social class.

Only late in the evening, when the entire detachment had jobs, did the general and Captain Kologrivov approach the pharmacy. The general leaned wearily against an electric streetlamp (in previous times it had used gas) by the entrance. He rummaged around in his pockets, fetched the keys, and began searching for the lock in the dying yellowy light. A minute later the door opened and a little bell jingled. The general enjoyed feeling the edges of the beveled glass on the door. The prisms reflected the evening's last lights. They reflected the soundness of a previous life. As it happened, in those November days, it had already been three years since that kind of glass had been made.

The general and Kologrivov entered the pharmacy and looked around. Unlike many abandoned places, the pharmacy had not been ransacked. Everything remained in place there. The general took Kologrivov by the shoulders and sat him down in a chair.

'The main thing is inner calm. Speak in a soft voice. The scrape of a little oak door, the smell of mint drops: nothing more is required here. That is the only way you will be able to exist organically in a pharmacy.'

'I'm calm,' said Kologrivov. 'And I speak in a soft voice.'

The general uncorked one of the little vials and stirred its contents with a glass pestle.

'I placed observers on the Alushtinsk road. They'll shoot a blank from a cannon when they sight the Reds. That will be the signal to start a new life. I won't be able to give further instruction because I'll be busy with my own matters. That, basically, is everything.'

The streetlamp was no longer burning when the general went outside. A cold autumn rain had begun. The pharmacy windows were all that prevented Morskaya Street from plunging into darkness.

The cannon struck at 9:30 in the morning. With that shot, they began playing Oginsky's *Polonaise* by the fence at the Tsar's Garden. A detachment of Tatars rode out to the Alushtinsk Road and energetic paving work began on Autskaya Street by the St. Theodor Tiron Church. Shoeshine booths opened in various parts of Yalta during those same minutes. The quantity of staff as well as the abundance of brushes and polish allowed them to shine shoes for the entire coastline but Yaltans preferred not to leave their homes that day. Even the shops did not open that morning, with the exception of a shoe store and a sweet shop. Yalta was at a standstill, awaiting the entrance of the Reds.

First to enter the city was an armored vehicle with the uneven inscription *Antichrist*. It did not notice the Tatar detachment and drove past at top speed. Shots were fired into the air from the armored vehicle. To the detachment's surprise, the armored vehicle did not notice a curve in the road, either. It did not brake until the place where the road's shoulder turned into a steep slope. The vehicle's front wheels went down and a belated reverse gear could no longer rectify anything. The vehicle rolled into the gorge, topsy-turvy, its armor knocking along the cliff's overhangs. Moans resounded in the gorge after the last echo had finished rumbling. Local residents—simple, god-fearing people—surrounded the vehicle. They had no love for the Reds but they did not plan to refuse them help. The residents began conferring when they saw the inscription on the armored vehicle. They did not know who lay ahead for them to save. Withered grass rustled in the wind. Nobody could bring themselves to come closer to the vehicle with the eschatological inscription. The moaning soon stopped.

The Reds' primary troops entered the city at that same time. Comrades Zhloba, Kun, and Zemlyachka were out front on well-fed horses. They met a Tatar detachment and even received kumys from them. Zemlyachka poured out kumys for representatives of the commanding personnel and passed the leftovers on to rank-and-file Red Armymen. Those entering the city praised the kumys, though they noted its sharp taste. Only Kun did not praise the kumys.

Surprised by his silence, Zemlyachka asked if he liked the kumys. Still on his horse, Kun vomited in answer and stated that this was because he was not accustomed to it. Zhloba jokingly proposed that Kun have his stomach pumped in the city hospital. Everyone laughed so as not to offend Zhloba. Kun blushed and said he was planning to inspect the hospital anyway. Zemlyachka recommended that he record how much blood was in stock. Seeing a shoe shiner, Kun asked the advance guard to wait while he had his spattered boots cleaned. In addition to the kumys, remnants of beet salad and poorly chewed veal were apparent on his boots. Zhloba's boots were not dirty but he dismounted to have his shined, too.

General Larionov was having his boots shined, too. This was happening at the other end of the city, by the St. Theodor Tiron Church. The mezzanine of the Chekhov house was visible about a hundred paces from the church. Maria Pavlovna Chekhova was opening the shutters. As he watched how deftly the brush moved in a shoe shiner's hands, the general said, 'Chekhov died only sixteen years ago but an entirely new epoch has arrived.'

The roadway was being repaired not far from the church. The knocking of wooden tampers, which pressed the paving stones, spread over Autskaya Street. The stones were laid in a fan shape on a sand foundation. The wind was tearing the last leaves from the trees in a front yard. Blackened and crumpled, they rolled along the brand-new paving stone, settling in a gutter.

The general stopped next to one of the houses as he walked down Autskaya Street. The biting November wind had come this far, too. It sounded in a squeaking gate spring and in a little flapping runner rug that had been flung on the fence. It was quiet in the house. They were playing chess there. Two men sitting on bentwood chairs were considering positions on the board. Their words were inaudible. Their calm could be sensed. A woman with a pail came down the front steps. She went behind the corner of the house and the general could no longer see her. He heard when the well's door was set aside and the chain began unwinding. The gurgly dipping, the unhurried path up, the knock of the full pail against the well house. The general pressed his cheek to the fence. It was warm, rough wood. The woman wiped her feet and went out on the porch. Poured some water into a tank. Someone began coughing behind a curtain. The bell-like ring of the tank and the patter of water on the bottom of the basin. Everything was authentic, nothing was superfluous: a thin trill at the beginning (a little hysterically), then calmed and muted as it filled. The distant bark of dogs. The general was not worried about this house.

He turned on Botkinskaya Street and went to the pier by Alexander Square. Thick snow had begun to fall. It was wet and not even cold. The sea whipped against the embankment's stones. There was no ice in the sea but it was hopelessly wintry, from the distant breakers to the splashes that spread in the snow. The pier's pilings were entwined in its gray strands. The general sniffed the air—only the winter sea smelled like this.

He stopped by the gate at the Tsar's Garden when he caught sight of the musicians. Pensive, he admired how the snow was coating them, to musical accompaniment. The general put all his money—several million—in the open violin case. Occasional pedestrians donated to the musicians, too. The case gradually filled with snow and multicolored bills that had not yet managed to become old: the snow and the bills already had the same approximate value.

The general picked up another million on the sidewalk by the Frantsia Hotel and gave it to the porter. A horsecab driver bowed to him from the coachman's seat. The wheels turned snow into water to the sound of wet clopping; black furrows stretched sloppily behind the horsecab. A small dark blue spot was forming on the leaden sky. This was the unpredictable Yalta weather. The snowstorm had begun to subside.

The sun peeked out as the general approached the jetty. He stopped, closed his eyes, and the skin of his face felt the sun's warmth. After standing like that for a bit, he turned onto the jetty. The snow that had fallen on the concrete was melting at full speed. The general slowly walked the rest of the way to the lighthouse. A small tree was growing out of a crack in its base. The tree's leaves had fallen so it was difficult to tell what kind of tree it was. The general laid his palm on the base's dirty-gray stones. They were beginning to warm up, barely enough to feel. This was like a return to life. The general closed his eyes again and imagined it was now summer. The sounds of the sea muffling what might have carried from the embankment. The wheels of coaches, shouts of kvass sellers, cries of children. Rustling of palms. Hot weather.

He opened his eyes and saw people walking toward him. They were walking unhurriedly, even somehow peaceably: Zemlyachka, Kun, and a group of sailors. Their faces were not triumphant; they were most likely preoccupied. Expecting a ploy, they were not taking their eyes off the edge of the jetty where the general stood. Those walking realized that the general was one step from the irretrievable and they feared that step. They feared the general would take it on his own.

They exchanged a few words as they drew closer. They were not looking in the general's direction at all now. Their hearts were jumping out of their chests. Zemlyachka was striding ahead of them all. She was holding her half-fastened leather coat with her hand and its hem flapped in the wind. Kun walked a little behind her, his boots cleaned to a shine. His wooden gait gave away his flatfootedness. There was an extinguished cigarette between his teeth. He kicked pebbles as he walked but there was nothing carefree in that. Or in the sailors' feline movements. Those walking were genuine hunters and could not hide that.

The general did not move. He was half-sitting on the base of the lighthouse and watching seagulls stroll along the jetty. They were letting out shrill sounds that were sometimes similar to a duck's quacking, sometimes to a child's screech. The seagulls were searching for something among the wet rocks. They groomed their feathers and raised their heads, pensively examining a sea entirely lacking ships. Never before had they seen a sea like that. The seagulls did not even fly off when the group of people walking along the jetty neared the general. They were not afraid of people.

Zemlyachka was the first to approach the general. She neared him without rushing but it was noticeable even under her leather coat how quickly her breasts were moving. As before, the general was half-sitting on the base of the lighthouse, leaning on his hands. Those walking smelled of horse sweat and unwashed human bodies. The sailors froze, awaiting an order. Kun spat out the cigarette butt. Zemlyachka took out her pen knife and silently drove it into the back of the general's hand. She was overrun with feelings.

A bell struck on Polikurovsky Hill. It was ringing in the St. John Chrysostom bell tower. Zemlyachka and Kun were arguing about something in undertones. The sailors observed the general moving his lips, barely noticeably, and they felt sympathy toward him. His hand was still lying on the base of the lighthouse. A crimson dribble wound through cracks in the rocks. Zemlyachka was insisting that his execution had to be agonizing. Kun objected that the execution should demonstrate the humanism of Soviet power. The striking bell muted Zemlyachka's reply. Its sound floated over the sea, filling Yalta's entire bay. When the argument was over, they led the general to the outer side of the jetty. They placed him on the edge and tied a piece of debris from an anchor to his feet.

'Shoot for the stomach, not the heart,' Kun advised the sailors. 'Then he'll be able to drown after he's shot, too.'

The sailors nodded.

'I'll be the one to shoot,' said Zemlyachka. 'In the groin.'

The sailors nodded again. Far below, brown seaweed undulated in time with the waves. The water had turned emerald green under the bright sun. It no longer had a repulsive wintry look and it seemed warm from a distance. The general decided to look straight ahead so as not to feel dizzy. He could see part of the embankment behind the sailors' heads. Coaches were driving and people were walking. The embankment continued to live its own life but that life was no longer the general's life; they were separated by a short strip of water and a group standing on the jetty. Yalta's cozy amphitheater towered over the embankment. Smoke stretched from the chimneys of some houses. It was rising toward the sky and mixing with clouds at the very top of Ai-Petri. The sailors stepped aside. Nothing else blocked the marvelous picture. The clouds seemed motionless but in actuality they were not. They were slowly drifting toward Ai-Petri. This became particularly noticeable when the shadow of a large triangular cloud began moving along the peak. The cloud itself still did not touch the peak. It was moving more slowly than its shadow. When Zemlyachka's leather coat appeared in front of the general, he thought the cloud would not moor at the peak during his lifetime. That it could have hurried up if, of course, all its spectators were equally important to it. But the cloud was not hurrying. It was obviously imitating the cloud the future military commander had seen from deep within Vorontsov Park in 1889. At approximately 3:00 in the afternoon, when his father, who was keen on photography, decided to take his picture. That time was considered the best for taking a photograph. The sun was still bright but the shadows had already settled prettily on the grass. The boy was standing in a glade between Lebanese cedars. The camera was on a cumbersome wooden stand located a little way below, on a walkway. His father had shortened the legs of the stand so the boy would be photographed against the backdrop of Ai-Petri. A dragonfly froze uneasily over the camera. It was not flying out of the lens; it simply hovered in one place. Its wings were indiscernible and seemed like a light thickening of air. His father needed that peak, suffused with sun, but the shadow of a cloud had already appeared on it. His father kept looking out from under the black cloth but the cloud was not thinking about moving. Only its shadow was migrating. It was creeping ever closer to Ai-Petri, depriving the peak of its last signs of luminescence. Zemlyachka energetically shook her right wrist. Larionov had been posed just as carefully in 1889 as now. Only then he was standing with his back to Ai-Petri. He had been watching the cloud then, looking around the entire time. He saw cedar branches rocking slightly in the wind. Felt the mountain's icy freshness mixing with the aromas of the park among the cedar branches. The boy inhaled that air and his nostrils moved. Caterpillars hung down from trees on thin threads; some were transforming into butterflies. The shrubs were scattered with ripe red berries. Cones dropped slowly from cedar crowns. The cones hit, muted, against the grass, stirring up grasshoppers who jumped together like fountains, then they bounced several times before falling still. The cones had been changing places, unnoticed, when he had turned around. An ant crawled along his knee. Zemlyachka raised the hand with the revolver. The general attempted to see himself from a distance but the image turned out to be a negative. A shot rang out from the opposite side of the jetty. The seagulls began taking off with a shriek but came right back down. The general turned his head and saw Zhloba. Zhloba's meager gestures asked Kun and Zemlyachka to approach him. Zemlyachka expressed dissatisfaction, like a person who has been interrupted at the most interesting part. She jabbed the revolver in the general's direction but Zhloba shook his head in the negative. As if foreseeing disappointment, Kun and

Zemlyachka were in no hurry to make their way to Zhloba.
The sailors took sunflower seeds from their pockets and
tossed them to the gulls. They liked observing the gulls
beating each other with their wings in their struggle for
the seeds. Zhloba's conversation with his comrades-in-arms
turned out to be anything but simple. Isolated exclamations
that the wind carried, and their gestures, spoke to that.
Zhloba took a paper folded into quarters from his map
case. He unfolded it, showed it to both his conversation
partners in turn, and placed it back in the case. The sailors
laughed about the birds' basic instincts. This spectacle enno-
bled them in some way. Zhloba was, perceptibly, beginning
to lose patience. He took out the paper once again, pressed
it up against Bela Kun's face and held it like that for several
seconds. Bela Kun did not resist. Zemlyachka turned around
abruptly and left the jetty. The men went after her. The
general's gaze followed them but not one of them turned
around. The sailors understood nothing. After tossing the
rest of the seeds to the seagulls, they began trudging uncertainly after their commanders. One of them returned,
untied the general's feet, and bolted off to catch up to the
others. The general took several steps away from the edge.
The wind was intensifying. The general flung open his
overcoat to greet the wind, just as people greet someone
they already said goodbye to for the last time, someone
who brings joy by simply existing. The general looked at
the sun without squinting. Tears welled up from rays that
were still bright but already orange. The sun was hanging
over the other side of the embankment, illuminating masses
of ice that had frozen on the streetlamps after the night's
storm. They glistened like a dazzling Christmas garland.

The size of the sun exceeded the boundaries of what is reasonable. Jolting as it moved, the sun disappeared behind the mountain at unexpected speed. The sun was setting in his presence.

ACKNOWLEDGEMENTS

Although *Solovyov and Larionov* is Eugene Vodolazkin's debut novel, it's the third of his books that I've translated for Oneworld. Like Eugene's *Laurus* and *The Aviator*, *Solovyov and Larionov* is a complex novel, both in terms of language, since the narrative voice is very defined, and content, which blends two time periods and includes a fair bit of history. Those complexities mean that Eugene's patient help—reading my manuscript, answering my questions, and simply being his usual humorous and thoughtful self—was more necessary than ever. The three novels fit together so beautifully, forming a sort of triptych, that each one is my favorite in its own right.

Part of the fun of *Solovyov and Larionov* is in the details, which Eugene cleverly plants throughout the novel so they can come together at the end of the book. Eugene often refers to me as his co-author and this book gave me more opportunities than *Laurus* and *The Aviator*, thanks to several passages that we changed significantly, often because translated humor and irony just aren't very funny when they have to be explained. (Fortunately, nearly all Eugene's humor and irony translates very nicely into English.) I also adapted the hundreds of footnotes that appeared in the Russian *Solovyov and Larionov*. Eugene warned me from the start that he was pretty sure I'd need to get rid of them and I confess that I (foolishly) told him most of them could likely stay. That meant it took an epiphany (in the shower) to realize I was wrong and that the novel would maintain its tone, not to mention its continuity, best if I incorporated the footnote information into the text.

Solovyov and Larionov is my fourth book for Oneworld and, as always, I'm grateful to Juliet Mabey for her love of Russian contemporary fiction, and to the team at Oneworld for all their editorial help.

My colleague Liza Prudovskaya read an entire draft of *Solovyov and Larionov*, comparing it to Eugene's original. She also answered hundreds of questions about language, tone, and usage, saving me from dozens and dozens of errors of all kinds. I can never thank her enough for her contributions to my translations. Any blunders are, of course, mine, not hers. Finally, *Solovyov and Larionov* contains quotes from a number of other texts. I'm particularly grateful to Katherine Young, a poet, translator, and friend, who transformed my draft work on lines by Semyon Nadson and Vasily Zhukovsky into real poetry.

Oneworld, Many Voices

Bringing you exceptional writing
from around the world

Umami by Laia Jufresa (Spanish)
Translated by Sophie Hughes

The Hermit by Thomas Rydahl (Danish)
Translated by K. E. Semmel

The Peculiar Life of a Lonely Postman by Denis Thériault
(French) Translated by Liedewy Hawke

Three Envelopes by Nir Hezroni (Hebrew)
Translated by Steven Cohen

Fever Dream by Samanta Schweblin (Spanish)
Translated by Megan McDowell

The Invisible Life of Euridice Gusmao by Martha Batalha
(Brazilian Portuguese) Translated by Eric M. B. Becker

The Temptation to Be Happy by Lorenzo Marone
(Italian) Translated by Shaun Whiteside

Sweet Bean Paste by Durian Sukegawa (Japanese)
Translated by Alison Watts

They Know Not What They Do by Jussi Valtonen (Finnish)
Translated by Kristian London

The Tiger and the Acrobat by Susanna Tamaro (Italian)
Translated by Nicoleugenia Prezzavento and Vicki Satlow

The Woman at 1,000 Degrees by Hallgrímur Helgason
(Icelandic) Translated by Brian FitzGibbon

Frankenstein in Baghdad by Ahmed Saadawi (Arabic)
Translated by Jonathan Wright

Back Up by Paul Colize (French)
Translated by Louise Rogers Lalaurie

Damnation by Peter Beck (German)
Translated by Jamie Bulloch

Oneiron by Laura Lindstedt (Finnish)
Translated by Owen Witesman

The Baghdad Clock by Shahad Al Rawi (Arabic)
Translated by Luke Leafgren

The Aviator by Eugene Vodolazkin (Russian)
Translated by Lisa C. Hayden

Lala by Jacek Dehnel (Polish)
Translated by Antonia Lloyd-Jones

Bogotá 39: New Voices from Latin America
(Spanish and Portuguese) Short story anthology

Last Instructions by Nir Hezroni (Hebrew)
Translated by Steven Cohen

Solovyov and Larionov by Eugene Vodolazkin (Russian)
Translated by Lisa C. Hayden

In/Half by Jasmin B. Frelih (Slovenian)
Translated by Jason Blake

What Hell Is Not by Alessandro D'Avenia (Italian)
Translated by Jeremy Parzen

Zuleikha by Guzel Yakhina (Russian)
Translated by Lisa C. Hayden

Mouthful of Birds by Samanta Schweblin (Spanish)
Translated by Megan McDowell

City of Jasmine by Olga Grjasnowa (German)
Translated by Katy Derbyshire

Things that Fall from the Sky by Selja Ahava (Finnish)
Translated by Emily Jeremiah and Fleur Jeremiah

Mrs Mohr Goes Missing by Jacek Dehnel and Piotr Tarczyński
(Polish) Translated by Antonia Lloyd-Jones

In the Shadow of Wolves by Alvidas Slepikas (Lithuanian)
Translated by Romas Kïnka

Humiliation by Paulina Flores (Spanish)
Translated by Megan McDowell

© Ilya Tolstoy

Eugene Vodolazkin was born in Kiev and has worked in the department of Old Russian Literature at Pushkin House since 1990. He is an expert in medieval Russian history and folklore, and in 2019 he was the recipient of the prestigious Aleksandr Solzhenitsyn Literature Prize. His novel *Laurus* (Oneworld, 2015) won the National Big Book Award and the Yasnaya Polyana Award, and has been translated into eighteen languages. *The Aviator* (Oneworld, 2018) was shortlisted for the Russian Booker Prize and the National Big Book Award. He lives in St Petersburg.

Lisa C. Hayden's translations from the Russian include Eugene Vodolazkin's *Laurus*, which won the Read Russia Award in 2016 and was also shortlisted for the Oxford-Weidenfeld Prize along with her translation of Vadim Levental's *Masha Regina*. Her blog, Lizok's Bookshelf, examines contemporary Russian fiction. She lives in Maine.

ALSO BY EUGENE VODOLAZKIN
LAURUS

Winner of the National Big
Book Award and the Yasnaya
Polyana Award

Winner of the Read Russia
Prize 2016

Shortlisted for the Oxford-
Weidenfeld Prize 2016

In fifteenth-century Russia a young healer, skilled in the art
of herbs and remedies, finds himself overcome with grief and
guilt when he fails to save the one he loves. Leaving behind his
village, his possessions and his name, he sets out on a quest for
redemption, penniless and alone. But this is no ordinary journey.

Winner of two of the biggest literary prizes in Russia, *Laurus* is a
remarkably rich novel about the eternal themes of love, loss, self-
sacrifice and faith, from one of the country's most experimental
and critically acclaimed novelists.

'At once stylistically ornate and compulsively readable...
delivered with great aplomb and narrative charm.'
Times Literary Supplement

'With flavours of Umberto Eco and *The Canterbury
Tales*, this affecting, idiosyncratic novel...is an
impressive achievement.' *Kirkus*

ALSO BY EUGENE VODOLAZKIN

THE AVIATOR

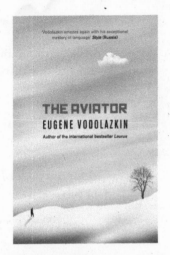

**Shortlisted for the Russian
Booker Prize**

**Shortlisted for the National
Big Book Award**

A man wakes up in a hospital bed, with no idea who he is or how
he came to be there. The only information the doctor shares with
him is his name: Innokenty Petrovich Platonov.

As memories slowly resurface, Innokenty begins to build a vivid
picture of his former life as a young man in Russia in the early
twentieth century, living through the turbulence of the Russian
Revolution and its aftermath. Soon, only one question remains:
how can he remember the start of the twentieth century, when
the pills by his bedside were made in 1999?

Reminiscent of the great works of twentieth-century Russian
literature, with nods to Dostoevsky's *Crime and Punishment* and
Bulgakov's *The White Guard*, *The Aviator* cements Vodolazkin's
position as the rising star of Russia's literary scene.

'Vodolazkin's grip on this narrative is iron-tight... We should
expect nothing less from an author whose previous novel, *Laurus*,
was a barnstorming thriller about medieval virtue.' *Guardian*

ONEWORLD